POOLE QUAY
BOAT HAVEN
PORT OF POOLE
MARINA
CW01550035
HOME OF
Pip Hare
OCEAN RACING
MARINA
OF THE YEAR
2016 - 2017 - 2019 - 2020
POOLE
A SEA OF DISCOVERY AWAITS
THE SOUTH
COAST'S PREMIER
MARINA
NGING MOORINGS
with a glass of wine, on a
afternoon, on your own
ing mooring in Poole
our overlooking Brownsea
. Away from the madding
, these offer you ultimate
y, peace & tranquillity.
Medallia
VISITOR MARINA
125 visitor berths all year for
vessels up to 75m in length
and up to 4.8m draft
On the Port estate we can
accommodate vessels
up to 210m in length with
a maximum draft of 9m.
GOLD ANCHOR
e Town Quay, Poole, Dorset BH15 1HJ
202 649488 | poolequayboathaven.co.uk
VHF Channel 80 call sign
"Poole Quay Boat Haven"

NEW
NOT ALL CHARTS
ARE CREATED
EQUAL
LIGHTHOUSE
CHARTS
Superior visual presentation, combined with rich detail and accurate navigation from official hydrographic sources. Subscribe to LightHouse Premium and unlock data-rich points of interest including marinas, restaurants and fuel berths as well as high-resolution satellite image aerial overlays.
Lighthouse Charts, discover the detail.
REEDS ALMANAC
NOW WITH
REEDS PREMIUM POI
Raymarine

REEDS WESTERN ALMANAC 2024

ADLARD COLES

EDITORS Perrin Towler and Mark Fishwick

Free updates are available at www.reedsalmanacs.co.uk

IMPORTANT SAFETY NOTE AND LEGAL DISCLAIMER

This Almanac provides basic navigational data for planning and executing passages. The tidal prediction data has been reproduced by permission of national hydrographic offices. Chartlets illustrate items in the text, orientate the user and highlight key features; they should not be relied on for navigational purposes and must always be used in conjunction with a current, corrected navigational chart. Any waypoint or position listed in this Almanac must first be plotted on the appropriate chart to assess its accuracy, safety in the prevailing circumstances and relevance to the Skipper's intentions.

Navigational guidance or suggestions are based on the accumulated experience of editors, agents, harbour masters and users. They are generic and in compiling a passage plan or pilotage notebook all other available publications and information should be consulted. They take no account of the characteristics of individual vessels nor the actual or forecast meteorological conditions, sea or tidal state. These need to be checked with appropriate local authorities for the intended area of operation prior to departure.

While every care has been taken in compiling the Almanac, it is a human endeavour with many contributors. Despite rigorous checking there may be inadvertent errors or inaccuracies, and omissions resulting from the time of notification in relation to the publication date. To the extent that the editors or publishers become aware of these, corrections will be published on the website www.reedsalmanacs.co.uk (requires registration). Readers should therefore regularly check the website between January and June for any such corrections. Data in this Almanac is corrected up to Weekly Edition 25/2023 of Admiralty Notices to Mariners.

The publishers, editors and their agents accept no responsibility for any errors or omissions, or for any accident, loss or damage (including without limitation any indirect, consequential, special or exemplary damages) arising from the use or misuse of, or reliance upon, the information contained in this Almanac.

The use of any data in this Almanac is entirely at the discretion of the Skipper or other individual with responsibility for the command, conduct or navigation of the vessel in which it is relied upon.

Managing editor Chris Stevens

Reeds Nautical Almanac
An imprint of Bloomsbury Publishing Plc
50 Bedford Square, London, WC1B 3DP

29 Earlsfort Terrace, Dublin 2, Ireland

Tel: +44 (0)20 7631 5600
info@reedsalmanacs.co.uk
editor.britishisles@reedsalmanacs.co.uk
editor.continental@reedsalmanacs.co.uk
www.reedsalmanacs.co.uk

REEDS, ADLARD COLES NAUTICAL and the Buoy logo are trademarks of Bloomsbury Publishing Plc

First published 2023

Reeds Western Almanac 2024 – ISBN 978 1 3994 0953 7

British Library Cataloguing-in-Publication Data
A catalogue record for this book is available from the British Library.

Library of Congress Cataloguing-in-Publication data has been applied for.

FSC www.fsc.org MIX Paper from responsible sources FSC® C007785

Typeset in Frutiger

Printed and bound in the UK by Bell & Bain Ltd

Reference Contents

Navigational Contents

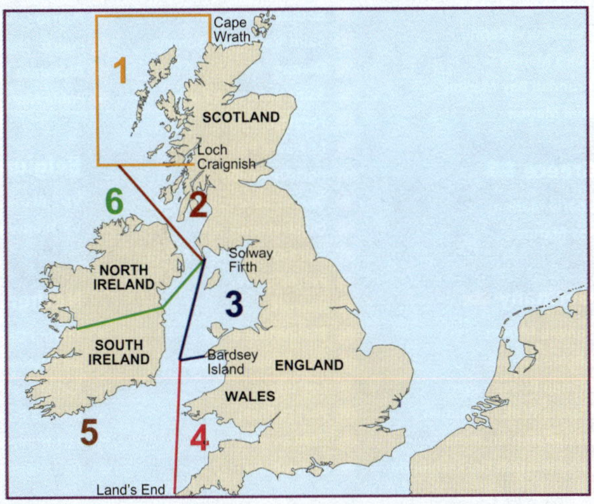

COWES
THE PERFECT BOATING DESTINATION
© Paul Wyeth
© Martin Allen/CWL
© Smoking Lobster, Cowes
REGATTAS AND RELAXATION
COWES WELCOMES EVERYONE
ISLE OF WIGHT FOOD & DRINK
MARINAS · YACHT CLUBS · BOATYARDS
ART · CHANDLERIES · CLOTHING
COWES HARBOUR
COMMISSION
www.cowesharbourcommission.co.uk

NEW
NOT ALL CHARTS
ARE CREATED
EQUAL
LIGHTHOUSE
CHARTS
Superior visual presentation, combined with rich detail and accurate navigation from official hydrographic sources. Subscribe to LightHouse Premium and unlock data-rich points of interest including marinas, restaurants and fuel berths as well as high-resolution satellite image aerial overlays.
Lighthouse Charts, discover the detail.
REEDS
ALMANAC
NOW WITH
REEDS PREMIUM POI
Raymarine

clarkeandcarter.co.uk
INTERNATIONAL YACHT BROKERS
Suffolk Yacht Harbour
Neptune Marina
Shotley Marina
Burnham Yacht Harbour
• International sailing yacht and motor boat brokerage with dedicated, highly experienced sales team
• Comprehensive marketing package including Yachtworld, The Yacht Market, BS24 group, Apollo Duck and more
• FREE storage deals available at our premium, fully serviced locations on dedicated sales areas
• Jeanneau Sail main agents with spares support service
October 4th - 6th
Burnham Yacht Harbour
CM0 8BL
clarkeandcarter.co.uk
USED BOAT SHOWS
October 25th - 27th
Suffolk Yacht Harbour
IP10 0LN
Essex - 01621 785600
essex@clarkeandcarter.co.uk
CLARKE + CARTER
INTERYACHT LTD
Suffolk - 01473 659681
suffolk@clarkeandcarter.co.uk

SAIL TO ORKNEY
ORKNEY MARINAS
The Orkney islands are an exciting cruising destination with an abundance of wildlife, history and outstanding coastal scenery.
Westray
Mainland
Stromness
Kirkwall
Hoy
+44 (0)1856 871313 | info@orkneymarinas.co.uk | www.orkneymarinas.co.uk
Orkney Marinas Ltd, Dunkirk, Shore Street, Kirkwall.

PORT CHANTEREYNE

YACHTING IN THE HEART OF A SURPRISING TOWN

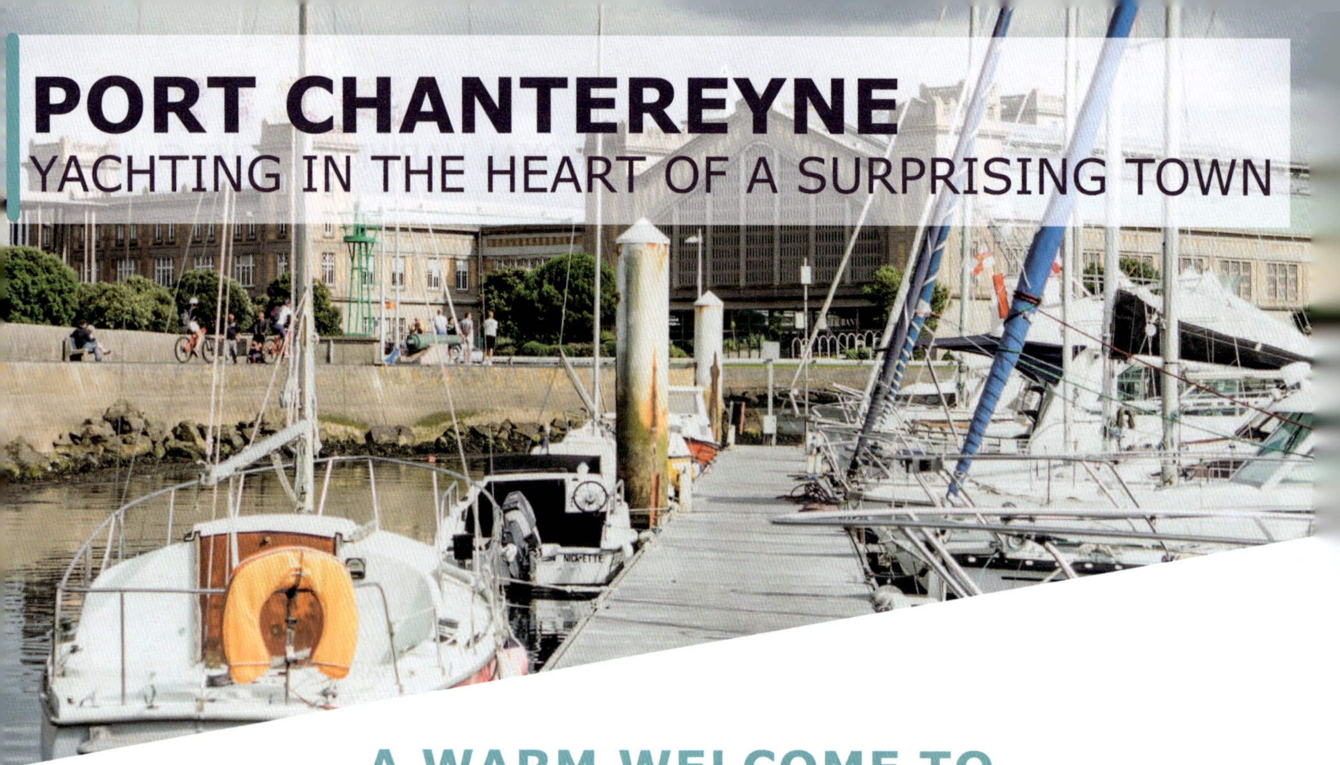

A WARM WELCOME TO CHERBOURG-EN-COTENTIN

- Largest marina on the Normandy Channel coast with a total of 1,600 berths, 190 of which are designated for visitors
- Ideally positioned on the Channel coast, close to England, the Channel Islands and Brittany
- Deep water harbour accessible 24 hours a day with no tide or weather restrictions
- Awarded service quality labels : Pavillon Bleu, Qualité Plaisance and 5 Gold Anchors
- Many services and facilities
- A large choice of nautical professionals in the marina
- Close to the town centre and its large selection of shops, restaurants, tourist sites and attractions

Tel: +33 (0)2 33 87 65 70
portchantereyne@cherbourg.fr
VHF Channel 9

Port Chantereyne CHERBOURG

www.portchantereyne.fr

CHERBOURG en Cotentin

Reference data

0.1 THE ALMANAC

• Acknowledgements

The Editors thank the many official bodies and individuals for information and advice given in the compilation of this Almanac. These include: UKHO, Trinity House, HM Nautical Almanac Office, SHOM, HMSO, HM Revenue & Customs, Meteorological Office, BBC, IBA, MCA, RNLI, ABP, countless Harbourmasters and our many individual Harbour Agents.

• Permissions

Chartlets, tidal stream diagrams and curves are reproduced from Admiralty charts and publications (ALL, ASD, ATT and ALRS) by permission of the UKHO (Licence No GB DQ – 001 – Adlard Coles) and the Controller of HMSO.

UK and foreign tidal predictions are supplied by and with the permission of UKHO.

Extracts from the *International Code of Signals 1969* and *Meteorological Office Weather Services for Shipping* are published by permission of the Controller of HMSO.

Ephemerides are derived from HM Nautical Almanac by permission of HM Nautical Almanac Office and the Council for the Central Laboratory of the Research Councils.

• Disclaimer

No National HO has verified the information in this product and none accepts liability for the accuracy of reproduction or any modifications made thereafter. No National HO warrants that this product satisfies national or international regulations regarding the use of the appropriate products for navigation.

Chartlets in this Almanac are not intended to be used for navigation. Always consult fully corrected official charts. See 0.30, Harbour Information, for more details.

• Improvements

Suggestions, however minor, for improving or correcting this Almanac are always welcome, especially if based on personal experience. All will be carefully considered. Please send your comments by email, if possible, direct to the relevant Editor (see below) or to info@reedsalmanacs.co.uk. Otherwise, a note to Adlard Coles Nautical (see page v) will be forwarded as necessary.

Perrin Towler (editor.britishisles@reedsalmanacs.co.uk) is responsible for all the Areas in this Almanac; Mark Fishwick (editor.continental@reedsalmanacs.co.uk) is responsible for the sections on weather and communications in the Reference Data chapter.

• Notifying errors

Although every care has been taken in compiling this Almanac, errors may still occur. Please let us know if you spot any.

• Harbour Agents

Our harbour agents provide invaluable local information which may not appear in official sources. If this is of interest and you would like to earn a free copy of Reeds Nautical Almanac please apply to the relevant editor, giving brief details of your experience and the area(s) you would be able cover.

• Sources of corrections

This Almanac is corrected to Weekly edition No. 25/2023 of Admiralty Notices to Mariners.

Corrections to Admiralty charts and publications can be downloaded from the UKHO website or obtained from Admiralty Chart Agents (ACA) and certain Port Authorities.

• Updates

Monthly updates from January to June are free to Almanac purchasers who provide their receipt or a photo of the imprint page to adlardcoles@bloomsbury.com or www.reedsnauticalalmanac.co.uk/update.

0.2 SYMBOLS AND ABBREVIATIONS

The following more common Symbols and Abbreviations feature in Reeds Almanacs and in some Admiralty charts and publications. Those symbols in the tinted box immediately below are frequently used within the text describing each port.

	Alongside berth
©	Automatic telling machine (ATM), cashpoint
Ⓑ	Bank
	Bottled gas available, Calor Gas, Camping Gaz,or Kosangas
	Boatyard
	Boat hoist (+tons)
	Crane (+ tons)
	Chandlery
	Customs
	Diesel (supply by hose)
	Diesel (in cans)
	Electrical repairs
Ⓔ	Electronic repairs
	Fresh water supply
	Food shop/supermarket
H	Hospital
≠	In transit with, ie ldg marks/lts
@	Internet café/access
	Landing place/steps/ladder
	Laundry facilities available
LB,	Lifeboat, inshore lifeboat
	Light float, minor
	Lt float, major; Light vessel or Lanby
	Licensed bar, Public house, Inn
©	National Coastwatch Institution (NCI)
	Marine engineering repairs
	Mooring buoy
	Petrol (supply by hose)
	Petrol (in cans)
✉	Post Office
	Pump out facility
✕	Restaurant/cafe
	Rigger
	Sailmaker
	Shipwright (esp wooden hulls)
	Shower
	Shore power (electrical)
	Slipway
Ⓥ	Visitors' berths
	Visitors' mooring
	Wind turbine
	Weather forecast available
	Yacht Club/(YC), Sailing Club(SC)

abm	Abeam
ABP	Associated British Ports
ACA	Admiralty Chart, AC Agent
ACN	Adlard Coles Nautical (Publisher)
Aff Mar	Affaires Maritimes
AIS	Automatic Identification System
aka	Also known as
ALL	Admiralty List of Lights
ALRS	Admiralty List of Radio Signals
Al	Alternating light
ANWB	Association of road & waterway users (Dutch)

ATT	Admiralty Tide Tables
ATT	Atterisage (landfall/SWM) buoy
Auto	Météo Répondeur Automatique
B.	Bay, Black
BE	Belgian chart
Bk	Broken (nature of seabed)
Bkwtr	Breakwater
BMS	Bulletin Météorologique Spécial (Strong wind/Gale warning)
	Bn, bcn(s) Beacon, beacon(s)
BSH	German Hydrographic Office/chart(s)
BST	British Summer Time (= DST)
Bu	Blue
By(s)	Buoy, buoys
C.	Cape, Cabo, Cap
c	Coarse (sand; nature of seabed)
ca	Cable (approx 185m long)
Cas	Castle
CD	Chart datum (tidal)
CEVNI	Code Européen de Voies de la Navigation Intérieure (inland waterway signs etc)
cf	Compare, cross-refer to
CG	Coast Guard, HM Coastguard (in the UK)
CGOC	Coast Guard Operations Centre (UK)
chan	Channel (navigational)
Ch	Channel (VHF)
Ch, ✠	Church
Chy	Chimney
Co	Coral (nature of seabed)
Col	Column, pillar, obelisk
CPA	Closest Point of Approach
CROSS	Centre Régional Opérationnel de Surveillance et Sauvetage (= MRCC)
CRS	Coast Radio Station
CRT	Canal and River Trust
C/S	COSPAS/SARSAT (satellite)
Cy	Clay (nature of seabed)
Dec	Declination (of the Sun) abbr: December
Defib	Automated External Defibrillator
dest	Destroyed
DF, D/F	Radio Direction Finding
DG	De-gaussing (range)
DGPS	Differential GPS
Dia	Diaphone (fog signal)
Dir Lt	Directional light
discont	Discontinued
DLR	Dockland Light Railway
Dn(s)	Dolphin(s)
DR	Dead Reckoning or Dries (secondary tides)
DSC	Digital Selective Calling
DST	Daylight Saving Time
DW	Deep Water (route)
DYC	Dutch Yacht Chart(s)
DZ	Danger Zone (buoy)
E	East
ECM	East cardinal mark (buoy/beacon)
ED	Existence doubtful. European Datum
EEA	European Economic Area
Elev	Elevation
Ent	Entrance, entry, enter
EP, △	Estimated position
ETA	Estimated Time of Arrival
ETD	Estimated Time of Departure
F	Fixed light
f	Fine (eg sand; nature of seabed)
F&A	Fore and aft (berth/mooring)
FFL	Fixed and Flashing light

Fl	Flashing light
FM	Frequency Modulation
Foc	Free of charge
Fog Det lt	Fog Detector light
Freq, Fx	Frequency
FS	Flagstaff, Flagpole
ft	Foot, feet
Ft,	Fort
FV	Fishing vessel
G	Gravel (nature of seabed), Green
GC	Great Circle
GDOP	Geometric Dilution of Precision (GPS)
GHA	Greenwich Hour Angle
GLA	General Lighthouse Authority
GMDSS	Global Maritime Distress & Safety System
grt	Gross Registered Tonnage
Gy	Grey
H, h, Hrs	Hour(s)
H–, H+	Minutes before, after the whole hour
H24	Continuous
Hd,hd	Headland, head (breakwater/mole)
HAT	Highest Astronomical Tide
HF	High Frequency
HFP	High Focal Plane (buoy)
HIE	Highlands & Islands Enterprise
HJ	Day service only, sunrise to sunset
HM	Harbour Master
HMRC	HM Revenue & Customs
HMSO	Her Majesty's Stationery Office
HN	Night service only, sunset to sunrise
HO	Office hours, Hydrographic Office
(hor)	Horizontally disposed (lights)
hPa	Hectopascal (= 1millibar)
HT	High Tension (overhead electricity line)
HW	High Water
HX	No fixed hours
IALA	International Association of Marine Aids to Navigation and Lighthouse Authorities
iaw	In accordance with
IDM	Isolated Danger Mark (buoy/beacon)
IHO	International Hydrographic Organisation
IMO	International Maritime Organisation
INMARSAT	International Maritime Satellite Organisation
intens	Intensified (light sector)
IPTS	International Port Traffic Signals
IQ	Interrupted quick flashing light
IRPCS	International Regulations for the Prevention of Collisions at Sea
Is, I	Island, Islet
ISAF	International Sailing Federation
Iso	Isophase light
ITU	International Telecommunications Union
ITZ	Inshore Traffic Zone (TSS)
IUQ	Interrupted ultra quick flashing light
IVQ	Interrupted very quick flashing light
kn	Knot(s)
kW	Kilowatts
L	Lake, Loch, Lough
Lat	Latitude
LAT	Lowest Astronomical Tide
Lanby,	Large automatic navigational buoy
Ldg	Leading (light)
LF	Low frequency
L Fl	Long flash
LH	Left hand
LNG	Liquefied Natural Gas
LNTM	Local Notice To Mariners

LOA	Length overall
Long, lng	Longitude
LPG	Liquefied Petroleum Gas
LT	Local time
Lt(s), ☆ ☆	Light(s)
M	Moorings. Nautical (sea) mile(s). Mud
m	Metre(s)
Mag	Magnetic. Magnitude (of star)
Mb, mb	Millibar (= 1 hectopascal, hPa)
MCA	Maritime and Coastguard Agency
Met/Météo	Meteorology/Météorologie (weather)
MHWN	Mean High Water Neaps
MHWS	Mean High Water Springs
MHz	Megahertz
ML	Mean Level (tidal)
MLWN	Mean Low Water Neaps
MLWS	Mean Low Water Springs
MMSI	Maritime Mobile Service Identity
Mo	Morse
Mon	Monument. Abbrev: Monday
MRCC	Maritime Rescue Co-ordination Centre
MRSC	Maritime Rescue Sub-Centre (not in the UK)
MSI	Maritime Safety Information
N	North
Navi	Navicarte (French charts)
NB	Nota Bene. Notice Board
NCM	North Cardinal Mark (buoy/beacon)
ND	No Data (secondary tides)
NGS	Naval Gunfire Support (buoy)
NM	Notice(s) to Mariners
NMOC	National Maritime Operations Centre (HMCG)
np	Neap tides
NP	Naval Publication (plus number)
NRT	Net registered tonnage
NT	National Trust (land/property)
Obscd	Obscured
Obstn	Obstruction
Oc	Occulting light
ODAS	Ocean Data Acquisition System (buoy)
Or	Orange (see also Y)
OT	Other times
P	Pebbles
(P)	Preliminary (NM)
PA	Position approximate
Pax	Passenger(s)
PC	Portuguese chart
PD	Position doubtful
PHM	Port-hand Mark (buoy/beacon)
PLA	Port of London Authority
Pos	Position
Prog	Prognosis (weather charts)
prom	Prominent
PSSA	Particularly Sensitive Sea Area
Pt(e).	Point(e)
Pta	Punta (point)
Q	Quick flashing light
QHM	Queen's Harbour Master
qv	Refer to (quod vide)
R	Red. River.
Racon	Radar transponder beacon
Ramark	Radar beacon
RCD	Recreational Craft Directive
RG	Emergency RDF station
RH	Right hand
Rk, Rky	Rock, Rocky (nature of seabed)
RNLI	Royal National Lifeboat Institution
ROI	Republic of Ireland
R/T	Radiotelephony
Ru	Ruins
RYA	Royal Yachting Association
S	South, Sand (nature of seabed)
S, St, Ste	Saint(s)
SAMU	Service d'Aide Médicale Urgente (ambulance)
SAR	Search and Rescue
SBM	Single buoy mooring
SC	Sailing Club. Spanish chart
SCM	South Cardinal Mark (buoy/beacon)
SD	Sailing Directions,Semi-diameter (of sun) Sounding of doubtful depth
sf	Stiff (nature of seabed)
Sh	Shells (nature of seabed). Shoal
SHM	Starboard-hand Mark (buoy/beacon); Simplified Harmonic Method (tides)
SHOM	Service Hydrographique et Océanographique de la Marine (FrenchHO/Chart)
Si	Silt (nature of seabed)
SIGNI	Signalisation de la Navigation Intérieure
SMS	Short Message Service (mobile texting)
so	Soft (eg mud; nature of seabed)
SOLAS	Safety of Life at Sea (IMO Convention)
Sp	Spire
sp	Spring tides
SPM	Special Mark (buoy/beacon)
SR	Sunrise
SRR	Search and Rescue Region
SS	Sunset. Signal Station
SSB	Single Sideband (radio)
St	Stones (nature of seabed)
Stbd	Starboard
subm	Submerged
SWM	Safe Water Mark (buoy/beacon)
sy	Sticky (eg mud; nature of seabed)
(T), (Temp)	Temporary
tbc	To be confirmed
tbn	To be notified
TD	Temporarily Discontinued (fog signal)
TE	Temporarily Extinguished (light)
tfn	Till further notice
Tr, twr	Tower
T/R	Traffic Report (route notification)
TSS	Traffic Separation Scheme
uncov	Uncovers
UQ	Ultra Quick flashing light
UT	Universal Time (= approx GMT)
Var	Variation (magnetic)
(vert)	Vertically disposed (lights)
Vi	Violet
vis	Visibility, visible
VLCC	Very large crude carrier (Oil tanker)
VNF	Voie Navigable de France (canals)
VQ	Very Quick flashing light
VTS	Vessel Traffic Service
W	West. White
WCM	West Cardinal Mark (buoy/beacon)
Wd	Weed (nature of seabed)
wef	With effect from
WGS	World Geodetic System (GPS datum)
wi-fi	Wireless Fidelity (internet access)
WIG	Wing in ground effect (craft)
WIP	Work in progress
Wk,	Wreck (see also Fig 1(1))
WMO	World Meteorological Organisation
WPT, ⊕	Waypoint
WZ	Code for UK coastal navigation warning
Y	Yellow, Amber, Orange

0.3 PASSAGE PLANNING FORM

DATE:............................ FROM: .... TO: .... DIST: ....nm

ALTERNATIVE DESTINATION(S): ....

WEATHER FORECAST: ....

....

FORECASTS AVAILABLE DURING PASSAGE: ....

....

TIDES

DATE:	DATE:	DATE: ....
PLACE:	PLACE:	PLACE: ....
HW	HW	HW ....
LW	LW	LW ....
HW	HW	HW ....
LW	LW	LW ....
COEFFICIENT:	....	....
HEIGHT OF TIDE AT:	....	....
............hrs ....m	............hrs ....m	............hrs ....m

DEPTH CONSTRAINTS: ....

TIDAL STREAMS AT: ....

TURNS .... AT .... TOTAL SET (FM .... TO ....): ....° .... M

TURNS .... AT .... TOTAL SET (FM .... TO ....): ....° .... M

NET TIDAL STREAM FOR PASSAGE: ....° .... M

ESTIMATED TIME: ....hrs ETD: .... ETA: ....

SUN/MOON SUNRISE: .... SUNSET: ....

MOONRISE: .... MOONSET: .... PHASE: ....

WAYPOINTS

NO	NAME	TRACK/DISTANCE (TO NEXT WAYPOINT)
....	....	.... / ....
....	....	.... / ....
....	....	.... / ....
....	....	.... / ....
....	....	.... / ....

DANGERS CLEARING BEARINGS/RANGES/DEPTHS

....

....

LIGHTS/MARKS EXPECTED ....

....

....

COMMUNICATIONS PORT/MARINA .... VHF .... ☎ ....

PORT/MARINA .... VHF .... ☎ ....

NOTES (CHARTS PREPARED & PAGE NUMBERS OF RELEVANT PILOTS / ALMANACS / ETC): ....

....

....

0.4 PASSAGE PLANNING

All passages by any vessel that goes to sea *must* be planned. This is defined as proceeding beyond sheltered waters. Full passage planning requirements may be found in Chapter V of the International Convention for Safety of Life at Sea (SOLAS), but more digestible guidance for small craft is in the MCA's website at: **https://www.gov.uk/** - the guide formerly issued has been withdrawn.

Although the passage plan does not have to be recorded on paper, in the event of legal action a written plan is clear proof that the required planning has been completed. A suggested passage planning form is on the previous page. When completed this would constitute a reasonable passage plan. The blank form may be photocopied and/or modified.

Although spot checks on small craft are unlikely, the MCA could, following an accident or incident, take action under the Merchant Shipping Act if it could be proved that the skipper did not have a reasonable passage plan.

All passage plans should at least consider the following:

- **Weather.** Check the weather forecast and know how to get regular updates during the passage.
- **Tides.** Check tidal predictions and determine if there are any limiting depths at your port of departure, during the passage and at the port of arrival (and at alternative ports, if applicable). Tidal streams will almost certainly affect the plan.
- **Vessel.** Confirm she is suitable for the intended trip, is properly equipped, and has sufficient fuel, water and food on board.
- **Crew.** Take into account your crew's experience, expertise and stamina. Cold, tiredness and seasickness can be debilitating – and skippers are not immune.
- **Navigation.** Make sure you are aware of all navigational dangers by consulting up to date charts, pilot books and this Almanac. Never *rely* on GPS for fixing your position.
- **Contingency plan.** Consider bolt holes which can be entered *safely* in an emergency.
- **Information ashore.** Make sure someone ashore knows your plans, when they should become concerned and what action to take if necessary. Be sure to join the Coastguard Voluntary Identification Scheme.

0.5 POSITIONS FROM GPS

GPS employs World Geodetic System 84 (WGS84). Galileo works to the ETRS 89. With the exception of some areas of Ireland and the west coast of Scotland, AC of UK waters use the ETRS 89 datum. Harbour chartlets reflect this.

If the chart in use is not referenced to ETRS 89/WGS84, positions read from the GPS receiver must be converted to the datum of the chart in use. This is printed on the chart and gives the Lat/Long corrections to be applied. They can be significant. There are two options:

- Set the receiver to WGS84. Before plotting positions, manually apply the corrections given on the chart. This option is advised by UKHO.
- Set the receiver to the datum of the chart in use; the datum corrections will be applied by the receiver's software. This method is not the most accurate due to the random nature of the differences.

0.6 VHF COMMUNICATIONS

Radio Telephony (R/T)

VHF radio (Marine band 156·00–174·00 MHz) is used by most vessels. Range is slightly better than the line of sight between aerials, typically about 20M between yachts and up to 65M to a shore station depending on aerial heights. It always pays to fit a good aerial, as high as possible.

VHF sets may be **Simplex**, ie transmit and receive on the same frequency, so only one person can talk at a time. **Semi-Duplex** (most modern sets), transmit and receive on different frequencies, or **full Duplex**, ie simultaneous Semi-Duplex, so conversation is normal, but two aerials are needed.

Marine VHF frequencies are known by their international channel number (Ch), as shown below.

Channels are grouped according to three main purposes, but some have more than one purpose.

Public correspondence: **(via Coast radio stations)**
Ch 26, 27, 25, 24, 23, 28, 04, 01, 03, 02, 07, 05, 84, 87, 86, 83, 85, 88, 61, 64, 65, 62, 66, 63, 60, 82, 78, 81.
All channels can be used for Duplex.

Inter-ship:
Ch 06*, 08*, 10, 13, 09, 72*, 73, 69, 77*, 15, 17.
These are all Simplex channels. * for use in UK.

Port Operations:
Simplex: Ch 12, 14, 11, 13, 09, 68, 71, 74, 69, 73, 17, 15.
Duplex: Ch 20, 22, 18, 19, 21, 05, 07, 02, 03, 01, 04, 78, 82, 79, 81, 80, 60, 63, 66, 62, 65, 64, 61, 84.

The following channels have one specific purpose:

Ch 0 (156·00 MHz): SAR ops, not available to yachts.

Ch 10 (156·50 MHz), **62** (160·725 MHz), **63** (160·775 MHz) and **64** (160·825 MHz): MSI broadcasts. The optimum channel number is stated on Ch 16 in the announcement prior to the broadcast itself.

Ch 13 (156·650 MHz): Inter-ship communications relating to safety of navigation; a possible channel for calling a merchant ship if no contact on Ch 16.

Ch 16 (156·80 MHz): Distress, Safety and calling. Ch 16, in parallel with DSC Ch 70, will be monitored by ships, CG rescue centres (and, in some areas, any remaining Coast Radio Stations) for Distress and Safety until further notice. Yachts should monitor Ch 16. After an initial call, stations concerned **must** switch to a working channel, except for Distress and Safety matters.

Ch 67 (156·375 MHz): Small craft safety channel used by all UK CG centres, accessed via Ch 16.

Ch 70 (156·525 MHz): Digital Selective Calling for Distress and Safety purposes under GMDSS.

Ch 80 (157·025 MHz): Primary working channel between yachts and UK marinas.

Ch M (157·85 MHz): Secondary working channel, formerly known as Ch 37. For use in UK territorial waters only.

Ch M2 (161·425 MHz): for race control, with Ch M as stand-by. YCs often use Ch M2. For use in UK waters only

Your position should be given as Lat/Long or the vessel's bearing and distance *from* a charted object, eg 'My position 225° Fastnet Rock 4M' means you are 4M SW of the Fastnet Rock (*not* 4M NE). Use the 360° True bearing notation and the 24-hour clock (0001–2359), specifying UT or LT.

0.7 DISTRESS CALLS

A distress call may only be made with the skipper's authority. The initial call may be made by DSC or voice. A distress call may also be madefor another vessel unable to make its own call. A man overboard usually justifies a distress call.

IMO IAMSAR Manual Vol III is the recognised reference.

0.7.1 MAYDAY call by voice

Brief your crew so they are all able to send a distress message; the MAYDAY message format below should be displayed near the radio. A MAYDAY call by voice should usually be sent on VHF Ch 16 or MF 2182 kHz, but any frequency may be used if help would thus be obtained more quickly. A distress call has priority over all other transmissions. If you hear a MAYDAY call, immediately cease all transmissions that may interfere with the call, listen on the frequency concerned and note down the details.

Before making the call check that the main battery switch and the radio are both ON, and that HIGH POWER (25 watts) and Ch 16 (or 2182 kHz for MF) are selected.

Press and hold the transmit button, and say slowly and distinctly:

- **MAYDAY MAYDAY MAYDAY**
- **THIS IS** ....
  (name of boat, spoken three times)
- **MAYDAY** ....
  (name of boat spoken once)
- **CALLSIGN / MMSI Number** ....
  (Following a DSC alert)
- **MY POSITION IS** ....
  (latitude and longitude, true bearing and distance *from* a known point, or general location)
- **Nature of distress** ....
  (sinking, on fire etc)
- **Help required** ....
  (immediate assistance)
- **Number of persons on board** ....
- **Any other important, helpful information** ....
  (you are taking to the liferaft; distress rockets are being fired etc)
- **OVER**

On completion of the distress message, release the transmit button and listen. The boat's position is of vital importance and should be repeated if time allows. If an acknowledgement is not received, check the set and repeat the distress call.

0.7.2 MAYDAY acknowledgement

In coastal waters an immediate acknowledgement should be expected, as follows:

MAYDAY ....
(name of vessel sending the distress message, spoken three times)

THIS IS ....
(name of station acknowledging, spoken three times)
RECEIVED MAYDAY

If you hear a distress message, write down the details and, if you can help, acknowledge accordingly but only after giving an opportunity for the nearest Coastguard station or more suitable vessel to do so.

0.7.3 MAYDAY relay

If you hear a distress message from a vessel, and it is not acknowledged, you should pass on the message as follows:

MAYDAY RELAY ....
(spoken 3 times)

THIS IS ....
(name of vessel re-transmitting the distress message, said 3 times), followed by the intercepted message.

0.7.4 Control of MAYDAY traffic

A MAYDAY call imposes general radio silence until the vessel concerned or some other authority (eg the nearest Coastguard station) cancels the distress. If necessary the station controlling distress traffic may impose radio silence as follows:

SEELONCE MAYDAY, followed by its name or other identification, on the distress frequency.

If some other station nearby believes it necessary to do likewise, it may transmit:

SEELONCE DISTRESS, followed by its name or other identification.

0.7.5 Cancelling radio silence

When the problem is resolved, the distress call must be cancelled by the coordinating station using the prowords SEELONCE FEENEE as follows:

MAYDAY

ALL STATIONS, ALL STATIONS, ALL STATIONS

THIS IS ....
(name or callsign)

The time ....
The name of the vessel in distress ....
SEELONCE FEENEE

0.7.6 Distress alert by DSC

Depending on the layout and switches fitted to your particular VHF DSC radio, a distress alert is typically sent as follows:

- Briefly press the red, guarded Distress button. The set will automatically switch to Ch 70. Press *again* for 5 seconds to transmit a basic distress alert with position and time. The set then reverts to Ch l6.
- If time permits, select the nature of the distress from the menu (eg Collision, Fire, Flooding) then press the Distress button for 5 seconds to send a full distress alert.

A CG/CRS should automatically send a distress acknowledgement on Ch 70 before replying on Ch 16. Ships in range should reply directly on Ch 16. If a distress acknowledgement is not received from a CG/CRS, the distress alert will automatically be repeated by the radio every four minutes.

When a DSC distress acknowledgement has been received, or after about 15 seconds, the vessel in distress should transmit a MAYDAY message by voice on Ch 16. This should include the **MMSI / callsign** after the vessel's name to correlate with the digital message.

0.7.7 False alerts

If a distress alert is inadvertently transmitted, an All Stations voice message on VHF Ch 16 cancelling the false alert must be sent at once. The message should include the name of the vessel, MMSI number, position, and the words 'Cancel my Distress Alert of (date/time (GMT/UT)'.

0.8 URGENCY AND SAFETY CALLS

Urgency signal - PAN PAN

The radio Urgency prefix, consisting of the words PAN PAN spoken three times, indicates that a vessel, or station, has ***a very urgent message concerning the safety of a ship or person***. It may be used when urgent medical advice is needed.

This is an example of an Urgency call:

> **PAN PAN, PAN PAN, PAN PAN**
>
> **ALL STATIONS, ALL STATIONS, ALL STATIONS**
>
> **THIS IS YACHT SEABIRD, SEABIRD, SEABIRD**
>
> Zero eight five degrees Ballagan Point one point five miles
>
> Dismasted and propeller fouled
>
> Drifting north west towards Limestone Rocks
>
> Require urgent tow
>
> **OVER**

PAN PAN messages take priority over all traffic except Distress, and are sent on Ch 16 or 2182 kHz. They should be cancelled when the urgency is over.

If the message is long (eg a medical call) or communications traffic is heavy, it may be passed on a working frequency after an initial call on Ch 16 or 2182 kHz. At the end of the initial call you should indicate that you are switching to a working frequency.

If you hear an Urgency call react in the same way as for a Distress call.

0.8.1 Safety signal - SÉCURITÉ

The word SÉCURITÉ (pronounced SAY-CURE-E-TAY) spoken three times, indicates that the station is about to transmit an important navigational or meteorological warning. Such messages usually originate from a CG Centre or a Coast Radio Station, and are transmitted on a working channel after an announcement on the distress/calling channel (Ch 16 or 2182 kHz).

Safety messages are usually addressed to 'All stations', and are often transmitted at the end of the first available silence period. An example of a Sécurité message is:

> **SÉCURITÉ, SÉCURITÉ, SÉCURITÉ** ....
>
> **THIS IS** ....
>
> (CG Centre or Coast Radio Station callsign, spoken three times)
>
> **ALL STATIONS** ....
>
> (spoken three times) followed by instructions to change channel, then the message.

0.9 GMDSS

The Global Maritime Distress and Safety System (GMDSS) came into force in 1999. Most seagoing vessels over 300 tons are required by SOLAS to comply with GMDSS, but it is not compulsory for yachts. However, it is important that the principles of the system are understood, and you should at least consider fitting compliant equipment depending on your cruising area. Full details may be found in ALRS Vol 5 (NP 285).

0.9.1 Purpose

GMDSS enables a coordinated SAR operation to be mounted rapidly and reliably anywhere at sea. To this end, terrestrial and satellite communications and navigation equipment is used to alert SAR authorities ashore and ships in the vicinity to a Distress incident or Urgency situation. GMDSS also promulgates MSI (Maritime Safety Information).

0.9.2 Sea areas

The type of equipment carried by a vessel depends of her operating area. The four GMDSS Areas are:

A1 An area within R/T coverage of at least one VHF Coastguard or Coast radio station in which continuous VHF alerting is available via DSC. Range: 20–50M from the CG/CRS.

A2 An area, excluding sea area A1, within R/T coverage of at least one MF CG/CRS in which continuous DSC alerting is available. Range: approx 50–250M from the CG/CRS.

A3 An area between 76°N and 76°S, excluding sea areas A1 and A2, within coverage of HF or an Inmarsat satellite in which continuous alerting is available.

A4 An area outside sea areas A1, A2 and A3, ie the polar regions, within coverage of HF.

In each Area, in addition to a Navtex receiver, certain types of radio equipment must be carried by GMDSS vessels: In A1, VHF DSC; A2, VHF and MF DSC; A3, VHF, MF and HF or SatCom; A4, VHF, MF and HF.

0.9.3 Digital Selective Calling (DSC)

GMDSS comprises 'sub-systems' which are coordinated through Maritime Rescue Coordination Centres (MRCC) to ensure safety at sea. DSC is one of the 'sub-systems' of GMDSS. It uses terrestial communications for making initial contact and, in a distress situation, provides the vessel's identity, nature of distress and position (entered manually or automatically if linked with the GPS). In all DSC messages every vessel and relevant shore station has a 9-digit Maritime Mobile Service Identity (MMSI) which is in effect an automatic electronic callsign. Dedicated frequencies are: VHF Ch 70, MF 2187·5 kHz. A thorough working knowledge of the following procedure is needed.

0.10 HM COASTGUARD - CONTACT DETAILS OF CG CENTRES

† MILFORD HAVEN COASTGUARD (MRCC)
51°42'N 05°03'W. MMSI 002320017
Gorsewood Drive, Hakin, Milford Haven, SA73 2HD.
☎ 01646 690909. 📠 01646 692176.
Area: Friog to Marsland Mouth (near Bude).

† HOLYHEAD COASTGUARD (MRCC)
53°19'N 04°38'W. MMSI 002320018
Prince of Wales Rd, Holyhead, Anglesey LL65 1ET.
☎ 01407 762051. 📠 01407 764373.
Area: Mull of Galloway to Friog (1·6M S of Barmouth).

†* BELFAST COASTGUARD (MRCC)
54°40'N 05°40'W. MMSI 002320021
Bregenz House, Quay St, Bangor, Co Down BT20 5ED.
☎ 02891 463933. 📠 02891 469886.
Area: L Foyle to Carlingford inc Firth of Clyde and islands.

†* STORNOWAY COASTGUARD (MRCC)
58°12'N 06°22'W. MMSI 002320024
Battery Point, Stornoway, Isle of Lewis H51 2RT.
☎ 01851 702013. 📠 01851 704387.
Area: Cape Wrath to Mull, Western Isles and St Kilda.

†Monitors DSC MF 2187.5 kHz. *Broadcasts Gunfacts/Subfacts.

0.11 NATIONAL COASTWATCH INSTITUTION

The National Coastwatch Institution (NCI) – www.nci.org.uk a national charity, is a voluntary organisation keeping visual watch along the coast of England and Wales, assisting the preservation and protection of life at sea and along the shore. The National Office is 17 Dean St, Liskeard, Cornwall, PL14 4AB ☎(01579) 347392. There were 58 operational stations (2023) manned by over 2600 volunteers. They are marked on the Area maps by the symbol © and maintain direct contact with HM CG, which also certify NCI stations and watchkeepers. Stations monitor VHF Ch **65** 16, HM CG channels and local operational VHF channels. **65** is the NCI dedicated channel.

Seafarers can call directly for radio checks, AIS checks, actual weather, sea state, current hazards and local information. Call sign: name of selected station, (see full list at: www.nci.org.uk) plus abbreviation NCI, e.g: *Froward Point NCI.* Do **not** call on Ch 16 or use call sign *National Coastwatch*.

0.12 THE SEA SAFETY GROUP

The Sea Safety Group – www.seasafetygroup.org – a charity, is an association of independent coastal watch stations, each authorised by HM CG (MCA) to provide additional lookout and communications cover around the UK. They are similar in ethos but separate from the NCI.

0.13 REPUBLIC OF IRELAND (COAST GUARD)

The Irish Coast Guard co-ordinates SAR operations around the coast of Eire via Dublin MRCC, Malin Head and Valentia MRSCs and remote sites.

It may liaise with the UK and France during any rescue operation within 100M of the Irish coast. It is part of the Dept of Marine, Leeson Lane, Dublin 2. ☎ (01) 6783454; 📠 (01) 6783459. The Irish EPIRB Registry is at the same address; ☎ (01) 6199280; 📠 (01) 6621571.

The MRCC/MRSCs are co-located with the Coast radio stations of the same name and manned by the same staff.

All stations keep watch H24 on VHF Ch 16 and DSC Ch 70. If ashore dial 999 or 112 in an emergency and ask for Marine Rescue. Details of the MRCC/MRSCs are as follows:

DUBLIN (MRCC)
53°20'N 06°15W. DSC MMSI 002500300 (+2187·5 kHz).
☎ +353 1 662 0922/3; 📠 +353 1 662 0795.
Area: Carlingford Lough to Youghal.

VALENTIA (MRSC)
51°56'N 10°21'W.DSC MMSI 002500200 (+2187·5 kHz).
☎ +353 669 476 109; 📠 +353 669 476 289.
Area: Youghal to Slyne Head.

MALIN HEAD (MRSC)
55°22'N 07°20W. DSC MMSI 002500100 (+2187·5 kHz).
☎ +353 74 9370103; 📠 +353 74 9370221.
Area: Slyne Head to Lough Foyle.

0.13.1 SAR resources

The Irish Coast Guard provides some 50 units around the coast and is on call H24. The RNLI maintains four stations around the coast and operates 42 lifeboats. Additionally, six community-run inshore rescue boats are available.

Sikorsky S-61 helicopters, based at Dublin, Waterford, Shannon and Sligo, can respond within 15 to 45 minutes and operate to a radius of 200M. They are equipped with infrared search equipment and can uplift 30 survivors.

Military and civilian aircraft and vessels, together with the Garda (police) and lighthouse service, can also be called upon.

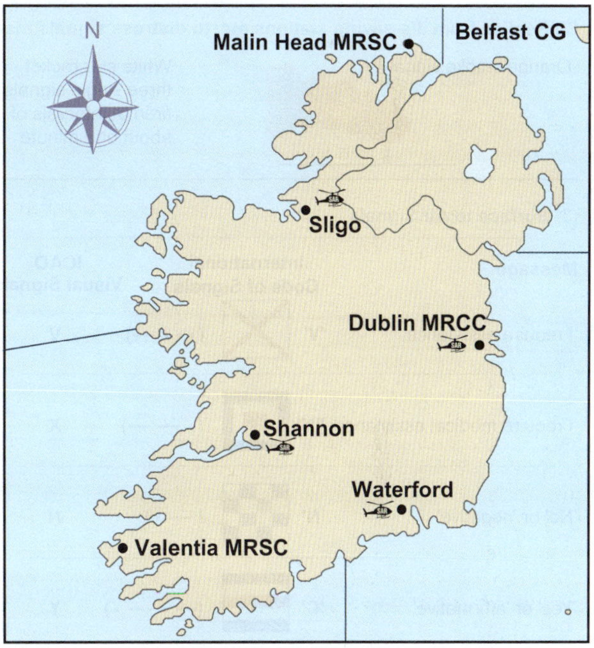

Fig 0(1) Irish CG centres and boundaries

Some stations provide specialist cliff climbing services. They are manned by volunteers, who are trained in first aid and equipped with inflatables, breeches buoys, cliff ladders etc. Their ☎ numbers (the Leader's residence) are given, where appropriate, under each port.

Fig 0(2) Distress and life saving signals

(1) Signals to be used by Ships, Aircraft or Persons in Distress

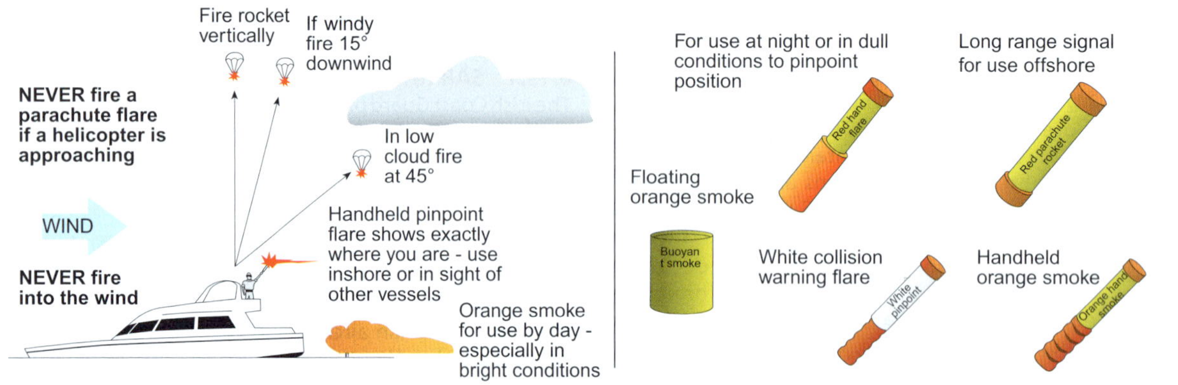

(2) Replies from life-saving stations etc. to distress signals made by ships or persons

Orange smoke signal

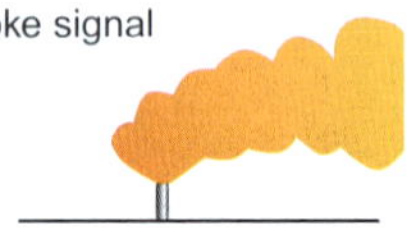

White star rocket - three single signals fired at intervals of about one minute

Meaning
'You are seen - assistance will be given as soon as possible'

(3) Surface to Air Signals

Message	**International Code of Signals**			**ICAO Visual Signals**
'I require assistance'	**'V'**		(• • • —)	**V**
'I require medical assistance'	**'W'**		(• — —)	**X**
'No' or 'negative'	**'N'**		(— •)	**N**
'Yes' or 'affirmative'	**'C'**		(— • — •)	**Y**
'Proceed in this direction'				↑

(4) Air to Surface replies

'Message understood'

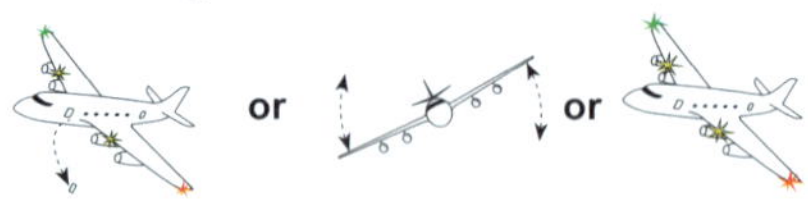

Drop a message **or** Rocking wings **or** Flash landing or navigation lights twice **or 'T'** (—) **or 'R'** (• — •) Morse code signal by light

'Message not understood - repeat'

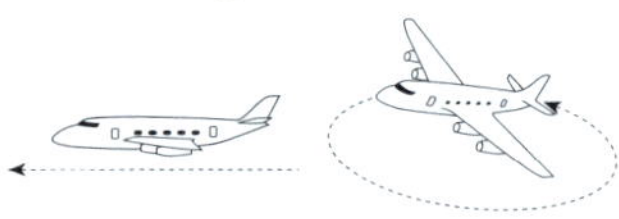

Straight and level flight

Circling

or 'RPT' (• — • • — — • —) Morse code signal by light

(5) Air to Surface Direction Signals

Sequence of 3 manœuvres meaning proceed in this direction

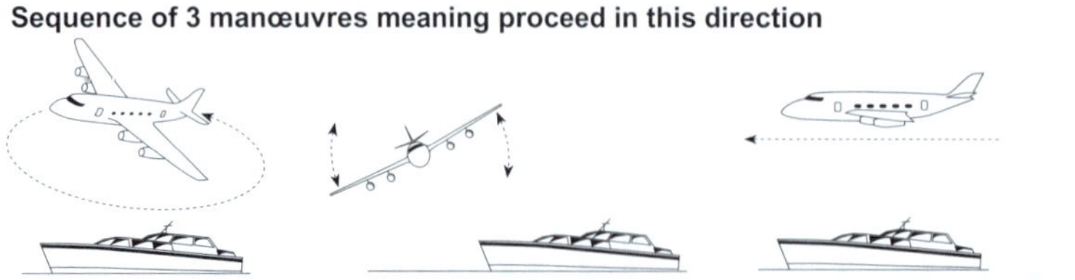

(1) Circle Vessel at least once

(2) Cross low ahead of vessel, rocking wings

(3) Overfly vessel and head in required direction

Your assistance is no longer required

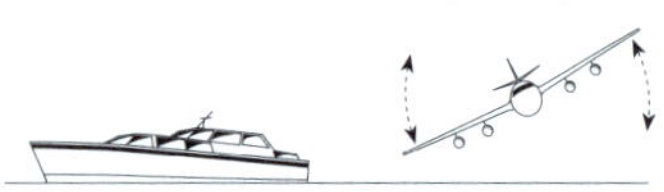

Cross low astern of vessel rocking wings

Note: as an alternative to rocking wings, the aircraft engine pitch or volume may be varied

(6) Surface to Air replies

'Message understood - I will comply'

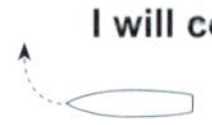

Change course or direction

or

'T' (—) Morse Code signal by light

or

Code and answering pennant 'Close up'

'I am unable to comply'

'N' (— •) Morse Code signal by light

or

International flag 'N'

0.14 NAVTEX

NAVTEX is the prime method of disseminating MSI to at least 200 miles offshore. A dedicated aerial and receiver with an LCD screen (or integrated printer) are required. The user selects which stations and message categories are recorded for automatic display or printing.

Two frequencies are used. On the international frequency, 518kHz, messages are always available in English with excellent coverage of Europe. Interference between stations is minimised by scheduling time slots and and by limiting transmission power. NAVTEX information applies only to the geographical area for which each station is responsible.

On the national frequency 490kHz (for clarity shown in red throughout this section) the UK/ROI issues inshore waters forecasts and coastal station actuals. Elsewhere it is used mainly for transmissions in the national language. 490khz stations have different identification letters from 518kHz. NAVTEX is particularly useful when preoccupied handling your vessel as you will not miss potentially important information.

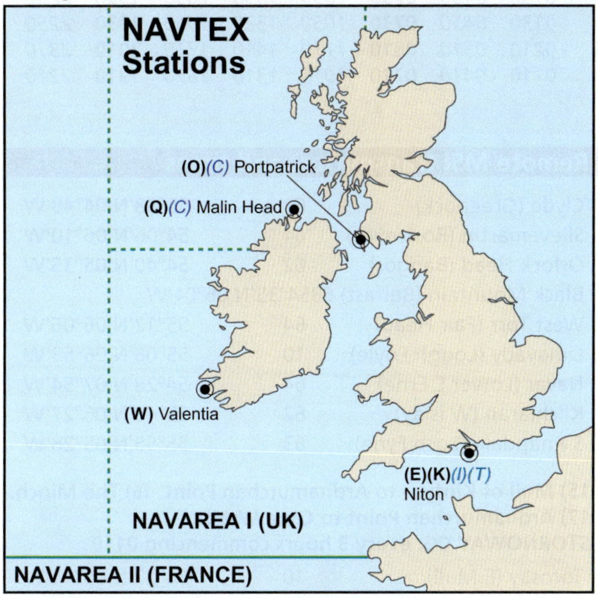

Fig 0(3) NAVTEX stations/areas – UK & Ireland

0.14.1 Message numbering

Each message is prefixed by a four-character group:

The first character is the code letter of the transmitting station (eg **E** for Niton).

The 2nd character is the message category, see 0.12.2.

The third and fourth are message serial numbers, running from 01 to 99 and then re-starting at 01.

The serial number 00 denotes urgent messages which are always printed.

Messages which are corrupt or have already been printed are rejected. Weather messages are dated and timed. All NAVTEX messages end with NNNN.

0.14.2 Message categories

A*	Navigational warnings
B*	Meteorological warnings
C	Ice reports
D*	SAR info and Piracy attack warnings
E	Weather forecasts
F	Pilot service
G	AIS
H	LORAN
I	Spare
J	SATNAV
K	Other electronic Navaids
L	Navwarnings additional to **A**
M-U	Spare
V-Y	Special services – as allocated
Z	No messages on hand

* These categories cannot be rejected by the receiver.

0.14.3 UK/ROI 518 kHz stations

Weather message times (UT) are in bold. Extended outlook times (2-3 days beyond the shipping forecast period) are in italics.

O	–	**Portpatrick** Lundy clockwise to SE Iceland.	**0220**	**0620**	**1020**	**1420**	**1820**	**2220**
Q	–	**Malin Head** sea areas Shannon, Rockall, Malin & Bailey,		**0640**			**1840**	
E	–	**Niton** Thames clockwise to Fastnet, excluding Trafalgar.	*0040*	0440	**0840**	1240	1640	**2040**

0.14.4 UK/ROI 490 kHz stations

These provide forecasts for UK inshore waters (to 12M offshore), a national 3 day outlook for inshore waters and, at times in bold, reports of actual weather at the places listed below. To receive these reports select message category 'V' (0.12.2) on your NAVTEX receiver. Times (UT) of transmissions are listed in chronological order.

Actual Met data includes: Sea level pressure (mb), wind direction and speed (kn), weather, visibility (M), air and sea temperatures (°C), dewpoint temperature (°C) and mean wave height (m).

C	–	**Portpatrick** Land's End to Shetland	**0020**	**0420**	0820	**1220**	**1620**	2020

North Rona, Stornoway, South Uist, Lusa (Skye bridge), Tiree, Macrihanish, Belfast, Malin Head, Belmullet, St Bees Head, Ronaldsway, Crosby (Liverpool), Valley, Aberporth, Roches Point, Valentia, St Mawgan.

0.14.5 NAVTEX broadcast times in Ireland

Times of weather messages are shown in **bold**. Gale warnings are usually transmitted 4 hourly.

METAREA I (Co-ordinator – UK)			**Transmission times (UT)**					
Q	–	**Malin Head,** Ireland	0240	**0640**	**1040**	1440	**1840**	**2240**
W	–	**Valentia,** Ireland	0340	**0740**	**1140**	1540	**1940**	**2340**

0.15 MSI BROADCASTS BY HM COASTGUARD

MRCC routinely broadcast Maritime Safety Information (MSI) every 3 hours from the start times in the Table below, but these can sometimes vary during busy operational times and emergencies. The VHF broadcast channel, either 10, 62, 63 or 64 is announced first on Ch 16. Each broadcast contains one of 3 different Groups of MSI:

Group A, the full broadcast, contains the Shipping forecast, a new Inshore waters forecast and 24 hrs outlook, Gale warnings, a Fisherman's 3 day forecast* (1 Oct-31 Mar), Navigational (WZ) warnings and Subfacts & Gunfacts ‡ where appropriate. Times of '**A**' broadcasts are in bold.

Group B contains a new Inshore waters forecast, plus the previous outlook, and Gale warnings. '**B**' broadcast times are in plain type.

Group C is a repeat of the Inshore forecast and Gale warnings (as per the previous Group A or B) plus new Strong wind warnings. '**C**' broadcast times are italicised.

Broadcasts of shipping and inshore waters forecasts by HM Coastguard

Coastguard	Shipping forecast areas	Inshore areas	Broadcast times LT							
			B	C	A	C	B	C	A	C
Milford Haven	Lundy, Fastnet, Irish Sea, Shannon	9, 10	0150	*0450*	**0750**	*1050*	1350	*1650*	**1950**	*2250*
Holyhead	Irish Sea	10,11,12	0130	*0450*	**0730**	*1050*	1330	*1650*	**1930**	*2250*
Belfast‡	Irish Sea, Rockall Malin	13, 14,15	0210	*0510*	**0810**	*1110*	1410	*1710*	**2010**	*2310*
Stornoway‡*	Rockall, Malin, Hebrides, Bailey, Fair Is, Faeroes, SE Iceland	15,16,17	0110	*0410*	**0710**	*1010*	1310	*1610*	**1910**	*2210*

Inshore waters forecast areas - Remote MSI transmitters and times

9) Land's End to St David's Head, inc the Bristol Channel. MILFORD HAVEN CG, every 3 hours commencing 0150

Hartland Point	64	51°01'N 04°31'W
Combe Martin (N Devon)	63	51°12'N 04°03'W
Severn Bridges	64	51°12'N 04°03'W
St Hilary (Barry)	63	51°27'N 03°25'W
Mumbles (Swansea)	64	51°42'N 04°41'W
Tenby	62	51°41'N 05°10'W
St Ann's Head	62	51°40'N 05°11'W
Dinas Hd (Fishguard)	64	52°00'N 04°54'W
Blaenplwyf (Aberystwyth)	62	52°22'N 04°06'W

10) St David's Head to Great Orme Head inc St George's Channel. HOLYHEAD CG (A) every 3 hours commencing 0150

South Stack (Holyhead)	63	53°19'N 04°41'W
Great Orme Head	64	53°20'N 03°51'W

11) Great Orme Head to Mull of Galloway. 12) Isle of Man. HOLYHEAD CG (B) every 3 hours commencing, 0130

Moel-y-Parc (NE Wales)	63	53°13'N 04°28'W
Langthwaite (Lancaster)	62	54°02'N 02°46'W
Caldbeck (Carlisle)	63	54°46'N 03°07'W
Snaefell (Isle of Man)	64	54°16'N 04°28'W

13) Lough Foyle to Carlingford Lough. 14) Mull of Galloway to Mull of Kintyre inc the Firth of Clyde and North Channel. BELFAST CG, every 3 hours commencing 0210

Rhu Staffnish (Kintyre)	10	55°22'N 05°32'W
Lawhill (Ardrossan)	64	55°42'N 04°50'W
Clyde (Greenock)	62	55°58'N 04°48'W
Slievemartin (Rostrevor)	64	54°06'N 06°10'W
Orlock Head (Bangor)	62	54°40'N 05°35'W
Black Mountain (Belfast)	63	54°35'N 06°01'W
West Torr (Fair Head)	64	55°12'N 06°06'W
Limavady (Lough Foyle)	10	55°06'N 06°53'W
Navar (Lower L Erne)	64	54°28'N 07°54'W
Kilchiaran (W Islay)	62	55°46'N 06°27'W
S Knapdale (Loch Fyne)	63	55°55'N 05°28'W

15) Mull of Kintyre to Ardnamurchan Point. 16) The Minch. 17) Ardnamurchan Point to Cape Wrath. STORNOWAY CG, every 3 hours commencing 0110

Torosay (E Mull)	10	56°27'N 05°43'W
Glengorm (N Mull)	62	56°38'N 06°08'W
Tiree (*MF 1883kHz*)	63	56°31'N 06°57'W
Arisaig (S of Mallaig)	64	56°55'N 06°50'W
Drumfearn (SE Skye)	63	57°12'N 05°48'W
Skriag (Portree, Skye)	10	57°23'N 06°15'W
Rodel (S Harris)	62	57°45'N 06°57'W
Melvaig (Loch Ewe)	64	57°50'N 05°47'W
Portnaguran (Stornoway)	63	58°15'N 06°10'W
Barra	10	57°01'N 07°30'W
Clettreval (N Uist)	63	57°37'N 07°26'W
Forsnaval (W Lewis)	62	58°13'N 07°00'W
Butt of Lewis (*MF 1743kHz*)	10	58°28'N 06°14'W

NOTE: Information on this page remains subject to potential change. Users are advised to check the MCGA Maritime Safety Information leaflet (MCA/064) available at www.mcga.gov.uk, and the monthly pdf updates from January to June free to Almanac subscribers and available for download at www.reedsnauticalalmanac.co.uk/update

0.16 OTHER UK WEATHER BROADCASTS

BBC Radio 4 Shipping forecast

BBC Radio 4 broadcasts shipping forecasts at:

0048, 0520 LT[1]		LW, FM
1201 LT	weekdays only	LW FM
1754 LT		LW only
0048, 0520, 1754 LT	Sat/ Sun	LW FM

[1]Includes weather reports from coastal stations

Frequencies

LW		198 kHz
FM	**England:**	92·4–94·6 MHz
	Scotland:	91·3–96·1 MHz 103·5–104·9 MHz
	Wales:	92·8–96·1 MHz & 103·5–104·9 MHz
	N Ireland	93·2–96·0 MHz 103·5–104·6 MHz

The Shipping Forecast contains:

Time of issue; summary of gale warnings in force at that time; a general synopsis of weather systems and their expected development and movement over the next 24 hours; sea area forecasts for the same 24 hours, including wind direction/ force, weather and visibility in each; and an outlook for the following 24 hours.

Gale warnings for all affected areas are broadcast at the earliest break in Radio 4 programmes after receipt, as well as after the next news bulletin.

Weather reports from coastal stations follow the 0048 and 0520 shipping forecasts. They include wind direction and force, present weather, visibility, and sealevel pressure and tendency, if available. The stations are shown in Fig 0(5).

0.16.1 BBC Radio 4 Inshore waters forecast

A forecast for UK inshore waters (up to 12M offshore), valid for 24 hrs, is broadcast after the 0048 and 0520 coastal station reports. It includes forecasts of wind direction and force, weather, visibility and sea state.

Reports of actual weather are broadcast from all the stations below after the 0048 inshore waters forecast and also after the 0520 forecast, except those in italics: Scilly*, Valentia, *Milford Haven, Aberporth, Valley, Liverpool(Crosby),* Ronaldsway, Malin Head; *Machrihanish*;* Stornoway. An asterix* denotes an automatic station.

0.16.2 Terms used in weather bulletins

Speed of movement of pressure systems

Slowly	< 15 knots
Steadily	15–25 knots
Rather quickly	25–35 knots
Rapidly	35–45 knots
Very rapidly	> 45 knots

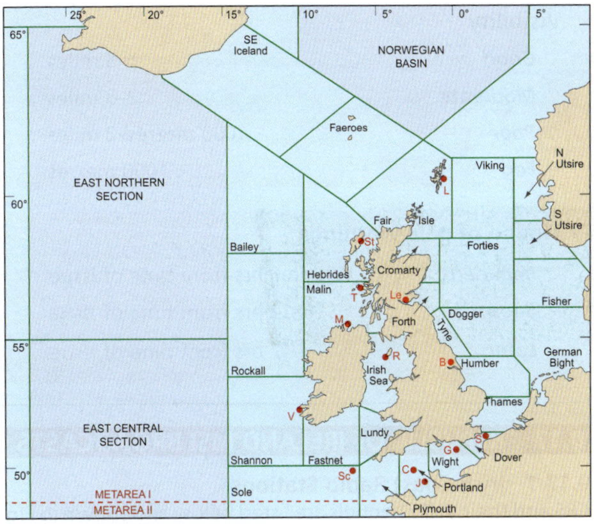

Fig 0(4) UK – Forecast areas

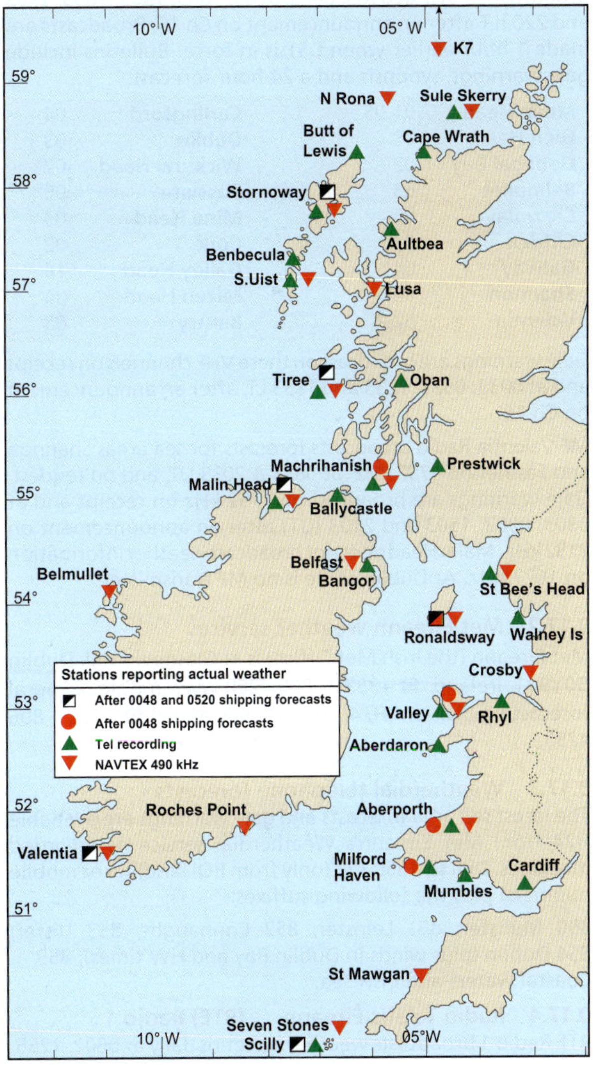

Fig 0(5) Stations reporting actual weather via BBC Radio 4, telephone recordings or NAVTEX

Visibility

Good	> 5 miles
Moderate	2–5 miles
Poor	1000 metres–2 miles
Fog	< 1000 metres

Timing of gale warnings

Imminent:	Within 6 hrs from time of issue
Soon:	6–12 hrs from time of issue
Later:	> 12 hrs from time of issue

Barometric pressure changes (tendency)

Rising or falling slowly: Pressure change of 0·1 to 1·5 hPa/mb in the preceding 3 hours.

Rising or falling: Pressure change of 1·6 to 3·5 hPa/mb in the preceding 3 hours.

Rising or falling quickly: Pressure change of 3·6 to 6 hPa/mb in the preceding 3 hours.

Rising or falling very rapidly: Pressure change of more than 6 hPa/mb in the preceding 3 hours.

Now rising (or falling): Pressure has been falling (rising) or steady in the preceding 3 hours, but at the observation time was definitely rising (falling).

0.17 REPUBLIC OF IRELAND MSI BROADCASTS

0.17.1 Irish Coast Radio Stations

CRS and their VHF channels are listed below and shown in Fig 0(7). See also: www.malinheadcoastguardradio.com/index.htm. Weather bulletins for 30M offshore and the Irish Sea are broadcast on VHF at 0103, 0403, 0703, 1003, 1303, 1603, 1903 and 2203LT after an announcement on Ch 16. Broadcasts are made 1 hour earlier when DST is in force. Bulletins include gale warnings, synopsis and a 24-hour forecast.

Malin Head	01,05	**Carlingford**	04
Glen Head	03	**Dublin**	03
Donegal Bay	02	**Wicklow Head**	02
Belmullet	63	**Rosslare**	05
Clew Bay	05	**Mine Head**	03
Clifden	03	**Cork**	02
Galway	04	**Galley Head**	16
Shannon	64	**Mizen Head**	04
Valentia	62	**Bantry**	05

Gale warnings are broadcast on these VHF channels on receipt and at 0033, 0633, 1233 and 1833 LT, after an announcement on Ch 16.

MF Valentia Radio broadcasts forecasts for sea areas Shannon and Fastnet on 1752 kHz at 0833 & 2033 UT, and on request. Gale warnings are broadcast on 1752 kHz on receipt and at 0303, 0903, 1503 and 2103 (UT) after an announcement on 2182 kHz. Malin Head does not broadcast weather information on 1677 kHz. At Dublin there is no MF transmitter.

0.17.2 Met Éireann weather services

Met Éireann (the Irish Met Office) is at Glasnevin Hill, Dublin D0Y921, Ireland. ☎ +353 1 806 4200 www.met.ie. General forecasting division (H24, charges may apply) ☎ +353 1 806 4255.

0.17.3 Weatherdial telephone forecasts

The latest sea area forecasts and gale warnings are available H24 from Met Éireann's Weatherdial service as recorded messages. Dial ☎ 1550 123 (only from ROI landline or mobile numbers) plus the following suffixes:

850 Munster; 851 Leinster; 852 Connaught; 853 Ulster; 854 Dublin (plus winds in Dublin Bay and HW times); 855 Coastal waters and Irish Sea.

0.17.4 Radio Telefís Éireann (RTE) Radio 1

RTE Radio 1 broadcasts weather bulletins daily at 0602, 1255, 1657 & 2355LT (1hr earlier when DST is in force) on 525kHz LW Summerhill, (15M west of Dublin airport) and FM (88·2–95·2MHz). Situation forecast and coastal reports for Irish Sea and coastal waters. The forecast includes: wind, weather, vis, swell (if higher than 4m) and a 24 hrs outlook.

Gale warnings are included in hourly news bulletins on FM & MF.

Coastal reports include wind, weather, visibility, pressure, with pressure change over the last 3 hrs described as:

Steady	=	0–0·4 hPa/mb change
Rising/falling slowly	=	0·5–1·9
Rising/falling	=	2·0–3·4
Rising/falling rapidly	=	3·5–5·9
Rising/falling very rapidly	=	> 6·0

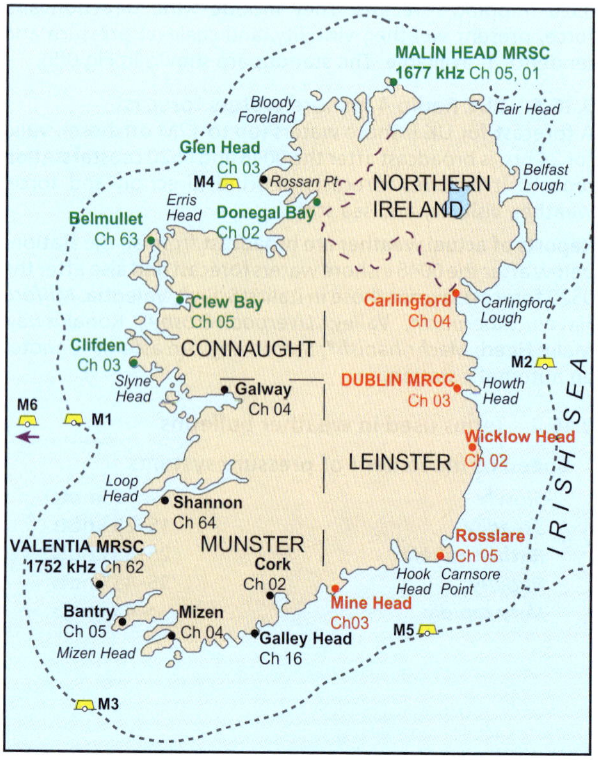

Fig 0(6) shows CRS, Met buoys M1–M6, PROVINCES and headlands named in forecasts

0.18 AUTOMATIC IDENTIFICATION SYSTEM (AIS)

Automatic Identification System (AIS) allows information to be provided to other ships and shore authorities; it is required by SOLAS to be fitted to most vessels over 300 GRT. AIS is widely used to automatically and continuously identify, track and display other vessels and their movements.

Each ship's course and speed vector is shown by a symbol on an AIS screen or overlaid on radar, chart plotter or PC. This data may also appear in a text box as heading, COG & SOG, range, CPA, position, ship's name, and her status – under power or sail, anchored, constrained by draught, restricted in her ability to manoeuvre, not under command, fishing etc.

Many lights, buoys and other aids to navigation (AtoN) are now fitted with AIS, and the number is growing rapidly. On Admiralty charts, these are shown by a magenta circle and the notation 'AIS'. Not all transmitted information is available to all users; it depends on the display system fitted.

AIS Class B transmitters/transceivers for non-SOLAS vessels are available, but are not mandatory. Later sets can receive aids to navigation (A2N) data, showing virtual marks and MMSI numbers from buoys and lighthouses.

Caveats: Many vessels are not fitted with AIS, and some may not have it switched on; some only display 3 lines of text, not a plot; in busy areas only the strongest signals may be shown; AIS may distract a bridge watchkeeper from his visual and radar watch; unlike eyes and radar, AIS does not yet feature in the Colregs; GPS/electronic failures invalidate AIS.

In areas of traffic concentration Class B transmitters may be excluded from the network if no time slots are available.

It is not a radar despite what some advertisements may imply.

0.19 TIDE TABLES / COMPUTER PREDICTIONS

The Almanac uses UKHO Standard Port tide prediction curves prepared for Admiralty Tide Tables. Standard Port predictions are replacing some established Secondary Ports in ATT to better support offshore activity. The Almanac continues to replicate the existing differences to provide the data in a compact format for planning. These are in italics where alternative information is available at reedstides.co.uk. The printed tidal curve is drawn to a mean Spring curve and, in dashed line, a mean Neap curve, with boxes for associated times of HW and LW. The curve does not take account of the differing arguments (geometrical positions) of the sun, moon and planets on a daily basis. Nor does it take account of differences which owe to the differing volume passing constrictions or obstructions.

The printed tables give condensed planning information. This is refinable from computer generated predictions, such as Easytide, which are accessible on-line and easy to use.

0.19.1 Clearances Below Overhead Objects

A diagram often helps when calculating vertical clearance below bridges, power cables etc. Fig 0(7) shows the relationship to CD. The height of such objects as shown on the chart is usually measured above HAT, so the actual clearance will almost always be more. The height of HAT above CD is given at the foot of each page of the tide tables. Most Admiralty charts now show clearances above HAT, but check the **Heights** block below the chart title.

To calculate clearances, insert the dimensions into the following formula, carefully observing the conventions for brackets:

> Masthead clearance = (Height of object above HAT + height of HAT above CD) minus (height of tide at the time + height of the masthead above waterline)

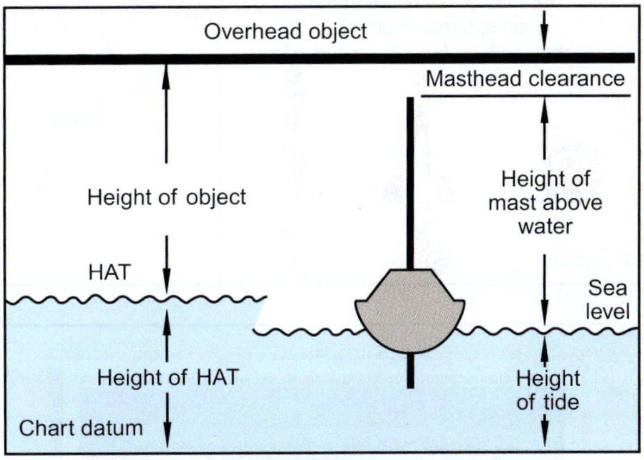

Fig 0(7) Calculating masthead clearance

0.20 IALA BUOYAGE

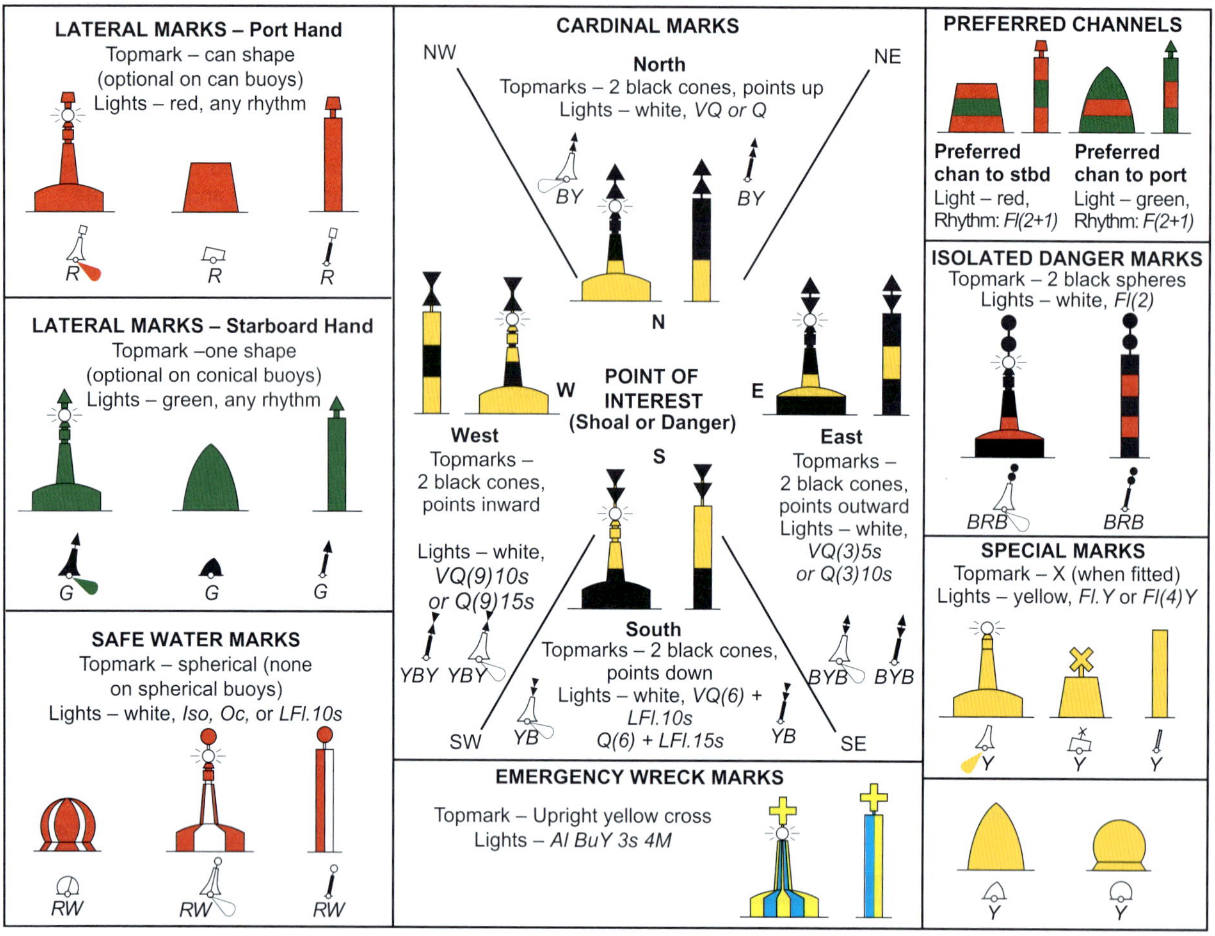

0.21 FLAGS AND ENSIGNS

UK WHITE ENSIGN

UK BLUE ENSIGN

UK RED ENSIGN

AUSTRALIA

AUSTRIA

BASQUE FLAG

BELGIUM

CANADA

CYPRUS

DENMARK

FINLAND

FRANCE

GERMANY

GREECE

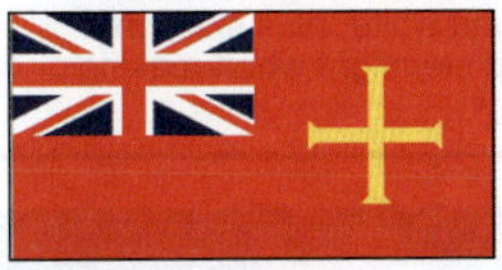
GUERNSEY

JERSEY

IRELAND

ISRAEL

ITALY

LIBERIA

MALTA

MONACO

MOROCCO

NETHERLANDS

NEW ZEALAND

NORWAY

PANAMA

POLAND

PORTUGAL

SOUTH AFRICA

SPAIN

SWEDEN

SWITZERLAND

TUNISIA

TURKEY

USA

0.22 LIGHTS AND SHAPES

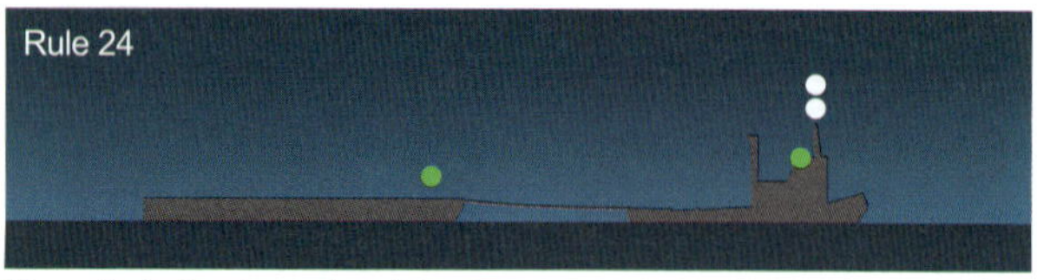

Vessels being towed and towing

Vessel towed shows sidelights (forward) and sternlight

Tug shows two masthead lights, sidelights, sternlight, white towing light

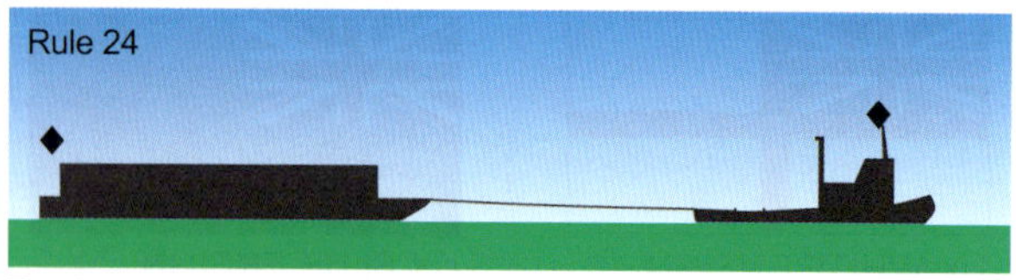

Towing by day — Length of tow more than 200m

Towing vessel and tow display diamond shapes. By night, the towing vessel shows three masthead lights instead of two as for shorter tows

Motor sailing

Cone point down, forward. At night the lights of a power-driven vessel underway

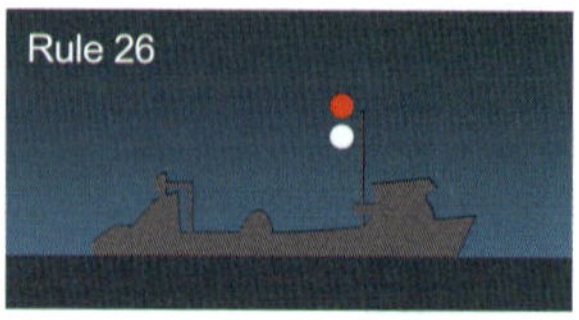

Vessel fishing

All-round red light over all-round white, plus sidelights and sternlight when making way

Fishing/Trawling

A shape consisting of two cones point to point in a vertical line one above the other

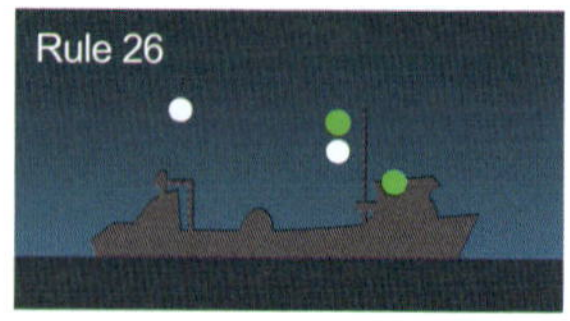

Vessel trawling

All-round green light over all-round white, plus sidelights and sternlight when making way

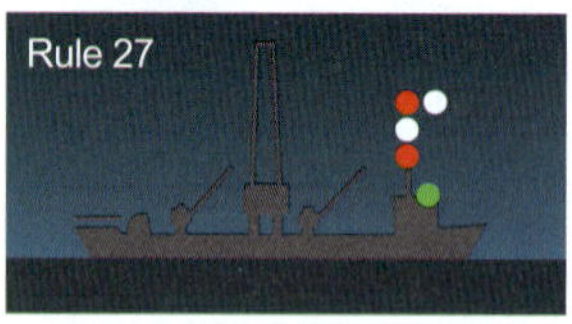

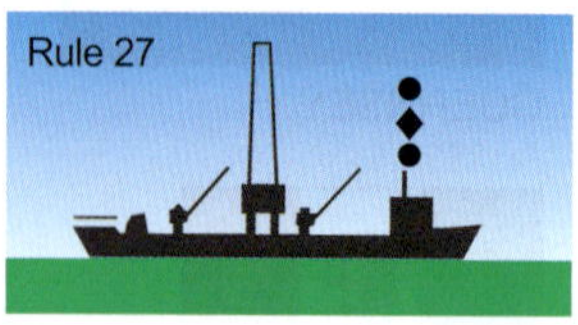

Vessel restricted in her ability to manoeuvre

All-round red, white, red lights vertically, plus normal steaming lights when making way

Three shapes in a vertical line: ball, diamond, ball

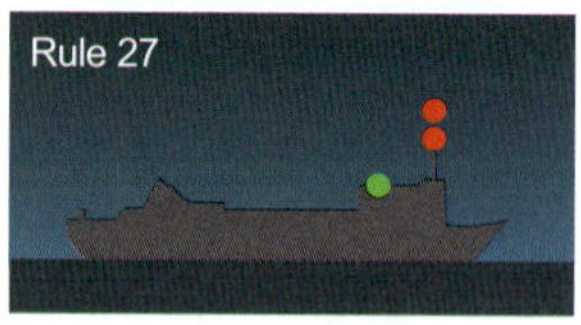

Not under command

Two all-round red lights, plus sidelights and sternlight when making way

Two balls vertically

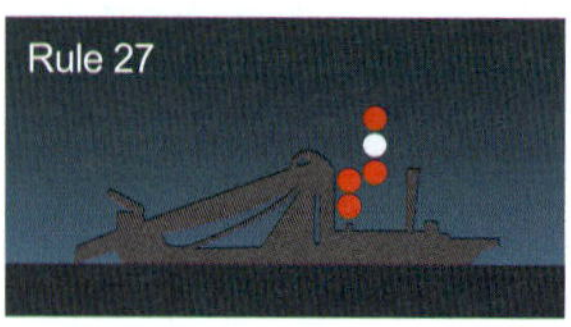

Dredger

All round red, white, red lights vertically, plus two all-round red lights (or two balls) on foul side, and two all-round green (or two diamonds) on clear side

Divers down

Letter 'A' International Code

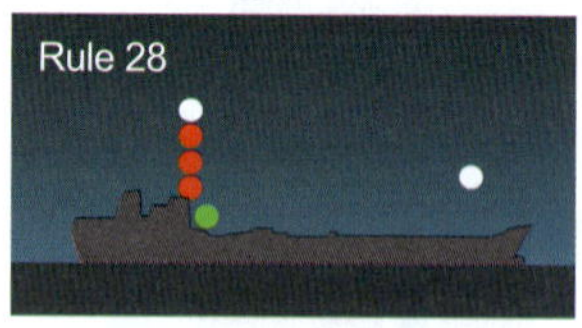

Constrained by draught

Three all-round red lights in a vertical line, plus normal steaming lights. By day — a cylinder

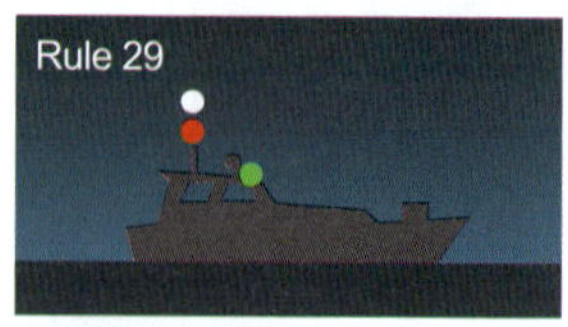

Pilot boat

All-round white light over all-round red, plus sidelights and sternlight when underway, or anchor light

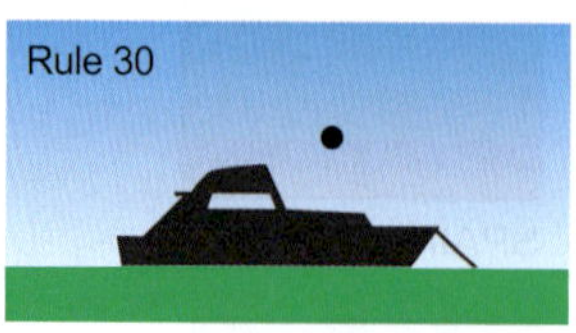

Vessel at anchor

All-round white light; if over 50m, a second light aft and lower

Ball forward

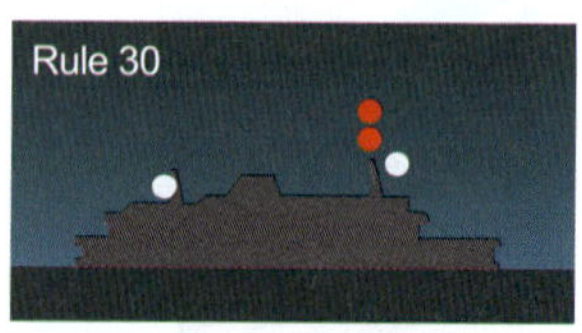

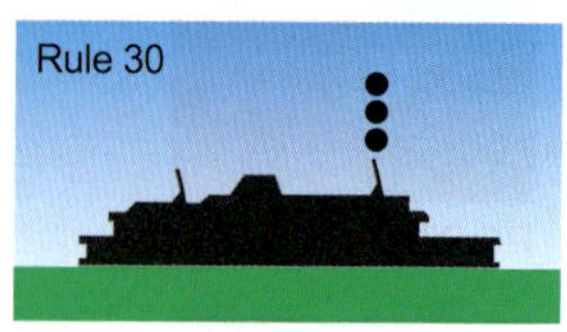

Vessel aground

Anchor light(s), plus two all-round red lights in a vertical line

Three balls in a vertical line

0.23 NAVIGATION LIGHTS

LIGHTS FOR TYPICAL YACHT WITH 3 OPTIONAL VARIANTS

C: If < 12m LOA: Masthead and sternlights may be combined into one all-round light.

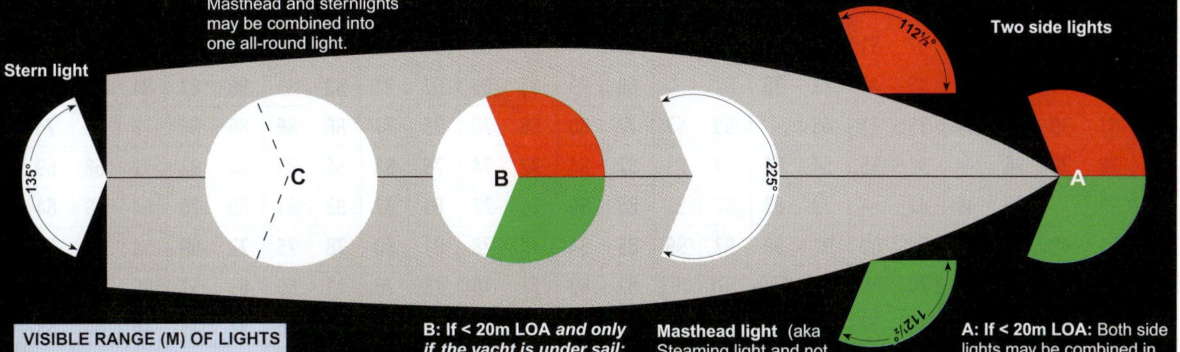

VISIBLE RANGE (M) OF LIGHTS (Rule 22)			
Light/LOA	<12m	<50m	>50m
All-round	2	2	3
Masthead	2	3*, 5	6
Side	**1**	**2**	**3**
Stern	2	2	3
		*<20m	

B: If < 20m LOA *and only if the yacht is under sail:* The side and sternlights may be combined in a single tricolour light atop the mast

Masthead light (aka Steaming light and not usually placed at the masthead) *Shown by vessels under power only*

A: If < 20m LOA: Both side lights may be combined in one centreline R/G light

PLAN VIEWS OF LIGHTS FOR SAILING VESSELS UNDERWAY AND UNDER SAIL ONLY

Note: If motor-sailing, the lights appropriate for a power-driven vessel must be shown, as below

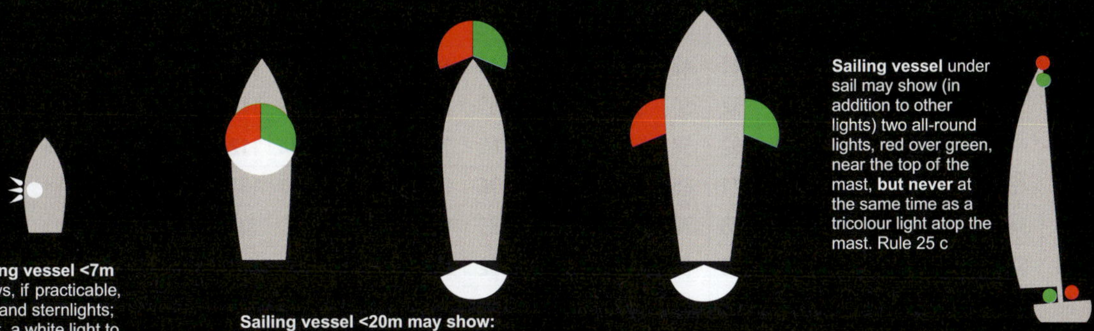

Sailing vessel under sail may show (in addition to other lights) two all-round lights, red over green, near the top of the mast, **but never** at the same time as a tricolour light atop the mast. Rule 25 c

Sailing vessel <7m shows, if practicable, side and sternlights; if not, a white light to prevent collision. Rule 25 d i

Sailing vessel <20m may show:

Either tricolour light atop the mast. Rule 25 b

Or combined centreline side lights plus stern light. Rule 25 a

Sailing vessel >20m Separate sidelights and sternlight. Rule 25 a

PLAN VIEWS OF LIGHTS FOR POWER-DRIVEN VESSELS UNDERWAY AND SAILING CRAFT UNDER POWER

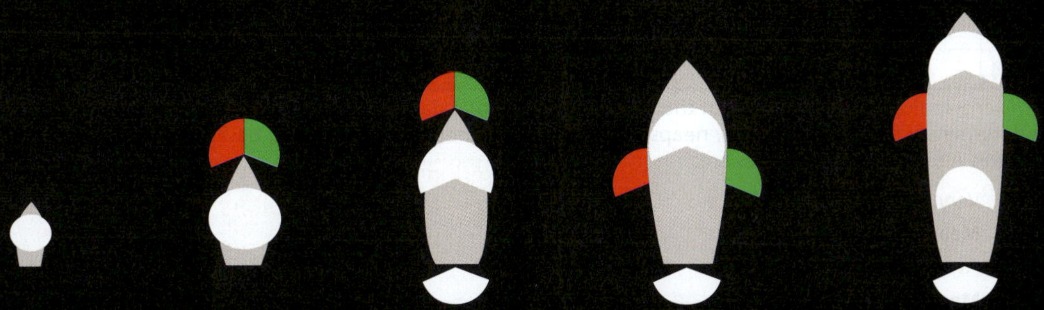

<7m and <7 knots (all-round light and, if practicable, side lights). Rule 23 d ii

<12m (combined masthead & sternlight). Rule 23 d i

<20m (sidelights combined in one centreline light). Rule 21 b

>20m showing masthead, stern and separate sidelights. Rule 21 a, b, c

>50m with two masthead lights, the aft one higher. Rule 23 a i & ii

0.24 TIDAL COEFFICIENTS 2024

Date	Jan		Feb		Mar		Apr		May		June		July		Aug		Sept		Oct		Nov		Dec	
	am	pm	am	pm	am	pm	am	pm	am	pm	am	pm	am	pm	am	pm	am	pm	am	pm	am	pm	am	pm
1	61	58	59	55	67	62	47	41	42	40	57	61	58	51	55		68	73	77	81	81	82	75	76
2	54	51	50	46	57	51	36	33	42	46	65	---	59	60	59	63	77	80	83	85	82	82	77	77
3	47	44	42	38	45	40	33	38	52	---	69	73	63	65	67	71	83	85	86	87	81	80	76	75
4	41	39	35	34	35	31	45	---	59	67	77	80	68	70	75	77	86	86	86	86	78	75	74	72
5	38	38	36	---	31	35	54	64	74	81	82	84	72	74	79	81	86	85	84	82	72	68	69	67
6	39	---	39	45	42	---	73	83	87	93	85	86	76	77	81	82	83	81	80	76	64	59	64	61
7	41	45	52	59	50	60	91	99	97	99	85	84	78	78	81	80	78	75	72	68	54	49	58	55
8	49	54	67	76	70	80	105	109	101	101	82	80	77	76	78	76	71	66	63	57	45	42	54	53
9	59	65	83	91	89	97	112	113	100	97	77	74	75	72	73	69	61	56	52	45	40	40	53	54
10	70	76	97	103	104	110	112	109	93	89	70	66	70	67	65	61	50	44	40	34	43	48	56	60
11	80	85	107	109	114	116	105	99	84	77	62	58	64	60	57	52	39	33	31	31	54	---	64	---
12	89	92	110	110	117	115	93	85	71	64	54	50	56	53	47	42	29	28	34	41	61	69	68	72
13	95	96	107	103	111	106	76	67	58	51	46	43	49	45	38	34	31	---	49	---	76	83	77	80
14	97	96	97	90	99	90	58	49	45	40	41	39	42	39	32	32	37	45	59	68	89	94	84	86
15	94	91	83	74	82	72	42	35	37	35	38	39	37	36	34	---	54	64	78	86	98	101	88	89
16	87	82	65	56	62	52	31	30	34	36	40	42	37	38	38	45	74	83	95	101	102	102	89	89
17	76	70	48	42	44	36	32	---	38	---	45	---	41	---	52	60	91	99	107	110	101	98	87	85
18	64	59	37	35	31	30	36	41	42	46	48	51	45	50	68	75	105	110	112	112	94	89	82	79
19	54	50	37	---	32	---	47	52	50	54	55	59	55	60	83	90	113	115	111	108	83	77	75	71
20	48	---	41	46	37	43	58	62	58	62	62	66	65	71	96	101	114	112	103	97	71	64	66	62
21	47	48	52	58	50	56	67	71	66	69	69	72	76	81	105	107	107	102	89	81	57	51	57	52
22	51	54	63	68	62	67	75	78	72	74	74	76	85	89	108	107	94	86	72	63	46	42	48	44
23	58	62	73	77	72	76	80	82	76	77	78	80	92	94	104	100	77	67	54	47	39	38	41	39
24	66	70	80	82	80	83	83	84	78	79	80	81	95	94	94	88	57	48	40	35	38	39	37	37
25	73	76	84	86	85	87	84	84	78	78	80	79	93	91	80	71	40	35	34	35	42	---	38	---
26	78	79	86	86	88	88	82	80	76	74	78	76	87	82	62	54	33	34	38	---	45	49	40	43
27	80	81	86	84	87	86	77	74	71	69	73	70	77	71	46	41	39	---	43	48	53	57	46	50
28	80	80	82	79	85	82	70	65	65	62	67	65	65	59	37	37	45	51	54	59	60	64	54	58
29	78	76	76	72	79	75	60	55	59	56	62	60	54	50	41	---	57	64	64	68	67	70	62	66
30	74	71			70	65	49	45	54	53	58	58	47	---	45	52	69	73	72	75	72	74	69	72
31	67	64			59	53			53	55			47	48	57	63			78	80			75	78

Tidal coefficients indicate the magnitude of the tide on any particular day without having to look up and calculate the range, and thus determine whether it is springs, neaps or somewhere in between. This table, based on Brest, is valid for all areas covered by this Almanac. Typical values are:

120	Very big spring tide
95	**Mean spring tide**
70	Average tide
45	**Mean neap tide**
20	Very small neap tide

0.25 CALCULATING TIDAL STREAM RATES

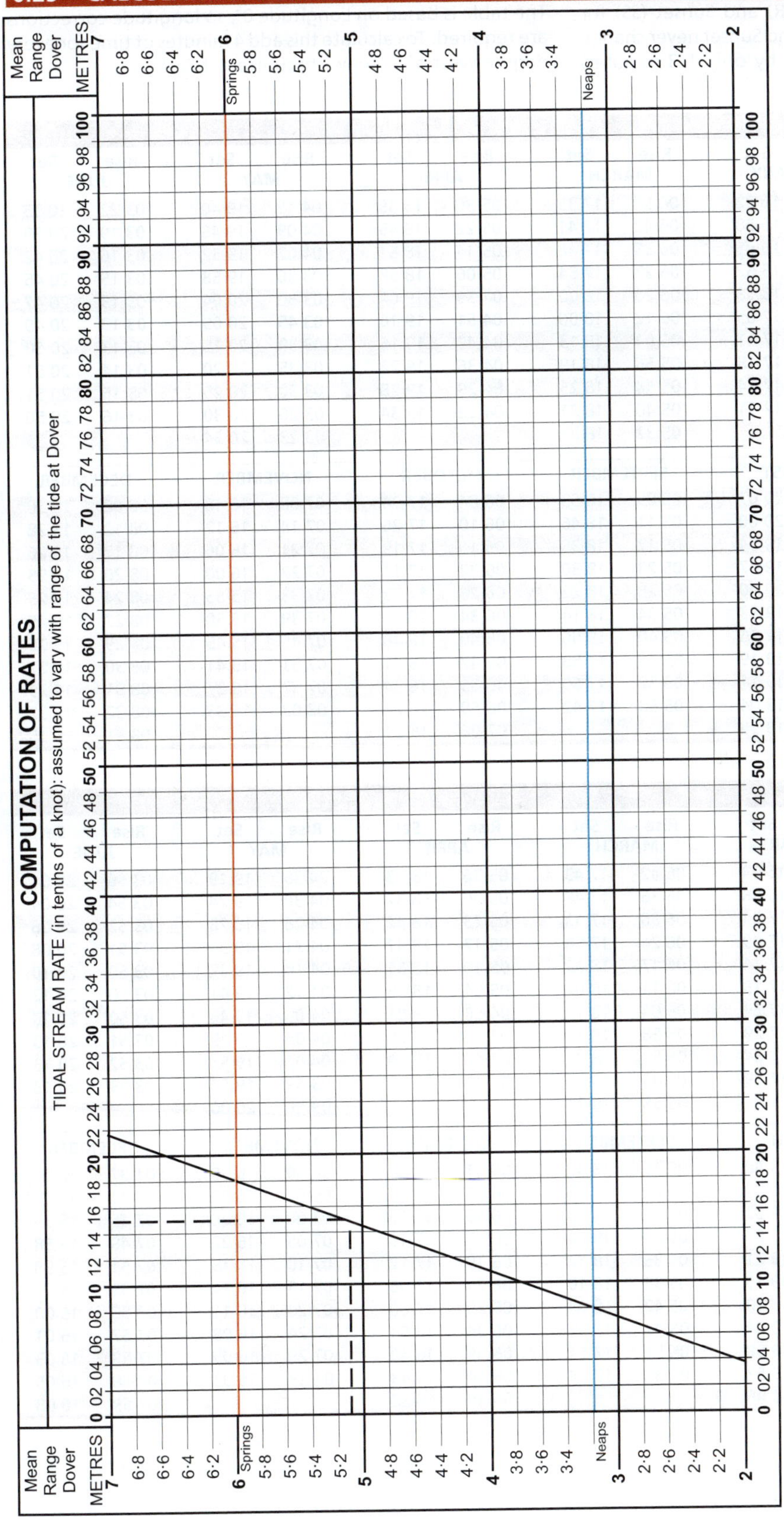

The tidal stream rate at any time may be calculated, assuming that it varies with the range of the tide at Dover. In tidal stream atlases, and on the tidal stream chartlets in this Almanac, the rates are shown in tenths of a knot. Thus '05,27' translates as 0·5k at Neaps and 2·7kn at Springs.

Example: Calculate the tidal stream rate off the north tip of Skye at 0420 UT on a day when the tide at Dover is:

UT	Ht (m)
0328	1·4
0819	6·3
1602	1·1
2054	6·4

The tidal stream chartlet for Skye [Dover HW–4] shows '08,18'. This is a mean Neap rate of 0·8kn and Spring rate of 1·8kn.

On the left hand figure identify the Spring (Red) and Neap (Blue) axes. On these mark the rate of 1.8kn and 0.8kn respectively, using the upper or lower scales.

Draw a diagonal line through these.

Calculate the tidal ranges for Dover:

(6·3 -1·4) = 4·9m   (6·4-1·1)=5·3m

The mean range = (4·9+5·3)/2 = 5·1m

On the vertical axis identify 5·1m and draw a horizontal line cutting the diagonal just drawn. From this intersection read off the required rate on either horizontal axis.

In the example this is 15 (1·5kn).

Times are in UT - add 1 hour in non-shaded areas to convert to BST

0.26 SUNRISE/SET TIMES 2024

The table shows times of Sunrise (SR) and Sunset (SS) for every 3rd day as the times of Sunrise and Sunset never change by more than 8 minutes (and often by only 1–3 minutes) between the given dates.

The table is based on Longitude 0°, so longitude corrections are required. To calculate this add 4 minutes of time for every degree West of Greenwich; subtract if East.

LATITUDE 56°N

	JANUARY Rise	JANUARY Set	FEBRUARY Rise	FEBRUARY Set	MARCH Rise	MARCH Set	APRIL Rise	APRIL Set	MAY Rise	MAY Set	JUNE Rise	JUNE Set
1	08 31	15 36	07 56	16 32	06 50	17 35	05 30	18 39	04 15	19 40	03 22	20 35
4	08 30	15 39	07 50	16 38	06 43	17 41	05 22	18 45	04 09	19 46	03 19	20 39
7	08 29	15 44	07 44	16 45	06 35	17 48	05 14	18 51	04 02	19 52	03 16	20 42
10	08 27	15 48	07 38	16 52	06 27	17 54	05 06	18 58	03 56	19 58	03 15	20 45
13	08 24	15 54	07 31	16 58	06 20	18 00	04 59	19 04	03 50	20 04	03 13	20 47
16	08 21	15 59	07 24	17 05	06 12	18 06	04 51	19 10	03 45	20 09	03 13	20 49
19	08 17	16 05	07 17	17 11	06 04	18 13	04 43	19 16	03 39	20 15	03 13	20 50
22	08 13	16 11	07 10	17 18	05 56	18 19	04 36	19 22	03 35	20 20	03 14	20 51
25	08 08	16 17	07 03	17 24	05 48	18 25	04 29	19 28	03 30	20 25	03 15	20 51
28	08 03	16 23	06 55	17 31	05 40	18 31	04 22	19 34	03 26	20 30	03 16	20 50
31	07 58	16 30			05 32	18 37			03 23	20 34		

	JULY Rise	JULY Set	AUGUST Rise	AUGUST Set	SEPTEMBER Rise	SEPTEMBER Set	OCTOBER Rise	OCTOBER Set	NOVEMBER Rise	NOVEMBER Set	DECEMBER Rise	DECEMBER Set
1	03 19	20 49	04 05	20 07	05 05	18 53	06 04	17 34	07 08	16 18	08 08	15 30
4	03 22	20 47	04 10	20 00	05 11	18 46	06 10	17 26	07 14	16 12	08 12	15 28
7	03 25	20 45	04 16	19 54	05 17	18 38	06 16	17 19	07 21	16 06	08 17	15 26
10	03 29	20 42	04 22	19 47	05 23	18 30	06 22	17 11	07 27	16 00	08 20	15 25
13	03 33	20 38	04 28	19 40	05 28	18 22	06 28	17 03	07 33	15 55	08 24	15 25
16	03 37	20 34	04 34	19 33	05 34	18 14	06 34	16 56	07 39	15 50	08 27	15 25
19	03 42	20 30	04 40	19 26	05 40	18 06	06 40	16 48	07 45	15 45	08 29	15 26
22	03 47	20 25	04 45	19 19	05 46	17 58	06 47	16 41	07 51	15 41	08 30	15 27
25	03 52	20 20	04 51	19 11	05 52	17 50	06 53	16 34	07 57	15 37	08 31	15 29
28	03 57	20 14	04 57	19 04	05 58	17 42	06 59	16 27	08 02	15 33	08 32	15 32
31	04 03	20 09	05 03	18 56			07 06	16 21			08 31	15 35

LATITUDE 50°N

	JANUARY Rise	JANUARY Set	FEBRUARY Rise	FEBRUARY Set	MARCH Rise	MARCH Set	APRIL Rise	APRIL Set	MAY Rise	MAY Set	JUNE Rise	JUNE Set
1	07 59	16 08	07 34	16 53	06 42	17 43	05 36	18 33	04 36	19 19	03 56	20 01
4	07 58	16 11	07 30	16 58	06 36	17 48	05 29	18 37	04 30	19 24	03 54	20 04
7	07 57	16 15	07 25	17 04	06 30	17 53	05 23	18 42	04 26	19 28	03 52	20 06
10	07 56	16 19	07 20	17 09	06 24	17 58	05 17	18 47	04 21	19 33	03 51	20 08
13	07 54	16 23	07 15	17 14	06 17	18 02	05 10	18 51	04 16	19 37	03 50	20 10
16	07 52	16 27	07 10	17 19	06 11	18 07	05 04	18 56	04 12	19 41	03 50	20 12
19	07 50	16 32	07 04	17 24	06 04	18 12	04 58	19 01	04 08	19 46	03 50	20 13
22	07 47	16 37	06 58	17 29	05 58	18 17	04 52	19 05	04 05	19 49	03 51	20 13
25	07 43	16 41	06 53	17 34	05 51	18 22	04 47	19 10	04 02	19 53	03 52	20 13
28	07 40	16 46	06 47	17 39	05 45	18 26	04 41	19 15	03 59	19 57	03 53	20 13
31	07 36	16 52			05 38	18 31			03 56	20 00		

	JULY Rise	JULY Set	AUGUST Rise	AUGUST Set	SEPTEMBER Rise	SEPTEMBER Set	OCTOBER Rise	OCTOBER Set	NOVEMBER Rise	NOVEMBER Set	DECEMBER Rise	DECEMBER Set
1	03 55	20 12	04 30	19 42	05 16	18 43	06 01	17 38	06 50	16 36	07 37	16 01
4	03 57	20 11	04 34	19 37	05 20	18 37	06 05	17 31	06 55	16 31	07 41	15 59
7	04 00	20 10	04 38	19 32	05 25	18 30	06 10	17 25	07 00	16 26	07 45	15 59
10	04 03	20 08	04 43	19 27	05 29	18 24	06 15	17 18	07 05	16 22	07 48	15 58
13	04 06	20 05	04 47	19 21	05 33	18 17	06 19	17 12	07 10	16 18	07 51	15 58
16	04 09	20 02	04 52	19 16	05 38	18 10	06 24	17 06	07 15	16 14	07 53	15 59
19	04 13	19 59	04 56	19 10	05 42	18 04	06 29	17 00	07 20	16 11	07 55	16 00
22	04 16	19 56	05 01	19 04	05 47	17 57	06 34	16 54	07 24	16 08	07 57	16 01
25	04 20	19 52	05 05	18 58	05 51	17 51	06 39	16 49	07 29	16 05	07 58	16 03
28	04 24	19 48	05 10	18 52	05 56	17 44	06 44	16 43	07 33	16 03	07 58	16 05
31	04 28	19 43	05 14	18 45			06 49	16 38			07 59	16 08

0.27 MOONRISE/SET TIMES 2024

The table gives the times of Moonrise (MR) and Moonset (MS) for every 3rd day; interpolation is necessary for other days. The aim is simply to indicate whether the night in question will be brightly moonlit, partially moonlit or pitch black – depending, of course, on the level of cloud cover. The table is based on Longitude 0°. To correct for longitude, add 4 minutes of time for every degree West; subtract if East.
** Indicates that the phenomenon does not occur.

LATITUDE 56°N

	JANUARY Rise	JANUARY Set	FEBRUARY Rise	FEBRUARY Set	MARCH Rise	MARCH Set	APRIL Rise	APRIL Set	MAY Rise	MAY Set	JUNE Rise	JUNE Set
1	21 45	11 16	** **	09 44	** **	08 06	02 54	07 52	02 44	09 49	01 29	13 51
4	00 15	11 30	03 23	10 13	03 54	09 08	04 37	12 11	03 14	14 38	01 51	18 38
7	04 21	11 55	07 13	12 30	06 15	13 04	05 05	17 10	03 34	19 31	03 04	22 49
10	08 34	13 43	08 26	17 34	06 50	18 13	05 27	22 11	04 29	** **	06 44	** **
13	10 09	18 31	08 49	22 28	07 11	23 09	06 35	01 17	07 43	01 33	10 48	00 25
16	10 34	23 19	09 16	01 37	08 02	02 19	10 04	03 31	11 49	02 11	14 35	00 39
19	10 57	02 21	10 51	05 42	11 00	05 04	14 06	04 02	15 37	02 25	18 46	01 01
22	12 06	06 42	14 36	07 15	15 02	05 45	17 53	04 15	19 42	02 43	22 20	02 31
25	15 29	08 51	18 32	07 40	18 50	06 00	22 01	04 34	23 39	03 47	23 23	06 53
28	19 29	09 24	22 20	07 53	22 50	06 16	00 45	05 49	00 49	07 34	23 44	11 37
31	23 15	09 39			01 40	07 07			01 23	12 19		

	JULY Rise	JULY Set	AUGUST Rise	AUGUST Set	SEPTEMBER Rise	SEPTEMBER Set	OCTOBER Rise	OCTOBER Set	NOVEMBER Rise	NOVEMBER Set	DECEMBER Rise	DECEMBER Set
1	** **	16 17	** **	19 25	02 35	18 52	04 20	17 18	07 13	15 49	09 06	14 45
4	00 58	20 37	03 27	20 34	06 32	19 07	08 08	17 32	11 20	16 42	11 52	17 46
7	04 21	22 15	07 31	20 52	10 21	19 22	12 13	18 08	13 49	19 58	12 35	22 22
10	08 30	22 39	11 17	21 06	14 28	20 05	15 19	20 45	14 27	** **	12 54	01 25
13	12 17	22 52	15 24	21 39	17 19	23 10	16 11	** **	14 46	03 50	13 27	06 18
16	16 21	23 19	18 49	** **	18 03	02 30	16 31	04 49	15 26	08 57	15 47	10 25
19	20 12	00 18	19 48	03 30	18 23	07 31	17 04	09 57	18 15	12 36	20 11	11 34
22	21 30	04 25	20 08	08 29	19 01	12 35	19 17	14 04	22 34	13 28	** **	11 52
25	21 53	09 20	20 38	13 22	21 33	16 08	23 30	15 12	01 09	13 43	02 39	12 07
28	22 17	14 03	22 31	17 25	00 21	17 02	02 08	15 29	04 57	13 59	06 46	12 45
31	23 39	18 29	01 10	18 43			05 54	15 43			09 52	15 28

LATITUDE 50°N

	JANUARY Rise	JANUARY Set	FEBRUARY Rise	FEBRUARY Set	MARCH Rise	MARCH Set	APRIL Rise	APRIL Set	MAY Rise	MAY Set	JUNE Rise	JUNE Set
1	21 54	11 03	** **	09 56	** **	08 32	01 57	08 48	02 07	10 24	01 27	13 49
4	00 10	11 38	02 47	10 52	03 01	10 02	04 05	12 42	03 06	14 42	02 15	18 07
7	03 50	12 27	06 20	13 23	05 36	13 41	05 01	17 10	03 52	19 05	03 56	21 55
10	07 39	14 37	08 04	17 53	06 42	18 17	05 50	21 39	05 18	23 12	07 21	23 40
13	09 42	18 55	08 53	22 18	07 29	22 44	07 28	00 25	08 26	00 49	10 59	00 12
16	10 34	23 14	09 48	01 07	08 51	01 31	10 44	02 50	12 05	01 53	14 24	00 46
19	11 22	01 58	11 45	04 48	11 45	04 18	14 18	03 47	15 30	02 28	18 07	01 32
22	12 57	05 51	15 08	06 42	15 20	05 25	17 43	04 21	19 09	03 09	21 28	03 26
25	16 07	08 11	18 39	07 30	18 45	06 01	21 24	05 03	22 44	04 41	23 02	07 23
28	19 42	09 09	22 05	08 03	22 20	06 39	** **	06 44	00 10	08 12	23 48	11 37
31	23 06	09 44			00 50	07 58			01 12	12 26		

	JULY Rise	JULY Set	AUGUST Rise	AUGUST Set	SEPTEMBER Rise	SEPTEMBER Set	OCTOBER Rise	OCTOBER Set	NOVEMBER Rise	NOVEMBER Set	DECEMBER Rise	DECEMBER Set
1	00 19	15 49	00 33	18 32	03 03	18 31	04 26	17 16	06 51	16 14	08 18	15 33
4	01 48	19 43	04 01	20 07	06 36	19 07	07 51	17 51	10 29	17 34	11 05	18 31
7	05 02	21 42	07 39	20 48	10 01	19 43	11 28	18 55	13 04	20 41	12 18	22 37
10	08 43	22 30	11 03	21 22	13 40	20 54	14 28	21 36	14 12	** **	13 01	01 21
13	12 08	23 04	14 42	22 22	16 32	23 56	15 51	00 22	14 57	03 43	14 03	05 44
16	15 46	23 56	17 57	** **	17 48	02 53	16 38	04 47	16 08	08 16	16 39	09 33
19	19 17	01 12	19 28	03 58	18 34	07 24	17 40	09 23	19 03	11 46	20 34	11 09
22	21 05	05 00	20 15	08 27	19 43	11 54	20 10	13 10	22 53	13 06	** **	11 50
25	21 55	09 23	21 13	12 49	22 24	15 17	23 55	14 45	01 12	13 44	02 23	12 25
28	22 45	13 37	23 26	16 30	00 52	16 39	02 16	15 25	04 38	14 20	06 01	13 31
31	** **	17 35	01 48	18 13			05 40	15 59			09 02	16 17

0.28 INTERNATIONAL CODE OF SIGNALS

Code flags, phonetic alphabet (NATO/ITU), Morse code, single-letter signals. INTERNATIONAL PORT TRAFFIC SIGNALS.

A – Alfa
I have a diver down; keep well clear at slow speed
• —

***B – Bravo**
I am taking in, or discharging, or carrying dangerous goods
— • • •

***C – Charlie**
Yes
— • — •

***D – Delta**
Keep clear of me; I am manoeuvring with difficulty
— • •

***E – Echo**
I am altering course to starboard
•

F – Foxtrot
I am disabled; communicate with me
• • — •

***G – Golf**
I require a pilot. When made by fishing vessels 'I am hauling in nets'
— — •

***H – Hotel**
I have a pilot on board
• • • •

***I – India**
I am altering my course to port
• •

J – Juliett
I am on fire and have dangerous cargo aboard; keep well clear of me
• — — —

K – Kilo
I wish to communicate with you
— • —

L – Lima
You should stop your vessel instantly
• — • •

***M – Mike**
My vessel is stopped and making no way through the water
— —

N – November
No
— •

O – Oscar
Man overboard
— — —

P – Papa
Vessel about to put to sea. By fishing vessels 'My nets are caught fast'
• — — •

Q – Quebec
My vessel is 'healthy' and I request free pratique
— — • —

R – Romeo
• — •

***S – Sierra**
My engines are going astern
• • •

***T – Tango**
Keep clear of me; I am engaged in pair trawling
—

U – Uniform
You are running into danger
• • —

V – Victor
I require assistance
• • • —

W – Whiskey
I require medical assistance
• — —

X – X-ray
Stop carrying out your intentions and watch for my signals
— • • —

Y – Yankee
I am dragging my anchor
— • — —

***Z – Zulu**
I require a tug. By fishing vessels 'I am shooting nets'
— — • •

1 Wun • — — — —

2 Too • • — — —

3 Tree • • • — —

4 Fow-er • • • • —

5 Fife • • • • •

6 Six — • • • •

7 Sev-en — — • • •

8 Ait — — — • •

9 Nin-er — — — — •

0 Zero — — — — —

Code and answering pennant

First Substitute
Second Substitute
Third Substitute

INTERNATIONAL PORT TRAFFIC SIGNALS

No	Lights		Main message
1		Flashing	Serious emergency – all vessels to stop or divert according to instructions
2		Fixed or Slow Occulting	Vessels shall not proceed (*Note:* Some ports may use an exemption signal, as in 2a below)
3		Fixed or Slow Occulting	Vessels may proceed. One-way traffic
4		Fixed or Slow Occulting	Vessels may proceed. Two-way traffic
5		Fixed or Slow Occulting	A vessel may proceed only when she has received specific orders to do so. (*Note:* Some ports may use an exemption signal, as in 5a below)
			Exemption signals and messages
2a		Fixed or Slow Occulting	Vessels shall not proceed, except that vessels which navigate outside the main channel need not comply with the main message
5a		Fixed or Slow Occulting	A vessel may proceed when she has received specific orders to do so, except that vessels which navigate outside the main channel need not comply with the main message
			Auxiliary signals and messages
White and/or yellow lights, displayed with the main lights			Local meanings, as promulgated in local port orders

Signals marked * when made by sound may only be used in compliance with the Collision Regulations Rules 34 and 35.

0.29 AREA INFORMATION

The 6 geographic Areas are arranged as follows:

An Area map which includes harbours, principal lights, TSS, MRCC's, NCI stations, airports, main ferry routes, magnetic variation and a distance table. Wind farms and other offshore energy installations are not routinely shown.

Tidal stream chartlets showing hourly rates and set.

Lights, buoys and waypoints (LBW) listing positions and characteristics of selected lights and other marks, their daytime appearance, fog signals and Racons. Arcs of visibility and alignment of sector/leading lights are true bearings as seen from seaward. Lights are white unless otherwise stated; any colours are shown between the bearings of the relevant arcs. AIS is widely fitted to navigational marks, but not normally shown in LBW. See the relevant official charts/publications for details.

Passage Information (PI) is at Section 4 in each Area. Further information is geographically arranged between the harbour entries.

Special notes giving data specific to a country or area.

Harbour information (see below).

0.30 HARBOUR INFORMATION

Each harbour entry is arranged as follows:

HARBOUR NAME followed by the County or Unitary Council (or foreign equivalent) and the lat/long of the harbour entrance, or equivalent, for use as the final waypoint.

Harbour ratings (❁ ♁ ✿), inevitably subjective, which grade a port based on the following criteria:

Ease of access:

❁❁❁ *Can be entered in almost any weather from most directions and at all states of tide, by day or night.*

❁❁ *Accessible in strong winds from most directions; possible tidal or pilotage constraints.*

❁ *Only accessible in calm, settled conditions by day with little or no swell; possible bar and difficult pilotage.*

Facilities available:

♁♁♁ *Good facilities for vessel and crew.*

♁♁ *Most domestic needs catered for, but limited boatyard facilities.*

♁ *Possibly some domestic facilities, but little else.*

Ambience:

✿✿✿ *An attractive place; well worth visiting.*

✿✿ *Average for this part of the coast.*

✿ *Holds no particular attraction.*

CHARTS show Admiralty (AC), Imray, and foreign charts, all smallest scale first. Admiralty Leisure Folios (56XX), which cover most of the UK, Channel Islands and Ireland, and Imray 2000 series folios (2X00) are also shown.

TIDES include a time difference (usually on Dover in the UK), ML, Duration and the harbour's Standard Port. Time and height differences for Secondary Ports are also shown. Computer prediction is replacing some Secondary Port data in ATT. The Almanac continues to replicate these differences in italics when alternative information can be found. Tidal coefficients are at 0.24.

SHELTER assesses how protected a harbour is from wind, sea, surge and swell. It warns of any access difficulties and advises on safe berths and anchorages.

NAVIGATION gives guidance on the approach and entry, and shows the position of the approach waypoint with its bearing and distance to the harbour entrance or next significant feature. Some waypoints may not be shown on the chartlet. Access times are only stated where a lock, gate, sill or other obstruction restricts entry. Otherwise the minimum charted depth of water in the approaches, where it is less than 2m, is usually shown, but always consult up to date official charts.

Chartlets are based on official charts augmented with local information. Due to their scale, they may not cover the whole area referred to in the text nor do they show every depth, mark, light or feature.

The chartlets are not intended to be used for navigation; *positions taken from them should not be used as waypoints in chart plotters.* The publisher and editors disclaim any responsibility for resultant accidents or damage if they are so used. The largest scale official chart, properly corrected, should always be used.

Drying areas and an indicative 5m depth contour are shown as: Dries <5m >5m

Wrecks around the UK which are of archaeological or historic interest are protected by law. Sites are listed under harbour entries or in Passage Information. Unauthorised interference, including anchoring and diving on these sites, may lead to a substantial fine.

LIGHTS AND MARKS describes, in more detail than is shown on the chartlets, any unusual characteristics of marks, their appearance by day and features not listed elsewhere.

COMMUNICATIONS shows the telephone area code followed by local telephone and VHF contact details for: CG, weather, police, doctor/medical, harbourmaster/office, other. Marina contact details are not usually duplicated if they are shown under the marina entry. International telephone calls from/to the UK are described in Special Notes, as are national numbers for emergency services: normally 112 in the EU; 999 in the UK. Radio callsigns, if not obvious, are in *italics*.

FACILITIES describes berthing options and facilities in harbours, marinas and yacht clubs (see the **Reeds Marina Guide** for detailed marina plans in the UK, Channel Islands and Ireland). Water, electricity, showers and toilets are available in marinas unless otherwise stated. Most yacht clubs welcome visiting crews who belong to a recognised club and arrive by sea. Any rail and air links are also shown.

The overnight cost of a visitor's alongside berth (AB) *is for comparison only and based on information supplied at the time of going to press (Summer 2023)* is the average charge per metre LOA (unless otherwise stated) during high season, usually June to Sept. It includes VAT, harbour dues and, where possible, any tourist taxes (per head). The cost of pile moorings, 🅐s or ⚓s, where these are the norm, may also be given. Shore electricity is usually free abroad but extra in the UK.

The number of Ⓥ berths is a marina's estimate of how many visitors may be accommodated at any one time. It is always advisable to call the marina beforehand.

TransEurope Marinas (www.transeuropemarinas.com) is a group of independent marinas in the UK and abroad. Many hold Blue Flags and 4 or 5 Gold Anchor Awards; it is a condition of membership that they are well-equipped and maintain high standards. They operate a discounted reciprocal berthing scheme and are shown by the symbol ⊗.

Rover Tickets, offering good discounts, are available for many berthing facilities in Scotland and the offlying islands.

0.31 ENVIRONMENTAL GUIDANCE

- Comply with regulations for navigation and conduct within Marine Nature Reserves, Particularly Sensitive Sea Areas (PSSA) and National Water Parks.
- In principle never ditch rubbish at sea, keep it on board and dispose of it in harbour refuse bins.
- Readily degradable foodstuffs may be ditched at sea when >3M offshore (>12M in the English Channel).
- Foodstuffs and other materials which are not readily degradable should never be ditched at sea.
- Sewage. If you do not have a holding tank, only use the onboard heads when well offshore. A holding tank should be fitted as soon as possible as many countries require them. Pump-out facilities (♁) are shown in the text. Do not pump out holding tanks until more than 3M offshore.
- Do not discharge foul water into a marina, anchorage or moorings area and minimise on washing-up water.
- Deposit used engine oil and oily waste ashore at a recognised facility. Do not allow an automatic bilge pump to discharge oily bilge water overboard.
- Dispose of toxic waste, (eg some antifoulings, cleaning chemicals, old batteries) at an approved disposal facility.
- Row ashore whenever possible – to minimise noise, wash and disturbance. Land at recognised places.
- Respect wild birds, plants, fish and marine animals. Avoid protected nesting sites and breeding colonies.
- Do not anchor or dry out on vulnerable seabed species, eg soft corals, eel grass.

0.32 DISTANCES (M) ACROSS THE IRISH SEA

Approximate distances in nautical miles are by the most direct route, avoiding dangers and allowing for TSS.

Scotland / England / Wales → ; Ireland ↓	Port Ellen (Islay)	Campbeltown	Troon	Portpatrick	Mull of Galloway	Kirkcudbright	Maryport	Fleetwood	Pt of Ayre (IOM)	Port St Mary (IOM)	Liverpool	Holyhead	Pwllheli	Fishguard	Milford Haven	Swansea	Avonmouth	Ilfracombe	Padstow	Longships
Tory Island	75	107	132	119	134	170	185	215	156	167	238	207	260	279	307	360	406	372	372	399
Malin Head	45	76	101	88	103	139	154	184	125	136	207	176	229	248	276	329	375	341	341	368
Lough Foyle	33	61	86	73	88	124	139	169	110	121	192	161	214	233	261	314	360	320	326	353
Portrush	31	50	76	64	80	116	131	161	102	113	184	153	206	225	253	306	352	308	318	345
Carnlough	42	35	57	32	45	81	96	126	67	78	149	115	168	187	215	268	314	265	280	307
Larne	51	39	58	24	37	72	88	118	58	70	141	106	159	178	206	259	305	254	271	298
Carrickfergus	64	48	65	26	34	69	85	115	55	66	138	101	154	173	201	254	300	249	266	293
Bangor	63	48	64	22	30	65	81	111	51	62	134	97	150	169	197	250	296	245	262	289
Strangford L.	89	72	84	36	30	63	76	97	41	37	107	69	121	141	167	219	265	214	231	258
Carlingford L.	117	100	112	64	60	90	103	112	70	51	118	67	111	124	149	202	248	197	214	241
Dun Laoghaire	153	136	148	100	93	119	126	120	93	69	119	56	82	94	109	162	208	157	174	201
Wicklow	170	153	165	117	108	133	140	127	108	83	123	56	67	71	90	143	189	138	155	182
Arklow	182	165	177	129	120	144	149	133	117	93	131	64	71	65	79	132	179	128	144	167
Rosslare	215	202	208	161	154	179	180	164	152	125	156	90	83	55	58	109	157	110	119	137
Tuskar Rock	216	203	209	162	155	179	182	165	152	126	152	91	82	48	51	105	150	103	112	130
Dunmore East	250	237	243	196	189	213	216	199	186	160	189	127	116	79	76	130	177	124	127	136
Youghal	281	268	274	227	220	244	247	230	217	191	220	158	147	110	103	156	200	148	139	138
Crosshaven	300	287	293	246	239	263	266	249	236	210	239	177	166	131	118	170	216	163	151	144
Baltimore	346	333	339	292	285	309	312	295	282	256	285	223	212	172	160	209	254	198	178	161
Fastnet Rock	354	341	347	300	293	317	320	303	290	264	293	231	220	181	169	216	260	207	185	170

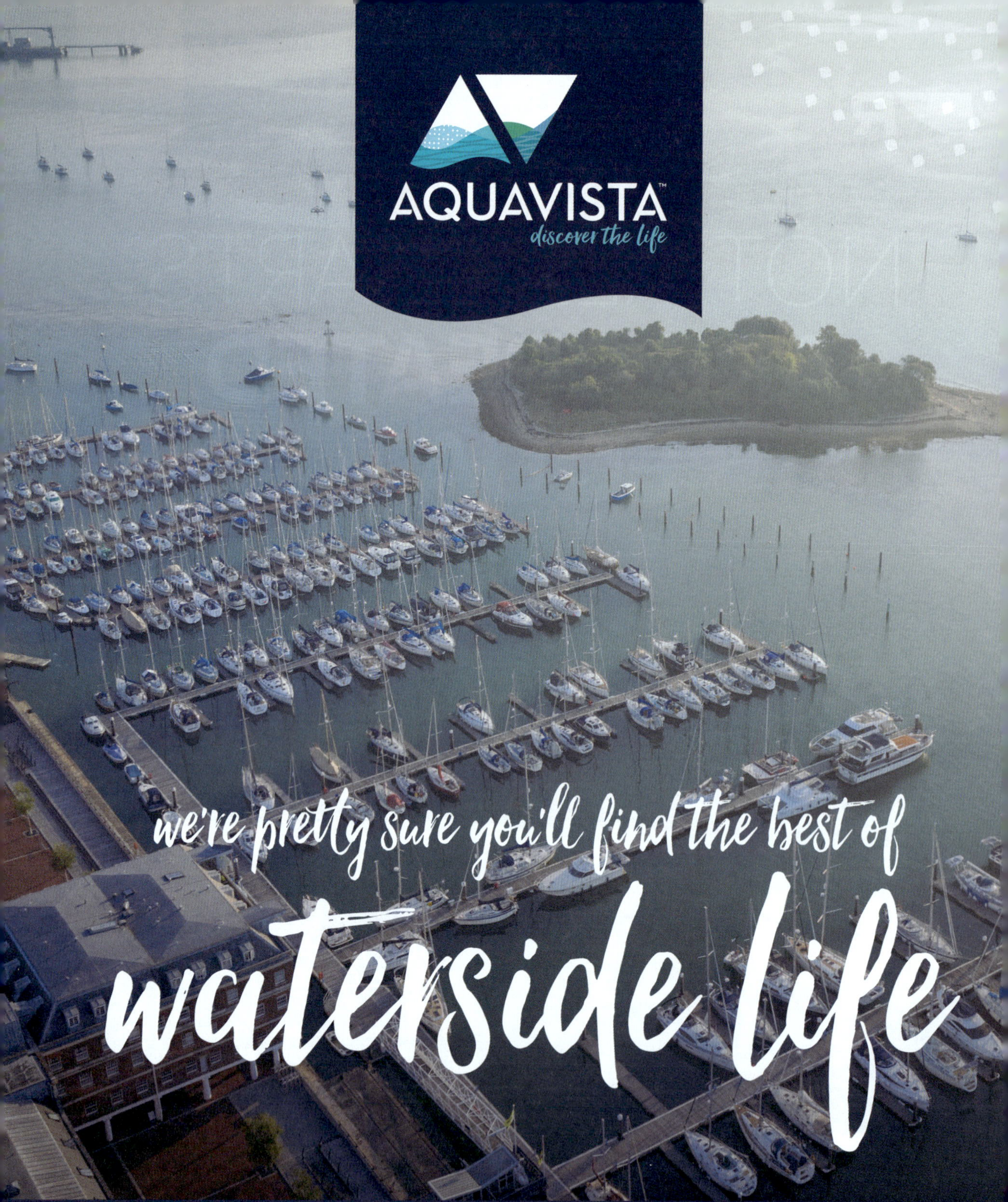
AQUAVISTA™
discover the life
we're pretty sure you'll find the best of
waterside life

West Scotland

Cape Wrath to Solway Firth

No.	Place	20	19	18	17	16	15	14	13	12	11	10	9	8	7	6	5	4	3	2	1
1	*Mull of Kintyre*	232	203	224	189	159	153	143	121	120	93	89	87	98	76	72	62	57	54	51	**1**
2	Crinan	187	157	179	158	112	105	95	74	97	46	42	30	54	29	25	14	9	6	**2**	
3	Loch Craignish	188	158	180	159	118	106	96	76	98	48	44	31	55	30	26	17	14	**3**		
4	Craobh Haven	184	155	176	155	114	102	92	70	93	44	40	27	50	25	21	5	**4**			
5	Loch Melfort	184	154	176	155	114	103	93	69	92	44	40	27	45	22	18	**5**				
6	Oban	169	138	161	139	100	87	77	56	77	28	24	13	29	4	**6**					
7	Dunstaffnage	171	140	163	141	102	89	79	58	79	30	26	15	28	**7**						
8	Fort William	198	161	190	162	121	108	98	75	96	47	43	34	**8**							
9	Loch Aline	157	127	149	128	87	76	66	45	66	17	13	**9**								
10	Tobermory	144	114	136	115	74	63	53	32	53	3	**10**									
11	Loch Sunart	147	117	139	118	77	66	56	35	56	**11**										
12	Castlebay (Barra)	133	105	125	92	97	86	76	59	**12**											
13	Mallaig	112	82	104	83	42	31	21	**13**												
14	Loch Alsh	91	63	83	62	21	10	**14**													
15	Plockton	95	66	87	64	23	**15**														
16	Portree	83	57	75	53	**16**															
17	Stornoway	53	45	46	**17**																
18	Kinlochbervie	14	46	**18**																	
19	Ullapool	54	**19**																		
20	Cape Wrath	**20**																			

DISTANCE TABLE
Approximate distances in nautical miles are by the most direct route, keeping East of Skye and Mull where appropriate, and avoiding dangers. Places in italics are in adjoining areas.

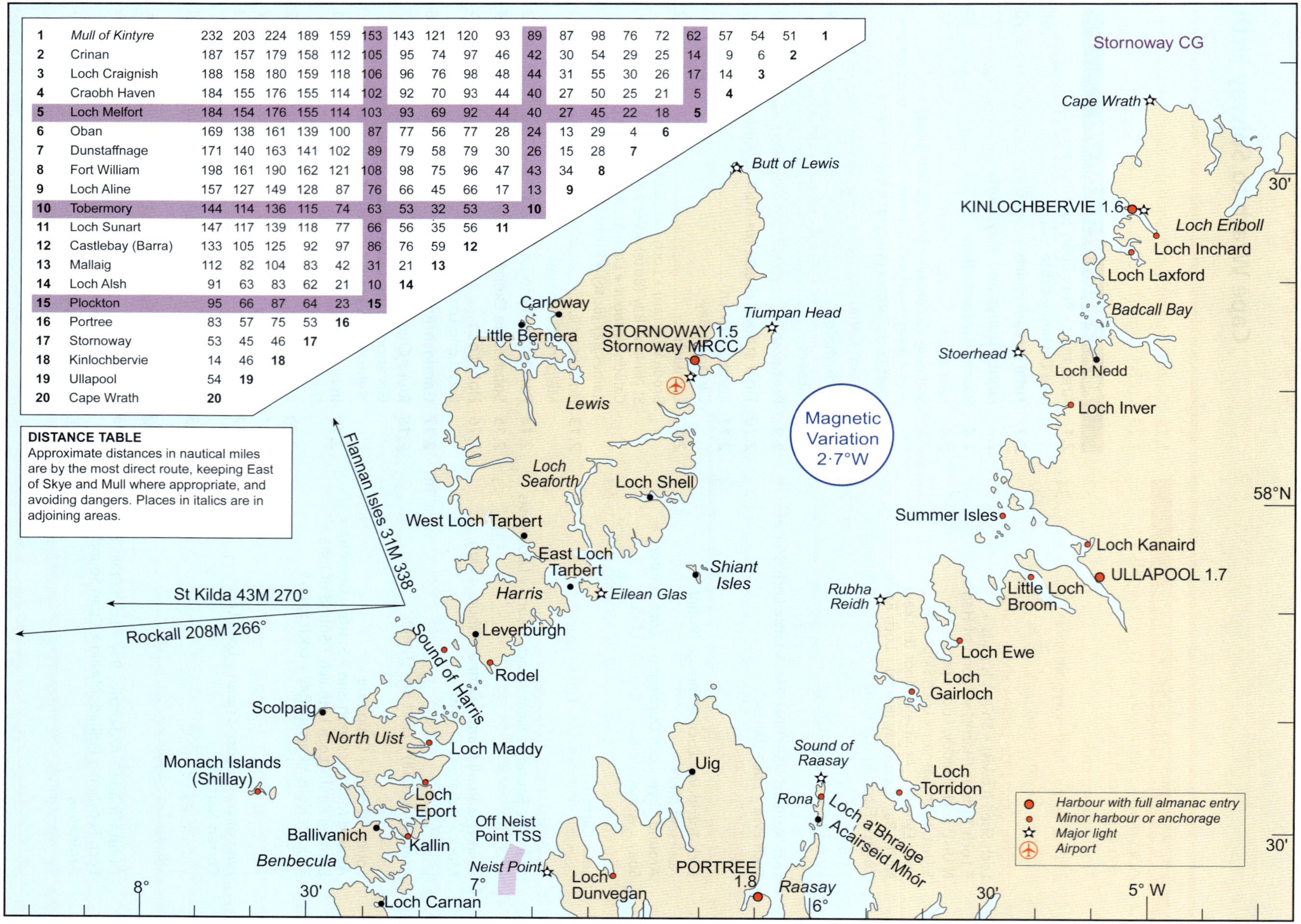

1.1
North West Scotland
Cape Wrath to Crinan Canal
EMERGENCY 999
HMCG NATIONAL – 02392 552100
HMCG STORNOWAY – 01851 702013
HM CUSTOMS – 0845 010 9000
POLICE - 101 MEDICAL - 111
Magnetic Variation 2·8°W
57°N
30'
5° W
6°
7°
8°
PLOCKTON 1.9
Kyle of Loch Alsh
LOCH ALSH 1.10
Kyle Rhea
Kyle Akin
Crowlin Is
Loch Hourn
Loch Nevis
MALLAIG 1.11
Sound of Sleat
Armadale Bay
Loch Harport
Skye
Soay
Rum
Canna
Hyskeir
Eigg
Muck
Arisaig
Loch Moidart
Ardnamurchan Point
CALEDONIAN CANAL 1.16
FORT WILLIAM/ CORPACH 1.15
Corran Narrows
Loch Leven
Loch Linnhe
LOCH SUNART 1.12
LOCH ALINE 1.14
Rubha nan Gall
TOBERMORY 1.13
Arinagour
Coll
Sound of Mull
Salen
Ulva Sound
Loch na Keal
Mull
Craignure
Lismore I
Loch Creran
Lynn of Lorn
Bonawe
Loch Etive
Dunstaffnage
OBAN 1.17
Loch Feochan
Puilladobhrain
Cuan Sound
LOCH MELFORT 1.18
CRAOBH MARINA 1.19
LOCH CRAIGNISH 1.20
Crinan Canal (2.6)
Gulf of Corryvreckan
Jura
Seil I
Ardinamar
Loch Spelve
Carsaig B
Loch Lathaich
Gometra
Staffa
Treshnish Is
Iona
Tinkers Hole
Colonsay
Oronsay
Dubh Artach
Gott Bay
Tiree
Skerryvore
Loch Skiport
South Uist
Loch Eynort
Loch Boisdale
Acairseid Mhór
Eriskay
North Bay
Barra
Castle Bay
Barra Head

1.2 AREA 1 TIDAL STREAMS

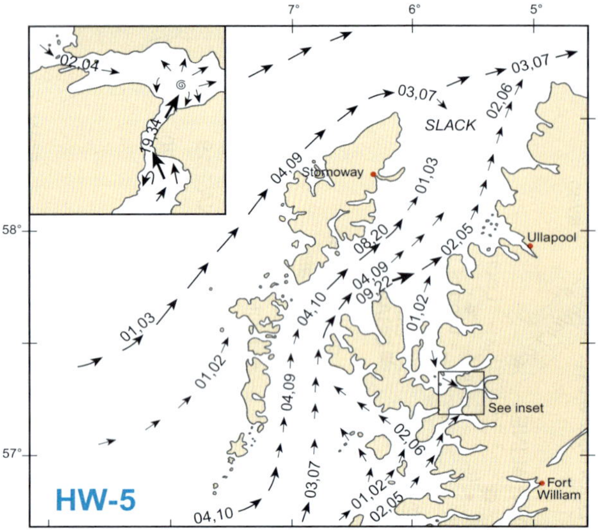

5 Hours before HW Dover (0050 before HW Ullapool)

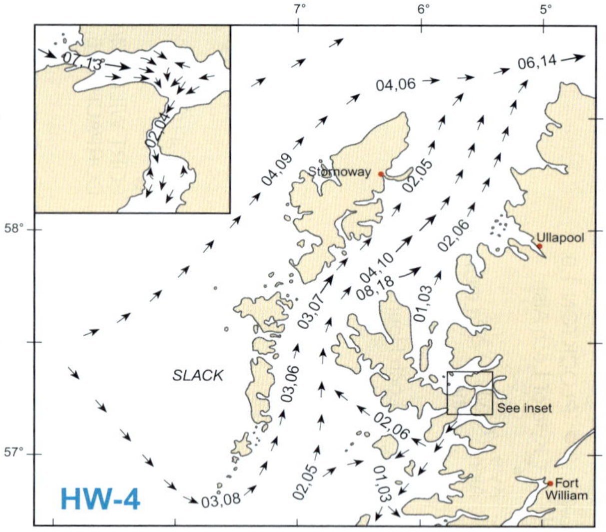

4 Hours before HW Dover (0010 after HW Ullapool)

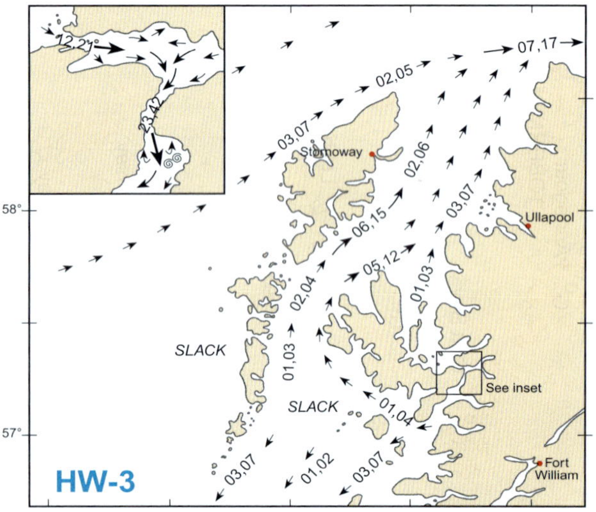

3 Hours before HW Dover (0110 after HW Ullapool)

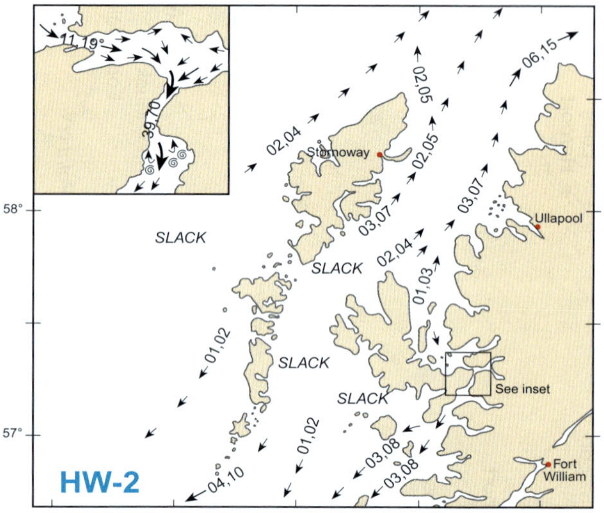

2 Hours before HW Dover (0210 after HW Ullapool)

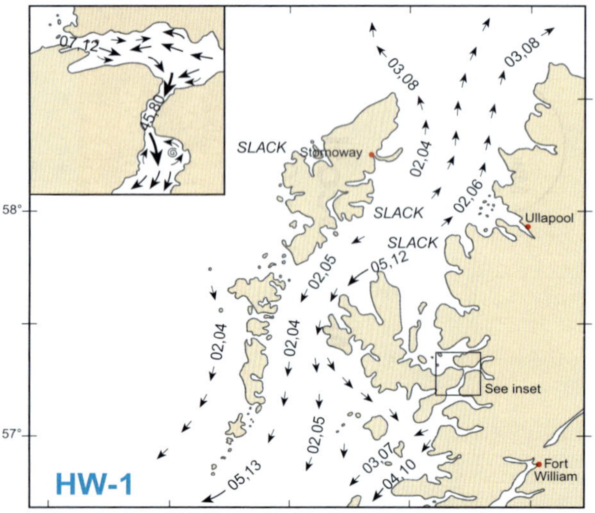

1 Hour before HW Dover (0310 after HW Ullapool)

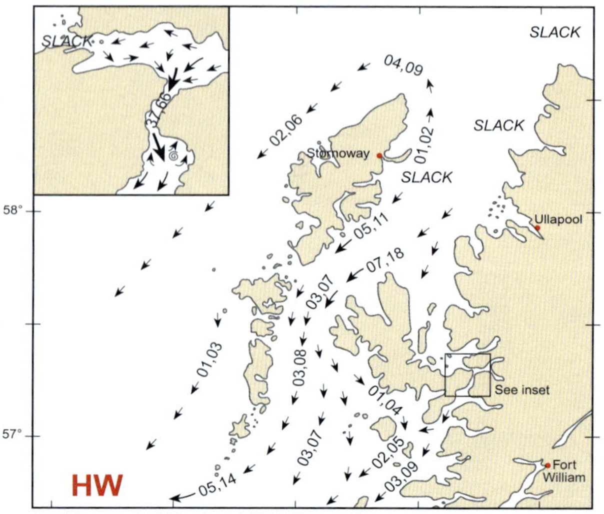

HW Dover (0410 after HW Ullapool)

Southward 2.2   Mull of Kintyre 2.10

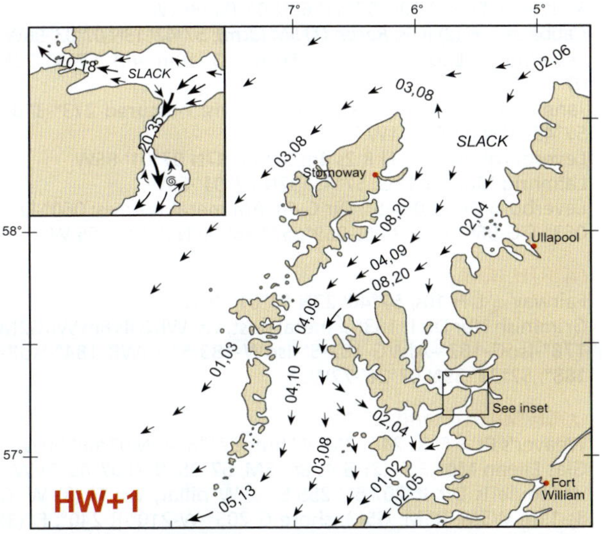

1 Hour after HW Dover (0510 after HW Ullapool)

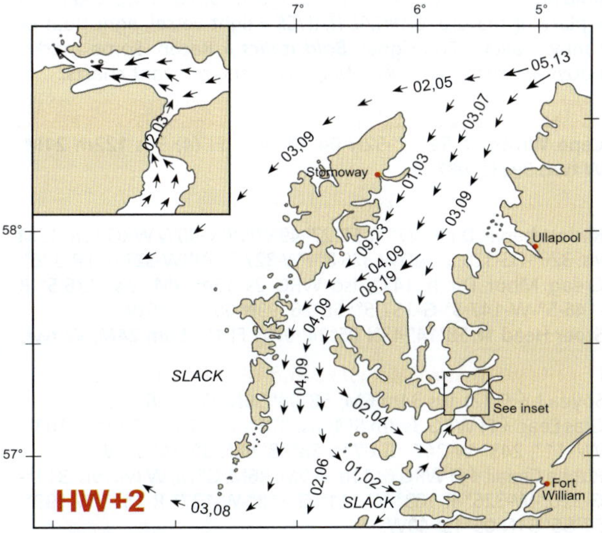

2 Hours after HW Dover (0615 before HW Ullapool)

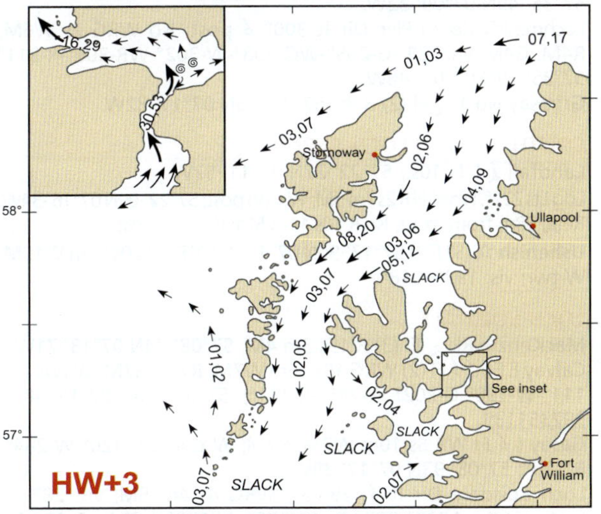

3 Hours after HW Dover (0515 before HW Ullapool)

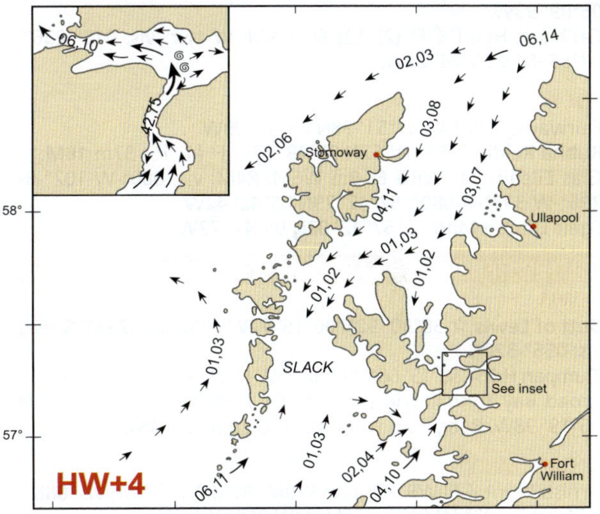

4 Hours after HW Dover (0415 before HW Ullapool)

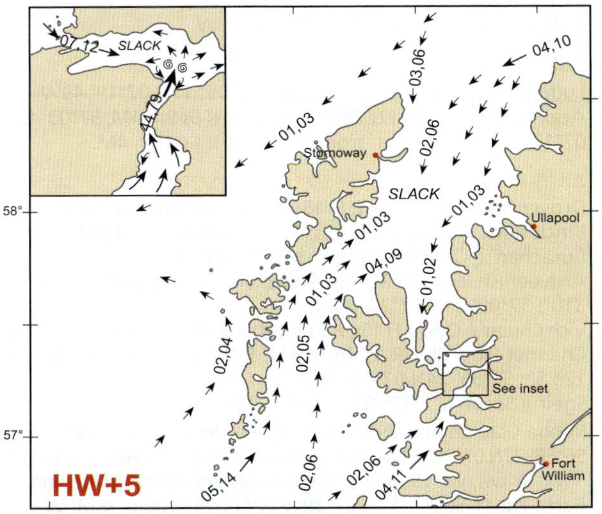

5 Hours after HW Dover (0315 before HW Ullapool)

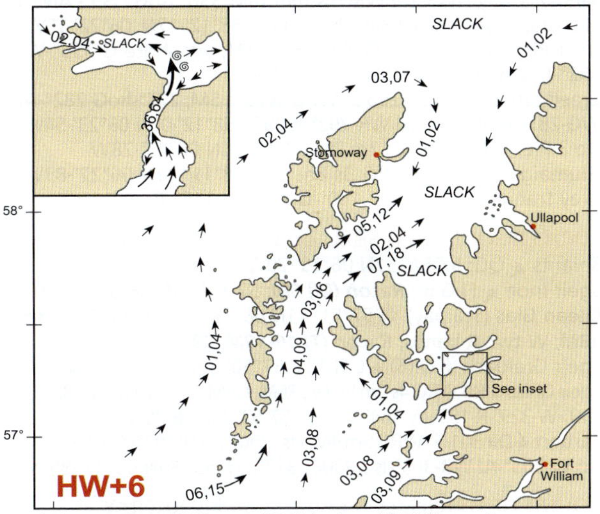

6 Hours after HW Dover (0215 before HW Ullapool)

1.3 LIGHTS, BUOYS AND WAYPOINTS

Bold print = light with a nominal range of 15M or more. CAPITALS = place or feature. *CAPITAL ITALICS* = light-vessel, light float or Lanby. *Italics* = Fog signal. ***Bold italics*** = Racon. Some marks/ buoys are fitted with AIS (MMSI No); see relevant charts.

CAPE WRATH TO LOCH TORRIDON

Cape Wrath ☆ 58°37′·52N 04°59′·94W Fl (4) 30s 122m **21M**; W twr; 992351087.

LOCH INCHARD and LOCH LAXFORD

Kinlochbervie Dir lt 327° ☆ 58°27′·49N 05°03′·08W WRG 15m **16M** vis: 326°-FG-326·5°-AlGW-326·8°-FW-327·3°-AlRW-327·5°-FR-328°.
Creag Mhòr Dir lt 147°; Iso WRG 2s 16m 4M; vis: 136·5°-R -146·5°-W-147·5°-G-157·5°; 58°26′·99N 05°02′·45W.
Stoer Head ☆ 58°14′·43N 05°24′·07W Fl 15s 59m **24M**; W twr.

LOCH INVER, SUMMER ISLES and ULLAPOOL

Soyea I ☆ Fl (2) 10s 34m 6M; 58°08′·56N 05°19′·67W.
Glas Leac ☆ Fl WRG 3s 7m 5M; vis: 071°- W-078°-R-090°-G-103°-W-111°, 243°-W-247°-G-071°; 58°08′·68N 05°16′·36W.
Rubha Cadail ☆ Fl WRG 6s 11m W9M, R6M, G6M; W twr; vis: 311°-G-320°-W-325°-R-103°-W-111°-G-118°-W-127°-R-157°-W-199°; 57°55′·51N 05°13′·40W.
Ullapool Pt ☆ Iso R 4s 8m 6M; W twr; vis: 258°-108°; 57°53′·59N 05°09′·93W.
Cailleach Head ☆ Fl (2) 12s 60m 9M; W twr; vis: 015°-236°; 57°55′·81N 05°24′·23W.

LOCH EWE and LOCH GAIRLOCH

Fairway L Fl 10s; 57°51′·98N 05°40′·09W.
Rubha Reidh ☆ 57°51′·52N 05°48′·72W Fl (4) 15s 37m **18M**.
Glas Eilean ☆ Fl WRG 6s 9m W6M, R4M; vis: 080°-W-102°-R-296°-W-333°-G-080°; 57°42′·79N 05°42′·42W.
Sgeir Dhubh Mhór; 57°42′·02N 05°42′·72W.

OUTER HEBRIDES – EAST SIDE

LEWIS

Butt of Lewis ☆ 58°30′·92N 06°15′·72W Fl 5s 52m **25M**; R twr; vis: 056°-320°.
Tiumpan Hd ☆ 58°15′·66N 06°08′·29W Fl (2)15s 55m **18M**; W twr.
Broad Bay Tong ⚓ Ldg Lts 320°, Oc R 8s 8m 4M; 58°14′·48N 06°19′·98W. Rear, 70m from front, Oc R 8s 9m 4M.

STORNOWAY

Arnish Point ☆ Fl WR 10s 17m W9M, R7M; W ○ twr; vis: 088°-W-198°-R-302°-W-013°; 58°11′·50N 06°22′·16W.
Sandwick Bay, NW ☆ Dir WRG 4s 10m 10M; 336°-IsoG -339°- AlWG -341°-IsoW-347°-AlWR-349°-Iso-R-352°; 58°12′·17N 06°22′·15W.
No 1 Pier SW corner ☆ Q WRG 5m 11M; vis: shore-G-335°-W-352°-R-shore; 58°12′·36N 06°23′·43W.
Creed Estuary Dir Lt ☆ 288·5° WRG 4s 23m 5M; 277°-IsoG-282°-Al WG-287°-IsoW-290°-Al WR-292°-R-295°; 58°12′·00N 06°23′·54W.
No 3 Pier ☆ Q (2) G 10s 7m 2M 58°12′·31N 06°23′·28W.
Glumaig Hbr ☆ Iso WRG 3s 8m 3M; 58°11′·29N 06°22′·83W; grey framework twr; vis: 150°-G-174°-W-185°-R-205°.

LOCH ERISORT, LOCH SHELL and EAST LOCH TARBERT

Shiants QG; 57°54′·57N 06°25′·70W.
Sgeir Inoe Fl G 6s; ***Racon (M) 5M***; 57°50′·93N 06°33′·93W.
Eilean Glas (Scalpay) ☆ 57°51′·41N 06°38′·55W Fl (3) 20s 43m **18M**; W twr, R bands; ***Racon (T) 16-18M***; 992356014.
Sgeir Graidach Q (6) + L Fl 15s; 57°50′·36N 06°41′·37W.
Sgeir Ghlas ☆ Iso WRG 4s 9m W9M, R6M, G6M; W ○ twr; vis: 282°-G-319°-W-329°-R-153°-W-164°-G-171°; 57°52′·36N 06°45′·24W.
Tarbert ☆ Dir 301·5° WRG 9m 4M; vis : 290°-Iso G-297°-Al WG-300°-Iso W-303°-Al WR-306°-Iso R306°-313°; 57°53′·80N 06°47′·85W.

SOUND OF HARRIS, LEVERBURGH and BERNERAY

No 1 QG; 57°41′·20N 07°02′·67W.
No 3 Fl G 5s; 57°41′·86N 07°03′·44W.
No 4 Fl R 5s; 57°41′·76N 07°03′·63W.
Suilven Fl (3)R 10s; 57°41′·68N 07°04′·36W.
Cabbage Fl (2) R 6s; ***Racon (T) 5M (3cm)***; 57°42′·13N 07°03′·96W.
Leverburgh Ldg Lts 014·7°. Front, Q 10m 4M 57°46′·23N 07°02′·04W. Rear, Oc 3s 12m 4M.
Jane's Tower Q (2) G 5s 6m 4M; vis: obscured 273°-318°; 57°45′·76N 07°02′·11W.
Leverburgh Reef Fl R 2s 4m 57°45′·97N 07°01′·86W.
Laimhrig Mhor ☆ Q G; 57°45′·92N 07°01′·65W.
Leverburg Dir Lt 064·5°; Dir G 4m 6M metal twr; vis: 060°-QG-063°-F G-066°-OcG 2·25s-069°; 57° 46′·00 N 07° 01′·55 W.

NORTH UIST

Fairway L Fl 10s; 57°40′·23N 07°01′·39W.
Griminish Hbr Dir lt 183° ☆ metal post; vis: WRG 4s 6m WRG2M 178°-IsoG-182°-AlWG-182·5°-IsoW-183·5°-AlWR-184°-IsoR-188°; 57°39′·39N 07°26′·72W.

LOCH MADDY and GRIMSAY

Weaver's Pt ☆ Fl 3s 24m 7M; W hut; 57°36′·49N 07°06′·00W.
Glas Eilean Mòr ☆ Fl (2) G 4s 8m 5M; 57°35′·95N 07°06′·70W.
Vallaquie Is Dir lt 207·5°/ 255·5° ☆ W pillar; vis: Fl (3) WRG 8s 11m W5M, R5M, G5M; shore-G-205°-W-210°-R-240°; Fl (3) WRG 8s 11m W8M, R8M, G8M; 249°-G-254°-W-257°-R-262° 57°35′·49N 07°09′·32W.
Lochmaddy Ro-Ro Pier, Dir lt 300° ☆ post; Iso WRG 2s W6M, R4M, G4M; vis: 288°-G-295°-WG-298°-W-302°-WR-305°-R-311° 57°35′·79N 07°09′·46W.
Grimsay No 1 Fl (2) R 8s; 57°28′·26N 07°11′·82W.

SOUTH UIST and LOCH CARNAN

Landfall L Fl 10s.; 57°22′·27N 07°11′·52W.
Ldg Lts 222°. Front Fl R 2s 7m 5M; W ◊ on post; 57°22′·00N 07°16′·34W. Rear, 58m from front, Iso R 10s 11m 5M; W ◊ on post.
Ushenish ☆ (S Uist) 57°17′·90N 07°11′·57W Fl W 20s 54m **W19M**; W twr; vis: 193°- 018°.

LOCH BOISDALE

MacKenzie Rk Fl (3) R 15s 3m 4M; 57°08′·24N 07°13′·71W.
Calvay E End ☆ Fl (2) WRG 10s 16m W7M, R7M, G7M; W twr; vis: 111°-W-190°-G-202°-W-286°-R-111°; 57°08′·53N 07°15′·38W; 992351139.
Gasay I ☆ Fl WR 5s 10m W7M, R7M; W twr; vis: 120°-W-284°-R-120°; 57°08′·93N 07°17′·39W.
Loch Boisdale Dir lt ☆, 292·5°; WRG 4s 4m 5M; vis: 287·5°-IsoG-290·5°-AlWG-292°-IsoW-293°-AlW-294·5°-IsoR-298·5°; 57°09′·19N 07°18′·24W.
2 FG 8m 3M on dn; 57°09′·13N 07°18′·18W.

LUDAIG and ERISKAY

Ludaig Bwtr ☆ 2 FR (vert) 6m 3M; 57°06′·17N 07°19′·49W.
Acairseid Mhor Ldg Lts 285°. Front, Oc R 6s 9m 4M; 57°03′·89N 07°17′·25W. Rear, 24m from front, Oc R 6s 10m 4M.

BARRA, CASTLEBAY and VATERSAY SOUND

Drover Rocks Q (6) + L Fl 15s; 57°04′·08N 07°23′·54W.
Binch Rock Q (6) + L Fl 15s; 57°01′·60N 07°17′·12W.
Curachan Q (3) 10s; 56°58′·56N 07°20′·51W.
Ardveenish ☆ Oc WRG 6m 9/6M; vis: 300°-G-304°-W-306°-R-310°; 57°00′·21N 07°24′·43W.
Vich Chuan Q(6)+LFl 15s; ***Racon (M) 5M***; 56°56′·15N 07°23′·31W.
Channel Rk ☆ Fl WR 6s 4m W6M, R4M; vis: 121·5°-W-277°-R-121·5°; 56°56′·24N 07°28′·94W.
Sgeir a Scape Fl (2) G 8s; 56°56′·25N 07°27′·21W.
Rubha Glas. Ldg Lts 295°. Front FBu 9m 6M; Or △ on W twr; 56°56′·77N 07°30′·64W. Rear, 457m from front, FBu 15m 6M; Or ▽ on W twr; vis: 15° and 8° respectively either side of ldg line.
Barra Hd ☆ 56°47′·12N 07°39′·21W Fl 15s 208m **18M**; W twr; obsc by islands to NE; 992351095.

OUTER HEBRIDES – WEST SIDE

Flannan I ☆, Eilean Mór Fl (2) 30s 101m **20M**; W twr; 58°17′·29N 07°35′·29W, obsc in places by Is to W of Eilean Mór.
Rockall ☆ Fl 15s 19m 8M (unreliable); 57°35′·76N 13°41′·27W.
Gasker Lt ☆ Fl (3) 10s 38m 10M; 57°59′·05N 07°17′·20W.
Whale Rock Q (3) 10s 5m 5M; ***Racon (T)***; 57°54′·40N 07°59·91W.
Haskeir I ☆ 57°41′·96N 07°41·31W Fl 20s 44m **22M**; W twr; ***Racon (M) 17–15M***; 992351140.
Monach Is ☆ Fl (2)15s 47m **18M**; red brick twr; 57°31′·55N 07°41′·68W.

EAST LOCH ROAG

Aird Laimishader Carloway ☆ Fl 6s 63m 8M; W hut; obsc on some brgs; 58°17′·06N 06°49′·50W.
Ardvanich Pt ☆ Fl G 3s 4m 2M; 58°13′·48N 06°47′·68W.
Tidal Rk ☆ Fl R 3s 2m 2M (sync with Ardvanich Pt above); 58°13′·45N 06°47′·57W.
Grèinam ☆ Fl WR 6s 8m W8M, R7M; W bn; vis: R143°-169°, W169°-143°; 58°13′·30N 06°46′·16W.

LOCH ROAG

Rubha Domhain ☆ Fl G 5s 9m 1M; post; 58°12′·96N 06°45′·40W.
Bogha na Muilne Fl (2) 10s; 58°12′·70N 06°54′·23W.
Mia Vaig Bay Fl G 2s 2m 1M; bn; 58°11′·83N 06°56′·60W.

NORTH UIST and SOUTH UIST

Falconet twr ☆ FR 25m 8M (3M by day); shown 1hr before firing, changes to Iso R 2s 15 min before firing until completion; 57°22′·04N 07°23′·58W.

ST KILDA

Ldg Lts 270°. Front, Oc 5s 26m 3M; 57°48′·32N 08°34′·31W. Rear, 100m from front, Oc 5s 38m 3M; sync.

LOCH TORRIDON TO MALLAIG

LITTLE MINCH and W SKYE

Eugenie Rock Q 6 + LF 15s; 57°46′·47N 06°27′·28W.
Eilean Trodday ☆ Fl (2) WRG 10s 52m W12M, R9M, G9M; W Bn; vis: W062°-R088°-130°-W-322°-G-062°; 57°43′·63N 06°17′·93W; 992351084.
Uig, Edward Pier Hd ☆ 57°35′·09N 06°22′·29W Iso WRG 4s 9m W7M, R4M, G4M; vis: 180-W-006°-G-050°-W-073°-R-180°.
Waternish Pt ☆ Fl 20s 21m 8M; W twr; 57°36′·48N 06°37′·99W.
Loch Dunvegan, Uiginish Pt ☆ Fl WRG 3s 16m W7M,R5M,G5M; W lattice twr; vis: 041°-G-132°-W-145°-R-148°-W-253°-R-263°-W-273°-G-306°, (>148° obsc by Fiadhairt Pt); 57°26′·84N 06°36′·53W.
Neist Point ☆ 57°25′·41N 06°47′·30W Fl 5s 43m **16M**; W twr.
Loch Harport, Ardtreck Pt ☆ 57°20′·38N 06°25′·80W Fl 6s 18m 9M; small W twr.

RONA, LOCH A'BHRAIGE and INNER SOUND

Na Gamhnachain Q; 57°35′·89N 05°57′·71W.
Rona NE Point ☆ 57°34′·69N 05°57′·54W Fl 12s 69m 12M; W twr; vis: 050°-358°; 992351045.
Loch A'Bhraige, Sgeir Shuas ☆ Fl R 2s 6m 3M; vis: 070°-199°; 57°35′·02N 05°58′·61W.
Ldg bn 136·5° Q WRG3m W4M RG 3M 57° 34′·41N 5° 58′·08W.
Rubha Ard Ghlaisen Fl R 3s; 57°29′·67N 05°58′·71W.
Screapadal Fl R (2) 5s; 57°25′·54N 06°01′·90W.

SOUND OF RAASAY, PORTREE and CROWLIN ISLANDS

Sgeir Mhór Fl G 5s; 57°24′·57N 06°10′·53W.
Eilean Beag ☆ Fl 6s 32m 6M; W Bn; 57°21′·21N 05°51′·42W.
Eyre Pt ☆ Fl WR 3s 6m WR8M; W clad framework twr; vis: 215°-W-267°-R-288°-W-063°; 57°20′·01N 06°01′·28W.
Sgeir Thraid ☆ Q 12m 3M; metal twr; 57°19′·82N 05°56′·50W.
Sgeir Ghobhlach ☆ Fl(3)10s 10m 3M; metal twr; 57°15′·69N 05°52′·25W.

LOCH CARRON

Sgeir Golach ☆ Fl 10s 5m 3M; 57°21′·20N 05°39′·01W.
Eilean a Chait Lt ho (dis) 13M; 57°20′·96N 05°38′·87W.
Bogha Dubh Sgeir Fl (2)R 6s 4m 2M; 57°20′·92N 05°37′·85W.

RAASAY and LOCH SLIGACHAN

Suisnish ☆ 2 FG (vert) 8m 2M; 57°19′·87N 06°03′·91W.
Eyre Point ☆ Fl WR 3s 6m WR 8M; W twr; vis: 215°-W-267°-R-288°-W-063°; 57°20′·01N 06°01′·29W.

KYLEAKIN and KYLE OF LOCH ALSH

Carragh Rk Fl (2) G 12s; ***Racon (T) 5M***; 57°17′·18N 05°45′·36W.
Bow Rk Fl (2) R 12s; 57°16′·71N 05°45′·85W.
Fork Rks Fl G 6s; 57°16′·85N 05°44′·93W.
Black Eye Rk Fl R 6s; 57°16′·68N 05°45′·20W.
Eileanan Dubha East ☆ Fl (2) 10s 9m 8M; vis: obscured 104°-146°; 57°16′·56N 05°42′·32W.
8 Metre Rock ☆ Fl G 6s 5m 4M; 57°16′·60N 05°42′·69W.
String Rock Fl R 6s; 57°16′·50N 05°42′·89W.
Sgeir-na-Caillich ☆ Fl (2) R 6s 3m 4M; 57°15′·59N 05°38′·90W.

SOUND OF SLEAT

Kyle Rhea ☆ Fl WRG 3s 7m W8M, R5M, G5M; W Bn; vis: shore-R-219°-W-228°-G-338°-W-346°-R-shore; 57°14′·22N 05°39′·93W.
Sandaig I, NW point ☆ Fl 6s 13m 8M; W twr; 57°10′·05N 05°42′·29W.
Ornsay ☆ Oc 8s 18m 12M; vis: 157°-030°; 57°08′·60N 05°46′·85W.
Pt. of Sleat ☆ Fl 3s 20m9M; W twr; 57°01′·08N 06°01′·08W.

MALLAIG and LOCH NEVIS ENTRANCE

Sgeir Dhearg QG; 57°00′·74N 05°49′·50W.
Northern Pier E end ☆ Iso WRG 4s 6m W9M, R6M, G6M; Gy twr; vis: 181°-G-185°-W-197°-R-201°. Fl G 3s 14m 6M; same structure; 57°00′·47N 05°49′·50W.
Sgeir Dhearg ☆ 57°00′·63N 05°49′·61W Fl (2) WG 8s 6m 5M; Gy Bn; vis: 190°-G-055°-W-190°.

SMALL ISLES AND WEST OF MULL

CANNA and RUM

Sanday ☆ Fl 10s 32m 9M; vis: 152°-061°; 57°02′·82N 06°28′·02W.
Loch Scresort Q; 57°00′·79N 06°14′·61W.

HYSKEIR, EIGG, MUCK and ARISAIG

Humla Fl G 6s 3m 4M 57°00′·46N 06°37′·39W.
Hyskeir ☆ 56°58′·16N 06°40′·83W Fl (3) 30s 41m **24M**; W twr. ***Racon (T) 14-17M***; 992351094.
SE point Eigg (Eilean Chathastail) ☆ Fl 6s 24m 8M; W twr; vis: 181°-shore; 56°52′·25N 06°07′·28W.
Eigg, Sgeir nam Bagh (Ferry Terminal) ☆ Dir 245°; Fl WRG 3s 9m W14, R11, G11; H24; steel pole; vis: 242·5°-G-244°-W-246°-R-247·5°. 2FR(vert) on same structure; 56°52′·79N 06°07′·56W.
Isle of Muck ☆ Dir 319·5° Fl WRG 3s 7m W14 RG11, by day WRG1; twr; vis: 317°-G-318·5°-W-320·5°-R-322°; 56°49′·94N 06°13′·71W.
Bogha Ruadh ☆ Fl G 5s 4m 3M; 56°49′·56N 06°13′·04W.
Dubh Sgeir ☆ Fl (2) R 10s 4m 3M; 56°49′·54N 06°13′·13W.
Bo Faskadale Fl (3) G 18s; 56°48′·18N 06°06′·37W.
Ardnamurchan ☆ 56°43′·63N 06°13′·58W Fl (2) 20s 55m **18M**; Gy twr; vis: 002°-217°.
Suil Ghorm ☆ Fl 12s 23m 10M; W twr; 56°42′·26N 06°26′·75W.

TIREE, COLL and ARINAGOUR

Loch Eatharna, Pier Head ☆ Dir 325°; Oc WRG 7s 6m 2M; vis: 316°-G-322°-W-328°-R-334°; 56°36′·86N 06°31′·29W.
Loch Eatharna, Bogha Mór Fl G 6s; 56°36′·65N 06°30′·90W.
Roan Bogha Q (6) + L Fl 15s 3m 5M; 56°32′·23N 06°40′·18W.
Placaid Bogha Fl G 4s; 56°33′·22N 06°44′·06W.
Scarinish ☆ Fl 3s 11m 12M; W □ twr; vis: 210°-030°; S side of ent, 56°30′·02N 06°48′·26W.
Cairn na Burgh More (Treshnish Is), Fl (3) 15s 36m 8M; solar panels on framework tr; 56°31′·05N 06°22′·95W.
Gott Bay Ldg Lts 286·5°. Front FR 8m; 56°30′·61N 06°47′·82W. Rear 30m from front FR 11m.

Skerryvore ☆ Fl 10s 46m **23M**; Gy twr; ***Racon (M) 18M***. 56°19′·36N 07°06′·88W; 992351091.

LOCH NA KEAL, LOCH NA LÀTHAICH and IONA

Sgeir a Charraigein Q(6) + LFl 15s; 56°28′·29N 06°07′·71W.
Eileanan na Liathanaich, SE end Fl WR 6s 12m W8M, R6M; vis: R088°- W108°-088°; 56°20′·56N 06°16′·38W.
Bo na Sliganach Q(6) + LFl 15s; 56°19′·45N 06°23′·12W.
Bogha hun a Chuhoil Q(6) + LFl 15s; 56°16′·57N 06°24′·86W.

DUBH ARTACH

Dubh Artach ☆ 56°07′·94N 06°38′·08W Fl (2) 30s 44m **20M**; Gy twr, R band; 992351088.

SOUND OF MULL

LOCH SUNART, TOBERMORY and LOCH ALINE

Ardmore Pt Fl (2) 10s 18m 13M; 56°39′·37N 06°07′·70W.
Salen Bay 56°42′·67N 05°46′·57W.
New Rks Q (9) 15s; 56°39′·07N 06°03′·55W; AIS.
Little Stirk Q(6)+L Fl 15s; 56°38′·50N 06°01′·50W.
Rubha nan Gall ☆ 56°38′·33N 06°04′·00W Fl 3s 17m **15M**; W twr.
Tobermory Slip Iso WRG 3s 5m 4M; vis: 220°-G-232°-W-244°-R-256° (sectors± 2°); metal column; 56°37′·41N 06°03′·77W.
Dearg Sgeir Fl 6s 7m 8M; W ○ twr; 56°32′·25N 05°54′·80W.
Fiunary Spit Fl G 6s; 56°32′·66N 05°53′·17W.
Fishnish Ferry Slip Iso WRG 3s 5m 4M; vis: 158°-G-170°-W-195°-R-230° (sectors± 4°); metal column; 56°30′·89N 05°48′·61W.
Loch Aline, Dir 357°; Oc WRG 6s 2m 4M; vis: 353°-G-356°-W-358°-R-002°; Or concrete plinth; 56°32′·38N 05°46′·47W.
Ardtornish Pt Fl (2) WRG 10s 8m W8M, R6M, G6M; W twr; vis: G shore- 301°-W-308°-R-342°-W-057°-R-095°-W-108°-G-shore; 56°31′·09N 05°45′·21W.
Craignure Ldg Lts 240·9°. Front, FR 10m; 56°28′·26N 05°42′·28W. Rear, 150m from front, FR 12m; vis: 225·8°-255·8°.

MULL TO CALEDONIAN CANAL AND OBAN

Lismore ☆, SW end 56°27′·34N 05°36′·45W Fl 10s 31m **17M**; W twr; vis: 237°-208°.
Lady's Rk Fl 6s 12m 5M; Red clad lattice tower on W base 56°26′·92N 05°37′·05W; 992351093.
Duart Pt Fl (3) WR 18s 14m W5M, R3M; vis: 162°-W-261°-R-275°-W-353°-R-shore; 56°26′·84N 05°38′·77W.

LOCH LINNHE

Corran Shoal QR 56°43′·69N 05°14′·39W.
Corran Pt Iso WRG 4s 12m W10M, R7M, G7M; W twr; vis: shore-R-195°-W-215°-G-020-W-030°-R-shore; 56°43′·25N 05°14′·54W.
Corran Narrows NE Fl 5s 4m 4M; W twr; vis: S shore-214°; Dir lt 033° Iso WRG 2s 4m 4M (1M day), vis: 028·5°- Iso G -030·5° - Alt W/G -031·5°- Iso W -032·5°- Alt W/R - 033·5°- Iso R -035·5°; co-located 56°43′·62N 05°13′·90W.
Clovullin Spit Fl (2) R 15s; 56°42′·29N 05°15′·56W.
Cuil-cheanna Spit Fl G 6s; 56°41′·17N 05°15′·72W.
Mc Lean Rk QR 56°49′·80N 05°07′·04W.
Eilean na Creiche Fl (2) 5s; 56°50′·25N 05°07′·02W.
Eilean na Craobh Fl (2) R 6s 4m 2M; 56°50′·43N 05°07′·95W.

FORT WILLIAM and CALEDONIAN CANAL

Corpach, Caledonian Canal Lock ent Iso WRG 4s 6m 5M; W twr; vis: G287°- W310°- R335°-030°; 56°50′·52N 05°07′·44W.
Rubha Cuil-Cheanna Dir 194°; WRG 2s 12m 5M; vis: 190·5°- Iso R -192·5° - Alt W/R -193·5°- Iso W -194·5°- Alt W/G -195·5°- Iso G -197·5°; W clad framework twr; 56°42′·31N 05°14′·80W.

LYNN OF LORN

Sgeir Bhuidhe Appin Fl (2) WR 7s 8m W9M R6M; W Bn; vis: W013·5°- R184°-220°; 56°33′·63N 05°24′·65W.
Appin Point Fl G 6s; 56°32′·69N 05°25′·97W.
Dearg Sgeir, off Aird's Point Fl WRG 2s 2m W3M, R1M, G1M; vis: 196°-R-246°-W-258°-G-041°-W-058°-R-093°-W-139°; 56°32′·20N 05°25′·22W.
Rubha nam Faoileann (Eriska) QG 2m 2M; G col; vis 128°-329°; 56°32′·20N 05°24′·11W.
Branra Rk Fl(2) 10s 4m 5M; metal frame on W twr; 56°32′·02N 05°26′·60W.

OBAN

N spit of Kerrera Fl R 3s 9m 5M; W col; 56°25′·49N 05°29′·56W.
Dunollie Fl (2) WRG 6s 6m W8M, R6M, G6M; vis: 351°-G- 020°-W-047°-R-120°-W-138°-G-143°; twr; 56°25′·37N 05°29′·05W.
Rubh'a'Chruidh Q R 3m 2M; W post; 56°25′·32N 05°29′·29W.
N Channel 1 Fl G 2s (sync); 56°25′·33N 05°29′·08W.
N Channel 2 Fl R 2s (sync); 56°25′·35N 05°29′·25W.
N Channel 3 Fl G 2s (sync); 56°25′·28N 05°29′·08W.
N Channel 4 Fl R 2s (sync); 56°25′·27N 05°29′·25W.
N Channel 5 Fl G 2s (sync); 56°25′·22N 05°29′·09W.
N Channel 7 Fl G 2s (sync); 56°25′·16N 05°29′·06W.
N Channel 9 Fl G 2s (sync); 56°25′·10N 05°29′·95W.
Transit Marina Fl G 2m 2M; post; 56°25′·00N 05°28′·57W.
Oban Bay Q; 56°24′·92N 05°29′·23W.
Sgeir Rathaid Q(6)+L Fl 15s; 56°24′·75N 05°29′·37W.
North Pier 2 F G (vert); metal post; 56°24′·89N 05°28′·49W.
Ro-Ro Jetty 2 F G (vert); post on dn; 56°24′·69N 05°28′·65W.
North'n Lt Pier 2 FG (vert); metal post; 56°24′·71N 05°28′·91W.

OBAN TO LOCH CRAIGNISH

Heather Is Fl R 2·5s 11m 2M; 56°24′·41N 05°30′·24W.
Ferry Rks NW Q G; 56°24′·11N 05°30′·69W.
Kerrera Q R; 56°24′·15N 05°30′·81W.
Ferry Rks SE Q (3) 10s; 56°23′·99N 05°30′·53W.
Ferry Pier 2 FL (vert); 56 23′.92N 005 31′.02W.
Little Horseshoe Fl R 12 s; 56 23′.22N 005 31′.83W.
Sgeirean Dubha Fl (2) 12s 7m 5M; W ○ twr; 56°22′·81N 05°32′·27W.
Sgeir an Fheuran Fl G 3s; 56°22′·80N 05°31′·94W.
Bogha Nuadh Q(6)+LFl 15s; 56°21′·69N 05°37′·87W; 992351090.
Bogha Ghair Q (3) 10s; 56°16′·50N 05°40′·44W.
Bono Rock Q (9) 15s; 56°16′·21N 05°41′·22W.
Fladda Fl (2) WRG 9s 13m W11M, R9M, G9M; W twr; vis: 169°-R-186°-W-337°-G-344°-W-356°-R-026°; 56°14′·89N 05°40′·83W.
Dubh Sgeir (Luing) Fl WRG 6s 9m W6M, R4M. G4M; W twr; vis: W002°-R012°-W030°-G201°-002°; ***Racon (M) 5M***; 56°14′·76N 05°40′·20W.
The Garvellachs, Eileach an Naoimh, SW end Fl 6s 21m 9M; W Bn; vis: 240°-215°; 56°13′·04N 05°49′·06W.

LOCH MELFORT and CRAOBH HAVEN

Melfort Pier Dir FR 6m 3M; (Apr -Nov); 56°16′·14N 05°30′·19W.
56°12′·88N 05°33′·59W.
Craobh Marina Bkwtr Hd Iso WRG 5s 10m, W5M, R3M, G3M; vis:114°-G-162°-W-183°-R-200°; 56°12′·78N 05°33′·52W.

1.4 PASSAGE INFORMATION

It is essential to carry large scale charts and current pilot books for this area. Admiralty Leisure Folio 5616 only partially covers the waters between Ardnamurchan Pt and the Shiant Isles. **Bibliography:** *Clyde Cruising Club Sailing Directions-Kintyre to Ardnamurchan, CCC Sailing Directions-Ardnamurchan to Cape Wrath, CCC Sailing Directions-Outer Hebrides* (all Imray/ Clyde Cruising Club, Lawrence). *The Yachtsman's Pilot to Skye and Northwest Scotland* (Imray/Lawrence). The *North West Coast of Scotland Pilot* (Admiralty NP66B) covers the area.

Scotland's west coast provides splendid, if boisterous, sailing and matchless scenery. In summer the long daylight hours and warmth of the Gulf Stream compensate for the lower air temperatures and higher wind speeds experienced when depressions run typically north of Scotland. Inshore winds are often unpredictable due to the topography of islands, lochs and mountains; calms and squalls can alternate rapidly.

Good anchors, especially on kelp/weed, are essential. Øs are listed but availability is not guaranteed. Facilities are very dispersed, particularly in N of area. A key for fuel pumps in the W Isles is available from Comhairlenan Eilean Siar (Hbr Authority) ☎01870 604992 harbourmaster@cne-siar.gov.uk. A *'Rover Ticket'* from Highland Council allows berthing for 15 days; the scheme includes: Kinlochbervie, Lochinver, Gairloch, Kyle of Lochalsh, Kyleakin, Portree and Uig. VHF communications with shore stations is restricted by high ground. Beware ever more fish farms in many inlets. Local magnetic anomalies occur in Kilbrannan Sound, Passage of Tiree, Sound of Mull, Canna, and East Loch Roag. Submarines exercise throughout these waters.

OUTER HEBRIDES

(AC 1785, 1794, 1795) The E sides of these Is have many good, sheltered ⚓s, but W coasts give little shelter. The CCC's *Outer Hebrides SDs* or *The Western Isles* (Imray) are advised.

▶ *The Minches and Sea of the Hebrides can be very rough, particularly in the Little Minch between Skye and Harris, and around Shiant Is where tide runs 4kn at Sp, and heavy overfalls occur. The NE-going stream on both shores begins at HW Ullapool -0340 (HW Dover +0430), with the strongest flow from mid-channel to the Skye coast. A W-going counter tide runs E of Vaternish Pt.*

The SW-going stream on both shores begins at HW Ullapool +0240 (HW Dover –0130), with the strongest flow from mid-channel to the Skye coast, Sp rates 2·5kn. The E-going stream in Sound of Scalpay runs at up to 2kn.The E-going flood and W-going ebb in Sound of Scalpay run at up to 2kn.◀

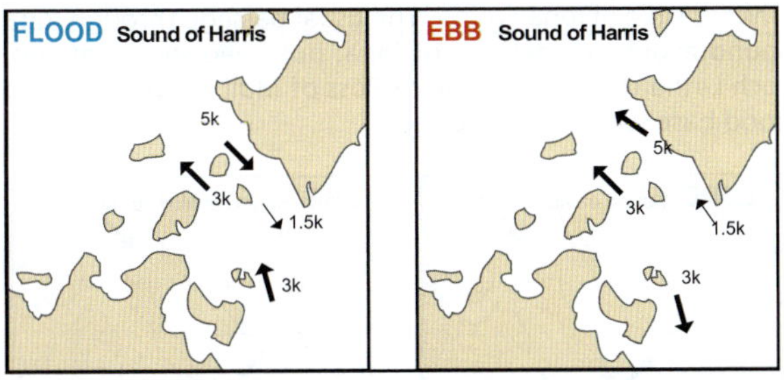

▶ **Sound of Harris.** *The behaviour of tidal streams is complicated and varies from day to night, Springs to Neaps, and winter to summer. In the NE part of the Sound, at Sp, the stream sets SE from Ullapool +0535 to –0035. At Np, in the summer, the stream sets SE during the day and NW at night. To the SW of the Sound, the NW stream starts at Ullapool –0545; the SE stream starts at Ullapool +0025. Approximate maximum rates are as shown. For more detailed information refer to the Admiralty West Coast of Scotland Pilot.*◀

From N to S, better harbours in the Outer Hebrides include:

Lewis. Stornoway; Loch Grimshader (beware Sgeir a'Chaolais, dries in entrance); Loch Erisort; Loch Odhairn; Loch Shell. Heading S from here, or to E Loch Tarbert beware Sgeir Inoe (dries 2·3m) 3M ESE of Eilean Glas lt ho (SE end of Scalpay).

Harris. E Loch Tarbert; Loch Scadaby; Loch Stockinish; Loch Finsby; W Loch Tarbert; Loch Rodel (Ø). A well-marked ferry channel connects Leverburgh (South Harris) to Berneray.

North Uist. Loch Maddy (Ø); Loch Eport, Kallin Hbr (Ø).

South Uist. Loch Carnan (Ø); Loch Skiport; Loch Eynort; Loch Boisdale (Ø).

Barra. Castlebay (Ø), and Berneray, on N side, E of Shelter Rk.

There are numerous ⚓s. Bratanish Mor in Loch Roag is very sheltered and provides respite on W coast. Yachts should register in advance at www.cne-siar.gov.uk.

Activity at the Hebrides Range, S Uist ☎(01870) 604441, is broadcast daily at 0950LT and Mon-Fri 1100-1700LT on VHF Ch **12** (Ch 73 in emergency) and on MF 2660 kHz.

CAPE WRATH TO ULLAPOOL

(AC 1785, 1794) C Wrath (lt AIS) is a steep headland (110m).

▶ *To N of it the E-going stream begins at HW Ullapool – 0350, and W-going at HW Ullapool + 0235, sp rates 3kn. Eddies close inshore cause almost continuous W-going stream E of Cape, and N-going stream SW of it. Where they meet is turbulence, with dangerous seas in bad weather.* ◀

Duslic Rk, 7ca NE of lt ho, dries 3·4m. 6M SW of C Wrath, islet of Am Balg (45m) is foul for 2ca around.

There are ⚓ in Loch Inchard (AC 2503), the best shelter being in Kinlochbervie on N shore; also good ⚓s among Is along S shore of Loch Laxford, entered between Ardmore Pt and Rubha Ruadh. Handa Is to WSW is a bird sanctuary. Handa Sound is navigable with care, but beware Bogha Morair in mid-chan and associated overfalls.

▶ *Tide turns 2hrs earlier in the Sound than offshore. Strong winds against tide raise a bad sea off Pt of Stoer.*◀

The best shelter is 8M S at Loch Inver (AC 2504), with good ⚓ off hotel near head of loch. ⚓s to the N of Loch Inver may be found at Kylesku, Culkein Drumbeg, Drumbeg, Loch Nedd and Loch Roe. To the S lies Enard Bay.

ULLAPOOL TO LOCH TORRIDON

(AC 1794, 2210, 5616) The Summer Isles (AC 2501), 12M NW of the major fishing port of Ullapool, offer some sheltered ⚓s and tight approaches. The best include the bay on E side of Tanera Mor; off NE of Tanera Beg (W of Eilean Fada Mor); and in Caolas Eilean Ristol, between the island and mainland.

Loch Ewe (AC 3146) provides good shelter and easy access. Best ⚓s are in Poolewe Bay (beware Boor Rks off W shore) and in SW corner of Loch Thuirnaig (entering, keep close to S shore to avoid rocks extending from N side). Off Rubha Reidh (lt) seas can be dangerous.

▶ *The NE-going stream begins at HW Ullapool –0335; the SW-going at HW Ullapool +0305. Sp rates 3kn, but slacker to SW of point.* ◀

Longa Is lies N of ent to Loch Gairloch (AC 2528). The channel N of it is navigable but narrow at E end. The Outer loch is free of dangers, but exposed to swell. Best ⚓ is on S side of loch in Caolas Bad a' Chrotha, W of Eilean Horrisdale.

NW Scotland

Entering L Torridon (AC 2210) from S or W beware Murchadh Breac (dries 1·5m) 3ca NNW of Rubha na Fearna. Best ⚓s are SW of Eilean Mor (to W of Ardheslaig); in Loch a' Chracaich, 7ca further SE; E of Shieldaig Is; and head of Upper L Torridon.

▶ *Streams are weak except where they run 2-3kn in narrows between L Shieldaig and Upper L Torridon.* ◀

SKYE AND THE INNER SOUND

(AC 1795, 2210, 2209, 2208, 2207, 5616) Skye and the islands around it provide many good and attractive ⚓s, of which the most secure are: Acairseid Mhor on the W side of Rona; Portree (1.8); Oronsay, Portnalong, near the entrance to Loch Harport, and Carbost at the head; Loch Dunvegan; and Uig Bay in Loch Snizort. Ⓥs at Stein (Loch Dunvegan), Portree, Acairseid Mhor (Rona), Churchton Bay (Raasay) and Armadale Bay (S tip).

▶ *Tides are strong off Rubha Hunish at N end of Skye; heavy overfalls occur with tide against fresh or strong winds.* ◀

⚓ behind Fladday Is near the N end of Raasay can be squally and uncomfortable; and Loch Scavaig (S. Skye, beneath the Cuillins) more so, though the latter is so spectacular as to warrant a visit in fair weather. Soay Is has a small, safe hbr on its N side, but the bar at entrance almost dries at LW springs.

Between N Skye and the mainland there is the choice of Sound of Raasay or Inner Sound. The direction of buoyage in both Sounds is Northward. In the former, coming S from Portree, beware Sgeir Chnapach (3m) and Ebbing Rk (dries 2·9m), both NNW of Oskaig Pt. Beware McMillan's Rk (0·4m depth) in mid-channel, marked by SHM lt buoy.

▶ *At the Narrows (chart 2534) the SE-going stream begins at HW Ullapool –0605, and the NW-going at HW Ullapool +0040; Sp rate 1·4kn in mid-chan, but more near shoals each side.* ◀

The channel between Scalpay and Skye narrows to 2.5ca with drying reefs each side and least depth 0·1m.

▶ *Here the E-going stream begins at HW Ullapool +0550, and W-going at HW Ullapool –0010, Sp rate 1kn.* ◀

Inner Sound, which is a Submarine exercise area, is wider and easier than Sound of Raasay; the two are connected by Caol Rona and Caol Mor, respectively N and S of Raasay. Dangers extend about 1M N of Rona, and Cow Is lies off the mainland 8M to S; otherwise approach from N is clear to Crowlin Is, which should be passed to W. There is a good ⚓ between Eilean Mor and Eilean Meadhonach.

A military torpedo range in the Inner Sound does not normally restrict passage, but vessels may be requested to keep to the E side of the Sound if it is active. Range activity is broadcast at 0800 and 1800LT first on VHF Ch 16 and then on Ch 8, and is indicated by Red Flags flown on the range building at Applecross, by range vessels and at the naval pier at Kyle of Lochalsh, ☎(01599) 534262.

KYLE AKIN TO MALLAIG

Approaching Kyle Akin (AC 2540) from W, beware dangerous rks to N, off Bleat Is (at S side of entrance to Loch Carron); on S side of chan, Bogha Beag (dries 1·2m) and Black Eye Rk (depth 3·2m), respectively 6ca and 4ca W of bridge. Pass at least 100m N or S of Eileanan Dubha in Kyle Akin. On S side of chan String Rk (dries) is marked by PHM lt buoy. Kyle Rhea connects Loch Alsh with NE end of Sound of Sleat.

▶ *The tidal streams are very strong: N-going stream begins HW Ullapool + 0600, sp rate 6-7kn; S-going stream begins at HW Ullapool, sp rate 8kn. N-going stream in Kyle Rhea begins HW Dover +0140 (HW Ullapool +0555) and runs for 6hrs. The E-going stream in Kyle Akin begins (Sp) HW Dover +0350 (HW Ullapool –0415). (Nps) HW Dover –0415 (HW Ullapool).*

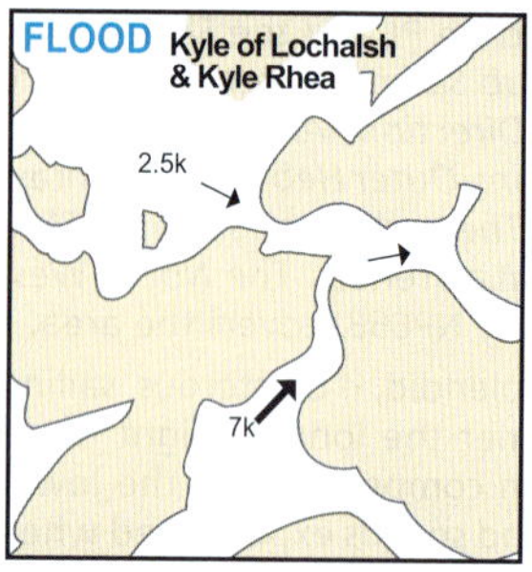

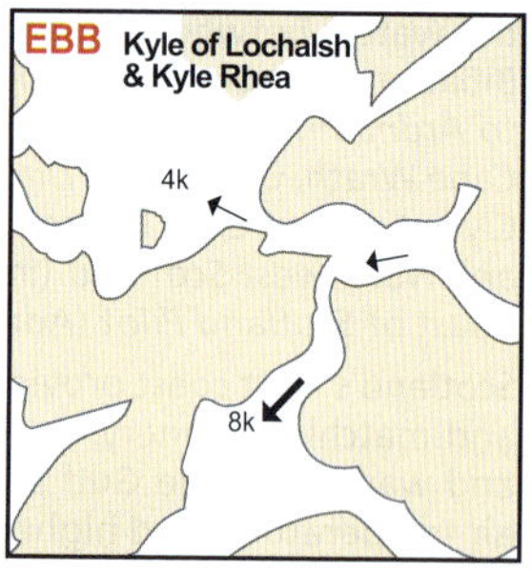

S-going stream in Kyle Rhea begins HW Dover –0415 (HW Ullapool) and runs for 6hrs. The W-going stream in Kyle Akin begins (Sp) HW Dover –0015 (HW Ullapool +0400). (Nps) HW Dover +0140 (HW Ullapool +0555). Eddies form both sides of the Kyle with dangerous overfalls off S end in fresh S'ly winds on S-going stream. ◀

Temp ⚓ in Sandaig Bay, 3M to SW. The Sound of Sleat widens to 4M off Point of Sleat and is exposed to SW winds unless Eigg and Muck give a lee. Mallaig is a busy fishing and ferry harbour, convenient for supplies. Further S the lochs require intricate pilotage. 6M NE of Ardnamurchan Pt (lt, fog sig) are Bo Faskadale rks, drying 0·5m and marked by SHM lt buoy, and Elizabeth Rock with depth of 0·7m.

▶ *Ardnamurchan Pt is an exposed headland onto which the ebb sets. With onshore winds, very heavy seas extend 2M offshore and it should be given a wide berth. Here the N-going stream begins at HW Oban – 0525, and the S-going at HW Oban + 0100, Sp rates 1·5kn.* ◀

ARDNAMURCHAN TO CRINAN

(AC 2171, 2169, 5616) S of Ardnamurchan the route lies either W of Mull via Passage of Tiree (where headlands need to be treated with respect in bad weather); or via the more sheltered Sound of Mull and Firth of Lorne. The former permits a visit to Coll and Tiree, where best ⚓s are at Arinagour (Ⓥs) and Gott Bay respectively. Beware Cairns of Coll, off the N tip.

The W coast of Mull is rewarding in settled weather, but careful pilotage is needed. Beware tide rip off Caliach Pt (NW corner) and Torran Rks off SW end of Mull (large-scale AC 2617 required). Apart from the attractions of Iona and of Staffa (Fingal's Cave), the remote Treshnish Is are worth visiting. The best ⚓s in this area are at Ulva, Gometra, Bull Hole and Tinker's Hole in Iona Sound. The usual passage through Iona Sound avoids overfalls W of Iona, but heed shoal patches. Loch Lathaich on the N side of Ross of Mull is 5M to the E; a good base with ⚓ at Bunessan.

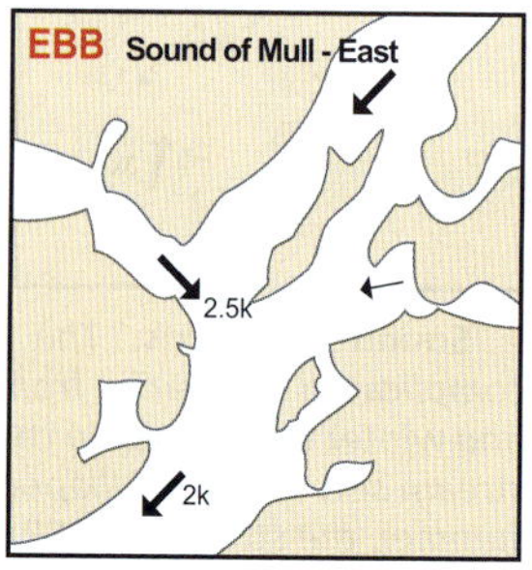

The Sound of Mull gives access to Tobermory, Dunstaffnage Bay, Oban, and up Loch Linnhe through Corran Narrows (where tide runs strongly) to Fort William and to Corpach for the Caledonian Canal. Apart from these places, there are dozens of ⚓s in the sheltered lochs inside Mull, as for example in Loch Sunart with 🅜s at Kilchoan.

FIRTH OF LORNE AND SOUND OF LUING

▶ **Firth of Lorne:** *the N-going stream begins at HW Oban +0430 (HW Dover –0100). The W-going stream in the Sound of Mull begins at HW Oban –0550 (HW Dover +0105). The ingoing tides at Lochs Feochan, Etive and Creran begin at HW Oban –0350, +0430 and +0600. The S-going stream in the Firth of Lorne begins at HW Oban –0155 (HW Dover +0500). The E-going stream in the Sound of Mull begins at HW Oban –0025 (HW Dover +0555).*◀

On the mainland shore Puilladobhrain is a sheltered ⚓. Cuan Sound is a useful short cut to Loch Melfort, and Craobh Marina. Good shelter may be found, draught permitting, in Ardinamar Bay, SW of Torsa.

Sound of Luing (AC 2326) between Fladda (lt), Lunga and Scarba on the W side, and Luing and Dubh Sgeir (lt) on the E side, is the normal chan to or from Sound of Jura, despite dangers at the N end and strong tidal streams.

▶ *The N- and W-going flood begins at HW Oban + 0430; the S- and E-going ebb at HW Oban –0155. Sp rates are 2·5kn at S end of Sound, increasing to 6kn or more in Islands off N entrance, where there are eddies, races and overfalls. The N- or W-going stream begins in the following sequence:* ◀

Dorus Mor:	*HW Oban +0330. Sp: 8kn.*
Corryvreckan:	*HW Oban +0410. Sp: 8.5kn.*
Cuan Sound:	*HW Oban +0420. Sp: 6kn.*
Sound of Jura:	*HW Oban +0400. Sp: 4kn.*
Sound of Luing:	*HW Oban +0430. Sp: 7kn.*

The S- or E-going stream begins as follows:

Dorus Mor:	*HW Oban –0215. Sp: 8kn.*
Corryvreckan:	*HW Oban –0210. Sp: 8.5kn.*
Cuan Sound:	*HW Oban –0200. Sp: 6kn.*
Sound of Jura:	*HW Oban –0205. Sp: 4kn.*
Sound of Luing:	*HW Oban –0155. Sp: 7kn.*

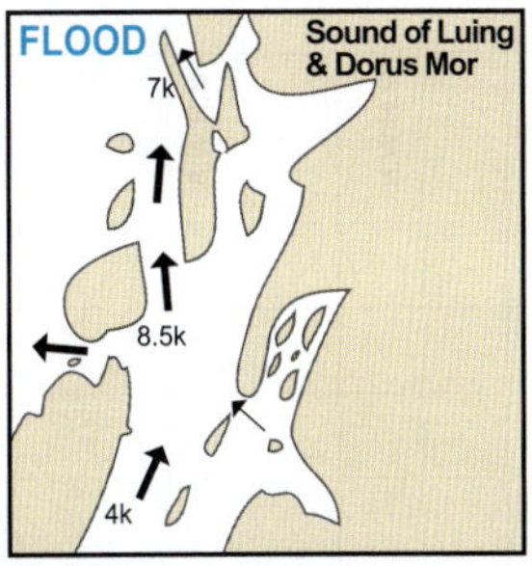

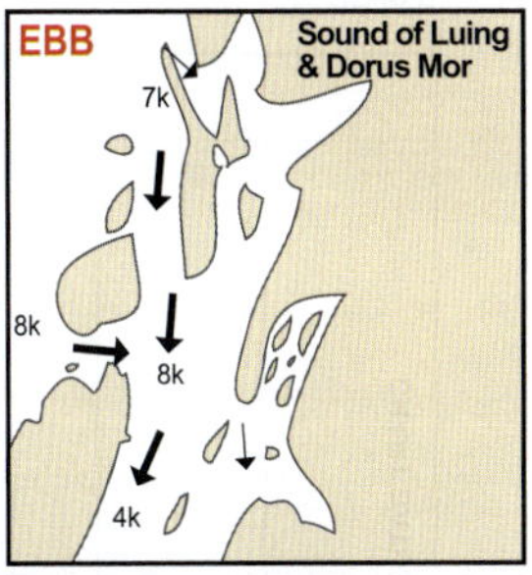

▶ *From the N, beware very strong streams, eddies and whirlpools in Dorus Mór, off Craignish Pt. Streams begin to set W and N away from Dorus Mór at HW Oban +0345, and E and S towards Dorus Mór at HW Oban –0215, Sp rates 7kn.*◀

At N end of Sound of Jura (AC 2326) is Loch Craignish. For Gulf of Corryvreckan, Colonsay, Islay, Loch Crinan and passage south through the Sound of Jura, see 2.4.

THE SMALL ISLES

(AC 2207, 2208, 5616) These consist of Canna, Rum, Eigg and Muck. The hbrs at Eigg (SE end), Rhum (Loch Scresort) and Canna (between Canna and Sanday) are all exposed to E'lies; Canna has best shelter and is useful for the Outer Hebrides. Dangers extend SSW from Canna: at 1M Jemina Rk (depth 1·5m) and Belle Rk (depth 3·6m); at 2M Humla Rk (5m high), marked by buoy and with offlying shoals close W of it; at 5M Hyskeir (lt, fog sig), the largest of a group of small islands; and at 7M Mill Rks (with depths of 1·8m).

▶ *The tide runs hard here, and in bad weather the sea breaks heavily up to 15M SW of Canna. Between Skerryvore and Neist Pt the stream runs generally N and S, starting N-going at HW Ullapool + 0550, and S-going at HW Ullapool –0010. It rarely exceeds 1kn, except near Skerryvore, around headlands of The Small Isles, and over rks and shoals.* ◀

1M off the N side of Muck are Godag Rks, some above water but with submerged dangers extending 2ca further N. Most other dangers around the Small Isles are closer inshore, but there are banks on which the sea breaks heavily in bad weather. A local magnetic anomaly exists about 2M E of Muck.

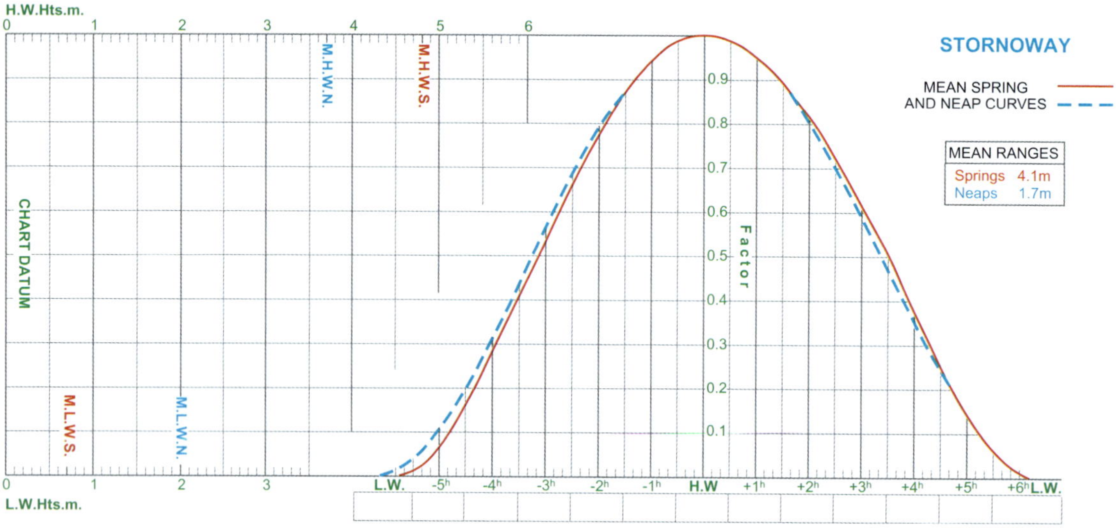

1.5 STORNOWAY

Lewis (Western Isles) **58°11′·58N 06°21′·82W** ✿✿✿◊◊✿✿

CHARTS AC 1785, 1794, 2529; Imray C67

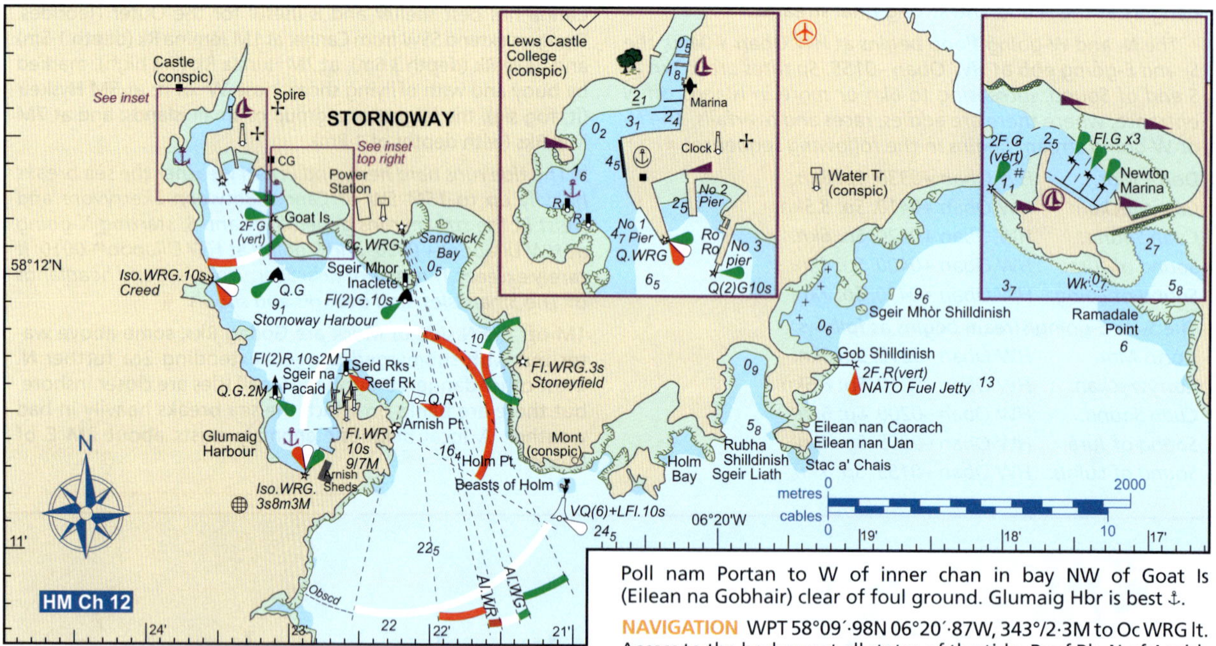

Poll nam Portan to W of inner chan in bay NW of Goat Is (Eilean na Gobhair) clear of foul ground. Glumaig Hbr is best ⚓.

TIDES

Standard Port STORNOWAY (⟶)

Times				**Height (metres)**			
High Water		Low Water		MHWS	MHWN	MLWN	MLWS
0100	0700	0300	0900	4·8	3·7	2·0	0·7
1300	1900	1500	2100				
Differences CARLOWAY (W Lewis)							
−0040	+0020	−0035	−0015	−0·7	−0·5	−0·3	0·0
LITTLE BERNERA (W Lewis)							
−0021	−0011	−0017	−0027	−0·5	−0·6	−0·4	−0·2
WEST LOCH TARBERT (W Harris)							
−0015	−0015	−0046	−0046	−1·1	−0·9	−0·5	0·0

SHELTER Good. Inner Hbr marina (LOA 24m) has depths to 3m. Newton Marina inside Goat Is depths to 2.5m. Visitors should report to Stornoway Port Authority; large boats may request berth on 80m pontoon on Esplanade Quay. Ferries use W side No 3 pier, and commercial vessels on Nos 1 and 2 Piers. South'ly swells can make anchoring uncomfortable. ⚓ on chartlet at:

NAVIGATION WPT 58°09′·98N 06°20′·87W, 343°/2·3M to Oc WRG lt. Access to the harbour at all states of the tide. Reef Rk, N of Arnish Pt to W of entrance, indicated by PHM, QR. To E side of ent unlit G bn marks the Beasts of Holm, a rky patch. This lies off Holm Pt, on which is a conspic memorial. A local magnetic anomaly exists over a small area in mid-hbr, 1·75ca N of Seid Rks PHM bn.

LIGHTS AND MARKS Arnish sheds conspic 3ca SW of Arnish Pt lt, W sector 302°-013° covers ent. In turn follow W sectors of: Sandwick Bay lt (close E of water tr, 3 power stn chys; all conspic), then Creed Estuary, Dir WRG 4s, across the harbour, and No 1 Pier, Q WRG. Lit bns in inner hbr mark appr chan to marina.

COMMUNICATIONS (Code 01851) Dr 703145; ⊖ 703626. HM 702688. HM VHF Ch 12 16 (H24).

FACILITIES **Hbr Marina** 80⊆, 8Ⓥ £2·92 inc ⚡, 🚰 ⛽ wi-fi.

Newton Marina 83⊆ seasonal berths £43·20/mth.

Piers 1 & 2 🚰 ⛽(10t) ⛴. **Pier 3** 🚰 ⛽(mob) ⛽(road tanker).

Services ⚒ 🔧 ACA.

Town ✉ Ⓑ ✕ ⇌ (Ferry to Ullapool, bus to Garve), ✈.

STANDARD TIME (UT)
For Summer Time add ONE hour in **non-shaded areas**

STORNOWAY

LAT 58°12'N LONG 6°23'W

TIMES AND HEIGHTS OF HIGH AND LOW WATERS

Dates in red are SPRINGS
Dates in blue are NEAPS

YEAR **2024**

JANUARY

Date	Day	Time	m	Time	m	Time	m	Time	m	Moon
1	M	0351	1.7	0948	4.4	1636	1.6	2229	3.9	
2	TU	0430	1.8	1028	4.2	1718	1.8	2317	3.8	
3	W	0512	2.0	1117	4.0	1805	1.9			
4	TH	0017	3.6	0603	2.2	1218	3.9	1901	2.0	◑
5	F	0126	3.6	0705	2.3	1331	3.8	2006	2.1	
6	SA	0234	3.7	0818	2.3	1441	3.8	2113	2.0	
7	SU	0333	3.8	0930	2.2	1543	3.9	2213	1.9	
8	M	0425	4.1	1031	2.0	1638	4.1	2304	1.7	
9	TU	0509	4.3	1124	1.7	1727	4.2	2350	1.5	
10	W	0551	4.6	1212	1.4	1814	4.5			
11	TH	0033	1.3	0633	4.8	1258	1.1	1900	4.6	●
12	F	0116	1.1	0715	5.0	1344	0.9	1945	4.7	
13	SA	0159	1.0	0757	5.2	1430	0.7	2030	4.7	
14	SU	0243	0.9	0842	5.2	1515	0.7	2116	4.6	
15	M	0327	1.0	0929	5.1	1601	0.8	2205	4.5	
16	TU	0412	1.2	1019	4.9	1649	1.0	2258	4.2	
17	W	0500	1.4	1115	4.7	1739	1.2			
18	TH	0000	4.0	0555	1.7	1219	4.4	1835	1.5	◐
19	F	0112	3.8	0700	1.9	1333	4.2	1942	1.8	
20	SA	0230	3.8	0819	2.1	1449	4.0	2101	1.9	
21	SU	0344	3.9	0946	2.0	1603	4.0	2218	1.9	
22	M	0446	4.1	1059	1.9	1704	4.1	2316	1.8	
23	TU	0534	4.3	1154	1.6	1753	4.2			
24	W	0003	1.6	0614	4.5	1239	1.4	1834	4.3	
25	TH	0042	1.5	0649	4.6	1319	1.3	1909	4.4	○
26	F	0118	1.3	0720	4.7	1354	1.1	1941	4.4	
27	SA	0152	1.3	0748	4.8	1427	1.1	2011	4.4	
28	SU	0224	1.2	0816	4.8	1459	1.1	2041	4.4	
29	M	0255	1.2	0845	4.7	1530	1.1	2111	4.3	
30	TU	0327	1.3	0914	4.6	1602	1.3	2143	4.1	
31	W	0359	1.5	0946	4.4	1635	1.4	2220	4.0	

FEBRUARY

Date	Day	Time	m	Time	m	Time	m	Time	m	Moon
1	TH	0433	1.6	1022	4.2	1710	1.6	2305	3.8	
2	F	0511	1.9	1105	4.0	1751	1.9			◑
3	SA	0005	3.6	0559	2.1	1204	3.8	1845	2.1	
4	SU	0125	3.6	0704	2.3	1333	3.6	2002	2.2	
5	M	0245	3.6	0835	2.3	1508	3.6	2134	2.1	
6	TU	0355	3.8	1005	2.1	1624	3.8	2244	1.9	
7	W	0451	4.1	1111	1.8	1721	4.1	2337	1.6	
8	TH	0537	4.5	1204	1.3	1808	4.4			
9	F	0023	1.2	0620	4.9	1250	0.9	1850	4.7	●
10	SA	0106	0.9	0700	5.2	1333	0.5	1931	4.9	
11	SU	0147	0.7	0741	5.4	1416	0.3	2011	4.9	
12	M	0228	0.6	0822	5.4	1457	0.3	2052	4.8	
13	TU	0308	0.6	0904	5.3	1538	0.4	2134	4.6	
14	W	0350	0.8	0950	5.0	1620	0.7	2219	4.3	
15	TH	0433	1.1	1041	4.7	1703	1.1	2313	4.0	
16	F	0521	1.5	1144	4.2	1751	1.6			◐
17	SA	0027	3.8	0621	1.9	1305	3.9	1852	2.0	
18	SU	0158	3.6	0747	2.2	1435	3.7	2025	2.2	
19	M	0328	3.7	0944	2.1	1559	3.7	2210	2.2	
20	TU	0437	3.9	1101	1.9	1702	3.8	2311	1.9	
21	W	0525	4.1	1150	1.6	1747	4.0	2354	1.7	
22	TH	0601	4.4	1229	1.3	1821	4.2			
23	F	0030	1.4	0632	4.5	1303	1.1	1851	4.4	
24	SA	0102	1.2	0659	4.7	1334	1.0	1918	4.5	○
25	SU	0133	1.1	0724	4.8	1403	0.9	1944	4.5	
26	M	0202	1.0	0749	4.8	1431	0.8	2010	4.5	
27	TU	0230	1.0	0814	4.7	1459	0.9	2036	4.4	
28	W	0259	1.0	0841	4.6	1526	1.0	2105	4.3	
29	TH	0328	1.2	0909	4.5	1555	1.2	2136	4.1	

MARCH

Date	Day	Time	m	Time	m	Time	m	Time	m	Moon
1	F	0359	1.4	0941	4.2	1626	1.4	2213	4.0	
2	SA	0435	1.6	1019	4.0	1702	1.7	2303	3.7	
3	SU	0517	1.9	1111	3.7	1747	2.0			◑
4	M	0023	3.6	0615	2.2	1249	3.5	1859	2.2	
5	TU	0205	3.5	0755	2.3	1449	3.5	2106	2.2	
6	W	0327	3.7	0951	2.0	1613	3.7	2230	1.9	
7	TH	0429	4.1	1100	1.6	1709	4.1	2323	1.5	
8	F	0517	4.5	1149	1.1	1752	4.4			
9	SA	0006	1.1	0559	4.9	1232	0.6	1831	4.8	
10	SU	0047	0.7	0638	5.3	1313	0.2	1908	5.0	●
11	M	0127	0.4	0717	5.5	1353	0.0	1945	5.0	
12	TU	0206	0.3	0757	5.5	1432	0.1	2023	4.9	
13	W	0245	0.3	0838	5.3	1510	0.3	2102	4.7	
14	TH	0326	0.6	0922	4.9	1549	0.7	2143	4.4	
15	F	0408	0.9	1013	4.5	1629	1.1	2232	4.0	
16	SA	0454	1.4	1119	4.0	1713	1.7	2347	3.7	
17	SU	0552	1.8	1249	3.6	1808	2.1			◐
18	M	0130	3.6	0728	2.2	1421	3.4	1950	2.4	
19	TU	0302	3.6	0940	2.1	1546	3.5	2155	2.3	
20	W	0414	3.8	1046	1.8	1647	3.7	2252	2.0	
21	TH	0502	4.0	1129	1.5	1726	3.9	2332	1.7	
22	F	0536	4.2	1204	1.2	1757	4.1			
23	SA	0006	1.4	0605	4.4	1235	1.0	1824	4.3	
24	SU	0037	1.2	0631	4.6	1304	0.9	1849	4.4	
25	M	0106	1.0	0655	4.6	1332	0.8	1914	4.5	○
26	TU	0134	0.9	0719	4.7	1359	0.7	1939	4.5	
27	W	0202	0.9	0744	4.6	1426	0.8	2004	4.5	
28	TH	0231	0.9	0810	4.5	1453	0.9	2032	4.4	
29	F	0300	1.0	0840	4.4	1521	1.1	2103	4.3	
30	SA	0333	1.2	0913	4.2	1552	1.3	2140	4.1	
31	SU	0409	1.5	0955	3.9	1628	1.6	2231	3.8	

APRIL

Date	Day	Time	m	Time	m	Time	m	Time	m	Moon
1	M	0453	1.7	1058	3.6	1714	1.9	2355	3.6	
2	TU	0554	2.0	1252	3.4	1828	2.2			◑
3	W	0137	3.6	0742	2.1	1436	3.4	2045	2.2	
4	TH	0258	3.8	0933	1.8	1553	3.7	2206	1.9	
5	F	0401	4.1	1037	1.3	1647	4.1	2258	1.4	
6	SA	0450	4.5	1124	0.8	1729	4.4	2342	1.0	
7	SU	0532	4.9	1207	0.4	1806	4.7			
8	M	0022	0.6	0612	5.2	1247	0.2	1843	4.9	●
9	TU	0103	0.4	0652	5.3	1326	0.1	1919	5.0	
10	W	0143	0.3	0733	5.3	1405	0.2	1956	4.9	
11	TH	0223	0.4	0815	5.0	1443	0.4	2034	4.7	
12	F	0304	0.6	0902	4.6	1521	0.8	2116	4.4	
13	SA	0348	1.0	0956	4.2	1600	1.3	2205	4.1	
14	SU	0436	1.4	1107	3.8	1643	1.7	2319	3.8	
15	M	0536	1.8	1230	3.5	1738	2.1			◐
16	TU	0056	3.6	0709	2.0	1352	3.3	1911	2.4	
17	W	0221	3.6	0903	2.0	1512	3.4	2109	2.3	
18	TH	0332	3.7	1008	1.8	1612	3.6	2213	2.0	
19	F	0423	3.9	1052	1.5	1653	3.8	2256	1.8	
20	SA	0500	4.0	1127	1.3	1724	4.0	2332	1.5	
21	SU	0530	4.2	1200	1.1	1752	4.2			
22	M	0004	1.3	0558	4.4	1229	0.9	1818	4.4	
23	TU	0035	1.1	0623	4.5	1258	0.8	1844	4.5	○
24	W	0105	1.0	0649	4.5	1326	0.8	1910	4.5	
25	TH	0135	0.9	0717	4.5	1354	0.8	1937	4.5	
26	F	0206	0.9	0747	4.4	1423	0.9	2008	4.5	
27	SA	0238	1.0	0822	4.2	1455	1.1	2044	4.3	
28	SU	0314	1.2	0904	4.0	1529	1.3	2127	4.1	
29	M	0355	1.4	0959	3.8	1610	1.6	2227	3.9	
30	TU	0446	1.6	1117	3.6	1702	1.9	2348	3.8	

Chart Datum: 2·71 metres below Ordnance Datum (Newlyn). HAT is 5·5 metres above Chart Datum.

STANDARD TIME (UT)
For Summer Time add ONE hour in **non-shaded areas**

STORNOWAY

LAT 58°12′N LONG 6°23′W

TIMES AND HEIGHTS OF HIGH AND LOW WATERS

Dates in red are SPRINGS
Dates in blue are NEAPS

YEAR **2024**

MAY

Date	Day	Time	m	Time	m	Time	m	Time	m	Moon
1	W	0555	1.8	1250	3.5	1825	2.1			◑
2	TH	0113	3.8	0733	1.8	1413	3.5	2014	2.1	
3	F	0226	3.9	0901	1.5	1523	3.8	2130	1.8	
4	SA	0327	4.2	1003	1.2	1617	4.1	2225	1.4	
5	SU	0419	4.5	1054	0.8	1701	4.4	2313	1.0	
6	M	0505	4.8	1138	0.5	1741	4.6	2357	0.8	
7	TU	0548	5.0	1221	0.4	1818	4.8			
8	W	0040	0.6	0631	5.0	1301	0.4	1857	4.8	●
9	TH	0123	0.5	0715	4.9	1340	0.5	1935	4.8	
10	F	0206	0.6	0801	4.7	1419	0.8	2016	4.6	
11	SA	0250	0.8	0851	4.3	1459	1.1	2100	4.4	
12	SU	0335	1.1	0946	4.0	1540	1.4	2150	4.1	
13	M	0425	1.4	1049	3.7	1624	1.7	2253	3.9	
14	TU	0522	1.7	1157	3.5	1716	2.0			
15	W	0008	3.7	0633	1.8	1305	3.4	1827	2.2	◐
16	TH	0123	3.6	0755	1.9	1414	3.4	1955	2.2	
17	F	0231	3.6	0906	1.8	1517	3.5	2111	2.1	
18	SA	0328	3.7	0959	1.6	1606	3.7	2205	1.9	
19	SU	0413	3.9	1041	1.4	1644	3.9	2248	1.7	
20	M	0450	4.0	1118	1.3	1716	4.1	2327	1.5	
21	TU	0522	4.1	1152	1.1	1746	4.2			
22	W	0002	1.3	0554	4.2	1224	1.0	1816	4.4	
23	TH	0036	1.2	0625	4.3	1256	1.0	1846	4.5	○
24	F	0111	1.1	0659	4.3	1328	1.0	1919	4.5	
25	SA	0147	1.0	0736	4.3	1403	1.1	1956	4.5	
26	SU	0225	1.0	0820	4.2	1439	1.2	2038	4.4	
27	M	0307	1.1	0910	4.0	1520	1.3	2128	4.3	
28	TU	0354	1.2	1010	3.9	1606	1.5	2227	4.2	
29	W	0448	1.4	1118	3.7	1703	1.7	2335	4.1	
30	TH	0553	1.4	1231	3.7	1815	1.9			◑
31	F	0044	4.1	0708	1.5	1341	3.7	1936	1.8	

JUNE

Date	Day	Time	m	Time	m	Time	m	Time	m	Moon
1	SA	0152	4.1	0821	1.4	1448	3.8	2048	1.7	
2	SU	0254	4.2	0925	1.2	1546	4.0	2150	1.5	
3	M	0351	4.4	1021	1.0	1636	4.2	2246	1.3	
4	TU	0444	4.5	1112	0.9	1720	4.4	2337	1.1	
5	W	0533	4.6	1158	0.9	1802	4.6			
6	TH	0025	0.9	0621	4.6	1241	0.9	1843	4.7	●
7	F	0111	0.8	0708	4.5	1323	0.9	1924	4.7	
8	SA	0157	0.9	0755	4.4	1404	1.1	2006	4.6	
9	SU	0241	0.9	0842	4.2	1444	1.2	2048	4.5	
10	M	0326	1.1	0930	4.0	1524	1.4	2132	4.3	
11	TU	0411	1.3	1018	3.8	1606	1.6	2218	4.1	
12	W	0458	1.5	1109	3.6	1651	1.8	2310	3.9	
13	TH	0548	1.6	1204	3.5	1743	2.0			
14	F	0010	3.8	0645	1.8	1305	3.4	1843	2.1	◐
15	SA	0116	3.7	0747	1.8	1409	3.5	1952	2.1	
16	SU	0220	3.7	0849	1.8	1507	3.6	2059	2.1	
17	M	0317	3.7	0945	1.7	1558	3.7	2158	1.9	
18	TU	0406	3.8	1033	1.6	1640	3.9	2248	1.8	
19	W	0450	3.9	1115	1.5	1718	4.1	2332	1.6	
20	TH	0530	4.0	1155	1.3	1753	4.3			
21	F	0013	1.4	0611	4.1	1233	1.2	1830	4.5	
22	SA	0055	1.2	0652	4.2	1312	1.1	1908	4.6	○
23	SU	0136	1.0	0735	4.3	1351	1.1	1949	4.7	
24	M	0220	0.9	0821	4.3	1433	1.1	2033	4.7	
25	TU	0304	0.9	0909	4.2	1516	1.2	2121	4.6	
26	W	0351	0.9	1001	4.1	1603	1.3	2213	4.5	
27	TH	0441	1.0	1058	4.0	1654	1.4	2310	4.4	
28	F	0535	1.1	1159	3.9	1751	1.6			◑
29	SA	0013	4.3	0634	1.3	1305	3.8	1857	1.7	
30	SU	0119	4.2	0738	1.4	1413	3.8	2008	1.7	

JULY

Date	Day	Time	m	Time	m	Time	m	Time	m	Moon
1	M	0226	4.1	0846	1.4	1519	3.9	2120	1.7	
2	TU	0332	4.1	0953	1.4	1619	4.0	2229	1.6	
3	W	0435	4.2	1054	1.4	1711	4.2	2329	1.4	
4	TH	0530	4.2	1146	1.3	1756	4.4			
5	F	0021	1.2	0621	4.3	1231	1.2	1839	4.6	●
6	SA	0109	1.1	0705	4.3	1314	1.2	1917	4.6	
7	SU	0152	1.0	0746	4.3	1353	1.2	1954	4.6	
8	M	0232	1.0	0825	4.3	1431	1.2	2029	4.6	
9	TU	0311	1.0	0902	4.2	1507	1.3	2104	4.5	
10	W	0348	1.1	0938	4.0	1544	1.4	2139	4.3	
11	TH	0425	1.2	1016	3.9	1621	1.5	2216	4.1	
12	F	0503	1.4	1100	3.7	1700	1.7	2259	4.0	
13	SA	0545	1.6	1153	3.6	1744	1.9	2352	3.8	◐
14	SU	0632	1.8	1258	3.5	1838	2.1			
15	M	0101	3.6	0730	1.9	1405	3.5	1946	2.2	
16	TU	0215	3.6	0839	2.0	1509	3.6	2103	2.2	
17	W	0324	3.6	0948	1.9	1606	3.8	2213	2.0	
18	TH	0426	3.7	1045	1.8	1654	4.0	2310	1.8	
19	F	0517	3.9	1134	1.6	1736	4.3	2359	1.5	
20	SA	0603	4.1	1218	1.4	1816	4.5			
21	SU	0044	1.2	0646	4.3	1300	1.1	1856	4.8	○
22	M	0128	0.9	0727	4.5	1342	1.0	1937	4.9	
23	TU	0211	0.6	0809	4.6	1423	0.9	2018	5.0	
24	W	0254	0.5	0852	4.6	1505	0.8	2102	5.0	
25	TH	0337	0.5	0937	4.4	1548	0.9	2149	4.9	
26	F	0421	0.7	1026	4.3	1633	1.1	2240	4.7	
27	SA	0507	0.9	1122	4.0	1722	1.4	2340	4.4	
28	SU	0557	1.2	1229	3.8	1820	1.6			◑
29	M	0050	4.1	0657	1.6	1344	3.7	1934	1.9	
30	TU	0208	3.9	0811	1.8	1502	3.8	2104	1.9	
31	W	0328	3.8	0937	1.9	1613	3.9	2230	1.8	

AUGUST

Date	Day	Time	m	Time	m	Time	m	Time	m	Moon
1	TH	0438	3.9	1049	1.8	1709	4.2	2333	1.5	
2	F	0534	4.0	1142	1.6	1753	4.4			
3	SA	0021	1.3	0618	4.2	1225	1.4	1831	4.6	
4	SU	0103	1.1	0655	4.3	1304	1.3	1904	4.7	●
5	M	0140	0.9	0728	4.4	1339	1.2	1934	4.7	
6	TU	0214	0.9	0758	4.4	1412	1.1	2002	4.7	
7	W	0246	0.9	0828	4.3	1444	1.1	2030	4.6	
8	TH	0317	0.9	0857	4.3	1515	1.2	2059	4.5	
9	F	0348	1.1	0929	4.1	1547	1.3	2129	4.3	
10	SA	0420	1.3	1003	4.0	1620	1.5	2203	4.1	
11	SU	0453	1.5	1045	3.8	1657	1.8	2244	3.9	
12	M	0531	1.7	1143	3.6	1741	2.0	2341	3.6	◐
13	TU	0618	2.0	1304	3.5	1840	2.2			
14	W	0115	3.5	0728	2.2	1425	3.6	2010	2.3	
15	TH	0254	3.5	0907	2.2	1536	3.7	2149	2.2	
16	F	0411	3.6	1026	2.0	1633	4.0	2257	1.8	
17	SA	0507	3.9	1119	1.7	1718	4.3	2347	1.4	
18	SU	0551	4.2	1204	1.3	1759	4.7			
19	M	0030	1.0	0631	4.5	1245	1.0	1837	5.0	○
20	TU	0112	0.6	0708	4.7	1325	0.7	1916	5.3	
21	W	0152	0.3	0746	4.9	1405	0.6	1955	5.4	
22	TH	0232	0.2	0825	4.9	1444	0.5	2036	5.3	
23	F	0312	0.3	0906	4.7	1525	0.7	2120	5.1	
24	SA	0353	0.5	0950	4.5	1607	0.9	2209	4.7	
25	SU	0435	0.9	1042	4.2	1654	1.3	2311	4.3	
26	M	0521	1.4	1153	3.9	1751	1.7			◑
27	TU	0033	3.9	0618	1.9	1324	3.7	1912	2.0	
28	W	0204	3.7	0742	2.2	1453	3.7	2111	2.1	
29	TH	0331	3.7	0937	2.2	1607	3.9	2237	1.8	
30	F	0440	3.8	1047	2.0	1701	4.2	2330	1.5	
31	SA	0528	4.0	1133	1.7	1741	4.4			

Chart Datum: 2·71 metres below Ordnance Datum (Newlyn). HAT is 5·5 metres above Chart Datum.

STANDARD TIME (UT)
For Summer Time add ONE hour in **non-shaded areas**

STORNOWAY

LAT 58°12′N LONG 6°23′W

TIMES AND HEIGHTS OF HIGH AND LOW WATERS

Dates in red are SPRINGS
Dates in blue are NEAPS

YEAR 2024

SEPTEMBER

Date	Day	Time	m
1		0010	1.3
		0604	4.2
	SU	1211	1.5
		1813	4.6
2		0045	1.1
		0634	4.4
	M	1245	1.3
		1841	4.7
3		0117	0.9
		0702	4.5
	TU	1316	1.1
		● 1907	4.8
4		0146	0.8
		0728	4.5
	W	1346	1.0
		1932	4.8
5		0215	0.8
		0753	4.5
	TH	1415	1.0
		1957	4.7
6		0242	0.9
		0820	4.5
	F	1444	1.1
		2022	4.6
7		0310	1.0
		0847	4.4
	SA	1513	1.2
		2050	4.4
8		0339	1.2
		0918	4.2
	SU	1545	1.4
		2121	4.2
9		0409	1.5
		0953	4.0
	M	1619	1.7
		2158	3.9
10		0443	1.8
		1042	3.8
	TU	1700	2.0
		2250	3.6
11		0525	2.1
		1206	3.6
	W	1755	2.2
		◐	
12		0038	3.4
		0629	2.3
	TH	1349	3.6
		1932	2.4
13		0236	3.4
		0838	2.4
	F	1508	3.7
		2135	2.1
14		0355	3.6
		1008	2.1
	SA	1608	4.1
		2240	1.7
15		0449	4.0
		1100	1.7
	SU	1654	4.4
		2327	1.2
16		0530	4.4
		1143	1.3
	M	1734	4.9
17		0008	0.8
		0608	4.7
	TU	1222	0.9
		1812	5.2
18		0048	0.4
		0643	5.0
	W	1301	0.6
		○ 1850	5.5
19		0127	0.1
		0719	5.1
	TH	1340	0.4
		1929	5.5
20		0206	0.1
		0756	5.1
	F	1420	0.4
		2010	5.4
21		0244	0.3
		0835	4.9
	SA	1501	0.6
		2054	5.1
22		0324	0.6
		0917	4.6
	SU	1544	0.9
		2145	4.6
23		0404	1.1
		1007	4.2
	M	1631	1.4
		2253	4.1
24		0449	1.6
		1123	3.9
	TU	1730	1.8
		◑	
25		0026	3.7
		0545	2.1
	W	1306	3.8
		1903	2.1
26		0158	3.6
		0720	2.4
	TH	1436	3.8
		2114	2.1
27		0324	3.6
		0927	2.4
	F	1549	4.0
		2224	1.8
28		0427	3.8
		1029	2.1
	SA	1640	4.2
		2309	1.5
29		0509	4.0
		1111	1.8
	SU	1717	4.4
		2345	1.3
30		0540	4.2
		1146	1.5
	M	1746	4.5

OCTOBER

Date	Day	Time	m
1		0016	1.1
		0607	4.4
	TU	1218	1.3
		1813	4.7
2		0046	0.9
		0632	4.6
	W	1248	1.1
		● 1837	4.8
3		0114	0.9
		0657	4.6
	TH	1317	1.1
		1901	4.8
4		0141	0.9
		0721	4.7
	F	1346	1.0
		1926	4.7
5		0208	0.9
		0747	4.6
	SA	1414	1.1
		1952	4.6
6		0235	1.1
		0814	4.5
	SU	1444	1.2
		2020	4.4
7		0303	1.3
		0844	4.4
	M	1516	1.4
		2053	4.2
8		0334	1.5
		0919	4.2
	TU	1552	1.7
		2133	3.9
9		0408	1.8
		1008	3.9
	W	1635	1.9
		2235	3.6
10		0451	2.1
		1132	3.7
	TH	1733	2.2
		◐	
11		0032	3.4
		0559	2.4
	F	1316	3.7
		1915	2.3
12		0214	3.5
		0811	2.4
	SA	1435	3.9
		2108	2.0
13		0329	3.8
		0939	2.1
	SU	1536	4.2
		2211	1.6
14		0422	4.1
		1031	1.7
	M	1624	4.6
		2258	1.1
15		0504	4.5
		1114	1.3
	TU	1706	5.0
		2340	0.7
16		0541	4.8
		1156	0.9
	W	1745	5.3
17		0020	0.4
		0617	5.0
	TH	1236	0.6
		○ 1825	5.5
18		0059	0.3
		0653	5.2
	F	1316	0.5
		1906	5.5
19		0139	0.3
		0731	5.1
	SA	1358	0.5
		1949	5.3
20		0218	0.5
		0810	5.0
	SU	1441	0.7
		2036	4.9
21		0258	0.9
		0853	4.7
	M	1526	1.1
		2132	4.4
22		0339	1.4
		0945	4.4
	TU	1617	1.5
		2244	4.0
23		0425	1.8
		1101	4.1
	W	1719	1.8
24		0010	3.7
		0522	2.2
	TH	1237	3.9
		◑ 1849	2.1
25		0133	3.6
		0649	2.5
	F	1401	3.9
		2038	2.1
26		0253	3.6
		0841	2.4
	SA	1513	3.9
		2146	1.9
27		0354	3.8
		0949	2.2
	SU	1605	4.1
		2232	1.6
28		0437	4.0
		1035	1.9
	M	1644	4.3
		2309	1.4
29		0508	4.2
		1112	1.7
	TU	1715	4.4
		2341	1.3
30		0536	4.4
		1146	1.5
	W	1742	4.5
31		0012	1.1
		0603	4.5
	TH	1218	1.3
		1809	4.6

NOVEMBER

Date	Day	Time	m
1		0041	1.1
		0629	4.6
	F	1248	1.2
		● 1835	4.7
2		0109	1.0
		0655	4.7
	SA	1319	1.2
		1902	4.6
3		0138	1.1
		0722	4.7
	SU	1350	1.2
		1931	4.5
4		0207	1.2
		0751	4.6
	M	1422	1.3
		2004	4.4
5		0237	1.4
		0825	4.5
	TU	1457	1.4
		2044	4.2
6		0311	1.6
		0906	4.3
	W	1537	1.6
		2134	3.9
7		0349	1.8
		1000	4.1
	TH	1625	1.8
		2245	3.7
8		0437	2.1
		1116	4.0
	F	1727	2.0
9		0016	3.6
		0549	2.3
	SA	1241	4.0
		◐ 1855	2.0
10		0140	3.7
		0732	2.3
	SU	1355	4.1
		2025	1.8
11		0251	3.9
		0855	2.1
	M	1458	4.3
		2131	1.5
12		0348	4.2
		0954	1.7
	TU	1551	4.6
		2223	1.1
13		0435	4.5
		1043	1.4
	W	1638	4.9
		2310	0.9
14		0515	4.7
		1129	1.1
	TH	1722	5.1
		2353	0.7
15		0554	5.0
		1214	0.9
	F	1806	5.2
		○	
16		0035	0.6
		0633	5.1
	SA	1258	0.8
		1852	5.2
17		0117	0.7
		0713	5.1
	SU	1343	0.8
		1939	5.0
18		0158	0.9
		0755	5.0
	M	1429	0.9
		2029	4.7
19		0239	1.2
		0841	4.8
	TU	1516	1.2
		2124	4.4
20		0322	1.5
		0932	4.5
	W	1607	1.4
		2226	4.0
21		0408	1.8
		1033	4.3
	TH	1705	1.7
		2333	3.8
22		0500	2.1
		1147	4.1
	F	1812	1.9
23		0043	3.6
		0606	2.3
	SA	1303	3.9
		◑ 1928	2.0
24		0153	3.6
		0726	2.4
	SU	1413	3.9
		2041	2.0
25		0259	3.7
		0843	2.3
	M	1513	4.0
		2139	1.9
26		0351	3.8
		0944	2.2
	TU	1600	4.1
		2224	1.7
27		0431	4.0
		1031	2.0
	W	1639	4.2
		2303	1.6
28		0505	4.2
		1112	1.8
	TH	1713	4.3
		2338	1.4
29		0536	4.4
		1149	1.6
	F	1745	4.4
30		0010	1.3
		0606	4.6
	SA	1223	1.5
		1817	4.4

DECEMBER

Date	Day	Time	m
1		0043	1.3
		0636	4.7
	SU	1258	1.4
		● 1849	4.5
2		0115	1.3
		0707	4.7
	M	1333	1.3
		1924	4.4
3		0148	1.3
		0741	4.7
	TU	1410	1.3
		2003	4.4
4		0223	1.4
		0820	4.7
	W	1450	1.4
		2048	4.2
5		0301	1.5
		0904	4.6
	TH	1533	1.4
		2138	4.1
6		0343	1.7
		0955	4.5
	F	1622	1.5
		2238	4.0
7		0433	1.9
		1055	4.3
	SA	1719	1.6
		2346	3.9
8		0534	2.0
		1203	4.3
	SU	1825	1.7
		◐	
9		0058	3.8
		0649	2.1
	M	1312	4.3
		1937	1.7
10		0208	3.9
		0805	2.0
	TU	1418	4.3
		2046	1.5
11		0312	4.1
		0913	1.8
	W	1519	4.5
		2148	1.4
12		0407	4.3
		1014	1.6
	TH	1616	4.6
		2243	1.2
13		0456	4.5
		1109	1.4
	F	1709	4.7
		2333	1.1
14		0541	4.7
		1201	1.2
	SA	1759	4.8
15		0019	1.1
		0624	4.9
	SU	1250	1.0
		○ 1848	4.8
16		0103	1.1
		0707	5.0
	M	1338	1.0
		1936	4.7
17		0146	1.1
		0749	4.9
	TU	1424	1.0
		2023	4.6
18		0228	1.3
		0832	4.9
	W	1509	1.1
		2109	4.4
19		0309	1.4
		0915	4.7
	TH	1554	1.3
		2154	4.2
20		0351	1.6
		0958	4.5
	F	1639	1.5
		2242	3.9
21		0434	1.8
		1045	4.3
	SA	1727	1.7
		2334	3.8
22		0521	2.0
		1141	4.1
	SU	1818	1.9
		◑	
23		0035	3.6
		0615	2.2
	M	1248	3.9
		1917	2.0
24		0143	3.6
		0720	2.3
	TU	1359	3.8
		2022	2.1
25		0249	3.7
		0832	2.4
	W	1504	3.8
		2127	2.0
26		0346	3.8
		0941	2.3
	TH	1600	3.9
		2221	1.9
27		0433	4.0
		1037	2.1
	F	1648	4.0
		2307	1.8
28		0513	4.2
		1124	1.9
	SA	1729	4.1
		2347	1.6
29		0549	4.4
		1206	1.7
	SU	1807	4.2
30		0024	1.5
		0624	4.6
	M	1245	1.5
		● 1845	4.4
31		0101	1.4
		0658	4.7
	TU	1325	1.3
		1922	4.4

Chart Datum: 2·71 metres below Ordnance Datum (Newlyn). HAT is 5·5 metres above Chart Datum.

HARBOURS/ANCHORAGES ON THE EAST OF THE OUTER HEBRIDES

Facilities are in the main managed by the local authority Comhairle nan Eilean Siar. www.cne-siar.gov.uk/roads-travel-and-parking/ports-piers-and-harbours/harbour-facilities. See AC 5616.

TIDES

Standard Port STORNOWAY (⟵)

Times				Height (metres)			
High Water		Low Water		MHWS	MHWN	MLWN	MLWS
0100	0700	0300	0900	4·8	3·7	2·0	0·7
1300	1900	1500	2100				
Differences East side of Outer Hebrides, N to S							
LOCH SHELL (Harris)							
–0013	0000	0000	–0017	0·0	–0·1	–0·1	0·0
EAST LOCH TARBERT (Harris)							
–0025	–0010	–0010	–0020	+0·2	0·0	+0·1	+0·1
LOCH MADDY (N Uist)							
–0044	–0014	–0016	–0030	0·0	–0·1	–0·1	0·0
LOCH CARNAN (S Uist)							
–0050	–0010	–0020	–0040	–0·3	–0·5	–0·1	–0·1
LOCH SKIPORT (S Uist)							
–0100	–0025	–0024	–0024	–0·2	–0·4	–0·3	–0·2
LOCH BOISDALE (S Uist)							
–0055	–0030	–0020	–0040	–0·7	–0·7	–0·3	–0·2
BARRA (North Bay)							
–0103	–0031	–0034	–0048	–0·6	–0·5	–0·2	–0·1
CASTLE BAY (Barra)							
–0115	–0040	–0045	–0100	–0·5	–0·6	–0·3	–0·1
BARRA HEAD (Berneray)							
–0115	–0040	–0045	–0055	–0·8	–0·7	–0·2	+0·1

SHELTER

LOCH SHELL, Lewis, **57°59′·00N 06°25′·50W**. AC 1794. HW –0437 on Dover; ML 2·7m. See 1.5. Pass S of Eilean Iuvard; beware rks to W of Is. ⚓ in Tob Eishken, 2½M up loch on N shore (beware rk awash on E side of ent), or at head of loch (exposed to E winds; dries some distance). Facilities: ✉/Stores at Lemreway.

SHIANT ISLANDS, Lewis, **57°53′·68N 06°21′·37W**. AC 1794, 1795. Tides as Loch Shell 1.5. Beware strong tidal streams and overfalls in Sound of Shiant. Strictly a fair weather ⚓; in W winds ⚓ E of Mol Mor, isthmus between Garbh Eileen (159m) and Eileen an Tighe. In E winds ⚓ W of Mol Mor. No lights or facilities.

EAST LOCH TARBERT, Harris, **57°49′·98N 06°41′·07W**. AC 2905. HW –0446 on Dover; ML 3·0m; Duration 0605. See 1.5. Appr via Sound of Scalpay; beware Elliot Rk (2m) 2½ca SSW of Rubha Crago. A bridge (57°52′·80N 06°41′·73W) joins Scalpay to Harris (20m ht). Bridge lts: Centre Oc 6s; N side Iso G 4s 35m; S side Iso R 4s 35m. Eilean Glas lt ho at E end of Scalpay, Fl (3) 20s 43m 23M; W tr, R bands. In Sound of Scalpay, stream sets W from HW +3, and E from HW –3. **Harris Hub Marina** www.isleofharrismarina.co.uk ☎ 01859 502 216 5Ⓐs £13, pontoon 10Ⓥ⌓ £2/m/day ⛽ ⛿ ▣ Ⓟ Ⓟ ✉ 🛒 ✕ ⛵ wi-fi, ferry to Uig. Secluded ⚓ 1½M SE in Loch Ceann Dibig W of Scotasay. Alternatively, Scalpay N Hbr gives good shelter. Beware rock 5ca off Aird an Aiseig, E side of ent. SHM buoy marks wk off Coddem; 5ca E of the buoy is a rk, depth 1·1m. ⚓ 7ca N in 3m or in South Hbr. Tarbert Ldg Lt Dir Iso WRG 4s 6m 5M. Piers have R/G lts Fl (2) 6s. Facilities: pontoon 8Ⓥ⌓ (1.5m) ⛽ ⛿ wi-fi, ✉ 🛒.

LOCH STOCKINISH, Harris. AC 1757. Enter via Loch Chlual; metal bn Fl R 2s at 57°48′·49N 06°48′·79W and SCM Q(6)+L Fl 15s atop B/Y perch at 57°48′·56N 06°48′·81W; pier landing and fish farms in loch.

LOCH RODEL, Harris. AC 2802. 3Ⓐs at **57°44′·2N 06°57′·4W** in Poll an Tigh-mhàil; enter from SW past jetties. No lts.

SOUND OF HARRIS, 57°43′N 06°58′W. Passages through this difficult Sound are detailed in the *W Coast of Scotland Pilot*. The Stanton and Outer Stromay Chans off the Harris shore are most feasible for yachts. AC 2802 shows the ferry routes from Leverburgh to Berneray.

LOCH MADDY, North Uist, **57°35′·98N 07°06′·07W**. AC 2825. HW –0500 on Dover. See 1.5. With strong wind against tide there can be bad seas off ent. Appr clear, but from S beware submerged rk ½ca N of Leacnam Madadh. Lts: Weaver's Pt Fl 3s 21m 7M; Glas Eilean Mor Fl (2) G 4s 8m 5M; Rubna Nam Pleac Fl R 4s 7m 5M. Inside loch: Ruigh Liath QG 6m 5M; Vallaquie Is Dir Fl (3) WRG 8s. RoRo pier Iso WRG 2s 6M dir sector light. Pontoon lit Fl R 3s. 2Ⓐs Bagh Aird nam Madadh ☎(01870) 602425; 2Ⓐs E of Oronsay. ⚓s: clear S of ferry pier; NE of Vallaquie Is; Charles Hbr; Oronsay (⚓ not advised due to moorings), tidal berth on private pier; Sponish Hbr; Loch Portain. VHF Ch **12** 16. Port Manager ☎(01876) 5003337(day), 5003226(night). Facilities: Lochmaddy, 26⌓ 18Ⓥ on lit pontoon (Fl R 3s 2M) £2/night inc ⏚, ⛽ Ⓟ Ⓟ ▮ 🛒; WC ⛿ (hotel). Loch Portain ✉ shop, bus to Benbecula.

LOCH EPORT, North Uist, **57°33′·45N 07°08′·12W**. AC 2825, but not the head of loch. Tides, approx as L Maddy; 3kn sp stream. On the S side of ent are rks, some drying. The ent proper is clean but very narrow (about 100m) for 5ca, then widens. Follow the charted clearing line 082°. Best ⚓s are: Bàgh a' Bhiorain (S of chan; line up cairn and Bu boulder on 129°); and Acairseid Lee (N bank) E or W of Deer Is. ✉ 🛒 ✕ ⛵ at Clachan, head of loch.

KALLIN, Grimsay. **57°28′·9N 07°12′·2W**. AC 2904. 1Ⓐ in NE of hbr. 3 chan lt buoys and 2 FR (vert) on hbr bkwtr. ☎(01870) 602425.

LOCH CARNAN, South Uist, **57°22′·03N 07°16′·39W**. AC 2825. Tides, see 1.5. SWM buoy, L Fl 10s, at 57°22′·30N 07°11′·57W is almost 2M E of app chan proper, marked by Nos 1 and 2 buoys, Fl G 2·5s and Fl R 2s, at 57°22′·45N 07°14′·90W. Round No 3 PHM buoy, Fl R 5s, between Gasay and Taigh lamain, then pick up ldg lts 222° to Sandwick Quay; front Fl R 2s, rear Iso R 10s, both 5M, W ◊s on posts. Power stn and 2 chys are conspic close to SE of quay. ☎(01870) 602425 for permission to berth on the quay (MoD property). ⚓ or 2Ⓐs about 2ca WNW of the quay in deep water. ☎(01870) 610238. The passage S of Gasay is unmarked and needs careful pilotage.

LOCH SKIPPORT, South Uist, **57°19′·98N 07°13′·67W**. AC 2904, 2825. HW –0602 on Dover; see 1.5. Easy ent 3M NNE of Hecla (604m). No lights, but 2¼M SSE is Usinish lt ho Fl WR 20s 54m 19/15M. ⚓s at: Wizard Pool in 7m; beware Float Rk, dries 2·3m; on N side of Caolas Mor in 7m; Bagh Charmaig in 5m. Linne Arm has narrow ent, many fish farms and poor holding. No facilities.

LOCH EYNORT, South Uist, **57°13′·13N 07°16′·87W**. AC 2825. Tides: interpolate between Lochs Skipport and Boisdale, see 1.5. ⚓s in the outer loch at Cearcdal Bay and on the N side just before the narrows are exposed to the E. The passage to Upper L Eynort is very narrow and streams reach 5-7kn; best not attempted unless local fishermen offer guidance. Good ⚓ inside at Bàgh Lathach.

LOCH BOISDALE, South Uist, **57°08′·78N 07°16′·07W**. AC 2770. HW –0455 on Dover; ML 2·4m; Duration 0600. See 1.5. Good shelter except in SE gales when swell runs right up the 2M loch. From N, approach between Rubha na Cruibe and Calvay Is leading line 245°: Hollisgeir (0·3m) on with pier (ru). From S beware Clan Ewan Rk, dries 1·2m, and McKenzie Rk (2·4m), lit PHM Fl (3) R 15s. Harbour with marina ☎(01870) 700830, VHF Ch 80, 52⌓ inc 40Ⓥ £2·70/m with ⏚ formed by a causeway from Rubha Bhuailt to Gasay, has two breakwaters (Fl G 6s & Fl R 6s with traffic sigs). Entrance to the N accessed from the channel to Boisdale Hbr which lies N of Gasay Is. Off E end beware rock. ⚓ off pier in approx 4m, or SW of Gasay Is in approx 9m. 4Ⓐs NE of pier; ☎(01870) 602425. There are fish cages W of Rubha Bhuailt. Lts: Dir Lt 292·5° WRG 4s 4m 5M, RoRo jetty hd Iso RG 4s 8m 2M; close SE, Eilean Dubh Fl (2) R 5s. E Calvay Is Fl (2) WRG 10s 16m 7M. Gasay Is Fl WR 5s 10m 7M, opposite shore, Fl G 6s 3m 3M; See 1.3. ☎(01870) 700288. Facilities: ⛽ ⛿ ▣ Ⓟ ✉ ✕ ⛵. Ferry to mainland.

ACAIRSEID MHÓR, Eriskay, ⊕ **57°03′·78N 07°16′·35W**. AC 2770. Tides approx as for North Bay (Barra), see 1.5. Ben Scrien (183m) is a conspicuous, pointed peak N of the harbour. Leading lts 285°, both Oc R 6s 9/10m 4M, W △ ▽ on orange posts, lead for 0·5M from the waypoint between two drying rocks into the outer loch. A SHM buoy, Fl G 6s, marks a rock drying 3m. Possible ⌓ on pontoon; 2Ⓐs (perhaps submerged at HW) are at 57°03′·95N 07°17′·40W on S side of inner loch, opp pier, 2 FG (vert). ☎(01870) 602425, ✉ 🛒 ✕ ⛵ at Haun, 1·5M at N end of island.

NORTH BAY, Barra, **57°00′·11N 07°24′·67W**. AC 2770. Tides see 1.5. Well-marked approach to inlet sheltered from both S and W winds. There are Ⓐs in N part of Bay Hirivagh, ⚓ 1ca WNW of Black Island or temporarily ⌓ on the quay in 4·5m. WPT 56°58′·68N 07°20′·31W is about 200m NE of Curachan ECM buoy, Q (3) 10s, and in the white sector (304°-306°) of Ardveenish Dir ☆ 305°, Oc WRG 3s, 2·5M to the WNW. ⛽ 🛒 ⛵ bus to Castlebay.

CASTLEBAY, Barra, **56°56´·78N 07°29´·67W**. AC 2769. HW –0525 on Dover; ML 2·3m; Duration 0600. See 1.5. Very good shelter & holding. A lit jetty extends from the old pier. Best ⚓ is in approx 8m NW of Kiessimul Castle; NE of castle are rocks. ⚓ in fairway, ferry keeps to port on entry to berth at Castlebay Pier www.calmac.co.uk.

MARINA www.castlebaymarina.com ☎(01871) 810925 20Ⓥs £30/nt lies W of pier with ⛽, 🚰 WC 🚿 🧺. **Town** ✉ 🛒 ✕ 🛍. Bus/Ferry.

⚓ in Vatersay Bay in approx 9m. W end of Vatersay Sound is closed by a causeway. Beware rocks NNW of Sgeir Dubh a conspic W/G tower, Q(3)G 6s 6m 5M, which leads 283° in transit with Sgeir Liath bn. Channel Rock lies 2ca South (Fl WR 6s 4m 6/4M). Leading lts 295°, FBu 6M on W framework towers: front 9m Or △ on Rubha Glas; rear 457m fm front, 15m Or ▽, vis: 15° and 8° each side of ldg line. Vatersay Community Hall ☎(01871) 810237 🚰 WC ✕ 🚿. Bus - not Sun.

ISLANDS WEST OF THE OUTER HEBRIDES (N TO S)

TIDES

Standard Port STORNOWAY (⟵)

Times				Height (metres)			
High Water		Low Water		MHWS	MHWN	MLWN	MLWS
0100	0700	0300	0900	4·8	3·7	2·0	0·7
1300	1900	1500	2100				
Differences West side of Outer Hebrides, N to S							
SCOLPAIG (W North Uist)							
–0033	–0033	–0040	–0040	–1·0	–0·9	–0·5	0·0
BALIVANICH (W Benbecula)							
–0103	–0017	–0031	–0045	–0·7	–0·6	–0·5	–0·2
FLANNAN ISLES							
–0026	–0016	–0016	–0026	–0·9	–0·7	–0·6	–0·2
VILLAGE BAY (St Kilda)							
–0040	–0040	–0045	–0045	–1·4	–1·1	–0·8	–0·3
ROCKALL							
–0055	–0055	–0105	–0105	–1·8	–1·5	–0·9	–0·2
SHILLAY (Monach Islands)							
–0103	–0043	–0047	–0107	–0·6	–0·7	–0·7	–0·3

SHELTER

FLANNAN ISLES, Western Isles, centred on **58°17´·28N 07°35´·27W** (Eilean Mór). AC 2524, 2721. Tides, as above. Uninhabited group of several rky islets, 18M WNW of Gallan Head (Lewis). The main islet is Eilean Mór where landing can be made on SW side in suitable conditions. Lt ho, Fl (2) 30s 101m 20M, is a 23m high W tr on NE tip of Eilean Mór; the lt is obscured by islets to the W which are up to 57m high. No recommended ⚓s and the few charted depths are by lead-line surveys.

ST KILDA, Western Isles, **57°48´·28N 08°33´·07W**. AC 2721, 2524. Tides at Village Bay, Hirta: HW –0510 on Dover; ML 1·9m; Duration 0615; see above. A group of four isles and three stacks, the main island is Hirta. The facility is now manned by a civilian company, Qinetiq ☎(01870) 604443, based at South Uist. Hirta is owned by National Trust for Scotland, who employ a Seasonal Warden, ☎01870 604628. ⚓ in Village Bay, SE-facing, in approx 5m about 1·5ca off the pier. Ldg lts 270°, both Oc 5s 26/38m 3M. If wind is between NE and SSW big swells enter the bay; good holding, but untenable if winds strong. Levenish Is (55m) is 1·5M E of Hirta with offlying rks. Courtesy call to *Kilda Radio* VHF Ch 16 **12** 73 (HJ) before landing; or Qinetic ☎(01870) 604406 (HO), 604612 (OT). Alternative ⚓ at Glen Bay on N side is only safe in S and E winds. Facilities: 🚰 from wells near landings.

ROCKALL, 57°35´·7N 13°41´·2W. AC 1128, 2524. Tides, as above. A 19m high granite rock, 200M W of N Uist. Best access by helicopter. Lt, Fl 15s 13M, is often extinguished for long periods due to weather damage. Helen's Reef, 1·4m, on which the sea breaks is 2M ENE.

MONACH ISLANDS (Heisker Is), centred on **57°31´·28N 07°38´·07W**. AC 2721, 2722. Tides, see 1.5 Shillay. The group lies 5M SW of N Uist and 8M WNW of Benbecula. The 5 main islands (W-E) are Shillay, Ceann Iar, Shivinish, Ceann Ear and Stockay; all uninhabited. Many rky offliers from NW through N to SE of the group. On Shillay there is a conspic red brick lt ho, Fl (2) 15s. ⚓s at: E of lt ho; Croic Hbr, bay N of Shivinish; and S Hbr on W side of Shivinish.

1.6 KINLOCHBERVIE

Highland **58°27′·26N 05°02′·78W**

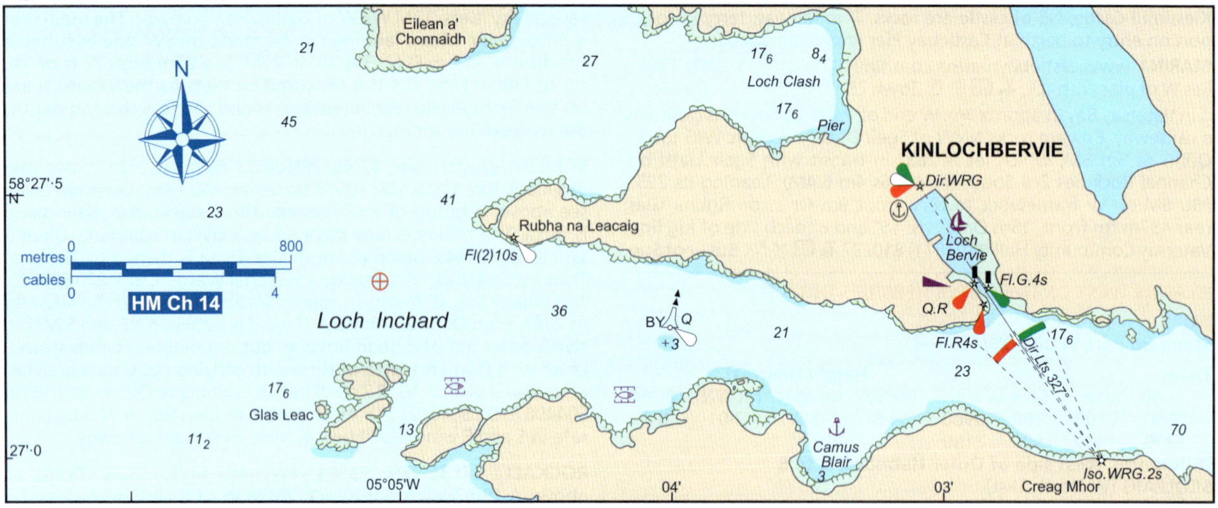

CHARTS AC 1954, 1785, 2503; Imray C67

TIDES –0400 Dover; ML 2·7; Duration 0610

Standard Port ULLAPOOL (⟶)

Times				Height (metres)			
High Water		Low Water		MHWS	MHWN	MLWN	MLWS
0000	0600	0300	0900	5·2	3·9	2·1	0·7
1200	1800	1500	2100				
Differences LOCH BERVIE							
+0017	+0020	+0015	+0015	–0·4	–0·2	–0·1	+0·1

SHELTER Very good in Kinlochbervie Hbr off the N shore of Loch Inchard. A useful passage port, only 14.5 track miles S of Cape Wrath. It is an active FV port, but yachts on pontoon (contact HM for details); NE side is shoal/foul. If full, ⚓ at Loch Clash, open to W, but sheltered in winds n through SE; landing jetty in 2·7m. Other ⚓s at: Camus Blair on S shore, 5ca SW of hbr ent, and up the loch at L Sheigra, Achriesgill Bay and 5ca short of the head of the loch.

NAVIGATION WPT 58°27′·34N 05°05′·08W (at mouth of Loch Inchard), 100°/1·3M to hbr ent. The sides of the loch are clean, but keep to N side of Loch Inchard to clear Bodha Ceann na Saile NCM and rk (3m depth) almost in mid-chan.

LIGHTS AND MARKS From offshore in good vis Ceann Garbh, a conspic mountain 900m (6M inland), leads 110° towards ent of Loch Inchard. Rubha na Leacaig, Fl (2) 10s 30m 8M, marks N side of loch ent. Dir ☆ WRG (H24) 15m 16M, Y framework tr (floodlit) leads 327° into hbr; see 1.3 for vis sectors. The 25m wide ent chan (and hbr) is dredged 4m and marked by 2 PHM poles, Fl R 4s and QR, and by a SHM pole, Fl G 4s. On S shore of loch Creag Mhòr, Dir Oc lt WRG 2.8s 16m 9M, is aligned 147°/327° with hbr ent chan; see 1.3.

COMMUNICATIONS (Code 01971) ⊜ (0141) 887 9369 (H24); Dr 502002. HM 521235, mob 07901 514350.

VHF Ch **14** 16 HX. Ch 06 is used by FVs in the Minches.

FACILITIES harbours@highland.gov.uk (pontoon) £1.50 <10m for 48hrs to E side of hbr; 8 Ⓥ in new development with and to W side. at FV quay, (Mission & Hbr Office), . In summer, bus to Inverness.

ANCHORAGES & HBRS BETWEEN KINLOCHBERVIE & ULLAPOOL

LOCH LAXFORD Highland, **58°24′·78N 05°07′·18W**. AC 2503. HW –0410 on Dover. ML 2·7m. See 1.6. Ent between Rubha Ruadh and Ardmore Pt, 1M ENE, clearly identified by 3 isolated mountains (N–S) Ceann Garbh, Ben Arkle and Ben Stack. The many ⚓s in the loch include: Loch a'Chadh-fi, on N/NE sides of islet (John Ridgway's Adventure School on Pt on W side of narrows has moorings); Bagh nah-Airde Beag, next bay to E, (beware rk 5ca off SE shore which covers at MHWS); Weaver's Bay on SW shore, 3M from ent (beware drying rk off NW Pt of ent); Bagh na Fionndalach Mor on SW shore (4-6m); Fanagmore Bay on SW shore (beware head of bay foul with old moorings). Beware many fish farming cages. Facilities: None, nearest stores at Scourie (5M).

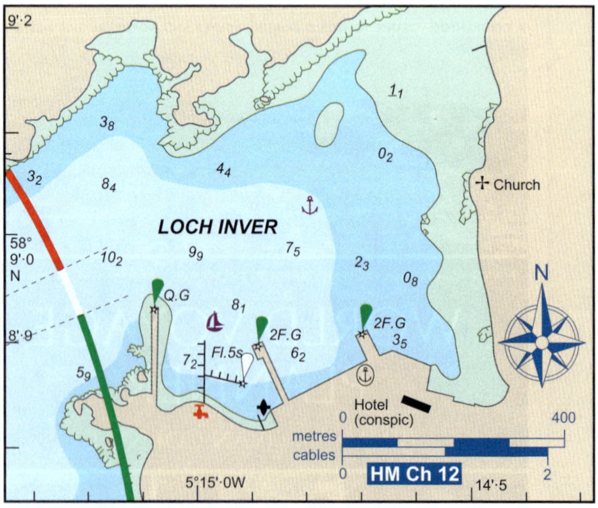

LOCH INVER Highland, **58°08′·98N 05°15′·08W**. AC 2504. HW –0433 on Dover; ML 3·0m. See 1.6. Good shelter in all weathers at head of loch in busy fishing hbr on S side. Appr N or S of Soyea Is, Fl (2) 10s 34m 6M; beware rock drying 1·7m about 50m off Kirkaig Point (S side of ent). Glas Leac, a small islet 7ca WSW of hbr, may be passed on either side. ☆, Fl WRG 3s, has 3 different approaches (see 1.3) covering the chans N and S of Soyea Is and into the hbr. The church, hotel (S side) and white ho (N side) are all conspic. A 22-berth marina is between the breakwater (QG) and the first FV pier. Or, in W'ly gales, ⚓ in the lee of bkwtr in about 8m; or where HM directs. Other ⚓s on S shore of Loch Inver. VHF Ch 12 16. HM ☎(01571) 844247; mob 07958 734610. Health Centre 01571 844452. Facilities: (Leisure Centre), .

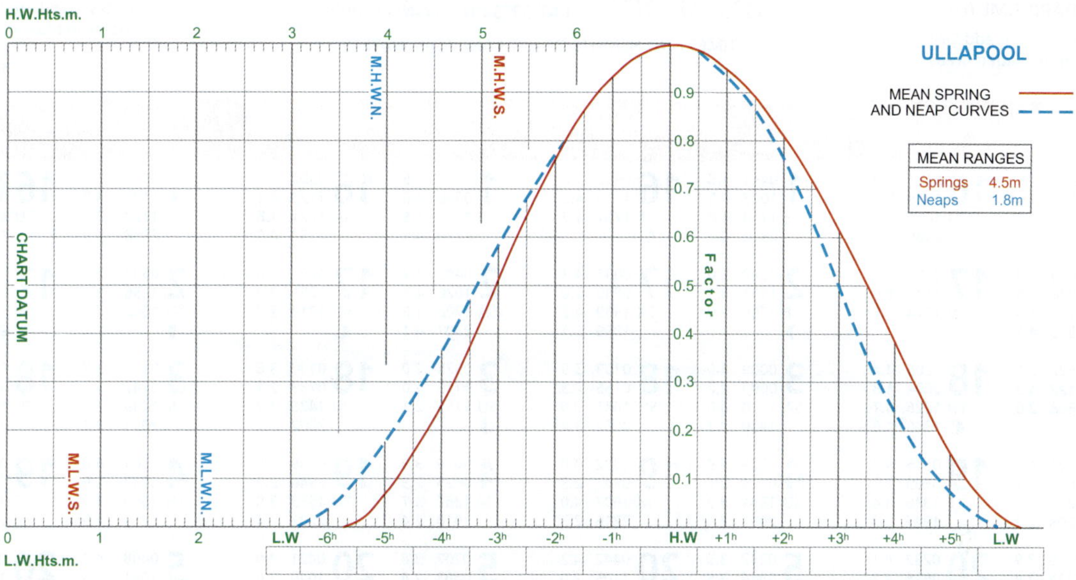

1.7 ULLAPOOL

Highland **57°53´·70N 05°09´·38W**

CHARTS AC 1794, 2500, 2501, 2509; Imray C67

TIDES –0415 Dover; ML 3·0; Duration 0610

Standard Port ULLAPOOL (⟶)

Times				Height (metres)			
High Water		Low Water		MHWS	MHWN	MLWN	MLWS
0000	0600	0300	0900	5·2	3·9	2·1	0·7
1200	1800	1500	2100				
Differences LOCH LAXFORD							
+0015	+0015	+0005	+0005	–0·3	–0·4	–0·2	0·0
BADCALL BAY							
+0005	+0005	+0005	+0005	–0·7	–0·5	–0·5	+0·2
LOCH NEDD							
0000	0000	0000	0000	–0·3	–0·2	–0·2	0·0
LOCH INVER							
–0005	–0005	–0005	–0005	–0·2	0·0	0·0	+0·1
SUMMER ISLES (Tanera Mor)							
–0005	–0005	–0010	–0010	–0·1	+0·1	0·0	+0·1
LOCH EWE (Mellon Charles, 57°51'N 05°38'W)							
–0005	–0010	–0005	–0005	–0·1	–0·1	–0·1	+0·1
LOCH GAIRLOCH							
–0012	–0011	–0011	–0011	–0·2	+0·1	–0·2	+0·2

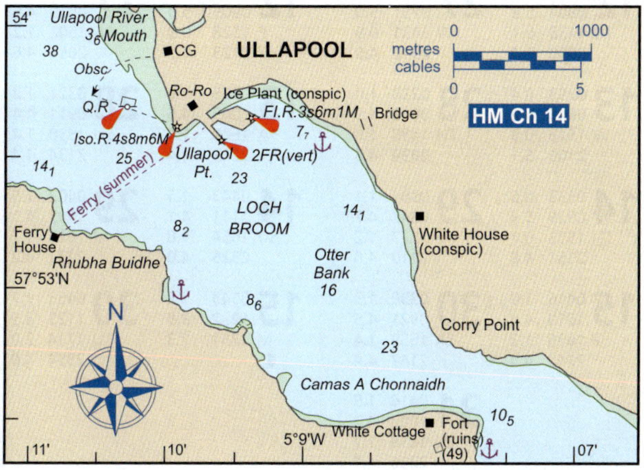

SHELTER A commercial port but yachts welcome. Good ⚓ E of pier, 8 🅐 or possible on pier (consult HM). Convenient landing inside pier, which may be busy with tourist vessels. Loch Kanaird (N of ent to Loch Broom) has good ⚓ E of Isle Martin. Possible ⚓s 6ca S of Ullapool Pt, and beyond the narrows 3ca ESE of W cottage. The upper loch is squally in strong winds.

NAVIGATION WPT L Broom ent 57°55´·78N 05°15´·08W, 129°/3.5M to Ullapool Pt lt. N of Ullapool Pt extensive drying flats off the mouth of Ullapool R are marked by QR buoy. Beware fish pens and unlit buoys SE of narrows off W shore. A wreck which may be hazardous lies in 21m of water 1·5ca SE of the tip of the E ferry wharf.

LIGHTS AND MARKS Rhubha Cadail, N of L. Broom ent, Fl WRG 6s 11m 9/6M. Cailleach Hd, W of ent, Fl (2) 12s 60m 9M. Ullapool Pt Iso R 4s 8m 6M; grey mast, vis 258°-108°.

COMMUNICATIONS (Code 01854) CG (non-emergency) 613076; Dr 08454 242424; Dentist 613289 or 612660; ⊖ (0141) 887 9369. HM 612724, mob 07734 004843.

Ullapool Harbour Ch 14 16 (H24).

FACILITIES **Pier** ; **Loch Broom SC Services** & GRP repairs Mobile Marine Services ☎633719, mob 07866 516067, Ⓔ A.Morgan ☎666383; **Town** (0700-2100), @ at Captains Cabin, Library and Ceilidh Place Hotel, all domestic facilities, at swimming pool, ⇌ (bus to Garve). Daily buses to Inverness (✈)(no Sunday bus service). **Ferries** Stornoway; 2-3/day; 2¾hrs; Calmac (www.calmac.co.uk).

ADJACENT ANCHORAGES

LOCH KANAIRD, 57°56´·60N 05°12´·20W. AC 2500. HW –0425 Dover; See 1.7; streams are weak and irreg. Situated E of the entrance to Loch Broom, S of the Summer Is and protected by Isle Martin. Good ⚓ (tripping line recommended) ENE of Sgeir Mhor or E of Isle Martin, N of Rubha Beag (also on pontoon). Beware cables and marine farms. Ent from S (1ca wide) between two rocky spits, leading line E extremity of Isle Martin in transit with dark streak on cliff behind brg 000°. Ent from N, deep and clear of dangers. Facilities: Ardmair Boat Centre P. Fraser ☎(01854) 612054, some repairs. Isle Martin, landing permitted (voluntary donation to Trust ☎(01854) 612531).

STANDARD TIME (UT)
For Summer Time add ONE hour in **non-shaded areas**

ULLAPOOL

LAT 57°54′N LONG 5°09′W

TIMES AND HEIGHTS OF HIGH AND LOW WATERS

Dates in red are SPRINGS
Dates in blue are NEAPS

YEAR **2024**

JANUARY

Date	Day	Time	m	Time	m	Time	m	Time	m	Moon
1	M	0401	1.8	0953	4.6	1640	1.7	2235	4.3	
2	TU	0439	2.0	1033	4.5	1721	1.9	2323	4.1	
3	W	0522	2.1	1122	4.3	1808	2.0			
4	TH	0021	4.0	0612	2.3	1224	4.1	1903	2.2	◑
5	F	0130	3.9	0715	2.4	1337	4.0	2009	2.2	
6	SA	0236	4.0	0828	2.5	1447	4.1	2117	2.2	
7	SU	0336	4.1	0938	2.3	1549	4.2	2218	2.0	
8	M	0428	4.4	1038	2.1	1644	4.4	2309	1.8	
9	TU	0514	4.6	1130	1.8	1734	4.6	2356	1.6	
10	W	0556	4.9	1218	1.5	1821	4.8			
11	TH	0040	1.4	0639	5.2	1305	1.2	1906	5.0	●
12	F	0124	1.2	0721	5.4	1350	0.9	1951	5.1	
13	SA	0208	1.0	0804	5.5	1436	0.8	2037	5.1	
14	SU	0251	1.0	0849	5.5	1521	0.7	2123	5.1	
15	M	0335	1.1	0935	5.4	1607	0.8	2212	4.9	
16	TU	0421	1.2	1026	5.2	1654	1.0	2305	4.6	
17	W	0509	1.5	1122	5.0	1744	1.3			
18	TH	0005	4.4	0604	1.8	1226	4.7	1840	1.6	◐
19	F	0115	4.2	0709	2.0	1338	4.4	1947	1.9	
20	SA	0232	4.1	0828	2.2	1456	4.3	2105	2.1	
21	SU	0348	4.2	0953	2.1	1611	4.3	2223	2.1	
22	M	0450	4.4	1104	2.0	1712	4.4	2323	1.9	
23	TU	0539	4.6	1200	1.7	1800	4.5			
24	W	0010	1.7	0620	4.8	1244	1.5	1841	4.7	
25	TH	0051	1.6	0654	4.9	1324	1.3	1917	4.8	○
26	F	0127	1.4	0726	5.0	1359	1.2	1949	4.8	
27	SA	0201	1.3	0755	5.1	1432	1.1	2019	4.8	
28	SU	0233	1.3	0823	5.1	1504	1.1	2048	4.8	
29	M	0304	1.3	0851	5.0	1535	1.2	2118	4.7	
30	TU	0335	1.4	0920	4.9	1606	1.3	2150	4.5	
31	W	0407	1.6	0952	4.7	1638	1.5	2226	4.3	

FEBRUARY

Date	Day	Time	m	Time	m	Time	m	Time	m	Moon
1	TH	0441	1.8	1028	4.5	1714	1.8	2310	4.1	
2	F	0520	2.0	1111	4.3	1756	2.0			◑
3	SA	0009	4.0	0609	2.2	1210	4.0	1850	2.2	
4	SU	0128	3.9	0714	2.4	1341	3.9	2007	2.4	
5	M	0247	3.9	0844	2.5	1512	3.9	2139	2.3	
6	TU	0358	4.1	1011	2.2	1629	4.1	2250	2.0	
7	W	0456	4.4	1116	1.9	1727	4.4	2344	1.7	
8	TH	0543	4.8	1209	1.4	1814	4.8			
9	F	0030	1.3	0626	5.2	1255	0.9	1857	5.1	●
10	SA	0114	1.0	0707	5.5	1339	0.6	1937	5.3	
11	SU	0155	0.7	0747	5.7	1422	0.3	2017	5.4	
12	M	0236	0.6	0829	5.8	1503	0.3	2058	5.3	
13	TU	0317	0.6	0911	5.6	1544	0.4	2140	5.1	
14	W	0358	0.8	0956	5.4	1625	0.8	2226	4.8	
15	TH	0441	1.1	1047	5.0	1709	1.2	2320	4.4	
16	F	0530	1.6	1150	4.5	1757	1.7			◐
17	SA	0031	4.1	0630	2.0	1309	4.2	1859	2.1	
18	SU	0159	3.9	0755	2.3	1441	3.9	2032	2.4	
19	M	0332	4.0	0947	2.3	1607	4.0	2216	2.3	
20	TU	0442	4.2	1105	2.0	1709	4.2	2318	2.1	
21	W	0530	4.4	1155	1.7	1753	4.4			
22	TH	0001	1.8	0608	4.6	1234	1.4	1828	4.6	
23	F	0038	1.5	0638	4.8	1308	1.2	1858	4.7	
24	SA	0111	1.3	0706	5.0	1339	1.0	1925	4.9	○
25	SU	0141	1.2	0731	5.1	1408	0.9	1951	4.9	
26	M	0210	1.1	0756	5.1	1436	0.9	2017	4.9	
27	TU	0238	1.1	0821	5.1	1504	1.0	2044	4.8	
28	W	0306	1.1	0847	4.9	1531	1.1	2112	4.7	
29	TH	0335	1.3	0916	4.8	1600	1.3	2143	4.5	

MARCH

Date	Day	Time	m	Time	m	Time	m	Time	m	Moon
1	F	0407	1.5	0948	4.6	1632	1.5	2220	4.3	
2	SA	0442	1.7	1026	4.3	1708	1.8	2307	4.1	
3	SU	0525	2.0	1119	4.0	1755	2.1			◑
4	M	0026	3.9	0625	2.3	1257	3.7	1910	2.4	
5	TU	0207	3.8	0803	2.4	1452	3.8	2113	2.4	
6	W	0332	4.0	0955	2.2	1618	4.0	2237	2.1	
7	TH	0436	4.4	1104	1.7	1715	4.4	2330	1.6	
8	F	0524	4.8	1154	1.1	1758	4.8			
9	SA	0014	1.1	0606	5.2	1238	0.6	1837	5.2	
10	SU	0055	0.7	0645	5.6	1319	0.3	1914	5.4	●
11	M	0135	0.4	0724	5.8	1359	0.1	1952	5.5	
12	TU	0214	0.3	0804	5.8	1438	0.1	2030	5.4	
13	W	0253	0.4	0845	5.6	1516	0.3	2109	5.1	
14	TH	0333	0.6	0929	5.3	1555	0.7	2151	4.8	
15	F	0416	1.0	1019	4.8	1636	1.2	2240	4.4	
16	SA	0502	1.5	1125	4.3	1721	1.8	2352	4.0	
17	SU	0601	2.0	1251	3.9	1819	2.2			◐
18	M	0130	3.8	0733	2.3	1426	3.7	2002	2.5	
19	TU	0309	3.8	0940	2.2	1553	3.8	2202	2.4	
20	W	0421	4.0	1049	2.0	1652	4.0	2300	2.1	
21	TH	0508	4.3	1133	1.6	1732	4.2	2340	1.8	
22	F	0543	4.5	1209	1.4	1803	4.5			
23	SA	0014	1.5	0612	4.7	1240	1.1	1831	4.7	
24	SU	0045	1.2	0638	4.9	1310	0.9	1856	4.8	
25	M	0114	1.1	0702	5.0	1338	0.8	1921	4.9	○
26	TU	0142	1.0	0726	5.0	1405	0.8	1946	4.9	
27	W	0210	0.9	0751	5.0	1431	0.8	2012	4.9	
28	TH	0238	1.0	0818	4.9	1458	1.0	2039	4.8	
29	F	0307	1.1	0847	4.7	1527	1.2	2110	4.6	
30	SA	0339	1.3	0921	4.5	1559	1.4	2147	4.4	
31	SU	0416	1.5	1003	4.2	1636	1.7	2236	4.1	

APRIL

Date	Day	Time	m	Time	m	Time	m	Time	m	Moon
1	M	0501	1.8	1105	3.9	1724	2.1	2358	3.9	
2	TU	0603	2.1	1256	3.7	1842	2.4			◑
3	W	0141	3.8	0747	2.2	1439	3.7	2054	2.3	
4	TH	0304	4.0	0937	1.9	1558	4.0	2214	1.9	
5	F	0408	4.4	1041	1.4	1652	4.4	2306	1.5	
6	SA	0457	4.8	1130	0.9	1734	4.8	2350	1.0	
7	SU	0540	5.2	1213	0.5	1812	5.1			
8	M	0030	0.6	0620	5.5	1253	0.2	1849	5.3	●
9	TU	0110	0.4	0659	5.7	1332	0.1	1925	5.4	
10	W	0150	0.3	0740	5.6	1411	0.2	2002	5.3	
11	TH	0231	0.4	0822	5.4	1449	0.5	2041	5.1	
12	F	0312	0.7	0909	5.0	1528	0.9	2123	4.7	
13	SA	0355	1.0	1003	4.5	1609	1.4	2213	4.4	
14	SU	0443	1.5	1111	4.1	1654	1.8	2325	4.0	
15	M	0543	1.9	1232	3.8	1751	2.3			◐
16	TU	0056	3.8	0711	2.2	1357	3.6	1927	2.5	
17	W	0229	3.8	0901	2.1	1518	3.7	2119	2.4	
18	TH	0341	3.9	1010	1.9	1617	3.9	2222	2.1	
19	F	0431	4.1	1055	1.6	1657	4.1	2304	1.8	
20	SA	0507	4.3	1132	1.4	1730	4.3	2340	1.5	
21	SU	0538	4.5	1205	1.2	1758	4.6			
22	M	0012	1.3	0605	4.7	1235	1.0	1825	4.7	
23	TU	0042	1.1	0631	4.8	1304	0.9	1850	4.8	○
24	W	0112	1.0	0657	4.8	1332	0.9	1917	4.9	
25	TH	0142	1.0	0725	4.8	1401	0.9	1944	4.9	
26	F	0213	1.0	0755	4.7	1430	1.0	2015	4.8	
27	SA	0245	1.1	0830	4.6	1502	1.2	2051	4.6	
28	SU	0321	1.2	0911	4.4	1538	1.4	2134	4.4	
29	M	0402	1.5	1005	4.1	1620	1.7	2232	4.2	
30	TU	0453	1.7	1123	3.9	1714	2.0	2354	4.0	

Chart Datum: 2·75 metres below Ordnance Datum (Newlyn). HAT is 5·9 metres above Chart Datum.

STANDARD TIME (UT)
For Summer Time add ONE hour in **non-shaded areas**

ULLAPOOL LAT 57°54′N LONG 5°09′W

TIMES AND HEIGHTS OF HIGH AND LOW WATERS

Dates in red are SPRINGS
Dates in blue are NEAPS

YEAR **2024**

MAY

Date	Day	Time	m	Date	Day	Time	m
1		0601	1.9	16		0128	3.8
		1254	3.8			0757	2.0
	W	1838	2.2		TH	1420	3.7
	◑					2010	2.3
2		0119	4.0	17		0241	3.8
		0737	1.9			0909	1.9
	TH	1416	3.9		F	1523	3.8
		2025	2.1			2122	2.2
3		0233	4.2	18		0338	3.9
		0905	1.6			1003	1.7
	F	1527	4.1		SA	1611	4.0
		2139	1.8			2215	2.0
4		0336	4.4	19		0422	4.1
		1008	1.3			1046	1.6
	SA	1622	4.4		SU	1649	4.2
		2234	1.4			2257	1.7
5		0428	4.8	20		0458	4.3
		1059	0.9			1124	1.4
	SU	1706	4.7		M	1722	4.4
		2321	1.1			2334	1.5
6		0513	5.1	21		0530	4.4
		1144	0.6			1158	1.2
	M	1746	5.0		TU	1752	4.6
7		0005	0.8	22		0009	1.4
		0556	5.3			0601	4.5
	TU	1226	0.5		W	1230	1.1
		1824	5.2			1822	4.7
8		0048	0.6	23		0043	1.2
		0639	5.3			0633	4.6
	W	1307	0.4		TH	1303	1.1
	●	1903	5.2		○	1853	4.8
9		0130	0.5	24		0118	1.1
		0723	5.2			0707	4.6
	TH	1347	0.6		F	1336	1.1
		1942	5.1			1926	4.8
10		0213	0.6	25		0154	1.1
		0808	5.0			0744	4.6
	F	1427	0.8		SA	1411	1.1
		2023	4.9			2002	4.8
11		0256	0.8	26		0232	1.1
		0858	4.7			0828	4.5
	SA	1508	1.1		SU	1448	1.2
		2107	4.7			2045	4.7
12		0342	1.1	27		0314	1.2
		0953	4.3			0918	4.4
	SU	1549	1.5		M	1530	1.4
		2157	4.4			2134	4.6
13		0431	1.5	28		0400	1.3
		1054	4.0			1017	4.2
	M	1635	1.8		TU	1617	1.6
		2259	4.1			2234	4.4
14		0527	1.8	29		0454	1.4
		1159	3.8			1124	4.1
	TU	1729	2.1		W	1715	1.8
						2342	4.3
15		0011	3.9	30		0558	1.5
		0636	2.0			1235	4.0
	W	1308	3.7		TH	1826	1.9
	◐	1842	2.3		◑		
				31		0052	4.3
						0712	1.6
					F	1345	4.0
						1946	1.9

JUNE

Date	Day	Time	m	Date	Day	Time	m
1		0159	4.3	16		0227	3.9
		0825	1.5			0854	1.9
	SA	1451	4.1		SU	1512	3.9
		2058	1.8			2110	2.2
2		0302	4.5	17		0325	3.9
		0930	1.3			0950	1.8
	SU	1550	4.3		M	1602	4.0
		2159	1.5			2207	2.0
3		0359	4.6	18		0414	4.0
		1027	1.1			1038	1.7
	M	1640	4.6		TU	1644	4.2
		2254	1.3			2255	1.8
4		0452	4.8	19		0457	4.2
		1118	1.0			1121	1.6
	TU	1725	4.8		W	1722	4.4
		2344	1.1			2338	1.6
5		0540	4.9	20		0538	4.3
		1205	0.9			1201	1.4
	W	1807	4.9		TH	1759	4.6
6		0032	0.9	21		0020	1.4
		0628	4.9			0618	4.5
	TH	1249	0.9		F	1240	1.3
	●	1849	5.0			1836	4.8
7		0118	0.9	22		0101	1.2
		0716	4.9			0659	4.6
	F	1331	1.0		SA	1320	1.2
		1931	5.0		○	1915	4.9
8		0203	0.9	23		0143	1.1
		0803	4.7			0743	4.6
	SA	1413	1.1		SU	1400	1.2
		2013	4.9			1956	4.9
9		0248	1.0	24		0226	1.0
		0850	4.6			0828	4.6
	SU	1454	1.3		M	1442	1.2
		2055	4.7			2041	4.9
10		0332	1.1	25		0311	0.9
		0937	4.4			0917	4.6
	M	1535	1.5		TU	1526	1.2
		2138	4.5			2128	4.9
11		0416	1.3	26		0357	1.0
		1024	4.2			1008	4.5
	TU	1617	1.7		W	1613	1.3
		2224	4.3			2221	4.8
12		0502	1.5	27		0447	1.1
		1114	4.0			1104	4.4
	W	1703	1.9		TH	1704	1.5
		2316	4.1			2318	4.7
13		0552	1.7	28		0540	1.2
		1209	3.8			1205	4.2
	TH	1755	2.1		F	1801	1.6
					◑		
14		0016	4.0	29		0021	4.5
		0649	1.9			0639	1.3
	F	1309	3.7		SA	1309	4.1
	◐	1856	2.2			1907	1.8
15		0122	3.9	30		0126	4.4
		0751	1.9			0743	1.5
	SA	1413	3.8		SU	1416	4.1
		2004	2.2			2017	1.8

JULY

Date	Day	Time	m	Date	Day	Time	m
1		0233	4.4	16		0221	3.8
		0851	1.5			0843	2.1
	M	1522	4.2		TU	1511	3.9
		2129	1.8			2111	2.3
2		0340	4.4	17		0330	3.8
		0959	1.5			0953	2.1
	TU	1622	4.4		W	1609	4.1
		2236	1.6			2219	2.1
3		0442	4.4	18		0432	4.0
		1100	1.5			1051	1.9
	W	1715	4.5		TH	1658	4.3
		2335	1.4			2315	1.8
4		0538	4.5	19		0524	4.2
		1153	1.4			1141	1.7
	TH	1802	4.7		F	1742	4.5
5		0027	1.3	20		0004	1.5
		0628	4.6			0610	4.4
	F	1240	1.3		SA	1225	1.4
	●	1845	4.8			1823	4.8
6		0114	1.1	21		0050	1.2
		0713	4.7			0652	4.7
	SA	1323	1.3		SU	1308	1.2
		1924	4.9		○	1903	5.1
7		0158	1.0	22		0134	0.9
		0754	4.7			0734	4.8
	SU	1403	1.2		M	1350	1.0
		2001	4.9			1944	5.2
8		0238	1.0	23		0217	0.7
		0832	4.6			0816	4.9
	M	1440	1.3		TU	1432	0.9
		2036	4.8			2026	5.3
9		0316	1.1	24		0300	0.6
		0909	4.5			0859	4.9
	TU	1517	1.3		W	1514	0.9
		2110	4.7			2109	5.3
10		0353	1.2	25		0342	0.6
		0945	4.4			0944	4.8
	W	1553	1.5		TH	1557	1.0
		2145	4.6			2156	5.2
11		0430	1.3	26		0426	0.7
		1023	4.2			1032	4.6
	TH	1630	1.6		F	1642	1.2
		2222	4.4			2248	4.9
12		0507	1.5	27		0512	1.0
		1106	4.1			1128	4.4
	F	1710	1.8		SA	1732	1.4
		2305	4.2			2348	4.6
13		0548	1.7	28		0603	1.3
		1158	3.9			1233	4.2
	SA	1754	2.0		SU	1830	1.7
	◐	2359	4.0		◑		
14		0636	1.9	29		0057	4.4
		1301	3.8			0702	1.7
	SU	1848	2.2		M	1346	4.1
						1943	2.0
15		0108	3.9	30		0214	4.2
		0734	2.1			0817	1.9
	M	1407	3.8		TU	1504	4.1
		1956	2.3			2111	2.0
				31		0335	4.1
						0943	2.0
					W	1617	4.2
						2234	1.9

AUGUST

Date	Day	Time	m	Date	Day	Time	m
1		0446	4.2	16		0416	3.9
		1056	1.9			1032	2.1
	TH	1714	4.4		F	1638	4.2
		2337	1.6			2300	1.9
2		0541	4.4	17		0513	4.2
		1150	1.7			1126	1.8
	F	1759	4.6		SA	1724	4.6
						2351	1.5
3		0026	1.4	18		0557	4.5
		0625	4.5			1212	1.4
	SA	1234	1.5		SU	1805	5.0
		1837	4.8				
4		0108	1.2	19		0035	1.0
		0702	4.7			0636	4.9
	SU	1313	1.3		M	1253	1.0
	●	1910	4.9		○	1844	5.3
5		0145	1.0	20		0117	0.6
		0735	4.7			0714	5.1
	M	1348	1.2		TU	1333	0.8
		1940	5.0			1923	5.6
6		0219	0.9	21		0158	0.3
		0806	4.8			0753	5.3
	TU	1421	1.2		W	1413	0.6
		2009	5.0			2002	5.7
7		0251	0.9	22		0238	0.2
		0835	4.7			0832	5.3
	W	1452	1.2		TH	1452	0.6
		2037	4.9			2043	5.6
8		0322	1.0	23		0318	0.3
		0905	4.6			0912	5.1
	TH	1523	1.2		F	1533	0.7
		2106	4.8			2127	5.4
9		0353	1.1	24		0359	0.6
		0936	4.5			0956	4.8
	F	1555	1.4		SA	1616	1.0
		2136	4.6			2217	5.0
10		0424	1.3	25		0441	1.0
		1010	4.3			1048	4.5
	SA	1628	1.6		SU	1703	1.4
		2210	4.4			2318	4.6
11		0458	1.6	26		0528	1.5
		1051	4.1			1158	4.2
	SU	1705	1.9		M	1759	1.8
		2252	4.1		◑		
12		0536	1.9	27		0038	4.2
		1147	3.9			0626	2.0
	M	1750	2.1		TU	1324	4.0
	◐	2348	3.9			1919	2.1
13		0624	2.1	28		0208	4.0
		1305	3.8			0750	2.3
	TU	1850	2.3		W	1456	4.0
						2112	2.2
14		0122	3.7	29		0338	3.9
		0734	2.3			0943	2.3
	W	1425	3.8		TH	1613	4.2
		2017	2.4			2240	2.0
15		0257	3.7	30		0446	4.1
		0913	2.3			1055	2.1
	TH	1538	4.0		F	1707	4.4
		2153	2.3			2334	1.6
				31		0534	4.3
						1142	1.8
					SA	1747	4.6

Chart Datum: 2·75 metres below Ordnance Datum (Newlyn). HAT is 5·9 metres above Chart Datum.

STANDARD TIME (UT)
For Summer Time add ONE hour in **non-shaded areas**

ULLAPOOL   LAT 57°54'N   LONG 5°09'W

TIMES AND HEIGHTS OF HIGH AND LOW WATERS

Dates in red are SPRINGS
Dates in blue are NEAPS

YEAR **2024**

SEPTEMBER

Date	Day	Time	m	Time	m	Time	m	Time	m
1	SU	0014	1.4	0611	4.5	1219	1.5	1819	4.8
2	M	0050	1.1	0641	4.7	1253	1.3	1847	5.0
3	TU ●	0122	1.0	0708	4.8	1325	1.1	1913	5.1
4	W	0152	0.9	0735	4.9	1355	1.1	1938	5.1
5	TH	0220	0.9	0800	4.9	1423	1.1	2003	5.0
6	F	0248	0.9	0827	4.8	1451	1.1	2029	4.9
7	SA	0315	1.1	0854	4.7	1521	1.3	2058	4.7
8	SU	0344	1.3	0924	4.5	1552	1.5	2129	4.5
9	M	0414	1.5	1000	4.3	1627	1.8	2206	4.2
10	TU	0449	1.9	1046	4.1	1708	2.1	2258	3.9
11	W ◐	0533	2.2	1206	3.9	1805	2.3		
12	TH	0043	3.7	0641	2.5	1349	3.8	1939	2.5
13	F	0237	3.7	0846	2.5	1511	4.0	2136	2.3
14	SA	0400	3.9	1015	2.2	1614	4.3	2243	1.8
15	SU	0454	4.3	1107	1.8	1701	4.7	2331	1.3
16	M	0536	4.7	1150	1.3	1741	5.2		
17	TU	0013	0.8	0613	5.1	1230	0.9	1819	5.5
18	W ○	0053	0.4	0649	5.4	1309	0.6	1857	5.8
19	TH	0132	0.2	0725	5.5	1348	0.4	1936	5.9
20	F	0211	0.1	0802	5.5	1428	0.4	2017	5.7
21	SA	0250	0.3	0841	5.3	1508	0.6	2101	5.4
22	SU	0330	0.7	0923	5.0	1551	1.0	2152	4.9
23	M	0411	1.2	1014	4.6	1639	1.4	2259	4.4
24	TU ◑	0457	1.7	1128	4.2	1738	1.9		
25	W	0028	4.0	0556	2.2	1306	4.0	1908	2.3
26	TH	0202	3.9	0732	2.6	1443	4.0	2113	2.2
27	F	0330	3.9	0934	2.5	1557	4.2	2227	1.9
28	SA	0432	4.1	1037	2.2	1647	4.4	2312	1.7
29	SU	0513	4.4	1119	1.9	1723	4.6	2349	1.4
30	M	0545	4.6	1154	1.6	1753	4.8		

OCTOBER

Date	Day	Time	m	Time	m	Time	m	Time	m
1	TU	0021	1.2	0613	4.8	1226	1.3	1820	5.0
2	W ●	0051	1.0	0639	4.9	1256	1.2	1844	5.1
3	TH	0120	0.9	0704	5.0	1325	1.1	1908	5.1
4	F	0147	0.9	0728	5.0	1353	1.1	1933	5.0
5	SA	0214	1.0	0754	5.0	1421	1.2	1959	4.9
6	SU	0241	1.1	0821	4.9	1451	1.3	2028	4.8
7	M	0309	1.3	0850	4.7	1522	1.5	2101	4.5
8	TU	0340	1.6	0926	4.5	1558	1.7	2141	4.2
9	W	0416	1.9	1013	4.2	1642	2.0	2241	3.9
10	TH ◐	0501	2.2	1133	4.0	1741	2.3		
11	F	0034	3.7	0612	2.5	1319	3.9	1918	2.4
12	SA	0215	3.8	0821	2.5	1440	4.1	2110	2.1
13	SU	0333	4.1	0947	2.2	1543	4.4	2215	1.7
14	M	0427	4.4	1039	1.7	1631	4.8	2303	1.2
15	TU	0508	4.8	1122	1.3	1713	5.3	2345	0.8
16	W	0545	5.2	1203	0.9	1752	5.6		
17	TH ○	0025	0.4	0622	5.4	1243	0.6	1832	5.8
18	F	0105	0.3	0659	5.6	1324	0.5	1913	5.8
19	SA	0145	0.3	0736	5.5	1405	0.5	1956	5.6
20	SU	0225	0.6	0816	5.3	1448	0.8	2043	5.2
21	M	0305	0.9	0900	5.0	1533	1.1	2138	4.8
22	TU	0348	1.4	0951	4.7	1623	1.5	2249	4.3
23	W	0435	1.9	1105	4.3	1725	2.0		
24	TH ◑	0011	4.0	0534	2.3	1238	4.1	1851	2.2
25	F	0137	3.9	0704	2.6	1409	4.0	2036	2.2
26	SA	0258	3.9	0851	2.5	1522	4.2	2148	2.0
27	SU	0359	4.1	0958	2.3	1613	4.3	2235	1.8
28	M	0441	4.3	1043	2.0	1651	4.5	2313	1.6
29	TU	0514	4.5	1121	1.7	1722	4.7	2347	1.4
30	W	0542	4.7	1154	1.5	1750	4.8		
31	TH	0017	1.2	0609	4.9	1225	1.4	1816	4.9

NOVEMBER

Date	Day	Time	m	Time	m	Time	m	Time	m
1	F ●	0047	1.1	0635	5.0	1256	1.3	1842	5.0
2	SA	0115	1.1	0701	5.0	1326	1.2	1910	5.0
3	SU	0144	1.2	0728	5.0	1356	1.3	1939	4.9
4	M	0213	1.3	0758	5.0	1429	1.4	2012	4.7
5	TU	0244	1.5	0831	4.8	1504	1.5	2051	4.5
6	W	0319	1.7	0912	4.6	1543	1.7	2140	4.3
7	TH	0358	1.9	1004	4.4	1631	1.9	2249	4.1
8	F	0448	2.2	1119	4.2	1733	2.1		
9	SA ◐	0019	3.9	0601	2.4	1246	4.2	1859	2.2
10	SU	0142	4.0	0742	2.4	1401	4.3	2028	2.0
11	M	0255	4.2	0904	2.2	1505	4.6	2136	1.6
12	TU	0352	4.5	1002	1.8	1558	4.9	2228	1.3
13	W	0439	4.8	1051	1.4	1645	5.2	2315	1.0
14	TH	0519	5.1	1137	1.1	1729	5.4	2359	0.7
15	F ○	0559	5.3	1221	0.9	1813	5.6		
16	SA	0041	0.7	0639	5.4	1305	0.8	1858	5.5
17	SU	0123	0.7	0719	5.4	1350	0.8	1945	5.3
18	M	0205	0.9	0802	5.3	1435	1.0	2036	5.0
19	TU	0248	1.2	0847	5.1	1523	1.2	2131	4.7
20	W	0331	1.6	0938	4.8	1613	1.5	2231	4.4
21	TH	0418	1.9	1038	4.5	1709	1.8	2336	4.1
22	F	0512	2.2	1150	4.3	1815	2.1		
23	SA ◑	0045	3.9	0619	2.5	1307	4.1	1931	2.2
24	SU	0159	3.9	0740	2.5	1422	4.1	2043	2.1
25	M	0305	4.0	0855	2.4	1522	4.2	2142	2.0
26	TU	0356	4.2	0954	2.2	1609	4.3	2229	1.8
27	W	0436	4.4	1040	2.0	1647	4.5	2308	1.7
28	TH	0511	4.6	1120	1.9	1721	4.6	2344	1.6
29	F	0542	4.7	1156	1.7	1753	4.7		
30	SA	0017	1.5	0612	4.9	1230	1.5	1824	4.8

DECEMBER

Date	Day	Time	m	Time	m	Time	m	Time	m
1	SU ●	0049	1.4	0642	5.0	1305	1.4	1857	4.8
2	M	0122	1.4	0713	5.0	1340	1.4	1932	4.8
3	TU	0155	1.4	0747	5.0	1417	1.4	2010	4.7
4	W	0231	1.5	0826	5.0	1456	1.4	2054	4.6
5	TH	0309	1.6	0909	4.9	1539	1.5	2144	4.5
6	F	0352	1.8	1000	4.7	1627	1.6	2243	4.3
7	SA	0443	2.0	1100	4.6	1723	1.7	2350	4.2
8	SU ◐	0544	2.1	1209	4.5	1829	1.8		
9	M	0101	4.2	0658	2.2	1319	4.5	1941	1.8
10	TU	0211	4.2	0814	2.1	1425	4.6	2050	1.7
11	W	0315	4.4	0922	1.9	1526	4.8	2153	1.5
12	TH	0411	4.6	1022	1.7	1623	4.9	2248	1.3
13	F	0500	4.9	1116	1.4	1716	5.1	2339	1.2
14	SA	0545	5.1	1208	1.2	1806	5.2		
15	SU ○	0026	1.1	0630	5.2	1256	1.1	1855	5.2
16	M	0111	1.1	0713	5.3	1344	1.0	1943	5.1
17	TU	0154	1.2	0756	5.3	1430	1.1	2030	5.0
18	W	0237	1.3	0838	5.2	1515	1.2	2115	4.8
19	TH	0319	1.5	0921	5.0	1559	1.4	2201	4.5
20	F	0401	1.7	1004	4.7	1644	1.6	2248	4.3
21	SA	0444	1.9	1051	4.5	1731	1.8	2339	4.1
22	SU ◑	0531	2.2	1145	4.3	1822	2.0		
23	M	0039	4.0	0627	2.3	1252	4.1	1921	2.2
24	TU	0147	3.9	0732	2.5	1405	4.0	2027	2.2
25	W	0254	4.0	0844	2.5	1511	4.1	2131	2.2
26	TH	0351	4.1	0950	2.4	1608	4.2	2226	2.1
27	F	0438	4.3	1044	2.2	1655	4.3	2312	1.9
28	SA	0518	4.5	1130	2.0	1736	4.4	2353	1.8
29	SU	0554	4.7	1212	1.8	1814	4.6		
30	M ●	0031	1.6	0630	4.9	1251	1.6	1852	4.7
31	TU	0108	1.5	0705	5.1	1331	1.4	1929	4.8

Chart Datum: 2·75 metres below Ordnance Datum (Newlyn). HAT is 5·9 metres above Chart Datum.

ADJACENT ISLANDS

SUMMER ISLES, 58°01'N 05°25'W. AC 2509, 2501. HW –0425 Dover; See 1.7; streams are weak and irregular. In the N apps to Loch Broom some 30 islands and rks, the main ones being Eilean Mullagrach, Isle Ristol, Glas-leac Mor, Tanera Beg, Eilean a' Char, Eilean Fada Mor. Beware rocks at S end of Horse Sound. ⚓s:

Isle Ristol, ⚓ to S of drying causeway and clear of moorings; beware landings frequented by local FVs. Close to slip is lt Fl G 3s. Facilities: 🛒(at Polbain 2M).

Tanera Beg, ⚓ in the chan to the E inside Eilean Fada Mor.

Tanera Mor, on E side, ⚓ in bay to N off pier or in W corner off stone jetty; beware many moorings and fish pens. Also poss ⚓ close NW of Is and close E of Eilean na Saille, but N of drying rock. Facilities: ☎(01854) 622272 B Wilder for ▲ 🚰 🚿 tea room.

Badentarbat Bay, Temp'y ⚓ NW part of bay ESE of pier which is busy with marina farm activity. Beware N part of bay is shoal. Suitable for Achiltibuie or Polbain on mainland. Facilities: ⛽ 🚰 ⛽ (emerg) ☎(01854) 622261, 🛒 ✕.

LITTLE LOCH BROOM, 57°54'·98N 05°24'·68W. AC 2500. HW –0415 Dover as per Ullapool, see 1.7; streams are weak (approx 1kn). Between Loch Broom and Gruinard Bay, entered S of Cailleach Hd it is deep (115m in centre) and shoreline steep to. In approaches beware of Ardross Rk (depth 0.6m) 0.38M ENE of Stattic Pt.

Camusnagaul, on S side of loch 1.6M from head and Dundonnel Hotel, ⚓ to E of hamlet.

Scoraig, inside narrows on N shore in N'lies, ⚓ off jetty clear of submarine cables and marine farm. ⚒ C.Dawson ☎01845 613380.

ANCHORAGES BETWEEN LITTLE LOCH BROOM & LOCH GAIRLOCH

LOCH EWE, 57°52'·0N 05°40'·0W (SWM buoy, L Fl 10s). AC 2509, 3146. Tides: See 1.7; HW –0415 on Dover; ML 2·6m; Duration 0610. Shelter in all winds. Easy ent with no dangers in loch. Rhubha Reidh lt, Fl (4) 15s 37m 24M, W tr, is 4·5M W of ent. No 1 buoy Fl (3) G 10s. Loch approx 7M long with Isle Ewe and 2 small islets about 2M from ent in centre; can be passed on either side. Temp ⚓ in bay of Isle of Ewe. Beware unlit buoy A2 between E side Isle Ewe and Aultbea Pier, 2 FG (vert); NATO fuelling jetty 2 FG (vert) and dolphins Fl G 4s.

Loch Thurnaig, 1.7M SSE of Isle of Ewe, sheltered ⚓ off Ob na Bà Rùaidhe, SE of pier to W of drying reef. Beware of numerous marine farms in approaches.

Aultbea, ⚓ off Aultbea Hotel on E shore or in NW'lies close E of pier; avoid moorings in bay, northern part of which is shoal. Facilities: Dr, ⓟ ✉ 🛒 ✕ ◻.

Poolewe Bay, ⚓ in SW part of bay in 3·5m, at head of loch: Boor Rks(3m) with drying rocks extending 1ca NW lie off W shore about 9ca NW of Poolewe. Head of Loch dries for a considerable distance. Facilities: ⛴ 🚰 ⛽ on pier, ⓟ (at garage) ⛽ ✉ 🛒 ✕ ◻. Landing difficult at E side of bay.

Inverewe Gdns on NE side of bay, ⚓ to SW of Jetty at Port na Cloiche Gile.

LOCH GAIRLOCH, 57°43'N 05°45'W. AC 228, 2528. HW –0440 on Dover. See 1.7. A wide loch facing W. Ent clear of dangers but Submarine Exercise Area to S of Longa Is. Quite heavy seas enter in bad weather. Lts: Glas Eilean Fl WRG 6s 9m 6/4M, Gairloch Pier Hd, QR 9m. HM ☎(01445) 712140.

Badachro, good shelter SW of Eilean Horrisdale on SW side of loch but busy with FVs and local craft. 6🅐s SE of Portree £15/nt ☎07775 652911. Unlit PHM/SHM mark rock ledges in approach. Passage to S of of Eilean Horrisdale is possible with caution. ⚓ on E side NNW of Sgeir Dhubh Bhea. ✕ ◻(Bad Inn). HM ☎(01445) 741255 for availability.

Loch Shieldaig, At SE end of the loch many moorings for local craft. 🅐 in Ob Na Acarseid when vacant £10/night. If unavailable ⚓ to SSW of Eilean an t-Sabhail. Beware marine farms.

Flowerdale Bay, ⚓ in approx 6m near Gairloch pier or berth on pontoons (2m depth N side, 3m S side) at pier. HM ☎(01445) 712140. VHF Ch 16 (occas). Gairloch Pier: ⛵ fees charged. 🚰 🚿 ⛽ ⓟ ⛽ ⓖ ✉ 🛒 ◻ SC, Hotel.

SUBMARINE EXERCISE INFORMATION

Details of submarine activity in the Exercise Areas north of Mull are broadcast at 0710 and1910 UT by Stornoway CG on a specified VHF Ch after an initial announcement on Ch 16. Areas are referred to by the names given below, rather than by the numbers indicated on the chartlet. For Areas 22–85 (South of Mull), see page 84.

SUBFACTS

General information on SUBFACTS is also broadcast twice daily at 0620 and 1820 UT on Navtex. Stornoway CGOC will provide SUBFACTS on request; call on Ch 16.

A 'Fisherman's hotline' (☎(01436) 677201) is available on a 24hr basis and may be used for any queries relating to SUBFACTS from any mariner.

Submarines on the surface and at periscope depth always listen on Ch 16.

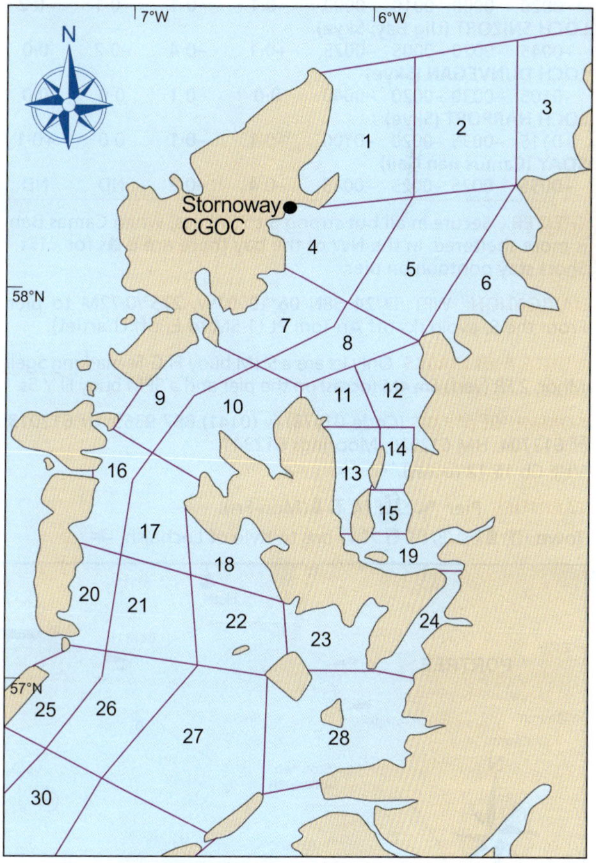

1	Tolsta	16	Wiay
2	Pulteney	17	Pooltiel
3	Eddrachillis	18	Bracadale
4	Erisort	19	Crowlin
5	Clynelish	20	Boisdale
6	Broom	21	Dalwhinnie
7	Shiant	22	Canna
8	Balbair	23	Rum
9	Hermitray	24	Sleat
10	Waternish	25	Hellisayl
11	Flodigarry	26	Edradour
12	Longa	27	Hawes
13	Portree	28	Eigg
14	Rona	29	Sandray
15	Raasay	30	Glenturret

1.8 PORTREE

Skye (Highland) **57°24′·73N 06°11′·07W**

CHARTS AC 2209, 2534, 5616; Imray C66

TIDES –0445 Dover; ML no data; Duration 0610

Standard Port ULLAPOOL (⟵)

Times				Height (metres)			
High Water		Low Water		MHWS	MHWN	MLWN	MLWS
0000	0600	0300	0900	5·2	3·9	2·1	0·7
1200	1800	1500	2100				
Differences PORTREE (Skye)							
–0025	–0025	–0025	–0025	+0·1	–0·2	–0·2	0·0
SHIELDAIG (Loch Torridon)							
–0020	–0020	–0015	–0015	+0·4	+0·3	+0·1	0·0
LOCH A'BHRAIGE (Rona)							
–0020	0000	–0010	0000	–0·1	–0·1	–0·1	–0·2
LOCH SNIZORT (Uig Bay, Skye)							
–0045	–0020	–0005	–0025	+0·1	–0·4	–0·2	0·0
LOCH DUNVEGAN (Skye)							
–0105	–0030	–0020	–0040	0·0	–0·1	0·0	0·0
LOCH HARPORT (Skye)							
–0115	–0035	–0020	–0100	–0·1	–0·1	0·0	+0·1
SOAY (Camus nan Gall)							
–0055	–0025	–0025	–0045	–0·4	–0·2	ND	ND

SHELTER Secure in all but strong S to SW'lies, when Camas Bàn is more sheltered. In the NW of the bay there are 8 🅐s for <15t. Short stay pontoon on pier.

NAVIGATION WPT 57°24′·58N 06°10′·07W, 275°/0·72M to pier. From the S, avoid rks off An Tom Pt (1·5M to E, off chartlet).

LIGHTS AND MARKS Only lts are a SHM buoy Fl G 5s marking Sgeir Mhór, 2 FR (vert) 6m 4M (occas) on the pier and a SPM buoy Fl Y 5s.

COMMUNICATIONS (Code 01478) ⊜ (0141) 887 9369; Dr 612013; Ⓗ 612704. HM 612926; Moorings 612341.

VHF Ch 16 12 (occas).

FACILITIES **Pier** £14 (Mon-Fri).

Town bus to Kyle of Lochalsh, ⇌.

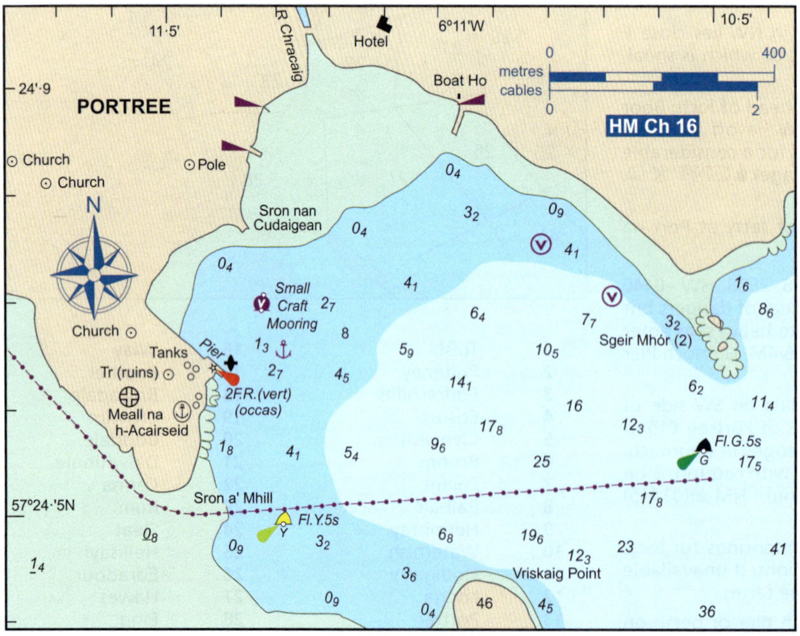

ANCHORAGES AROUND OR NEAR SKYE

LOCH TORRIDON Highland, **57°36′N 05°49′W**. AC 2210. Tides, see 1.8. Three large lochs: ent to outer loch (Torridon) is 3M wide, with isolated Sgeir na Trian (2m) almost in mid-chan; ⚓s on SW side behind Eilean Mór and in L Beag. L Sheildaig is middle loch with good ⚓. 2🅐s SE of Portree £20/nt. 1M to the N, a 2ca wide chan leads into Upper L Torridon; many fish cages and prone to squalls. Few facilities, except Shieldaig: Garage; Diabeg: ✕.

LOCH A'BHRAIGE Rona (Highland), **57°34′·6N 05°57′·9W**. AC 2479, 2534. HW –0438 on Dover; ML 2·8m; Duration 0605. See 1.8. A good ⚓ in NW of the island, safe except in NNW winds. Beware rks on NE side up to 1ca offshore. Hbr in NE corner of loch head. Ldg lts 137°, see 1.3. Facilities: jetty, and a helipad, all owned by MOD (DRA). Before ent, call *Rona* Range Control VHF Ch 13.

Acarseid Mhór is ⚓ on W of Rona. 6🅐, ☎07831 293963. App S of Eilean Garbh marked by W arrow. SD sketch of rks at ent is necessary. **Churchton Bay**, SW tip of Raasay ✕.

LOCH DUNVEGAN 4 🅐s off Stein, **57°30′·9N 06°34′·5W**. Pontoon in 1m and 6🅐 off Dunvegan, 57°26′·3N 06°35′·2W. (garage), ✕. ☎(01478) 612341.

LOCH HARPORT Skye (Highland), **57°20′·6N 06°25′·8W**. AC 1795. HW –0447 (sp), –0527 (np) on Dover. See 1.8. On E side of Loch Bracadale, entered between Oronsay Is and Ardtreck Pt (W lt ho, Fl 6s 18m 9M). SW end of Oronsay has conspic rk pillar, called The Castle; keep ¼M offshore here and off E coast of Oronsay which is joined to Ullinish Pt by drying reef. ⚓ Oronsay Is, N side of drying reef (4m), or on E side, but beware rk (dries) 0·5ca off N shore of Oronsay. Fiskavaig Bay 1M S of Ardtreck (7m); Loch Beag on N side of loch, exposed to W winds; Port na Long E of Ardtreck, sheltered except from E winds (beware fish farm); pontoon off the distillery and 5🅐 off *The Old Inn* at Carbost on SW shore. Facilities: Carbost ✕. Port na Long.

LOCH SLIGACHAN Skye (Highland), **57°19′·0N 06°06′·0W**. AC 2534. Tides see 1.8. Differences as for Portree. Steep sided sheltered Loch S of Narrows of Raasay. In sheltered weather ⚓ outside in Balmeanach Bay. Entr marked by ECM and SHM. Sconser harbour with pier and pontoon (lit Fl R 3s 2m 3M) inside narrows used to service fish farms and shellfish beds, which should be avoided.

SOAY HARBOUR Skye (Highland), **57°09′·5N 06°13′·4W**. AC 2208. Tides see 1.8. Narrow inlet on NW side of Soay; enter from Soay Sound above half flood to clear bar, dries 1·0m. Appr on 135° from 5ca out to avoid reefs close each side of ent. Cross bar slightly E of mid-chan, altering 20° stbd for best water; ent is 15m wide between boulder spits marked by W poles with Or tops. ⚓ in 3m mid-pool or shoal draught boats can enter inner pool. Good shelter and holding. Camas nan Gall (poor holding); no other facilities.

ARMADALE BAY Skye (Highland), 4M NW of Mallaig. AC 2208. 🅐s £15 at **57°04′·0N 05°53′·6W**, moorarmadale@btinternet.com. Bay is sheltered from SE to N winds but subject to swell in winds from N to SE. From S, beware the Eilean Maol and Sgorach rocks. Ferry pier, Oc R 6s 6m 6M, with conspic W shed. Facilities: at pontoon (not Sun), free pontoon for tenders, ferry to Mallaig for ⇌. Ardvasar ¾ mile: HW±3, (not Sun) ✕.

CROWLIN ISLANDS Highland, **57°21′·1N 05°50′·6W**. AC 2209, 2498. HW –0435 on Dover, –0020 on Ullapool; HW +0·3m on Ullapool. See 1.7. ⚓ between Eilean Meadhonach and Eilean Mor, appr from N, keep E of Eilean Beg. Excellent shelter except in strong N winds. There is an inner ⚓ with 3½m but ent chan dries. Eilean Beg lt ho Fl 6s 32m 6M, W tr. No facilities.

1.9 PLOCKTON

Highland **57°20´·52N 05°38´·47W** ❁❁◊◊✿✿✿

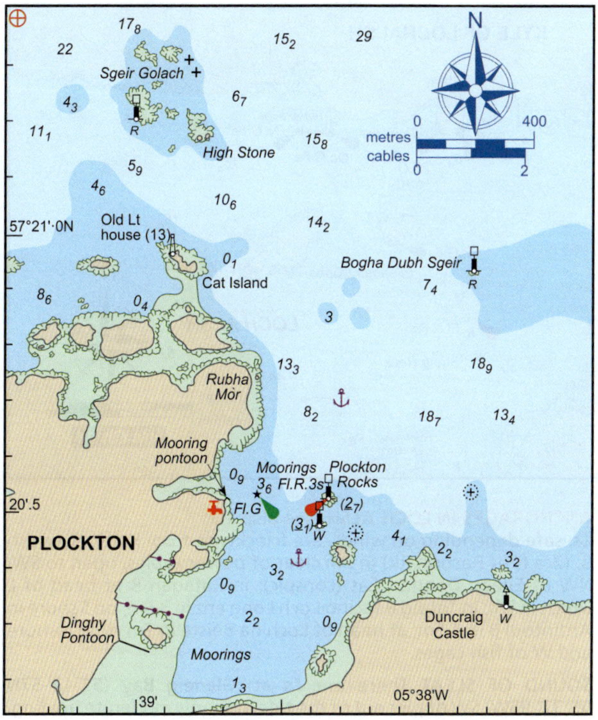

CHARTS AC 2209, 2498, 2528, 5616; Imray C66

TIDES −0445 Dover; ML no data; Duration 0610

Standard Port ULLAPOOL (⟵)

Times				Height (metres)			
High Water		Low Water		MHWS	MHWN	MLWN	MLWS
0000	0600	0300	0900	5·2	3·9	2·1	0·7
1200	1800	1500	2100				
Differences PLOCKTON							
+0005	−0025	−0005	−0010	+0·5	+0·5	+0·5	+0·2

SHELTER Good, exposed only to N/NE'lies. 15 Y Øs or ⚓ in centre of bay in approx 3·5m. Inner part of bay shoals and dries to the SW.

NAVIGATION WPT 57°21´·16N 05°39´·44W; thence towards Bogha Dubh Sgeir Bn, between Eilean a Chait disused Lt ho and Sgeir Golach Bn / High Stone (1m) to the North. Hawk Rock (0.1m) will be cleared when Duncraig Castle bears 158°. Alter S to the ⚓. Beware Plockton Rks (3·1m) on E side of bay.

LIGHTS AND MARKS See 1.3 and chartlet. Old lt ho (13m) on Eilean a Chait is conspic, as is Duncraig Castle. Sgeir Golach Bn a twr with W panels Fl W 10s, Dubh Sgeir Bn a tower with R panels Fl(2) R 6s and Plockton Rks a PHM Bn Fl R 3s.

COMMUNICATIONS HM (01599) 534589, ✉ 534167, Mobile 07802 367253 (at Kyle of Lochalsh); ⊜ (0141) 887 9369; Dr via HM.

FACILITIES **Village** 20Øs £15, tap, slip at 50m dinghy pontoon (H24 except MLWS), Ⓔ, ✉, 🛒, ✕, 🍴, ⇉ airstrip (bus to Kyle of Lochalsh).

ADJACENT MOORINGS

LOCH CARRON Strome Narrows are not buoyed or lit. Appr on 328° between Sgeir Chreagach and Sgeir Fhada. Fish farms on W shore of Loch Kishorn.

WESTERN ISLE FERRY SERVICES

Many ferries ply between mainland and island harbours. This summary may prove useful when plans or crews change in remote places. It covers Areas 1 and 2. The major operator is Caledonian MacBrayne: Head Office, The Ferry Terminal, Gourock PA19 1QP. For reservations: ☎08000 665000; www.calmac.co.uk. Many routes are very short and may not be pre-bookable; seasonal routes are marked *.

CalMac From	To	Time	Remarks
Area 1			
Berneray	Leverburgh	1¼ hrs	
Ullapool	Stornoway	2¾ hrs	
Uig (Skye)	Tarbert (Harris)	1¾ hrs	Not Sun
Uig	Lochmaddy (N Uist)	1¾ hrs	
Oban	Castlebay/Lochboisdale	5-7 hrs	
Sconser (Skye)	Raasay	15 mins	Not Sun
Mallaig*	Armadale (Skye)	20 mins	
Mallaig	Eigg–Muck–Rum–Canna	Varies	Not Sun
Oban	Coll-Tiree	Varies	Not Thurs
Tobermory	Kilchoan	35 mins	
Fionnphort	Iona	5 mins	
Lochaline	Fishnish (Mull)	15 mins	
Oban	Craignure (Mull)	45 mins	
Oban	Lismore	50 mins	Not Sun
Areas 1/2			
Oban	Colonsay	2¼ hrs	Sun/W/Fri
Area 2			
Kennacraig	Port Askaig/Colonsay	Varies	Wed
Kennacraig	Port Ellen	2 hrs 10m	
Kennacraig	Port Askaig	2 hrs	
Tayinloan	Gigha	20 mins	
Ardrossan	Brodick	55 mins	
Claonaig	Lochranza (Arran)	30 mins	
Largs	Cumbrae Slip	10 mins	
Tarbert (L Fyne)	Portavadie*	25 mins	
Colintraive	Rhubodach (Bute)	5 mins	
Wemyss Bay	Rothesay (Bute)	35 mins	
Gourock	Dunoon	20 mins	

Other Island Ferry Operators From	To	Operator	Telephone
Area 1			
Corran – V	Ardgour	Highland Council	01855 841243
Easdale – P	Seil	Area Manager	01631 562125
Firth of Lorn – P	Colonsay Uisken (Ross of Mull) Scalasaig (Colonsay) Tarbert (Jura) Port Askaig (Islay)	K & C Byrne	01951 200320
Jura – V	Port Askaig (Islay)	Serco Denholm	01496 840681
Kerrara – P	Oban	Oban Yachts	01631 565333
Kilgregan – P	Gourock	Clyde Marine Motoring	01475 721281
Lismore – P	Port Appin	Area Manager	01631 562125
Loch Nevis – P	Mallaig	Bruce Watt	01687 462233
Luing – P/V	Seil	Area Manager	01631 562125
Morvern	Sunart	Pre-book via	01688 302851
Mull	Drimnin	Sound of Mull	or mobile
Ardnamurchan	Tobermory Kilchoan	Transport	07799 608199
Skye – V	Glenelg	IOSFCIC	01599 522236
Staffa – P	Iona	D Kirkpatrick	01681 700373
Staffa – P	Mull	Gordon Grant	01681 700338
Staffa – P	Mull	Turus Mara	01688 400242

P = Passenger only V = Cars and Passengers

1.10 LOCH ALSH

Highland **57°16′·68N 05°42′·87W**

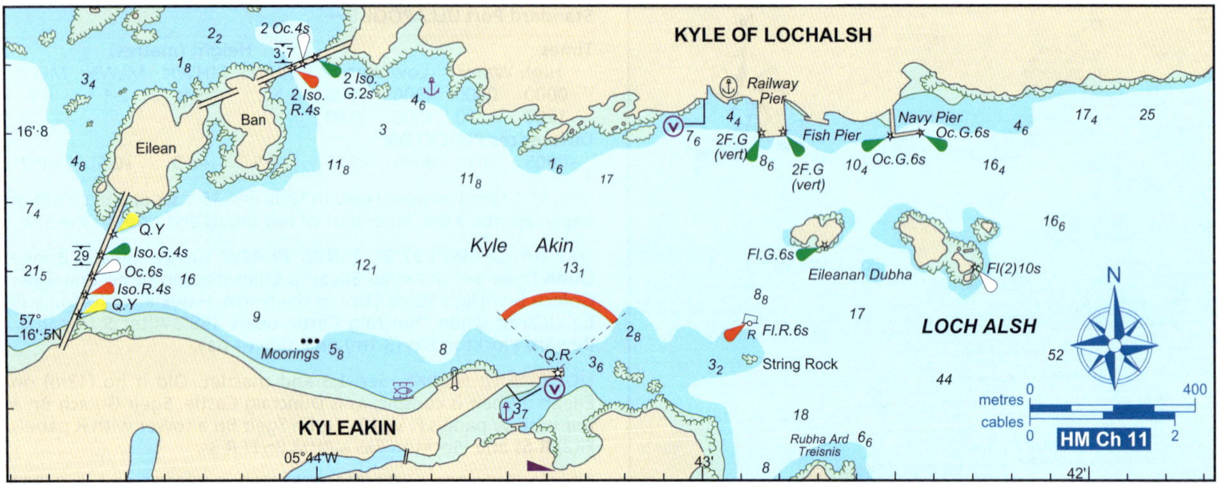

CHARTS AC 2540, 5616; Imray C66

TIDES –0450 Dover; ML 3·0m; Duration 0555; See 1.8

Standard Port ULLAPOOL (⟵)

Times				Height (metres)			
High Water		Low Water		MHWS	MHWN	MLWN	MLWS
0000	0600	0300	0900	5·2	3·9	2·1	0·7
1200	1800	1500	2100				
Differences KYLE OF LOCHALSH							
–0040	–0020	–0005	–0025	+0·1	0·0	0·0	–0·1
DORNIE BRIDGE (Loch Alsh)							
–0040	–0010	–0005	–0020	+0·1	–0·1	0·0	0·0
GLENELG BAY (Kyle Rhea)							
–0105	–0035	–0035	–0055	–0·4	–0·4	–0·9	–0·1
LOCH HOURN							
–0125	–0050	–0040	–0110	–0·2	–0·1	–0·1	+0·1

SHELTER **Kyle of Lochalsh:** on Railway Pier, with FVs, or on 40m L-shaped pontoon (seasonal), close W of Railway Pier; or ⚓ off the hotel in 11m. **Kyle Akin:** 3 Ⓐs in bay E of N span of viaduct. Lit Ⓥ seasonal pontoon on NW side of hbr for yachts, shoal on N side.

NAVIGATION WPT (from Inner Sound) 57°16′·98N 05°45′·77W, 123°/0·75M to bridge. Chan to bridge is marked by 2 PHM and 2 SHM lt buoys. Bridge to Skye, 29m clearance, is lit Oc 6s in centre of main span, Iso R 4s on S pier and Iso G4s on N pier. The secondary NE span is lit, but has only 3.7m clearance. Beware traffic coming to/from new pier on Skye shore close W of bridge.

LIGHTS AND MARKS See chartlet. Direction of buoyage is N in Kyle Rhea, thence E up Loch Alsh; but W through Kyle Akin and the bridge, ie SHMs are on N side of channel. Iso G.4s shown on SW corner of seasonal Ⓥ pontoon at Kyle of Localsh Mar-Oct.

COMMUNICATIONS (Code 01599) ⊜ (0141) 887 9369; HM 534306, Mobile 07990 971161, Deputy 07771 816900. Skye br 534844. VHF Ch **11** 16.

FACILITIES **Kyle of Lochalsh**: www.kyleandlochalsh.org.uk/index.asp pontoon, £15 1st night then £10, (Fish pier via HM, Mon-Fri) Ⓔ Ⓑ £2 (honesty box). ⇌ (useful railhead), Bus to Glasgow & Inverness; buses every ½hr to/from Kyleakin.

Kyleakin: ☎534167 or VHF Ch 11, 120m (£14/craft) depth varies from 3m to drying.

ANCHORAGES IN LOCH ALSH (see also 1.8)

⚓s, safe depending on winds, are (clockwise from Kyle): Avernish B, (2ca N of Racoon Rk) in 3m clear of power cables, open to SW; NW of Eilean Donnan Cas (conspic); in Ratagan B at head of L Duich in 7m; in Totaig B facing Loch Long ent in 3·5m; on S shore in Ardintoul B in 5·5m; at head of Loch na Béiste in 7m close inshore and W of fish cages.

SOUND OF SLEAT There are ⚓s at: **Glenelg Bay (57°12′·57N 05°37′·95W)** SW of pier out of the tide, but only moderate holding. Usual facilities in village. At **Sandaig Bay** (57°10′·0N 05°41′·4W), exposed to SW. Sandaig Is are to NW of the bay; beware rks off Sgeir nan Eun. Eilean Mór lit Fl 6s. At **Isleornsay Hbr** (57°09′N 05°48′W) 5Ⓐs at Duisdale (NW corner) 2ca N of pier, 2FR (vert) and floodlit. Give drying N end of Ornsay Is a wide berth. Lts: SE tip of Ornsay, Oc 8s 18m 15M, W tr; N end, Fl R 6s 8m 4M. Facilities: Hotels.

LOCH HOURN Highland, **57°08′N 05°42′W**. AC 2208, 2541. Tides see 1.8. Ent is S of Sandaig Is and opposite Isle Ornsay, Skye. Loch extends 11M inland via 4 narrows to Loch Beag; it is scenically magnificent, but violent squalls occur in strong winds. Sgeir Ulibhe, drying 2·1m, bn, lies almost in mid-ent; best to pass S of it to clear Clansman Rk, 2·1m, to the N. ⚓s on N shore at Eilean Ràrsaidh and Camas Bàn, within first 4M. For pilotage further E, consult SDs. Facilities at Arnisdale (Camas Bàn). Doune Marine (01687 462667), 2Ⓐs.

LOCH NEVIS Highland, **57°02′·2N 05°43′·3W**. AC 2208, 2541. HW –0515 on Dover. See 1.8. Beware rocks Bogha cas Sruth (1·8m), Bogha Don and Sgeirean Glasa both marked by bns. Good ⚓ NE of Eilean na Glaschoille, except in S winds; 7 Or Ⓐs off Inverie, £15 (free if dining), 10m max LOA. Call *Old Forge* VHF Ch 16, 12. In strong winds expect violent unpredictable squalls. Enter the inner loch with caution, and ⚓ N or SE of Eilean Maol.

ARISAIG (Loch nan Ceall), Highland, **56°53′·64N 05°55′·77W** (ent). AC 2207. HW –0515 on Dover; +0030 and +0·9m on Oban. Exposed to strong winds, especially from SE to NW. SDs essential. W mark on Rubh' Arisaig on S side of ent. S Chan is winding, marked by 8 perches. Appr HW±4 to avoid strongest streams LW±1½. Caution: many unmarked rks; no lts. Sheltered ⚓ at head of loch, clear of moorings. Call **Arisaig Marine** ☎(01687) 450224, VHF Ch 16, M; few Ⓐs, pontoon (loading, & fuel) (10t). **Village** at hotel, ⇌.

1.11 MALLAIG

Highland **57°00´·47N 05°49´·47W**

CHARTS AC 2208, 2541, 5616; Imray C65, C66

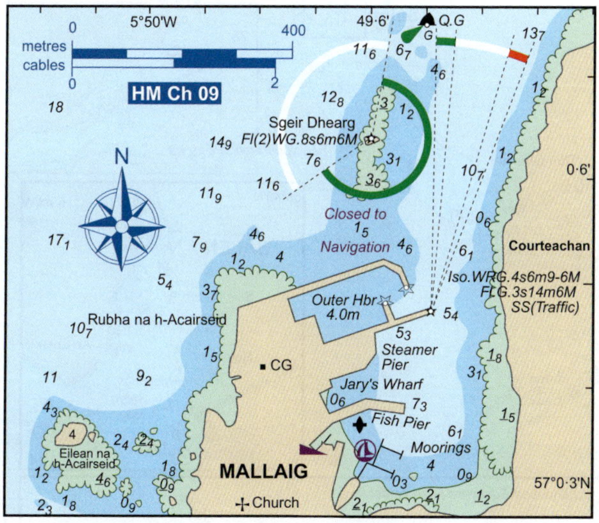

TIDES –0515 Dover; ML 2·9; Duration 0605

Standard Port OBAN (⟶)

Times				Height (metres)			
High Water		Low Water		MHWS	MHWN	MLWN	MLWS
0000	0600	0100	0700	4·0	2·9	1·8	0·7
1200	1800	1300	1900				
Differences MALLAIG							
+0017	+0017	+0030	+0024	+1·0	+0·7	+0·3	+0·1
INVERIE BAY (Loch Nevis)							
+0030	+0020	+0035	+0020	+1·0	+0·9	+0·2	0·0
BAY OF LAIG (Eigg)							
+0015	+0030	+0040	+0005	+0·7	+0·6	–0·2	–0·2
LOCH MOIDART							
+0015	+0015	+0040	+0020	+0·8	+0·6	–0·2	–0·2
LOCH EATHARNA (Coll)							
+0025	+0010	+0015	+0025	+0·4	+0·3	ND	ND
GOTT BAY (Tiree)							
0000	+0010	+0005	+0010	0·0	+0·1	0·0	0·0

SHELTER Good in SW'lies but open to N. Access H24. Small marina or 9 ⚓s in SE part of hbr. Mallaig is a reasonably busy FV harbour. It is also a hub for Skye, Small Isles and S Uist ferries.

NAVIGATION WPT 57°00´·75N 05°49´·40W, 191°/0·3m to Steamer Pier lt, passing E of Sgeir Dhearg lt bn. The former W chan is permanently closed to navigation.

LIGHTS AND MARKS As chartlet and 1.3. Town lts may obscure Sgeir Dhearg lt. Outer Hbr Pier Hds floodlit. IPTS (3 FR vert at pier hd) when ferries manoeuvring, no other traffic allowed except with HM's permission.

COMMUNICATIONS (Code 01687) ⊜ (0141) 887 9369; HM 462154, outside office hours 462411, Marina 07824 331031 (0800-2000); Dr 462202.

Mallaig Hbr Radio VHF Ch 09 16 (HO).

FACILITIES in marina, £2·70/m/night, short stay <4hrs £15. £3.90 /night. If marina full berth on Fish Pier with HM permission. ⚓ £18/night. (mob 10t) ACA, wi-fi.

Town ✕ ⊠ Ⓑ ⇌.

ANCHORAGES IN THE SMALL ISLES

CANNA The Small Isles, **57°03´·3N 06°29´·4W**. AC 1796, 2208. HW –0457 (Sp), –0550 (Np) on Dover; HW –0035 and –0·4m on Ullapool; Duration 0605. Good shelter, except in strong E'lies, in hbr between Canna and Sanday Is. 10⚓s (£10) around edge of the bay and middle is clear to ⚓ but holding is poor due to kelp. Appr along Sanday shore, keeping N of Sgeir a' Phuirt, dries 4·6m. Ldg marks as in SDs. ⚓ in 3–4m W of Canna pier, off which beware drying rky patch. ⚓ Lt advised due to FVs. Conspic bn, Fl W10s 32m 9M, vis 152°-061°, at E end of Sanday Is. Magnetic anomaly off NE Canna. Facilities: shower at farm (01687 462963), limited ⊠ (H24-honesty) free wi-fi, ✕. NTS manage island HM ☎ 01687 310733 (HO) or 01687 462818 (OOH).

RUM The Small Isles, **57°00´·1N 06°15´·7W**. AC 2207, 2208. HW –0500 on Dover; –0035 and –0·3m on Ullapool; ML 2·4m; Duration 0600. SNH owns Is. The mountains (809m) are unmistakable. Landing is only allowed at Loch Scresort on E side; no dogs beyond village limit. Beware drying rocks 1ca off Northern point of entrance and almost 3ca off South point. The head of the loch dries 2ca out; ⚓ off slip on S side or further in, to NE of jetty. Hbr is open to E winds/swell. Facilities: 10⚓s (£15) WC (eco) at hostel ☎07824 036305, ⊠ (limited) ✕ ferry to Mallaig.

EIGG HARBOUR The Small Isles, **56°52´·6N 06°07´·6W**. AC 2207. HW –0523 on Dover. See 1.11. Entering from N or E use Sgeir nam Bagh (Ferry Terminal) Dir lt 245° Fl WRG 3s, leads between Garbh Sgeir Bn Fl (2) G 10s & Flod Sgeir Bn Fl R 5s. An Sgùrr is a conspic 391m high peak/ridge brg 281°/1·3M from Sgeir nam Bagh. Most of hbr dries, but good ⚓ 1ca NE of Galmisdale Pt pier, except in NE winds when yachts should go through the narrows and ⚓ in South Bay in 6–8m; tide runs hard in the narrows. Also ⚓ in 2·5m at Poll nam Partan, about 2ca N of Flod Sgeir. SE point of Eilean Chathastail Fl 6s 24m 8M, vis 181°-shore, W tr. VHF Ch 08 *Eigg Hbr*. HM ☎ via (01687) 482428. repairs. **Pierhead** ⊠ ✕ ☎01687 482487. **Cleadale village** (2M to N).

MUCK The Small Isles, **56°49'·8N 06°13'·3W**. AC 2207. Tides approx as Eigg, 1.11. Port Mór at SE end is the main hbr, with a deep pool inside offlying rks, but open to S'lies. Approach: Dir lt Fl WRG 3s 7m 11M (vis 1M by day) leads between Dubh Sgeir (Fl(2) R 10s) and Bogha Ruadh (Fl(2) G 10s) rks; see 1.3. ⚓ towards the NW side of inlet; NE side has drying rks. To N of Is, Bagh a' Ghallanaich is ⚓ protected from S. Few facilities.

NW Scotland

1.12 LOCH SUNART

Highland **56°39'·49N 06°00'·07W**

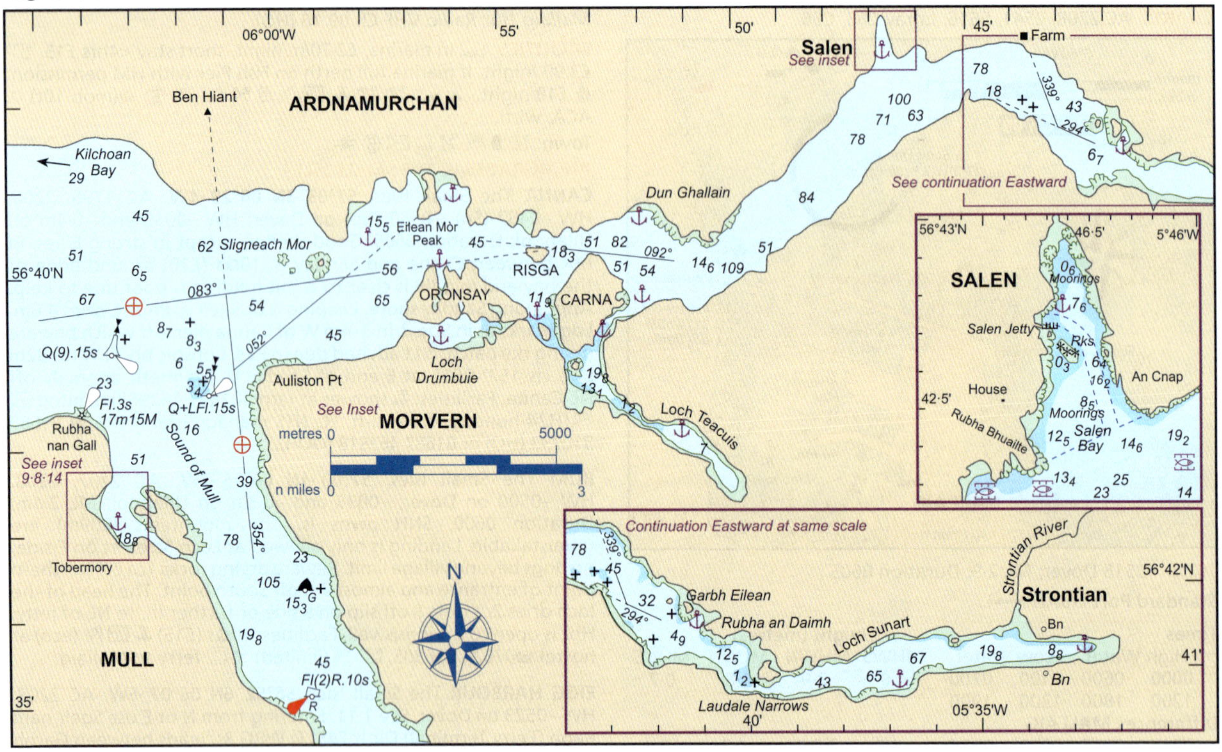

CHARTS AC 2171, 2392, 2394, 5611; Imray C65, 2800

TIDES Salen –0500 Dover; ML 2·0

Standard Port OBAN (⟶)

Times				Height (metres)			
High Water		Low Water		MHWS	MHWN	MLWN	MLWS
0100	0700	0100	0800	4·0	2·9	1·8	0·7
1300	1900	1300	2000				
Differences SALEN (Loch Sunart)							
–0015	+0015	+0010	+0005	+0·6	+0·5	–0·1	–0·1

SHELTER Ⓐs at Kilchoan Bay (2M N of Ardmore Pt). ⚓s in Loch Drumbuie (S of Oronsay) sheltered in all winds; in Sailean Mór (N of Oronsay) convenient and easy ent; between Oronsay and Carna; in Loch Teacuis (very tricky ent); E of Carna; Salen Bay, with Ⓐs and pontoon, open only to SSE (see facilities); Garbh Eilean (NW of Rubha an Daimh), and E of sand spit by Strontian R.

NAVIGATION **West WPT**, 56°39'·69N 06°03'·07W, 083°/3·7M to Creag nan Sgarbh (NW tip of Orinsay). **South WPT**, 56°38'·00N 06°00'·65W, 1M S of Auliston Pt; there are extensive rky reefs, The Stirks W of this pt. AC 2394 and detailed directions are needed to navigate the 17M loch, particularly its upper reaches. Beware Ross Rk, S of Risga; Broad Rk, E of Risga; Dun Ghallain Rk; shoals extending 3ca NNW from Eilean mo Shlinneag off S shore; drying rock 1ca W of Garbh Eilean and strong streams at Sp in Laudale Narrows. Fish farms on both sides of the loch.

LIGHTS AND MARKS Unlit. Transits as on the chart: from W WPT, Risga on with N tip of Oronsay at 083°; N pt of Carna on with top of Risga 092°. From S WPT, Ben Hiant bearing 354°, thence Eilean Mor Peak at 052°. Further up the loch, 339° and 294°, as on chartlet, are useful. Other transits are shown on AC 2394.

COMMUNICATIONS (Code 01967) ⊖ (0141) 887 9369; Dr 431231.

FACILITIES

Kilchoan Bay (56°41'·5N 06°07'·3W); ☎(01972) 510305, 4 Ⓐs £13/night, hotel (1M).

Salen Bay (56°42'·39N 05°46'·17W); www.salenjetty.co.uk ☎(01967) 431510, mob 07909944494. VHF Ch 80 (occas). Keep on E side of entrance to avoid a drying reef on W side. Pontoon 8 Ⓥ, O/night £10< 6m <£2·40 /m, £5 <4hrs; 4 R Ⓐs(15t) (other moorings private); buoy advised, as bottom is generally foul.

Acharacle (2½M), (bus to L. Ailort/Ft William), ✈ Oban.

Strontian hotel, bus to Ft William.

ANCHORAGES IN COLL AND TIREE (Argyll and Bute)

COLL, Loch Eatharna, **ARINAGOUR, 56°37'·0N 06°31'·2W**. AC 2171, 2474, 5611. HW –0530 on Dover; ML 1·4m; Duration 0600; see 1.11. Good shelter except with SE swell or strong winds from ENE to SSW in which case consider ⚓ in Loch Breachacha to SW. Enter at SHM buoy, Fl G 6s, marking Bogha Mòr; thence NW to Arinagour ferry pier, 2 FR(vert) 10m 3M and Dir Oc WRG 7s 6m 2M. Beware McQuarrie's Rk (dries 2·9m) 1ca E of pier hd and unmarked drying rks further N on E side of fairway. ✠ and hotel are conspic. Continue N towards old stone pier; ⚓ S of it or use 12Ⓐs S of Dgeir Dubh for boats <10t at £10/night (pay at ferry terminal). If set fair ⚓ ESE of Eilean Eatharna. Piermaster ☎(01879) 230347; VHF Ch 31.

Facilities: **HIE** Trading Post ☎230349.

Village Ferry to Oban (⇌).

TIREE, GOTT BAY, 56°30'·74N 06°48'·07W. AC 2474, 5611. Tides as 1.11; HW –0540 on Dover. HM ☎(01879) 230337, VHF Ch 31. Adequate shelter in calm weather at NE end of island, but in winds ENE to S use Wilson Hbr in Balephetrish B 2½M W, Ldg lts F/ Occ G. Gott Bay can be identified by conspic lattice twr at Scarinish about 8ca SW of entr, with lt Fl 3s 11m 16M close by (obscd over hbr). Appr on NW track, keeping to its SW side. To NE side lies Soa Is and drying rks. Ferry pier to S side of entrance FR ldg lts 286½°. 10Ⓐs 15t £12/night (www.isleoftiree.com) North of terminal (MacLennan Motors on pier) or ⚓ 1ca further NW of pier head in 3m on sand; at pier. Road over headland to **SCARINISH** where a newly restored stone pier gives 3 drying for small craft/RIBs £10/craft for 24hrs (honesty box). Access via narrow chan to S of drying rks Bogha Chorr-eilean.

Facilities: (Scarinish ½M), Ferry to Oban (⇌).

1.13 TOBERMORY

Mull (Argyll and Bute) **56°37′·19N 06°03′·87W** ❀❀❀◊◊✿✿✿

CHARTS AC 2171, 2390, 2474, 5611; Imray C65, 2800

TIDES –0519 Dover; ML 2·4; Duration 0610

Standard Port OBAN (⟶)

Times				Height (metres)			
High Water		Low Water		MHWS	MHWN	MLWN	MLWS
0100	0700	0100	0800	4·0	2·9	1·8	0·7
1300	1900	1300	2000				
Differences TOBERMORY (Mull)							
+0025	+0010	+0015	+0025	+0·5	+0·6	+0·1	+0·2
CARSAIG BAY (S Mull)							
–0015	–0005	–0030	+0020	+0·1	+0·2	0·0	–0·1
IONA (SW Mull)							
–0010	–0005	–0020	+0015	0·0	+0·1	–0·3	–0·2
BUNESSAN (Loch Lathaich, SW Mull)							
–0015	–0015	–0010	–0015	+0·3	+0·1	0·0	–0·1
ULVA SOUND (W Mull)							
–0010	–0015	0000	–0005	+0·4	+0·3	0·0	–0·1

SHELTER Good, but some swell in strong N/NE winds. 26 ⚲s are marked by a blue ⌂ with a Y pick-up. ⚓ clear of fairway, where marked; at SE end of The Doirlinn. Tobermory Harbour Association (THA) manages local and visitor's moorings and ⊆ on pontoon.

NAVIGATION WPT 56°37′·59N 06°03′·17W, 224°/0·5M to moorings. N ent is wide and clear of dangers. S ent via The Doirlinn is only 80m wide at HW, and dries at LW; at HW±2 least depth is 2m. The clear channel is N of the central rock and is marked with 2 metal perches. Take care to avoid fishing pier chan. No ⚓ in harbour fairway (buoyed). Keep wash to a minimum.

LIGHTS AND MARKS Rhubha nan Gall, Fl 3s 17m 15M, W tr is 1M N of ent. Ch spire and hotel turret are both conspic.

COMMUNICATIONS (Code 01688) Local CG 302200; Dr 302013. Cal-Mac Piermaster 302017;
THA Moorings Officer ☎302876, mob 07917 832497.
VHF Ch 16 12 (HO), M.

FACILITIES www.tobermoryharbour.co.uk 25⚲s from £14, ⊿ <25′; pontoon 50⊆ £3.00 inc ⊅ ⚲ ♟; **Taigh Solais** (THA Harbour Building) WC ⚑ ⊡ wi-fi, ⊡ in car park.

Western Isles YC ☎302371. **Town** ♟ ✎ ⊡ ⊡ ACA ✉ Ⓑ Ⓒ ⊡ ✕ ⊡ ⇄ (ferry to Oban), ✈ (helipad on golf course).

SOUND OF MULL Dearg Sgeir Fl 6s 7m 8M marks Eileann Glasa, 2·3M to SE Rubha na Leitrach, 2 F R (vert), marks N ent to Fishnish Bay.

SALEN BAY (Mull, **56°31′·44N 05°56′·82W**). Beware Bogha, drying rks 6ca E of the bay; ⚲s £10; ⊿ at Salen Jetty, fee £1/person. **Facilities** ⚲ ♟. **Village** Dr, ✎ Ⓔ ⊡ ✉ ⊡ ✕.

CRAIGNURE (Mull, **56°28′·37N 05°42′·25W**) ldg lts 241°, both FR 10/12m. Facilities: ♟ ✉ ⊡ ⊡ Ferry to Oban. Tides, see 1.14.

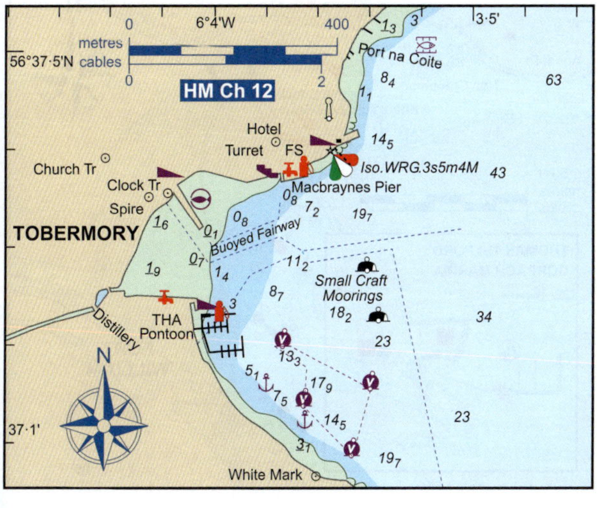

ANCHORAGES on WEST and SOUTH COASTS OF MULL
(Anti-clockwise from the north) SDs essential Tides as 1.13.

TRESHNISH ISLES 56°29′N 06°31′W. AC 2652. Main Is (N to S) are: Cairn na Burgh, Fladda, Lunga, Bac Mòr and Bac Beag. Tides run hard and isles are exposed to swell, but merit visit in calm weather. Appr cautiously on ldg lines (CCC SDs) temp ⚓ off Lunga N tip in 4m.

STAFFA 56°25′·96N 06°20′·34W. AC 2652. Spectacular isle with Fingal's Cave, but same caveats as above. Very temp ⚓ off SE tip where there is landing; beware unmarked rks.

GOMETRA 56°28′·85N 06°23′W. AC 2652. Except in S'lies, narrow inlet between Gometra and Ulva offers sheltered ⚓. Appr 020° between Staffa and Little Colonsay, or N of the former. Beware rks drying 3·2m, to stbd and 5ca S of ent. E side is cleaner.

LOCH NA KEAL 56°26′N 06°18′W (ent). AC 2652. Appr S of Geasgill Is and N of drying rks off **Inch Kenneth**, MacQuarrie's Rk, dries 0·8m. ⚓s E of this Is, in Cragaig B and **Sound of Ulva** are exposed to S'lies. **Ulva Ferry** www.ulvaferrypontoon.co.uk ☎ 07557378953; 8⊆ in 4m on walk-ashore pontoon, £2·50; ⊅ ⚲ ♟ wi-fi, ✕ ⚑ at Ballgown. Hire bikes, bus to Loch na Keal and Salen for ⊡. Ferry to Ulva (seasonal ✕). Appr via Sound of Ulva shelves to 2m at LW.

LOCH LATHAICH Mull, **56°19′·29N 06°15′·47W**. AC 2617. HW –0545 on Dover; ML 2·4. Excellent shelter with easy access; good base for cruising W Mull. Eilean na Liathanaich (a group of islets) lie off the ent, marked by a W bn at the E end, Fl WR 6s 12m 8/6M, R088°-108°, W108°-088°. Keep to W side of loch and ⚓ off Bendoran BY in SW, or SE of Eilean Ban off the pier in approx 5m keeping clear of creeler moorings to the E side. Facilities: (Bunessan) ⚲ ✉ ⊡ ✕ ⊡.

SOUND OF IONA 56°19′·45N 06°23′·12W. AC 2617. From N, enter in mid-chan; from S keep clear of Torran Rks. Cathedral brg 012° closes the Iona shore past 2 SHM buoys and SCM buoy. Beware a bank 0·1m in mid-sound, between cathedral and Fionnphort; also tel cables and ferries. ⚓ S of ferry close in to Iona, or in Bull Hole. Consult SDs. Crowded in season; limited facilities.

TINKER'S HOLE Ross of Mull, **56°17′·49N 06°23′·07W**. AC 2617. Beware Torran Rks, reefs extending 5M S and SW of Erraid. Usual app from S, avoiding Rankin's Rks, drying 0·8m, and rk, dries 2·3m, between Eilean nam Muc and Erraid. Popular ⚓ in mid-pool between Eilean Dubh and Erraid.

CARSAIG BAY Ross of Mull, **56°19′·19N 05°59′·07W**. AC 2386. Temp, fair weather ⚓s to N of Gamhnach Mhòr, reef 2m high, or close into NW corner of bay. ⊿ at stone quay on NE side.

LOCH SPELVE Mull, **56°23′N 05°41′W**. AC 2387. Tides as Oban. Landlocked water, prone to squalls off surrounding hills. Ent narrows to ½ca due to shoal S side and drying rk N side marked by G pole, Fl G 5s 3m 2M, 56°23′·24N 05°42′·04W. CCC SDs give local ldg lines. ⚓s in SW and NW arms, clear of fish farms. Pier at Croggan; no facilities.

ANCHORAGES ALONG LOCH LINNHE (AC 2378, 2379, 2380, 5611)
LYNN OF LORN 56°33′N 05°25′·2W. At NE end are ⚓s off **Port Appin**, clear of ferry and cables (beware Appin Rks); and in Airds Bay, open to SW. At NW tip of Lismore, Port Ramsey offers good ⚓s between the 3 main islets.
Linnhe Marina ☎(01631) 730401 offers pontoon and moorings.

LOCH CRERAN 56°32′·14N 05°25′·22W. Tides 1.15. Enter at Airds Pt, Dir lt 050°, Fl WRG 2s, W vis 041-058°. Chan turns 90° stbd with streams of 4kn. Sgeir Callich, rky ridge extends NE to SHM By, Fl G 3s; ⚓ W of it. ⚲s (max LOA 7m) off Barcaldine; also 3⚲s (max LOA 9m) off Creagan Inn, ☎(01631) 573250. Bridge has 12m clearance. Beware of extensive marine farms in loch.

LOCH A'CHOIRE 56°22′.2N 05°18′.6W on west side of Loch Linnhe. Entrance offers no difficulties, fish farm on north side and restaurant moorings (condition unknown) , ⚲ in SW corner or anchor as depths permit. Sheltered from west but beware downdrafts in strong winds.

LOCH LEVEN 56°42′N 05°12′W. Tides 1.15. Ballachulish Bay ⚓s: N shore Onich and off St Brides, S shore Kentallen Bay (deep). Approach Ballachullish Bridge (16m clnce) on 114°. Moorings are 4ca to ENE with sheltered ⚓ at Poll an Dùnan, ent W of perch. Loch navigable 7M to Kinlochleven. **Ballachulish**: Hotels, ✉ Ⓑ ⊡ ✕.

CORRAN NARROWS 56°43′·27N 05°14′·34W. AC 2372. Sp rate 6kn. Well buoyed; Corran Pt lt ho, Iso WRG 4s, and lt bn 5ca NE. ⚓ 5ca NW of Pt, off Camas Aiseig pier/slip.

1.14 LOCH ALINE

Highland **56°32′·09N 05°46′·47W**

CHARTS AC 2390, 5611; Imray C65, 2800

TIDES –0523 Dover; Duration 0610

Standard Port OBAN (⟶)

Times				Height (metres)			
High Water		Low Water		MHWS	MHWN	MLWN	MLWS
0100	0700	0100	0800	4·0	2·9	1·8	0·7
1300	1900	1300	2000				
Differences LOCH ALINE							
+0012	+0012	ND	ND	+0·5	+0·3	ND	ND
SALEN (Sound of Mull)							
+0045	+0015	+0020	+0030	+0·2	+0·2	–0·1	0·0
CRAIGNURE (Sound of Mull)							
+0030	+0005	+0010	+0015	0·0	+0·1	–0·1	–0·1

SHELTER Very good. ⚓s in SE end of loch and in N and E part of loch. Temp berth on old stone slip on W side of ent, depth and ferries permitting. Walk ashore pontoons N of sand mine pier with 10 Y 🔘 for boats <12m and 4 Crown Estate 🔘 on E side of loch.

NAVIGATION WPT 56°31′·49N 05°46′·37W, 176°/0·9M toldg bn. Bn (bright orange) leads 357°, 100m W of Bogha Lurcain, drying rk off Bolorkle Pt on E side of ent. Buoyed ent is easy, but narrow with a bar (min depth 2·1m); stream runs 2½kn at springs. Beware coasters (which completely fill the ent) going to/from the active sand mine jetty and ferries to/from Mull. Last 5ca of loch dries.

LIGHTS AND MARKS Ardtornish Pt lt ho, 1M SSE of ent, Fl (2) WRG 10s 8m 8/6M. Lts and buoys as chartlet. War memorial, 9m high (inconspic), stands on W side of ent. Dir Ldg lt, Oc WRG 6s 4M, 357°, co-located with front ldg bn (Or). 1M up the loch on E side a bn with rusty ● topmark marks a reef; ½M further up a similar bn marks a larger reef on W side. Clock tr is very conspic at head of loch.

COMMUNICATIONS (Code 01967) Ⓗ (01631) 563727; Dr 421252. No VHF.

FACILITIES Pontoons, www.lochalineharbour.co.uk ☎07583 800500, 26 inc Ⓥ £3·00, 🔘 £15/night, WC. **Village** at pier, ✉ ✕ (Ⓑ ⇌ ✈ at Oban), Ferry to Fishnish Bay (Mull).

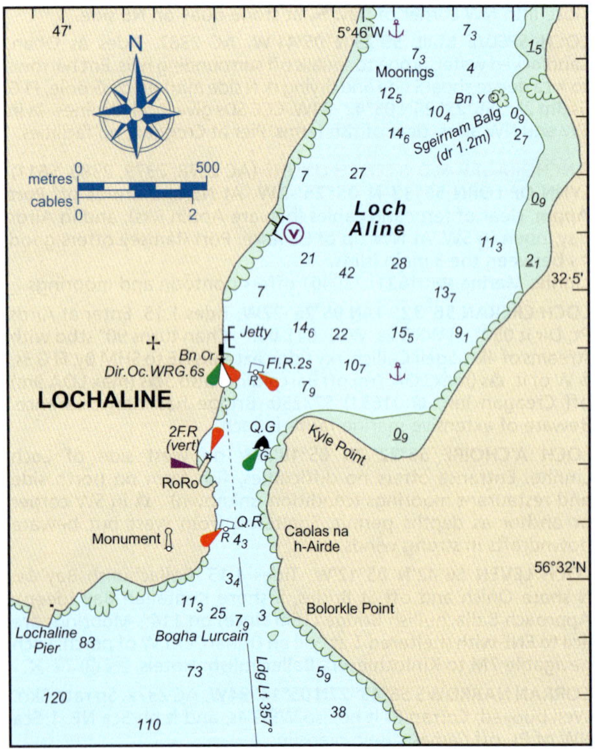

1.15 FORT WILLIAM/CORPACH

Highland 56°48′·99N 05°07′·07W (off Fort William)

CHARTS AC 5611, 2372, 2380, 5617; Imray C65, C63, 2800

TIDES –0535 Dover; ML 2·3; Duration 0610

Standard Port OBAN (⟶)

Times				Height (metres)			
High Water		Low Water		MHWS	MHWN	MLWN	MLWS
0100	0700	0100	0800	4·0	2·9	1·8	0·7
1300	1900	1300	2000				
Differences CORPACH							
0000	+0020	+0040	0000	0·0	0·0	–0·2	–0·2
LOCH EIL (Head)							
+0025	+0045	+0105	+0025	ND	ND	ND	ND
CORRAN NARROWS							
+0007	+0007	+0004	+0004	+0·4	+0·4	–0·1	0·0
LOCH LEVEN (Head)							
+0045	+0045	+0045	+0045	ND	ND	ND	ND
LOCH LINNHE (Port Appin)							
–0005	–0005	–0030	0000	+0·2	+0·2	+0·1	+0·1
LOCH CRERAN (Barcaldine Pier)							
+0010	+0020	+0040	+0015	+0·1	+0·1	0·0	+0·1
LOCH CRERAN (Head)							
+0015	+0025	+0120	+0020	–0·3	–0·3	–0·4	–0·3

SHELTER ⚓ off Fort William pier exposed to winds SW thro' N to NE. Other ⚓ in Camus na Gall and SSW of Eilean A Bhealaidh. At Corpach Basin there is a marina W of sea lock; the transit jetty is usually available LW±2 during canal hrs (see 1.16).

NAVIGATION Corpach WPT 56°50′·29N 05°07′·07W, 315°/0·32M to lock ent.

Beware McLean Rk, dries 0·3m, buoyed, 8ca N of Fort William. Lochy Flats dry 3ca off the E bank. In Annat Narrows at ent to Loch Eil streams reach 5kn.

LIGHTS AND MARKS Corpach Iso WRG 4s lt at N jetty of sea lock, W310°-335°. Marina bwtr Fl(2) G 8s. Jetty NE of Eileann nan Craobh lit Fl(2) R 6s 4m 2M. At Ft William long pier/viaduct is unlit.

COMMUNICATIONS (Code 01397) Dr 703136. **HM** 772249, mob 07917348025. **Marina** corpachmarina.co.uk

Corpach Lock VHF Ch **74** 16 (during canal hours).

FACILITIES **Fort William Pier** ☎703881. **Town** ACA ✉ Ⓑ ✕ YC Ⓗ ⇌.

Thomas Telford Marina mob 07760166970 45 inc Ⓥ £3/nt s/stay (<4hrs) £12, £18/wk; WC ✕.

Corpach Basin ☎772249 mob 07917348025.

Lochaber YC ☎703576. **Services** Divers.

Village ✉ Ⓑ ✕ ⇌.

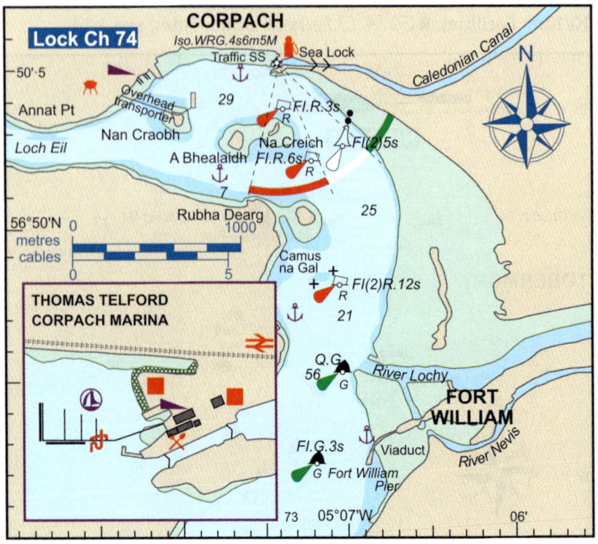

1.16 CALEDONIAN CANAL

Highland

CHARTS AC 1791, 5617; Imray C63; *Scottish Canals Skippers Guide*

TIDES Tidal differences: Corpach –0455 on Dover; See 1.15. Clachnaharry: +0116 on Dover.

SHELTER Corpach is at the SW ent of the Caledonian Canal, see 1.15; the sea locks at both ends do not open LW±2 at springs. For best shelter transit the sea lock and lie above the double lock. Numerous pontoons along the canal; cost is included in the canal dues.

NAVIGATION The 60M canal consists of 38M through Lochs Lochy, Oich and Ness, connected by 22M of canal.

Loch Oich is part of a hydro-electric scheme which varies the water level. Minimum passage time is 3½ days but allow longer. Speed limit is 5kn in the canal sections. There are 11 swing bridges; road traffic has priority at peak hrs. Do not pass bridges without the keeper's instructions.

LOCKS There are 29 locks: 14 between Loch Linnhe (Corpach), via Lochs Lochy and Oich to the summit (106ft above sea level) and 15 from the summit down via Loch Ness to Inverness. **The Canal has endured winter closures in the recent past: check www.scottishcanals.co.uk for works in progress**

Operating hours are often subject to change see www.scottishcanals.co.uk for latest information.

Dues Payable at Corpach and Clachnaharry sea locks: see www.scottishcanals.co.uk for latest prices, licence information & Skipper's Guide.

LIGHTS AND MARKS See 1.15 for ent lts. Channel is marked by posts, cairns and unlit buoys, PHM on the NW side and SHM on the SE side.

CHARGES

1. Transit Licence (7 nts/192 hrs)

a) Outward journey £24·35/m

b) Return journey £43·50/m

c) Additional days £1·80/m – max of 3 days.

2. Fixed Period Licence – 2 wks

a) Licence – £36·85/m

b) Overnight haven – £4·50/m

c) Additional days – £1·65/m – max of 3 days.

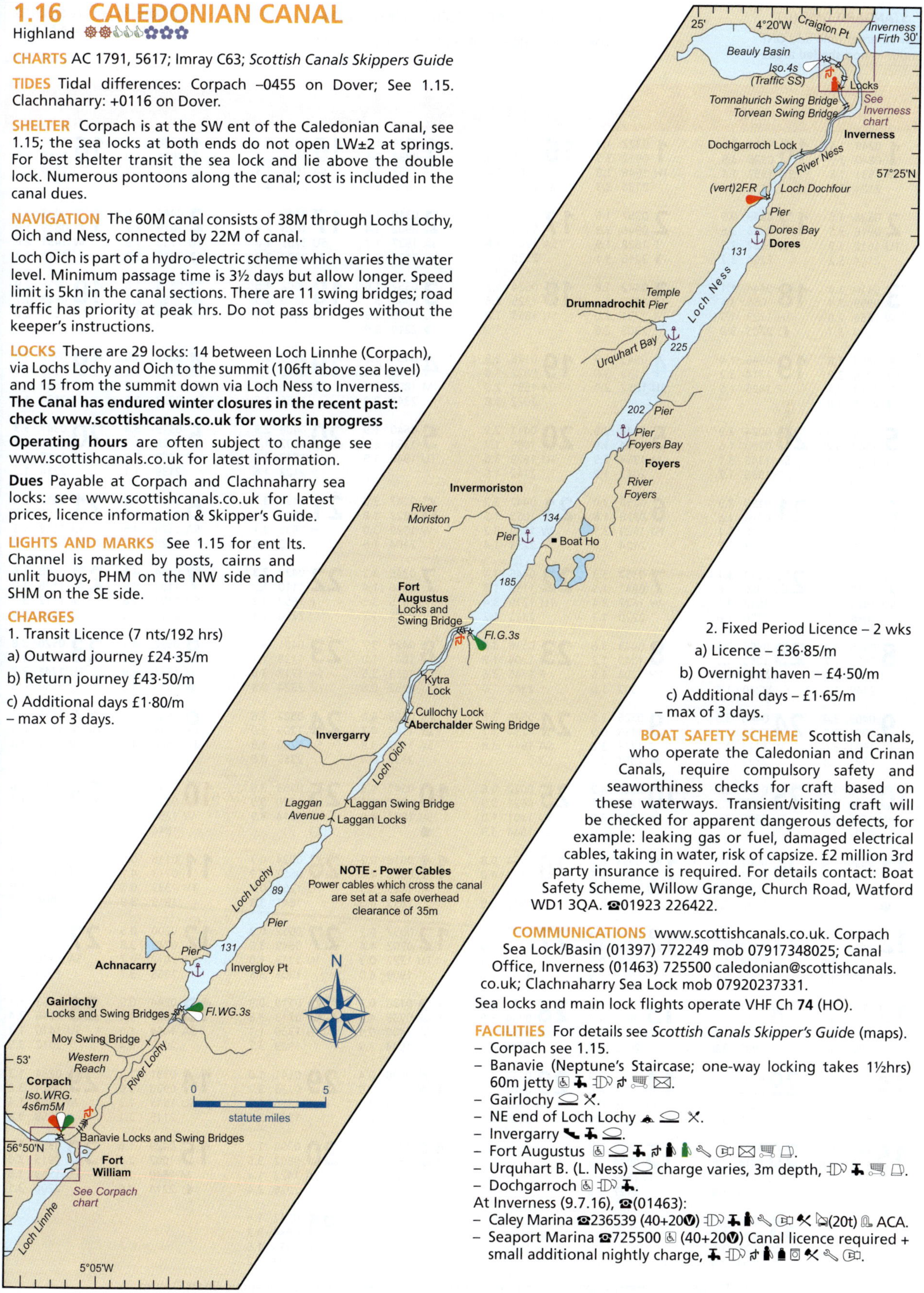

BOAT SAFETY SCHEME Scottish Canals, who operate the Caledonian and Crinan Canals, require compulsory safety and seaworthiness checks for craft based on these waterways. Transient/visiting craft will be checked for apparent dangerous defects, for example: leaking gas or fuel, damaged electrical cables, taking in water, risk of capsize. £2 million 3rd party insurance is required. For details contact: Boat Safety Scheme, Willow Grange, Church Road, Watford WD1 3QA. ☎01923 226422.

COMMUNICATIONS www.scottishcanals.co.uk. Corpach Sea Lock/Basin (01397) 772249 mob 07917348025; Canal Office, Inverness (01463) 725500 caledonian@scottishcanals.co.uk; Clachnaharry Sea Lock mob 07920237331.

Sea locks and main lock flights operate VHF Ch **74** (HO).

FACILITIES For details see *Scottish Canals Skipper's Guide* (maps).

- Corpach see 1.15.
- Banavie (Neptune's Staircase; one-way locking takes 1½hrs) 60m jetty.
- Gairlochy.
- NE end of Loch Lochy.
- Invergarry.
- Fort Augustus.
- Urquhart B. (L. Ness) charge varies, 3m depth.
- Dochgarroch.

At Inverness (9.7.16), ☎(01463):

- Caley Marina ☎236539 (40+20Ⓥ) (20t) ACA.
- Seaport Marina ☎725500 (40+20Ⓥ) Canal licence required + small additional nightly charge.

STANDARD TIME (UT)
For Summer Time add ONE hour in **non-shaded areas**

OBAN LAT 56°25′N LONG 5°29′W

TIMES AND HEIGHTS OF HIGH AND LOW WATERS

Dates in red are SPRINGS
Dates in blue are NEAPS

YEAR **2024**

JANUARY

Date	Day	Time	m	Time	m	Time	m	Time	m
1	M	0249	1.4	0840	3.7	1531	1.8	2104	3.4
2	TU	0328	1.5	0918	3.5	1612	1.9	2144	3.2
3	W	0410	1.6	0959	3.4	1659	2.0	2230	3.1
4	TH	0455	1.8	1046	3.2	1754	2.1	◑ 2328	3.0
5	F	0546	1.9	1147	3.2	1856	2.1		
6	SA	0052	3.0	0645	1.9	1313	3.1	2000	2.0
7	SU	0216	3.0	0749	1.8	1434	3.2	2058	1.8
8	M	0315	3.2	0853	1.7	1532	3.4	2149	1.6
9	TU	0403	3.4	0955	1.5	1621	3.6	2234	1.4
10	W	0448	3.6	1050	1.3	1705	3.7	2317	1.1
11	TH	0530	3.8	1142	1.0	1747	3.8	●	
12	F	0000	0.9	0613	4.0	1229	0.9	1828	3.9
13	SA	0043	0.7	0655	4.1	1316	0.8	1908	3.8
14	SU	0128	0.6	0737	4.1	1402	0.8	1949	3.7
15	M	0213	0.6	0821	4.0	1449	0.9	2031	3.6
16	TU	0300	0.7	0906	3.9	1537	1.1	2116	3.4
17	W	0349	0.9	0956	3.6	1627	1.3	2204	3.2
18	TH	0444	1.1	1055	3.4	1723	1.5	◐ 2303	3.0
19	F	0546	1.4	1214	3.2	1826	1.6		
20	SA	0024	2.9	0700	1.6	1348	3.1	1936	1.7
21	SU	0158	2.9	0826	1.6	1510	3.1	2048	1.7
22	M	0313	3.1	0950	1.6	1612	3.2	2150	1.6
23	TU	0407	3.3	1050	1.5	1654	3.4	2240	1.4
24	W	0448	3.5	1136	1.4	1728	3.5	2322	1.2
25	TH	0527	3.7	1215	1.3	1800	3.6	○	
26	F	0001	1.1	0604	3.9	1250	1.3	1832	3.7
27	SA	0039	1.0	0639	3.9	1324	1.3	1904	3.8
28	SU	0115	1.0	0712	4.0	1356	1.3	1935	3.8
29	M	0149	1.0	0744	3.9	1426	1.4	2005	3.7
30	TU	0221	1.1	0814	3.8	1455	1.5	2034	3.6
31	W	0251	1.3	0843	3.7	1521	1.6	2103	3.4

FEBRUARY

Date	Day	Time	m	Time	m	Time	m	Time	m
1	TH	0322	1.4	0912	3.5	1548	1.8	2136	3.3
2	F	0357	1.6	0946	3.3	1628	1.9	◑ 2216	3.1
3	SA	0442	1.8	1030	3.2	1731	2.0	2309	2.9
4	SU	0545	1.9	1133	3.0	1852	2.1		
5	M	0048	2.9	0704	1.9	1354	2.9	2013	1.9
6	TU	0256	3.0	0828	1.8	1529	3.1	2124	1.7
7	W	0357	3.3	0947	1.5	1622	3.4	2220	1.3
8	TH	0443	3.6	1049	1.2	1704	3.6	2307	1.0
9	F	0525	3.9	1139	0.9	1743	3.8	● 2351	0.7
10	SA	0605	4.2	1224	0.6	1820	3.9		
11	SU	0033	0.4	0645	4.3	1305	0.5	1856	4.0
12	M	0115	0.3	0724	4.3	1346	0.5	1933	3.9
13	TU	0157	0.3	0803	4.2	1426	0.6	2010	3.8
14	W	0241	0.4	0842	4.0	1508	0.8	2047	3.6
15	TH	0325	0.7	0924	3.6	1552	1.1	2127	3.3
16	F	0414	1.0	1011	3.3	1641	1.4	◐ 2212	3.1
17	SA	0511	1.4	1114	2.9	1740	1.6	2320	2.8
18	SU	0624	1.7	1325	2.8	1853	1.8		
19	M	0128	2.8	0822	1.8	1531	2.8	2022	1.8
20	TU	0411	2.9	1005	1.7	1629	3.0	2142	1.6
21	W	0442	3.2	1055	1.5	1659	3.2	2233	1.4
22	TH	0446	3.4	1132	1.3	1719	3.4	2313	1.2
23	F	0516	3.6	1204	1.2	1745	3.6	2348	1.0
24	SA	0548	3.8	1234	1.1	1814	3.8	○	
25	SU	0022	0.8	0621	3.9	1301	1.0	1844	3.9
26	M	0054	0.8	0651	4.0	1329	1.1	1911	3.9
27	TU	0123	0.8	0719	3.9	1355	1.1	1937	3.8
28	W	0150	0.9	0744	3.9	1416	1.2	2001	3.7
29	TH	0214	1.1	0808	3.7	1432	1.4	2026	3.6

MARCH

Date	Day	Time	m	Time	m	Time	m	Time	m
1	F	0239	1.2	0832	3.6	1453	1.5	2055	3.4
2	SA	0310	1.4	0902	3.4	1527	1.7	2131	3.2
3	SU	0352	1.6	0941	3.1	1619	1.9	◑ 2219	3.0
4	M	0457	1.9	1039	2.9	1801	2.0	2346	2.8
5	TU	0640	1.9	1354	2.7	1940	1.9		
6	W	0247	3.0	0822	1.8	1529	3.0	2104	1.6
7	TH	0345	3.3	0946	1.4	1615	3.3	2205	1.2
8	F	0429	3.7	1041	1.0	1653	3.5	2252	0.8
9	SA	0509	4.0	1126	0.7	1727	3.8	2335	0.4
10	SU	0547	4.3	1207	0.4	1801	4.0	●	
11	M	0016	0.2	0625	4.4	1245	0.3	1835	4.0
12	TU	0057	0.1	0702	4.4	1322	0.3	1909	4.0
13	W	0138	0.1	0738	4.2	1400	0.4	1944	3.9
14	TH	0220	0.4	0815	3.9	1438	0.7	2019	3.7
15	F	0303	0.7	0852	3.6	1520	1.0	2055	3.4
16	SA	0350	1.1	0934	3.2	1608	1.3	2135	3.1
17	SU	0446	1.5	1028	2.8	1707	1.6	◐ 2233	2.8
18	M	0602	1.8	1320	2.5	1820	1.8		
19	TU	0110	2.7	0842	1.9	1522	2.7	1956	1.8
20	W	0408	2.9	1002	1.7	1612	2.9	2122	1.6
21	TH	0432	3.1	1040	1.5	1635	3.1	2212	1.3
22	F	0424	3.3	1110	1.3	1652	3.3	2250	1.1
23	SA	0451	3.6	1138	1.1	1717	3.6	2324	0.9
24	SU	0522	3.8	1205	1.0	1746	3.8	2355	0.8
25	M	0553	3.9	1230	0.9	1814	3.9	○	
26	TU	0024	0.7	0622	3.9	1255	0.9	1841	3.9
27	W	0052	0.8	0649	3.9	1319	1.0	1905	3.8
28	TH	0118	0.9	0713	3.8	1339	1.1	1929	3.7
29	F	0141	1.0	0736	3.7	1356	1.2	1956	3.6
30	SA	0208	1.2	0802	3.5	1422	1.4	2026	3.4
31	SU	0242	1.4	0834	3.3	1459	1.5	2104	3.2

APRIL

Date	Day	Time	m	Time	m	Time	m	Time	m
1	M	0328	1.6	0914	3.0	1551	1.7	2157	3.0
2	TU	0442	1.8	1019	2.7	1732	1.9	◑ 2338	2.8
3	W	0635	1.8	1352	2.7	1914	1.8		
4	TH	0221	3.0	0816	1.6	1506	2.9	2037	1.5
5	F	0319	3.4	0928	1.3	1552	3.2	2139	1.1
6	SA	0403	3.8	1019	0.9	1629	3.5	2228	0.7
7	SU	0444	4.1	1101	0.6	1701	3.8	2312	0.4
8	M	0522	4.3	1141	0.4	1734	3.9	● 2355	0.2
9	TU	0559	4.3	1219	0.3	1808	4.0		
10	W	0036	0.2	0637	4.3	1255	0.3	1844	4.0
11	TH	0118	0.3	0713	4.1	1333	0.5	1919	3.9
12	F	0200	0.5	0749	3.8	1412	0.7	1955	3.7
13	SA	0244	0.9	0827	3.4	1454	1.0	2032	3.4
14	SU	0331	1.2	0908	3.0	1543	1.3	2115	3.1
15	M	0429	1.6	1002	2.7	1640	1.6	◐ 2214	2.9
16	TU	0548	1.9	1258	2.5	1750	1.7		
17	W	0033	2.7	0819	1.9	1431	2.6	1915	1.7
18	TH	0256	2.9	0928	1.7	1521	2.8	2040	1.6
19	F	0322	3.0	1005	1.5	1549	3.0	2134	1.4
20	SA	0347	3.3	1035	1.3	1613	3.3	2214	1.2
21	SU	0417	3.5	1102	1.2	1642	3.5	2248	1.0
22	M	0448	3.6	1128	1.0	1712	3.7	2320	0.9
23	TU	0520	3.8	1153	1.0	1741	3.8	○ 2350	0.8
24	W	0550	3.8	1219	0.9	1809	3.8		
25	TH	0019	0.8	0618	3.8	1245	0.9	1836	3.8
26	F	0049	0.9	0645	3.7	1309	1.0	1904	3.7
27	SA	0119	1.0	0713	3.6	1336	1.1	1935	3.6
28	SU	0153	1.2	0746	3.4	1410	1.3	2012	3.5
29	M	0234	1.3	0824	3.2	1453	1.4	2058	3.3
30	TU	0330	1.5	0915	3.0	1553	1.6	2200	3.1

Chart Datum: 2·10 metres below Ordnance Datum (Newlyn). HAT is 4·5 metres above Chart Datum.

STANDARD TIME (UT)
For Summer Time add ONE hour in **non-shaded areas**

OBAN LAT 56°25'N LONG 5°29'W

TIMES AND HEIGHTS OF HIGH AND LOW WATERS

Dates in red are SPRINGS
Dates in blue are NEAPS

YEAR **2024**

MAY

Date	Day	Time	m	Time	m	Time	m	Time	m
1	W	0452	1.7	1034	2.7	1717	1.7	◑ 2339	3.0
2	TH	0626	1.6	1305	2.7	1844	1.6		
3	F	0140	3.2	0751	1.5	1428	2.9	2003	1.4
4	SA	0243	3.5	0857	1.2	1517	3.2	2107	1.1
5	SU	0332	3.7	0948	0.9	1556	3.4	2200	0.8
6	M	0415	4.0	1032	0.7	1632	3.7	2248	0.6
7	TU	0456	4.1	1113	0.6	1707	3.9	2333	0.4
8	W ●	0535	4.1	1152	0.5	1744	3.9		
9	TH	0017	0.5	0614	4.0	1230	0.6	1822	3.9
10	F	0101	0.6	0652	3.9	1309	0.7	1900	3.9
11	SA	0145	0.8	0731	3.6	1350	0.9	1939	3.7
12	SU	0230	1.1	0810	3.3	1434	1.1	2019	3.5
13	M	0318	1.4	0854	3.0	1522	1.3	2104	3.3
14	TU	0414	1.7	0948	2.8	1615	1.5	2159	3.0
15	W	0524	1.9	1131	2.6	1715	1.6	◐ 2317	2.9
16	TH	0704	1.9	1324	2.7	1821	1.7		
17	F	0111	2.9	0827	1.8	1417	2.8	1932	1.6
18	SA	0217	3.0	0914	1.7	1456	3.0	2034	1.5
19	SU	0258	3.2	0949	1.5	1530	3.2	2122	1.4
20	M	0335	3.3	1019	1.4	1603	3.3	2201	1.2
21	TU	0411	3.5	1047	1.2	1637	3.5	2238	1.1
22	W	0446	3.6	1115	1.1	1710	3.6	2314	1.0
23	TH	0521	3.7	1145	1.0	1742	3.7	○ 2351	1.0
24	F	0554	3.7	1217	1.0	1814	3.7		
25	SA	0028	1.0	0628	3.6	1250	1.0	1849	3.7
26	SU	0108	1.0	0704	3.5	1327	1.0	1928	3.6
27	M	0152	1.1	0744	3.4	1408	1.1	2011	3.5
28	TU	0241	1.2	0830	3.2	1456	1.2	2102	3.4
29	W	0339	1.3	0925	3.0	1552	1.3	2203	3.3
30	TH	0447	1.4	1032	2.9	1658	1.4	◑ 2319	3.2
31	F	0601	1.4	1159	2.8	1811	1.4		

JUNE

Date	Day	Time	m	Time	m	Time	m	Time	m
1	SA	0051	3.3	0715	1.4	1332	2.9	1925	1.3
2	SU	0204	3.4	0819	1.3	1434	3.1	2033	1.1
3	M	0301	3.6	0914	1.1	1523	3.3	2133	1.0
4	TU	0351	3.7	1003	1.0	1605	3.5	2227	0.9
5	W	0436	3.8	1047	0.9	1646	3.7	2317	0.8
6	TH ●	0519	3.8	1129	0.8	1727	3.8		
7	F	0004	0.8	0601	3.8	1210	0.8	1808	3.8
8	SA	0050	0.9	0641	3.7	1252	0.9	1848	3.8
9	SU	0135	1.1	0721	3.5	1334	1.0	1929	3.7
10	M	0220	1.3	0801	3.4	1417	1.1	2009	3.6
11	TU	0305	1.5	0843	3.2	1501	1.2	2051	3.4
12	W	0353	1.6	0928	3.0	1546	1.4	2136	3.3
13	TH	0444	1.8	1020	2.9	1635	1.5	2227	3.1
14	F	0542	1.9	1127	2.8	1726	1.6	◐ 2326	3.0
15	SA	0646	1.9	1248	2.8	1820	1.7		
16	SU	0037	3.0	0751	1.8	1351	2.9	1917	1.7
17	M	0147	3.0	0844	1.7	1441	3.0	2013	1.6
18	TU	0245	3.2	0928	1.6	1525	3.2	2107	1.5
19	W	0335	3.3	1006	1.4	1607	3.3	2158	1.4
20	TH	0420	3.4	1043	1.3	1647	3.5	2246	1.2
21	F	0502	3.5	1120	1.1	1726	3.6	2332	1.1
22	SA ○	0542	3.6	1158	1.0	1805	3.7		
23	SU	0018	1.0	0622	3.6	1238	0.9	1846	3.8
24	M	0104	0.9	0702	3.6	1319	0.9	1927	3.8
25	TU	0151	0.9	0744	3.5	1403	0.8	2011	3.8
26	W	0240	1.0	0828	3.4	1449	0.9	2058	3.7
27	TH	0331	1.1	0916	3.2	1540	1.0	2151	3.5
28	F	0426	1.2	1010	3.1	1635	1.1	◑ 2251	3.4
29	SA	0527	1.3	1114	3.0	1738	1.2		
30	SU	0003	3.3	0632	1.4	1231	2.9	1848	1.3

JULY

Date	Day	Time	m	Time	m	Time	m	Time	m
1	M	0125	3.3	0738	1.4	1352	3.0	2002	1.3
2	TU	0237	3.3	0842	1.4	1458	3.1	2113	1.3
3	W	0339	3.4	0939	1.3	1552	3.3	2218	1.2
4	TH	0433	3.4	1030	1.2	1639	3.5	2313	1.2
5	F ●	0519	3.5	1116	1.1	1721	3.7		
6	SA	0001	1.1	0600	3.6	1159	1.0	1802	3.8
7	SU	0045	1.1	0638	3.6	1240	0.9	1841	3.8
8	M	0127	1.2	0714	3.6	1320	0.9	1918	3.8
9	TU	0207	1.3	0749	3.5	1359	1.0	1955	3.8
10	W	0244	1.4	0824	3.4	1437	1.1	2030	3.6
11	TH	0321	1.5	0858	3.3	1514	1.2	2106	3.5
12	F	0358	1.6	0935	3.2	1553	1.4	2142	3.3
13	SA	0439	1.8	1015	3.1	1634	1.6	◐ 2222	3.2
14	SU	0527	1.9	1104	2.9	1721	1.7	2309	3.1
15	M	0624	1.9	1213	2.9	1816	1.8		
16	TU	0015	3.0	0730	1.9	1345	2.9	1918	1.8
17	W	0155	3.0	0836	1.8	1457	3.0	2025	1.8
18	TH	0312	3.1	0935	1.6	1551	3.2	2132	1.6
19	F	0409	3.3	1023	1.4	1637	3.4	2232	1.3
20	SA	0456	3.4	1106	1.1	1720	3.7	2325	1.1
21	SU ○	0539	3.6	1147	0.9	1801	3.8		
22	M	0013	0.9	0619	3.7	1227	0.7	1841	4.0
23	TU	0058	0.7	0656	3.7	1308	0.6	1921	4.0
24	W	0142	0.7	0734	3.7	1350	0.5	2001	4.0
25	TH	0226	0.7	0812	3.6	1434	0.6	2043	3.9
26	F	0310	0.8	0854	3.4	1521	0.7	2127	3.7
27	SA	0357	1.0	0939	3.3	1611	0.9	2218	3.5
28	SU	0450	1.2	1031	3.1	1708	1.2	◑ 2321	3.2
29	M	0550	1.4	1143	2.9	1817	1.4		
30	TU	0054	3.0	0700	1.6	1323	2.9	1939	1.6
31	W	0232	3.0	0816	1.6	1458	3.0	2116	1.6

AUGUST

Date	Day	Time	m	Time	m	Time	m	Time	m
1	TH	0353	3.1	0928	1.5	1607	3.2	2231	1.5
2	F	0446	3.2	1024	1.3	1645	3.4	2321	1.3
3	SA	0524	3.4	1110	1.1	1719	3.6		
4	SU	0001	1.2	0556	3.5	1149	1.0	● 1754	3.8
5	M	0037	1.1	0627	3.6	1227	0.9	1828	3.9
6	TU	0111	1.1	0657	3.7	1303	0.8	1900	3.9
7	W	0143	1.1	0727	3.7	1336	0.9	1932	3.9
8	TH	0214	1.2	0755	3.7	1408	1.0	2001	3.8
9	F	0244	1.3	0823	3.6	1439	1.1	2030	3.7
10	SA	0312	1.5	0852	3.4	1510	1.3	2058	3.5
11	SU	0341	1.6	0923	3.3	1544	1.5	2127	3.3
12	M	0417	1.8	1001	3.1	1626	1.7	◐ 2204	3.1
13	TU	0515	2.0	1052	2.9	1724	1.9	2256	2.9
14	W	0634	2.0	1244	2.8	1840	2.0		
15	TH	0113	2.8	0758	1.9	1450	2.9	2004	1.9
16	F	0314	3.0	0915	1.7	1547	3.2	2127	1.7
17	SA	0409	3.2	1010	1.4	1630	3.5	2231	1.3
18	SU	0451	3.4	1054	1.0	1710	3.8	2320	1.0
19	M ○	0529	3.7	1133	0.7	1748	4.1		
20	TU	0002	0.7	0604	3.8	1212	0.5	1826	4.3
21	W	0043	0.5	0638	3.9	1252	0.3	1903	4.3
22	TH	0122	0.4	0712	3.9	1333	0.3	1940	4.2
23	F	0202	0.5	0748	3.8	1415	0.4	2018	4.0
24	SA	0242	0.7	0825	3.6	1459	0.6	2058	3.8
25	SU	0326	0.9	0905	3.4	1547	0.9	2143	3.4
26	M	0415	1.2	0951	3.1	1644	1.3	◑ 2241	3.0
27	TU	0515	1.5	1059	2.9	1754	1.6		
28	W	0042	2.8	0628	1.7	1318	2.8	1936	1.8
29	TH	0255	2.8	0758	1.7	1543	3.0	2144	1.7
30	F	0408	3.0	0922	1.6	1632	3.2	2238	1.5
31	SA	0447	3.2	1015	1.3	1644	3.5	2315	1.3

Chart Datum: 2·10 metres below Ordnance Datum (Newlyn). HAT is 4·5 metres above Chart Datum.

STANDARD TIME (UT)
For Summer Time add ONE hour in **non-shaded areas**

OBAN LAT 56°25′N LONG 5°29′W

TIMES AND HEIGHTS OF HIGH AND LOW WATERS

Dates in red are SPRINGS
Dates in blue are NEAPS

YEAR **2024**

SEPTEMBER

Date	Time	m	Date	Time	m
1 SU	0509 1056 1704 2346	3.4 1.1 3.7 1.2	16 M	0433 1032 1648 2302	3.5 0.9 4.0 0.8
2 M	0532 1133 1733	3.6 0.9 3.9	17 TU	0507 1112 1724 2341	3.8 0.6 4.3 0.5
3 TU	0015 0600 1206 ● 1804	1.1 3.8 0.8 4.0	18 W	0538 1152 1800 ○	3.9 0.3 4.4
4 W	0043 0629 1238 1834	1.0 3.9 0.7 4.0	19 TH	0019 0611 1231 1837	0.4 4.1 0.2 4.5
5 TH	0111 0657 1308 1902	1.0 3.9 0.8 4.0	20 F	0056 0645 1312 1913	0.3 4.1 0.2 4.3
6 F	0139 0722 1337 1928	1.1 3.9 0.9 3.9	21 SA	0134 0720 1354 1950	0.4 4.0 0.4 4.1
7 SA	0205 0747 1403 1953	1.2 3.7 1.1 3.8	22 SU	0214 0756 1438 2028	0.6 3.8 0.7 3.7
8 SU	0226 0813 1428 2016	1.4 3.6 1.3 3.6	23 M	0257 0835 1527 2110	0.9 3.5 1.1 3.3
9 M	0245 0842 1457 2043	1.5 3.4 1.6 3.4	24 TU	0346 0920 1625 ◑ 2205	1.3 3.2 1.5 2.9
10 TU	0313 0917 1536 2115	1.7 3.2 1.8 3.2	25 W	0446 1027 1741	1.6 2.9 1.8
11 W	0400 1004 1638 ◐ 2203	1.9 3.0 2.0 2.9	26 TH	0049 0601 1346 2011	2.6 1.8 2.8 1.9
12 TH	0548 1138 1821	2.1 2.8 2.1	27 F	0252 0737 1536 2142	2.7 1.8 3.1 1.7
13 F	0144 0728 1441 2001	2.7 2.0 3.0 2.0	28 SA	0350 0901 1614 2221	3.0 1.6 3.3 1.5
14 SA	0311 0853 1531 2125	2.9 1.7 3.3 1.6	29 SU	0420 0952 1615 2250	3.2 1.3 3.5 1.3
15 SU	0356 0949 1611 2218	3.2 1.3 3.7 1.2	30 M	0436 1031 1635 2318	3.4 1.1 3.7 1.2

OCTOBER

Date	Time	m	Date	Time	m
1 TU	0459 1106 1703 2344	3.6 0.9 3.9 1.1	16 W	0437 1046 1656 2313	3.8 0.6 4.4 0.6
2 W	0527 1138 1733 ●	3.8 0.8 4.0	17 TH	0508 1128 1732 ○ 2351	4.0 0.4 4.5 0.5
3 TH	0009 0556 1208 1802	1.0 3.9 0.8 4.1	18 F	0543 1210 1809	4.1 0.3 4.4
4 F	0036 0623 1237 1830	1.0 4.0 0.9 4.0	19 SA	0028 0619 1252 1847	0.4 4.1 0.4 4.3
5 SA	0103 0649 1304 1855	1.0 3.9 1.0 4.0	20 SU	0107 0656 1335 1924	0.5 4.1 0.6 4.0
6 SU	0127 0714 1329 1919	1.2 3.8 1.2 3.8	21 M	0148 0734 1421 2004	0.8 3.9 1.0 3.6
7 M	0148 0741 1355 1943	1.3 3.7 1.4 3.6	22 TU	0232 0815 1512 2046	1.0 3.6 1.3 3.3
8 TU	0210 0811 1426 2011	1.5 3.5 1.6 3.4	23 W	0322 0902 1611 2141	1.3 3.3 1.7 2.9
9 W	0241 0848 1509 2046	1.7 3.3 1.9 3.2	24 TH	0420 1008 1730 ◑	1.6 3.1 2.0
10 TH	0329 0939 1621 ◐ 2140	1.9 3.1 2.1 2.9	25 F	0030 0531 1308 1948	2.7 1.8 3.0 2.0
11 F	0508 1124 1813	2.0 2.9 2.1	26 SA	0208 0656 1448 2105	2.8 1.8 3.1 1.8
12 SA	0133 0652 1410 1951	2.7 2.0 3.2 1.9	27 SU	0304 0819 1520 2145	2.9 1.7 3.3 1.7
13 SU	0244 0816 1501 2102	2.9 1.7 3.5 1.5	28 M	0333 0914 1536 2215	3.2 1.5 3.5 1.5
14 M	0329 0916 1542 2152	3.2 1.3 3.8 1.2	29 TU	0356 0957 1600 2242	3.4 1.3 3.6 1.3
15 TU	0405 1003 1619 2234	3.5 0.9 4.1 0.8	30 W	0423 1032 1629 2308	3.6 1.1 3.8 1.2
			31 TH	0453 1104 1700 2334	3.8 1.1 3.9 1.1

NOVEMBER

Date	Time	m	Date	Time	m
1 F	0523 1135 1730 ●	3.9 1.1 4.0	16 SA	0519 1152 1748	4.1 0.7 4.2
2 SA	0001 0553 1205 1800	1.1 4.0 1.1 4.0	17 SU	0004 0559 1237 1828	0.7 4.1 0.7 4.1
3 SU	0030 0621 1235 1828	1.1 3.9 1.2 3.9	18 M	0046 0639 1323 1908	0.8 4.1 0.9 3.9
4 M	0057 0650 1306 1856	1.2 3.9 1.3 3.8	19 TU	0128 0721 1410 1949	0.9 3.9 1.2 3.6
5 TU	0124 0721 1337 1926	1.3 3.7 1.5 3.6	20 W	0213 0804 1500 2033	1.1 3.7 1.5 3.3
6 W	0154 0756 1416 2000	1.5 3.6 1.7 3.4	21 TH	0302 0851 1556 2124	1.3 3.5 1.8 3.0
7 TH	0233 0838 1507 2044	1.6 3.4 1.8 3.2	22 F	0355 0947 1703 2240	1.5 3.3 2.0 2.8
8 F	0325 0936 1622 2150	1.8 3.3 2.0 2.9	23 SA	0454 1104 1831 ◑	1.7 3.1 2.0
9 SA	0441 1105 1753 ◐ 2338	1.9 3.2 2.0 2.8	24 SU	0054 0600 1310 1958	2.8 1.8 3.1 2.0
10 SU	0608 1318 1918	1.8 3.3 1.8	25 M	0155 0711 1411 2052	2.9 1.8 3.2 1.9
11 M	0157 0729 1420 2025	3.0 1.6 3.6 1.5	26 TU	0238 0817 1448 2130	3.1 1.7 3.3 1.7
12 TU	0249 0836 1507 2117	3.2 1.4 3.8 1.2	27 W	0313 0908 1521 2202	3.3 1.6 3.5 1.6
13 W	0329 0931 1549 2202	3.5 1.1 4.1 1.0	28 TH	0347 0950 1555 2231	3.4 1.5 3.6 1.5
14 TH	0404 1020 1629 2244	3.7 0.8 4.2 0.8	29 F	0421 1027 1630 2300	3.6 1.4 3.7 1.3
15 F	0441 1107 1708 ○ 2324	3.9 0.7 4.3 0.7	30 SA	0455 1103 1705 2332	3.7 1.3 3.8 1.3

DECEMBER

Date	Time	m	Date	Time	m
1 SU	0529 1139 1740 ●	3.8 1.3 3.8	16 M	0549 1231 1820	4.0 1.0 3.9
2 M	0004 0603 1216 1813	1.2 3.9 1.3 3.8	17 TU	0032 0632 1317 1901	0.9 4.0 1.1 3.8
3 TU	0037 0637 1254 1847	1.2 3.8 1.3 3.7	18 W	0115 0713 1402 1941	1.0 4.0 1.3 3.6
4 W	0112 0713 1334 1923	1.2 3.8 1.4 3.6	19 TH	0158 0755 1447 2021	1.0 3.9 1.5 3.5
5 TH	0149 0753 1418 2003	1.3 3.7 1.5 3.4	20 F	0242 0836 1533 2102	1.2 3.7 1.7 3.3
6 F	0230 0838 1508 2050	1.4 3.6 1.6 3.3	21 SA	0327 0919 1620 2147	1.3 3.5 1.8 3.1
7 SA	0319 0931 1608 2146	1.5 3.5 1.7 3.1	22 SU	0413 1006 1712 ◑ 2240	1.5 3.3 2.0 3.0
8 SU	0417 1037 1717 ◐ 2254	1.5 3.4 1.7 3.0	23 M	0503 1101 1811 2352	1.7 3.2 2.0 2.9
9 M	0526 1201 1830	1.6 3.4 1.7	24 TU	0557 1210 1916	1.8 3.1 2.1
10 TU	0019 0641 1328 1938	3.0 1.5 3.5 1.6	25 W	0116 0655 1329 2020	3.0 1.9 3.1 2.0
11 W	0147 0754 1432 2038	3.1 1.4 3.6 1.4	26 TH	0220 0756 1435 2112	3.1 1.9 3.2 1.9
12 TH	0249 0901 1525 2131	3.3 1.3 3.8 1.3	27 F	0311 0856 1525 2156	3.2 1.8 3.3 1.7
13 F	0338 1000 1612 2219	3.6 1.1 3.9 1.1	28 SA	0355 0950 1610 2234	3.4 1.7 3.5 1.5
14 SA	0423 1053 1656 2305	3.8 1.0 4.0 1.0	29 SU	0437 1039 1652 2311	3.5 1.5 3.6 1.4
15 SU	0506 1143 1739 ○ 2349	3.9 1.0 4.0 0.9	30 M	0517 1124 1732 ● 2348	3.7 1.4 3.7 1.2
			31 TU	0555 1207 1809	3.8 1.3 3.7

Chart Datum: 2·10 metres below Ordnance Datum (Newlyn). HAT is 4·5 metres above Chart Datum.

1.17 OBAN

Argyll and Bute **56°24'·99N 05°29'·07W** ❀❀❀◊◊◊✿✿

CHARTS AC 2171, 2387, 2388, 1790, 5611; Imray C65, 2800

TIDES –0530 Dover; ML 2·4; Duration 0610

Standard Port OBAN (⟵)

Times				**Height (metres)**			
High Water		Low Water		MHWS	MHWN	MLWN	MLWS
0100	0700	0100	0800	4·0	2·9	1·8	0·7
1300	1900	1300	2000				
Differences DUNSTAFFNAGE BAY							
+0005	0000	0000	+0005	+0·1	+0·1	+0·1	+0·1
CONNEL							
+0020	+0005	+0010	+0015	–0·3	–0·2	–0·1	+0·1
ARDCHATTAN PT							
+0150	+0150	+0215	+0200	–2·0	–1·3	–1·0	–0·3
BONAWE							
+0150	+0205	+0240	+0210	–2·0	–1·7	–1·3	–0·5
RUBHA Na CREIGE							
+0200	+0200	+0230	+0215	–1·9	–1·3	–1·0	–0·3

SHELTER Good shelter in bay except in strong SW/NW winds, but Oban Marina in Ardantrive Bay (Kerrera) is well sheltered from all directions. ⚓s convenient for town are in deep water NW of Sailing Club, beware of moorings. Alternatively ⚓ at N end of Kerrera to S of Rubh'a Chruidh Is or Horseshoe and Little Horseshoe Bay, Kerrera Sound. Beware fish farms S of Ardantrive Bay.

NAVIGATION **WPT (N)** 56°25'·85N 05°30'·0W, 132°/0·7M to Dunollie lt; **WPT (S)** 56°22'N 05°33'W, 035°/1M to 1·5ca E of Sgeirean Dubha, thence through Kerrera Sound to Oban Bay. Ferry Rks can be passed on either side. Direction of the buoyage is **NE**, thus pass to the East of ECM Q (3) 10s, or to West of the SH QG buoy. The N'ly SHM must be passed to the West. In Oban Bay beware Sgeir Rathaid (buoyed) and ferries running to/from Railway Pier. Yachts should follow the Code of Practice at www.obanharbour.scot.

LIGHTS AND MARKS See 1.3 and chartlet.

COMMUNICATIONS (Code 01631) Dr 563175; N Pier ☎562892. *North Pier* Ch **12** 16 (0900-1700); Railway Pier, *CalMac* Ch 06 12 16; *Oban Marina* Ch 80.

FACILITIES **North Pier** ⛴ ▬ ⛽.

Railway Pier ⛴ ⛽ ⛽(H24, ☎562849) ⛽ ⛽ ACA 🔧 ⛽ divers.

Oban Sailing Club 16 ⚓s £15/night, pay at Y honesty box £5 until 1600; short stay ⚓ (with ⛽), £2/half hour; free for 30 mins.

Oban Transit Marina ☎07388 808061 walk ashore pontoons on N Pier for up to 3 days. ⚓ £3.20, short stay £12.50; ⛽ ⛽ WC ⛽.

Kerrara Marina (Ardantrive Bay) www.kerraramarina.com

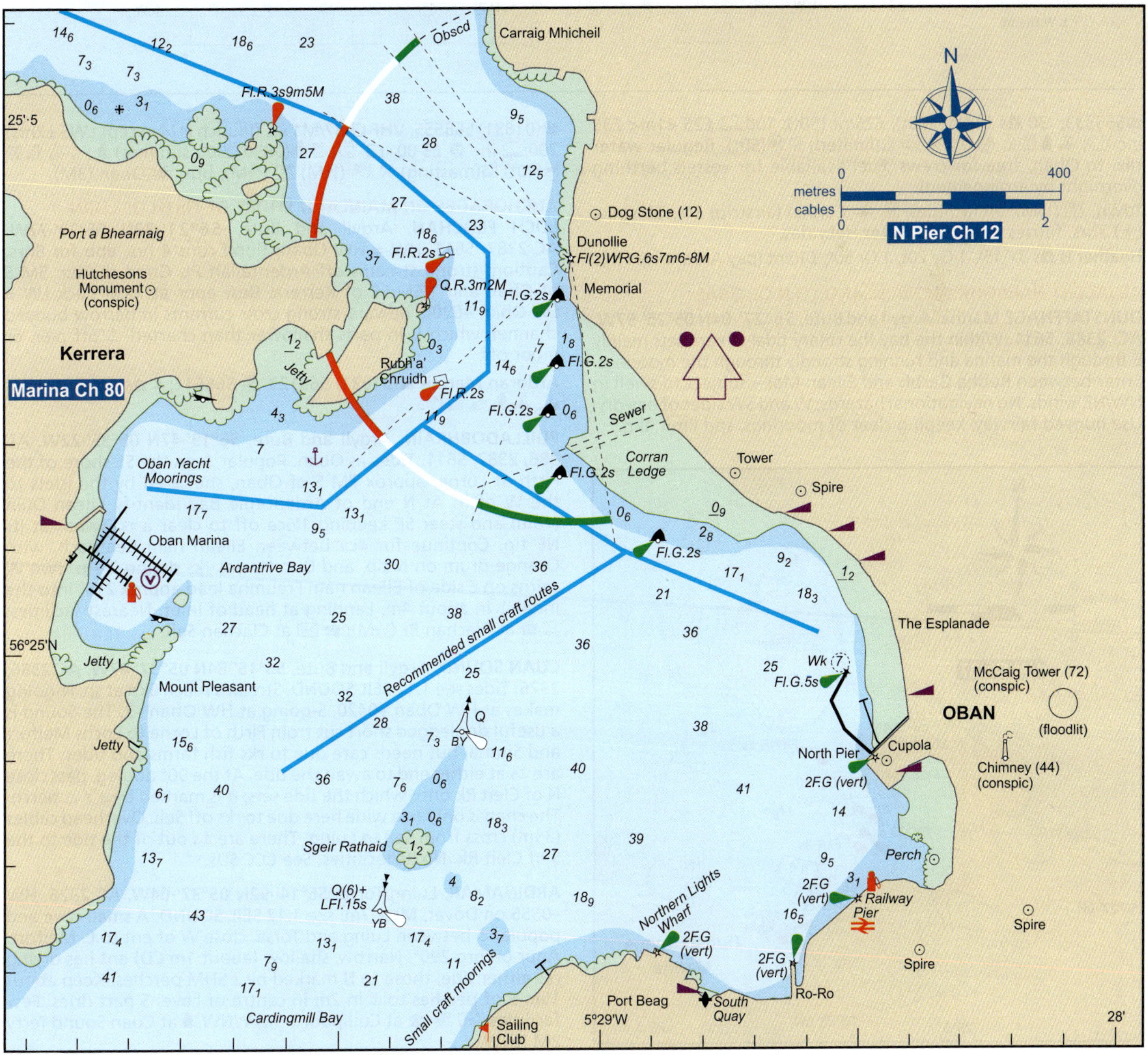

NW Scotland

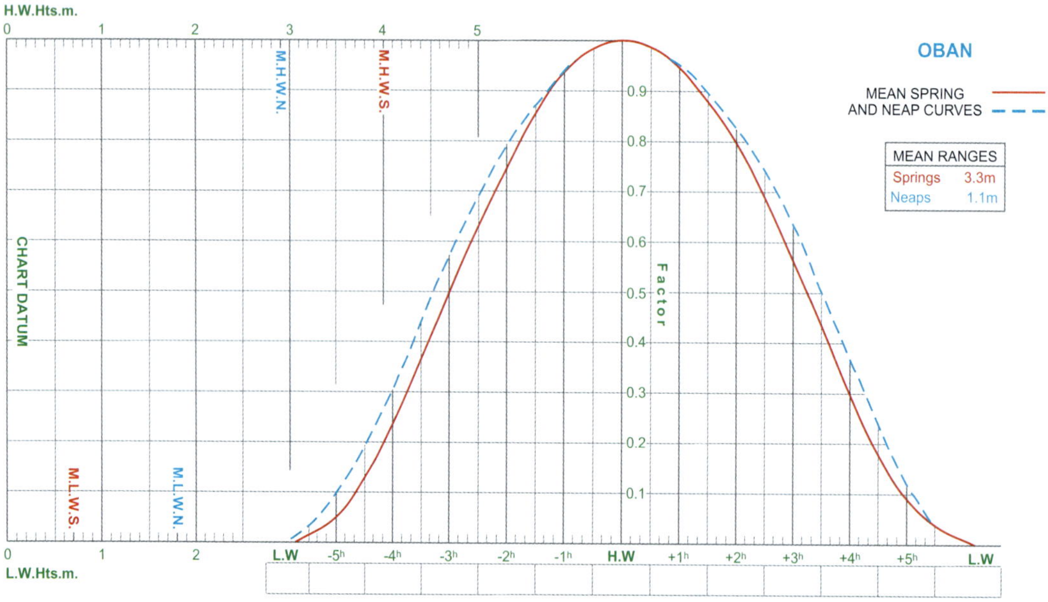

☎565333; 30 ⚓s £14/nt (20t), £25/nt (50t); 100 £25 <1m< £35 inc ; (limited) (50t). Regular water taxi to Oban, free for crews. Fuel available for vessels berthing overnight by arrangement.

Town (½M), all facilities, Ⓗ, ⇌ Connel (airstrip) 3M, Glasgow (✈) 3hrs, ferries to Inner & Outer Hebrides.

Heather Is ⚓s 3Y 15t, 1 Gy 20t, 1 Or 50t; £10/nt (pay Ardantrive Fm).

ADJACENT HARBOUR ON MAINLAND TO N OF OBAN

DUNSTAFFNAGE Marina, Argyll and Bute, **56°27′·04N 05°25′·97W**. AC 2388, 5611. Within the bay the rotary tidal stream sets mainly E through the marina and running strongly through the moorings. Enter between Rubha Garbh and Eilean Mór – subject to swell in NW/NE winds. No navigational hazards; W and SW sides of bay dry. Use buoyed fairway, keeping clear of moorings, spd limit 4kn.

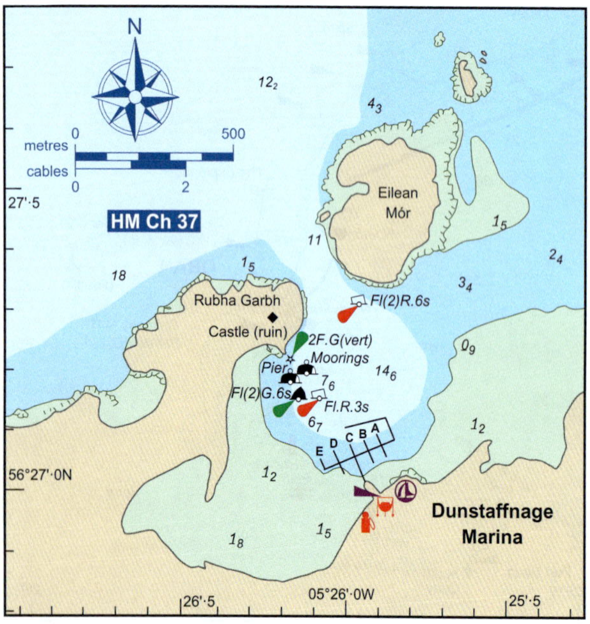

☎(01631) 566555, VHF Ch37/M1 (launch H24 except LWS ±2hrs) 200 inc Ⓥ £3·00+£3 (0830-2000 summer) (40t) (masting) (½M) (¾M), bus, ⇌ Oban (3M).

ANCHORAGES ON MAINLAND SHORE OF FIRTH OF LORN

LOCH FEOCHAN, Argyll and Bute, **56°21′·39N 05°29′·77W**. AC 2387, 5611. HW = HW Oban; flood runs 4 hrs, ebb for 8hrs. Caution: strong streams off Ardentallan Pt. Good shelter, 5M S of Oban and 1·5M SE of Kerrera. Best appr at local slack LW = LW Oban +0200; beware strong cross currents in narrow buoyed channel, which is in parts shallower than charted. ⚓ off pier, or moor off.

Ardoran Marine ☎(01631) 566123, 566611; 4 ⚓s £16·00 <11m, .

PUILLADOBHRAIN, Argyll and Bute, **56°19′·47N 05°35′·22W**. AC 386, 2387, 5611. Tides as Oban. Popular ⚓ on the SE shore of the Firth of Lorne, approx 7M S of Oban, sheltered by the islets to the W of it. At N end of Ardencaple Bay identify Eilean Dùin (18m) and steer SE keeping 1½ca off to clear a rk awash at its NE tip. Continue for 4ca between Eilean nam Beathach, with Orange drum on N tip, and Dun Horses rks drying 2·7m. Two W cairns on E side of Eilean nam Freumha lead approx 215° into the inner ⚓ in about 4m. Landing at head of inlet. Nearest facilities: ☎ at Clachan Br (½M); ☎ ✉ at Clachan Seil.

CUAN SOUND, Argyll and Bute, **56°15′·84N 05°37′·47W**. AC 2386, 2326. Tides see 1.17 SEIL SOUND. Streams reach 6kn at sp; N-going makes at HW Oban +0420, S-going at HW Oban –2. The Sound is a useful doglegged short cut from Firth of Lorne to Lochs Melfort and Shuna, but needs care due to rks fish farms and tides. There are ⚓s at either end to await the tide. At the 90° dogleg, pass close N of Cleit Rk onto which the tide sets; it is marked by a Y △ perch. The chan is only ¾ca wide here due to rks off Seil. Overhead cables (35m) cross from Seil to Luing. There are ⚓s out of the tide to the S of Cleit Rk. No lts/facilities. See CCC SDs.

ARDINAMAR, Luing/Torsa, **56°14′·92N 05°37′·04W**. AC 2326. HW –0555 on Dover; ML 1·7m; see 1.17 SEIL SOUND. A small cove and popular ⚓ between Luing and Torsa, close W of ent to L. Melfort. Appr on brg 290°. Narrow, shallow (about 1m CD) ent has drying rks either side, those to N marked by 2 SHM perches. Keep about 15m S of perches to ⚓ in 2m in centre of cove; S part dries. Few facilities: ✉ ☎ at Cullipool 1·5M WNW. at Cuan Sound ferry 2M NNW.

1.18 LOCH MELFORT

Argyll and Bute **56°14′·59N 05°34′·07W**

CHARTS AC 2169, 2326, 5611; Imray C65, 2800

TIDES Loch Shuna –0615 Dover; ML Loch Melfort 1·7; Duration Seil Sound 0615

Standard Port OBAN (⟵)

Times				Height (metres)			
High Water		Low Water		MHWS	MHWN	MLWN	MLWS
0100	0700	0100	0800	4·0	2·9	1·8	0·7
1300	1900	1300	2000				
Differences LOCH MELFORT							
–0055	–0025	–0040	–0035	–1·2	–0·8	–0·5	–0·1
SEIL SOUND							
–0035	–0015	–0040	–0015	–1·3	–0·9	–0·7	–0·3

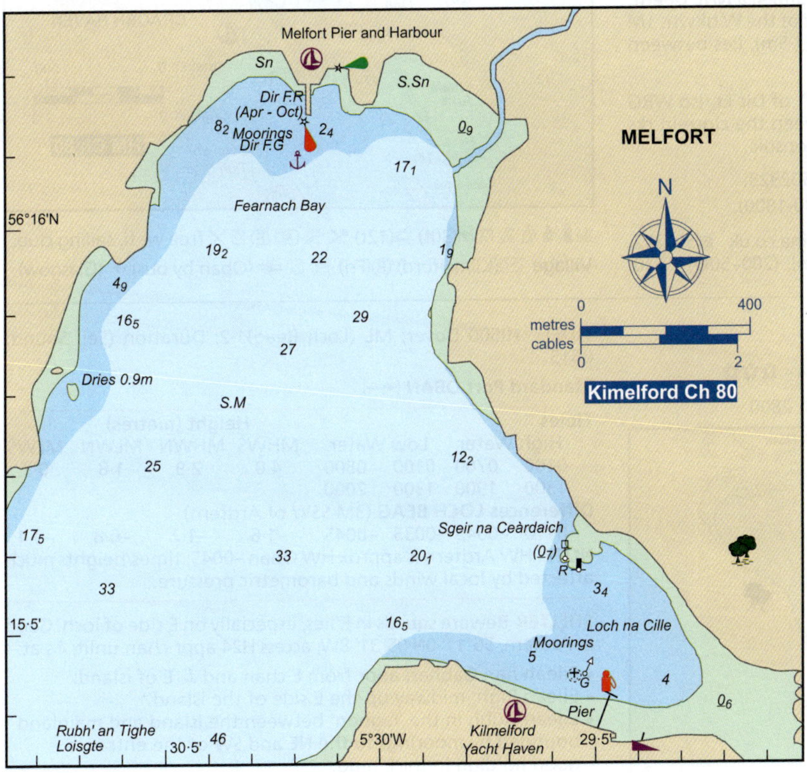

SHELTER Good at Kilmelford Yacht Haven in Loch na Cille; access at all tides for 3m draught, W lts at end of pier and along its length. Or lt at Melfort Pier (Fearnach Bay at N end of loch): pier/pontoon in 2m, but chan to inner hbr dries; good ⚓ in N winds. ⚓'ge sheltered from S to W at Kames Bay clear of moorings and rocks. Beware extensive marine farm activity inshore NE of Arduaine Point.

NAVIGATION WPT 56°13′·90N 05°34′·80W, 000°/3·5ca to Eilean Gamhna. Pass either side of Eilean Gamhna. 8ca NE lies Campbell Rk (1·8m). A rk drying 1m lies 1½ca ESE of the FS on Eilean Coltair. The S side of L Melfort is mostly steep-to, except in Kames Bay. At Loch na Cille, beware drying reef ¾ca off NE shore (PHM perch), and rk near S shore (SHM perch); boats may obscure perches.

LIGHTS AND MARKS A Dir FR ☆ 6m 3M on Melfort pier (also depth gauge) and a Dir FG ☆ close NE on the shore are not ldg lts, nor do they form a safe transit. Approach on a N'ly track keeping them an equal angle off each bow.

COMMUNICATIONS (Code 01852) Ⓗ (01631) 567500.

Kilmelford VHF Ch **80** M (HO).

FACILITIES

Melfort Pier melharbour@aol.com ☎200333, < 6m or £15/day, @ wi-fi, hotel accommodation.

Kilmelford Yacht Haven ☎ 200248 HW±4; £21/craft (any LOA) (Mon-Sat 0800-2000) (20t).

Kilmelford Village (1¼M).

1.19 CRAOBH MARINA (L SHUNA)

Argyll & Bute **56°12'·80N 05°33'·54W**

CHARTS AC 2169, 2326, 5611; Imray C65, 2800

TIDES HW Loch Shuna –0100 Oban; –0615 Dover; Seil Sound Duration 0615, ML 1·4. For tidal figures see 1.18.

SHELTER Very good. Craobh (pronounced Croove) Marina (access H24) on SE shore of Loch Shuna is enclosed by N and S causeways between islets. The ent is between 2 bkwtrs on the N side. In the marina, a shoal area S of the E bkwtr is marked by 9 PHM and 2 SHM buoys. A Y perch in W corner of hbr marks a spit; elsewhere ample depth. There are ⚓s in Asknish Bay 1M to the N, and in the bays E of Eilean Arsa and at Bàgh an Tigh-Stòir, S of Craobh.

NAVIGATION WPT 56°13'·01N 05°33'·57W, 173°/2ca to ent. Tidal streams in Loch Shuna are weak. Beware fish farm 2ca N of Shuna, lobster pots in appr's and unmarked rks (dr 1·5m) 4ca NNE of ent. An unlit SHM buoy marks a rk (1m) 150m NNW of the W bkwtr. 1M N of marina, Eich Donna, an unmarked reef (1·5m), lies between Eilean Creagach and Arduaine Pt.

LIGHTS AND MARKS The W sector, 162°-183°, of Dir Lt, Iso WRG 5s 10m 5/3M, on E bkwtr hd leads 172° between the close-in rks above. Multi-coloured marina buildings are conspic.

COMMUNICATIONS (Code 01852) Ⓗ (01546) 602323. VHF Ch M 80 (summer 0830-2000; winter 0830-1800).

FACILITIES **Craobh Marina** www.craobhmarina.co.uk ☎500222, mob 07917 805386; ▬ (launch/recover £3.70/m); (200+50Ⓥ) £3·10; (30t) (12t) Ⓔ free wi-fi, sailing club.
Village ✉(Kilmelford) Ⓑ(Fri) (Oban by bus) ✈ (Glasgow).

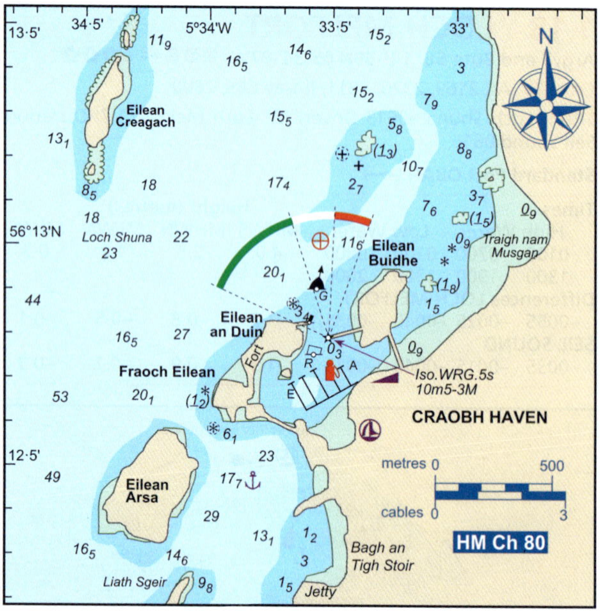

1.20 LOCH CRAIGNISH

Argyll and Bute **56°07'·99N 05°35'·07W**

CHARTS AC 2169, 2326, 5611; Imray C65, C63, 2800

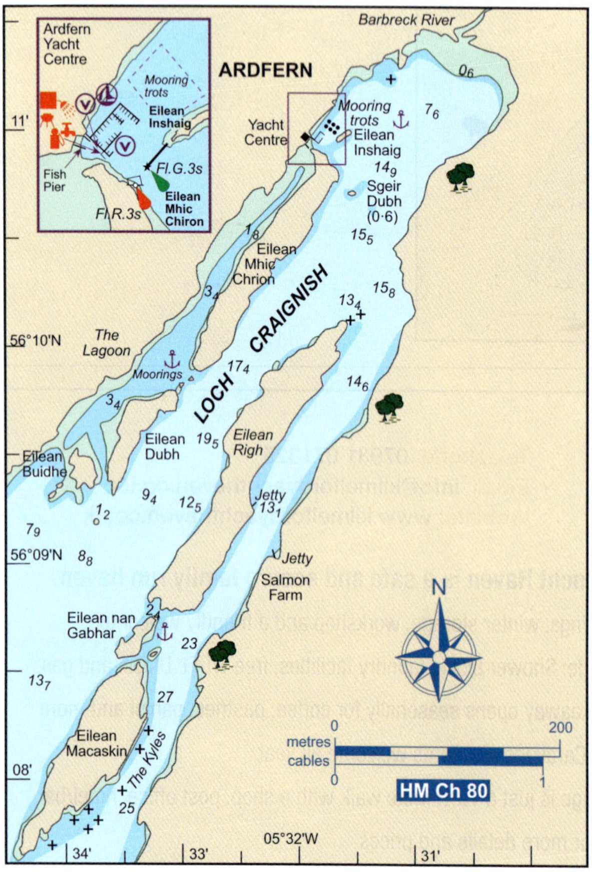

TIDES +0600 Dover; ML (Loch Beag)1·2; Duration (Seil Sound) 0615

Standard Port OBAN (⟵)

Times				Height (metres)			
High Water		Low Water		MHWS	MHWN	MLWN	MLWS
0100	0700	0100	0800	4·0	2·9	1·8	0·7
1300	1900	1300	2000				
Differences LOCH BEAG (3M SSW of Ardfern)							
–0110	–0045	–0035	–0045	–1·6	–1·2	–0·8	–0·4

NOTE: HW Ardfern is approx HW Oban –0045; times/heights much affected by local winds and barometric pressure.

SHELTER Beware squalls in E'lies, especially on E side of loch. Good at Ardfern, 56°11'·0N 05°31'·8W, access H24 appr chan unlit; ⚓s at:

- Eilean nan Gabhar; appr from E chan and ⚓ E of island.
- Eilean Righ; midway up the E side of the island.
- Eilean Dubh in the 'lagoon' between the island and mainland bounded by moorings to the NE and SW of the entrance – good holding in thick mud.

NAVIGATION WPT 56°07'·59N 05°35'·37W (off chartlet) between Dorus Mór and Liath-sgier Mhòr.

Beware: strong tidal streams (up to 8kn) in Dorus Mór; a reef extending 1ca SSW of Eilean Macaskin; rk 1½ca SSW of Eilean Dubh; fish cages especially on E side of loch; a drying rock at N end of Ardfern ⚓ with a rock awash ¼ca E of it. (These 2 rks are ½ca S of the more S'ly of little islets close to mainland.) The main fairway is free from hazards, except for Sgeir Dhubh (0·6m), an unmarked rk 3½ca SSE of Ardfern, with a reef extending about ½ca all round. Ardfern is 1ca W of Eilean Inshaig.

LIGHTS AND MARKS Ent to Ardfern Yacht Centre marked by PHM buoy, Fl R 3s, and end of floating bkwtr, Fl G 3s, which extends 90m SW from Eilean Inshaig.

COMMUNICATIONS Dr (01546) 602921; Ⓗ (01546) 602449.
Ardfern Yacht Centre VHF Ch 80 M (office hrs).

FACILITIES **Ardfern Yacht Centre** www.ardfernyacht.co.uk ☎ 01852 500247; 12 £1·85) 87+20 Ⓥ £2·75; ▬ (HW±3, £1.75/m) (HO) (40t) (25t) ACA.
Village ✉ Ⓑ(Fri) (Oban) ✈(Glasgow).

2.1
South West Scotland
Crinan Canal to Mull of Galloway
EMERGENCY 999
HMCG NATIONAL – 02392 552100
HMCG BELFAST – 02891 463933
HM CUSTOMS – 0845 010 9000
POLICE – 101 MEDICAL – 111
Harbour with full almanac entry
Minor harbour or anchorage
Major light
Ferry route
Airport
AREA 1
AREA 2
Loch Fyne
Inveraray
Loch Long
Loch Goil
Gareloch
GARELOCH/RHU 2.17
RIVER CLYDE 2.18
Dumbarton & Bowling
Glasgow
Greenock
INVERKIP 2.19
Toward Pt
PORT BANNATYNE 2.14
Dunoon
HOLY LOCH 2.16
Loch Riddon
Burnt Is
Caladh
West Kyle
PORTAVADIE 2.9
ROTHESAY 2.13
Bute
LARGS 2.20
FAIRLIE QUAY 2.21
Millport
Cumbraes
Little Cumbrae
Kilchattan Bay
ARDROSSAN 2.22
Irvine
FIRTH OF CLYDE
Loch Ranza
Arran
Brodick
ARDRISHAIG 2.7
CRINAN CANAL 2.6
Loch Fyne
TARBERT 2.8
West Loch Tarbert
Carradale Bay
Loch Sween
Oban
See 1.1
Gulf of Corryvreckan
Sound of Jura
Scarba
Craignure
Mull
Loch Spelve
Carsaig Bay
Glengarrisdale Bay
Jura
Loch Tarbert
Rubha A'Mhail
Craighouse
Gigha Is
Sound of Islay
PORT ELLEN 2.5
Port Askaig
Islay
Loch Indaal
Orsay I
Ardnave Pt
Scalasaig
Colonsay
Oronsay
Iona
Loch Lathaich
Magnetic Variation 2·3°W
4°
30'
5°W
6°
56°N

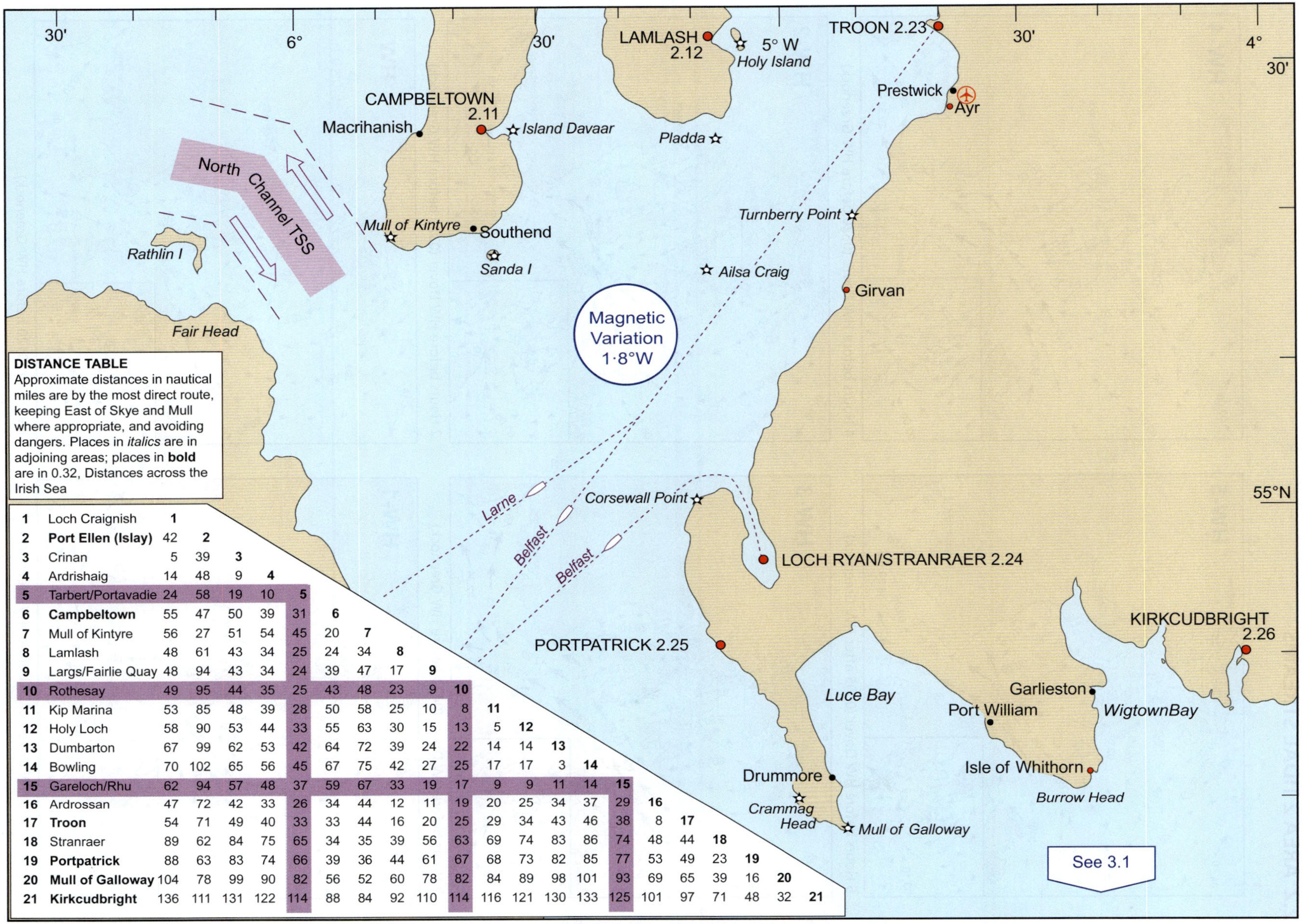

DISTANCE TABLE

Approximate distances in nautical miles are by the most direct route, keeping East of Skye and Mull where appropriate, and avoiding dangers. Places in *italics* are in adjoining areas; places in **bold** are in 0.32, Distances across the Irish Sea

		1	2	3	4	5	6	7	8	9	10	11	12	13	14	15	16	17	18	19	20	21
1	Loch Craignish	**1**																				
2	**Port Ellen (Islay)**	42	**2**																			
3	Crinan	5	39	**3**																		
4	Ardrishaig	14	48	9	**4**																	
5	Tarbert/Portavadie	24	58	19	10	**5**																
6	**Campbeltown**	55	47	50	39	31	**6**															
7	Mull of Kintyre	56	27	51	54	45	20	**7**														
8	Lamlash	48	61	43	34	25	24	34	**8**													
9	Largs/Fairlie Quay	48	94	43	34	24	39	47	17	**9**												
10	Rothesay	49	95	44	35	25	43	48	23	9	**10**											
11	Kip Marina	53	85	48	39	28	50	58	25	10	8	**11**										
12	Holy Loch	58	90	53	44	33	55	63	30	15	13	5	**12**									
13	Dumbarton	67	99	62	53	42	64	72	39	24	22	14	14	**13**								
14	Bowling	70	102	65	56	45	67	75	42	27	25	17	17	3	**14**							
15	Gareloch/Rhu	62	94	57	48	37	59	67	33	19	17	9	9	11	14	**15**						
16	Ardrossan	47	72	42	33	26	34	44	12	11	19	20	25	34	37	29	**16**					
17	**Troon**	54	71	49	40	33	33	44	16	20	25	29	34	43	46	38	8	**17**				
18	Stranraer	89	62	84	75	65	34	35	39	56	63	69	74	83	86	74	48	44	**18**			
19	**Portpatrick**	88	63	83	74	66	39	36	44	61	67	68	73	82	85	77	53	49	23	**19**		
20	**Mull of Galloway**	104	78	99	90	82	56	52	60	78	82	84	89	98	101	93	69	65	39	16	**20**	
21	**Kirkcudbright**	136	111	131	122	114	88	84	92	110	114	116	121	130	133	125	101	97	71	48	32	**21**

2.2 AREA 2 TIDAL STREAMS

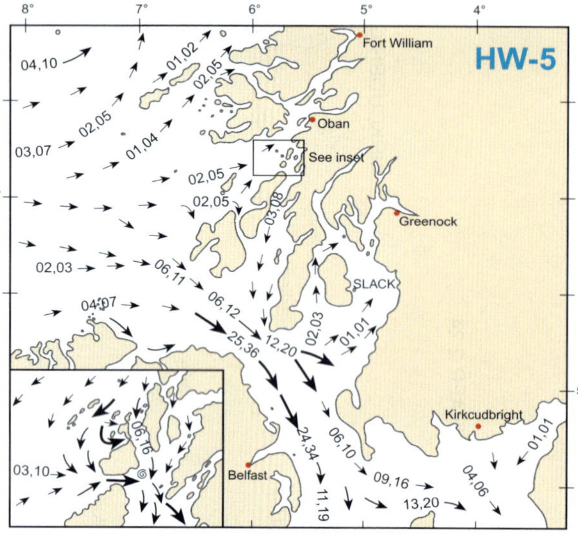

5 Hours before HW Dover (0605 after HW Greenock)

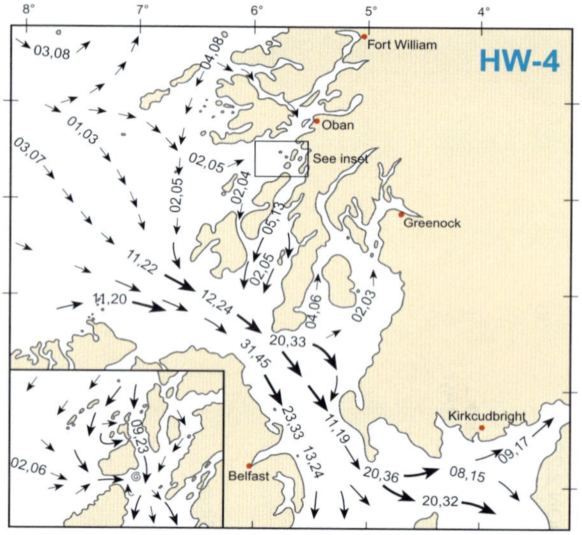

4 Hours before HW Dover (0520 before HW Greenock)

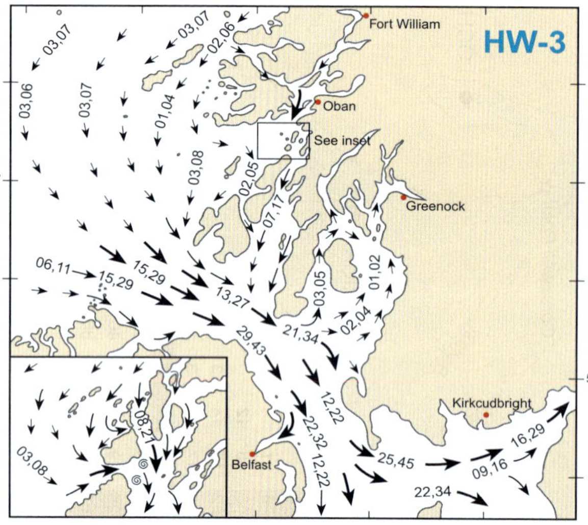

3 Hours before HW Dover (0420 before HW Greenock)

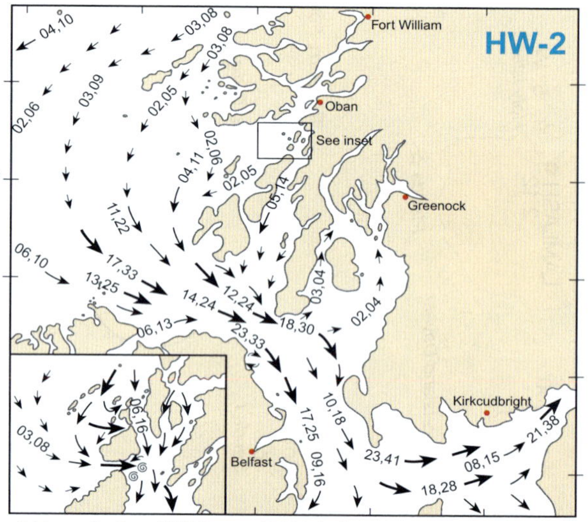

2 Hours before HW Dover (0320 before HW Greenock)

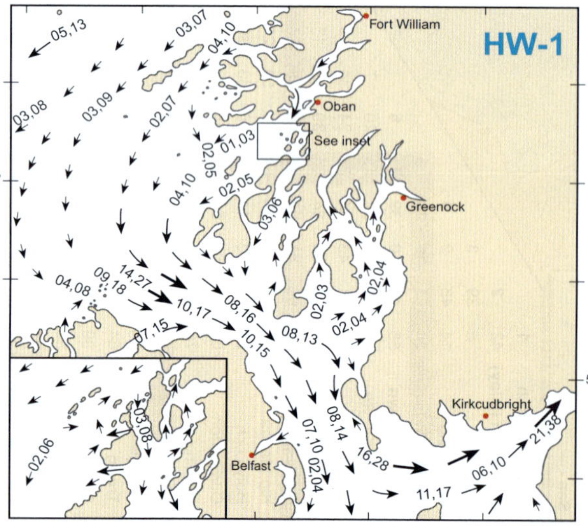

1 Hour before HW Dover (0220 before HW Greenock)

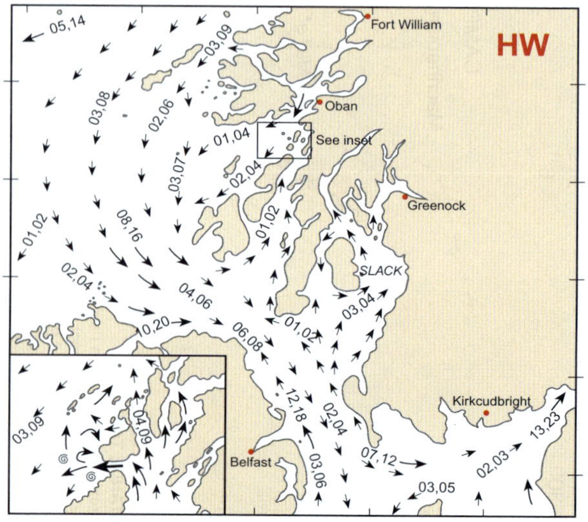

HW Dover (0120 before HW Greenock)

Northward 1.2 Mull of Kintyre 2.10 Irish Sea 3.2 North Ireland 6.2

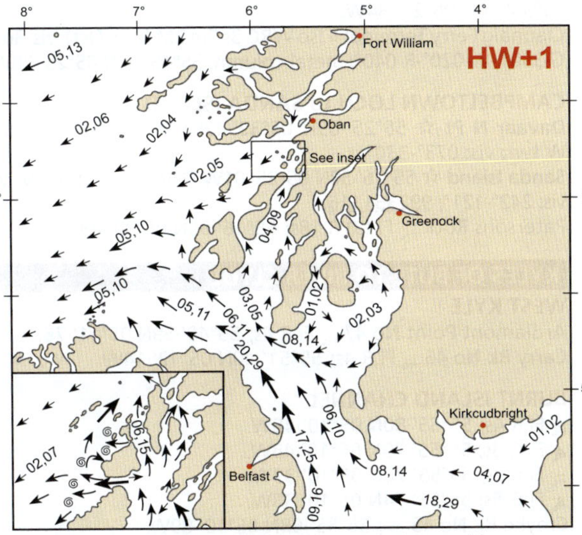

1 Hour after HW Dover (0020 before HW Greenock)

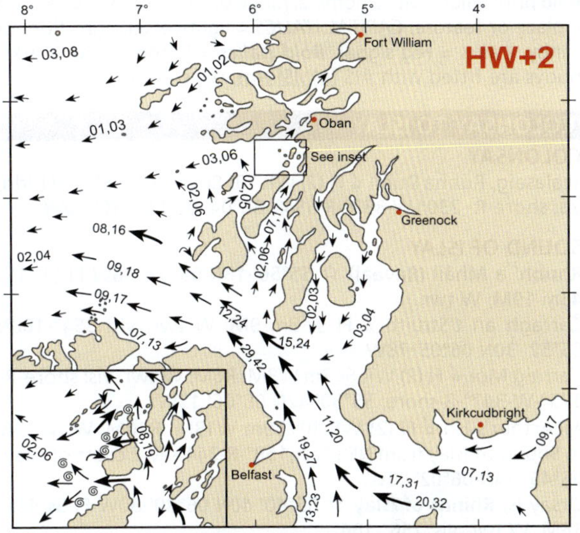

2 Hours after HW Dover (0040 after HW Greenock)

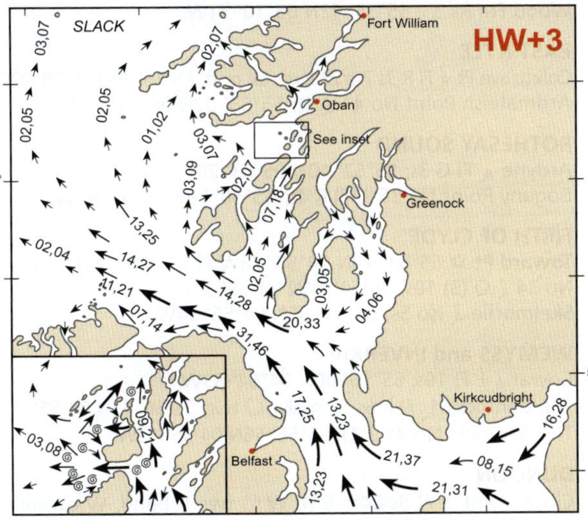

3 Hours after HW Dover (0140 after HW Greenock)

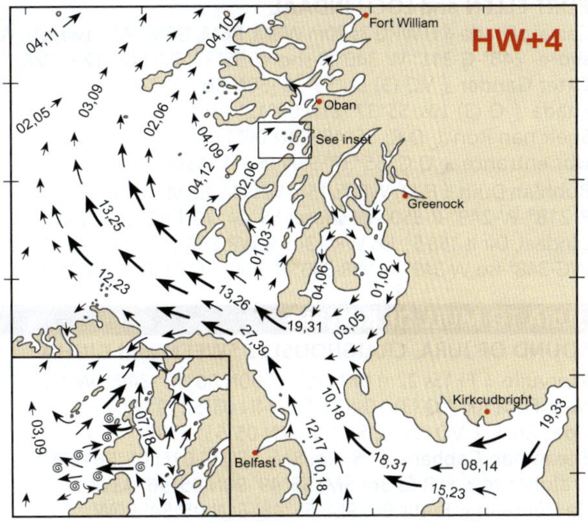

4 Hours after HW Dover (0240 after HW Greenock)

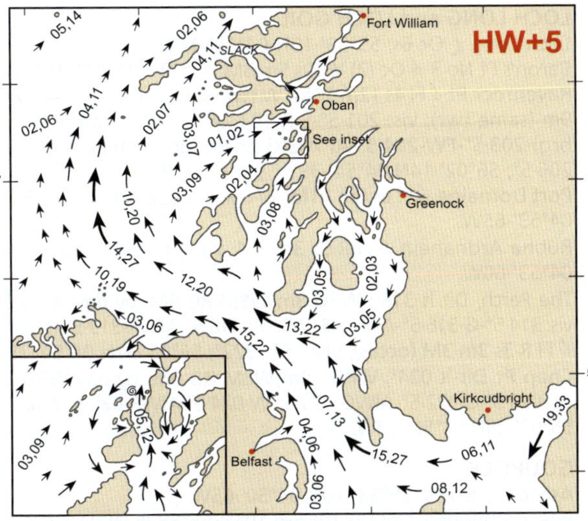

5 Hours after HW Dover (0340 after HW Greenock)

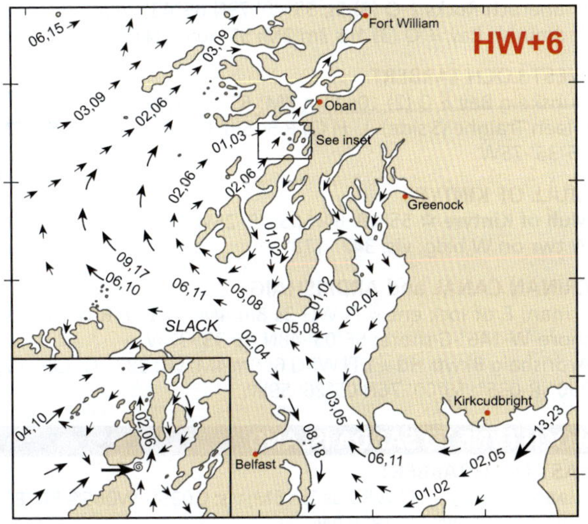

6 Hours after HW Dover (0440 after HW Greenock)

2.3 LIGHTS, BUOYS AND WAYPOINTS

Bold print = light with a nominal range of 15M or more. CAPITALS = place or feature. *CAPITAL ITALICS* = light-vessel, light float or Lanby. *Italics* = Fog signal. ***Bold italics*** = Racon. Some marks/buoys are fitted with AIS (MMSI No); see relevant charts.

COLONSAY TO ISLAY

COLONSAY

Scalasaig, Rubha Dubh ✧ Fl (2) WR 10s 8m W8M, R6M; W bldg; vis: shore-R- 230°-W-337°-R-354°; 56°04′·01N 06°10′·90W.

SOUND OF ISLAY

Rhubh' a Mháil (Ruvaal) ☆ 55°56′·18N 06°07′·46W Fl (3) 15s 45m **19M**; W twr.
Carragh an t'Struith ✧ Fl 3s 8m 9M; W twr; vis: 354°-180°; 55°52′·30N 06°05′·78W.
Carraig Mòr ✧ Fl (2) WR 6s 7m W8M, R6M; W twr; vis: shore-R-175°-W-347°-R-shore; 55°50′·42N 06°06′·13W.
McArthur's Hd ✧ Fl (2) WR 10s 39m W13M, R10M; W twr; W in Sound of Islay from NE coast,159°-R-244°-W-E coast of Islay; 55°45′·84N 06°02′·90W.
Orsay Is, **Rhinns of Islay** ☆ 55°40′·40N 06°30′·80W Fl 5s 46m **18M**; W twr; vis: 256°-184°.

PORT ELLEN and LOCH INDAAL

Carraig Fhada ✧ Fl WRG 3s 20m W8M, R6M, G6M; W □ twr; vis: W shore- 248°-G-311°-W-340°-R-shore; 55°37′·22N 06°12′·71W.
Otter Gander VQ (3) 5s; 55°36′·60N 06°12′·34W.
Fhada Q (3) 10s; 55°37′·21N 06°12′·41W.
Sgeir nan Ron Q R; 55°45′·53N 06°17′·32W.
Hbr entrance Q G; 55°37′·55N 06°11′·45W.
Rubh'an Dùin ✧ Fl (2) WR 7s 15m W11M, R8M; W twr; vis: shore-R-218°-W-249°-R-350°-W-shore; 55°44′·70N 06°22′·28 W.
L Indaal, Dir lt 168·5°; Iso WRG 3m 4s WRG 5M, vis: 343°-G-347°-Al WG-348°-Iso W-349°-Al WR-350°-R-354°; 55°46′·01N 06°21′·63W.

JURA TO MULL OF KINTYRE

SOUND OF JURA, CRAIGHOUSE, L SWEEN and GIGHA

Skervuile ✧ Fl 15s 22m 9M; 55°36′·60N 06°12′·34W; W twr.
Nine Foot Rk Q (3) 10s; 55°52′·44N 05°52′·91W.
Goat Rock VQ (3) 5s; 55°50′·12N 05°55′·67W.
Eilean nan Gabhar ✧ Fl 5s 9m 8M; 55°50′·01N 05°56′·25W.
Craighouse ✧ Fl R 6s 3m 5M; 55°49′·98N 05°56′·43W.
Na Cùiltean ✧ Fl 10s 9m 9M; 55°48′·64N 05°54′·90W.
Gamhna Gigha ✧ Fl (2) 6s 7m 5M; 55°43′·78N 05°41′·08W.
Bhanarach Rocks Q (3) 5s; 55°40′·73N 05°43′·29W.
Ardminish Bay, ✧ Q (3) 10s 3m 2M; 55°40′·56N 05°43′·99W.

WEST LOCH TARBERT

Dunskeig Bay ✧ Q (2) 10s 11m 8M; 55°45′·22N 05°35′·00W.
Eileen Tráighe (S side) Fl (2) R 5s 5m 3M; R post; 55°45′·37N 05°35′·75W.

MULL OF KINTYRE

Mull of Kintyre ☆ 55°18′·64N 05°48′·25W Fl (2) 20s 91m **18M**; W twr on W bldg; vis: 347°-178°.

CRINAN CANAL and ARDRISHAIG

Crinan, E of lock ent ✧ Fl WG 3s 8m 4M; W twr, R band; vis: shore-W-146°-G-shore; 56°05′·48N 05°33′·37W.
Ardrishaig Bkwtr Hd ✧ L Fl WRG 6s 9m 4M; vis: 287°-G-339°-W-350°-R-035°; 56°00′·76N 05°26′·59W.

LOCH FYNE TO SANDA ISLAND

EAST LOCH TARBERT

Eilean na Beithe ✧ Fl WRG 3s 7m 5M; vis: G036°- W065°- R078°-106°; 55°52′·68N 05°19′·62W.

KILBRANNAN SOUND, CRANNAICH and CARRADALE BAY

Port Crannaich Bkwtr Hd ✧ Fl R 10s 5m 6M; vis: 099°-279°; 55°35′·60N 05°27′·84W.
Claonaig Ferry Terminal ✧ Iso WRG 3s 5m 2M (Apr-Oct); vis: 305°-G-350° -W-020°-R-040°; metal column; 55°45′·04N 05°23′·28W.

CAMPBELTOWN LOCH to SANDA ISLAND

Davaar N Pt ☆ 55°25′·69N 05°32′·42W Fl (2) 10s 37m **15M**; W twr; vis: 073°-330°.
Sanda Island ☆ 55°16′·50N 05°35′·01W Fl 10s 50m **15M**; W twr; vis: 242°-121°; 992351116.
Patersons Rock Fl (3) R 18s; 55°16′·90N 05°32′·48W.

KYLES OF BUTE TO RIVER CLYDE

WEST KYLE

Ardlamont Point No 47 Fl R 4s; 55°49′·59N 05°11′·76.
Carry Rk No 46 Fl R 4s; 55°51′·40N 05°12′·14W.

BURNT ISLAND CHANNEL

Fl R 4s; 55°55′·80N 05°10′·46W.
Fl G 3s; 55°55′·79N 05°10′·48W.
Fl R 2s; 55°55′·76N 05°10′·39W.
Fl G 5s; 55°55′·74N 05°10′·38W.
Creyke Rk No 45 ; 55°55′·68N 05°10′·89W.
Beere Rk No 44 ; 55°55′·10N 05°10′·63W.
Wood Fm Rk ; 55°55′·42N 05°10′·31W.

EAST KYLE

Colintrave Pt ✧ Fl R 3s 7m 2M; metal post; 55°55′·39N 05°09′·22W.
Ardmaleish Point No 41 Q; 55°53′·02N 05°04′·70W.

ROTHESAY SOUND

Ardyne Fl G 3s; 55°52′·10N 05°03′·20W.
Bogany Point No 36 Fl R 4s; 55°50′·78N 05°01′·41W.

FIRTH OF CLYDE

Toward Pt ☆ 55°51′·73N 04°58′·78W Fl 10s 21m **22M**; W twr.
No 34 Q (3) 10s; 55°51′·44N 04°59′·11W.
Skelmorlie Iso 5s; 55°51′·65N 04°56′·34W.

WEMYSS and INVERKIP

Cowal L Fl 10s; 55°56′·00N 04°54′·83W.
The Gantocks Fl R 6s 12m 6M; ○ twr; 55°56′·45N 04°55′·08W.
The Gantocks No 31 Q; 55°56′·56N 04°55′·13W.

DUNOON

Cloch Point ✧ Fl 3s 24m 8M; W ○ twr, B band, W dwellings; 55°56′·55N 04°52′·74W.

LOCH LONG and LOCH GOIL

Loch Long Oc 6s; 55°59′·15N 04°52′·42W.
Baron's Pt No 3 ✧ Oc (2) Y 10s 5m 3M; 55°59′·18N 04°51′·12W.
Ravenrock Pt ✧ Fl 4s 12m 10M; W twr on W col. Dir lt 204°, WRG 9m (same twr); vis: 201·5°-F R-203°-Al WR(W phase incr with brg)-203·5°-FW-204·5°-Al WG(G phase incr with brg)-205°-FG-206·5°; 56°02′·14N 04°54′·39W; 992351319
Port Dornaige ✧ Fl 6s 8m 11M; W col; vis: 026°-206°; 56°03·75N 04°53′·65W.
Rubha Ardnahein ✧ Fl R 5s 3m 3M; vis: 132°-312°; 56°06′·15N 04°53′·60W.
The Perch, Dir lt 318°; WRG 3m W8M RG 6M, by day WRG 3M; vis: 314·5°-G-316·5°-Al WG-317·5°-W-318·5°-AlWR-319·5°-R-324·5°; ✧ Fl R 3s 3m 3M (occas); vis: 187°-322°; 56°06′·91N 04°54′·29W.
Cnap Pt Dir lt 024°; WRG 10m W8M RG 6M, by day WRG 3M; vis: 020·5°-G-022·5°-AlWG-023·5°-W-024·5°-AlWR-025·5°-R-027·5°; 56°07′·38N 04°50′·19W.

GOUROCK

Ashton Iso 5s; 55°58′·10N 04°50′·65W.
Rosneath Patch Fl (2) 10s 5m 10M; 55°58′·52N 04°47′·45W.

ROSNEATH, RHU NARROWS and GARELOCH

Ldg Lts 356°. **Front, No 7N** ⚓ 56°00′·05N 04°45′·36W Dir lt 356°. WRG 5m **W16M**, R13M, G13M; vis: 353°-Al WG-355°-FW-357°-Al WR-000°-FR-002°.

Dir lt 115° WRG 5m **W16M**, R13M, G13M; vis: 111°-Al WG-114°-FW- 116°-Al WR-119°-FR-121°. Passing lt Oc G 6s 6m 3M; G △ on G pile. Rear, Ardencaple Castle Centre ☆ 56°00′·54N 04°45′·43W 2 FG (vert) 26m 12M; twr on Castle NW corner; vis: 335°-020°.

No 8N Lt Bn ⚓ 55°59′·09N 04°44′·21W Dir lt 080° WRG 4m; **W16M**, R13M,G13M;vis: 075°-FG-077·5°-Al WG-079·5°-FW-080·5°-AltWR-082·5°-FR-085°. **Dir lt 138°** WRG 4m **W16M**, R13M, G13M; vis: 132°-FG-134°-Al WG-FW137°-139°-Al WR-142°. Passing lt Fl Y 3s 6m 3M.

Gareloch No 1 Lt Bn ☆ VQ (4) Y 5s 9m; Y 'X' on Y structure; 55°59′·12N 04°43′·89W.

No 3N Lt Bn ⚓ 56°00′·07N 04°46′·72W Dir lt 149° WRG 9m **W16M**, R13M, G13M F & Al; vis: 144°-FG-145°-Al WG-148°-FW-150°-Al WR-153°-FR-154°. Passing lt Oc R 8s 9m 3M.

Rosneath DG Jetty ☆ 2 FR (vert) 5M; W col; vis: 150°-330°; 56°00′·39N 04°47′·51W.

Rhu Pt ⚓ Dir lt 318° WRG **W16M**, R13M, G13M; vis: 315°-Al WG-317°-F-319°-Al WR-321°-FR-325°; Dir W; vis: 325°-QW-340°-FW-345°-OcW-350°; 56°00′·95N 04°47′·20W.

Limekiln No 2N Lt Bn ⚓ 56°00′·67N 04°47′·64W Dir lt 295° WRG 5m **W16M**, R13M, G13M F & Al; R □ on R Bn; vis: 291°-Al WG-294°-FW- 296°-Al WR-299°-FR-301°.

Carraig an Roin ☆ Fl Y 5s 2m 2M; Y post with 'x' topmark; 56°00′·99N 04°48′·40W.

Mambeg Dir lt 331°, Q (4) WRG 8s 10m 14M; vis: 328·5°-G-330°-W- 332°-R-333°; H24; 56°03′·74N 04°50′·47W.

GREENOCK and PORT GLASGOW

Anchorage Lts in line 196°. Front, FG 7m 12M; Y col; 55°57′·62N 04°46′·58W. Rear, 32m from front, FG 9m 12M. Y col.

Lts in line 194·5°. Front, FG 18m; 55°57′·45N 04°45′·91W. Rear, 360m from front, FG 33m.

Steamboat Quay, W end ☆ FG 12m 12M; B&W chequered col; vis 210°-290°; 55°56′·25N 04°41′·44W.

CLYDE TO MULL OF GALLOWAY

HUNTERSTON CHANNEL

'C' ▲ Fl G 5s; 55°48′·10N 05°55′·30W.

Hun 1 ⚓ (Y) Fl (4) Y 15s; 55°48′·10N 04°54′·21W.

Hun 3 ⚓ Fl R 2s; 55°47′·60N 04°53′·52W.

LARGS and FAIRLIE

Approach ⚓ L Fl 10s; 55°46′·40N 04°51′·85W.

Fairlie Patch ▲ Fl G 1·5s; 55°45′·38N 04°52′·34W.

MILLPORT and GREAT CUMBRAE

Tomont End Daymark 55°47′·56N 04°54′·10W.

Tattie Pier ☆ WRG 3s 5m 4M; vis: 222°-G-234°-W-246°-R-258°; metal column; 55°47′·20N 04°53′·89W.

Ldg Lts 333°. Pier Head front, 55°45′·04N 04°55′·85W FR 7m 5M. Rear, 137m from front, FR 9m 5M.

Mountstuart ⚓ L Fl 10s; 55°48′·00N 04°57′·57W.

Runnaneun Pt (Rubha'n Eun) ☆ Fl R 6s 8m 12M; W twr; 55°43′·79N 05°00′·23W.

Little Cumbrae Is, Cumbrae Elbow ☆ Fl 6s 28m 14M; W twr; vis: 334°-193°; 55°43′·22N 04°58′·06W.

ARDROSSAN

Approach Dir lt 055°, WRG 15m W14M, R11M, G11M; vis: 050°-F G-051·2°-Alt WG(W phase inc with Brg)-053·8°-FW-056·2°-Alt WR(R phase inc with brg)-058·8°-FR-060°; 55°38′·66N 04°49′·22W. Same structure FR 13m 6M; vis: 325°-145°.

Lt ho Pier Hd ☆ Iso WG 4s 11m 9M; W twr; vis: 035°-W-317°-G-035°; 55°38′·47N 04°49′·57W.

IRVINE

Ldg Lts 051°. Front, FG 10m 5M; 55°36′·40N 04°41′·57W. Rear, 101m from front, FR 15m 5M; G masts, both vis: 019°-120°.

TROON

Troon Approach ▲ Fl G 4s; 55°33′·08N 04°41′·42W.

W Pier Hd ☆ Fl (2) WG 5s 11m 9M; W twr; vis: 036°-G-090°-W-036°; 55°33′·07N 04°41′·02W.

Lady I ☆ Fl 2s 19m 11M; W Tr R vert stripes; ***Racon (T) 13-11M***; 55°31′·63N 04°44′·05W.

ARRAN, RANZA, LAMLASH and BRODICK

Pillar Rk Pt ☆ (Holy Island), 55°31′·04N 05°03′·65W Fl (2) 20s 38m **18M**; W □ twr.

Holy Is SW end ☆ Fl G 3s 14m 6M; W twr; vis: 282°-147°; 55°30′·73N 05°04′·21W.

Pladda ☆ 55°25′·50N 05°07′·12W Fl (3) 30s 40m **17M**; W twr.

AYR and AILSA CRAIG

S Pier Hd ☆ Q 7m 7M; R twr; vis: 012°-161°. Also Fl G 4s 5m 5M; vis: 012°-082°; 55°28′·17N 04°38′·74W.

Ldg Lts 098°. Front, FR 10m 5M; Tfc sigs; 55°28′·15N 04°38′·38W. Rear, 130m from front Oc R 10s 18m 9M.

Maidens Hbr, E side ☆ Fl G 5s 4m 3M; 55°20′·24N 04°49′·20W.

Maidens Hbr, W side ☆ Fl R 3s 4m 2M; 55°20′·23N 04°49′·19W.

Turnberry Point ☆, near castle ruins 55°19′·57N 04°50′·69W Fl 15s 29m 12M; W twr.

Ailsa Craig ☆ 55°15′·12N 05°06′·52W Fl 4s 18m **17M**; W twr; vis: 145°-028°.

GIRVAN

S Pier Hd ☆2 FG (vert) 8m 4M; W twr; 55°14′·72N 04°51′·90W.

LOCH RYAN and STRANRAER

Milleur Point ⚓ Q; 55°01′·28N 05°05′·66W.

Fairway ⚓ Iso 4s; 54°59′·77N 05°03′·82W.

Forbes Shoal ⚓ QR; 54°59′·47N 05°02′·96W.

Loch Ryan W ▲QG;54°59′·23N 05°03′·24W.

Cairn Pt ☆ Fl (2) R 10s 14m 12M; W twr; 54°58′·46N 05°01′·85W.

Cairnryan ☆ Fl R 5s 5m 5M; 54°57′·77N 05°00′·99W.

Stranraer No 1 ⚓ Oc G 6s; 54°56′·67N 05°01′·32W.

No 3 ⚓ QG; 54°55′·87N 05°01′·60W.

No 5 ⚓ Fl G 3s; 54°55′·08N 05°01′·86W.

E Pier Hd ☆ 2 FR (vert) 9m; 54°54′·61N 05°01′·60W.

Corsewall Point ☆ 55°00′·41N 05°09′·58W Fl (5) 30s 34m **22M**; W twr; vis: 027°-257°.

Black Hd Old Lt Ho; W tower, 22m; 54°51′·70N 05°08′·80W.

PORTPATRICK

Ldg Lts 050·5°. Front, FG (occas); 54°50′·50N 05°07′·02W. Rear, 68m from front, FG 8m (occas).

Crammag Hd ☆ 54°39′·90N 04°57′·92W Fl 10s 35m **18M**; W twr.

Mull of Galloway ☆, SE end 54°38′·11N 04°51′·45W Fl 20s 99m **18M**; W twr; vis: 182°-105°.

MULL OF GALLOWAY and WIGTOWN BAY

Port William Ldg Lts 105°. Front, Pier Hd Fl G 3s 7m 3M; 54°45′·66N 04°35′·28W. Rear, 130m from front, FG 10m 2M.

Isle of Whithorn ☆ Fl WR 3s 20m 6/4M; vis: 310°-W-005°- R-040°; 54°41′·79N 04°21′·54W.

Whithorn Ldg Lts 335°. Front, Oc R 8s 7m 7M; Or ♦; 54°42′·01N 04°22′·05W. Rear, 35m from front, Oc R 8s 9m 7M; Or ♦, synch.

Little Ross ☆ Fl 5s 50m 12M; W twr; obsc in Wigtown B when brg more than 103°; 54°45′·93N 04°05′·10W.

KIRKCUDBRIGHT BAY and KIPPFORD

Little Ross NNE end of Is ☆ Fl (2) 5s 21m 5M; Stone bcn; 54°46′·06N 04°05′·02W.

Hestan I, E end ☆ Fl (2) 10s 42m 9M; 54°49′·95N 03°48′·53W.

2.4 PASSAGE INFORMATION

Conditions are generally less rugged south of Mull but good charts and up to date Pilots are still essential. Admiralty Leisure Folio 5611 covers the Mull of Kintyre to Point of Ardnamurchan; 5610 the Firth of Clyde. Folio 5613, Irish Sea eastern part, covers the Scottish coast south of the Clyde to Kirkcudbright. **Bibliography:** *The Yachtsman's Pilot, Clyde to Colonsay* (Imray/Lawrence). *Clyde Cruising Club Sailing Directions-Firth of Clyde including Solway Firth and North Channel* (Imray/Clyde Cruising Club, Lawrence). The *South West Coast of Scotland Pilot* (Admiralty NP66A) covers the whole area.

Submarines exercise in this area, see **2.15, SUBMARINE EXERCISE AREAS** and SUBFACTS for information on this.

Some more common *Gaelic* terms may help with navigation: *Acairseid*: anchorage. *Ailean*: meadow. *Aird, ard*: promontory. *Aisir, aisridh*: passage between rocks. *Beag*: little. *Beinn*: mountain. *Bo, boghar, bodha*: rock. *Cala*: harbour. *Camas*: channel, bay. *Caol*: strait. *Cladach*: shore, beach. *Creag*: cliff. *Cumhamn*: narrows. *Dubh, dhubh*: black. *Dun*: castle. *Eilean, eileanan*: island. *Garbh*: rough. *Geal, gheal*: white. *Glas, ghlas*: grey, green. *Inis*: island. *Kyle*: narrow strait. *Linn, Linne*: pool. *Mor, mhor:* large. *Mull*: promontory. *Rinn, roinn*: point. *Ruadh*: red, brown. *Rubha, rhu*: cape. *Sgeir*: rock. *Sruth*: current. *Strath*: river valley. *Tarbert*: isthmus. *Traigh*: beach. *Uig*: bay.

CORRYVRECKAN TO CRINAN

(AC 2326, 2343) Between Scarba and Jura is the Gulf of Corryvreckan (AC 2343) which is best avoided, and should never be attempted by small craft except at slack water and in calm conditions. (In any event the Sound of Luing is always a safer and not much longer alternative.) The Gulf has a least width of 6ca and is free of dangers apart from its very strong tides which, in conjunction with a very uneven bottom, cause extreme turbulence. This is particularly dangerous with strong W winds over a W-going (flood) tide which spews out several miles to seaward of the gulf, with overfalls extending 5M from the W of ent (The Great Race). Keep to the S side to avoid the worst turbulence and The Hag, a whirlpool in 29m, as opposed to more than 100m in the fairway.

▶ *The W-going stream in the gulf begins at HW Oban + 0410, and the E-going at HW Oban – 0210. Sp rate W-going is 8·5kn, and E-going about 6kn. The range of tide at Sp can vary nearly 2m between the E end of the gulf (1·5m) and the W end (3·4m), with HW 30 mins earlier at the E end. Slack water occurs at HW Oban +0400 and –0230 and lasts almost 1hr at Nps, but only 15 mins at Sps. On the W-going (flood) stream eddies form both sides of the gulf, but the one on the N (Scarba) shore is more important. Where this eddy meets the main stream off Camas nam Bairneach there is violent turbulence, with heavy overfalls extending W along the division boundary.* ◀

There are temp ⚓s with the wind in the right quarter in Bàgh Gleann a' Mhaoil in the SE corner of Scarba, and in Bàgh Gleann nam Muc at N end of Jura but the latter has rks in approaches E and SW of Eilean Beag.

SE of Corryvreckan is Loch Crinan, which leads to the Crinan Canal. Beware Black Rk, 2m high and 2ca N of the canal sea lock, and dangers extending 100m from the rock.

WEST OF JURA TO ISLAY

(AC 2481, 2168) The W coasts of Colonsay and Oronsay (AC 2169) separated by a narrow drying channel crossed by a cable (10m) are fringed with dangers up to 2M offshore.

The Sound of Islay presents no difficulty; hold to the Islay shore, where all dangers are close in. ⚓s in the Sound, have mostly poor holding. The best places are alongside at Port Askaig, or ⚓ off the distillery in Bunnahabhain Bay, 2·5M to the North.

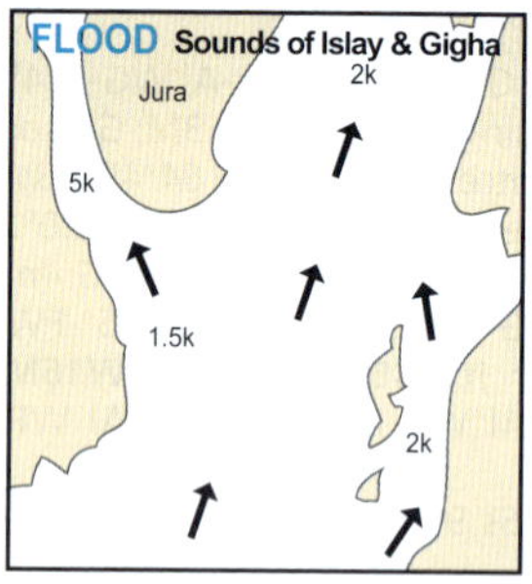

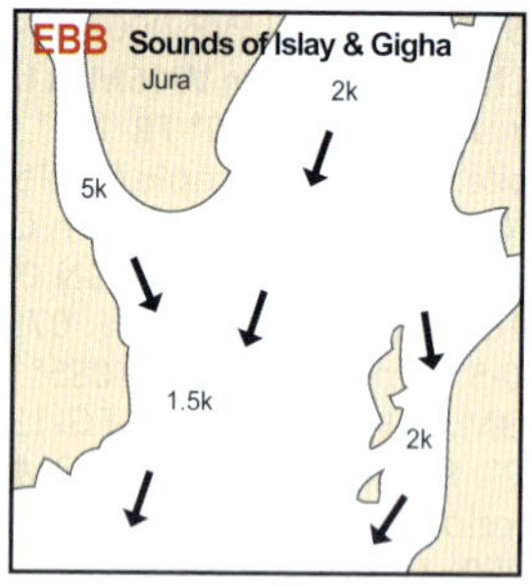

▶ *The N-going stream begins at HW Oban + 0440, and the S-going at HW Oban – 0140. Main flood begins HW Oban +0545. Streams turn approx 1hr earlier in Gigha Sd and at Kintyre and Jura shores. S-going stream for 9hrs close inshore between Gigha and Machrihanish starting HW Oban –0530.*

Main ebb begins HW Oban –0015. Streams turn 1hr earlier in Gigha Sd, off Kintyre and Jura shores. Sp rates are 2·5kn at N entrance and 1·5kn at S entrance, ***but reach 5kn in the narrows off Port Askaig.*** *There are overfalls off McArthur's Hd (Islay side of S ent) during the S-going stream.* ◀

The N coast of Islay and Rhinns of Islay are very exposed. In the N there is an ⚓ SE of Nave Island at entrance to Loch Gruinart; beware Balach Rks which dry, just to N.

▶ *To the SW off Orsay (lt), Frenchman's Rks and W Bank is a race and overfalls which should be cleared by 3M. Here the NW-going stream begins at HW Oban +0530, and the SE-going at HW Oban -0040;* ***Sp rates are 6-8kn inshore,*** *but decrease to 3kn 5M offshore.* ◀

Loch Indaal gives some shelter; beware rks extending from Laggan Pt on E side of ent. Off the Mull of Oa there are overfalls. Port Ellen, the main hbr on Islay, has HIE Ⓞs; there are some dangers in approach, and it is exposed to S; see AC 2474.

SOUND OF JURA TO GIGHA

(AC 2397, 2396, 2168) From Crinan to Gigha the Sound of Jura is safe if a mid-chan course is held. Ruadh Sgeir (lit) are rocky ledges in mid-fairway, about 3M W of Crinan. Loch Sween (AC 2397) can be approached N or SE of MacCormaig Islands; there is an attractive ⚓ NE of Eilean Mor, exposed to the NE. Coming from N beware Keills Rk and Danna Rk. Sgeirean a Mhain is a rock in the fairway 1·5M NE of Castle Sween (conspic on SE shore). ⚓ at Tayvallich, near the head of loch on W side.

On W side of Sound, near S end of Jura, The Small Is (AC 2396) lie across the mouth of Loch na Mile. Beware Goat Rk (dries 0·3m) 1.5ca off S'most Is, Eilean nan Gabhar. Behind this is a good ⚓ and it one can go alongside Craighouse Pier (HIE Ⓞ). Another ⚓ is in Lowlandman's B, about 3M to N, but is exposed to S winds; Ninefoot Rks with depth of 2·4m and lit ECM lie off the ent. Skervuile (lit) is a reef in middle of the Sound. W Loch Tarbert (AC 2477) is long and narrow, with good ⚓s but unmarked shoals. On entry (lit) give a berth of at least 2½ca to Eilean Traighe off N shore, E of Ardpatrick Pt. Dun Skeig, an isolated hill, is conspic on S shore. Good ⚓ near head of the loch, 1M by road to E Loch Tarbert, Loch Fyne.

S of W Loch Tarbert, and about 2M off the Kintyre shore, is Gigha Is (AC 2475). Good ⚓s on E side in Druimyeon B and Ardminish Bay (HIE Ⓞs), respectively N and S of Ardminish Pt. Outer and Inner Red Rks (least depth 2m) lie 2M SW of N end of Gigha Is. Dangers extend 1M W off S Gigha Is and Gigalum

Is and Cara Is lie off the S end. Gigha Sound needs careful pilotage; there are dangerous rks, some buoyed/lit, others not.

▶ *The N-going stream begins at HW Oban + 0430, and S-going at HW Oban – 0155, Sp rates 1·3kn.* ◀

MULL OF KINTYRE

(AC 2126, 2199, 2798) From Crinan to Mull of Kintyre is 50M. Passage round the Mull of Kintyre within 2M or 3M of the coast requires great care. Races exist S and SW of the Mull, and fresh to strong S winds cause dangerous breaking seas especially during E-going (flood) tidal streams. Best to keep at least 3M offshore and S of Sanda Island.

▶*In Sanda Sound the W-going stream starts HW Dover –0110, and the E-going stream starts HW Dover +0500. Sp rates 5kn. Close W of the Mull the N-going stream starts at HW Dover –0130, and the S-going stream at HW Dover +0430. Sp rates 5kn. Careful timing is needed, especially W-bound.*◀

The TSS in North Channel, 2M W of the Mull, restricts the ITZ. Sanda Sound separates Sanda Island and its rocks and islets from Kintyre. On the mainland shore beware Macosh Rks (dry, PHM lt buoy), forming part of Barley Ridges, 2ca offshore; and Arranman's Barrels, drying and submerged, marked by PHM lt buoy. Sanda Is provides useful stopping point while waiting for the tide. Beware Paterson's Rk (9ca E, dries). There is a good ⚓ on N side in Sanda Roads. Approach with Boat Ho bearing 155°; beware strong tidal stream across entrance, and drying rocks in middle of bay. See Plan on AC 2126.

MULL OF KINTYRE TO UPPER LOCH FYNE

(AC 2126, 2383, 2381, 2382). Campbeltown is entered N of Island Davaar (lit). 1·5M N of lt ho lies Otterard Rk, 3·8m ECM. Long Rk 5ca W of it dries 1·1m.

▶*E of Island Davaar tide runs 3kn at Sp, and there are overfalls. There are few dangers apart from overfalls off Carradale Pt and on Erins Bank, 10M S of Skipness, on S-going stream.*◀

Kilbrannan Sound runs 21M from Island Davaar to Skipness Pt, where it joins Inchmarnock Water, Lower Loch Fyne and Bute Sound. Good ⚓ in Carradale Bay, off Torrisdale Castle. Lower L Fyne (AC 2381) is mainly clear S to East L Tarbert. On E shore beware rks off Ardlamont Pt; 4M to NW is Skate Is, best passed to the W. 3M S of Ardrishaig beware Big Rk (2·1m). Further N, at entrance to L Gilp (mostly dries), note shoals (least depth 1·5m) round Gulnare Rk (lit PHM); also Duncuan Is with dangers extending SW to Sgeir Sgalag (depth 0·6m), buoyed. The Narrows is partly obstructed by Otter Spit (dries 0·9m), extending 8ca WNW from E shore. The stream runs up to 2kn here. A buoyed rk, depth less than 2m, lies about 7ca SW of Otter Spit bn. In Upper L Fyne (AC 2382) off Minard Pt, the fairway between rocks and islands is buoyed and lit.

ARRAN, BUTE AND FIRTH OF CLYDE

(AC1906, 1907) Arran's mountains may cause squalls, but there are good ⚓s at Lamlash, Brodick and Loch Ranza. Sannox Rock (1·5m) is 2½ca off Arran coast 8M N of Lamlash. 1ca off W side of Inchmarnock is Tra na-h-Uil drying 1·5m. In Inchmarnock Sound, Shearwater Rk (0·9m) lies in middle of S entry.

The Kyles of Bute are attractive channels N of Bute, and straightforward. At the Burnt Islands it is best to take the north chan, passing between Eilean Buidhe and Fraoich. ▶***Sp stream may reach 5kn.***◀ Caladh Hbr is a beautiful ⚓. The N lochs in Firth of Clyde are less attractive. Loch Goil is worth a visit; Loch Long is squally with few ⚓s but no hidden dangers. There are marinas at Inverkip, Largs, Holy Loch, Gareloch, Portavadie and Rothesay Hbr. Kilchattan Bay (⚓ 6M to S) is sheltered from SSE to WNW.

▶ *Navigation in Firth of Clyde is straightforward since tidal streams are weak. It is busy with many large commercial vessel movements and extensive naval training involving submarines, ships and aircraft. All users should read The CLYDE LEISURE NAVIGATION GUIDE www.clydeport.co.uk* ◀

FIRTH OF CLYDE TO MULL OF GALLOWAY

(AC 2131, 2126, 2199, 2198) Further S the coast is less inviting, with mostly commercial harbours until Ardrossan and Troon, NW of which there are various dangers: Troon Rk (depth 5·6m, but sea can break), Lappock Rk (dries 0·6m, bn), and Mill Rk (dries 0·4m, buoyed). Lady Isle is 2M WSW of Troon.

▶ *There is a severe race off Bennane Hd (8M SSE of Ailsa Craig, conspic) when tide is running strongly.*◀

Loch Ryan offers little for yachtsmen; there is a small marina at Stranraer and ⚓ S of Kirkcolm Pt, inside the drying spit which runs in SE direction 1·5M from the point. There is also a useful ⚓ in Lady Bay, sheltered except from NE. Portpatrick is a useful passage harbour, but not in onshore winds.

▶ **North Channel South:** *Irish coast – the S-going flood begins HW Belfast –0600 (HW Dover +0610). Counter tide off Donaghadee and Island Magee for last 3hrs of flood. Ebb (N'ly stream) begins at HW Belfast (HW Dover –0015). Scottish coast between Corsewall Pt and Mull of Galloway – S'ly flood HW Greenock +0310 (HW Dover +0430), Sp rate off Corsewall Pt 2–3kn, increasing* ***to 5kn off/S of Black Hd.*** *Flood begins 2hrs early close inshore N of Mull of Galloway. N bound ebb HW Greenock –0250 (HW Dover –0130).*

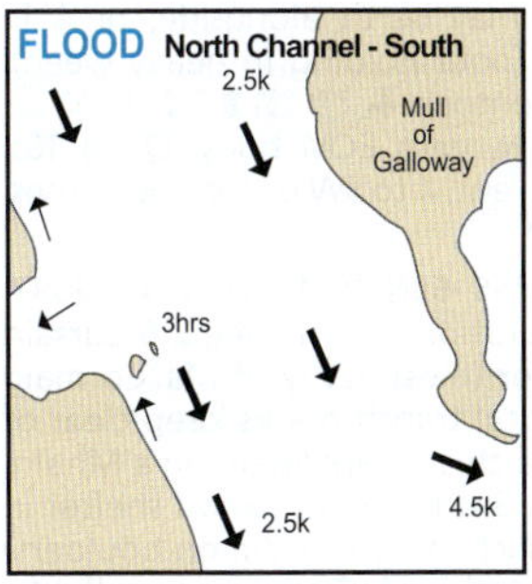

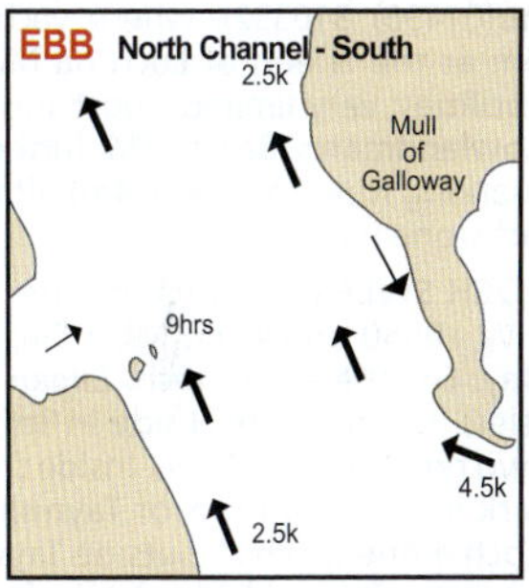

Races occur off Copeland Is. Morroch B, Money Hd and Mull of Logan. A race SSE of Crammag Hd is bad in wind against tide. Mull of Galloway. (lt) is a high (82m), steep-to headland with ***a dangerous race extending nearly 3M to S.*** *On E-going stream it extends NNE into Luce B; on W-going stream it extends SW and W. Give the race a wide berth, or pass close inshore at slack water Nps and calm weather. In SW wind >F4 against W-going stream, do not attempt inshore route.*◀

SCOTLAND – SW COAST

The Scares, 2 groups of rocks, lie at the mouth of Luce Bay. Luce Bay Firing Range (D402/403) marked by 12 DZ SPM lit buoys occupies the bay. For info on activity ☎(01776) 888792. Good ⚓ at E Tarbert Bay awaiting the tide around Mull of Galloway, or good shelter in drying harbour of Drummore.

▶ *A race forms off Burrow Hd in strong wind against tide.*◀

In Wigtown Bay the best ⚓ is in Isle of Whithorn Bay, but it is exposed to S. It is also possible to dry out in Garlieston.

A firing range, between the E side of ent to Kirkcudbright Bay and Abbey Hd, 4M to E, extends 14M offshore. If unable to avoid, cross at N end close inshore. For information contact range safety boat 'Gallovidian' on VHF Ch 16/73. The range operates 0900-1600LT Mon-Fri, but weekend and night firing may also occur.

HARBOURS AND ANCHORAGES IN COLONSAY, JURA, ISLAY AND THE SOUND OF JURA

SCALASAIG, Colonsay, **56°04′·14N 06°10′·86W**. AC 2169. HW +0542 on Dover; ML 2·2m. See 2.5. Conspic monument ½M SW of hbr. Beware group of rks N of pier hd marked by bn. 2 berths run by CMAL on N side of pier, inner end approx 2·5m. Inner hbr to SW of pier is safe, but dries. Ldg lts 262°, both FR 8/10m on pier. Also ⚓ clear of cable in **Loch Staosnaig**; SW of Rubha Dubh lt, Fl (2) WR 10s 8m 8/6M; shore-R-230°-W-337°-R-354°. Facilities: (all at ✉), Hotel ☎(01951) 200316, Dr (0951) 200328.

LOCH TARBERT, W Jura, **55°57′·69N 06°00′·06W**. AC 2169, 2481. Tides as Rubha A'Mhàil (N tip of Islay). See 2.5. HW –0540 on Dover; ML 2·1m; Duration 0600. Excellent shelter inside the loch, but subject to squalls in strong winds; ⚓ outside in Glenbatrick Bay in approx 6m in S winds, or at Bagh Gleann Righ Mor in approx 2m in N winds. To enter inner loch via Cumhann Beag, there are four pairs of ldg marks (W stones) at approx 120°, 150°, 077°, and 188°, the latter astern, to be used in sequence; pilot book required. There are no facilities.

PORT ASKAIG, Islay, **55°50′·87N 06°06′·26W**. AC 2168, 2481. HW +0610 on Dover; ML 1·2m. See 2.5. Hbr on W side of Sound of Islay. ⚓ close inshore in 4m or secure to ferry pier. Beware strong tide/eddies. ☆ FR at LB. Facilities: (on pier) ✉ ✕ Hotel ferries to Jura and Kintyre. Other ⚓s in the Sound at: Bunnahabhain (2M N); Whitefarland Bay, Jura, opp Caol Ila distillery; NW of Am Fraoch Eilean (S tip of Jura); Aros Bay, N of Ardmore Pt.

CRAIGHOUSE, SE Jura, **55°49′·99N 05°56′·31W**. AC 2168, 2481, 2396. HW +0600 on Dover; ML 0·5m; Duration 0640 np, 0530 sp. See 2.5. Good shelter, but squally in strong W winds with uncomfortable swell in ⚓ in winds from E–S. Enter between lit bn on SW end of Eilean nan Gabhar, Fl 5s 7m 8M vis 225°-010°, and unlit bn close SW. There are 16 Jura Dev Trust s (£10/night) N of pier (☎(01496) 810332), where yachts may berth alongside; or ⚓ in 5m at the N end of Loch na Mile (poor holding in heavy weed). Facilities: very limited, short stay pontoon ✉ ✕. **Lowlandman's Bay** is 1M further N, with ECM buoy, Q (3) 10s, marking Nine Foot Rk (2·4m) off the ent. ⚓ to SW of conspic houses, off stone jetty.

LOCH SWEEN, Argyll and Bute, **55°55′·69N 05°41′·26W**. AC 2397. HW +0550 on Dover; ML 1·5m; Duration = 0610. See 2.6 Carsaig Bay. Off the ent to loch, **Eilean Mòr** (most SW'ly of MacCormaig Isles) has tiny ⚓ on N side in 3m; local transit marks keep clear of two rks, 0·6m and 0·9m. Inside the loch, beware Sgeirean a'Mhain, a rk in mid-chan to S of Taynish Is, 3M from ent. Good shelter in Loch a Bhealaich (⚓ outside **Tayvallich** in approx 7m on boulders) or enter inner hbr to ⚓ W of central reef. There are no lights. Facilities: ✉ with ✕. Close to NE are ⚓s at **Caol Scotnish** and **Fairy Is**, the former obstructed by rks 3ca from ent.

WEST LOCH TARBERT, Argyll and Bute, (Kintyre), **55°45′N 05°36′W**. AC 2476. Tides as Gigha Sound, 2.5. Good shelter. Ent S of Eilean Traighe, Fl (2) R 5s, and NW of Dun Skeig, Q (2) 10s, where there is conspic conical hill (142m). Avoid shallows inshore to each side. Loch is lit for 5M by 3 bns, QG, QR and QG in sequence, up to Kennacraig ferry pier, 2FG (vert). PHM buoy, QR, is 2½ca NW of pier. Caution: many drying rks and fish farms outside the fairway and near head of loch. ⚓s are NE of Eilean Traighe (beware weed and ferry wash); near Rhu Pt, possible s; NE of Eilean dà Gallagain, and at loch hd by pier (ru). Tarbert (2.8) is 1·5M walk/bus.

GIGHA ISLAND, Argyll and Bute, **55°40′·6N 05°44′·0W**. AC 2168, 2475. HW +0600 on Dover; ML 0·9m; Duration 0530. See 2.5. **Ardminish Bay**: 23 Gigha Heritage Trust s in the centre (£10) 17 rated at 15t and 6 at 25t or ⚓ NE of Ferry Jetty. Refurbished pontoon and walkway for landing marked by seasonal lts Fl R 3s. Reefs extend off both points, the S'ly reef is marked by a NCM. Sgeir na h-Atho (Kiln Rk) NE of pontoon marked by ECM dries 1·5m. **Druimyeon Bay** is more sheltered in E'lies, but care needed entering from S. ⚓s sheltered from winds in Kilnaughton Bay, Port Mór (S–W), Bàgh na Dòirlinne (SE–S), W Tarbert Bay (NE). Caolas Gigalum (⚓ 50m SE of pier) is safe in all but NE-E winds. Beware many rks in Gigha Sound. Lts: Fl (2) 6s, on Gamhna Gigha (off NE tip); WCM buoy Fl (9) 15s marks Gigalum Rks, at S end of Gigha. **Ardminish** ☎(01583) 505254, ✉ ✕.

2.5 PORT ELLEN

Islay (Argyll and Bute) **55°37′·29N 06°12′·26W**

CHARTS AC 2168, 2476, 5611; Imray C64

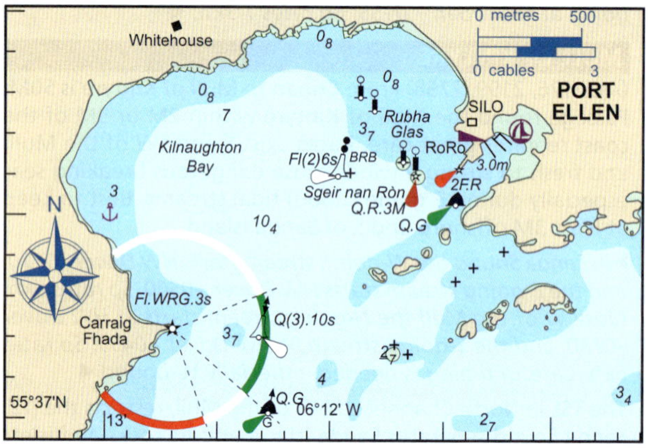

TIDES HW +0620 np, +0130 sp on Dover; ML 0·6. Sea level is much affected by the weather, rising by 1m in S/E gales; at nps the tide is sometimes diurnal and range negligible.

Standard Port OBAN (⟵)

Times				Height (metres)			
High Water		Low Water		MHWS	MHWN	MLWN	MLWS
0100	0700	0100	0800	4·0	2·9	1·8	0·7
1300	1900	1300	2000				
Differences PORT ELLEN (S Islay)							
–0530	–0050	–0045	–0530	–3·1	–2·1	–1·3	–0·4
SCALASAIG (E Colonsay)							
–0020	–0005	–0015	+0005	–0·3	–0·2	–0·3	0·0
GLENGARRISDALE BAY (N Jura)							
–0020	0000	–0010	0000	–0·4	–0·2	0·0	–0·2
CRAIGHOUSE (SE Jura)							
–0230	–0250	–0150	–0230	–3·0	–2·4	–1·3	–0·6
RUBHA A'MHÀIL (N Islay)							
–0020	0000	+0005	–0015	–0·3	–0·1	–0·3	–0·1
ARDNAVE POINT (NW Islay)							
–0035	+0010	0000	–0025	–0·4	–0·2	–0·3	–0·1
ORSAY ISLAND (SW Islay)							
–0110	–0110	–0040	–0040	–1·4	–0·6	–0·5	–0·2
BRUICHLADDICH (Islay, Loch Indaal)							
–0105	–0035	–0110	–0110	–1·8	–1·3	–0·4	+0·3
PORT ASKAIG (Sound of Islay)							
–0030	–0035	–0015	–0025	–1·8	–1·3	–0·7	–0·2
GIGHA SOUND (Sound of Jura)							
–0450	–0210	–0130	–0410	–2·8	–1·9	–1·3	–0·4
MACHRIHANISH							
–0520	–0350	–0340	–0540	Mean range 0·5 metres.			

SHELTER Good shelter on 2 of 3 pontoons (3m at MLWS), most NE'ly for shallow local boats. In S winds swell sets into the bay. In W'lies ⚓ in Kilnaughton Bay, N of Carraig Fhada lt ho; or 4M ENE at Loch-an-t-Sàilein.

NAVIGATION WPT 55°36′·69N 06°12′·06W, 326°/0·63M to Carraig Fhada lt ho. Beware Otter Rk 4M SE of hbr marked by ECM, rks on both sides of ent and in NE corner of bay. W of Rubha Glas rocks marked by 3 bns with reflective topmarks. Keep close to pier.

LIGHTS AND MARKS On W side 10 radio masts (103m) and Carraig Fhada lt ho (conspic), Fl WRG 3s 20m 8/6M; keep in W sector until past the SHM lt buoy. Inbound, Sgeir nan Ròn Bn Q R, dolphin off Ro-Ro Pier 2 FG (vert), SHM Iso G 2s and marina pontoon Fl G 4s. Dredged area around pier and pontoons area marked by buoys.

COMMUNICATIONS CGOC (02891) 463933. Moorings are run by local community – Marina ☎07464151200 portellenmarina.co.uk

FACILITIES **Marina** in bay, 60 inc 20, dredged to 3m, many on 10m fingers, £2 approx; (HO) wi-fi (☎300301). **Village** ✉ ✕.

2.6 CRINAN CANAL

Argyll and Bute **56°05′·50N 05°33′·38W** Crinan

CHARTS AC 2326, 2476, 5611; Imray C65, C63.

TIDES –0608 Dover; ML 2·1; Duration 0605; HW Crinan is at HW Oban –0045

Standard Port OBAN (⟵)

Times				Height (metres)			
High Water		Low Water		MHWS	MHWN	MLWN	MLWS
0100	0700	0100	0800	4·0	2·9	1·8	0·7
1300	1900	1300	2000				
Differences CARSAIG BAY (56°02′N 05°38′W)							
–0105	–0040	–0050	–0050	–2·1	–1·6	–1·0	–0·4

NOTE: In the Sound of Jura, S of Loch Crinan, the rise of tide occurs mainly during the 3½hrs after LW; the fall during the 3½ hrs after HW. At other times the changes in level are usually small and irregular.

SHELTER Complete shelter in canal basin; yachts are welcome. Good shelter in Crinan Hbr (E of Eilean da Mheinn) but full of moorings, contact Crinan Boatyard. Except in strong W/N winds, ⚓ E of the canal ent, clear of fairway or SW of Eilean da Mheinn. Good holding in Gallanach Bay on N side of L Crinan in about 3m.

NAVIGATION WPT 56°05′·70N 05°33′·64W, 146°/0·27M to Fl WG 3s lt. Beware Black Rock (2m high) in appr NE of ldg line 146° to dir Fl WG 3s lt.

CANAL Canal is 9M (14.5km) long with 15 locks and 7 opening bridges. Transit time is at least 6hrs, observing the 4kn speed limit. Entry at all tides. Max LOA: 26·82m, 6.09m beam, 2·7m draught (add 0.10m to salt water draught. If >2.2m contact Canal Office or Sea Locks 24hrs in advance to confirm canal level will allow passage – there may be some delay to raise water levels) mast 28.95m. The canal operates Mon-Fri in winter months increasing to 6/7 days in peak season. Contact Crinan Canal Office for timings or consult www.scottishcanals.co.uk. Periods of closure may be expected during winter months. It is closed between Christmas and New Year. Long warps and fenders are essential; sea locks can be turbulent at low tide and care is to be taken handling warps – always take a turn round a suitable cleat. Do not pump out bilges or heads in the canal. Water points are supplied but not hoses. Bellanoch pontoons / moorings are reserved for long term berth holders and should not be used by those in transit.

BOAT SAFETY SCHEME Transit craft may be subject to random safety checks on gas systems. £1M 3rd party insurance is required. See also 1.16.

LIGHTS AND MARKS Crinan Hotel is conspic W bldg. A conspic chy, 3ca SW of hotel, leads 187° into Crinan Hbr. E of sea-lock: Dir Fl WG 3s 8m 4M, vis 114°-W-146°-G-280°. Ent: 2 FG (vert) and 2FR (vert).

COMMUNICATIONS (Code 01546) Dr 462001. Canal Office 603210 (HO). Sea lock 830285 (for advice at w/e and if no response to VHF – staff carry phone).
VHF Ch **74** 16 only at sea locks, Ch 12.

FACILITIES **Canal Office** (Mon-Fri), www.scottishcanals.co.uk. All fees are under review; contact office for details. *Skippers Guide* is essential reading; **Sea Basin** (overnight rate available). Use shore toilets, not yacht heads, whilst in canal.

Services Crinan Boatyard www.crinanboatyard.co.uk ☎830232, (5t) ✕.

Village ✕ (Ardrishaig), ⇌ (Oban), ✈ (Glasgow).

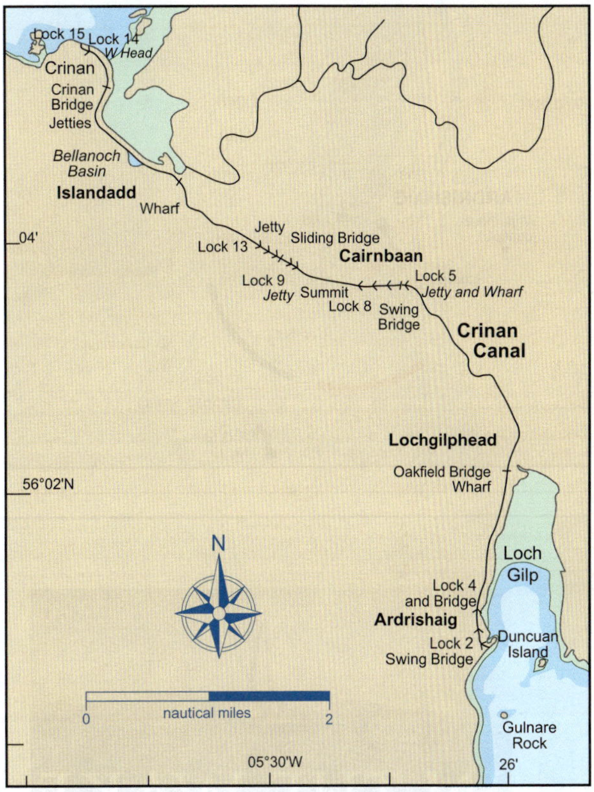

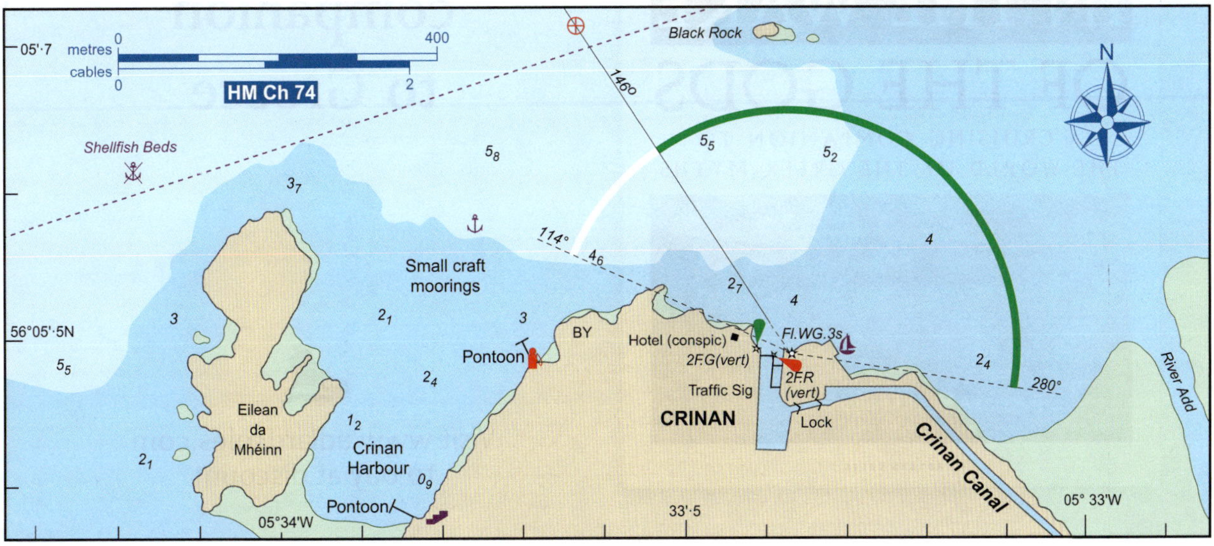

2.7 ARDRISHAIG

Argyll and Bute **56°00′·78N 05°26′·62W**

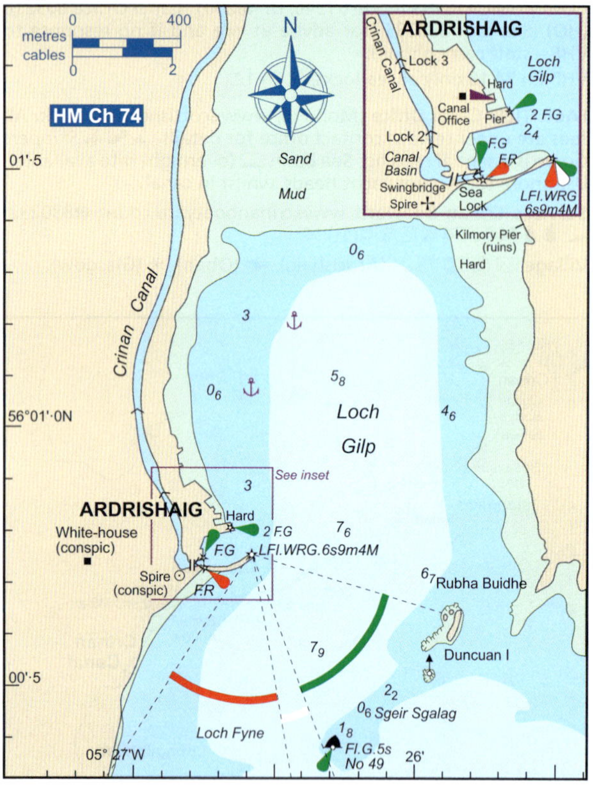

CHARTS AC 2131, 2381, 5610; Imray C63, 2900

TIDES +0120 Dover; ML 1·9; Duration 0640

Standard Port GREENOCK (⟶)

Times				Height (metres)			
High Water		Low Water		MHWS	MHWN	MLWN	MLWS
0000	0600	0000	0600	3·4	2·8	1·0	0·3
1200	1800	1200	1800				
Differences ARDRISHAIG							
+0006	+0006	-0015	+0020	0·0	0·0	+0·1	–0·1
INVERARAY							
+0011	+0011	+0034	+0034	–0·1	+0·1	–0·5	–0·2

SHELTER Hbr is sheltered except from strong E'lies; do not berth on pier or ⚓ due to commercial vessels H24. Sea lock into the Crinan Canal is usually left open, with a waiting pontoon outside the lock, in restricted depth, for use in fair weather only. Access at all tides. Complete shelter in the canal basin, or beyond lock No 2. Also ⚓ 2ca N of hbr, off the W shore of L Gilp, but S'ly gales raise a significant swell. Head of Loch dries for nearly 1M.

NAVIGATION WPT No 48 PHM buoy, Fl R 4s, 56°00′·18N 05°26′·31W, 345°/0·6M to bkwtr lt. Dangerous drying rocks to E of appr chan are marked by No 49 Fl.G.5s SHM buoy.

LIGHTS AND MARKS Conspic W Ho on with block of flats leads 315° between Nos 48 and 49 buoys. Bkwtr lt, L Fl WRG 6s, W339°-350°. Pier is floodlit. Other lights as plan.

COMMUNICATIONS (Code 01546) Dr 462001. Canal Office 603210 (Mon-Fri); Sea lock 602458.

VHF Ch **74** 16.

FACILITIES **Pier/Hbr** ☎603210, (fees under review).

Crinan Canal www.scottishcanals.co.uk

Sea Lock ☎602458; dues, see 2.6.

Services

Village (Oban), ✈ (Glasgow or Campbeltown).

2.8 TARBERT

Entrance **55°52'·05N 05°24'·22W**

CHARTS AC 2131, 2381, 5610; Imray C63, 2900

TIDES +0120 Dover; ML 1·9; Duration 0640

Standard Port GREENOCK (⟶)

Times				Height (metres)			
High Water		Low Water		MHWS	MHWN	MLWN	MLWS
0000	0600	0000	0600	3·4	2·8	1·0	0·3
1200	1800	1200	1800				
Differences EAST LOCH TARBERT							
−0005	−0005	0000	−0005	+0·2	+0·1	0·0	0·0

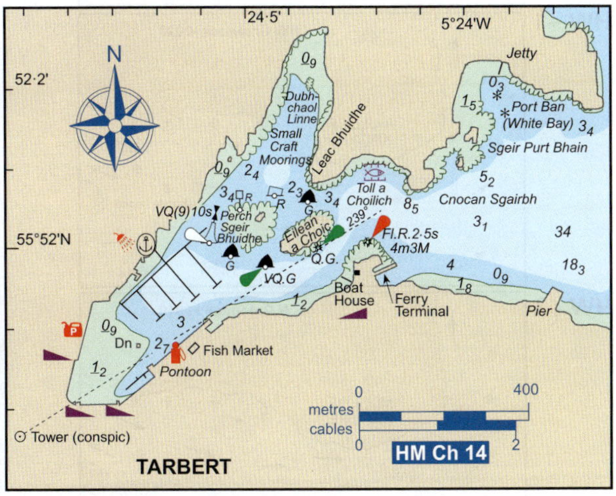

SHELTER Very good in all weathers on new pontoons. Access H24. 00 inc ⓥ on hammerheads, pontoons A and G (call on VHF Ch 14 for berth); only use Fish Quay if directed by HM.

NAVIGATION WPT 55°52'·02N 05°23'·03W, 270°/0·7M to Fl R 2·5s lt. Ent is 60m wide and well marked. Cock Isle divides the ent in half: Main hbr to the S, Buteman's Hole to the N, where ⚓s are fouled by heavy moorings and lost chains. Speed limit 3kn.

LIGHTS AND MARKS Outer ldg lts 252° to S ent: Fl R 2·5s on with Cock Is lt QG. Inner ldg line 239°: same QG, G column, on with conspic ✠ tr. Note: The W sector, 065°-078°, of Eilean na Beithe ☆, Fl WRG 3s 7m 5M (on E shore of Lower Loch Fyne), could be used to position for the initial appr to Tarbert.

COMMUNICATIONS (Code 01880) HM www. tarbertharbour.co.uk ☎820344, Ⓗ (01546) 602323.
VHF Ch **14** (0900-1700LT).

FACILITIES **Yacht Berthing Facility**, www.tarbertharbour.co.uk, ⓥs £15 < 12m, £2·80.

Fish Quay (Mon-Fri 0800-1800); **Tarbert YC**.

Town (0800-1800) ACA, ⓑ (bus to Glasgow), ✈ (Glasgow/Campbeltown).

ANCHORAGES IN LOCH FYNE

• ***Beware discarded wires on seabed throughout the area.***

In Lower L Fyne there is a ⓥ at Kilfinan Bay, ☎(01700) 821201. In Upper Loch Fyne: 10ⓥs for patrons of the Oyster Bar at Cairndow 6M N of Inverary; ⚓ SSW of pier in 4m or dry out NW of the pier; (on pier), bus to Glasgow. On NW bank at Port Ann, Loch Gair, Minard Bay and Union Bay; and on SE bank at Otter Ferry, Sailors' Bothy (Otter Ferry Pier Association) with dinghy pontoon WC. 15ⓥs at Oyster Catcher uncomfortable swell in S/SW winds, Strachur Bay (pontoon and 5ⓥs off Creggans Inn, ☎(01369) 860279) and St Catherine's.

2.9 PORTAVADIE

55°52'·23N 05°18'·98W

CHARTS AC 2131, 2381, 5610; Imray C63, 2900

TIDES +0120 Dover; ML 1·9; Duration 0640

Standard Port GREENOCK (⟶)

Times				Height (metres)			
High Water		Low Water		MHWS	MHWN	MLWN	MLWS
0000	0600	0000	0600	3·4	2·8	1·0	0·3
1200	1800	1200	1800				
Differences PORTAVADIE							
−0005	−0005	0000	−0005	+0·2	+0·1	0·0	0·0

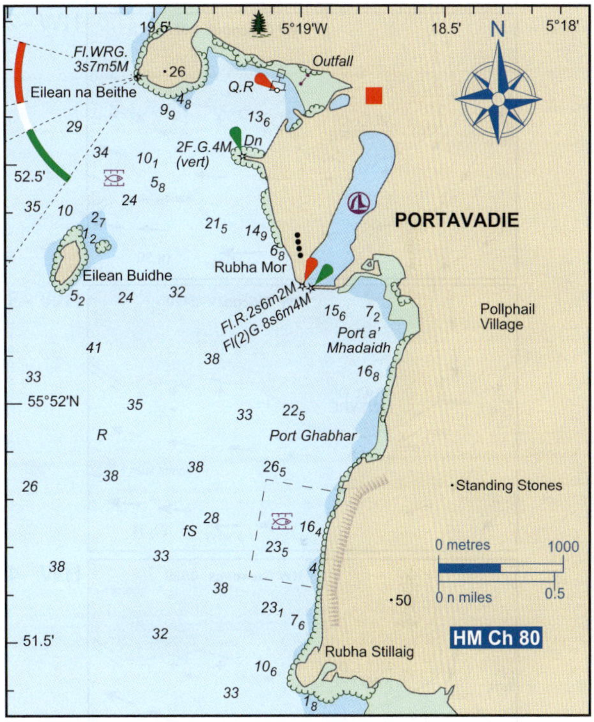

SHELTER Very good in a well protected deep water facility. Access H24. ⓥ on pontoons with assistance available (call on VHF Ch 80). If arriving after hours use S, or lie alongside concrete b'water.

NAVIGATION WPT 55°52'·00N 05°19'·20W, 027°/0·27M to entrance. When approaching from north pass SW of Eilean Buidhe which has fish farm to the NE. Inshore passage may be used with local knowledge. From the S Clear Sgat Mor and round Rubha Stillaig avoiding fish farm inshore. Harbour has a narrow entrance between lit bwaters off which is a 4m deep bar. Speed limit 3kn.

LIGHTS AND MARKS Eilean na Beithe to North Fl WRG 3s 7m 5M 036°-G-065°-W-078°-R-106° marks access to Glenan Bay and inshore passage NE of Eilean Buidhe. Sgat Mor Fl 3s 9m 12M. Entrance marked by beacons PH Fl R 2s 6m 2M; SH Fl (2) G 8s 6m 4M.

COMMUNICATIONS. (01700) .
VHF Ch **80** (0900-1700LT).

FACILITIES **Marina**, www.portavadiemarina.com ☎811075, 230 inc 40ⓥ £3·30, (12t) wi-fi, small shop, ✈ (Glasgow). Other local shops at Kames (2.5M).

ADJACENT ANCHORAGES

Glenan Bay to NW ⚓ in 15m steep to bay open to SW.

Asgog B 1.5M to S entered between Sgat Mor and Sgat Beag. ⚓ in 15M to E of Eilean Aoidhe.

2.10 TIDAL STREAMS AROUND THE MULL OF KINTYRE

HW –1

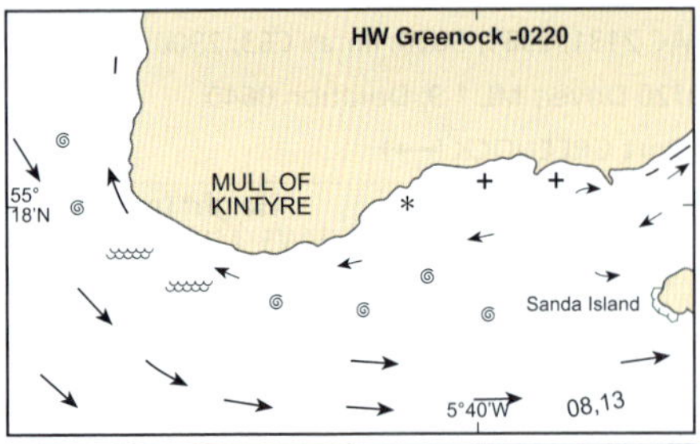

HW –2

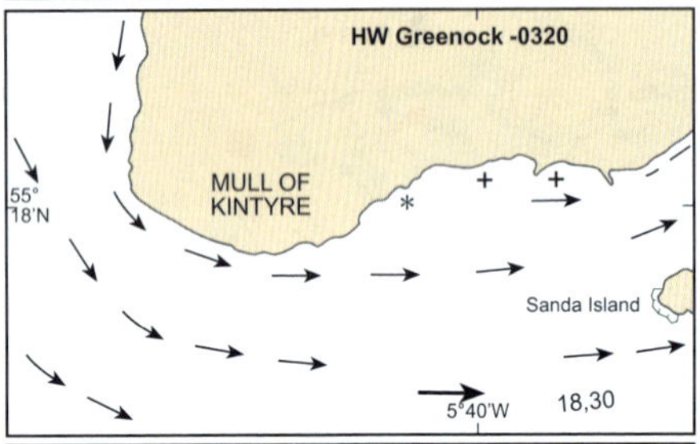

HW –3

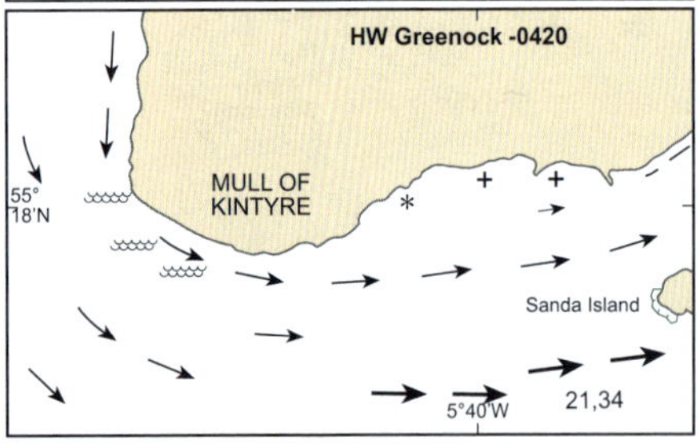

HW –4

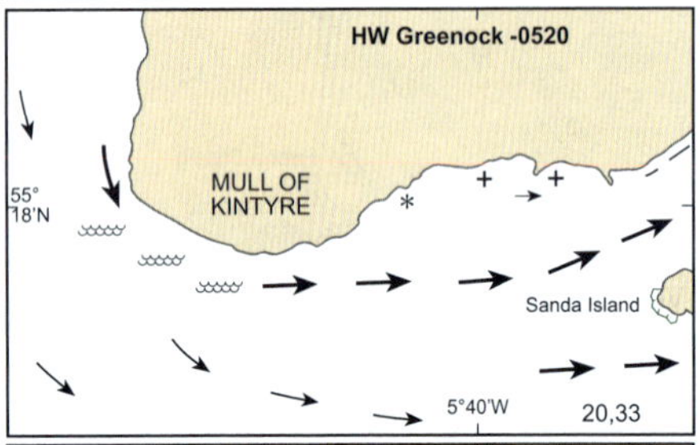

HW –5

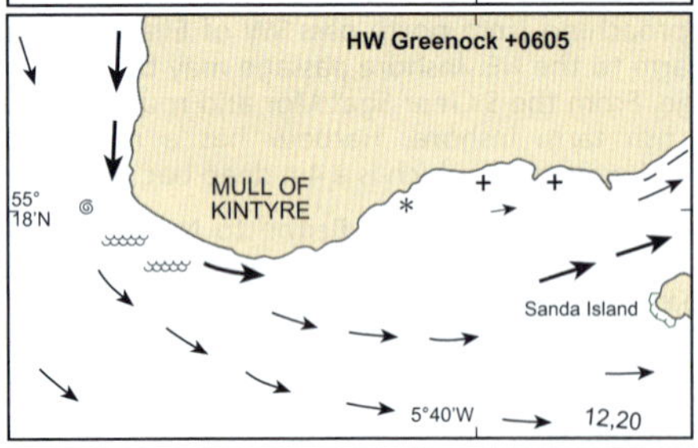

HW –6

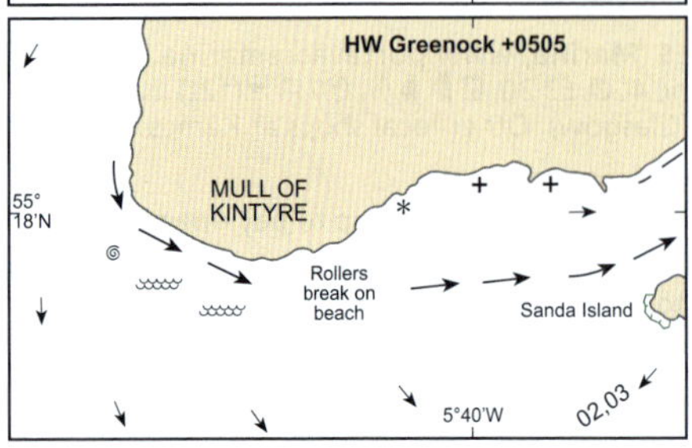

HW DOVER

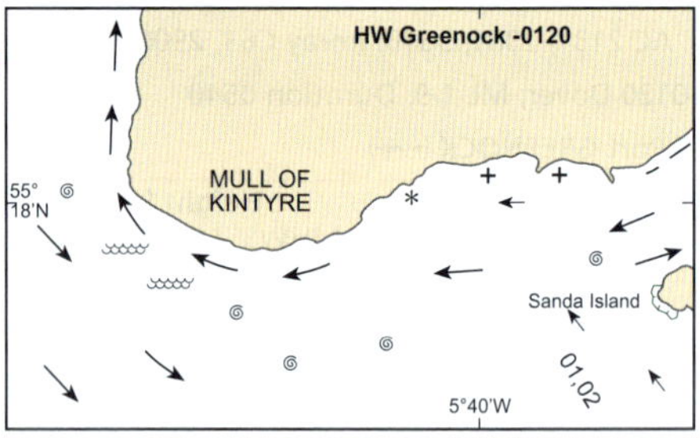

HW +1

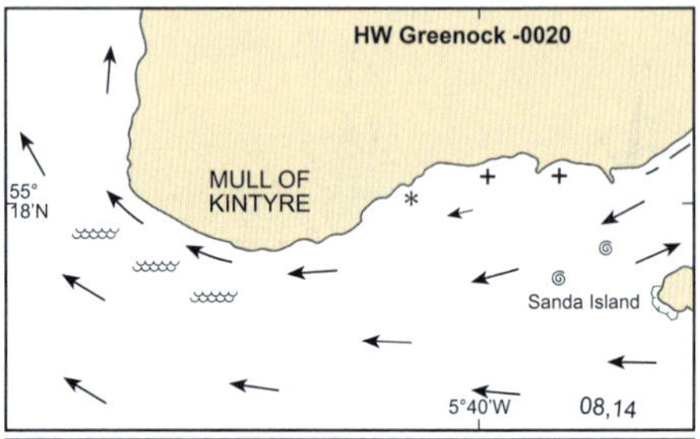

HW +2

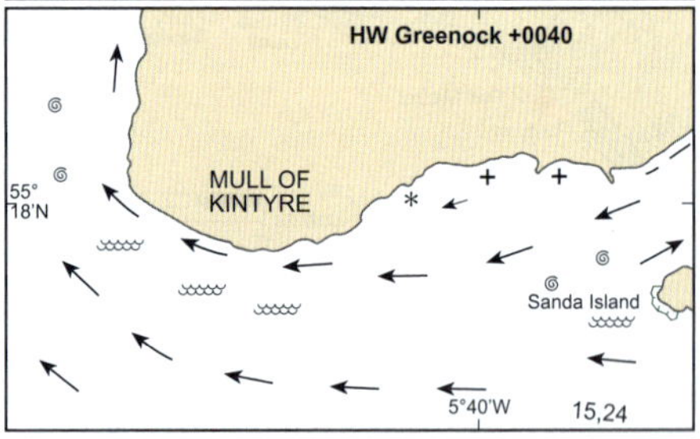

HW +3

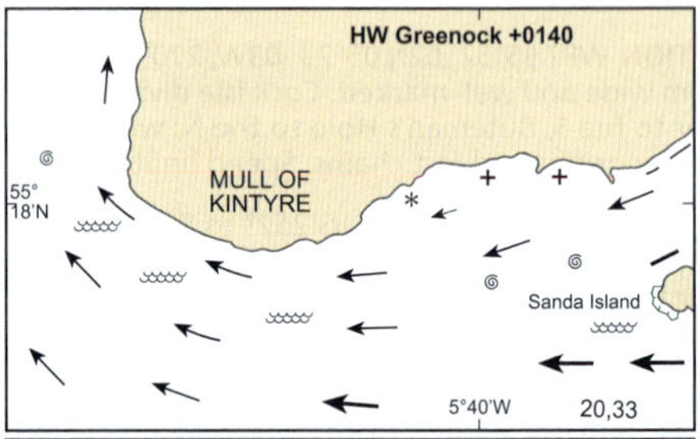

HW +4

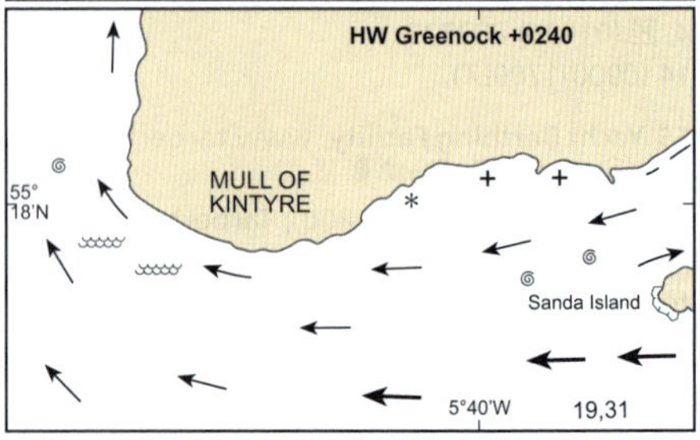

HW +5

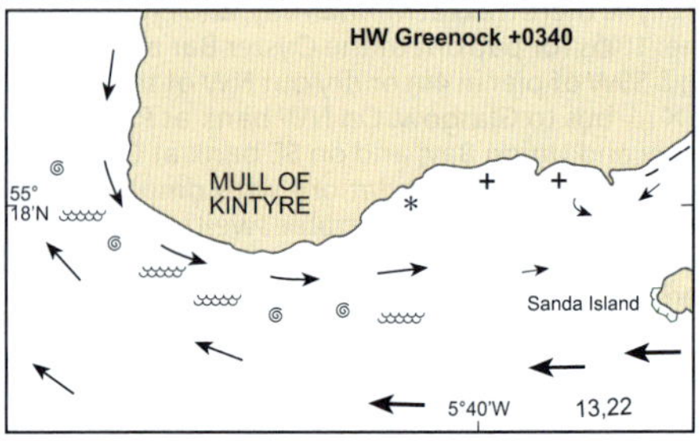

2.11 CAMPBELTOWN

Argyll & Bute **55°25'·90N 05°32'·56W** Hbr ent ❀❀❀◊◊✿✿✿

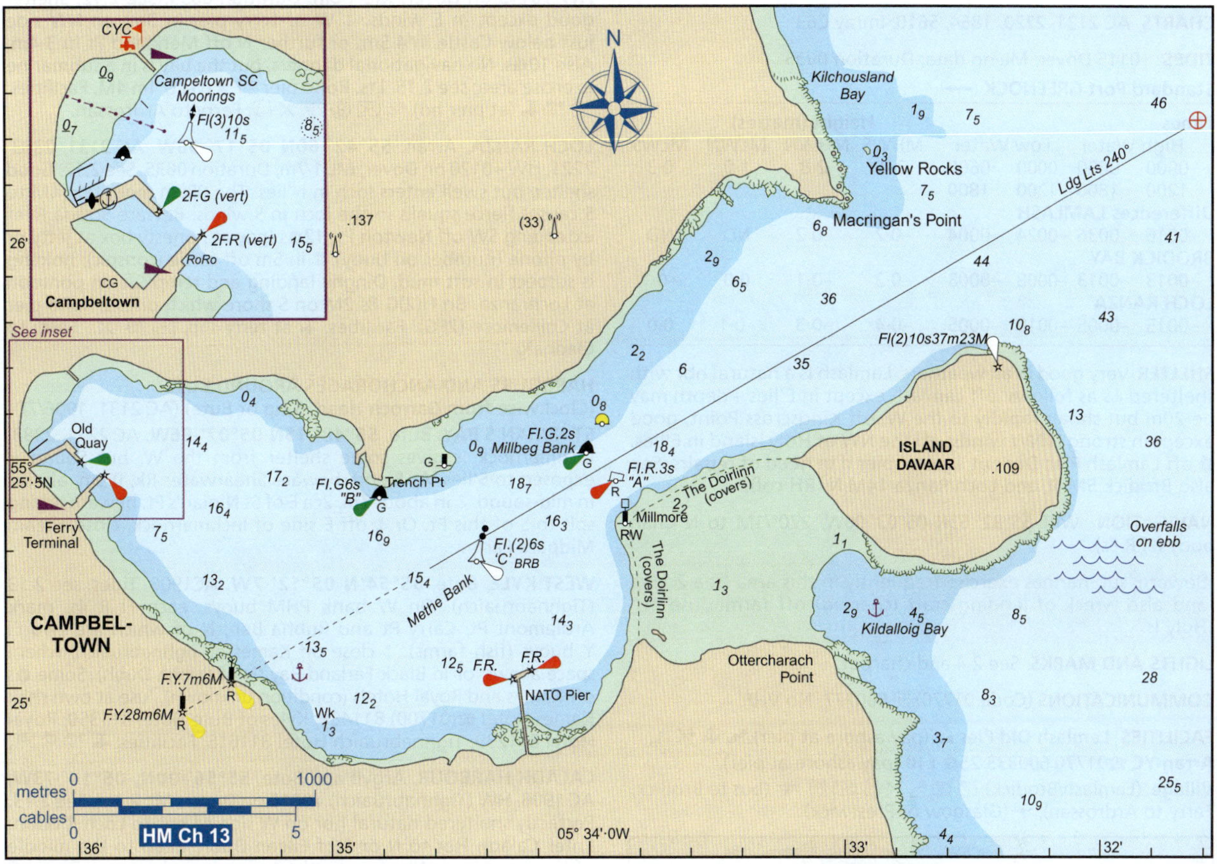

CHARTS AC 2126, 1864, 5610; Imray C63

TIDES +0125 Dover; ML 1·8; Duration 0630

Standard Port GREENOCK (⟶)

Times				Height (metres)			
High Water		Low Water		MHWS	MHWN	MLWN	MLWS
0000	0600	0000	0600	3·4	2·8	1·0	0·3
1200	1800	1200	1800				
Differences *CAMPBELTOWN*							
–0025	*–0005*	*–0015*	*+0005*	*–0·5*	*–0·3*	*+0·1*	*+0·2*
CARRADALE BAY							
–0015	–0005	–0005	+0005	–0·3	–0·2	+0·1	+0·1
SOUTHEND, (Mull of Kintyre)							
–0030	–0010	+0005	+0035	–1·3	–1·2	–0·5	–0·2

SHELTER Good, but gusts off the hills in strong SW'lies. Main harbour dredged to 9m for commercial vessels. Yacht pontoon dredged 3·0m is close NW of Old Quay and gives excellent sheltered berthing with some swell on outside in strong E'ly winds. Yachts >12m LOA should notify ETA to the berthing master by ☎. Good ⚓ on S side of loch, E of front leading light. ⚓ possible in N of harbour, but is exposed to SE winds. Holding is poor and great care must be taken not to foul local moorings (large Y buoys). S of Island Davaar temp ⚓ in Kildalloig Bay, but no access to the loch.

NAVIGATION WPT 55°26'·24N 05°31'·61W, 240°/1·4M to first chan buoys. The ent is easily identified by radio masts N and NE of Trench Pt and conspic lt ho on N tip of Island Davaar off which streams are strong (4kn sp). Caution: The Doirlinn, a bank drying 2·5m which covers at HW, is close S of the ldg line.

LIGHTS AND MARKS See 2.4 and chartlet. Otterard Rk (3·8m depth, off chartlet, 1·5M NNE of Island Davaar), is marked by ECM lt buoy. Small, unlit SHM guards shallows on marina approach.

COMMUNICATIONS (Code 01586) Dr 552105 HM 552552 mobile 07825 732862, Asst HM mobile 07500 294920.

VHF Ch 13 16 (Mon-Fri 0900-1700).

FACILITIES Yacht pontoon ☎07798 524821, ⛴ £1·50/m (20+30Ⓥ) £3·00/m, ⛽ WC on pier, keypad entry, payment to berthing master or at honesty box using payment envelopes in toilet block.

Old Quay D (and by cans from across road, opposite pontoon), ⛽ LB.

Ferry Terminal used by commercial vessels. No berthing alongside without HM's permission. The attached public slipway has a drying out berth (with timber keel blocks and upright leaning posts) for FVs and yachts, ⛽.

Campbeltown SC ⛴ (dinghies), regular racing.

Town Ⓔ (10t) ACA, (2) ✕ ✉ Ⓑ; WC about 100m from yacht pontoon (keypad, number displayed on pontoon). Bus 3/day to Glasgow, ✈ twice daily to Glasgow, (nearest ⇄ Arrochar, 90 miles N by road). Car hire/taxi.

ADJACENT ANCHORAGE IN KILBRANNAN SOUND

CARRADALE BAY, Argyll and Bute, **55°34'·40N 05°28'·66W**. AC 5610, 2131, HW+0115 on Dover. ML 1·8m. See 2.11. Good ⚓ 1 M S in 7m off Torrisdale Castle in SW corner, or in middle of bay in 5m. Beware shoal on S edge of Torrisdale Bay. In N & E winds ⚓ in NE corner of bay, W of Carradale Pt. 3ca E of this Pt, a PHM buoy Fl (2) R 12s marks Crubon Rk.

In S and E winds a swell sets into bay, when good shelter can be found 1M N in **Carradale Harbour** (Port Crannaich); use 4Ⓥ immediately to N or ⚓ 100m N of Hbr. Bkwtr lt, Fl R 10s 5m 6M. Call HM Campbeltown for overnight berth, £10 pay in honesty box. Facilities: ⛴ to SW of hbr, ⛽ on pier, ✉ ✕.

2.12 LAMLASH

Isle of Arran, N Ayrshire **55°32'·00N 05°07'·06W**

CHARTS AC 2131, 2220, 1864, 5610; Imray C63

TIDES +0115 Dover; ML no data; Duration 0635

Standard Port GREENOCK (⟶)

Times				Height (metres)			
High Water		Low Water		MHWS	MHWN	MLWN	MLWS
0000	0600	0000	0600	3·4	2·8	1·0	0·3
1200	1800	1200	1800				
Differences LAMLASH							
–0016	–0036	–0024	–0004	–0·2	–0·2	ND	ND
BRODICK BAY							
–0013	–0013	–0008	–0008	–0·2	–0·1	0·0	+0·1
LOCH RANZA							
–0015	–0005	–0010	–0005	–0·4	–0·3	–0·1	0·0

SHELTER Very good in all weathers. Lamlash is a natural hbr with sheltered ⚓s as follows: off Lamlash except in E'lies – depth may be 20m but shoals rapidly to the W; off Kingscross Point, good except in strong N/NW winds; off the NW of Holy Island in E'lies. Ⓥ off Lamlash Pier. Dry out against pier if in need of repairs. See also Brodick 5M N, and Loch Ranza 14M N (RH col).

NAVIGATION WPT 55°32'·63N 05°03'·06W, 270°/1M to N Chan buoy (Fl R 6s).

Beware: submarines exercise frequently in this area (see 2.15), and also wreck of landing craft (charted) off farmhouse on Holy Is.

LIGHTS AND MARKS See 2.4 and chartlet.

COMMUNICATIONS (Code 01770) Ⓗ 600777. No VHF.

FACILITIES **Lamlash Old Pier** (pay ashore at pier). **Arran YC** ☎01770 600333 25Ⓥ £10 (pay ashore at pier). **Village** (Lamlash/Brodick) (bus to Brodick, Ferry to Ardrossan), ✈ (Glasgow or Prestwick).

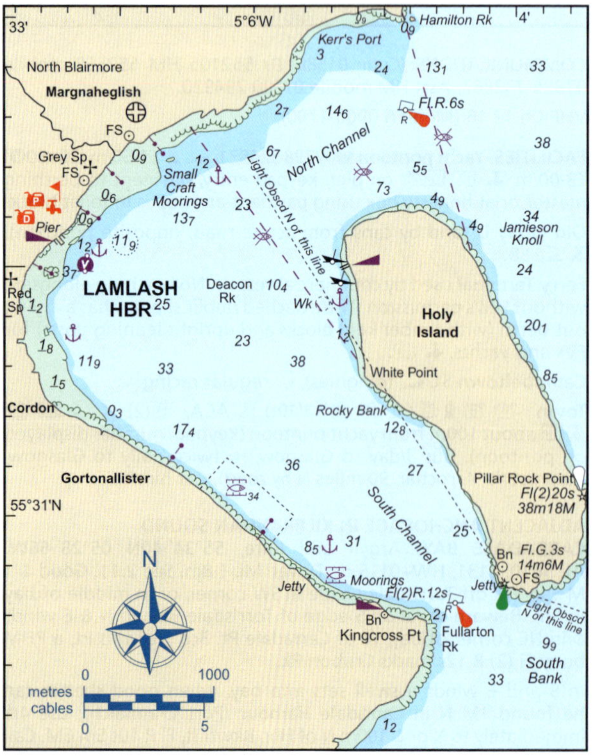

OTHER HARBOURS ON ARRAN (AC 2724, 2131, 2126)

BRODICK, Arran, **55°35'·50N 05°08'·66W**. AC 2131, 2220, 1864. HW +0115 on Dover; ML 1·8m; Duration 0635. See 2.12. Shelter good except in E winds. ⚓ W of ferry pier in 3m; on NW side just below Castle in 4·5m, or further N off Merkland Pt in 3-4m. Also 10Ⓥs. No navigational dangers, but the bay is in a submarine exercise area; see 2.15. Lts: RoRo pier 2 F R (vert) 4m 4M. Facilities: (at pier hd) Ⓑ. Ferry to Ardrossan.

LOCH RANZA, Arran, **55°42'·60N 05°17'·96W**. AC 2131, 2383, 2221. HW +0120 on Dover; ML 1·7m; Duration 0635. See 2.12. Good shelter, but swell enters loch in N'lies. The 850m mountain 4M to S causes fierce squalls in the loch in S winds. Beware Screda Reef extending SW off Newton Pt. 12Ⓥs (pay at honesty box at jetty or by phone (number on buoy). ⚓ in 5m off castle (conspic); holding is suspect in soft mud. Dinghy landing and temp on pontoon at Lochranza. Bn Fl(2)G 8s 2M on S shore which dries.2 RoRo pier at Coillemore (2FG). Facilities: at ferry slip, . Ferry to Claonaig.

HARBOURS AND ANCHORAGES AROUND BUTE

(Clockwise from Garroch Head, S tip of Bute) (AC 2131, 1906/7)

ST NINIAN'S BAY, Bute, **55°48'·15N 05°07'·86W**. AC 2221, 2383. Inchmarnock Is gives some shelter from the W, but Sound is exposed to S'lies. At S end, beware Shearwater Rk, 0·9m, almost in mid-sound. ⚓ in about 7m, 2ca E of St Ninian's Pt; beware drying spit to S of this Pt. Or ⚓ off E side of Inchmarnock, close abeam Midpark Farm.

WEST KYLE, Bute, **55°54'N 05°12'·7W**. AC1906. Tides, see 2.13 (Tighnabruaich). On W bank PHM buoys, each Fl R 4s, mark Ardlamont Pt, Carry Pt and Rubha Ban; N of which are two Fl Y buoys (fish farms). ⚓ close off Kames or Tighnabruaich, where space allows; or in Black Farland Bay (N of Rubha Dubh). Some Ⓥs off Kames and Royal Hotels (condition unknown), 'use at own risk': Kames Hotel ☎(01700) 811489; Kyles of Bute Hotel 811350; Royal Hotel 811239; Tighnabruaich Hotel 811615. Facilities: .

CALADH HARBOUR, Argyll and Bute, **55°56'·00N, 05°11'·73W**. AC 1906. HW (Tighnabruaich) +0015 on Dover; ML 2·1m. See 2.13. Perfectly sheltered natural hbr on W side of ent to Loch Riddon. Enter Caladh Hbr to N or S of Eilean Dubh; keep to the middle of the S passage. When using the N ent, keep between R and G bns to clear a drying rk marked by perch. ⚓ in the middle of hbr clear of moorings. No facilities/stores or shore access in hbr; see West Kyle above.

LOCH RIDDON, Argyll and Bute, **55°57'N 05°11'·6W**. AC 1906. Tides, see 2.13. Water is deep for 1·3M N of Caladh and shore is steep-to; upper 1·5M of loch dries. ⚓ on W side close N of Ormidale pier; on E side at Salthouse; off Eilean Dearg (One Tree Is); and at NW corner of Fearnoch Bay.

BURNT ISLANDS, Bute, **55°55'·76N 05°10'·39W**. AC 1906. Tides, see 2.16. The three islands (Eilean Mor, Fraoich and Buidhe) straddle the East Kyle. There are 2 channels: North, between Buidhe and the other 2 islets, is narrow, short and marked by 2 SHM buoys (the NW'ly one is Fl G 3s), and one PHM buoy, Fl R 2s. South chan lies between Bute and Fraoich/Mor; it is unlit, but marked by 2 lateral buoys and a NCM (bn). Depths may be less than charted. A SHM buoy, Fl G 3s, is off Rubha a' Bhodaich, 4ca ESE. Direction of buoyage is to SE. Sp streams reach 5kn in N Chan and 3kn in S Chan. ⚓ in Wreck Bay, Balnakailly Bay or in the lee of Buidhe and Mor in W'lies; also W of Colintraive Pt, clear of ferry and cables. There are 6Ⓥs north of ferry slip, owned by and reserved for customers of Colintraive Hotel ☎(01700) 841207.

KILCHATTAN BAY, Bute, **55°45'N 05°01'·1W**. AC 1907. Bay is deep, but dries 3ca off the W shore. Temp ⚓s only in offshore winds: off the village on SW side, or on N side near Kerrytonlia Pt. Rubh' an Eun Lt, Fl R 6s, is 1·1M to SSE. Facilities: bus to Rothesay.

2.13 ROTHESAY

Isle of Bute, Argyll and Bute **55°50′·32N 05°03′·08W**

CHARTS AC 2131, 1907, 1906, 1867, 5610; Imray C63, 2900

TIDES +0100 Dover; ML 1·9; Duration 0640

Standard Port GREENOCK (⟶)

Times				Height (metres)			
High Water		Low Water		MHWS	MHWN	MLWN	MLWS
0000	0600	0000	0600	3·4	2·8	1·0	0·3
1200	1800	1200	1800				
Differences ROTHESAY BAY							
–0020	–0015	–0010	–0002	+0·2	+0·2	+0·2	+0·2
RUBHA A'BHODAICH (Burnt Is)							
–0020	–0010	–0007	–0007	–0·2	–0·1	+0·2	+0·2
TIGHNABRUAICH							
+0007	–0010	–0002	–0015	0·0	+0·2	+0·4	+0·5

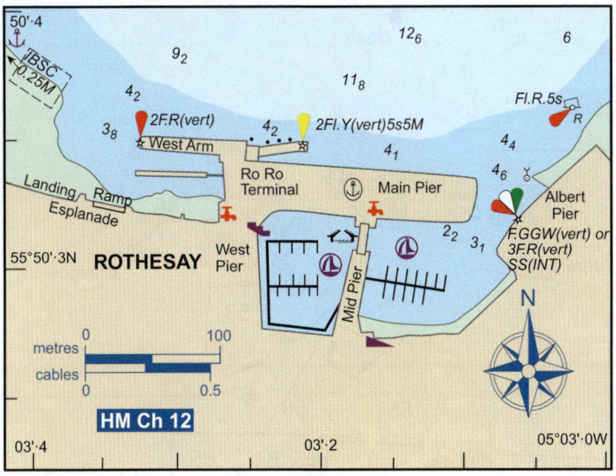

SHELTER Good in Outer and Inner Harbours (max 2m draught and very limited space for LOA > 40ft), but beware very strong easterly flow towards the rocks on the E side of the harbour and swell in outer hbr due to wash during ferry manoeuvres. No berthing on north and east faces of Main Pier, or on pontoon S of West Arm. Good ⚓ off Isle of Bute SC in west side of bay. Exposed to N/NE; **Port Bannatyne Marina** (Kames Bay) offers better shelter.

NAVIGATION WPT 55°51′·00N 05°02′·76W, 194°/0·69M to Outer hbr ent. From E keep 1ca off Bogany Pt PHM buoy, Fl R 4s. Call HM for bridge openings to Inner Harbour. Entry/exit to/from hbr controlled by traffic lights. Extreme care needed; very limited room to manoeuvre.

LIGHTS AND MARKS Lts as chartlet, hard to see against shore lts. Conspicuous church spire leads 190° to outer harbour. Port Sigs:

● (3 vert) = Harbour closed to all traffic movements.

● (2 vert) + ○ = Harbour open.

COMMUNICATIONS (Code 01700) Dr 503985; Ⓗ 503938. HM 503842; Bute Berthing Co mob 07799 724225.
Rothesay Harbour Ch **12** 16; *Bute Berthing* **M**.

FACILITIES 68 ⊆ ⓥ (Bute Berthing Co) call ahead for availability. £2·60/m, short stay £6, on Pier; by arrangement weekdays (min 200 galls).

Town (Wed – early closing) (closes 1800) @(0900-1700) ✉ Ⓑ ✕ ⇌ (ferry to Wemyss Bay) ✈(Glasgow). Ferries to Wemyss Bay and Skelmorlie N.

2.14 PORT BANNATYNE

Isle of Bute, Argyll and Bute **55°51′·75N 05°05′·17W**

CHARTS AC 2131, 1907, 1906, 1867, 5610; Imray C63, 2900

TIDES As for Rothesay

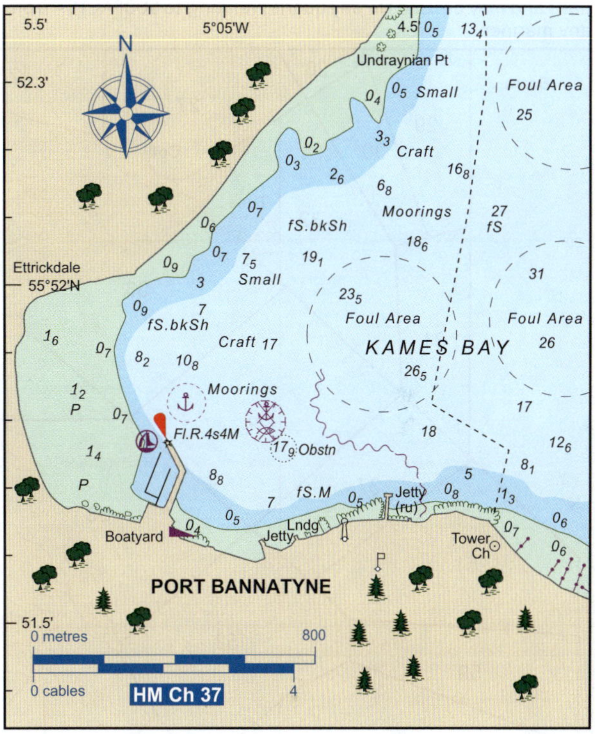

SHELTER Well sheltered from westerly winds and protected by stone breakwater. Marina situated in SW corner of Kames Bay provides secure alonside berth in 2.4m. Alternatively ⚓ in 11m to NE of b'water clear of small craft along N shore. moorings NE of marina – beware sunken fishing boat. Beware drying rks 1ca off Ardbeg Pt, and shoal water, marked by a row of piles, close W of marina breakwater.

NAVIGATION WPT 55°52′·00N 05°04′·00W, 252°/0·7M to marina entrance, which is accessible at all states of the tide. Approach marina keeping at least 20m clear of the end of the breakwater. Avoid no ⚓/fishing areas to ENE of breakwater.

LIGHTS AND MARKS Breakwater lt Fl R 4s 2M.

COMMUNICATIONS (Code 01700) Ⓗ 503938.
Marina VHF Ch 37 (M1).

FACILITIES **Marina**, www.portbannatynemarina.co.uk, ☎503116, 105⊆ inc ⓥ in 2·5m, £2·60/m, £6 for short stay (4hrs) ✕ wi-fi.

Port Boatyard ☎502719, Ⓔ (25t).

Town ✉ ✕ bus to Rothesay.

GREAT CUMBRAE ISLAND

MILLPORT, Great Cumbrae, N Ayrshire, **55°45′·00N 04°55′·82W**. AC 5610, 1867, 1907. HW +0100 on Dover; ML 1·9m; Duration 0640. See 2.20. Good shelter, except in S'lies. ⚓ in approx 3m S of pier or E of the Eileans. 12 Ⓜs 1½ca SSE of pier. Ldg marks: pier hd on with ✠ twr 333°; or ldg lts 333°, both FR 7/9m 5M, between the Spoig and the Eileans, QG. Unmarked, drying rk is close E of ldg line. HM ☎(01475) 530826.

Town ✉ ✕.

SW Scotland

2.15 SUBMARINE EXERCISE AREAS

Submarines keep a constant listening watch on Ch 16. Submarines on the surface comply strictly with IRPCS; submarines at periscope depth will not close to within 1500 yds of a FV without her express agreement.

A 'Fisherman's hotline' (☎(01436) 677201) is available on a 24hr basis and may be used for any queries relating to SUBFACTS – from any mariner.

SUBFACTS broadcasts detail submarine activity in the exercise areas between Barra and the Isle of Man. They are transmitted by CGOC Belfast at 0710 and 1910 on a specified VHF Ch after an initial announcement on Ch 16.

The areas are referred to by the names given in the table for Areas 1–25 (North of Mull), see 1.8.

General information on SUBFACTS is also broadcast twice daily at 0620 and 1820 UT on Navtex.

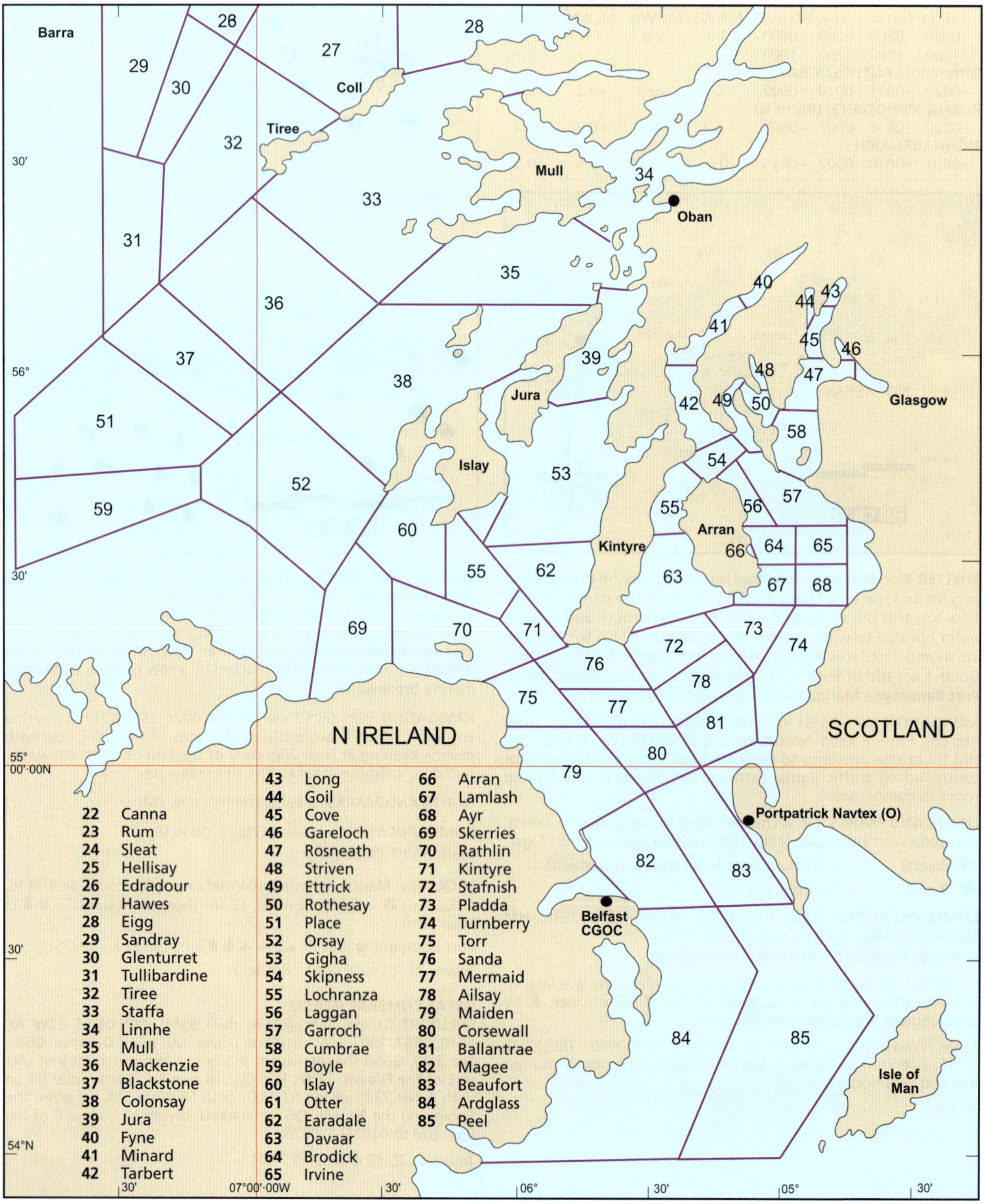

2.16 HOLY LOCH

Argyll **55°59'·03N 04°56'·82W** ❀❀❀◊◊◊✿✿✿

CHARTS AC 2131, 1994, 5610; Imray C63, 2900

TIDES +0122 Dover; ML 2·0; Duration 0640

Standard Port GREENOCK (⟶)

SHELTER Good, but exposed to to E/NE.

NAVIGATION WPT 55°59'·03N 04°55'·75W 270° to marina ent 0·60M. No offshore dangers. Holy Loch is controlled by QHM Clyde but navigation is not restricted; keep well clear of ferries when entering or leaving the loch.

LIGHTS AND MARKS No 30 SCM 55°58'·75N 04°53'·82W off Strone Pt. 2FR at SE end of pier. Marina floodlit.

COMMUNICATIONS (Code 01369) Dr 703279; H 704341. *Holy Loch Marina* Ch 80 M.

FACILITIES **Marina** www.holylochmarina.co.uk ☎701800, 270+ ⓥ in 3m £3·45. (25t) wi-fi. Possible on bkwtr pontoon for larger yachts in depth >5m, but open to the E. Commercial timber yard operating alongside marina facilities. **Holy Loch SC** ☎702707.

Sandbank (town) PO, ✕ Ferries from Hunter's Quay to McInroy's Pt, Gourock, connecting with trains and coaches to Glasgow Airport. Good local area bus service.

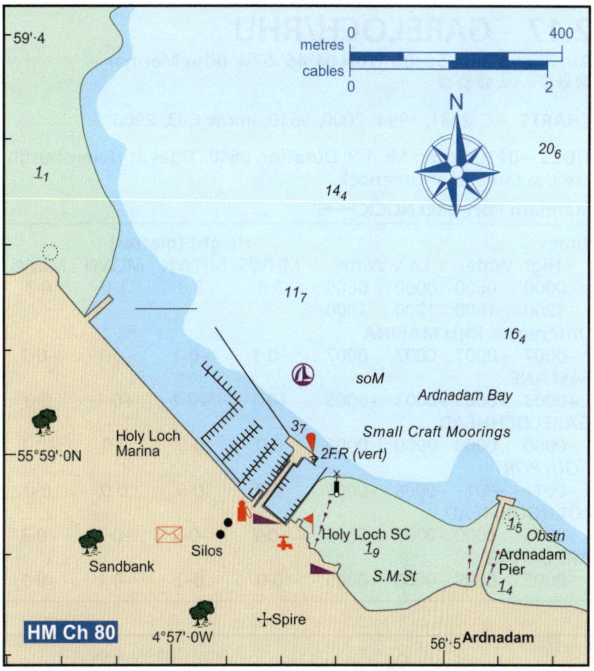

LOCH LONG and LOCH GOIL, Argyll and Bute, approx 56°00'N 04°52'·5W to 56°12'·00N 04°45'·00W. AC 3746, 5610. Tides: See 2.17 for differences. ML 1·7m; Duration 0645.

SHELTER Loch Long is about 15M long. Temp ⚓s (south to north) at: Cove, Blairmore (not in S'lies), Ardentinny, Portincaple, Coilessan (about 1M S of Ardgartan Pt), and near head of loch (Arrochar) on either shore. In Loch Goil ⚓ at Swines Hole and off Carrick Castle (S of the pier, in N'lies a swell builds). Avoid ⚓ near Douglas Pier. The head of the loch is crowded with private/dinghy moorings, and is either too steep-to or too shallow to ⚓. The loch is frequently closed to navigation due to the trial range half way down.

LIGHTS Coulport Jetty, 2FG (vert) each end; Covered Berth L Fl G (SW corner) with 3F G(vert) and F G to NE; Port Dornaige Fl 6s 8m 11M, vis 026°-206°; Dog Rock (Carraig nan Ron) Fl 2s 11M; Finnart Oil Terminal has FG lts and ldg lts 031° QW/FW on Cnap Pt. Upper Loch Long is unlit. Loch Goil ent is marked by 2 PHM buoys (Fl R 3s and QR), a SHM buoy (QG) and ldg lts 318°: front (The Perch) Dir FWRG and Fl R 3s; rear FW. Rubha Ardnahein Fl R5s.

FACILITIES Loch Long (Cove), Cove SC, ; (pier); (Portincaple) hotel, ; (Ardentinny) shop, ✕ hotel, ; (Blairmore) ; (Arrochar) shops, hotel, . Loch Goil (Carrick Castle) has 2 blue s (£10/night, max 15t, free wi-fi), WC. Lochgoilhead: .

2.17 GARELOCH/RHU

Argyll and Bute **56°00′·70N 04°46′·57W** (Rhu Marina)

CHARTS AC 2131, 1994, 2000, 5610; Imray C63, 2900

TIDES +0110 Dover; ML 1·9; Duration 0640. Tides at Helensburgh are the same as at Greenock.

Standard Port GREENOCK (⟶)

Times				Height (metres)			
High Water		Low Water		MHWS	MHWN	MLWN	MLWS
0000	0600	0000	0600	3·4	2·8	1·0	0·3
1200	1800	1200	1800				
Differences RHU MARINA							
–0007	–0007	–0007	–0007	–0·1	–0·1	–0·1	–0·2
FASLANE							
+0003	+0003	+0003	+0003	+0·1	+0·1	+0·1	0·0
GARELOCHHEAD							
0000	0000	0000	0000	0·0	0·0	0·0	–0·1
COULPORT							
–0011	*–0011*	*–0008*	*–0008*	*0·0*	*0·0*	*0·0*	*0·0*
LOCHGOILHEAD							
+0015	0000	–0005	–0005	–0·2	–0·3	–0·3	–0·3
ARROCHAR							
–0005	–0005	–0005	–0005	0·0	0·0	–0·1	–0·1

BYELAWS Loch Long and Gareloch are Dockyard Ports under the jurisdiction of the King's Harbour Master. All submarines and other warships at anchor or underway have an Exclusion Zone around them enforced by MOD Police.

SHELTER Rhu Marina rock bkwtr 1m above MHWS, now extended with submerged section (end marked by SHM Fl G 5s) replacing floating wavebreak, protects the berths from strong winds from E to S. Helensburgh Pier is a temp'y drying berth, rather exposed, used by occas steamers. ⚓ E of marina or in Rosneath Bay. Moorings N of the narrows at Stroul B & Clynder; and at the head of the loch. Clyde Naval Base at Faslane must be avoided by yachts.

NAVIGATION WPT 55°59′·29N 04°45′·26W, 356°/1·3M to bn No 7. Beaches between Cairndhu Pt and Helensburgh Pier are strewn with large boulders above/below MLWS. Gareloch ent is via Rhu Narrows. Marina entrance not easy to find at night between pontoon breakwater and Fl G Bn of marina entrance; beware cross-tides. There are large unlit MoD buoys and barges off W shore of Gareloch; for Garelochhead keep to W shore until well clear of Faslane Naval Base.

LIGHTS AND MARKS Ldg/dir lts into Gareloch 356°, 318°, 295°, 329° and 331°. SS at Rosneath Pt. Conspic ✠ tr at Rhu Point.

COMMUNICATIONS (Code 01436) Ⓗ (01389) 754121; Dr 672277. KHM 674321.

MoD Police/KHM Ch 16/**73**. Rhu Marina Ch **80** M (H24 in season).

FACILITIES **Rhu Marina,** rhu@boatfolk.co.uk ☎820238; (235) £3·25 pontoons A-J, (35t) wi-fi.

Royal Northern and Clyde YC ☎820322; club s, ; **Helensburgh SC** ☎672778 (dinghies) . **Town** All services, ✈ (Glasgow). **DRB Marine** (Rosneath) ☎831231, use jetty only to load, some s, (40t). **Silvers Yard** private moorings.

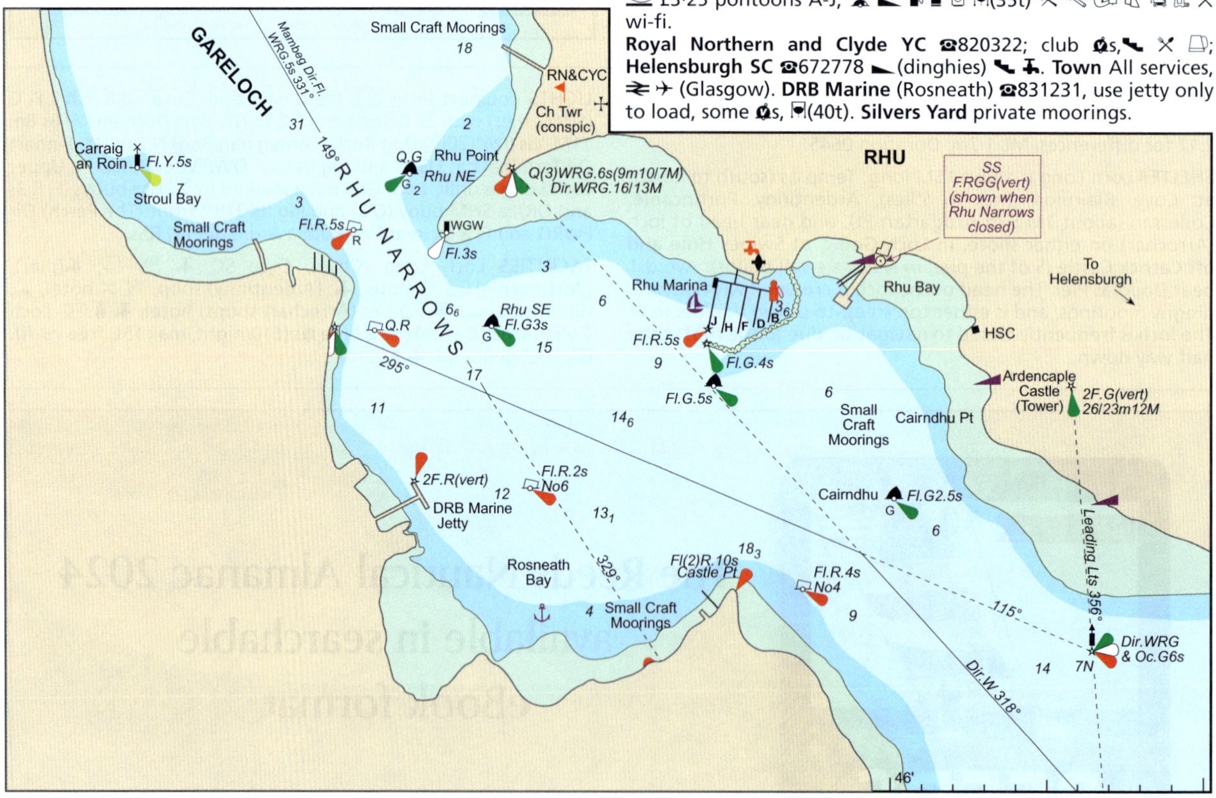

Naval activity: Beware submarines from Faslane Base. See 2.15 for submarine activity (Subfacts) in the Clyde and offshore or call FOSNNI Ops ☎(01436) 674321 Ext 3206 and monitor Ch 73.

Protected Areas: Vessels are never allowed within 150m of naval shore installations at Faslane and Coulport.

Restricted Areas (Faslane, Rhu Chan and Coulport): These are closed to all vessels during submarine movements (see opposite and *W Coast of Scotland Pilot*, App 2). MoD Police patrols enforce areas which are shown on charts. The S limit of Faslane Restricted area is marked by two Or posts with X topmarks on Shandon foreshore. The W limit is marked by Iso WRG 4s, vis W356°-006°, at Gareloch Oil fuel depot N jetty. The following signals are shown when restrictions are in force:

Entrance to Gareloch

Day & Night: ● ● ● (vert), supplemented by R flag with W diagonal bar.

Faslane and Coulport (Barons Pt)

Day & Night: ● ● ● (vert), supplemented by International Code pendant over pendant Nine.

2.18 RIVER CLYDE

Dunbartonshire **55°57'·50N 04°45'·70W** (Tail of the Bank)

CHARTS AC 2131, 1994, 2007, 5610: *BW Skipper's Guide for Forth and Clyde Canal, BW Skipper's Handbook for Lowland Canals*; Imray C63, 2900

TIDES +0122 Dover; ML 2·0; Duration 0640

Standard Port GREENOCK (⟶)

Times				Height (metres)			
High Water		Low Water		MHWS	MHWN	MLWN	MLWS
0000	0600	0000	0600	3·4	2·8	1·0	0·3
1200	1800	1200	1800				
Differences PORT GLASGOW (55°56'·10N 04°40'·50W)							
+0010	+0005	+0010	+0020	+0·2	+0·1	0·0	0·0
DUMBARTON							
+0015	+0010	+0020	+0040	+0·4	+0·3	+0·1	0·0
BOWLING							
+0020	+0010	+0030	+0055	+0·6	+0·5	+0·3	+0·1
RENFREW							
+0025	+0015	+0035	+0100	+0·9	+0·8	+0·5	+0·2
GLASGOW							
+0025	*+0015*	*+0035*	*+0105*	*+1·4*	*+1·1*	*+0·8*	*+0·4*

SHELTER Good at Greenock (James Watt Dock Marina), Dumbarton (Sandpoint Marina) Bowling Harbour and city centre pontoons.

NAVIGATION WPT 55°57'·50N 04°45'·70W, 1·2M to James Watt Dock (JWD), which experiences strong tidal streams flowing in the dredged channel across the entrance. Sandpoint Marina and Bowling Harbour are, respectively, about 6M and 9M upriver. The density of shipping and numerous ferries in the Clyde warrant particular attention. Large vessels manoeuvre at the Greenock Container/Ocean Terminal and masters are to maintain communication with Harbour Control.

Speed limit above Cloch Pt is 12kn but 5kn where boards mark Dead Slow. Sailing vessels must conform to Rules for Narrow Channels and E of Bowling may proceed under power alone.

All vessels planning an upriver passage are to contact their berth or destination before proceeding. Keep just inboard of chan lateral marks as depths shoal rapidly outboard. For Dumbarton cross the river at 90° at No 39 SHM buoy. Depths in R Leven may be less than charted. For Bowling Hbr cross at No 45 SHM buoy.

LIGHTS AND MARKS The River Clyde is well buoyed/lit. Upstream from Steamboat Quay S bank lts are Fl G and N bank lts are Fl R

COMMUNICATIONS (Codes: Greenock 01475; Glasgow 0141) Dr 634617; Ⓗ 01389 754121. HM 725775; Estuary Control 726221; Scottish Canals 332 6936.

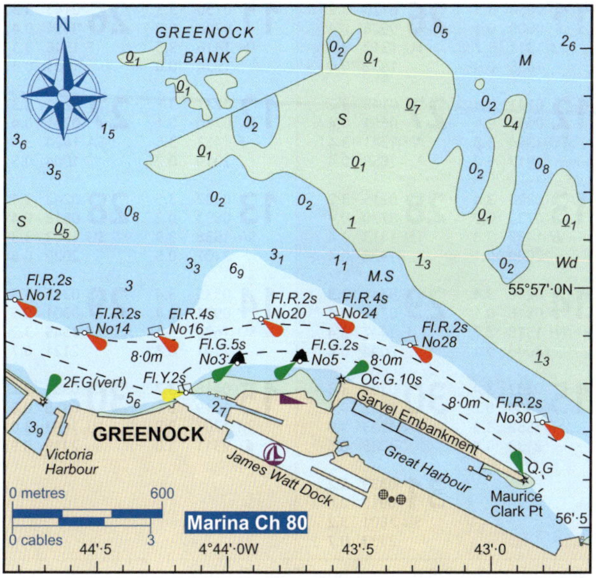

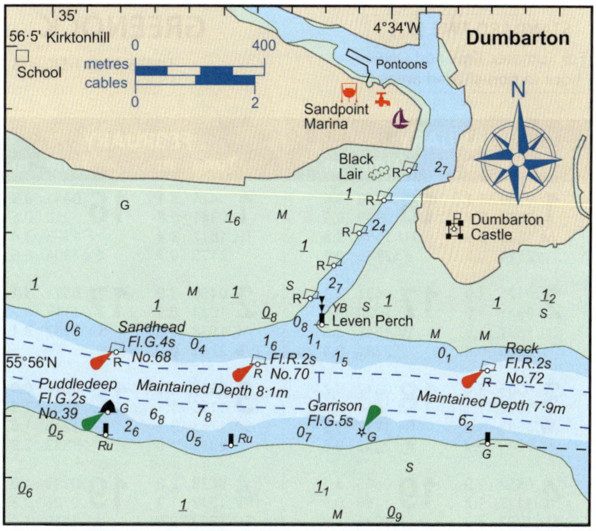

All vessels seeking passage upstream beyond No 1 buoy are to seek permission from *Clyde Harbour Control* Ch **12** 16 (H24) at charted reporting points. Weather/traffic info on request. James Watt Dock Ch 80; Marinas Ch M. Bowling lockkeeper Ch 74, HW±2.

FACILITIES James Watt Dock Marina 55°56'·72N 04°44'·01W. info@jwdmarina.co.uk ☎729838, mob 07710 611117; 65 inc Ⓥ in 4.5m, £3·00; at entrance.

Greenock . Pontoon in E India Harbour.

Sandpoint Marina 55°56'·48N 04°34'·07W www.sandpoint-marina.co.uk ☎01389 762396/731500. Limited Ⓥ, £10 per night. VHF Ch **M**. (40t) ☎01389 742438. **Town** Ⓑ.

Bowling Basin 55°55'·8N 04°29'·0W, W end of Forth & Clyde Canal. ☎01389 877969. Basin Lock access dries 0·7m. Call VHF Ch 74 for lock schedule. *Skipper's Brief* www.scottishcanals.co.uk. Facilities: £3.75, by prior notice, (mast).

Town Ⓑ.

GLASGOW 55°55'·94N 04°34'·25W www.glasgow.gov.uk ☎2879650. Pontoons are at Govan (Water Row), Yorkhill Quay, Broomielaw Quay and Plantation Quay for stays of up to 3 nts. Millennium Br (3.2m) opens ☎4205030 as does Bells Br (3.5m) ☎01436 831222. Boats may also berth at Braehead Shopping Centre.

Clyde Yacht Clubs Association is at 8 St James St, Paisley. ☎8878296. Clyde CC Suite 408, Pentagon Centre, 36 Washington St, Glasgow, G3 8AZ, ☎221 2774.

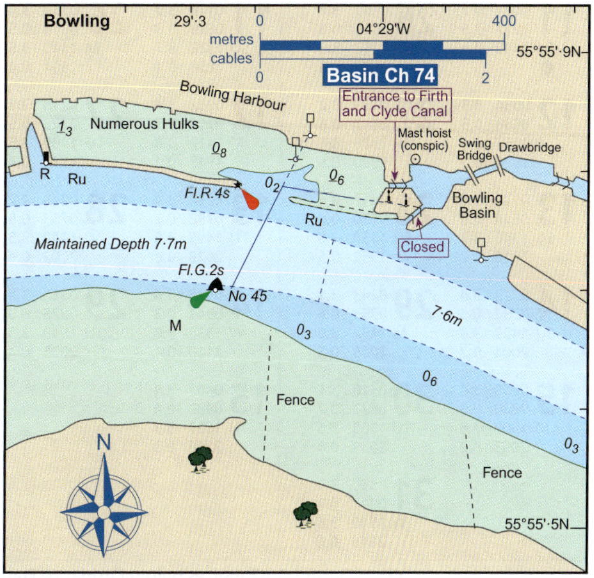

SW Scotland

STANDARD TIME (UT)
For Summer Time add ONE hour in **non-shaded areas**

GREENOCK LAT 55°57′N LONG 4°46′W

TIMES AND HEIGHTS OF HIGH AND LOW WATERS

Dates in red are SPRINGS
Dates in blue are NEAPS

YEAR **2024**

JANUARY

Day	Time	m	Day	Time	m
1	0340	3.1	16	0346	3.4
	0858	0.9		0909	0.5
M	1528	3.6	TU	1554	3.8
	2114	0.7		2145	0.2
2	0421	3.0	17	0431	3.3
	0941	1.0		1000	0.6
TU	1607	3.5	W	1642	3.6
	2200	0.8		2241	0.4
3	0505	3.0	18	0517	3.2
	1026	1.1		1054	0.8
W	1649	3.3	TH	1733	3.5
	2249	0.9	◐	2342	0.5
4	0552	2.9	19	0605	3.1
	1117	1.2		1156	0.9
TH	1737	3.2	F	1831	3.3
◑	2344	1.0			
5	0644	2.8	20	0048	0.7
	1215	1.3		0701	3.0
F	1831	3.1	SA	1309	1.0
				1943	3.1
6	0044	1.0	21	0156	0.8
	0746	2.8		0817	2.9
SA	1319	1.3	SU	1426	1.0
	1933	3.0		2113	3.0
7	0145	1.0	22	0300	0.8
	0855	2.9		0940	3.0
SU	1425	1.2	M	1532	0.9
	2041	3.0		2230	3.0
8	0243	1.0	23	0357	0.8
	0958	3.0		1044	3.1
M	1524	1.0	TU	1627	0.7
	2148	3.1		2329	3.1
9	0336	0.9	24	0446	0.7
	1050	3.2		1133	3.3
TU	1614	0.8	W	1712	0.6
	2248	3.2			
10	0425	0.8	25	0018	3.2
	1135	3.3		0531	0.7
W	1700	0.6	TH	1215	3.4
	2343	3.3	○	1752	0.5
11	0511	0.7	26	0101	3.2
	1217	3.5		0611	0.6
TH	1745	0.4	F	1252	3.5
●				1827	0.5
12	0034	3.3	27	0139	3.2
	0558	0.6		0647	0.6
F	1257	3.6	SA	1326	3.6
	1830	0.3		1900	0.5
13	0124	3.4	28	0212	3.1
	0644	0.5		0720	0.6
SA	1340	3.7	SU	1359	3.6
	1916	0.2		1932	0.5
14	0212	3.4	29	0243	3.1
	0732	0.5		0753	0.6
SU	1423	3.8	M	1432	3.6
	2004	0.2		2005	0.5
15	0259	3.4	30	0316	3.1
	0820	0.5		0827	0.7
M	1508	3.8	TU	1505	3.6
	2053	0.2		2039	0.6
			31	0350	3.1
				0903	0.7
			W	1540	3.5
				2115	0.6

FEBRUARY

Day	Time	m	Day	Time	m
1	0424	3.1	16	0441	3.3
	0941	0.8		1020	0.5
TH	1617	3.4	F	1705	3.4
	2155	0.7	◐	2304	0.6
2	0459	3.0	17	0521	3.1
	1024	0.9		1117	0.7
F	1658	3.3	SA	1752	3.1
◑	2241	0.8			
3	0539	2.9	18	0013	0.8
	1115	1.1		0607	2.9
SA	1745	3.1	SU	1236	1.0
	2336	1.0		1853	2.8
4	0628	2.8	19	0133	1.0
	1217	1.2		0706	2.8
SU	1842	2.9	M	1410	1.0
				2113	2.7
5	0040	1.1	20	0245	1.0
	0740	2.7		0918	2.8
M	1331	1.2	TU	1521	0.9
	1955	2.8		2232	2.8
6	0155	1.1	21	0344	0.9
	0914	2.8		1032	3.0
TU	1451	1.0	W	1615	0.7
	2119	2.9		2325	3.0
7	0309	1.0	22	0434	0.7
	1025	3.0		1121	3.2
W	1556	0.8	TH	1659	0.5
	2236	3.0			
8	0409	0.8	23	0008	3.1
	1117	3.2		0517	0.6
TH	1646	0.4	F	1202	3.4
	2336	3.2		1736	0.4
9	0459	0.6	24	0046	3.1
	1201	3.4		0554	0.5
F	1731	0.2	SA	1238	3.4
●			○	1808	0.4
10	0027	3.3	25	0120	3.1
	0545	0.4		0627	0.5
SA	1245	3.6	SU	1311	3.5
	1815	0.0		1837	0.4
11	0116	3.3	26	0150	3.1
	0629	0.3		0656	0.5
SU	1328	3.7	M	1340	3.5
	1858	-0.1		1904	0.4
12	0202	3.4	27	0218	3.1
	0714	0.3		0723	0.5
M	1412	3.8	TU	1409	3.5
	1943	-0.1		1932	0.4
13	0244	3.4	28	0246	3.2
	0758	0.2		0753	0.5
TU	1455	3.8	W	1440	3.5
	2028	0.0		2002	0.4
14	0325	3.4	29	0315	3.2
	0844	0.3		0825	0.5
W	1538	3.8	TH	1513	3.5
	2116	0.1		2035	0.4
15	0403	3.4			
	0930	0.4			
TH	1621	3.7			
	2206	0.3			

MARCH

Day	Time	m	Day	Time	m
1	0344	3.2	16	0407	3.3
	0902	0.6		0947	0.4
F	1548	3.4	SA	1639	3.3
	2114	0.5		2228	0.7
2	0414	3.1	17	0446	3.2
	0944	0.7		1043	0.7
SA	1626	3.2	SU	1724	2.9
	2159	0.7	◐	2341	1.0
3	0447	2.9	18	0529	2.9
	1035	0.9		1212	0.9
SU	1709	3.0	M	1821	2.6
◑	2253	0.9			
4	0527	2.8	19	0110	1.1
	1136	1.0		0626	2.7
M	1803	2.8	TU	1352	0.9
	2359	1.1		2114	2.5
5	0627	2.6	20	0223	1.1
	1254	1.1		0850	2.7
TU	1918	2.7	W	1500	0.8
				2219	2.7
6	0119	1.2	21	0323	0.9
	0826	2.6		1009	2.9
W	1427	0.9	TH	1552	0.6
	2103	2.7		2304	2.9
7	0250	1.1	22	0412	0.7
	1002	2.9		1057	3.1
TH	1537	0.6	F	1634	0.4
	2230	2.9		2343	3.0
8	0354	0.8	23	0453	0.5
	1056	3.2		1137	3.3
F	1628	0.2	SA	1709	0.4
	2326	3.1			
9	0443	0.5	24	0018	3.1
	1142	3.4		0529	0.5
SA	1711	0.0	SU	1212	3.3
				1740	0.4
10	0014	3.3	25	0050	3.1
	0527	0.3		0559	0.4
SU	1226	3.6	M	1244	3.3
●	1753	-0.2	○	1807	0.4
11	0058	3.3	26	0120	3.2
	0609	0.1		0626	0.4
M	1311	3.7	TU	1312	3.3
	1835	-0.3		1832	0.4
12	0141	3.4	27	0148	3.2
	0651	0.1		0651	0.4
TU	1354	3.8	W	1341	3.4
	1917	-0.2		1858	0.4
13	0220	3.4	28	0215	3.2
	0733	0.0		0720	0.4
W	1437	3.8	TH	1413	3.4
	2000	-0.1		1928	0.4
14	0256	3.4	29	0241	3.3
	0816	0.1		0754	0.4
TH	1518	3.7	F	1447	3.4
	2045	0.1		2004	0.4
15	0332	3.4	30	0309	3.3
	0900	0.2		0832	0.4
F	1558	3.5	SA	1523	3.3
	2133	0.4		2045	0.5
			31	0339	3.2
				0917	0.6
			SU	1601	3.2
				2133	0.7

APRIL

Day	Time	m	Day	Time	m
1	0411	3.1	16	0502	3.0
	1010	0.7		1147	0.8
M	1644	3.0	TU	1810	2.5
	2229	0.9			
2	0451	2.9	17	0035	1.2
	1115	0.9		0600	2.8
TU	1739	2.8	W	1319	0.9
◑	2337	1.1		2040	2.5
3	0549	2.7	18	0148	1.2
	1236	0.9		0746	2.7
W	1858	2.7	TH	1424	0.7
				2143	2.7
4	0059	1.2	19	0249	1.0
	0748	2.7		0928	2.8
TH	1405	0.7	F	1516	0.6
	2056	2.7		2227	2.8
5	0229	1.0	20	0339	0.8
	0932	2.9		1019	3.0
F	1512	0.4	SA	1557	0.5
	2214	2.9		2305	3.0
6	0333	0.7	21	0421	0.6
	1029	3.2		1100	3.2
SA	1603	0.1	SU	1633	0.4
	2305	3.1		2341	3.1
7	0422	0.4	22	0456	0.5
	1117	3.4		1136	3.2
SU	1646	-0.2	M	1704	0.4
	2351	3.3			
8	0505	0.2	23	0014	3.1
	1203	3.6		0528	0.4
M	1728	-0.3	TU	1208	3.2
●			○	1733	0.4
9	0032	3.4	24	0046	3.2
	0547	0.1		0555	0.4
TU	1248	3.6	W	1238	3.2
	1810	-0.2		1759	0.4
10	0113	3.4	25	0115	3.2
	0628	0.0		0623	0.4
W	1333	3.7	TH	1311	3.3
	1851	-0.1		1828	0.4
11	0150	3.5	26	0143	3.3
	0708	0.0		0654	0.4
TH	1416	3.6	F	1346	3.3
	1934	0.0		1903	0.4
12	0227	3.5	27	0211	3.3
	0750	0.1		0731	0.4
F	1457	3.5	SA	1424	3.3
	2019	0.2		1944	0.5
13	0302	3.5	28	0242	3.4
	0833	0.2		0813	0.4
SA	1538	3.3	SU	1503	3.3
	2107	0.5		2029	0.6
14	0339	3.4	29	0315	3.3
	0921	0.4		0901	0.5
SU	1620	3.1	M	1545	3.2
	2201	0.8		2121	0.7
15	0418	3.2	30	0351	3.2
	1019	0.6		0958	0.6
M	1707	2.8	TU	1633	3.0
◐	2311	1.0		2219	0.9

Chart Datum: 1·62 metres below Ordnance Datum (Newlyn). HAT is 3·9 metres above Chart Datum.

STANDARD TIME (UT)
For Summer Time add ONE hour in **non-shaded areas**

GREENOCK LAT 55°57′N LONG 4°46′W

TIMES AND HEIGHTS OF HIGH AND LOW WATERS

Dates in red are SPRINGS
Dates in blue are NEAPS

YEAR **2024**

MAY

Date	Day	Time	m	Time	m	Time	m	Time	m
1	W	0435	3.0	1106	0.7	1732	2.8	◑ 2326	1.0
2	TH	0538	2.8	1224	0.6	1851	2.7		
3	F	0042	1.1	0724	2.8	1339	0.5	2031	2.8
4	SA	0200	0.9	0857	3.0	1442	0.2	2142	3.0
5	SU	0304	0.7	0958	3.2	1533	0.0	2234	3.1
6	M	0356	0.4	1049	3.4	1619	-0.1	2320	3.2
7	TU	0442	0.2	1137	3.5	1703	-0.1		
8	W	0003	3.3	0525	0.1	1224	3.5	● 1746	0.0
9	TH	0044	3.4	0607	0.1	1311	3.5	1829	0.1
10	F	0123	3.5	0648	0.1	1356	3.4	1913	0.3
11	SA	0200	3.5	0729	0.1	1439	3.3	1959	0.4
12	SU	0238	3.5	0813	0.2	1522	3.1	2048	0.6
13	M	0315	3.4	0902	0.4	1607	2.9	2140	0.8
14	TU	0356	3.3	0959	0.6	1657	2.7	2240	1.0
15	W	0440	3.1	1109	0.7	1800	2.6	◐ 2347	1.1
16	TH	0535	2.9	1227	0.8	1921	2.5		
17	F	0056	1.1	0650	2.8	1332	0.7	2037	2.6
18	SA	0200	1.0	0820	2.8	1426	0.6	2131	2.8
19	SU	0255	0.9	0923	2.9	1511	0.5	2216	2.9
20	M	0341	0.7	1010	3.0	1550	0.5	2257	3.0
21	TU	0420	0.6	1050	3.1	1626	0.5	2336	3.1
22	W	0455	0.5	1127	3.1	1658	0.5		
23	TH	0012	3.2	0527	0.5	1203	3.2	○ 1731	0.5
24	F	0045	3.3	0600	0.4	1242	3.2	1806	0.5
25	SA	0116	3.3	0637	0.4	1324	3.2	1847	0.5
26	SU	0148	3.4	0717	0.4	1406	3.2	1932	0.5
27	M	0223	3.4	0803	0.4	1450	3.2	2022	0.6
28	TU	0301	3.4	0854	0.4	1537	3.1	2115	0.7
29	W	0342	3.3	0952	0.4	1629	3.0	2212	0.8
30	TH	0431	3.2	1056	0.4	1728	2.9	◑ 2313	0.8
31	F	0534	3.1	1204	0.4	1837	2.9		

JUNE

Date	Day	Time	m	Time	m	Time	m	Time	m
1	SA	0018	0.9	0657	3.0	1309	0.3	1952	2.9
2	SU	0126	0.8	0819	3.1	1409	0.2	2100	3.0
3	M	0232	0.7	0925	3.2	1504	0.2	2158	3.1
4	TU	0330	0.5	1022	3.3	1554	0.1	2250	3.2
5	W	0421	0.4	1115	3.4	1642	0.2	2337	3.3
6	TH ●	0508	0.3	1206	3.3	1727	0.2		
7	F	0020	3.4	0552	0.2	1255	3.3	1813	0.3
8	SA	0101	3.4	0634	0.2	1342	3.2	1858	0.5
9	SU	0140	3.5	0715	0.2	1427	3.1	1944	0.6
10	M	0218	3.5	0758	0.3	1511	3.0	2030	0.7
11	TU	0257	3.4	0844	0.4	1555	2.9	2117	0.7
12	W	0336	3.3	0933	0.5	1642	2.8	2206	0.8
13	TH	0418	3.2	1028	0.6	1732	2.7	2257	0.9
14	F	0505	3.1	1127	0.7	1825	2.7	◐ 2353	1.0
15	SA	0600	3.0	1228	0.7	1921	2.7		
16	SU	0053	1.0	0701	2.9	1325	0.7	2020	2.8
17	M	0155	1.0	0806	2.9	1418	0.7	2118	2.8
18	TU	0252	0.9	0907	2.9	1505	0.7	2211	2.9
19	W	0341	0.8	1001	3.0	1548	0.6	2258	3.1
20	TH	0425	0.7	1049	3.1	1629	0.6	2341	3.2
21	F	0505	0.5	1135	3.1	1709	0.6		
22	SA	0018	3.3	0545	0.4	1221	3.1	○ 1751	0.6
23	SU	0054	3.4	0625	0.3	1307	3.2	1836	0.5
24	M	0132	3.5	0709	0.3	1355	3.2	1923	0.5
25	TU	0211	3.5	0755	0.2	1443	3.2	2013	0.5
26	W	0252	3.5	0844	0.2	1532	3.2	2103	0.5
27	TH	0336	3.5	0938	0.2	1622	3.1	2156	0.6
28	F	0424	3.4	1035	0.2	1713	3.1	◑ 2250	0.6
29	SA	0519	3.3	1136	0.3	1807	3.0	2349	0.7
30	SU	0624	3.2	1238	0.3	1906	3.0		

JULY

Date	Day	Time	m	Time	m	Time	m	Time	m
1	M	0053	0.8	0739	3.1	1340	0.4	2012	2.9
2	TU	0202	0.8	0854	3.1	1440	0.4	2121	3.0
3	W	0309	0.7	1003	3.1	1536	0.4	2224	3.1
4	TH	0408	0.6	1104	3.1	1628	0.5	2318	3.2
5	F ●	0458	0.4	1159	3.1	1717	0.5		
6	SA	0005	3.3	0544	0.3	1250	3.1	1803	0.5
7	SU	0047	3.4	0625	0.3	1337	3.1	1847	0.5
8	M	0126	3.4	0703	0.3	1420	3.0	1928	0.6
9	TU	0203	3.5	0741	0.3	1458	3.0	2008	0.6
10	W	0239	3.5	0820	0.4	1535	2.9	2048	0.6
11	TH	0315	3.4	0901	0.4	1613	2.9	2128	0.7
12	F	0352	3.3	0944	0.5	1653	2.9	2211	0.8
13	SA	0431	3.2	1031	0.6	1735	2.9	◐ 2257	0.9
14	SU	0515	3.1	1124	0.7	1820	2.8	2348	1.0
15	M	0605	3.0	1220	0.8	1911	2.8		
16	TU	0048	1.1	0705	2.9	1319	0.9	2012	2.8
17	W	0156	1.1	0811	2.8	1419	0.9	2122	2.8
18	TH	0304	1.0	0919	2.9	1515	0.8	2224	3.0
19	F	0401	0.8	1022	2.9	1606	0.7	2314	3.1
20	SA	0448	0.6	1117	3.0	1652	0.6	2357	3.3
21	SU ○	0531	0.4	1209	3.1	1737	0.6		
22	M	0037	3.4	0613	0.2	1258	3.2	1823	0.5
23	TU	0118	3.5	0655	0.1	1346	3.2	1908	0.4
24	W	0159	3.6	0739	0.0	1433	3.2	1955	0.4
25	TH	0242	3.7	0825	0.0	1519	3.2	2043	0.4
26	F	0325	3.7	0914	0.0	1603	3.2	2131	0.4
27	SA	0410	3.6	1006	0.2	1646	3.2	2222	0.5
28	SU	0457	3.4	1104	0.3	1730	3.1	◑ 2317	0.6
29	M	0550	3.2	1207	0.5	1818	3.0		
30	TU	0021	0.8	0655	3.0	1316	0.6	1917	2.9
31	W	0140	0.9	0829	2.8	1424	0.7	2045	2.9

AUGUST

Date	Day	Time	m	Time	m	Time	m	Time	m
1	TH	0259	0.9	1004	2.9	1526	0.7	2212	3.0
2	F	0402	0.7	1108	3.0	1621	0.7	2311	3.1
3	SA	0453	0.5	1200	3.0	1709	0.6	2358	3.3
4	SU ●	0536	0.4	1247	3.1	1752	0.6		
5	M	0038	3.4	0613	0.3	1327	3.0	1831	0.5
6	TU	0114	3.5	0646	0.3	1403	3.0	1906	0.6
7	W	0147	3.5	0718	0.4	1434	3.0	1939	0.6
8	TH	0218	3.5	0750	0.4	1504	3.0	2013	0.6
9	F	0250	3.5	0823	0.4	1536	3.0	2048	0.6
10	SA	0323	3.4	0858	0.5	1610	3.0	2125	0.7
11	SU	0358	3.4	0936	0.6	1645	3.0	2206	0.8
12	M	0437	3.2	1020	0.7	1724	2.9	◐ 2253	0.9
13	TU	0522	3.0	1113	0.9	1810	2.8	2351	1.1
14	W	0618	2.8	1218	1.1	1910	2.7		
15	TH	0104	1.2	0729	2.7	1333	1.1	2031	2.7
16	F	0232	1.1	0850	2.7	1449	1.0	2155	2.9
17	SA	0342	0.8	1009	2.9	1549	0.9	2252	3.1
18	SU	0431	0.5	1110	3.0	1637	0.7	2337	3.3
19	M ○	0513	0.2	1200	3.2	1721	0.5		
20	TU	0019	3.5	0554	0.0	1246	3.2	1804	0.4
21	W	0101	3.6	0634	-0.1	1331	3.3	1847	0.3
22	TH	0144	3.7	0716	-0.1	1414	3.3	1931	0.2
23	F	0227	3.8	0759	-0.1	1455	3.3	2016	0.2
24	SA	0309	3.8	0845	0.0	1534	3.4	2102	0.3
25	SU	0351	3.7	0934	0.2	1612	3.3	2151	0.4
26	M	0433	3.5	1030	0.5	1653	3.2	◑ 2245	0.7
27	TU	0519	3.2	1139	0.8	1737	3.1	2356	0.9
28	W	0616	2.8	1301	1.0	1831	2.9		
29	TH	0132	1.0	0840	2.6	1415	1.0	2013	2.8
30	F	0253	0.9	1011	2.8	1517	0.9	2205	3.0
31	SA	0353	0.7	1105	3.0	1609	0.8	2259	3.2

Chart Datum: 1·62 metres below Ordnance Datum (Newlyn). HAT is 3·9 metres above Chart Datum.

STANDARD TIME (UT)
For Summer Time add ONE hour in **non-shaded areas**

GREENOCK LAT 55°57′N LONG 4°46′W

TIMES AND HEIGHTS OF HIGH AND LOW WATERS

Dates in red are SPRINGS
Dates in blue are NEAPS

YEAR 2024

SEPTEMBER

Date	Day	Time	m	Time	m	Time	m	Time	m
1	SU	0440	0.5	1149	3.1	1654	0.6	2343	3.4
2	M	0519	0.4	1229	3.1	1734	0.5		
3	TU ●	0020	3.5	0553	0.4	1304	3.1	1809	0.5
4	W	0054	3.5	0622	0.4	1334	3.1	1839	0.5
5	TH	0124	3.5	0649	0.4	1401	3.1	1907	0.6
6	F	0152	3.5	0716	0.4	1428	3.2	1936	0.6
7	SA	0222	3.5	0745	0.5	1458	3.2	2008	0.6
8	SU	0254	3.5	0816	0.5	1528	3.2	2044	0.6
9	M	0329	3.4	0852	0.6	1600	3.2	2125	0.8
10	TU	0405	3.3	0934	0.8	1635	3.0	2212	0.9
11	W ◐	0447	3.1	1026	1.0	1717	2.9	2311	1.1
12	TH	0541	2.8	1133	1.2	1817	2.8		
13	F	0027	1.2	0656	2.7	1257	1.3	1946	2.7
14	SA	0208	1.1	0833	2.7	1428	1.2	2126	2.9
15	SU	0320	0.7	1003	2.9	1531	0.9	2227	3.2
16	M	0408	0.4	1058	3.1	1617	0.6	2313	3.4
17	TU	0449	0.1	1143	3.3	1700	0.4	2357	3.6
18	W ○	0529	-0.1	1226	3.4	1741	0.3		
19	TH	0040	3.7	0609	-0.2	1307	3.4	1823	0.2
20	F	0124	3.8	0649	-0.1	1347	3.5	1905	0.2
21	SA	0207	3.8	0732	0.0	1426	3.5	1948	0.2
22	SU	0249	3.8	0816	0.2	1503	3.5	2034	0.3
23	M	0330	3.6	0904	0.4	1541	3.4	2122	0.5
24	TU ◑	0412	3.4	0959	0.7	1621	3.3	2218	0.8
25	W	0458	3.1	1115	1.1	1706	3.1	2343	1.0
26	TH	0556	2.7	1246	1.2	1802	2.9		
27	F	0123	1.0	0852	2.6	1358	1.2	1957	2.8
28	SA	0235	0.9	0959	2.8	1458	1.0	2142	3.0
29	SU	0331	0.7	1045	3.0	1548	0.8	2233	3.3
30	M	0415	0.5	1123	3.2	1631	0.7	2315	3.4

OCTOBER

Date	Day	Time	m	Time	m	Time	m	Time	m
1	TU	0452	0.4	1159	3.2	1709	0.6	2352	3.5
2	W ●	0524	0.4	1230	3.3	1741	0.5		
3	TH	0024	3.5	0552	0.5	1258	3.3	1809	0.6
4	F	0054	3.5	0617	0.5	1326	3.3	1835	0.6
5	SA	0123	3.5	0643	0.5	1354	3.3	1903	0.6
6	SU	0154	3.5	0711	0.6	1422	3.4	1935	0.6
7	M	0227	3.5	0744	0.6	1452	3.4	2013	0.7
8	TU	0303	3.4	0822	0.7	1523	3.3	2055	0.8
9	W	0341	3.3	0907	0.9	1558	3.2	2146	1.0
10	TH ◐	0423	3.1	1001	1.1	1639	3.0	2248	1.1
11	F	0516	2.9	1108	1.3	1737	2.9		
12	SA	0006	1.1	0633	2.8	1232	1.4	1909	2.8
13	SU	0140	1.0	0819	2.8	1401	1.2	2050	3.0
14	M	0248	0.7	0943	3.0	1504	1.0	2155	3.3
15	TU	0338	0.3	1034	3.2	1553	0.7	2244	3.5
16	W	0421	0.1	1117	3.4	1636	0.4	2331	3.7
17	TH ○	0502	-0.1	1159	3.5	1718	0.3		
18	F	0016	3.8	0543	-0.1	1239	3.5	1800	0.2
19	SA	0102	3.8	0625	0.0	1319	3.6	1842	0.2
20	SU	0147	3.8	0708	0.2	1358	3.6	1925	0.3
21	M	0231	3.7	0753	0.4	1436	3.6	2010	0.4
22	TU	0313	3.5	0841	0.7	1516	3.6	2100	0.6
23	W	0357	3.3	0937	1.0	1557	3.4	2159	0.8
24	TH ◑	0446	3.0	1050	1.2	1644	3.2	2325	1.0
25	F	0555	2.7	1215	1.4	1742	3.0		
26	SA	0055	1.0	0820	2.7	1326	1.3	1919	2.9
27	SU	0203	0.9	0924	2.9	1426	1.2	2059	3.1
28	M	0256	0.8	1008	3.0	1518	0.9	2154	3.3
29	TU	0341	0.6	1046	3.2	1601	0.8	2238	3.4
30	W	0418	0.6	1120	3.3	1639	0.7	2315	3.4
31	TH	0451	0.6	1153	3.4	1711	0.6	2349	3.5

NOVEMBER

Date	Day	Time	m	Time	m	Time	m	Time	m
1	F ●	0520	0.6	1224	3.4	1740	0.6		
2	SA	0021	3.5	0548	0.6	1255	3.5	1808	0.7
3	SU	0053	3.5	0615	0.7	1324	3.5	1838	0.7
4	M	0128	3.5	0647	0.7	1354	3.5	1913	0.7
5	TU	0205	3.5	0723	0.7	1425	3.5	1953	0.7
6	W	0244	3.4	0805	0.8	1459	3.5	2038	0.8
7	TH	0324	3.3	0853	1.0	1536	3.4	2131	0.9
8	F	0409	3.2	0949	1.2	1619	3.2	2234	1.0
9	SA ◐	0504	3.0	1053	1.3	1716	3.1	2348	1.0
10	SU	0616	2.9	1208	1.3	1838	3.1		
11	M	0105	0.8	0748	2.9	1325	1.2	2009	3.2
12	TU	0211	0.6	0906	3.1	1431	1.0	2119	3.4
13	W	0305	0.4	1001	3.3	1525	0.8	2214	3.6
14	TH	0353	0.2	1048	3.4	1613	0.5	2305	3.7
15	F ○	0437	0.1	1132	3.5	1657	0.4	2355	3.7
16	SA	0521	0.2	1214	3.6	1740	0.3		
17	SU	0043	3.7	0605	0.3	1255	3.7	1824	0.3
18	M	0131	3.7	0650	0.4	1336	3.7	1908	0.4
19	TU	0217	3.5	0737	0.6	1416	3.7	1954	0.5
20	W	0302	3.4	0826	0.8	1457	3.7	2044	0.6
21	TH	0348	3.2	0919	1.0	1540	3.5	2140	0.8
22	F	0440	3.0	1018	1.2	1626	3.4	2248	0.9
23	SA ◑	0543	2.8	1126	1.3	1722	3.2		
24	SU	0004	1.0	0703	2.7	1237	1.3	1831	3.1
25	M	0113	1.0	0817	2.8	1342	1.3	1950	3.1
26	TU	0210	0.9	0912	3.0	1437	1.1	2057	3.2
27	W	0258	0.8	0957	3.1	1525	1.0	2149	3.2
28	TH	0339	0.8	1039	3.3	1606	0.9	2233	3.3
29	F	0416	0.7	1118	3.4	1643	0.8	2313	3.3
30	SA	0451	0.7	1154	3.5	1716	0.8	2351	3.4

DECEMBER

Date	Day	Time	m	Time	m	Time	m	Time	m
1	SU ●	0523	0.8	1229	3.5	1749	0.7		
2	M	0028	3.4	0556	0.8	1301	3.6	1823	0.7
3	TU	0108	3.4	0631	0.8	1333	3.6	1901	0.7
4	W	0149	3.4	0712	0.8	1407	3.6	1942	0.7
5	TH	0231	3.4	0756	0.9	1444	3.6	2029	0.7
6	F	0314	3.3	0845	0.9	1524	3.6	2121	0.7
7	SA	0401	3.2	0938	1.0	1609	3.5	2219	0.7
8	SU ◐	0453	3.1	1035	1.1	1703	3.4	2322	0.7
9	M	0552	3.1	1138	1.1	1809	3.3		
10	TU	0028	0.7	0703	3.0	1246	1.1	1927	3.3
11	W	0133	0.6	0817	3.1	1354	1.0	2042	3.3
12	TH	0233	0.5	0923	3.2	1457	0.9	2147	3.4
13	F	0327	0.4	1019	3.3	1552	0.7	2245	3.5
14	SA	0418	0.4	1109	3.4	1642	0.5	2340	3.5
15	SU ○	0506	0.4	1156	3.6	1729	0.4		
16	M	0032	3.5	0553	0.5	1240	3.6	1814	0.4
17	TU	0123	3.5	0639	0.6	1322	3.7	1858	0.4
18	W	0210	3.4	0725	0.7	1403	3.7	1942	0.5
19	TH	0255	3.3	0810	0.8	1444	3.7	2027	0.5
20	F	0340	3.1	0856	0.9	1525	3.6	2114	0.7
21	SA	0424	3.0	0944	1.0	1608	3.5	2205	0.8
22	SU ◑	0511	2.9	1034	1.1	1653	3.4	2301	0.9
23	M	0600	2.9	1130	1.2	1743	3.2		
24	TU	0001	1.0	0655	2.9	1233	1.3	1838	3.1
25	W	0104	1.0	0755	2.9	1339	1.2	1938	3.0
26	TH	0203	1.0	0857	3.0	1441	1.2	2043	3.0
27	F	0256	1.0	0955	3.1	1533	1.1	2145	3.1
28	SA	0344	0.9	1045	3.2	1618	0.9	2239	3.1
29	SU	0426	0.9	1129	3.4	1658	0.8	2327	3.2
30	M ●	0505	0.8	1208	3.5	1736	0.7		
31	TU	0011	3.3	0543	0.8	1243	3.5	1813	0.6

Chart Datum: 1·62 metres below Ordnance Datum (Newlyn). HAT is 3·9 metres above Chart Datum.

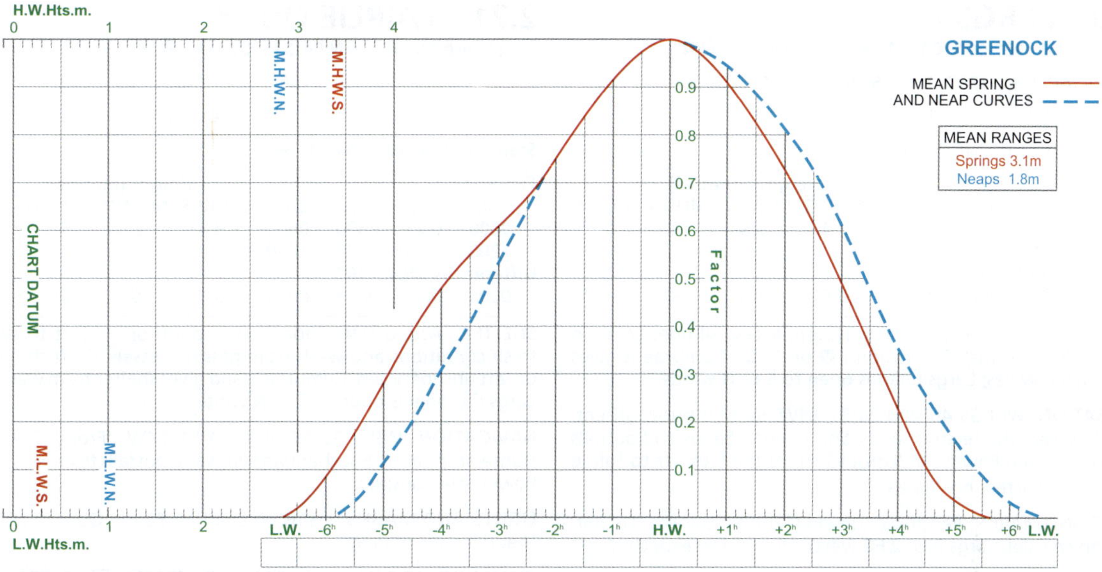

2.19 INVERKIP (KIP MARINA)

Inverclyde **55°54'·50N 04°53'·00W**

CHARTS AC 2131, 1907, 5610; Imray C63, 2900

TIDES +0110 Dover; ML 1·8; Duration 0640

Standard Port GREENOCK (⟵)

Times				Height (metres)			
High Water		Low Water		MHWS	MHWN	MLWN	MLWS
0000	0600	0000	0600	3·4	2·8	1·0	0·3
1200	1800	1200	1800				
Differences WEMYSS BAY							
–0005	–0005	–0005	–0005	0·0	0·0	+0·1	+0·1

SHELTER Excellent inside marina. Chan and marina are dredged 3·5m; accessible H24. Inverkip Bay is exposed to SW/NW winds.

NAVIGATION WPT 55°54'·49N 04°52'·95W, Kip SHM buoy, Fl G 5s, at ent to buoyed chan; beware shifting bank to the N.

LIGHTS AND MARKS SHM 55°54'·55N 04°54'·47W Fl G 1·06M 093° to entrance. SPM buoy marks sewer outfall off Ardgowan Pt. From Kip SHM buoy, 3 SHM and 3 PHM buoys mark 365m long appr channel.

COMMUNICATIONS (Code 01475) Dr 520248; Ⓗ 33777. *Kip Marina* Ch **80** M (H24). *Clydeport Estuary Radio* VHF Ch **12** 16 (H24). Info on weather and traffic available on request.

FACILITIES Kip Marina www.scottishmarinas.co.uk ☎521485; 625 inc Ⓥ, £2·70, £16 <5hrs, Ⓔ (50t) Diver, YC. **Town** ⓑ (Gourock), ⇄ ✈ (Glasgow).

ADJACENT ANCHORAGE

DUNOON, Argyll and Bute, **55°56'·70N 04°55'·20W**. AC 5610, 2131, 1907, 1994. Use Greenock tides. Temp ⚓ in West or East Bays (S and N of Dunoon Pt). The former is open to the S; the latter more shoal. The Gantocks, drying rks 3ca SE of Dunoon Pt, have W ○ bn tr, Fl R 6s 12m 6M. 2FR (vert) on ferry pier. Facilities: ferry to Gourock. 3 Ⓥs off Innellan, 3·7M S of Dunoon, ☎(01369) 830445.

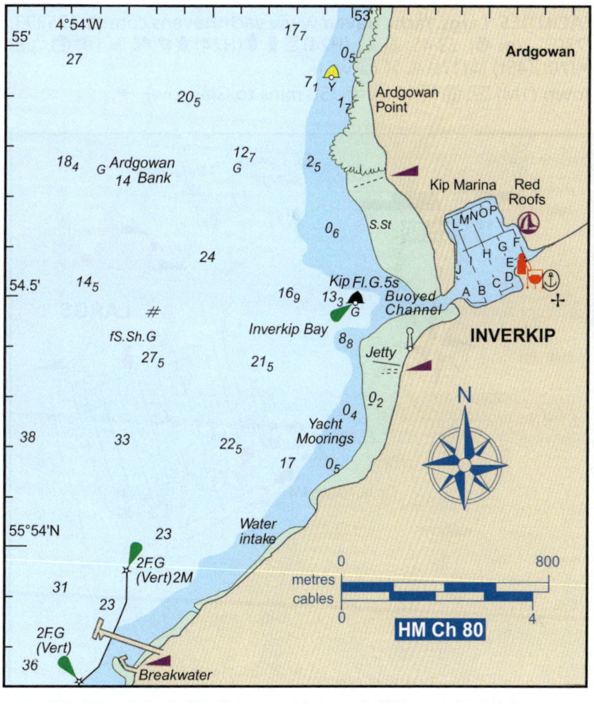

ANCHORAGE IN THE UPPER FIRTH OF CLYDE

GOUROCK, Inverclyde, **55°58'·00N 04°49'·00W**. AC 2131, 1994, 5610 Imray C63, 2900 Series; OS 63. Use Greenock tides. ⚓ in W of Gourock Bay, beware of moorings and foul ground. It is exposed in NW/NE'lies. No navigational dangers, but much shipping and ferries in the Clyde. The S edge of the Firth of Clyde recommended channel lies 2ca N of Kempock Pt. The pier at the S end of Gourock Bay is disused and unsafe. Facilities: Royal Gourock YC ☎632983, 2 Ⓥs serviced by Club launch.

Town ⓑ ⇄ Ferry (hourly to Dunoon, passes close to Club moorings with significant wake/wash) ✈ (Glasgow).

2.20 LARGS

N Ayrshire **55°46'·40N 04°51'·84W**

CHARTS AC 2131, 1907, 1867, 5610; Imray C63, 2900

TIDES +0105 Dover; ML 1·9; Duration 0640

Standard Port GREENOCK (←)

Times				Heights (metres)			
High Water		Low Water		MHWS	MHWN	MLWN	MLWS
0000	0600	0000	0600	3·4	2·8	1·0	0·3
1200	1800	1200	1800				
Differences *MILLPORT*							
−0005	*−0025*	*−0025*	*−0005*	*0·0*	*−0·1*	*0·0*	*+0·1*

SHELTER Excellent in Largs Yacht Haven, access all tides (2·5m in ent; 3m deep berths). 7 pontoons; Ⓥ on 'C/D'. Cumbrae Is gives shelter from W'lies; Largs Chan is open to S or N winds.

NAVIGATION WPT 55°46'·40N 04°51'·84W, SWM lt buoy, off ent. From S beware Hunterston Sands, Southannan Sands and outfalls from Hunterston Power Stn (conspic). From the S bkwtr to Fairlie Quay is a restricted, no ⚓ area.

LIGHTS AND MARKS 'Pencil' monument (12m) conspic 4ca N of ent. Lts as on chartlet. Largs Pier, 2 FG (vert) when vessel expected.

COMMUNICATIONS (Code 01475) Dr 673380; Ⓗ 733777; Largs SC 670000.
Largs Yacht Haven Ch **80** M (H24).

FACILITIES **Largs Yacht Haven** www.yachthavens.com ☎ 675333, (730 inc Ⓥ), £3·45; (H24) (H24) Ⓔ (70t)(45t) (17t) wi-fi.
Town (1M) Ⓑ (50 mins to Glasgow), ✈.

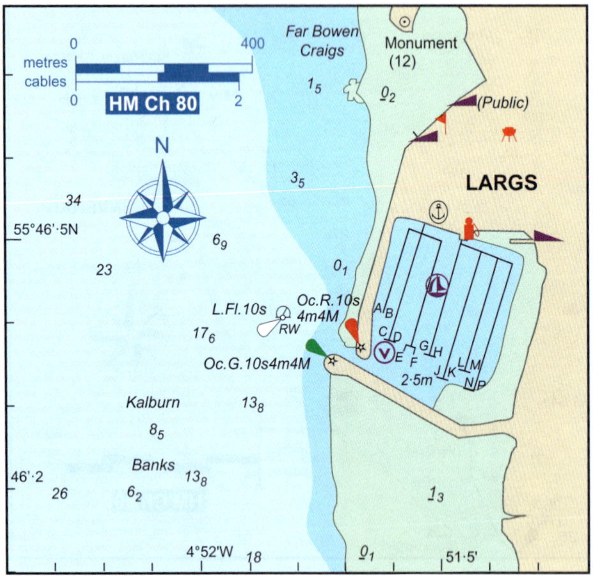

2.21 FAIRLIE QUAY

N Ayrshire **55°46'·07N 04°51'·78W**

CHARTS AC 2131, 1907, 1867, 5610; Imray C63, 2900

TIDES +0105 Dover; ML 1·9; Duration 0640

Standard Port GREENOCK (←)

Times				Height (metres)			
High Water		Low Water		MHWS	MHWN	MLWN	MLWS
0000	0600	0000	0600	3·4	2·8	1·0	0·3
1200	1800	1200	1800				
Differences *MILLPORT*							
−0005	*−0025*	*−0025*	*−0005*	*0·0*	*−0·1*	*0·0*	*+0·1*

SHELTER Access H24. Poor shelter; pontoon subject to swell in fresh conditions and wash from passing vessels. Craft should not be left unsupervised. Cumbrae Island gives shelter from westerlies; Largs Channel is open to S or N winds.

NAVIGATION WPT 55°46'·08N 04°51'·84W. From S beware Hunterston Sands, Southannan Sands and outfalls from Hunterston Power Stn (conspic).

LIGHTS AND MARKS Lts as on chartlet. Fairlie Quay, 2 FG (vert) N and S ends of Pier.

COMMUNICATIONS (Code 01475) Dr 673380; Ⓗ 733777; Fairlie Quay 568267.
Fairlie Quay Marina Ch **80** M (H24).

FACILITIES **Fairlie Quay** s £15 Fuel H24: (80t) . **Fairlie YC; Town** Ⓑ (Fairlie & Largs; 50 mins to Glasgow), ✈.

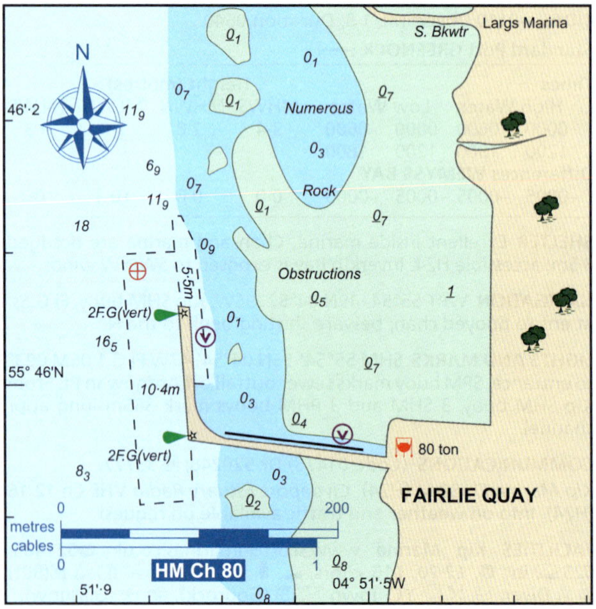

2.22 ARDROSSAN

N Ayrshire **55°38'·50N 04°49'·61W**

CHARTS AC 2126, 2221, 2491, 1866, 5610; Imray C63

TIDES +0055 Dover; ML 1·9; Duration 0630

Standard Port GREENOCK (⟵)

Times				Height (metres)			
High Water		Low Water		MHWS	MHWN	MLWN	MLWS
0000	0600	0000	0600	3·4	2·8	1·0	0·3
1200	1800	1200	1800				
Differences ARDROSSAN							
−0020	−0010	−0010	−0010	−0·2	−0·2	+0·1	+0·1
IRVINE							
−0020	−0020	−0030	−0010	−0·3	−0·3	−0·1	0·0

SHELTER Good in marina (formerly Eglinton Dock), access at all tides over sill, 5·2m least depth. A storm gate is fitted; max acceptable beam is 8·6m (28ft). Strong SW/NW winds cause heavy seas in the apprs and the hbr may be closed in SW gales. Ferries berth on both sides of Winton Pier.

NAVIGATION WPT 55°38'·13N 04°50'·55W, 055°/0·65M to hbr ent. From the W/NW keep clear of low-lying Horse Isle (conspic W tower on its S end) ringed by drying ledges. The passage between Horse Isle and the mainland is obstructed by unmarked drying rks and should not be attempted. Be aware of following dangers: From the S/SE, Eagle Rk 3ca S of hbr ent, marked by SHM buoy, Fl G 5s. 3ca SE of Eagle Rk lies unmarked Campbell Rk (0·2m). W Crinan Rk (1·1m) is 300m W of hbr ent, marked by PHM buoy, Fl R 4s.

LIGHTS AND MARKS Dir lt WRG 15m W14M, R/G11M (see 2.3); W sector leads 055° to hbr ent between lt ho and detached bkwtr. Lt ho Iso WG 4s 11m 9M, 317°-G-035°, W elsewhere. On S end of detached bkwtr, Fl R 5s 7m 5M.

Traffic Signals, shown H24 from control twr at ent to marina:

3 F ● lts (vert) = hbr and marina closed; no entry/exit for commercial and pleasure vessels.

3 F ● lts (vert) = marina open, hbr closed; pleasure craft may enter/exit the marina, no commercial movements.

2 F ● lts over 1 F ● = hbr open, marina closed; in severe weather marina storm gate is closed. Commercial vessels may enter/exit hbr, subject to approval by Hbr Control on VHF. Pleasure craft must clear the approach channel, ferry turning area (between the detached bkwtr and Winton Pier) and the outer basin. Yachts may not manoeuvre under sail alone until seaward of the outer breakwater.

COMMUNICATIONS (Code 01294) Dr 463011.
Clyde Marina VHF Ch **80** M. *Hbr Control* Ch 12 14 16 (H24).

FACILITIES Clyde Marina www.clyde marina.com ☎607077 252 inc 50 £3·10 <25m, £10·00 < 4hrs, access H24, office hrs 0900-1800 Ⓔ (50t) ✕.

Town ✉ Ⓑ ✕. ⇌ ✈ (Prestwick/Glasgow). Ferry to Brodick (Arran).

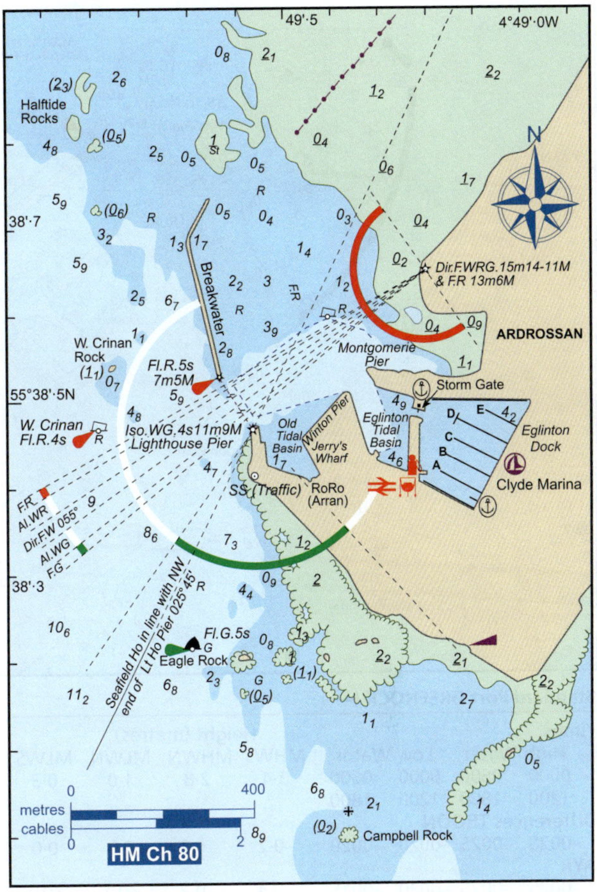

ADJACENT HARBOURS

IRVINE, N Ayrshire, **55°36'·17N 04°42'·07W**. AC 2126, 2220, 1866. HW +0055 on Dover. Tides: see 2.22.

Do not attempt entrance in heavy onshore weather. Good shelter once across the bar which carries approx 0·5m. The IB-B SPM buoy, Fl Y 3s, is 1·15M from hbr ent, close NW of ldg line. 5 blocks of flats and chimneys are conspic ENE of entrance. Channel is not maintained, local knowledge essential. Ent made across Irvine Bar, [Bn (Ru) now destroyed] passing between groynes inside which have unlit perches. W tidal stn twr conspic 3ca inside entrance.

HM ☎(01294) 487286, 487111, VHF Ch 12 (0800-1600 Tues and Thurs; 0800-1300 Wed).

⚓ prohib. Visitors' pontoons on S side at Scottish Maritime Museum visitors' quay (2·2m). Berths available above opening footbridge which opens at 5 mins notice ☎08708 403123 or VHF Ch 12 (call *Irvine Bridge*). **Quay** , 5poa, (3t).

Town (1·5km), ✕ ⇌ ✈ (Prestwick).

AYR, S Ayrshire, **55°28'·22N 04°38'·78W**. AC 5610, 2126, 2220, 1866. HW +0050 on Dover; ML 1·8m. Duration 0630. See 2.23.

Good shelter in S dock although berth space limited. Heavy rains may wash large amounts of debris down the R Ayr. From the W, harbour ent lies between conspic gasholder to the N and townhall spire to the S.

St Nicholas SHM, Fl G 2s and Inner St Nicholas, Iso G, guard shoals and a drying rk (0·8m) 150m S of ent. PHM, FL R 2s marks rk awash at LW 120m NW of N Bkwtr.Ldg lts 098°: front, by Pilot Stn, FR 10m 5M R tower, rear (130m from front), Oc R 10s 18m 9M. Traffic signals (near front ldg lt):

2 ● (vert) = hbr closed to incoming traffic.

N Bkwtr Hd, QR 9m 5M. S Pier Hd, Q 7m 7M, vis 012°-161°, and Fl G 4s 5m 5M, same structure, vis 012°-082°, over St Nicholas Rk.

HM ☎(01292) 281687; VHF Ch 14 16.

Ayr Y & CC at S dock dredged 2021, limited on pontoon on N side of harbour (access key, £10 deposit, from Ship Inn).

Services .

Town ✉ Ⓑ ✕ ⇌.

2.23 TROON

S Ayrshire **55°33'·10N 04°40'·97W** ❁❁◊◊◊✿✿

CHARTS AC 2126, 2220, 1866, 5610; Imray C63

TIDES +0050 Dover; ML 1·9; Duration 0630

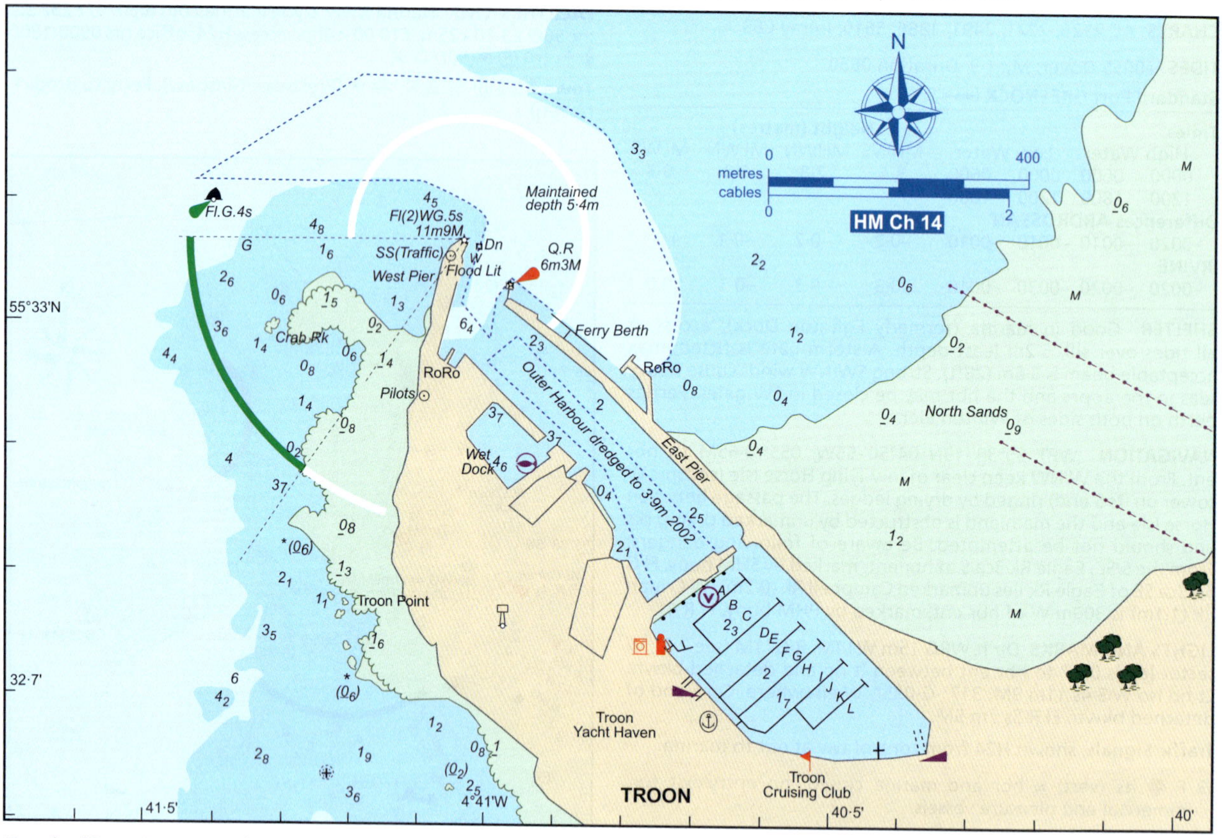

Standard Port GREENOCK (⟵)

Times				Height (metres)			
High Water		Low Water		MHWS	MHWN	MLWN	MLWS
0000	0600	0000	0600	3·4	2·8	1·0	0·3
1200	1800	1200	1800				
Differences TROON							
–0025	–0025	–0020	–0020	–0·2	–0·2	0·0	0·0
AYR							
–0025	–0025	–0030	–0015	–0·4	–0·3	+0·1	+0·1
GIRVAN							
–0025	–0040	–0035	–0010	–0·3	–0·3	–0·1	0·0

SHELTER Complete in marina (2·4m at ent, 1·6m at SE end); speed limit 5kn. *Strong W winds cause heavy seas in the hbr approach.*

NAVIGATION WPT 55°33'·20N 04°42'·00W, 103°/0·6M to W pier lt. Appr in sector SW to NW. Beware Lady Isle, Fl (4) 30s 19m 8M, W bn, 2·2M SW; Troon Rock (5·6m, occas breaks) 1·1M W; Lappock Rock (0̲·6m, bn with G barrel topmark) 1·6M NNW; Mill Rock (0̲·4m) ½M NNE of hbr ent, marked by lit PHM.

LIGHTS AND MARKS No ldg lts. 4 x SPM Fl Y.4s mark limit of dredged appr. W pier hd lt, Fl (2) WG 5s. Traffic signals (H24) on W Pier: 3 F●(vert) + ●(strobe) = hbr closed to fishing/pleasure vessels during commercial moves. SHM Q.G marks marina entrance.

COMMUNICATIONS (Code 01292) Dr 313593; Ⓗ 610555 (Ayr). HM 281687; Troon CC 311865; Troon YC 316770.
HM Ch **14**. Marina Ch **80** M.

FACILITIES Troon Yacht Haven www.yachthavens.com ☎315553 all tide access 300+50Ⓥ, £3·00 (short stay £10). Ⓥ berth on pontoon **A**, first to stbd. 36m x 3m draught at hammerheads. (H24) Ⓔ (daily pick-up) (50t) (25t) ✕ ☎311523.
Town ✉ Ⓑ ⇌ ✈ (Prestwick/Glasgow).

HARBOUR ON THE FIRTH OF CLYDE SOUTH OF TROON

GIRVAN, S Ayrshire, **55°14'·77N 04°51'·87W**. AC 2199, 1866. HW +0043 on Dover; ML 1·8m; Duration 0630. See 2.23.

Good shelter. Brest Rks, 3·5M N of the harbour extend 6ca offshore. Beware Girvan Patch, 1·7m, 4ca SW of ent. Bar carries approx 1·5m. Entry not advised LW±2. River silts, local knowledge advised. S'ly of 2 Ch spires (110°) leads between N Bwtr, Fl R 4s 5m 2M, and S pier (deeper water), 2 FG (vert) 8m 4M in dredged channel 1·2m (2017). Inner N groyne, Iso 4s 3m 4M.

Traffic sig at root of S pier: 2 B discs (hor)/ 2 ● (hor) = hbr shut. HM ☎(01465) 713648; VHF Ch **12** 16 (HO)

35 (£2·70) on fingers around perimeter of inner hbr (1·7m). Coasters and FVs berth on adjacent quay.

Town Ⓑ ✉ ✕ ⇌.

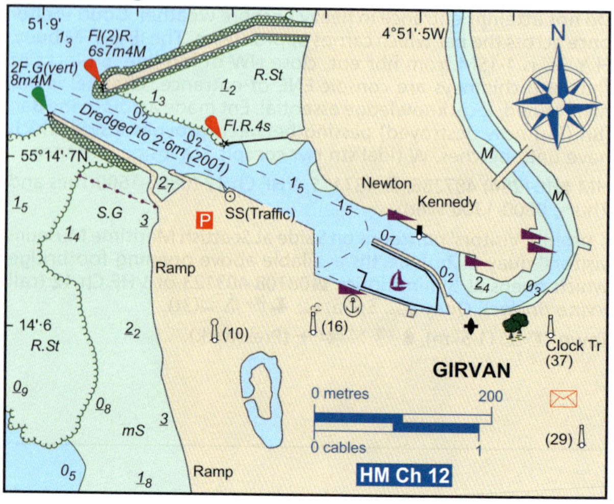

2.24 LOCH RYAN/STRANRAER

Dumfries and Galloway **55°01´N 05°05´W**

CHARTS AC 2198, 1403, 5610

TIDES HW (Stranraer) +0055 Dover; ML 1.6m; Duration 0640

Standard Port GREENOCK (⟵)

Times				Heights (metres)			
High Water		Low Water		MHWS	MHWN	MLWN	MLWS
0000	0600	0200	0800	3.4	2.8	1.0	0·3
1200	1800	1400	2000				
LOCH RYAN/STRANRAER							
–0030	*–0025*	*–0010*	*–0010*	*–0·2*	*–0·1*	*0·0*	*+0·1*

SHELTER Very good shelter except in strong NW winds. ⚓s in Lady Bay, 1·3M SSE of Milleur Pt, but exposed to heavy wash from HSS; in The Wig in 3m (avoid weed patches and old moorings); Stranraer Marina good shelter, but exposed to strong NE winds.

NAVIGATION LOCH RYAN: (see chartlet rhs). Ent between Milleur Pt and Finnarts Pt. Beware The Beef Barrel rock, 1m high 6ca SSE of Milleur Pt, Forbes Shoal ⍊ Fl(2)5s and The Spit running 1·5M to SE from W shore opposite Cairn Pt lt ho Fl (2) R10s 14m 12M. Frequent conventional and high-speed ferries run from Cairnryan and Loch Ryan Port, a new facility on NE shore to the NE of Cairn Pt. They operate in buoyed channels and areas, in which anchoring is prohibited. 3 x G bns mark the approach to STRANRAER. On reaching the harbour bear to starboard to pass between lateral marks immediately to the E of a rubble breakwater. Marina lies on SE side of West Pier with Ⓥ at seaward end.

LIGHTS AND MARKS Milleur Pt NCM Q; Loch Ryan Port ldg lts Iso 2s 9M; Cairn Pt Fl(2) R 10s 14m; Cairnryan ferry terminal Fl R 5s 5m 5M.

COMMUNICATIONS (Code 01776) HM ☎702460. VHF Ch **14** (H24)

FACILITIES **Marina** ☎706565, hbr off 707500; mob 07734 073421 or 07827 277247. 8 Ⓥ £3·25/m. Max LOA 27m; craft >23m must book in advance (30t).

Town .

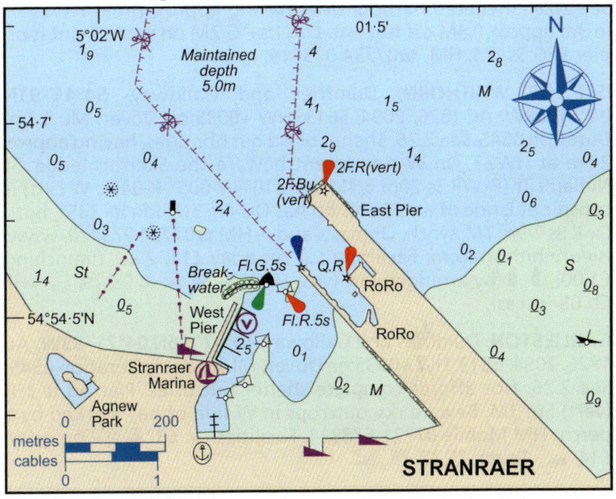

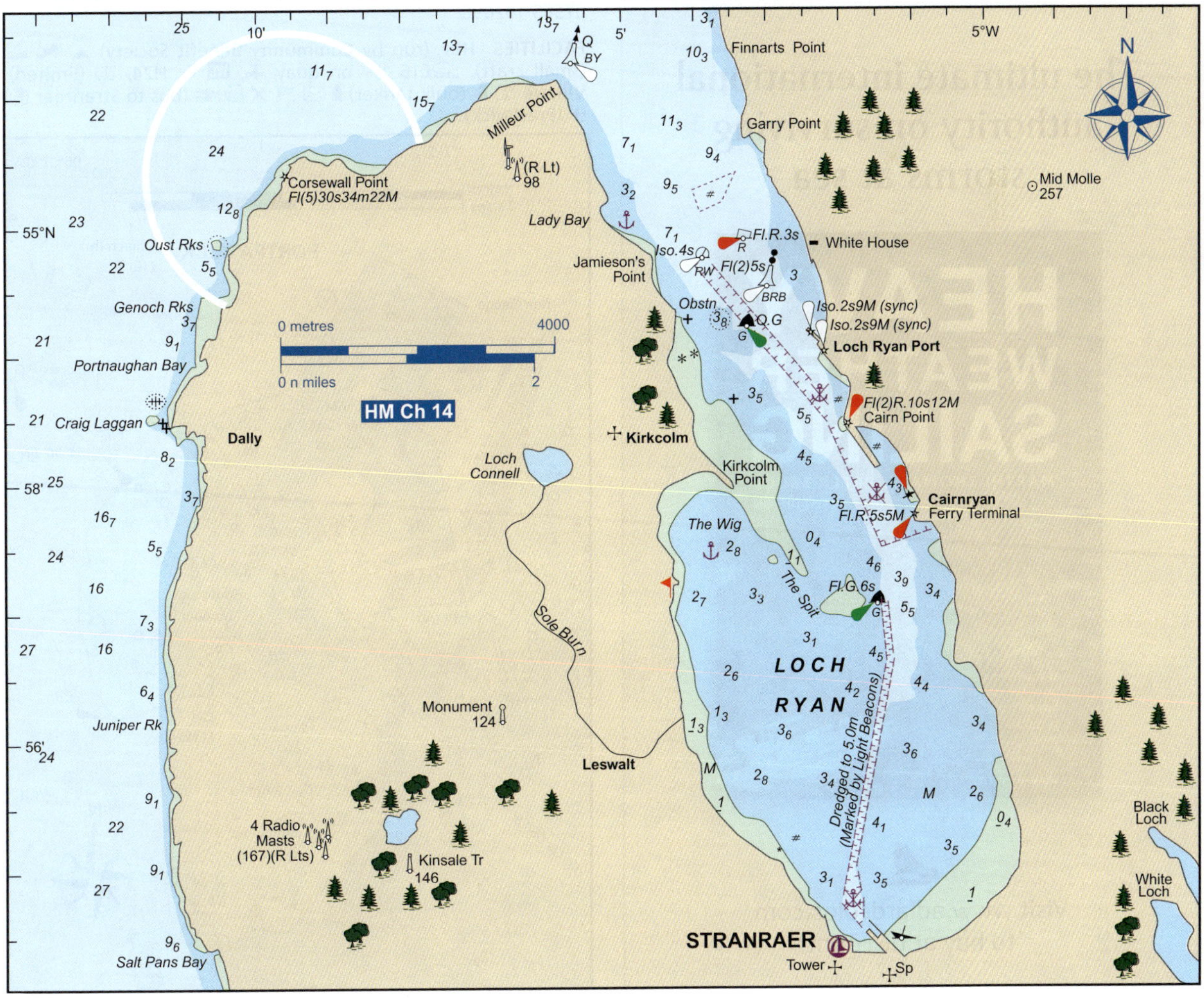

HARBOURS FROM MULL OF GALLOWAY TO WIGTOWN BAY

DRUMMORE, Dumfries and Galloway, **54°41′·57N 04°53′·49W.** AC 2094, 5613. HW +0040m on Dover; ML 3.3m; Duration 0610. Owned by Drummore Hbr Trust the small drying harbour has now silted almost entirely rendering it of little interest to passing mariners. Temp'y ⚓ 5.5ca NNE of hbr ent in 4m. Facilities in village: (bus to Stranraer), ✈ (Carlisle).

PORT WILLIAM, Dumfries and Galloway, **54°45′·70N 04°35′·10W.** AC 1826, 2094, 5613. HW +0035 on Dover; ML 3·7m; Duration 0545. See 2.26. Sheltered harbour dries having approx 1m at HW±2. ⚓ in 3m approx 0.4M off hbr ent. Ldg lts F G 2M on shore front lt on pier Fl G 3s 3M. HM ☎07734 073419.

ISLE OF WHITHORN, Dumfries and Galloway, **54°41′·91N 04°21′·88W.** AC 1826, 2094, 5613. HW +0035 on Dover; ML 3·7m; Duration 0545. See 2.26. Shelter good but hbr dries, having approx 2·5m at HW±3. On W side of ent beware the Skerries ledge. St Ninian's Tr (Fl WR 3s 20m 6/4M viz: 310°-W-005°-R-040°; W □ tr) is conspic at E side of ent. E pier hd has QG 4m 5M; ldg lts 335°, both Oc R 8s 7/9m 7M, synch, Or masts and ◊. HM ☎07734 073420, www.isleofwhithorn.com; Facilities: on quay £14, 2 (launching £1.00), (by arrangement with HM), VHF Ch 08 (occas).

GARLIESTON, Dumfries and Galloway, **54°47′·36N 04°21′·83W.** AC 1826, 2094, 5613. HW +0035 on Dover; ML no data; Duration 0545. See 2.26. Hbr affords complete shelter but dries. Pier hd lt 2FR (vert) 5m 3M. Beware rky outcrops in W side of bay marked by a perch. HM Mobile 07771 678824. Facilities: £3, on quay, £14, . **Town** .

2.25 PORTPATRICK

Dumfries and Galloway **54°50′·42N 05°07′·18W**

CHARTS AC 2724, 2198; Imray C62

TIDES +0032 Dover; ML 2·1; Duration 0615

Standard Port LIVERPOOL (⟶)

Times				Heights (metres)			
High Water		Low Water		MHWS	MHWN	MLWN	MLWS
0000	0600	0200	0800	9·4	7·5	3·2	1·1
1200	1800	1400	2000				
Differences PORTPATRICK							
+0038	+0032	0009	−0008	−5·5	−4·4	−2·0	−0·6

SHELTER Good in tiny Inner harbour (on rough stone wall), but entrance is difficult in strong SW/NW winds. Buoys protect ladders/yachts. Depth on wall reported as not more than 1.5m (2017).

NAVIGATION WPT 54°50′·00N 05°08′·07W, 050°/0·7M to ent. Ent to outer hbr by short narrow chan with hazards either side, including rky shelf covered at HW. Beware cross tides off ent, up to 3kn springs. Barrel buoy (a mooring buoy) marks end of Half Tide Rk; do not cut inside.

LIGHTS AND MARKS Old Lt Ho (W tower, 22m) on Black Head is conspic 1·6M north of entrance. Ldg lts 050·5°, FG (H24) 6/8m: Front on sea wall; rear on bldg; 2 vert orange stripes by day. Conspic features include: TV mast 1M NE, almost on ldg line; large hotel on cliffs about 1½ca NNW of hbr ent; Dunskey Castle (ru) 4ca SE of hbr.

COMMUNICATIONS (Code 01776) Ⓗ 702323; HM 810355, mob 07565 102096.

FACILITIES **Hbr** (run by Community Benefit Society) (small craft), £16 on quay, H24, (limited). **Village** (bulk tanker) (bus to Stranraer Ⓑ) ✈ (Prestwick).

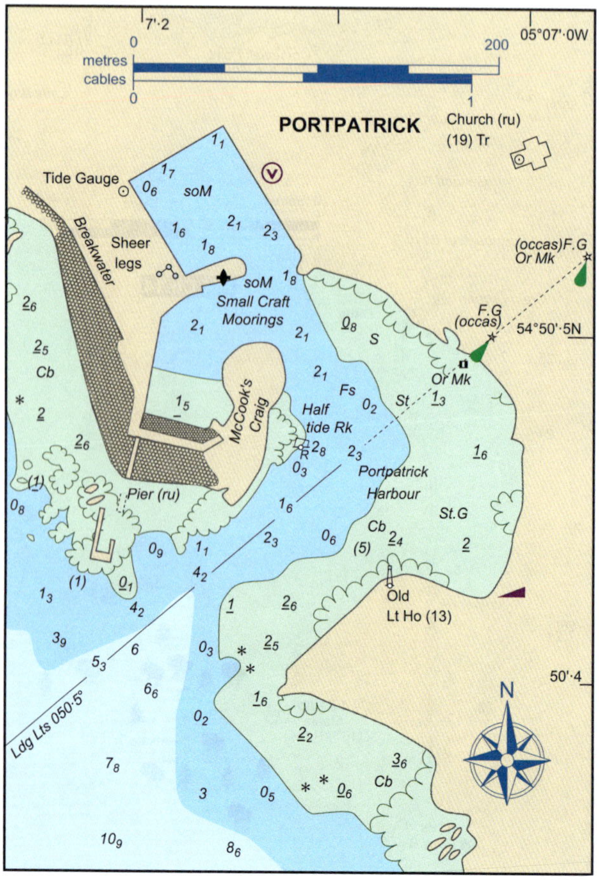

2.26 KIRKCUDBRIGHT

Dumfries and Galloway **54°50′·33N 04°03′·47W**

CHARTS AC 1826, 2094, 1346, 1344, 5613; Imray C62

TIDES +0030 Dover; ML 4·1; Duration 0545

Standard Port LIVERPOOL (3.16) (⟶)

Times				Height (metres)			
High Water		Low Water		MHWS	MHWN	MLWN	MLWS
0000	0600	0200	0800	9·4	7·5	3·2	1·1
1200	1800	1400	2000				
Differences KIRKCUDBRIGHT BAY							
+0020	+0020	+0005	−0005	−1·9	−1·6	−0·8	−0·3
DRUMMORE							
+0035	+0045	+0010	+0015	−3·5	−2·6	−1·2	−0·5
PORT WILLIAM							
+0035	+0035	+0020	−0005	−3·0	−2·3	−1·1	ND
GARLIESTON							
+0030	+0040	+0025	0000	−2·4	−1·8	−0·8	ND
ISLE OF WHITHORN							
+0025	+0030	+0020	0000	−2·5	−2·1	−1·1	−0·4
HESTAN ISLET (Kippford)							
+0030	+0030	+0015	+0020	−1·1	−1·2	−0·8	−0·2
SOUTHERNESS POINT							
+0035	+0035	+0025	+0005	−0·8	−0·8	ND	ND
ANNAN WATERFOOT							
+0055	+0110	+0215	+0305	−2·3	−2·7	−3·0	CD+
TORDUFF POINT							
+0110	+0145	+0515	+0405	−4·2	−5·0	CD+	CD+
REDKIRK							
+0115	+0220	+0710	+0440	−5·6	−6·3	CD+	CD+

NOTES: At Annan Waterfoot, Torduff Pt and Redkirk the LW time differences are for the start of the rise, which at sp is very sudden. CD+ = At LW the tide does not usually fall below CD; ND = No Data.

SHELTER Very good. Depths at LW: 1·0–2·0m at the floating pontoon 300m below quay, visitors should always berth/raft on N side of it between piles 9 and 11 marked by white line. Craft drawing 2·0–3·0m, and drying out against Town Quay (used H24 by FVs) by advance arrangement with HM. Downriver there are good ⚓s close W, N, and NE of Little Ross and ½ca N of Torrs Pt, except in S'lies which raise heavy swell.

NAVIGATION WPT 54°45′·51N 04°04′·08W, 005°/1·4M to Torrs Pt. The Bar is 1ca N of Torrs Pt; access HW±2½. R Dee has depths of 0·1m to 4·3m. Spring tides run up to 3–4kn. A firing range straddles the ent but no restrictions on transit of firing area; call Range Safety Officer ☎(01557) 500271 (out of hours), 830236 HO or Range Safety Craft, Gallavidian, monitoring VHF Ch **73** 16.

LIGHTS AND MARKS Little Ross Lt ho, W of ent, Fl 5s 50m 12M, NNE end of Is, Stone bn Fl (2) 5s 21m 5M. Fl 3s 7m 3M, on shed (54°47′·70N). River well lit/marked, 2 Fl G lts at pontoon.

COMMUNICATIONS (Code 01557) Dr 330755; HM 331135 Mobile 07709 479663; GM Marine Services (Fuel) 07970 109814. Ch 12 (0730-1700). *Range Control* Ch **73** 16.

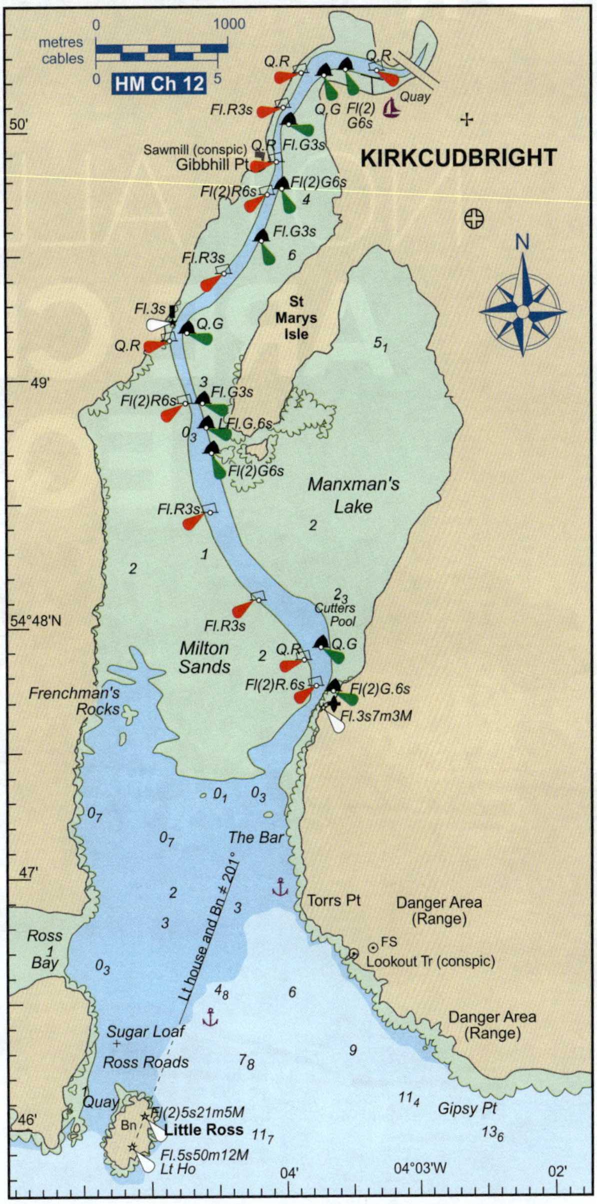

FACILITIES Pontoon/jetty max LOA 20m £3·25/m inc **Town Quay** (by arrangement with HM) (15t).
KYC ☎330963; **SC** ☎330032.
Town ✉ Ⓑ ⇌ (Dumfries 30M), ✈ (Glasgow 100M).

HARBOUR IN THE SOLWAY FIRTH APPROACHES

KIPPFORD, Dumfries and Galloway, **54°52′·36N 03°48′·93W**.
AC 1826, 1346, 5613. HW +0040 on Dover; ML 4·2m (Hestan Is). Good shelter on drying /pontoons off Kippford, 2·75M up drying Urr Estuary from Hestan Is lt ho Fl (2) 10s 42m 9M. Temp ⚓s NE or W of Hestan Is to await tide. Navigation Access via drying, marked, unlit chan. *Clyde Cruising Club* or *Solway Sailing Directions* (from Solway YC) are strongly advised. Beware Craig Roan on E side of entrance. Comms Ch M call *Kippford Startline* (YC) HW±2 in season. *Kippford Slipway* (Pilotage) Ch 16. **Solway YC** www.thesyc.com ☎(01556) 620312; . **Services:** £10 *Kippford Slipway Ltd* (01556) 620249. **Town** ✉.

West England, IoM & Wales

Solway Firth to Land's End

North West England, Isle of Man and North Wales
EMERGENCY 999
HMCG NATIONAL – 02392 552100
HMCG HOLYHEAD – 01407 762051
HM CUSTOMS – 0845 010 9000
POLICE – 101 MEDICAL – 111
Harbour with full almanac entry
Minor harbour or anchorage
Major light
NCI station
Ferry route
Airport
See 2.1
Luce Bay
Port William
Garlieston
Wigtown Bay
Kirkcudbright
Little Ross
Kipperford
Hestan I
Solway Firth
Silloth
3.1
Robin Rigg Wind Farm
MARYPORT 3.5
WORKINGTON 3.6
Harrington
WHITEHAVEN 3.7
St Bees Head
Ravenglass
Tarn Point
Duddon Bar
Barrow-in-Furness
Ulverston
Arnside
Morecambe
Lancaster
Heysham
GLASSON DOCK 3.13
FLEETWOOD 3.14
Walney I
Ormonde Wind Farm
Duddon Sands Wind Farm
Barrow Wind Farm
Walney Wind Farm
Heysham
Magnetic Variation 1·1°W
Liverpool
Dublin
Belfast
Belfast CG
Holyhead CG
Drummore
Crammag Head
Mull of Galloway
Burrow Head
Isle of Whithorn
Point of Ayre
RAMSEY 3.12
Maughold Head
Laxey
DOUGLAS 3.11
Douglas Head
ISLE OF MAN 9.10.9
Derby Haven
Langness
Castletown
Port Erin
PEEL 3.9
PORT ST MARY 3.10
Chicken Rock
54°N
30'
5°W
30'
4°
30'
3°

DISTANCE TABLE
Approximate distances in nautical miles are by the most direct route, whilst avoiding dangers and allowing for Traffic Separation Schemes. Places in *italics* are in adjoining areas; places in **bold** are in 0.32, Distances across the Irish Sea.

1	***Fishguard***	158	175	175	169	163	153	140	126	134	144	153	147	142	136	100	88	78	89	45	**1**
2	*Bardsey Island*	113	129	129	123	117	107	94	80	88	98	107	101	96	90	53	41	31	43	**2**	
3	**Holyhead**	81	94	96	90	84	68	62	46	50	65	79	73	74	68	36	32	26	**3**		
4	Menai (Caernarfon)	103	104	105	99	93	81	73	68	68	80	76	70	68	59	22	10	**4**			
5	Menai (Beaumaris)	93	94	95	89	83	71	73	58	58	70	66	60	58	49	12	**5**				
6	**Conwy/Deganwy**	95	95	92	86	80	72	72	57	59	68	62	56	55	46	**6**					
7	**Liverpool**	102	97	89	83	77	80	86	76	70	77	52	46	30	**7**						
8	River Ribble Ent	86	76	68	62	56	65	89	69	61	62	32	27	**8**							
9	**Fleetwood**	79	68	59	53	47	58	80	63	57	55	10	**9**								
10	Glasson Dock	85	74	66	60	54	64	85	69	63	61	**10**									
11	Ramsey	28	34	41	35	32	6	24	27	15	**11**										
12	Douglas	42	46	50	44	39	19	30	13	**12**											
13	**Port St Mary**	41	61	63	57	51	35	18	**13**												
14	Peel	26	46	55	49	49	18	**14**													
15	**Point of Ayre**	22	28	37	31	31	**15**														
16	Whitehaven	44	23	12	7	**16**															
17	Workington	47	25	6	**17**																
18	**Maryport**	49	26	**18**																	
19	**Kirkcudbright**	32	**19**																		
20	***Mull of Galloway***	**20**																			

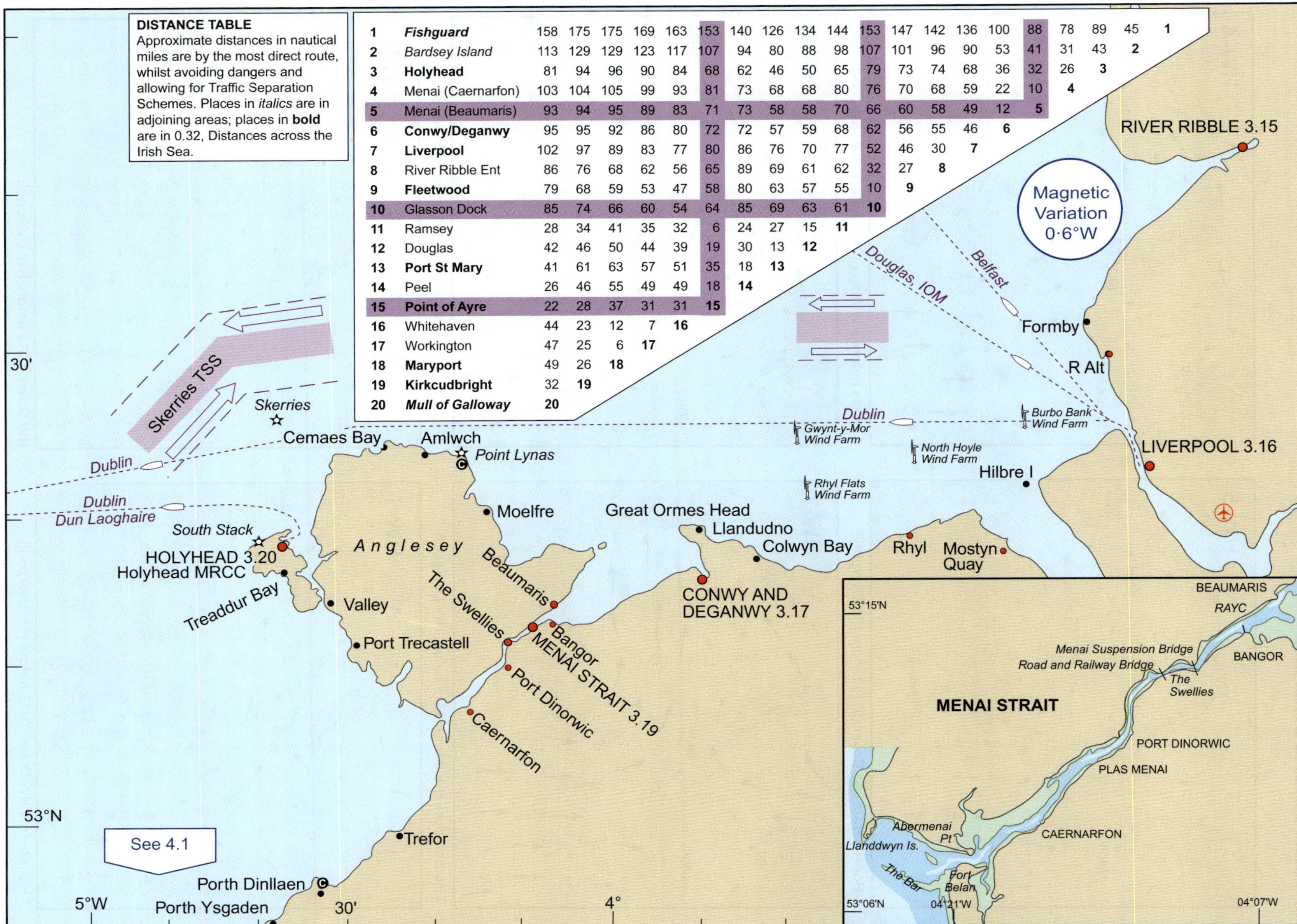

NW England

3.2 AREA 3 TIDAL STREAMS

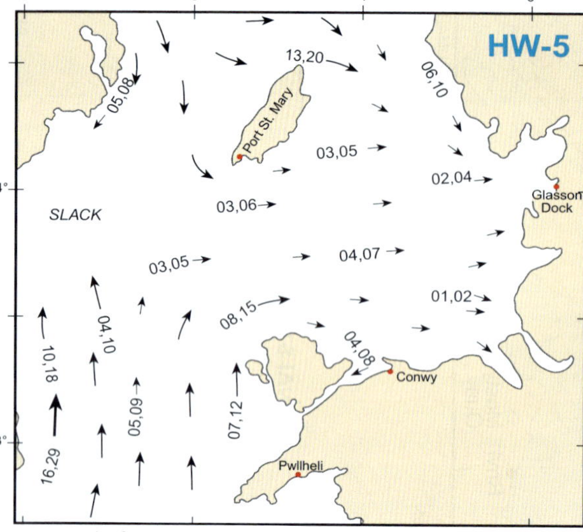

5 Hours before HW Dover (0515 before HW Liverpool)

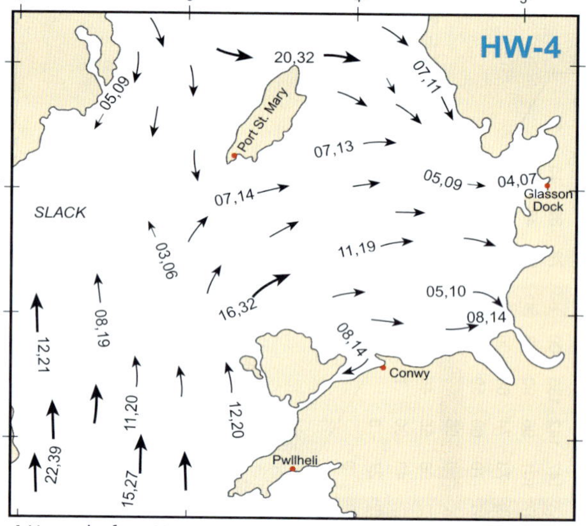

4 Hours before HW Dover (0415 before HW Liverpool)

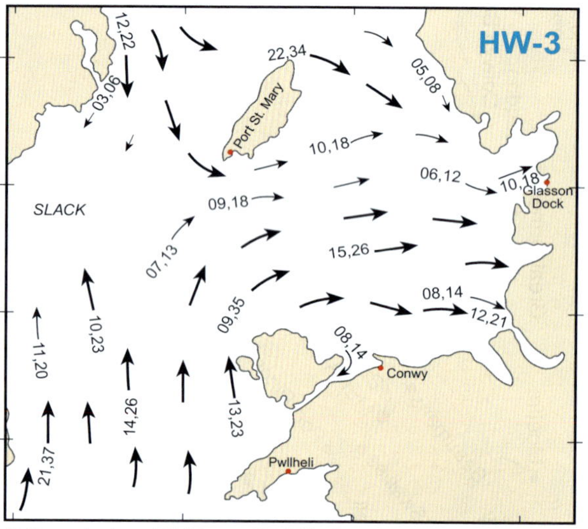

3 Hours before HW Dover (0315 before HW Liverpool)

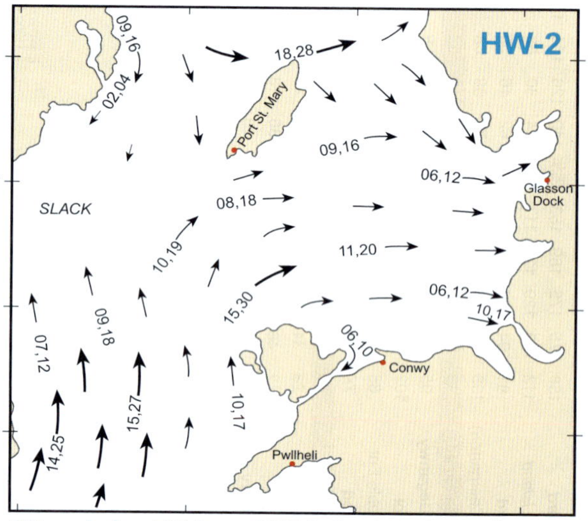

2 Hours before HW Dover (0215 before HW Liverpool)

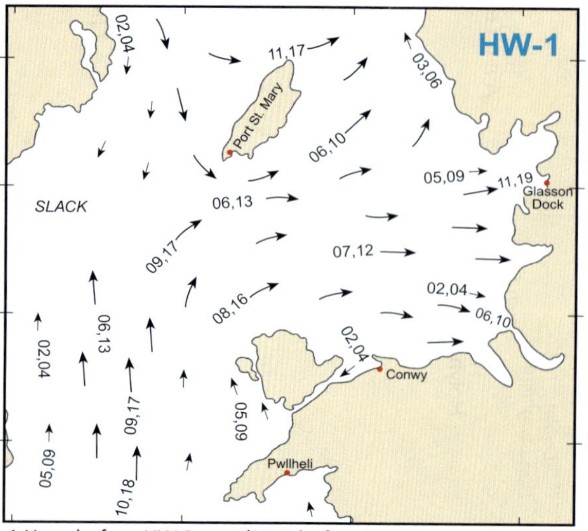

1 Hour before HW Dover (0115 before HW Liverpool)

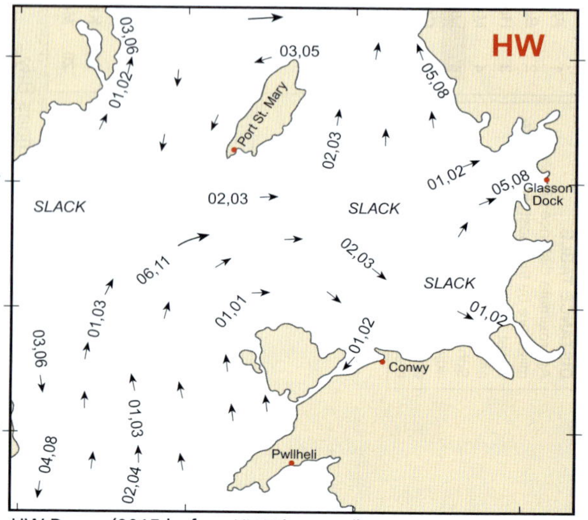

HW Dover (0015 before HW Liverpool)

Northward 2.2 Southward 4.2 North Ireland 6.2 Mull of Kintyre 2.10 South Ireland 5.2

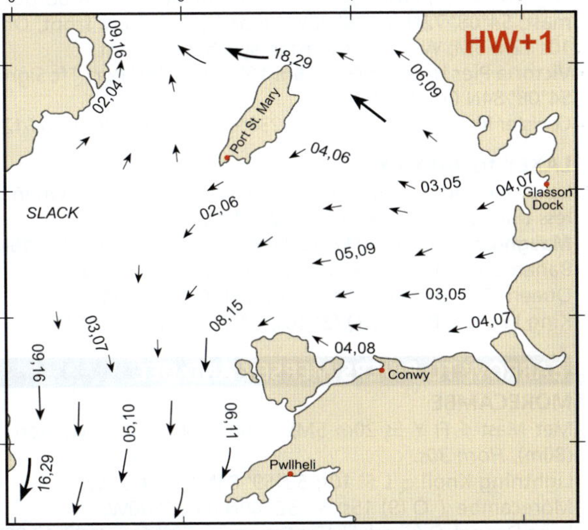

1 Hour after HW Dover (0045 after HW Liverpool)

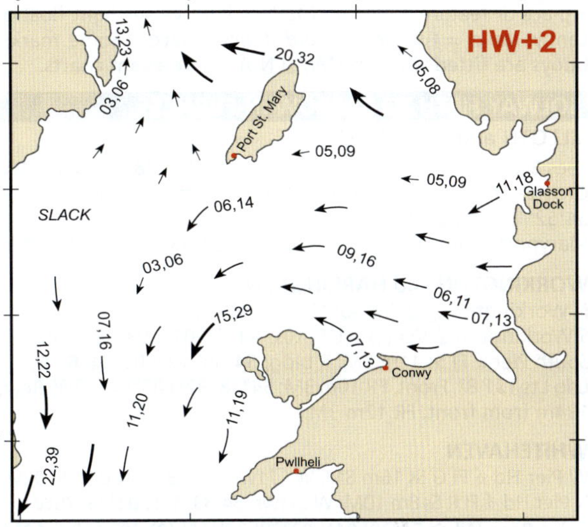

2 Hours after HW Dover (0145 after HW Liverpool)

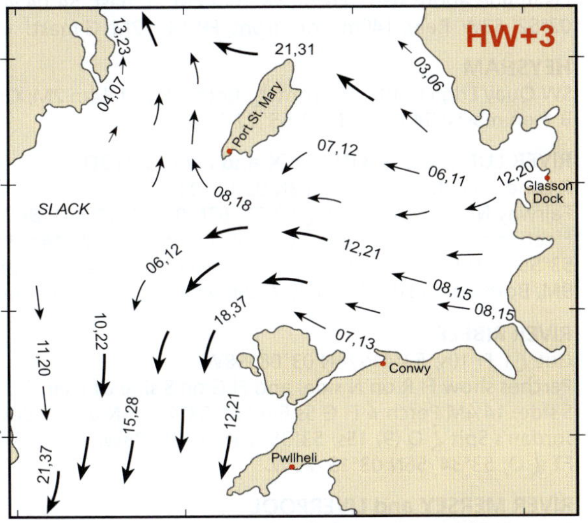

3 Hours after HW Dover (0245 after HW Liverpool)

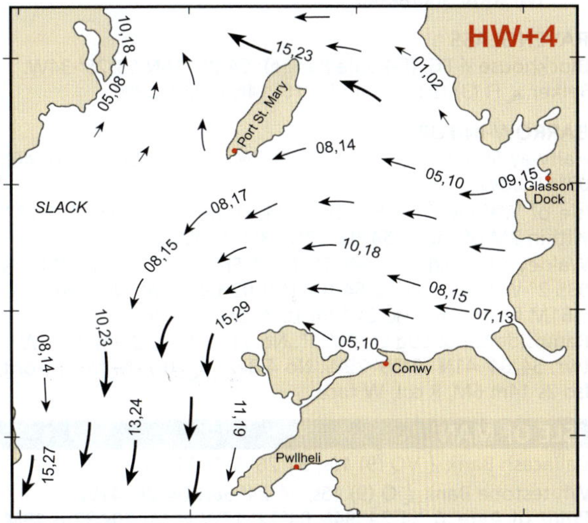

4 Hours after HW Dover (0345 after HW Liverpool)

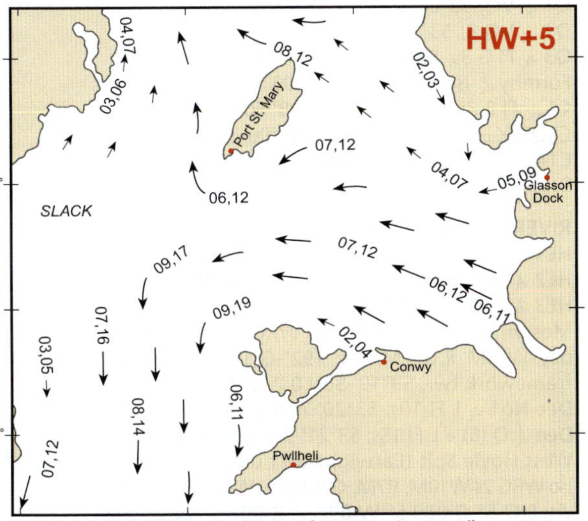

5 Hours after HW Dover (0445 after HW Liverpool)

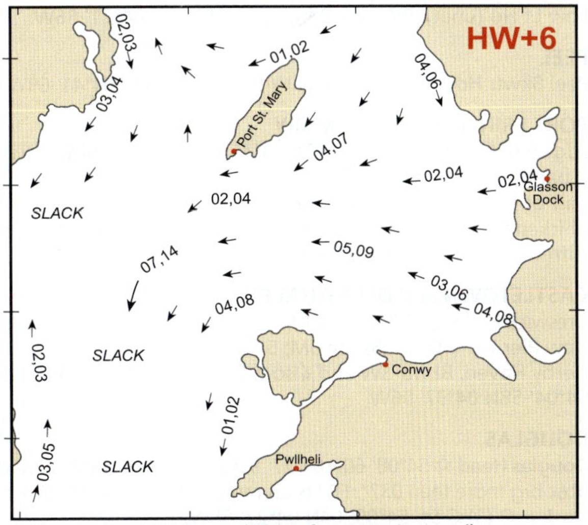

6 Hours after HW Dover (0545 after HW Liverpool)

3.3 LIGHTS, BUOYS AND WAYPOINTS

Bold print = light with a nominal range of 15M or more. CAPITALS = place or feature. *CAPITAL ITALICS* = light-vessel, light float or Lanby. *Italics* = Fog signal. ***Bold italics*** = Racon. Some marks/ buoys are fitted with AIS (MMSI No); see relevant charts.

SOLWAY FIRTH TO BARROW-IN-FURNESS

SILLOTH and MARYPORT

Lees Scar ☆ Fl G 5s 11m 4M; W piles; 54°51′·78N 03°24′·79W.
Groyne Hd ☆ 2 FG (vert) 4m 4M; Fl Bu tfc signals close by; 54°52′·14N 03°23′·93W.
Maryport S Pier Hd ☆.Fl 1·5s 10m 6M; 54°43′·07N 03°30′·64W.

WORKINGTON and HARRINGTON

N Workington Q; 54°40′·10N 03°38′·18W.
S Workington VQ (6) + L Fl 10s; 54°37′·01N 03°38′·58W.
South Pier ☆ Fl 5s 11m 5M; R bldg; 54°39′·12N 03°34′·67W.
Ldg Lts 131·8°. Front, FR 10m 3M; 54°38′·92N 03°34′·19W. Rear, 134m from front, FR 12m 3M.

WHITEHAVEN

W Pier Hd ☆ Fl G 5s 16m 8M; W ○ twr; 54°33′·17N 03°35′·92W.
N Pier Hd ☆ Fl R 5s 8m 10M; W ○ twr; 54°33′·17N 03°35′·75W.
Saint Bees Hd ☆ 54°30′·81N 03°38′·23W Fl (2) 20s 102m **18M**; W○ twr; obsc shore-340°.

RAVENGLASS

Blockhouse ☆ FG; (Eskdale Range); 54°20′·16N 03°25′·34W.
Selker Fl (3) G 10s; *Bell;* 54°16′·14N 03°29′·58W.

BARROW-IN-FURNESS

Halfway Shoal QR 19m 10s; R&W chequer Bn; 54°01′·46N 03°11′·88W.
Isle of Walney ☆ Fl 15s 21m 10M; stone twr; obsc 122°-127° within 3M of shore; 54°02′·92N 03°10′·64W.
Walney Chan Ldg Lts 040·7°. No 1 Front, Q 7m 10M; vis: 035·2°-W-046·2°; Or □; 54°03′·19N 03°09′·22W. No 2 Rear, 0·61M from front, Iso 2s 13m 10M; Or □ on Pile.
Rampside Sands Ldg Lts 005·1°. No 3 Front, Q 9m10M; W ○ twr; 54°04′·41N 03°09′·79W. No 4 Rear, 0·77M from front, Iso 2s 14m 6M; R col, W face.

ISLE OF MAN

Ballacash Bank VQ (9) 10s; 54°26′·50N 04°16′·70W.
Whitestone Bank Q (9) 15s; 54°24′·58N 04°20′·41W.
Point of Ayre ☆ 54°24′·94N 04°22′·13W Fl (4) 20s 32m **19M**; W twr, two R bands, ***Racon (M) 13-15M***.
Low Lt Ho (unlit), RW twr, B base, 54°25′·03N 04°21′·86W.

PEEL

Peel Bkwtr Hd ☆ Oc 7s 11m 6M; W twr; 54°13′·67N 04°41′·69W.

PORT ERIN and PORT ST MARY

Ldg Lts 099·1°. Front, 54°05′·23N 04°45′·57W FR 10m 5M; W twr, R band. Rear, 39m from front, FR 19m 5M; W col, R band.
Calf of Man Lighthouse (disused), white 8-sided tower.
Chicken Rk ☆ Fl 5s 38m **18M**; ***Racon (C)*** 54°02′·27N 04°50′·32W
Alfred Pier Hd ☆ Oc R 10s 8m 6M; 54°04′·33N 04°43′·82W.

CASTLETOWN and DERBY HAVEN

Dreswick Pt ☆ Fl (2) 30s 23m 12M; W twr; 54°03′·29N 04°37′·45W.
New Pier Hd ☆ Oc R 15s 8m 5M; 54°04′·33N 04°38′·97W.
Derby Haven, Bkwtr SW end ☆Iso G 2s 5m 5M; W twr, G band; 54°04′·58N 04°37′·06W.

DOUGLAS

Douglas Head ☆ 54°08′·60N 04°27′·95W Fl 10s 32m **15M**; W twr; obsc brg more than 037°. FR Lts on radio masts 1 and 3M West.
No 1 Q (3) G 5s; 54°09′·04N 04°27′·68W.
Princess Alexandra Pier Hd ☆ Fl R 5s 16m 8M; R mast; *Whis (2) 40s;* 54°08′·84N 04°27′·85W.
Ldg Lts 229·3°, Front, Oc Bu 10s 9m 5M; W △ R border on mast; 54°08′·72N 04°28′·25W. Rear, 62m from front, Oc Bu 10s 12m 5M; W ▽ on R border; synch with front.
Victoria Pier Hd ☆ Iso G 10s 6m 10M; Post; Intl Port Tfc Signals; 54°08′·84N 04°28′·08W.
Conister Rk Refuge Q 3M; vis: 234°-312°; 54°09′·03N 04°28′·12W.

LAXEY to RAMSEY

Laxey Pier Hd ☆ Oc R 3s 7m 5M; W twr, R band; obsc when brg less than 318°; 54°13′·50N 04°23′·43W.
Maughold Head ☆ 54°17′·72N 04°18′·58W Fl (3) 30s 65m **15M**.
Bahama VQ (6) + L Fl 10s; 54°20′·01N 04°08′·57W.
Queens Pier Dn ☆ Fl R 5s; 54°19′·28N 04°21′·95W.
King William Bank Q (3) 10s; 54°26′·01N 04°00′·08W.

BARROW TO RIVERS MERSEY AND DEE

MORECAMBE

Met Mast ☆ Fl Y 5s 20m 5M*;* 54°00′·13N 03°33′·38W; Aero FR (80m), *Horn 30s.*
Lightning Knoll L Fl 10s; 53°59′·84N 03°14′·28W.
Morecambe Q (9) 15s; 53°52′·00N 03°22′·00W.
Lune Deep Q (6) + L Fl 15s; ***Racon (T);*** 53°56′·07N 03°12·90W.
Lts in line about 090°. Front, FR 10m 2M; G mast; 54°04′·41N 02°52′·63W. Rear, 140m from front, FR 14m 2M; G mast.

HEYSHAM

SW Quay Ldg Lts 102·2°. Front, both F Bu 11/14m 2M; Or & B ♦ on masts; 54°01′·91N 02°55′·22W.

RIVER LUNE, GLASSON DOCK and FLEETWOOD

R Lune Q (9) 15s; 53°58′·63N 03°00′·03W.
Fairway No 1(Fleetwood) 53°57′·67N 03°02′·03W Q; *Bell.*
Fleetwood Esplanade Ldg Lts 156°. Front, Iso G 2s 14m 9M; 53°55′·71N 03°00′·56W. Rear, 320m from front, Iso G 4s 28m 9M. Both vis on Ldg line only. (H24) (chan liable to change).

RIVER RIBBLE

Gut L Fl 10s; 53°41′·74N 03°08′·98W.
Perches show Fl R on N side, and Fl G on S side of chan.
S side, 14¼M Perch ☆ Fl G 5s 6m 3M; 53°42′·75N 03°04′·90W.
Jordan's Spit Q (9) 15s; 53°35′·76N 03°19′·28W.
FT Q; 53°34′·56N 03°13′·20W.

RIVER MERSEY and LIVERPOOL

Bar Fl.5s 12M; ***Racon (T) 10M***; 53°32′·02N 03°20′·98W, AIS.
Q1 VQ; 53°31′·01N 03°16′·70W.
Q2 VQ R; 53°31′·48N 03°14′·94W.
Q3 Fl G 3s; 53°30′·97N 03°15′·08W.
Formby Iso 4s; 53°31′·14N 03°13′·48W.
C4 Fl R 3s; 53°31′·83N 03°08′·50W.
CROSBY Oc 5s; 53°30′·74N 03°06′·30W.
C14 Fl R 3s; 53°29′·93N 03°05′·35W.
Brazil QG; G hull,53°26′·85N 03°02′·23W.

RIVER DEE, MOSTYN and CONNAH'S QUAY

HE1 Q (9) 15s; 53°26′·33N 03°18′·08W.
HE2 Fl G 2·5s; 53°24′·90N 03°12′·88W.
HE3 Q G; 53°24′·55N 03°12′·74W.
Mostyn Dir Lt ☆ 194·5°; Iso WRG 2s 11m W 10M R,G 7M, by day W 3M R,G 2M; vis: 192°-G-194°-W-195°-R-197°; H24; Y framework twr; 53°19′·55N 03°15′·69W.
Dee No1 L Fl 10s; 53°20′·70N 03°12′·46W.
Dee Q (6) + L Fl 15s; 53°21′·90N 03°18·20W.
West Hoyle Spit (Earwig) Dir Lt 090. 53°21′·21N 03°24′·07W; Iso WRG 2s W10M, R7M, G7M (day W3M, R2M, G2M); vis: 087·5°-G-089·5°-W-090·5°-R-092·5°; occasional.
S Hoyle Outer Fl R 2·5s; 53°21′·26N 03°26′·95W.

WALES – NORTH COAST AND INNER PASSAGE

South Hoyle Outer Fl R 2·5s; 53°21'·47N 03°24'·70W.
Prestatyn Q; 53°21'·37N 03°29'·00W.
Inner Passage Fl R 5s; 53°21'·91N 03°31'·95W.
Mid Patch Spit QR; 53°22'·25N 03°32'·67W.
Mast Fl Y 5s 18m 5M; Mast (80); 53°28'·84N 03°30'·50W.
W Constable Q (9) 15s; ***Racon (M) 10M***; 53°23'·14N 03°49'·26W.

RHYL, LLANDUDNO and CONWY

River Clwyd Outfall Q R 7m 2M; 53°19'·45N 03°30'·34W.
Llandudno Pier Hd 2 FG (vert) 8m 4M; 53°19'·90N 03°49'·51W.
Great Ormes Hd Lt Ho, (unlit); 53°20'·56N 03°52'·17W.
Conwy Fairway L Fl 10s; 53°17'·95N 03°55'·58W.
C1 Fl G 10s; 53°17'·83N 03°54'·58W.
C2 Fl (2) R 10s; 53°17'·94N 03°54'·52W.
River Conwy ent, L Fl G 15s 5m 2M; 53°18'·03N 03°50'·86W.

ANGLESEY

Point Lynas ☆ 53°24'·98N 04°17'·35W Oc 10s 39m **18M**; W castellated twr; vis: 109°-315°; H24.

AMLWCH to HOLYHEAD BAY

Main Bkwtr Fl G 15s 11m 3M; W mast; vis: 141°-271°; 53°25'·02N 04°19'·91W.
Furlong Fl G 2·5s; 53°25'·41N 04°30'·47W.
Archdeacon Rock Q; 53°26'·71N 04°30'·87W.
Victoria Bank VQ; 53°25'·61N 04°31'·37W.
Coal Rk Q (6) + L Fl 15s; 53°25'·91N 04°32'·79W.
Ethel Rk VQ; 53°26'·64N 04°33'·67W.
The Skerries ☆ 53°25'·27N 04°36'·50W Fl (2) 15s 36m **20M**; W ○ twr, R band; ***Racon (T) 25M***. Iso R 4s 26m 10M; same twr; vis: 233°-252°, sector unreliable > 4M; *Horn (2) 60s*. H24 in periods of reduced visibility; 992351084.
Langdon Q (9) 15s; 53°22'·74N 04°38'·74W.
Bolivar FL G 2·5s; 53°21'·51N 04°35'·33W.
Wk Fl (2) R 10s; 53°20'·43N 04°36'·60W.

HOLYHEAD to SOUTH STACK

Bkwtr Head Fl (3) G 10s 21m 14M; W □ twr, B band; Fl Y vis: 174°-226°; *Siren 20s;* 53°19'·86N 04°37'·16W.
Spit Fl G 3s; 53°19'·79N 04°37'·15W.
South Stack ☆ 53°18'·41N 04°41'·98W Fl 10s 60m **24M**; (H24); W ○ twr; obsc to N by N Stack and part obsc in Penrhos bay; *Horn 30s*. Fog Det lt vis: 145°-325°.

MENAI STRAIT TO BARDSEY ISLAND

Ten Feet Bank QR; 53°19'·47N 04°02'·82W.
Dinmor QG; 53°19'·34N 04°03'·32W.
Trwyn-Du Fl 5s 19m 12M; W ○ castellated twr, B bands; vis: 101°-023°; *Horn (3) 30s*, sounded continuously; 53°18'·77N 04°02'·45W.

MENAI STRAIT
(Direction of buoyage NE to SW)

Perch Rock Fl R 5s; 53°18'·73N 04°02'·09W.
Port Dinorwic Pier Hd 53°11'·21N 04°12'·60W F WR 5m 2M; vis: 225°-R-357°-W-225°.

(Direction of buoyage SW to NE)

Caernarfon N Pier 2 FG(vert) 5m 2M; 53°08'·72N 04°16'·56W.
Abermenai Point Fl WR 3·5s 6m 3M; W mast; vis: 065°-R-245°-W-065°; 53°07'·62N 04°19'·72W.
C1 Fl G 5s; 53°07'·18N 04°24'·60W.
C2 Fl R 10s; 53°07'·38N 04°24'·33W.
Caernarfon Bar L Fl 10s; 53°07'·00N 04°25'·00W.
Llanddwyn I Fl WR 2·5s 12m W7M, R4M; W twr; vis: 280°-R-015°-W-120°; 53°08'·05N 04°24'·79W.

PORTH DINLLÄEN

CG Stn FR when firing 10M N; 52°56'·82N 04°33'·89W.
Careg y Chwislen Fl(2) 10s 2M 52°56'·99N 04°33'·51W.
Bardsey I ☆ 52°44'·97N 04°48'·02W Fl R 10s 39m **18M**; W □ twr, R bands; obsc by Bardsey Is 198°-250° and in Tremadoc B when brg < 260°.

3.4 PASSAGE INFORMATION

Admiralty Leisure Folio 5613, Irish Sea eastern part including Isle of Man, covers the Mull of Galloway to Great Ormes Head including the Isle of Man. Folio 5609, North West Wales including Menai Strait, covers Colwyn Bay to Aberystwyth, including Anglesey. **Bibliography:** *Irish Sea Pilot* (Imray/Rainsbury). *Cruising Anglesey and Adjoining Waters* (Imray/Morris). (Imray/Clyde Cruising Club): *Firth of Clyde West Coasts of England and Wales Pilot* (Admiralty NP37).

SOLWAY FIRTH

(AC 1346) Between Abbey Hd and St Bees Hd lies the Solway Firth, most of which is encumbered by shifting sandbanks. *Solway SDs* are essential. Off the entrances to the Firth, and in the approaches to Workington, beware shoals over which strong W winds raise a heavy sea. The area N of Silloth is unsurveyed but channels are navigable as far as Dumfries and Annan (N shore). Buoys are primarily for the aid of pilots.

▶ *Local knowledge is required, particularly in the upper Firth, where streams run very strongly in channels when the banks are dry, and less strongly when they are covered. In Powfoot Channel the flood stream begins at HW L'pool – 0300, and the ebb at HW L'pool + 0100,* ***Sp rates up to 6kn.*** ◀

The River Nith, approached between Borron Point and Blackshaw Spit, leads to Carsethorn, Glencaple, Kingholm Quay and Dumfries. There are 2 ⚓s at Caresthorn; Kingholm Quay offers drying berths, and on pontoons. Local knowledge is essential, but pilotage for visiting yachts is available. Contact Nith navigation ☎07801 321457 / 07860 522598.

On the south side of the Solway Firth are Maryport, Workington, Harrington and Whitehaven. South of St Bees Head lies the nuclear processing plant at Sellafield. The large shallow drying harbour at Ravenglass lies south again with Eskmeals Firing Range. Selker rocks and Black Leg Rk are notable shoals between Ravenglass and the Duddon Estuary. This dries at LW and is only navigable by small shoal draught craft. The Isle of Walney has an airfield and shelters Barrow-in-Furness which is reached by Walney Channel on rounding South East Point.

Morecambe Bay is shallow and mostly dries. Heysham harbour is exclusively for commercial traffic. The R Lune gives access to Port Glasson and the R Wyre to Fleetwood. The Channels which traverse the extensive offshore sandbanks are buoyed and shift frequently. Shell Flat extends 11M off the beach at Blackpool.

WIND FARMS

Robin Rigg wind farm is approximately 7M WNW of Maryport. Be aware of Walney, Ormonde Barrow and West of Duddon Sands wind farms between 6M and 12M off Walney Island. Burbo Bank wind farm (57 turbines) is directly S of the approaches to Liverpool extending W of the Bar light vessel. North Hoyle, Gwynt y Mor (160 turbines) and Rhyl Flats wind farms lie between 6M and 12M off the coast of N Wales.

ISLE OF MAN

(Charts 2094, 2696, 5613) Pilotage information and harbours see *IOM Sailing Directions, Tidal Streams and Anchorages,* (Hunter Pubs); *FIRTH OF CLYDE-Including Solway Firth and North Channel* (Imray). Crossing the Irish Sea, see 6.4.

There are four choices rounding S of IoM:

- In bad weather, or at night, keep south of Chicken Rk.
- If benign pass between Chicken Rk and Calf of Man.
- By day, with winds <F3 and a reliable engine giving >5kn, Calf Sound between Calf of Man and IoM is navigable. Pass between Kitterland Is and Thousla Rk(FIR 3s 9m).
- Little Sound – unmarked chan – runs E of Kitterland Is.

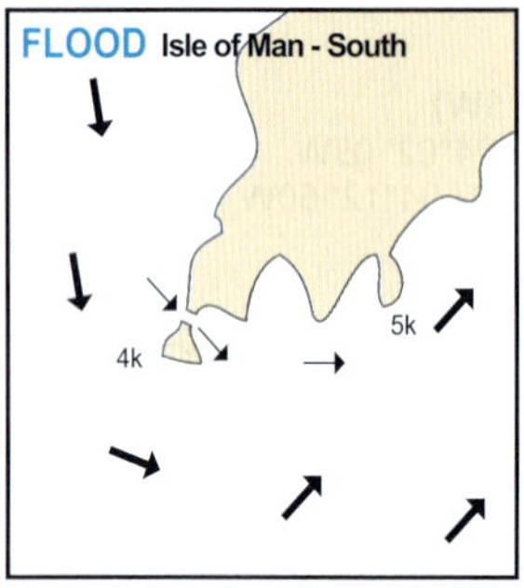

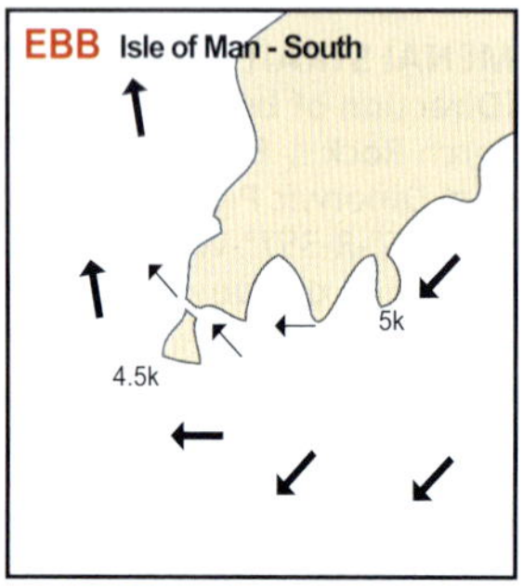

▶ *The stream runs strongly through Calf Sound, N-going at HW Liverpool –0145, and S-going at HW Liverpool +0345, Sp rate 3·5kn. W of Calf of Man the stream runs N/S, but changes direction off Chicken Rk running E/W between Calf of Man and Langness Pt. Overfalls extend E from Chicken Rk on E-going stream, beginning at HW L'pool +0610, and N from the rock on W-going stream, starting at HW L'pool. The Skerranes (drying) extend 1ca SW Of Langness Pt (lit). Tidal streams here run strongly, with eddies and a race. In strong winds a dangerous sea builds to the E of Langness peninsula. The NE-going stream begins at HW L'pool +0545, and the SW-going at HW L'pool –0415, Sp rates 2·25kn.* ◀

⚓ (exposed to the E) in Derby Haven, N of St Michael's Is. From here to Douglas and on to Maughold Hd (lt), there are no dangers more than 4ca offshore.

▶ *Inshore the SW-going stream runs for 9hrs and the NE-going for 3hrs, a back eddy forming during the NE'ly stream. Off Maughold Hd the NE'ly stream begins at HW L'pool +0500, and SW'ly at HW L'pool –0415.* ◀

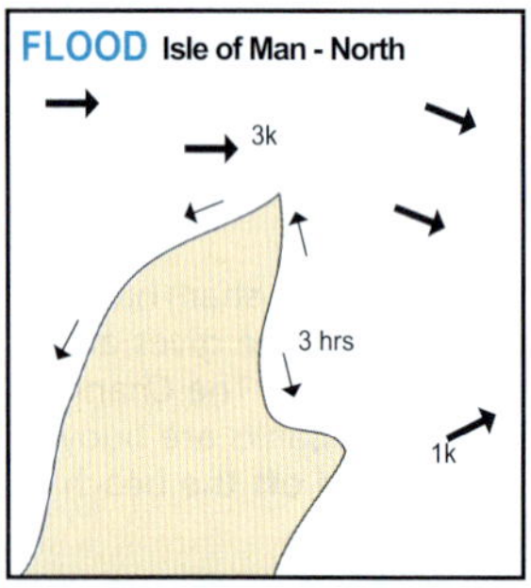

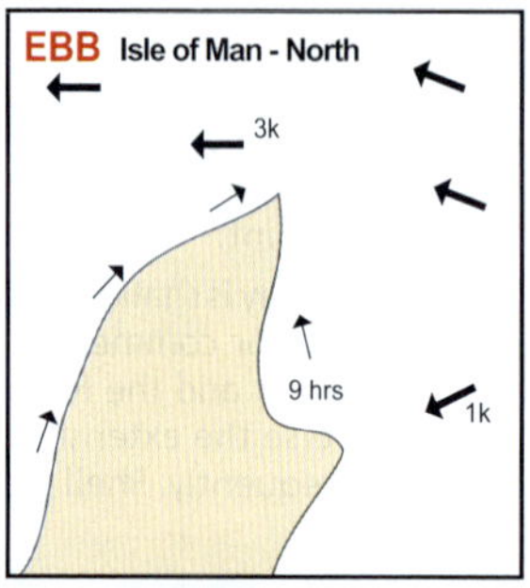

SE, E and NW of Pt of Ayre are dangerous banks, on which seas break in bad weather. These are Whitestone Bank (least depth 2·0m), Bahama Bank (1·5m), Ballacash Bank (1·8m), King William Banks (3·3m), and Strunakill Bank (6·7m). A clearing line brg < 225° on Pt of Ayre Lt clears these.

▶ *At Point of Ayre E-going stream begins HW Liverpool –0600 (HW Dover –0545) and the W-going stream at HW L'pool (HW Dover +0015). A counter tide runs inside the banks to the East. In Ramsey Bay the S-going tide runs for 3hrs from HW L'pool +0515 (Dover +0530). In Ramsey Bay the N-going tide runs for 9hrs from HW L'pool –0345 (Dover –0330).* ◀

The W coast of IOM has few pilotage hazards. A spit with depth of 1·4m runs 2ca offshore from Rue Pt. Jurby Rock (depth 2·7m) lies 3ca off Jurby Head. Craig Rock (depth 4m) and shoals lie 2·5M NNE of Peel.

BARROW TO CONWY

(AC 2010, 1981, 1978, 5613) Ent to Barrow-in-Furness (AC 3164) is about 1M S of Hilpsford Pt at S end of Walney Island (lt ho conspic). W winds cause rough sea in the entrance. Moorings and ⚓ off Piel and Roa Islands, but space is limited.

▶ *The stream sets across the narrow channel, which is well marked, but shallow in patches. Stream runs hard on ebb. Coming from the S it is possible with sufficient rise of tide to cross the sands between Fleetwood and Barrow.* ◀

Barrow Wind Farm (30 turbines) marked by FR and Fl Y lights and fog signals is centred 7·6M SSW of Barrow-in-Furness. Further west lies W Duddon Sands Wind Farm (108 turbines). Its west extremity is marked by a Met Mast. To the north Walney (102 turbines) and Ormonde (30 turbines) straddle the northern approaches to Barrow and the R Lune.

Lune Deep, 2M NW of Rossall Pt, Morecambe Bay (AC 2010), gives access to the commercial ports of Heysham, Glasson Dock, and Fleetwood; it is well buoyed. The bay is encumbered with drying sands, intersected by chans subject to frequent change. S of Morecambe B, beware shoals and drying outfall (2·0m) extending 3M W of Rossall Pt. Further S, the R Ribble gives access via long drying chan to the marina at Preston.

Queen's Channnel and Crosby Chan (AC 1951, 1978) are entered E of the Bar light float. They are well buoyed, dredged and preserved by training banks, giving access to R Mersey and Liverpool. Keep clear of commercial shipping. From the N the old Formby chan is abandoned, but possible near HW. Towards HW in moderate winds a yacht can cross the training bank (level varies 2–3m above CD) E of Great Burbo Bank. If coming from the W; Rock Chan, which is unmarked and dries in parts, may also be used, but beware wrecks. W of Bar Lt Float Douglas oil field (Area to be Avoided), centred on 53°32´·23N 03°34´·70W, divides the lanes of a TSS.

In good weather at neaps, the Dee Estuary (AC 1953, 1978) is accessible for boats able to take the ground. Most of the estuary dries and banks extend 6M seaward. Channels shift, and buoys are moved as required. Stream runs hard in channels when banks are dry. Main entry is Welsh Chan, but if coming from N, Hilbre Swash runs west of Hilbre Is.

Sailing W from the Dee on the ebb, it is feasible to take the Inner Passage (buoyed) S of West Hoyle Spit, which gives some protection from onshore winds at half tide or below. Rhyl hbr, marked by SWM, is not accessible in strong onshore winds and tidal, giving shelter for yachts able to take the ground. Abergele Road, Colwyn and Llandudno Bays are possible ⚓s in settled weather and S winds. Conwy and Deganwy harbours offer good shelter in marinas.

▶ *Between Point of Ayr and Great Ormes Head the E-going stream begins at HW Liverpool +0600, and the W-going at HW Liverpool –0015, Sp rates 3kn.* ◀

MENAI STRAIT

(AC 1464, Imray C52) From NE to SW the main features of this narrow, 16 mile channel are: Puffin Is, where the Strait begins at its North-East entrance; Beaumaris; Garth Pt at Bangor; Menai Suspension Bridge (29m); The Swellies, a narrow 1M stretch with strong tidal streams and dangers mid-stream;

Britannia Bridge, both road and rail (26m), with cables close W (21m); Port Dinorwic; Caernarfon; Abermenai Pt and Fort Belan, at the SW ent and Caernarfon Bar. The following brief notes cover only very basic pilotage. For detailed directions see the UKHO *West Coasts of England and Wales Pilot*, or *Cruising Anglesey and Adjoining Waters* by Ralph Morris.

▶ *The Swellies should be passed about local HW (slack). An understanding of tidal streams is essential. The tide is about 1hr later, and Sp range 2·7m more, at the NE end of the Strait than the SW end. Levels differ most 1hr after HW at the NE end where sea level is > 1·8m above the level at the SW end and at about 4¾hrs before HW at the NE end where sea level is >1·8m below the level at the SW end. Normally the stream runs as follows (intervals referred to HW Dover).*

–0110 to +0340	SW between Garth Pt and Abermenai Pt.
+0340 to +0510	Outwards from The Swellies. (NE towards Garth Pt / SW towards Abermenai Pt)
+0510 to -0110	NE between Abermenai Pt and Garth Pt.

Sp rates are about 3kn, ***but more in narrows, eg 5kn off Abermenai Pt, 6kn between the bridges, and 8kn through The Swellies.*** *Timings and rates may be affected by any strong winds and storm surges in the Irish Sea.* ◀

Note: Direction of buoyage becomes NE off Caernarfon.

From SW to NE, aim to arrive at the Swellies early HW Dover –0300 to take the last of the E-going tidal stream to pass Menai bridge between HW Dover –0230 to –0200. Better to arrive too early, and wait, than too late and risk not making it through the narrows before the stream turns to the W. Approach the S arch of Britannia Bridge keeping the white pyramid in line with the centre of the arch. Once through the bridge run parallel to the shore until abeam the pyramid. At this point, look astern and keep the white leading marks (beneath the S arch of the bridge) in line. When Price's Point is abeam, turn to starboard to pass 20-30m S of Swelly Perch rock, then head just S of the Anglesey (ie N) pillar of the Menai Suspension Bridge until clear of the Platters (cottage abeam to starboard). Then head for the centre of the bridge.

From the NE, pilotage is the reverse of the above, passing Beaumaris in time to arrive at the Swellies at HW Dover –0200, though the timing is not quite so critical. If too early, passage will be slow until the stream turns; if too late the strong, but favourable, stream may prove difficult.

▶ *Caernarfon Bar is impassable even in moderately strong winds against the ebb, and the narrows at Abermenai Pt demand a fair tide, or slackish water, since the tide runs strongly here. Going seaward on first of the ebb, when there is water over the banks, it may not be practicable to return to the Strait if conditions on the bar are bad.*◀

Leaving Abermenai Pt on the last of the ebb there is little water in channel or over the bar.

ANGLESEY TO BARDSEY ISLAND

(AC 1977, 1970, 1971 Imray C52) On N coast of Anglesey a race extends 5ca off Pt Lynas (Oc 10s) on the E-going stream. Amlwch is a small hrbr (partly dries) 1·5M to the W. A drying rock lies 100m offshore on W side of approach, which should not be attempted in strong onshore winds. From here to Carmel Head beware E Mouse (and shoals to SE), Middle Mouse, Harry Furlong's Rocks (dry) marked by SHM Fl G 2½s, Victoria Bank (least depth 1·8m) and W Mouse (with dangers to W & SW). Further offshore are the shoals of Archdeacon Rk, Coal Rk and Ethel Rk marked by cardinal buoys in the red sector of Skerries Lt Ho. The outermost of these is 2M offshore. Overfalls and races occur at headlands and over the many rocks and shoals along this coast.

In good conditions by day and at slack water, Carmel Hd can be rounded close inshore following a track outside East Mouse, inshore of Middle and West Mouse, staying N of Furlong SHM and passing S of Victoria Bank. Short, steep seas break here in even moderate winds against tide and can be dangerous. The best passage at night or in bad weather, is to pass 1M off Skerries, in the TSS ITZ. Holyhead is accessible H24 in all weathers. The marina is within New Harbour; beware fast ferries across the entrance and the TSS.

▶*Between Carmel Hd and The Skerries the NE'ly stream begins at HW Dover +0530 (HW Holyhead +0615), and SW'ly at HW Dover –0045 (HW Holyhead +0005)* ***Sp rate 5kn.*** *1M NW of Skerries the stream turns 0130 later, running less strongly.* ***Sp Flood and Ebb tides close to the coast run at over 5kn,*** *and at about 2.5kn 7M offshore. Brief slack water offshore at HW Dover –0100 and +0500. There is no real counter tide in Holyhead Bay, but slack water lasts longer. Races occur off N and S Stack. There is dangerous race off South Stack starting at HW–0600 on the flood* ***(Sp rate 5kn)*** *extending 8M to the Skerries and off Carmel Hd* ***(Sp rate 6kn).*** *Races are less extensive on SSW-going stream, which begins at HW Holyhead +0020,* ***(Sp rate 5kn).***◀

The W coast of Anglesey is rugged with rks, some drying, up to 1·5M offshore. Races run off Penrhyn Mawr and Rhoscolyn Hd. between which is Maen Piscar a drying rock (1·2m).

▶*A W-going eddy forms E of Penrhyn Mawr during the SE'ly stream with others in Abraham's Bosom and Gogarth Bay.*◀

E of Llanddwyn Is, Pilot's Cove is a good ⚓ to await a window. On the Lleyn Peninsula Porth Dinllaen is a good ⚓, but exposed from NW through N to SE. Braich y Pwll is the steep, rky point at end of Lleyn Peninsula (AC 1971). About 1M N of it and up to 1M offshore lie The Tripods, a bank on which there are overfalls and steep seas when wind is against tide.

▶ *Use Bardsey Sound, 1·5M wide, by day in moderate winds.* ***Stream reaches 8kn at Sp, and make passage at slack water,*** *which occurs about 2¼hrs after local HW/LW: HW Dover –0100 (HW Holyhead –0010) going E, or westbound LW Dover –0100 (LW Holyhead +0030). An eddy ('Young flood') flows W from N of Carreg Ddu 2hrs before the tide turns allowing approach to the Sound at HW Dover +0500.*◀

Avoid Carreg Ddu on N side and Maen Bugail Rk (dries 4·1m) on S side of Sound, where there are dangerous races. If passing outside Bardsey Is make a good offing to avoid overfalls which extend 1·5M W and 2·5M S of the island. Turbulence occurs over Bastram Shoal, Devil's Tail and Devil's Ridge, which lie SSE and E of Bardsey Island respectively.

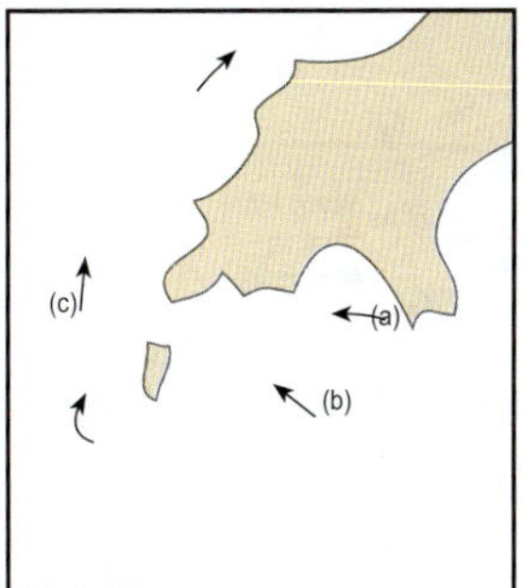

FLOOD Bardsey Sound

The tide turns to the NW or NE (flood) as follows
(a): Dover +0300;
(b): Dover +0500;
(c): Dover +0600.
These times are approximate.

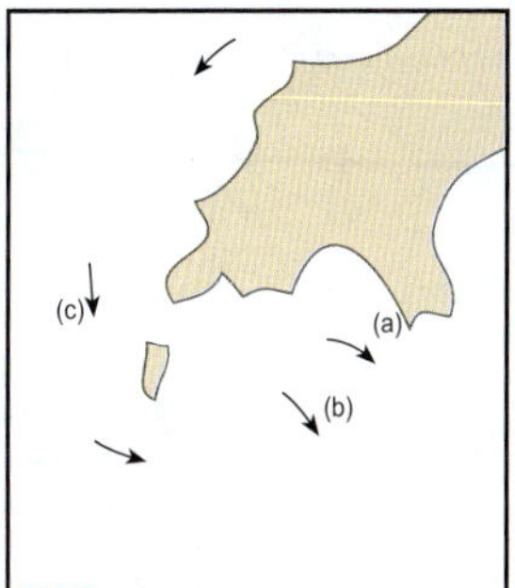

EBB Bardsey Sound

The tide turns to the SW or SE (ebb) as follows
(a): Dover –0300;
(b): Dover –0100;
(c): Dover +0030.
These times are approximate.

NOTE: There is a strong eddy down tide off Bardsey Island and overfalls throughout the area.

3.5 MARYPORT

Cumbria **54°43′·03N 03°30′·38W**

CHARTS AC 1826, 1346, 2013, 5613; Imray C62

TIDES +0038 Dover; ML no data; Duration 0550

Standard Port LIVERPOOL (⟶)

Times				Height (metres)			
High Water		Low Water		MHWS	MHWN	MLWN	MLWS
0000	0600	0200	0800	9·4	7·5	3·2	1·1
1200	1800	1400	2000				
Differences MARYPORT							
+0021	+0036	+0017	+0002	−0·8	−0·9	−0·7	−0·2
SILLOTH							
+0035	+0045	+0040	+0050	−0·2	−0·4	−0·9	−0·3

SHELTER Good in marina, sill 3·1m above CD, 2.5m above sill for entry; at other times Workington is a refuge. Elizabeth Dock gates u/s. Elizabeth Basin dries 2m; commercial, not used by yachts.

NAVIGATION WPT 54°43′·09N 03°32′·47W, 090°/1M to S pier. Overfalls at ent in W/SW winds over ebb. At HW–3 1·8m over bar at ent and in river chan; mudbanks cover HW –2. Max speed 4kn.

LIGHTS AND MARKS SHM bn Fl G 5s marks outfall 6ca SW of S pier. SSS displays IPTS signals 2 and 5 (see IPTS 5.20)

COMMUNICATIONS (Code 01900) Dr 815544; Ⓗ 812634. HM 817440; Hbr Authority 604351.
Port VHF Ch **12** 16. Marina (H24) Ch **12** 16.

FACILITIES **Maryport Marina** www.maryportmarina.com ☎814431, 190 inc Ⓥ £1·95/m + (card) (±3HW) (25t)
Maryport Yachting Association www.maryportyachting.co.uk.
Town Ⓑ ✕ ⇄ ✈ (Manchester/Newcastle).

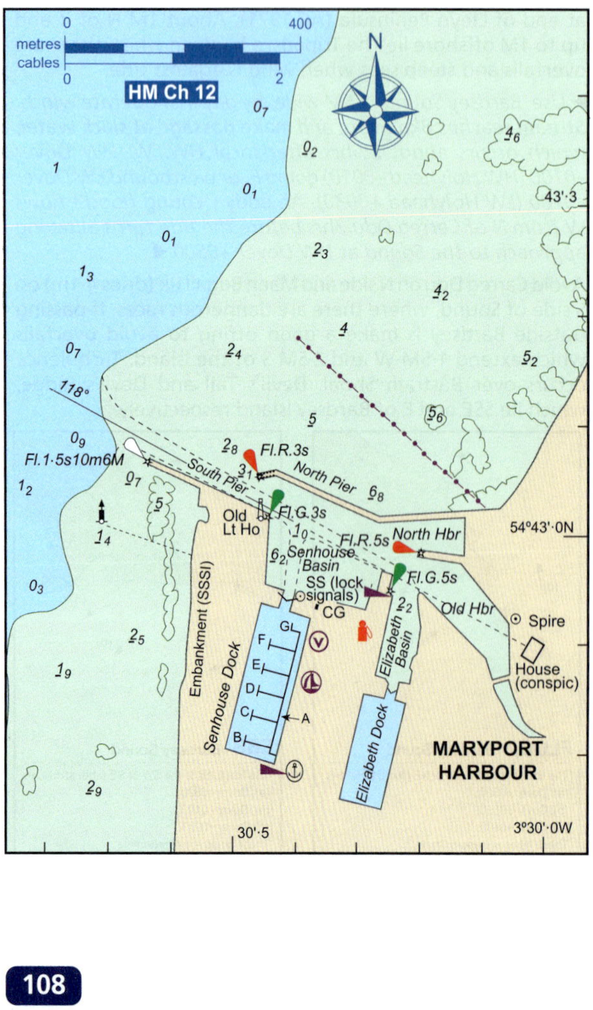

3.6 WORKINGTON

Cumbria 54°39′·03N 03°34′·38W

CHARTS AC 1826, 1346, 2013, 5613; Imray C62

TIDES +0025 Dover; ML 4·5; Duration 0545

Standard Port LIVERPOOL (⟶)

Times				Height (metres)			
High Water		Low Water		MHWS	MHWN	MLWN	MLWS
0000	0600	0200	0800	9·4	7·5	3·2	1·1
1200	1800	1400	2000				
Differences WORKINGTON							
+0029	+0027	+0014	+0004	−1·1	−1·1	−0·5	−0·1

SHELTER Good. Ent and chan to Prince of Wales Dock are maintained at 1·2m. Berth/moor by prior arrangement with Vanguard SC (☎07707 785328) in drying Tidal Dock; no ⚓ in Turning Basin. Prince of Wales Dock for commercial vessels only.

NAVIGATION WPT 54°39′·59N 03°35′·38W, 131°/1M to front ldg lt.

- Tide sets strongly across ent. In periods of heavy rain a strong freshet from R Derwent may be encountered in the hbr ent.

LIGHTS AND MARKS Workington Bank, least depth 5·5m, is 2M W of hbr ent; and is marked by NCM and SCM lt buoys (see 3.3). Ldg lts 132°, both FR 10/12m 3M, on W pyramidal trs with R bands. Two sets of F Bu lts in line mark NE and SW edges of chan. There are 16 wind-turbines on shore between ¾M and 2M NE of hbr ent.

COMMUNICATIONS (Code 01900) Dr 64866; Ⓗ 602244; HM 602301. VHF Ch 14 16 (HW–2½ to HW+2 approx).

FACILITIES **Dock**

Vanguard SC www.vanguard-workington.co.uk ☎01228 674238,

Town Ⓑ ✕ ⇄ ✈ (Carlisle).

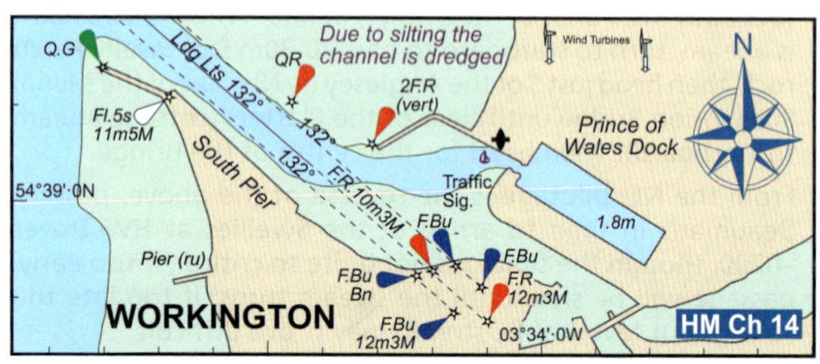

MINOR HARBOUR 10M NNE OF MARYPORT

SILLOTH, Cumbria, **54°52′·16N 03°23′·86W**. AC 1826, 1346, 2013, 5613. HW –0050 on Dover; ML no data; Duration 0520. See 3.5. Commercial harbour which welcomes occasional visiting yachts. Appr via English or Middle Chans; requires local knowledge, Beware constantly shifting chans and banks, and unsurveyed areas. East Cote Dir lt 052° FG 15m 12M; vis 046°-058°, intens 052°. Ldg lts, both F, 115°. Middle dn 2 FG (vert). Outer hbr dries 2·8m; lock into New Dock (4m) HW-1½ to HW+½. Ent marked by Oc R/G lts. Subtract 1m from height of tide to calculate draught over sill. Traffic sigs on mast at New Dock; must receive permission before proceeding. VHF Ch 16 12. HM ☎(01697) 331358. ⚓ WSW of ent in about 4m off Lees Scar, Fl G 5s 11m 4M; exposed to SW winds. Facilities: Ⓑ ✕.

MINOR HARBOUR 2M S OF WORKINGTON

HARRINGTON, Cumbria, **54°36′·77N 03°34′·29W**. AC 1826, 1346, 2013, 5613. HW +0025 on Dover; Duration 0540; Use Diff's Workington 3.6. Good shelter in small hbr only used by local FVs and yachts; dries 3ca offshore. Ent, marked by PHM perches on N side, difficult in strong W winds. Berth on N wall of inner hbr (free) 1Ⓥ. Call ☎(01946) 823741 Ext 148 for moorings. Limited facilities. **SC** ☎(01946) 830600.

3.7 WHITEHAVEN

Cumbria **54°33'·18N 03°35'·82W**

CHARTS AC 1826, 1346, 2013, 5613; Imray C62

TIDES +0015 Dover; ML 4·5; Duration 0550

Standard Port LIVERPOOL (⟶)

Times				Height (metres)			
High Water		Low Water		MHWS	MHWN	MLWN	MLWS
0000	0600	0200	0800	9·4	7·5	3·2	1·1
1200	1800	1400	2000				
Differences WHITEHAVEN							
+0010	+0020	+0005	0000	–1·4	–1·2	–0·8	–0·1
TARN POINT (54°17'N 03°25'W)							
+0010	+0010	+0005	–0005	–1·1	–1·1	–0·7	–0·2
DUDDON BAR (54°09'N 03°20'W)							
+0007	+0007	+0005	–0001	–0·9	–0·9	–0·6	–0·2

SHELTER Very good, entry safe in most weathers. One of the more accessible ports of refuge in NW England, with a marina in the Inner Hbr. Appr chan across the outer hbr is dredged to 1·0m above CD. Sea lock (30m x 13.7m), with sill at CD, maintains 7m within inner hbr. N Hbr is for commercial and FV use.

NAVIGATION WPT 54°33'·34N 03°36'·21W, 133°/4½ca to W pier hd. There are no hazards in the offing. Hold closer to the North Pier, and beware bar at end of W Pier.

LIGHTS AND MARKS Several tall chimneys are charted within 1·5M S of hbr. St Bees Head Lt ho is 2·7M SSW of hbr ent. SHM bn, Fl G 2·5s, 4½ca S of W pierhead marks sewer outfall. IPTS sigs 1-3 shown from N side of lock ent to seaward only at present: priority to inward-bound vessels.

COMMUNICATIONS (Code 01946) HM 692435; Sealock 694672. HM VHF Ch 12 16.

FACILITIES Marina www.whitehavenmarina.co.uk ☎692435 285 inc Ⓥ in Inner Harbour (Lowther Marina) and Queen's Dock (Queen's Marina) £2·84, Ⓔ SC.
Town Market days Thurs, Sat; Ⓑ.

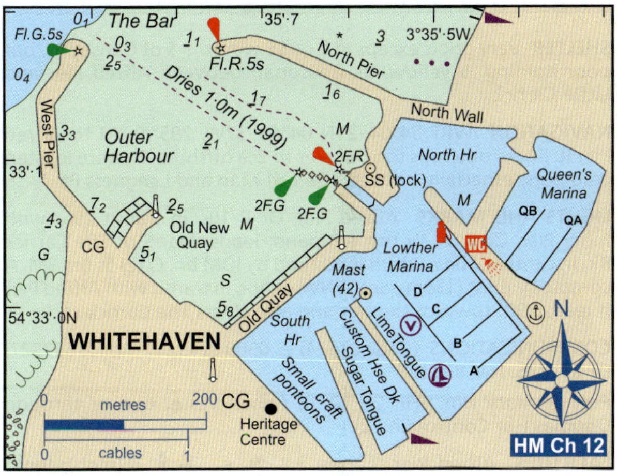

MINOR HARBOUR BETWEEN ST BEES HD AND MORECAMBE BAY

RAVENGLASS, Cumbria, **54°20'·00N 03°26'·80W** (drying line). AC 1346, 1826, 5613. HW +0020 on Dover; ML no data; Duration 0545. See 3.7 (Tarn Pt). Large drying hbr, into which R's Mite, Irt and Esk flow; approx 2·5m in ent at HW–2. Sellafield power stn with WCM lt buoy and outfall buoys are 5M NNW. FG ☆ (occas) on blockhouse at S side of ent. *Solway Sailing Directions* with pilotage notes by Ravenglass Boating Ass'n, local knowledge advisable. From N beware Drigg Rk and from S Selker Rks, SHM lt buoy, 5M SSW of ent. Firing range D406 close S at Eskmeals; Mon-Thur 0800-1600LT (1500 Fri). When in use R flags flown, R lts at night; *Eskmeals Gun Range* VHF Ch 16 11, ☎(01229) 712245/5.
Village.

3.8 ISLE OF MAN

Charts AC Irish Sea 1826, 1411; 2094 (small scale); 2696 (ports), 5613; Imray C62, Y70

The Isle of Man a British Island, set in the Irish Sea roughly equidistant from England, Scotland, Wales and Ireland but is not part of the UK. It has a large degree of self-government. Lights are maintained by the Northern Lighthouse Board. Manx harbours are administered by the IoM Government, see www.gov.im/harbours/

Distances See 3.1 for distances between ports in Area 3 and 0.32 for distances across the Irish Sea, North Channel and St George's Channel.

Harbours and anchorages Most of the harbours are on the E and S sides, but a visit to the W coast with its characteristic cliffs is worthwhile. The four main harbours are described in an anti-clockwise direction from Peel on the W coast to Ramsey in the NE. There are good ⚓s at: Port Erin in the SW, Castletown and Derby Haven in the SE, and Laxey Bay in the E. All IOM harbours charge the same overnight berthing depending on berth location and type. Outer Hbr £1·36/m, Inner Hbr £2·05/m (2021/22)

Multihulls are charged at 1.5 times the usual monohull rate.
A 90 day pass for all harbours (except marina berths) is available.

R/T If contact with local Harbour Offices cannot be established on VHF, vessels should call *Douglas Hbr Control* Ch **12** 16 for urgent messages or other info.

Coastguard Call Holyhead CGOC Ch 16 67 86; the Snaefell (IoM) aerial is linked to the CG network.

Customs The IOM is under the same customs umbrella as the rest of the UK, and there are no formalities on arriving from or returning to the UK.

Weather Forecasts can be obtained direct from the forecaster at Ronaldsway Met Office ☎0900 6243 3200, H24. **Douglas Hbr Control** (3.11) can supply visibility and wind info on request.

MINOR HARBOURS ON THE ISLE OF MAN

PORT ERIN, Isle of Man, **54°05'·31N 04°46'·34W**. AC 2094, 2696, 5613. HW –0020 on Dover; ML 2·9m; Duration 0555. See 3.10. From S and W, Milner's Twr on Bradda Hd is conspic. Ldg lts, both FR 10/19m 5M, lead 099° into the bay. Beware the ruined bkwtr (dries 2·9m) extending N from the SW corner, marked by an unlit SHM buoy. A small hbr on the S side dries 0·8m. Raglan Pier (E arm of hbr), Oc G 5s 8m 5M. 2Ⓥs W of Raglan Pier. Good ⚓ in 3-8m N of Raglan Pier, but exposed to W'lies. Call Port St. Mary Harbour (VHF Ch 12) ☎833205.

CASTLETOWN BAY, Isle of Man, **54°03'·51N 04°38'·57W**. AC 2094, 2696, 5613. HW +0025 on Dover; ML 3·4m; Duration 0555. The bay gives good shelter except in SE to SW winds. From the E, keep inside the race off Dreswick Pt, or give it a wide berth. Beware Lheeah-rio Rks in W of bay, marked by PHM buoy, Fl R 3s, Bell. Hbr dries 3·1m to level sand. Berth in outer hbr or go via swing footbridge (manually opened) into inner hbr below fixed bridge. ⚓ between Lheeah-rio Rks and pier in 3m; or NW of Langness Pt. Lts: Langness lt, on Dreswick Pt, Fl (2) 30s 23m 12M. Hbr S (New) Pier, Oc R 15s 8m 5M; Inner S pier (Irish Quay), Oc R 4s 5m 5M, vis 142°-322°. 150m NW is swing bridge marked by 2 FR (hor). N pier, Oc G 4s 3m (W metal post on concrete column). VHF Ch 12 16 (when vessel due). HM ☎823549; Dr 823597. Facilities: **Outer hbr** (mob); **Irish Quay**; **Inner hbr**; **Town**.

LAXEY, Isle of Man, **54°13'·46N 04°23'·32W**. AC 2094, 5613. HW +0025 on Dover; +0010 and –2·0m on Liverpool; ML 4m; Duration 0550. The bay gives good shelter in SW to N winds. 2 yellow Ⓥs (seasonal) are close E of hbr ent; 2 more are 1M S in Garwick Bay. ⚓ about 2ca S of pier hds or in Garwick Bay. The hbr dries 3·0m to rk and is only suitable for small yachts. Beware rks on N side of the narrow ent. Keep close to pier after entering to avoid training wall on NE side. on inside of pier; inner basin is full of local boats. Pier hd lt Oc R 3s 7m 5M, obsc when brg <318°. Bkwtr hd lt Oc G 3s 7m. Harbour Office ☎861663. Facilities: Ⓑ.

3.9 PEEL

Isle of Man 54°13′·61N 04°41′·68W

CHARTS AC 2094, 2696, 5613; Imray C62; Y70

TIDES +0005 Dover; ML 2·9; Duration 0545

Standard Port LIVERPOOL (⟶)

Times				Height (metres)			
High Water		Low Water		MHWS	MHWN	MLWN	MLWS
0000	0600	0200	0700	9·4	7·5	3·2	1·1
1200	1800	1400	1900				
Differences PEEL							
+0010	+0010	-0020	–0030	–4·2	–3·2	–1·7	–0·7

SHELTER Good, except in strong NW to NE winds when ent should not be attempted. 4 Y ⚓s (seasonal) off S groyne in about 2m. Fin keelers may be able to berth on N bkwtr in 5m. Marina is in the Inner Harbour with berthing on pontoons and alongside harbour wall for boats up to 15m LOA. Pass dimensions on Ch 12. Approach dries 1·4m; access approx HW±2 when flapgate lowered and through swing bridge. Depth generally 2m, around pontoons.

NAVIGATION WPT 54°14′·00N 04°41′·78W, 207°/5ca to groyne lt. Beware groyne on S side of harbour ent, submerged at half tide.

LIGHTS AND MARKS Power stn chy (83m, grey with B top) at S end of inner hbr is conspic from W and N; chy brg 203° leads to hbr ent. Groyne lt and Clock Tr (conspic) in transit 200° are almost on same line. Peel Castle and 2 twrs are conspic on St Patrick's Isle to NW of hbr. 207° ldg lts, Fl R 5s. The E and W abutments to the Inner Hbr ent are marked by lts Fl R 3s and Fl G 3s respectively. Traffic signals at marina entrance. Swing bridge has FR lts at centre span. Fl Y lts = flap gate being raised lowered; bridge opening/closing.

COMMUNICATIONS (Code 01624) 0900 6243 322; Police 697327; Dr 843636. Harbour Office 842338, Mobile 07624 495036.

Peel Hbr VHF Ch **12** 16 (HW±2), HO for Swing Bridge – other times call *Douglas Hbr Control* Ch 12 for remote bridge opening.

FACILITIES **Outer Hbr,** see 3.8; **Marina** 120 inc ♥; access via flapgate; (mob); **Peel Sailing** & **Cruising Club** ☎842390, (key from Harbour Office), . **Town** ACA Ⓑ (bus to Douglas & ferry), ✈ Ronaldsway.

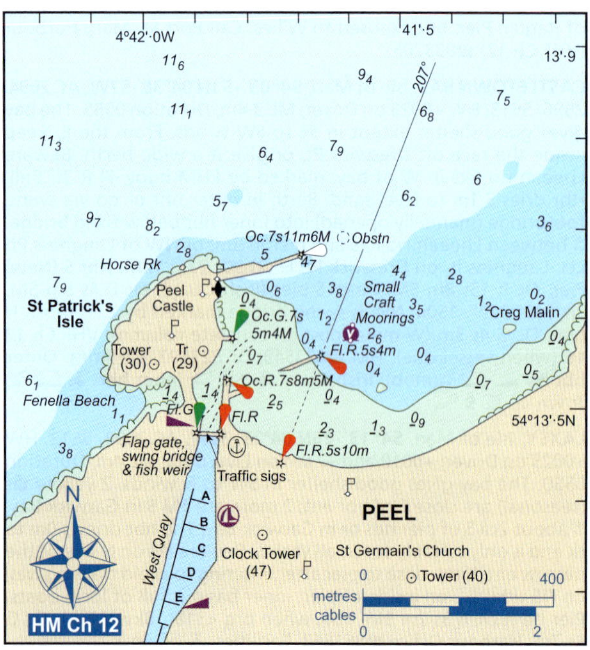

3.10 PORT ST MARY

Isle of Man **54°04′·43N 04°43′·73W**

CHARTS AC 2094, 2696, 5613; Imray C62; Y70

TIDES +0020 Dover; ML 3·2; Duration 0605

Standard Port LIVERPOOL (⟶)

Times				Height (metres)			
High Water		Low Water		MHWS	MHWN	MLWN	MLWS
0000	0600	0200	0700	9·4	7·5	3·2	1·1
1200	1800	1400	1900				
Differences PORT ST MARY							
+0010	+0020	–0015	–0035	–3·5	–2·7	–1·6	–0·6
CALF SOUND							
+0010	+0010	–0020	–0030	–3·3	–2·7	–1·2	–0·5
PORT ERIN							
+0018	+0010	–0013	–0028	–4·1	–3·3	–1·6	–0·6

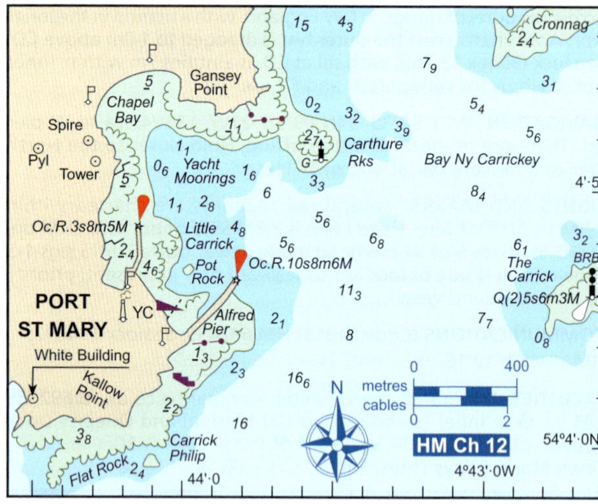

SHELTER Very good except in E or SE winds. ⚓ S of Gansey Pt, but poor holding. 5 yellow ⚓s (seasonal) between Alfred Pier and Little Carrick.

NAVIGATION WPT 54°04′·21N 04°43′·37W, 295°/0·3M to Alfred Pier lt. Rocky outcrops to SE of pier to 2ca offshore. Beware lobster/crab pots, especially between Calf of Man and Langness Pt.

LIGHTS AND MARKS Alfred Pier, Oc R 10s, in transit 295° with Inner Pier, Oc R 3s, W twr + R band, leads clear S of The Carrick Rk, in centre of bay, which is marked by IDM bn, Q (2) 5s 6m 3M. A conspic TV mast (133m), 5ca WNW of hbr, in transit with Alfred Pier lt leads 290° towards the hbr and also clears The Carrick rock.

COMMUNICATIONS (Code 01624) 0900 6243 322, Police 697327; Dr 832226. HM 833205.

Port St Mary Hbr VHF Ch 12 16 (when vessel due or through Douglas Hbr Control Ch 12).

FACILITIES **Alfred Pier** see 3.8, (mob); **Inner Hbr** dries 2·4m on sand; ; **Isle of Man YC** ☎832088, . **Town** Ⓑ (bus to Douglas, qv for ferries), ✈ Ronaldsway.

MINOR HARBOUR EAST OF CASTLETOWN

DERBY HAVEN, Isle of Man, **54°04′·65N 04°36′·45W.** Tides & charts as above. Rather remote bay exposed only to NE/E winds. ⚓ in centre of bay, NW of St Michael's Island, in 3-5m. A detached bkwtr on NW side of the bay gives shelter to craft able to dry out behind it. Lts: Iso G 2s on S end of bkwtr. Aero FR (occas) at Ronaldsway airport, NW of bay. Facilities: at Castletown (1½M) or Port St Mary.

3.11 DOUGLAS

Isle of Man **54°08'·87N 04°27'·96W** ❁❁❁◌◌✿✿✿

CHARTS AC 2094, 2696, 5613; Imray C62; Y70

TIDES +0009 Dover; ML 3·8; Duration 0600

Standard Port LIVERPOOL (⟶)

Times				Height (metres)			
High Water		Low Water		MHWS	MHWN	MLWN	MLWS
0000	0600	0200	0700	9·4	7·5	3·2	1·1
1200	1800	1400	1900				
Differences *DOUGLAS*							
+0010	*+0020*	*–0020*	*–0030*	*–2·5*	*–2·1*	*–0·8*	*–0·3*

SHELTER Good except in NE winds. Very heavy seas run in during NE gales. Outer hbr: Victoria and King Edward VIII piers are for commercial vessels/ferries. At inner end of Battery Pier in summer about 18 boats can raft up on pontoon; untenable in NE/E winds. Complete shelter in inner hbr, with possible pontoon berths, flapgate lowers on the flood and rises on the ebb at 4·4m above CD, lifting bridge opens every ½hr subject to tide/road traffic conditions (request opening on VHF Ch12). Depths 2m or less.

NAVIGATION WPT 54°09´·01N 04°27´·67W (abeam No 1 SHM buoy, Q (3) G 5s), 229°/0·47M to front ldg lt. Appr from NE of No 1 buoy (to avoid overfalls E of Princess Alexandra Pier) and await port entry sig, or call on VHF Ch 12. There is no bar. Keep clear of large vessels and ferries. Beware concrete step at end of dredged area (◊ mark on King Edward VIII Pier) and sill at ent to inner hbr.

LIGHTS AND MARKS Douglas Head Fl 10s 32m 18M. Ldg lts 229°, both Oc Bu 10s 9/12m 5M, synch; front W △; rear W ▽, both on R border. IPTS Nos 2, 3 and 5 shown from mast on Victoria Pier. Dolphin at N end of Alexandra Pier 2FR (vert).

COMMUNICATIONS (Code 01624) ☼ 0900 6243 322, Police 697327; Ⓗ 650000. Harbour Control 686628 (H24).

Douglas Hbr Control VHF Ch **12** 16 (H24); also broadcasts nav warnings for IoM ports and coastal waters on Ch 12 including weather and tidal info on request.

FACILITIES Outer Hbr ⛵ see 3.8, ⛴ ⛵ ⛽ at pontoon, ▮ ⛵(mob); **Inner Hbr** (Pontoons, N and S Quays) 110⛵; ❶ according to space, ⛵ ⛽ ⛵ ⛵; **Douglas Bay YC** ☎673965, ⛵ ⛵ ⛵ 0930-2300 ⛵. **Services** ⛵ ⚒ 🔧 ⛵ ACA, Kos. **Town** www.gov.im ▮ ✉ Ⓑ ⛵ ⛵ ✕ ⛵ ✈ Ronaldsway. **Ferries** Liverpool; 16/week; 2½ hrs; IoM. Heysham; 16/week; 3½hrs; Steam Packet (www.steam-packet.com). Also to Dublin and Belfast.

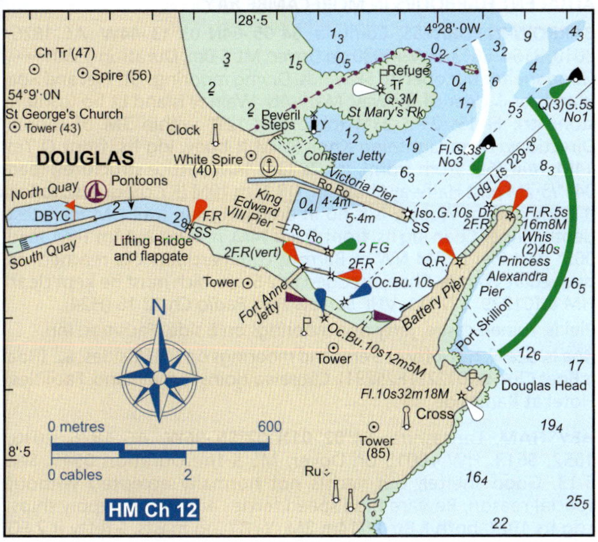

3.12 RAMSEY

Isle of Man **54°19'·44N 04°22'·49W** ❁❁◌◌✿✿

CHARTS AC 2094, 2696, 5613; Imray C62; Y70

TIDES +0020 Dover; ML 4·2; Duration 0545

Standard Port LIVERPOOL (⟶)

Times				Height (metres)			
High Water		Low Water		MHWS	MHWN	MLWN	MLWS
0000	0600	0200	0700	9·4	7·5	3·2	1·1
1200	1800	1400	1900				
Differences RAMSEY							
+0010	+0020	–0010	–0020	–2·0	–1·6	–0·9	–0·2

SHELTER Very good in inner harbour but entrance difficult in strong NE-E winds. Hbr dries 1·8m – 6m. Access approx HW –2½ to HW +2. Berth on Town quay (S side) or as directed by HM on entry. 5 yellow ⛵s are close to Queen's Pier hd (seasonal). Note: landing on Queen's Pier is prohibited.

NAVIGATION WPT 54°19´·44N 04°21´·89W, 270°/0·37M to ent. The foreshore dries out 1ca to seaward of the pier hds.

LIGHTS AND MARKS No ldg lts/marks. Relative to hbr ent, Pt of Ayre, Fl (4) 20s 32m 19M, is 5·5M N; Maughold Hd, Fl (3) 30s 65m 21M, is 3M SE; Albert Tr (□ stone tr 14m, on hill 130m) is conspic 7ca S; and Snaefell (617m) bears 220°/5M. Inside the hbr an Iso G 4s, G SHM post, marks the S tip of Mooragh Bank; it is not visible from seaward. 2FR (hor) on each side mark the centre of swing bridge.

COMMUNICATIONS (Code 01624) ☼ 0900 6243 322, Police 812234; Dr 813881; Ⓗ 811811. Harbour Office 812245, mob 07624 460304.

Ramsey Hbr VHF Ch **12** 16 (0800-1600LT and when a vessel is due); Other times call *Douglas Hbr Control* Ch **12**.

FACILITIES Outer Hbr: E Quay ☎812245, only for commercial vessels (frequent movements H24); **Town Quay** (S side) ⛵ see 3.8, ⛽ ⛵. **Inner Hbr, W Quay** ⛵ ⛵ ⛽ ⛵ (Grid); **N Quay** ⛵ ▮ ⛽; **Shipyard Quay** ⛵; **Old Hbr** ⛵ ⛵ ⛵; **Manx S&CC** ☎813494, ⛵; **Services** ⛵ ⚒ 🔧 ⛵ Ⓔ. **Town** ▮ Kos, ✉ Ⓑ ⛵ ⛵ ✕ ⛵ @ in Library, ⇌ (bus to Douglas for ferries), ✈ Ronaldsway.

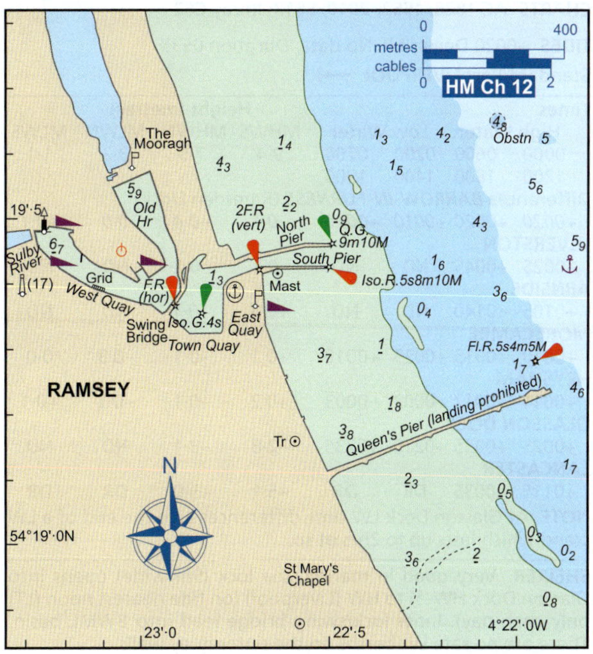

Isle of Man

3.13 GLASSON DOCK

Lancashire **53°59'·98N 02°50'·93W**

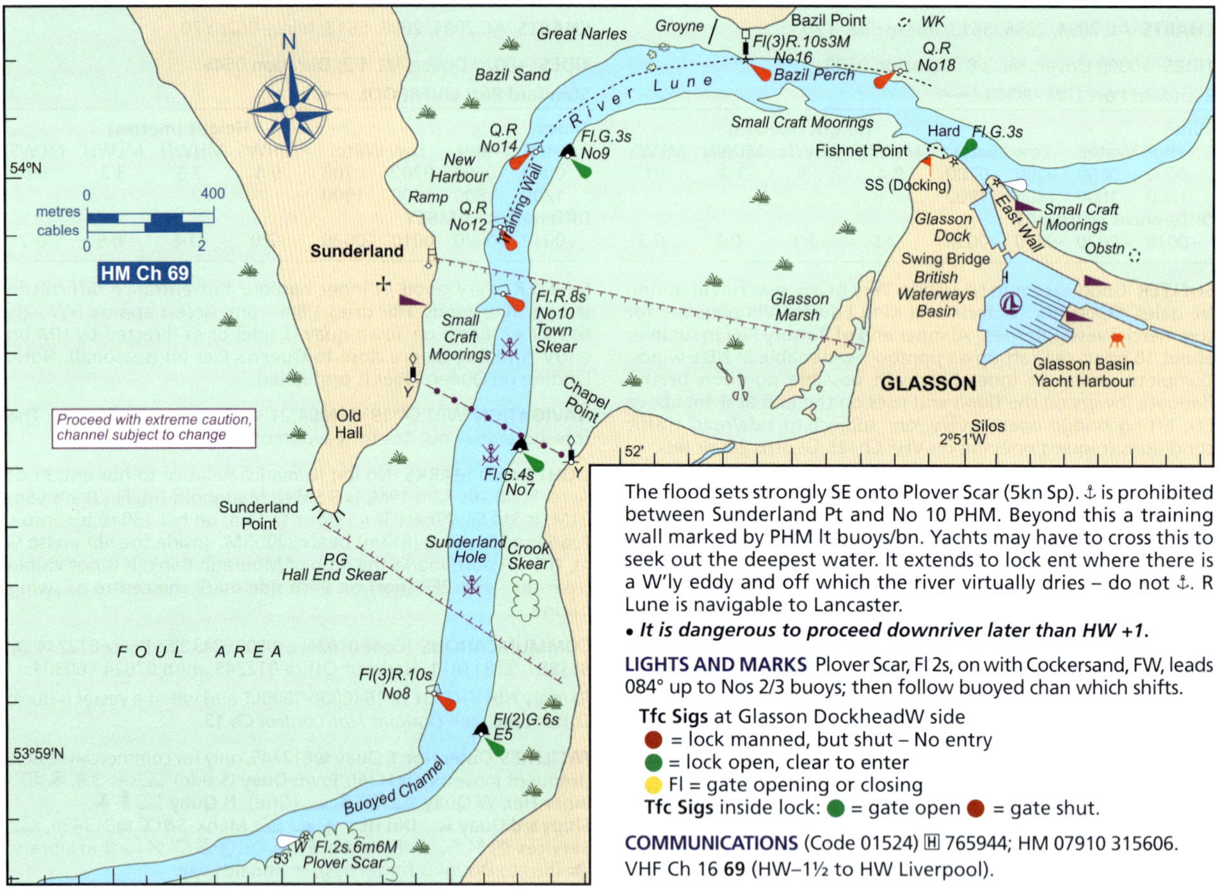

The flood sets strongly SE onto Plover Scar (5kn Sp). ⚓ is prohibited between Sunderland Pt and No 10 PHM. Beyond this a training wall marked by PHM lt buoys/bn. Yachts may have to cross this to seek out the deepest water. It extends to lock ent where there is a W'ly eddy and off which the river virtually dries – do not ⚓. R Lune is navigable to Lancaster.

- ***It is dangerous to proceed downriver later than HW +1.***

LIGHTS AND MARKS Plover Scar, Fl 2s, on with Cockersand, FW, leads 084° up to Nos 2/3 buoys; then follow buoyed chan which shifts.

Tfc Sigs at Glasson DockheadW side
● = lock manned, but shut – No entry
● = lock open, clear to enter
● Fl = gate opening or closing
Tfc Sigs inside lock: ● = gate open ● = gate shut.

COMMUNICATIONS (Code 01524) Ⓗ 765944; HM 07910 315606. VHF Ch 16 **69** (HW–1½ to HW Liverpool).

FACILITIES Glasson Marina www.aquavista.com ☎751491; 156 inc Ⓥ (poa); (50t) .
Glasson SC ☎751089, ; **Lune CC** Access only near HW.
Town (bus to Lancaster 4M), ✈ (Blackpool).

CHARTS AC 1826, 1552, 2010, 5613; Imray C62

TIDES +0020 Dover; ML No data; Duration 0535

Standard Port LIVERPOOL (⟶)

Times				Height (metres)			
High Water		Low Water		MHWS	MHWN	MLWN	MLWS
0000	0600	0200	0700	9·4	7·5	3·2	1·1
1200	1800	1400	1900				
Differences *BARROW-IN-FURNESS* (Ramsden Dock)							
+0020	*+0020*	*+0010*	*+0010*	*–0·1*	*–0·4*	*0·0*	*+0·1*
ULVERSTON							
+0025	+0045	ND	ND	–0·1	–0·2	ND	ND
ARNSIDE							
+0105	+0140	ND	ND	+0·4	+0·1	ND	ND
MORECAMBE							
+0010	+0015	+0025	+0010	+0·1	–0·1	–0·3	0·0
HEYSHAM							
+0014	+0012	+0002	–0003	+0·2	–0·1	–0·1	+0·1
GLASSON DOCK							
+0025	+0035	+0215	+0235	–2·8	–3·1	ND	ND
LANCASTER							
+0115	+0035	DR	DR	–5·1	–5·0	DR	DR

NOTE: At Glasson Dock LW time differences give the end of a LW stand which lasts up to 2hrs at sp.

SHELTER Very good in marina, sea lock (9m wide) opens into Glasson Dock HW–¾ to HW (Liverpool) (on tide nearest noon (LT) only each day). Inner lock/swing bridge lead into BWML basin. There are no safe LW berths on the outer quay walls.

NAVIGATION WPT 53°58'·63N 03°00'·03W (Lune WCM), 4·2M to Plover Scar. Enter buoyed chan at HW–1½ (–1¼ Nps). It changes frequently. For latest info call Port Commission (☎01524 751724).

ADJACENT HARBOURS IN MORECAMBE BAY

BARROW-IN-FURNESS, Cumbria, **54°05'·64N 03°13'·44W**. AC 1826, 2010, 3164, 5613. HW +0030 on Dover; ML 5·0m; Duration 0530 (⟵). Good shelter but open to SE winds. Drying moorings off Piel and Roa Islands or ⚓ clear of fairway. Marks/lts: Walney Island Lt ho (conspic stone tr), Fl 15s 21m 23M (obsc 122°-127° within 3M of shore). Directions: From Lightning Knoll SWM lt buoy, ldg lts, front Q 7m 14M; rear (6ca from front), Iso 2s 13m 14M (lattice structures) lead 041°/3·7M past Halfway Shoal bn, QR 16m 10M (RY chequers), to Bar lt buoy abeam Walney Is lt ho in dredged chan (call HM for latest depth). Inner Chan ldg lts, front Q 9m 14M, rear Iso 2s 14m 14M, lead 005° past Piel Is. 3M NW at Barrow, commercial docks reached via buoyed/lit Walney Chan, dredged to 2·5m, which must be kept clear. HM ☎(01229) 822911; VHF *Barrow Port Radio* Ch 12 16 (H24).

Piel Is, ruined castle, jetty and moorings on E side. Facilities: Inn.

Roa Is, 5ca N, has jetty at S end and moorings on E & W sides. (Roa Is Boat Club ☎(01229) 825291). Causeway joins to mainland. Facilities: Hotel at Rampside, .

HEYSHAM, Lancashire, **54°02'·01N 02°55'·96W**. AC 1826, 2010, 1552, 5613. HW +0015 on Dover; ML 5·1m; Duration 0545. See 3.13. Good shelter, but yachts not normally accepted without special reason. Beware high speed ferries and oil rig supply ships. Ldg lts 102°, both F Bu 11/14m 2M, Y+B ◊ on masts. S jetty lt 2 FG (vert), Siren 30s. S pier hd, Oc G 7·5s 9m 6M. N pier hd, 2FR (vert) 11m, obsc from seaward. Ent sigs: R flag or ● = no entry; no sig = no dep; 2 R flags or 2 ● = no ent or dep. VHF Ch 14 74 16 (H24). HM ☎(01524) 852373. Facilities: at Morecambe (2M).

3.14 FLEETWOOD

Lancashire **53°55′·49N 03°00′·15W**

CHARTS AC 1826, 2010, 1552, 5613; Imray C62

TIDES +0015 Dover; ML 5.2; Duration 0530

Standard Port LIVERPOOL (⟶)

Times				**Height (metres)**			
High Water		Low Water		MHWS	MHWN	MLWN	MLWS
0000	0600	0200	0700	9·4	7·5	3·2	1·1
1200	1800	1400	1900				
Differences WYRE LIGHTHOUSE							
−0005	−0005	0000	−0005	−0·2	−0·2	ND	ND
FLEETWOOD							
−0004	−0004	−0006	−0006	0·0	−0·2	−0·1	+0·1
BLACKPOOL							
−0010	0000	−0010	−0020	−0·5	−0·5	−0·4	−0·1

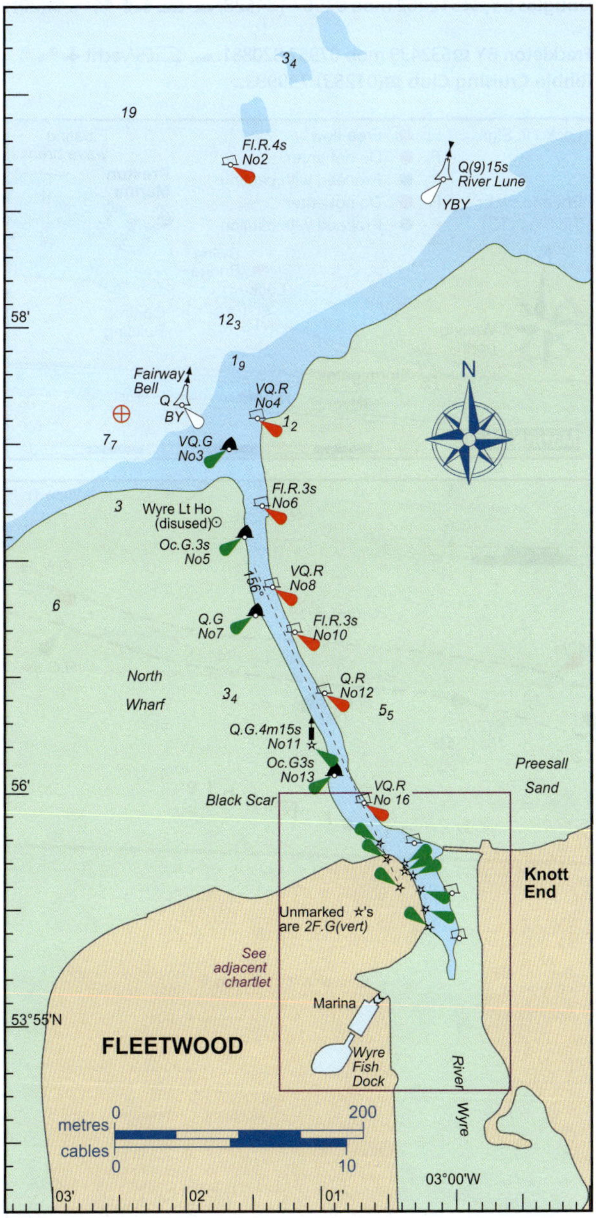

SHELTER Excellent in Fleetwood Haven Marina. Sheltered ⚓, clear of turning circle, off Knott End pier on E bank to await tide. Passage upriver to Skippool (5M) needs local knowledge and is only possible with shoal draught.

NAVIGATION WPT 53°57′·67N 03°02′·05W, Fairway NCM buoy, Q, 134°/3ca to No 3 SHM buoy, VQ.G. Regular dredging is no longer undertaken to maintain Fleetwood channel. Depths are liable to frequent change owing to siltation. Call HM for latest info.

Ideally arrive at WPT about HW–1½ if bound for Wyre Dock marina, 3M upriver, which can be entered during freeflow on all tides. Call *Fleetwood Dock Radio* before entering buoyed Dock Channel. Waiting pontoon outside lock on East Jetty.

LIGHTS AND MARKS Chan is well buoyed/lit. Ldg lts, front Iso G 2s; rear Iso G 4s, 156° (only to be used between Nos 8 buoy and 11 perch bn). Lock sigs: ● lights = 'Stop'; ● lights = 'Go'.

COMMUNICATIONS (Code 01253) Dr 873312. HM (ABP) 872323. *Fleetwood Dock Radio*, Ch 12 (HW±2), before entering channel.

FACILITIES

Fleetwood Haven Marina ☎879062, 340 inc Ⓥ (max 20m LOA) in two basins, £2·65, (0800-1700) (75t).

River Wyre YC ☎811948, 1Ⓥ.

Blackpool & Fleetwood YC (Skippool) ☎884205.

Services Ⓔ(☎823535).

Town Ⓑ (Poulton-le-Fylde or Blackpool), ✈ (Blackpool).

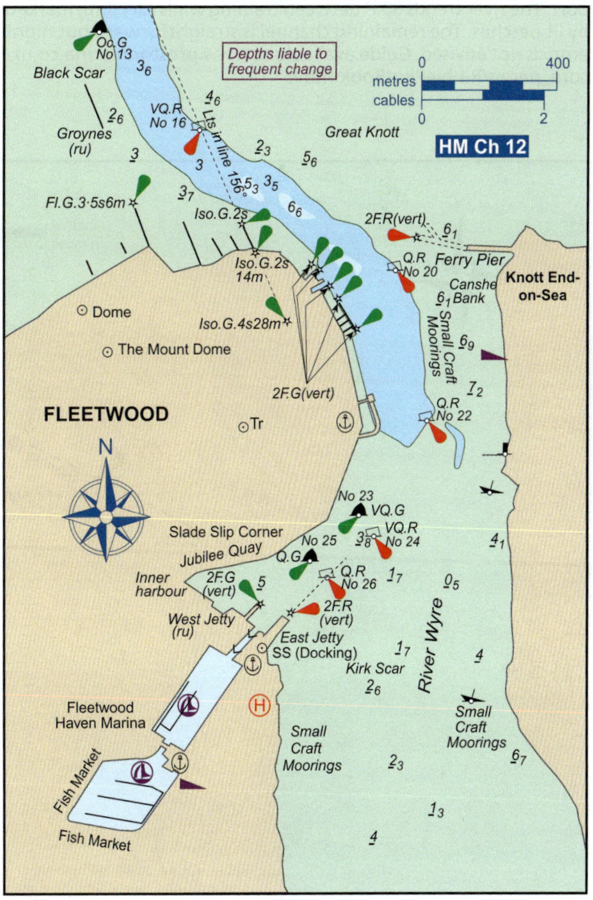

3.15 RIVER RIBBLE/PRESTON

Lancashire **53°43´·51N 03°00´·08W**

CHARTS AC 1826, 1981, 5613; Imray C62

TIDES +0013 Dover; ML No data; Duration 0520

Standard Port LIVERPOOL (⟶)

Times				Height (metres)			
High Water		Low Water		MHWS	MHWN	MLWN	MLWS
0000	0600	0200	0700	9·4	7·5	3·2	1·1
1200	1800	1400	1900				
Differences PRESTON							
+0015	+0015	+0330	+0305	–4·1	–4·2	–3·1	–1·0
LW time differences give the end of a LW stand lasting 3½ hrs.							
SOUTHPORT							
–0015	–0005	ND	ND	–0·4	–0·4	ND	ND
FORMBY							
–0010	–0005	–0025	–0025	–0·4	–0·2	–0·3	–0·1

SHELTER Good in Preston Marina (5m depth) 15M upriver. Possible drying berths on the N bank at Lytham or Freckleton, or 2M up R Douglas access only near HW.

NAVIGATION WPT **A** 53°41'·75N 03°08'·90W, Gut SWM lt buoy. The chartlet shows only the outer 6M of the estuary. Due to changes to the Gut Channel and South Gut, best water is now in the Gut Channel which almost dries but not to the extent shown on AC 1981. It is navigable approx HW±2. South Gut is no longer discernible and should not be used without local knowledge.

Leave WPT **A** at HW Liverpool –2 then track 070°/2·6M to WPT **B** (53°42'·90N 03°05'·00W). Continue up Gut Channel leaving the first 3 perches about 100m to starboard. Leave 11½M perch 100m to port. The river trends 080° between training walls (dry 3m), marked by lit perches. The remaining channel is straightforward but night entry is not advised. Guide available at www.prestonmarina.co.uk/core_pages/RibblePilotBook.html.

LIGHTS AND MARKS 14½M perch is the most seaward channel mark. Upriver of 11½M perch there is a PHM buoy and perch (off chartlet), both Fl R 5s. 4 SHM perches, Fl G 5s, lead to 5M perch, Fl (2) G 10s, marking mouth of unlit R Douglas. 3M and 2M perches are Fl G 5s; 1M perch is Fl G 10s. Warton airfield beacon, Mo (WQ) G 9s occas, is N abeam 6M perch, Fl G 5s.

COMMUNICATIONS (Code 01772) 710408. Preston locks 726871. At Preston, for locks call *Riversway* Ch **16** 14 (HW –1½ to +2); Marina Ch 80 (HO); Douglas BY Ch 16 when vessel due.

FACILITIES Waiting berth (2m) outside storm gates (usually open). Traffic lts at marina lock; plan below. Lockmaster on duty HW±2, on daylight tides (0700-2000 Apr-Sep by Lavers Liverpool Tide Tables). This and tidal height should permit locking from –1 HW +2 on demand. Swing bridge opens in unison with locks. From 1 Oct–31 Mar contact marina to book locking 24hrs in advance.

Preston Marina www.prestonmarina. co.uk ☎733595, mob 07770 505094, £1·60 (£10 specials), (25t), ACA.

Douglas BY, ☎812462 mob 07967 184528, (20t).

Freckleton BY ☎632439 mob 07957 820881, £5/yacht.

Ribble Cruising Club ☎(01253) 739983.

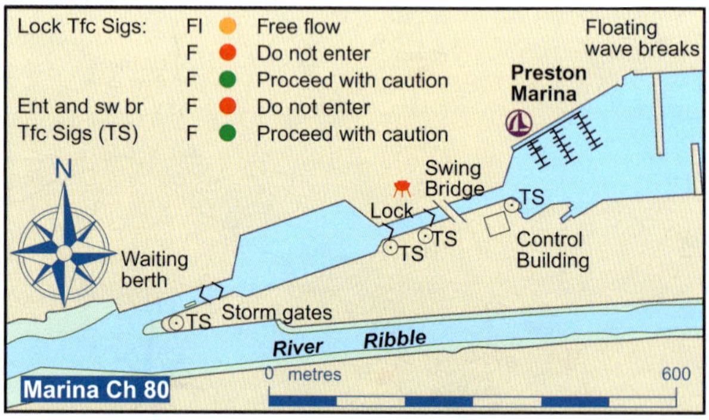

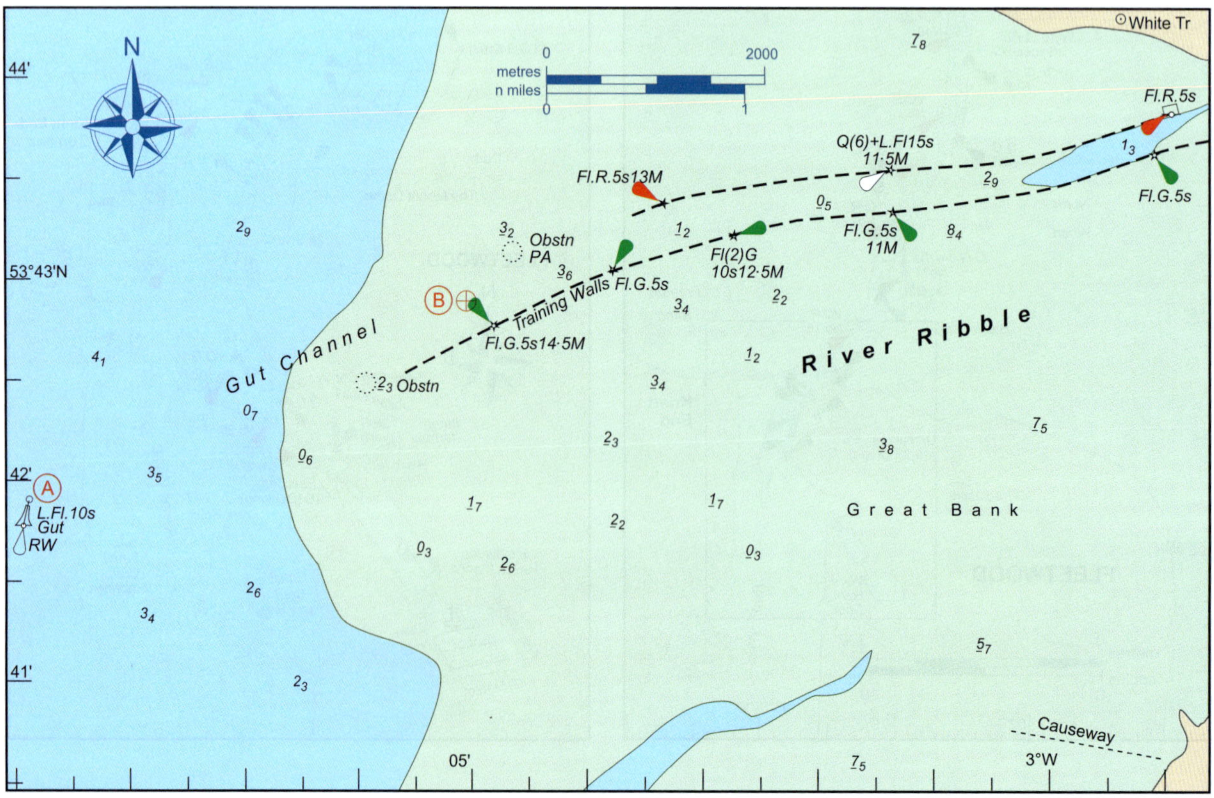

STANDARD TIME (UT)
For Summer Time add ONE hour in **non-shaded areas**

LIVERPOOL (GLADSTONE DOCK) LAT 53°27'N LONG 3°01'W

TIMES AND HEIGHTS OF HIGH AND LOW WATERS

Dates in red are SPRINGS
Dates in blue are NEAPS

YEAR **2024**

JANUARY

Date	Day	Time	m	Time	m	Time	m	Time	m
1	M	0200	8.2	0826	2.6	1413	8.4	2106	2.5
2	TU	0239	7.9	0903	2.9	1453	8.1	2144	2.7
3	W	0321	7.6	0945	3.1	1538	7.8	2228	3.0
4	TH ◑	0410	7.4	1035	3.4	1630	7.6	2322	3.2
5	F	0507	7.2	1135	3.6	1732	7.4		
6	SA	0028	3.3	0614	7.2	1247	3.5	1840	7.4
7	SU	0139	3.2	0720	7.4	1400	3.3	1946	7.6
8	M	0242	2.9	0820	7.8	1504	2.9	2045	7.9
9	TU	0337	2.5	0913	8.2	1601	2.4	2137	8.3
10	W	0428	2.1	1001	8.7	1653	2.0	2226	8.7
11	TH ●	0516	1.8	1047	9.1	1744	1.6	2314	9.0
12	F	0604	1.5	1133	9.4	1834	1.2		
13	SA	0000	9.2	0651	1.4	1219	9.6	1922	1.0
14	SU	0047	9.3	0736	1.3	1306	9.7	2009	0.9
15	M	0135	9.2	0821	1.4	1353	9.6	2054	1.1
16	TU	0222	9.0	0905	1.6	1441	9.4	2140	1.4
17	W	0310	8.7	0951	2.0	1532	9.0	2227	1.8
18	TH ◐	0402	8.3	1042	2.3	1627	8.6	2320	2.2
19	F	0501	7.9	1141	2.7	1730	8.2		
20	SA	0022	2.7	0611	7.6	1251	3.0	1842	7.9
21	SU	0134	2.9	0727	7.6	1410	2.9	1957	7.8
22	M	0245	2.8	0837	7.8	1523	2.7	2104	8.0
23	TU	0348	2.7	0934	8.2	1625	2.4	2200	8.2
24	W	0440	2.4	1022	8.5	1716	2.1	2246	8.5
25	TH ○	0524	2.2	1103	8.7	1759	1.8	2325	8.6
26	F	0602	2.1	1139	8.9	1836	1.7		
27	SA	0000	8.7	0635	2.0	1212	9.0	1909	1.7
28	SU	0031	8.7	0705	2.0	1243	9.0	1939	1.7
29	M	0102	8.7	0734	2.0	1314	8.9	2007	1.8
30	TU	0133	8.5	0804	2.1	1345	8.7	2035	2.0
31	W	0205	8.3	0836	2.3	1416	8.5	2106	2.3

FEBRUARY

Date	Day	Time	m	Time	m	Time	m	Time	m
1	TH	0238	8.1	0910	2.6	1448	8.2	2140	2.6
2	F ◑	0314	7.8	0948	2.9	1526	7.9	2220	3.0
3	SA	0359	7.5	1035	3.3	1616	7.5	2314	3.3
4	SU	0500	7.2	1142	3.5	1729	7.2		
5	M	0036	3.5	0622	7.1	1311	3.5	1859	7.2
6	TU	0203	3.3	0743	7.4	1434	3.1	2020	7.5
7	W	0312	2.8	0851	8.0	1541	2.5	2124	8.1
8	TH	0410	2.2	0946	8.6	1641	1.8	2217	8.7
9	F ●	0504	1.7	1035	9.2	1735	1.2	2305	9.2
10	SA	0554	1.2	1121	9.6	1824	0.7	2350	9.5
11	SU	0640	0.9	1206	10.0	1910	0.4		
12	M	0033	9.6	0724	0.7	1249	10.1	1953	0.3
13	TU	0116	9.6	0805	0.8	1332	10.0	2034	0.6
14	W	0158	9.3	0845	1.1	1416	9.7	2113	1.0
15	TH	0240	8.9	0925	1.5	1500	9.2	2153	1.7
16	F ◐	0325	8.4	1009	2.1	1550	8.5	2238	2.4
17	SA	0418	7.8	1103	2.7	1651	7.8	2337	3.0
18	SU	0529	7.3	1219	3.2	1812	7.3		
19	M	0101	3.4	0700	7.2	1354	3.2	1945	7.3
20	TU	0230	3.3	0824	7.5	1517	2.9	2100	7.6
21	W	0342	3.0	0925	7.9	1620	2.4	2154	8.0
22	TH	0434	2.6	1011	8.4	1707	2.0	2235	8.4
23	F	0514	2.2	1048	8.7	1745	1.7	2309	8.6
24	SA ○	0548	2.0	1121	8.9	1817	1.5	2340	8.8
25	SU	0617	1.8	1151	9.0	1845	1.4		
26	M	0008	8.9	0644	1.6	1219	9.1	1912	1.4
27	TU	0036	8.9	0712	1.6	1248	9.0	1938	1.5
28	W	0104	8.8	0740	1.6	1315	8.9	2005	1.7
29	TH	0132	8.6	0810	1.8	1342	8.7	2033	1.9

MARCH

Date	Day	Time	m	Time	m	Time	m	Time	m
1	F	0201	8.4	0841	2.2	1410	8.4	2102	2.3
2	SA	0233	8.1	0913	2.6	1445	8.1	2135	2.8
3	SU ◑	0313	7.7	0954	3.0	1531	7.6	2221	3.2
4	M	0410	7.3	1055	3.4	1641	7.1	2341	3.6
5	TU	0538	7.0	1233	3.5	1827	7.0		
6	W	0129	3.5	0715	7.3	1410	3.1	2002	7.4
7	TH	0250	2.9	0830	7.9	1524	2.3	2110	8.1
8	F	0353	2.2	0928	8.6	1626	1.5	2203	8.8
9	SA	0448	1.5	1017	9.3	1719	0.8	2248	9.3
10	SU ●	0537	0.9	1101	9.8	1806	0.3	2330	9.7
11	M	0621	0.6	1144	10.2	1849	0.1		
12	TU	0011	9.8	0703	0.4	1226	10.2	1929	0.1
13	W	0051	9.7	0742	0.5	1307	10.1	2007	0.5
14	TH	0130	9.4	0821	0.8	1348	9.6	2043	1.0
15	F	0209	9.0	0859	1.4	1431	9.0	2119	1.8
16	SA	0251	8.4	0941	2.1	1518	8.3	2200	2.6
17	SU ◐	0342	7.8	1034	2.8	1620	7.5	2257	3.3
18	M	0454	7.2	1156	3.3	1747	7.0		
19	TU	0030	3.7	0632	7.0	1339	3.3	1929	7.0
20	W	0213	3.6	0801	7.3	1500	2.9	2045	7.4
21	TH	0324	3.1	0902	7.8	1558	2.3	2134	7.9
22	F	0413	2.6	0946	8.2	1641	1.9	2211	8.3
23	SA	0450	2.2	1022	8.6	1716	1.6	2243	8.6
24	SU	0521	1.9	1053	8.8	1746	1.5	2312	8.8
25	M ○	0549	1.6	1122	9.0	1813	1.3	2339	8.9
26	TU	0616	1.5	1151	9.0	1840	1.3		
27	W	0006	8.9	0646	1.4	1218	9.0	1908	1.3
28	TH	0034	8.9	0716	1.5	1245	8.9	1936	1.5
29	F	0102	8.7	0746	1.7	1313	8.7	2005	1.8
30	SA	0131	8.5	0817	2.0	1344	8.4	2034	2.2
31	SU	0204	8.3	0850	2.4	1421	8.1	2107	2.7

APRIL

Date	Day	Time	m	Time	m	Time	m	Time	m
1	M	0246	7.9	0932	2.8	1512	7.6	2156	3.2
2	TU ◑	0347	7.4	1035	3.1	1627	7.1	2315	3.5
3	W	0517	7.2	1212	3.2	1810	7.0		
4	TH	0101	3.4	0652	7.4	1347	2.8	1942	7.5
5	F	0224	2.8	0805	8.1	1501	2.0	2048	8.2
6	SA	0329	2.1	0903	8.8	1602	1.3	2139	8.9
7	SU	0424	1.4	0951	9.4	1654	0.7	2223	9.4
8	M ●	0512	0.9	1036	9.8	1740	0.3	2305	9.6
9	TU	0556	0.5	1119	10.1	1822	0.2	2345	9.7
10	W	0638	0.4	1201	10.0	1901	0.3		
11	TH	0024	9.6	0719	0.5	1242	9.8	1939	0.7
12	F	0103	9.3	0758	0.9	1324	9.3	2015	1.3
13	SA	0142	8.9	0838	1.5	1407	8.7	2051	2.0
14	SU	0224	8.4	0921	2.1	1455	8.0	2131	2.8
15	M ◐	0315	7.8	1015	2.8	1556	7.3	2225	3.4
16	TU	0425	7.3	1135	3.2	1719	6.9	2355	3.8
17	W	0555	7.0	1308	3.2	1853	6.9		
18	TH	0134	3.7	0719	7.2	1420	2.9	2007	7.3
19	F	0243	3.2	0821	7.6	1516	2.5	2057	7.7
20	SA	0332	2.8	0907	8.0	1559	2.1	2135	8.1
21	SU	0410	2.4	0945	8.4	1635	1.8	2207	8.4
22	M	0443	2.0	1018	8.6	1707	1.6	2237	8.7
23	TU ○	0515	1.7	1049	8.8	1738	1.4	2306	8.8
24	W	0546	1.5	1120	8.8	1808	1.4	2336	8.9
25	TH	0619	1.4	1150	8.8	1839	1.4		
26	F	0006	8.9	0653	1.5	1220	8.7	1911	1.6
27	SA	0037	8.8	0726	1.6	1253	8.6	1943	1.9
28	SU	0111	8.6	0801	1.9	1330	8.4	2016	2.2
29	M	0150	8.4	0839	2.2	1414	8.0	2056	2.6
30	TU	0238	8.0	0927	2.5	1511	7.6	2149	3.0

Chart Datum: 4·93 metres below Ordnance Datum (Newlyn). HAT is 10·3 metres above Chart Datum.

NW England

STANDARD TIME (UT)
For Summer Time add ONE hour in **non-shaded areas**

LIVERPOOL (GLADSTONE DOCK) LAT 53°27′N LONG 3°01′W

TIMES AND HEIGHTS OF HIGH AND LOW WATERS

Dates in red are SPRINGS
Dates in blue are NEAPS

YEAR **2024**

MAY

Date	Day	Time m	Time m	Time m	Time m
1	W	0343 7.7	1033 2.8	1626 7.3	◑ 2306 3.2
2	TH	0506 7.6	1158 2.7	1754 7.4	
3	F	0035 3.1	0626 7.8	1320 2.4	1914 7.8
4	SA	0151 2.6	0735 8.3	1430 1.8	2018 8.3
5	SU	0256 2.1	0833 8.8	1530 1.3	2110 8.8
6	M	0353 1.5	0923 9.3	1623 1.0	2155 9.2
7	TU	0443 1.1	1010 9.6	1710 0.8	2238 9.4
8	W	0530 0.9	1055 9.7	1753 0.7	● 2320 9.4
9	TH	0614 0.8	1139 9.6	1834 0.9	
10	F	0000 9.4	0657 0.9	1222 9.3	1913 1.2
11	SA	0041 9.1	0740 1.2	1305 8.9	1951 1.7
12	SU	0122 8.8	0822 1.7	1350 8.4	2028 2.3
13	M	0205 8.4	0907 2.2	1437 7.9	2108 2.8
14	TU	0254 7.9	0959 2.7	1533 7.4	2158 3.3
15	W	0356 7.5	1103 3.0	1640 7.0	◐ 2306 3.6
16	TH	0509 7.3	1216 3.1	1755 7.0	
17	F	0028 3.7	0621 7.3	1322 3.0	1906 7.1
18	SA	0138 3.4	0724 7.5	1419 2.7	2003 7.5
19	SU	0233 3.0	0817 7.8	1506 2.4	2047 7.8
20	M	0319 2.7	0900 8.1	1547 2.1	2125 8.2
21	TU	0400 2.3	0939 8.3	1625 1.9	2200 8.4
22	W	0438 2.0	1015 8.5	1702 1.7	2234 8.6
23	TH	0516 1.8	1050 8.6	1738 1.6	○ 2308 8.8
24	F	0555 1.6	1125 8.6	1814 1.6	2343 8.8
25	SA	0633 1.6	1203 8.6	1851 1.7	
26	SU	0020 8.8	0713 1.6	1242 8.6	1929 1.9
27	M	0100 8.7	0754 1.8	1326 8.4	2008 2.1
28	TU	0146 8.6	0838 1.9	1415 8.2	2054 2.4
29	W	0238 8.4	0930 2.1	1512 8.0	2148 2.6
30	TH	0340 8.2	1031 2.2	1618 7.8	◑ 2254 2.8
31	F	0448 8.1	1139 2.2	1729 7.8	

JUNE

Date	Day	Time m	Time m	Time m	Time m
1	SA	0005 2.7	0557 8.2	1248 2.1	1840 7.9
2	SU	0114 2.5	0702 8.4	1354 1.9	1943 8.2
3	M	0220 2.2	0802 8.7	1456 1.7	2039 8.5
4	TU	0321 1.9	0857 8.9	1552 1.5	2129 8.8
5	W	0417 1.6	0948 9.0	1642 1.4	2216 9.0
6	TH	0508 1.4	1037 9.1	1729 1.4	● 2301 9.1
7	F	0557 1.3	1124 9.0	1812 1.5	2344 9.0
8	SA	0643 1.3	1209 8.9	1853 1.7	
9	SU	0025 8.9	0728 1.5	1252 8.6	1933 2.0
10	M	0106 8.7	0810 1.8	1335 8.3	2010 2.3
11	TU	0148 8.5	0852 2.1	1417 8.0	2048 2.7
12	W	0232 8.2	0935 2.4	1503 7.7	2128 3.0
13	TH	0321 7.9	1020 2.7	1554 7.4	2216 3.2
14	F	0417 7.6	1112 2.9	1651 7.2	◐ 2313 3.4
15	SA	0517 7.4	1210 3.0	1753 7.1	
16	SU	0017 3.4	0619 7.4	1310 3.0	1855 7.3
17	M	0123 3.3	0718 7.5	1407 2.8	1952 7.5
18	TU	0223 3.0	0812 7.7	1459 2.6	2040 7.8
19	W	0316 2.7	0900 7.9	1546 2.3	2124 8.1
20	TH	0405 2.3	0944 8.1	1630 2.1	2205 8.4
21	F	0451 2.0	1026 8.4	1713 1.9	2245 8.7
22	SA	0536 1.8	1108 8.6	1755 1.7	○ 2326 8.9
23	SU	0621 1.6	1151 8.7	1838 1.7	
24	M	0009 9.0	0707 1.4	1235 8.8	1922 1.7
25	TU	0054 9.1	0753 1.4	1322 8.7	2006 1.7
26	W	0141 9.0	0839 1.4	1411 8.6	2052 1.9
27	TH	0231 8.9	0927 1.5	1502 8.4	2141 2.1
28	F	0324 8.7	1018 1.7	1557 8.2	◑ 2234 2.3
29	SA	0421 8.6	1113 1.9	1657 8.0	2333 2.4
30	SU	0523 8.4	1213 2.1	1802 7.9	

JULY

Date	Day	Time m	Time m	Time m	Time m
1	M	0037 2.5	0629 8.3	1318 2.2	1910 7.9
2	TU	0147 2.5	0735 8.3	1425 2.2	2014 8.1
3	W	0257 2.3	0839 8.3	1527 2.2	2112 8.3
4	TH	0400 2.1	0937 8.5	1623 2.0	2204 8.6
5	F	0457 1.8	1029 8.6	1713 1.9	● 2251 8.8
6	SA	0549 1.6	1117 8.7	1758 1.9	2334 8.9
7	SU	0635 1.5	1200 8.6	1839 1.9	
8	M	0014 8.9	0718 1.6	1239 8.6	1917 2.0
9	TU	0051 8.8	0755 1.7	1316 8.4	1951 2.2
10	W	0127 8.7	0830 1.9	1351 8.3	2023 2.3
11	TH	0204 8.5	0902 2.1	1428 8.1	2056 2.5
12	F	0242 8.2	0934 2.4	1508 7.8	2133 2.8
13	SA	0324 7.9	1010 2.6	1552 7.5	◐ 2216 3.1
14	SU	0411 7.6	1056 2.9	1643 7.3	2308 3.3
15	M	0506 7.3	1154 3.1	1744 7.1	
16	TU	0014 3.4	0613 7.2	1304 3.2	1853 7.2
17	W	0129 3.3	0722 7.3	1413 3.0	1958 7.5
18	TH	0238 3.0	0826 7.5	1512 2.7	2054 7.9
19	F	0338 2.6	0921 7.9	1605 2.4	2143 8.3
20	SA	0432 2.1	1011 8.3	1654 2.0	2229 8.8
21	SU	0523 1.7	1056 8.7	1742 1.7	○ 2313 9.1
22	M	0613 1.3	1141 9.0	1829 1.4	2357 9.4
23	TU	0700 1.0	1226 9.1	1914 1.3	
24	W	0042 9.6	0746 0.8	1310 9.2	1958 1.2
25	TH	0127 9.6	0829 0.8	1355 9.1	2040 1.4
26	F	0212 9.4	0911 1.1	1440 8.8	2123 1.6
27	SA	0259 9.2	0954 1.4	1528 8.5	2208 2.0
28	SU	0350 8.8	1041 1.9	1622 8.1	◑ 2301 2.4
29	M	0448 8.3	1137 2.4	1726 7.7	
30	TU	0006 2.7	0559 7.9	1246 2.8	1843 7.6
31	W	0126 2.9	0718 7.7	1405 2.9	2000 7.7

AUGUST

Date	Day	Time m	Time m	Time m	Time m
1	TH	0248 2.7	0833 7.8	1517 2.7	2106 8.0
2	F	0358 2.3	0936 8.1	1617 2.5	2159 8.4
3	SA	0456 2.0	1027 8.4	1708 2.2	2244 8.7
4	SU	0544 1.7	1110 8.6	1750 2.0	● 2323 8.9
5	M	0624 1.5	1146 8.7	1826 1.9	2358 9.0
6	TU	0700 1.5	1219 8.7	1858 1.9	
7	W	0030 9.0	0731 1.5	1250 8.7	1927 1.9
8	TH	0101 8.9	0759 1.7	1321 8.6	1955 2.0
9	F	0131 8.8	0825 1.8	1352 8.4	2024 2.2
10	SA	0202 8.5	0852 2.1	1424 8.2	2056 2.4
11	SU	0234 8.2	0923 2.4	1459 7.8	2132 2.8
12	M	0310 7.8	1000 2.8	1541 7.5	◐ 2216 3.2
13	TU	0356 7.4	1049 3.3	1637 7.2	2317 3.5
14	W	0503 7.0	1203 3.5	1756 7.0	
15	TH	0042 3.6	0636 6.9	1332 3.5	1921 7.3
16	F	0208 3.2	0800 7.3	1445 3.0	2030 7.8
17	SA	0317 2.7	0905 7.8	1545 2.5	2125 8.4
18	SU	0416 2.0	0957 8.4	1639 1.9	2212 9.0
19	M	0510 1.4	1043 8.9	1728 1.5	○ 2256 9.5
20	TU	0559 0.9	1125 9.3	1815 1.1	2339 9.8
21	W	0645 0.5	1208 9.6	1858 0.8	
22	TH	0021 10.0	0728 0.4	1249 9.6	1940 0.8
23	F	0104 10.0	0808 0.5	1330 9.4	2020 1.0
24	SA	0147 9.8	0846 0.9	1412 9.1	2059 1.4
25	SU	0231 9.3	0925 1.5	1456 8.6	2142 1.9
26	M	0319 8.7	1008 2.2	1547 8.1	◑ 2233 2.5
27	TU	0418 8.0	1102 2.9	1654 7.5	2344 3.0
28	W	0537 7.4	1222 3.3	1823 7.3	
29	TH	0120 3.2	0712 7.3	1357 3.4	1952 7.5
30	F	0248 2.8	0835 7.6	1515 3.0	2100 8.0
31	SA	0356 2.3	0933 8.0	1613 2.6	2150 8.4

Chart Datum: 4·93 metres below Ordnance Datum (Newlyn). HAT is 10·3 metres above Chart Datum.

STANDARD TIME (UT)
For Summer Time add ONE hour in **non-shaded areas**

LIVERPOOL (GLADSTONE DOCK) LAT 53°27′N LONG 3°01′W

TIMES AND HEIGHTS OF HIGH AND LOW WATERS

Dates in red are SPRINGS
Dates in blue are NEAPS

YEAR **2024**

SEPTEMBER

Date	Day	Time	m
1	SU	0447	1.9
		1017	8.4
		1657	2.2
		2229	8.8
2	M	0528	1.6
		1053	8.7
		1733	2.0
		2303	9.0
3	TU	0602	1.5
		1124	8.8
		1803	1.8
		● 2334	9.1
4	W	0631	1.4
		1153	8.9
		1831	1.7
5	TH	0002	9.1
		0659	1.4
		1220	8.9
		1858	1.7
6	F	0031	9.1
		0724	1.5
		1248	8.8
		1925	1.8
7	SA	0058	8.9
		0749	1.7
		1316	8.6
		1954	2.0
8	SU	0126	8.7
		0816	2.0
		1345	8.4
		2025	2.3
9	M	0154	8.3
		0845	2.4
		1416	8.1
		2058	2.7
10	TU	0227	8.0
		0918	2.9
		1454	7.7
		2138	3.1
11	W	0310	7.5
		1001	3.4
		1547	7.3
		◐ 2235	3.5
12	TH	0415	7.0
		1113	3.7
		1711	7.0
13	F	0006	3.7
		0600	6.8
		1258	3.7
		1850	7.2
14	SA	0143	3.3
		0739	7.2
		1421	3.2
		2006	7.8
15	SU	0256	2.5
		0847	7.9
		1524	2.5
		2103	8.6
16	M	0357	1.8
		0938	8.7
		1619	1.8
		2150	9.2
17	TU	0450	1.1
		1021	9.2
		1708	1.3
		2233	9.8
18	W	0537	0.6
		1103	9.6
		1753	0.8
		○ 2315	10.1
19	TH	0621	0.3
		1143	9.8
		1836	0.6
		2357	10.3
20	F	0702	0.3
		1223	9.8
		1916	0.6
21	SA	0038	10.1
		0741	0.5
		1303	9.6
		1956	0.9
22	SU	0120	9.8
		0818	1.0
		1343	9.2
		2036	1.4
23	M	0204	9.2
		0856	1.7
		1426	8.6
		2120	2.0
24	TU	0253	8.5
		0938	2.5
		1518	8.0
		◑ 2214	2.7
25	W	0355	7.7
		1034	3.3
		1629	7.4
		2334	3.2
26	TH	0522	7.1
		1204	3.7
		1805	7.2
27	F	0114	3.3
		0703	7.1
		1346	3.6
		1936	7.5
28	SA	0235	2.8
		0822	7.5
		1500	3.1
		2040	8.0
29	SU	0335	2.3
		0914	8.0
		1552	2.7
		2126	8.4
30	M	0421	1.9
		0953	8.4
		1632	2.3
		2203	8.8

OCTOBER

Date	Day	Time	m
1	TU	0458	1.7
		1026	8.7
		1704	2.0
		2235	9.0
2	W	0529	1.5
		1054	8.9
		1732	1.8
		● 2304	9.1
3	TH	0556	1.5
		1122	9.0
		1759	1.7
		2333	9.1
4	F	0623	1.5
		1149	9.0
		1827	1.7
5	SA	0000	9.1
		0650	1.5
		1217	8.9
		1857	1.7
6	SU	0028	8.9
		0717	1.7
		1244	8.8
		1928	1.9
7	M	0056	8.7
		0746	2.0
		1313	8.6
		1959	2.2
8	TU	0126	8.4
		0816	2.4
		1345	8.3
		2033	2.6
9	W	0201	8.0
		0849	2.9
		1425	7.9
		2114	3.0
10	TH	0248	7.5
		0934	3.4
		1521	7.5
		◐ 2213	3.4
11	F	0357	7.1
		1045	3.7
		1646	7.2
		2343	3.5
12	SA	0537	7.0
		1228	3.7
		1821	7.4
13	SU	0117	3.0
		0712	7.4
		1352	3.1
		1936	8.0
14	M	0230	2.3
		0820	8.1
		1456	2.4
		2034	8.7
15	TU	0329	1.6
		0910	8.8
		1551	1.8
		2122	9.4
16	W	0422	1.0
		0954	9.3
		1641	1.3
		2206	9.9
17	TH	0509	0.6
		1036	9.7
		1727	0.9
		○ 2249	10.1
18	F	0553	0.5
		1116	9.8
		1810	0.7
		2332	10.2
19	SA	0634	0.5
		1157	9.8
		1853	0.8
20	SU	0015	10.0
		0714	0.9
		1237	9.5
		1935	1.1
21	M	0059	9.5
		0753	1.4
		1319	9.1
		2018	1.6
22	TU	0144	8.9
		0832	2.1
		1403	8.6
		2105	2.2
23	W	0235	8.2
		0915	2.8
		1456	8.0
		2202	2.8
24	TH	0337	7.5
		1012	3.5
		1607	7.5
		◑ 2321	3.2
25	F	0459	7.1
		1139	3.9
		1734	7.3
26	SA	0047	3.2
		0630	7.1
		1312	3.7
		1857	7.5
27	SU	0159	2.9
		0746	7.4
		1421	3.3
		2001	7.8
28	M	0256	2.5
		0839	7.8
		1512	2.9
		2049	8.2
29	TU	0340	2.2
		0918	8.2
		1552	2.5
		2127	8.6
30	W	0417	1.9
		0951	8.6
		1626	2.2
		2201	8.8
31	TH	0449	1.8
		1021	8.8
		1657	2.0
		2233	8.9

NOVEMBER

Date	Day	Time	m
1	F	0519	1.7
		1051	8.9
		1728	1.8
		● 2303	8.9
2	SA	0549	1.7
		1120	9.0
		1800	1.8
		2334	8.9
3	SU	0619	1.7
		1150	9.0
		1833	1.8
4	M	0004	8.8
		0651	1.9
		1220	8.9
		1907	2.0
5	TU	0036	8.6
		0723	2.1
		1253	8.7
		1942	2.2
6	W	0111	8.4
		0756	2.5
		1329	8.4
		2020	2.5
7	TH	0152	8.1
		0834	2.8
		1414	8.1
		2105	2.8
8	F	0243	7.7
		0923	3.2
		1512	7.8
		2206	3.0
9	SA	0351	7.4
		1032	3.5
		1629	7.6
		◐ 2324	3.1
10	SU	0514	7.3
		1157	3.4
		1749	7.8
11	M	0045	2.7
		0636	7.7
		1314	3.0
		1900	8.2
12	TU	0154	2.2
		0744	8.2
		1420	2.5
		2000	8.8
13	W	0256	1.7
		0838	8.7
		1518	1.9
		2052	9.3
14	TH	0350	1.3
		0926	9.2
		1612	1.5
		2140	9.6
15	F	0440	1.0
		1010	9.4
		1701	1.2
		○ 2227	9.8
16	SA	0526	0.9
		1053	9.6
		1748	1.0
		2313	9.8
17	SU	0609	1.0
		1136	9.6
		1834	1.1
		2359	9.6
18	M	0651	1.3
		1219	9.4
		1920	1.3
19	TU	0044	9.2
		0733	1.7
		1302	9.1
		2007	1.7
20	W	0131	8.7
		0814	2.3
		1348	8.7
		2055	2.2
21	TH	0220	8.2
		0858	2.8
		1439	8.2
		2149	2.6
22	F	0316	7.7
		0949	3.3
		1539	7.8
		2252	3.0
23	SA	0420	7.3
		1055	3.7
		1648	7.5
		◑	
24	SU	0000	3.1
		0532	7.1
		1211	3.8
		1758	7.5
25	M	0104	3.1
		0644	7.2
		1319	3.6
		1904	7.6
26	TU	0201	2.9
		0745	7.5
		1416	3.3
		1959	7.9
27	W	0249	2.6
		0833	7.9
		1503	2.9
		2046	8.1
28	TH	0331	2.4
		0912	8.2
		1544	2.6
		2126	8.4
29	F	0409	2.2
		0948	8.5
		1623	2.3
		2203	8.5
30	SA	0445	2.0
		1022	8.7
		1700	2.1
		2238	8.6

DECEMBER

Date	Day	Time	m
1	SU	0520	1.9
		1055	8.8
		1737	2.0
		● 2313	8.7
2	M	0555	1.9
		1129	8.9
		1815	1.9
		2348	8.7
3	TU	0631	2.0
		1204	8.9
		1854	1.9
4	W	0025	8.6
		0709	2.1
		1242	8.9
		1935	2.0
5	TH	0105	8.5
		0747	2.3
		1323	8.7
		2017	2.2
6	F	0149	8.3
		0830	2.5
		1410	8.5
		2104	2.3
7	SA	0240	8.1
		0918	2.8
		1504	8.3
		2158	2.5
8	SU	0339	7.9
		1016	2.9
		1607	8.2
		◐ 2300	2.5
9	M	0445	7.8
		1123	3.0
		1714	8.2
10	TU	0007	2.5
		0556	7.8
		1231	2.9
		1821	8.4
11	W	0114	2.3
		0704	8.1
		1340	2.6
		1925	8.6
12	TH	0220	2.1
		0806	8.4
		1446	2.3
		2025	8.8
13	F	0320	1.8
		0901	8.7
		1547	1.9
		2121	9.1
14	SA	0415	1.6
		0951	9.0
		1642	1.6
		2213	9.2
15	SU	0505	1.5
		1039	9.2
		1735	1.4
		○ 2303	9.2
16	M	0552	1.5
		1125	9.3
		1825	1.4
		2351	9.1
17	TU	0636	1.7
		1210	9.2
		1912	1.4
18	W	0036	8.9
		0720	1.9
		1252	9.1
		1958	1.6
19	TH	0120	8.7
		0800	2.2
		1335	8.8
		2042	1.9
20	F	0203	8.3
		0840	2.6
		1417	8.5
		2125	2.3
21	SA	0246	8.0
		0919	2.9
		1503	8.2
		2209	2.7
22	SU	0333	7.7
		1002	3.2
		1554	7.9
		◑ 2256	3.0
23	M	0426	7.4
		1053	3.5
		1651	7.6
		2350	3.2
24	TU	0526	7.2
		1155	3.6
		1753	7.4
25	W	0050	3.2
		0632	7.2
		1302	3.6
		1858	7.4
26	TH	0150	3.1
		0735	7.4
		1407	3.4
		1959	7.6
27	F	0244	2.9
		0830	7.7
		1502	3.1
		2051	7.8
28	SA	0332	2.7
		0916	8.0
		1552	2.7
		2138	8.1
29	SU	0416	2.4
		0958	8.4
		1637	2.4
		2219	8.3
30	M	0458	2.2
		1037	8.7
		1721	2.1
		● 2259	8.5
31	TU	0539	2.0
		1115	8.9
		1805	1.8
		2338	8.7

Chart Datum: 4·93 metres below Ordnance Datum (Newlyn). HAT is 10·3 metres above Chart Datum.

NW England

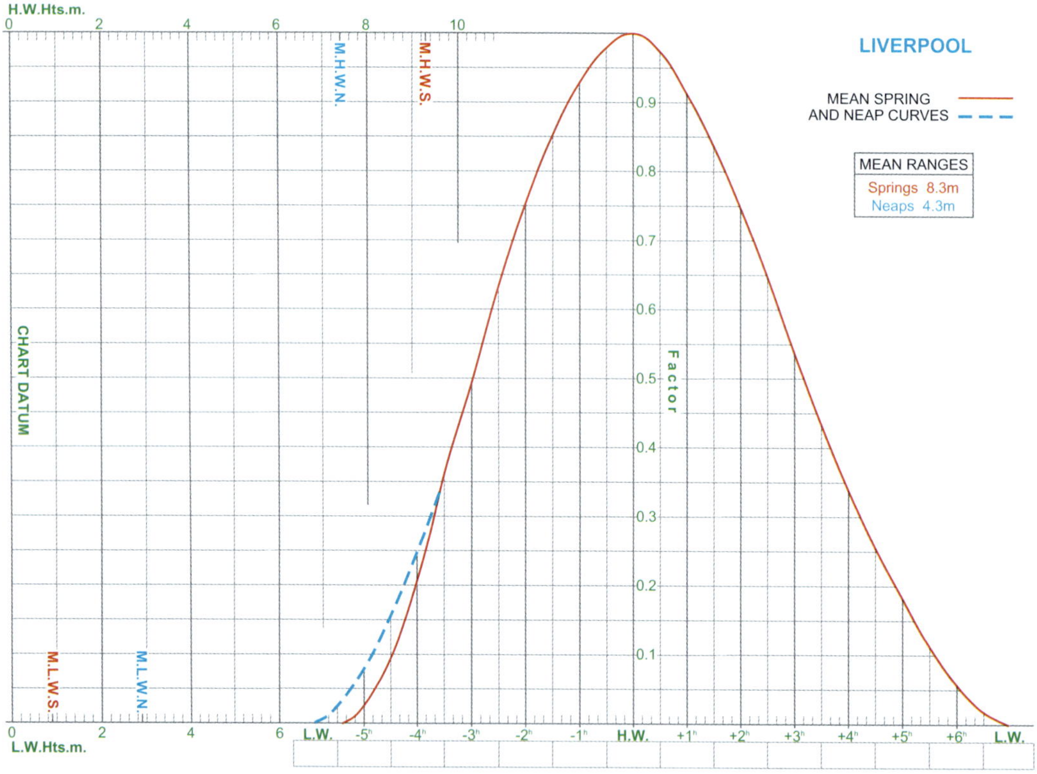

3.16 LIVERPOOL

Merseyside **53°24′·22N 03°00′·28W** (Liver Bldg)

CHARTS AC 1826, 1978, 1951, 3490, 5613; Imray C62, C52

TIDES +0015 Dover; ML 5·2; Duration 0535

Standard Port LIVERPOOL (GLADSTONE DOCK) (⟵)

Times				Height (metres)			
High Water		Low Water		MHWS	MHWN	MLWN	MLWS
0000	0600	0200	0700	9·4	7·5	3·2	1·1
1200	1800	1400	1900				
Differences SEACOMBE (ALFRED DK)							
+0007	+0007	+0000	+0000	–0·1	–0·1	–0·3	–0·2
GARSTON							
+0026	+0022	+0017	+0020	+0·3	+0·1	–0·4	–0·5
EASTHAM (River Mersey)							
+0014	*+0014*	*+0006*	*+0006*	*+0·2*	*0·0*	*0·0*	*+0·2*
HALE HEAD (River Mersey)							
+0035	+0030	ND	ND	–2·5	–2·6	ND	ND
WIDNES (River Mersey)							
+0045	*+0050*	*+0355*	*+0340*	*–4·3*	*–4·5*	*–2·8*	*–0·6*
FIDDLER'S FERRY (River Mersey)							
+0105	+0120	+0535	+0445	–6·0	–6·4	–2·7	–0·6
HILBRE ISLAND (River Dee)							
–0011	–0008	–0013	–0018	–0·4	–0·3	+0·1	+0·2
MOSTYN DOCKS (River Dee)							
–0015	*–0010*	*–0025*	*–0025*	*–0·9*	*–0·8*	*ND*	*ND*
CONNAH'S QUAY (River Dee)							
+0005	+0020	+0350	+0335	–4·7	–4·5	DR	DR
CHESTER (River Dee)							
+0110	+0110	+0455	+0455	–5·4	–5·5	DR	DR
COLWYN BAY							
–0015	–0015	ND	ND	–1·6	–1·4	ND	ND
LLANDUDNO							
–0009	–0021	–0031	–0038	–1·7	–1·6	–0·9	–0·6

NOTE: LW time differences at Connah's Quay give the end of a LW stand lasting about 3¾hrs at sp and 5hrs at nps. A bore occurs in the R Dee at Chester.

SHELTER Good at marinas in Brunswick/Coburg docks and in Canning/Albert Docks. Fair weather ⚓ on the SW side of river. Strong winds from any direction raise a swell on the bar. Wind against tide causes steep, breaking seas in outer reaches of R Mersey with disturbed waters into the Crosby Channel.

NAVIGATION WPT 53°32′·02N 03°20′·98W, Bar light float, 111°/2·8M to Q1 NCM lt F. From Q1 to marina is 15·5M via Queens and Crosby Channels. Both have training banks which cover and it is unsafe to navigate between these and the floats/buoys. Sp tidal streams exceed 5kn within the river. Elsewhere great caution is needed as the whole area (R Dee, R Mersey to R Alt and N to Morecambe Bay) is littered with sandbanks and damaged training walls. Local knowledge is advisable inshore outside marked passages.

Leeds and Liverpool Canal (BWB) gives access to E Coast, ent at Stanley Dock. Max draught 1·0m, air draught 2·2m, beam 4·3m, LOA 18·3m. Liverpool to Goole 161M, 103 locks.

Manchester Ship Canal, ent at Eastham Locks (outer wall bn Iso YR 4s), leads 31M to Salford Quays or R Weaver for boatyards at Northwich. Obtain info pack from Peel Ports https://www.peelports.com/media/2259/mpf3-pleasure-craft-induction-pack-2017-2018.pdf.

R Dee: WPT 53°25′·13N 03°13′·17W, Hilbre Swash HE2 ECM buoy, Q (3) 10s, (chan shifts). From the W use Welsh Chan. The Dee estuary mostly dries.

LIGHTS AND MARKS Bar SWM lt float, Fl 5s Racon. Keep 5ca clear of SPM, 5ca W of Bar lt float. Formby SWM buoy, Iso 4s, is at the ent to Queen's Chan which is marked by light floats and buoys, and 3 NCM buoys, numbered Q1–Q12. Crosby Chan is similarly marked, C1–C23. From Crosby SWM buoy, Oc 5s, the track upriver is approx 145°. The Liver Bldg (twin spires) and Port of Liverpool Bldg (dome) are conspic on the E bank opposite Birkenhead Docks.

COMMUNICATIONS (Code 0151) C Ⓗ 709 0141. Port Ops 949 6134/5; ⛅949 6095.

Contact *Mersey VTS* Ch **12** 16 (H24) before Bar lt and maintain listening watch in fairway for traffic info, nav and gale warnings. Movements, and weather are b/cast on Ch 09 at HW–3 and –2.

Canning Dock/Liverpool Marina Ch **M**. Eastham Locks Ch 07 (H24). Manchester Ship Canal Ch 14. Liverpool NTM for further detail.

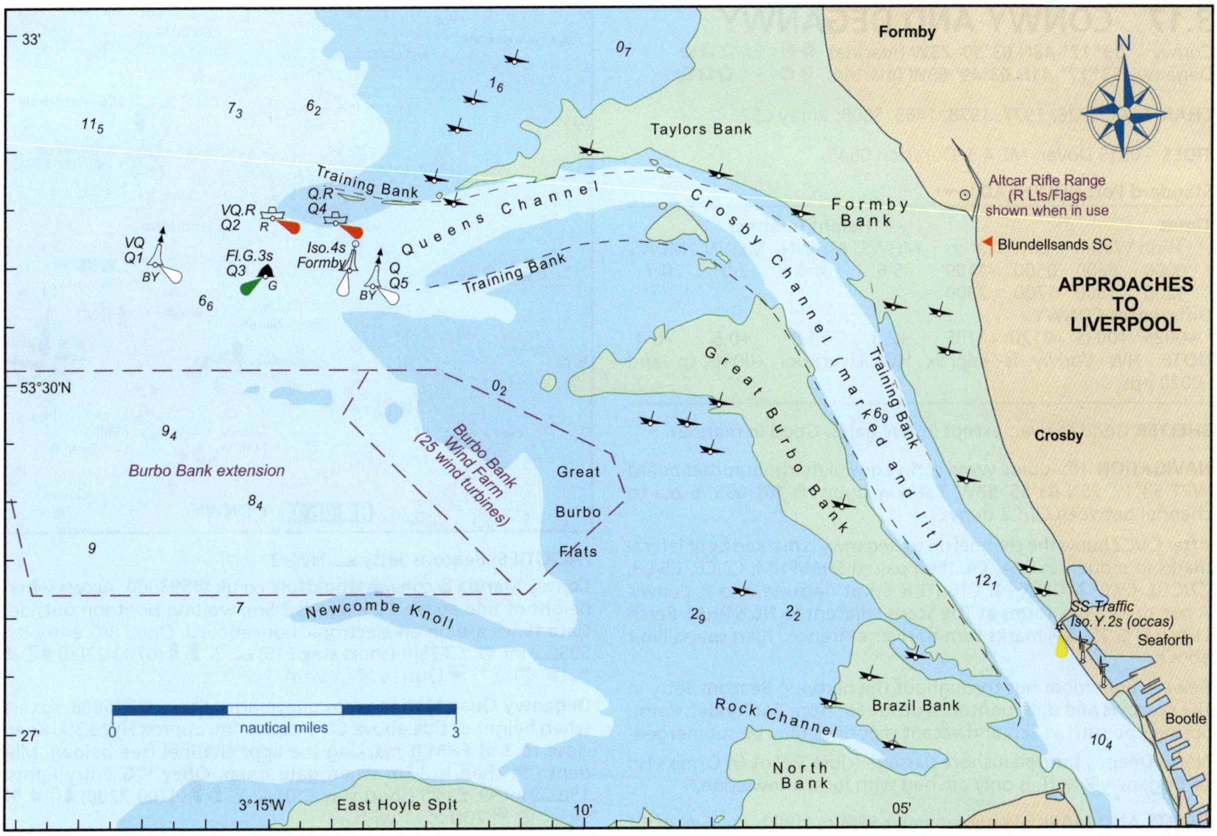

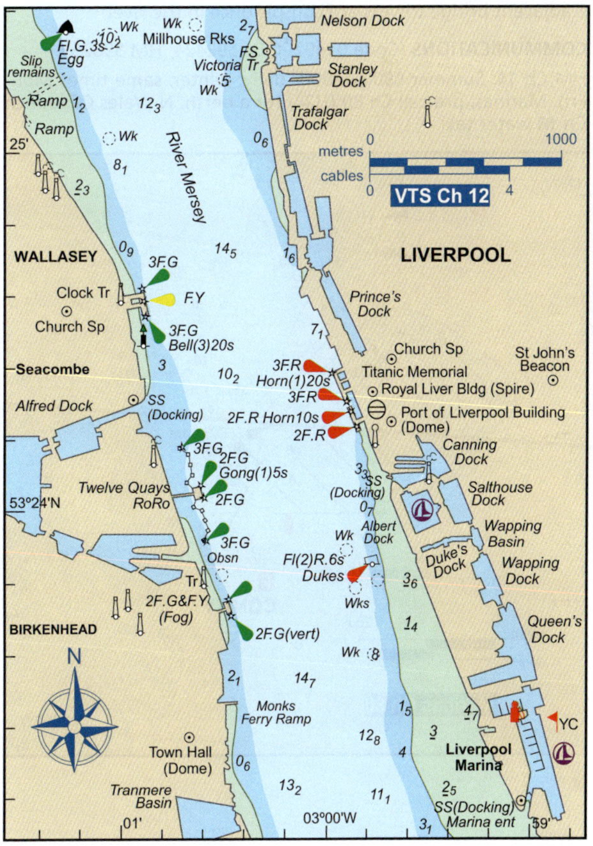

FACILITIES **Liverpool Marina** ent is 1M S of the Liver Bldg, abeam Pluckington Bank WCM buoy. **IPTS** (sigs 2, 3 and 5) from conspic black control bldg at lock ent. 2m depth over sill at Brunswick Dock lock (width 8m) approx HW ±2¼ sp, ±1½ nps, 0600-2200 Mar-Oct. Pontoons inside, depth generally 2·5m, but less in places; night locking by arrangement. www.liverpoolmarina.co.uk ☎7076777 (0500-2200 Mar–Oct). 350, £2·70, lock fee c. £25; (½M) (60t), (☎7076888) wi-fi.

Albert Dock ☎7096558; access HW–2 to HW via Canning Dock, but not on every tide. VHF Ch M when manned.

Royal Mersey YC ☎6453204.

W Kirby SC ☎6255579, M (in Dee Est) (at HW), (30t).

Hoylake SC ☎6322616.

City all facilities.

ADJACENT ANCHORAGE

RIVER ALT, Merseyside, **53°31′·42N 03°03′·80W**. AC 1978, 1951, 5613. HW –0008 on Dover. Good shelter but only for LOA <8·5m x 1·2m draught on a HW of at least 8m. Mersey E training wall can be crossed HW±2. Entrance to channel (shifts frequently) is E of C14 PHM lt float. The channel runs NW of, and parallel to the large fixed marks on the training wall (outer is a R basket; inner a Y cross), then between R and G perches. Inadvisable to ⚓ in R Alt without local knowledge; pick up a free mooring off the SC and contact club. Facilities are very limited. **Blundell Sands SC** ☎(0151) 9292101 (occas), (at HW).

ADJACENT HARBOUR

RHYL, Denbigh, **53°19′·0N 03°30′·4W**. AC 1978, 1951, 5613. Good shelter for vessels able to take the ground on pontoons in outer hbr. Inner hbr dries. Strong tides rip across ent between SWM and Hope's Nose, but training and harbour walls make entry achievable with care. Training wall marked by 4 lit bns Fl(2) R 4s with outer PHM Q R 7m 2M. Lifting bridge divides hbr opening on req Ch 14. Contact HM prior to visit: ☎01824 708400.

3.17 CONWY AND DEGANWY

Conwy 53°17′·48N 03°50′·23W (marina)
Deganwy 53°17′·41N 03°49′·66W (marina)

CHARTS AC 1826, 1977, 1978, 1463, 5609; Imray C52

TIDES –0015 Dover; ML 4·3; Duration 0545

Standard Port HOLYHEAD (⟶)

Times				Height (metres)			
High Water		Low Water		MHWS	MHWN	MLWN	MLWS
0000	0600	0500	1100	5·6	4·4	2·0	0·7
1200	1800	1700	2300				
Differences CONWY							
+0025	+0035	+0120	+0105	+2·3	+1·8	+0·6	+0·4

NOTE: HW Conwy is approx HW Liverpool –0040 sp and –0020 nps.

SHELTER Good in river, except in NW gales. Good in marinas.

NAVIGATION Hbr guide www.conwy.gov.uk/harbourandseaboard WPT 53°17′·95N 03°55′·58W, Fairway buoy LFl 10s; 095°/6·2ca to channel between C1/C2 buoys.

After C1/C2 buoys the channel up to Deganwy is marked by lit lateral marks in sequence: C2A, C4, then paired SHM/PHM: C3/C6, C5/C8, C7/C10, C9/C12, C11/C14. C16 (Fl R 6s) at narrows into R Conwy. A bar, dries 1·0m, forms at The Scabs adjacent to No 6 PHM. Perch Lt bcn Fl G 15s 5M marks turn to river entrance. 10kn speed limit above.

Beware unlit moorings throughout the harbour, Beacons Jetty in the narrows and unlit pontoons upstream from Bodlondeb Point. Spring ebb runs at 5kn and vacant moorings may be submerged.

North Deep, a buoyed inshore passage (close SW of Gt Orme's Hd to Deganwy Point), is only advised with local knowledge.

LIGHTS AND MARKS Penmaenmawr SPM outfall buoy (SW of C1 buoy) is not a channel mark. The 4 towers of Conwy Castle and the 2 adjacent bridge towers are conspic once in the river.

COMMUNICATIONS (Code 01492) C Dr 592424; HM 596253.

HM Ch **14**. Summer 0900-1700LT daily; winter, same times Mon-Fri). Marinas, pre-call Ch 80 (H24) for a berth. N Wales CC launch Ch **M** water taxi.

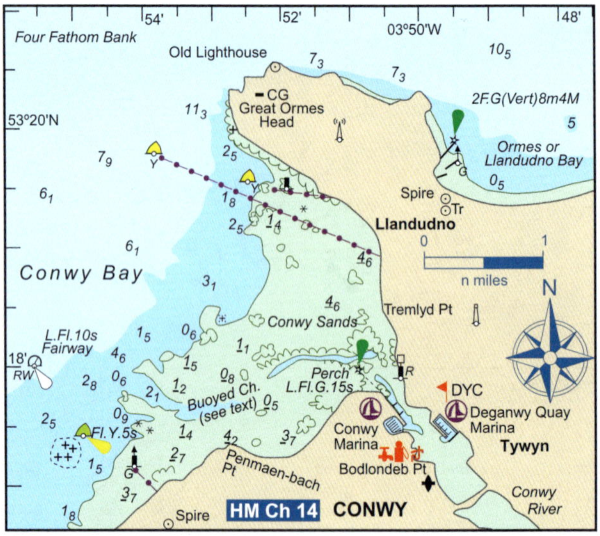

FACILITIES Beacons Jetty HW±3.

Conwy Marina conway@boatfolk.co.uk ☎593000. Access when height of tide above CD exceeds 3·5m; waiting pontoon outside. Gate times are on an electronic noticeboard. Obey R/G entry lts. 505 inc Ⓥ, £3·75m (short stay £15) (0700-2200) Ⓔ (30t) wi-fi.

Deganwy Quay Marina www.quaymarinas.com ☎576888. Access when height of tide above CD exceeds 4m, approx HW ±3¼. Keep close to 3 lit PHM lt marking the appr channel (see below). Min depth in chan is 2·5m when gate open. Obey R/G entry lights. 150 inc Ⓥ, £3·25 (short stay £10) (0700-2200) Ⓔ (20t) wi-fi.

Harbour contact HM for: 's, pontoon £13<8m +£1·82/m; **Town Quay** 3 drying £11<8m>£12·50<12·3m; (Town Quay HW±2, call Ch 14 to confirm).

N Wales Cruising Club (Conwy) ☎593481.

Conwy YC (Deganwy) ☎583690.

Town Ⓑ (Liverpool).

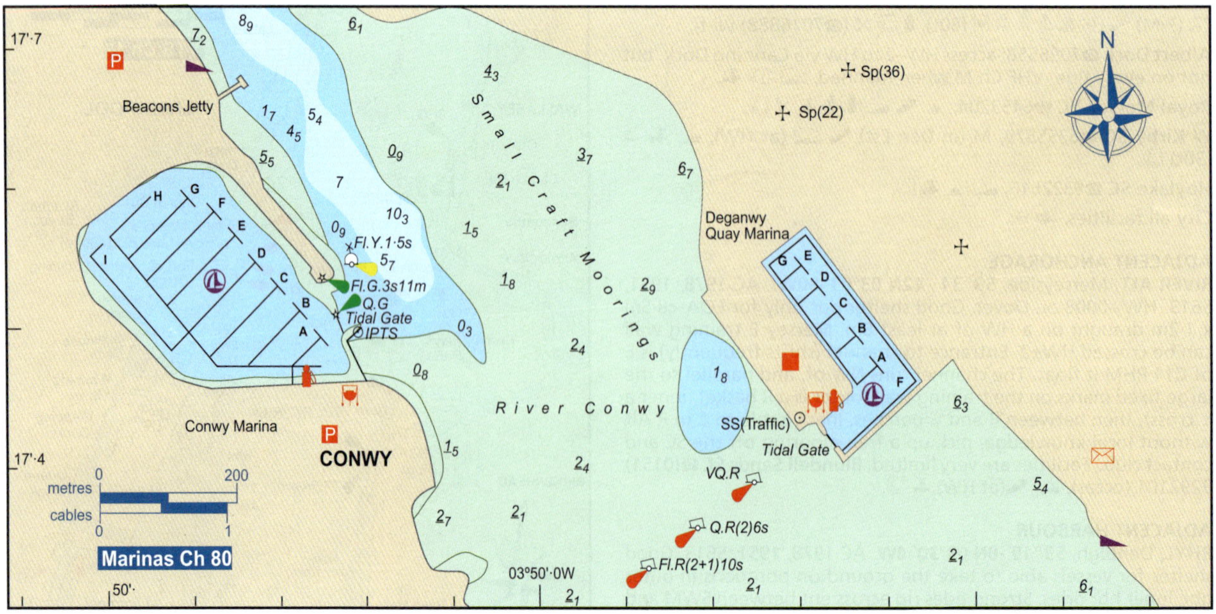

3.18 TIDAL STREAMS THROUGH THE MENAI STRAIT

FLOOD

(T): turning → : < 2k ➡ : 2-4k ➡ : 4k+

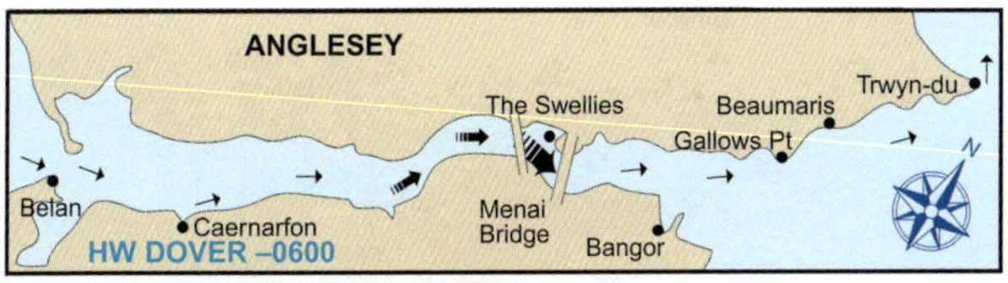

LOCAL LW: Caernarfon HW Dover –0555. Port Dinorwic –0620. Menai –0540. Beaumaris –0605.

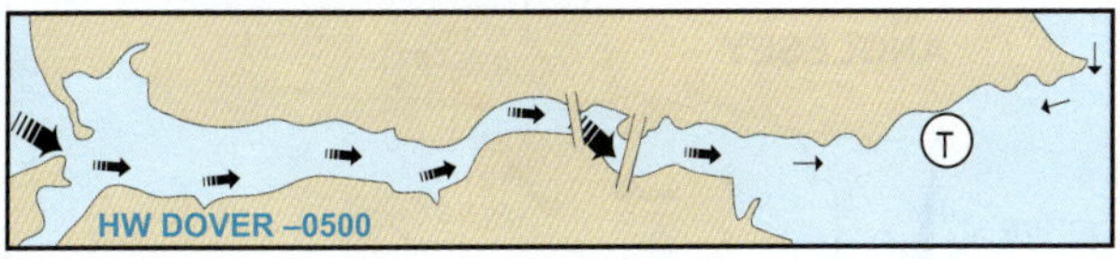

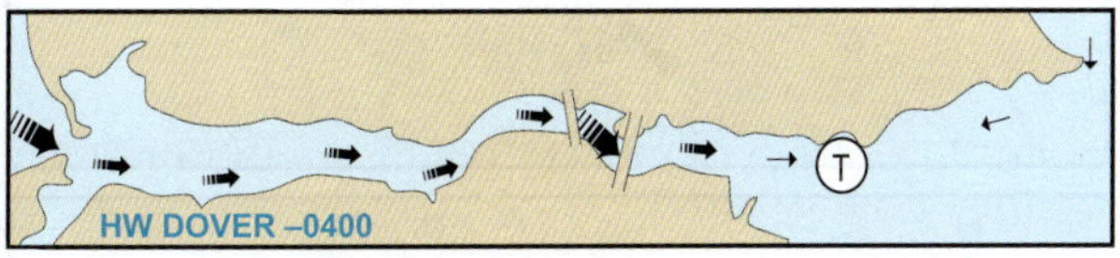

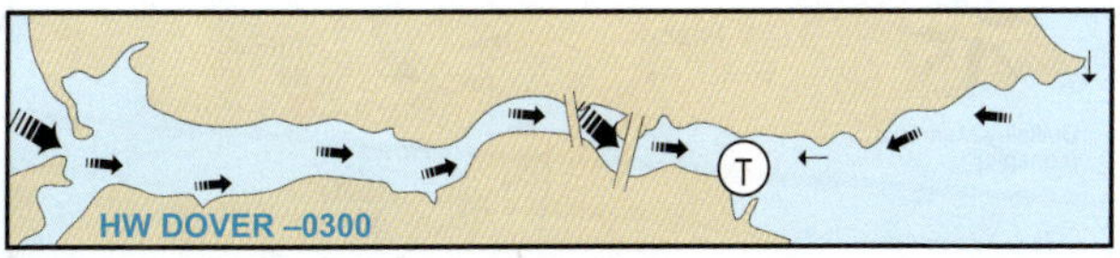

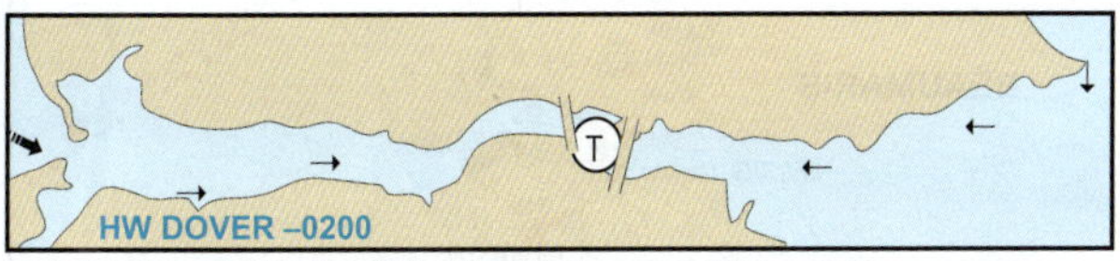

SLACK WATER IN THE SWELLIES: HW Dover –0200 to –0230.

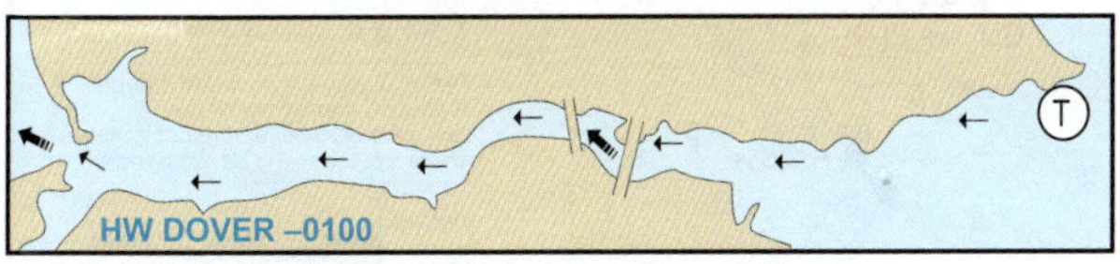

LOCAL HW: Belan: HW Dover –0115. Caernarfon: –0105. Port Dinorwic: –0050.

EBB

(T): turning → : < 2k ➡ : 2-4k ➡ : 4k +

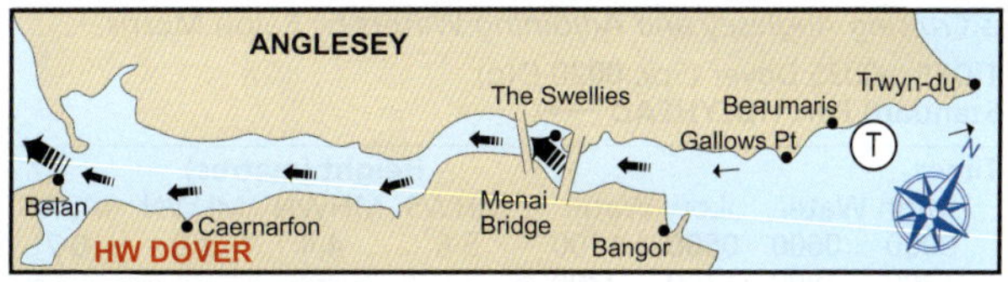

LOCAL HW: Menai –0005. Beaumaris –0010.

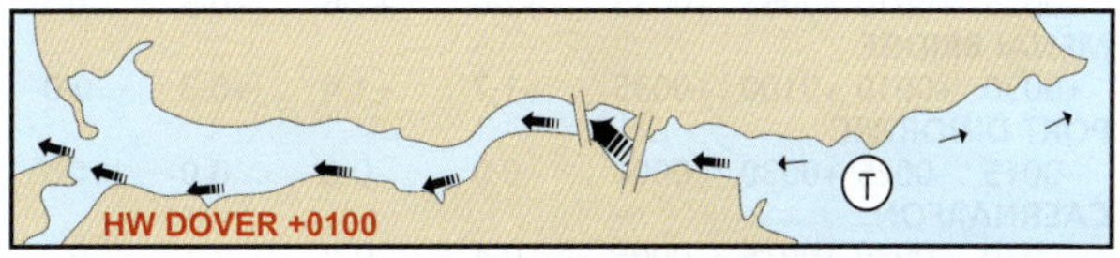

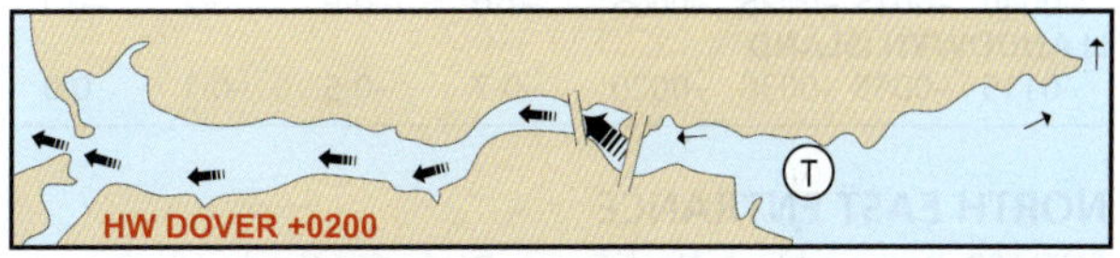

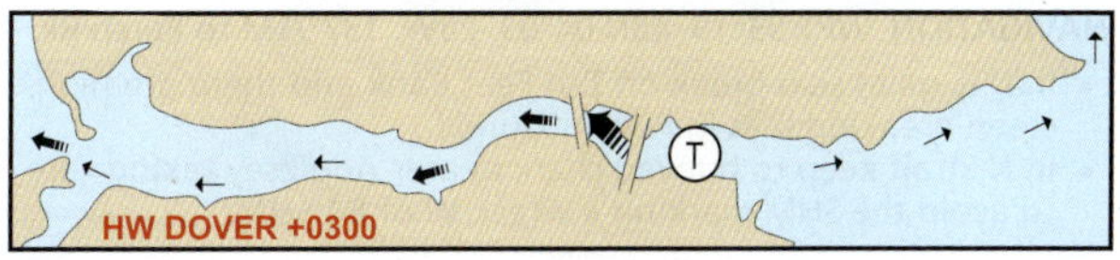

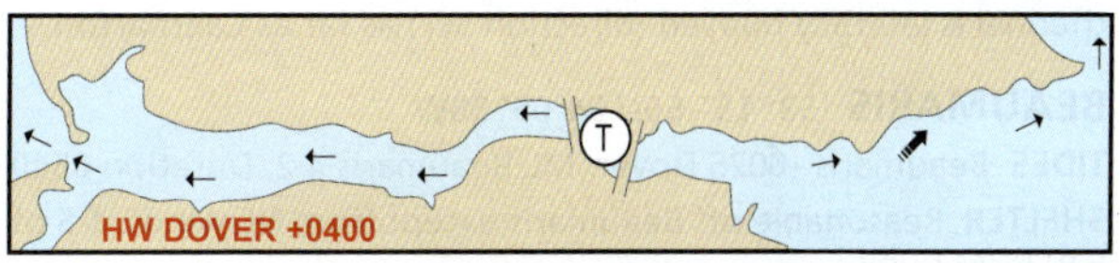

LOCAL LW: Belan: HW Dover +0520.

N Wales

3.19 MENAI STRAIT

Gwynedd/Isle of Anglesey

CHARTS AC 1464, 5609, Imray C52. NOTE: The definitive Pilot book is *Cruising Anglesey and Adjoining Waters* by Ralph Morris.

TIDES –0035 Dover (Sp), 0020 (Np)

Standard Port HOLYHEAD (⟶)

Times				Height (metres)			
High Water		Low Water		MHWS	MHWN	MLWN	MLWS
0000	0600	0500	1100	5·6	4·4	2·0	0·7
1200	1800	1700	2300				
Differences BEAUMARIS							
+0025	+0010	+0055	+0035	+2·0	+1·6	+0·5	+0·1
MENAI BRIDGE							
+0030	+0010	+0100	+0035	+1·7	+1·4	+0·3	0·0
PORT DINORWIC							
–0015	–0025	+0030	0000	0·0	0·0	0·0	+0·1
CAERNARFON							
–0030	–0030	+0015	–0005	–0·4	–0·4	–0·1	–0·1
FORT BELAN							
–0040	–0015	–0025	–0005	–1·0	–0·9	–0·2	–0·1
LLANDDWYN ISLAND							
–0115	–0055	–0030	–0020	–0·7	–0·5	–0·1	0·0

NORTH EAST ENTRANCE

SHELTER Reasonable ⚓ N of Trwyn Du in Southerly winds or in outer road in settled conditions to await a favourable tide.

NAVIGATION WPT 53°19′·48N 04°03′·28W, 137°/1M to Perch Rk.

- In N'ly gales seas break on Ten Feet Bank and there are high, steep breaking seas in Puffin Sound.
- In N Strait keep to buoyed chan, nearer Anglesey taking care to avoid the SHM marking a wreck W of B1 SHM.

LIGHTS AND MARKS See 3.3 and chartlet. At NE end of Strait, Trwyn-Du Lt ho, Conspic tr on Puffin Is and Perch Rk PHM bn. The channel is laterally buoyed (direction SW) as far as Caernarfon.

BEAUMARIS 53°15′·66N 04°05′·38W

TIDES Beaumaris –0025 Dover; ML Beaumaris 4·2; Duration 0540

SHELTER Reasonable off Beaumaris except from NE winds. ⚓ S of B10 PHM buoy.

LIGHTS AND MARKS Beaumaris pier has light 2Fl (3) G 10s 6M.

COMMUNICATIONS (Code 01248); Dr (emergency) 384001.

FACILITIES **Royal Anglesey YC** www.royalangleseyyc.org.uk ☎810295.

North West Venturers' YC, at Gallows Pt www.nwyc.org.uk.

Power Marine (20t) (2t).

Pier pontoon (access all tides) only with Piermasters permission.

Town Ⓑ (bus to Bangor), ✈ (Anglesey/Liverpool).

BANGOR 53°14′·46N 04°07′·58W

SHELTER Good, but open to winds from N to NE, at or Port Penrhyn dock. Dock and approaches dry approx 3m.

COMMUNICATIONS (Code 01248) Penrhyn HM ☎352525.

FACILITIES Port Penrhyn Dock, www.dickies.co.uk ☎363400, 5 £15/night, Ⓔ (30t).

Town (1M) Ⓑ ✈ (Anglesey/Liverpool).

MENAI BRIDGE 53°13′·20N 04°09′·79W

COMMUNICATIONS (Code 01248) Piermaster Menai Bridge 712312, mobile 07990 531595. At Menai Bridge, all moorings are private. Pier is owned and managed by Bangor University.

FACILITIES **St George's Pier** (Fl G 10s) at all tides (gated).

The Marine Club, Porth Daniel, ☎717484.

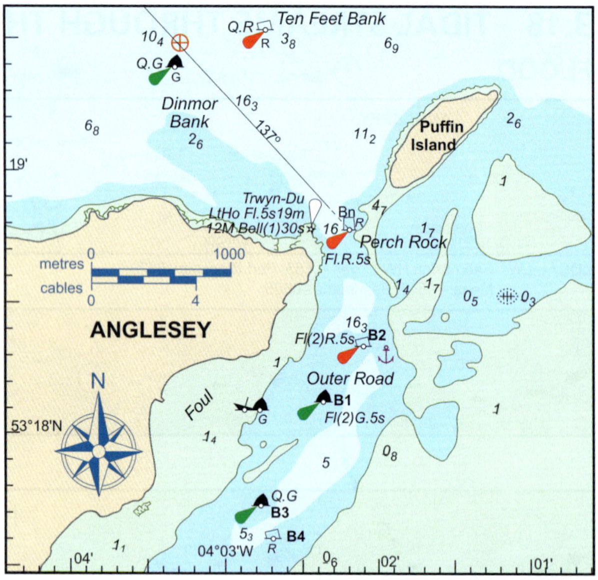

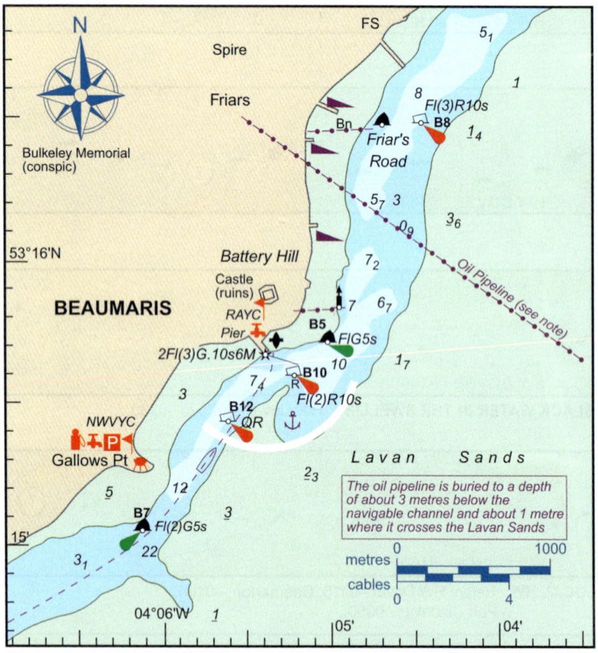

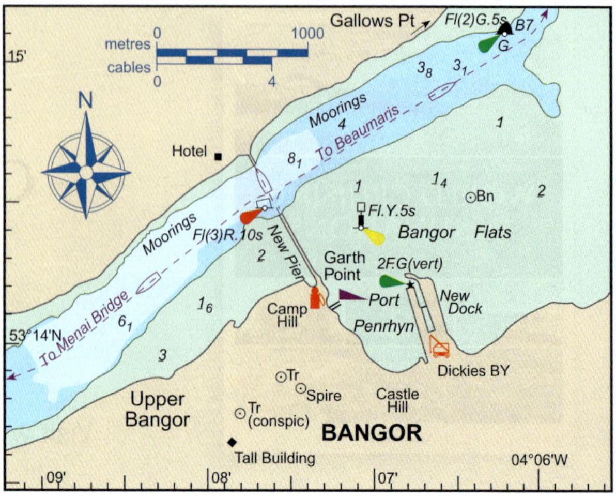

THE SWELLIES

NAVIGATION

- The passage should only be attempted at slack HW, which is –0145 HW Dover.
- The shallow rky narrows between the bridges may be dangerous for yachts at other times, when the stream can reach 8kn.
- At slack HW Sp there is 3m over The Platters and the outcrop off Price's Pt, which can be ignored.
- For shoal-draught boats passage is also possible at slack LW Nps, when there are depths of 0·5m close E of Britannia Bridge.
- Bridges and power cables have a least clearance of 21m at MHWS.
- Night passage is not recommended.

LIGHTS AND MARKS See 3.3. and chartlet. Britannia Bridge, E side ldg lts 231°, both FW. Br lts, both sides: Centre span Iso 5s 27m 3M; S end, FR 21m 3M; N end, FG 21m 3M.

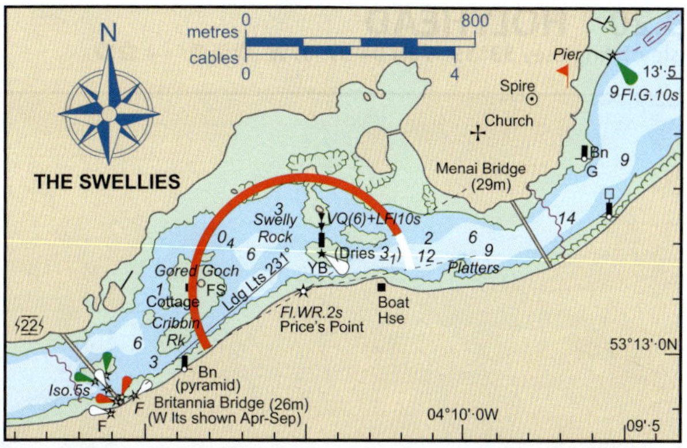

PORT DINORWIC/Y Felinheli 53°11'·20N 04°13'·70W

LIGHTS AND MARKS Pier Hd F WR 5m 2M, vis R225°- W357°-225°.

COMMUNICATIONS (Code 01248); Dr 670423. Marina 671500. *Dinorwic Marina* VHF Ch, Plas Menai Centre *Menai Base* Ch **80** M.

FACILITIES Port Dinorwic Marina www.themarinegroup.co.uk ☎671500; **Tidal basin** dries at Sp; lock (width 9·7m) opens HW±2. 180 £3·50 (15t).

Dinas Boatyard ☎671642, all facilities.

Town (Bangor or Caernarfon), (Bangor), ✈ (Liverpool).

Plas Menai (between Port Dinorwic and Caernarfon), Sailing and Sports Centre ☎670964, day moorings only. Shallow banks with **depths to 0·5m below CD** lie SW of Llanfair Belfry.

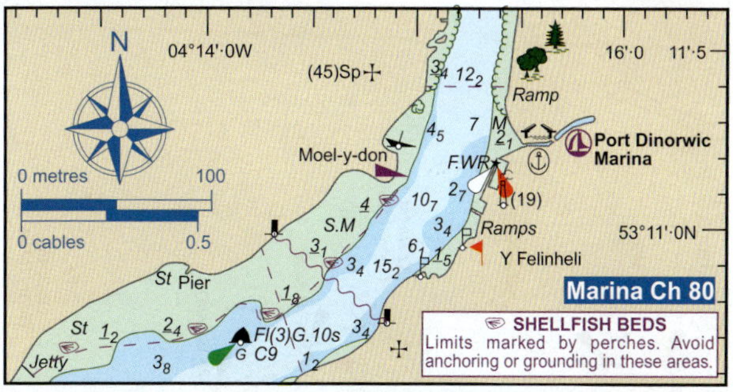

CAERNARFON 53°08'·51N 04°16'·83W

SHELTER Good in Victoria Dock Marina, access HW±2 via lifting sill, traffic lts (HO); pontoons at SW end in 2m, to starboard of ent. In river hbr (S of conspic castle) berth against wall, dries to mud/gravel, access HW±3 via swing bridge; for opening sound B (–···). ⚓ off Foel Ferry only with local knowledge; temp ⚓ off Abermenai Pt, sheltered from W, but strong streams. waiting 1½ca SW of C9.

COMMUNICATIONS (Code 01286) Ⓗ 01248 384384; Dr (emergency) 01248 384001. HM 672118, Mobile 07786 730865. *Victoria Dock Marina* Ch **80**. *Caernarfon Hbr* Ch **14** 16 (HJ).

FACILITIES River £9·60<20'<£13·20<30'<£18 /craft.
Victoria Dock ☎672346, 46 £2·95.
Caernarfon SC ☎(01248) 672861.
Royal Welsh YC ☎(01248) 672599.

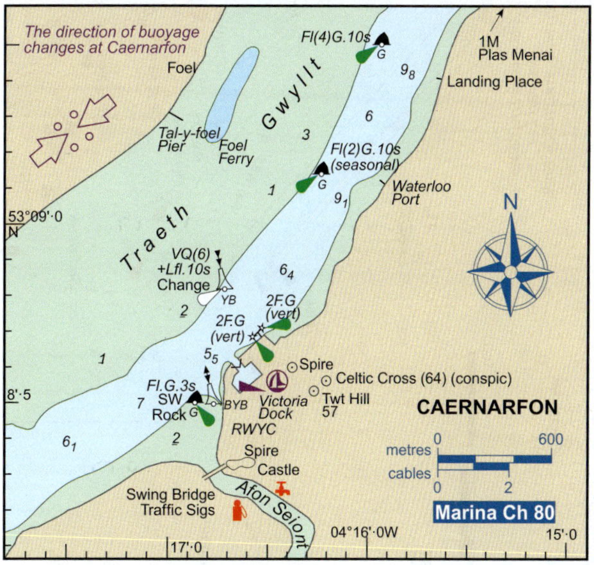

SOUTH WEST ENTRANCE – CAERNARFON BAR

NAVIGATION A dangerous sea can build in even a moderate breeze against tide, especially if a swell is running. Bar Chan should not be used at any time other than local HW-3 to HW+3. Caernarfon Bar shifts often and unpredictably see website at www.caernarfonharbour.org.uk.

Direction of buoyage changes to NE at Caernarfon.

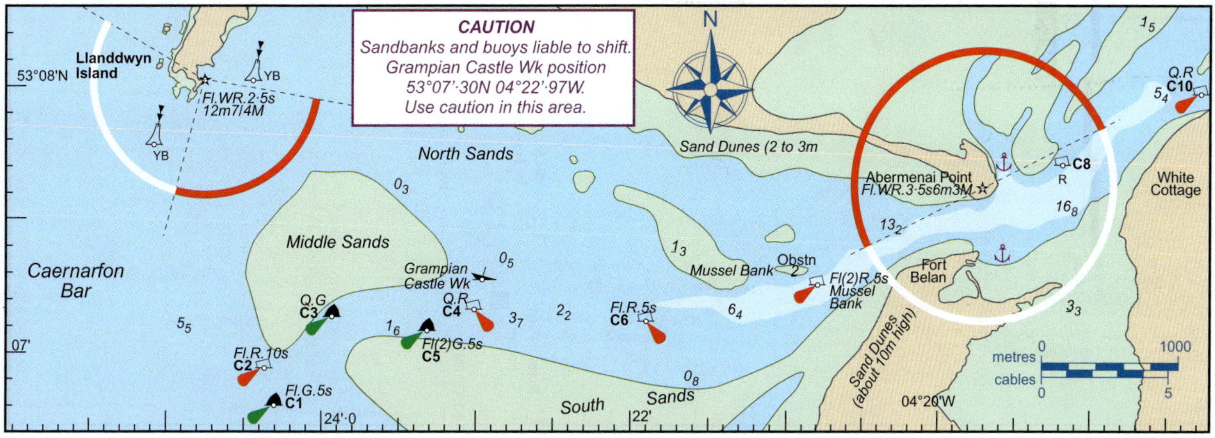

3.20 HOLYHEAD

Isle of Anglesey **53°19′·72N 04°37′·07W**

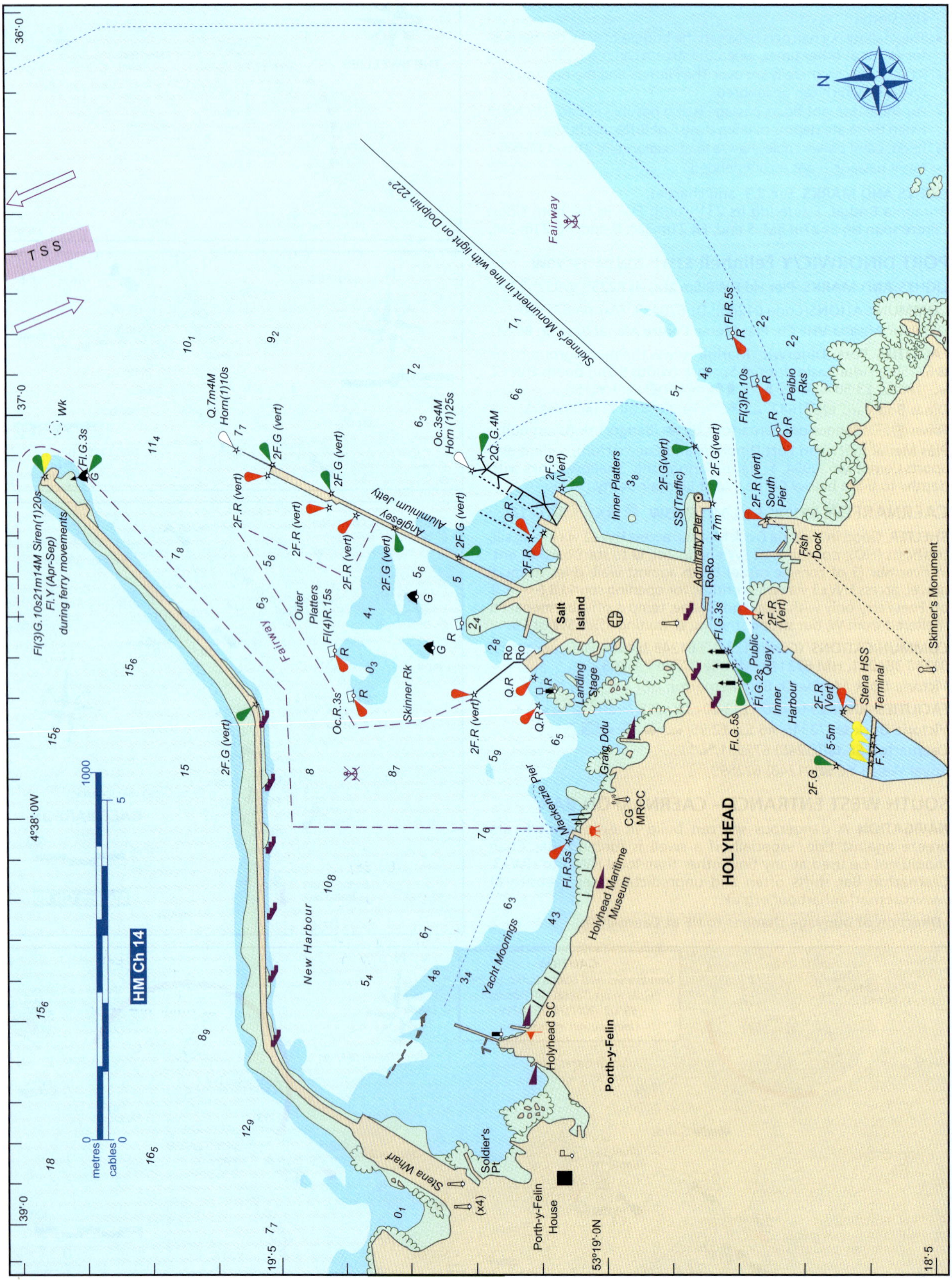

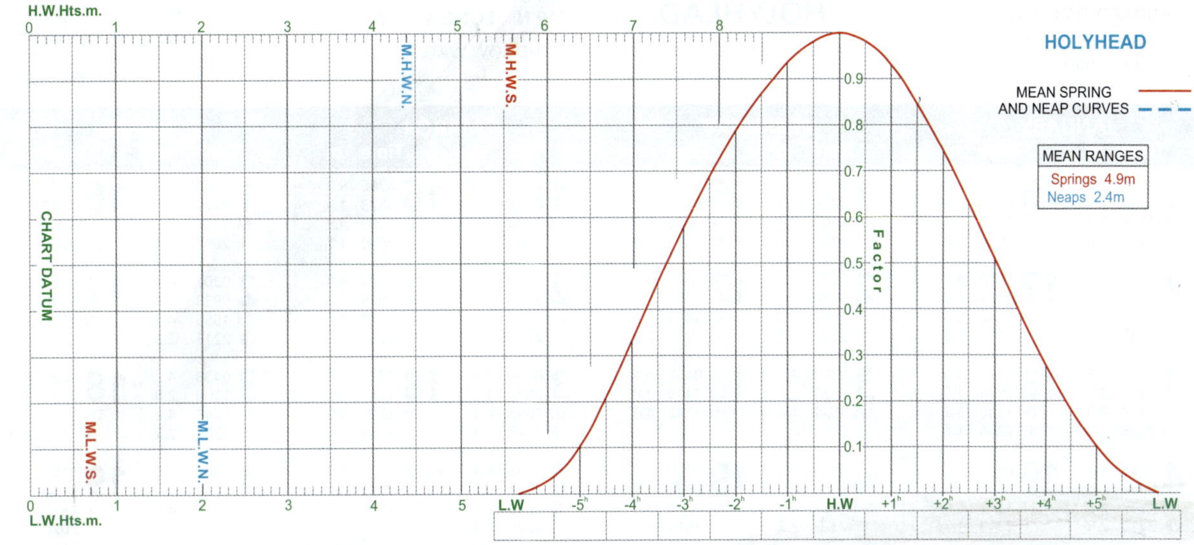

CHARTS AC 1826, 1970, 1977, 1413, 2011, 5609; Imray C61, C52

TIDES –0050 Dover; ML 3·2; Duration 0615

Standard Port HOLYHEAD (⟶)

Times				Height (metres)			
High Water		Low Water		MHWS	MHWN	MLWN	MLWS
0000	0600	0500	1100	5·6	4·4	2·0	0·7
1200	1800	1700	2300				
Differences TRWYN DINMOR (W of Puffin Is)							
+0025	+0015	+0050	+0035	+1·9	+1·5	+0·5	+0·2
MOELFRE (NE Anglesey)							
+0025	+0020	+0050	+0035	+1·9	+1·4	+0·5	+0·2
AMLWCH (N Anglesey)							
+0020	+0010	+0035	+0025	+1·6	+1·3	+0·5	+0·2
CEMAES BAY (N Anglesey)							
+0020	+0025	+0040	+0035	+1·0	+0·7	+0·3	+0·1
TREARDDUR BAY (W Anglesey)							
–0045	–0025	–0015	–0015	–0·4	–0·4	0·0	+0·1
PORTH TRECASTELL (SW Anglesey)							
–0045	–0025	–0005	–0015	–0·6	–0·6	0·0	0·0
TREFOR (Lleyn peninsula)							
–0115	–0100	–0030	–0020	–0·8	–0·9	–0·2	–0·1
PORTH DINLLAEN (Lleyn peninsula)							
–0120	–0105	–0035	–0025	–1·0	–1·0	–0·2	–0·2
PORTH YSGADEN (Lleyn peninsula)							
–0125	–0110	–0040	–0035	–1·1	–1·0	–0·1	–0·1
BARDSEY ISLAND							
–0220	–0240	–0145	–0140	–1·2	–1·2	–0·5	–0·1

SHELTER Accessible at all times. A single string pontoon landing is connected to shore, in the W corner of New Hbr least depth 2m. are available, ⚓ not recommended – foul ground. in fairways. Strong NW–NE winds raise an uncomfortable sea.

NAVIGATION WPT 53°20′·12N 04°37′·27W, 165°/0·28M to bkwtr lt. Small craft should leave Spit buoy to starboard and maintain a safe distance from breakwater to allow for obstns before heading for moorings. Yachts should keep clear of commercial shipping and the Outer Platters. Beware numerous fishing markers.

RoRo ferries to/from Ireland berth E of the 'Rio Tinto' aluminium jetty and in the Old Harbour complying with a mini-TSS off bkwtr.

LIGHTS AND MARKS Ldg marks 165°: bkwtr lt ho on with chy (127m, grey + B top; R lts); chy and Holyhead Mountain (218m) are conspic from afar. Cranes on aluminium jetty conspic closer to.

COMMUNICATIONS (Code 01407) Marina 764242; Port Control 606700.

Holyhead Marina and *Holyhead SC*: Ch **M**. Monitor *Holyhead* Ch **14** 16 (H24) for ferry traffic.

FACILITIES Marina www.holyheadmarina.co.uk, ☎764242. The plan to build a stone bkwtr to provide shelter to the marina location has been blocked and rival proposals submitted to redevelop the former marina site. The re-build of the marina has been set back indefinitely. Call ahead for availability.

Services (25t) wi-fi.

Inner Hbr used by HSS/Ferries; not advised for yachts.

Holyhead SC (HSC) ☎762526; £1·70/m, launch (call Ch M: 0900-2100, Fri/Sat to 2330).

Town ✈ (Anglesey/Liverpool). HSS/Ferry to Dublin (Irish Ferries/Stena Line).

MINOR HARBOURS (HW –0240 on Dover, see table (⟵)). May be useful, in settled conditions only, on passage N, see PI.

Trearddur Bay (3M south) **53°16′·66N 04°37′·50W.** AC 1970, 5609, Imray C52. (private, small craft only) or poss ⚓; open to prevailing SW'lies.

PORTH DINLLAEN, Gwynedd, **52°56′·68N 04°33′·66W**. AC 1971, 1512. Shelter good in S to W winds but strong NNW to NNE winds cause heavy seas in the bay. Beware Carreg-y-Chad (1·8m) 0·75M SW of the point, and Carreg-y-Chwislen (dries, with unlit IDM Bn) 2ca ENE of the point. From N, Garn Fadryn (369m) brg 182° leads into the bay. Best ⚓ 1ca S of LB ho in approx 2m.

HM ☎(01758) 720276. Facilities: by landing stage.

Morfa Nefyn (1M).

ABERDARON BAY, Gwynedd, **52°47′·75N 04°42′·82W**. AC 5609, 1410, 1411, 1971, 5609. In SE appr to bay are 2 islets Ynys Gwylan-fawr and Ynys Gwylan-bâch with a deep water passage between them, also passage between Ynys Gwylan-fawr and Trwyn Gwningaer (shore). ⚓ 4ca SSW of church in 5-10m, limited protection and subject to swell at times but sheltered in winds from W through N to NE. **Do not leave craft unattended due to poor holding ground.** Dinghy landing with care on shingle beach at Porth Simddy or Meudwy, W side of bay.

Village Limited facilities: (Pwllheli).

BARDSEY ISLAND – YNYS ENNLI, Gwynedd, **52°45′·00N 04°47′·40W.** AC 5609, 1410, 1411, 1971. Island of historical interest with ruined abbey and religious settlement since 6th century (now a managed farm and nature reserve, see 0.30). ⚓ W of Pen Cristin in appr to Henllwyn Cove in 4m is sheltered in winds from WSW through N to NE but is subject to swell at times. Small craft may ⚓ in the cove with caution, but beware isolated rocks and shoals. Landing at jetty in rocks marked by small boathouse at top of slip.

STANDARD TIME (UT)
For Summer Time add ONE hour in **non-shaded areas**

HOLYHEAD LAT 53°19'N LONG 4°37'W

TIMES AND HEIGHTS OF HIGH AND LOW WATERS

Dates in red are SPRINGS
Dates in blue are NEAPS

YEAR **2024**

JANUARY

Date	Day	Time	m	Time	m	Time	m	Time	m
1	M	0117	4.9	0713	1.7	1327	5.2	1952	1.6
2	TU	0157	4.7	0754	1.9	1408	5.0	2035	1.7
3	W	0241	4.6	0839	2.1	1453	4.8	2123	1.9
4	TH	0333	4.4	0931	2.3	1547	4.7	◑ 2219	2.0
5	F	0435	4.4	1033	2.4	1651	4.6	2321	2.1
6	SA	0543	4.4	1141	2.3	1800	4.6		
7	SU	0024	2.0	0648	4.5	1247	2.2	1906	4.7
8	M	0122	1.9	0744	4.8	1345	1.9	2004	4.8
9	TU	0214	1.7	0833	5.0	1437	1.6	2055	5.0
10	W	0301	1.4	0918	5.3	1525	1.3	2142	5.3
11	TH	0346	1.2	1001	5.5	1612	1.0	● 2228	5.4
12	F	0430	1.0	1044	5.8	1658	0.8	2313	5.5
13	SA	0515	0.9	1129	5.9	1744	0.6		
14	SU	0000	5.6	0600	0.9	1215	6.0	1831	0.6
15	M	0046	5.5	0647	0.9	1301	5.9	1920	0.7
16	TU	0135	5.3	0735	1.1	1350	5.8	2011	0.9
17	W	0225	5.1	0827	1.3	1442	5.5	2105	1.1
18	TH	0321	4.9	0924	1.6	1540	5.3	◐ 2206	1.4
19	F	0425	4.7	1031	1.8	1647	5.0	2314	1.7
20	SA	0539	4.6	1145	1.9	1803	4.8		
21	SU	0025	1.8	0654	4.6	1300	1.9	1921	4.8
22	M	0133	1.8	0800	4.8	1409	1.7	2026	4.9
23	TU	0232	1.7	0853	5.0	1505	1.5	2119	5.0
24	W	0320	1.6	0938	5.2	1551	1.3	2202	5.1
25	TH	0401	1.4	1016	5.4	1631	1.2	○ 2239	5.2
26	F	0436	1.3	1051	5.5	1706	1.1	2313	5.2
27	SA	0508	1.2	1123	5.5	1738	1.1	2345	5.2
28	SU	0540	1.2	1155	5.5	1810	1.1		
29	M	0015	5.2	0612	1.3	1226	5.4	1842	1.1
30	TU	0047	5.1	0644	1.3	1258	5.3	1915	1.3
31	W	0120	5.0	0718	1.5	1331	5.2	1950	1.4

FEBRUARY

Date	Day	Time	m	Time	m	Time	m	Time	m
1	TH	0155	4.8	0754	1.7	1407	5.0	2028	1.7
2	F	0235	4.6	0836	1.9	1448	4.8	◑ 2113	1.9
3	SA	0323	4.5	0929	2.1	1541	4.6	2211	2.1
4	SU	0429	4.3	1038	2.3	1657	4.4	2327	2.2
5	M	0553	4.3	1202	2.3	1827	4.4		
6	TU	0046	2.1	0711	4.5	1319	2.0	1945	4.6
7	W	0153	1.8	0813	4.8	1421	1.6	2044	4.9
8	TH	0247	1.5	0903	5.2	1514	1.2	2133	5.2
9	F	0334	1.1	0947	5.6	1600	0.7	● 2217	5.5
10	SA	0418	0.8	1030	5.9	1644	0.4	2300	5.7
11	SU	0500	0.6	1113	6.1	1728	0.2	2343	5.7
12	M	0542	0.5	1156	6.2	1811	0.2		
13	TU	0025	5.7	0626	0.5	1240	6.1	1856	0.4
14	W	0108	5.5	0710	0.7	1325	5.9	1941	0.7
15	TH	0153	5.3	0757	1.0	1412	5.6	2030	1.1
16	F	0241	4.9	0850	1.4	1506	5.2	◐ 2126	1.5
17	SA	0339	4.6	0955	1.8	1613	4.7	2236	2.0
18	SU	0457	4.4	1119	2.0	1742	4.4		
19	M	0000	2.2	0632	4.4	1248	2.0	1918	4.4
20	TU	0123	2.1	0751	4.6	1405	1.8	2028	4.6
21	W	0227	1.9	0847	4.9	1459	1.5	2116	4.8
22	TH	0312	1.7	0928	5.1	1540	1.3	2152	5.0
23	F	0348	1.4	1002	5.3	1614	1.1	2223	5.1
24	SA	0419	1.2	1032	5.4	1645	0.9	○ 2251	5.2
25	SU	0447	1.1	1101	5.5	1713	0.9	2319	5.3
26	M	0515	1.0	1129	5.5	1741	0.9	2347	5.3
27	TU	0544	1.0	1158	5.5	1809	0.9		
28	W	0015	5.2	0614	1.1	1228	5.4	1839	1.1
29	TH	0045	5.1	0645	1.2	1258	5.3	1910	1.3

MARCH

Date	Day	Time	m	Time	m	Time	m	Time	m
1	F	0117	5.0	0718	1.4	1330	5.1	1943	1.5
2	SA	0152	4.8	0756	1.6	1407	4.8	2023	1.8
3	SU	0234	4.6	0844	1.9	1455	4.5	◑ 2118	2.1
4	M	0333	4.4	0953	2.2	1610	4.3	2240	2.3
5	TU	0505	4.2	1128	2.2	1802	4.2		
6	W	0018	2.2	0642	4.4	1258	1.9	1932	4.5
7	TH	0134	1.9	0751	4.8	1404	1.4	2031	4.9
8	F	0230	1.4	0843	5.2	1456	0.9	2118	5.3
9	SA	0316	1.0	0927	5.6	1541	0.5	2159	5.6
10	SU	0358	0.6	1009	6.0	1623	0.2	● 2239	5.8
11	M	0438	0.3	1051	6.2	1704	0.0	2319	5.8
12	TU	0519	0.2	1133	6.3	1746	0.1	2359	5.8
13	W	0601	0.3	1216	6.1	1828	0.3		
14	TH	0040	5.6	0645	0.5	1300	5.8	1911	0.7
15	F	0122	5.3	0731	0.9	1346	5.4	1957	1.2
16	SA	0208	5.0	0823	1.3	1439	4.9	2050	1.7
17	SU	0303	4.6	0929	1.8	1547	4.5	◐ 2201	2.2
18	M	0420	4.3	1057	2.1	1727	4.2	2334	2.4
19	TU	0605	4.3	1233	2.0	1908	4.2		
20	W	0105	2.3	0731	4.5	1347	1.8	2014	4.5
21	TH	0208	2.0	0825	4.8	1438	1.5	2056	4.7
22	F	0251	1.7	0903	5.0	1515	1.2	2129	4.9
23	SA	0324	1.4	0935	5.2	1547	1.0	2157	5.1
24	SU	0353	1.2	1004	5.3	1615	0.9	2223	5.2
25	M	0420	1.0	1032	5.4	1642	0.8	○ 2249	5.3
26	TU	0447	0.9	1100	5.5	1709	0.8	2316	5.3
27	W	0516	0.9	1129	5.4	1737	0.9	2345	5.3
28	TH	0545	1.0	1159	5.4	1805	1.0		
29	F	0015	5.2	0617	1.1	1230	5.2	1836	1.2
30	SA	0047	5.1	0651	1.3	1303	5.0	1910	1.4
31	SU	0122	4.9	0731	1.5	1342	4.8	1953	1.7

APRIL

Date	Day	Time	m	Time	m	Time	m	Time	m
1	M	0206	4.7	0821	1.8	1434	4.5	2050	2.1
2	TU	0307	4.4	0933	2.0	1555	4.2	◑ 2216	2.3
3	W	0438	4.3	1109	2.0	1748	4.2	2356	2.2
4	TH	0614	4.5	1236	1.7	1912	4.6		
5	F	0110	1.8	0723	4.9	1340	1.2	2009	4.9
6	SA	0206	1.3	0816	5.3	1431	0.7	2054	5.3
7	SU	0251	0.9	0901	5.7	1515	0.4	2134	5.6
8	M	0333	0.5	0944	6.0	1557	0.2	● 2213	5.7
9	TU	0414	0.3	1026	6.1	1638	0.1	2253	5.8
10	W	0455	0.2	1110	6.1	1719	0.2	2334	5.8
11	TH	0538	0.3	1154	5.9	1801	0.5		
12	F	0015	5.6	0624	0.6	1239	5.6	1845	0.9
13	SA	0057	5.3	0711	0.9	1326	5.2	1931	1.4
14	SU	0143	5.0	0805	1.3	1420	4.7	2023	1.8
15	M	0237	4.7	0910	1.7	1528	4.3	◐ 2130	2.2
16	TU	0349	4.4	1032	2.0	1700	4.1	2259	2.4
17	W	0522	4.3	1158	2.0	1834	4.2		
18	TH	0025	2.4	0647	4.4	1308	1.8	1937	4.4
19	F	0129	2.1	0744	4.6	1359	1.5	2020	4.6
20	SA	0214	1.8	0825	4.9	1438	1.3	2053	4.8
21	SU	0249	1.5	0859	5.0	1511	1.1	2123	5.0
22	M	0320	1.3	0930	5.2	1540	1.0	2150	5.2
23	TU	0348	1.1	1000	5.3	1608	0.9	○ 2218	5.3
24	W	0418	1.0	1030	5.3	1637	0.9	2247	5.3
25	TH	0448	1.0	1102	5.3	1706	1.0	2318	5.3
26	F	0521	1.0	1134	5.2	1738	1.1	2351	5.3
27	SA	0555	1.1	1209	5.1	1812	1.2		
28	SU	0026	5.2	0635	1.2	1247	5.0	1852	1.5
29	M	0107	5.0	0720	1.4	1334	4.7	1940	1.7
30	TU	0156	4.8	0816	1.6	1433	4.5	2042	2.0

Chart Datum: 3·05 metres below Ordnance Datum (Newlyn). HAT is 6·3 metres above Chart Datum.

STANDARD TIME (UT)
For Summer Time add ONE hour in **non-shaded areas**

HOLYHEAD

LAT 53°19′N LONG 4°37′W

TIMES AND HEIGHTS OF HIGH AND LOW WATERS

Dates in red are SPRINGS
Dates in blue are NEAPS

YEAR **2024**

MAY

Date	Day	Time	m
1	W	0300 0928 1554 ◑ 2204	4.6 1.7 4.3 2.1
2	TH	0421 1052 1728 2329	4.6 1.7 4.4 2.0
3	F	0543 1209 1842	4.7 1.4 4.7
4	SA	0039 0650 1310 1939	1.7 5.0 1.1 5.0
5	SU	0134 0745 1402 2025	1.3 5.3 0.8 5.2
6	M	0223 0833 1448 2107	1.0 5.6 0.5 5.5
7	TU	0307 0919 1531 2149	0.7 5.8 0.4 5.6
8	W	0351 1005 1614 ● 2230	0.5 5.9 0.4 5.7
9	TH	0436 1051 1657 2312	0.5 5.8 0.6 5.6
10	F	0521 1137 1740 2356	0.5 5.6 0.8 5.5
11	SA	0608 1224 1824	0.7 5.3 1.1
12	SU	0039 0657 1311 1910	5.3 1.0 5.0 1.5
13	M	0125 0750 1403 2000	5.1 1.3 4.6 1.8
14	TU	0215 0848 1503 2058	4.8 1.6 4.4 2.1
15	W	0316 0956 1615 ◐ 2210	4.6 1.8 4.2 2.3
16	TH	0427 1107 1732 2326	4.4 1.9 4.2 2.3
17	F	0541 1213 1839	4.4 1.8 4.3
18	SA	0031 0644 1307 1929	2.2 4.5 1.7 4.5
19	SU	0123 0734 1351 2009	2.0 4.7 1.5 4.7
20	M	0205 0816 1429 2044	1.7 4.9 1.3 4.9
21	TU	0241 0853 1502 2116	1.5 5.0 1.2 5.0
22	W	0315 0928 1535 2148	1.3 5.1 1.2 5.2
23	TH	0350 1003 1608 ○ 2221	1.2 5.2 1.1 5.3
24	F	0425 1039 1642 2256	1.1 5.2 1.1 5.3
25	SA	0503 1117 1719 2334	1.1 5.2 1.2 5.3
26	SU	0543 1158 1800	1.1 5.1 1.2
27	M	0015 0628 1242 1845	5.3 1.1 5.0 1.4
28	TU	0101 0718 1333 1937	5.2 1.2 4.8 1.6
29	W	0153 0814 1433 2037	5.1 1.3 4.7 1.7
30	TH	0252 0919 1543 ◑ 2146	4.9 1.4 4.6 1.8
31	F	0400 1029 1657 2257	4.9 1.4 4.6 1.8

JUNE

Date	Day	Time	m
1	SA	0510 1137 1806	5.0 1.3 4.7
2	SU	0003 0616 1238 1905	1.6 5.1 1.1 4.9
3	M	0103 0715 1333 1957	1.4 5.2 1.0 5.1
4	TU	0157 0809 1424 2044	1.2 5.4 0.9 5.3
5	W	0247 0901 1511 2129	1.0 5.5 0.8 5.4
6	TH	0336 0950 1557 ● 2214	0.8 5.5 0.9 5.5
7	F	0424 1038 1641 2258	0.8 5.4 1.0 5.5
8	SA	0512 1126 1725 2341	0.8 5.3 1.1 5.4
9	SU	0558 1211 1807	0.9 5.1 1.3
10	M	0024 0644 1256 1850	5.3 1.1 4.9 1.5
11	TU	0106 0730 1341 1934	5.2 1.3 4.7 1.7
12	W	0150 0818 1428 2022	5.0 1.5 4.5 1.9
13	TH	0237 0909 1520 2114	4.8 1.7 4.4 2.1
14	F	0330 1005 1619 ◐ 2214	4.6 1.8 4.3 2.2
15	SA	0430 1105 1722 2319	4.5 1.9 4.3 2.2
16	SU	0533 1203 1822	4.5 1.8 4.4
17	M	0020 0634 1256 1916	2.2 4.5 1.8 4.5
18	TU	0114 0728 1343 2002	2.0 4.6 1.7 4.7
19	W	0202 0817 1426 2043	1.8 4.8 1.5 4.9
20	TH	0246 0900 1506 2122	1.6 4.9 1.4 5.1
21	F	0327 0942 1546 2200	1.4 5.0 1.3 5.2
22	SA	0409 1023 1626 ○ 2240	1.2 5.1 1.2 5.4
23	SU	0451 1106 1708 2322	1.0 5.2 1.1 5.5
24	M	0536 1151 1752	0.9 5.2 1.1
25	TU	0006 0622 1237 1838	5.5 0.9 5.1 1.2
26	W	0053 0711 1326 1928	5.5 0.9 5.1 1.3
27	TH	0142 0803 1419 2021	5.4 1.0 4.9 1.4
28	F	0235 0858 1517 ◑ 2119	5.3 1.1 4.8 1.5
29	SA	0333 0959 1620 2223	5.2 1.2 4.7 1.6
30	SU	0436 1103 1727 2330	5.1 1.3 4.7 1.6

JULY

Date	Day	Time	m
1	M	0543 1208 1833	5.0 1.4 4.7
2	TU	0036 0652 1310 1935	1.6 5.0 1.4 4.9
3	W	0140 0756 1408 2030	1.4 5.0 1.3 5.0
4	TH	0239 0854 1501 2119	1.3 5.1 1.3 5.2
5	F	0332 0946 1548 ● 2205	1.1 5.1 1.2 5.3
6	SA	0420 1033 1631 2248	1.0 5.2 1.2 5.4
7	SU	0504 1116 1712 2328	0.9 5.1 1.2 5.4
8	M	0545 1156 1750	1.0 5.1 1.3
9	TU	0006 0625 1233 1827	5.4 1.0 5.0 1.3
10	W	0042 0702 1310 1904	5.3 1.1 4.9 1.5
11	TH	0119 0741 1347 1943	5.2 1.3 4.7 1.6
12	F	0157 0820 1427 2024	5.0 1.5 4.6 1.8
13	SA	0238 0904 1512 ◐ 2111	4.8 1.7 4.5 2.0
14	SU	0325 0954 1607 2207	4.6 1.8 4.3 2.2
15	M	0423 1052 1711 2313	4.5 2.0 4.3 2.3
16	TU	0531 1157 1819	4.4 2.0 4.4
17	W	0023 0643 1259 1922	2.2 4.4 2.0 4.5
18	TH	0127 0747 1355 2015	2.0 4.5 1.8 4.8
19	F	0222 0841 1445 2102	1.7 4.7 1.6 5.0
20	SA	0311 0928 1530 2144	1.4 4.9 1.3 5.3
21	SU	0356 1012 1613 ○ 2226	1.1 5.2 1.1 5.5
22	M	0440 1055 1655 2309	0.8 5.3 0.9 5.7
23	TU	0523 1139 1738 2352	0.6 5.4 0.8 5.8
24	W	0608 1223 1822	0.5 5.4 0.8
25	TH	0036 0653 1307 1908	5.8 0.5 5.3 0.9
26	F	0122 0740 1354 1956	5.8 0.7 5.2 1.1
27	SA	0210 0830 1444 2048	5.6 0.9 5.0 1.3
28	SU	0303 0925 1542 ◑ 2149	5.3 1.2 4.8 1.6
29	M	0404 1029 1651 2302	5.0 1.5 4.6 1.8
30	TU	0519 1142 1809	4.8 1.7 4.6
31	W	0020 0642 1256 1925	1.8 4.7 1.8 4.7

AUGUST

Date	Day	Time	m
1	TH	0136 0758 1403 2027	1.7 4.7 1.7 4.9
2	F	0241 0858 1458 2116	1.5 4.9 1.6 5.1
3	SA	0332 0945 1543 2158	1.2 5.0 1.4 5.3
4	SU	0414 1025 1621 ● 2235	1.1 5.1 1.3 5.4
5	M	0451 1100 1655 2309	1.0 5.1 1.2 5.5
6	TU	0525 1133 1727 2342	0.9 5.2 1.1 5.5
7	W	0557 1204 1758	0.9 5.1 1.2
8	TH	0013 0629 1234 1831	5.4 1.0 5.1 1.3
9	F	0044 0701 1307 1904	5.3 1.2 5.0 1.4
10	SA	0117 0735 1341 1940	5.2 1.4 4.8 1.6
11	SU	0152 0811 1419 2020	5.0 1.6 4.7 1.9
12	M	0231 0853 1504 ◐ 2110	4.7 1.8 4.5 2.1
13	TU	0321 0947 1604 2215	4.5 2.1 4.3 2.3
14	W	0431 1059 1726 2339	4.3 2.3 4.3 2.3
15	TH	0605 1222 1847	4.2 2.2 4.4
16	F	0100 0727 1332 1952	2.1 4.4 2.0 4.7
17	SA	0204 0827 1427 2043	1.7 4.7 1.7 5.1
18	SU	0255 0915 1514 2126	1.3 5.0 1.3 5.4
19	M	0340 0957 1555 ○ 2207	0.9 5.3 1.0 5.8
20	TU	0421 1037 1636 2248	0.5 5.5 0.7 6.0
21	W	0503 1118 1717 2330	0.3 5.7 0.5 6.1
22	TH	0544 1159 1758	0.2 5.7 0.5
23	F	0012 0627 1241 1842	6.1 0.3 5.6 0.6
24	SA	0056 0712 1324 1928	6.0 0.6 5.4 0.9
25	SU	0143 0759 1411 2019	5.7 0.9 5.1 1.2
26	M	0235 0852 1507 ◑ 2122	5.3 1.4 4.8 1.6
27	TU	0339 0959 1620 2244	4.8 1.9 4.5 1.9
28	W	0506 1123 1754	4.5 2.1 4.5
29	TH	0015 0646 1250 1920	2.0 4.4 2.2 4.7
30	F	0137 0803 1400 2022	1.8 4.6 2.0 4.9
31	SA	0237 0856 1451 2107	1.5 4.8 1.7 5.2

Chart Datum: 3·05 metres below Ordnance Datum (Newlyn). HAT is 6·3 metres above Chart Datum.

N Wales

STANDARD TIME (UT)
For Summer Time add ONE hour in **non-shaded areas**

HOLYHEAD LAT 53°19′N LONG 4°37′W

TIMES AND HEIGHTS OF HIGH AND LOW WATERS

Dates in red are SPRINGS
Dates in blue are NEAPS

YEAR **2024**

SEPTEMBER

Date	Day	Time	m
1	SU	0321 0935 1529 2142	1.2 5.0 1.5 5.4
2	M	0357 1007 1602 2214	1.1 5.1 1.3 5.5
3	TU	0428 1036 1631 ● 2243	0.9 5.2 1.1 5.5
4	W	0457 1103 1659 2312	0.9 5.3 1.1 5.6
5	TH	0525 1131 1728 2341	0.9 5.3 1.1 5.5
6	F	0553 1200 1757	1.0 5.2 1.2
7	SA	0011 0622 1229 1829	5.4 1.1 5.2 1.3
8	SU	0041 0653 1301 1902	5.3 1.3 5.0 1.5
9	M	0113 0726 1336 1940	5.0 1.6 4.9 1.8
10	TU	0149 0804 1417 2027	4.8 1.9 4.6 2.1
11	W	0236 0856 1514 ◐ 2133	4.5 2.2 4.4 2.3
12	TH	0347 1013 1641 2306	4.2 2.4 4.3 2.4
13	F	0539 1152 1817	4.2 2.4 4.4
14	SA	0037 0711 1310 1928	2.1 4.4 2.1 4.8
15	SU	0143 0810 1406 2019	1.6 4.8 1.7 5.2
16	M	0233 0854 1451 2101	1.1 5.2 1.2 5.6
17	TU	0316 0934 1531 2142	0.7 5.5 0.8 6.0
18	W	0356 1012 1611 ○ 2222	0.3 5.7 0.5 6.2
19	TH	0436 1051 1651 2304	0.2 5.9 0.4 6.3
20	F	0517 1132 1732 2348	0.2 5.9 0.4 6.2
21	SA	0559 1213 1816	0.3 5.7 0.6
22	SU	0032 0643 1256 1904	6.0 0.7 5.5 0.9
23	M	0120 0730 1343 1957	5.6 1.2 5.2 1.3
24	TU	0213 0824 1439 ◑ 2104	5.1 1.7 4.8 1.8
25	W	0322 0933 1556 2232	4.6 2.2 4.6 2.0
26	TH	0501 1106 1737	4.3 2.4 4.5
27	F	0006 0643 1236 1904	2.0 4.4 2.3 4.7
28	SA	0123 0751 1343 2002	1.8 4.6 2.1 4.9
29	SU	0217 0837 1429 2043	1.5 4.8 1.8 5.2
30	M	0257 0911 1505 2116	1.3 5.0 1.5 5.3

OCTOBER

Date	Day	Time	m
1	TU	0329 0939 1535 2145	1.1 5.2 1.3 5.5
2	W	0358 1006 1602 ● 2213	1.0 5.3 1.2 5.5
3	TH	0425 1032 1630 2242	1.0 5.4 1.1 5.6
4	F	0451 1059 1658 2311	1.0 5.4 1.1 5.5
5	SA	0519 1128 1727 2341	1.1 5.4 1.2 5.4
6	SU	0547 1158 1759	1.2 5.3 1.3
7	M	0011 0618 1229 1833	5.3 1.4 5.2 1.5
8	TU	0044 0652 1304 1912	5.0 1.6 5.0 1.8
9	W	0122 0732 1347 2002	4.8 1.9 4.8 2.0
10	TH	0213 0826 1446 ◐ 2110	4.5 2.2 4.6 2.2
11	F	0328 0946 1611 2242	4.3 2.5 4.4 2.2
12	SA	0519 1124 1745	4.3 2.4 4.6
13	SU	0009 0645 1241 1855	1.9 4.6 2.1 4.9
14	M	0113 0742 1337 1948	1.5 5.0 1.6 5.4
15	TU	0204 0827 1423 2032	1.0 5.3 1.2 5.7
16	W	0247 0907 1504 2115	0.6 5.6 0.8 6.1
17	TH	0328 0946 1545 ○ 2157	0.4 5.8 0.5 6.2
18	F	0409 1025 1627 2241	0.3 5.9 0.4 6.3
19	SA	0451 1106 1711 2326	0.3 5.9 0.5 6.1
20	SU	0534 1149 1757	0.6 5.8 0.7
21	M	0013 0619 1234 1847	5.8 1.0 5.6 1.0
22	TU	0103 0707 1322 1943	5.4 1.4 5.3 1.4
23	W	0159 0801 1419 2050	4.9 1.9 4.9 1.8
24	TH	0309 0909 1532 ◑ 2212	4.5 2.3 4.7 2.0
25	F	0440 1036 1702 2336	4.3 2.5 4.6 2.0
26	SA	0611 1200 1824	4.4 2.5 4.7
27	SU	0047 0717 1306 1923	1.9 4.6 2.2 4.9
28	M	0140 0802 1354 2007	1.7 4.8 2.0 5.1
29	TU	0221 0837 1431 2042	1.5 5.0 1.7 5.2
30	W	0254 0907 1503 2113	1.3 5.2 1.5 5.4
31	TH	0324 0934 1532 2143	1.2 5.3 1.4 5.4

NOVEMBER

Date	Day	Time	m
1	F	0352 1002 1602 ● 2213	1.1 5.4 1.3 5.5
2	SA	0420 1031 1632 2244	1.2 5.5 1.2 5.4
3	SU	0450 1101 1704 2316	1.2 5.5 1.3 5.3
4	M	0521 1133 1738 2351	1.3 5.4 1.4 5.2
5	TU	0554 1208 1816	1.5 5.3 1.5
6	W	0028 0632 1247 1900	5.0 1.7 5.2 1.7
7	TH	0111 0716 1334 1952	4.8 1.9 5.0 1.9
8	F	0206 0813 1432 2059	4.6 2.2 4.8 2.0
9	SA	0319 0927 1547 ◐ 2218	4.4 2.3 4.7 1.9
10	SU	0450 1051 1708 2335	4.5 2.3 4.8 1.7
11	M	0608 1204 1816	4.7 2.0 5.1
12	TU	0038 0707 1302 1913	1.4 5.0 1.6 5.4
13	W	0131 0756 1352 2003	1.0 5.3 1.3 5.7
14	TH	0218 0839 1438 2050	0.8 5.6 1.0 5.9
15	F	0303 0921 1523 ○ 2137	0.6 5.7 0.7 6.0
16	SA	0347 1004 1609 2224	0.6 5.8 0.7 6.0
17	SU	0431 1048 1656 2312	0.7 5.9 0.7 5.8
18	M	0516 1133 1745	0.9 5.8 0.8
19	TU	0000 0602 1218 1837	5.6 1.2 5.6 1.1
20	W	0051 0650 1307 1931	5.3 1.5 5.4 1.4
21	TH	0145 0741 1359 2030	4.9 1.9 5.1 1.7
22	F	0245 0839 1459 2136	4.6 2.2 4.9 1.9
23	SA	0355 0947 1609 ◑ 2246	4.4 2.4 4.7 2.0
24	SU	0510 1102 1720 2352	4.3 2.5 4.6 2.0
25	M	0618 1210 1825	4.4 2.4 4.7
26	TU	0048 0712 1305 1918	1.9 4.6 2.2 4.8
27	W	0135 0754 1350 2002	1.7 4.8 2.0 5.0
28	TH	0215 0831 1428 2040	1.6 5.0 1.8 5.1
29	F	0250 0904 1504 2116	1.5 5.2 1.6 5.2
30	SA	0323 0935 1538 2150	1.4 5.3 1.5 5.3

DECEMBER

Date	Day	Time	m
1	SU	0355 1008 1613 ● 2225	1.4 5.4 1.4 5.3
2	M	0428 1041 1649 2301	1.4 5.5 1.3 5.3
3	TU	0503 1118 1727 2340	1.4 5.5 1.3 5.2
4	W	0541 1156 1808	1.4 5.5 1.4
5	TH	0021 0623 1238 1854	5.1 1.6 5.4 1.4
6	F	0107 0709 1326 1945	5.0 1.7 5.3 1.5
7	SA	0200 0803 1419 2043	4.8 1.9 5.1 1.6
8	SU	0301 0904 1520 ◐ 2148	4.7 2.0 5.1 1.6
9	M	0412 1013 1628 2256	4.7 2.0 5.1 1.5
10	TU	0523 1123 1736	4.7 1.9 5.2
11	W	0000 0629 1226 1840	1.4 4.9 1.7 5.3
12	TH	0100 0726 1325 1938	1.3 5.1 1.5 5.4
13	F	0154 0817 1419 2033	1.1 5.3 1.2 5.6
14	SA	0245 0905 1511 2126	1.0 5.5 1.0 5.6
15	SU	0333 0951 1602 ○ 2216	1.0 5.7 0.9 5.6
16	M	0420 1037 1651 2305	1.0 5.7 0.9 5.6
17	TU	0505 1122 1739 2352	1.1 5.7 0.9 5.4
18	W	0549 1207 1826	1.3 5.6 1.1
19	TH	0038 0633 1250 1912	5.2 1.4 5.5 1.2
20	F	0123 0717 1334 1959	5.0 1.7 5.3 1.5
21	SA	0209 0802 1419 2049	4.8 1.9 5.1 1.7
22	SU	0258 0852 1509 ◑ 2142	4.6 2.1 4.9 1.9
23	M	0353 0948 1605 2241	4.4 2.3 4.7 2.0
24	TU	0456 1053 1709 2342	4.3 2.4 4.6 2.1
25	W	0601 1200 1814	4.4 2.4 4.6
26	TH	0040 0701 1300 1916	2.0 4.5 2.3 4.7
27	F	0132 0752 1353 2008	1.9 4.7 2.1 4.8
28	SA	0218 0835 1438 2053	1.8 4.9 1.8 4.9
29	SU	0258 0914 1520 2134	1.7 5.1 1.6 5.0
30	M	0337 0951 1559 ● 2213	1.5 5.3 1.4 5.2
31	TU	0414 1028 1639 2252	1.4 5.5 1.2 5.2

Chart Datum: 3·05 metres below Ordnance Datum (Newlyn). HAT is 6·3 metres above Chart Datum.

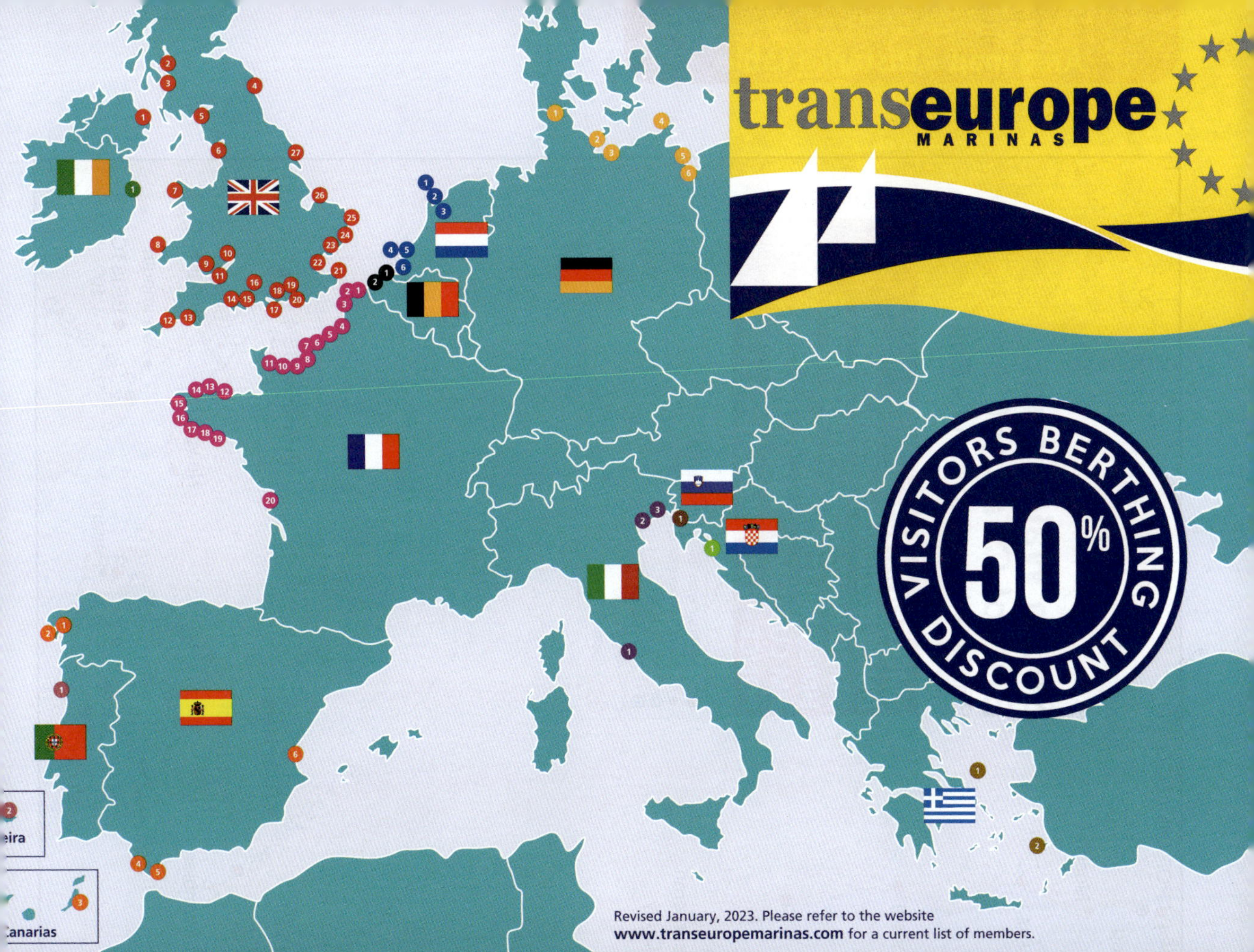
transeurope
MARINAS
VISITORS BERTHING 50% DISCOUNT
Revised January, 2023. Please refer to the website
www.transeuropemarinas.com for a current list of members.

4.1 South Wales and Bristol Channel

Bardsey Island to Land's End

EMERGENCY 999
HMCG NATIONAL – 02392 552100
HMCG HOLYHEAD – 01407 762051
HMCG MILFORD HAVEN – 01646 690909
HM CUSTOMS – 0845 010 9000
POLICE – 101 MEDICAL – 111

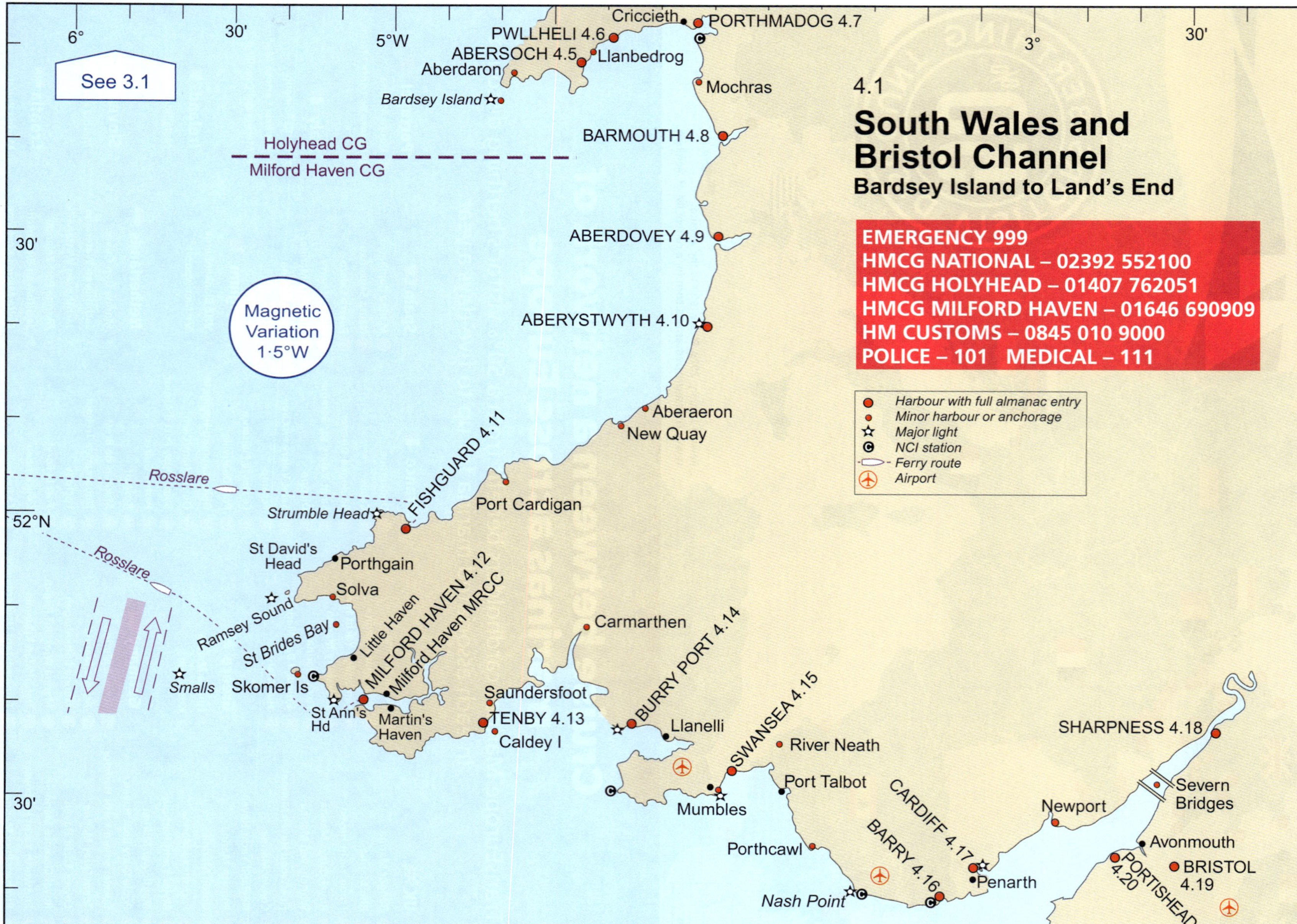

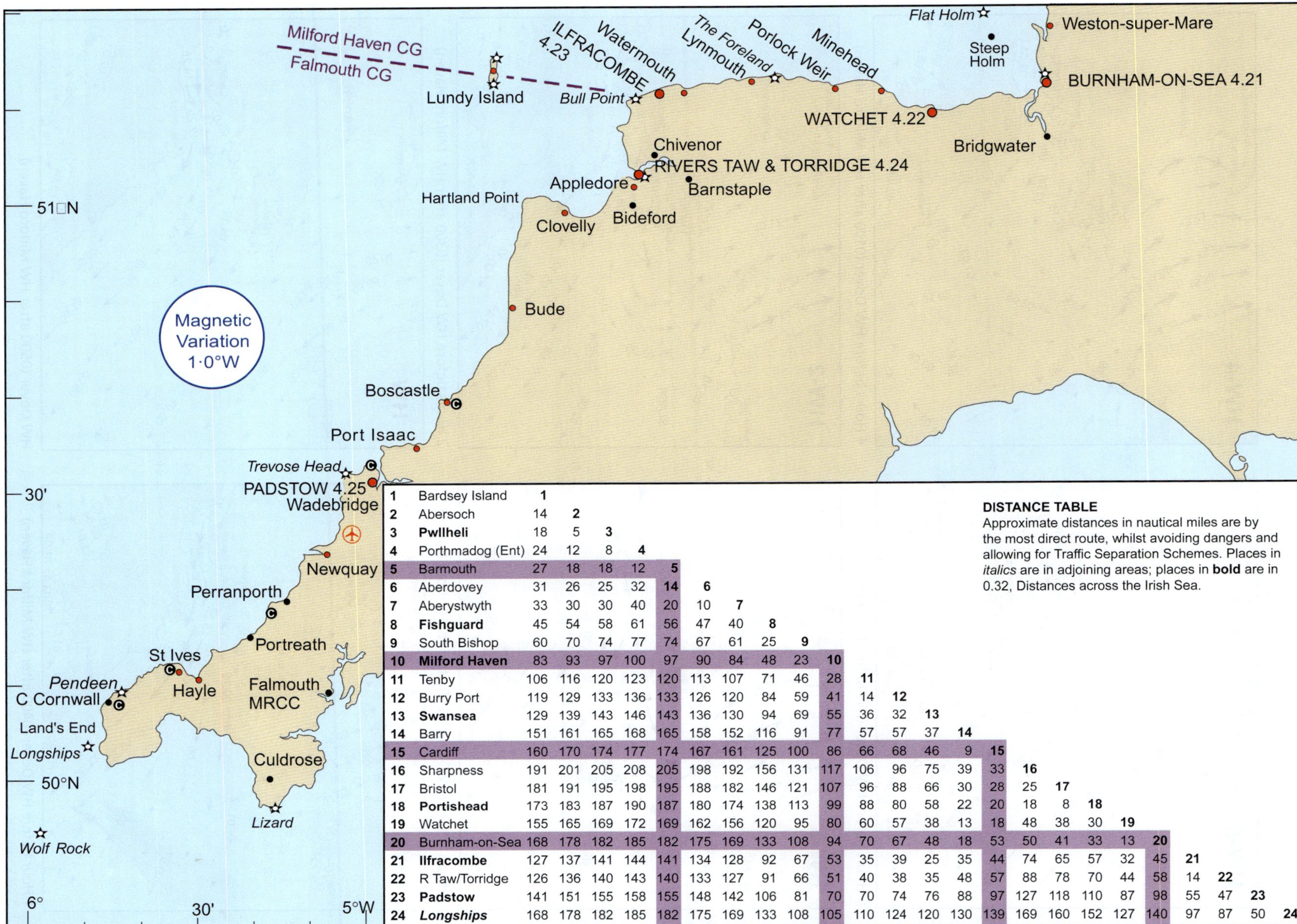

DISTANCE TABLE

Approximate distances in nautical miles are by the most direct route, whilst avoiding dangers and allowing for Traffic Separation Schemes. Places in *italics* are in adjoining areas; places in **bold** are in 0.32, Distances across the Irish Sea.

No	Place	1	2	3	4	5	6	7	8	9	10	11	12	13	14	15	16	17	18	19	20	21	22	23	24
1	Bardsey Island	**1**																							
2	Abersoch	14	**2**																						
3	**Pwllheli**	18	5	**3**																					
4	Porthmadog (Ent)	24	12	8	**4**																				
5	Barmouth	27	18	18	12	**5**																			
6	Aberdovey	31	26	25	32	14	**6**																		
7	Aberystwyth	33	30	30	40	20	10	**7**																	
8	**Fishguard**	45	54	58	61	56	47	40	**8**																
9	South Bishop	60	70	74	77	74	67	61	25	**9**															
10	**Milford Haven**	83	93	97	100	97	90	84	48	23	**10**														
11	Tenby	106	116	120	123	120	113	107	71	46	28	**11**													
12	Burry Port	119	129	133	136	133	126	120	84	59	41	14	**12**												
13	**Swansea**	129	139	143	146	143	136	130	94	69	55	36	32	**13**											
14	Barry	151	161	165	168	165	158	152	116	91	77	57	57	37	**14**										
15	Cardiff	160	170	174	177	174	167	161	125	100	86	66	68	46	9	**15**									
16	Sharpness	191	201	205	208	205	198	192	156	131	117	106	96	75	39	33	**16**								
17	Bristol	181	191	195	198	195	188	182	146	121	107	96	88	66	30	28	25	**17**							
18	**Portishead**	173	183	187	190	187	180	174	138	113	99	88	80	58	22	20	18	8	**18**						
19	Watchet	155	165	169	172	169	162	156	120	95	80	60	57	38	13	18	48	38	30	**19**					
20	Burnham-on-Sea	168	178	182	185	182	175	169	133	108	94	70	67	48	18	53	50	41	33	13	**20**				
21	**Ilfracombe**	127	137	141	144	141	134	128	92	67	53	35	39	25	35	44	74	65	57	32	45	**21**			
22	R Taw/Torridge	126	136	140	143	140	133	127	91	66	51	40	38	35	48	57	88	78	70	44	58	14	**22**		
23	**Padstow**	141	151	155	158	155	148	142	106	81	70	70	74	76	88	97	127	118	110	87	98	55	47	**23**	
24	***Longships***	168	178	182	185	182	175	169	133	108	105	110	124	120	130	139	169	160	152	127	140	97	87	50	**24**

4.2 AREA 4 TIDAL STREAMS

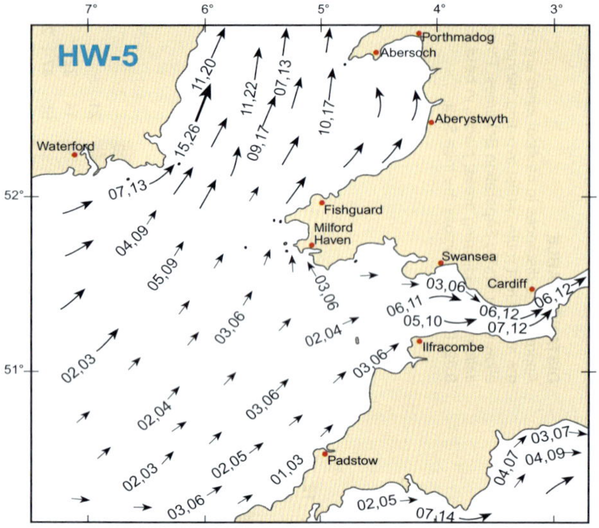

5 Hours before HW Dover (HW Milford Haven)

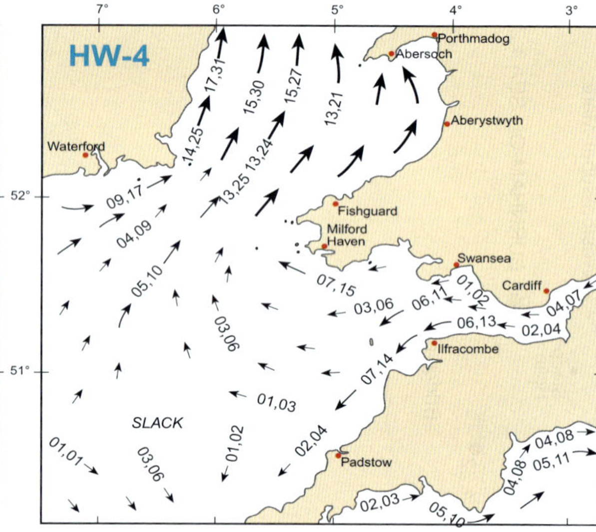

4 Hours before HW Dover (0100 after HW Milford Haven)

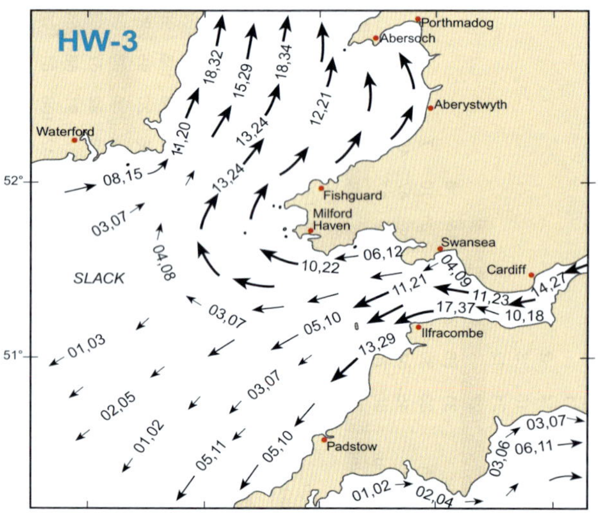

3 Hours before HW Dover (0200 after HW Milford Haven)

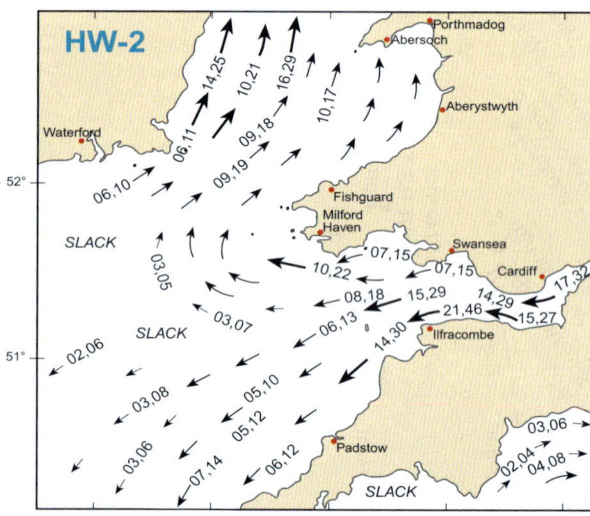

2 Hours before HW Dover (0300 after HW Milford Haven)

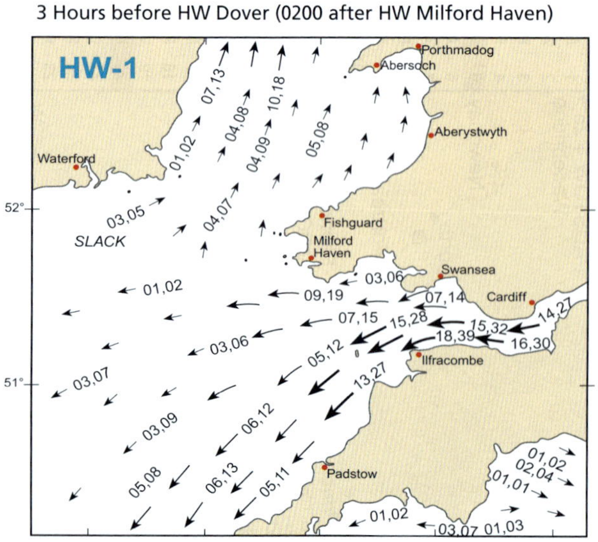

1 Hour before HW Dover (0400 after HW Milford Haven)

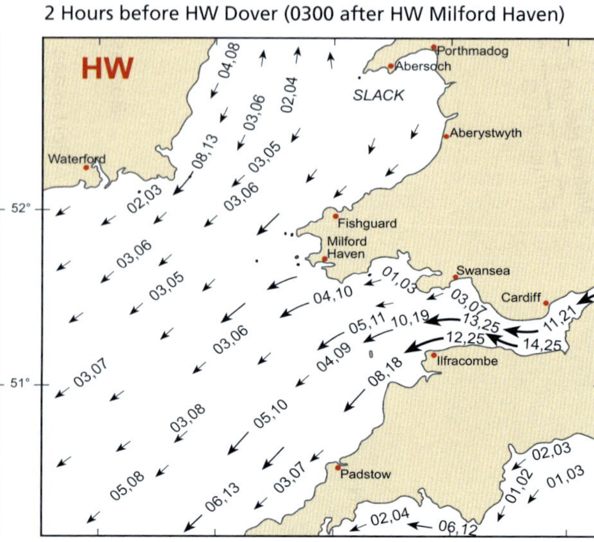

HW Dover (0500 after HW Milford Haven)

Northward 3.2 South Ireland 5.2

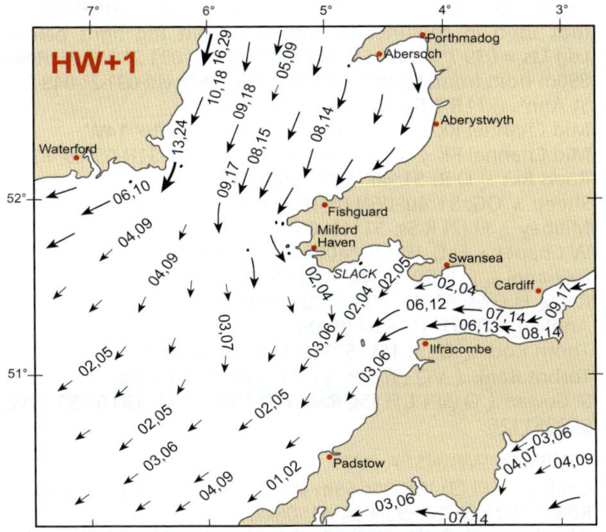

1 Hour after HW Dover (0600 after HW Milford Haven)

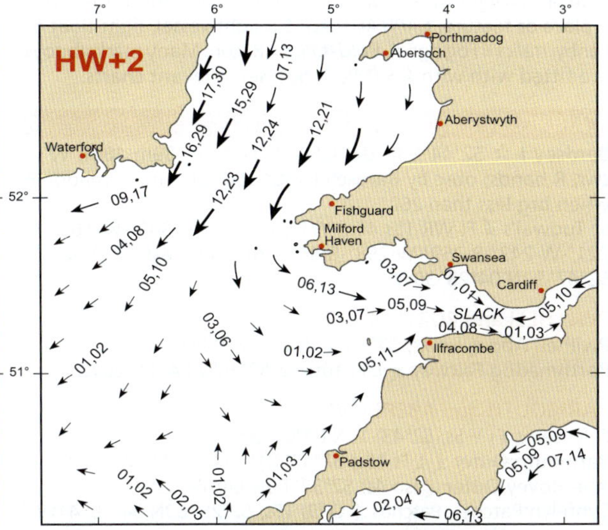

2 Hours after HW Dover (0525 before HW Milford Haven)

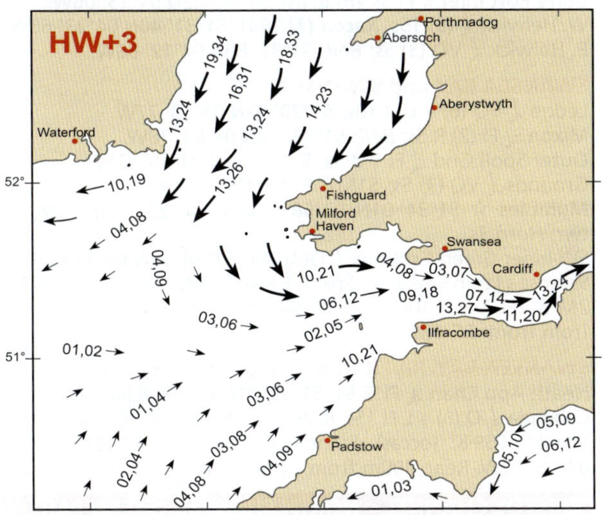

3 Hours after HW Dover (0425 before HW Milford Haven)

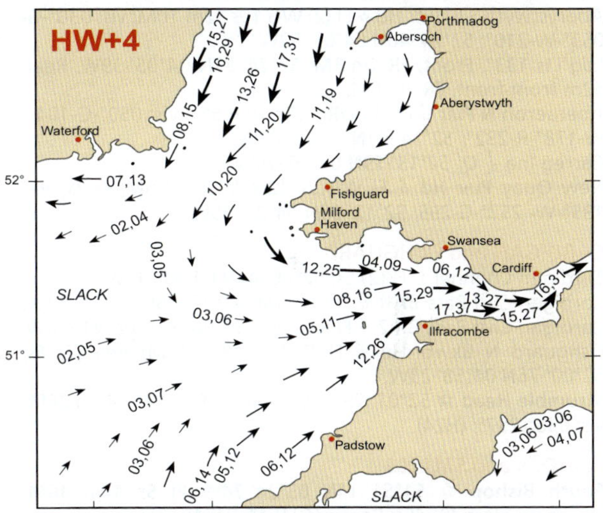

4 Hours after HW Dover (0325 before HW Milford Haven)

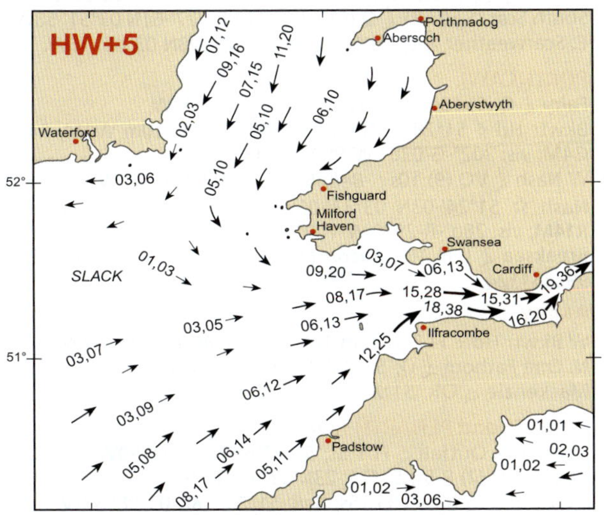

5 Hours after HW Dover (0225 before HW Milford Haven)

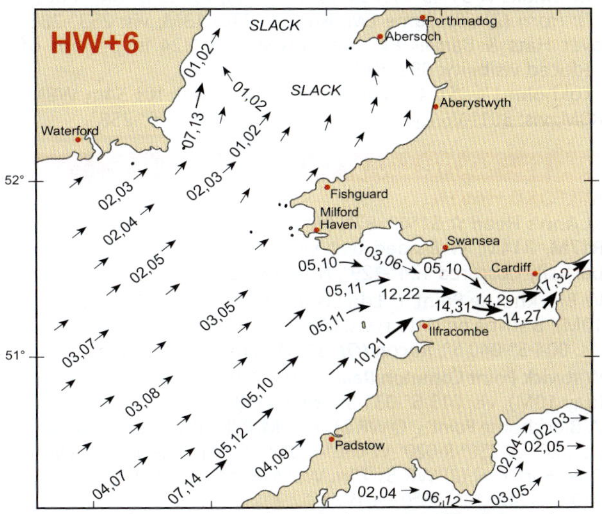

6 Hours after HW Dover (0125 before HW Milford Haven)

4.3 LIGHTS, BUOYS AND WAYPOINTS

Bold print = light with a nominal range of 15M or more. CAPITALS = place or feature. *CAPITAL ITALICS* = light-vessel, light float or Lanby. *Italics* = Fog signal. ***Bold italics*** = Racon. Many marks/buoys are fitted with with AIS (MMSI No); see relevant charts.

CARDIGAN BAY (SEE ALSO 3.3)

Bardsey I ☆ 52°44'·98N 04°48'·01W Fl R 10s 39m **18M**; W □ twr, R bands; obsc by Bardsey I 198°-250° and in Tremadoc B when brg less than 260°.
St Tudwal's Fl WR 15s 46m W14, R10M; vis: 349°-W-169°-R-221°-W-243°-R-259°-W-293°-R-349°; obsc by East I 211°-231°; 52°47'·92N 04°28'·30W.

PWLLHELI and PORTHMADOG

Pwllheli App Iso 2s; 52°53'·03N 04°22'·90W.
Porthmadog Fairway L Fl 10s; 52°52'·97N 04°11'·20W.

BARMOUTH and ABERDOVEY

Diffuser Fl Y 5s; 52°43'·19N 04°05'·38W.
Barmouth Outer L Fl 10s; 52°42'·81N 04°04'·89W.
Aberdovey Outer Iso 4s; 52°32'·00N 04°05'·55W.
Cynfelyn Patches, Patches Q (9) 15s; 52°25'·83N 04°16'·41W.

ABERYSTWYTH, ABERAERON and NEW QUAY

Aberystwyth S Bkwtr Hd Fl (2) WG 10s 12m 10M; vis: 030°-G-053°-W-210°; 52°24'·40N 04°05'·52W.
Ldg Lts 133°. Front, FR 4m 5M; 52°24'·37N 04°05'·39W. Rear, 52m from front, FR 7m 6M.
Aberaeron N Pier Fl (4) WRG 15s 10m 6M; vis: 050°-G-104°-W-178°-R-232°; 52°14'·61N 04°15'·87W.
Carreg Ina Q; 52°13'·19N 04°20'·70W.
New Quay Pier Hd Fl WG 3s 12m W8M, G5M; G △; vis: 135°-W- 252°-G-295; 52°12'·95N 04°21'·35W.

CARDIGAN and FISHGUARD

Cardigan Channel Fl (2) 5s; 52°06'·44N 04°41'·43W.
Cardigan Cliff Base Bn 1 Fl R 4s 3M; 52°07'·05N 04°41'·39W.
Cardigan Cliff Base Bn 2 Fl R 2s 3M; 52°06'·91N 04°41'·34W.
Fishguard N Bkwtr Hd Fl G 4·5s 18m 13M; *Bell (1) 8s;* 52°00'·76N 04°58'·23W.
Strumble Head ☆ 52°01'·79N 05°04'·43W Fl (4) 15s 45m **26M**; vis: 038°-257°; (H24).

BISHOPS and SMALLS

South Bishop ☆ 51°51'·14N 05°24'·74W Fl 5s 44m **16M**; W ○ twr; *Horn (3) 45s;* ***Racon (O)10M***; (H24).
The Smalls ☆ 51°43'·27N 05°40'·19W Fl (3) 15s 36m **18M**; ***Racon (T)***; *Horn (2) 60s*. Same twr, Iso R 4s 33m 13M; vis: 253°-285° over Hats & Barrels Rk; both Lts shown H24 in periods of reduced visibility; 992351123.
Skokholm I, 51°41'·64N 05°17'·22W Fl WR 10s 54m W8M, R8M; vis: 301°-W-154°-R-301°; partially obsc 226°-258°.

WALES – SOUTH COAST – BRISTOL CHANNEL

MILFORD HAVEN

St Ann's Head ☆ 51°40'·87N 05°10'·42W Fl WR 5s 48m **W18M, R17M**, R14M; W 8-sided twr; vis: 233°-W-247°-R-332°-W131°, partially obscured 124°-129°; *Horn (2) 60s*.
W Blockhouse Point Ldg Lts 022·5°. Front, F 54m 13M (day 10M); B stripe on W twr; vis: 004·5°-040·5°; intens on lead line. vis: 004·5°-040·5°; ***Racon (Q)***; 51°41'·31N 05°09'·56W.
Watwick Point Common Rear ☆, 0·5M from front, F 80m **15M** (day 10M); vis: 013·5°-031·5°; ***Racon (Y)***.
W Blockhouse Point Q WR 21m W9M, R7M; R lantern on W base: vis: 220°-W-250°-R-020°-W-036°-R-049°; 51°41'·31N 05°09'·56W.
Dale Fort Fl (2) WR 5s 20m W5M, R3M; vis: 222°-R-276°-W-019°; 51°42'·16N 05°09'·01W.
Gt Castle Hd F WRG 27m W5M, R3M, G3M; vis: 243°-R-281°-G-299°-W-029°; 51°42'·68N 05°07'·06W. Co-located Dir WRG (040°); vis: 038·25°-G-039°-AlWG-039·5°-W-040·5°-AlWR-041°-R-041·75° (**not** used in conjunction with the front ldg light below)
Ldg Lts ≠ 039·7° **Front,** Oc 4s 27m **15M**; vis: 031·2°-048·2°. **Rear,** 890m from front. Oc 8s 53m **15M** (day 10M); vis: 031·2°-048·2°.
St Ann's Fl R 2·5s; 51°40'·25N 05°10'·51W.
Mid Channel Rks Q (9) 15s; 51°40'·18N 05°10'·14W.
Mid Channel Rk Fl (3) G 7s 18m 8M; 51°40'·31N 05°09'·83W.
Rows Rks Q R; 51°40'·22N 05°09'·02W.
Sheep QG; 51°40'·06N 05°08'·31W.
Millbay Fl (2) R 5s; 51°41'·05N 05°09'·45W.
W Chapel Fl G 10s; 51°40'·98N 05°08'·67W.
E Chapel Fl R 5s; 51°40'·87N 05°08'·15W.
Rat Fl G 5s; 51°40'·80N 05°07'·86W.
Angle VQ; 51°41'·63N 05°08'·27W.
Thorn Rock Q (9) 15s; 51°41'·53N 05°07'·76W.
Turbot Bank VQ (9) 10s; 51°37'·41N 05°10'·08W.
St Gowan Q (6) + L Fl 15s, ***Racon (T) 10M***; 51°31'·93N 04°59'·77W; 992351126.

TENBY to SWANSEA BAY

Caldey I Fl (3) WR 20s 65m W13M, R9M; vis: R173°- W212°-R088°-102°; 51°37'·90N 04°41'·08W.
Woolhouse Q (6) + L Fl 15s; 51°39'·35N 04°39'·69W.
Burry Port Inlet Fl 5s 7m 6½M; 51°40'·62N 04°15'·06W.
W. Helwick (9) 15s; ***Racon (T) 10M***; 51°31'·40N 04°23'·65W.
E. Helwick VQ (3) 5s; *Bell;* 51°31'·80N 04°12'·68W.

SWANSEA BAY and SWANSEA

Ledge VQ (6) + L Fl 10s; 51°29'·93N 03°58'·77W.
Mixon Fl (2) R 5s; *Bell;* 51°33'·12N 03°58'·78W.
Outer Spoil Gnd Fl Y 2·5s; 51°32'·11N 03°55'·73W.
Grounds VQ (3) 5s; 51°32'·81N 03°53'·47W.
Mumbles ☆ 51°34'·01N 03°58'·27W Fl (4) 20s 35m **15M**; W twr; *Horn 3s*.
SW Inner Green Grounds Q(3) 10s; 51°34'·21N 03°57'·12W.
Swansea Lts in line 020°. Front: E Breakwater head, Oc G 4s 5m 2M & 2FG(vert) 10m 6M; 51°36'·38N 03°55'·62W. Rear, 3·1ca from front: FG 6M.

SWANSEA BAY, RIVER NEATH and PORT TALBOT

Neath App Chan Fl G 5s; 51°35'·71N 03°52'·83W.
Cabenda Q (6) + L Fl 15s; ***Racon (Q)***; 51°33'·36N 03°52'·23W.
Ldg Lts 059·8° (occas). Front, Oc R 3s 12m 6M; 51°34'·92N 03°48'·10W. Rear, 400m from front, Oc R 6s 32m 6M.

BRISTOL CHANNEL – NORTH SHORE (EASTERN PART)

W Scar Q (9) 15s, *Bell*, ***Racon (T) 10M***; 51°28'·31N 03°55'·57W.
South Scar (S SCAR) Q (6) + L Fl 15s; 51°27'·61N 03°51'·58W.
E. Scarweather Q (3) 10s; *Bell;* 51°27'·98N 03°46'·76W.

PORTHCAWL

Fairy Q (9) 15s; *Bell;* 51°27'·86N 03°42'·07W.
Bkwtr Hd 51°28'·39N 03°41'·98W F WRG 10m W6M, R4M, G4M; vis: 302°-G-036°-W-082°-R-116°.
W Nash VQ (9) 10s ; *Bell;* 51°25'·99N 03°45'·95W.
Nash ☆ 51°24'·03N 03°33'·06W Fl (2) WR 15s 56m **W19M, R14M**; vis: 280°-R-290°-W-100°-R-120°-W-128°.
Breaksea L Fl 10s; ***Racon (T) 10M***; 51°19'·88N 03°19'·08W; 992351124.

BARRY

W Bkwtr Hd Fl 2·5s 12m 10M; 51°23'·46N 03°15'·52W.
N. One Fathom Q; 51°20'·94N 03°12'·17W.
Mackenzie QR; 51°21'·75N 03°08'·24W.

CARDIFF and PENARTH ROADS

Lavernock Outfall Fl Y 5s; 51°23'·95N 03°09'·50W.
Ranie Fl (2) R 5s; 51°24'·23N 03°09'·39W.
S Cardiff Q (6) + L Fl 15s; *Bell;* 51°24'·18N 03°08'·57W.
Mid Cardiff Fl (3) G 10s; 51°25'·60N 03°08'·09W.

Cardiff Spit QR; 51°24′·57N 03°07′·12W.
N Cardiff QG; 51°26′·52N 03°07′·19W.
Wrach Chan Dir lt 348·5°. Oc WRG 10s 5m; W3M, R3M, G3M; vis: 344·5°-G-347°-W-350°-R-352°; H24; 51°27′·16N 03°09′·75W.
Outer Wrach Q (9) 15s; 51°26′·20N 03°09′·46W.

FLATHOLM to THE BRIDGE

Flat Holm ☆, SE Pt 51°22′·54N 03°07′·14W Fl (3) WR 10s 50m **W15M**, R12M; W ○ twr; vis: 106°-R-140°-W-151°-R-203°-W-106°; (H24).
Monkstone Fl 5s 13m 12M; R column on W ○ twr; 51°24′·89N 03°06′·01W.
Tail Patch QG; 51°23′·53N 03°03′·65W.
Hope Q (3) 10s; 51°24′·84N 03°02′·68W.
NW Elbow VQ (9) 10s; *Bell;* 51°26′·28N 02°59′·93W.
EW Grounds L Fl 10s 7M; *Bell;* ***Racon (T) 7M***; 51°27′·12N 02°59′·95W.

NEWPORT DEEP, RIVER USK and NEWPORT

Newport Deep Fl (3) G 10s; *Bell;*51°29′·36N 02°59′·12W.
East Usk ☆ 51°32′·40N 02°58′·01W; Oc WRG 10s 10m W11M, R9M, G9M; vis: 011°-G-015°-W- 017°-R-021°.
Julians Pill Ldg Lts 062°. Front, F Bu 5m 5M; 51°33′·32N 02°57′·94W. Rear, `44m from front, F Bu 8m 5M.

BRISTOL CHANNEL – SOUTH SHORE (EASTERN PART)

BRISTOL DEEP

N Elbow QG; *Bell;* 51°26′·97N 02°58′·65W.
S Mid Grounds VQ(6) + L Fl 10s; 51°27′·62N 02°58′·68W.
E Mid Grounds Fl R 5s; 51°27′·75N 02°54′·98W.
Clevedon VQ; 51°27′·39N 02°54′·93W.
Welsh Hook Q(6) + L Fl 15s; 51°28′·53N 02°51′·86W.
Avon Fl G 2·5s; 51°27′·92N 02°51′·73W.
Black Nore Pt Lt Ho; W ○ twr on frame; 51°29′·09N 02°48′·05W.
Newcome 51°30′·01N 02°46′·71W Fl (3) R 10s.
Denny Shoal VQ(6) + L Fl 10s; 51°30′·15N 02°45′·45W.
Cockburn 51°30′·45N 02°44′·10W Fl R 2·5s.
W Dock Middle 51°29.95′N 02°44′·20W Q G.
W Dock Outer 51°30′·00N 02°44′·85W Fl G 5s.
Firefly Fl(2) G 5s; 51°29′·96N 02°45′·35W.
Portishead Point ☆ 51°29′·68N 02°46′·42W Q (3) 10s 9m **16M**; B twr, W base; vis: 060°-262°; *Horn 20s.*

PORTISHEAD

Pier Hd Iso G 2s 5m 3M; 51°29′·69N 02°45′·27W.
Seabank ldg line 086·8°; W Mast, Q(8) 5M 16m; vis: 070·3°-103·3°; day 1M vis: 076·8°-096·8°; 51°30′·09N 02°43′·36W.
Knuckle Lts in line 099·6°, Oc G 5s 6m 6M; 51°29′·94N 02°43′·67W. Rear, 165m from front, FG 13m 6M; vis: 044°-134°.

AVONMOUTH

Royal Edward Dock N Pier Hd Fl 4s 15m 10M; vis: 060°-228·5°; 51°30′·49N 02°43′·09W.
King Road Ldg Lts 072·4°. N Pier Hd Front, Oc R 5s 5m 9M; W obelisk, R bands; vis: 062°-082°; 51°30′·49N 02°43′·09W. Rear, 546m from front, QR 15m 10M; vis: 066°-078°.

RIVER AVON, CUMBERLAND BASIN and AVON BRIDGE

S Pier Hd Oc RG 30s 9m 10M and FBu 4m 1M; vis: 294°-R-036°-G-194°; 51°30′·37N 02°43′·10W. *Bell(1) 10s.*
Ldg Lts 127·2°. Front, Iso R 2s 6m 3M, vis: 010°-160°; 51°30′·10N 02°42′·59W. Rear , Iso R 2s10m 3M, vis: 048°-138°.

BRISTOL CHANNEL (SOUTH SHORE)

WESTON-SUPER-MARE

Pier Hd 2 FG (vert) 6m; 51°20′·88N 02°59′·26W.
E Culver Q (3) 10s; 51°18′·00N 03°15′·44W.
W Culver VQ (9) 10s; 51°17′·47N 03°19′·00W.
E Hinkley 51°13.50′N 03°09′·26W Fl(4) G 10s.
W Hinkley 51°13′·67N 03°10′·76W Fl(3) R 10s.

BURNHAM-ON-SEA and RIVER PARRETT

Ent Fl 7·5s 7m 12M; vis: 074°-164°; 51°14′·89N 03°00′·36W; Dir lt 080°. F WRG 4m W12M, R10M, G10M; vis: 071°-G- 075°-W-085- R-095°.
DZ No 1 Fl Y 2·5s; 51°15′·28N 03°09′·49W.
DZ No 2 Fl Y 10s; 51°13′·77N 03°19′·86W.
DZ No 3 Fl Y 5s; 51°16′·34N 03°14′·98W.

WATCHET, MINEHEAD and PORLOCK WEIR

Watchet W Bkwtr Hd Oc G 3s 9m 9M; 51°11′·03N 03°19′·74W.
Watchet E Pier 2 FR (vert) 3M; 51°11′·01N 03°19′·71W.
Minehead Bkwtr Hd Fl(2) G 5s 4M; vis: 127°-262°; 51°12′·81N 03°28′·35W.
Lynmouth Foreland ☆ 51°14′·73N 03°47′·21W Fl (4) 15s 67m **18M**; W ○ twr; vis: 083°-275°.

LYNMOUTH and WATERMOUTH

River Training Arm 2 FR (vert) 6m 5M; 51°13′·90N 03°49′·83W.
Harbour Arm 2 FG (vert) 6m 5M; 51°13′·92N 03°49′·84W.
Sand Ridge Q G; 51°15′·01N 03°49′·77W.
Copperas Rock Fl G 2·5s; 51°13′·78N 04°00′·60W.
Watermouth Oc WRG 5s 1m 3M; W △; vis: 149·5°-G-151·5°-W-154·5°-R-156·5°; 51°12′·93N 04°04′·60W.

ILFRACOMBE to BAGGY POINT

Ldg Lts 188°. Front, Oc 10s 8m 3M; 51°12′·53N 04°06′·65W. Rear, Oc 10s 6m 3M.
Horseshoe Q; 51°15′·03N 04°12′·96W; AIS.
Bull Point ☆ 51°11′·94N 04°12′·09W Fl (3) 10s 54m **20M**; W ○ twr, obscd shore-056°. Same twr; FR 48m 12M; vis: 058°-096°.
Morte Stone Fl G 5s; 51°11′·30N 04°14′·95W.
Baggy Leap Fl(2) G 10s; 51°08′·92N 04°16′·97W.

BIDEFORD, RIVERS TAW and TORRIDGE

Bideford Fairway L Fl 10s; *Bell;* 51°05′·25N 04°16′·25W.
Bideford Bar Q G; 51°04′·89N 04°14′·62W.
Instow ☆ Ldg Lts 118°. **Front**, 51°03′·62N 04°10′·66W Oc 6s 22m **15M**; vis: 103·5°-132°. **Rear**, 427m from front, Oc 10s 38m **15M**; vis: 103°-132·5°; (H24).
Crow Pt Fl WR 2. 5s 8m W6M R5M; vis: 225°-R-232°-W-237°-R-358°-W- 015°-R-045°; 51°03′·96N 04°11′·39W.

LUNDY

North Pt ☆ 51°12′·10N 04°40′·65W Fl 15s 48m **18M**; vis: 009°-285°.
South East Pt ☆ 51°09′·72N 04°39′·37W Fl 5s 53m **15M**; vis: 170°-073°.
Hartland Point 51°01′·3N 04°31′·6W Fl (6) 15s 30m 8M; adjacent to Hartland Point Light House (disused).

NORTH CORNWALL

BUDE, PADSTOW and NEWQUAY

Compass Pt twr 50°49′·71N 04°33′·42W.
Stepper Pt (Padstow) LFl 10s 12m 4M; 50°34′·12N 04°56′·72W.
Middle Gnd (Padstow) Fl(2+1)R 10s; 50°32′·84N 04°55′·96W.
Trevose Head ☆ 50°32′·94N 05°02′·13W Fl 7·5s 62m **21M**.
North Pier Hd (Newquay) 2 FG (vert) 5m 2M; 50°25′·07N 05°05′·19W.

HAYLE and ST IVES

The Stones Q; 50°15′·64N 05°25′·51W.
Godrevy I Fl WR 10s 28m 8M; metal post; vis: 022°-W-101°-R-145°-W-272°; 50°14′·56N 05°24′·01W;
adjacent to Godrevy Light House (disused).
Hayle App Q; 50°12′·28N 05°26′·20W.
St Ives App 50°12′·85N 05°28′·42W.
Bann Shoal Fl G 2.5s; ***Racon (B) 10M***; 50°20′·03N 05°51′·11W; 992351053.
Pendeen ☆ 50°09′·90N 05°40′·30W Fl (4) 15s 59m **16M**; vis: 042°-240°; between Gurnard Hd and Pendeen it shows to coast.

4.4 PASSAGE INFORMATION

See Admiralty Leisure Folios 5620 SW Wales, 5608 The Bristol Channel and 5603 The Bristol Channel from Land's End. For additional tidal information E of Ilfracombe/Swansea see *Arrowsmith's Bristol Channel Tide Tables* J.W. Arrowsmith Ltd ☎(0117) 9667545. **Bibliography:** *Bristol Channel and River Severn Cruising Guide*, (Imray/Cumberlidge). The *West Coasts of England and Wales Pilot* (Admiralty NP37).

Below are some Welsh words with navigational significance.

Aber: estuary	*Afon:* river
Bach, bychan, fach: little	*Borth:* cove
Bryn: hill	*Careg, craig:* rock
Coch, goch: red	*Dinas:* fort
Ddu: black	*Fawr, Mawr:* big
Ffrydiau: tide rip	*Llwyd:* grey
Moel: bare conical hill	*Mor:* sea
Morfa: sandy shore	*Mynydd:* mountain
Penrhyn: headland	*Porth:* cove.
Ynys, Ynysoedd: island(s)	

CARDIGAN BAY

(AC 1971, 1972, 1973) Harbours are mostly on a lee shore, and/or have bars which make them dangerous to approach in bad weather. Abersoch and Pwllheli offer best shelter from the prevailing westerlies. Overfalls occur off Trwyn Cilan, SW of St Tudwal's Is (lit). The bay has three main offshore dangers: St Patrick's Causeway (Sarn Badrig) runs SW 12M from Mochras Pt. Mostly of large, loose stones, it dries (up to 1·5m) for much of its length and seas break heavily at all states of tide in strong winds. The outer end is marked by a lit WCM. A channel, 5ca offshore, can be taken with care at half tide.

Sarn-y-Bwch runs 4M WSW from Pen Bwch Pt. It consists of rocky boulders, which dry close inshore and with least depth of 0·3m over 1M offshore. There is a lit WCM off the W end.

NW of Aberystwyth, Sarn Cynfelyn / Cynfelyn Patches extend 6·5M offshore, with depths of 1·5m in places. A WCM buoy is at the outer end. About halfway along the bank is Main Channel, 3ca wide, running roughly N/S but not marked.

Aberporth MoD Range occupies much of Cardigan Bay. Beware of targets and buoys in the danger area, some unlit. It is usually active Mon-Fri 0900-1630LT, and some weekends. Both the times and extent of active danger areas are subject to change and may include the area to the west of Aberporth. Range activity is broadcast on VHF Ch 16 one hour before live firings. Flags are flown either side of the Range head to signify activity in the inner (yellow flags) or outer (red flags) danger areas. On passage contact *Aberporth Marine Control* on Ch 16 or Ch 13. Further information may be obtained from Aberporth Marine Control, ☎ (01239) 813760, or Aberporth Range Control ☎(01239) 813480.

If on passage N/S through St George's Channel (not bound for Cardigan Bay or Milford Haven) the easiest route, and always by night, is W of the Bishops and the Smalls, noting the TSS. If bound to/from Milford Haven or Cardigan Bay, passage inside both the Smalls and Grassholm is possible with care.

RAMSEY IS, BISHOPS, SMALLS TO MILFORD HAVEN

(AC 1478, 1482) The Bishops and Clerks are islets / rocks 2·5M W / NW of Ramsey Is, a bird sanctuary SSW of St David's Head. N Bishop is the N'ly of the group, 3ca ENE of which is Bell Rock (depth 1·9m). S Bishop (Lt, fog sig) is 3M to the SSW. Between S Bishop and Ramsey Is dangers include Daufraich with offlying dangers to the E and heavy overfalls; Llech Isaf and Llech Uchaf drying rocks are further ENE. Carreg Rhoson and other dangers lie between Daufraich and N Bishop. The navigable routes between these outcrops trend NE/SW. Use only by day, in good visibility and with local knowledge. The N/S route close W of Ramsey Is is easier than Ramsey Sound.

▶ *2M W of The Bishops the S-going flood begins at Milford Haven +0400, and N-going ebb at Milford Haven –0230, Sp rate 2kn. Between The Bishops and Ramsey Is the SW-going stream begins at Milford Haven +0330, and NE-going at Milford Haven –0300,* ***Sp rate 5kn.*** *Ramsey Sound should be taken at slack water. S-going stream begins at Milford Haven +0300, and the N-going at Milford Haven –0330;* ***Sp rates 6kn at The Bitches,*** *where the chan is narrow (2ca).* ◀

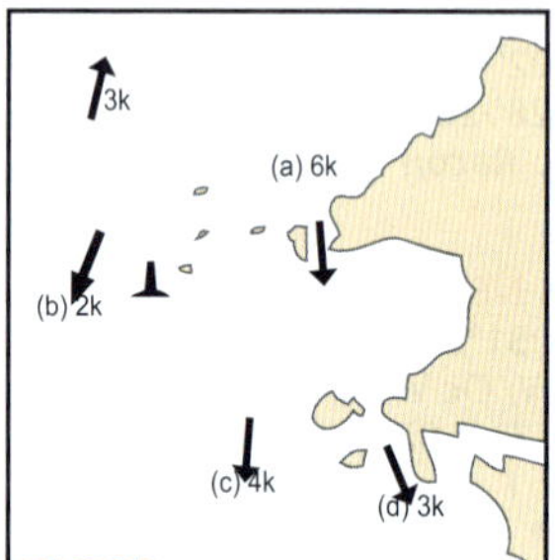

FLOOD SW Wales

The tide turns to the S or SE (Bristol Channel flood) as follows:
(a): Milford Haven +0330;
(b) & (c): Milford Haven +0400;
(d): Milford Haven +0200.

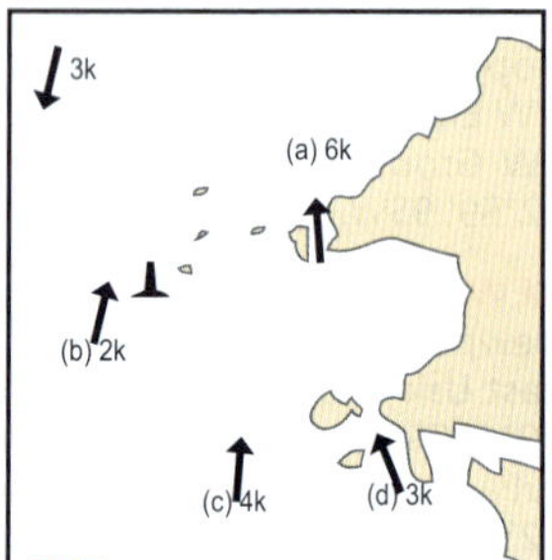

EBB SW Wales

The tide turns to the N or NW (Bristol Channel ebb) as follows:
(a): Milford Haven –0300;
(b) & (c): Milford Haven –0230 ;
(d): Milford Haven –0430.

Gwahan and Carreg-gafeiliog, both 3m high, lie to W and E at N end of Sound; a tidal turbine is 2ca off Trwyn Ogof Hen and Horse Rock (dries 0·9m) almost in mid-channel about 5ca NNE of The Bitches. These are rocks up to 4m high extending 2ca from E side of Ramsey Island with associated overfalls. Rocks extend 5ca SSE from S end of Ramsey Is. Shoe Rock (dries 3m) at SE end of channel, off mainland. Porthlysgi bay provides a passage ⚓ in 12m, but open to SW'ly wind/swell.

St Brides Bay is a regular anchorage for tankers, but ⚓ only in settled weather/offshore winds as it is a trap in westerlies. Solva is a little hbr with shelter for boats able to take the ground, or ⚓ behind Black Rk (dries 3·6m) in the middle of the entrance.

The Smalls Lt, where there is a Historic Wreck (see 0.30), is 13M W of the Welsh mainland (Wooltack Pt). The Hats and Barrels, rocky patches on which the sea breaks, lie 2M and 4M E of The Smalls respectively.

▶ *7M E of The Smalls Grassholm Island has a race either end and strong tidal eddies. It is advisable to pass about 1M off. The chan between Barrels and Grassholm is 2·5M wide, and there the S-going stream begins at Milford Haven +0440, and the N-going at Milford Haven –0135,* ***Sp rates 5kn.*** ◀

Five miles of clear water lie between Grassholm and Skomer Is/Skokholm Is to the E. Wildgoose Race, which forms W of Skomer and Skokholm is very dangerous, so keep 2M W of these two Islands. At the E end of Skomer Is lies The Neck guarding North and South haven passage ⚓. Close E lies Midland Island, separated from Wooltack Point by Jack Sound, least width 1ca. Do not attempt it without AC 1482, detailed pilotage directions, and only at slack water neaps.

▶ *Correct timing is important. The S-going stream begins at Milford Haven +0200, and the N-going at Milford Haven –0430,* ***Sp rates 6-7kn.*** ◀

Rocks which must be identified include, from N to S: On E side of chan off Wooltack Pt, Tusker Rock (2m), steep-to on its W side; and off Anvil Point, The Cable (2·4m), The Anvil and Limpet Rocks (3·7m). On the W side lie the Crabstones (3·7m) and the Blackstones (1·5m).

MILFORD HAVEN TO MUMBLES HEAD

(AC 1179, 1076) Milford Haven is a long natural, all-weather harbour with marinas beyond the oil terminals. Beware Turbot Bank (lit WCM) 3M S of the entrance. Further East 5ca SSE of Linney Hd, Crow Rk dries 5·5m, and The Toes are dangerous submerged rocks close W and SE. There is a passage inshore of these dangers. There are overfalls on St Gowan Shoals which extend 4M SW of St Govan's Hd, and the sea breaks on the shallow patches in bad weather. There are firing areas from Linney Hd to Carmarthen Bay.

Caldey Is (lit) lies S of Tenby. Off its NW pt is St Margaret's Is connected by a rocky reef. Caldey Sound, between St Margaret's Is and Giltar Pt (AC 1482), is buoyed, but beware Eel Spit near W end of Caldey Is where there can be a nasty sea with wind against tide, and Woolhouse Rocks (dry 3·6m) 1ca NE of Caldey Is. Saundersfoot harbour (dries) is 2M N of Tenby, with ⚓ well sheltered from N/W but subject to swell. Streams are weak here. Carmarthen Bay has no offshore dangers for yachts, other than the extensive drying sands at the head of the bay and on its E side off Burry Inlet.

S of Worms Head, Helwick Sands (buoyed at each end) extend 7M W from Port Eynon Pt; least depth of 1·3m is near their W end. Stream sets NE/SW across the sands. There is a narrow channel inshore, close to Port Eynon Pt.

► *Between here and Mumbles Hd the stream runs roughly along the coast, Sp rates 3kn off headlands, but there are eddies in Port Eynon Bay and Oxwich Bay (both yacht anchorages), and overfalls SSE of Oxwich Pt.* ◄

FIRING RANGES – LINNEY HEAD TO BURRY INLET

For daily info on all range firing times call *Milford Haven CG* Ch 16/67 or ☎01646 690909.

Castlemartin Range extends 12M WNW from Linney Hd, thence anti-clockwise to a point 12M S of St Govan's Head. It is primarily a tank range. When firing is in progress red flags are flown (Fl R lts at night) along from Freshwater West to Linney Head to St Govan's Head. Yachts are requested to keep clear of active areas. Firing takes place on weekdays 0900-1630, exceptionally to 1700. Night firing takes place on Mon to Thurs, up to 2359, depending on the hrs of darkness. In Jan small arms are fired and the danger area is often reduced. Days/times of firing are published locally and can be obtained from *Castlemartin Range* Ch 16 or ☎01646 662367 (H24); also from the Range Office ☎(01646) 662287 or Warren Tower 01646 662336. Range safety launches listen Ch 16/12.

Manorbier Range (further E) covers a sector arc radius 12M centred on Old Castle Hd between St Govan's Hd and Caldey Is (see AC Q6402). It is usually active Mon-Fri 0900-1700LT, occas Sat / Sun. Primarily a missile range, areas vary on any given day. On firing days warnings are broadcast on VHF Ch 16, 73 at 0830, 1430 and on completion; Red flags are flown either side of Old Castle Hd. Yachts on passage should either keep 12M offshore or transit close inshore via Stackpole Hd, Trewent Pt, Priest's Nose and Old Castle Hd. For further info call: *Manorbier Range Control* Ch 16, 73 (also manned by Range safety launches); *Milford Haven CG* Ch 16; or Range Control ☎(01834) 871282 ext 209.

Penally Range (at Giltar Pt) for small arms seldom interferes with passage through Caldey Sound. Info ☎(01834) 843522.

Pendine Range (W of Burry Inlet) is a MoD explosives range. It is usually possible to steer the rhumb line course from Tenby to Worms Hd without interference. Info ☎(01994) 453243. Broadcasts on VHF Ch 16, 73 at 0900 and 1400LT.

Pembrey Range (approx 5M NW of Burry Inlet) is used for bombing practice by the RAF. Info ☎(01554) 891224.

MUMBLES HEAD TO CARDIFF

(AC 1165, 1182) Off Mumbles Hd (Lt, fog sig) beware Mixon Shoal (dries 0·3m), marked by lit PHM. In good conditions pass N of shoal, 1ca off Mumbles Hd. ⚓ N of Mumbles Hd, good holding but exposed to swell. At W side of Swansea Bay, Green Grounds, rocky shoals, lie in approaches to Swansea.

Scarweather Sands, much of which dry (up to 3·3m) with seas breaking heavily, extend 7M W from Porthcawl (4.15) and are well buoyed (AC 1161). There is a channel between the sands and coast to E, but beware Hugo Bank (dries 2·6m) and Kenfig Patches (0·5m) with overalls up to 7ca offshore between Sker Pt and Porthcawl.

Nash Sands extend 7·5M WNW from Nash Pt. Depths are least at inshore end (dries 3m), but Nash Passage, 1ca wide, runs close inshore between E Nash ECM and ledge off Nash Pt.

► *On E-going stream there are heavy overfalls off Nash Pt and at W end of Nash Sands. Between Nash Pt and Breaksea Pt the E-going stream begins at HW Avonmouth +0535, and the W-going at HW Avonmouth –0035, Sp rates 3kn. Off Breaksea Pt there may be overfalls.* ◄

From Rhoose Pt to Lavernock Pt the coast is fringed with foul ground. Lavernock Spit extends 1·75M S of Lavernock Pt, and E of the spit lies the main channel to Cardiff. On the other side of the channel is Cardiff Grounds, a bank drying 5·4m. This lies parallel with the shore about 1·5M from it.

SEVERN ESTUARY

(AC 1176, 1166) Near the centre of the Bristol Channel, either side of the buoyed fairway, are the islands of Flat Holm (Lt, fog sig) and Steep Holm. 7M SW of Flat Holm lies Culver Sand (0·9m), 3M in length, buoyed with W and ECM. Monkstone Rk (Lt, dries) is 2M NW of the buoyed channel to Avonmouth and Bristol. Extensive drying banks cover the N shore of the estuary, beyond Newport and the Severn bridges (AC 1176). Call Bristol VTS VHF Ch 12 when passing reporting points inwards/outwards.

► *The tidal range in the Bristol Channel is exceptional, 12·2m at Sp and 6·0m Np. Care must be taken to understand the changes in chart datum in the upper reaches of the estuary. Tidal streams are very powerful, particularly above Avonmouth. Between Flat and Steep Holm the E-going stream begins at HW Avonmouth –0610, Sp rate 3kn, and the W-going at HW Avonmouth +0015, Sp rate 4kn.* ◄

The entrance to the R Avon is S of Avonmouth S Pier Head. Bristol City Docks lie some 6M upriver. Approach the entrance via King Road and the Newcombe and Cockburn lit buoys and thence via the Swash channel into the Avon. The entrance dries at LW but the river is navigable at about half tide.

► *Tidal streams are strong in the approaches to Avonmouth, up to **5kn at Sp**. The tide is also strong in the R Avon which is best entered no earlier than HW Avonmouth – 0200.* ◄

From Avonmouth it is 16M to Sharpness, which you should aim to reach at about HW Avonmouth. The passage between Avonmouth and Sharpness requires considerable attention to timing and tidal conditions if it is to be undertaken safely. Plan your passage to arrive off Sharpness no earlier than HW Sharpness –1 and no later than HW Sharpness. Information to assist passage planning is available from Gloucester Harbour Trustees (see entry for Sharpness). Pilots are available (see entry for Sharpness). To ensure the safety of navigation of all vessels, the fairway between Avonmouth approaches and Sharpness old Dock entrance must be recognised as a 'Narrow Channel' and attention is drawn to the provisions of Rule 9 of the Regulations for the Prevention of Collisions.

▶ ***Sp rates 6kn at the Severn bridges****. At the Shoots the flood begins at HW Avonmouth –0430* ***Sp streams 8kn*** *and the ebb at HW Avonmouth +0045. The Severn Bore may be seen if Avonmouth range is 13·5m or more.* ◀

AVONMOUTH TO HARTLAND POINT

(AC 1152, 1165) From Avonmouth to Sand Pt, the part-drying English Grounds extend 3M off the S shore. Portishead Quays Marina offers good shelter. Extensive mudflats fill the bays S to Burnham-on-Sea. Westward, the S shore of Bristol Chan is cleaner than N shore. But there is less shelter since the approaches to harbours such as Watchet, Minehead, Porlock Weir and Watermouth dry out.

▶ *In bad weather dangerous overfalls occur NW and NE of Foreland Pt. 5M to W there is a race off Highveer Pt. Between Ilfracombe and Bull Pt the E-going stream begins at HW Milford Haven +0540, and the W-going at HW Milford Haven –0025, Sp rates 3kn. Overfalls occur up to 1·5M N of Bull Pt and over Horseshoe Rks, which lie 3M N. There is a dangerous race off Morte Pt, 1·5M to W of Bull Pt.* ◀

Shelter is available under the lee of Lundy Island; but avoid bad races to NE (White Horses), NW (Hen and Chickens), and SE; also beware overfalls over NW Bank.

▶ *W of Lundy streams are moderate. They are strong around the Is and much stronger in the Bristol Channel proper.* ◀

Proceeding WSW from Rivers Taw/Torridge, keep 3M off to avoid the race N of Hartland Pt (Lt, fog sig, conspic radome). There is shelter off Clovelly in S/SW winds.

HARTLAND POINT TO LAND'S END

(AC 1156, 1149) The N coast of Cornwall is very exposed. Yachts need to be sturdy and well equipped, since, if bad weather develops, no shelter may be at hand.

Bude dries, and is not approachable in W winds; it is only accessible in calm weather or offshore winds. Boscastle is a tiny drying hbr 3M NE of Tintagel Hd. Only approach it in good weather or offshore winds; ⚓ off or dry out alongside.

Padstow can be a refuge, but in strong NW winds the sea breaks on Doom Bar and prevents entry. Off Trevose Head beware Quies Rocks which extend 1M to W. From here South the coast is relatively clear to Godrevy Is, apart from Bawden Rks 1M N of St Agnes Hd. Newquay Bay is a good ⚓ in offshore winds, and the hbr (dries) is sheltered but uncomfortable in N winds. Off Godrevy Is are The Stones, drying rocky shoals extending 1·5M offshore, marked by a lit NCM.

In St Ives Bay (AC 1168), Hayle is a commercial port which dries; the bottom is mostly sand. Seas break heavily on bar at times, especially with a ground swell. Entry is advised just before HW to maximise depth and minimise streams.

St Ives (dries) gives shelter from winds E to SW, but is very exposed to the N; a heavy breaking sea may form with a ground swell. Avoid the renewable energy test area centred approx 325°/10M from St Ives Bay (see AC 2565).

From St Ives to Land's End coast is rugged and exposed. There are overfalls SW of Pendeen Pt. Vyneck Rks lie awash about 3ca NW of C Cornwall and The Brisons are two high rocky islets 5ca SW of C Cornwall, with outlying rocky ledges inshore and to the S. Longships Rocks lie about 1M W of Land's End. The inshore passage (001° on Brisons) is about 4ca wide with unmarked drying rocks on the W side; only to be considered in calm weather and beware of fishing gear marker buoys.

4.5 ABERSOCH

Gwynedd **52°49'·29N 04°29'·20W** (⚓)

CHARTS AC 1410, 1411, 1971, 1512, 5609; Imray C61, C52, C51

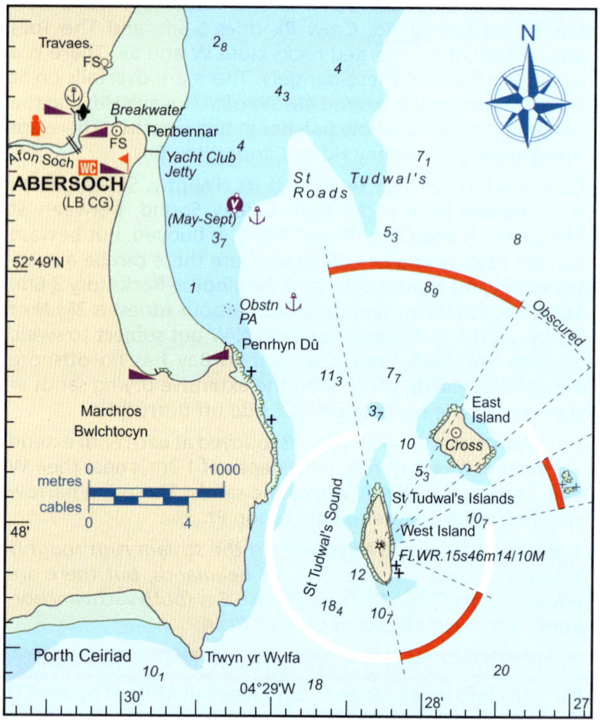

TIDES –0315 Dover; ML 2·5; Duration 0520; Zone 0 (UT)

Standard Port MILFORD HAVEN (⟶)

Times				Height (metres)			
High Water		Low Water		MHWS	MHWN	MLWN	MLWS
0100	0800	0100	0700	7·0	5·2	2·5	0·7
1300	2000	1300	1900				
Differences ST TUDWAL'S ROADS							
+0155	+0145	+0240	+0310	–2·2	–1·9	–0·7	–0·2
ABERDARON							
+0210	+0200	+0240	+0310	–2·4	–1·9	–0·6	–0·2

SHELTER There are few moorings for visitors. Apply to HM or SC. ⚓ in St Tudwal's Roads clear of moored yachts; sheltered from SSE through S to NE.

NAVIGATION WPT 52°48'·52N 04°26'·13W, 293°/2·4M to YC jetty. There are no navigational dangers, but steer well clear of the drying rks to the E of East Island; Carred y Trai buoy FlR 2·5s is 2ca E of these rks (just off chartlet). St Tudwal's islands themselves are fairly steep-to, except at N ends. St Tudwal's Sound is clear of dangers.

LIGHTS AND MARKS The only lt is on St Tudwal's West Island, Fl WR 15s 46m 14/10M (see chartlet and 4.3).

COMMUNICATIONS (Code 01758) Dr 612535. HM 712203.

S Caernarfon YC Ch **80** M.

FACILITIES **South Caernarvonshire YC** ☎712338, (May-Sept).

Abersoch Power Boat Club ☎812027.

Services (12t).

Town ACA, ✉ Ⓑ (Pwllheli), ✈ (Chester).

4.6 PWLLHELI

Gwynedd **52°53′·23N 04°23′·75W**

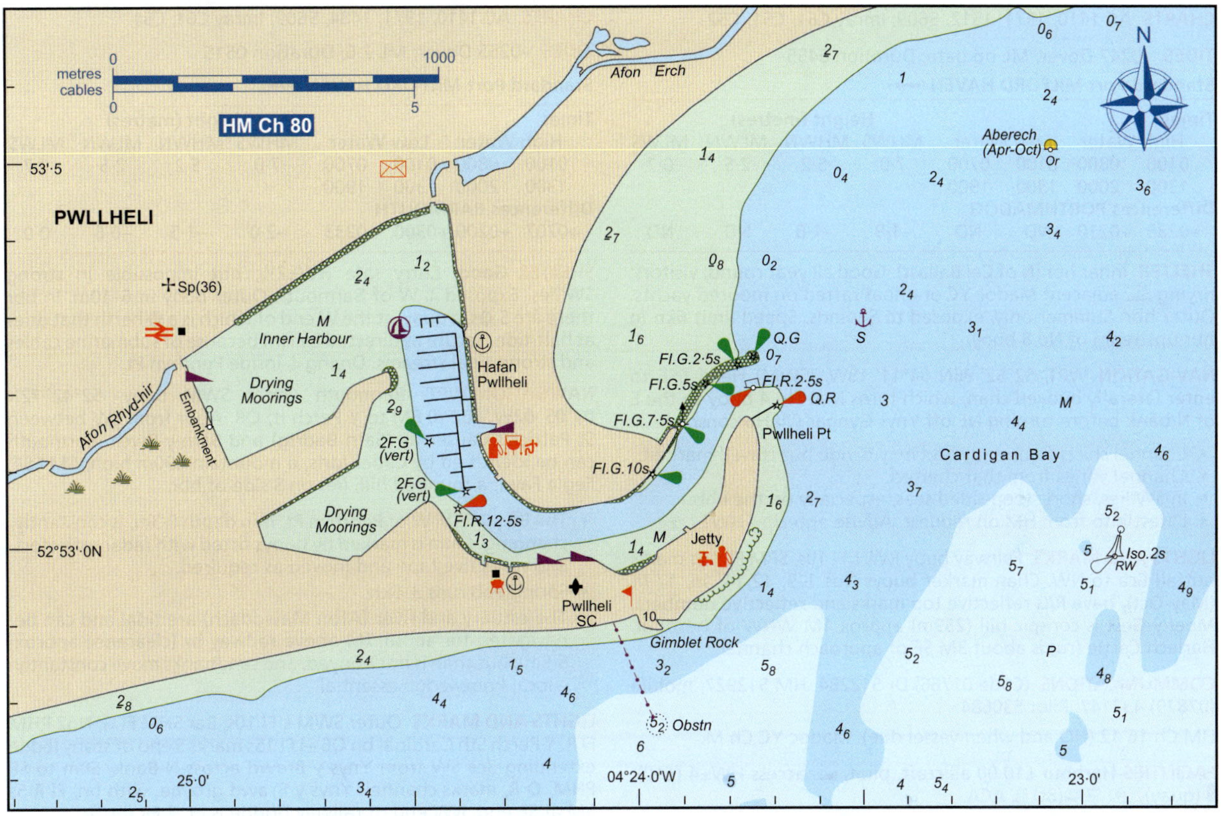

CHARTS AC 1410, 1971, 1512, 5609; Imray C61, C52, C51

TIDES –0315 Dover; ML 2·6; Duration 0510

Standard Port MILFORD HAVEN (⟶)

Times				Height (metres)			
High Water		Low Water		MHWS	MHWN	MLWN	MLWS
0100	0800	0100	0700	7·0	5·2	2·5	0·7
1300	2000	1300	1900				
Differences PWLLHELI							
+0210	+0150	+0245	+0320	–1·9	–1·6	–0·6	–0·1
CRICCIETH							
+0210	+0155	+0255	+0320	–2·0	–1·8	–0·7	–0·3

SHELTER Good in hbr and marina. Drying moorings in inner hbr (SW and NW bights).

NAVIGATION WPT 52°53′·02N 04°23′·07W, SWM lt buoy 299°/ 0·47M to QG lt at head of Training Arm.

- Ent is safe in most winds, but in strong E–SW winds sea breaks on offshore shoals.
- Ent subject to silting; 3 tide gauges. Average tidal stream 2kn.
- No ⚓ in hbr; 4kn speed limit.

LIGHTS AND MARKS See 4.3 and chartlet. Gimblet Rock (30m) is conspic conical rock 3ca SW of ent.

COMMUNICATIONS (Code 01758) Ⓗ Bangor (A&E) 01248 384384; Dr 701457. HM ☎704081.

Marina: Ch **80** M H24. HM: VHF Ch **16** (0900-1715).

FACILITIES Marina www.hafanpwllheli.co.uk ☎701219; 420, £2·94 (sail) £3·60 (power) + short stay £15·36. Pontoons are numbered 4–12 from S–N; Pile berths on S side of appr channel.

Services Ⓔ (50t) (14t) wi-fi.

Marina Boat Club ☎612271.

Harbour 6, £8/craft/day.

Town Ⓑ (Chester).

YACHT CLUBS

South Caernarvonshire YC ☎712338.

Pwllheli SC pwllhelisailingclub@btinternet.com ☎614442.

Marina Boat Club ☎612271.

ADJACENT HARBOURS AND ANCHORAGES

LLANBEDROG, Gwynedd, **52°51′·14N 04°28′·09W**. AC 5609, 1410, 1411, 1971, 1512. HW –0245 on Dover, see 4.5 (St Tudwal's Roads). Good ⚓ N of Trwyn Llanbedrog (steep sided headland 131m) 1.0ca ENE of Bcn PHM in 2-3m. Beach has numerous conspicuous bathing huts. Sheltered in winds from N through W to SW. ⚓ well clear of local craft moorings as they have a long scope. Dinghy landing near boathouse.

Village limited facilities: (½M) (Pwllheli).

MOCHRAS, Gwynedd, **52°49′·57N 04°07′·77W**. AC 1971, 1512. HW –0310 on Dover. Small yacht hbr in drying Mochras lagoon on SE side of Shell Is. Bar, about 2ca seaward. Appr advised HW±2, but HW±1 at Sp. 3 grey posts, R topmarks, mark NE side of chan. Ebb tide runs strongly in the narrow ent between the sea wall and Shell Is (lt Fl WRG 4s, 079°-G-124°-W-134°-R-179°; Mar-Nov); at sp beware severe eddies inside. Inside ent, buoyed chan runs WSW to Shell Island Yacht Hbr ☎01341 241453.

Facilities: . Shifting chan, marked by posts and buoys, runs NE to Pensarn, where permanent moorings limit space. Drying.

4.7 PORTHMADOG

Gwynedd **52°55'·32N 04°07'·77W**

CHARTS AC 1410, 1971, 1512, 5609; Imray C61, C51, C52

TIDES –0247 Dover; ML no data; Duration 0455

Standard Port MILFORD HAVEN (⟶)

Times				Height (metres)			
High Water		Low Water		MHWS	MHWN	MLWN	MLWS
0100	0800	0100	0700	7·0	5·2	2·5	0·7
1300	2000	1300	1900				
Differences PORTHMADOG							
+0235	+0210	ND	ND	–1·9	–1·8	ND	ND

SHELTER Inner hbr (N of Cei Ballast): Good all year round; visitors' drying berths adjacent Madoc YC or afloat rafted on moored yachts. Outer hbr: Summer only, exposed to S winds. Speed limit 6kn in hbr upstream of No 8 buoy.

NAVIGATION WPT, 52°52'·96N 04°11'·18W, (SWM) Head ESE to enter laterally buoyed chan, which turns N at No 4 buoy to the E of N bank before turning NE off Ynys Gyngar (W Ho conspic).

- Channel shifts frequently and may divide but is well marked.
- Channel varies from that charted.
- In SW'lies, short steep-sided seas, especially on the ebb.
- Latest info from HM on request. Advise entering HW±1½.

LIGHTS AND MARKS Fairway buoy RW, L Fl 10s. SPM Fl Y 5s marks outfall 6ca to NW. Chan marker buoys Nos 1–9, 12,14, 15, 17 lit (May-Oct), have R/G reflective top marks and reflective numbers. Moel-y-Gest is conspic hill (259m) approx 1M WNW of harbour. Harlech Castle (ru) is about 3M SE of approach channel.

COMMUNICATIONS (Code 01766) Dr 512284. HM 512927, mobile (07879) 433147; Pilot 530684.

HM Ch 16 **12** (HO and when vessel due). Madoc YC Ch M.

FACILITIES **Harbour** £10·00 all craft, pilot, slip access HW±4 (£10), (quay), (8t) ACA.

Porthmadog SC ☎513546.

Madoc YC ☎512976.

Town (Chester).

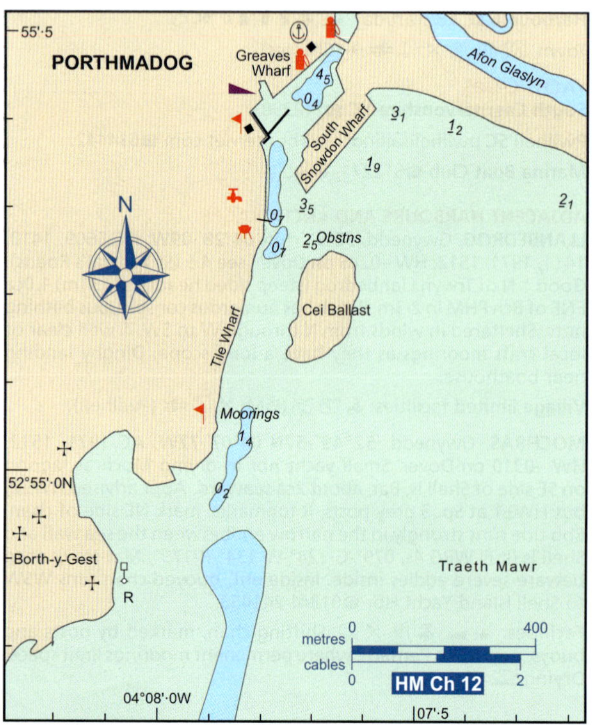

4.8 BARMOUTH

Gwynedd **52°42'·97N 04°03'·07W**

CHARTS AC 1410, 1971, 1484, 5609; Imray C61, C51

TIDES –0255 Dover; ML 2·6; Duration 0515

Standard Port MILFORD HAVEN (⟶)

Times				Height (metres)			
High Water		Low Water		MHWS	MHWN	MLWN	MLWS
0100	0800	0100	0700	7·0	5·2	2·5	0·7
1300	2000	1300	1900				
Differences BARMOUTH							
+0207	+0200	+0300	+0233	–2·0	–1·5	–0·6	0·0

SHELTER Good. Entry safe HW±2½, but impossible in strong SW'lies. Exposed ⚓ W of Barmouth Outer buoy in 6–10m. In hbr there are 5 buoys, a quay, at the W end of which is a berth that dries at half-tide. Secure as directed by HM because of submarine cables and strong tidal streams. Drying ⚓ inside Penrhyn Pt.

NAVIGATION WPT, Barmouth Outer SWM buoy, 52°42'·72N 04°05'·02W, 082°/0·8M to Y Perch lt, QR. Appr from SW between St Patrick's Causeway (Sarn Badrig) and Sarn-y-Bwch. Barmouth can be identified by Cader Idris, a mountain 890m high, 5M ESE. Fegla Fawr, a rounded hill, lies on S side of hbr.

- The Bar, 0·75M W of Penrhyn Pt, min depth 0·3m, is constantly changing. Chan is marked by buoys fitted with radar reflectors and reflective tape and moved as required.
- Spring ebb runs 3–5kn.
- The estuary and river (Afon Mawddach) are tidal and can be navigated for about 7M above railway br (clearance approx 5·5m); but chan is not buoyed, and sandbanks move constantly – local knowledge essential.

LIGHTS AND MARKS Outer SWM L Fl 10s; Bar SHM Fl G; No2 PHM Fl R. Y Perch Sth Cardinal bn Q6 +LFl 15s marks S end of stony ledge extending 3ca SW from Ynys y Brawd across N Bank, 50m to SE PHM, Q R, marks channel. Ynys y Brawd groyne, with bn, Fl R 5s 5M at SE end. NW end of railway bridge is lit, 2 FR (hor).

COMMUNICATIONS (Code 01341) Dr 280521. HM 280671 mob 07795 012747; Local information www.barmouthwebcam.co.uk

Call *Barmouth Hbr* VHF Ch **12** 16 (Apr-Sep 0900-1700 later for HW; Oct-Mar 0900-1600); wind and sea state are available.

FACILITIES 3 drying buoys M (call HM in advance for deep water buoy), 2 berths on quay £10/£6 yacht (inc), 2 slip (HW±3, £10/day). at . **Merioneth YC** ☎280000.

Town (Manchester/ L'pool); Ferry to Penrhyn Pt for **Fairbourne** .

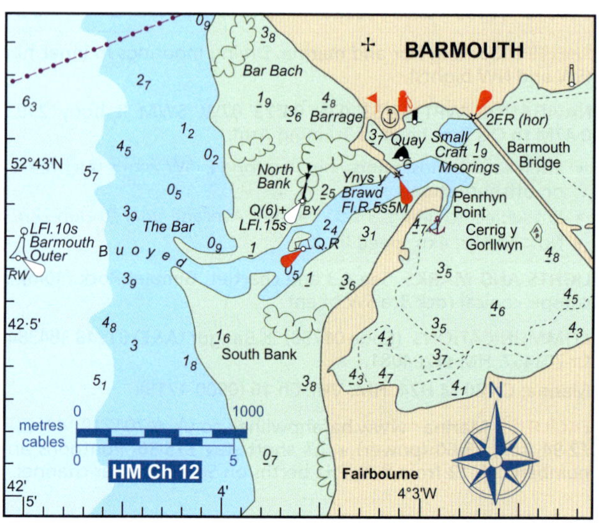

4.9 ABERDOVEY

Gwynedd **52°32'·57N 04°02'·72W** (Jetty)

CHARTS AC 1410, 1972, 1484, 5609; Imray C61, C51

TIDES –0257 Dover; ML 2·6; Duration 0535. For differences see 4.10.

SHELTER Good except in strong W/SW winds. Berth on jetty in 3m; to the E there is heavy silting.

NAVIGATION WPT Aberdovey Outer SWM buoy, 52°32'·00N 04°05'·56W, 093°/0.43M to Bar buoy.

- Bar and channel constantly shift and are hazardous below half-tide; buoys moved accordingly.
- Enter channel at gateway between Bar SHM and PHM Fl R 5s. Visitors should call HM on VHF before entering.

LIGHTS AND MARKS See 4.3 and chartlet. No daymarks. Lts may be unreliable. Submarine cables (prohib ⚓s) marked by bns with R ◊ topmarks.

COMMUNICATIONS (Code 01654) Dr 710414; Ⓗ 710411. HM 767626, mob 07879 433148.

Call *Aberdovey Hbr* VHF Ch **12** 16.

FACILITIES **Jetty/Wharf** 5 £10·00.
Dovey YC ☎767607, (£4·50 if engine <10hp).
Ynyslas BY (S shore) (16t).
Town (Birmingham).

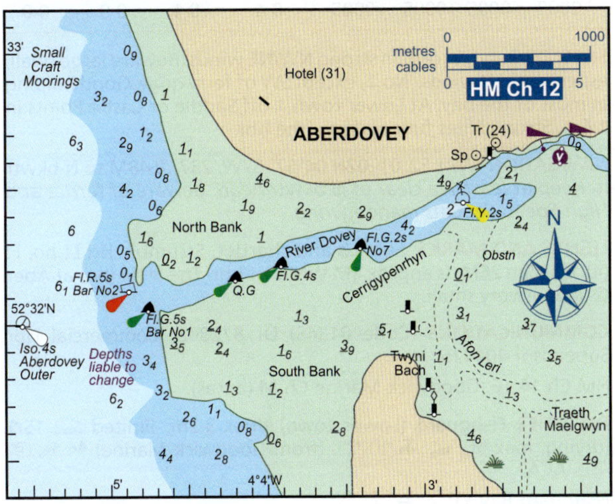

OTHER HARBOURS IN SOUTH PART OF CARDIGAN BAY

ABERAERON, Ceredigion, **52°14'·62N 04°15'·94W.** AC 1410, 1972, 1484. HW –0325 on Dover; +0140 and –1·9m on Milford Haven; ML 2·7m; Duration 0540. A small, popular drying hbr at the mouth of the R Aeron. Short drying piers extend each side of river ent. In strong NW'lies there is little shelter. £8·50/craft on NW wall, only in calm conditions. Foul ground with depths of 1·5m extend 3ca offshore to SW of Aberaeron. Beware Carreg Gloyn (0·3m) 4ca WSW of hbr, and Sarn Cadwgan (1·8m) shoals 5ca N of the hbr ent. Lts (see 4.3 for sectors): N pier Fl (4) WRG 15s 10m 6M. S pier Fl (3) G 10s 11m 6M. VHF **14** 16. HM ☎(01545) 571645, (from fishermen). **YC** ☎570077. **Town**.

NEW QUAY, Ceredigion, **52°12'·92N 04°21'·22W.** AC 1410, 1972, 1484. HW –0335 on Dover; Duration 0540; see 4.10. Good shelter in offshore winds, but untenable in North Westerlies. Carreg Ina, rks drying 1·3m, are marked by NCM buoy, Q, on E side of bay. 2 Y bns mark sewer outfall running 7ca NNW from Ina Pt. The hbr (dries 1·6m) is protected by a pier; Lt, Fl WG 3s 12m 8/5M; 135°-W-252°-G-295°. Groyne extends 80m SSE of pier head to a starboard bn; close ENE of which is a ECM bn, Q (3) 10s. HM ☎(01545) 560368; Dr ☎560203; YC ☎560516. VHF Ch **14** 16. Facilities: (from fishermen) (£8·50). **Town** (3M).

4.10 ABERYSTWYTH

Ceredigion **52°24'·42N 04°05'·47W**

CHARTS AC 5620, 1410, 1972, 1484, 5609; Imray C61, C51

TIDES – 0330 Dover; ML 2·7; Duration 0540

Standard Port MILFORD HAVEN (⟶)

Times				Height (metres)			
High Water		Low Water		MHWS	MHWN	MLWN	MLWS
0100	0800	0100	0700	7·0	5·2	2·5	0·7
1300	2000	1300	1900				
Differences ABERDOVEY							
+0215	+0200	+0230	+0305	–2·0	–1·7	–0·5	0·0
ABERYSTWYTH							
+0145	+0130	+0210	+0245	–2·0	–1·7	–0·7	0·0
NEW QUAY							
+0150	+0125	+0155	+0230	–2·1	–1·8	–0·6	–0·1
ABERPORTH							
+0135	+0120	+0150	+0220	–2·1	–1·8	–0·6	–0·1

SHELTER Good, in marina (1·7m) on E side of chan; or dry against Town Quay.

NAVIGATION WPT 52°24'·83N 04°06'·22W,133/0·6M° to ent. Appr dangerous in strong on-shore winds. The Bar, close off S pier hd, has 0·7m least depth. From N, beware Castle Rks, in R sector of N bkwtr lt; also rks drying 0·5m W of N bkwtr and boulders below S pier hd. Turn 90° port inside narrow ent. E edge of inner hbr chan 0·3m is defined by WCM bn which in line with Y daymark gives a daytime lead into the harbour.

LIGHTS AND MARKS N Bkwtr Hd ≠ 140° Wellington Mon't (on top Pendinas, conspic hill 120m high) clears to S of Castle Rks. Ldg lts 133°, both FR on Ystwyth Bridge, white daymarks. WCM bn on with Y daymark leads 100° across bar into harbour entrance.

COMMUNICATIONS (Code 01970) Dr 624855. HM 611433, Mobile 07974 023965; Marina 611422.

HM Ch **14** 16. Marina Ch 80.

FACILITIES **Marina (Y Lanfa),** www.themarinegroup.co.uk ☎611422 (launch £18), 88+15 £3·20 +£3 (10t) (15t by arrangement) wi-fi.
Town Quay (25t).
YC ☎612907.
Town (Swansea).

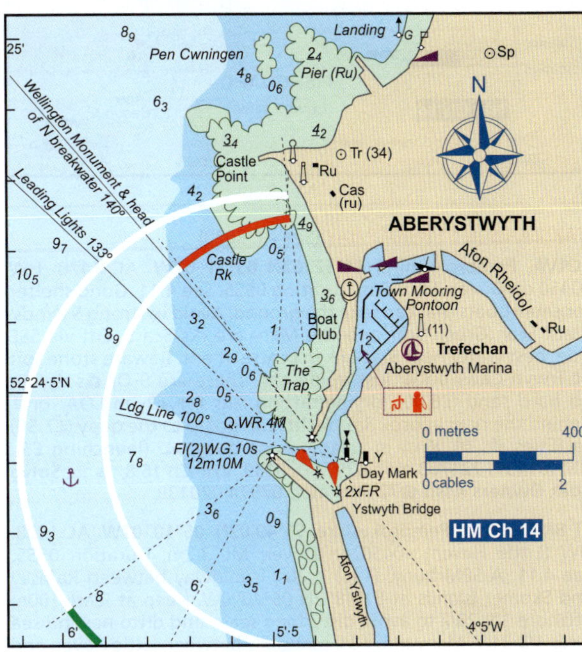

MINOR HARBOUR, 12M NE of Fishguard

PORT CARDIGAN, Ceredigion, **52°07´·02N 04°42´·07W**. AC 1973, 1484. HW –0405 on Dover; ML 2·4m; Duration 0550. Good shelter, but ent dangerous in strong N/NW winds. **Large scale charts are essential**; contact Afon Teifi Fairways Ltd, www.afonteififairways.com or Mooring Master (see below) in advance. The bar has 0·5m or less. ⚓ near Hotel (conspic) on E side of ent (2 bns Fl.R.4s, Fl.R.2s). Chan is usually close to E side marked by W posts; IDM (Fl (2) 5s) should be left to stbd when clear of the bar. ⚓ off Pen-yr-Ergyd. Inside spit pontoon or 🅐s off Teifi Boating Club, Mooring Master ☎(01239) 613966, mob 07799 284206. Upstream to Bryn-Du chan is marked by SWM but shifts constantly. St Dogmaels chan lies between 🅐s and pontoon, Mooring Master ☎07909 830752. Above the Ferry Inn chan runs up to the old bridge (3m clearance)through Netpool with deeper water moorings, Mooring Master ☎07814 035438.

Teifi Boating Club ☎613846; Services.

Town Ⓑ.

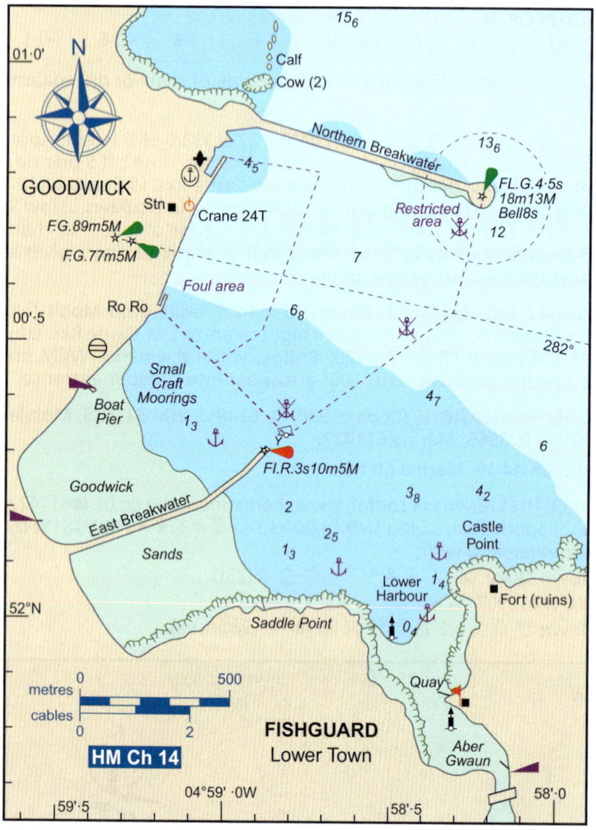

4.11 FISHGUARD

Pembrokeshire **52°00'·12N 04°58'·40W**
Commercial Hbr; Lower Hbr

CHARTS AC 1178, 1410, 1973, 1484, 5620; Imray C61, C51, C60

TIDES –0400 Dover; ML 2·6; Duration 0550

Standard Port MILFORD HAVEN (⟶)

Times				Height (metres)			
High Water		Low Water		MHWS	MHWN	MLWN	MLWS
0100	0800	0100	0700	7·0	5·2	2·5	0·7
1300	2000	1300	1900				
Differences ***FISHGUARD***							
+0115	*+0100*	*+0110*	*+0135*	*–2·2*	*–1·8*	*–0·5*	*+0·1*
PORT CARDIGAN							
+0140	+0120	+0220	+0130	–2·3	–1·8	–0·5	0·0
CARDIGAN (Town)							
+0220	+0150	ND	ND	–2·2	–1·6	ND	ND
PORTHGAIN							
+0055	+0045	+0045	+0100	–2·5	–1·8	–0·6	0·0
RAMSEY SOUND							
+0030	+0030	+0030	+0030	–1·9	–1·3	–0·3	0·0
SOLVA							
+0015	+0010	+0035	+0015	–1·5	–1·0	–0·2	0·0
LITTLE HAVEN							
+0010	+0010	+0025	+0015	–1·1	–0·8	–0·2	0·0
MARTIN'S HAVEN							
+0010	+0010	+0015	+0015	–0·8	–0·5	+0·1	+0·1
SKOMER IS							
–0005	–0005	+0005	+0005	–0·4	–0·1	0·0	0·0

SHELTER Good, except in strong NW/NE winds. Beware large swell, especially in N winds. No ⚓, except SW of ferry quay. Good holding in most of the bay. At Lower town ⚓ off Saddle or Castle Points in 1·4m. Strong S'lies funnel down the hbr.

NAVIGATION WPT 52°01´·02N 04°57´·57W, 237°/0·48M to N bkwtr lt. *Keep at least 1ca clear of N bkwtr head; beware of ferries and High-Speed SeaCats manoeuvring.*

LIGHTS AND MARKS See 4.3 and chartlet. Strumble Hd Lt ho, Fl (4) 15s 45m 26M, is approx 4M WNW of hbr. The SHM (bn) at Aber Gwaun is very small.

COMMUNICATIONS (Code 01348) Dr 872802. Commercial Hbr Supervisor 404425.

HM Ch **14** 16. Goodwick Marine Ch M (occas).

FACILITIES **Fishguard** (Lower town) dries 3·2m; limited 15🅐 (drying, max 5t), (from Goodwick Marine) ACA.

Fishguard Bay YC.

Town Ⓑ @ ✈ (Cardiff), Ferry to Rosslare; 2/day; 1¾hrs; Stena Line (www.stenaline.ie).

HARBOURS IN ST BRIDES BAY (See AC 5620)

SOLVA, Pembrokeshire, **51°52´·02N 05°11´·67W**. AC 1478. HW –0450 on Dover; ML 3·2m; Duration 0555. See 4.11. Good shelter for small boats that can take the ground. Avoid in strong S winds. Black Scar, Green Scar and The Mare are rks 5ca S. Ent via SSE side; best water near Black Rk in centre of ent. Beware stone spit at Trwyn Caws on W just inside ent. There are 9 Or 🅐s drying on hard sand (£6.00), drying/rafting ABs for <9·5m LOA; or ⚓ behind the rk in approx 3m. Yachts can go up to the quay (£7.50) Facilities: in village. on quay, (launching £5). HM (01437) 721703 mob 07974 020139, VHF Ch 16 8. **Solva Boat Owners Assn** ☎721489 mob 07974 020139.

ST BRIDES BAY, Pembrokeshire, **51°49'02N 05°10´·07W**. AC 1478. HW (Little Haven) –0450 on Dover; ML 3·2m; Duration 0555. See 4.11. A SPM buoy, Fl (5) Y 20s, is midway between Ramsey and Skomer islands at 51°48'·2N 05°20'·0W. Keep at least 100m offshore 1/9-28/2 to avoid disturbing seals, and ditto nesting sea birds 1/3-31/7. Many good ⚓s, especially between Little Haven and Borough Head in S or E winds or between Solva and Dinas Fawr in N or E winds. In W'lies boats should shelter in Solva (above), Skomer (below) or Pendinas Bach. Tankers ⚓ in mouth of bay. For apprs from the N or S see 4.4. Facilities: (Little Haven) (cans).

SKOMER, Pembrokeshire, **51°44´·42N 05°16´·77W**. AC 1478, 2878. HW –0455 Dover. See 4.11. The island is a National Nature Reserve (fee payable to Warden on landing or Welsh Wildlife Trust directly) and also a Marine Nature Reserve, extending to Marloes Peninsula. Keep at least 100m offshore 1/9-28/2 to avoid disturbing seals and ditto nesting sea birds 1/3-31/7. There is a 5kn speed limit within 100m of the island. ⚓ in S Haven (N Haven ⚓ prohibited due to eel grass). Enter N Haven close to W shore, and land on W side of bay on beach or at steps. In N Haven pick up 🅐s provided. No access to the island from S Haven. For Jack Sound see 4.4. There are no lts, marks or facilities. For info, Marine Conservation Officer ☎(01646) 636736.

4.12 MILFORD HAVEN

Pembrokeshire **51°40'·13N 05°08'·16W**

CHARTS AC 1410, 1178, 1478, 2878, 3273/4/5, 5620; Imray C60, C13, 2600

TIDES –0500 Dover; ML 3·8; Duration 0605

Standard Port MILFORD HAVEN (⟶)

Times				Height (metres)			
High Water		Low Water		MHWS	MHWN	MLWN	MLWS
0100	0800	0100	0700	7·0	5·2	2·5	0·7
1300	2000	1300	1900				
Differences DALE ROADS							
–0005	–0005	–0008	–0008	0·0	0·0	0·0	–0·1
NEYLAND							
+0002	*+0010*	*0000*	*0000*	*0·0*	*0·0*	*0·0*	*0·0*
HAVERFORDWEST							
+0010	+0025	DR	DR	–4·8	–4·9	DR	DR
LLANGWM (Black Tar)							
+0010	+0020	+0005	0000	+0·1	+0·1	0·0	–0·1

SHELTER Very good in various places round the hbr, especially in Milford Marina and Neyland Yacht Haven. ⚓s in Dale Bay; off Chapel Bay and Angle Pt on S shore; off Scotch Bay, E of Milford marina; and others beyond Pembroke Dock. Free pontoons (May-Oct) include: Dale Bay, Gelliswick Bay; waiting pontoons off Milford Dock and Hobbs Pt (for Pembroke Dock); and drying pontoons at Dale Beach, Hazelbeach, Neyland and Burton; mainly intended for tenders. It is possible to dry out safely at inshore areas of Dale, Sandy Haven and Angle Bay, depending on weather.

NAVIGATION WPT (W) 51°40'·25N 05°10'·65W. WPT (E) 51°40'·05N 05°08'·06W.

- The tide sets strongly across the ent to the Haven particularly at sp. In bad weather avoid passing over Mid Chan Rks and St Ann's Hd shoal, where a confused sea and swell will be found. Give St Ann's Head a wide berth especially on the ebb, when East Chan by Sheep Island is better.
- Beware large tankers entering/departing the Haven and ferries moving at high speed in the lower Haven. **Keep outside the main shipping channels if possible.**
- Milford Haven Port Authority has a jetty, Port Control and offices near Hubberston Pt. Their launches have G hulls and W upperworks with 'PILOT' in black letters and fly a Pilot flag while on patrol; Fl Bu lt at night. Their instructions must be obeyed. No vessel may pass within 100m of any terminal or any tanker, whether at ⚓ or under way.

River Cleddau is navigable 6M to Picton Pt, at junction of West and East arms, at all tides for boats of moderate draught. Clearance under Cleddau Bridge above Neyland is 36m; and 25m under power cable 1M upstream. Chan to Haverfordwest has 2m at HW and clearances of only 6m below cables and bridge; only feasible for shoal draught/lifting keel and unmasted craft.

Firing Ranges to the S and SE, see 4.13 and AC 1076.

LIGHTS AND MARKS See 4.3 and chartlets. Y SPM have been established in W Angle, Gelliswick, Dale Bays and off Jenkins Pt to prohibit high speed craft and water skiing.

Milford Haven leading lights are specifically for VLCCs entering/leaving hbr and proceeding to/from the oil refineries. The Haven is very well buoyed and lit as far as Cleddau bridge.

Milford Dock ldg lts 348°, both F.Bu, with W ○ daymarks. Dock entry sigs on E side of lock: 2 FG (vert) = gates open, vessels may enter. VHF Ch 18 is normally used for ent/exit by day and night.

COMMUNICATIONS (Code 01646) Lock 696310; Ⓗ Haverfordwest (01437) 764545; Dr 690674. Port Control 696136/7.

Monitor *Milford Haven Port Control* Ch 12 (H24) while underway in the Haven. *Milford Haven Patrol* launches Ch11/12 (H24). To lock in to Milford Dock marina call *Pierhead*, Ch 14, for clearance, then call *Milford Marina*, Ch ▲ for a berth. Neyland Yacht Haven Ch 80/M.

Broadcasts: Nav warnings on Ch 12 14 at 0300 and 1500 (both UT). Gale warnings on receipt. Tide hts and winds on request. Bcsts on Ch 16 67 at 0335 then every 4hrs to 2335.

FACILITIES Marinas/Berthing (from seaward):

Dale Bay YC Pontoon.

Milford Haven Port Authority jetty ☎696133 (occas use by visitors with approval from HM).

Milford Marina ☎696312, Pierhead ☎696310. VHF Ch 14, 80/M. Lock hrs summer (Apr–Sep): ent HW–5, exit HW–4, free flow HW–2¼ to HW–¼, ent+3½, exit+4½; winter (Oct–Mar): ent HW–3¼, free flow HW–2¼ to HW–¼, ent+2½, exit+3; waiting pontoon or shelter in lock, 3·5m water at MLWS. 280 inc Ⓥ, £2·80. (H24) (14t) Ⓔ Ⓑ ice, wi-fi.

Lawrenny Yacht Station ☎651212/651065, £17·50, 100; (launch £5) (15t).

Neyland Yacht Haven, www.yachthavens.com ☎601601, 420 inc Ⓥ £3·50+£5 in lower basin, Ⓔ (20t); Access lower basin H24, but upper basin depth limited (sill + depth gauges and R/G lit perches); marina and approaches dredged annually Oct/March – proceed with extreme caution.

Dale Sailing Co (at Neyland) LPG (35t).

East Llannion Marine: access HW±3, scrubbing piles (30t).

Rudder's BY, small but useful, is just upstream of Burton Pt.

Yacht Clubs: Dale YC ☎636362; Pembrokeshire YC ☎692799; Neyland YC ☎600267; Pembroke Haven YC ☎684403; Lawrenny YC ☎651212.

Towns: Milford Haven, Ⓑ. Pembroke Dock; Ⓑ Ⓗ. Neyland, Ⓑ. Haverfordwest, Ⓗ Ⓑ ✈ (Swansea or Cardiff). Ferry: Pembroke Dock–Rosslare; 2/day; Irish Ferries.

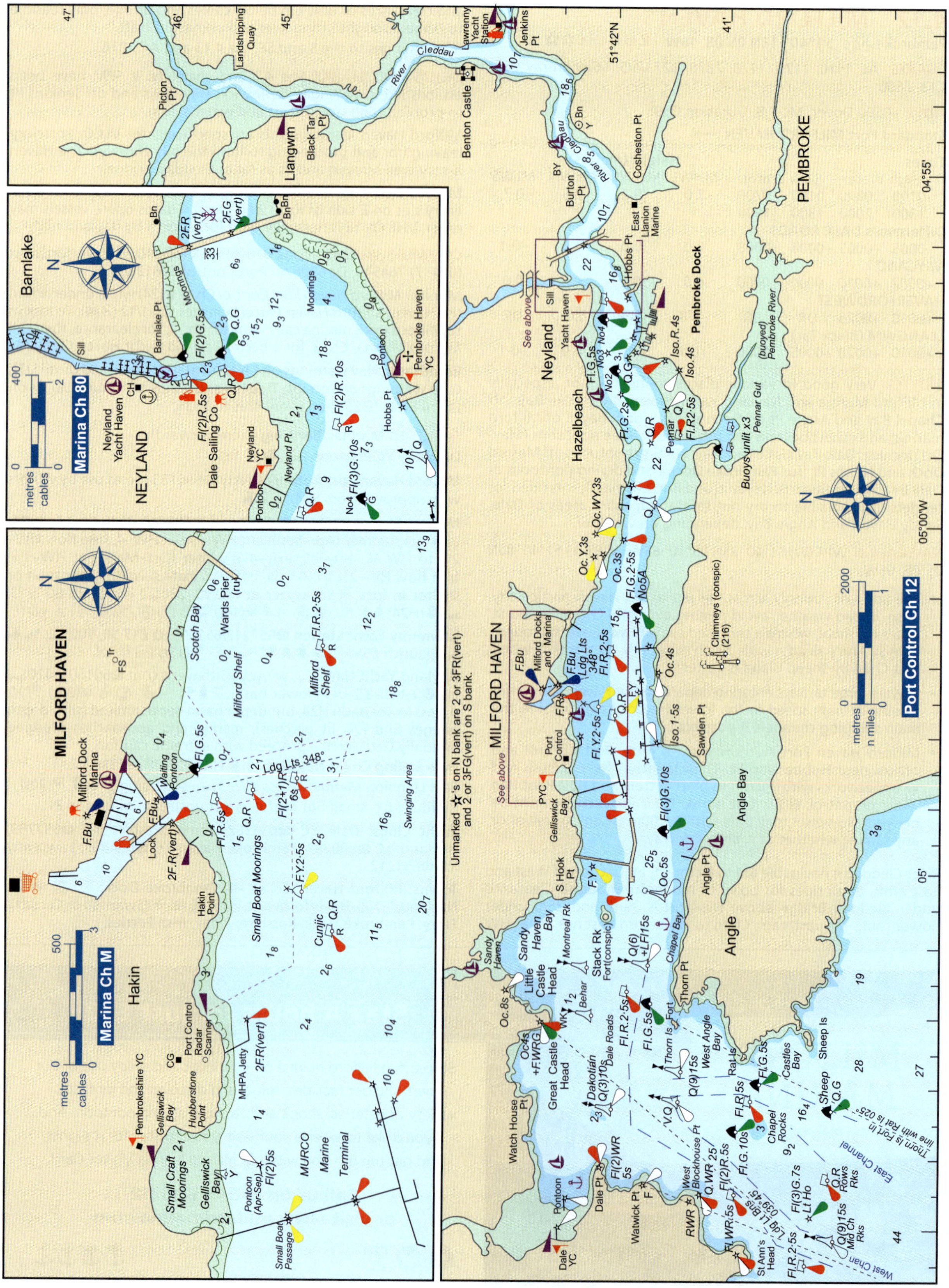
MILFORD HAVEN
Milford Dock Marina
Marina Ch M
metres 0 500
cables 0 3
Hakin
Pembrokeshire YC
Gelliswick Bay
Hubberstone Point
Port Control Radar Scanner
MHPA Jetty
Small Craft Moorings
Small Boat Moorings
Small Boat Passage
Pontoon (Apr-Sep)
MURCO Marine Terminal
Hakin Point
Lock
Waiting Pontoon
Scotch Bay
Wards Pier (ru)
Milford Shelf
Cunjic
Swinging Area
Ldg Lts 348°
NEYLAND
Marina Ch 80
metres 0 400
cables 0 2
Neyland Yacht Haven
Dale Sailing Co
Barnlake
Barnlake Pt
Sill
Moorings
Neyland YC
Neyland Pt
Hobbs Pt
Pontoon
Pembroke Haven YC
Picton Pt
Landshipping Quay
River Cleddau
Llangwm
Black Tar Pt
Benton Castle
Lawrenny Yacht Station
Jenkins Pt
Burton Pt
Cosheston Pt
East Llanion Marine
PEMBROKE
Pembroke Dock
Pembroke River (buoyed)
Pennar Gut
Buoys unlit x3
Pennar
Hazelbeach
Neyland
Yacht Haven
See above
MILFORD HAVEN
Milford Docks and Marina
Port Control
PYC
Gelliswick Bay
S Hook Pt
Sandy Haven Bay
Sandy Haven
Little Castle Head
Great Castle Head
Watch House Pt
Dale Pt
Dale YC
Watwick Pt
West Blockhouse Pt
St Ann's Head
Dale Roads
Montreal Rk
Stack Rk Fort(conspic)
Behar
Dakotian
Thorn Is
Chapel Bay
Thorn Pt
Angle
Angle Pt
Angle Bay
Sawden Pt
Chimneys (conspic) (216)
West Angle Bay
Rat Is
Castles Bay
Sheep Is
Chapel Rocks
Sheep
Mid Ch Rks
Rows Rks
Lt Ho
Ldg Lts 039·5°
East Channel
West Chan
Thorn Is Fort In line with Rat Is 025°
Unmarked ☆'s on N bank are 2 or 3FR(vert) and 2 or 3FG(vert) on S bank.
metres 0 2000
n miles 0 1
Port Control Ch 12
51°42'N
05°00'W
04°55'
05'

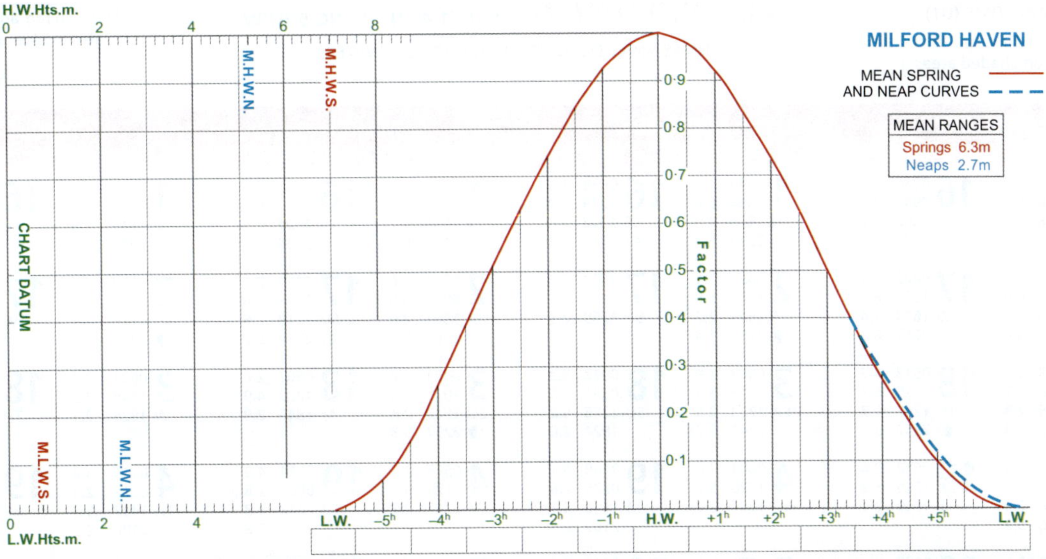
MILFORD HAVEN
MEAN SPRING AND NEAP CURVES
MEAN RANGES
Springs 6.3m
Neaps 2.7m
H.W.Hts.m.
L.W.Hts.m.
CHART DATUM
M.H.W.N.
M.H.W.S.
M.L.W.S.
M.L.W.N.
Factor
L.W.
H.W.
L.W.

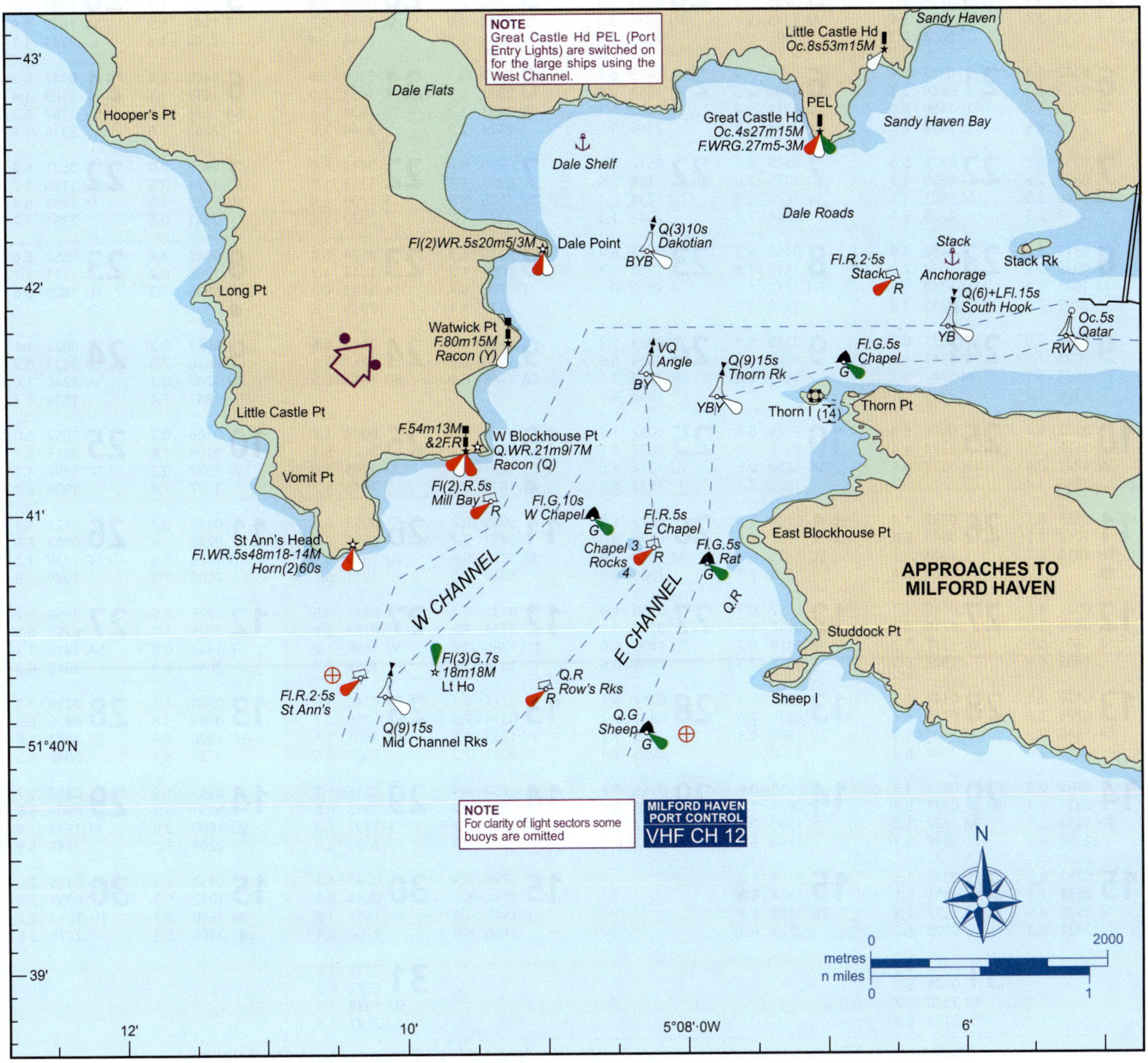
NOTE
Great Castle Hd PEL (Port Entry Lights) are switched on for the large ships using the West Channel.
Sandy Haven
Little Castle Hd
Oc.8s53m15M
Dale Flats
Hooper's Pt
PEL
Great Castle Hd
Oc.4s27m15M
F.WRG.27m5-3M
Sandy Haven Bay
Dale Shelf
Dale Roads
Q(3)10s
Dakotian
BYB
Fl(2)WR.5s20m5/3M
Dale Point
Stack Anchorage
Stack Rk
Fl.R.2·5s
Stack
Long Pt
Q(6)+LFl.15s
South Hook
YB
Oc.5s
Qatar
RW
Watwick Pt
F.80m15M
Racon (Y)
VQ
Angle
BY
Q(9)15s
Thorn Rk
YBY
Fl.G.5s
Chapel
Thorn I
Thorn Pt
Little Castle Pt
F.54m13M
&2F.R
W Blockhouse Pt
Q.WR.21m9/7M
Racon (Q)
Vomit Pt
Fl(2).R.5s
Mill Bay
Fl.G.10s
W Chapel
Fl.R.5s
E Chapel
St Ann's Head
Fl.WR.5s48m18-14M
Horn(2)60s
Chapel Rocks
Fl.G.5s
Rat
East Blockhouse Pt
APPROACHES TO MILFORD HAVEN
W CHANNEL
E CHANNEL
Q.R
Studdock Pt
Fl(3)G.7s
18m18M
Lt Ho
Fl.R.2·5s
St Ann's
Q(9)15s
Mid Channel Rks
Q.R
Row's Rks
Q.G
Sheep
Sheep I
NOTE
For clarity of light sectors some buoys are omitted
MILFORD HAVEN PORT CONTROL
VHF CH 12
metres
n miles
51°40'N
5°08'·0W

STANDARD TIME (UT)
For Summer Time add ONE hour in **non-shaded areas**

MILFORD HAVEN LAT 51°42′N LONG 5°03′W

TIMES AND HEIGHTS OF HIGH AND LOW WATERS

Dates in red are SPRINGS
Dates in blue are NEAPS

YEAR **2024**

JANUARY

Date	Time	m	Date	Time	m
1 M	0308 0918 1536 2139	1.8 6.2 1.9 5.8	16 TU	0336 0945 1606 2208	1.0 7.0 1.0 6.5
2 TU	0343 0955 1613 2218	2.0 6.0 2.1 5.6	17 W	0422 1033 1654 2257	1.3 6.7 1.4 6.1
3 W	0423 1036 1656 2302	2.3 5.7 2.3 5.4	18 TH ◐	0513 1125 1747 2352	1.7 6.3 1.7 5.8
4 TH ◑	0510 1124 1748 2356	2.5 5.5 2.5 5.2	19 F	0612 1225 1849	2.0 5.9 2.1
5 F	0610 1222 1853	2.6 5.3 2.6	20 SA	0057 0725 1334 2004	5.5 2.3 5.6 2.3
6 SA	0102 0723 1330 2005	5.1 2.7 5.3 2.6	21 SU	0212 0846 1450 2119	5.4 2.3 5.6 2.3
7 SU	0213 0835 1440 2112	5.3 2.5 5.5 2.3	22 M	0328 0959 1601 2223	5.6 2.2 5.7 2.1
8 M	0317 0939 1541 2209	5.6 2.2 5.7 2.0	23 TU	0432 1058 1700 2315	5.9 1.9 5.9 1.8
9 TU	0412 1035 1636 2300	6.0 1.9 6.1 1.7	24 W	0523 1147 1747 2359	6.2 1.6 6.2 1.6
10 W	0502 1126 1727 2348	6.4 1.5 6.4 1.4	25 TH ○	0606 1228 1827	6.4 1.4 6.4
11 TH ●	0551 1214 1815	6.7 1.2 6.7	26 F	0037 0644 1304 1903	1.4 6.6 1.3 6.4
12 F	0034 0638 1301 1903	1.1 7.0 0.9 6.9	27 SA	0112 0718 1337 1936	1.3 6.7 1.2 6.5
13 SA	0120 0725 1348 1950	0.9 7.2 0.7 7.0	28 SU	0144 0750 1408 2008	1.3 6.7 1.3 6.4
14 SU	0205 0811 1434 2036	0.8 7.3 0.7 6.9	29 M	0215 0821 1437 2038	1.3 6.6 1.3 6.3
15 M	0251 0858 1520 2122	0.9 7.2 0.8 6.8	30 TU	0244 0851 1506 2108	1.4 6.5 1.5 6.2
			31 W	0314 0921 1536 2139	1.5 6.3 1.7 6.0

FEBRUARY

Date	Time	m	Date	Time	m
1 TH	0346 0954 1608 2213	1.8 6.0 1.9 5.7	16 F ◐	0438 1049 1704 2310	1.5 6.2 1.8 5.8
2 F ◑	0421 1030 1645 2253	2.1 5.8 2.2 5.4	17 SA	0528 1143 1759	2.0 5.7 2.3
3 SA	0503 1116 1733 2349	2.4 5.4 2.5 5.2	18 SU	0012 0641 1256 1924	5.3 2.5 5.2 2.6
4 SU	0604 1220 1847	2.6 5.2 2.7	19 M	0140 0825 1430 2102	5.1 2.6 5.1 2.6
5 M	0106 0736 1345 2025	5.1 2.7 5.1 2.6	20 TU	0316 0953 1556 2215	5.3 2.4 5.3 2.3
6 TU	0235 0906 1511 2144	5.2 2.5 5.4 2.3	21 W	0425 1053 1652 2306	5.7 2.0 5.7 1.9
7 W	0349 1016 1620 2244	5.7 2.0 5.8 1.8	22 TH	0512 1138 1734 2347	6.1 1.6 6.1 1.5
8 TH	0448 1113 1716 2336	6.2 1.4 6.3 1.3	23 F	0551 1214 1810	6.4 1.3 6.4
9 F ●	0539 1203 1805	6.8 0.9 6.8	24 SA ○	0021 0626 1245 1843	1.3 6.6 1.1 6.5
10 SA	0023 0627 1250 1852	0.8 7.2 0.5 7.1	25 SU	0052 0657 1314 1913	1.1 6.7 1.0 6.6
11 SU	0108 0712 1335 1936	0.5 7.5 0.2 7.3	26 M	0122 0726 1342 1941	1.0 6.8 1.0 6.6
12 M	0152 0756 1418 2018	0.3 7.6 0.2 7.3	27 TU	0150 0754 1409 2008	1.0 6.8 1.0 6.6
13 TU	0234 0839 1500 2100	0.4 7.6 0.3 7.1	28 W	0217 0821 1435 2035	1.1 6.7 1.2 6.4
14 W	0315 0921 1540 2140	0.6 7.3 0.7 6.7	29 TH	0245 0848 1502 2103	1.2 6.5 1.4 6.2
15 TH	0355 1004 1620 2223	1.0 6.8 1.2 6.3			

MARCH

Date	Time	m	Date	Time	m
1 F	0313 0917 1530 2133	1.5 6.2 1.7 6.0	16 SA	0407 1017 1627 2234	1.5 6.1 1.9 5.8
2 SA	0344 0949 1601 2208	1.8 5.9 2.0 5.7	17 SU ◐	0454 1108 1718 2334	2.1 5.4 2.5 5.2
3 SU ◑	0421 1029 1642 2257	2.2 5.5 2.4 5.3	18 M	0607 1223 1846	2.6 4.9 2.9
4 M	0515 1129 1747	2.5 5.1 2.7	19 TU	0111 0807 1412 2043	4.9 2.8 4.8 2.8
5 TU	0015 0648 1305 1948	5.0 2.7 4.9 2.8	20 W	0258 0937 1539 2156	5.1 2.4 5.2 2.4
6 W	0203 0843 1451 2124	5.1 2.5 5.2 2.3	21 TH	0404 1033 1631 2244	5.6 2.0 5.6 1.9
7 TH	0330 0959 1606 2227	5.6 1.9 5.8 1.7	22 F	0448 1113 1709 2322	6.0 1.6 6.0 1.5
8 F	0431 1056 1700 2319	6.3 1.2 6.4 1.1	23 SA	0524 1146 1743 2355	6.4 1.3 6.3 1.3
9 SA	0521 1146 1748	6.9 0.6 6.9	24 SU	0557 1217 1814	6.6 1.1 6.5
10 SU ●	0005 0608 1231 1832	0.6 7.4 0.2 7.3	25 M ○	0024 0627 1245 1843	1.1 6.7 1.0 6.7
11 M	0049 0651 1314 1914	0.2 7.7 0.0 7.5	26 TU	0053 0656 1312 1911	0.9 6.8 0.9 6.7
12 TU	0131 0734 1355 1954	0.1 7.8 0.0 7.5	27 W	0121 0723 1338 1938	0.9 6.8 1.0 6.7
13 W	0211 0814 1433 2033	0.1 7.6 0.2 7.2	28 TH	0149 0750 1405 2005	1.0 6.7 1.1 6.6
14 TH	0250 0854 1511 2111	0.4 7.2 0.7 6.8	29 F	0218 0818 1432 2033	1.1 6.5 1.3 6.4
15 F	0328 0934 1547 2150	0.9 6.7 1.3 6.3	30 SA	0247 0848 1501 2104	1.4 6.3 1.6 6.1
			31 SU	0319 0922 1533 2141	1.7 6.0 1.9 5.8

APRIL

Date	Time	m	Date	Time	m
1 M	0359 1004 1617 2232	2.1 5.6 2.3 5.4	16 TU	0544 1155 1813	2.6 4.8 2.9
2 TU ◑	0456 1108 1726 2354	2.4 5.1 2.7 5.1	17 W	0038 0732 1336 2002	5.0 2.7 4.8 2.8
3 W	0631 1248 1926	2.6 4.9 2.7	18 TH	0215 0857 1459 2115	5.1 2.5 5.1 2.5
4 TH	0141 0822 1432 2100	5.2 2.3 5.3 2.2	19 F	0322 0952 1552 2205	5.5 2.1 5.5 2.1
5 F	0306 0936 1543 2204	5.7 1.7 5.9 1.6	20 SA	0409 1033 1632 2244	5.9 1.7 5.9 1.7
6 SA	0406 1032 1636 2255	6.4 1.1 6.5 1.0	21 SU	0447 1108 1707 2319	6.2 1.4 6.2 1.4
7 SU	0457 1121 1723 2341	7.0 0.6 7.0 0.5	22 M	0521 1140 1738 2351	6.4 1.2 6.4 1.2
8 M ●	0542 1206 1806	7.4 0.2 7.3	23 TU ○	0552 1211 1809	6.6 1.1 6.6
9 TU	0024 0626 1247 1847	0.2 7.6 0.1 7.4	24 W	0022 0623 1240 1839	1.1 6.7 1.0 6.7
10 W	0106 0708 1327 1927	0.2 7.6 0.2 7.4	25 TH	0052 0653 1309 1909	1.0 6.7 1.1 6.7
11 TH	0146 0749 1406 2006	0.3 7.4 0.5 7.2	26 F	0123 0723 1339 1939	1.1 6.6 1.2 6.6
12 F	0225 0829 1443 2044	0.6 7.0 0.9 6.8	27 SA	0156 0755 1410 2012	1.2 6.5 1.3 6.5
13 SA	0304 0909 1520 2124	1.1 6.5 1.4 6.3	28 SU	0230 0829 1444 2048	1.4 6.3 1.6 6.2
14 SU	0345 0951 1600 2209	1.6 5.9 2.0 5.7	29 M	0308 0909 1523 2132	1.7 5.9 1.9 5.9
15 M ◐	0433 1042 1650 2308	2.2 5.3 2.5 5.3	30 TU	0355 0959 1614 2230	2.0 5.6 2.2 5.6

Chart Datum: 3·71 metres below Ordnance Datum (Newlyn). HAT is 7·9 metres above Chart Datum.

STANDARD TIME (UT)
For Summer Time add ONE hour in **non-shaded areas**

MILFORD HAVEN LAT 51°42′N LONG 5°03′W

TIMES AND HEIGHTS OF HIGH AND LOW WATERS

Dates in red are SPRINGS
Dates in blue are NEAPS

YEAR **2024**

MAY

Date	Day	Time	m	Time	m	Time	m	Time	m	Moon
1	W	0458	2.2	1108	5.3	1727	2.5	2350	5.4	◑
2	TH	0626	2.3	1238	5.2	1906	2.4			
3	F	0119	5.5	0755	2.0	1404	5.5	2029	2.1	
4	SA	0235	6.0	0905	1.6	1511	5.9	2132	1.6	
5	SU	0335	6.4	1002	1.1	1606	6.4	2225	1.1	
6	M	0427	6.9	1052	0.8	1653	6.8	2314	0.8	
7	TU	0515	7.1	1138	0.6	1738	7.1	2359	0.6	
8	W	0600	7.2	1221	0.5	1821	7.2			●
9	TH	0042	0.5	0644	7.2	1302	0.6	1903	7.1	
10	F	0124	0.7	0726	7.0	1342	0.8	1944	6.9	
11	SA	0206	0.9	0808	6.7	1421	1.2	2024	6.6	
12	SU	0247	1.3	0850	6.2	1501	1.6	2106	6.2	
13	M	0330	1.7	0934	5.8	1542	2.0	2152	5.8	
14	TU	0418	2.1	1023	5.4	1630	2.4	2246	5.5	
15	W	0518	2.5	1124	5.0	1736	2.7	2355	5.2	◐
16	TH	0634	2.6	1241	4.9	1857	2.7			
17	F	0114	5.2	0751	2.5	1357	5.0	2012	2.5	
18	SA	0222	5.4	0853	2.2	1457	5.3	2110	2.3	
19	SU	0316	5.6	0941	2.0	1543	5.6	2156	2.0	
20	M	0400	5.9	1023	1.7	1623	6.0	2237	1.7	
21	TU	0439	6.1	1100	1.5	1700	6.2	2314	1.5	
22	W	0515	6.3	1135	1.4	1735	6.4	2351	1.3	
23	TH	0551	6.4	1210	1.3	1809	6.6			○
24	F	0026	1.2	0627	6.5	1244	1.2	1845	6.6	
25	SA	0103	1.2	0703	6.5	1320	1.3	1922	6.6	
26	SU	0142	1.2	0742	6.4	1358	1.4	2001	6.5	
27	M	0222	1.3	0823	6.3	1438	1.5	2045	6.4	
28	TU	0307	1.5	0910	6.0	1524	1.7	2135	6.2	
29	W	0358	1.7	1004	5.8	1618	1.9	2233	6.0	
30	TH	0459	1.8	1107	5.6	1723	2.1	2340	5.9	◑
31	F	0609	1.9	1217	5.6	1839	2.1			

JUNE

Date	Day	Time	m	Time	m	Time	m	Time	m	Moon
1	SA	0051	5.9	0722	1.8	1329	5.7	1952	1.9	
2	SU	0159	6.1	0828	1.6	1434	5.9	2057	1.7	
3	M	0301	6.3	0928	1.4	1533	6.2	2155	1.4	
4	TU	0358	6.5	1022	1.2	1625	6.5	2248	1.2	
5	W	0450	6.7	1112	1.1	1715	6.7	2338	1.0	
6	TH	0540	6.7	1158	1.0	1801	6.8			●
7	F	0024	1.0	0627	6.7	1242	1.1	1846	6.8	
8	SA	0109	1.0	0712	6.6	1324	1.2	1929	6.7	
9	SU	0152	1.2	0754	6.4	1405	1.4	2011	6.5	
10	M	0234	1.4	0836	6.2	1445	1.6	2052	6.3	
11	TU	0316	1.7	0917	5.9	1525	1.9	2134	6.0	
12	W	0357	1.9	1000	5.6	1606	2.1	2218	5.8	
13	TH	0443	2.1	1046	5.3	1654	2.3	2308	5.5	
14	F	0535	2.3	1140	5.2	1751	2.5			◐
15	SA	0004	5.4	0635	2.4	1242	5.1	1856	2.5	
16	SU	0108	5.3	0738	2.4	1347	5.2	2000	2.5	
17	M	0211	5.4	0838	2.3	1446	5.4	2100	2.3	
18	TU	0307	5.6	0931	2.1	1536	5.6	2152	2.0	
19	W	0356	5.8	1019	1.9	1622	5.9	2240	1.8	
20	TH	0441	6.0	1103	1.7	1704	6.2	2324	1.6	
21	F	0524	6.2	1145	1.5	1746	6.4			
22	SA	0007	1.4	0608	6.4	1226	1.3	1829	6.6	○
23	SU	0050	1.2	0651	6.5	1308	1.2	1912	6.7	
24	M	0134	1.1	0736	6.5	1351	1.2	1957	6.8	
25	TU	0219	1.1	0821	6.5	1436	1.2	2043	6.7	
26	W	0305	1.1	0908	6.4	1522	1.3	2132	6.6	
27	TH	0354	1.2	0958	6.2	1611	1.5	2223	6.4	
28	F	0446	1.4	1051	6.0	1705	1.7	2319	6.3	◑
29	SA	0542	1.6	1148	5.8	1806	1.8			
30	SU	0019	6.1	0644	1.7	1251	5.7	1913	1.9	

JULY

Date	Day	Time	m	Time	m	Time	m	Time	m	Moon
1	M	0124	6.0	0751	1.8	1358	5.7	2023	1.9	
2	TU	0230	5.9	0858	1.8	1504	5.8	2131	1.8	
3	W	0335	6.0	1000	1.7	1606	6.0	2233	1.6	
4	TH	0436	6.1	1056	1.6	1702	6.3	2327	1.5	
5	F	0530	6.3	1145	1.4	1752	6.5			●
6	SA	0016	1.3	0618	6.4	1230	1.3	1837	6.6	
7	SU	0100	1.3	0702	6.4	1312	1.3	1919	6.6	
8	M	0141	1.3	0742	6.4	1351	1.3	1957	6.6	
9	TU	0219	1.3	0819	6.3	1427	1.4	2034	6.4	
10	W	0254	1.5	0854	6.1	1501	1.6	2109	6.3	
11	TH	0328	1.6	0929	5.9	1535	1.8	2144	6.1	
12	F	0402	1.8	1005	5.7	1611	2.0	2222	5.8	
13	SA	0439	2.0	1045	5.5	1652	2.2	2304	5.6	◐
14	SU	0523	2.3	1132	5.3	1742	2.4	2354	5.4	
15	M	0619	2.5	1229	5.1	1847	2.6			
16	TU	0056	5.2	0728	2.6	1339	5.1	2001	2.6	
17	W	0208	5.2	0840	2.5	1449	5.3	2111	2.4	
18	TH	0316	5.4	0943	2.2	1550	5.7	2212	2.1	
19	F	0415	5.7	1038	1.9	1642	6.1	2304	1.7	
20	SA	0507	6.1	1127	1.6	1730	6.4	2353	1.3	
21	SU	0555	6.4	1213	1.2	1816	6.8			○
22	M	0039	1.0	0641	6.7	1257	1.0	1902	7.0	
23	TU	0124	0.8	0726	6.8	1342	0.8	1947	7.2	
24	W	0209	0.6	0811	6.9	1425	0.8	2032	7.2	
25	TH	0253	0.6	0855	6.8	1509	0.9	2117	7.1	
26	F	0337	0.8	0939	6.6	1553	1.1	2202	6.8	
27	SA	0421	1.1	1025	6.3	1639	1.4	2251	6.5	
28	SU	0509	1.5	1115	6.0	1730	1.8	2345	6.0	◑
29	M	0604	1.9	1214	5.6	1836	2.1			
30	TU	0050	5.7	0715	2.2	1326	5.4	1958	2.3	
31	W	0206	5.5	0836	2.3	1447	5.5	2122	2.2	

AUGUST

Date	Day	Time	m	Time	m	Time	m	Time	m	Moon
1	TH	0326	5.5	0950	2.1	1601	5.8	2230	1.9	
2	F	0433	5.8	1050	1.9	1659	6.1	2325	1.6	
3	SA	0526	6.1	1139	1.6	1746	6.4			
4	SU	0010	1.4	0610	6.3	1220	1.4	1827	6.6	●
5	M	0049	1.2	0648	6.4	1257	1.2	1903	6.7	
6	TU	0123	1.2	0722	6.5	1331	1.2	1936	6.7	
7	W	0155	1.2	0754	6.5	1402	1.2	2008	6.7	
8	TH	0225	1.2	0825	6.4	1432	1.3	2038	6.5	
9	F	0253	1.4	0854	6.2	1501	1.5	2107	6.3	
10	SA	0322	1.6	0924	6.0	1531	1.7	2138	6.1	
11	SU	0352	1.8	0956	5.8	1604	2.0	2212	5.8	
12	M	0426	2.2	1033	5.5	1643	2.3	2253	5.5	◐
13	TU	0509	2.5	1123	5.2	1738	2.7	2350	5.1	
14	W	0613	2.8	1234	5.0	1904	2.8			
15	TH	0112	5.0	0753	2.8	1407	5.1	2041	2.6	
16	F	0246	5.2	0918	2.5	1526	5.5	2152	2.2	
17	SA	0357	5.6	1020	2.0	1625	6.0	2249	1.6	
18	SU	0453	6.1	1111	1.5	1715	6.6	2338	1.1	
19	M	0541	6.6	1157	1.0	1801	7.1			○
20	TU	0023	0.7	0626	7.0	1241	0.7	1845	7.4	
21	W	0108	0.4	0709	7.2	1324	0.5	1929	7.6	
22	TH	0150	0.3	0751	7.3	1406	0.4	2011	7.6	
23	F	0232	0.3	0832	7.2	1447	0.6	2053	7.4	
24	SA	0312	0.6	0912	6.9	1528	0.9	2135	7.0	
25	SU	0352	1.1	0954	6.5	1610	1.4	2220	6.4	
26	M	0435	1.6	1040	6.0	1658	1.9	2312	5.8	◑
27	TU	0527	2.2	1139	5.5	1805	2.4			
28	W	0020	5.3	0645	2.6	1303	5.2	1949	2.6	
29	TH	0155	5.1	0828	2.7	1443	5.3	2125	2.4	
30	F	0328	5.3	0948	2.4	1559	5.7	2230	2.0	
31	SA	0429	5.7	1044	1.9	1651	6.1	2318	1.6	

Chart Datum: 3·71 metres below Ordnance Datum (Newlyn). HAT is 7·9 metres above Chart Datum.

S Wales

STANDARD TIME (UT)
For Summer Time add ONE hour in **non-shaded areas**

MILFORD HAVEN LAT 51°42′N LONG 5°03′W

TIMES AND HEIGHTS OF HIGH AND LOW WATERS

Dates in red are SPRINGS
Dates in blue are NEAPS

YEAR **2024**

SEPTEMBER

Date	Day	Time	m	Time	m	Time	m	Time	m
1	SU	0514	6.1	1127	1.6	1731	6.5	2355	1.3
2	M	0552	6.4	1203	1.3	1807	6.7		
3	TU ●	0027	1.2	0625	6.6	1234	1.2	1839	6.8
4	W	0057	1.1	0656	6.7	1304	1.1	1909	6.8
5	TH	0125	1.1	0724	6.7	1333	1.1	1937	6.8
6	F	0152	1.1	0752	6.6	1400	1.2	2004	6.7
7	SA	0218	1.3	0819	6.5	1427	1.3	2031	6.5
8	SU	0244	1.5	0846	6.3	1455	1.6	2059	6.3
9	M	0312	1.8	0915	6.0	1526	1.9	2129	5.9
10	TU	0342	2.1	0948	5.7	1601	2.3	2207	5.5
11	W ◐	0420	2.5	1033	5.3	1652	2.7	2301	5.1
12	TH	0519	2.9	1145	5.0	1819	2.9		
13	F	0032	4.9	0716	3.0	1335	5.0	2018	2.7
14	SA	0225	5.1	0857	2.6	1505	5.5	2134	2.1
15	SU	0341	5.7	1001	2.0	1605	6.2	2230	1.5
16	M	0434	6.3	1051	1.4	1654	6.8	2318	0.9
17	TU	0520	6.8	1137	0.8	1739	7.3		
18	W ○	0002	0.4	0603	7.3	1219	0.5	1822	7.7
19	TH	0044	0.2	0645	7.5	1301	0.3	1905	7.8
20	F	0126	0.1	0725	7.5	1342	0.3	1946	7.7
21	SA	0206	0.3	0805	7.3	1422	0.5	2027	7.4
22	SU	0245	0.7	0845	7.0	1502	1.0	2109	6.9
23	M	0323	1.3	0926	6.5	1544	1.5	2153	6.3
24	TU ◑	0405	1.9	1012	6.0	1633	2.1	2245	5.6
25	W	0457	2.5	1112	5.4	1747	2.7	2359	5.1
26	TH	0624	2.9	1247	5.1	1945	2.8		
27	F	0146	4.9	0819	2.9	1433	5.3	2117	2.5
28	SA	0317	5.3	0935	2.4	1542	5.7	2213	2.0
29	SU	0410	5.7	1024	2.0	1628	6.2	2254	1.6
30	M	0450	6.2	1103	1.6	1705	6.5	2328	1.4

OCTOBER

Date	Day	Time	m	Time	m	Time	m	Time	m
1	TU	0524	6.5	1136	1.4	1738	6.7	2358	1.2
2	W ●	0555	6.6	1206	1.2	1809	6.8		
3	TH	0026	1.1	0625	6.8	1234	1.1	1838	6.9
4	F	0053	1.1	0653	6.8	1302	1.1	1905	6.8
5	SA	0120	1.1	0720	6.8	1330	1.2	1932	6.8
6	SU	0146	1.3	0747	6.6	1358	1.4	1959	6.6
7	M	0213	1.5	0814	6.5	1427	1.6	2028	6.3
8	TU	0241	1.8	0844	6.2	1459	1.9	2100	6.0
9	W	0312	2.1	0920	5.9	1537	2.3	2140	5.6
10	TH ◐	0353	2.5	1007	5.5	1632	2.7	2238	5.2
11	F	0456	2.9	1123	5.2	1801	2.8		
12	SA	0012	5.0	0652	2.9	1309	5.2	1954	2.6
13	SU	0201	5.2	0831	2.5	1437	5.7	2108	2.0
14	M	0314	5.8	0934	1.9	1537	6.3	2203	1.4
15	TU	0407	6.4	1025	1.3	1627	6.9	2251	0.9
16	W	0453	6.9	1111	0.8	1712	7.4	2336	0.5
17	TH ○	0536	7.3	1155	0.5	1756	7.7		
18	F	0018	0.3	0619	7.5	1237	0.4	1840	7.7
19	SA	0100	0.3	0700	7.5	1319	0.4	1922	7.6
20	SU	0140	0.6	0740	7.3	1401	0.7	2004	7.2
21	M	0220	1.0	0822	7.0	1443	1.2	2047	6.7
22	TU	0301	1.5	0904	6.5	1527	1.7	2133	6.1
23	W	0344	2.1	0953	6.0	1619	2.3	2226	5.5
24	TH ◑	0437	2.6	1054	5.5	1733	2.7	2339	5.0
25	F	0601	2.9	1221	5.2	1917	2.8		
26	SA	0115	4.9	0745	2.9	1355	5.3	2040	2.6
27	SU	0238	5.2	0857	2.6	1503	5.7	2135	2.2
28	M	0334	5.6	0947	2.2	1551	6.0	2217	1.8
29	TU	0415	6.0	1027	1.8	1630	6.3	2252	1.6
30	W	0450	6.3	1102	1.6	1704	6.6	2324	1.4
31	TH	0522	6.5	1134	1.4	1736	6.7	2354	1.3

NOVEMBER

Date	Day	Time	m	Time	m	Time	m	Time	m
1	F ●	0552	6.7	1205	1.3	1806	6.7		
2	SA	0023	1.3	0622	6.8	1235	1.3	1836	6.7
3	SU	0052	1.3	0652	6.8	1305	1.3	1906	6.7
4	M	0121	1.4	0722	6.7	1337	1.5	1937	6.5
5	TU	0151	1.6	0754	6.5	1411	1.7	2010	6.3
6	W	0224	1.8	0828	6.3	1448	1.9	2047	6.0
7	TH	0301	2.1	0909	6.0	1532	2.2	2133	5.7
8	F	0348	2.4	1002	5.7	1630	2.4	2236	5.4
9	SA ◐	0453	2.7	1116	5.5	1750	2.5	2359	5.2
10	SU	0626	2.7	1242	5.6	1920	2.3		
11	M	0126	5.4	0754	2.4	1400	5.9	2032	1.9
12	TU	0237	5.9	0900	1.9	1503	6.4	2131	1.5
13	W	0334	6.4	0955	1.4	1556	6.8	2222	1.1
14	TH	0424	6.8	1044	1.1	1646	7.2	2310	0.8
15	F ○	0510	7.1	1131	0.8	1733	7.3	2355	0.7
16	SA	0555	7.3	1217	0.7	1818	7.4		
17	SU	0038	0.7	0639	7.3	1301	0.8	1904	7.2
18	M	0121	0.9	0723	7.1	1346	1.0	1949	6.9
19	TU	0203	1.2	0807	6.9	1431	1.3	2033	6.5
20	W	0245	1.6	0852	6.5	1517	1.7	2120	6.0
21	TH	0330	2.0	0939	6.1	1607	2.2	2210	5.6
22	F	0420	2.4	1033	5.7	1707	2.5	2309	5.3
23	SA ◑	0523	2.7	1138	5.5	1820	2.7		
24	SU	0020	5.1	0640	2.8	1253	5.4	1935	2.6
25	M	0135	5.2	0754	2.7	1402	5.5	2037	2.4
26	TU	0238	5.4	0854	2.5	1459	5.7	2127	2.2
27	W	0328	5.7	0942	2.2	1545	6.0	2210	1.9
28	TH	0410	6.0	1024	1.9	1626	6.2	2247	1.7
29	F	0447	6.3	1102	1.7	1703	6.4	2323	1.6
30	SA	0523	6.5	1138	1.6	1739	6.5	2357	1.5

DECEMBER

Date	Day	Time	m	Time	m	Time	m	Time	m
1	SU ●	0557	6.6	1214	1.5	1813	6.5		
2	M	0030	1.5	0632	6.7	1249	1.4	1849	6.5
3	TU	0104	1.5	0707	6.7	1325	1.5	1925	6.5
4	W	0140	1.5	0744	6.6	1404	1.5	2004	6.4
5	TH	0219	1.7	0825	6.5	1446	1.6	2047	6.2
6	F	0301	1.8	0910	6.3	1532	1.8	2135	6.0
7	SA	0349	2.0	1002	6.1	1626	1.9	2231	5.8
8	SU ◐	0446	2.2	1103	6.0	1729	2.0	2336	5.6
9	M	0554	2.3	1210	5.9	1840	2.0		
10	TU	0046	5.6	0710	2.2	1319	6.0	1950	1.9
11	W	0156	5.8	0820	2.0	1426	6.2	2055	1.7
12	TH	0259	6.1	0924	1.7	1527	6.4	2154	1.5
13	F	0357	6.4	1021	1.5	1623	6.6	2248	1.3
14	SA	0450	6.7	1115	1.2	1717	6.8	2337	1.2
15	SU ○	0540	6.9	1205	1.1	1807	6.9		
16	M	0024	1.1	0628	7.0	1252	1.1	1855	6.8
17	TU	0109	1.2	0714	7.0	1338	1.1	1940	6.7
18	W	0152	1.3	0758	6.8	1422	1.3	2023	6.5
19	TH	0233	1.5	0840	6.6	1505	1.5	2105	6.2
20	F	0314	1.8	0922	6.4	1546	1.8	2146	5.9
21	SA	0355	2.0	1005	6.1	1629	2.1	2230	5.6
22	SU ◑	0438	2.3	1050	5.8	1716	2.3	2318	5.4
23	M	0529	2.5	1142	5.5	1811	2.5		
24	TU	0016	5.2	0630	2.7	1243	5.4	1915	2.6
25	W	0123	5.2	0738	2.7	1350	5.3	2021	2.6
26	TH	0229	5.3	0845	2.6	1453	5.5	2121	2.4
27	F	0325	5.5	0943	2.3	1547	5.7	2211	2.2
28	SA	0414	5.8	1032	2.1	1634	5.9	2256	1.9
29	SU	0458	6.1	1117	1.8	1717	6.1	2336	1.7
30	M ●	0539	6.4	1158	1.6	1758	6.3		
31	TU	0015	1.5	0619	6.6	1238	1.4	1839	6.5

Chart Datum: 3·71 metres below Ordnance Datum (Newlyn). HAT is 7·9 metres above Chart Datum.

4.13 TENBY

Pembrokeshire **51°40′·42N 04°41′·93W**

CHARTS AC 1179, 1076, 1482, 5620; Imray C60, 2600

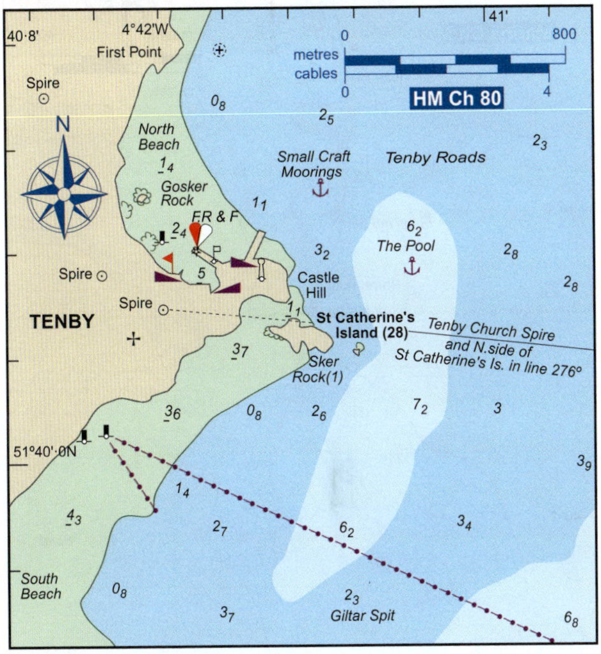

TIDES –0510 Dover; ML 4·5; Duration 0610

Standard Port MILFORD HAVEN (⟵)

Times				Height (metres)			
High Water		Low Water		MHWS	MHWN	MLWN	MLWS
0100	0800	0100	0700	7·0	5·2	2·5	0·7
1300	2000	1300	1900				
Differences TENBY							
–0015	–0010	–0015	–0020	+1·4	+1·1	+0·5	+0·2
STACKPOLE QUAY (7M W of Caldey Island)							
–0005	+0025	–0010	–0010	+0·9	+0·7	+0·2	+0·3

SHELTER Good, but hbr dries up to 5m. 12 cylindrical GRP fitted with mooring eyes, but not strops in deep water off North Beach. Sheltered ⚓s, depending on wind direction, to NE in Tenby Roads, in Lydstep Haven (2·5M SW), and around Caldey Is as follows: Priory Bay to the N but shallow, Jones Bay (NE), Drinkim Bay (E) or Sandtop Bay (W).

NAVIGATION WPT 51°40′·02N 04°38′·08W, 279°/2·2M to monument on Castle Hill. The ⊕ WPT (off chartlet) is 2ca W of DZ2 SPM lit buoy. Beware Woolhouse Rks (3·6m) 1·5M SExE of the Hbr, marked by lit SCM buoy; and Sker Rk (1m high) closer in off St Catherine's Island (28m). From the W, Caldey Sound is navigable with care between Eel Pt SHM and Giltar Spit PHM lit buoys. Approaching Tenby Roads, keep outside the line of mooring buoys and look out for swimmers. Tenby is a popular triathlon training destination. For adjacent Firing ranges, see overleaf. Caldey Island is private and no landing without permission from the Abbot.

LIGHTS AND MARKS See 4.3 and chartlet. Church spire transit N side of St Catherine's Is 276°. FR 7m 7M on pier hd. Inside hbr, FW 6m 1M marks landing steps PHM beacon (unlit) marks outcrop from Gosker Rk on beach close N of hbr ent. Hbr is floodlit.

COMMUNICATIONS (Code 01834) Dr 844161; Ⓗ 842040. HM 842717 (end May-end Sept), Mobile 07977 609947.
Ch 16, 80 (listening during HO).

FACILITIES Hbr (<4·2m). **Town** (Swansea; and a small airfield at Haverfordwest).

OTHER ADJACENT HARBOURS (See AC 5620)

SAUNDERSFOOT, Pembrokeshire, **51°42′·60N 04°41′·76W**. AC 1179, 1076, 1482. HW –0510 on Dover; ML 4·4m; Duration 0605. See 4.13. A half-tide hbr with good shelter, but there may be a surge in prolonged E winds. On appr, beware buoys marking restricted area (power boats, etc) between Coppett Hall Pt and Perry's Pt. Keep a lookout for swimmers especially those triathlon training. may be available (see HM), or moorings in the middle. Pier hd lt Fl R 5s 6m 7M on stone cupola. VHF: HM 11 16. HM ☎(01834) 812094/(Home 831389). Facilities: 6 (on SW wall). **Town** Ⓑ (Tenby/Saundersfoot).

CARMARTHEN, Carmarthenshire, **51°46′·27N 04°22′·53W**. AC 1179, 1076. HW –0455 on Dover. See 4.14. R Towy and Taf dry. Beware Carmarthen Bar in S winds F4 and over with strong sp streams. Nav info is available from Carmarthen Bar Navigation Committee ☎ (01267) 231250 or YC's. Appr on N'ly hdg toward Wharley Pt, leaving DZ8 & 9 buoys 5ca to stbd. Chan shifts frequently and is unmarked so local knowledge reqd unless conditions ideal. ⚓ in mid-stream or s at R Towy YC off Ferryside (7M below Carmarthen) or R Towey Boat Club 1M N on W bank. 4 power lines cross in last 2·5M before Carmarthen, clearance 7·4m. **R Towy YC** ☎(01267) 238356, . **R Towy BC** ☎(01267) 238316. **Town** Ⓑ (Cardiff).

4.14 BURRY PORT

Carmarthenshire **51°40′·52N 04°14′·93W** (Burry Port) ✿✿◊◊✿

CHARTS AC 5608 1179, 1076, 5620; Imray C59, C60, 2600

TIDES –0500 Dover; ML 4·7; Duration 0555

Standard Port MILFORD HAVEN (⟵)

Times				Height (metres)			
High Water		Low Water		MHWS	MHWN	MLWN	MLWS
0100	0800	0100	0700	7·0	5·2	2·5	0·7
1300	2000	1300	1900				
Differences BURRY PORT							
+0003	+0003	+0007	+0007	+1·6	+1·4	+0·5	+0·4
LLANELLI							
–0003	–0003	+0150	+0020	+0·8	+0·6	ND	ND
FERRYSIDE							
0000	–0010	+0220	0000	–0·3	–0·7	–1·7	–0·6
CARMARTHEN							
+0010	0000	DR	DR	–4·4	–4·8	DR	DR

SHELTER Good in Burry Port Marina via lock with flapgate controlled by R/G lts. Access HW±2 (max) over sill depth 2·5m. Sp tides run hard. Note: If bad weather precludes access, especially in W'lies, see 4.13 for ⚓s around Caldey Island.

NAVIGATION WPT 51°36′·50N 04°23′·00W, 090°/2·5M to Burry Holms, then about 5M to Burry Port over Lynch Sands which dry approx 1·5m. Carmarthen Bar and the approaches to Burry Port should not be attempted in W winds >F5, nor at night. Depths are changeable. Pendine Range may be active (look for red flags) but clear range procedures are in force and there are no restrictions on navigation.

From close NW of Burry Holms, with sufficient rise of tide, track 015° for 2·5M with the W edge of Burry Holms in transit astern with Worms Head. When Whiteford lighthouse (disused) bears 086° alter to approx 065° until Barrel Post bears 015°.

Near approaches to the harbour are marked by a buoyed channel, dries 3.2m. Barrel Post should not be rounded too close.

LIGHTS AND MARKS Whiteford lt ho is conspic, but no longer lit. On head of W bkwtr is Barrel post; 1½ca N is conspic old lt ho (W tr, R top) Fl 5s 7m 6½M, and flagstaff.

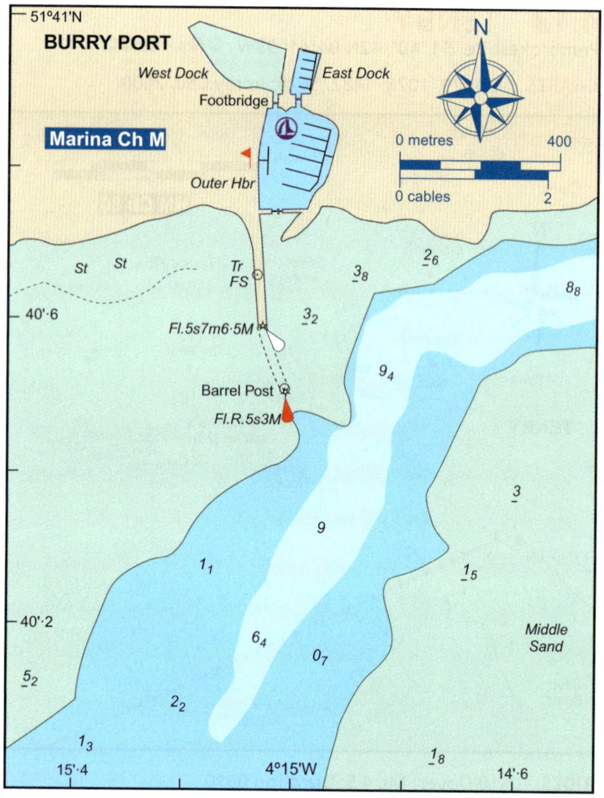

COMMUNICATIONS (Code 01554); Pendine Range (01994) 453243 Ext 240; Dr 832240. HM 835691, mob (emergencies only) 07817 395710. Marina Ch M (HO).

FACILITIES **Burry Port Marina** 450 inc ♥, £2·25, max LOA 11m, max draught 1·5m; **Burry Port YC**; **Services**. **Town** (approx 1M), ⓑ ✕ ⇌ ✈ (Cardiff).

4.15 SWANSEA

Swansea 51°36′·43N 03°55′·67W

CHARTS AC 1179, 1165, 1161, 5608; Imray C59, 2600

TIDES –0500 Dover; ML 5·2; Duration 0620

Standard Port MILFORD HAVEN (⟵)

Times				Height (metres)			
High Water		Low Water		MHWS	MHWN	MLWN	MLWS
0100	0800	0100	0700	7·0	5·2	2·5	0·7
1300	2000	1300	1900				
Differences *SWANSEA*							
+0004	*+0006*	*–0006*	*–0003*	*+2·6*	*+2·1*	*+0·7*	*+0·3*
MUMBLES							
+0001	+0003	–0012	–0005	+2·5	+2·0	+0·8	+0·4
PORT TALBOT							
0000	*+0005*	*–0010*	*–0005*	*+2·7*	*+2·1*	*+1·0*	*+0·4*
PORTHCAWL							
+0005	+0010	–0010	–0005	+2·9	+2·3	+0·8	+0·3

SHELTER Very good in marina.

NAVIGATION WPT 51°35′·53N 03°56′·08W (SHM buoy) 020°/0·92M to E bkwtr lt. Keep seaward of Mixon Shoal. When N of SW Inner Green Grounds (SWIGG) SCM lt buoy keep to W of dredged chan and clear of commercial ships. *Yachts must motor in approaches and in harbour*, max speed 4kn. In Swansea Bay tidal streams flow anti-clockwise for 9½hrs (Swansea HW–3½ to +6), with at times a race off Mumbles Hd. From HW–6 to –3 the stream reverses, setting N past Mumbles Hd towards Swansea.

LOCKS Enter via R Tawe barrage locks, which operate on request HW±4½ (co-ordinated with the marina lock), 0700-2200BST; out of season, 0700-1900UT, but to 2200 at w/ends. There are pontoons in both locks.

Vessels usually exit Tawe barrage locks at H+00, and enter at H+30. Locks are closed when ht of tide falls to 1·5m above CD, usually at MLWS. At sp, do not enter river until LW+1½. Two large Or holding buoys below barrage in mid-stream; also, at W side of barrage lock, a landing pontoon (dries, foul ground).

LIGHTS AND MARKS See 4.3 and chartlet. Mumbles Hd, Fl (4) 20s 35m 16M, is 3M SSW of hbr ent. A conspic TV mast (R lts) NNE of hbr is almost aligned with the fairway. Ldg lts 020° mark E side of chan dredged 3m. When N of Swansea Middle West (QR) and Swansea Middle East (QG) chan buoys stay inside dredged chan. Barrage lock lit by 2FR/FG (vert) to seaward.

Port Traffic sigs are conspic at W side of ent to King's Dock; there are 9 lts, ● or ●, arranged in a 3 x 3 frame. Yachts arriving must obey the middle lt in left column:

- [Red] = Do not enter the river; hold SW of W Pier.
- [Green] = Yachts may enter the river, keeping to mid-chan, then to W of holding buoys.

Lock Master will advise on tfc movements Ch 18.

Lock sigs for barrage and marina locks alike are:

- [Red over Red] = Lock closed. Do not proceed
- [Red] = Wait
- [Green] = Enter with caution
- [Red over Green] = Free flow operating; proceed with caution

COMMUNICATIONS (Code 01792) 205666; Dr 653452; DVLA (for SSR) 783355. HM 653787; Barrage 456014.

Barrage, *Tawe Lock* Ch 18. *Swansea Marina* Ch **80**. For commercial docks call *Swansea Docks Radio* VHF Ch14 (H24).

FACILITIES Swansea Marina (340+50) ☎470310, £2·75, lock 9m wide (25t) (1t) ACA, ice, wi-fi.

Swansea Yacht & Sub Aqua Club (SY & SAC) ☎654863, No visitors, (5t static).

City

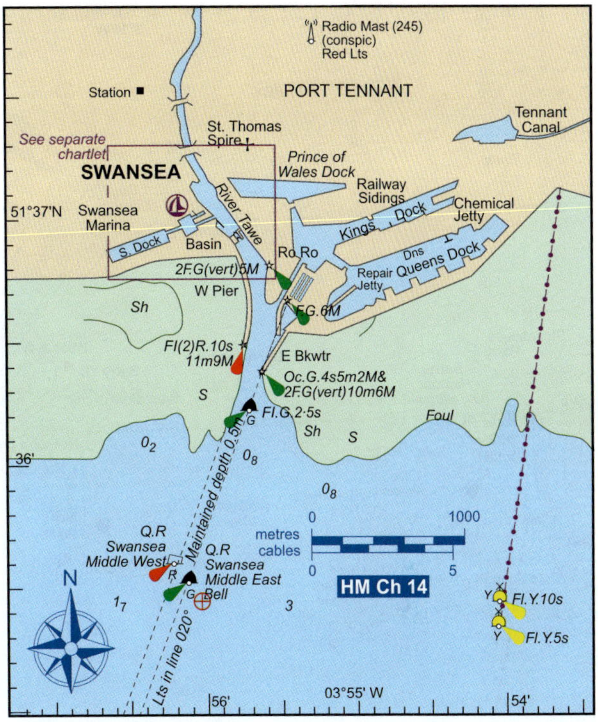

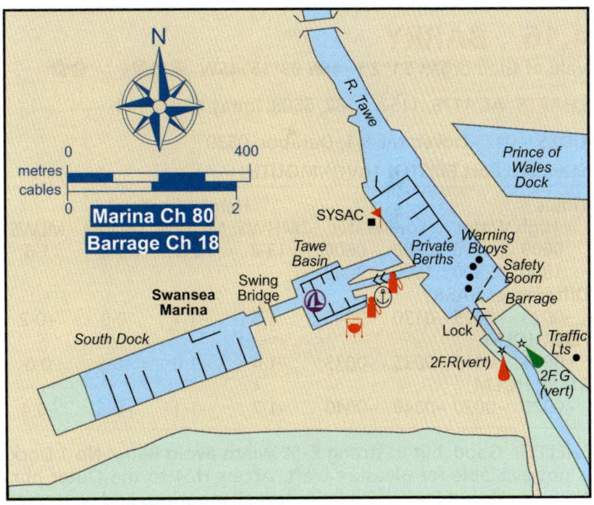

ADJACENT HARBOURS AND ANCHORAGES

Mumbles, 51°34′·2N 03°58′·2W. Good ⚓ in W'lies 5ca N of Mumbles **Bristol Chan YC** ☎(01792) 366000; **Mumbles YC** ☎369321, (hire).

R Neath, 51°37′·88N 03°49′·97W. Ent over bar HW±2½ via 1·5M chan, marked/lit training wall to stbd. Tfc info from *Neath Pilot* VHF Ch 77, if on stn. **Monkstone Marina,** W bank just S of bridge, dries 4m: , 2 Y s, (15t) . Visitors welcome. **Monkstone C & SC,** ☎(01792) 812229; VHF Ch **M** (occas).

PORTHCAWL, Bridgend, **51°28′·48N 03°42′·02W.** AC 1165, 1169. HW –0500 on Dover; ML 5·3m. See 4.15. Hbr protected by bkwtr running SE from Porthcawl Pt. Beware rk ledges and appr drying 5m above CD. Porthcawl lt ho, F WRG (see 4.3). Tidal streams off bkwtr can reach 6kn at Sp. 3 s or ⚓ approx 3ca SSE of lt ho. Look out for swimmers. Marina access gate opens HW±3, R/G tfc lts, sill 3.5m above CD; by arrangement, HM ☎(01656) 815715 VHF Ch 80. Facilities: 70 . **Porthcawl Hbr B C** ☎782342. **Town** (Bridgend) ✈(Cardiff).

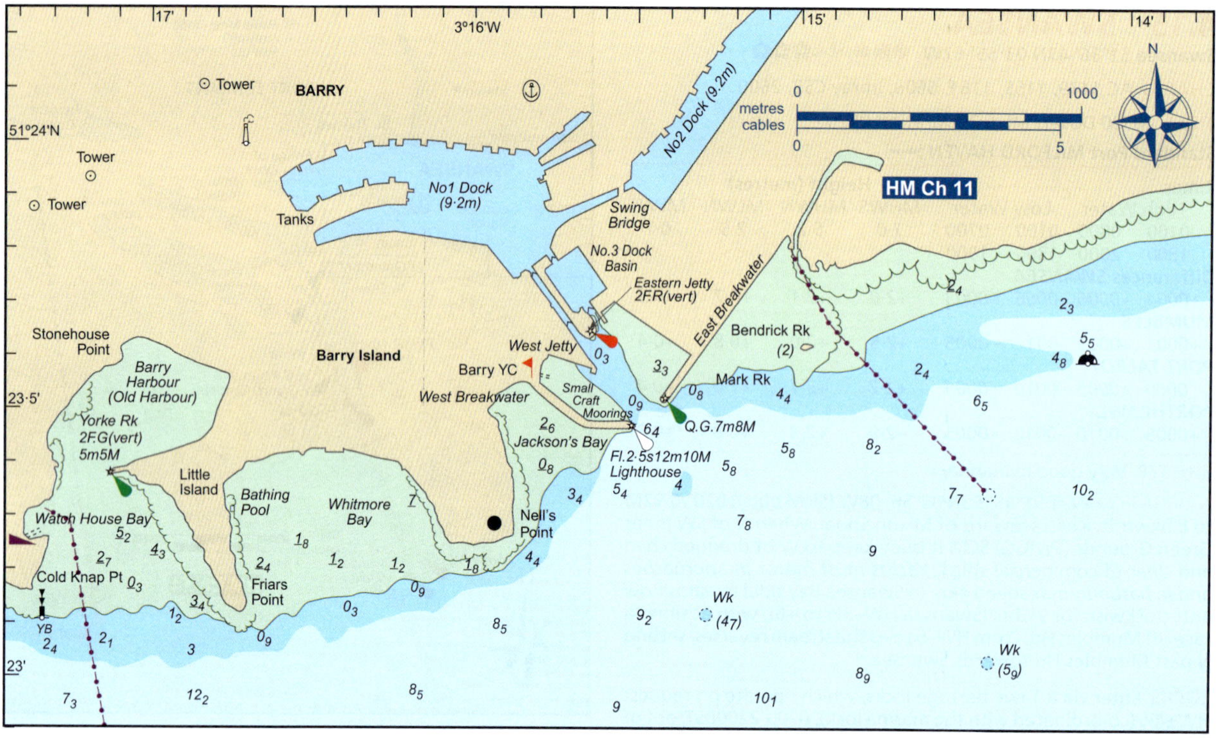

4.16 BARRY

Vale of Glamorgan **51°23'·48N 03°15'·45W**

CHARTS AC 1179, 1152, 1182, 5608; Imray C59, 2600

TIDES –0423 Dover; ML 6·1; Duration 0630

Standard Port BRISTOL (AVONMOUTH) (⟶)

Times				Height (metres)			
High Water		Low Water		MHWS	MHWN	MLWN	MLWS
0600	1100	0300	0800	13·2	9·8	3·8	1·0
1800	2300	1500	2000				
Differences BARRY							
–0025	–0025	–0130	–0045	–1·5	–1·1	0·0	+0·2
FLAT HOLM							
–0015	–0015	–0035	–0035	–1·4	–1·0	–0·5	0·0
STEEP HOLM							
–0020	–0020	–0040	–0040	–1·7	–1·1	–0·5	–0·4

SHELTER Good, but in strong E–SE winds avoid Barry; No 1 Dock is not available for pleasure craft. Access H24 to the Outer hbr. No mooring or anchorage, but Barry YC administers all moorings and welcomes visitors. Temporary mooring may be available from Bristol Pilots on request.

NAVIGATION WPT 51°23'·03N 03°15'·08W, 332°/0·53M to entrance. Beware heavy commercial traffic. Approaching from E keep well out from the shore. Strong tidal stream across entrance.

LIGHTS AND MARKS Welsh Water Barry West PHM buoy, Fl R 5s, and Merkur PHM buoy, Fl R 2·5s, lie respectively 217°/1·5M and 191°/1·65M from harbour entrance. W bkwtr Fl 2·5s 10M. E bkwtr QG 8M.

COMMUNICATIONS (Code 01446) Dr 733355. HM 0870 609 6699. BY 678186.

Barry Radio VHF Ch **11** 10 16 (HW–4 to HW+3); tidal info on request. *Bristol Pilot* via Ch 16 may advise on vacant moorings.

FACILITIES **Barry YC** (130) ☎735511, approaches dry approx 2m; (50t).

Town (2M) (2M) Ⓑ ✈ (Cardiff).

4.17 CARDIFF/PENARTH

Vale of Glamorgan **51°26'·74N 03°09'·92W** (marina)

CHARTS AC 1179, 1176, 1182, 5608; Imray C59, 2600

TIDES –0425 Dover; ML 6·4; Duration 0610

Standard Port BRISTOL (AVONMOUTH) (⟶)

Times				Height (metres)			
High Water		Low Water		MHWS	MHWN	MLWN	MLWS
0600	1100	0300	0800	13·2	9·8	3·8	1·0
1800	2300	1500	2000				
Differences CARDIFF							
–0015	*–0015*	*–0035*	*–0030*	*–0·9*	*–0·7*	*+0·2*	*+0·2*
NEWPORT							
–0005	*–0010*	*–0015*	*–0015*	*–0·9*	*–0·9*	*–0·2*	*–0·2*
CHEPSTOW (River Wye)							
+0020	+0020	ND	ND	ND	ND	ND	ND

NOTE: At Newport the ht of LW does not normally fall below MLWS. Tidal hts are based on a minimum river flow; max flow may raise ht of LW by as much as 0·3m.

SHELTER Very good in marinas. See above for barrage locks. Waiting trot berths in outer hbr; or ⚓ off Penarth seafront in W'lies; in E'lies cramped ⚓ off Alexandra Dock ent in 2m.

NAVIGATION WPT 51°24'·03N 03°08'·81W (2½ca SW of S Cardiff SCM lt buoy), 349°/2·9M to barrage locks.

The outer approaches from W or SW are via Breaksea lt float and N of One Fathom Bk. Keep S of Lavernock Spit SCM lt buoy and NW of Flat Holm and Wolves NCM lt buoy drying rk. From NE, drying ledges and shoals extend >1M offshore. From E, appr via Monkstone Lt ho and S Cardiff SCM buoy. Ranny Spit (dries 0·4m) is 3½ca to the W, and Cardiff Grounds (dries 5·4m) 3½ca to the E.

The Wrach Chan is buoyed/lit and dredged 1·2m; it passes 1½ca E of Penarth Hd. The locks appr chan, is dredged 0·7m below CD. Pont Y Werin Br opens on request to Barrage Control. Closed air draught 4.5m. IPTS control traffic.

Do not impede merchant ships, especially those entering/leaving Alexandra Dock.

Cardiff Bay Barrage and Marina lock

- Call *Barrage Control* VHF Ch 18 or ☎02920 700234 to request lock-in or lock-out. Waiting berth on a barge in outer hbr.
- If entering near LW ask Barrage Control for up-to-date depths.
- Subject to VHF instructions, enter the outer hbr (Wpt 51°26′·71N 03°09′·84W) and lock in.
- IPTS (sigs 1, 2, 3, 5) are shown at lock ent.
- Departures on H and H +30. Arrivals at H +15 and H +45.
- Lock into marina operates H24 on free-flow from the bay.

LIGHTS AND MARKS Directional light, Oc WRG 10s 5m3M, on a W metal post marks Wrach Channel. SPM Fl Y 3s mark the 5kn limit.

COMMUNICATIONS (Code 02920) 397020; Dr 415258; HM 400500; Barrage control 700234; Cardiff Bay Authority 877900.

Port VHF Ch **14** 16 (HW–4 to HW+3). *Barrage Control* Ch 18 H24. Penarth Quays Marina Ch 80 H24. Cardiff Marina Ch M.

FACILITIES **Penarth Marina** penarth@boatfolk.co.uk ☎705021, H24, 350+Ⓥ welcome, £3·50 (short stay £17), max draught 3m, lock width 7·3m; (0930-1630, E pontoon) Ⓔ (20t) (20t) ACA.

Penarth YC ☎ 708196.

Mermaid Quay Ⓥ on pontoons (£1/craft/hr) near city centre; many Rs and Bars.

Cardiff Marina www.themarinegroup.co.uk ☎396078, mob 07784 928592; 320 inc 50Ⓥ £3·85, short stay £15, Ⓔ (50t) (4½t) (short walk).

Cardiff YC ☎463697, (floating pontoon).

Cardiff Bay YC ☎226575.

City Ⓑ (15 mins).

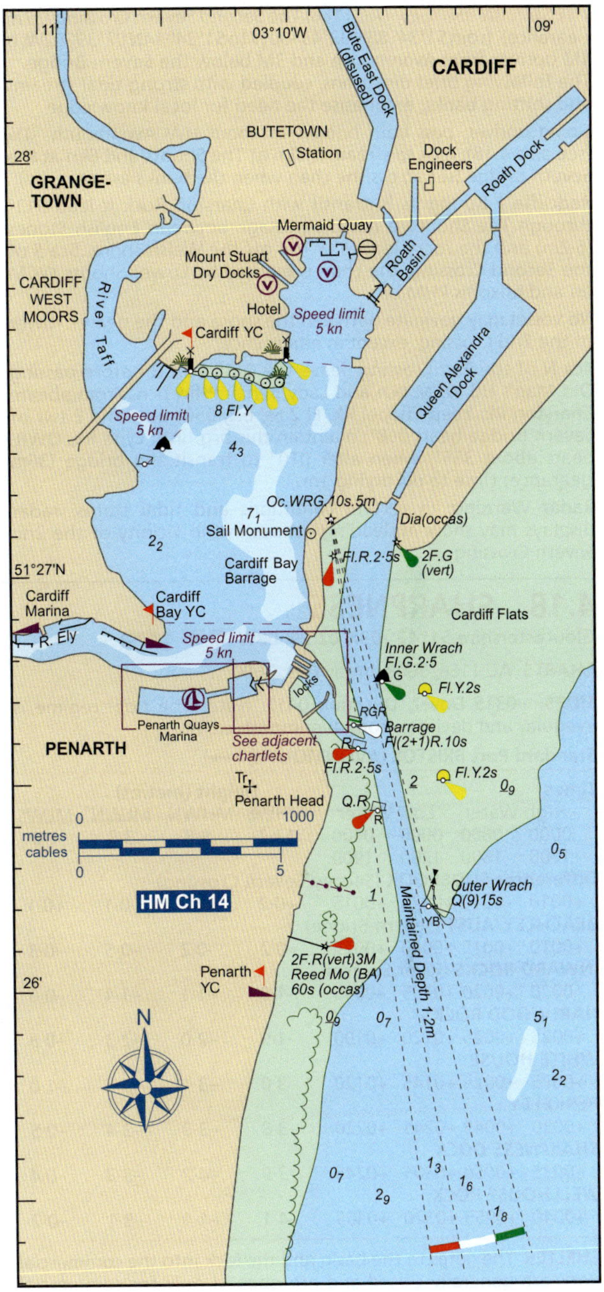

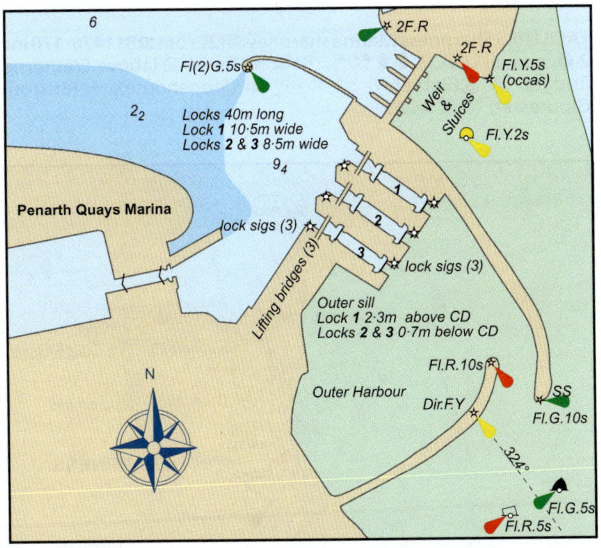

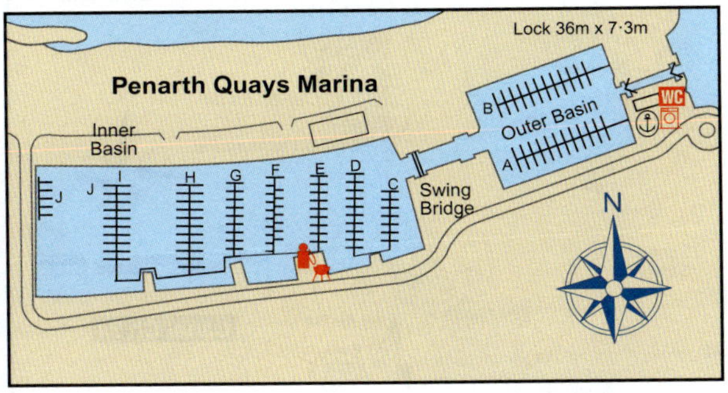

ADJACENT HARBOUR

NEWPORT, Newport, **51°32′·95N 02°59′·13W**. AC 1179, 1152, 1176, 5608. HW –0425 on Dover; ML 6·0m; Duration 0620. See 4.17. A commercial port controlled by ABP, but a safe shelter for yachts. Enter R Usk over bar (approx 0·5m) E of West Usk buoy, QR, and follow buoyed and lit chan to S Lock ent; turn NE (ldg lts 062°) for yacht moorings on S side between power stn pier and YC. Beware overhead cables in Julian's Pill, clearance 3·8m.

Lights, see 4.3. East Usk lt ho Fl (2) WRG 10s. Ldg lts 062°, both FG. Alexandra Dock, S lock W pier head 2 FR (vert) 9/7m 6M. E pier head 2 FG (vert) 9/7m 6M.

Port VHF, *Newport Radio,* and VTS: Ch 09, **71**, 74 (HW ±4). HM (ABP) ☎0870 609 6699. Facilities: Ⓔ. **Newport and Uskmouth SC** M. **Town** All facilities.

THE SEVERN BRIDGES (AC 1166) The Second Severn Crossing (37m clearance), from 51°34'·88N 02°43'·80W to 51°34'·14N 02°39'·82W, is 4M upriver from Avonmouth and 3M below the Severn Bridge. The following brief directions, coupled with strong tidal streams and shifting banks, emphasise the need for local knowledge.

Going upriver, pass both bridges at about HW Avonmouth –1¼ (see also 4.18); max sp stream is 8kn at The Shoots and 6kn at the Severn Bridge (set across the chan when the banks are covered).

Redcliffe F Bu ldg lts in transit with Charston Rock lt lead 013° through The Shoots, a narrow passage between English Stones (6·2m) and the rocky ledges (5·1m) off the Welsh shore. 5ca S of the Second Crossing, the chan is marked by Lower Shoots WCM bn and Mixoms PHM bn.

No vessel may navigate between the shore and the nearer Tower of the 2nd Crossing, except in emergency.

4ca N of the 2nd Crossing, leave the 013° transit before passing Old Man's Hd WCM bcn and Lady Bench PHM bcn. From abeam Charston Rk, keep Chapel Rk, Fl 2·6s, brg 050° until the E twr of Severn Bridge bears 068°; maintain this brg until Lyde Rk, QWR, bears about 355°, when alter 010° to transit the bridge (36m clearance) close to rks drying 1m.

Radar Warning. In certain conditions and tidal states, radar displays may show misleading echoes in the vicinity of the 2nd Severn Crossing.

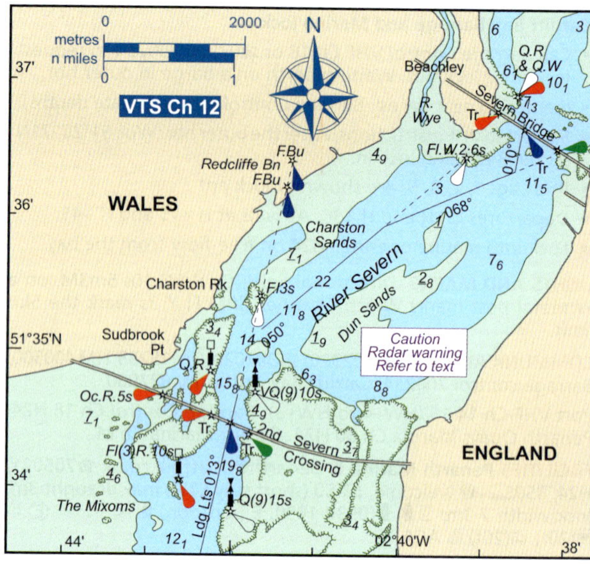

4.18 SHARPNESS

Gloucestershire **51°43'·03N 02°29'·08W**

CHARTS AC 1166, 5608, Imray C59, 2600

TIDES –0315 Dover; Duration 0415. Note: The tidal regime is irregular and deviates from Avonmouth curve.

Standard Port BRISTOL (AVONMOUTH) (⟶)

Times				Height (metres)			
High Water		Low Water		MHWS	MHWN	MLWN	MLWS
0000	0600	0000	0700	13·2	9·8	3·8	1·0
1200	1800	1200	1900				
Differences SUDBROOK (Second Severn Crossing)							
+0010	+0010	+0025	+0015	+0·2	+0·1	–0·1	+0·1
BEACHLEY/AUST (Severn Bridge)							
+0010	+0015	+0040	+0025	–0·2	–0·2	–0·5	–0·3
INWARD ROCKS (River Severn)							
+0020	+0020	+0105	+0045	–1·0	–1·1	–1·4	–0·6
NARLWOOD ROCKS							
+0025	+0025	+0120	+0100	–1·9	–2·0	–2·3	–0·8
WHITE HOUSE							
+0025	+0025	+0145	+0120	–3·0	–3·1	–3·6	–1·0
BERKELEY							
+0030	+0045	+0245	+0220	–3·8	–3·9	–3·4	–0·5
SHARPNESS DOCK							
+0035	*+0050*	*+0305*	*+0245*	*–3·9*	*–4·2*	*–3·3*	*–0·4*
WELLHOUSE ROCK							
+0040	+0055	+0320	+0305	–4·1	–4·4	–3·1	–0·2

SHELTER The gates to the basin and the lock into the commercial dock are generally closed and are opened only for commercial shipping movements and other craft which have made the required booking and given appropriate notice (min. 24hrs). It is essential for arrangements to be made by contacting the Pierhead office which is generally manned during daylight tides, HW-4 to HW+1 (if unmanned leave a message). Plan your passage to arrive no sooner than HW–1 and no later than HW. Detailed information on lock fees and canal licences is available from the Pierhead office. Comprehensive information on the passage from Avonmouth is available from Gloucester Harbour Trustees. Fog signals are available from Sharpness Radio on VHF Ch 13 or Pierhead office.

NAVIGATION Use transits shown on AC 1166. Study guidance notes from Gloucester Harbour Trustees in good time.

- Leave King Road, Avonmouth (17M downriver) not before HW Sharpness –3, to be off Hbr ent about HW –½. Stem strong flood S of F Bu lt; beware tidal eddy.
- Do not proceed above the Severn Bridge except HW–1¼ /+2. There is a 5hr flood and a 7hr ebb.

LIGHTS AND MARKS Lights as chartlet, but night passage not advised without local knowledge/pilot (07774 226143).

COMMUNICATIONS (Code 01453) Ⓗ 810777. Pierhead 511968 (HW–4 to HW+1). Gloucester Harbour Trustees www.gloucesterharbourtrustees.org ☎811913 (HO).

Call Gloucester and Sharpness Canal Ch 74 for bridges (no locks). Call *Bristol VTS* VHF Ch 12 when passing reporting points inwards/outwards E/W Grounds PHM, Welsh Hook SCM and at Lower Shoots Bcn.

FACILITIES Sharpness Marina sharpness@f2s.com ☎811476. 170 inc 2 Ⓥ, poa all LOA. **Town** (above Fretherne Bridge), ✉ Ⓑ(Berkeley), ✕, ⇌ (Stonehouse), ✈ (Bristol). Gloucester: ACA.

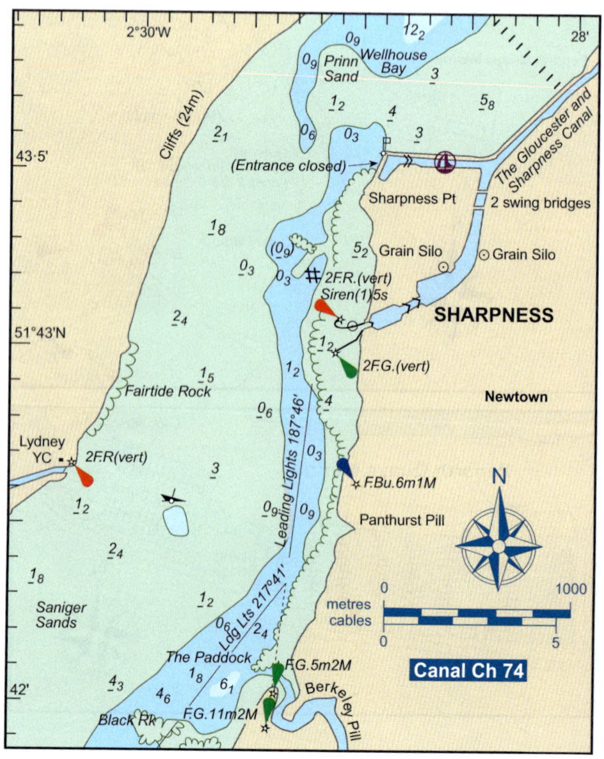

STANDARD TIME (UT)
For Summer Time add ONE hour in **non-shaded areas**

BRISTOL (AVONMOUTH) LAT 51°30′N LONG 2°44′W

TIMES AND HEIGHTS OF HIGH AND LOW WATERS

Dates in red are SPRINGS
Dates in blue are NEAPS

YEAR **2024**

JANUARY

Date	Time	m	Time	m	Time	m	Time	m
1 M	0416	2.7	1010	11.5	1635	2.9	2231	11.1
2 TU	0445	2.8	1043	11.1	1706	3.0	2304	10.7
3 W	0519	3.0	1119	10.8	1743	3.2	2343	10.4
4 TH ◑	0601	3.3	1203	10.4	1829	3.5		
5 F	0032	10.0	0654	3.7	1300	10.1	1926	3.8
6 SA	0135	9.8	0802	3.9	1409	10.1	2040	3.9
7 SU	0251	10.0	0923	3.8	1524	10.3	2202	3.7
8 M	0405	10.5	1038	3.3	1633	10.9	2314	3.1
9 TU	0507	11.2	1142	2.7	1732	11.5		
10 W	0013	2.5	0601	12.0	1238	2.1	1826	12.2
11 TH	0107	2.0	0650	12.7	1333	1.7	● 1917	12.7
12 F	0200	1.7	0738	13.1	1427	1.4	2006	13.0
13 SA	0251	1.5	0826	13.4	1518	1.2	2053	13.2
14 SU	0337	1.3	0912	13.5	1604	1.1	2139	13.2
15 M	0419	1.3	0957	13.4	1645	1.1	2222	13.0
16 TU	0457	1.5	1041	13.1	1722	1.4	2304	12.6
17 W	0533	1.8	1126	12.6	1759	1.8	2348	12.0
18 TH ◐	0611	2.3	1214	11.9	1839	2.4		
19 F	0037	11.2	0654	2.9	1312	11.1	1927	3.0
20 SA	0139	10.6	0750	3.5	1424	10.5	2032	3.6
21 SU	0256	10.2	0920	3.9	1538	10.4	2203	3.7
22 M	0409	10.4	1048	3.6	1646	10.7	2316	3.3
23 TU	0512	10.9	1152	3.0	1744	11.2		
24 W	0014	2.7	0606	11.5	1245	2.5	1836	11.7
25 TH	0106	2.2	0654	12.1	1336	2.1	○ 1922	12.1
26 F	0155	1.9	0736	12.4	1423	1.9	2003	12.3
27 SA	0239	1.8	0816	12.5	1505	2.0	2040	12.3
28 SU	0318	1.9	0851	12.5	1540	2.1	2112	12.1
29 M	0348	2.1	0922	12.3	1605	2.3	2141	11.9
30 TU	0408	2.2	0950	12.0	1622	2.4	2207	11.7
31 W	0427	2.3	1017	11.8	1642	2.4	2234	11.4

FEBRUARY

Date	Time	m	Time	m	Time	m	Time	m
1 TH	0452	2.4	1045	11.5	1709	2.5	2304	11.1
2 F	0524	2.6	1119	11.1	1743	2.8	◑ 2342	10.6
3 SA	0604	3.1	1204	10.5	1826	3.3		
4 SU	0032	10.1	0656	3.7	1304	10.0	1926	3.9
5 M	0142	9.7	0815	4.1	1424	9.8	2101	4.1
6 TU	0316	9.8	0959	3.8	1559	10.2	2242	3.6
7 W	0441	10.6	1118	3.0	1714	11.1	2354	2.8
8 TH	0544	11.7	1224	2.2	1814	12.0		
9 F	0055	2.1	0638	12.7	1324	1.5	● 1906	12.9
10 SA	0153	1.4	0728	13.5	1421	1.0	1955	13.5
11 SU	0245	0.9	0814	14.0	1511	0.5	2041	13.9
12 M	0331	0.6	0859	14.2	1555	0.3	2123	13.9
13 TU	0411	0.6	0941	14.2	1632	0.5	2202	13.7
14 W	0444	0.8	1020	13.8	1702	0.9	2239	13.2
15 TH	0511	1.3	1059	13.0	1729	1.5	2315	12.3
16 F	0538	2.0	1138	12.0	1758	2.3	◐ 2354	11.3
17 SA	0610	2.8	1224	10.8	1836	3.2		
18 SU	0043	10.2	0655	3.7	1335	9.8	1932	4.0
19 M	0211	9.4	0809	4.5	1513	9.4	2111	4.5
20 TU	0346	9.5	1030	4.3	1629	9.8	2257	3.8
21 W	0456	10.3	1137	3.4	1731	10.7	2357	2.9
22 TH	0552	11.2	1230	2.5	1821	11.5		
23 F	0048	2.1	0639	12.0	1318	1.9	1905	12.1
24 SA	0136	1.6	0720	12.5	1404	1.6	○ 1944	12.5
25 SU	0221	1.4	0756	12.7	1447	1.5	2018	12.5
26 M	0301	1.4	0829	12.7	1522	1.7	2048	12.4
27 TU	0333	1.7	0859	12.5	1549	2.0	2115	12.2
28 W	0353	1.9	0924	12.3	1602	2.2	2139	12.0
29 TH	0405	2.0	0948	12.1	1613	2.2	2202	11.8

MARCH

Date	Time	m	Time	m	Time	m	Time	m
1 F	0424	2.0	1014	11.8	1636	2.2	2230	11.5
2 SA	0452	2.2	1046	11.4	1706	2.4	2305	11.0
3 SU	0526	2.7	1127	10.8	1743	3.0	◑ 2352	10.3
4 M	0610	3.4	1224	10.0	1835	3.8		
5 TU	0057	9.6	0720	4.1	1344	9.5	2001	4.4
6 W	0237	9.5	0928	4.1	1538	9.8	2223	3.9
7 TH	0423	10.4	1106	3.1	1702	10.9	2342	2.8
8 F	0530	11.7	1214	2.1	1800	12.2		
9 SA	0044	1.8	0623	12.9	1312	1.2	1851	13.2
10 SU	0139	1.0	0711	13.8	1406	0.5	● 1937	13.9
11 M	0229	0.5	0756	14.4	1453	0.1	2020	14.3
12 TU	0313	0.2	0838	14.6	1534	0.0	2100	14.3
13 W	0351	0.2	0918	14.4	1608	0.3	2137	13.9
14 TH	0421	0.6	0955	13.8	1634	0.9	2211	13.2
15 F	0444	1.3	1030	12.9	1656	1.6	2243	12.3
16 SA	0505	2.0	1105	11.7	1720	2.4	2316	11.1
17 SU	0533	2.9	1144	10.4	1754	3.4	◐ 2359	9.9
18 M	0614	3.9	1247	9.2	1847	4.3		
19 TU	0129	9.0	0729	4.7	1452	8.8	2030	4.8
20 W	0325	9.2	1014	4.5	1608	9.5	2237	4.0
21 TH	0434	10.1	1116	3.4	1708	10.5	2334	2.9
22 F	0528	11.1	1205	2.4	1756	11.5		
23 SA	0023	2.0	0613	12.0	1251	1.7	1837	12.2
24 SU	0109	1.5	0652	12.5	1336	1.4	1914	12.5
25 M	0154	1.2	0727	12.7	1418	1.3	○ 1947	12.6
26 TU	0234	1.3	0800	12.7	1454	1.5	2018	12.5
27 W	0307	1.5	0829	12.5	1522	1.8	2045	12.4
28 TH	0329	1.8	0855	12.3	1536	2.1	2109	12.2
29 F	0341	1.9	0920	12.2	1546	2.1	2133	12.0
30 SA	0400	1.9	0948	11.9	1609	2.1	2203	11.7
31 SU	0427	2.0	1022	11.5	1639	2.3	2240	11.2

APRIL

Date	Time	m	Time	m	Time	m	Time	m
1 M	0501	2.5	1105	10.8	1716	2.9	2328	10.4
2 TU ◑	0546	3.2	1202	10.0	1807	3.7		
3 W	0035	9.7	0655	4.0	1325	9.4	1934	4.4
4 TH	0219	9.6	0910	3.9	1523	9.9	2207	3.8
5 F	0403	10.5	1048	2.9	1642	11.1	2323	2.6
6 SA	0508	11.9	1153	1.8	1739	12.3		
7 SU	0021	1.6	0601	13.0	1248	1.0	1828	13.4
8 M	0114	0.9	0648	13.9	1339	0.4	● 1912	14.0
9 TU	0202	0.4	0732	14.3	1426	0.1	1954	14.2
10 W	0246	0.2	0814	14.4	1506	0.2	2033	14.1
11 TH	0324	0.4	0853	14.1	1540	0.6	2110	13.7
12 F	0355	0.9	0930	13.4	1606	1.2	2144	12.9
13 SA	0418	1.6	1005	12.4	1627	1.9	2216	12.0
14 SU	0439	2.3	1039	11.3	1651	2.6	2249	10.9
15 M	0508	3.0	1117	10.1	1725	3.5	◐ 2330	9.8
16 TU	0550	3.9	1217	9.0	1818	4.4		
17 W	0059	9.0	0706	4.6	1420	8.8	1956	4.8
18 TH	0252	9.2	0917	4.5	1533	9.4	2156	4.1
19 F	0357	10.0	1038	3.5	1630	10.3	2258	3.1
20 SA	0450	10.9	1128	2.6	1718	11.2	2347	2.3
21 SU	0535	11.7	1215	2.0	1800	11.9		
22 M	0033	1.7	0615	12.2	1258	1.6	1837	12.3
23 TU	0117	1.5	0652	12.4	1340	1.5	○ 1912	12.5
24 W	0157	1.5	0726	12.5	1418	1.6	1944	12.5
25 TH	0232	1.6	0758	12.4	1448	1.8	2014	12.4
26 F	0300	1.8	0829	12.3	1510	2.0	2043	12.2
27 SA	0321	1.9	0859	12.1	1528	2.1	2113	12.1
28 SU	0345	1.9	0932	11.9	1553	2.1	2147	11.8
29 M	0415	2.1	1011	11.5	1626	2.4	2229	11.3
30 TU	0453	2.5	1057	10.9	1707	2.9	2320	10.6

Chart Datum: 6·50 metres below Ordnance Datum (Newlyn). HAT is 14·7 metres above Chart Datum.

STANDARD TIME (UT)
For Summer Time add ONE hour in **non-shaded areas**

BRISTOL (AVONMOUTH) LAT 51°30′N LONG 2°44′W

TIMES AND HEIGHTS OF HIGH AND LOW WATERS

Dates in red are SPRINGS
Dates in blue are NEAPS

YEAR 2024

MAY

Date	Day	Time m	Time m	Time m	Time m	Moon
1	W	0542 3.1	1156 10.2	1803 3.6		◑
2	TH	0030 10.1	0657 3.6	1317 9.9	1934 4.0	
3	F	0206 10.2	0847 3.4	1456 10.3	2135 3.4	
4	SA	0332 10.9	1014 2.6	1610 11.2	2249 2.5	
5	SU	0437 11.9	1119 1.8	1708 12.2	2348 1.7	
6	M	0531 12.8	1216 1.2	1758 13.1		
7	TU	0041 1.1	0620 13.5	1307 0.8	1844 13.6	
8	W	0131 0.8	0706 13.7	1354 0.6	1927 13.7	●
9	TH	0217 0.7	0749 13.7	1436 0.7	2007 13.6	
10	F	0257 0.9	0831 13.3	1513 1.1	2046 13.1	
11	SA	0332 1.4	0910 12.7	1543 1.7	2123 12.5	
12	SU	0359 2.0	0947 11.9	1608 2.2	2157 11.7	
13	M	0424 2.6	1024 11.0	1635 2.8	2233 10.9	
14	TU	0455 3.1	1103 10.2	1710 3.4	2317 10.1	
15	W	0539 3.7	1156 9.5	1800 4.0		◐
16	TH	0024 9.5	0642 4.1	1320 9.1	1915 4.3	
17	F	0158 9.4	0759 4.1	1439 9.4	2036 4.1	
18	SA	0305 9.9	0915 3.7	1538 10.0	2151 3.5	
19	SU	0400 10.5	1025 3.1	1629 10.7	2253 2.8	
20	M	0448 11.1	1122 2.6	1715 11.4	2346 2.3	
21	TU	0532 11.6	1212 2.2	1756 11.9		
22	W	0033 1.9	0613 12.0	1257 1.9	1836 12.2	
23	TH	0116 1.7	0652 12.2	1339 1.8	1913 12.4	○
24	F	0157 1.7	0730 12.2	1416 1.9	1949 12.4	
25	SA	0234 1.7	0808 12.2	1450 1.9	2025 12.3	
26	SU	0308 1.8	0847 12.1	1520 2.0	2103 12.2	
27	M	0342 1.9	0927 11.9	1552 2.2	2144 11.9	
28	TU	0418 2.1	1011 11.6	1629 2.4	2230 11.6	
29	W	0501 2.3	1059 11.3	1714 2.7	2323 11.2	
30	TH	0553 2.6	1156 10.9	1811 3.1		◑
31	F	0026 10.9	0659 2.8	1303 10.7	1926 3.2	

JUNE

Date	Day	Time m	Time m	Time m	Time m	Moon
1	SA	0142 10.9	0814 2.8	1420 10.8	2052 3.1	
2	SU	0256 11.2	0930 2.5	1531 11.2	2208 2.6	
3	M	0401 11.7	1040 2.2	1633 11.8	2313 2.1	
4	TU	0500 12.2	1141 1.8	1728 12.3		
5	W	0009 1.7	0553 12.6	1235 1.5	1817 12.7	
6	TH	0102 1.5	0642 12.8	1325 1.4	1903 12.9	●
7	F	0151 1.4	0729 12.8	1411 1.4	1947 12.9	
8	SA	0236 1.6	0813 12.5	1453 1.6	2029 12.6	
9	SU	0317 1.9	0856 12.2	1529 2.0	2109 12.2	
10	M	0351 2.3	0936 11.7	1559 2.4	2146 11.7	
11	TU	0420 2.6	1013 11.2	1627 2.7	2223 11.2	
12	W	0449 2.9	1050 10.7	1700 3.0	2302 10.7	
13	TH	0526 3.2	1130 10.2	1740 3.3	2348 10.3	
14	F	0611 3.4	1218 9.9	1831 3.6		◐
15	SA	0044 10.0	0705 3.5	1318 9.7	1933 3.8	
16	SU	0150 9.9	0806 3.6	1424 9.9	2040 3.7	
17	M	0253 10.1	0911 3.4	1527 10.2	2148 3.4	
18	TU	0352 10.5	1019 3.1	1624 10.7	2253 2.9	
19	W	0446 11.0	1122 2.7	1716 11.3	2349 2.4	
20	TH	0536 11.5	1216 2.3	1803 11.8		
21	F	0040 2.0	0623 11.8	1305 2.0	1847 12.2	
22	SA	0129 1.8	0709 12.1	1352 1.9	1931 12.5	○
23	SU	0216 1.7	0755 12.3	1437 1.9	2015 12.6	
24	M	0302 1.7	0841 12.3	1520 1.9	2059 12.6	
25	TU	0346 1.7	0926 12.4	1600 1.9	2144 12.5	
26	W	0428 1.7	1011 12.3	1640 2.0	2229 12.4	
27	TH	0510 1.7	1056 12.1	1722 2.1	2317 12.1	
28	F	0554 1.9	1144 11.7	1807 2.3		◑
29	SA	0009 11.7	0642 2.2	1237 11.4	1900 2.7	
30	SU	0110 11.4	0736 2.5	1340 11.0	2004 3.0	

JULY

Date	Day	Time m	Time m	Time m	Time m	Moon
1	M	0218 11.1	0841 2.8	1450 10.9	2124 3.1	
2	TU	0327 11.1	0959 2.9	1559 11.0	2240 2.9	
3	W	0432 11.3	1109 2.7	1701 11.4	2344 2.6	
4	TH	0531 11.6	1209 2.4	1756 11.8		
5	F	0040 2.2	0625 11.9	1303 2.1	1847 12.2	●
6	SA	0132 2.0	0715 12.1	1354 1.9	1933 12.4	
7	SU	0222 1.9	0802 12.1	1440 1.9	2017 12.4	
8	M	0308 2.0	0845 12.1	1521 2.0	2057 12.3	
9	TU	0347 2.2	0923 11.9	1555 2.2	2133 12.0	
10	W	0417 2.4	0957 11.6	1621 2.4	2206 11.7	
11	TH	0440 2.6	1027 11.3	1645 2.6	2237 11.4	
12	F	0505 2.7	1058 11.0	1714 2.7	2310 11.0	
13	SA	0535 2.8	1132 10.6	1749 3.0	2348 10.6	◐
14	SU	0613 3.0	1214 10.3	1833 3.3		
15	M	0036 10.2	0702 3.4	1307 9.9	1933 3.7	
16	TU	0138 10.0	0805 3.7	1417 9.8	2049 3.8	
17	W	0251 10.0	0924 3.7	1533 10.1	2207 3.5	
18	TH	0403 10.4	1040 3.3	1641 10.7	2315 2.9	
19	F	0507 11.0	1145 2.7	1738 11.5		
20	SA	0014 2.3	0603 11.6	1242 2.3	1829 12.2	
21	SU	0110 1.9	0655 12.2	1338 1.9	1918 12.7	○
22	M	0206 1.6	0744 12.6	1431 1.7	2005 13.1	
23	TU	0259 1.3	0832 12.9	1520 1.4	2051 13.3	
24	W	0346 1.1	0917 13.1	1603 1.3	2135 13.4	
25	TH	0427 1.0	1000 13.1	1640 1.3	2217 13.2	
26	F	0504 1.1	1041 12.8	1714 1.5	2259 12.8	
27	SA	0538 1.5	1122 12.3	1748 1.9	2344 12.2	
28	SU	0613 2.0	1206 11.6	1825 2.5		◑
29	M	0034 11.4	0655 2.6	1259 10.9	1914 3.2	
30	TU	0140 10.6	0750 3.3	1412 10.2	2029 3.9	
31	W	0259 10.2	0917 3.8	1533 10.1	2218 3.8	

AUGUST

Date	Day	Time m	Time m	Time m	Time m	Moon
1	TH	0414 10.3	1047 3.5	1644 10.6	2329 3.2	
2	F	0519 10.8	1153 2.9	1745 11.3		
3	SA	0027 2.6	0616 11.4	1248 2.3	1836 11.9	
4	SU	0119 2.1	0705 11.9	1339 1.9	1922 12.4	●
5	M	0209 1.8	0749 12.2	1427 1.7	2003 12.6	
6	TU	0255 1.7	0828 12.3	1509 1.7	2040 12.6	
7	W	0334 1.8	0903 12.2	1544 1.8	2113 12.4	
8	TH	0404 2.1	0932 12.0	1608 2.1	2141 12.1	
9	F	0423 2.3	0958 11.8	1624 2.3	2207 11.8	
10	SA	0436 2.5	1023 11.5	1643 2.4	2232 11.5	
11	SU	0457 2.5	1050 11.1	1709 2.6	2302 11.0	
12	M	0526 2.8	1123 10.7	1743 3.0	2340 10.5	◐
13	TU	0604 3.2	1208 10.1	1829 3.7		
14	W	0035 9.9	0657 3.8	1312 9.6	1943 4.2	
15	TH	0153 9.5	0824 4.2	1446 9.6	2130 4.1	
16	F	0331 9.8	1009 3.9	1616 10.3	2253 3.3	
17	SA	0448 10.7	1125 3.1	1721 11.4		
18	SU	0000 2.4	0549 11.6	1229 2.3	1815 12.4	
19	M	0100 1.7	0642 12.5	1328 1.7	1904 13.2	○
20	TU	0157 1.2	0730 13.1	1422 1.3	1950 13.8	
21	W	0249 0.8	0816 13.6	1510 0.9	2034 14.1	
22	TH	0334 0.5	0859 13.7	1551 0.8	2116 14.1	
23	F	0412 0.6	0939 13.6	1625 0.9	2156 13.8	
24	SA	0444 0.9	1016 13.2	1654 1.3	2235 13.2	
25	SU	0511 1.5	1053 12.5	1719 1.9	2314 12.2	
26	M	0538 2.2	1131 11.6	1748 2.7	2358 11.0	◑
27	TU	0612 3.1	1218 10.5	1829 3.7		
28	W	0103 9.9	0703 4.0	1340 9.6	1940 4.6	
29	TH	0245 9.4	0844 4.6	1520 9.5	2214 4.4	
30	F	0405 9.7	1038 4.0	1634 10.2	2320 3.4	
31	SA	0509 10.6	1139 3.0	1732 11.2		

Chart Datum: 6·50 metres below Ordnance Datum (Newlyn). HAT is 14·7 metres above Chart Datum.

STANDARD TIME (UT)
For Summer Time add ONE hour in **non-shaded areas**

BRISTOL (AVONMOUTH)

LAT 51°30'N LONG 2°44'W

TIMES AND HEIGHTS OF HIGH AND LOW WATERS

Dates in red are SPRINGS
Dates in blue are NEAPS

YEAR **2024**

SEPTEMBER

Date	Day	Time	m	Time	m	Time	m	Time	m
1	SU	0012	2.5	0602	11.5	1231	2.2	1821	12.1
2	M	0101	1.8	0647	12.2	1319	1.6	1903	12.7
3	TU	0147	1.4	0726	12.6	1405	1.3	● 1941	12.9
4	W	0231	1.3	0802	12.7	1446	1.3	2015	12.9
5	TH	0309	1.5	0834	12.5	1521	1.6	2045	12.7
6	F	0339	1.8	0901	12.3	1546	2.0	2111	12.3
7	SA	0357	2.3	0925	12.0	1557	2.3	2133	12.0
8	SU	0403	2.4	0947	11.7	1611	2.4	2156	11.7
9	M	0420	2.4	1012	11.4	1634	2.5	2224	11.3
10	TU	0447	2.6	1043	10.9	1705	2.9	2302	10.7
11	W	0520	3.1	1126	10.2	1744	3.6	◐ 2354	9.9
12	TH	0606	3.9	1228	9.5	1845	4.4		
13	F	0111	9.3	0722	4.6	1407	9.3	2059	4.5
14	SA	0310	9.5	0949	4.3	1557	10.2	2241	3.5
15	SU	0434	10.6	1114	3.2	1704	11.5	2348	2.4
16	M	0533	11.9	1216	2.2	1756	12.7		
17	TU	0045	1.5	0623	12.9	1311	1.5	1844	13.6
18	W	0138	0.8	0709	13.7	1402	0.9	○ 1929	14.2
19	TH	0227	0.4	0752	14.1	1448	0.6	2012	14.5
20	F	0311	0.3	0834	14.1	1528	0.6	2053	14.4
21	SA	0347	0.5	0912	13.9	1602	0.9	2131	13.9
22	SU	0417	1.0	0949	13.3	1628	1.5	2208	13.0
23	M	0440	1.8	1024	12.4	1650	2.2	2245	11.9
24	TU	0504	2.6	1100	11.3	1716	3.1	◑ 2326	10.5
25	W	0536	3.5	1144	10.1	1755	4.1		
26	TH	0032	9.3	0626	4.5	1322	9.1	1910	5.0
27	F	0234	8.9	0828	5.1	1506	9.4	2204	4.6
28	SA	0347	9.6	1023	4.1	1613	10.2	2301	3.4
29	SU	0447	10.6	1117	3.0	1708	11.3	2348	2.4
30	M	0536	11.6	1205	2.1	1754	12.2		

OCTOBER

Date	Day	Time	m	Time	m	Time	m	Time	m
1	TU	0033	1.6	0618	12.3	1250	1.5	1834	12.8
2	W	0117	1.3	0655	12.7	1334	1.2	● 1910	13.0
3	TH	0159	1.2	0729	12.8	1415	1.3	1943	12.9
4	F	0237	1.4	0800	12.7	1450	1.6	2013	12.7
5	SA	0307	1.8	0828	12.4	1516	2.0	2039	12.4
6	SU	0325	2.2	0853	12.1	1529	2.3	2103	12.1
7	M	0333	2.4	0915	11.9	1544	2.4	2127	11.8
8	TU	0352	2.4	0942	11.6	1608	2.5	2159	11.4
9	W	0419	2.6	1016	11.1	1640	2.9	2238	10.7
10	TH	0453	3.1	1101	10.4	1720	3.5	◐ 2331	9.9
11	F	0538	3.9	1204	9.7	1820	4.3		
12	SA	0048	9.3	0653	4.6	1342	9.5	2030	4.5
13	SU	0248	9.6	0927	4.3	1533	10.3	2219	3.4
14	M	0411	10.8	1051	3.2	1638	11.6	2324	2.3
15	TU	0509	12.0	1151	2.1	1731	12.8		
16	W	0019	1.4	0558	13.1	1243	1.4	1819	13.7
17	TH	0110	0.8	0643	13.8	1333	0.9	○ 1904	14.3
18	F	0158	0.5	0726	14.1	1419	0.7	1947	14.4
19	SA	0241	0.5	0807	14.1	1500	0.8	2028	14.2
20	SU	0318	0.8	0846	13.8	1535	1.2	2108	13.6
21	M	0349	1.4	0924	13.1	1604	1.8	2147	12.7
22	TU	0415	2.1	1000	12.2	1629	2.5	2225	11.5
23	W	0440	2.9	1037	11.2	1657	3.4	2307	10.3
24	TH	0513	3.7	1124	10.1	1739	4.2	◑	
25	F	0012	9.3	0605	4.6	1301	9.3	1853	4.9
26	SA	0205	9.0	0742	5.0	1436	9.5	2124	4.6
27	SU	0314	9.6	0944	4.3	1538	10.2	2223	3.7
28	M	0410	10.4	1040	3.3	1631	11.1	2312	2.7
29	TU	0459	11.3	1128	2.4	1717	11.9	2356	2.0
30	W	0541	12.0	1214	1.8	1757	12.4		
31	TH	0039	1.6	0619	12.5	1256	1.6	1835	12.7

NOVEMBER

Date	Day	Time	m	Time	m	Time	m	Time	m
1	F	0121	1.5	0654	12.7	1337	1.6	● 1909	12.7
2	SA	0159	1.6	0727	12.6	1414	1.7	1942	12.5
3	SU	0231	1.9	0758	12.5	1444	2.0	2012	12.3
4	M	0255	2.2	0826	12.2	1506	2.2	2041	12.1
5	TU	0313	2.4	0854	12.0	1528	2.4	2111	11.8
6	W	0336	2.5	0926	11.7	1556	2.5	2147	11.4
7	TH	0406	2.7	1005	11.3	1631	2.8	2231	10.9
8	F	0444	3.1	1053	10.7	1716	3.3	2325	10.3
9	SA	0533	3.7	1156	10.2	1819	3.8	◐	
10	SU	0036	9.9	0646	4.2	1320	10.1	1957	3.9
11	M	0210	10.1	0841	4.0	1454	10.7	2135	3.3
12	TU	0333	10.9	1011	3.2	1603	11.6	2246	2.5
13	W	0435	11.9	1115	2.4	1700	12.6	2345	1.7
14	TH	0528	12.7	1211	1.7	1751	13.3		
15	F	0038	1.2	0616	13.4	1302	1.3	○ 1839	13.7
16	SA	0127	0.9	0700	13.7	1350	1.1	1924	13.8
17	SU	0212	0.9	0743	13.7	1435	1.2	2008	13.6
18	M	0253	1.2	0825	13.4	1514	1.5	2051	13.0
19	TU	0329	1.7	0906	12.8	1549	2.1	2133	12.3
20	W	0359	2.3	0946	12.1	1619	2.7	2213	11.5
21	TH	0429	2.9	1026	11.3	1651	3.3	2256	10.6
22	F	0503	3.5	1112	10.5	1731	3.9	2348	9.8
23	SA	0549	4.1	1216	9.9	1827	4.3	◑	
24	SU	0105	9.4	0654	4.4	1342	9.7	1939	4.4
25	M	0220	9.6	0812	4.3	1448	10.1	2057	4.0
26	TU	0320	10.0	0929	3.8	1542	10.6	2208	3.5
27	W	0411	10.7	1033	3.2	1632	11.2	2305	2.9
28	TH	0458	11.3	1126	2.6	1716	11.6	2354	2.4
29	F	0540	11.9	1213	2.2	1758	12.0		
30	SA	0038	2.1	0620	12.2	1257	1.9	1837	12.2

DECEMBER

Date	Day	Time	m	Time	m	Time	m	Time	m
1	SU	0120	1.9	0657	12.4	1338	1.9	● 1915	12.3
2	M	0158	2.0	0733	12.4	1416	2.0	1952	12.2
3	TU	0233	2.1	0809	12.3	1451	2.1	2029	12.1
4	W	0304	2.3	0845	12.2	1524	2.2	2108	11.9
5	TH	0334	2.4	0924	12.0	1559	2.4	2148	11.7
6	F	0409	2.6	1006	11.7	1638	2.6	2232	11.4
7	SA	0449	2.8	1053	11.4	1723	2.8	2322	11.1
8	SU	0537	3.1	1148	11.1	1818	3.0	◐	
9	M	0019	10.8	0637	3.4	1254	10.9	1924	3.2
10	TU	0129	10.7	0751	3.5	1409	11.0	2041	3.1
11	W	0246	10.8	0919	3.3	1522	11.4	2201	2.9
12	TH	0357	11.3	1037	2.9	1627	11.9	2310	2.4
13	F	0458	11.9	1140	2.4	1725	12.4		
14	SA	0008	2.0	0551	12.5	1235	1.9	1818	12.8
15	SU	0101	1.6	0640	12.9	1327	1.7	○ 1907	12.9
16	M	0150	1.5	0727	13.1	1417	1.6	1955	12.9
17	TU	0236	1.6	0812	13.0	1503	1.8	2040	12.7
18	W	0318	1.8	0855	12.7	1543	2.1	2123	12.3
19	TH	0354	2.2	0936	12.3	1617	2.5	2203	11.8
20	F	0424	2.6	1015	11.8	1646	2.9	2240	11.2
21	SA	0454	2.9	1053	11.3	1717	3.1	2317	10.7
22	SU	0528	3.2	1133	10.8	1755	3.4	◑ 2358	10.2
23	M	0611	3.5	1222	10.3	1841	3.6		
24	TU	0050	9.9	0704	3.8	1322	10.0	1937	3.8
25	W	0155	9.8	0807	3.9	1429	10.0	2042	3.9
26	TH	0305	10.0	0917	3.8	1533	10.3	2153	3.6
27	F	0407	10.4	1027	3.4	1631	10.7	2301	3.1
28	SA	0501	11.0	1128	2.8	1723	11.2	2358	2.6
29	SU	0549	11.6	1221	2.3	1810	11.7		
30	M	0047	2.2	0633	12.1	1309	2.0	● 1855	12.0
31	TU	0134	2.0	0716	12.4	1357	1.9	1939	12.3

Chart Datum: 6·50 metres below Ordnance Datum (Newlyn). HAT is 14·7 metres above Chart Datum.

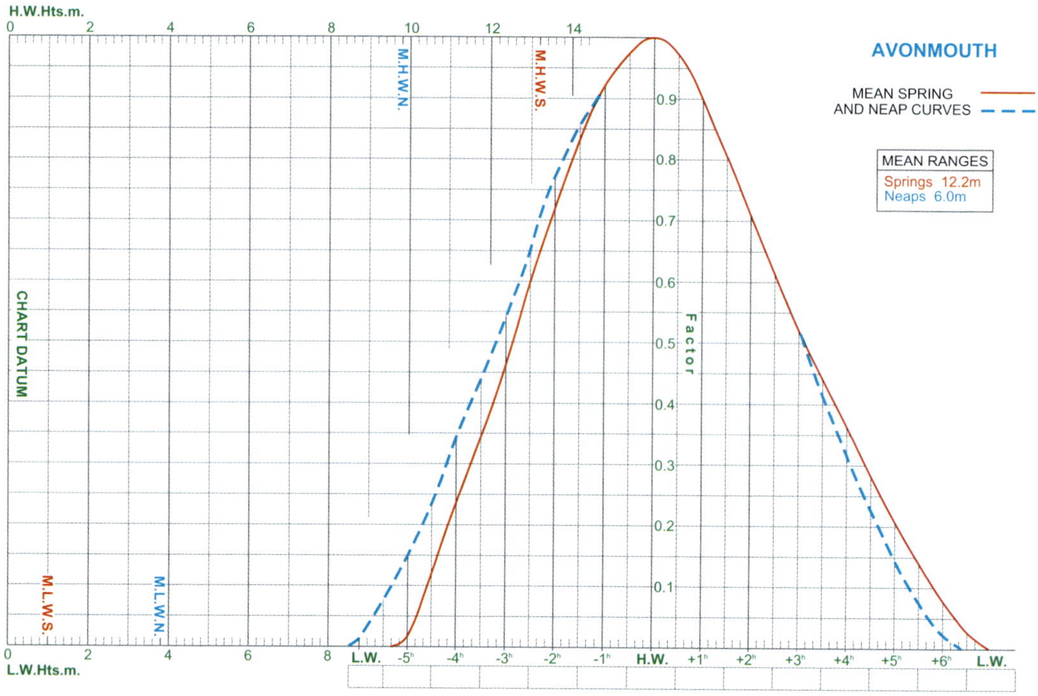

4.19 BRISTOL (CITY DOCKS)

Ent to R Avon **51°30'·44N 02°43'·31W**

CHARTS AC 1179, 1176, 1859, 5608; Imray C59, 2600

TIDES –0410 on Dover; ML 7·0; Duration 0620. NB very large range

Standard Port BRISTOL (AVONMOUTH) (⟵)

Times				Height (metres)			
High Water		Low Water		MHWS	MHWN	MLWN	MLWS
0200	0800	0300	0800	13·2	9·8	3·8	1·0
1400	2000	1500	2000				
Differences SHIREHAMPTON (R Avon, 51°29'N 02°41'W)							
0000	0000	+0035	+0010	–0·7	–0·7	–0·8	0·0
SEA MILLS (R Avon, 51°29'N 02°39'W)							
+0005	+0005	+0105	+0030	–1·4	–1·5	–1·7	–0·1
CUMBERLAND BASIN (Ent)							
+0010	*+0010*	*DR*	*DR*	*–2·9*	*–3·0*	*DR*	*DR*

SHELTER Excellent in Bristol Floating Harbour. Avonmouth and Royal Portbury Docks are prohib to yachts, except in emergency. If early/late on the tide, ⚓ as close inshore as depth allows in Portishead Pool between Portishead Dock and Royal Portbury Dock, but avoid in onshore winds.

NAVIGATION **From the south and west**: from Avon SHM buoy (51°27'·92N 02°51'·73W) either follow the Bristol Deep shipping channel taking care not to impede the safe passage of commercial traffic or stay well clear to the S passing close to Portishead Pt. If to the north, cross the shipping channel by the most direct route keeping clear of inbound/outbound traffic.

From the north: Conform to the channel taking care not to impede the safe passage of commercial traffic.

- Beware large ships transiting/turning in the main channel.
- Beware ships and tugs leaving the docks at any time.
- When on passage up/down the Severn estuary without stopping at Bristol or Portishead, use the *Offshore Route*.

Entering R Avon keep N of shallows (Swash Bank) between Royal Portbury Dock and Avonmouth Docks. Speed limit in river: 6kn if draught >2m; 9kn if draught <2m.

LIGHTS AND MARKS Ldg lts 127°, both Iso R 2s, to R Avon ent abeam S pier lt, Oc RG 30s. St George ldg lts 173°, both Oc G 5s, front/rear W/Or posts, clear Swash Bank (dries). Upriver, G or R ☆s mark the outside of bends.

Entry signals to Bristol Hbr may be shown from E bank, 1½ and 2½ca S of Clifton Suspension Bridge: ● = continue with caution; ● = stop and await orders.

LOCKS Floating Harbour (approx 7M upriver) is accessed via Entrance Lock into Cumberland Basin and Junction Lock into Floating Hbr. Aim to reach the Ent lock no later than HW –0015. Ent lock opens approx HW –2½, –1½ and –¼hr for arrivals; departures approx 15 mins after these times. Plimsoll swing bridge opens in unison with lock, except weekday rush hours 0800–0900 and 1700-1800.

Junction lock is always open, unless ht of HW is >9·6m ('stopgate' tide) when it closes; read special instructions. If you miss the last lock-in, call Ch 12 for advice.

BRIDGES Prince St Bridge opens (by arrangement only) summer 0915–2130, winter 0915–1830. Call Duty Office ☎9031484 or VHF Ch 73. Same for Redcliffe Bridge, but only opened in exceptional circumstances. Clearances above HAT: St Augustine's Reach 1·8m and 0·7m; Prince St 0·7m; Redcliffe 2·1m; Bristol 2·6m. The R Avon leads to Netham lock ☎9776590, Keynsham, Bath and the Kennett and Avon canal.

COMMUNICATIONS (Code 0117) Cumberland Basin Dock Master 9273633 Ⓗ 923 0000.

Bristol VTS, Ch 12, ☎0117 980 2638.

- All vessels are to maintain a listening watch on Ch 12 in Bristol VTS area and monitor commercial ship movements.
- At Black Rks (1M to run) call City Docks Radio Ch 14, 11 low power, (HW–3 to HW+1) for locking instructions.
- For berth: Bristol Floating Hbr Ch 73; Bristol Marina Ch 80.

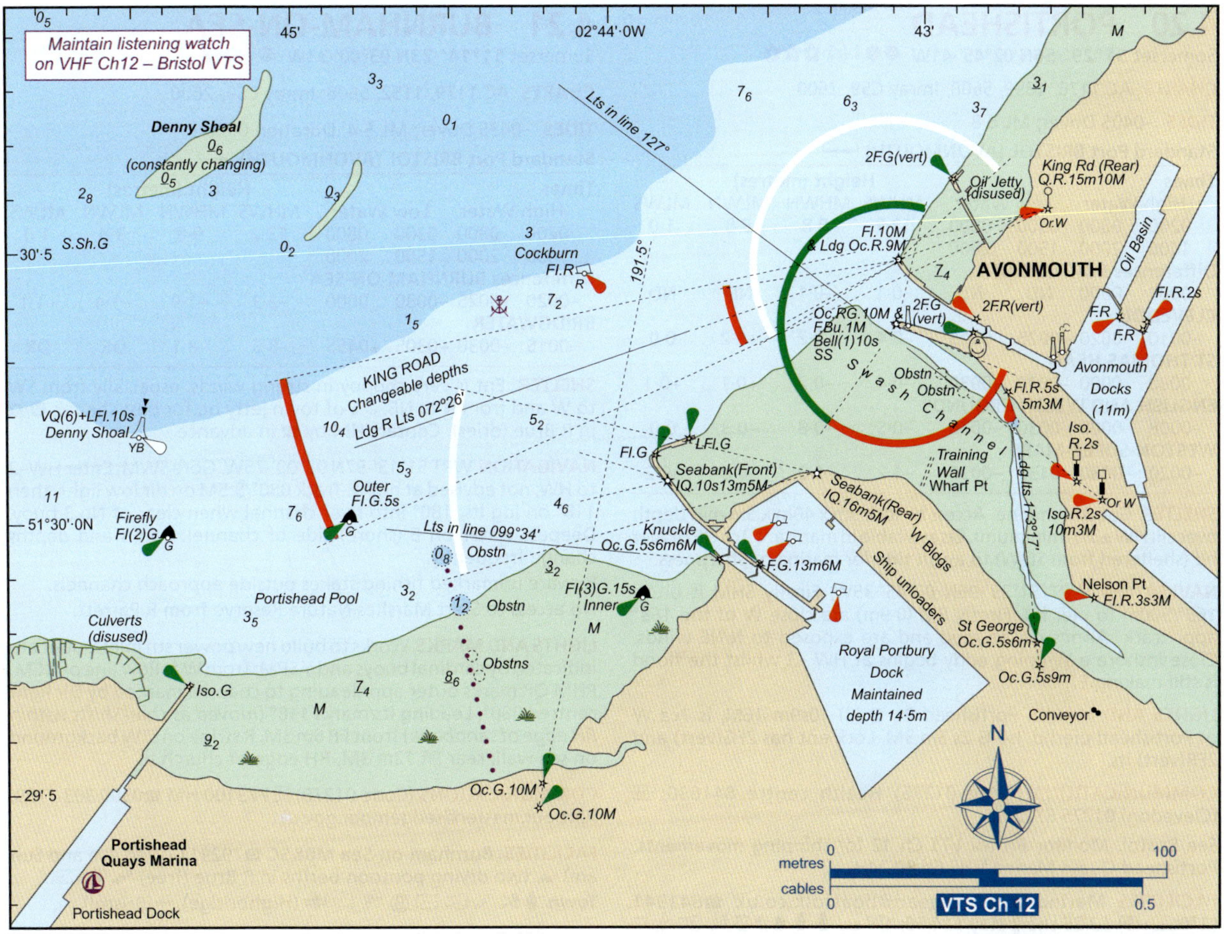

FACILITIES (from seaward) **Portishead Cruising Club** at Crockerne Pill, S bank, 5ca above M5 bridge; www.portisheadcruisingclub.org.uk ☎01275 373988, Drying (soft mud) grid (£5/day).

Bristol Hbr HM, Underfall Yard, Cumberland Rd, Bristol BS1 6XG. www.bristol-city.gov.uk ☎9031484; approx 40 consult website and HM in advance for detailed info on lock and bridge opening times near ent to St Augustine's Reach, £2.67 inc licence fee. ; ferries ply between various landing stages around the hbr.

Baltic Wharf Leisure Centre contact HM ☎9031484.

Bristol Marina Access –3 HW +1. www.bristolmarina.co.uk ☎9213198, 170, inc about 5 (21m max LOA) £2·75. (6/12t) (50t).

Bathurst Basin. **Cabot CC** ☎9268318.

City All domestic facilities, ACA.

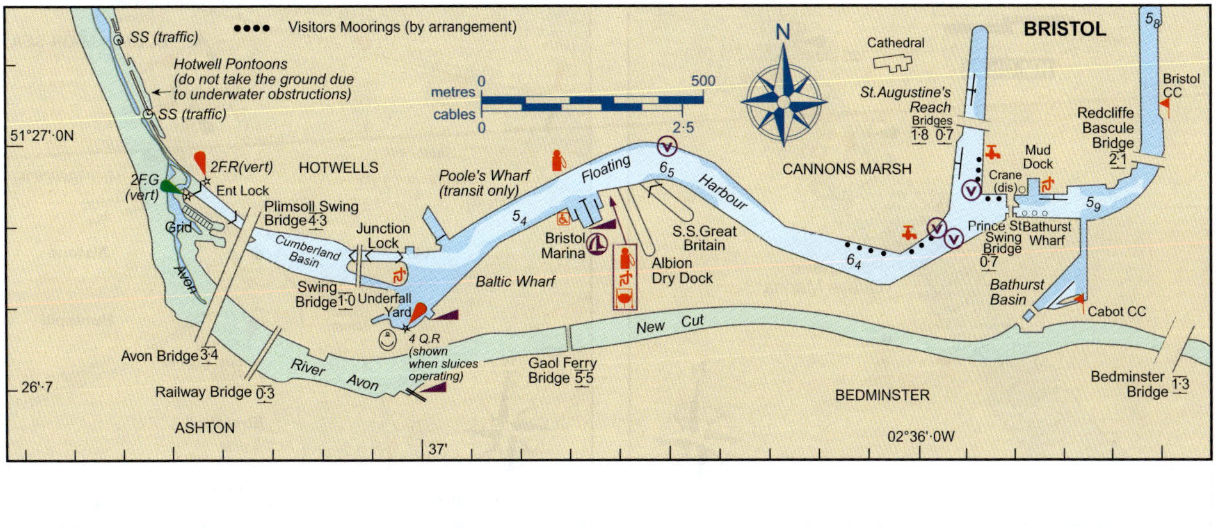

4.20 PORTISHEAD

Somerset **51°29′·56N 02°45′·41W**

CHARTS AC 1176, 1859, 5608; Imray C59, 2600

TIDES –0405 Dover; ML 6·8

Standard Port BRISTOL (AVONMOUTH) (⟵)

Times				Height (metres)			
High Water		Low Water		MHWS	MHWN	MLWN	MLWS
0200	0800	0300	0800	13·2	9·8	3·8	1·0
1400	2000	1500	2000				
Differences PORTISHEAD							
–0002	0000	ND	ND	–0·1	–0·1	ND	ND
CLEVEDON							
–0010	–0020	–0025	–0015	–0·4	–0·2	+0·2	0·0
ST THOMAS HEAD							
0000	0000	–0030	–0030	–0·4	–0·2	+0·1	+0·1
ENGLISH AND WELSH GROUNDS							
–0008	–0008	–0030	–0030	–0·5	–0·8	–0·3	0·0
WESTON-SUPER-MARE							
–0020	–0030	–0130	–0030	–1·2	–1·0	–0·8	–0·2

SHELTER Good in marina. Access by lock 9m x 40m x 5m min depth over cill HW ±3½ (minimum). Vs available in marina. ⚓ 1ca NE of pier hd (sheltered from SE-W) to await tide for marina or Sharpness.

NAVIGATION WPT 51°29′·96N 02°45′·35W, Firefly SHM lt buoy, 168°/500m to pier hd. Firefly Rks (0·9m) are close W of the 168° appr track. Appr's dry to mud and are exposed to N/NE winds. Close inshore a W-going eddy begins at HW –3 whilst the flood is still making E.

LIGHTS AND MARKS Portishead Pt, Q (3) 10s9m 16M, is 7ca W of Portishead pierhd, Iso G 2s 5m 3M. Lock ent has 2FG(vert) and 2FR(vert) lts.

COMMUNICATIONS (Code 01275) Health centre 841630; Ⓗ (Clevedon) 01275 872212.

See Bristol. Monitor *Bristol VTS* Ch **12** for shipping movements. Portishead Quays Marina VHF Ch 80 24H.

FACILITIES **Marina** portishead@boatfolk.co.uk ☎841941 (270+V) £3·25 short stay £14·50; (35t) wi-fi.

Portishead Cruising Club ☎373988.

Town Ⓑ ⇌ ✈ (Bristol). 3M to Junction 19 of M5.

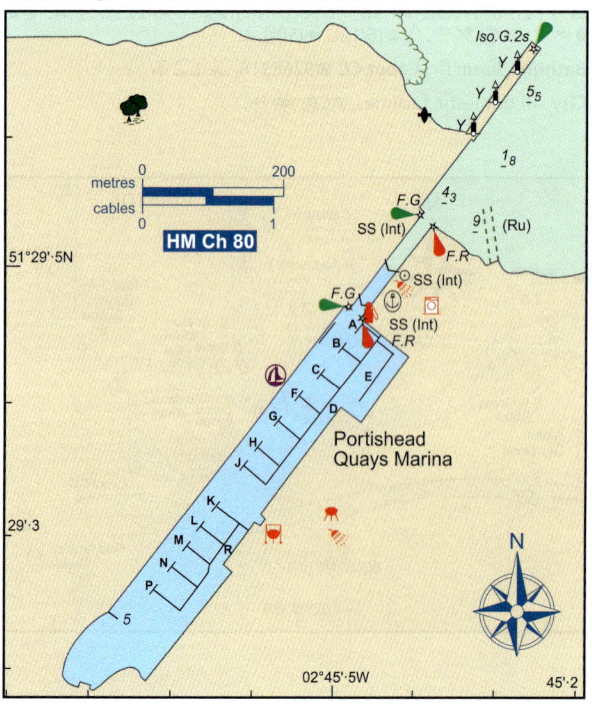

4.21 BURNHAM-ON-SEA

Somerset **51°14′·23N 03°00′·33W**

CHARTS AC 1179, 1152, 5608; Imray C59, 2600

TIDES –0435 Dover; ML 5·4; Duration 0620

Standard Port BRISTOL (AVONMOUTH) (⟵)

Times				Height (metres)			
High Water		Low Water		MHWS	MHWN	MLWN	MLWS
0200	0800	0300	0800	13·2	9·8	3·8	1·0
1400	2000	1500	2000				
Differences BURNHAM-ON-SEA							
–0020	–0025	–0030	0000	–2·3	–1·9	–1·4	–1·1
BRIDGWATER							
–0015	–0030	+0305	+0455	–8·6	–8·1	DR	DR

SHELTER Ent is very choppy in strong winds, especially from SW to W and from N to NE. ⚓ S of town jetty or, for best shelter, in R Brue (dries). Contact HM by ☎ in advance.

NAVIGATION WPT 51°13′·97N 03°09′·75W, Gore SWM. Enter HW–2 to HW; not advised at night. Track 080°/5.5M on dir low light, then 118° on ldg lts, 180° into river channel when clear of No 3 buoy. Deepest water on E (shore) side of channel. Banks and depths change frequently.

Beware unmarked fishing stakes outside approach channels.

No access to Stert Marshes Nature Reserve from R Parrett.

LIGHTS AND MARKS Works to build new power stn inlet/outlet are indicated by cardinal buoys and Y SPM; from W follow line of NCM. PHM QR marks outer appr leading to channel marked by Dir light centred 080°. Leading lts/marks 118° (*moved as chan shifts within RH edge of sandbank*) front FR 6m 3M, R stripe on □ W background on sea wall; rear FR 12m 3M, RH edge of church tr.

COMMUNICATIONS (Code 01278) Ⓗ 773100 HM ☎0300 303 7799; harbour.master@sedgemoor.gov.uk.

FACILITIES **Burnham-on-Sea MB&SC** ☎792911 (Wed eve and Sun am) two drying pontoon berths in R Brue (free).

Town Ⓑ ⇌ (Highbridge), ✈(Bristol).

ADJACENT FACILITY

Combwich A cargo wharf has been constructed to facilitate the inload of large indivisible loads to Hinkley Pt C Power Station. The approaches can be busy on appropriate tides.

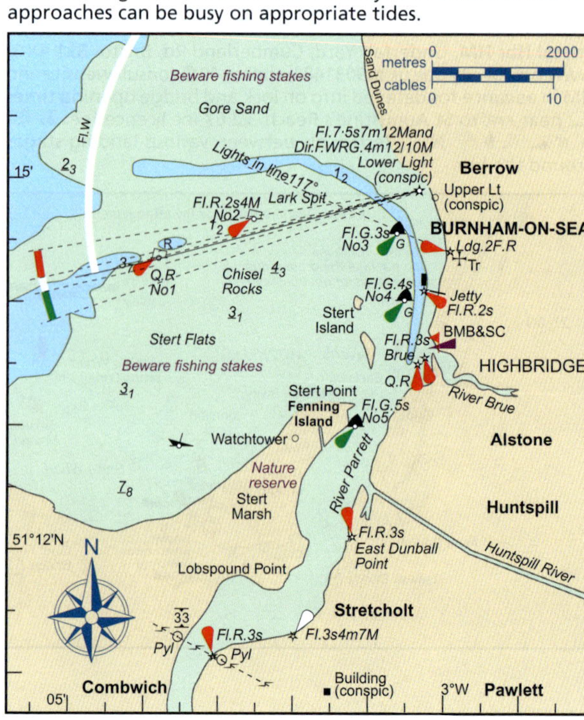

4.22 WATCHET

Somerset **51°11´·03N 03°19´·72W** ⚙🍃🍃✿✿

CHARTS AC 1179, 1152, 1160, 5608; Imray C59, 2600

TIDES –0450 Dover; ML 5·9; Duration 0655

Standard Port BRISTOL (AVONMOUTH) (⟵)

Times				Height (metres)			
High Water		Low Water		MHWS	MHWN	MLWN	MLWS
0200	0800	0300	0800	13·2	9·8	3·8	1·0
1400	2000	1500	2000				
Differences HINKLEY POINT							
–0032	–0028	–0055	–0049	–1·4	–1·1	–0·1	0·0
WATCHET							
–0035	–0050	–0145	–0040	–1·9	–1·5	+0·1	+0·1
MINEHEAD							
–0037	–0052	–0155	–0045	–2·6	–1·9	–0·2	0·0
PORLOCK BAY							
–0045	–0055	–0205	–0050	–3·0	–2·2	–0·1	–0·1
LYNMOUTH							
–0055	–0115	ND	ND	–3·6	–2·7	ND	ND

SHELTER Good, but open to N and E winds. Outer hbr (controlled by HM on VHF) dries 6·5m, but has about 6m depth at MHWS. Marina subject to silting, some berths allow boats to settle in soft mud; some berths have limited accessibility. Approx gate opening times HW ±2½H Sp, HW ±1½H Np. **Outer harbour** 6 drying ⊆ on W wall, also used by commercial shipping.

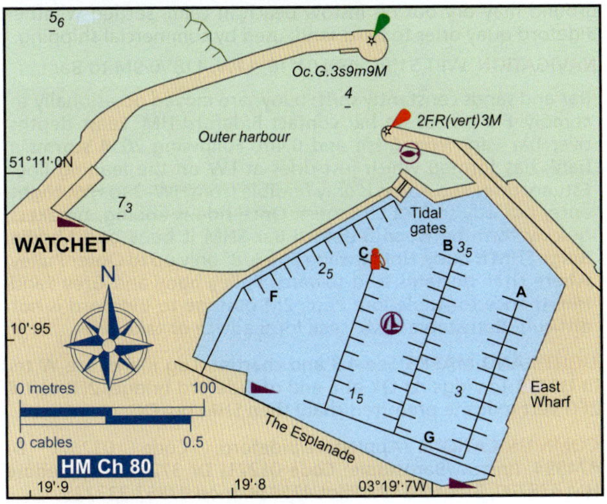

NAVIGATION WPT 51°12´·03N 03°18´·88W, 208°/1·1M to hbr ent. Rks/mud dry 5ca to seaward. Beware tidal streams 4-5kn at sp offshore and around W pier hd. Marina entered through a dropping sill gate (width 7m) which opens when tide level is at least CD +6.92m (retained water level). Entrance is controlled by automatic stop/go R/G lts. Min clearance over the gate is 2.5m. Min retained water depths vary 1.5–3.0m. 3kn speed limit in marina.

LIGHTS AND MARKS Two lit (FR) radio masts (206m) bearing 208° Station is conspic 7·5M to the E. W pier hd Oc G 3s 9m 9M on Red (R) tr. E pier hd 2 FR (vert) 3M.

COMMUNICATIONS (Code 01984) **Marina** ☎631264 mob below; Watchet Boat Owners Association (01643) 702569. Harbour/Marina Ch 80.

FACILITIES **Watchet Harbour Marina** www.watchetharbour.co.uk ☎631264 mob 07957208980 (H24) contact prior to arrival for berth. 250⊆ inc Ⓥ £3·00 inc ⚡, 🚿🚻 ⊡ ⚓ (20t) ACA.

Town ✉ 🛒 ✕ 🍺. At Williton (2M): ⛽ ⊡ 🚿; Ⓗ (Minehead 8M), ⇌ (Taunton 18M), ✈ (Bristol).

ADJACENT JETTY

Hinkley Pt C Power Station. The redevelopment includes the construction of a jetty and dolphins on Hinkley Pt (Lit *G (Gp) Fl*). Craft are not allowed within 100m except in emergency.

4.23 ILFRACOMBE

Devon **51°12´·65N 04°06´·65W** ⚙⚙🍃🍃✿✿

CHARTS AC *1179, 1165,* 1160, 5608; Imray C59, 2600

TIDES –0525 Dover; ML 5·0; Duration 0625

Standard Port MILFORD HAVEN (⟵)

Times				Height (metres)			
High Water		Low Water		MHWS	MHWN	MLWN	MLWS
0100	0700	0100	0700	7·0	5·2	2·5	0·7
1300	1900	1300	1900				
Differences ILFRACOMBE							
–0016	–0016	–0041	–0031	+2·2	+1·7	+0·6	+0·3
LUNDY ISLAND							
–0025	–0025	–0035	–0030	+1·0	+0·8	+0·2	+0·1

SHELTER Good except in NE/E winds. SW gales can cause surge in hbrs, which dry. 8 ⚓s in outer hbr, dries 2·7m. Or ⚓ clear of pier. Visitors ⊆ on N snd S walls of Inner Hbr, dries approx 4m, or dry out on chains off foot of N Pier. Call beforehand to confirm berth availability.

NAVIGATION WPT 51°13´·23N 04°06´·67W, 180°/0·55M to pier hd. From E, beware Copperas Rks (4M to E), and tide rips on Buggy Pit, 7ca NE of ent. On entry keep toward Pier to clear drying ledges and lobster keep-pots obstructing Hbr ent on SE side.

LIGHTS AND MARKS See 4.3 and chartlet.

COMMUNICATIONS (Code 01271) Dr 863119. HM 862108 mob 07775 532606.

Ilfracombe Hbr VHF Ch 12 16 (not H24).

FACILITIES **Hbr** ⛵(launching £7·70/day, £23·11/week) ⊆ and ⚓s £1·672 (inc use of 🚿) ⛽ ⚡(S Quay) 🚿 ⚒ 🔧 ⊡ ⊡. **Ilfracombe YC** ☎863969, ⛵ ⊡ ⚓(35t as arranged) 🍺.

Town ✉ Ⓑ 🛒 ✕ 🍺 bus to Barnstaple (⇌), ✈ (Exeter).

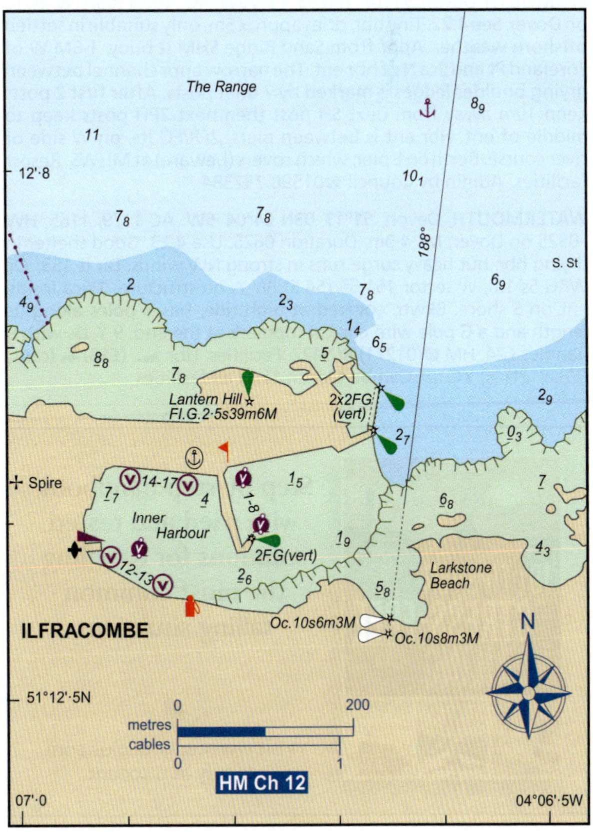

HARBOURS ON THE SOUTH SHORE OF THE BRISTOL CHANNEL

WESTON-SUPER-MARE, Somerset, **51°21´·03N 02°59´·28W**. AC 1179, 1176,1152, 5608. HW –0435 on Dover; Duration 0655; ML 6·1m. See 4.20. Good shelter, except in S'lies, in Knightstone Hbr (dries) at N end of bay; access HW±1½. Causeway at ent marked by bn. Grand Pier hd 2 FG (vert) 6/5m. Or ⚓ in good weather in R Axe (dries), enter only near HW.

Weston Bay YC (sited on beach) ☎01934 413366, VHF Ch 80.

Uphill Boat Centre ☎01934 418617. (lower R Axe-drying) (10t).

Town.

MINEHEAD, Somerset, **51°12´·79N 03°28´·37W**. AC 1179, 1165, 1160. HW –0450 on Dover. ML 5·7m. See 4.22. Small hbr, dries 7·5m. Good shelter within pier curving E and then SE, over which seas may break in gales at MHWS; exposed to E'lies. Best appr from N or NW; beware The Gables, shingle bank (dries 3·7m) about 5ca ENE of pier. Keep E of a sewer outfall which passes ½ca E of pier hd and extends 1¾ca NNE of it; outfall is protected by rk covering, drying 2·8m and N end marked by SHM Bn QG 6m 7M. Shingle bank extends 20m all round pierhead, lit Fl (2) G 5s 4M, vis 127°-262°. There are 2 R 🅐s at hbr ent just seaward of 3 posts or Med moor on quay at inner end of pier; £16·30/day. Hbr has live webcam. Holiday camp conspic 6ca SE.

HM ☎(01984) 634594, mob 07528 208758.

Facilities: **Hbr** (launching £13·15/day), at.

Town (Taunton).

PORLOCK WEIR, Somerset, **51°13´·17N 03°37´·64W**. AC 1179, 1165, 1160. HW –0500 on Dover; ML 5·6m. See 4.22. Access only near HW. Ent chan (250°), about 15m wide marked by withies (3 PHM and 1 SHM), between shingle bank/wood pilings to stbd and sunken wooden wall to port is difficult in any seas. A small pool (1m) just inside ent is for shoal draught boats; others dry out on pebble banks. Or turn 90° stbd, via gates (but opening bridge usually closed), into inner drying dock with good shelter. No lts. HM ☎01643 863187 (not local). **Porlock Weir SC**. Facilities: and limited.

LYNMOUTH, Devon, **51°14´·16N 03°49´·79W**. AC 1160, 1165. HW –0515 on Dover. See 4.22. Tiny hbr, dries approx 5m, only suitable in settled offshore weather. Appr from Sand Ridge SHM lt buoy, 1·6M W of Foreland Pt and 9ca N of hbr ent. The narrow appr channel between drying boulder ledges is marked by 7 unlit posts. After first 2 posts keep 10m away from next SH post then next 2PH posts keep to middle of ent. Hbr ent is between piers, 2FR/FG lts, on W side of river course. Berth on E pier, which covers (beware) at MHWS. Resort facilities. Admin by Council ☎01598 752384.

WATERMOUTH, Devon, **51°13´·03N 04°04´·6W**. AC 1179, 1165. HW –0525 on Dover; ML 4·9m; Duration 0625. Use 4.23. Good shelter in drying hbr, but heavy surge runs in strong NW winds. Dir lt 153° Oc WRG 5s 1m, W sector 151·5°-154·5°, W △ on structure, 1½ca inside ent on S shore. Bkwtr, covered at high tide, has Y poles along its length and a G pole with conical topmark at the end. 9 Y 🅐s with B handles £24. HM ☎(01271) 865422. Facilities: Hbr (£18) (cans) (12t); **YC**. **Combe Martin** 1½M all facilities.

4.24 RIVERS TAW AND TORRIDGE

Devon **51°04´·37N 04°12´·88W**

CHARTS AC 1179, 1164, 1160, 5608; Imray C58, 2600

TIDES –0525 (Appledore) Dover; ML 3·6; Duration 0600

Standard Port MILFORD HAVEN (⟵)

Times				Height (metres)			
High Water		Low Water		MHWS	MHWN	MLWN	MLWS
0100	0700	0100	0700	7·0	5·2	2·5	0·7
1300	1900	1300	1900				
Differences APPLEDORE							
–0020	–0025	+0015	–0045	+0·5	0·0	–0·9	–0·5
YELLAND MARSH (R Taw)							
–0010	–0015	+0100	–0015	+0·1	–0·4	–1·2	–0·6
FREMINGTON (R Taw)							
–0010	–0015	+0030	–0030	–1·1	–1·8	–2·2	–0·5
BARNSTAPLE (R Taw)							
0000	–0015	–0155	–0245	–2·9	–3·8	–2·2	–0·4
BIDEFORD (R Torridge)							
–0020	–0025	0000	0000	–1·1	–1·6	–2·5	–0·7
CLOVELLY							
–0030	–0030	–0020	–0040	+1·3	+1·1	+0·2	+0·2

SHELTER Very well protected, but ent is dangerous in strong on-shore winds and/or swell. Yachts can ⚓ or pick up RNLI buoy (please donate to RNLI, Boathouse ☎473969) in Appledore Pool N of Skern Pt where spring stream can reach 5kn. Yachts that can take the ground may dry out on Instow beach in calm, settled weather. Bideford quay dries to hard sand; used by commercial shipping.

NAVIGATION WPT 51°05´·43N 04°16´·11W, 118°/0·9M to Bar.

Bar and sands constantly shift; buoys are moved occasionally to comply. For advice on bar contact Bideford HM. Least depths over bar vary from 0·1m and 0·4m. Following 2014 storms a bank has formed which just dries at LW on the leading line. Estuary dries and access is only feasible from HW–2 to HW. Night entry not advised for strangers. Once tide is ebbing, breakers quickly form between Bideford Bar SHM lt buoy and Middle Ridge SHM lt buoy. Hold the ldg line 118° only up to Outer Pulley where chan deviates stbd towards Pulley buoy and Grey Sand Hill, thence to Appledore Pool. 2M passage to Bideford is not difficult. Barnstaple (7M): seek local advice or take pilot.

LIGHTS AND MARKS See 4.3 and chartlet. Ldg marks are W trs, lit H24. R Torridge: Lt QY at E end of Bideford bridge, 2FR vert & 2FG vert indicate preferred chan; then SHM bn, QG, on W bank.

COMMUNICATIONS (Appledore/Bideford: Code 01237) Dr 474994. (Instow/Barnstaple: Code 01271) Dr 372672. Appledore HM 428700; Bideford HM/Pilot 475834, mob 07967 333725.

2 Rivers Port/Pilots VHF Ch 12 16 (From HW–2 occasional).

FACILITIES

APPLEDORE: no; slips at town quay. **Services** Ⓔ (70t).

BIDEFORD: some (contact HM). Ferry to Lundy Is.

INSTOW: North Devon YC, ☎861390; **Services** via Instow Marine ☎861081, Ⓔ (4t). **Town**.

BARNSTAPLE: Access above Fremlington Quay advisable only with local knowledge or after recce in dinghy. (free for short stay): limited facilities.

Towns ✉ (all four), Ⓑ (Barnstaple, Bideford) ⇌ (Barnstaple) ✈ (Exeter).

CLOVELLY, Devon, **51°00´·18N 04°23´·77W**. AC 1164. Tides see above. HW –0524 on Dover. Tiny drying hbr, 5M E of Hartland Pt, is sheltered from S/SW winds; useful to await the tide into Bideford or around Hartland Pt. Some (max LOA 12m) on pier, access only near HW; or ⚓ off in 5m. Lt Fl G 5s 5m 5M on hbr wall. HM mob: 07975 501830. Facilities: ✉ limited.

ISLAND IN BRISTOL CHANNEL, 10M NNW of Hartland Pt

LUNDY ISLAND, Devon, **51°09′·83N 04°39′·27W**. AC 1179, 1164, 5608. HW –0530 on Dover; ML 4·3m; Duration 0605. See 4.23. Shore Office ☎01237 470074, Island ☎01237 431831. Beware bad tide races, esp on E-going flood, off the N and SE tips of the island; and to the SW on the W-going ebb. A violent race forms over Stanley Bank 3M NE of the N tip. Shelter good in lee of island's high ground (145m). In SSW to NW winds, usual ⚓ is close inshore to NW of SE Pt and Rat Island, clear of ferry. In N'lies ⚓ in The Rattles, small bay on S side. In E'lies Jenny's Cove is safe if no W'ly swell. Lts: NW Pt, Fl 15s 48m 17M, vis 009°-285°, W ○ tr. On SE Pt, Fl 5s 53m 15M, vis 170°-073°, W ○ tr. Two Historic Wrecks (see 0.30) lie on the E side of island, at 51°11′N 04°39′·4W, and 4ca further E. Facilities: Landing by the ⚓ off SE end of island or using N side of jetty to disembark passengers only, boats may not remain alongside; £5.00/person landing fee. The waters around Lundy are a Marine Nature Reserve. **Lundy Co**: ⛽ ✉ 📖 limited stores.

MINOR HARBOURS ON THE NW COAST OF CORNWALL

BUDE, Cornwall, **50°49′·93N 04°33′·37W**. AC 1156, 5608. HW –0540 on Dover. Duration 0605. See 4.25. Limited shelter in drying hbr, access near HW in daylight, quiet weather, no swell conditions but sea lock gives access to canal basin with 2m. Conspic W radar dish aerials 3·3M N of hbr. Outer ldg marks 075°, front W spar with Y ◊ topmark, rear W flagstaff; hold this line until inner ldg marks in line at 131°, front W pile, rear W spar, both with Y △ topmarks. There are no lts. VHF Ch 16 12 (when vessel expected). Advise HM of ETA with 24hr notice ☎(01288) 353111; 🏗 on quay; **Town** (½M); ⛽ ✉ Ⓑ 🛒 ✕ 📖.

BOSCASTLE, Cornwall, **50°41′·48N 04°42·17W**. AC 1156, 5608. HW –0543 on Dover; see 4.25. A tiny, picturesque hbr, almost a land-locked cleft in the cliffs. Access near HW, but not in onshore winds when swell causes surge inside. An E'ly appr, S of Meachard Rk (37m high, 2ca NW of hbr), is best. 2 short bkwtrs at ent; moor as directed on drying S quay. HM ☎01840 250200.

4.25 PADSTOW

Cornwall **50°32′·51N 04°56′·17W**

CHARTS AC 1156, 1168, 5608; Imray C58, 2400

TIDES –0550 Dover; ML 4·0; Duration 0600

Standard Port MILFORD HAVEN (⟵)

Times				Height (metres)			
High Water		Low Water		MHWS	MHWN	MLWN	MLWS
0100	0700	0100	0700	7·0	5·2	2·5	0·7
1300	1900	1300	1900				
Differences BUDE							
–0040	–0040	–0035	–0045	+0·7	+0·6	ND	ND
BOSCASTLE							
–0045	–0010	–0110	–0100	+0·3	+0·4	+0·2	+0·2
PADSTOW							
–0055	–0050	–0040	–0050	+0·3	+0·4	+0·1	+0·1
WADEBRIDGE (R Camel)							
–0052	–0052	+0235	+0245	–3·8	–3·8	–2·5	–0·4
NEWQUAY							
–0100	*–0110*	*–0105*	*–0050*	*0·0*	*+0·1*	*0·0*	*–0·1*
PERRANPORTH							
–0100	–0110	–0110	–0050	–0·1	0·0	0·0	+0·1
ST IVES							
–0050	–0115	–0105	–0040	–0·4	–0·3	–0·1	+0·1
CAPE CORNWALL							
–0130	–0145	–0120	–0120	–1·0	–0·9	–0·5	–0·1

NOTE: At Wadebridge LW time differences give the start of the rise, following a LW stand of about 5hrs.

SHELTER Good in inner hbr 3m+, access approx HW±2 Sp, ±1½ Np via tidal gate. If too late for gate, moor in the Pool. Drying moorings available for smaller craft. Good at Wadebridge 4.5M up R Camel.

NAVIGATION WPT 50°34′·56N 04°56′·07W, 044° Stepper Pt 6ca. From SW, beware Quies Rks, Gulland Rk, The Hen, Gurley Rk, Chimney Rks and a wreck 5ca W of Stepper Pt (all off the chartlet). From N, keep well off Newland Island and its offlying reef.

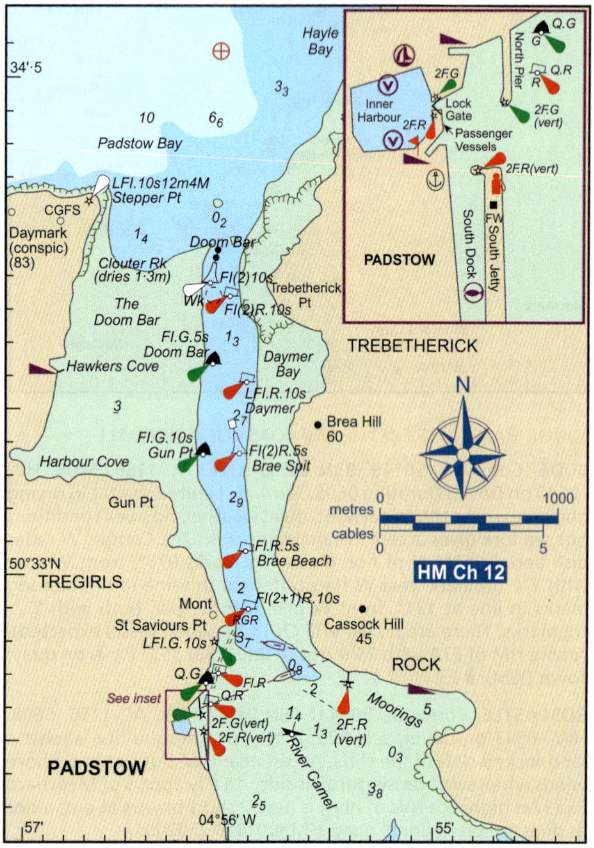

- Best appr HW–2½, do not try LW±2; least depth on the bar is 0·5m at MLWS. Waiting ⚓s in Port Quin Bay in lee of Rumps Pt and Mother Ivey's Bay 3M WSW Stepper Pt.
- Shifting banks in estuary require care and a rising tide (ditto the drying R Camel to Wadebridge, 4M). In doubt, consult HM.
- Identify the first 2 chan buoys before entry. In strong onshore winds or heavy ground swell, seas can break on Doom Bar and in the adjacent chan. Beware Wk marked by IDM Fl (2) 10s.
- S of St Saviour's Pt the chan lies very close to W shore.

LIGHTS AND MARKS See 4.3 and chartlet.

COMMUNICATIONS (Code 01841) Dr 532346. HM padstowharbour@btconnect.com, ☎532239; **Ferry** to Rock, 07773081574 – it also acts as water taxi.

HM VHF Ch **12** 16 (Mon-Fri 0800-1700 and HW±2). Ferry Ch 12.

FACILITIES Hbr £2·14, 🅐s £1·18, (£4·50 <10 hp engine< £6·50) (extra) . **Services** (60t) .

Town Ⓑ Bus (to Bodmin ⇄/✈ Newquay).

Rock SC ☎(01208) 862431, .

Wadebridge HM as Padstow; only; **Town** Ⓑ .

MINOR HBRS BETWEEN BOSCASTLE AND LAND'S END

PORT ISAAC, Cornwall, **50°35′·75N 04°49′·57W**. AC 1156, 1168. HW –0548 on Dover; ML 4·0m. Small drying hbr. Conspic ✠ tr bears 171°/1·3M. Rks close E of 50m wide ent between short bkwtrs. LB.

NEWQUAY, Cornwall, **50°25′·06N 05°05′·19W**. AC 1149, 1168. HW –0604 on Dover; ML 3·7m; see 4.25. Ent to drying hbr ('The Gap'), between two walls, is 23m wide. Beware Old Dane Rk and Listrey Rk outside hbr towards Towan Hd. Swell causes a surge in the hbr. Enter HW±2 but not in strong onshore winds. Lts: N pier 2 FG (vert) 2M; S pier 2 FR (vert) 2M. HM ☎07816 077755 (also St Ives) VHF Ch 08 16 14. Facilities: . Note: Shoal draught boats can dry out in Gannel Creek, close S of Newquay, but only in settled weather. Beware causeway bridge halfway up creek.

PORTREATH, Cornwall, **50°15′·88N 05°17′·57W**. AC 1149. HW –0600 on Dover. Conspic W daymark (38m) at E side of ent to small drying hbr. Gull Rk (23m) is 3ca W of ent and Horse Rk is close N. Keep close to pier on W side of chan. in either of 2 basins, both dry. contact: secretary@portreath-harbour.org ; .

HAYLE, Cornwall, **50°12′·14N 05°26′·13W** (NCM) . AC 1149, 1168. HW –0605 on Dover; ML 3·6m; Duration 0555. See 4.25. Drying hbr gives very good shelter, but is not advised for yachts. In ground swell dangerous seas break on the bar, drying 2·7m; approx 4m at ent @ MHWS. Cross in good weather HW±1. Marks do not necessarily indicate best water. Ldg marks/lts 180°: both W □ R horiz band, ☆ FW 17/23m 4M. NCM buoy, Q is about 7ca N of the front ldg lt. Training wall on W side of ent chan is marked by 5 lit perches, all Oc G 4s. The hbr is divided by long central island (about 700m long, with lt bn QG at NW end) which should be left to stbd. Follow the SE arm of hbr to Hayle; the S arm leads to Lelant Quay. Visitors must contact HM ☎(01736) 754043, Mob 07500 993867, VHF Ch 16 prior to arrival. . Facilities: (can) Ⓑ ⇄.

ST IVES, Cornwall, **50°12′·79N 05°28′·67W** . AC 1149, 1168. HW –0610 on Dover; ML 3·6m; Duration 0555. See 4.25. Drying hbr with about 4·5m @ MHWS. Good shelter except in onshore winds when heavy swell works in. ⚓ in 3m between the hbr and Porthminster Pt to S and drying Or 🅐s in hbr. From the NW beware Hoe Rk off St Ives Hd, and obstn drying 0·9m at collapsed b'water E of Smeaton pier inshore of SHM Fl(2) G.4s. From SE off Porthminster Pt avoid The Carracks and obstn drying 1·0m in Carbis Bay. Keep E of SHM buoy about 1½ ca ENE of E pier. Lts: E pier hd 2 FG (vert) 8m 5M. W pier hd 2 FR (vert) 5m 3M. VHF Ch **12** 16 (occas). HM ☎07816 077755 (Newquay). Facilities: 🅐s £17.

E Pier . **Town** Ⓑ ⇄.

Ireland

All Ireland

AREA 5 – SOUTH IRELAND

AREA 6 – NORTH IRELAND

10°W
9°W
53°N
52°N
Malin CG
Valentia CG
Galway
Galway Bay
Black Head
Rock Island
Inishmore
Kilronan
Aran Islands
Inisheer
See 5.1
Liscannor Bay
KILRUSH 5.35
Limerick
Loop Head
SHANNON ESTUARY 5.34
Kerry Head
Little Samphire Island
FENIT HARBOUR 5.33
Tralee Bay
Smerwick Harbour
Brandon Bay
Ventry
DINGLE 5.32
Inishtearaght
DINGLE BAY 5.30
VALENTIA HARBOUR 5.31
Portmagee
Great Skellig
KENMARE RIVER 5.29
Glengariff
Adrigole
CASTLETOWN BEARHAVEN 5.28
Lonehort Hbr
Bantry
Bull Rock
DUNMANUS/BANTRY BAY 5.27
Sheep Head
Dunmanus Bay
Mizen Head
CROOKHAVEN 5.26
Fastnet
Clear I
SCHULL 5.25
Roaringwater Bay
BALTIMORE 5.24
Barlogue Creek
CASTLETOWNSHEND 5.23
GLANDORE/UNIONHALL 5.22
Galley Head
COURTMACSHERRY 5.21
Old Head of Kinsale
KINSALE 5.20
Oyster Haven
Roscoff
CORK HARBOUR 5.19
Fastnet TSS
Magnetic Variation 2·8°W

5.1

South Ireland

Malahide clockwise to Liscannor Bay

Harbour with full almanac entry
Minor harbour or anchorage
Major light
Ferry route
Airport

DISTANCE TABLE
See page 175

EMERGENCY 112 or 999
JRCC DUBLIN (+353) 01 662 0922
MRCC VALENTIA (+353) 066 947 6109

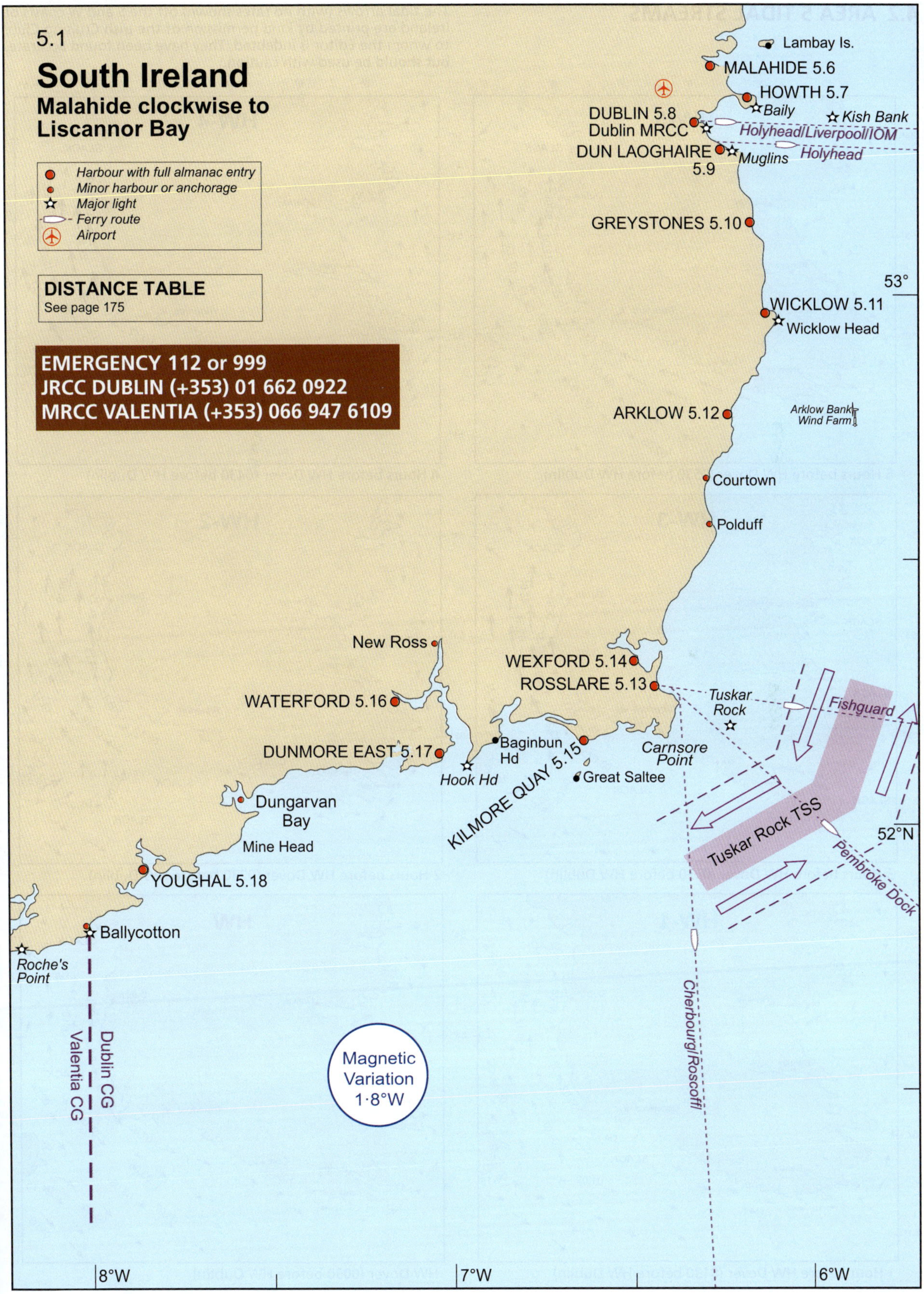

4.2 AREA 5 TIDAL STREAMS

The tidal arrows (with no rates shown) off the S and W coasts of Ireland are printed by kind permission of the Irish Cruising Club, to whom the Editor is indebted. They have been found accurate, but should be used with caution.

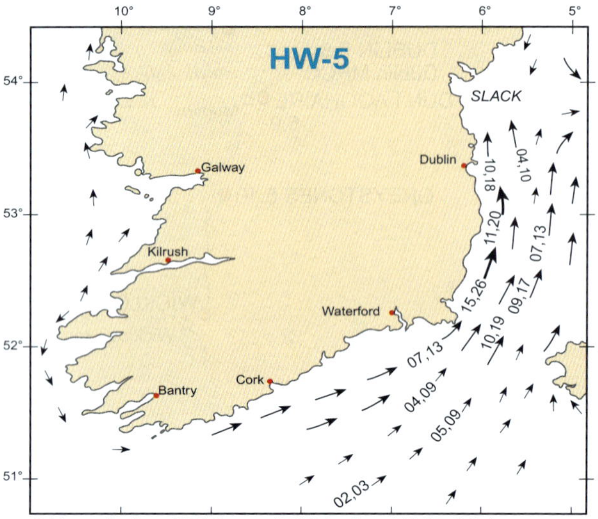

5 Hours before HW Dover (0530 before HW Dublin)

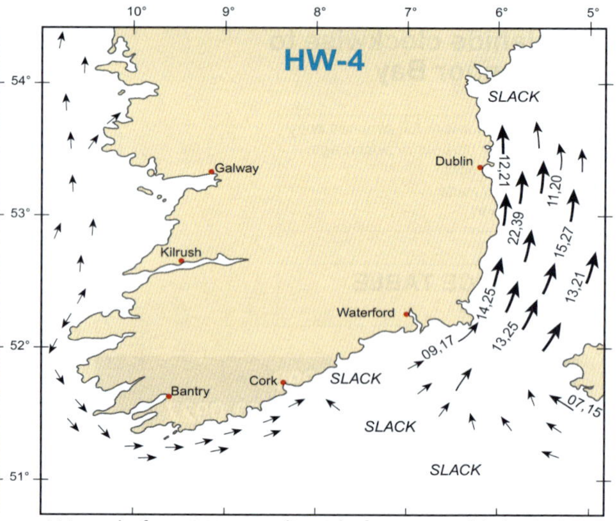

4 Hours before HW Dover (0430 before HW Dublin)

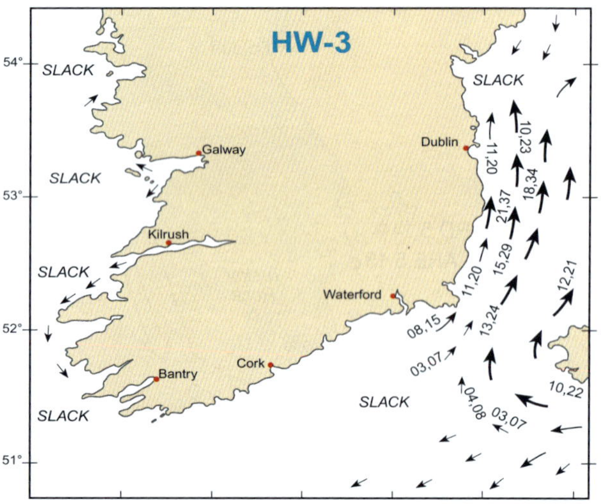

3 Hours before HW Dover (0330 before HW Dublin)

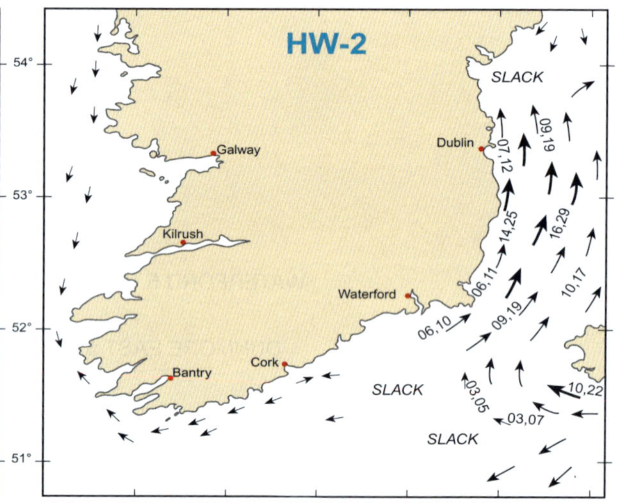

2 Hours before HW Dover (0230 before HW Dublin)

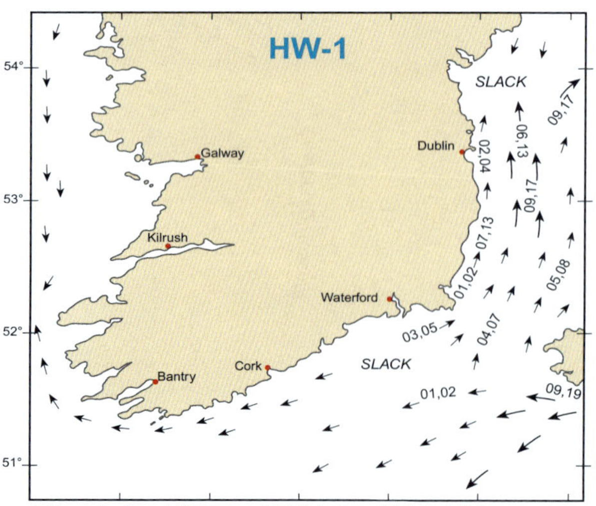

1 Hour before HW Dover (0130 before HW Dublin)

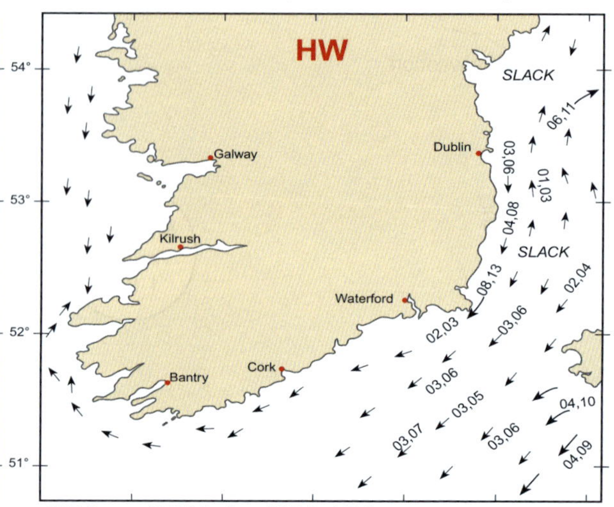

HW Dover (0030 before HW Dublin)

Northward 6.2 South Irish Sea 4.2

The tidal arrows (with no rates shown) off the S and W coasts of Ireland are printed by kind permission of the Irish Cruising Club, to whom the Editor is indebted. They have been found accurate, but should be used with caution.

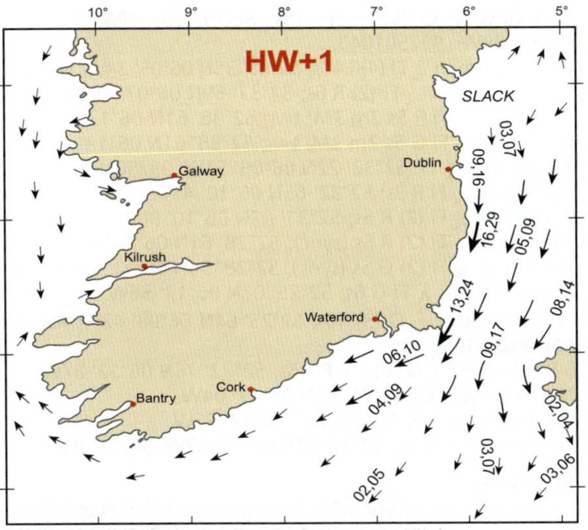

1 Hour after HW Dover (0030 after HW Dublin)

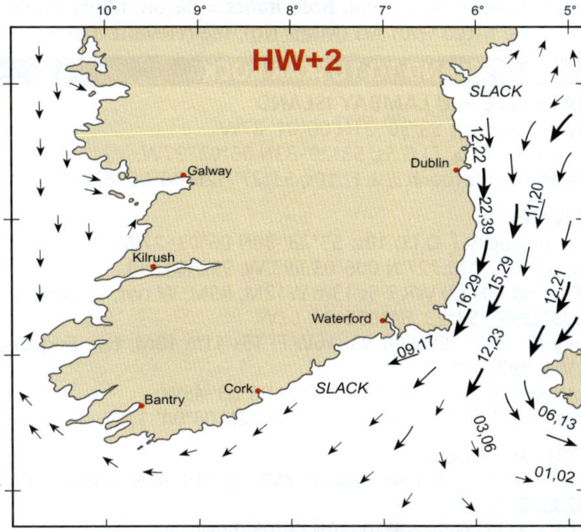

2 Hours after HW Dover (0130 after HW Dublin)

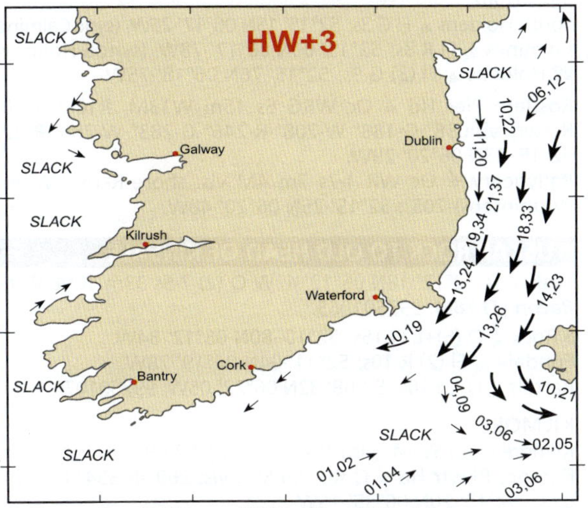

3 Hours after HW Dover (0230 after HW Dublin)

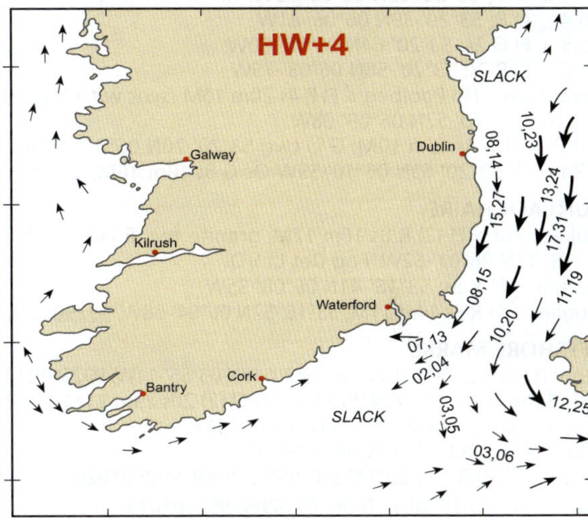

4 Hours after HW Dover (0330 after HW Dublin)

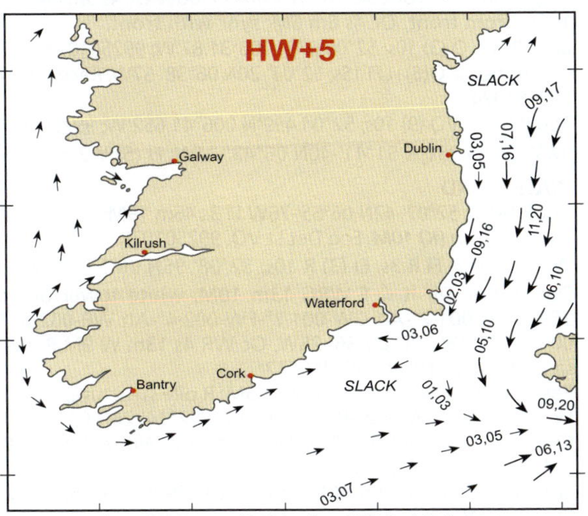

5 Hours after HW Dover (0430 after HW Dublin)

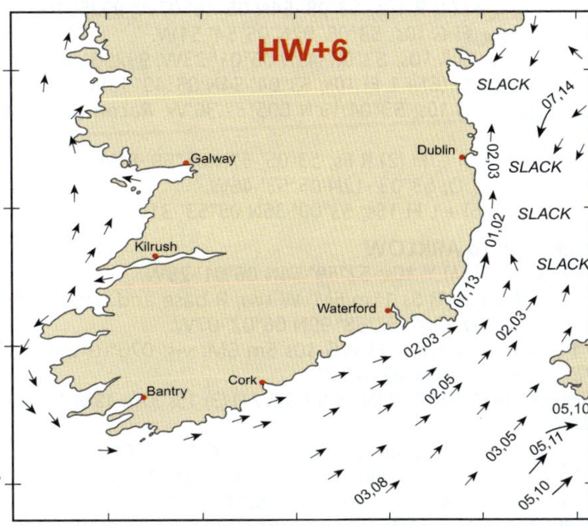

6 Hours after HW Dover (0530 after HW Dublin)

5.3 LIGHTS, BUOYS AND WAYPOINTS

Bold print = light with a nominal range of 15M or more. CAPITALS = place or feature. *CAPITAL ITALICS* = light-vessel, light float or Lanby. *Italics* = Fog signal. ***Bold italics*** = Racon. Many marks/ buoys are fitted with AIS (MMSI No); see relevant charts.

LAMBAY ISLAND TO TUSKAR ROCK

MALAHIDE and LAMBAY ISLAND

Taylor Rks Q; 53°30′·21N 06°01′·87W.
Burren Rocks Fl G 5s; 53°29′·33N 06°02′·37W.
Malahide approach L Fl 10s; 53°27′·12N 06°06′·87W.

HOWTH

Rowan Rocks Q (3) 10s; 53°23′·88N 06°03′·27W.
Howth 53°23.727′N 006°03.593′W; 992501250.
E Pier Hd Fl (2) WR 7·5s 13m W12M, R9M; W twr; vis: W256°-R295°-256°; 53°23′·64N 06°04′·02W.
Baily ☆ 53°21′·69N 06°03′·16W Fl 15s 41m **18M**; twr. Fog Det Lt VQ; 992501010.
Rosbeg E Q (3) 10s; 53°21′·02N 06°03′·45W.
Rosbeg S Q (6) + L Fl 15s; 53°20′·22N 06°04′·17W.

PORT OF DUBLIN

Dublin Bay Iso 4s; ***Racon (M)***; 53°19′·92N 06°04′·65W; 992351301.
No 1 Fl (3) G 5s; 53°20′·30N 06°05′·56W.
No 3 Q G; 53°20′·59N 06°06′·78W.
No 4 Q R; 53°20′·39N 06°06′·81W.
No 5 Fl G 2s; 53°20′·64N 06°08′·60W.
No 6 Fl R 2s; 53°20′·56N 06°08′·75W.
Great S Wall Hd Poolbeg Fl R 4s 20m 10M *(sync with N.Bull)*; R ○ twr; 53°20′·52N 06°09′·08W.
N Bull Fl G 4s 15m 10M; G ○ twr; 53°20′·70N 06°08′·98W.
N Bank ☆ 53°20′·69N 06°10′·59W Oc G 8s 10m **16M**; G □ twr.

DUN LAOGHAIRE

E Bkwtr Hd Fl (2) R 8s 16m **17M**; granite twr, R lantern 7M; 53°18′·14N 06°07′·62W. Fog Det Lt VQ.
Outfall Fl Y 5s; 53°18′·41N 06°08′·35W.
Muglins Fl R 5s 14m 11M; 53°16′·52N 06°04′·58W; 992501019.

OFFSHORE MARKS

Bennett Bank Q(6)+ L Fl 15s; 53°20′·17N 05°55′·11W; 992501012.
Kish Bank ☆ 53°18′·65N 05°55′·54W Fl (2) 20s 29m **21M** (H24); W twr, R band; ***Racon (T) 15M***; 992501017.
N Kish VQ; 53°18′·56N 05°56′·44W.
E Kish Fl (2) R 10s; 53°14′·35N 05°53′·56W; 992501020.
N Burford Q 53°20.51′N 06° 01′.49W; 992501016.
S Burford VQ(6)+L Fl 10s; 53°18′.06N 06° 01.30′W; 992501018.
E Codling Fl (4) R 10s; 53°08′·54N 05°46′·07W; 992501024.
W Codling Fl G 10s; 53°06′·97N 05°54′·51W.
Moulditch Fl R 10s; 53°08′·43N 06°01′·23W; 992501022.
S Codling VQ (6) + L Fl 10s; 53°04′·54N 05°49′·13W.
Codling Q(3) 10s; 53°04.19′N 005°37.36′W, ***Racon (G) 10M***, 992501028.
Breaches Shoal Fl (2) R 6s; 53°05′·67N 05°59′·81W.
North India Q; 53°03′·12N 05°53′·46W.
S India Q (6) + L Fl 15s; 53°00′·36N 05°53′·31W; 992501030.

WICKLOW to ARKLOW

Wicklow Fl (4) Y 10s; 52°59′·54N 06°01′·29W.
E Pier Hd Fl WR 5s 11m 6M; W twr, R base and cupola; vis: 136°-R-293°-W-136°; 52°58′·99N 06°02′·07W.
W Packet Quay Hd Fl WG 10s 5m 6M; vis: 076°-G-256°-W-076°; 52°58′·88N 06°02′·08W.
Wicklow Hd ☆ 52°57′·93N 05°59′·93W Fl (3) 15s 37m **18M**; W twr; 992501031.
Horseshoe Fl R 3s; 52°56′·84N 05°58′·47W; 992501032.
N Arklow Q; 52°53′·86N 05°55′·21W; 992501034.
Arklow Bank Wind Farm from 52°48′·47N 05°56′·57W to 52°46′·47N 05°57′·11W, N and S Turbines Fl Y 5s14m 10M. No 7 Turbine 992501302. Other turbines Fl Y 5s. See 5.4.

ARKLOW to WEXFORD

S Pier Hd Fl WR 6s 11m 13M; twr; vis: R shore- W223°- R350°-shore; 52°47′·61N 06°08′·22W.
Roadstone Bkwtr Hd QY; 52°46′·65N 06°08′·23W.
S Arklow Q (6) + LFl 15s; ***Racon (O) 10M***; 52°40′·20N 05°58′·89W; 992501040.
2 Glassgorman Fl (4)R 10s; 52°45′·35N 06°05′·34W; 992501038
1 Glassgorman Fl (2) R 6s; 52°37′·69N 06°07′·46W.
Courtown Fl R 5s 2m 3M; twr; 52°38′·61N 06°13′·45W.
Courtown Fl G 5s 2m 3M; twr; 52°38′·61N 06°13′·45W.
Blackwater Q; 52°32′·22N 06°09′·51W; 992501046.
No 6 Rusk Fl R 3s; 52°32′·65N 06°10′·41W.
No 4 Rusk Fl (2) R 5s; 52°31′·07N 06°10′·86W.
No 2 Rusk Fl (2) R 5s (sync); 52°28′·61N 06°12′·66W.
No 1 Rusk Fl (2) G 5s (sync); 52°28′·56N 06°11′·78W; AIS.
W Blackwater Fl G 6s; 52°25′·87N 06°13′·56W.
SE Blackwater Q (3) 10s, 52°25′·64N 06°08′·42W; ***Racon (M) 6M***; 992501050.
S Blackwater Q (6) + L Fl 15s; 52°22′·76N 06°12′·87W.
North Long Q; 52°21′·44N 06°17′·04W.
West Long QG; 52°18′·18N 06°17′·96W.
Lucifer VQ (3) 5s; 52°17′·02N 06°12′·67W; 992501054.

ROSSLARE

S Long Fl G 6s (sync with Splaugh); 52°14′·74N 06°15′·80W.
Splaugh Fl R 6s (sync with S Long); 52°14′·36N 06°16′·78W; 992501062.
South Holdens Fl G 3s; 52°15′·15N 06°17′·25W. (sync Calmines).
Calmines Fl R 3s; 52°15′·00N 06°17′·78W. (sync S Holdens).
W Holdens Fl (3) G 9s; 52°15′·76N 06°18′·75W.
Rosslare Pier Hd Oc WRG 5s 15m W13M, R10M, G10M; R twr; vis:098°-G-188°-W-208°-R-246°-G-283°-W-286°-R-320°; 52°15′·43N 06°20′·29W.
Ballygeary Oc WR 1·7s 7m 4M vis: shore-R-152°-W-200°-W(unintens)-205°; 52°15′·25N 06°20′·48W.

TUSKAR ROCK TO OLD HEAD OF KINSALE

Tuskar ☆ 52°12′·18N 06°12′·42W Q (2) 7·5s 33m **18M**; W twr; ***Racon (T) 18M***; 992501065.
S Rock Q (6)+L Fl 15s; 52°10′·80N 06°12′·84W.
Fundale Fl (2) R 10s; 52°11′·04N 06°19′·78W.
Barrels Q (3) 10s; 52°08′·32N 06°22′·05W; 992501070.

KILMORE

Kilmore Quay SWM Iso 10s; (Apr-Sep); 52°09′·20N 06°35′·30W.
Kilmore Bkwtr Hd Q RG 7m 5M; vis: 269°-R-354°-G-003°-R-077°; 52°10′·20N 06°35′·15W.
Ldg lts 007·9°, Front 52°10′·37N 06°35′·08W Oc 4s 3m 6M. Rear, 100m from front, Oc 4s 6m 6M; sync with front.
Bore Rks Q (3) 10s; 52°06.07′N 006°31.87′W; 992501072.
Coningbeg Q(6)+LFl 15s; 52°03′·20N 06°38′·57W; ***Racon (G) 9M***; 992501074.
Red Bank VQ (9) 10s; 52°04.499′N 006°41.652′W; 992501076.
'M5' ODAS 35 51°41′·40N 06°42′·24W; Fl (5) Y 20s.

WATERFORD

Hook Hd ☆ 52°07′·42N 06°55′·76W Fl 3s 46m **18M**; W twr, two B bands; ***Racon (K) 10M***. Fog Det Lt VQ. 992501079.
Waterford Fl R 3s. Fl (3) R 10s; 52°08′·95N 06°57′·00W.
Duncannon Dir lt F WRG 13m 10M, white tower on fort, 359·5°-FG-001·2°-Alt GW-001·7°-FW-002·4°-Alt WR-002·9°-FR-004·5°; 52°13′·23N 06°56′·25W; Oc WR 4s 13m W 9M R 7M on same tower, 119°-R-149°-W-172°.
Passage Pt Fl WR 5s 7m W6M, R5M; R pile structure; vis: 114°-W-127°-R-180°-W-302°-R-021° (shore); 52°14′·26N 06°57′·77W.
Cheek Pt Q WR 6m 5M; W mast; vis: W007°-R289°-007°; 52°16′·12N 06°59′·38W.
Sheagh Fl R 3s 29m 3M; Gy twr; vis: 090°-318°; 52°16′·29N 06°59′·34W.
Snowhill Point Ldg lts 255°. Front, Fl WR 2·5s 5m 3M; vis:

W222°- R020°- W057°-107°; 52°16'·39N 07°00'·91W. Rear, Flour Mill, 750m from front, Q 12m 5M.
Queen's Chan Ldg lts 098°. Front, QR 8m 5M; B twr, W band; vis: 030°-210°;52°15'·32N 07°02'·38W. Rear, 550m from front, Q 15m 5M; W mast.
Beacon Quay Fl G 3s 9m; vis: 255°-086°; 52°15'·50N 07°04'·21W.
Cove Fl WRG 6s 6m 2M; W twr; vis: R111°-G161°-W234°-111°; 52°15'·05N 07°05'·16W.
Smelting Ho Pt Q 8m 3M; W mast; 52°15'·15N 07°05'·27W.
Ballycar Fl RG 3s 5m; vis: G127°-R212°-284°; 52°15'·06N 07°05'·51W.

DUNMORE EAST

East Pier Head ☆ 52°08'·93N 06°59'·34W Fl WR 8s 13m **W17M**, R13M; Gy twr, vis: W225°- R310°-004°.
Dunmore East 1 Q G; 52°09'·06N 06°59'·38W.
Dunmore East 2 Fl G 2s; 52°09'·00N 06°59'·47W.
W Wharf Fl G 2s 6m 4M; vis: 165°-246°; 52°08'·97N 06°59'·45W.

DUNGARVAN

Ballinacourty Pt Fl (2) WRG 10s 16m W10M, R8M, G8M; W twr; vis: G245°- W274°- R302°- W325°-117°; 52°04'·69N 07°33'·18W.
Helvick Q (3) 10s; 52°03'·61N 07°32'·25W.
Mine Head 51°59'·56N 07°35'·23W Fl (4) 30s 87m 12M; W twr, B band; vis: 228°-052°; 992501085.

YOUGHAL

Bar Rocks Q (6) + L Fl 15s; 51°54'·85N 07°50'·05W.
Blackball Ledge Q (3) 10s, 51°55'·34N 07°48'·53W.
W side of ent ☆ 51°56'·57N 07°50'·53W Fl WR 2·5s 24m **W17M**, R13M; W twr; vis: W183°- R273°- W295°- R307°- W351°-003°.

BALLYCOTTON

Ballycotton ☆ 51°49'·50N 07° 59'·13W; Fl WR 10s 59m **W18M**, R14M; B twr, within W walls, B lantern; vis: 238°-W-041°-R-238°; 992501093.
The Smiths Fl (3) R 10s; 51°48'·43N 08°00'·60W.
Power Q (6) + L Fl 15s; 51°45'·59N 08°06'·67W; 992501098.

CORK

Cork L Fl 10s; 51°42'·92N 08°15'·60W; ***Racon (T) 7M***; 992501100.
Daunt Rock Fl (2) R 6s; 51°43'·53N 08°17'·50W; 992501102.
Fort Davis Ldg lts 354·5°. Front, 51°48'·83N 08°15'·79W, H24 Dir WRG 25m **17M**; vis: 351·5°-FG-352·5°-QG-353·5°-FW-355·5°-QR-356·5°-FR-357·5°. Rear, Dognose Quay, 203m from front, Oc 5s 37m 10M; Or 3, sync with front.
Roche's Pt ☆ 51°47'·58N 08°15'·29W Fl WR 3s 30m **W18M**, R12M; vis: shore-R-292°-W-016°-R-033°, 033°- W (unintens)-159°-R-shore; 992501099.
Outer Hbr Rk E2 Fl R 2·5s; 51°47'·52N 08°15'·67W.
Chicago Knoll E1 Fl G 5s; 51°47'·66N 08°15'·54W.
W1 Fl G 10s; 51°47'·69N 08°16'·05W.
W2 Fl R 10s; 51°47'·69N 08°16'·34W.
White Bay Ldg lts 034·6°. Front, Oc R 5s 11m 5M; W hut; 51°48'·53N 08°15'·22W. Rear, 113m from front, Oc R 5s 21m 5M; W hut; synch with front.
Spit Bank Pile Iso WR 4s 10m W10M, R7M; W house on R piles; vis: R087°- W196°- R221°- 358°; 51°50'·72N 08°16'·45W.

KINSALE and OYSTER HAVEN

Bulman Q (6) + L Fl 15s; 51°40'·14N 08°29'·74W; 992501104.
Charlesfort Fl WRG 5s 18m W9M, R6M, G7M; vis: G348°- W358°- R004°-168°; H24; 51°41'·75N 08°29'·84W.

OLD HEAD OF KINSALE TO MIZEN HEAD

Old Head of Kinsale ☆, S point 51°36'·29N 08°32'·02W Fl (2) 10s 72m **20M**; B twr, two W bands; 992501107.

COURTMACSHERRY

Barrel Rock 51°37'·01N 08°37'·30W.
Black Tom Fl G 5s; 51°36'·41N 08°37'·95W; 992501110.

Wood Pt (Land Pt) Fl (2) WR 5s 15m 5M; vis: W315°-R332°-315°; 51°38'·16N 08°41'·00W.
Galley Head ☆ summit 51°31'·80N 08°57'·21W Fl (5) 20s 53m **23M**; W twr; vis: 256°-065°.

GLANDORE and CASTLETOWNSHEND

Glandore Dir lt Oc WRG 37m 7M, metal tower, vis: 294°-G-304°-W-312°-R-342°; 51°33'·33N 09°07'·08W.
Reen Point Fl WRG 10s 9m W5M, R3M, G3M; W twr; vis: shore-G-338°-W-001°-R-shore; 51°30'·98N 09°10'·50W.
Kowloon Bridge Q(6)+LFl 15s; 51°27'·58N 09°13'·75W; 992501118.

BALTIMORE and FASTNET

Barrack Pt Fl (2) WR 6s 40m W6M, R3M; vis: R168°- W294°-038°; 51°28'·33N 09°23'·65W.
Loo Rock Fl G 3s; 51°28'·44N 09°23'·46W; 992501119.
Lousy Rks Q(6)+LFl 15s; 51°28'·93N 09°23'·39W.
Wallis Rk Fl (3) R 10s; 51°28'·93N 09°22'·99W.
Lettuce Pt VQ (3) 5s; 51°29'·32N 09°23'·81W.
Mealbeg Q(6) + LFl 15s; 51°29'·68N 09°24'·69W.
Inane Pt Q(6) + LFl 15s; 51°30'·02N 09°23'·66W.
Hare Is Q; 51°30'·17N 09°25'·38W.
Fastnet ☆, W end 51°23'·36N 09°36'·18W Fl 5s 53m **18M**; Gy twr, ***Racon (G) 18M***. Fog Det Lt VQ; 992501123.

SCHULL and LONG ISLAND CHANNEL

Amelia ; 51°29.979'N 009°31.461'W; 992501120.
Copper Point 51°30'·25N 09°32'·06W Q (3) 10s 16m 8M.
Ldg lts 346° Front, Oc 5s 5m 11M, W mast; 51°31'·68N 09°32'·43W. Rear, 91m from front, Oc 5s 8m11M; W mast.

CROOKHAVEN

Rock Is Pt L Fl WR 8s 20m W13M, R11M; W twr; vis: W over Long Is B to 281°-R-340°; inside harbour 281°-R-348°- towards N shore; 51°28'·59N 09°42'·27W; 992501124.

MIZEN HEAD TO DINGLE BAY

Mizen Head Iso 4s 55m 12M; vis: 313°-133°; 51°26'·99N 09°49'·23W; 992501127.
Sheep's Hd ☆ 51°32'·59N 09°50'·92W Fl (3) WR 15s 83m **W15M** R9M; W bldg; vis: 011·3°-R-016·6°-W-212·5°-(partially obs) 233° (shore); 992501129.

BANTRY BAY, CASTLETOWN BEARHAVEN, WHIDDY IS

Carrigavaddra VQ (3) 5s, 51°38'·72N 09°45'·91W.
Roancarrigmore Fl WR 5s 13m W11M, R9M, R5M; s/steel twr; vis: 312°-W-050°-R-122°-R(unintens)-207°-obsc-246°-R-312°; 51°39'·18N 09°44'·82W. Old Lt ho W twr, B band; 992501130.
Ardnakinna Pt 51°37'·10N 09°55'·09W Fl (2) WR 10s 62m W14M, R9M; W ○ twr; vis: 319°-R-348°-W-066°-R-shore; 992501131.
Walter Scott Rk Q (6) + L Fl 15s; 51°38'·52N 09°54'·20W; 992501128.
Castletownbere Dir lt 023·25° Oc WRG 5s 5·7m WRG15M; Twr; vis: 020·5°-G-023°-W-023·5°-R-025·5°; 51°38'·73N 09°54'·35W; 992501125.
Castletown Ldg lts 008°. Front, Oc Bu 6s 4m 6M; W col, R stripe; vis: 005°-013°; 51°39'·16N 09°54'·40W. Rear, 80m from front, Oc Bu 6s 7m 6M; W with R stripe; vis: 005°-013°.
Bull Rock ☆ 51°35'·52N 10°18'·07W Fl 15s 91m **18M**; W twr; 992501131.

KENMARE RIVER, DARRYNANE and BALLYCROVANE

Illaunnameanla (Ballycrovane) Fl R 3s; 51°42'·60N 09°57'·50W.
Book Rks Fl(2) R 10s; 51°46'·54N 09°49'·74W.
Cuskeal Fl R 5s; 51°46'·45N 09°48'·85W.
Bunaw Ldg Lts 041°. Front, Oc R 3s 9m 2M; B col, Y bands; 51°46'·80N 09°48'·40W. Rear, 200m from front Iso R 2s 11m 2M.
Maiden Rk Fl G 5s; 51°49'·00N 09°47'·99W; 992501134.
Bat Rk Fl G 5s; 51°50'·89N 09°40'·89W.
Carrignaronebeg Fl R 5s; 51°50'·99N 09°41'·39W.

No1 ▲ Fl G 5s; 51°52′·09N 09°36′·35W.
Carrignarone (Seal Rk) Fl 5s 2m 2M; 51°48′·58N 09°52′·65W.
Castlecove Ldg Lts 045°. Front, Oc 2s 5m 6M; concrete post W front; 51°46′·29N 10°02′·04W. Rear, 400m from front Oc 2s 18m 6M.
West Cove Hbr ☆ Fl R 3s; post W front; 51°46′·00N 10°02′·93W.
West Cove Hbr Ldg Lts 312°. Front, Fl 2s 2m 6M; concrete post; 51°46′·11N 10°03′·08W. Rear, 200m from front Fl 2s 4m 6M.
Darrynane Ldg lts 034°. Front, Oc 3s 10m 4M; 51°45′·90N 10°09′·20W. Rear, Oc 3s 16m 4M.

SKELLIG ISLANDS

Skelligs Rock ☆ Fl (3) 15s 53m 12M; W twr; vis: 262°-115°; part obsc within 6M 110°-115°; 51°46′·11N 10°32′·52W; 992501137.

VALENTIA and PORTMAGEE

Fort (Cromwell) Point ☆ 51°56′·02N 10°19′·27W Fl WR 2s 16m **W17M, R10M**; W twr; vis: 304°-R-351°,104°-W-304°; obsc from seaward by Doulus Head when brg more than 180°; 992501141.

Dir lt 141° ☆ Oc WRG 4s 25m W11M, R8M, G8M (by day: W3M, R2M, G2M); W twr, R stripe; vis:136°-G-140°-W-142°-R-146°; 51°55′·51N 10°18′·42W.

The Foot ⚓ VQ (3) 5s; 51°55′·72N 10°17′·07W; 992501140.

DINGLE BAY TO LOOP HEAD

DINGLE BAY, VENTRY and DINGLE

Lt Twr ☆ Fl WRG 3s 20m WRG 6M; W metal twr; vis: 310°-G-328°-W-000°-R-024°; 52°07′·30N 10°15′·51W.
Dingle Hbr ☆ Fl (2) 3s 6m 3M, 52 07·24 N 10 15·71 W.
Foheragh Dir Lt ☆ 182° Oc WRG 5s 8 2 Pole; vis:177°-Oc R-181°-Oc W-183°-Oc G-187°, 52 07·43 N 10 16·59 W.
Dingle Dir Lt ☆ 002° Oc WRG 5s 14 3 Mast; vis: 354°-Oc G-001°-Oc W-003°-Oc R-009°, 52 08·34 N 10 16·52 W.

Inishtearaght ☆, W end Blasket Islands 52°04′·54N 10°39′·67W Fl (2) 20s 84m **18M**; W twr; vis: 318°-221°; ***Racon (O)***; 992501143.

BRANDON BAY, TRALEE BAY and FENIT HARBOUR

Lit Samphire Is ☆ Fl WRG 5s 17m W14M, RG11M; Bu ○ twr; vis: 262°-R-275°, 280°-R-090°-G-140°-W-152°-R-172°; 52°16′·26N 09°52′·91W.

Gt Samphire Is ☆ QR 15m 3M; vis: 242°-097°; 52°16′·15N 09°51′·81W.

Fenit Hbr Pier Hd ☆ 2 FR (vert) 12m 3M; vis: 148°-058°; 52°16′·24N 09°51′·55W.

SHANNON ESTUARY

Ballybunnion ⚓ VQ; ***Racon (M) 6M***; 52°32′·52N 09°46′·93W; 992501146.
Kilstiffin ◬ Fl R 3s; 52°33′·80N 09°43′·83W; 992501148.
Kilcredaun ◬ Q R (sync); 52°34′·42N 09°41′·16W.
Tail of Beal ▲ Q G (sync); 52°34′·37N 09°40′·71W; 992501150.
Kilcredaun Head ◬, W twr; 52°34′·78N 09°42′·58W.
Carrigaholt ◬ Fl (2) R 6s (sync); 52°34′·90N 09°40′·47W.
Beal Spit ▲ Fl (2) G 6s (sync); 52°34′·80N 09°39′·94W.
Beal Bar ▲ Fl G 3s (sync); 52°35′·18N 09°39′·05W.
Doonaha ◬ Fl R 3s (sync); 52°35′·54N 09°39′·01W; 992501154.
Corlis Pt (Ldg lts 046·4° H24) ☆ Front, Iso 4s 9m 7M(day) 10M; hut; 52°37′·10N 09°36′·36W; 992501156.
Querrin Pt ☆ Rear, Iso 4s 28m 7M(day) 10M; lattice mast; 52°37′·69N 09°35′·34W.
Letter Point ◬ Fl R 7s; 52°35′·44N 09°35′·89W.
Asdee ◬ Fl R 5s; 52°35′·09N 09°34′·55W.
Rineanna ◬ QR; 52°35′·59N 09°31′·24W.
North Carraig ⚓ Q; 52°35′·60N 09°29′·76W.

Scattery Is, Rineanna Pt ☆ Fl (2) 8s 15m 10M; W twr; vis: 208°-092°; 52°36′·35N 09°31′·07W.

KILRUSH

Marina Ent Chan Ldg lts 355°. Front, Oc 3s; 52°37′·99N 09°30′·27W. Rear, 75m from front, Oc 3s.
Tarbert Is N Point ☆ Q WR 4s 18m W14M, R10M; W ○ twr; vis: W069°-R277°-W287°-339°; 52°35′·52N 09°21′·83W.
Tarbert (Ballyhoolahan Pt) Ldg lts 128·2° ⚓. Front, Iso 3s 13m 3M; △ on W twr; vis: 123·2°-133·2°; 52°34′·35N 09°18′·80W. Rear, 400m from front, Iso 5s 18m 3M; G stripe on W Bn.
Garraunbaun Pt ☆ Fl (3) WR 10s 16m W8M, R5M; W □ col, vis: R shore - W072°- R242°- shore; 52°35′·62N 09°13′·94W.
Rinealon Pt ☆ Fl 2·5s 4m 7M; B col, W bands; vis: 234°-088°; 52°37′·12N 09°09′·82W.

FOYNES

W Chan Ldg lts 107·9° (may be moved for changes in chan). Front, Oc 4s 34m 12M; 52°36′·91N 09°06′·59W . Rear, Oc 4s 39m 12M.

RIVER SHANNON

Beeves Rock ☆ Fl WR 5s 12m W12M, R9M; vis: 064·5°-W-091°-R-238°-W-265°-W(unintens)-064·5°; 52°39′·01N 09°01′·35W .
North Channel Ldg lts 093°. Front, Tradree Rock Fl R 2s 6m 5M; W Trs; vis: 246°-110°; 52°41′·00N 08°49′·87W. Rear 0·65M from front, Iso 6s 14m 5M; W twr, R bands; vis: 327°-190°.

N side, Ldg lts 061°. Front, 52°40′·72N 08°45′·27W, Crawford Rock 490m from rear, Fl R 3s 6m 5M. Crawford No 2, Common Rear, Iso 6s 10m 5M; 52°40′·85N 08°44′·88W.
Ldg lts 302·1°, Flagstaff Rock, 670m from rear, Fl R 7s 7m 5M; 52°40′·66N 08°44′·40W.
Ldg lts 106·5°. Meelick Rk, Front Iso R 4s 6m 5M; 52°40′·24N 08°42′·32W. Meelick No 2, rear 275m from front Iso R 4s 9m 5M; both W beacons.

LOOP HEAD

Loop Head ☆ 52°33′·67N 09°55′·92W Fl (4) 20s 84m **23M**; vis: 280°-218°; 992501161.
Mal Bay ◬ Fl(5) Y 20s 52°46.42′N 009°35.15′W; *AIS.*

5.4 PASSAGE INFORMATION

The latest editions of Irish Cruising Club Sailing Directions are recommended for Irish waters (www.irishcruisingclub.com). They are particularly useful on the N and W coast where information is scarce and published in two volumes, *E and N coasts of Ireland* and *S and W coasts of Ireland* – available from Todd Chart Services, Bangor, Co Down, ☎028 9146 6640 (www.toddchart.com) or Imray. See also *Cruising Cork and Kerry* (Imray/Swanson). For notes on crossing the Irish Sea, see 6.4; and for distances across it see 0.32.

MALAHIDE TO DUN LAOGHAIRE

(AC 1468) Malahide, 4M from both Lambay Is and Howth, given adequate tidal height, can be entered in most weather except strong onshore winds. The channel, shallow at points, runs between drying banks marked by R & G fixed perches.

Ireland's Eye, a rky island which rises steeply to a height of 99m, lies about 7½ca N of Howth with reefs running SE and SW from Thulla Rk at its SE end. This provides some shelter to the ent to Howth but following strong ENE'ly winds heavy seas can pile up in the approach channel.

Ben of Howth, on the N of Dublin Bay, a prominent landmark, is steep-to, with no dangers over 1ca offshore.

Dublin Bay is protected by the offshore shoals of Bennet and Kish Banks, the main passage between which is marked by N/S cardinal buoys. Closer inshore, SE of Baily Lt, lies Burford Bank, on which the sea breaks in E gales. Rosbeg Bank lies on the N side of Dublin Bay marked by cardinal buoys guarding the approach to the R Liffey.

A TSS ½M long at either end of the Burford Bank leads to/ from an anti-clockwise 'roundabout' radius 2·3ca centred on Dublin Bay SWM lt buoy 2·75M ESE of Dublin Port. Do not impede large vessels and keep clear of the TSS and fairway.

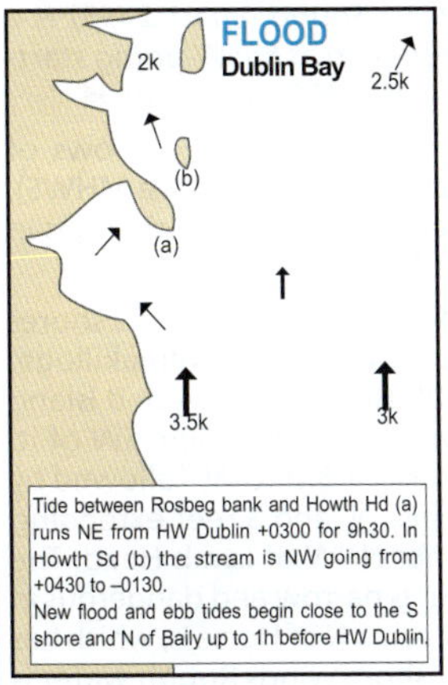

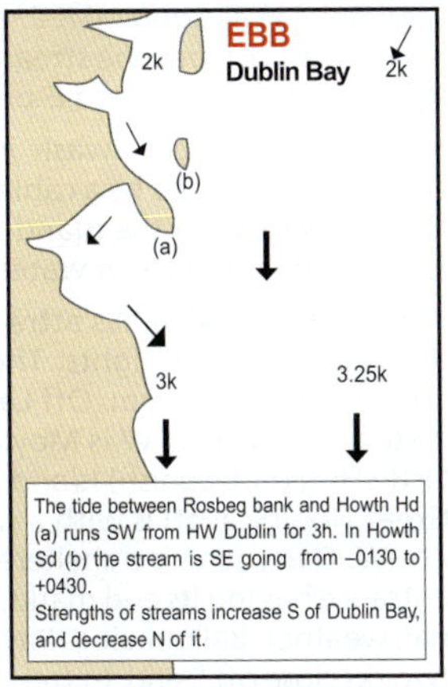

▶ *The N-going stream begins at HW Dublin – 0600, and the S-going at HW Dublin, Sp rate 3kn. Strong tidal streams run SE–NW through Muglin and Dalkey Snds (2.5Kn at Sp).* ◀

The bay between Dublin and Dun Laoghaire is shallow but otherwise clear of obstacles. To the E Dalkey Is and Muglins (lit) lie close under Sorrento Pt. Dalkey Snd should be used only in fair weather and ⚓ made off the slip on the W shore.

DUN LAOGHAIRE TO TUSKAR ROCK

(AC 1468, 1787) From Dublin to Carnsore Pt shallow offshore banks cause dangerous overfalls and dictate the route most sheltered from the W winds. Arklow is safe in offshore winds; Wexford has a difficult entrance. Rosslare lacks yacht facilities, but provides good shelter to wait out a SW'ly blow.

▶ *Tidal streams run N-S, the N-going flood sets across the banks to the E, and the S-going ebb sets across them to the W.* ◀

Leaving Dublin Bay, yachts normally use Dalkey Sound, but with a foul tide or light wind it is better to use Muglins Sound. Muglins (lt) is steep-to with a rock about 1ca WSW of the lt. Beware Leac Buidhe (dries) 1ca E of Clare Rock. The inshore passage is best as far as Wicklow running W of Kish, Codling and India Banks. Waves break on these in heavy weather esp in vicinity of the extreme shoal portions and occas wrecks. Thereafter yachts may either route offshore, east of Arklow Bank to fetch Tuskar Rock or Greenore Pt, or keep inshore avoiding Glassgorman Banks. Arklow Bank Wind Farm, 7 miles east of Arklow, has 7 wind turbines, each 72.8m high with 104m diameter blades. They are lit, No 7 is fitted with an AIS transmitter. Only use Rusk Channel in settled weather. Otherwise, stay E of Blackwater Bank to Lucifer ECM buoy then pass W of Tuskar Rock to round Carnsore Point.

Dangerous rks lie up to 2ca NW and 6½ca SSW of Tuskar Rk and a dangerous race forms off Carnsore Pt. In bad weather or poor visibility, use the ITZ of the Tuskar Rock TSS, passing to seaward of Tuskar Rk, Barrels ECM and Coningbeg buoy.

TUSKAR ROCK TO COBH

(AC 2049) If taking the inshore passage from Greenore Pt, stay inside The Bailies to pass 2ca off Carnsore Pt. Beware of lobster pots. Steer WSW to pass N of Black Rk and the Bohurs, S of which are extensive overfalls. The small harbour at Kilmore Quay has been rebuilt with a marina, but beware rocks and shoals in the approaches.

Saltee Sound (AC 2740) is a safe passage, least width 3ca, between Great and Little Saltee, conspic islands to S and N.

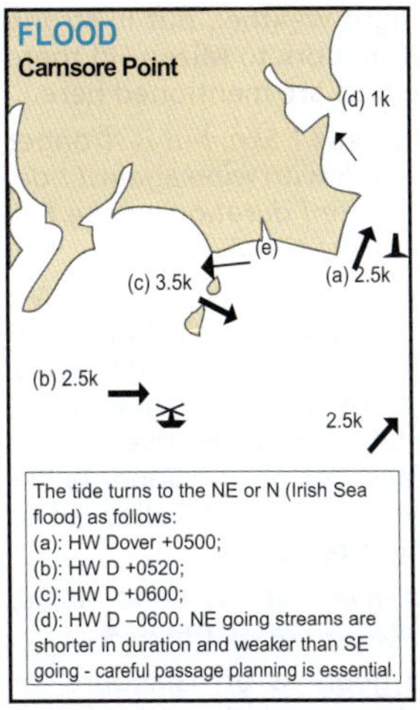

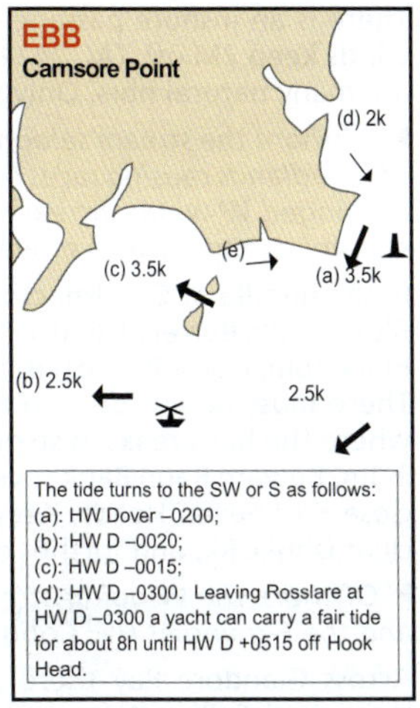

NOTE: The tide turns on St Patrick's Bridge (e) up to 2 hours earlier than in Saltee Sound

Sebber Bridge extends 7½ca N from the NE point of Great Saltee and Jackeen Rk is 1M NW of S end of Little Saltee.

▶ *Care is needed in the sound, with a Sp rate of 3·5kn.* ◀

S of the Saltees lie rocks interlaced with passages. There are no hazards on a rhumb line to a point 1M S of Hook Head. This clears Tower Race which can be violent in strong W'ly winds. Overfalls occur off Waterford Hbr (AC2046) when the W'ly stream from Hook Hd meets the strong outgoing stream.

Dunmore East (AC 2046) is a useful refuge at the mouth of Waterford Hbr. To the W, Falskirt, a dangerous rock, lies off Swines Pt. There are few offlying rocks from Tramore Bay to Ballinacourty Pt on the N side of Dungarvan Bay (AC 2017). Helvick is a small sheltered hbr approached along the S shore of the bay, keeping SE of Helvick Rk (ECM) and other dangers.

▶ *Here the W-going stream starts at HW Cobh +0230, and the E-going at HW Cobh –0215, Sp rates 1·5kn.* ◀

Mine Hd (lt) has two dangerous rks, The Rogue about 2½ca E and The Longship 1M SW. To the W is a submerged rock 100m SE of Ram Hd. The best appr to Youghal is E of East Bar (W Sect) and the hazards of Blackball Ledge and Bar Rocks. Heading W Pass 2ca off Capel Island; the sound between it and Knockadoon Hd is not recommended (overfalls). The N side of Ballycotton Bay is foul up to 5ca offshore. Ballycotton Hbr is small and crowded, but there is a sheltered ⚓ outside. Sound Rk and Small Is lie between the mainland and Ballycotton Is (lit). From Ballycotton to Cork keep at least 5ca off for dangers including The Smiths (PHM) 1·5M WSW of Ballycotton Island. Pass between Hawk Rk, close off Power Hd and Pollock Rk (SCM) 1.25M SE.

COBH TO MIZEN HEAD

Near the easy entrance and excellent shelter of Cork Harbour (AC 1777), Ringabella Bay offers temp ⚓ in good weather. 7ca SE of Robert's Hd is Daunt Rk (3·5m, PHM) on which seas break in bad weather. Little Sovereign ≠ with Reanies Hd 241° leads inshore of it. The Sovereigns are large rks off Oyster Haven, a good hbr prone to swell in S'lies. Harbour Rk, which must be left to the E, lies in the mouth. Bulman Rk (SCM) is 4ca S of Preghane Pt at the entry to Kinsale's fine harbour.

▶ *The tide on the Cork coast turns to the NE at HW Dover +0045. There is an eddy 5M ESE of Old Head of Kinsale at HW Dover +0400. The ingoing Cork Harbour tide begins at HW Dover +0055. The tide turns SW at HW Dover +0500. The outgoing Cork Harbour tide begins at HW Dover –0540. Old Head of Kinsale (lt, fog sig) is quite steep-to; a race extends 1M SW on W-going stream, and to SE on E-going stream.* ◀

There is an inshore passage in light weather, but in strong winds keep 2M off. (AC 2424) From Cork to Mizen Hd there are many natural hbrs. Only the best are mentioned here.

► *Offshore the stream seldom exceeds 1·5kn, but is stronger off headlands causing races / overfalls with wind against tide. Prolonged W winds increase the rate / duration of the E-ly stream; strong E winds similarly effect the W-ly stream.* ◄

In the middle of Courtmacsherry Bay dangers, from E to W: Blueboy Rk, Barrel Rk (with Inner Barrels closer inshore), and Black Tom; Horse Rk is off Barry's Pt at the W side of the bay. These must be avoided going to or from Courtmacsherry, where the bar breaks in strong S/SE winds. The river carries 2·3m. Beware Baun Bank (overfalls) Cotton and Shoonta Rks close E of Seven Heads. Keep at least 5ca off Galley Hd to clear Dhulic Rk, and further off in fresh winds.

► *Offshore the W-going stream makes at HW Cobh +0200, and the E-going at HW Cobh –0420, Sp rates 1·5kn.* ◄

Across Glandore Bay there are good ⚓s off Glandore, or Union Hall. Sailing W from Glandore, pass either side of High and Low Is; if inside beware Belly Rk (awash) about 3ca S of Rabbit Is. Castle Haven, a sheltered and attractive hbr, is entered between Reen Pt (lt) and Battery Pt. Toe Head has foul ground out to 100m S, and The Stags (rks) lie 7½ca S.

Fastnet Rk (lit) is nearly 4M WSW of Cape Clear; 2½ca NE of it is an outlying rk. An E/W TSS lies between 2 and 8M SSE of the Fastnet. Long Island Bay can be entered from Cape Clear or through Gascanane Sound, between Clear Is and Sherkin Is. Carrigmore Rks lie in the middle of this chan, with Gascanane Rk 1ca W of them. The channel between Carrigmore Rks and Badger Island is best. If bound for Crookhaven, beware Bullig Reef, N of Clear Is. Schull is N of Long Island, inside which passage can be made W'ward to Crookhaven. A well-sheltered hbr, it is accessible at all states of tide, entered between Rock Is lt Ho and Alderman Rks, ENE of Streek Hd. ⚓ off the village.

► *Off Mizen Hd (lt ho) the W-going stream starts at HW Cobh +0120, and the E-going at HW Cobh –0500 Sp rate 4kn. With wind against tide a dangerous race forms right to the shore, sometimes reaching to Brow Hd or Three Castle Hd.* ◄

THE WEST COAST

This coast offers wonderful cruising, although exposed to the Atlantic and any swell offshore; but this diminishes mid-summer. In bad weather the sea breaks dangerously on shoals with quite substantial depths. There is often a refuge nearby, but if caught out in deteriorating weather and poor vis, a stranger may need to make an offing until conditions improve. Even in mid-summer a gale may be met in a two-week cruise. Fog is less frequent than in the Irish Sea.

► *Tidal streams are weak, except round headlands.* ◄

The few lights inshore render navigation unwise after dark, but coastal navigation is feasible in good visibility.

MIZEN HEAD TO DINGLE BAY

(AC 2423) Three Castle Hd has rks 1ca W, and seas break on S Bullig 4ca off Hd. Dunmanus B (AC 2552) has three hbrs: Dunmanus, Kitchen Cove and Dunbeacon. It is best to keep N of Carbery, Cold and Furze Is. Sheep's Hd (lt) is at the S end of Bantry Bay (AC 1838, 1840) which has excellent hbrs, notably Glengariff and Castletown. There are few dangers offshore, except around Bear and Whiddy Islands.

► *Off Blackball Hd at W entrance to Bantry B there can be a nasty race, particularly on W-going stream against the wind. Keep 3ca off Crow Is to clear dangers.* ◄

Dursey Island is steep-to; beware rock 7½ca NE of Dursey Hd and Lea Rk (1·4m) 1½ca SW. Calf and Heifer Rks are 7½ca SW of Dursey Hd, where there is often broken water and tidal streams run strongly. The Bull (AIS, Racon) and two rocks W of it lie 2·5M WNW of Dursey Hd. The Cow is midway between Dursey Hd and The Bull with clear water each side.

► *2M W of The Bull the stream turns NW at HW Cobh +0150, and SE at HW Cobh –0420. Dursey Sound (chart 2495) is a good short cut, but the stream runs 4kn at Sp; W-going starts at HW Cobh +0135, and E-going at HW Cobh –0450.* ◄

Flag Rk lies almost awash in mid-chan at the narrows of Dursey Snd, crossed by a cable car (cables 25m above MHWS). Hold very close to the Island shore. Beware wind changes in the sound, and broken water at N entrance.

Kenmare (AC 2495) has attractive hbrs and ⚓s, but its shores are rocky, without lights. The best places are Kilmakilloge, Sneem and Ardgroom. Off Lamb's Head, Two Headed Island is steep-to; further W is Moylaun Is with a rk 300m SW of it. Little Hog (or Deenish) Island is rocky 1·5M to W, followed by Great Hog (Scariff) Is with a rk close N, and a reef extending 2ca W. Darrynane is a sheltered hbr NNW of Lamb Head. The entrance has ldg lts and marks, but is narrow and dangerous in bad weather. Ballinskelligs Bay has an ⚓ N of Horse Is, which has two rks close off E end. In fresh onshore winds Rough water is met between Bolus and Bray Hd. The SW end of Puffin Island is steep-to, but the sound to the E is rocky and not advised. Great Skellig (lit) is 6M, and Little Skellig 5M WSW of Puffin Is. Lemon Rk lies between Puffin Is and Little Skellig.

► *Tide turns N at HW Cobh+0500, and S at HW Cobh –0110.* ◄

There is a rock 3ca SW of Great Skellig. When very calm it is possible to go alongside at Blind Man's Cove on NE side of Great Skellig, where there are interesting ruins.

DINGLE BAY TO LISCANNOR BAY

(AC 2254) Dingle Bay (AC 2789, 2790) is wide and deep, with few dangers around its shores. Cahersiveen and Dingle have small marinas. The best ⚓ are at Portmagee and Ventry. At the NW ent to the bay, 2·5M SSW of Slea Hd, is Wild Bank (Three Fathom Pinnacle), a shallow patch with overfalls. 3M SW of Wild Bank is Barrack Rock, which breaks in strong winds. The Blasket Islands are very exposed, with strong tides and overfalls but worth a visit in settled weather (AC 2790).

Great Blasket and Inishvickillane each have ⚓ and landing on their NE side. Between lies Inishabro with a beach and impressive rock formations. Inishtearaght is the most W'ly Is (lt), but further W lie Tearaght Rks, and 3M S are Little Foze and Gt Foze Rks. Inishtooskert is the most N'ly. Blasket Sound is the most convenient N-S route, 1M wide, and easy in daylight and reasonable weather with fair wind or tide; extensive rks and shoals form its W side.

► *The N-going stream starts at HW Galway +0430, and the S-going at HW Galway –0155, with sp rate 3kn.* ◄

Between Blasket Sound and Sybil Pt there is a race in W or NW winds with N-going tide, and often a nasty sea. Sybil Pt has steep cliffs, and offlying rks extend 3½ca.

Smerwick hbr, entered between Duncapple Is and the E Sister, is sheltered, except from NW or N winds. From here the scenery is spectacular to Brandon Bay on the W side of which there is an ⚓, but exposed to N winds and swell.

From Inishtearaght to Loop Hd, Little Samphire Is is the sole lt in Tralee Bay, leading to Fenit the only secure refuge before the Shannon Estuary. The coast from Loop Hd to Liscannor Bay has no safe ⚓ and no lts, save SPM Fl(5)Y 20s 3M off Donegal Pt and an AIS buoy Fl(5)Y 20s in Mal Bay marking Doughmore Shoals. Take care not to be set inshore, although there are few offlying dangers except Grundel Rk near Mutton Is and Drumdeirg and Kilstiffin Rks in Liscannor Bay.

5.5 SPECIAL NOTES FOR IRELAND

Céad Míle Fáilte! One hundred thousand Welcomes!

LIFEJACKETS: It is mandatory to wear lifejackets in Irish waters on all craft of over 7m LOA. Children under 16 years must wear a lifejacket or personal flotation device at all times on deck when underway. Every vessel, irrespective of size, must carry a lifejacket or personal flotation device for each person on board.

Irish Customs: Ports of entry are: Dublin, Dun Laoghaire, Waterford, New Ross, Cork, Ringaskiddy, Bantry, Foynes, Limerick, Galway, Sligo and Killybegs. Yachts may, in fact, make their first call anywhere and if no Customs officer arrives within a reasonable time, the skipper should inform the nearest Garda (Police) station. Yachts from non-EU member states should fly flag Q or show ● over ○ lts on arrival. Passports are not required by UK citizens.

Telephone: To call the **Republic of Ireland (RoI)** from abroad, dial **+353**, the area code minus the initial 0, followed by the number. Northern Ireland telephone nos have 8 digits **028 90**12 3456.

Access by air: Intl airports in RoI are at Dublin, Cork and Shannon. Regional airports in Waterford, Farranfore (Kerry), Knock (Mayo) and Carrickfinn (Donegal) provide some scheduled flights between Ireland and Britain. For details, see http://www.irishairports.com/.

Currency is the Euro (€), readily available from ATMs. VAT is 23%.

Useful Irish websites:

Commissioners of Irish Lights (CIL) www.cil.ie
Irish Sailing Association www.sailing.ie
Irish Tourist Board www.discoverireland.com
Sea Area Forecast www.met.ie/forecasts/sea-area.asp

AIS stations: AIS stations have been established on navigational marks around the coast of Ireland under the control of the CIL. These are fitted at lighthouses, and in remote areas buoys offshore.

Liquefied petroleum gas: In RoI LPG is supplied by Kosan, a sister company of Calorgas Ltd, but the smallest bottle is taller than the Calor equivalent fitted in most yachts with different connections. Calor bottles can be filled in larger towns. Camping Gaz is widely available.

Diesel: The supply of marine diesel has been greatly reduced by changes in the fiscal regime and opportunities to fuel in remote areas limited.

Salmon drift nets are now illegal and should not be encountered. Draft netting (across a river or estuary) is still permitted, but is rare.

Northern Ireland: Belfast CG (MRCC) is at Bangor, Co Down, ☎(02891) 463933. HM Customs (⊜) should be contacted H24 on ☎0300 1232012, (National Yachtline) if a local Customs Officer is not available. Belfast (Aldergrove) is the main airport.

GAELIC: It helps to understand some of the more common words for navigational features (courtesy of the Irish Cruising Club):

Ail, alt	cliff, height	*Cladach*	shore	*Inish, illaun*	island	*Mara*	of the sea
Aird, ard	height, high	*Cuan, coon*	harbour	*Inver*	river mouth	*More, mor*	big
Anna, annagh	marsh	*Derg, dearg*	red	*Keal, keel*	narrow place,	*Rannagh*	point
Ath	ford	*Drum*	hill, ridge		sound	*Ron, roan*	seal
Bal, Bally	town	*Duff, dubh*	black	*Kill*	church, cell	*Roe, ruadh*	red
Barra	sandbank	*Dun, doon*	fort	*Kin, ken*	promontory,	*Scolt*	split, rky gut
Bel, beal	mouth, strait	*Ennis*	island		head	*Scrow*	boggy,
Beg	little	*Fad, fadda*	long	*Knock*	hill		grassy sward
Ben, binna	hill	*Fan*	slope	*Lag*	hollow	*Slieve*	mountain
Bo	sunken rock	*Fin*	white	*Lahan*	broad	*Slig*	shells
Boy, bwee	yellow	*Freagh, free*	heather	*Lea*	grey	*Stag, stac*	high rock
Bullig	shoal, round	*Gall*	stranger	*Lenan*	weed-	*Tawney*	low hill
	rock, breaker	*Glas, glass*	green		covered rock	*Tigh, ti*	house
Bun	end, river mouth	*Glinsk*	clear water	*Lis*	ancient fort	*Togher*	causeway
Caher	fort	*Gorm*	blue	*Long, luing*	ship	*Tra, traw*	strand
Camus	bay, river bend	*Gub*	point of land	*Maan*	middle	*Turlin*	boulder, beach
Carrick	rock	*Hassans*	swift current	*Maol, mwee*	bare	*Vad, bad*	boat

DISTANCE TABLE

Approximate distances in nautical miles are by the most direct route, whilst avoiding dangers and allowing for Traffic Separation Schemes. Places in *italics* are in adjoining areas; places in **bold** are in 0.32, Distances across the Irish Sea.

1	***Carlingford Lough***	**1**																											
2	Malahide	36	**2**																										
3	Howth	39	4	**3**																									
4	**Dublin/Dun Laoghaire**	48	12	8	**4**																								
5	**Wicklow**	63	29	25	21	**5**																							
6	**Arklow**	75	43	37	36	15	**6**																						
7	Wexford (Bar Buoy)	104	71	66	62	43	30	**7**																					
8	**Rosslare**	108	75	70	66	47	34	4	**8**																				
9	Kilmore Quay	128	95	90	86	67	54	25	21	**9**																			
10	Waterford	154	127	116	117	99	84	51	47	32	**10**																		
11	**Dunmore East**	139	112	101	102	84	69	36	32	17	15	**11**																	
12	**Youghal**	172	143	134	133	115	100	69	65	51	52	37	**12**																
13	**Crosshaven**	192	165	154	155	137	122	89	85	69	74	59	25	**13**															
14	Kinsale	202	178	164	168	150	135	99	95	79	84	69	35	17	**14**														
15	Courtmacsherry	201	177	163	167	149	136	109	105	85	90	75	44	26	13	**15**													
16	Glandore	213	189	175	179	161	148	121	117	97	102	87	56	38	25	23	**16**												
17	Castletownshend	224	200	186	190	172	159	132	128	108	113	98	67	49	36	26	6	**17**											
18	**Baltimore**	239	205	201	196	177	164	136	132	112	117	102	70	54	42	34	16	12	**18**										
19	**Fastnet Rock**	250	216	212	207	189	174	148	144	122	127	112	78	60	49	42	24	20	10	**19**									
20	Schull	256	222	218	213	195	180	154	150	128	133	118	84	66	55	48	30	26	14	9	**20**								
21	Crookhaven	256	222	218	213	195	180	154	150	128	133	118	84	66	55	47	29	25	16	8	10	**21**							
22	Bantry	286	252	237	243	225	210	184	180	158	163	148	114	96	85	78	60	56	45	36	41	35	**22**						
23	Kenmare R (Scariff Is)	285	251	236	242	224	209	183	179	157	162	147	113	95	84	77	59	55	44	35	40	34	42	**23**					
24	Valentia Hbr	295	261	257	252	242	227	192	188	175	180	165	131	113	102	96	78	74	56	54	60	53	55	20	**24**				
25	Dingle	308	274	270	265	246	233	205	201	181	186	171	139	123	111	104	86	82	69	62	67	61	63	28	13	**25**			
26	Fenit Hbr	344	310	306	301	283	268	242	238	216	221	206	172	154	143	136	118	114	105	95	99	93	100	60	47	45	**26**		
27	Kilrush	361	333	323	318	299	286	258	254	234	239	224	192	176	164	155	137	133	122	114	116	109	116	78	66	64	32	**27**	
28	*Slyne Head*	317	355	351	346	328	313	287	283	261	266	251	217	199	188	180	162	158	153	139	141	133	144	103	97	95	70	75	**28**

5.6 MALAHIDE

Dublin **53°27'·20N 06°08'·90W**

CHARTS AC 1468, 633, 5621; Imray C61, C62

TIDES +0030 Dover; ML 2·4; Duration 0615

Standard Port DUBLIN (NORTH WALL) (→)

Times				Height (metres)			
High Water		Low Water		MHWS	MHWN	MLWN	MLWS
0000	0700	0000	0500	4·1	3·4	1·5	0·7
1200	1900	1200	1700				
Differences MALAHIDE							
+0002	+0003	+0009	+0009	+0·1	–0·2	–0·4	–0·2

SHELTER Excellent in marina, dredged approx 2·3m. Visitor's berth on pontoon A. Moorings preclude ⚓ in the inlet.

NAVIGATION WPT: SWM LFl 10s 53°27'·12N 06°06'·87W. The approach channel, which is well marked by 12 lit PHM and SHM, lies between drying sandbanks. The entrance is straightforward, but there is less than 1m of water below CD at some points of the chan, so adequate height of tide is required for safe entry. The flood reaches 3kn sp, the ebb 3½kn and a strong flow may be experienced through the marina at some states of the tide. Steep seas are formed in strong onshore winds against the full ebb, during which extreme caution needs to be exercised. The speed limit is 5kn in the fairway and 4kn in the marina.

LIGHTS AND MARKS The marina and apartment blocks close S of it are visible from the WPT. The marina entrance is marked by occulting red and green lights to each side.

COMMUNICATIONS (Code 01) ⊜ 8746571; Police 666 4600; Dr 845 5994; Ⓗ 837 7755.

Malahide Marina, Ch **M** 80 (H24). MY: *Yacht Base* Ch **M** (occas).

FACILITIES Marina ☎8454129, 349 inc 20Ⓥ €4·10, €20·50 wkly (charge varies) /WC (H24) Kos Ⓔ (30t) ✕.

Malahide YC ☎8453372, (for craft <5.5m, launching HW ±2).

Town ✉ Ⓑ ≉ ✈ (Dublin).

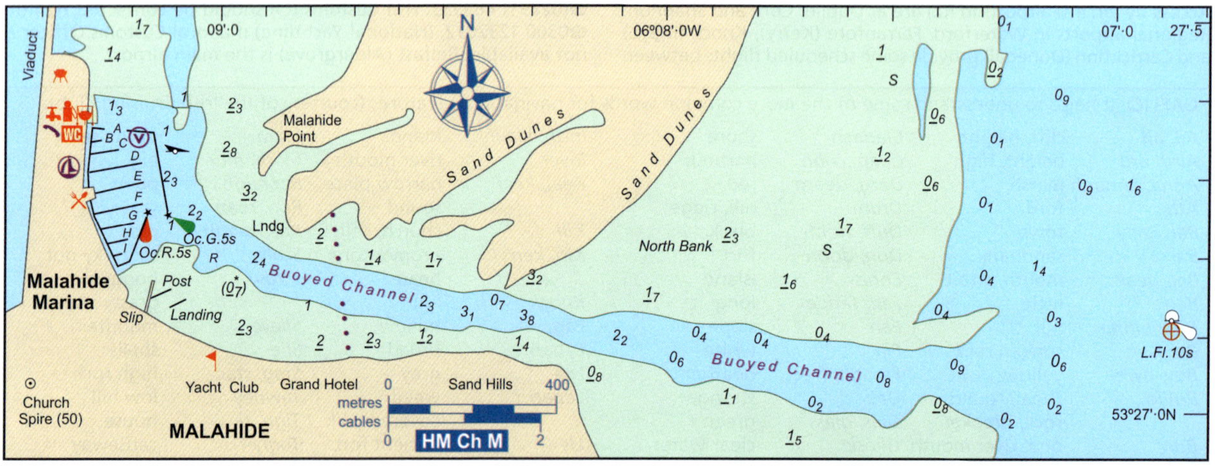

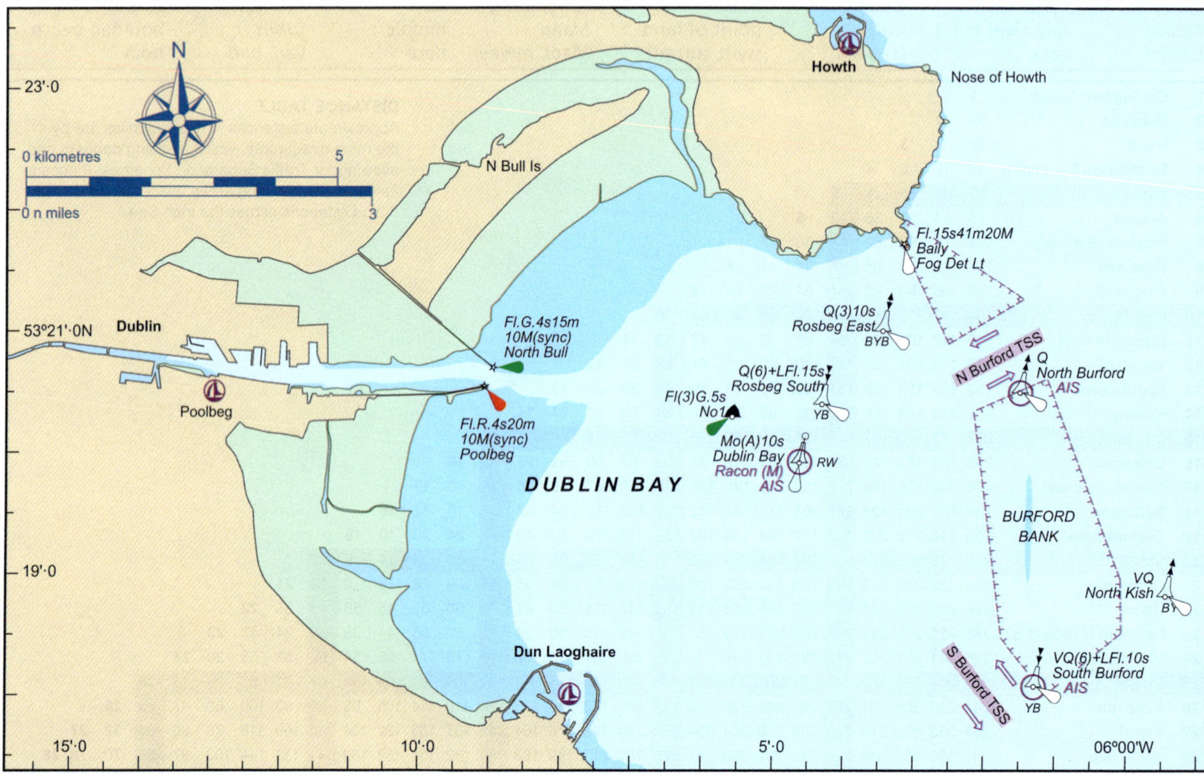

5.7 HOWTH

Dublin **53°23'·60N 06°04'·00W** ⚙⚙⚙◊◊◊✿✿✿

CHARTS AC 1468, 1415, 5621; Imray C61, C62

TIDES +0025 Dover; ML 2·4; Duration 0625

Standard Port DUBLIN (NORTH WALL) (⟶)

Times				Height (metres)			
High Water		Low Water		MHWS	MHWN	MLWN	MLWS
0000	0700	0000	0500	4·1	3·4	1·5	0·7
1200	1900	1200	1700				
Differences HOWTH							
–0007	–0005	+0001	+0005	0·0	–0·1	–0·2	–0·2

SHELTER Excellent in marina, at all states of tide. After ENE'ly storm, expect a dangerous scend in the approach. 11Ø, 6G and 5R. Caution: many moorings in E part of outer hbr. No ent to FV basin for yachts. Inside the inner hbr keep strictly to chan to avoid drying shoals either side and a substantial wavebreak (gabion). Marina approach channel 1·7m. R posts mark the outer limit of dredging around the marina. 4kn speed limit. There is a fair weather ⚓ in 2-3m at Carrigeen Bay, SW side of Ireland's Eye.

NAVIGATION WPT Howth SHM buoy, Fl G 5s, 53°23'·72N 06°03'·53W, 251°/0·27M to E pier lt. From the S beware Casana Rk 4ca S of the Nose of Howth and Puck's Rks extending about 50m off the Nose. Ireland's Eye is 0·6M N of hbr, with the Rowan Rks SE and SW, marked by Rowan Rks ECM, and S Rowan SHM. The usual approach passes S of Ireland's Eye, but beware lobster pots between the Nose and the hbr, and rocks off both pier hds. Howth Sound has 2·4m min depth; give way to FVs (constrained by draught). 2·5m in marina approach channel.

LIGHTS AND MARKS Baily Lt Ho, Fl 15s 41m 26M, is 1·5M S of Nose of Howth. Disused lt ho on E pier is conspic. E pier lt, Fl (2) WR 7·5s 13m 12/9M; 256°-W-295°, R elsewhere. W sector leads safely to NE pierhead which should be rounded 50m off. Trawler Dock moles are lit QR and Fl G 3s. Marina channel has 8 lit lateral marks.

COMMUNICATIONS (Code 01) ⊜ 8746571; Police 666 4900; Dr 832 3191; Ⓗ 837 7755. HM 8322252.

Marina Ch **M** 80. *Howth Harbour* VHF Ch 16 (Mon-Fri 0700–2300).

FACILITIES Howth Marina ☎8392777 (HO 0800-2130 Apr-Oct, 0900-1700 Nov-Mar) 350 inc Ⓥ €3·96 (inc ⚡) €19·57 wkly ♿ ⛵ ⛴(H24) 🗑 ⛽(OH) 🅿 ⛽ ⚓(15t).

Howth YC www.hyc.ie ☎8322141, ♿ 🗑 Scrubbing posts <20m LOA, ✕(☎8392100) 🍴(☎8320606).

Howth Boat Club (no facilities). **Services** LB, ⛽ Kos, 🔧 ⛵ ⚙ Ⓔ 🔨.

Town ✉ Ⓑ 🗑 ⇌ ✈ (Dublin).

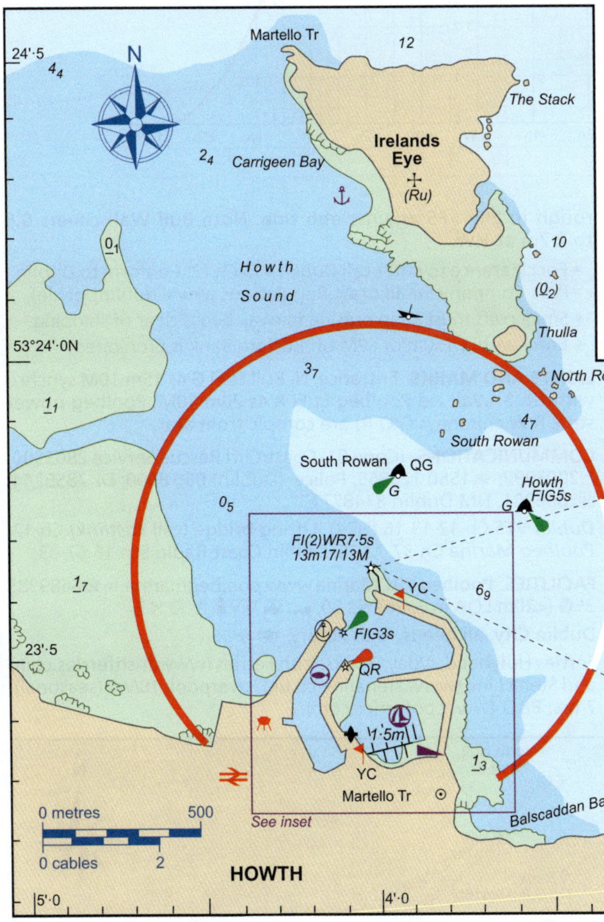

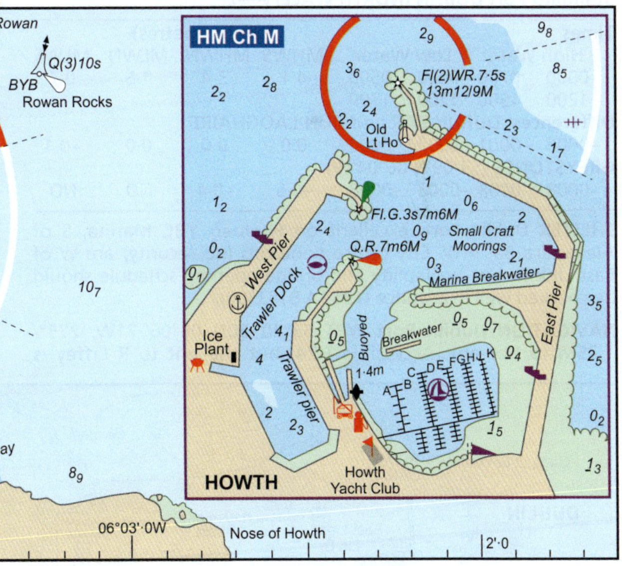

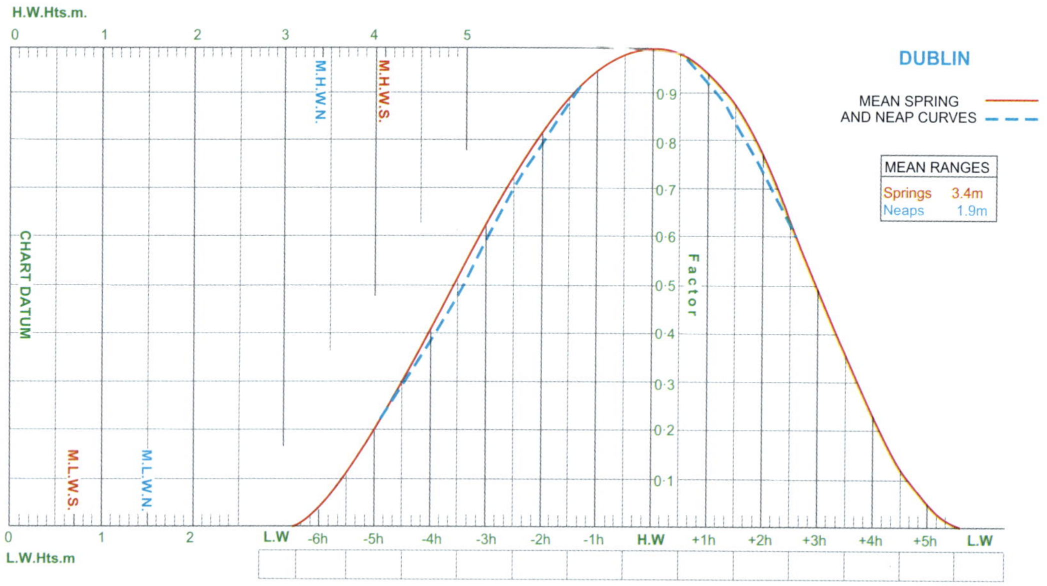

5.8 DUBLIN

Dublin **53°20'·85N 06°14'·80W**

CHARTS AC 1468, 1415, 1447, 5621; Imray C61, C62

TIDES +0042 Dover; ML 2·4; Duration 0640

Standard Port DUBLIN (NORTH WALL) (⟶)

Times				**Height (metres)**			
High Water		Low Water		MHWS	MHWN	MLWN	MLWS
0000	0700	0000	0500	4·1	3·4	1·5	0·7
1200	1900	1200	1700				
Differences DUBLIN BAR and DUN LAOGHAIRE							
–0006	–0001	–0002	–0003	0·0	0·0	0·0	+0·1
GREYSTONES (53°09'N 06°04'W)							
–0008	–0008	–0008	–0008	–0·5	–0·4	ND	ND

SHELTER **Dublin Port,** excellent on Poolbeg YBC Marina, S of Alexandra Basin W. City centre pontoons (no security) are W of East Link Br but availability and bridge opening schedule should be checked well in advance (+353 1 8183300).

NAVIGATION **Dublin Port** WPT 53°20'·50N 06°06'·71W, 275°/1·35M to hbr ent. Accessible H24, but the ent to R Liffey is rough in E'ly >F5 against ebb tide. Note Bull Wall covers 0.6 to 2.7m at HW.

- For clearance to enter call *Dublin VTS* Ch 12. Conform to Dublin Port Company Small Craft Regulations (www.dublinport.ie).
- Small craft must keep outside fairway buoys clear of shipping.
- Entry within 150m of SPM off Burford Bank is prohibited.

LIGHTS AND MARKS Entrance, N. Bull Lt Fl G 4s 15m 10M synchro with Gt. S. Wall Hd Poolbeg Lt Fl R 4s 20m 10M. Poolbeg power stn 2 R/W chimneys (VQ R) are conspic from afar.

COMMUNICATIONS (Code 01) Coast/Cliff Rescue Service 2803900; ⊜2803992; 1550 123855; Police (Dublin) 666 8000; Dr 2859244; Ⓗ2806901. HM Dublin 8748771.

Dublin VTS Ch **12** 13 16 (H24). Lifting bridge (call *Eastlink*) Ch 12. *Poolbeg Marina* Ch **37** 12 16. Dublin Coast Radio Stn 16 67 83.

FACILITIES **Poolbeg YBC Marina** www.poolbegmarina.ie ☎6689983 35Ⓥ (<20m LOA in 2.4m) €3·80.

Dublin City, all needs, @ at library.

Ferries Holyhead; 4/day; 3¼hrs; Irish Ferries (www.irishferries.com) and Stena Line (www.stenaline.co.uk). Liverpool; 18/wk (seasonal); 7 hrs; P&O (www.poferries.com).

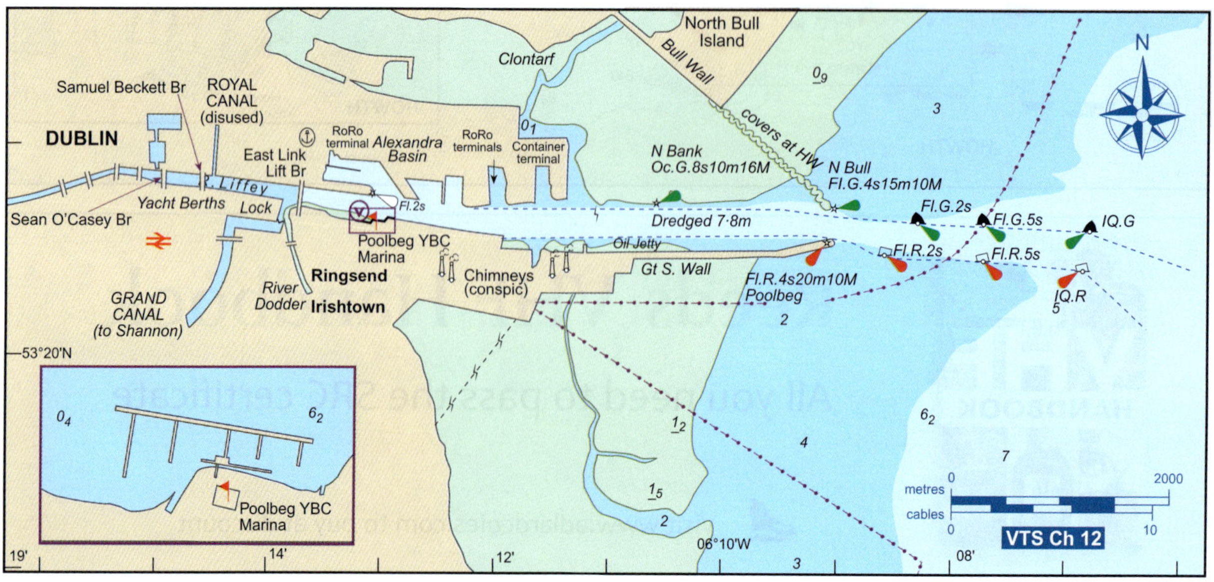

STANDARD TIME (UT)
For Summer Time add ONE hour in **non-shaded areas**

DUBLIN (NORTH WALL) LAT 53°21'N LONG 6°13'W

TIMES AND HEIGHTS OF HIGH AND LOW WATERS

Dates in red are SPRINGS
Dates in blue are NEAPS

YEAR **2024**

JANUARY

Date	Day	Time	m	Time	m	Time	m	Time	m
1	M	0241	3.5	0816	1.3	1454	3.8	2059	1.1
2	TU	0326	3.4	0901	1.4	1539	3.7	2145	1.2
3	W	0415	3.3	0951	1.5	1627	3.5	2233	1.3
4	TH	0510	3.3	1048	1.6	1720	3.4	◑ 2327	1.4
5	F	0611	3.3	1149	1.7	1821	3.4		
6	SA	0024	1.4	0713	3.3	1250	1.7	1927	3.4
7	SU	0121	1.4	0809	3.4	1347	1.6	2028	3.4
8	M	0216	1.3	0859	3.6	1440	1.4	2122	3.6
9	TU	0305	1.2	0944	3.7	1528	1.2	2212	3.7
10	W	0350	1.1	1027	3.9	1613	1.0	2258	3.8
11	TH	0433	0.9	1109	4.1	1658	0.7	● 2343	3.9
12	F	0515	0.8	1152	4.2	1743	0.5		
13	SA	0028	4.0	0558	0.8	1236	4.3	1830	0.4
14	SU	0114	4.0	0644	0.8	1324	4.3	1919	0.4
15	M	0204	3.9	0732	0.8	1414	4.3	2011	0.5
16	TU	0256	3.9	0825	0.9	1506	4.2	2105	0.6
17	W	0351	3.7	0921	1.1	1602	4.1	2203	0.8
18	TH	0450	3.6	1022	1.2	1702	3.9	◐ 2304	1.0
19	F	0556	3.5	1128	1.3	1810	3.7		
20	SA	0010	1.2	0705	3.5	1239	1.4	1923	3.6
21	SU	0124	1.3	0812	3.6	1354	1.4	2036	3.6
22	M	0236	1.4	0915	3.6	1503	1.3	2142	3.6
23	TU	0334	1.3	1011	3.8	1559	1.1	2239	3.6
24	W	0420	1.2	1058	3.9	1645	1.0	2323	3.7
25	TH	0459	1.1	1136	4.0	1724	0.9	○ 2358	3.7
26	F	0533	1.1	1208	4.0	1800	0.8		
27	SA	0026	3.6	0604	1.0	1237	4.0	1835	0.8
28	SU	0056	3.6	0635	1.0	1309	4.0	1908	0.8
29	M	0127	3.6	0705	1.0	1342	3.9	1940	0.8
30	TU	0202	3.6	0737	1.0	1418	3.8	2013	0.9
31	W	0239	3.6	0812	1.1	1457	3.7	2049	1.0

FEBRUARY

Date	Day	Time	m	Time	m	Time	m	Time	m
1	TH	0319	3.5	0852	1.2	1539	3.6	2128	1.1
2	F	0405	3.4	0936	1.4	1625	3.5	◑ 2214	1.3
3	SA	0457	3.3	1028	1.5	1720	3.3	2310	1.4
4	SU	0600	3.2	1138	1.6	1829	3.2		
5	M	0024	1.6	0716	3.2	1300	1.6	1952	3.2
6	TU	0140	1.5	0825	3.4	1412	1.4	2101	3.4
7	W	0244	1.3	0921	3.6	1512	1.1	2157	3.6
8	TH	0336	1.1	1010	3.9	1602	0.8	2246	3.8
9	F	0421	0.8	1054	4.1	1646	0.5	● 2329	4.0
10	SA	0502	0.6	1137	4.3	1729	0.2		
11	SU	0011	4.1	0543	0.5	1219	4.4	1813	0.1
12	M	0054	4.1	0625	0.4	1303	4.4	1858	0.1
13	TU	0138	4.0	0709	0.5	1350	4.4	1945	0.3
14	W	0224	3.9	0757	0.6	1439	4.2	2034	0.5
15	TH	0314	3.8	0850	0.8	1531	4.0	2127	0.8
16	F	0408	3.6	0948	1.0	1630	3.8	◐ 2224	1.1
17	SA	0513	3.4	1054	1.3	1741	3.5	2330	1.4
18	SU	0628	3.4	1210	1.4	1902	3.4		
19	M	0054	1.6	0744	3.4	1340	1.4	2023	3.3
20	TU	0225	1.6	0855	3.5	1457	1.3	2137	3.4
21	W	0325	1.4	0956	3.7	1550	1.1	2232	3.5
22	TH	0409	1.3	1044	3.8	1632	0.9	2313	3.6
23	F	0444	1.1	1121	3.9	1706	0.8	2342	3.6
24	SA	0514	1.0	1150	3.9	1738	0.7	○	
25	SU	0005	3.6	0543	0.9	1215	3.9	1808	0.7
26	M	0028	3.6	0609	0.8	1241	3.9	1835	0.7
27	TU	0054	3.7	0634	0.8	1311	3.9	1901	0.7
28	W	0124	3.7	0702	0.8	1345	3.8	1930	0.8
29	TH	0159	3.7	0735	0.9	1422	3.7	2004	0.8

MARCH

Date	Day	Time	m	Time	m	Time	m	Time	m
1	F	0238	3.6	0812	1.0	1503	3.6	2043	1.0
2	SA	0321	3.5	0854	1.1	1548	3.5	2128	1.2
3	SU	0410	3.3	0945	1.3	1642	3.3	◑ 2222	1.4
4	M	0510	3.2	1051	1.5	1752	3.1	2341	1.6
5	TU	0630	3.1	1228	1.5	1927	3.1		
6	W	0114	1.6	0755	3.3	1353	1.3	2045	3.3
7	TH	0228	1.4	0859	3.5	1458	0.9	2143	3.6
8	F	0322	1.0	0951	3.8	1547	0.6	2230	3.8
9	SA	0405	0.7	1036	4.1	1630	0.2	2311	4.0
10	SU	0445	0.5	1118	4.3	1711	0.0	● 2351	4.1
11	M	0523	0.3	1159	4.4	1752	0.0		
12	TU	0029	4.1	0604	0.2	1241	4.4	1834	0.0
13	W	0109	4.0	0646	0.3	1326	4.3	1918	0.2
14	TH	0152	3.9	0733	0.4	1414	4.1	2004	0.5
15	F	0239	3.8	0825	0.7	1506	3.9	2054	0.9
16	SA	0330	3.6	0923	0.9	1604	3.6	2150	1.2
17	SU	0432	3.4	1028	1.2	1718	3.3	◐ 2254	1.5
18	M	0553	3.3	1145	1.4	1843	3.2		
19	TU	0018	1.7	0715	3.3	1321	1.4	2009	3.2
20	W	0202	1.7	0831	3.4	1437	1.2	2122	3.3
21	TH	0303	1.5	0933	3.6	1528	1.0	2213	3.4
22	F	0345	1.3	1020	3.7	1607	0.8	2249	3.5
23	SA	0419	1.1	1055	3.8	1639	0.7	2315	3.6
24	SU	0449	0.9	1124	3.8	1708	0.7	2337	3.6
25	M	0516	0.8	1149	3.8	1735	0.6	○ 2358	3.7
26	TU	0540	0.7	1214	3.8	1759	0.6		
27	W	0021	3.7	0604	0.7	1242	3.8	1825	0.7
28	TH	0051	3.7	0631	0.7	1316	3.8	1855	0.7
29	F	0127	3.7	0705	0.8	1355	3.7	1931	0.8
30	SA	0207	3.7	0744	0.9	1437	3.6	2012	1.0
31	SU	0251	3.5	0829	1.0	1524	3.4	2059	1.2

APRIL

Date	Day	Time	m	Time	m	Time	m	Time	m
1	M	0341	3.4	0924	1.2	1621	3.3	2159	1.4
2	TU	0441	3.2	1038	1.3	1736	3.1	◑ 2321	1.6
3	W	0600	3.2	1212	1.3	1908	3.2		
4	TH	0052	1.5	0726	3.3	1334	1.1	2024	3.4
5	F	0204	1.3	0833	3.6	1437	0.7	2122	3.6
6	SA	0259	1.0	0927	3.9	1527	0.4	2209	3.8
7	SU	0343	0.7	1014	4.1	1610	0.2	2250	4.0
8	M	0424	0.4	1057	4.3	1650	0.0	● 2328	4.1
9	TU	0503	0.3	1139	4.3	1730	0.0		
10	W	0005	4.1	0544	0.2	1222	4.3	1811	0.2
11	TH	0044	4.0	0627	0.3	1307	4.2	1853	0.4
12	F	0126	3.9	0714	0.4	1356	4.0	1939	0.7
13	SA	0212	3.8	0807	0.6	1448	3.7	2028	1.0
14	SU	0303	3.6	0905	0.9	1547	3.5	2123	1.3
15	M	0403	3.5	1009	1.1	1658	3.2	◐ 2226	1.6
16	TU	0521	3.3	1120	1.2	1817	3.1	2341	1.7
17	W	0640	3.3	1245	1.3	1937	3.1		
18	TH	0115	1.7	0754	3.4	1358	1.2	2047	3.2
19	F	0223	1.5	0855	3.5	1451	1.0	2136	3.4
20	SA	0309	1.3	0943	3.6	1531	0.9	2211	3.5
21	SU	0346	1.1	1020	3.7	1605	0.8	2239	3.6
22	M	0417	0.9	1052	3.7	1634	0.7	2305	3.6
23	TU	0445	0.8	1120	3.8	1700	0.7	○ 2327	3.7
24	W	0509	0.8	1147	3.8	1725	0.7	2352	3.8
25	TH	0535	0.8	1218	3.8	1753	0.7		
26	F	0024	3.8	0606	0.7	1254	3.7	1827	0.8
27	SA	0102	3.8	0643	0.8	1335	3.7	1906	0.9
28	SU	0144	3.7	0727	0.9	1421	3.6	1952	1.1
29	M	0232	3.6	0819	1.0	1513	3.5	2046	1.2
30	TU	0325	3.5	0922	1.1	1613	3.3	2151	1.4

Chart Datum: 0·20 metres above Ordnance Datum (Dublin). HAT is 4·5 metres above Chart Datum.

STANDARD TIME (UT)
For Summer Time add ONE hour in **non-shaded areas**

DUBLIN (NORTH WALL)

LAT 53°21′N LONG 6°13′W

TIMES AND HEIGHTS OF HIGH AND LOW WATERS

Dates in red are SPRINGS
Dates in blue are NEAPS

YEAR **2024**

MAY

Date	Time	m	Date	Time	m
1	0427	3.4	16	0559	3.4
	1036	1.1		1158	1.2
	W 1726	3.3		TH 1849	3.1
	◑ 2307	1.5			
2	0541	3.4	17	0013	1.7
	1156	1.1		0707	3.4
	TH 1845	3.3		F 1304	1.2
				1951	3.2
3	0024	1.4	18	0123	1.6
	0657	3.5		0806	3.5
	F 1308	0.9		SA 1401	1.1
	1956	3.5		2042	3.3
4	0132	1.2	19	0219	1.4
	0803	3.7		0856	3.5
	SA 1409	0.7		SU 1446	1.0
	2053	3.6		2123	3.4
5	0228	1.0	20	0302	1.3
	0900	3.9		0939	3.6
	SU 1501	0.4		M 1523	0.9
	2143	3.8		2158	3.6
6	0317	0.7	21	0338	1.1
	0951	4.1		1016	3.6
	M 1547	0.3		TU 1556	0.9
	2226	3.9		2229	3.6
7	0402	0.5	22	0410	1.0
	1038	4.2		1050	3.7
	TU 1630	0.3		W 1626	0.9
	2307	4.0		2256	3.7
8	0445	0.4	23	0439	0.9
	1124	4.2		1122	3.7
	W 1711	0.3		TH 1656	0.9
	● 2346	4.0		○ 2327	3.8
9	0528	0.4	24	0511	0.9
	1209	4.1		1158	3.7
	TH 1752	0.5		F 1729	0.9
10	0026	4.0	25	0002	3.9
	0614	0.4		0548	0.8
	F 1254	4.0		SA 1237	3.7
	1834	0.6		1808	0.9
11	0108	3.9	26	0043	3.9
	0702	0.5		0630	0.8
	SA 1342	3.8		SU 1322	3.7
	1919	0.9		1851	1.0
12	0154	3.8	27	0129	3.9
	0754	0.7		0719	0.8
	SU 1434	3.6		M 1411	3.6
	2007	1.1		1940	1.1
13	0243	3.7	28	0219	3.8
	0850	0.8		0816	0.9
	M 1530	3.4		TU 1506	3.6
	2100	1.3		2037	1.2
14	0341	3.6	29	0314	3.8
	0949	1.0		0919	0.9
	TU 1632	3.3		W 1605	3.5
	2159	1.5		2139	1.3
15	0448	3.5	30	0414	3.7
	1052	1.1		1025	0.9
	W 1741	3.1		TH 1709	3.5
	◐ 2303	1.6		◑ 2245	1.3
			31	0519	3.7
				1133	0.9
				F 1817	3.5
				2352	1.3

JUNE

Date	Time	m	Date	Time	m
1	0626	3.7	16	0021	1.6
	1238	0.8		0711	3.4
	SA 1922	3.5		SU 1301	1.3
				1945	3.3
2	0056	1.2	17	0118	1.5
	0732	3.8		0805	3.4
	SU 1339	0.7		M 1352	1.2
	2022	3.6		2034	3.4
3	0156	1.1	18	0210	1.4
	0833	3.9		0855	3.5
	M 1435	0.7		TU 1437	1.2
	2116	3.7		2116	3.5
4	0252	0.9	19	0256	1.3
	0931	4.0		0940	3.5
	TU 1526	0.6		W 1518	1.1
	2206	3.8		2155	3.6
5	0343	0.8	20	0336	1.2
	1024	4.0		1022	3.6
	W 1613	0.6		TH 1556	1.1
	2251	3.9		2230	3.7
6	0432	0.7	21	0414	1.1
	1114	4.0		1102	3.7
	TH 1657	0.7		F 1633	1.0
	● 2333	3.9		2307	3.9
7	0519	0.7	22	0453	0.9
	1200	3.9		1142	3.7
	F 1739	0.8		SA 1712	0.9
				○ 2346	4.0
8	0012	4.0	23	0535	0.8
	0606	0.7		1225	3.8
	SA 1244	3.8		SU 1753	0.9
	1820	0.9			
9	0053	3.9	24	0029	4.0
	0653	0.7		0621	0.7
	SU 1329	3.7		M 1310	3.8
	1901	1.0		1838	0.9
10	0136	3.9	25	0115	4.1
	0741	0.8		0710	0.7
	M 1415	3.6		TU 1359	3.8
	1946	1.1		1926	0.9
11	0222	3.8	26	0205	4.1
	0831	0.8		0805	0.7
	TU 1504	3.5		W 1451	3.7
	2034	1.3		2019	1.0
12	0312	3.7	27	0258	4.0
	0923	1.0		0903	0.7
	W 1556	3.3		TH 1545	3.7
	2126	1.4		2116	1.1
13	0407	3.6	28	0354	4.0
	1016	1.1		1003	0.7
	TH 1652	3.2		F 1643	3.6
	2222	1.5		◑ 2216	1.1
14	0507	3.5	29	0453	3.9
	1110	1.2		1104	0.8
	F 1752	3.2		SA 1745	3.6
	◐ 2321	1.6		2318	1.2
15	0610	3.4	30	0557	3.8
	1206	1.2		1206	0.9
	SA 1851	3.2		SU 1849	3.6

JULY

Date	Time	m	Date	Time	m
1	0023	1.2	16	0020	1.6
	0705	3.8		0711	3.3
	M 1309	1.0		TU 1258	1.4
	1954	3.6		1943	3.3
2	0129	1.2	17	0121	1.6
	0813	3.8		0815	3.3
	TU 1412	1.0		W 1355	1.4
	2055	3.7		2038	3.4
3	0234	1.2	18	0219	1.5
	0918	3.8		0911	3.4
	W 1511	1.0		TH 1447	1.3
	2150	3.8		2126	3.6
4	0334	1.1	19	0310	1.3
	1017	3.8		1001	3.6
	TH 1602	1.0		F 1534	1.2
	2240	3.8		2209	3.8
5	0427	0.9	20	0356	1.1
	1109	3.8		1045	3.7
	F 1647	1.0		SA 1616	1.0
	● 2323	3.9		2250	3.9
6	0514	0.8	21	0439	0.8
	1153	3.8		1128	3.8
	SA 1728	1.0		SU 1656	0.9
				○ 2330	4.1
7	0000	4.0	22	0522	0.6
	0558	0.8		1210	3.9
	SU 1232	3.7		M 1737	0.8
	1805	1.0			
8	0037	4.0	23	0011	4.2
	0640	0.7		0606	0.5
	M 1309	3.7		TU 1253	3.9
	1842	1.0		1820	0.7
9	0114	3.9	24	0055	4.3
	0721	0.8		0653	0.4
	TU 1348	3.6		W 1338	3.9
	1920	1.1		1905	0.7
10	0154	3.9	25	0142	4.3
	0803	0.8		0743	0.4
	W 1428	3.5		TH 1426	3.9
	2000	1.1		1954	0.8
11	0235	3.8	26	0233	4.2
	0847	0.9		0836	0.5
	TH 1509	3.4		F 1516	3.8
	2043	1.2		2047	0.9
12	0319	3.7	27	0326	4.1
	0931	1.0		0932	0.7
	F 1554	3.3		SA 1610	3.7
	2130	1.3		2144	1.0
13	0406	3.6	28	0423	4.0
	1018	1.2		1030	0.9
	SA 1643	3.3		SU 1710	3.6
	◐ 2222	1.5		◑ 2246	1.2
14	0459	3.4	29	0528	3.8
	1108	1.3		1133	1.1
	SU 1739	3.2		M 1818	3.5
	2319	1.6		2355	1.3
15	0601	3.3	30	0644	3.6
	1202	1.4		1243	1.3
	M 1842	3.2		TU 1930	3.5
			31	0110	1.4
				0802	3.6
				W 1356	1.4
				2038	3.6

AUGUST

Date	Time	m	Date	Time	m
1	0227	1.3	16	0153	1.5
	0914	3.6		0850	3.3
	TH 1502	1.3		F 1425	1.5
	2140	3.7		2102	3.5
2	0333	1.2	17	0254	1.2
	1015	3.6		0944	3.5
	F 1555	1.2		SA 1517	1.2
	2232	3.8		2149	3.8
3	0424	1.0	18	0343	0.9
	1106	3.7		1029	3.8
	SA 1638	1.1		SU 1600	1.0
	2314	3.9		2231	4.0
4	0506	0.8	19	0425	0.6
	1146	3.7		1110	3.9
	SU 1714	1.0		M 1639	0.7
	● 2348	4.0		○ 2311	4.2
5	0543	0.8	20	0505	0.3
	1217	3.7		1150	4.0
	M 1747	1.0		TU 1718	0.6
				2351	4.4
6	0016	4.0	21	0546	0.2
	0619	0.7		1230	4.1
	TU 1244	3.6		W 1758	0.5
	1818	0.9			
7	0047	4.0	22	0031	4.4
	0653	0.7		0629	0.2
	W 1314	3.6		TH 1311	4.1
	1849	0.9		1841	0.5
8	0121	3.9	23	0116	4.4
	0726	0.8		0715	0.3
	TH 1348	3.6		F 1355	4.0
	1922	1.0		1926	0.6
9	0157	3.9	24	0204	4.3
	0801	0.9		0804	0.5
	F 1424	3.6		SA 1443	3.9
	1957	1.1		2017	0.8
10	0235	3.8	25	0256	4.1
	0837	1.0		0858	0.7
	SA 1502	3.5		SU 1535	3.7
	2035	1.2		2114	1.0
11	0317	3.6	26	0353	3.9
	0917	1.1		0956	1.0
	SU 1545	3.4		M 1634	3.6
	2118	1.3		◑ 2219	1.2
12	0404	3.5	27	0504	3.6
	1002	1.3		1101	1.3
	M 1634	3.3		TU 1748	3.4
	◐ 2209	1.5		2333	1.4
13	0500	3.3	28	0631	3.4
	1059	1.5		1218	1.6
	TU 1734	3.2		W 1908	3.4
	2316	1.7			
14	0614	3.2	29	0101	1.5
	1209	1.6		0756	3.4
	W 1851	3.2		TH 1346	1.6
				2024	3.5
15	0039	1.7	30	0227	1.3
	0742	3.2		0913	3.5
	TH 1321	1.6		F 1454	1.5
	2005	3.3		2129	3.7
			31	0327	1.1
				1012	3.6
				SA 1543	1.3
				2220	3.9

Chart Datum: 0·20 metres above Ordnance Datum (Dublin). HAT is 4·5 metres above Chart Datum.

STANDARD TIME (UT)
For Summer Time add ONE hour in **non-shaded areas**

DUBLIN (NORTH WALL)

LAT 53°21'N LONG 6°13'W

TIMES AND HEIGHTS OF HIGH AND LOW WATERS

Dates in red are SPRINGS
Dates in blue are NEAPS

YEAR **2024**

SEPTEMBER

Date	Time	m	Date	Time	m
1 SU	0412 1056 1621 2259	0.9 3.6 1.2 4.0	16 M	0325 1010 1541 2209	0.7 3.8 0.9 4.1
2 M	0448 1130 1654 2329	0.8 3.7 1.0 4.0	17 TU	0406 1049 1619 2249	0.4 4.0 0.6 4.4
3 TU	0521 1155 1724 ● 2354	0.7 3.7 0.9 4.0	18 W	0444 1127 1657 ○ 2328	0.1 4.1 0.4 4.5
4 W	0551 1217 1752	0.7 3.7 0.9	19 TH	0524 1204 1735	0.0 4.2 0.3
5 TH	0020 0620 1241 1819	4.0 0.7 3.7 0.9	20 F	0008 0605 1244 1817	4.5 0.1 4.1 0.3
6 F	0050 0647 1311 1847	3.9 0.8 3.7 0.9	21 SA	0052 0648 1326 1903	4.4 0.3 4.1 0.5
7 SA	0123 0715 1345 1919	3.9 0.8 3.7 1.0	22 SU	0139 0734 1413 1954	4.3 0.5 3.9 0.7
8 SU	0200 0748 1423 1955	3.8 1.0 3.6 1.1	23 M	0232 0826 1504 2052	4.0 0.9 3.8 1.0
9 M	0241 0827 1505 2036	3.6 1.1 3.5 1.2	24 TU	0332 0925 1605 ◑ 2159	3.7 1.2 3.6 1.2
10 TU	0327 0912 1552 2126	3.5 1.3 3.4 1.4	25 W	0449 1032 1722 2315	3.5 1.5 3.5 1.4
11 W	0421 1008 1650 ◐ 2232	3.3 1.6 3.2 1.6	26 TH	0618 1153 1845	3.3 1.7 3.4
12 TH	0536 1129 1807	3.1 1.7 3.2	27 F	0050 0747 1327 2003	1.4 3.3 1.7 3.6
13 F	0009 0717 1256 1933	1.7 3.1 1.7 3.3	28 SA	0212 0901 1433 2108	1.3 3.4 1.6 3.7
14 SA	0134 0831 1407 2037	1.5 3.3 1.5 3.6	29 SU	0306 0954 1519 2158	1.1 3.6 1.4 3.9
15 SU	0238 0926 1459 2126	1.1 3.6 1.2 3.9	30 M	0348 1034 1557 2235	0.9 3.7 1.2 4.0

OCTOBER

Date	Time	m	Date	Time	m
1 TU	0422 1104 1629 2305	0.8 3.7 1.0 4.0	16 W	0343 1024 1556 2225	0.3 4.1 0.6 4.4
2 W	0453 1127 1659 ● 2330	0.7 3.7 0.9 4.0	17 TH	0422 1103 1635 ○ 2307	0.2 4.2 0.4 4.5
3 TH	0521 1149 1726 2355	0.7 3.8 0.9 4.0	18 F	0502 1141 1716 2350	0.1 4.2 0.3 4.5
4 F	0546 1212 1751	0.7 3.8 0.9	19 SA	0542 1221 1759	0.2 4.2 0.4
5 SA	0023 0611 1240 1818	3.9 0.8 3.8 0.9	20 SU	0035 0625 1304 1846	4.3 0.4 4.1 0.5
6 SU	0055 0638 1314 1849	3.9 0.9 3.8 1.0	21 M	0124 0711 1351 1939	4.2 0.7 4.0 0.7
7 M	0133 0712 1353 1927	3.8 1.0 3.7 1.1	22 TU	0218 0802 1443 2037	3.9 1.1 3.9 0.9
8 TU	0215 0752 1436 2010	3.6 1.2 3.6 1.2	23 W	0320 0900 1544 2142	3.6 1.4 3.7 1.2
9 W	0302 0839 1524 2103	3.5 1.4 3.5 1.4	24 TH	0435 1006 1657 ◑ 2254	3.4 1.6 3.6 1.3
10 TH	0359 0940 1622 ◐ 2214	3.3 1.6 3.4 1.5	25 F	0556 1121 1814	3.3 1.8 3.5
11 F	0516 1104 1735 2347	3.1 1.8 3.3 1.5	26 SA	0018 0719 1247 1928	1.4 3.3 1.8 3.6
12 SA	0650 1230 1857	3.2 1.7 3.4	27 SU	0135 0829 1356 2032	1.3 3.4 1.6 3.7
13 SU	0109 0805 1339 2004	1.3 3.4 1.5 3.6	28 M	0232 0920 1446 2122	1.1 3.6 1.4 3.8
14 M	0212 0900 1432 2057	1.0 3.7 1.2 3.9	29 TU	0315 0959 1527 2202	1.0 3.7 1.2 3.9
15 TU	0300 0945 1515 2143	0.6 3.9 0.9 4.2	30 W	0350 1029 1601 2235	0.9 3.7 1.1 3.9
			31 TH	0421 1056 1632 2305	0.8 3.8 1.0 3.9

NOVEMBER

Date	Time	m	Date	Time	m
1 F	0450 1121 1701 ● 2333	0.8 3.8 1.0 3.9	16 SA	0444 1123 1703 2339	0.4 4.2 0.5 4.3
2 SA	0515 1146 1727	0.9 3.9 1.0	17 SU	0526 1205 1748	0.5 4.2 0.5
3 SU	0001 0541 1214 1756	3.8 0.9 3.9 1.0	18 M	0026 0609 1249 1837	4.2 0.7 4.2 0.6
4 M	0035 0611 1250 1829	3.8 1.0 3.9 1.0	19 TU	0115 0654 1336 1929	4.0 0.9 4.1 0.7
5 TU	0114 0647 1330 1910	3.7 1.1 3.8 1.1	20 W	0209 0743 1427 2024	3.8 1.2 4.0 0.9
6 W	0158 0730 1416 1957	3.6 1.3 3.7 1.2	21 TH	0307 0837 1523 2123	3.6 1.4 3.8 1.1
7 TH	0249 0821 1506 2055	3.5 1.4 3.7 1.3	22 F	0411 0937 1626 2225	3.4 1.6 3.7 1.2
8 F	0348 0924 1603 2203	3.4 1.6 3.6 1.3	23 SA	0520 1043 1734 ◑ 2332	3.3 1.7 3.6 1.3
9 SA	0458 1039 1709 ◐ 2321	3.3 1.7 3.5 1.3	24 SU	0629 1153 1840	3.3 1.8 3.6
10 SU	0616 1156 1820	3.4 1.6 3.6	25 M	0041 0733 1303 1942	1.3 3.4 1.7 3.6
11 M	0035 0726 1302 1926	1.1 3.5 1.4 3.8	26 TU	0143 0827 1403 2036	1.3 3.5 1.6 3.6
12 TU	0138 0824 1358 2023	0.9 3.7 1.2 4.0	27 W	0233 0911 1450 2122	1.2 3.6 1.4 3.7
13 W	0231 0914 1448 2116	0.7 3.9 1.0 4.1	28 TH	0314 0949 1530 2202	1.1 3.7 1.3 3.7
14 TH	0318 0959 1534 2205	0.5 4.0 0.8 4.3	29 F	0348 1023 1605 2239	1.1 3.8 1.2 3.8
15 F	0402 1041 1618 ○ 2252	0.4 4.1 0.6 4.3	30 SA	0419 1054 1637 2312	1.1 3.9 1.1 3.8

DECEMBER

Date	Time	m	Date	Time	m
1 SU	0449 1123 1707 ● 2345	1.1 3.9 1.1 3.8	16 M	0517 1156 1744	0.8 4.2 0.7
2 M	0519 1155 1740	1.1 3.9 1.1	17 TU	0021 0559 1238 1831	4.0 0.9 4.2 0.7
3 TU	0021 0553 1232 1817	3.8 1.1 4.0 1.0	18 W	0107 0641 1322 1917	3.9 1.0 4.1 0.7
4 W	0101 0631 1314 1900	3.7 1.1 4.0 1.0	19 TH	0154 0724 1407 2006	3.8 1.1 4.0 0.8
5 TH	0147 0716 1400 1949	3.7 1.2 3.9 1.0	20 F	0243 0811 1456 2056	3.6 1.3 3.9 0.9
6 F	0238 0807 1450 2044	3.6 1.3 3.9 1.0	21 SA	0334 0903 1547 2147	3.5 1.4 3.8 1.1
7 SA	0333 0905 1544 2144	3.6 1.4 3.8 1.0	22 SU	0430 0958 1642 ◑ 2241	3.4 1.5 3.6 1.2
8 SU	0434 1008 1642 ◐ 2249	3.5 1.5 3.8 1.0	23 M	0529 1058 1743 2339	3.3 1.7 3.5 1.4
9 M	0538 1115 1744 2356	3.5 1.5 3.8 1.0	24 TU	0630 1201 1844	3.3 1.7 3.4
10 TU	0644 1221 1848	3.6 1.4 3.8	25 W	0038 0728 1304 1944	1.4 3.3 1.7 3.4
11 W	0101 0747 1323 1952	1.0 3.7 1.3 3.9	26 TH	0137 0820 1405 2039	1.4 3.4 1.6 3.4
12 TH	0201 0844 1422 2053	0.9 3.8 1.1 4.0	27 F	0230 0908 1456 2129	1.4 3.6 1.5 3.5
13 F	0257 0937 1517 2151	0.8 3.9 1.0 4.0	28 SA	0315 0950 1539 2213	1.3 3.7 1.4 3.6
14 SA	0347 1026 1608 2245	0.8 4.0 0.8 4.1	29 SU	0353 1028 1616 2253	1.3 3.8 1.2 3.7
15 SU	0434 1112 1657 ○ 2334	0.8 4.1 0.7 4.1	30 M	0428 1103 1651 ● 2331	1.2 3.9 1.1 3.7
			31 TU	0502 1138 1726	1.1 4.0 1.0

Chart Datum: 0·20 metres above Ordnance Datum (Dublin). HAT is 4·5 metres above Chart Datum.

5.9 DUN LAOGHAIRE

Dublin (Port ent) **53°18'·16N 06°07'·68W**

CHARTS AC 1468, 1415, 1447, 5621; IMRAY C61, C62

TIDES +0042 Dover; ML 2·4; Duration 0640

Standard Port DUBLIN (NORTH WALL) (⟵)

Times				Height (metres)			
High Water		Low Water		MHWS	MHWN	MLWN	MLWS
0000	0700	0000	0500	4·1	3·4	1·5	0·7
1200	1900	1200	1700				
Differences DUBLIN BAR and DUN LAOGHAIRE							
0000	0000	+0002	+0003	0·0	+0·1	0·0	0·0
GREYSTONES (53°09'N 06°04'W)							
–0008	–0008	–0008	–0008	–0·5	–0·4	ND	ND

SHELTER Excellent. Breakwaters within main hbr protect 800+ berth marina. Ⓥ berths on end of pontoons or as directed. Additional berths inside Western Marina Breakwater. All YCs advertise Ⓥs and/or pontoon berths.

NAVIGATION Dun Laoghaire WPT 53°18'·40N 06°07'·00W, 240°/0·47M to ent. Accessible H24. Keep clear of commercial traffic turning off St Michael's Pier. Beware drying rks around E Pier Hd.

LIGHTS AND MARKS RoRo Berth 2 x Fl.W = 'Large vessel under way; small craft keep clear of No 1 Fairway (out to 600m seaward of ent). Traffic signals (Fl W) repeated at head of E Marina Breakwater. Marina Breakwater Hds marked by sync lts Fl G 2s and Fl R 2s.

COMMUNICATIONS (Code 01) Coast/Cliff Rescue Service 2803900; ⊜ 2803992; 1550 123855; Police 6665000; Dr 2859244; Ⓗ 2806901. HM Dun Laoghaire 2801130.

Dun Laoghaire Hbr VHF Ch **14** 16 (H24); Marina Ch **M** M2 16; YCs Ch M. Dublin Coast Radio Stn 16 67 83.

FACILITIES **Dun Laoghaire Harbour Marina,** www.dlmarina.com ☎2020040; 800 inc 20Ⓥ €3.50, €5.00<6hrs, (by card) (call on Ch M in advance) wi-fi.

Town Ⓔ ACA ✕ ⇌ ✈(Dublin).

YACHT CLUBS (E→W):

Irish National SC ☎28444195.

National YC ☎2805725, (12t) ✕ .

Royal St George YC ☎2801811, Boatman ☎2801208; by prior agreement, €3.60, (5t) ✕ .

Royal Irish YC ☎2809452, (5t) ✕ .

Dun Laoghaire Motor YC ☎2801371, ✕ .

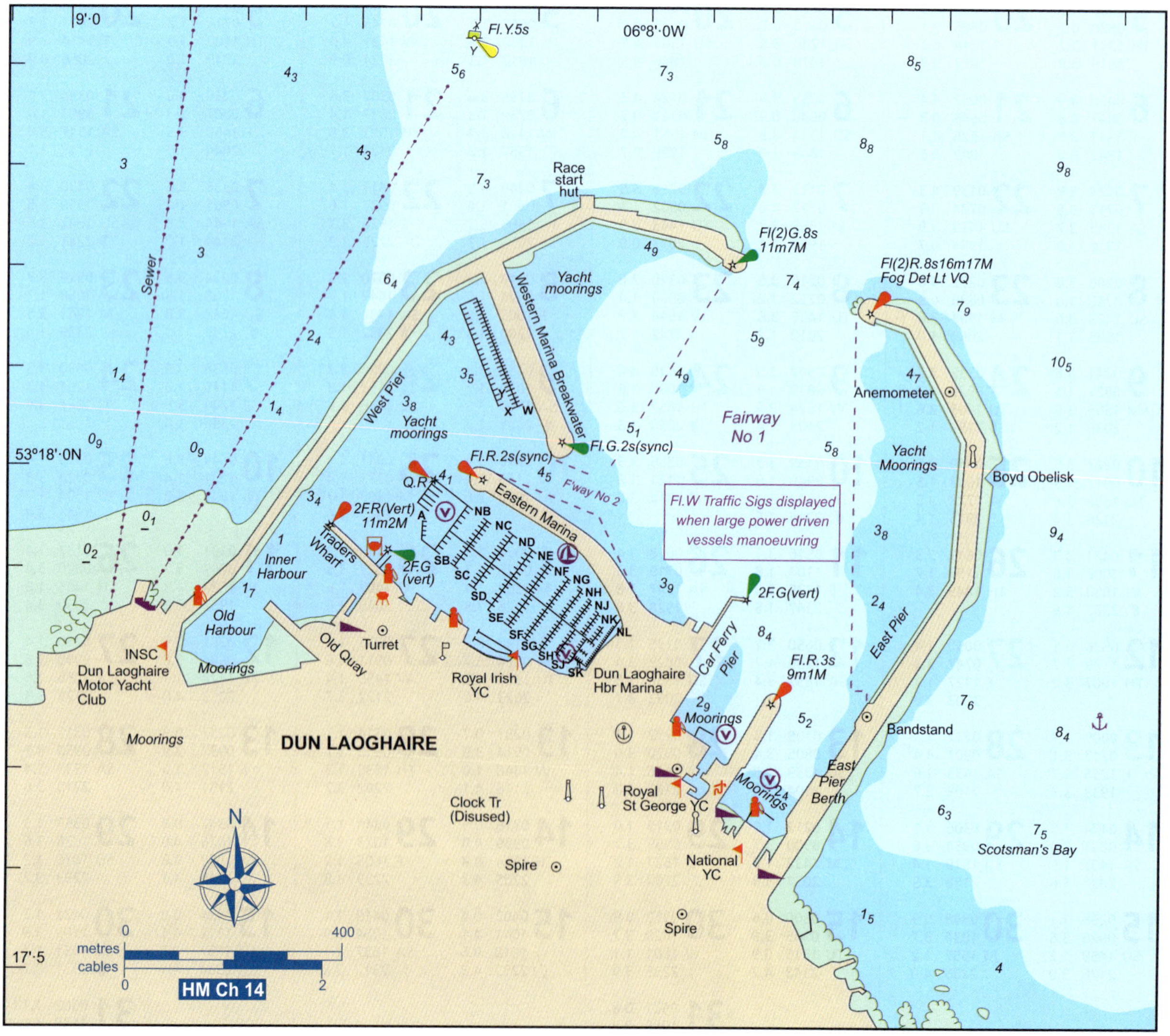

5.10 GREYSTONES

Greystones 53°09′·12N 06°03′·80W

CHARTS AC 1468, 633, 5621; Imray C61

TIDES +0042 Dover; ML 2·4; Duration 0640

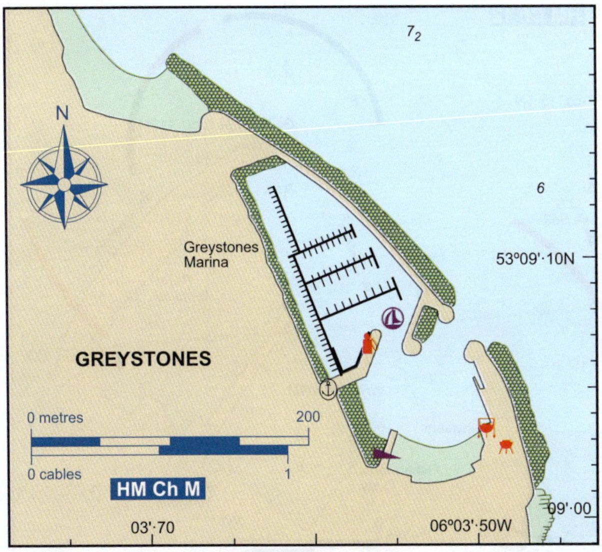

Standard Port DUBLIN (NORTH WALL) (⟵)

Times				Height (metres)			
High Water		Low Water		MHWS	MHWN	MLWN	MLWS
0000	0700	0000	0500	4·1	3·4	1·5	0·7
1200	1900	1200	1700				
GREYSTONES (53°09′N 06°04′W)							
–0008	–0008	–0008	–0008	–0·5	–0·4	ND	ND

SHELTER Midway between Dun Laoghaire and Wicklow, good shelter in all but winds from N–E. Harbour ent open to large seas in strong NE'ly winds, with large scend in outer basin, which can become untenable. Berthing on 3 of 5 pontoons in >5m. If marina full, in good weather ⚓ possible in bay N of hbr in 5-6m.

NAVIGATION If approaching from S beware Moulditch Bk marked by lit buoy Fl R 10s and sewerage outfall with Y SPM Fl Y 5s. Hbr accessible H24. Deepest water in approach lies close NE of the entrance. Pass between moles of outer hbr on a SSW'ly heading. Keeping N mole on starboard hand, a tight turn around its end gives access to the narrow ent to the marina with 'A' pontoon directly ahead.

LIGHTS AND MARKS Entrance marked by lateral bns on pier hds; Fl G 5s and Fl R 5s respectively.

COMMUNICATIONS (Code 01) Coast/Cliff Rescue Service 2803900; ⊜ 2803992; 1550 123855. HM 287 3131, 086 2718161.

Marina Ch 37, **M**; Dublin Coast Radio Stn 16 67 83.

FACILITIES **Greystones Marina**, info@greystonesharbourmarina.ie ☎353 (086) 2718161; 100 berths, Ⓥ facilities tbc in N Basin.

Town Ⓔ ACA.

5.11 WICKLOW

Wicklow **52°58′·98N 06°02′·70W**

CHARTS AC 1468, 633, 5621; Imray C61

TIDES –0010 Dover; ML 1·7; Duration 0640

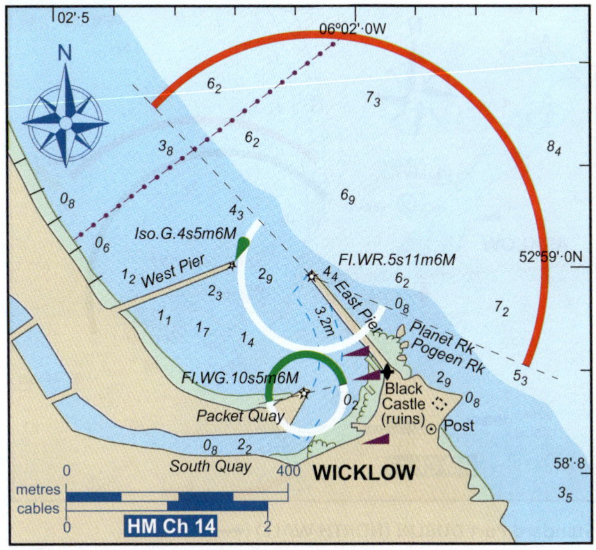

Standard Port DUBLIN (NORTH WALL) (⟵)

Times				Height (metres)			
High Water		Low Water		MHWS	MHWN	MLWN	MLWS
0000	0700	0000	0500	4·1	3·4	1·5	0·7
1200	1900	1200	1700				
Differences WICKLOW							
–0019	–0019	–0024	–0026	–1·4	–1·1	–0·4	0·0

SHELTER Very safe, access H24. Outer hbr is open to NE winds which cause a swell. Moorings in NW of hbr belong to SC and may not be used without permission. 4 berths on E Pier (2·5m) are convenient except in strong winds NW to NE, with fender boards/ladders provided. W pier is not recommended. ⚓ in hbr is restricted by ships' turning circle. Inner hbr (river) gives excellent shelter in 2·5m on N and S Quays, which are used by FVs. Packet Quay is for ships (2·5m), but may be used if none due; fender board needed. Yachts should berth on N or S quays as directed and/or space available.

NAVIGATION WPT 52°59′·20N 06°01′·80W, 220°/0·27M to ent. Appr presents no difficulty; keep in the R sector of the E pier lt to avoid Planet Rk and Pogeen Rk.

LIGHTS AND MARKS W pier head lt, Iso G 4s, is shown H24. ☆ Fl WG 10s on Packet Quay hd is vis 076°-G-256°-W-076°.

COMMUNICATIONS (Code 0404) Cliff Rescue Service 086 8686009; ⊜ 67222; Police 60140; Dr 67381. HM 67455.

Ch 12, **14**, 16. Wicklow SC Ch M 16 (occas).

FACILITIES **East Pier, S and N Quays,** €14.00/craft (bulk: see HM). **Wicklow SC** ☎67526, (except LWS).

Service Kos. **Town** Ⓑ ✈(Dublin).

5.12 ARKLOW

Wicklow **52°47'·60N 06°08'·20W**

CHARTS AC 1468, 633, 5621; Imray C61

TIDES –0150 Dover; ML 1·0; Duration 0640

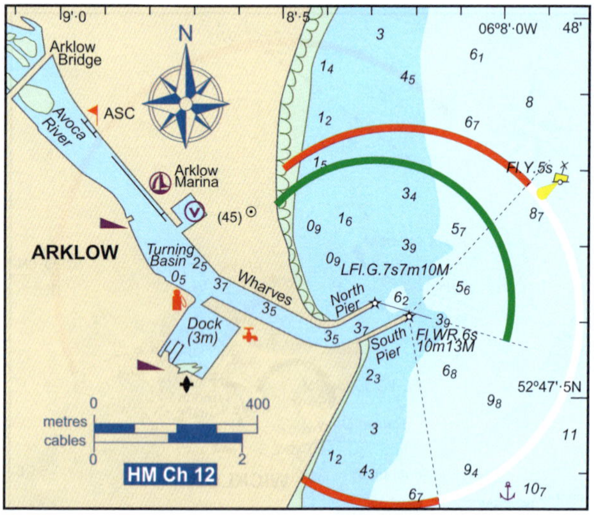

Standard Port DUBLIN (NORTH WALL) (⟵)

Times				Height (metres)			
High Water		Low Water		MHWS	MHWN	MLWN	MLWS
0000	0700	0000	0500	4·1	3·4	1·5	0·7
1200	1900	1200	1700				
Differences *ARKLOW* (Note small Range)							
–0315	*–0201*	*–0140*	*–0134*	*–2·7*	*–2·2*	*–0·6*	*–0·1*
COURTOWN							
–0328	–0242	–0158	–0138	–2·8	–2·4	–0·5	0·0

SHELTER Good, access H24 but river shoals above turning circle. **Arklow Roadstone Hbr**, 1M S of Arklow, is not for yachts.

- Strong E'ly winds make the entrance unsafe and cause significant turbulence in the river.

A 60 berth marina lies on NE side of river. New pontoon in sheltered dock S of the river. The basin is tight. Good ⚓ in bay; avoid whelk pots. One in 1.2m at ASC quay. on SE wall of Dock (ent is 13·5m wide; 3m depth) in perfect shelter, but amidst FVs.

NAVIGATION WPT 52°47'·60N 06°07'·50W, 270°/0·40M to ent. No navigational dangers, but beware ebb setting SE across hbr ent; give S pierhd a wide berth. Ent is difficult without power, due to blanking by piers. 3kn speed limit. Night entry, see below. Caution: Upriver of Dock ent keep to NE side of river.

LIGHTS AND MARKS No ldg lts/marks, see 5.3 and chartlet Conspic factory chy 2·5ca NW of piers.

- Beware the Pier Hd lts are very difficult to see due to powerful orange flood lts near the root of both piers shining E/ENE onto them (to assist pilotage of departing shipping).
- Best advice to visitors is to enter by day as the confined berthing areas are particularly challenging at night. If unavoidable approach harbour from the NE with R sector just showing.

COMMUNICATIONS (Code 0402) Cliff Rescue Service 32430; 67222; RNLI 32901; Police 32304; Dr 32421. HM 32466.
Marina Ch 16 12 (HJ); Arklow SC Ch 10.

FACILITIES **Arklow Marina** ☎087 258 8078, 60 inc €3·35 on N bank on ageing pontoons and in basin; (20t) Kos, also operates **South Dock** €30·00/craft/nt, discounts available WC/ in LB Ho, (Dock ent, HO).

Arklow SC (NE bank, 500m upriver) .

Town   limited   Ⓑ   @ ≈ ✈(Dublin).

5.13 ROSSLARE

Dublin **52°15'·30N 06°20'·90W**

CHARTS AC 1787, 1772, 5621; Imray C61, C57

TIDES –0510 Dover; ML 1·1; Duration 0640

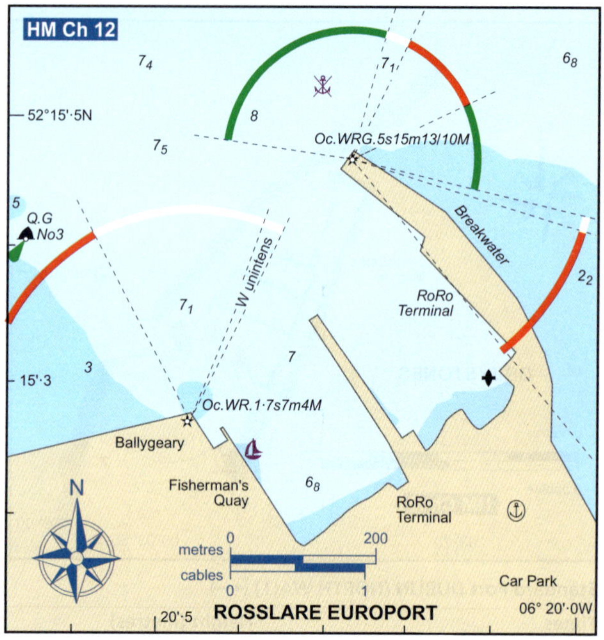

SHELTER Passage shelter from SW'lies, but few facilities for yachts berth on E wall of marshalling area (on the chartlet, 3·7m), use 3 s off Strand or ⚓ clear west of harbour. ***Small craft harbour (5ca W) is not recommended in onshore winds and can become dangerous if winds freshen.*** Rosslare Europort has 80 ferry movements/wk.

NAVIGATION WPT 52°14'·70N 06°15'·80W (abeam S Long SHM buoy, Fl(2) G 6s), 287°/2·9M to 1ca N of breakwater light. Main approach from E, S and W is via S Shear, buoyed/lit chan to S of Holden's Bed, a shoal of varying depth; the tide sets across the chan. From S, beware rks off Greenore Pt, and overfalls here and over The Baillies. From the N, appr via N Shear.

LIGHTS AND MARKS Water tr (R lt, 35m) is conspic 0·8M SSE of hbr ent. Bkwtr lt, Oc WRG 5s 15m 13/10M, see 5.3. Its two W sectors (188°-208° and 283°-286°) cover N and S Shear respectively. Note: Floodlights in the hbr can mask navigational lights.

COMMUNICATIONS (Code 053) LB Lookout Stn 9133205; 9149499; Police 9165200; Dr 9131154; Ⓗ 9142233. HM 9157921, mobile 087 2320251.
VHF Ch **12** (H24) – Call before entering harbour.

FACILITIES **Hbr Ops** ☎9157929, No dues, (hose on berths 2 and 3)   Kos   . **Village**   Ⓑ ≈ ✈ (Dublin). **Ferries** Irish Ferries (www.irishferries.com): Pembroke Dock, 4 hrs; Cherbourg, 2-3/wk, 18½hrs; Roscoff, 1-2/wk, 17½hrs (seasonal). Stena (www.stenaline.co.uk): Fishguard, 2/day, 3½hrs; Cherbourg 3/week.

MINOR HARBOURS S OF ARKLOW

COURTOWN, Wexford, **52°38'·55N 06°13'·50W**. AC 1787. 9·6M S of Arklow is feasible in settled weather and offshore winds. Caution: depth varies on appr and in ent esp in winter. Ent 10m wide between pierheads/lateral bns only 1m at MLWS due to silting. Shoaling/swell likely. Contact Courtown Hbr YC for mooring.

POLDUFF PIER, Wexford, **52°34'·15N 06°11'·97W**. AC 1787. 14M S of Arklow. Pier, extends 100m NE from shore. NW side of pier has slipway from shore and 1m depth alongside. Local moorings W of pier. Good shelter for small boats in S to W winds. Swell in winds E of S. Appr in daylight only. Appr is clear from NE to E. Rks extend from shore E'ward 200m N of pier but steering along line of pier will clear them. Pub near pier. **Village** (Ballygarrett) 1·25M W.

5.14 WEXFORD

Wexford **52°20'·10N 06°27'·00W**

CHARTS AC 1787, 1772, 5621; Imray C61

TIDES –0450 Dover; ML 1·3; Duration 0630

Standard Port COBH (⟶)

Times				Height (metres)			
High Water		Low Water		MHWS	MHWN	MLWN	MLWS
0500	1100	0500	1100	4·1	3·2	1·3	0·4
1700	2300	1700	2300				
Differences *ROSSLARE EUROPORT*							
+0045	*+0035*	*+0015*	*–0005*	*–2·2*	*–1·8*	*–0·5*	*–0·1*
WEXFORD							
+0126	+0126	+0118	+0108	–2·1	–1·7	–0·3	+0·1

SHELTER 250m of pontoon available just below bridge though silting occurs in 50m closest to the bridge. Sheltered ⚓ off town quays in 2·3m, but streams are strong. Ⓜs are provided by WHBTC, close N of Ballast Bank or proceed to quays. FVs use a new quay on E bank with ⛽ and space for tanker. Close upstream below the bridge is an all-tide slipway and trailer park.

NAVIGATION Wexford Bar SWM (52°19'·14N 06°19·39W): make good 214°/2·7M from North Long Buoy; from S make good 353°/3·4M from West Holdens Buoy. SWM is on 10m contour and marks the start of the buoyed channel to Wexford. Visitors are advised to obtain information from www.wexfordharbour.com.

- For strangers best entry is HW±2. It is difficult at any time for vessels with a draught >1.3m.
- Maintain a course on the rhumb line between marks as channel is narrow in places. Beware the S training wall (covers) and pass well S of Black Man SHM Bn at end of N training wall.
- Entry is hazardous in strong winds between SE and NE when the sea breaks on the bar.

LIGHTS AND MARKS The narrow channel frequently shifts and marks are moved accordingly; positions on the chartlet are not reliable. They are sequentially numbered from 2–30. Outer channel buoys Nos 2–9 in position from Apr–Oct are removed seasonally. The 2 church spires/Opera House (conspic) at Wexford give orientation. No ldg lts. Buoys continue upstream from Bridge.

COMMUNICATIONS (Code 053) ⊜ 9133116; Police 9122333; Dr 9122524; Ⓗ 9142233. HM 9122300.
www.wexfordharbour.info is run by local sailing enthusiasts
Wexford Hbr listening watch VHF 16, 09 (HO).

FACILITIES HM harbourmaster@wexfordcoco.ie Capt Murphy is the Marine Officer responsible for Co. Wexford harbours except Rosslare Europort.

Wexford Quays slipway 3 pontoon (free) ⛽ delivery by road tanker 🔧.

Wexford Harbour Boat & Tennis Club, www.whbtc.ie ☎914 7504 (office 0900-1700), 912 2039 (bar evenings), slipway (5t).

Town ✉ Ⓑ 🛒 ⇌ ✈ (Dublin).

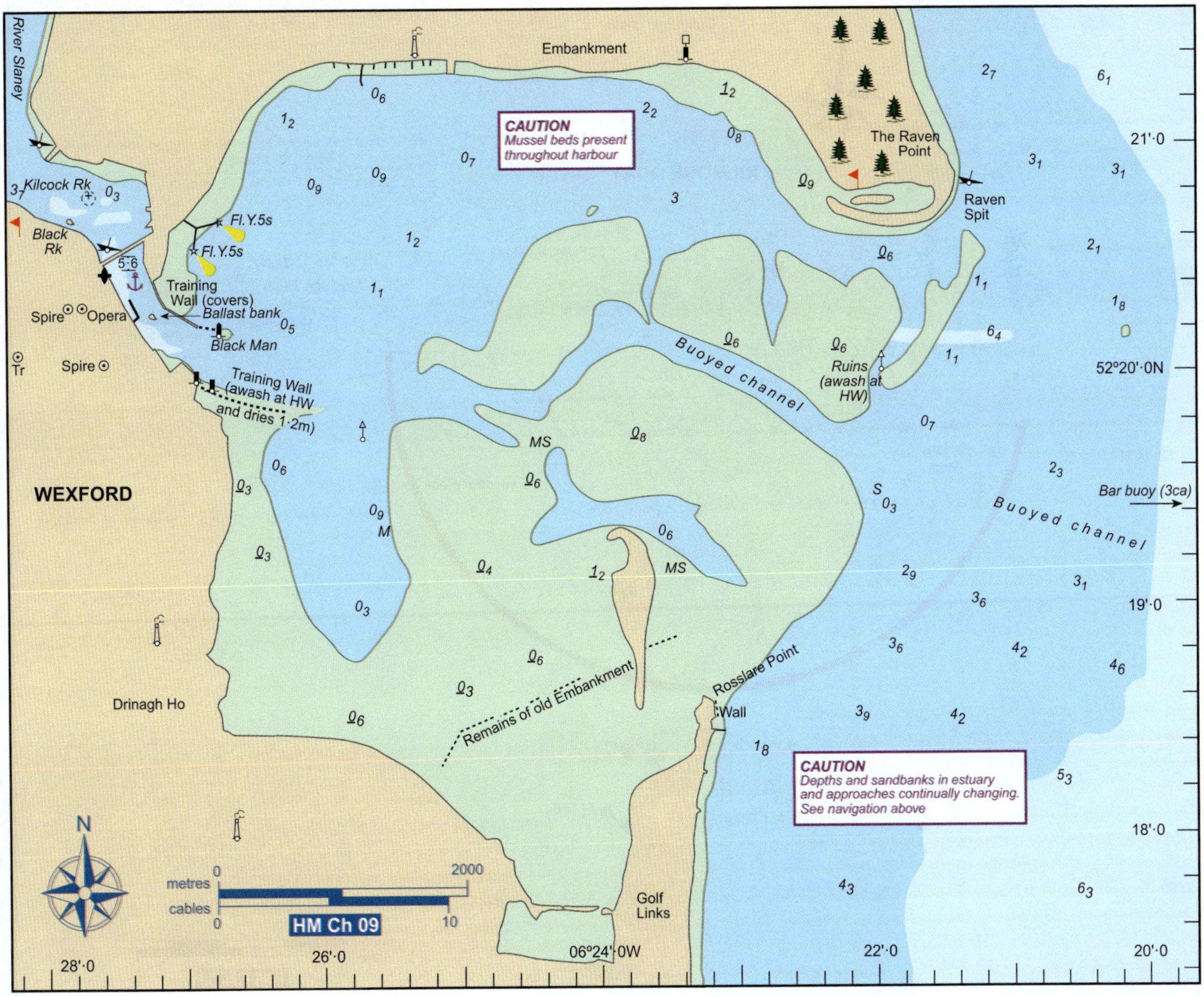

5.15 KILMORE QUAY

Wexford **52°10'·25N 06°35'·15W**

CHARTS AC 2049, 2740, 5621; Imray C61, C57

TIDES –0535 Dover; ML No data; Duration 0605

Standard Port COBH (⟶)

Times				Height (metres)			
High Water		Low Water		MHWS	MHWN	MLWN	MLWS
0500	1100	0500	1100	4·1	3·2	1·3	0·4
1700	2300	1700	2300				
Differences BAGINBUN HEAD (5M NE of Hook Hd)							
+0003	+0003	–0008	–0008	–0·2	–0·1	+0·2	+0·2
GREAT SALTEE							
+0019	+0009	–0004	+0006	–0·3	–0·4	ND	ND
CARNSORE POINT							
+0029	+0019	–0002	+0008	–1·1	–1·0	ND	ND

SHELTER Excellent in marina (3m depth) with 0.8m below CD at LAT in entrance. Harbour exposed to SE'lies. FVs berth on E and W piers close S of marina.

NAVIGATION WPT 52°09'·22N 06°35'·20W, E of SWM 000°/1·0M to pier head lt, remaining in G sector. Great (57m) and Little (35m) Saltee Islands lie respectively 3M SSW and 1·7M S, of hbr, separated by Saltee Sound. In bad weather seas break on the Bohurs and The Bore, rocks 2M E of Saltee Islands. From the W, appr is clear but keep at least 5ca off Forlorn Pt to avoid Forlorn Rk (1·5m).

From the E, safest approach is initially via Saltee Sound, then N to WPT. Beware, particularly on E-going stream, Goose Rk (2·6m) close W of L Saltee and Murroch's Rk (2·1m) 6ca NW of L Saltee. St Patrick's Bridge, 650m E of the WPT, is a 300m wide E/W chan used by FVs and yachts, carrying < 2m; indicated by lateral marks. Care is needed in strong SW winds when a standing wave can form.

LIGHTS AND MARKS See 5.3 and chartlet. A white-gabled church is conspic from afar, as are two 20m high flood lt pylons on the E quay. **Note**: Ldg marks lead 008° W of safe G sector and lead very close to 0.9m Rk on approach.

- From W, ldg lts are obscured by piers until S of hbr entrance. Turn 90° port into hbr ent, just past ☆ QRG at W Quay Hd; do not overshoot into shoal water ahead.
- R sectors of this ☆ QRG warn of Forlorn Rk, The Lings W of the ldg line and shingle banks drying 0·6m close E of the ldg line.

St Patrick's Bridge: Fl R 6s; 52°09'·30N 06°34'·71W
Fl G 6s; 52°09'·14N 06°34'·71W

COMMUNICATIONS (Code 053) HM 9129955, mob 087 9001037, 9149499.
VHF Ch 16, **09** (occas).

FACILITIES www.kilmorequaymarina.com or HM ☎(0800-2000) 20Ⓥ €2.50 (€25 min) (24/7) cycle hire.
Village .
Kilmore 3M inland, (Wexford 15M).

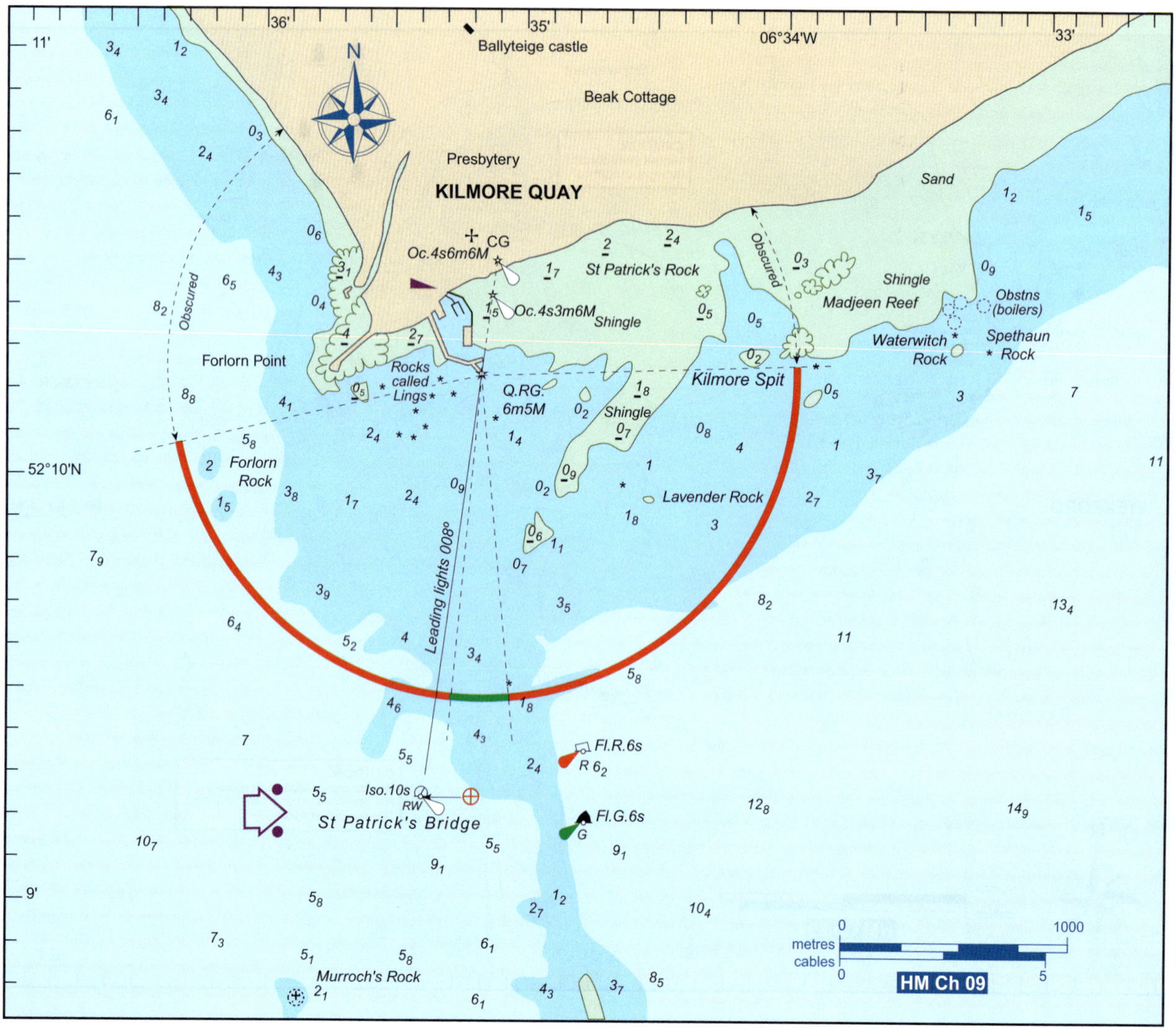

5.16 WATERFORD

Waterford **52°15'·50N 07°06'·00W** ❀❀❀◊◊✿✿

CHARTS AC 2049, 2046, 5621, 5622; Imray C61, C57

TIDES –0520 Dover; ML 2·4; Duration 0605

Standard Port COBH (⟶)

Times				Height (metres)			
High Water		Low Water		MHWS	MHWN	MLWN	MLWS
0500	1100	0500	1100	4·1	3·2	1·3	0·4
1700	2300	1700	2300				
Differences WATERFORD							
+0053	+0032	+0015	+0100	+0·6	+0·6	+0·4	+0·2
CHEEKPOINT							
+0026	+0021	+0019	+0022	+0·5	+0·4	+0·3	+0·2
KILMOKEA POINT							
+0026	*+0022*	*+0020*	*+0020*	*+0·2*	*+0·1*	*+0·1*	*+0·1*
NEW ROSS							
+0100	+0030	+0055	+0130	+0·3	+0·4	+0·3	+0·4

SHELTER Very good on 4 long marina pontoons after Nanny pontoon (first one/private) on S bank, abeam cathedral spire. All tide access, but beware strong tidal stream. There are many excellent ⚓: off S side of R Suir in King's Chan (only to be entered W of Little Is); and up the R Barrow near Marsh Pt (about 2M S of New Ross) and ½M S of New Ross fixed bridge.

NAVIGATION WPT 52°06'·50N 06°58'·50W, 002°/6·7M to Dir lt at Duncannon. From the E, keep clear of Brecaun reef (2M NE of Hook Hd). Keep about 1·5M S of Hook Hd to clear Tower Race and overfalls, especially HW Dover ±2. From the W beware Falskirt Rk (3m), 2ca off Swine Head and 2M WSW of Dunmore East (5.17). Marine Farms off Creadan Hd and Broomhill Pt; large ships go up to Waterford; beware ferry between Passage East and Ballyhack. Bridge N of Pink Pt, air draft 36m en-route New Ross.

LIGHTS AND MARKS Ent is between Dunmore East and Hook Hd. Duncannon dir lt, F WRG, leads 002° into the river. Estuary and R Suir are very well marked to Waterford. R Barrow is marked up to New Ross. Buoys lead across bar at river ent and change often. Disused railway swing bridge at the ent opens at its W end. Call bridgekeeper ☎086 8167826 when abeam Passage East (no VHF).

COMMUNICATIONS (Code 051) ⊜862141; Police 305300; Dr 855411; 🄷 848000. HM ☎899801 Mob 087 2224961 Asst HM ☎899804 Mob 087 278103; New Ross 421303.

Waterford and New Ross VHF Ch **14** 16. No VHF for marina.

FACILITIES **Marina** ☎309900, berth mob 087 2384944 (H24); 100 €16<7.6m>€20<10.7m>€30<13.7m; water, shore power €2·50/10Kw, showers, laundry at HM's office, fuel (from Dunmore East by Coast2Coast ☎382797, mob 0872512170) ✕ 🔧 (Ballyhack ☎389164).

New Ross Marina newrossmarina@wexfordcoco.ie mob 086 388 9652; water, shore power, 66 €10 (€50/wk) <9.5m; €20(€100/wk) <10.5m; €20 (€120/wk) <12.5m, €30 (€120/wk) <13.5m; wi-fi.

New Ross Boatyard 🔧.

Waterford Boatyard (R Suir), ☎857755 or 086 1727502 will arrange Rice bridge lift on approach as will Waterford CC ☎076 1102020.

City All facilities, bus to Rosslare for UK ferries.

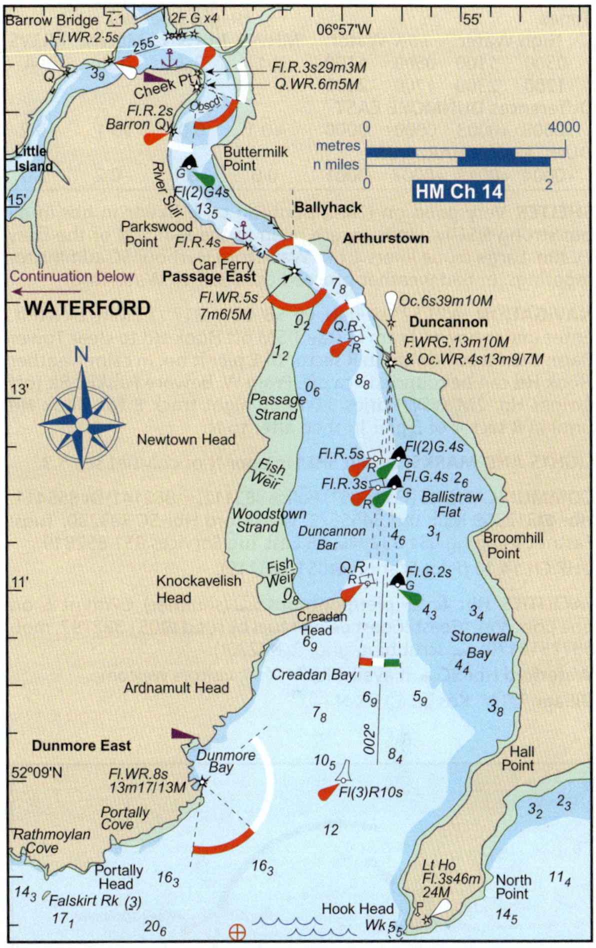

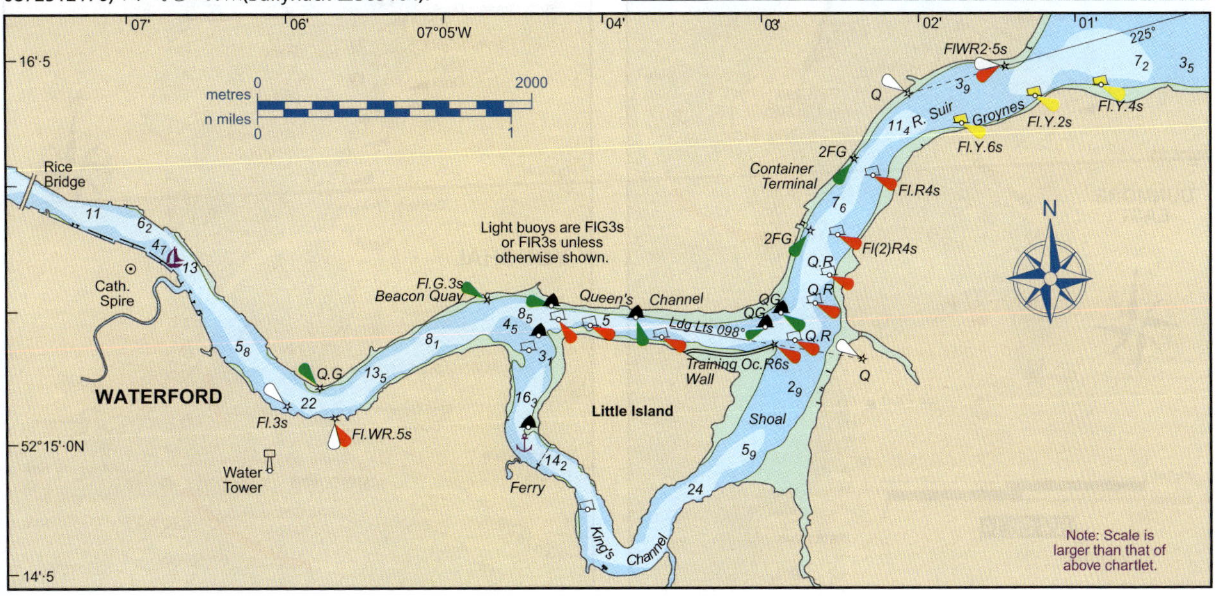

5.17 DUNMORE EAST

Waterford **52°08′·95N 06°59′·37W**

CHARTS AC 2049, 2046, 5621, 5622; Imray C61, C57

TIDES –0535 Dover; ML 2·4; Duration 0605

Standard Port COBH (⟶)

Times				Height (metres)			
High Water		Low Water		MHWS	MHWN	MLWN	MLWS
0500	1100	0500	1100	4·1	3·2	1·3	0·4
1700	2300	1700	2300				
Differences DUNMORE EAST							
+0008	+0003	0000	0000	+0·1	0·0	+0·1	+0·2
DUNGARVAN HARBOUR							
+0004	+0012	+0007	–0001	0·0	+0·1	–0·2	0·0

SHELTER Very good on (70m) pontoon on E bkwtr in hbr in all but strong S/SE′ly winds. ⛵ are open to the E or ⚓ N of the busy FV hbr. Large cruise liners ⚓ off. Waterford Harbour SC administer moorings. In bad weather proceed up R Suir to Waterford.

NAVIGATION WPT 52°08′·00N, 06°58′·00W, 317°/1·2M to bkwtr lt. Enter under power. From E, stay 1·5M off Hook Hd to clear Tower Race; then steer for hbr in R sector of E pier lt ho. In calm weather Hook Hd can be rounded 1ca off. From W, beware Falskirt Rk (off Swines Hd, 2M WSW) dries 3·0m. By night track E for Hook Hd until in R sector of E pier lt, then alter to N.

LIGHTS AND MARKS 2nd lit SHM in appr N of chartlet see 5.3.

COMMUNICATIONS (Code 051) Police 383112; ⊜862141; Dr 855411. Hbr ☎312359 Mob 087 3455623; Waterford Hbr SC 383230. Tugs: Fastnet shipping 051 832946, SE East Tug Services 051 852819.

VHF Ch **14** 16 (Pilot Station ☎051 383119).

FACILITIES **Hbr** pier/pontoons (summer) €2/m/nt on one pontoon. (Coast2Coast deliver fuel by road ☎051 382797, mob 0872512170) scrubbing grid, (220t).

Waterford Hbr SC if available, ✕; visitors welcome.

Village Kos ✉ Ⓒ ✕.

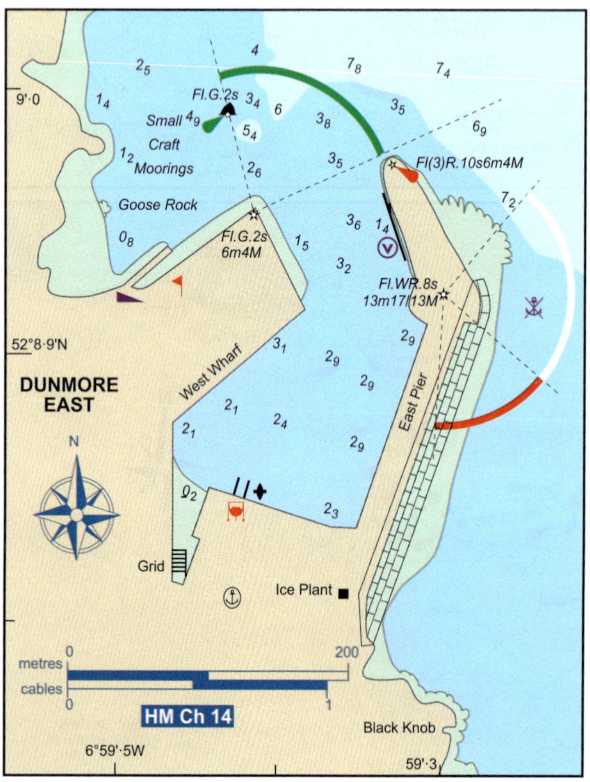

5.18 YOUGHAL

Cork **51°56′·54N 07°50′·20W**

CHARTS AC 2049, 2071, 5622; Imray C57

TIDES –0556 Dover; ML 2·1; Duration 0555

Standard Port COBH (⟶)

Times				Height (metres)			
High Water		Low Water		MHWS	MHWN	MLWN	MLWS
0500	1100	0500	1100	4·1	3·2	1·3	0·4
1700	2300	1700	2300				
Differences YOUGHAL							
0000	+0010	+0010	0000	–0·2	–0·1	–0·1	–0·1

SHELTER Good, but strong S′lies cause swell inside the hbr. Possible from Youghal Shipping in 1.3m (drying patches just off quay); walk ashore short-stay pontoon, with off quay N of Town Hall for boats on 8 s (see chartlet). ⚓ as chartlet; no dues. Strong tidal streams run throughout ⚓.

NAVIGATION WPT, East Bar, 51°55′·62N 07°48′·00W, 302°/1·8M to Fl WR 2·5s lt. Beware Blackball Ledge (ECM lt buoy) and Bar Rks (SCM lt buoy), both outside hbr ent in R sector of lt ho. From W, appr via West Bar (1·7m) is shorter route and E Bar has 2·0m.

- Both Bars in E to SSW′lies >F6 are likely to have dangerous seas.
- Red Bank is continually changing, now further E than charted it closes off E chan at N end – obtain local knowledge.

LIGHTS AND MARKS See 5.3 and chartlet. Water tr is conspic from seaward; clock tr and tr within hbr. Upriver, 175° transit of convent belfry tr/town hall clears W of Red Bank.

COMMUNICATIONS (Code 024) ⊜ (021) 4325000; Police 92200; Dr 92702. HM ☎92926 mob 086 7800878; Youghal Shipping ☎92577 (for poss).

VHF Ch 14 16 0900-1700 and when ships expected.

FACILITIES €20/night (HM, www.corkcoco.ie) .

Town ✉ Ⓑ ✕ Bus (Cork/W′ford) ✈(Cork).

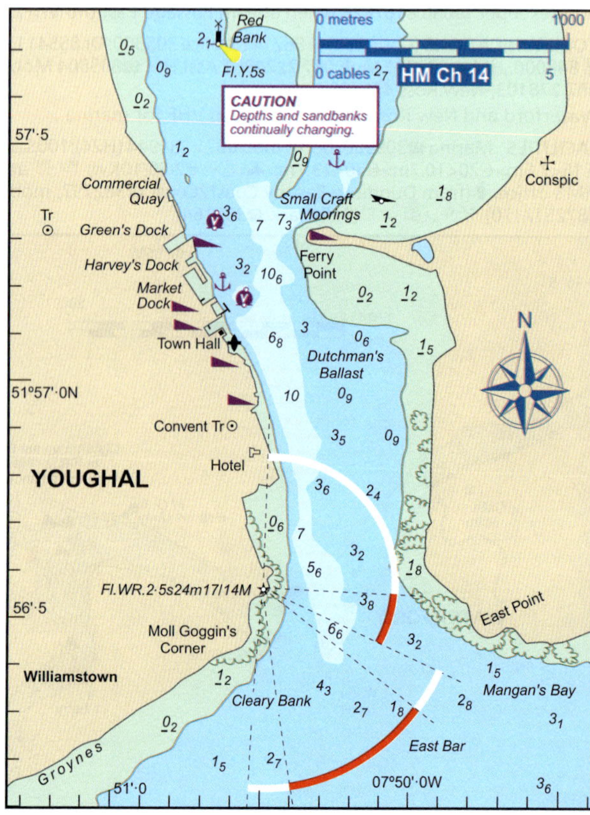

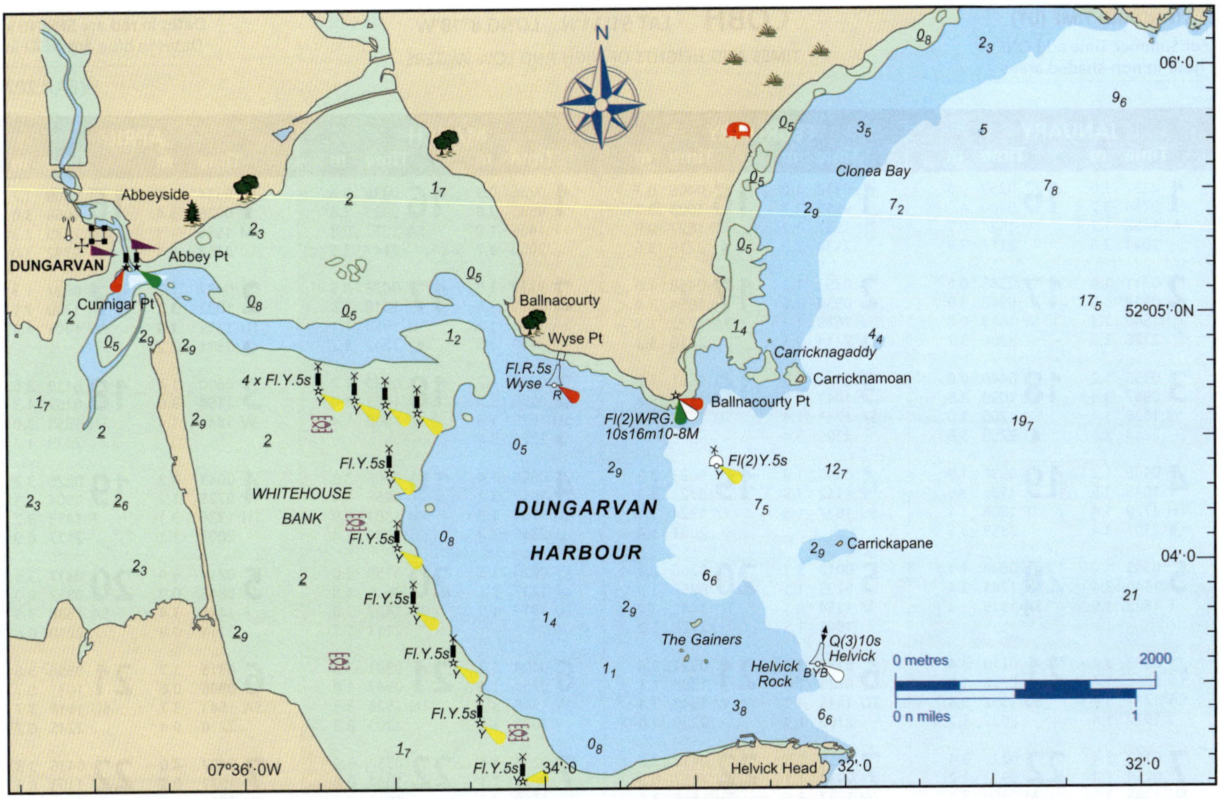

MINOR HARBOUR 16M ENE of YOUGHAL

DUNGARVAN BAY, Waterford, **52°05'·15N 07°36'·70W**. AC 2017, 5622. HW –0542 on Dover; Duration 0600. See 5.17. A large bay, drying to the W, entered between Helvick Hd to the S and Ballynacourty Pt to the N. Approach in W sector (274°-302°) of this lt to clear Carricknamoan islet to the N, and Carrickapane Rk and Helvick Rk (ECM buoy Q (3) 10s) to the S. 5ca W of this buoy are The Gainers, a large unmarked rocky patch (dries 0·8m). Beware salmon nets. Off Helvick harbour ⚓ in approx 4m. Dungarvan town harbour is accessible via buoyed chan which almost dries and shifts, the buoys being moved to suit. Approach is difficult in SE'lies >F6. ⚓ in the pool below the town or on pontoon (dries to soft mud), S bank below bridge; craft can stay overnight beyond double Y lines. Facilities: Kos ✉ Ⓑ ✕.

MINOR HARBOUR 15M ENE of ROCHE'S POINT

BALLYCOTTON, Cork, **51°49'·70N 08°00·19W**. AC 2424, 5622. HW –0555 on Dover; Duration 0550. See above. Small, NE-facing harbour at W end of bay suffers from scend in strong SE winds; 3m in entrance and about 1·5m against piers. Many FVs alongside piers, on which yachts should berth, rather than ⚓ in hbr, which is foul with old ground tackle. 6 Y✪s are outside harbour, or good ⚓ in offshore winds in 6m NE of pier, protected by Ballycotton Is. Lt ho Fl WR 10s 59m 21/17M, B tr in W walls; 238°-W-048°-R-238°. Facilities: HM Youghal; on pier. **Village** LB, Kos ✉ Hotel ✕.

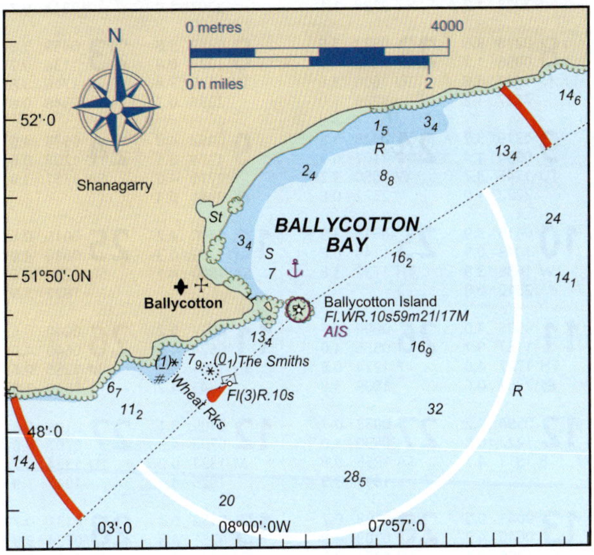

STANDARD TIME (UT)
For Summer Time add ONE hour in **non-shaded areas**

COBH LAT 51°51′N LONG 8°18′W

TIMES AND HEIGHTS OF HIGH AND LOW WATERS

Dates in red are SPRINGS
Dates in blue are NEAPS

YEAR **2024**

JANUARY

Date	Time	m	Date	Time	m
1 M	0232 0834 1458 2044	1.0 3.7 1.2 3.6	16 TU	0259 0900 1524 2117	0.5 4.1 0.7 3.9
2 TU	0311 0914 1540 2126	1.1 3.6 1.3 3.5	17 W	0348 0948 1613 2206	0.6 3.9 0.8 3.7
3 W	0355 0957 1626 2213	1.2 3.6 1.4 3.5	18 TH	0440 1039 1706 ◐ 2258	0.8 3.8 1.0 3.6
4 TH	0446 1045 1720 ◑ 2307	1.3 3.5 1.4 3.4	19 F	0538 1136 1806 2359	1.0 3.6 1.1 3.5
5 F	0545 1140 1822	1.4 3.4 1.5	20 SA	0644 1241 1915	1.1 3.4 1.2
6 SA	0007 0650 1241 1927	3.4 1.4 3.4 1.4	21 SU	0110 0758 1352 2029	3.4 1.2 3.4 1.2
7 SU	0113 0754 1345 2028	3.4 1.4 3.5 1.3	22 M	0225 0912 1500 2138	3.4 1.2 3.5 1.1
8 M	0218 0856 1447 2127	3.5 1.2 3.6 1.2	23 TU	0333 1016 1600 2236	3.6 1.0 3.6 1.0
9 TU	0319 0954 1545 2222	3.7 1.1 3.7 1.0	24 W	0429 1107 1650 2322	3.8 0.9 3.7 0.8
10 W	0415 1048 1638 2312	3.9 0.9 3.9 0.8	25 TH	0515 1149 1732 ○	3.9 0.8 3.8
11 TH	0506 1137 1727 ● 2357	4.0 0.7 4.0 0.6	26 F	0000 0555 1224 1809	0.7 4.0 0.8 3.9
12 F	0554 1222 1813	4.2 0.5 4.1	27 SA	0033 0630 1255 1842	0.7 4.0 0.8 3.9
13 SA	0041 0640 1306 1858	0.5 4.2 0.5 4.1	28 SU	0103 0703 1324 1913	0.7 4.0 0.8 3.9
14 SU	0126 0726 1351 1943	0.4 4.2 0.5 4.0	29 M	0132 0735 1353 1944	0.7 3.9 0.9 3.8
15 M	0212 0812 1437 2030	0.4 4.2 0.5 4.0	30 TU	0202 0806 1426 2016	0.8 3.9 1.0 3.8
			31 W	0235 0839 1500 2051	0.9 3.8 1.1 3.7

FEBRUARY

Date	Time	m	Date	Time	m
1 TH	0312 0915 1537 2130	1.0 3.7 1.2 3.6	16 F	0406 1003 1627 ◐ 2219	0.7 3.7 0.9 3.6
2 F	0353 0954 1619 ◑ 2214	1.2 3.6 1.3 3.5	17 SA	0458 1054 1722 2316	1.0 3.4 1.1 3.3
3 SA	0442 1042 1713 2309	1.3 3.5 1.4 3.4	18 SU	0601 1159 1832	1.2 3.2 1.3
4 SU	0546 1142 1827	1.4 3.3 1.5	19 M	0033 0723 1324 2001	3.2 1.3 3.1 1.4
5 M	0018 0705 1254 1948	3.3 1.5 3.3 1.5	20 TU	0206 0857 1445 2128	3.2 1.3 3.2 1.2
6 TU	0137 0823 1413 2100	3.3 1.4 3.3 1.3	21 W	0321 1008 1548 2229	3.4 1.1 3.4 1.0
7 W	0254 0934 1527 2203	3.5 1.1 3.5 1.0	22 TH	0416 1057 1636 2313	3.6 0.9 3.6 0.7
8 TH	0359 1034 1626 2257	3.8 0.8 3.8 0.7	23 F	0459 1136 1716 2348	3.8 0.7 3.8 0.6
9 F	0452 1124 1715 ● 2344	4.0 0.5 4.0 0.4	24 SA	0536 1208 1751 ○	4.0 0.6 3.9
10 SA	0540 1209 1800	4.2 0.3 4.1	25 SU	0016 0610 1234 1822	0.6 4.0 0.6 3.9
11 SU	0027 0624 1251 1843	0.2 4.3 0.2 4.2	26 M	0040 0640 1258 1850	0.6 4.0 0.6 3.9
12 M	0109 0708 1333 1925	0.1 4.3 0.2 4.2	27 TU	0104 0707 1324 1917	0.6 4.0 0.7 3.9
13 TU	0152 0751 1415 2007	0.2 4.3 0.3 4.1	28 W	0131 0734 1353 1946	0.7 3.9 0.8 3.8
14 W	0235 0834 1457 2049	0.3 4.1 0.4 4.0	29 TH	0202 0803 1424 2016	0.8 3.8 0.9 3.8
15 TH	0320 0917 1541 2132	0.4 4.0 0.6 3.8			

MARCH

Date	Time	m	Date	Time	m
1 F	0236 0835 1456 2050	0.9 3.8 1.0 3.7	16 SA	0338 0929 1557 2147	0.6 3.6 0.8 3.5
2 SA	0313 0911 1532 2130	1.0 3.6 1.2 3.6	17 SU	0428 1018 1650 ◐ 2242	0.9 3.3 1.1 3.2
3 SU	0358 0956 1620 ◑ 2223	1.2 3.5 1.4 3.4	18 M	0530 1123 1800	1.2 3.0 1.4
4 M	0500 1057 1735 2335	1.4 3.2 1.5 3.2	19 TU	0006 0655 1301 1936	3.0 1.4 2.9 1.4
5 TU	0624 1217 1910	1.5 3.1 1.5	20 W	0150 0838 1427 2111	3.0 1.3 3.0 1.2
6 W	0104 0754 1348 2033	3.2 1.4 3.1 1.3	21 TH	0301 0947 1528 2209	3.3 1.0 3.3 0.9
7 TH	0233 0911 1509 2141	3.4 1.1 3.4 0.9	22 F	0352 1034 1614 2250	3.6 0.8 3.6 0.7
8 F	0340 1013 1609 2236	3.7 0.7 3.7 0.5	23 SA	0434 1111 1652 2323	3.8 0.6 3.8 0.6
9 SA	0433 1104 1656 2323	4.0 0.4 4.0 0.2	24 SU	0510 1141 1726 2350	3.9 0.6 3.9 0.5
10 SU	0519 1148 1740 ●	4.2 0.1 4.2	25 M	0542 1206 1755 ○	3.9 0.5 3.9
11 M	0006 0602 1229 1821	0.0 4.4 0.0 4.3	26 TU	0011 0611 1228 1823	0.5 3.9 0.6 3.9
12 TU	0047 0644 1310 1901	0.0 4.4 0.0 4.3	27 W	0034 0636 1254 1849	0.6 3.9 0.6 3.9
13 W	0129 0725 1350 1941	0.0 4.3 0.1 4.2	28 TH	0102 0702 1322 1916	0.6 3.9 0.7 3.9
14 TH	0210 0805 1430 2021	0.1 4.1 0.3 4.0	29 F	0133 0730 1353 1947	0.7 3.8 0.8 3.8
15 F	0253 0846 1512 2102	0.4 3.9 0.5 3.8	30 SA	0208 0803 1427 2021	0.8 3.7 0.9 3.7
			31 SU	0247 0841 1505 2103	1.0 3.6 1.1 3.6

APRIL

Date	Time	m	Date	Time	m
1 M	0334 0928 1556 2158	1.1 3.4 1.3 3.4	16 TU	0509 1056 1739 2342	1.2 3.0 1.3 3.0
2 TU	0437 1032 1711 ◑ 2311	1.3 3.2 1.4 3.2	17 W	0627 1230 1905	1.3 2.9 1.3
3 W	0600 1154 1843	1.4 3.0 1.4	18 TH	0119 0757 1354 2029	3.0 1.3 3.0 1.2
4 TH	0043 0728 1326 2007	3.2 1.2 3.1 1.1	19 F	0226 0904 1453 2127	3.2 1.1 3.2 0.9
5 F	0210 0845 1445 2114	3.4 0.9 3.4 0.8	20 SA	0317 0952 1538 2210	3.5 0.9 3.5 0.8
6 SA	0315 0946 1543 2210	3.7 0.6 3.7 0.4	21 SU	0358 1031 1618 2245	3.6 0.7 3.7 0.7
7 SU	0407 1037 1631 2259	4.0 0.3 4.0 0.2	22 M	0435 1103 1652 2313	3.8 0.6 3.8 0.6
8 M	0453 1123 1715 ● 2343	4.2 0.1 4.2 0.0	23 TU	0508 1131 1723 ○ 2339	3.8 0.6 3.8 0.6
9 TU	0537 1205 1757	4.3 0.0 4.3	24 W	0538 1158 1752	3.8 0.6 3.9
10 W	0025 0619 1246 1837	0.0 4.3 0.0 4.2	25 TH	0006 0606 1227 1822	0.6 3.8 0.6 3.9
11 TH	0107 0700 1327 1917	0.0 4.2 0.1 4.1	26 F	0037 0634 1259 1853	0.6 3.8 0.7 3.9
12 F	0149 0740 1408 1957	0.2 4.0 0.3 4.0	27 SA	0112 0707 1334 1928	0.7 3.8 0.8 3.8
13 SA	0232 0821 1451 2038	0.4 3.8 0.6 3.7	28 SU	0150 0745 1413 2007	0.8 3.7 0.9 3.7
14 SU	0317 0903 1536 2124	0.7 3.5 0.8 3.5	29 M	0234 0828 1458 2054	0.9 3.6 1.0 3.6
15 M	0407 0952 1630 ◐ 2219	1.0 3.2 1.1 3.2	30 TU	0327 0920 1554 2151	1.0 3.4 1.1 3.5

Chart Datum: 0·13 metres above Ordnance Datum (Dublin). HAT is 4·5 metres above Chart Datum.

STANDARD TIME (UT)
For Summer Time add ONE hour in **non-shaded areas**

COBH LAT 51°51′N LONG 8°18′W

TIMES AND HEIGHTS OF HIGH AND LOW WATERS

Dates in red are SPRINGS
Dates in blue are NEAPS

YEAR 2024

MAY

Date	Time	m	Date	Time	m
1	0430	1.2	16	0552	1.3
	1024	3.2		1141	3.0
W	1705	1.2	TH	1823	1.2
	◑ 2302	3.3			
2	0545	1.2	17	0027	3.1
	1140	3.2		0702	1.2
TH	1824	1.2	F	1257	3.0
				1931	1.2
3	0024	3.4	18	0134	3.2
	0705	1.1		0803	1.1
F	1301	3.3	SA	1359	3.2
	1940	1.0		2027	1.0
4	0141	3.5	19	0227	3.4
	0815	0.8		0854	1.0
SA	1412	3.5	SU	1448	3.4
	2045	0.7		2114	0.9
5	0244	3.8	20	0312	3.5
	0915	0.6		0938	0.9
SU	1511	3.8	M	1531	3.5
	2142	0.4		2155	0.8
6	0338	4.0	21	0353	3.6
	1009	0.4		1017	0.8
M	1602	4.0	TU	1611	3.7
	2233	0.3		2232	0.7
7	0427	4.1	22	0430	3.7
	1057	0.2		1054	0.7
TU	1650	4.1	W	1649	3.8
	2321	0.2		2307	0.7
8	0513	4.2	23	0505	3.8
	1143	0.2		1130	0.7
W	1734	4.2	TH	1725	3.8
	●			○ 2343	0.7
9	0005	0.2	24	0540	3.8
	0557	4.1		1207	0.7
TH	1226	0.2	F	1801	3.9
	1817	4.1			
10	0048	0.2	25	0020	0.7
	0639	4.0		0616	3.8
F	1308	0.3	SA	1245	0.7
	1858	4.0		1839	3.9
11	0131	0.4	26	0100	0.7
	0720	3.9		0655	3.8
SA	1351	0.5	SU	1325	0.7
	1939	3.9		1919	3.8
12	0215	0.6	27	0143	0.7
	0801	3.7		0738	3.7
SU	1435	0.7	M	1409	0.8
	2022	3.7		2003	3.8
13	0300	0.8	28	0231	0.8
	0844	3.5		0826	3.6
M	1521	0.9	TU	1458	0.9
	2108	3.5		2053	3.7
14	0350	1.0	29	0324	0.9
	0932	3.3		0919	3.5
TU	1613	1.1	W	1553	0.9
	2201	3.3		2150	3.6
15	0446	1.2	30	0423	1.0
	1028	3.1		1018	3.4
W	1714	1.2	TH	1655	1.0
	◐ 2308	3.1		◑ 2253	3.5
			31	0528	1.0
				1124	3.4
			F	1802	0.9

JUNE

Date	Time	m	Date	Time	m
1	0001	3.5	16	0022	3.3
	0637	0.9		0700	1.2
SA	1231	3.5	SU	1248	3.2
	1911	0.8		1924	1.2
2	0109	3.6	17	0122	3.3
	0743	0.8		0754	1.2
SU	1337	3.6	M	1346	3.3
	2015	0.7		2017	1.1
3	0211	3.7	18	0216	3.4
	0844	0.7		0845	1.1
M	1437	3.7	TU	1439	3.4
	2114	0.6		2107	1.0
4	0308	3.8	19	0305	3.5
	0941	0.6		0935	1.0
TU	1534	3.8	W	1529	3.6
	2210	0.5		2156	0.9
5	0402	3.9	20	0353	3.6
	1034	0.5		1024	0.9
W	1627	3.9	TH	1617	3.7
	2302	0.4		2242	0.8
6	0452	3.9	21	0438	3.7
	1124	0.5		1109	0.8
TH	1716	4.0	F	1703	3.8
	● 2349	0.4		2327	0.7
7	0539	3.9	22	0522	3.8
	1210	0.5		1153	0.7
F	1801	4.0	SA	1746	3.9
				○	
8	0034	0.5	23	0009	0.6
	0623	3.9		0605	3.8
SA	1253	0.5	SU	1235	0.6
	1844	3.9		1829	3.9
9	0116	0.6	24	0053	0.6
	0705	3.8		0648	3.8
SU	1336	0.6	M	1318	0.6
	1925	3.8		1913	3.9
10	0159	0.7	25	0137	0.6
	0745	3.7		0734	3.8
M	1418	0.7	TU	1403	0.6
	2007	3.7		1959	3.9
11	0241	0.8	26	0225	0.6
	0826	3.5		0821	3.8
TU	1502	0.9	W	1451	0.6
	2050	3.6		2048	3.9
12	0326	1.0	27	0314	0.7
	0909	3.4		0911	3.7
W	1547	1.0	TH	1541	0.7
	2136	3.4		2139	3.8
13	0414	1.1	28	0406	0.7
	0956	3.3		1003	3.6
TH	1636	1.1	F	1634	0.7
	2226	3.3		◑ 2233	3.7
14	0506	1.2	29	0502	0.8
	1048	3.2		1058	3.6
F	1730	1.2	SA	1733	0.8
	◐ 2322	3.3		2331	3.6
15	0602	1.2	30	0603	0.9
	1147	3.2		1158	3.5
SA	1828	1.2	SU	1836	0.9

JULY

Date	Time	m	Date	Time	m
1	0034	3.6	16	0010	3.3
	0708	0.9		0656	1.3
M	1301	3.5	TU	1244	3.3
	1943	0.9		1923	1.3
2	0138	3.6	17	0115	3.3
	0813	0.9		0800	1.3
TU	1406	3.6	W	1351	3.3
	2049	0.8		2026	1.2
3	0242	3.6	18	0221	3.4
	0917	0.9		0901	1.2
W	1511	3.6	TH	1455	3.5
	2152	0.8		2127	1.1
4	0342	3.6	19	0323	3.5
	1018	0.8		0959	1.0
TH	1611	3.7	F	1553	3.6
	2249	0.7		2223	0.9
5	0438	3.7	20	0418	3.6
	1111	0.7		1051	0.8
F	1704	3.8	SA	1645	3.8
	● 2338	0.6		2312	0.7
6	0526	3.8	21	0507	3.8
	1158	0.6		1138	0.6
SA	1750	3.9	SU	1732	4.0
				○ 2358	0.5
7	0021	0.6	22	0553	3.9
	0610	3.8		1221	0.5
SU	1240	0.6	M	1817	4.1
	1831	3.9			
8	0101	0.7	23	0041	0.4
	0649	3.8		0637	3.9
M	1318	0.6	TU	1304	0.4
	1910	3.9		1901	4.1
9	0138	0.7	24	0124	0.4
	0726	3.7		0721	3.9
TU	1356	0.7	W	1347	0.3
	1947	3.8		1945	4.1
10	0215	0.8	25	0208	0.4
	0803	3.6		0806	3.9
W	1432	0.8	TH	1432	0.4
	2024	3.7		2030	4.0
11	0252	0.9	26	0253	0.5
	0840	3.6		0851	3.9
TH	1509	0.9	F	1518	0.5
	2102	3.6		2116	3.9
12	0330	1.0	27	0340	0.6
	0919	3.5		0938	3.8
F	1547	1.0	SA	1606	0.6
	2142	3.5		2204	3.8
13	0412	1.1	28	0429	0.7
	1001	3.4		1027	3.7
SA	1630	1.1	SU	1658	0.8
	◐ 2225	3.4		◑ 2257	3.6
14	0459	1.2	29	0524	0.9
	1048	3.4		1122	3.5
SU	1719	1.2	M	1758	1.0
	2313	3.4		2358	3.4
15	0554	1.3	30	0630	1.1
	1142	3.3		1228	3.4
M	1818	1.3	TU	1910	1.1
			31	0109	3.3
				0745	1.1
			W	1344	3.3
				2029	1.1

AUGUST

Date	Time	m	Date	Time	m
1	0224	3.3	16	0144	3.2
	0903	1.1		0832	1.3
TH	1500	3.4	F	1429	3.3
	2144	1.0		2102	1.2
2	0331	3.4	17	0300	3.4
	1011	0.9		0936	1.0
F	1603	3.6	SA	1534	3.6
	2243	0.8		2203	0.9
3	0427	3.6	18	0401	3.6
	1105	0.7		1031	0.7
SA	1654	3.8	SU	1627	3.9
	2330	0.7		2254	0.6
4	0514	3.7	19	0450	3.8
	1148	0.6		1118	0.5
SU	1737	3.9	M	1714	4.1
	●			○ 2339	0.4
5	0009	0.6	20	0534	4.0
	0555	3.8		1201	0.3
M	1224	0.6	TU	1757	4.2
	1815	3.9			
6	0042	0.6	21	0021	0.2
	0630	3.8		0617	4.1
TU	1256	0.6	W	1242	0.2
	1849	3.9		1839	4.3
7	0112	0.7	22	0102	0.2
	0703	3.8		0659	4.1
W	1326	0.6	TH	1324	0.1
	1921	3.9		1921	4.2
8	0141	0.8	23	0144	0.2
	0734	3.8		0741	4.1
TH	1355	0.7	F	1407	0.2
	1952	3.8		2004	4.1
9	0212	0.8	24	0226	0.3
	0806	3.7		0823	4.0
F	1425	0.8	SA	1450	0.4
	2024	3.7		2047	4.0
10	0245	0.9	25	0311	0.5
	0840	3.6		0907	3.8
SA	1458	0.9	SU	1536	0.6
	2057	3.7		2132	3.8
11	0320	1.1	26	0357	0.7
	0917	3.6		0954	3.6
SU	1535	1.1	M	1626	0.8
	2134	3.6		◑ 2222	3.5
12	0400	1.2	27	0451	1.0
	0958	3.5		1049	3.4
M	1619	1.2	TU	1726	1.1
	◐ 2218	3.4		2324	3.2
13	0449	1.3	28	0558	1.2
	1048	3.3		1202	3.2
TU	1716	1.4	W	1844	1.3
	2313	3.3			
14	0557	1.4	29	0048	3.1
	1153	3.2		0726	1.3
W	1831	1.4	TH	1336	3.2
				2022	1.3
15	0022	3.2	30	0215	3.2
	0718	1.4		0900	1.2
TH	1310	3.2	F	1455	3.3
	1951	1.4		2141	1.1
			31	0323	3.4
				1007	0.9
			SA	1554	3.6
				2235	0.9

Chart Datum: 0·13 metres above Ordnance Datum (Dublin). HAT is 4·5 metres above Chart Datum.

STANDARD TIME (UT)
For Summer Time add ONE hour in **non-shaded areas**

COBH LAT 51°51′N LONG 8°18′W

TIMES AND HEIGHTS OF HIGH AND LOW WATERS

Dates in red are SPRINGS
Dates in blue are NEAPS

YEAR **2024**

SEPTEMBER

Date	Day	Time	m	Date	Day	Time	m
1		0414	3.6	16		0338	3.7
		1055	0.7			1006	0.6
	SU	1639	3.8		M	1604	4.0
		2316	0.7			2231	0.5
2		0457	3.8	17		0426	4.0
		1133	0.6			1054	0.3
	M	1718	3.9		TU	1650	4.2
		2350	0.6			2315	0.3
3		0533	3.9	18		0510	4.2
		1204	0.5			1137	0.1
	TU	1752	4.0		W	1732	4.3
	●				○	2357	0.1
4		0017	0.6	19		0552	4.3
		0606	3.9			1219	0.1
	W	1229	0.5		TH	1814	4.4
		1823	4.0				
5		0041	0.6	20		0037	0.1
		0635	3.9			0633	4.3
	TH	1252	0.6		F	1300	0.1
		1850	3.9			1855	4.3
6		0106	0.7	21		0118	0.2
		0702	3.8			0714	4.2
	F	1317	0.7		SA	1342	0.2
		1917	3.9			1937	4.2
7		0133	0.8	22		0201	0.3
		0731	3.8			0756	4.1
	SA	1345	0.8		SU	1426	0.4
		1944	3.8			2019	4.0
8		0203	0.9	23		0245	0.6
		0801	3.7			0840	3.9
	SU	1417	0.9		M	1512	0.7
		2015	3.7			2103	3.7
9		0237	1.0	24		0332	0.8
		0835	3.6			0927	3.6
	M	1453	1.1		TU	1602	1.0
		2050	3.6		◑	2153	3.4
10		0314	1.2	25		0427	1.1
		0914	3.5			1024	3.3
	TU	1535	1.2		W	1704	1.2
		2133	3.5			2257	3.1
11		0401	1.4	26		0538	1.3
		1004	3.3			1147	3.1
	W	1631	1.4		TH	1828	1.4
	◐	2229	3.3				
12		0510	1.5	27		0033	3.0
		1112	3.2			0716	1.4
	TH	1751	1.5		F	1328	3.1
		2344	3.1			2014	1.3
13		0641	1.5	28		0203	3.1
		1238	3.1			0849	1.2
	F	1921	1.5		SA	1441	3.3
						2123	1.1
14		0115	3.1	29		0305	3.4
		0804	1.3			0947	0.9
	SA	1407	3.3		SU	1533	3.6
		2038	1.2			2212	0.9
15		0239	3.4	30		0352	3.6
		0912	1.0			1031	0.7
	SU	1513	3.7		M	1615	3.8
		2140	0.8			2250	0.7

OCTOBER

Date	Day	Time	m	Date	Day	Time	m
1		0432	3.8	16		0358	4.1
		1106	0.6			1027	0.3
	TU	1651	4.0		W	1623	4.3
		2322	0.6			2249	0.3
2		0506	3.9	17		0443	4.2
		1135	0.6			1113	0.2
	W	1724	4.0		TH	1707	4.4
	●	2347	0.6		○	2333	0.2
3		0537	3.9	18		0527	4.3
		1158	0.6			1157	0.1
	TH	1752	4.0		F	1750	4.4
4		0008	0.7	19		0015	0.2
		0605	3.9			0610	4.3
	F	1219	0.7		SA	1239	0.2
		1818	4.0			1832	4.3
5		0032	0.7	20		0057	0.3
		0631	3.9			0652	4.2
	SA	1243	0.7		SU	1323	0.3
		1843	3.9			1914	4.1
6		0100	0.8	21		0141	0.4
		0659	3.9			0735	4.1
	SU	1313	0.8		M	1408	0.5
		1910	3.9			1956	3.9
7		0130	0.9	22		0226	0.7
		0729	3.8			0820	3.8
	M	1346	1.0		TU	1455	0.8
		1941	3.8			2041	3.7
8		0204	1.0	23		0315	0.9
		0803	3.7			0909	3.6
	TU	1424	1.1		W	1547	1.1
		2018	3.7			2131	3.4
9		0244	1.2	24		0412	1.2
		0845	3.6			1008	3.3
	W	1509	1.3		TH	1649	1.3
		2103	3.5		◑	2235	3.1
10		0335	1.4	25		0523	1.4
		0938	3.4			1129	3.1
	TH	1609	1.4		F	1809	1.5
	◐	2202	3.3				
11		0446	1.5	26		0006	3.0
		1048	3.3			0652	1.4
	F	1727	1.5		SA	1300	3.2
		2319	3.2			1939	1.4
12		0614	1.5	27		0132	3.1
		1214	3.2			0813	1.2
	SA	1854	1.4		SU	1408	3.4
						2045	1.2
13		0049	3.2	28		0232	3.4
		0736	1.3			0909	1.0
	SU	1340	3.4		M	1458	3.6
		2011	1.1			2132	1.0
14		0210	3.5	29		0318	3.6
		0843	0.9			0952	0.9
	M	1445	3.8		TU	1540	3.8
		2112	0.8			2211	0.9
15		0309	3.8	30		0358	3.8
		0938	0.6			1029	0.8
	TU	1536	4.0		W	1617	3.9
		2203	0.5			2244	0.8
				31		0433	3.9
						1059	0.7
					TH	1651	4.0
						2312	0.8

NOVEMBER

Date	Day	Time	m	Date	Day	Time	m
1		0505	3.9	16		0506	4.3
		1125	0.7			1140	0.3
	F	1721	4.0		SA	1730	4.3
	●	2338	0.8			2358	0.4
2		0535	4.0	17		0552	4.3
		1151	0.8			1225	0.4
	SA	1748	4.0		SU	1814	4.2
3		0005	0.8	18		0042	0.4
		0605	4.0			0637	4.2
	SU	1219	0.8		M	1310	0.5
		1816	3.9			1858	4.1
4		0036	0.9	19		0126	0.6
		0636	3.9			0721	4.1
	M	1252	0.9		TU	1355	0.7
		1846	3.9			1941	3.9
5		0110	0.9	20		0212	0.8
		0709	3.9			0807	3.9
	TU	1329	1.0		W	1442	0.9
		1921	3.8			2025	3.7
6		0148	1.0	21		0301	1.0
		0748	3.8			0856	3.7
	W	1411	1.1		TH	1532	1.1
		2002	3.7			2113	3.4
7		0233	1.2	22		0355	1.1
		0833	3.7			0950	3.4
	TH	1500	1.3		F	1628	1.3
		2051	3.6			2208	3.2
8		0328	1.3	23		0456	1.3
		0928	3.5			1054	3.3
	F	1559	1.4		SA	1733	1.4
		2151	3.4		◑	2316	3.1
9		0434	1.4	24		0606	1.4
		1035	3.4			1207	3.3
	SA	1710	1.4		SU	1843	1.4
	◐	2303	3.3				
10		0551	1.3	25		0032	3.2
		1151	3.5			0715	1.3
	SU	1828	1.3		M	1314	3.3
						1946	1.3
11		0021	3.4	26		0137	3.3
		0706	1.2			0812	1.2
	M	1307	3.6		TU	1408	3.5
		1940	1.1			2038	1.2
12		0134	3.6	27		0229	3.5
		0812	0.9			0900	1.1
	TU	1411	3.8		W	1455	3.6
		2041	0.9			2122	1.1
13		0236	3.8	28		0314	3.6
		0910	0.7			0942	1.0
	W	1506	4.0		TH	1537	3.7
		2135	0.6			2202	1.0
14		0329	4.0	29		0355	3.8
		1003	0.5			1021	0.9
	TH	1556	4.2		F	1616	3.8
		2226	0.5			2239	0.9
15		0419	4.2	30		0434	3.9
		1052	0.4			1056	0.9
	F	1644	4.3		SA	1652	3.9
	○	2313	0.4			2314	0.9

DECEMBER

Date	Day	Time	m	Date	Day	Time	m
1		0511	4.0	16		0541	4.2
		1131	0.9			1216	0.6
	SU	1725	3.9		M	1803	4.1
	●	2348	0.8				
2		0546	4.0	17		0031	0.6
		1207	0.9			0627	4.1
	M	1759	3.9		TU	1300	0.6
						1846	4.0
3		0024	0.9	18		0115	0.6
		0623	4.0			0711	4.1
	TU	1243	0.9		W	1343	0.7
		1835	3.9			1927	3.9
4		0102	0.9	19		0158	0.7
		0701	4.0			0754	3.9
	W	1323	0.9		TH	1426	0.9
		1913	3.9			2008	3.7
5		0143	0.9	20		0242	0.9
		0743	3.9			0837	3.8
	TH	1407	1.0		F	1510	1.0
		1957	3.8			2050	3.6
6		0230	1.0	21		0327	1.0
		0830	3.8			0922	3.6
	F	1456	1.1		SA	1555	1.2
		2046	3.7			2134	3.5
7		0321	1.1	22		0415	1.2
		0922	3.8			1010	3.5
	SA	1549	1.2		SU	1644	1.3
		2141	3.6		◑	2223	3.4
8		0419	1.1	23		0507	1.3
		1020	3.7			1101	3.4
	SU	1649	1.2		M	1738	1.4
	◐	2242	3.5			2318	3.3
9		0523	1.2	24		0605	1.4
		1124	3.7			1159	3.4
	M	1755	1.2		TU	1836	1.4
		2348	3.5				
10		0631	1.1	25		0019	3.3
		1230	3.7			0704	1.4
	TU	1903	1.1		W	1300	3.4
						1935	1.4
11		0055	3.6	26		0124	3.4
		0738	1.0			0800	1.3
	W	1334	3.8		TH	1359	3.4
		2009	1.0			2030	1.3
12		0200	3.7	27		0223	3.5
		0841	0.9			0855	1.3
	TH	1435	3.9		F	1453	3.5
		2109	0.9			2122	1.2
13		0301	3.9	28		0317	3.6
		0941	0.8			0946	1.1
	F	1532	4.0		SA	1543	3.7
		2206	0.7			2211	1.1
14		0359	4.0	29		0407	3.8
		1037	0.7			1034	1.0
	SA	1627	4.0		SU	1629	3.8
		2258	0.6			2256	0.9
15		0452	4.1	30		0452	3.9
		1129	0.6			1117	0.9
	SU	1717	4.1		M	1711	3.9
	○	2347	0.6		●	2336	0.8
				31		0535	4.0
						1158	0.8
					TU	1750	3.9

Chart Datum: 0·13 metres above Ordnance Datum (Dublin). HAT is 4·5 metres above Chart Datum.

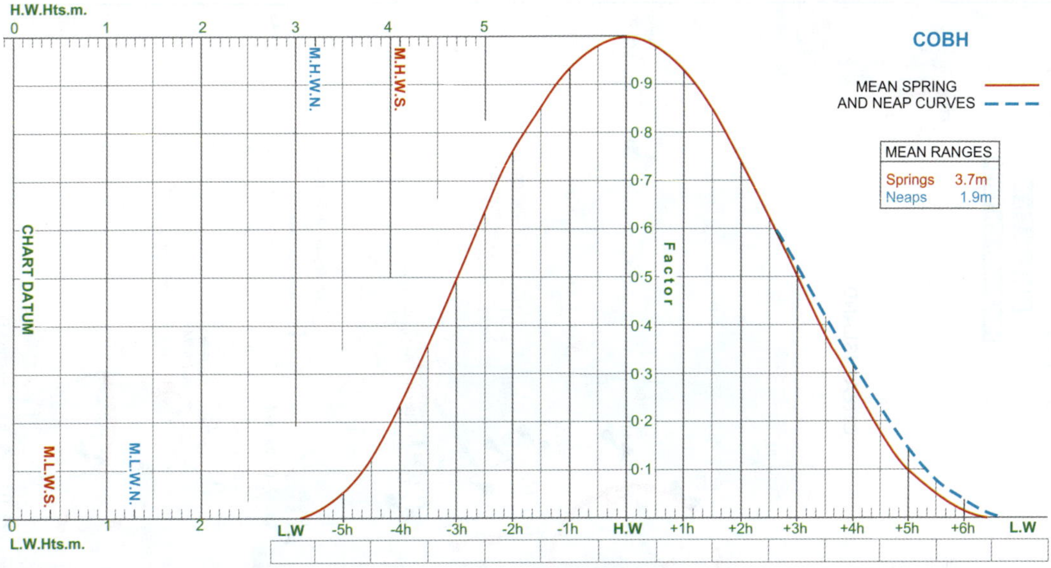

5.19 CORK HARBOUR

Cork **51°47'·50N 08°15'·54W**

CHARTS AC 1765, 1777, 1773, 5622; Imray C57, C56

TIDES –0523 Dover; ML 2·3; Duration 0555

Standard Port COBH (⟵)

Times				Height (metres)			
High Water		Low Water		MHWS	MHWN	MLWN	MLWS
0500	1100	0500	1100	4·1	3·2	1·3	0·4
1700	2300	1700	2300				
Differences BALLYCOTTON (15M ENE of Roche's Point)							
–0011	+0001	+0003	–0009	0·0	0·0	–0·1	0·0
RINGASKIDDY							
+0005	+0020	+0007	+0013	+0·1	+0·1	+0·1	+0·1
MARINO POINT							
0000	+0010	0000	+0010	+0·1	+0·1	0·0	0·0
CORK CITY							
+0005	+0010	+0020	+0010	+0·4	+0·4	+0·3	+0·2
ROBERTS COVE (approx 4M SW of Roche's Point)							
–0005	–0005	–0005	–0005	–0·1	0·0	0·0	+0·1

SHELTER Very good in all conditions, esp in Crosshaven and East Passage. There are 3 marinas at Crosshaven, plus a small marina and several ⚓s up the Owenboy River, notably at Drake's Pool. There are marinas at Cork City and at Monkstown. Cobh, Ringaskiddy and Cork City are commercial and ferry ports; contact HM/Port berthing Master for advice on berths. 100m yacht pontoon in 4·5m at Custom House Quay, Cork City. Additional Ⓥ pontoons are sited at Passage West, Aghada and Blackrock.

NAVIGATION WPT 51°46'·57N, 08°15'·39W, 005°/1M to Roche's Pt lt; also on 354°ldg line. Safe hbr with no dangers for yachts; ent is deep and well marked. Sp rate is about 1½kn in ent. Main chan up to Cork and the chan to E Ferry are marked, but shoal outside navigable chan. Ent to Crosshaven/Owenboy River carries at least 3m at LWS, and the chan is buoyed.

LIGHTS AND MARKS See 5.3. The 24·5m high hammerhead water tr S of Crosshaven and the R/W power stn chy NE of Corkbeg Is are conspic from seaward. Two set Ldg lts/marks lead through The Sound, either side of Hbr Rk (5·2m), not a hazard for yachts; but do not impede merchant ships. The chan to Crosshaven is marked by C1 SHM lt buoy, C1A SHM lt buoy; C2A PHM lt buoy, C2 PHM lt buoy; and C4 PHM lt buoy.

Haulbowline Br connecting Is to S shore is lit. N span Iso 6s (sync), S span Iso 10s (sync). These are synchronised with Spike Is pontoon E/W ends lit Iso G 6s.

COMMUNICATIONS (Code 021) HM www.corkcoco.ie ☎4772503, (4800048 OOH). Port Berthing Master 4273125, Port Ops 4811380. ⊜ 4311024; Police 4831222; Dr 4831716; Ⓗ 4546400.

Cork Hbr Radio (Port Ops) VHF Ch 12 14 16 (H24); *Crosshaven BY* Ch **M** (Mon–Fri: 0830–1730LT). *Royal Cork* YC Marina Ch **M** (0900-2359LT) and RCYC water taxi, *Salve Marine* Ch **M** 0830-1730.

FACILITIES Crosshaven BY Marina www.crosshavenboatyard.com ☎4831161, 100+20Ⓥ €2.50, Ⓔ (40t) (1½t) wi-fi.

Salve Marine ☎4831145, 45+12Ⓥ €2.50, Koz **Village**

Royal Cork YC Marina www.royalcork.com ☎4831023 170+30Ⓥ €3.00, wi-fi.

Crosshaven Pier/Pontoon €21.00 any size.

East Ferry Marina ☎(086) 7357785. Access all tides, max draught 5·5m (haul-out). Sailing Sch: www.sailcork.com

Crosshaven Village FV pier in 3·5m at Town quay, HW±4(for RIBs small power craft) Dr grid ✉ Ⓒ

Cobh E of cruise liner berth 50m pontoon in 3m at 'The Quays' Restaurant for free use by patrons.

Cork Harbour Marina, www.monkstownmarina.com ☎(087) 3669009, access all tides, max length 17m, 80 inc Ⓥ €2.40, facilities under development.

Cork City Marina, ☎423 0466 150m Ⓥ pontoon in 5m; €20 ≤12m > €35, charges inc after 3rd night;

Cork City All facilities. ✈, Ferries: Roscoff; weekly; 13hrs; Brittany (www.brittany-ferries.ie).

Aghada Pontoon with 0.4m at LAT. (enquire at petrol stn). Appr by 2 SHM 'A1' FL G 5s and 'A2' FL(2)G 10s which should be passed close to remaining on a steady straight track. Facilities:

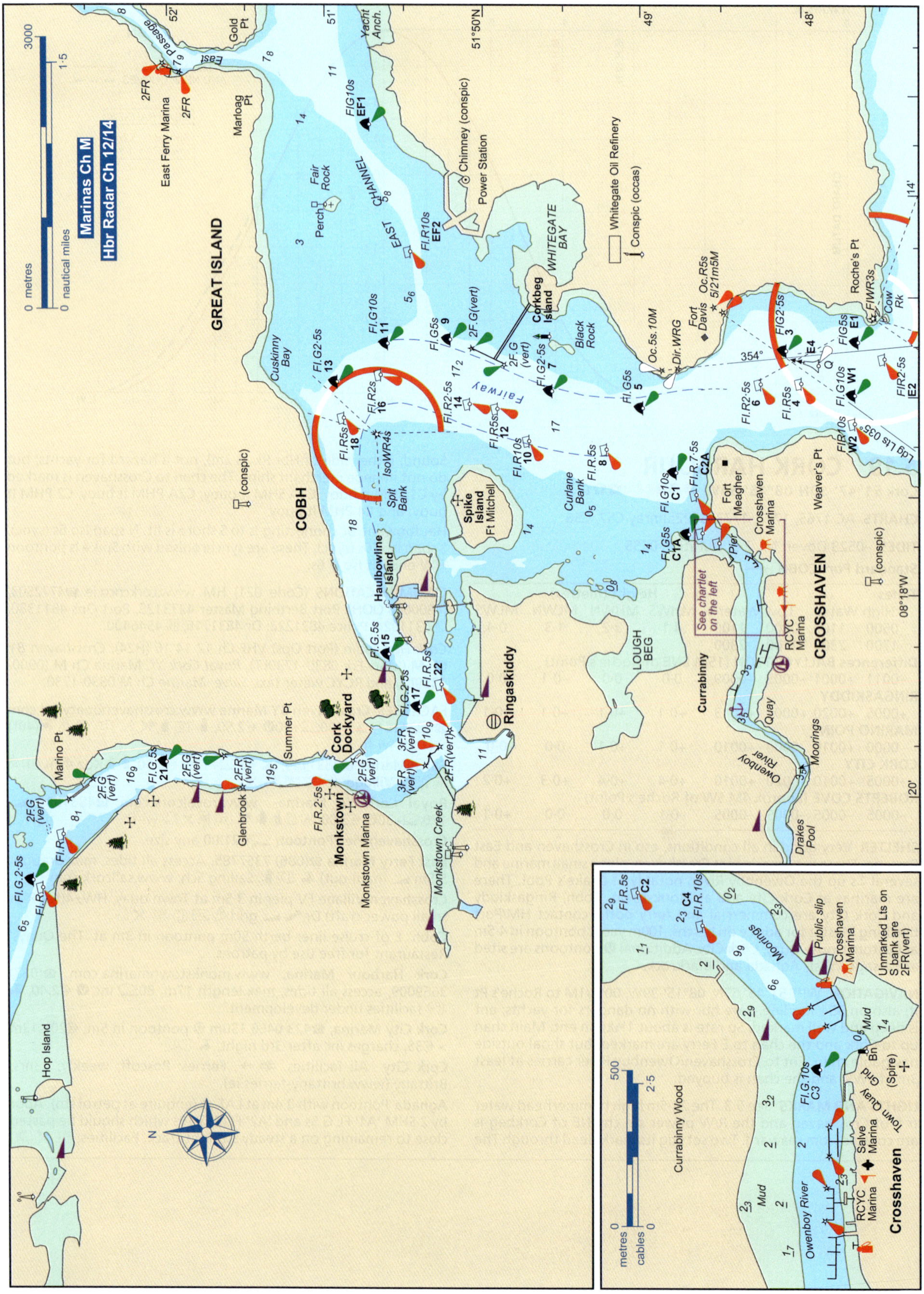
Marinas Ch M
Hbr Radar Ch 12/14
GREAT ISLAND
COBH
Cuskinny Bay
East Ferry Marina
Marloag Pt
Gold Pt
East Passage
Fair Rock
Perch
EAST CHANNEL
Chimney (conspic)
Power Station
WHITEGATE BAY
Corkbeg Island
Black Rock
Whitegate Oil Refinery
Conspic (occas)
Fort Davis
Roche's Pt
Cow Rk
Fairway
Spit Bank
Spike Island
Ft Mitchell
Curlane Bank
Haulbowline Island
Ringaskiddy
Cork Dockyard
Summer Pt
Marino Pt
Glenbrook
Monkstown
Monkstown Marina
Monkstown Creek
Hop Island
LOUGH BEG
Currabinny
Fort Meagher
Crosshaven Marina
Weaver's Pt
CROSSHAVEN
RCYC Marina
See chartlet on the left
Owenboy River
Drakes Pool
Moorings
Quay
Currabinny Wood
Public slip
Salve Marina
Town Quay
Unmarked Lts on S bank are 2FR(vert)
Crosshaven

ANCHORAGE 2M EAST OF KINSALE

OYSTERHAVEN, Cork, **51°41'·20N 08°26'·90W**. ❀❀◊✿✿✿. AC 1765, 2053, 5622. HW –0600 on Dover; ML 2·2m; Duration 0600. Use 5.19. Good shelter but ⚓'s subject to swell in S winds. Enter 0·5M N of Big Sovereign, a steep islet divided into two. Keep to S of Little Sovereign on E side of ent. There is foul ground off Ballymacus Pt on W side, and off Kinure Pt on E side. Pass W of Hbr Rk (0·9m) off Ferry Pt, the only danger within hbr. ⚓ NNW of Ferry Pt in 4–6m on soft mud/weed. NW arm shoals suddenly about 5ca NW of Ferry Pt. Also ⚓ up N arm of hbr in 3m off the W shore. Weed in higher reaches may foul ⚓. No lts, marks or VHF radio. Coast/Cliff Rescue Service ☎(021) 4770711. Oysterhaven Yacht Harbour (strictly private) 51°42'·10N 08°26'·58W, ☎(021) 4770878.

5.20 KINSALE

Cork **51°40'·80N 08°30'·00W** ❀❀❀◊◊◊✿✿✿

CHARTS AC 1765, 2053, 5622, 5623; Imray C56

TIDES –0600 Dover; ML 2·2; Duration 0600

Standard Port COBH (⟵)

Times				Height (metres)			
High Water		Low Water		MHWS	MHWN	MLWN	MLWS
0500	1100	0500	1100	4·1	3·2	1·3	0·4
1700	2300	1700	2300				
Differences KINSALE							
–0019	–0005	–0009	–0023	–0·2	0·0	+0·1	+0·2

SHELTER Excellent, except in very strong SE winds. Access H24 in all weathers/tides. Marinas at Kinsale YC and Castlepark; Ⓥ's berth on outside of pontoons in 10m in both cases; NNW of latter is FV pontoon and no ⚓ area. Possible ⊆ (Sun-Thurs) at Trident Hotel. 2 large ⚓s NE of Kinsale Bridge (contact HM). No ⚓ allowed in main channel or within 700m of Town Pier. Contact HM prior to ⚓. All craft have to pay harbour dues as well as berthing/launching fees.

NAVIGATION WPT 51°40'·00N 08°30'·00W, 001°/1·7M to Charles's Fort lt. Beware: Bulman Rk (0·9m; SCM lt buoy) 4ca S of Preghane Pt and Farmer Rk (0·6m) ¾ca off W bank. Harbour speed limit 6kn.

LIGHTS AND MARKS See 5.3 and chartlet. Chan is marked by PHM lt buoys. Marina lts are 2 FG or FR.

COMMUNICATIONS (Code 021) Coast/Cliff Rescue 0868 501804; ⊖ 6027700; Police 4779250; Dr 4772253; Ⓗ 4546400. HM ☎4772503 HO, ☎4800048 (OT) liam.keating@corkcoco.ie.

KYC VHF Ch M 16. Castlepark Marina 06 16 M. HM **14** 16.

FACILITIES **Kinsale BY** ☎4774774, Ⓥ ⛽ ⚒ 🔧 ⊡ ⛉(30t).

Kinsale YC Marina www.kyc.ie ☎4772196, mob 087 6787377, 170+50Ⓥ €3·20, ♿ ⊿ ⛽ ✕ ⊡.

Castlepark Marina www.castleparkmarina.com ☎4774959, mob 0877502737, 130⊆ inc 20Ⓥ €3·50, deals for longer stays, ⊿ ⊡ ⊡ ✕ ⊡ @.

Trident Hotel ⊆ ⚓ ⛽ Sovereign Sailing 4774145/087 6172555.

Services ⛽ ⛽ 🔧 ⊡ Ⓔ ⛵ Divers ⛉(30t).

Town LB ⊿ ⊡ ⊡ ✉ Ⓑ 🛒 ✕ ⊡ (bus to Cork, ⇌, ✈).

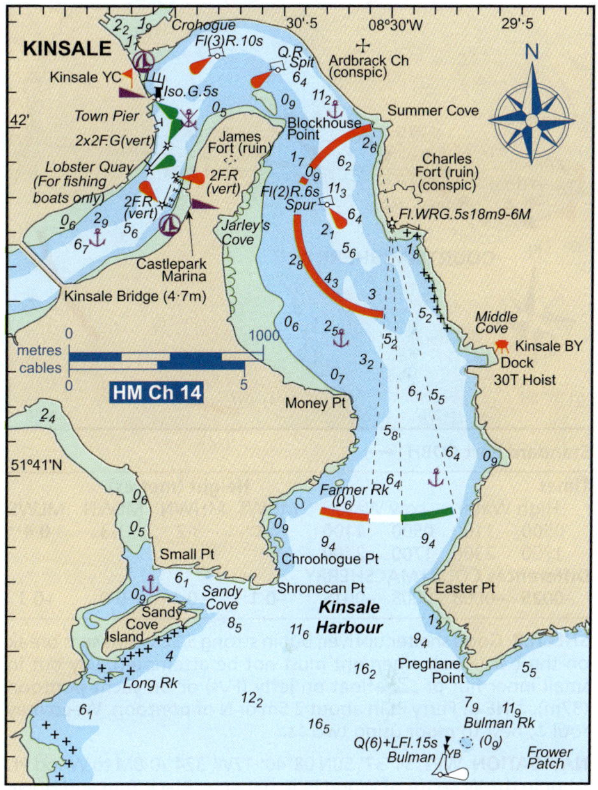

5.21 COURTMACSHERRY

Cork **51°38'·22N 08°40'·90W**

CHARTS AC 2092, 2081, 5622, 5623; Imray C56

TIDES HW –0610 on Dover; Duration 0545

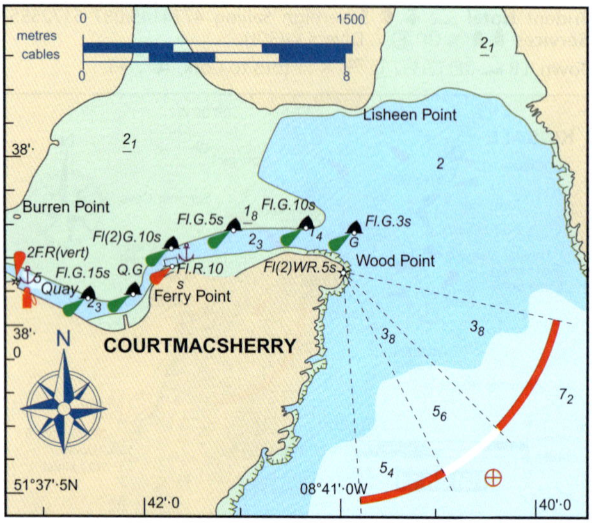

Standard Port COBH (⟵)

Times				Height (metres)			
High Water		Low Water		MHWS	MHWN	MLWN	MLWS
0500	1100	0500	1100	4·1	3·2	1·3	0·4
1700	2300	1700	2300				
Differences COURTMACSHERRY							
–0025	–0008	–0008	–0015	–0·1	–0·1	0·0	+0·1

SHELTER Good shelter upriver, but in strong S/SE winds seas break on the bar (<2m), when ent must not be attempted. Dry out in small inner hbr or afloat on jetty (FVs) or on yacht pontoon (37m). ⚓ NE of Ferry Pt in about 2·5m or N of pontoon. Weed may foul ⚓; best to moor using two ⚓s.

NAVIGATION WPT, 51°37'·50N 08°40'·17W, 324°/0·8M to Wood Pt. Appr in the W sector of Wood Pt lt, between Black Tom and Horse Rk (dries 3·6m); the latter is 3-4½ca E of Barry Pt on the W shore. Black Tom (2·3m), with SHM buoy Fl.G.5s 5ca SSE, is close NE of the appr. Further to NE, in centre of bay, Barrel Rk (dries 2·6m), has unlit perch (ruin). To NNW and E of it are Inner Barrels (0·5m) and Blueboy Rk. Hbr ent is between Wood Pt and SHM buoy 2ca NE, Fl G 3s. Chan (2m but 1·4m close inside ent) is marked by 5 SHM buoys and 1 PHM buoy (off Ferry Point). Upstream of Ferry Point there are moorings on both sides of the channel. The pier head is marked by 2 FR (vert) lights.

LIGHTS AND MARKS Wood Pt, Fl (2) WR 5s 15m 5M.

COMMUNICATIONS (023) Coast Rescue Service (Mob) 08685 01806; Dr 8846186 (HN 1850 335999); Police 8846122. HM (Mob) 0867394299; RNLI boathouse 8846600. No VHF.

FACILITIES Quay (min €15/craft) (Pier 0930-1800 on request) WC. **Village** (bus to Cork).

5.22 GLANDORE/UNIONHALL

Cork, **51°33'·70N 09°07'·20W**

CHARTS AC 2092, 5622, 5623; Imray C56

TIDES Approx as for 5.23 Castletownshend

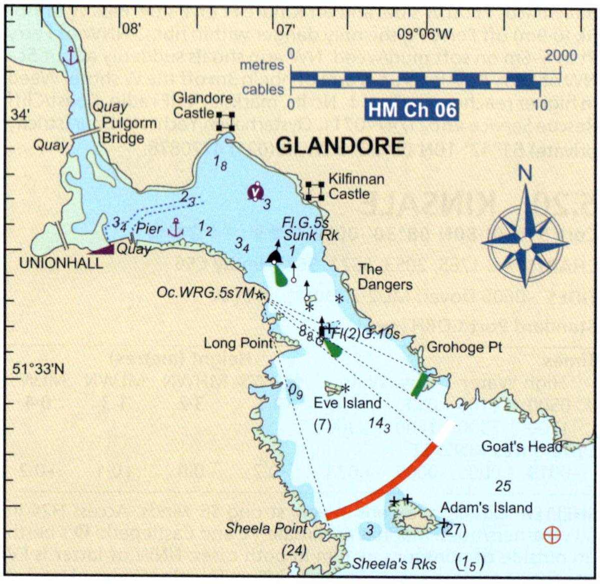

SHELTER Excellent. 12 Ys or ⚓ 1½ca E of the pier at Unionhall.

NAVIGATION WPT 51°32'·35N 09°05'·10W, 309°/1·2M to Outer Dangers. Approach between Adam Is and Goat's Hd, thence keep E of Eve Is and W of the chain of rocks: Outer, Middle and Inner Dangers and Sunk Rk. Before altering W for Unionhall, stand on to clear mudbank 1ca off S shore. Speed limit 3kn.

LIGHTS AND MARKS See 5.3. Galley Hd, Fl (5) 20s, is 5M E of ent. Middle and Inner Dangers are marked by 2 SHM bns; and Sunk Rk by a SHM lt buoy, Fl G 5s. Dir Lt 308° leads from W to E NW of *The Dangers*.

COMMUNICATIONS (Code 028) Coast Rescue 33115; Police (023) 23088; Dr 23456; HM Glandore/Unionhall 34737, mob 0866081944, garrett.mahony@corkcoco.ie.

HM Ch 06.

FACILITIES **Glandore** GHYC, s €14.00/craft (contact Glandore Inn ☎33468/33518), Kos. **Unionhall** (outside of FVs/ drying Old Quay) €15.00/craft, D(occ on quayside) or (Leap 2M) WC.

ADJACENT ANCHORAGES

RABBIT IS 51°32'·02N 09°07'·02W ⚓ in 8-10m of water in calm weather between Stack of Beans on Rabbit Is and shore. Ent to the E, S of Sheela's Rks. Narrow shallow passage to N of the Is should only be attempted with local knowledge.

SQUINCE HARBOUR 51°31'·81N 09°07'·75W to W of Rabbit Is best approached from Big Snd to S. Ent between Lamb Rk and South Rk with small ⚓ in pool in 7m.

ADJACENT ANCHORAGES

CLONAKILTY BAY 51°32'·46N 08°56'·36W Dunworthy Bay may be entered with care on its E side, avoiding Cow Rks and Horse Rk to the W. Sheltered from the N and E it is a secluded ⚓ in 8-10m of water. Appr to Clonakilty is shallow and drying. Ent at Ring Hd indicated by WCM Q(9) 15s marking Wind Rk. Channel between Wine Rock (unlit perch at the ent) and pier at South Ring is marked by two starboard-hand perches and two lit lateral buoys, PHM and SHM. ⚓ off Ring Hd exposed in all but calmest conditions.

DIRK BAY 51°34'·90N 08°45'·52W ⚓ under bluffs to W side of bay avoiding Carrigduff Rks to E side with shallow Wk to their S.

Mill Cove and **Tralong Bay** are isolated ⚓ in narrow steep to coves, which should be approached only in fair weather with care and local advice.

5.23 CASTLETOWNSHEND

Cork **51°30′·90N 09°10′·70W**

CHARTS AC 2092, 2129, 5623; Imray C56

TIDES +0605 Dover; ML 2·2; Duration 0605

Standard Port COBH (⟵)

Times				**Height (metres)**			
High Water		Low Water		MHWS	MHWN	MLWN	MLWS
0500	1100	0500	1100	4·1	3·2	1·3	0·4
1700	2300	1700	2300				
Differences CASTLETOWNSHEND							
–0020	–0030	–0020	–0050	–0·4	–0·2	+0·1	+0·3

SHELTER The outer part of hbr is subject to swell in S winds. Excellent ⚓ midstream SE of Castletownshend slip, protected from all weathers and available at all tides. ⚓ N of Cat Is upstream as depth permits. Caution: Underwater cables run E/W across the hbr from the slips close N of Reen Pier and town quay.

NAVIGATION WPT 51°30′·28N, 09°10′·26W, 349°/7ca to Reen Pt lt. Ent between Horse Is (35m) and Skiddy Is (9m) both of which have foul ground all round. Black Rk is off the SE side of Horse Is. Flea Sound, a narrow boat chan, is obstructed by rks. Colonel's Rk (0·5m) lies close to the E shore, 2ca N of Reen Pt. Beware salmon nets.

LIGHTS AND MARKS Reen Pt, Fl WRG 10s; a small slender W bn; vis shore-G-338°-W-001°-R-shore. A ruined tr is on Horse Is.

COMMUNICATIONS (Code 028) Coast Rescue Service 21039; ⊖ Bantry (027) 50061; Police 36144; 🄷 21677.

FACILITIES **Reen Pier** ⛴ ⛽; **Sailing Club** ☎36100.
Village ⛴ ⛽ ✉ Ⓑ(Skibbereen) 🛒 ✕ 🛈 ⇄ ✈ (Cork).

ADJACENT ANCHORAGE

BARLOGE CREEK, Cork, **51°29′·57N 09°17′·58W**. AC 2129. Tides approx as Castletownshend. A narrow creek, well sheltered except from S/SE winds. Appr with Gokane Pt brg 120°. Enter W of Bullock Is, keeping to the W side to clear rks S of the island. ⚓ W of the Is in 3m but weedy. No facilities.

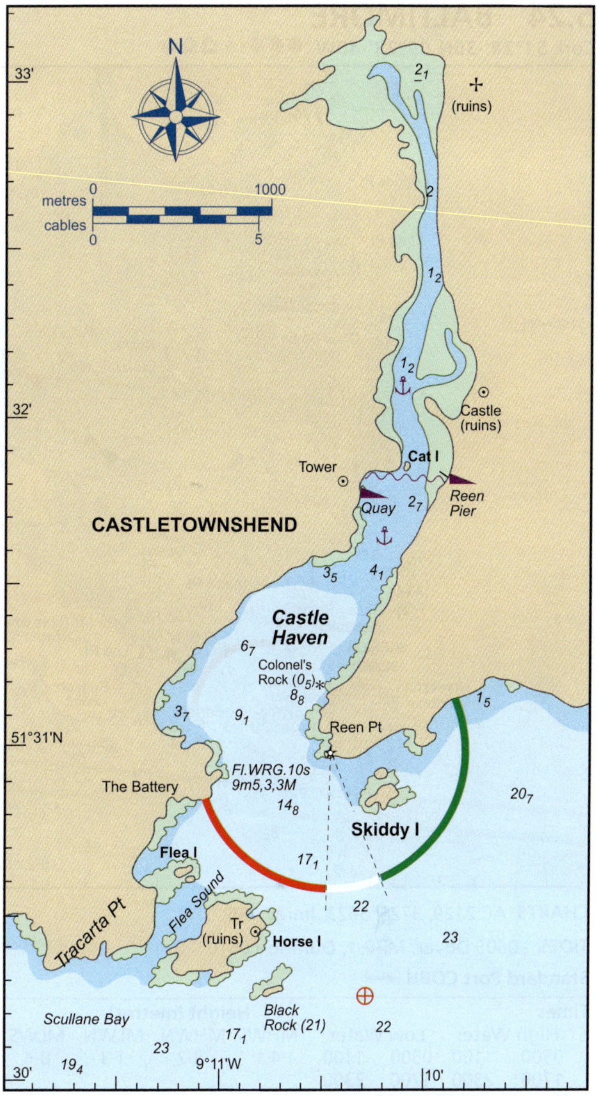

5.24 BALTIMORE

Cork **51°28′·30N 09°23′·40W** ❀❀❀◊◊✿✿✿

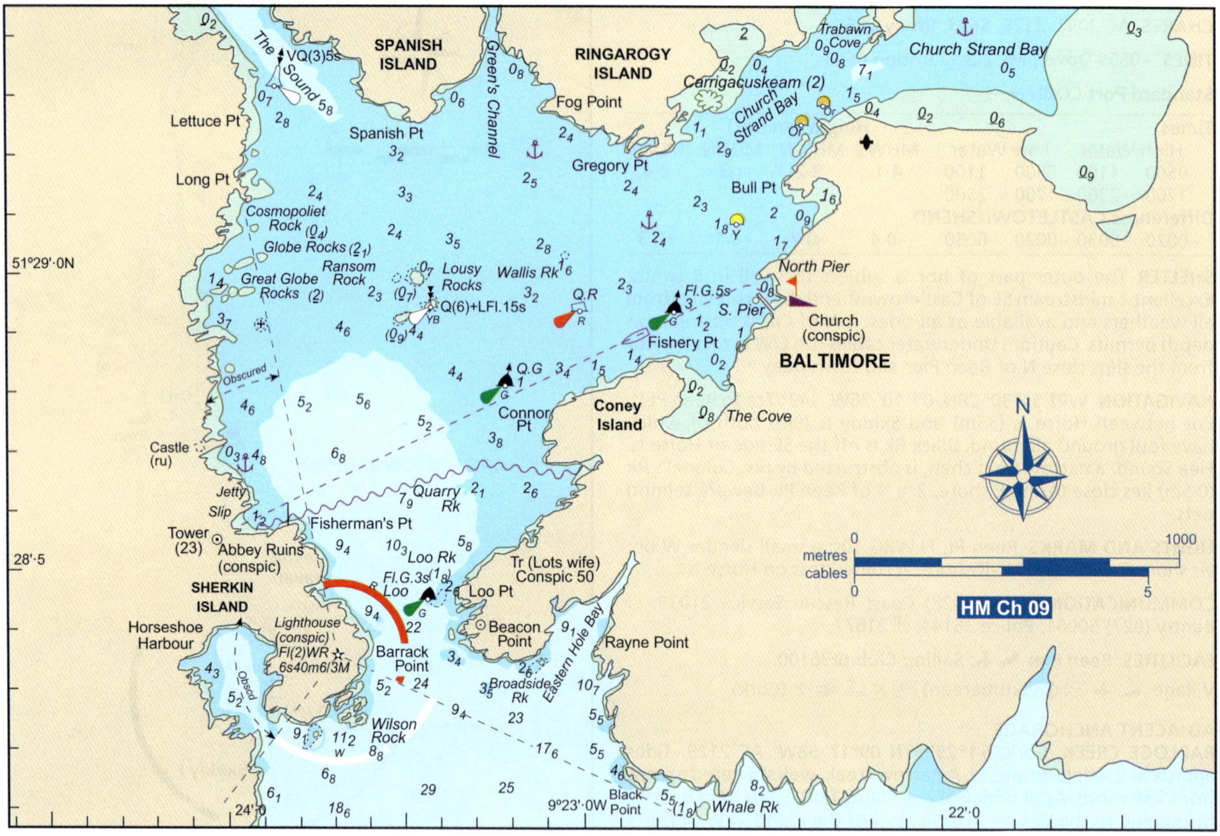

CHARTS AC 2129, 3725, 5623; Imray C56

TIDES –0605 Dover; ML 2·1; Duration 0610

Standard Port COBH (⟵)

Times				Height (metres)			
High Water		Low Water		MHWS	MHWN	MLWN	MLWS
0500	1100	0500	1100	4·1	3·2	1·3	0·4
1700	2300	1700	2300				
Differences BALTIMORE							
–0025	–0005	–0010	–0050	–0·6	–0·3	+0·1	+0·2

SHELTER Excellent. Access H24 from the S. At Baltimore, pontoon (May-Sep) on S Pier, ⛵ for up to 10 yachts rafted in 2·4m. Inner Hbr, partly dries between N and S piers, mostly used by ferries, local boats and FVs; the latter also berth on N pier. RoRo berth SE of Bull Pt. ⚓ about 200m W of S pier, or about 200m N of N Pier. Beware extensive moorings. In strong NW'lies ⚓ in Church Strand Bay. Lts are required. Do not ⚓ in dredged chan between Wallis Rk buoy and N Pier, or in chan to Church Strand Bay. In strong W winds ⚓ in lee of Sherkin Is off Castle ruins.

NAVIGATION WPT 51°27′·93N 09°23′·46W, 000°/5ca to Loo Rk SHM lt buoy. No passage between buoy and mainland. Beware Lousy Rks (SCM bn) and Wallis Rk (PHM lt buoy) in middle of the bay. Cardinal buoys mark rocks in The Sound, which demands care in pilotage; AC 3725 and ICC SDs essential. SCM marks isolated rk off Inane Pt in the R Ilen, which is navigable on the flood for at least 4M above The Sound. Speed limit 6kn in R Ilen and N/NE of Wallace Rock.

LIGHTS AND MARKS See 5.3 and chartlet. Ent easily identified by Barrack Pt lt ho and conspic W tr (Lot's Wife) on Beacon Pt.

COMMUNICATIONS (Code 028) ⊜ (027) 53210; Police 20102; Dr 23456/after hrs 1850 335999, 🄷 21677. HM ☎320560, mob 087 2351485.

VHF (HM) Ch 09, 16.

FACILITIES Berthing: May-Sept from €20/craft, ☎0872 351485 or www.atlanticboat.ie; ⛵ (☎20106) on pontoon; **Baltimore SC** ☎20426, visitors welcome; **Sherkin** Pontoon access to shore in season.

Services Gaz (on R Ilen at Old Court), ACA. **Village** bus to Cork for ✈.

ADJACENT ANCHORAGES

SHERKIN ISLAND on W side of harbour entrance. ⚓s: Horseshoe Harbour (keep well to the W in narrow entrance; unlit); and off Castle ruins, 5ca N.

CLEAR ISLAND, NORTH HARBOUR, 51°26′·60N 09°30′·20W. AC 2129, 5623. Tides approx as Schull, 5.25. A tiny, partly drying inlet on N coast of Clear Is, exposed to N'ly swell. Rks either side of outer appr 196°. Inside the narrow (30m), rky ent keep to the E. Lie to 2 ⚓s on E side in about 1·5m or drying berth above ferry berth. Storm gate and sill (1·3m) with pontoons (2·1m) in inner harbour. Facilities: ✉ ✕.

ROARINGWATER BAY, Long Island Bay AC 2129, 5623. Enter between Cape Clear and Mizen Hd, extends NE into Roaringwater Bay. *Beware extensive, low-lying unlit fish farms.* Safest appr, S of Schull, is via Carthy's Sound (51°30′N 09°30′W). From the SE appr via Gascanane Sound, but beware Toorane Rks, Anima Rk and outlying rks off many of the islands. Shelter in various winds at ⚓s clockwise from Horse Island: 3ca E and 7ca NE of E tip of Horse Is; in Ballydehob B 2m (Ballydehob has a good quay for tenders and most facilities); Poulgorm B 2m; 3ca SSW of Carrigvalish Rks in 6m. Rincolisky Cas (ru) is conspic on S side of bay. The narrow chan E of Hare Is and N of Sherkin Is has two ⚓s; also leads via The Sound into Baltimore hbr. Local advice useful. Temp'y fair weather ⚓s in Carthy's Islands. Rossbrin Cove safe ⚓ 2·5M E of Schull, but many local moorings; no access from E of Horse Is due to drying Horse Ridge.

5.25 SCHULL

Cork **51°30'·80N 09°32'·00W**

CHARTS AC 2184, 2129, 5623; Imray C56

TIDES +0610 Dover; ML 1·8; Duration 0610

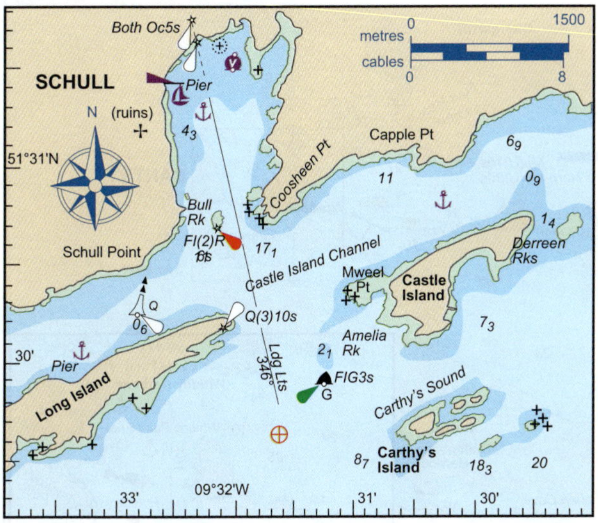

Standard Port COBH (⟵)

Times				Height (metres)			
High Water		Low Water		MHWS	MHWN	MLWN	MLWS
0500	1100	0500	1100	4·1	3·2	1·3	0·4
1700	2300	1700	2300				
Differences SCHULL							
–0040	–0015	–0015	–0110	–0·9	–0·6	–0·2	0·0

SHELTER Good, except in strong S/SE winds when best shelter is N of Long Island. Schull Hbr access H24. 12 Y 🅥s in NE part of hbr or ⚓ in 3m 1ca SE of pier, usually lit by street lts all night; keep clear of fairway marked by 8 unlit lateral buoys (summer time only).

NAVIGATION WPT 51°29'·60N 09°31'·60W, 346°/2·1M to front ldg lt. In hbr ent, Bull Rk (dries 1·8m), R iron perch, can be passed either side. Beware unmarked isolated rock, 0·5m, close to the visitors' buoys.

LIGHTS AND MARKS See 5.3 and chartlet. Ldg lts, lead 346° between Long Is Pt, W conical tr, and Amelia Rk SHM lt buoy; thence E of Bull Rk and towards head of bay. By day in good vis 2 W radomes conspic on Mt Gabriel (2M N of Schull) lead 355° with Long Is Pt lt ho in transit.

COMMUNICATIONS (Code 028) Coast/Cliff Rescue Service 35318; Inshore Rescue Service 086 236 0206: ⊖ (027) 51562; Police 28111; Dr 28311; Ⓗ (027) 50133. Water Sports Centre 28554; HM (027) 28136. No VHF.

FACILITIES **Schull Pier/Hbr** … (not at LWS) FV pier/pontoon for tenders, … tempy, 🅥s €10/night, … (by arrangement) … .
Sailing Club ☎37352; **Services** Kos … .
Village … (Ballydehob 5M), … @, Charts, ✉ Ⓑ ✕ … bus to Cork for ⇌ ✈ Ferries.

ADJACENT HARBOURS

GOLEEN (Kireal-coegea), Cork, **51°29'·65N 09°42'·21W**. AC 2184, 5623. Tides as Crookhaven. A narrow inlet 6ca N of Spanish Pt; good shelter in fair weather, except from SE. 2 churches are easily seen, but ent not visible until close. Keep to S side of ent and ⚓ fore-and-aft just below quay, where … also possible.
Facilities: … bus to Cork ✈ ⇌.

5.26 CROOKHAVEN

Cork **51°28'·50N 09°42'·00W**

CHARTS AC 2184, 5623; Imray C56

TIDES +0550 Dover; ML 1·8; Duration 0610

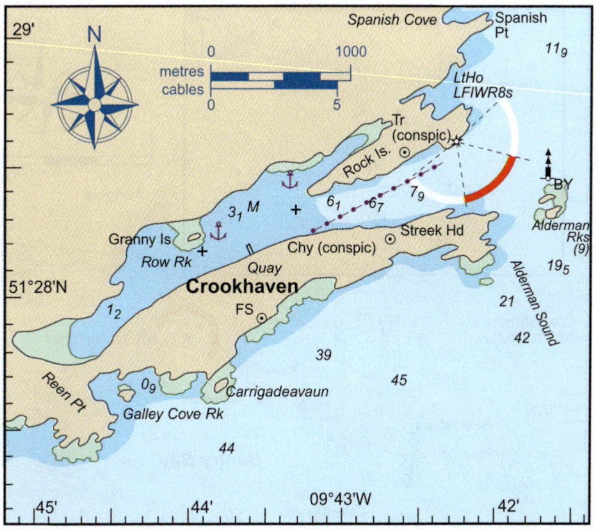

Standard Port COBH (⟵)

Times				Height (metres)			
High Water		Low Water		MHWS	MHWN	MLWN	MLWS
0500	1100	0500	1100	4·1	3·2	1·3	0·4
1700	2300	1700	2300				
Differences CROOKHAVEN							
–0057	–0033	–0048	–0112	–0·8	–0·6	–0·4	–0·1

SHELTER Excellent. There are 8 Y 🅥s and 10 dayglow R 🅥s. Short stay pontoon for up to 4 boats (…/stores/passengers). ⚓s in middle of bay in 3m; off W tip of Rock Is; and E of Granny Is; last two are far from the village. Holding is patchy, especially in strong SW'lies; beware weed, shellfish beds around shoreline and submarine pipeline from Rock Is to Crookhaven.

NAVIGATION WPT 51°28'·50N 09°40'·50W, 274°/1M to Rock Is lt ho. Ent between this lt and NCM bn on Black Horse Rks (3½ca ESE). From S, keep 1ca E of Alderman Rks and ½ca off Black Horse Rks bn. Passage between Streek Hd and Alderman Rks is not advised for strangers. Inside the bay the shores are steep-to. 1ca WSW of West end of Rock Is beware isolated rock, which is awash at LAT.

LIGHTS AND MARKS Lt ho on Rock Is (conspic W tr) L Fl WR 8s 20m 13/11M; vis outside hbr: W over Long Is Bay-281°-R-340°; vis inside hbr: 281°-R-348°-W-shore(N).

COMMUNICATIONS (Code 028) Coast/Cliff Rescue at Goleen 35318; ⊖ (027) 50061; Dr 35148; ✉ 35200. HM (O'Sullivan's Bar) 35319. No VHF.

FACILITIES **Village** 🅥s (☎086 356 7771) €8.00, pontoon for small craft … ✉ Ⓑ(Schull) … ✕ …, taxi to Goleen.

5.27 DUNMANUS / BANTRY BAY

Cork 51°34'N 09°57'W

CHARTS AC 2552, 1840, 1838, 5623; Imray C56

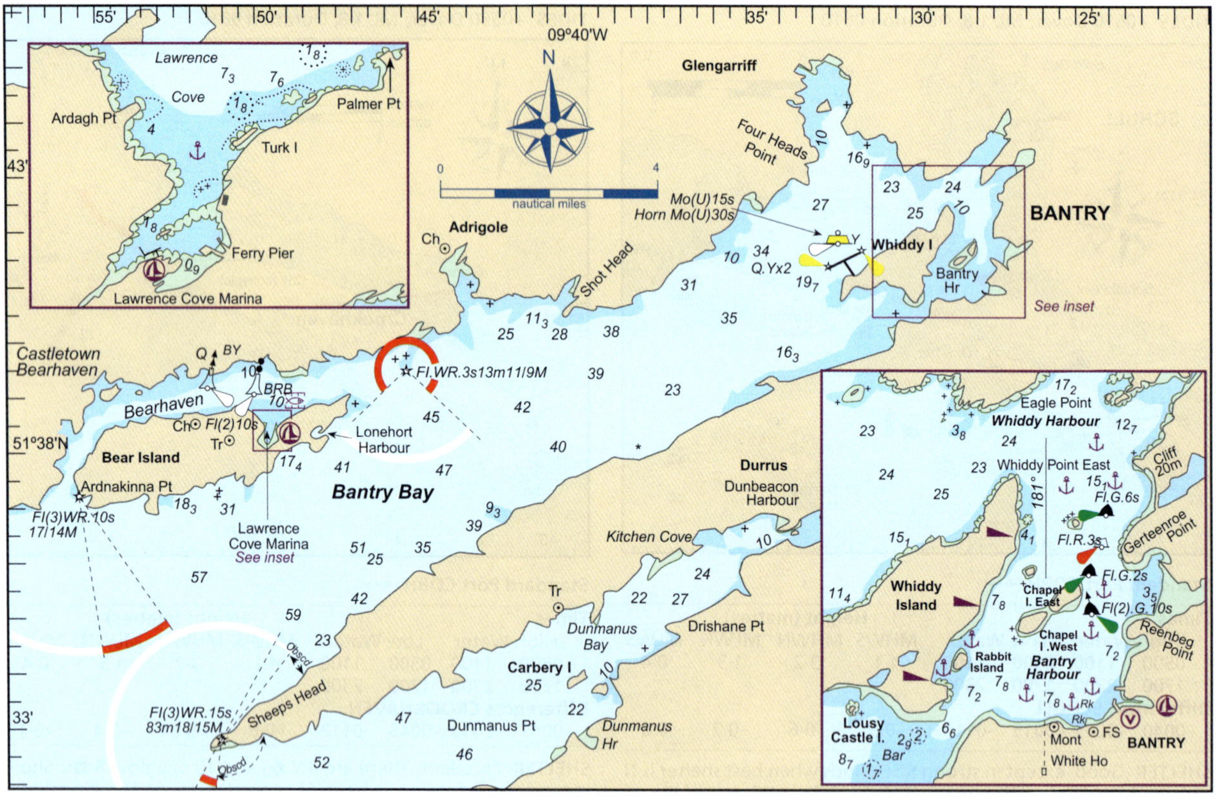

TIDES +0600 Dover; ML 1·8; Duration 0610

Standard Port COBH (⟵)

Times				Height (metres)			
High Water		Low Water		MHWS	MHWN	MLWN	MLWS
0500	1100	0500	1100	4·1	3·2	1·3	0·4
1700	2300	1700	2300				
Differences *BANTRY*							
–0045	*–0025*	*–0040*	*–0105*	*–0·7*	*–0·6*	*–0·2*	*+0·1*
CASTLETOWN (Bearhaven)							
–0048	–0012	–0025	–0101	–0·8	–0·6	–0·2	0·0
BLACK BALL HARBOUR (51°36N 10°02W)							
–0115	–0035	–0047	–0127	–0·7	–0·6	–0·1	+0·1
DUNMANUS BAY							
–0107	–0031	–0044	–0120	–0·7	–0·6	–0·2	0·0
DUNBEACON HARBOUR							
–0057	–0025	–0032	–0104	–0·8	–0·7	–0·3	–0·1

SHELTER/NAVIGATION Bantry Bay extends 20M ENE from Sheep's Hd, Fl (3) WR 15s 83m 18/15M. Access is easy, but the Bay is exposed to W'lies. The shore is clear everywhere except off Bear Is and Whiddy Is. Some of the many well-sheltered ⚓s on the N shore are detailed on this page. The S shore has few ⚓s.

DUNMANUS BAY, Cork. AC 2552, 5623. Tides see 5.27. Appr between Three Castle Hd and Sheep's Hd, Fl (3) WR 15s 83m 18/15M; no other lts. Ent to **Dunmanus Hbr**, 51°32'·70N 09°39'·86W, is 1ca wide; breakers both sides. ⚓ in 4m centre of B. **Kitchen Cove**, 51°35'·50N 09°38'·05W, best of the 3 hbrs; enter W of Owens Is and ⚓ 1ca NNW of it or 2ca further N in 3m. Exposed to S, but good holding. Quay at Ahakista village: (drying) ✕. **Dunbeacon Hbr**, 51°36'·35N 09°33'·60W, is shallow and rock-girt. Quay possible in 2m (used by FVs), ; ⚓ E or SE of Mannion Is. Durrus (¾M): ✕.

LONEHORT HARBOUR 51°38'·12N 09°47'·80W. AC 1840, 5623. At E tip of Bear Is, good shelter but keep S at ent to clear unmarked rks; then turn ENE to ⚓ in 2·7m at E end of cove. Be aware of Firing Practice Area to east of harbour entrance (full clear range procedure in force).

ADRIGOLE 51°40'·51N 09°43'·22W. AC 1840, 5623. Good shelter, but squally in W/N gales. Beware Doucallia Rk, dries 1·2m, 1M SSW of ent. Beyond the 2ca wide ent, keep E of Orthons Is (rks on W side). 7 Y 🅐s NE of Orthons Is. ⚓s to suit wind direction: off pier on E shore 4m; N or NW of Orthons Is. Drumlave (½M E): (sailing school) ⊠.

Trafrask Bay, 2M east, has Y🅐 at **51°40'·8N 09°40'·1W**; ✕.

GLENGARRIFF 51°44'·20N 09°31'·90W. AC 1838, 5623. Tides as Bantry. Beautiful ⚓ S of Bark Is in 7-10m; or to NE in 3m, where there are 6 Y 🅐s. Better for yachts than Bantry hbr. Ent between Big Pt and Gun Pt. Keep 1ca E of rks off Garinish Island (Illnacullen) and Ship Is; chan marked to either side by lateral marks LFl R/G 4s. Beware marine farms. HT cables removed allowing access N of Garinish with local knowledge; but rocky chan W of should not be attempted. Facilities: Eccles hotel, . **Village** (ferry berth 1800-1900) Kos ⊠ ✕.

BANTRY 51°40'·85N 09°27'·85W. AC 1838, 5623. Beware Gerane Rks ½M W of Whiddy Is. Appr via the buoyed/lit N chan to E of Horse and Chapel Is; keep 2ca off all islands to clear unlit marine farms. The S chan, fair weather only. Appr Relane Pt hdg 063° with HW mark S. Beach (seaward edge of airfield) ≠ Reenbeg Cliff (distant rounded hill) to clear Cracker Rk, then leave Blue Hill and S Beach to stbd. 🅐s call Bantry Hbr Ch 14 or ☎027 51253; VHF Ch 14 11 16 (H24). HM (027) 53277; ⊜ 50061; Police 50045; Dr 50405; Ⓗ 50133. MRCC (066) 9476109. Facilities: **Pier** (drying), Marina 50 €20<12 m>€30<15m /night ; **Bantry Bay SC** ☎51724, Kos ⊠ Ⓑ ✕ bus to Cork.

5.28 CASTLETOWN BEARHAVEN

Cork **51°34'N 09°57'W**

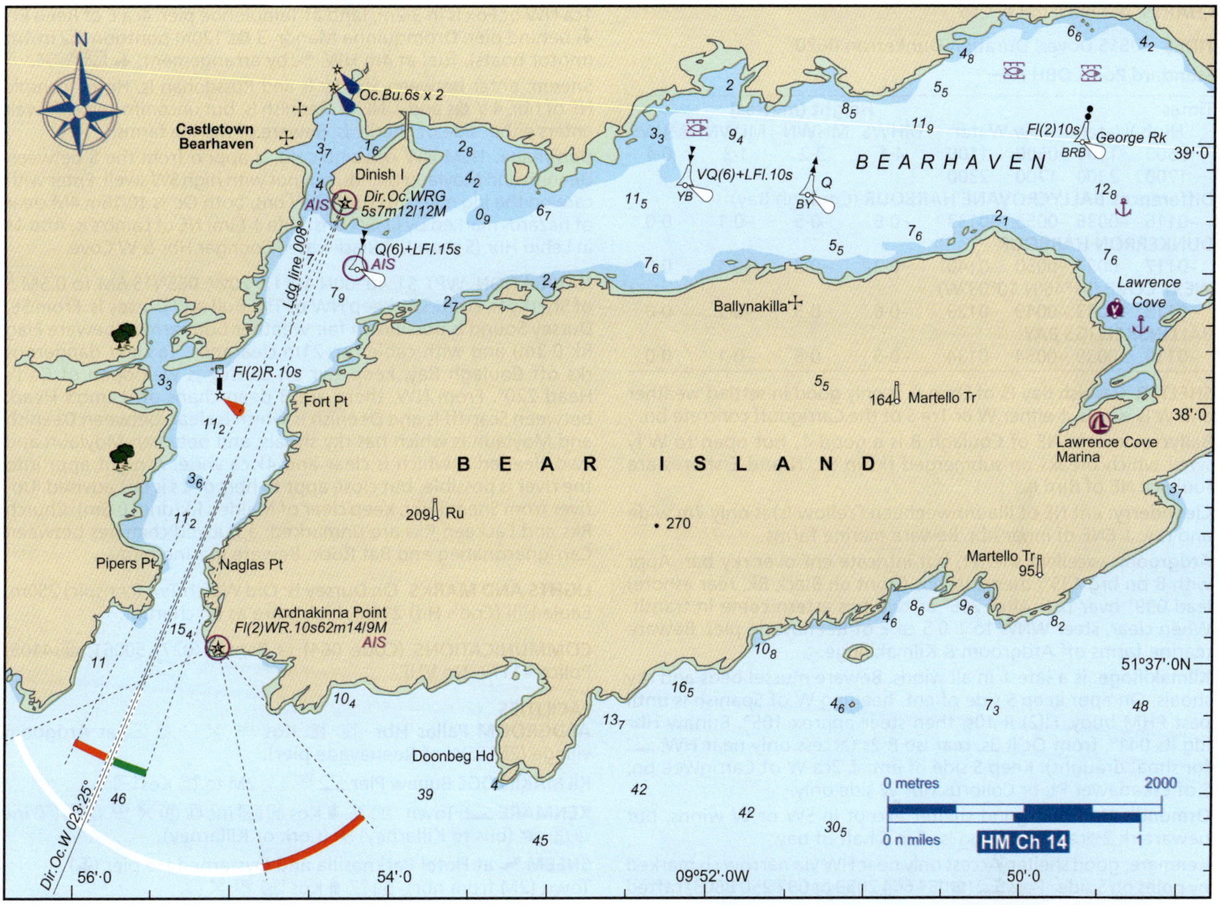

CHARTS AC 1840, 5623; Imray C56

TIDES +0600 Dover; ML 1·8; Duration 0610

Standard Port COBH (⟵)

Times				Height (metres)			
High Water		Low Water		MHWS	MHWN	MLWN	MLWS
0500	1100	0500	1100	4·1	3·2	1·3	0·4
1700	2300	1700	2300				
Differences *CASTLETOWN* (Bearhaven)							
–0048	*–0012*	*–0025*	*–0101*	*–0·8*	*–0·6*	*–0·2*	*0·0*

SHELTER Castletownbere Fishery Harbour lies between Dinish Is and the mainland. A pontoon with for yachts is at W end of Bere hbr, but also used by small fishing vessels. Recommend calling HM in advance(OH). ⚓ at **Dunboy Bay,** W of Piper Snd (open to E). 4 Y s are laid Apr-Sep 3ca E of Dinish Is.

NAVIGATION At W ent, Ardnakinna Pt, Fl (2) WR 10s 62m 17/14M, H24. At E ent to Bearhaven: Roancarrigmore, Fl WR 5s 13m 11/9M. Appr W of Bear Is on 023·25° Dir lt, Oc WRG 5s 7m 15/12M (023°-W-023·5°); then inner ldg lts 008°, both Oc Bu 6s 4/7m 6M, vis 005°-013°, via ent chan which narrows to 50m where it is marked by lit bcns and buoys. Beware Walter Scott Rk (2·7m), SCM lt buoy, and Carrigaglos (0·6m high) S of Dinish Is.

LIGHTS AND MARKS See 5.3 and chartlet.

COMMUNICATIONS (Code 028) Coast/Cliff Rescue Service 35318; Inshore Rescue Service 086 236 0206. HM (027) 70220.
VHF Ch **14** 16.

FACILITIES **Fishery Hbr** on quay; on Dinish Is.
Town Kos .
Rerrin (storage) bus to Cork.

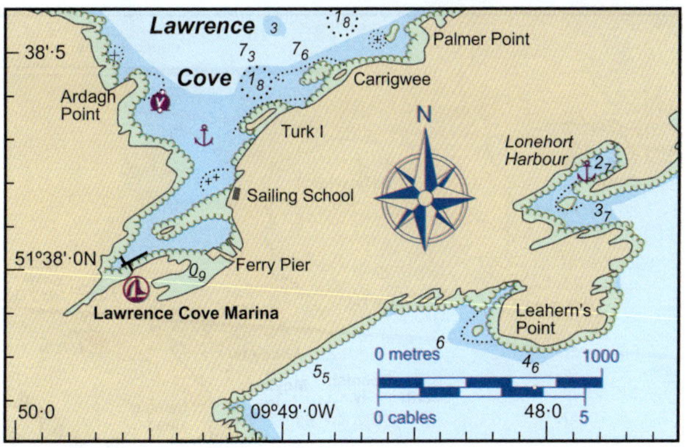

ADJACENT HARBOURS

BEAR (BERE) ISLAND Good shelter on N side of Bear Island. There are 4 yellow s in 3m close S of Ardagh Point, or ⚓ in 4m to W of Turk Is. A pontoon with for yachts is at W end of Bere hbr, but also used by small fishing vessels. Recommend calling HM in advance (HO). From E keep clear of Palmer Rock and a shoal patch, both 1·8m. Friendly welcome at the only marina between Kinsale and Cahersiveen/Dingle.

LAWRENCE COVE 51°38'·28N 09°49'·28W; Buoyed appr to Marina on S side of cove with 90m NE/SW pontoon in 3-3·5m. mob 087 9125930; VHF Ch 16 **M.** 40(€2·75), (€3/nt) .

5.29 KENMARE RIVER

Kerry **51°45'·00N 10°00'·00W** ✿✿✿✿✿✿✿

CHARTS AC 2495; Imray C56

TIDES +0515 Dover; Duration Dunkerron 0620

Standard Port COBH (⟵)

Times				Height (metres)			
High Water		Low Water		MHWS	MHWN	MLWN	MLWS
0500	1100	0500	1100	4·1	3·2	1·3	0·4
1700	2300	1700	2300				
Differences BALLYCROVANE HARBOUR (Coulagh Bay)							
−0116	−0036	−0053	−0133	−0·6	−0·5	−0·1	0·0
DUNKERRON HARBOUR							
−0117	−0027	−0050	−0140	−0·2	−0·3	+0·1	0·0
WEST COVE (51°46'N 10°03'W)							
−0113	−0033	−0049	−0129	−0·6	−0·5	−0·1	0·0
BALLINSKELLIGS BAY							
−0119	−0039	−0054	−0134	−0·5	−0·5	−0·1	0·0

SHELTER **Garnish Bay** (S of Long I): is only good in settled weather and W'ly winds. ⚓ either W or 1ca S of the Carrigduff concrete bn.

Ballycrovane: in NE of Coulagh B is a good ⚓, but open to W'ly swell which breaks on submerged rks in SE. N and E shores are foul 5ca NE of Bird Is.

Cleanderry: ent NE of Illaunbweeheen (Yellow Is) is only 7m wide and rky. ⚓ ENE of inner hbr. Beware marine farms.

Ardgroom: excellent shelter, but intricate ent over rky bar. Appr with B bn brg 135°; then 2 W bns (front on Black Rk, rear ashore) lead 099° over bar. Alter 206° as two bns astern come in transit. When clear, steer WNW to ⚓ 0·5 ca E of Reenavade pier. Beware marine farms off Ardgroom & Kilmakilloge.

Kilmakilloge: is a safe ⚓ in all winds. Beware mussel beds and rky shoals. On appr keep S side of ent, heading W of Spanish Is until past PHM buoy, Fl(2) R 10s, then steer approx 105°. Bunaw Hbr ldg lts 041°, front Oc R 3s, rear Iso R 2s (access only near HW; pontoon for shoal draught). Keep S side of ent; ⚓ 2ca W of Carrigwee bn; S of Eskadawer Pt; or Collorus Hbr W side only.

Ormond's Harbour: good shelter except in SW or W winds, but beware rk 2½ca ENE of Hog Is. ⚓ in S half of bay.

Kenmare: good shelter. Access only near HW via narrow ch marked by poles on S side. Poss pontoon (☎064 664 2059 or 087 250 8803) rafted at end of pier (water available) at N side of river, just below town. Beware very strong ebbs at springs and after heavy rains.

Dunkerron Harbour: enter between Cod Rocks and The Boar to ⚓ 1ca NW of Fox Is in 3·2m; land at Templenoe pier. 4ca E of Reen Pt. Water behind pier. Dromquinna Manor 3 ⚓s 120m pontoon in 1m (motor boats), fuel at 4m HW, 🔧 by arrangement; water WC showers ✕.

Sneem: enter between Sherky Is and Rossdohan Is. Hotel conspic NE of hbr. 4 Y ⚓s and ⚓ NE of Garinish Is, but uncomfortable if swell enters either side of Sherky Is. Beware of marine farms.

Darrynane: 1½M NW of Lamb's Hd, is appr'd from the S between Deenish and Moylaun Islands, but not with high SW swell. Enter with care on the ldg marks/lts 034°, 2 W bns, both Oc 3s 10/16m 4M clear of hazards marked by lit G/R bns. Safe ⚓ (3m) NE of Lamb's Is. Also ⚓s in Lehid Hbr (S shore), R Blackwater, Coongar Hbr & W Cove.

NAVIGATION WPT 51°40'·00N 10°17'·20W, 065°/15·6M to 0.5M S of Sherky Is. From SW, keep NW of The Bull and Dursey Is. From SE, Dursey Sound is possible in fair weather but narrow (beware Flag Rk 0·3m) and with cable car, 21m clearance. To clear dangerous rks off Coulagh Bay, keep twr on Dursey Is well open of Cod's Head 220°. From NW, there are 3 deep chans off Lamb's Head: between Scarriff Is and Deenish Is which is clear; between Deenish and Moylaun Is which has rky shoals; and between Moylaun and Two Headed Is which is clear and 4½ca wide. A night appr into the river is possible, but close appr to hbrs or ⚓s is not advised. Up-river from Sneem Hbr, keep clear of Maiden Rk(dries 0·5m); Church Rks and Lackeen Rks are unmarked; a buoyed chan lies between Carrignaronabeg and Bat Rock. Beware marine farms.

LIGHTS AND MARKS On Dursey Is: Old Watch Twr (conspic) 250m. Eagle Hill (Cod's Hd) 216m. Lights are as on chartlet.

COMMUNICATIONS (Code 064) ⊜ Bantry (027) 50061; Ⓗ 4108; Police 41177. No VHF.

FACILITIES

ARDGROOM Pallas Hbr Ⓟ Ⓓ Kos 🛒 ✕ ▭ @ ✉ at Ardgoom village (2M SSW of Reenavade pier).

KILMAKILLOGE Bunaw Pier pontoon 🛒 ▭; 2M to Ⓓ Kos ✉.

KENMARE pontoon. **Town** Ⓟ Ⓓ ▮ Kos Ⓗ ✉ inc @ Ⓑ ✕ 🛒 ▭ Ⓗ ✉ inc @ Ⓑ ⇄ (bus to Killarney) ✈ (Cork or Killarney).

SNEEM slip at Hotel Parknasilla and Oysterbed Ho pier (water). **Town** (2M from hbr), Ⓟ Ⓓ ▮ Kos ✉ 🛒 ✕ ▭.

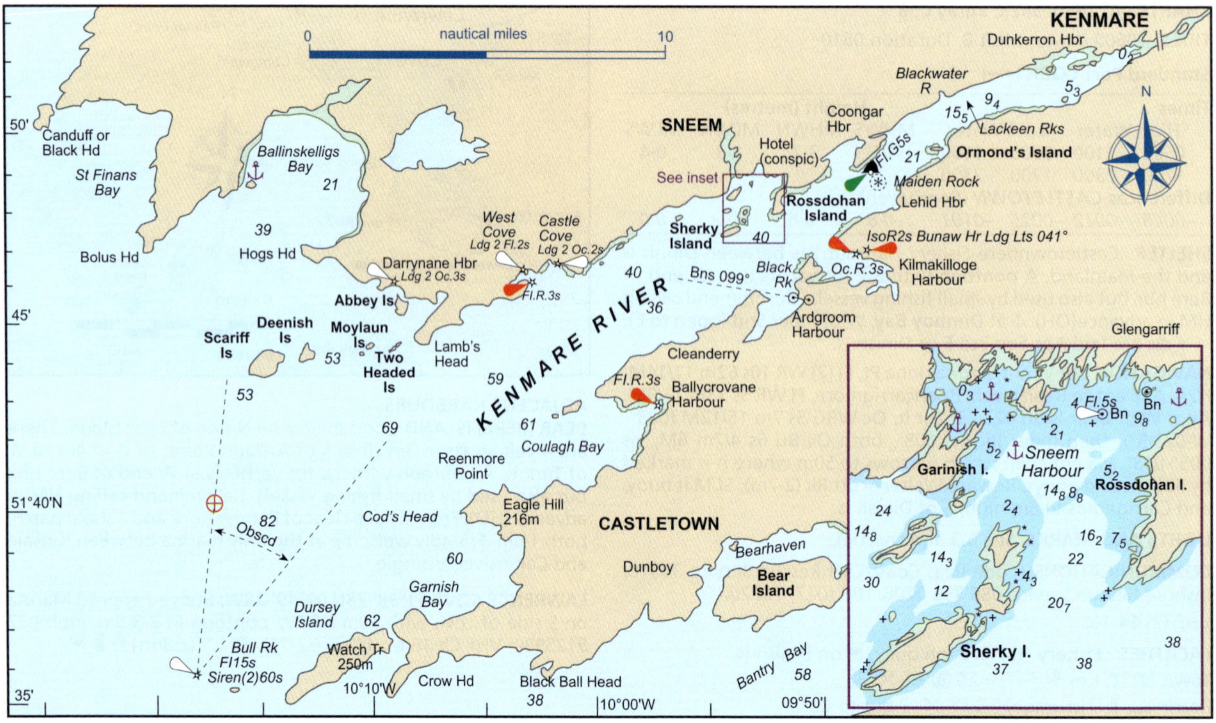

5.30 DINGLE BAY

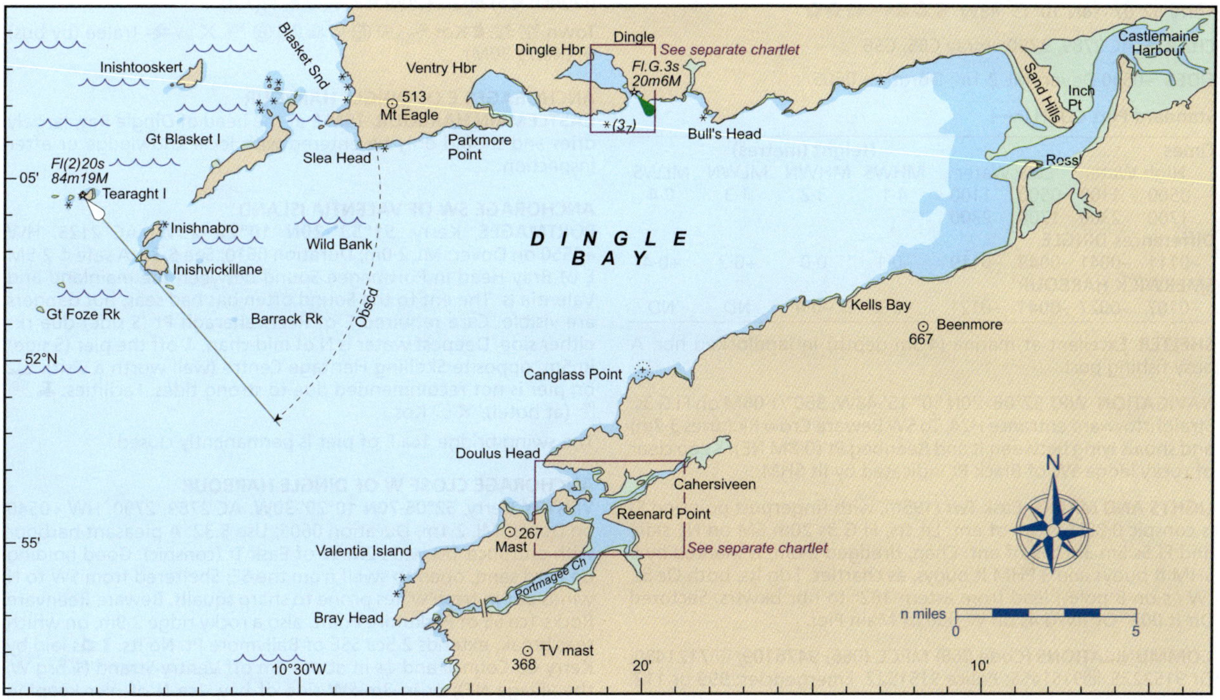

5.31 VALENTIA HARBOUR

Kerry **51°55'·7N 10°17'·1W** ❀❀◊◊✿✿✿

CHARTS AC 2125; Imray C56

TIDES +0515 Dover

Standard Port COBH (⟵)

Times				Height (metres)			
High Water		Low Water		MHWS	MHWN	MLWN	MLWS
0500	1100	0500	1100	4·1	3·2	1·3	0·4
1700	2300	1700	2300				
Differences VALENTIA HARBOUR (Knight's Town)							
−0118	−0038	−0056	−0136	−0·6	−0·4	−0·1	0·0

SHELTER Good ⚓s at: Glanleam B, 6ca S of Fort Pt in 4m; 1ca NW of LB slip in 2·5m (beware The Foot, spit drying 1·2m, marked by ECM lt buoy) SE of Ferry Pier at Knight's Town (E end of the island) in 4m; in bay on the S side of Beginish Is in 3m.

NAVIGATION WPT 51°56'·84N 10°20'·15W 147°/1M to Fort Pt lt. Beware rock outcrop 2.6m 1 Ca ENE Reenadrolaun Pt and other shoal patches within 10m contour. Appr NE end of Valentia Is via:

- Doulus Bay, N of Beginish Is (avoid if swell is running). Clear Black Rks by ½ca then head for E end of Beginish Is as soon as Reenard Pt opens to port. When Lamb Is and the N point of Beginish are about to open astern, steer to keep them so till Reenard Point opens to the E of Church Is. Then steer to pass between Church Is and the WCM buoy marking Passage Rk.
- Better ent, between Fort Pt and Beginish Is (easy access except in strong NW'lies). Beware Hbr Rk, 2·6m, 3ca SE of Fort Pt marked by ECM lt Bn.

For **Cahersiveen Marina** from Valentia Is start as early on the tide as possible to cross the Caher Bar, min depth 1·4m (buoyed), using the ldg lts/lines 019-199°, then keep to the middle of river.

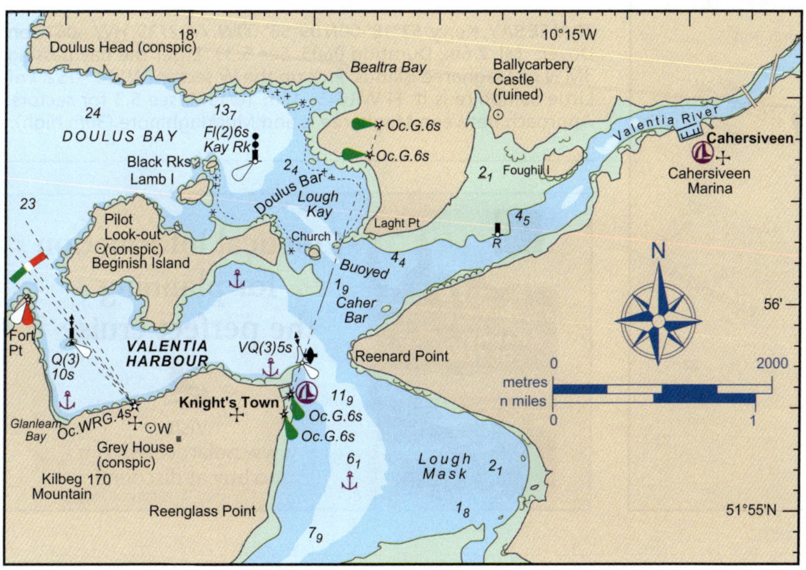

Passage S of the island via Portmagee chan is only for small craft which can pass under the closed bridge.

LIGHTS AND MARKS See 5.3.

COMMUNICATIONS ⊖ 7128540; Dr 9472121; Police 9472111; Ⓗ 9472100.

FACILITIES **Knight's Town** Kos ▣ ⚒ 🔧 ⛱ **Marina** ⛵ some with ⊐D in expanding facility. Ferry/bus to Cahersiveen (2½M) for shops; Bus to ⇌ (Tralee and Killarney) ✈ (Kerry, Shannon, Cork).

Cahersiveen Marina ☎947 2777, VHF Ch 24 www.cahersiveenmarina.ie 2M upriver, min depth 2.5m in basin, 93 inc Ⓥ €2.50, ▣ ⛽ ⛽ ⚓ ⚒ 🔧 ⊐D Ⓔ ⩚ ⛟(14t) ✉ Ⓑ 🛒 ✕ ☕.

Kells Bay 4 Ⓥs laid by Kerry Co Council.

5.32 DINGLE

Kerry **52°07'·14N 10°15'·48W**

CHARTS AC 2789, 2790; Imray C55, C56

TIDES +0540 Dover; ML 2·1m; Duration 0605

Standard Port COBH (⟵)

Times				Height (metres)			
High Water		Low Water		MHWS	MHWN	MLWN	MLWS
0500	1100	0500	1100	4·1	3·2	1·3	0·4
1700	2300	1700	2300				
Differences DINGLE							
–0111	–0041	–0049	–0119	–0·1	0·0	+0·3	+0·4
SMERWICK HARBOUR							
–0107	–0027	–0041	–0121	–0·3	–0·4	ND	ND

SHELTER Excellent at marina (4·5m depth) in landlocked hbr. A busy fishing port.

NAVIGATION WPT 52°06'·20N 10° 15'·48W, 360°/1·06M on Fl G 3s. Straightforward entrance H24. To SW Beware Crow Rk (dries 3·7m) and shoals lying between it and Reenbeg Pt (0·8M NE). Keep clear of rocky ledge SW of Black Pt indicated by lit SHM.

LIGHTS AND MARKS Eask Twr (195m, with fingerpost pointing E) is conspic 0·85M WSW of ent. Lit trs, Fl G 3s 20m 6M on NE side, and Fl 5s 5m 3M SW of ent. Chan, dredged 2·6m, is marked by 5 SHM lt buoys and 3 PHM lt buoys, as chartlet. Ldg lts, both Oc 3s, (W ◊s on B poles) lead from astern 182° to hbr bkwtrs. Sectored Dir lt 002° Oc RWG 4s on W side of Main Pier.

COMMUNICATIONS (Code 066) MRCC (066) 9476109; ⊜ 7121480; Dr 9152225; Ⓗ9151455; Police 9151522. Emergencies: 999 or 112.

Ch **14** 16 but no calls required. Valentia Radio (Ch 24 28) will relay urgent messages to Dingle HM.

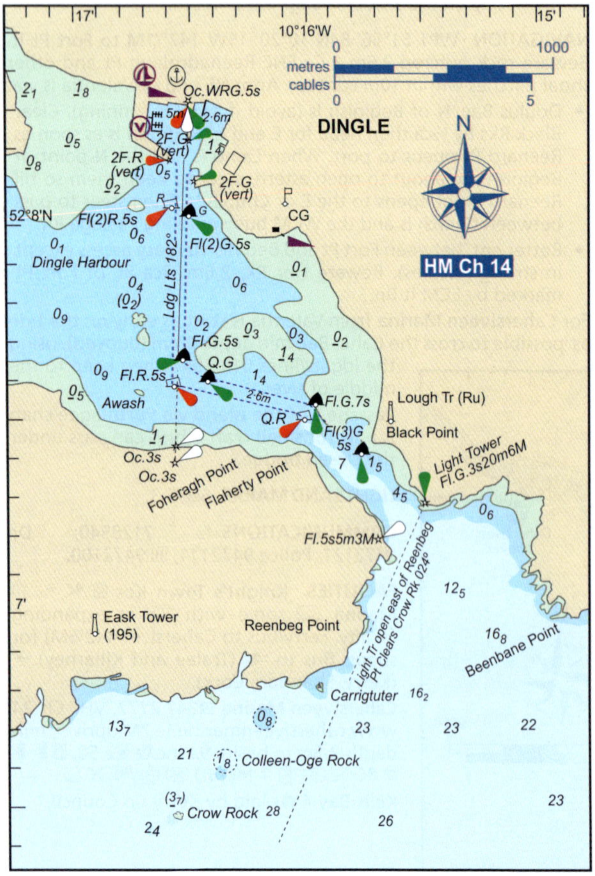

FACILITIES Marina www.dinglemarina.ie ☎087 9254115, (launch €5) 60+20 €2, (70t).

Town Kos ⓔ Ⓑ ✕ ⇌ Tralee (by bus) ✈ (Kerry 30M).

ANCHORAGES E OF DINGLE HARBOUR

CASTLEMAIN HARBOUR, 15M E at the head of Dingle Bay, largely dries and should only be entered with local knowledge or after inspection.

ANCHORAGE SW OF VALENTIA ISLAND

PORTMAGEE, Kerry, **51°53'·20N 10°22'·29W**. AC 2125. HW +0550 on Dover; ML 2·0m; Duration 0610; See 5.31. A safe ⚓ 2·5M E of Bray Head in Portmagee Sound between the mainland and Valentia Is. The ent to the Sound often has bad seas, but dangers are visible. Care required E of Reencaheragh Pt (S side) due rks either side. Deepest water is N of mid-chan. ⚓ off the pier (S side) in 5m, opposite Skelling Heritage Centre (well worth a visit). on pier is not recommended due to strong tides. Facilities: (at hotel), ✕ Kos.

The swing bridge 1ca E of pier is permanently closed.

ANCHORAGE CLOSE W OF DINGLE HARBOUR

VENTRY Kerry, **52°06·70N 10°20'·30W**. AC 2789, 2790. HW +0540 on Dover; ML 2·1m; Duration 0605; Use 5.32. A pleasant harbour with entrance 1M wide 2M W of Eask Tr (conspic). Good holding on hard sand, open to swell from the SE; Sheltered from SW to N winds but in fresh w'lies prone to sharp squalls. Beware Reenvare Rocks 1ca SE of Parkmore Point; also a rocky ridge 2·9m, on which seas break, extends 2·5ca SSE of Ballymore Pt. No lts. 3 s laid by Kerry Co Council and ⚓s in about 4m off Ventry Strand (brg W, the village NE); or in 3m SW side of bay, 1ca N of pier keeping clear of marine and seaweed farms. Both piers access HW±3 for landing. Facilities: Kos ✕ ⊠.

ANCHORAGES BETWEEN THE BLASKETS AND KERRY HD

SMERWICK HARBOUR, Kerry, **52°13'·00N 10°24'·00W**. AC 2789. Tides 5.32. Adequate shelter in 1M wide bay, except from NW'ly when considerable swell runs in. Ent between The Three Sisters (150m hill) and Dunacapple Is to the NE. Beacon Fl.R.3s at pier end at Ballynagall Pt. ⚓s at: the W side close N or S of the Boat Hr in 3-10m, avoiding Wk (8·8m); to the S, off Carrigveen Pt in 2·5m; or in N'lies at the bay in NE corner inside 10m line. Facilities at Ballynagall village on SE side: pier (0·5m), limited , bus.

BRANDON BAY, Kerry, **52°16'·10N 10°09'·92**W. AC 2739. Tides as Fenit 5.33. A 4M wide bay, very exposed to the N, but in moderate SW–W winds there is safe ⚓ in 6m close E of drying Brandon Pier, 2FG (vert). Cloghane Inlet in SW of Bay is not advised. Facilities at Brandon: limited (1M) ⊠ ✕ bus.

TRALEE BAY, Kerry, **52°18'·00N 09°56'·00W**. AC 2739. HW –0612 on Dover; ML 2·6m; Duration 0605. See 5.33. Enter the bay passing 3M N of Magharee Islands. Pick up the W sector (W140°–152°) of Little Samphire Is lt, Fl WRG 5s 17m 16/13M; see 5.3 for sectors. Approach between Magharee Is and Mucklaghmore (30m high).

5.33 FENIT HARBOUR

Kerry **52°16'·20N 09°51'·61W** ❀❀❀◊✿✿✿

CHARTS AC 2254, 2739; Imray C55

TIDES –0612 Dover; ML 2·6m; Duration 0605

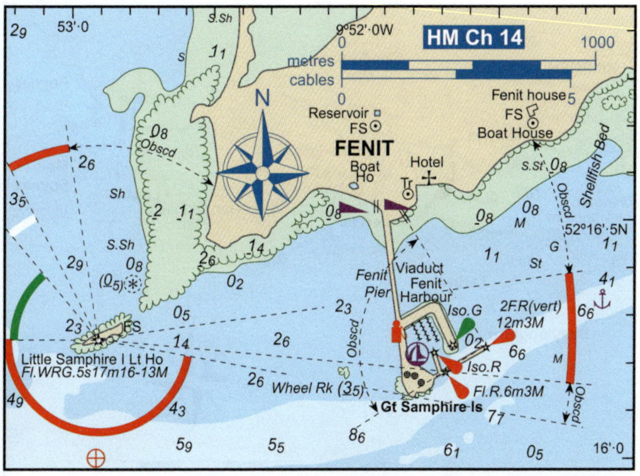

Standard Port COBH (⟵)

Times				Height (metres)			
High Water		Low Water		MHWS	MHWN	MLWN	MLWS
0500	1100	0500	1100	4·1	3·2	1·3	0·4
1700	2300	1700	2300				
Differences FENIT PIER (Tralee Bay)							
–0057	–0017	–0029	–0109	+0·5	+0·2	+0·3	+0·1

SHELTER Good shelter in marina (2.7m depth).

NAVIGATION Appr on 146° to WPT 52°16'·00N 09° 53'·00W, Little Samphire Is, conspic lt ho, Fl WRG 5s 17m 16/13M, thence 7ca E to Samphire Is; lt QR 15m 3M vis 242°–097°, leaving S breakwater bn FlR 6m 3M to N. Fenit Pier Hd 2 FR (vert) 12m 3M, vis 148°-058°. Easy ent H24.

LIGHTS AND MARKS See 5.3 and chartlet.

COMMUNICATIONS (Code 066) ⊜7121480. Port Manager ☎7136231. VHF Ch 16 **14 M** (0900-2100UT). *Neptune* (Tralee SC) VHF Ch 14.

FACILITIES Marina www.fenitharbour.com, ⟶ 130 inc 15Ⓥ; max LOA 25m, €2.30 (min €23.00/craft) ♿ ⊡ ⛽ (at LB stn) 🔧.

Village Ⓟ ⓑ ✕.

Tralee (bus, Fri only) Tralee SC ☎7136119. ✕ ⇄ ✈ (Kerry).

5.34 SHANNON ESTUARY

Clare (N); Kerry and Limerick (S) **52°35'·00N 09°40'·00W** ❁❁❁◊◊✿✿✿

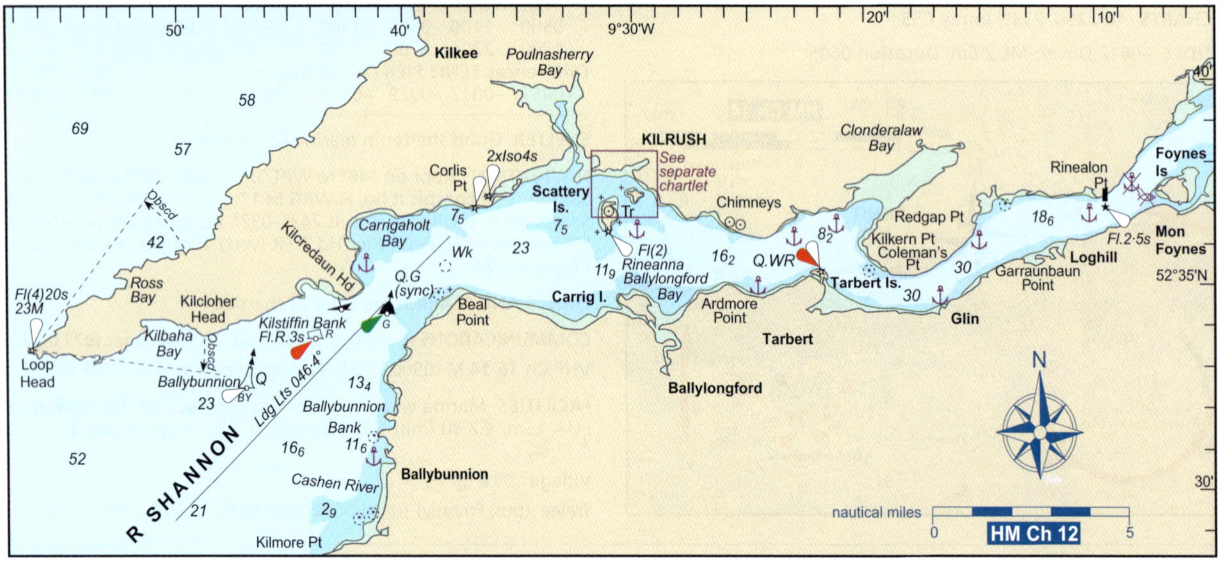

CHARTS AC 1819, 1547, 1548, 1549, 1540; L. Derg 5080; L. Ree 5078; Imray C55.

The ICC's *Sailing Directions for S & W Ireland* and/or Admiralty *Irish Coast Pilot* are essential.

TIDES

HW at	HW Tarbert Is	HW Dover
Kilbaha & Carrigaholt	–0030	+0605
Coney Island	+0045	–0500
Foynes	+0030	–0515
Limerick	+0110	–0435

At Limerick strong S–W winds increase the height and delay the times of HW; strong N–E winds do the opposite. The tides and streams have roughly equal duration and similar flood and ebb streams. In the entrance the flood stream begins at HW Tarbert Is –0555, and the ebb at HW Tarbert Is +0015. In the Shannon the stream is much affected by the wind. S and W winds increase the rate and duration of the flood stream, and reduce the ebb. Strong N or E winds have the opposite effect.

▶ *Off Kilcredaun Pt the Sp ebb reaches 4kn, and in strong winds between S and NW a race forms. This can be skirted keeping near the N shore, which is free from offlying dangers, cheating the worst of the tide. When leaving the Shannon in strong W winds, pass Kilcredaun Pt at slack water, and again keep near the N shore. Loop Hd (lt) marks the N side of Shannon Est, and should be passed 3ca off. Here the stream runs SW from HW Tarbert Is +0300, and NE from HW Tarbert Is –0300.* ◀

SHELTER The Shannon Estuary is 50M long and are tidal from its mouth between Loop Hd and Kerry Hd up to Limerick Dock, some 15M beyond the junction with R Fergus. For boats on N/S passage the nearest fine weather ⚓ is Kilbaha Bay (AC 1819), 3M inside Loop Hd; 🅥s not maintained and holding is poor. It is sheltered in winds from W to NE, but is exposed to SE and swell. 6M further E, Carrigaholt Bay (AC 1547) ent ent 1M N of Kilcredaun Pt, is sheltered from W'lies, ⚓ just N of the new quay, out of the tide; again 🅥s not maintained. In N winds ⚓ SE of Querrin Pt 4½M above Kilcredaun avoiding mussel/fish farms. At Kilrush 7M further E there are ⚓s E of Scattery Is and N of Hog Is and Kilrush Marina (5.35) with all facilities. From Kilcredaun Head in the W to the R Fergus ent (about 25M) there are ⚓, protected from all but E winds, at Tarbert Is, avoiding Wk (6·2m) Glin, Labasheeda, Killadysert (pontoon) and among the islands in the Fergus mouth. ⚓ is prohibited between Moneypoint and Ardmore owing to submarine cables. The reach is exposed in W'lies with overfalls on 'The Bridge' when winds are strong. There is a YC pontoon S of Foynes Is and drying quays at Ballylongford Creek (Saleen), Knock and Clarecastle (S of Ennis, off chartlet). Yachts may enter Limerick Dock, but it is a commercial port.

NAVIGATION WPT 52°32'·52N 09°46'·93W, Ballybunnion NCM Q 062°/4·0M to intercept Ldg lts, Oc. 5s, 046·4° on Corlis Pt, passing between Kilcredaun PHM Q.R(sync) and Tail of Beal buoy SHM, Q.G(sync). The lower estuary between Kerry and Loop Heads is 9M wide, narrowing to 2M off Kilcredaun Pt. Here the chan is well buoyed in mid-stream and then follows the Kerry shore, S of Scattery Is. Note that there are overfalls ¾M S of Scattery Is with W winds and ebb tide. From Tarbert Is to Foynes Is the river narrows to less than 1M in places. Abeam Shannon airport at the junction with R Fergus the characteristics become more riverine, ie the flood stream is stronger than the ebb, but it runs for a shorter time. Here the buoyed channel narrows and shelves although there is a minimum of 2m at LWS. AC 1540 is essential for the final 15M stretch to Limerick.

RIVER SHANNON The Shannon, the longest navigable river in the UK or Ireland, is managed by Shannon Foynes Port Company up to Limerick. Upstream it effectively becomes an inland waterway; progress is restricted by locks and bridges. Info on navigation and facilities can be obtained from Waterways Ireland, Western Regional Office, ☎(061) 922033; or from the Inland Waterways Association of Ireland, Kingston House, Ballinteer, Dublin 4, ☎01-983392; also from Tourist Offices and inland marinas.

LIGHTS AND MARKS See 5.3. There are QW (vert) aero hazard lts on tall chimneys at Money Pt power station 3M ESE of Kilrush. 2 chys at Tarbert Is are conspic (R lts).

COMMUNICATIONS. *Shannon Estuary Radio* Ch **11** for estuary transit/pilotage, 14 berthing/unberthing ops, 16 Emergency only.

FACILITIES Marine facilities are available at several communities on the Shannon; can be found at many villages. 🅥s are at Foynes and Glin Pier (pontoon). E of Aughanish Is on S shore, R Deal is navigable 3M to Askeaton. Deal BC may offer berths (tidal constraints). Ent, marked by RW bn, is 8ca SE of Beeves Rk with 1m in buoyed chan. at Massey's Pier ☎069) 73100, 🅥s.

Facilities upstream at Foynes and Limerick inc:

Shannon Foynes Port ☎(069) 73103 Ⓑ

Foynes YC ☎(069) 65261, (pontoon) .

City all usual city amenities, ⇌ ✈ (Shannon).

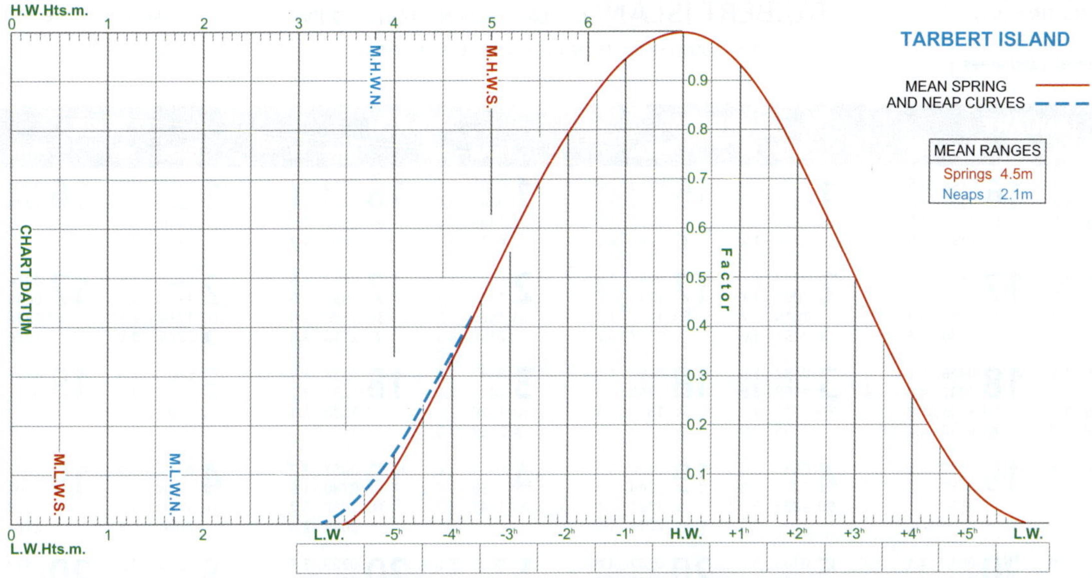

5.35 KILRUSH

Clare **52°37'·90N 09°29'·70W**

CHARTS AC 1819, 1547; Imray C55

TIDES –0555 Dover; ML 2·6; Duration 0610

Standard Port TARBERT ISLAND (⟶)

Times				Height (metres)			
High Water		Low Water		MHWS	MHWN	MLWN	MLWS
0500	1000	0000	0600	5·0	3·8	1·7	0·5
1700	2200	1200	1800				
Differences KILRUSH							
–0010	–0010	–0005	–0005	0·0	–0·1	0·0	0·0

SHELTER Excellent in Kilrush Marina (2·7m), access via lock (width 9m) H24. Day ⚓ in lee of Scattery Is.

NAVIGATION WPT 52°37'·18N 09°31'·64W, 063°/1M to SWM buoy. From seaward usual appr is N of Scattery Is (prominent Round Twr, 26m); beware Baurnahard Spit and Carrigillaun to the N. Follow ldg lts (355°) exactly in buoyed channel where the depth is dredged 1·5m (2016). Coming downriver between Hog Is and mainland, beware unmarked Wolf Rk.

LIGHTS AND MARKS SWM buoy, L Fl 10s, at ent to buoyed chan, with ldg lts 355°, both Oc 3s, to lock. Fl G 3s on S side of lock.

COMMUNICATIONS (Code 065 90) Coast/Cliff Rescue Service 51004; ⊜ (061) 415366; (061) 62677; Police 51017; Dr 51374. Marina 52072 Mobile 087 3712656; Lock 52155.
Marina Ch 80. Kilrush Ch 16, **12**.

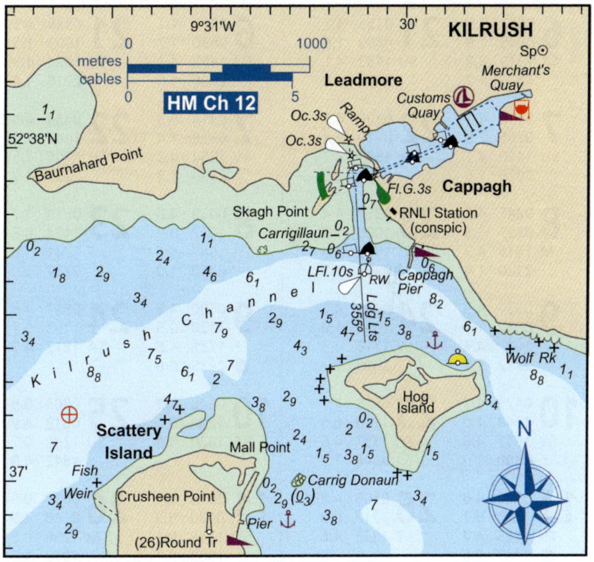

FACILITIES Marina kilrushmarina.ie 120 inc €1.90 (min €16/craft) Kos (45t) (26t).
Town @ (bus to Limerick) ✈ (Shannon).

STANDARD TIME (UT)
For Summer Time add ONE hour in **non-shaded areas**

TARBERT ISLAND

LAT 52°35′N LONG 9°21′W

TIMES AND HEIGHTS OF HIGH AND LOW WATERS

Dates in red are SPRINGS
Dates in blue are NEAPS

YEAR 2024

JANUARY

Date	Time	m	Date	Time	m
1	0218	1.3	16	0243	0.8
	0846	4.4		0900	4.8
M	1452	1.2	TU	1515	0.6
	2119	4.1		2137	4.5
2	0256	1.5	17	0331	1.0
	0926	4.3		0950	4.6
TU	1532	1.4	W	1605	0.9
	2202	4.0		2230	4.4
3	0339	1.6	18	0426	1.2
	1011	4.1		1047	4.4
W	1619	1.6	TH	1703	1.2
	2253	3.9		◐ 2330	4.2
4	0430	1.8	19	0530	1.5
	1107	4.0		1157	4.2
TH	1715	1.7	F	1808	1.4
	◑ 2352	3.9			
5	0532	1.9	20	0042	4.1
	1213	3.9		0644	1.6
F	1821	1.7	SA	1318	4.1
				1919	1.5
6	0053	3.9	21	0155	4.1
	0645	1.9		0800	1.6
SA	1319	3.9	SU	1433	4.1
	1926	1.7		2028	1.6
7	0152	4.1	22	0300	4.2
	0755	1.8		0910	1.4
SU	1420	4.1	M	1536	4.2
	2026	1.6		2130	1.5
8	0246	4.3	23	0357	4.4
	0857	1.5		1009	1.2
M	1515	4.2	TU	1630	4.4
	2120	1.4		2223	1.3
9	0337	4.5	24	0445	4.6
	0952	1.3		1058	1.0
TU	1607	4.4	W	1716	4.5
	2212	1.2		2308	1.2
10	0425	4.7	25	0528	4.7
	1044	1.0		1140	0.9
W	1657	4.6	TH	1757	4.6
	2300	1.0		○ 2348	1.1
11	0512	4.8	26	0605	4.8
	1132	0.7		1218	0.8
TH	1745	4.7	F	1833	4.6
	● 2347	0.8			
12	0558	5.0	27	0022	1.0
	1217	0.5		0640	4.9
F	1832	4.8	SA	1252	0.7
				1908	4.6
13	0031	0.7	28	0053	1.0
	0644	5.1		0714	4.8
SA	1301	0.3	SU	1324	0.8
	1918	4.8		1940	4.6
14	0115	0.6	29	0123	1.1
	0729	5.1		0746	4.8
SU	1344	0.3	M	1352	0.9
	2004	4.8		2012	4.5
15	0158	0.7	30	0153	1.1
	0814	5.0		0818	4.7
M	1429	0.4	TU	1422	1.1
	2049	4.7		2045	4.4
			31	0225	1.3
				0850	4.5
			W	1454	1.3
				2120	4.3

FEBRUARY

Date	Time	m	Date	Time	m
1	0300	1.5	16	0350	1.2
	0925	4.4		1014	4.4
TH	1531	1.5	F	1622	1.3
	2200	4.2		◐ 2246	4.2
2	0342	1.7	17	0448	1.6
	1008	4.1		1120	4.1
F	1615	1.7	SA	1727	1.7
	◑ 2251	4.0		2357	4.0
3	0432	1.9	18	0606	1.8
	1108	3.9		1252	3.9
SA	1713	1.9	SU	1851	1.9
	2355	3.9			
4	0539	2.0	19	0126	3.9
	1225	3.8		0744	1.8
SU	1827	2.0	M	1423	3.9
				2019	1.9
5	0105	4.0	20	0247	4.0
	0704	2.0		0907	1.6
M	1342	3.9	TU	1533	4.1
	1948	1.9		2127	1.7
6	0213	4.1	21	0349	4.3
	0830	1.7		1003	1.3
TU	1453	4.1	W	1624	4.3
	2100	1.6		2216	1.4
7	0314	4.3	22	0436	4.5
	0938	1.4		1047	1.0
W	1554	4.3	TH	1706	4.5
	2159	1.3		2257	1.2
8	0410	4.6	23	0514	4.7
	1032	0.9		1124	0.8
TH	1647	4.6	F	1741	4.6
	2250	1.0		2332	1.0
9	0500	4.9	24	0547	4.8
	1120	0.5		1159	0.7
F	1735	4.8	SA	1812	4.7
	● 2335	0.6		○	
10	0546	5.1	25	0003	0.9
	1204	0.2		0618	4.9
SA	1820	5.0	SU	1230	0.7
				1842	4.8
11	0018	0.4	26	0032	0.9
	0630	5.3		0648	4.9
SU	1245	0.1	M	1258	0.7
	1903	5.1		1910	4.8
12	0059	0.3	27	0059	0.9
	0713	5.4		0718	4.9
M	1326	0.0	TU	1323	0.9
	1944	5.1		1939	4.7
13	0140	0.4	28	0126	1.0
	0755	5.3		0746	4.8
TU	1406	0.2	W	1349	1.0
	2025	5.0		2009	4.7
14	0220	0.5	29	0154	1.1
	0837	5.1		0814	4.7
W	1447	0.5	TH	1417	1.2
	2107	4.8		2039	4.5
15	0302	0.8			
	0922	4.8			
TH	1531	0.9			
	2152	4.5			

MARCH

Date	Time	m	Date	Time	m
1	0225	1.3	16	0319	1.2
	0844	4.5		0946	4.3
F	1449	1.5	SA	1547	1.5
	2113	4.3		2209	4.2
2	0301	1.5	17	0413	1.6
	0922	4.3		1052	3.9
SA	1528	1.7	SU	1650	1.9
	2156	4.1		◐ 2318	3.8
3	0347	1.8	18	0534	1.9
	1014	4.0		1231	3.7
SU	1620	2.0	M	1830	2.1
	◑ 2257	3.9			
4	0451	2.0	19	0057	3.7
	1138	3.7		0730	1.9
M	1741	2.1	TU	1412	3.7
				2012	2.0
5	0020	3.8	20	0229	3.9
	0625	2.0		0854	1.6
TU	1315	3.7	W	1520	4.0
	1923	2.1		2113	1.7
6	0144	3.9	21	0330	4.1
	0811	1.7		0944	1.3
W	1441	4.0	TH	1606	4.2
	2049	1.7		2157	1.4
7	0256	4.2	22	0414	4.4
	0924	1.2		1023	1.0
TH	1544	4.3	F	1642	4.4
	2147	1.2		2234	1.1
8	0355	4.6	23	0449	4.6
	1017	0.7		1058	0.8
F	1634	4.7	SA	1714	4.6
	2235	0.8		2307	0.9
9	0444	5.0	24	0520	4.7
	1102	0.3		1130	0.7
SA	1719	5.0	SU	1742	4.7
	2319	0.4		2336	0.8
10	0529	5.3	25	0548	4.9
	1144	0.0		1159	0.7
SU	1800	5.2	M	1809	4.8
	●			○	
11	0000	0.2	26	0004	0.8
	0611	5.5		0617	4.9
M	1223	-0.1	TU	1226	0.7
	1840	5.3		1838	4.8
12	0038	0.1	27	0031	0.8
	0652	5.5		0646	4.9
TU	1302	-0.1	W	1252	0.8
	1920	5.3		1906	4.8
13	0117	0.2	28	0058	0.9
	0732	5.4		0714	4.8
W	1340	0.2	TH	1318	1.0
	1958	5.2		1936	4.8
14	0155	0.4	29	0126	1.0
	0813	5.1		0743	4.7
TH	1419	0.6	F	1345	1.2
	2037	4.9		2006	4.6
15	0235	0.7	30	0157	1.1
	0857	4.8		0815	4.5
F	1500	1.0	SA	1416	1.4
	2119	4.5		2040	4.4
			31	0233	1.3
				0855	4.3
			SU	1454	1.6
				2122	4.2

APRIL

Date	Time	m	Date	Time	m
1	0319	1.6	16	0502	1.8
	0948	3.9		1203	3.6
M	1548	1.9	TU	1756	2.1
	2221	3.9			
2	0424	1.8	17	0016	3.6
	1111	3.7		0648	1.8
TU	1714	2.1	W	1336	3.6
	◑ 2346	3.8		1936	2.0
3	0602	1.8	18	0145	3.7
	1256	3.7		0811	1.6
W	1905	2.0	TH	1442	3.8
				2037	1.7
4	0118	3.9	19	0248	3.9
	0748	1.5		0903	1.3
TH	1426	4.0	F	1528	4.1
	2030	1.6		2121	1.4
5	0235	4.2	20	0333	4.2
	0859	1.0		0943	1.1
F	1524	4.4	SA	1604	4.3
	2126	1.1		2158	1.2
6	0333	4.6	21	0410	4.4
	0951	0.5		1019	0.9
SA	1612	4.8	SU	1636	4.5
	2213	0.6		2231	1.0
7	0421	5.0	22	0442	4.6
	1036	0.2		1052	0.8
SU	1655	5.1	M	1706	4.6
	2256	0.3		2303	0.8
8	0506	5.3	23	0513	4.7
	1117	0.0		1123	0.7
M	1736	5.3	TU	1735	4.8
	● 2337	0.1		○ 2334	0.8
9	0548	5.4	24	0543	4.8
	1157	-0.1		1153	0.8
TU	1816	5.4	W	1805	4.8
10	0015	0.0	25	0004	0.8
	0630	5.4		0614	4.8
W	1236	0.1	TH	1221	0.8
	1855	5.3		1837	4.8
11	0054	0.2	26	0034	0.8
	0711	5.2		0647	4.7
TH	1314	0.3	F	1251	0.9
	1933	5.1		1909	4.8
12	0132	0.4	27	0105	0.9
	0753	5.0		0721	4.6
F	1352	0.7	SA	1322	1.1
	2012	4.8		1944	4.7
13	0212	0.7	28	0139	0.9
	0836	4.6		0800	4.4
SA	1432	1.1	SU	1357	1.3
	2053	4.5		2022	4.5
14	0255	1.1	29	0220	1.1
	0926	4.2		0845	4.2
SU	1518	1.6	M	1440	1.5
	2141	4.1		2108	4.2
15	0347	1.5	30	0309	1.3
	1030	3.8		0942	3.9
M	1619	1.9	TU	1538	1.7
	◐ 2245	3.8		2207	4.0

Chart Datum: 0·30 metres below Ordnance Datum (Dublin). HAT is 5·5 metres above Chart Datum.

STANDARD TIME (UT)
For Summer Time add ONE hour in **non-shaded areas**

TARBERT ISLAND LAT 52°35′N LONG 9°21′W

TIMES AND HEIGHTS OF HIGH AND LOW WATERS

Dates in red are SPRINGS
Dates in blue are NEAPS

YEAR **2024**

MAY

Date	Time	m	Date	Time	m
1 W	0416	1.4	16 TH	0546	1.6
	1059	3.7		1237	3.6
	1703	1.8		1829	1.9
	◑ 2322	3.9			
2 TH	0544	1.4	17 F	0041	3.7
	1235	3.8		0701	1.5
	1840	1.7		1342	3.7
				1936	1.7
3 F	0047	4.0	18 SA	0146	3.8
	0713	1.2		0800	1.4
	1358	4.0		1434	3.9
	1958	1.3		2027	1.5
4 SA	0204	4.2	19 SU	0238	4.0
	0821	0.8		0847	1.2
	1456	4.4		1516	4.1
	2055	0.9		2111	1.3
5 SU	0304	4.5	20 M	0321	4.2
	0916	0.5		0929	1.1
	1544	4.7		1553	4.3
	2145	0.6		2150	1.1
6 M	0354	4.8	21 TU	0359	4.3
	1004	0.3		1008	1.0
	1629	5.0		1627	4.5
	2230	0.3		2228	1.0
7 TU	0441	5.0	22 W	0435	4.5
	1049	0.2		1045	0.9
	1711	5.1		1701	4.6
	2313	0.2		2305	0.9
8 W	0526	5.1	23 TH	0511	4.6
	1131	0.2		1121	0.9
	1753	5.2		1736	4.7
	● 2355	0.2		○ 2341	0.8
9 TH	0610	5.1	24 F	0548	4.6
	1212	0.3		1156	0.9
	1833	5.1		1812	4.8
10 F	0035	0.3	25 SA	0017	0.7
	0654	4.9		0627	4.6
	1251	0.6		1232	0.9
	1913	4.9		1851	4.7
11 SA	0115	0.5	26 SU	0054	0.7
	0738	4.7		0709	4.5
	1331	0.9		1310	1.0
	1954	4.7		1931	4.7
12 SU	0155	0.7	27 M	0133	0.7
	0823	4.4		0753	4.4
	1411	1.2		1351	1.1
	2036	4.4		2014	4.5
13 M	0238	1.0	28 TU	0217	0.8
	0911	4.1		0842	4.2
	1456	1.5		1439	1.2
	2122	4.1		2102	4.4
14 TU	0327	1.3	29 W	0308	0.9
	1008	3.8		0938	4.1
	1550	1.8		1536	1.4
	2216	3.9		2157	4.2
15 W	0428	1.5	30 TH	0409	1.0
	1120	3.6		1045	3.9
	1704	1.9		1647	1.5
	◐ 2325	3.7		◑ 2301	4.1
			31 F	0520	1.0
				1204	3.9
				1806	1.4

JUNE

Date	Time	m	Date	Time	m
1 SA	0014	4.1	16 SU	0038	3.8
	0634	1.0		0651	1.5
	1321	4.1		1330	3.8
	1919	1.2		1927	1.7
2 SU	0127	4.2	17 M	0136	3.8
	0740	0.8		0747	1.5
	1422	4.3		1422	4.0
	2020	1.0		2021	1.6
3 M	0231	4.4	18 TU	0229	4.0
	0838	0.7		0838	1.4
	1515	4.6		1507	4.2
	2115	0.8		2110	1.4
4 TU	0327	4.6	19 W	0316	4.1
	0932	0.6		0925	1.2
	1603	4.8		1550	4.4
	2206	0.6		2157	1.2
5 W	0418	4.7	20 TH	0401	4.3
	1022	0.6		1011	1.1
	1649	4.9		1632	4.5
	2254	0.5		2241	1.0
6 TH	0508	4.7	21 F	0445	4.4
	1110	0.6		1055	1.0
	1734	4.9		1713	4.6
	● 2339	0.5		2324	0.8
7 F	0555	4.7	22 SA	0529	4.5
	1154	0.7		1138	0.9
	1817	4.9		1755	4.7
				○	
8 SA	0022	0.5	23 SU	0006	0.7
	0642	4.6		0615	4.5
	1236	0.8		1221	0.8
	1900	4.8		1838	4.8
9 SU	0104	0.6	24 M	0047	0.5
	0727	4.5		0701	4.5
	1316	1.0		1303	0.8
	1941	4.7		1921	4.8
10 M	0144	0.7	25 TU	0130	0.5
	0810	4.3		0747	4.5
	1356	1.1		1347	0.8
	2021	4.5		2005	4.7
11 TU	0224	0.9	26 W	0214	0.5
	0854	4.1		0836	4.4
	1436	1.3		1434	0.9
	2103	4.3		2052	4.6
12 W	0305	1.1	27 TH	0301	0.5
	0940	3.9		0927	4.3
	1520	1.5		1525	1.0
	2148	4.1		2142	4.5
13 TH	0351	1.3	28 F	0353	0.7
	1031	3.8		1023	4.2
	1612	1.7		1624	1.2
	2238	3.9		◑ 2238	4.4
14 F	0445	1.4	29 SA	0451	0.8
	1130	3.7		1128	4.1
	1716	1.8		1730	1.3
	◐ 2336	3.8		2342	4.2
15 SA	0547	1.5	30 SU	0555	1.0
	1233	3.7		1240	4.1
	1825	1.8		1840	1.3

JULY

Date	Time	m	Date	Time	m
1 M	0052	4.2	16 TU	0038	3.8
	0701	1.1		0641	1.7
	1347	4.2		1328	3.9
	1949	1.2		1931	1.8
2 TU	0202	4.2	17 W	0141	3.8
	0806	1.1		0748	1.7
	1449	4.4		1426	4.0
	2052	1.1		2036	1.6
3 W	0306	4.3	18 TH	0241	3.9
	0908	1.1		0850	1.5
	1544	4.5		1520	4.2
	2151	0.9		2133	1.4
4 TH	0405	4.4	19 F	0336	4.1
	1006	1.0		0947	1.3
	1635	4.6		1610	4.4
	2244	0.8		2224	1.1
5 F	0458	4.4	20 SA	0429	4.3
	1058	1.0		1038	1.1
	1723	4.7		1657	4.6
	● 2332	0.7		2312	0.8
6 SA	0547	4.5	21 SU	0518	4.5
	1145	0.9		1126	0.9
	1807	4.8		1742	4.8
				○ 2356	0.5
7 SU	0015	0.6	22 M	0605	4.6
	0632	4.5		1211	0.7
	1227	0.9		1826	4.9
	1848	4.8			
8 M	0055	0.6	23 TU	0038	0.3
	0714	4.5		0652	4.7
	1305	1.0		1254	0.5
	1926	4.7		1909	5.0
9 TU	0131	0.7	24 W	0119	0.2
	0752	4.4		0736	4.8
	1339	1.0		1337	0.5
	2003	4.6		1952	5.0
10 W	0206	0.8	25 TH	0201	0.2
	0829	4.3		0820	4.8
	1413	1.2		1420	0.6
	2039	4.5		2036	4.9
11 TH	0239	0.9	26 F	0244	0.3
	0905	4.2		0906	4.6
	1448	1.3		1505	0.8
	2116	4.3		2122	4.8
12 F	0313	1.1	27 SA	0329	0.6
	0944	4.1		0955	4.5
	1527	1.5		1556	1.0
	2156	4.1		2213	4.5
13 SA	0352	1.3	28 SU	0420	0.9
	1029	3.9		1051	4.3
	1613	1.7		1655	1.3
	◐ 2242	4.0		◑ 2313	4.2
14 SU	0439	1.5	29 M	0519	1.2
	1123	3.8		1201	4.1
	1709	1.8		1807	1.5
	2337	3.8			
15 M	0535	1.7	30 TU	0025	4.0
	1225	3.8		0630	1.4
	1818	1.9		1319	4.0
				1928	1.5
			31 W	0146	4.0
				0747	1.5
				1433	4.1
				2044	1.4

AUGUST

Date	Time	m	Date	Time	m
1 TH	0301	4.0	16 F	0218	3.8
	0902	1.5		0828	1.7
	1537	4.3		1459	4.1
	2148	1.2		2119	1.4
2 F	0404	4.2	17 SA	0324	4.0
	1004	1.3		0934	1.4
	1631	4.5		1554	4.4
	2240	0.9		2212	1.0
3 SA	0456	4.3	18 SU	0419	4.3
	1054	1.1		1027	1.0
	1717	4.7		1643	4.7
	2324	0.7		2258	0.6
4 SU	0540	4.4	19 M	0508	4.6
	1137	1.0		1114	0.7
	1756	4.8		1728	5.0
	●			○ 2341	0.2
5 M	0003	0.6	20 TU	0553	4.9
	0619	4.5		1157	0.4
	1214	0.9		1811	5.2
	1832	4.8			
6 TU	0039	0.6	21 W	0021	0.0
	0654	4.5		0636	5.0
	1247	0.9		1238	0.2
	1906	4.8		1853	5.3
7 W	0111	0.6	22 TH	0101	-0.1
	0726	4.5		0717	5.1
	1317	0.9		1318	0.2
	1938	4.7		1934	5.3
8 TH	0140	0.7	23 F	0140	0.0
	0757	4.5		0758	5.0
	1345	1.0		1359	0.4
	2010	4.6		2016	5.1
9 F	0207	0.9	24 SA	0220	0.3
	0828	4.4		0840	4.9
	1414	1.2		1441	0.6
	2041	4.5		2100	4.9
10 SA	0236	1.1	25 SU	0302	0.6
	0900	4.3		0925	4.6
	1447	1.4		1527	1.0
	2114	4.3		2149	4.5
11 SU	0308	1.3	26 M	0349	1.1
	0937	4.1		1017	4.3
	1525	1.6		1624	1.4
	2153	4.1		◑ 2249	4.1
12 M	0347	1.6	27 TU	0447	1.5
	1022	4.0		1127	4.0
	1612	1.8		1742	1.7
	◐ 2242	3.9			
13 TU	0436	1.8	28 W	0009	3.8
	1124	3.8		0608	1.8
	1715	2.0		1301	3.8
	2349	3.7		1923	1.7
14 W	0543	2.0	29 TH	0145	3.7
	1239	3.8		0748	1.9
	1841	2.0		1429	4.0
				2048	1.5
15 TH	0104	3.7	30 F	0306	3.9
	0707	1.9		0908	1.7
	1353	3.9		1535	4.2
	2011	1.8		2145	1.2
			31 SA	0404	4.1
				1001	1.4
				1624	4.5
				2229	0.9

Chart Datum: 0·30 metres below Ordnance Datum (Dublin). HAT is 5·5 metres above Chart Datum.

STANDARD TIME (UT)
For Summer Time add ONE hour in **non-shaded areas**

TARBERT ISLAND

LAT 52°35′N LONG 9°21′W

TIMES AND HEIGHTS OF HIGH AND LOW WATERS

Dates in red are SPRINGS
Dates in blue are NEAPS

YEAR 2024

SEPTEMBER

Date	Day	Time	m	Time	m	Time	m	Time	m
1	SU	0448	4.3	1044	1.1	1704	4.7	2308	0.7
2	M	0524	4.5	1121	0.9	1738	4.8	2343	0.6
3	TU	0556	4.6	1153	0.8	1809	4.9	●	
4	W	0014	0.6	0625	4.6	1222	0.8	1839	4.9
5	TH	0043	0.6	0653	4.7	1248	0.8	1908	4.8
6	F	0108	0.8	0721	4.7	1314	1.0	1937	4.7
7	SA	0133	0.9	0749	4.6	1342	1.1	2005	4.6
8	SU	0200	1.1	0819	4.5	1411	1.3	2036	4.4
9	M	0229	1.4	0851	4.3	1446	1.5	2112	4.2
10	TU	0304	1.6	0930	4.1	1529	1.8	2159	3.9
11	W	0350	1.9	1027	3.9	1631	2.0	◐ 2309	3.7
12	TH	0500	2.1	1154	3.7	1805	2.0		
13	F	0038	3.6	0641	2.1	1326	3.8	1954	1.8
14	SA	0207	3.8	0817	1.8	1441	4.1	2103	1.3
15	SU	0314	4.1	0921	1.3	1538	4.5	2153	0.8
16	M	0405	4.5	1011	0.8	1625	4.8	2237	0.3
17	TU	0450	4.8	1055	0.5	1709	5.1	2319	0.0
18	W	0533	5.1	1137	0.2	1751	5.4	○ 2359	-0.1
19	TH	0613	5.2	1217	0.1	1832	5.4		
20	F	0037	-0.1	0654	5.3	1256	0.1	1913	5.4
21	SA	0116	0.1	0733	5.2	1335	0.3	1955	5.1
22	SU	0154	0.4	0813	4.9	1417	0.6	2039	4.8
23	M	0235	0.8	0856	4.6	1502	1.0	2128	4.4
24	TU	0320	1.3	0947	4.2	1558	1.4	◑ 2231	3.9
25	W	0419	1.8	1059	3.8	1723	1.7	2359	3.6
26	TH	0552	2.1	1243	3.7	1920	1.7		
27	F	0141	3.6	0748	2.0	1417	3.8	2035	1.4
28	SA	0255	3.9	0855	1.7	1517	4.1	2125	1.1
29	SU	0345	4.1	0941	1.4	1601	4.4	2205	0.9
30	M	0423	4.3	1019	1.1	1638	4.6	2240	0.7

OCTOBER

Date	Day	Time	m	Time	m	Time	m	Time	m
1	TU	0456	4.5	1053	0.9	1710	4.7	2313	0.6
2	W	0524	4.6	1123	0.8	1739	4.8	● 2343	0.6
3	TH	0551	4.7	1152	0.8	1807	4.8		
4	F	0010	0.7	0618	4.8	1219	0.8	1836	4.8
5	SA	0036	0.8	0646	4.8	1246	0.9	1905	4.7
6	SU	0102	1.0	0716	4.7	1314	1.0	1935	4.6
7	M	0129	1.1	0746	4.6	1344	1.2	2008	4.4
8	TU	0159	1.3	0820	4.4	1419	1.4	2046	4.2
9	W	0235	1.6	0900	4.2	1504	1.6	2137	3.9
10	TH	0323	1.8	0956	3.9	1607	1.8	◐ 2246	3.6
11	F	0436	2.0	1118	3.7	1742	1.8		
12	SA	0018	3.6	0621	2.0	1257	3.8	1927	1.5
13	SU	0151	3.8	0756	1.6	1417	4.1	2035	1.1
14	M	0253	4.2	0857	1.2	1513	4.5	2125	0.6
15	TU	0342	4.6	0946	0.7	1601	4.9	2210	0.3
16	W	0426	4.9	1031	0.4	1645	5.2	2252	0.0
17	TH	0508	5.2	1113	0.1	1728	5.3	○ 2332	-0.1
18	F	0549	5.3	1154	0.1	1810	5.4		
19	SA	0012	0.0	0630	5.3	1234	0.1	1853	5.2
20	SU	0051	0.3	0710	5.1	1315	0.4	1937	5.0
21	M	0131	0.6	0750	4.8	1357	0.7	2023	4.6
22	TU	0212	1.0	0834	4.5	1443	1.0	2113	4.2
23	W	0257	1.4	0924	4.1	1539	1.4	2215	3.8
24	TH	0354	1.8	1031	3.8	1658	1.6	◑ 2337	3.6
25	F	0522	2.0	1206	3.7	1839	1.7		
26	SA	0107	3.6	0707	2.0	1335	3.8	1955	1.5
27	SU	0216	3.8	0815	1.7	1437	4.0	2045	1.2
28	M	0305	4.0	0902	1.4	1522	4.2	2126	1.0
29	TU	0344	4.2	0941	1.2	1600	4.4	2202	0.9
30	W	0417	4.4	1016	1.0	1634	4.6	2235	0.8
31	TH	0447	4.6	1049	0.9	1705	4.7	2307	0.8

NOVEMBER

Date	Day	Time	m	Time	m	Time	m	Time	m
1	F	0516	4.7	1121	0.8	1735	4.7	● 2337	0.8
2	SA	0545	4.8	1152	0.8	1806	4.7		
3	SU	0007	0.9	0617	4.8	1223	0.9	1839	4.7
4	M	0037	1.0	0650	4.7	1255	1.0	1913	4.5
5	TU	0108	1.1	0725	4.6	1328	1.1	1951	4.4
6	W	0142	1.3	0803	4.5	1407	1.2	2035	4.2
7	TH	0222	1.5	0847	4.3	1455	1.4	2127	3.9
8	F	0313	1.6	0942	4.0	1557	1.5	2232	3.8
9	SA	0423	1.8	1053	3.9	1719	1.5	◐ 2355	3.7
10	SU	0552	1.8	1220	3.9	1845	1.3		
11	M	0119	3.9	0718	1.5	1341	4.2	1954	1.0
12	TU	0221	4.3	0822	1.1	1441	4.5	2049	0.7
13	W	0313	4.6	0915	0.8	1532	4.8	2137	0.4
14	TH	0359	4.9	1004	0.5	1620	5.0	2223	0.3
15	F	0443	5.1	1050	0.3	1706	5.1	○ 2307	0.3
16	SA	0526	5.1	1134	0.3	1752	5.1	2350	0.4
17	SU	0609	5.1	1217	0.3	1837	5.0		
18	M	0031	0.6	0652	5.0	1300	0.5	1924	4.8
19	TU	0112	0.8	0734	4.8	1344	0.7	2010	4.5
20	W	0154	1.1	0819	4.5	1429	1.0	2059	4.2
21	TH	0238	1.4	0906	4.2	1520	1.2	2153	3.9
22	F	0329	1.6	1001	4.0	1623	1.4	2257	3.7
23	SA	0434	1.8	1111	3.8	1736	1.5	◑	
24	SU	0008	3.7	0555	1.9	1229	3.8	1846	1.5
25	M	0115	3.7	0706	1.8	1337	3.9	1945	1.4
26	TU	0209	3.9	0804	1.6	1430	4.0	2033	1.3
27	W	0255	4.1	0852	1.4	1515	4.2	2115	1.2
28	TH	0334	4.3	0934	1.3	1555	4.4	2155	1.1
29	F	0409	4.5	1014	1.1	1631	4.5	2232	1.0
30	SA	0443	4.6	1053	1.0	1707	4.5	2308	1.0

DECEMBER

Date	Day	Time	m	Time	m	Time	m	Time	m
1	SU	0518	4.7	1131	0.9	1743	4.6	● 2344	1.0
2	M	0555	4.8	1208	0.9	1820	4.6		
3	TU	0019	1.0	0633	4.7	1244	0.9	1900	4.5
4	W	0056	1.1	0712	4.7	1322	0.9	1942	4.4
5	TH	0134	1.1	0753	4.6	1403	0.9	2027	4.3
6	F	0217	1.2	0838	4.4	1450	1.0	2117	4.1
7	SA	0306	1.4	0929	4.3	1545	1.1	2214	4.0
8	SU	0406	1.5	1029	4.2	1650	1.2	◐ 2321	4.0
9	M	0516	1.5	1140	4.1	1800	1.2		
10	TU	0035	4.1	0633	1.4	1256	4.2	1909	1.1
11	W	0142	4.3	0742	1.3	1405	4.4	2010	1.0
12	TH	0240	4.5	0843	1.0	1504	4.6	2106	0.8
13	F	0332	4.7	0939	0.8	1558	4.7	2158	0.8
14	SA	0421	4.8	1032	0.7	1650	4.8	2248	0.7
15	SU	0508	4.9	1121	0.6	1739	4.8	○ 2335	0.8
16	M	0554	4.9	1208	0.5	1827	4.8		
17	TU	0018	0.8	0639	4.9	1251	0.6	1913	4.7
18	W	0100	0.9	0722	4.8	1334	0.7	1957	4.5
19	TH	0140	1.1	0804	4.7	1415	0.8	2040	4.3
20	F	0219	1.2	0846	4.5	1458	1.0	2124	4.2
21	SA	0301	1.4	0930	4.3	1543	1.2	2210	4.0
22	SU	0347	1.6	1019	4.1	1635	1.4	◑ 2302	3.9
23	M	0442	1.7	1117	3.9	1735	1.6		
24	TU	0000	3.8	0550	1.8	1223	3.9	1838	1.6
25	W	0101	3.9	0659	1.8	1328	3.9	1937	1.6
26	TH	0158	4.0	0801	1.7	1426	4.0	2030	1.6
27	F	0249	4.2	0856	1.6	1517	4.1	2118	1.5
28	SA	0334	4.4	0946	1.4	1603	4.3	2203	1.3
29	SU	0417	4.5	1032	1.2	1646	4.4	2246	1.2
30	M	0458	4.6	1115	1.0	1727	4.5	● 2328	1.1
31	TU	0539	4.7	1156	0.9	1808	4.5		

Chart Datum: 0·30 metres below Ordnance Datum (Dublin). HAT is 5·5 metres above Chart Datum.

No.	Place	21	20	19	18	17	16	15	14	13	12	11	10	9	8	7	6	5	4	3	2	1
1	*Kilrush*	318	361	364	335	332	323	309	291	276	274	270	251	220	203	191	183	142	119	75	76	**1**
2	Galway	348	366	338	309	307	297	284	266	253	251	245	227	192	178	166	163	104	94	49	**2**	
3	Slyne Head	352	317	289	260	257	248	234	217	201	199	195	178	143	128	117	114	55	44	**3**		
4	Westport	337	323	295	266	249	240	226	207	193	191	187	168	137	120	108	100	57	**4**			
5	Eagle Island	297	262	234	205	198	193	175	162	147	145	136	123	88	72	62	59	**5**				
6	Sligo	281	246	218	189	179	177	156	146	123	121	117	107	72	51	30	**6**					
7	Killybegs	267	232	204	175	171	163	148	132	115	113	109	93	58	43	**7**						
8	Burtonport	218	182	153	130	130	116	108	90	74	72	68	49	18	**8**							
9	**Tory Island**	209	174	146	117	113	105	90	74	57	55	51	35	**9**								
10	L Swilly (Fahan)	200	166	138	109	104	96	81	65	48	46	42	**10**									
11	**Lough Foyle**	157	121	92	72	73	55	47	30	11	9	**11**										
12	River Bann	155	120	92	63	65	53	40	24	5	**12**											
13	**Portrush**	150	115	87	58	60	48	35	19	**13**												
14	Altacarry Head	135	102	74	45	45	31	21	**14**													
15	**Carnlough**	118	78	50	25	26	11	**15**														
16	**Larne**	108	73	45	16	16	**16**															
17	**Carrickfergus**	101	66	39	6	**17**																
18	**Bangor**	96	61	34	**18**																	
19	**Strangford L**	71	36	**19**																		
20	**Carlingford L**	50	**20**																			
21	***Dun Laoghaire***	**21**																				

DISTANCE TABLE
Approximate distances in nautical miles are by the most direct route, whilst avoiding dangers and allowing for Traffic Separation Schemes. Places in *italics* are in adjoining areas; places in **bold** are in 0.32, Distances across the Irish Sea.

REPUBLIC OF IRELAND
EMERGENCY 112 or 999
MRCC MALIN HEAD (+353) 074 937 0103
JRCC DUBLIN (+353) 01 662 0922
MRCC VALENTIA (+353) 066 947 6109

UK
EMERGENCY 999
HMCG NATIONAL – 02392 552100
HMCG BELFAST – 028 9146 3933
HMCG MILFORD HAVEN – 01646 690909
HM CUSTOMS – 0845 010 9000
POLICE – 101 MEDICAL – 111

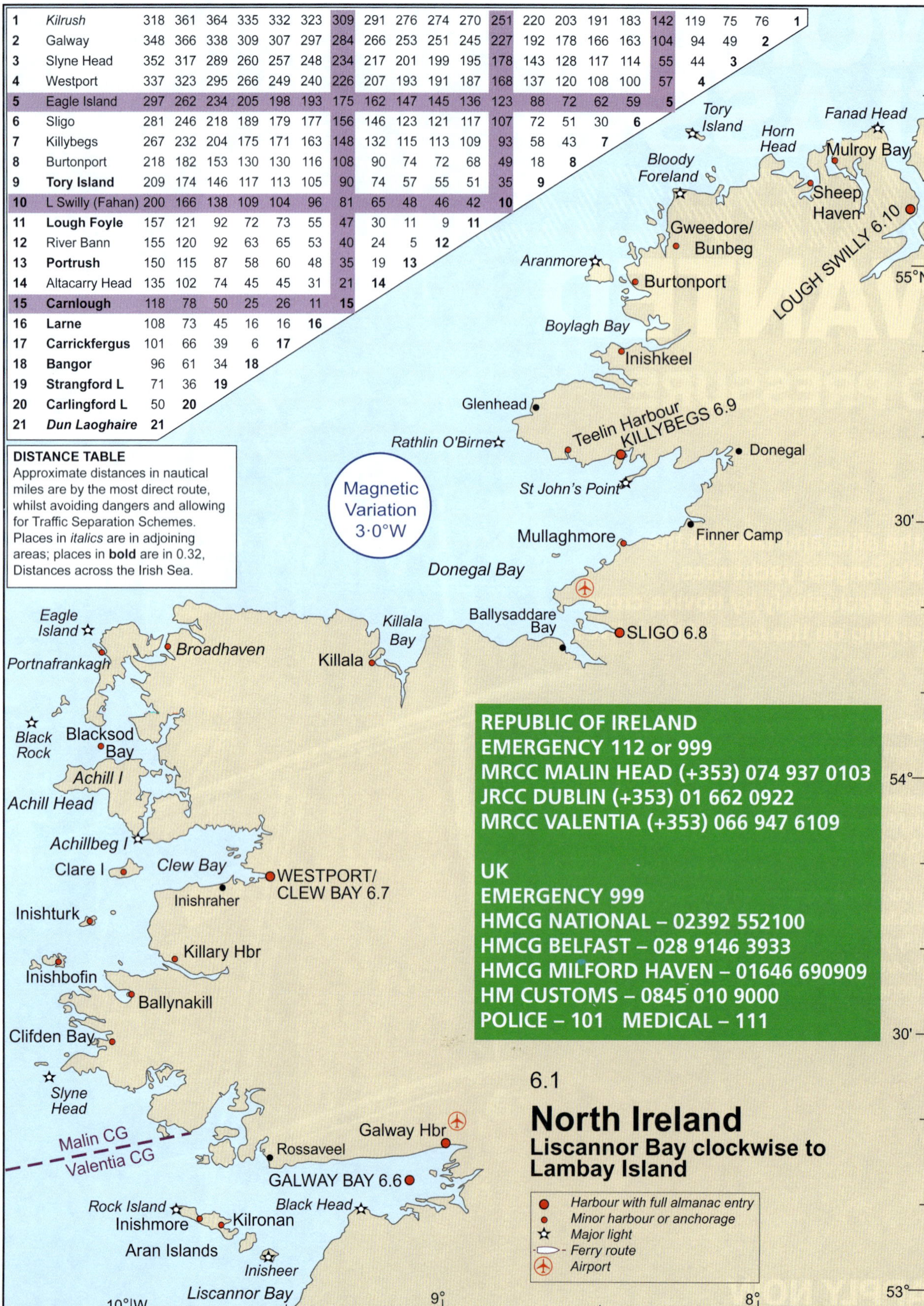

6.1

North Ireland

Liscannor Bay clockwise to Lambay Island

- Harbour with full almanac entry
- Minor harbour or anchorage
- Major light
- Ferry route
- Airport

Malin Head
Inishtrahull
MRCC
Malin CG
Belfast CG
Inishowen
Moville
LOUGH FOYLE 6.11
PORTRUSH 6.13
Portstewart
RIVER BANN 6.12
Ballycastle
Rathlin I
Fair Head
N Chan
TSS
Campbeltown
Mull of Kintyre
Sanda I
Lamlash
Firth of Clyde
Troon
Ailsa Craig
Cushendun Bay
Red Bay
Carnlough
Glenarm
Maidens
Stranraer
Troon
55°N
Loch Ryan
Portpatrick
LARNE 6.15
Black Head
Mew Island
BELFAST LOUGH 6.16
Carrickfergus
Belfast MRCC
Bangor
Donaghadee
Lough Neagh
Liverpool/IOM
30'
Portavogie
Magnetic Variation 1·3°W
STRANGFORD LOUGH 6.17
ARDGLASS 6.18
St John's Point
Peel
I of Man
Dundrum Bay
Annalong
Warrenpoint
Kilkeel
CARLINGFORD LOUGH 6.19
Port St Mary
54°
Dundalk
Haulbowline
Belfast CG
Dublin CG
Dunany Pt
Port Oriel
Clogher Head
DROGHEDA 6.20
R. Boyne
Balbriggan
Skerries
Rockabill
Off Skerries TSS
30'
Lambay I
Malahide
See 5.1
The Skerries
Howth
Baily
Dublin
Kish Bank
Holyhead
Dun Laoghaire
Muglins
Magnetic Variation 1·3°W
53°
Wicklow
7°
6°
5°W

N Ireland

6.2 AREA 6 TIDAL STREAMS

The tidal arrows (with no rates shown) off the S and W coasts of Ireland are printed by kind permission of the Irish Cruising Club. They have been found accurate, but should be used with caution.

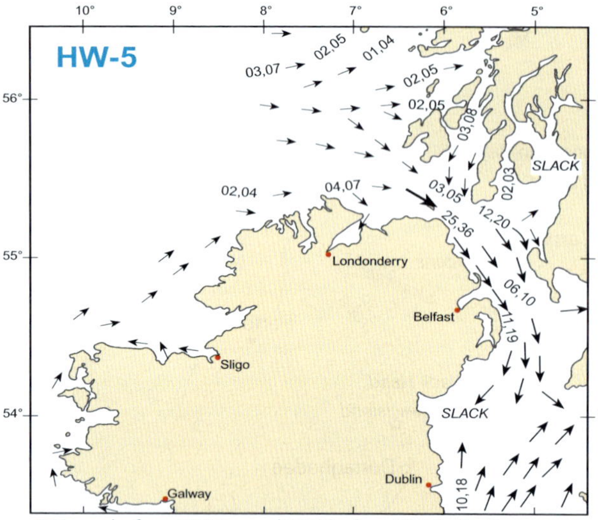

5 Hours before HW Dover (0450 before HW Belfast)

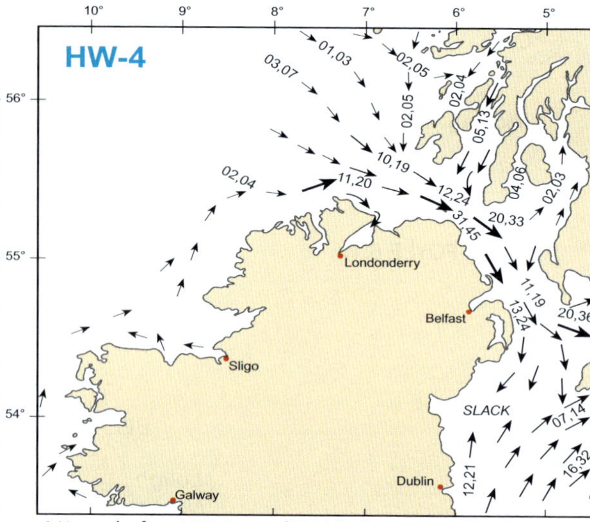

4 Hours before HW Dover (0350 before HW Belfast)

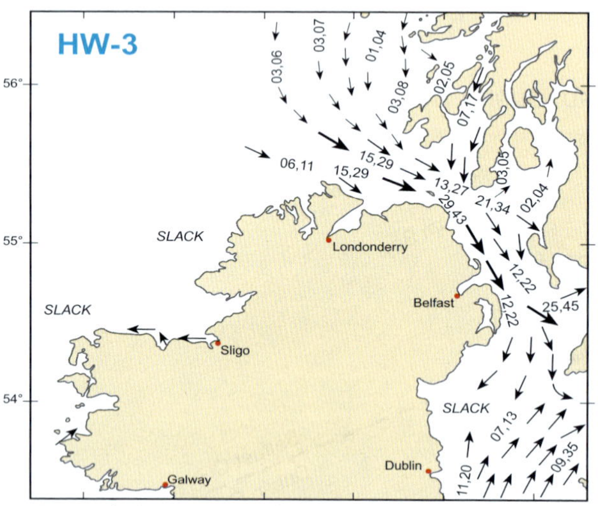

3 Hours before HW Dover (0250 before HW Belfast)

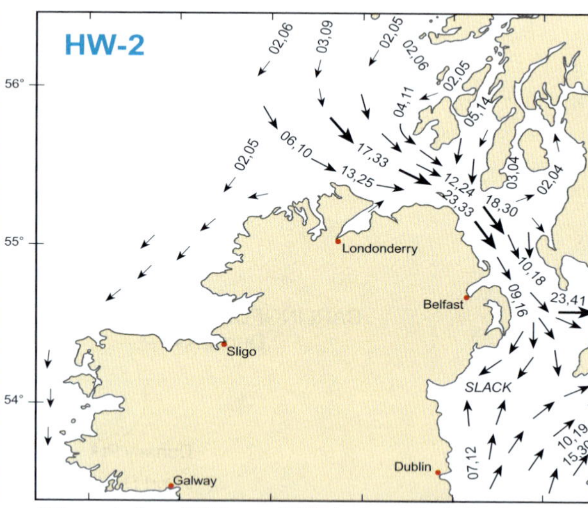

2 Hours before HW Dover (0150 before HW Belfast)

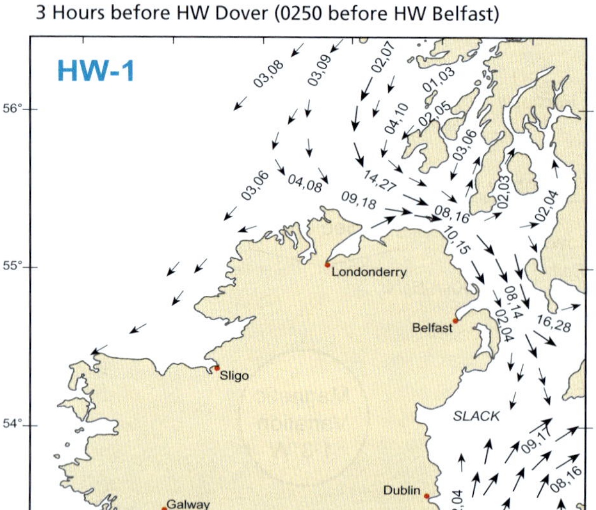

1 Hour before HW Dover (0050 before HW Belfast)

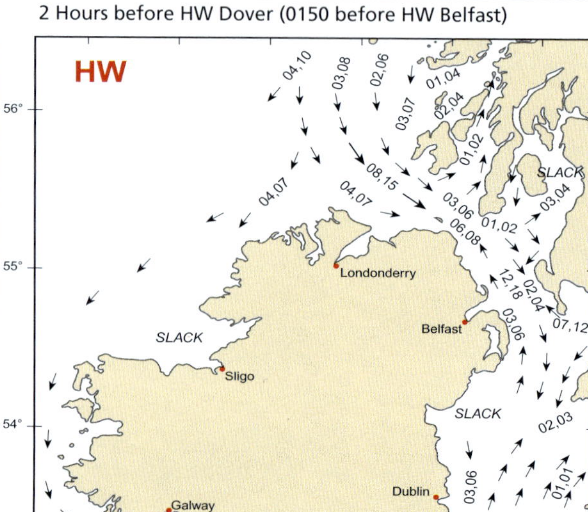

HW Dover (0010 after HW Belfast)

Rathlin Island 6.14
Mull of Kintyre 2.10
North Irish Sea 3.2
SW Scotland 2.2
South Ireland 5.2

The tidal arrows (with no rates shown) off the S and W coasts of Ireland are printed by kind permission of the Irish Cruising Club. They have been found accurate, but should be used with caution.

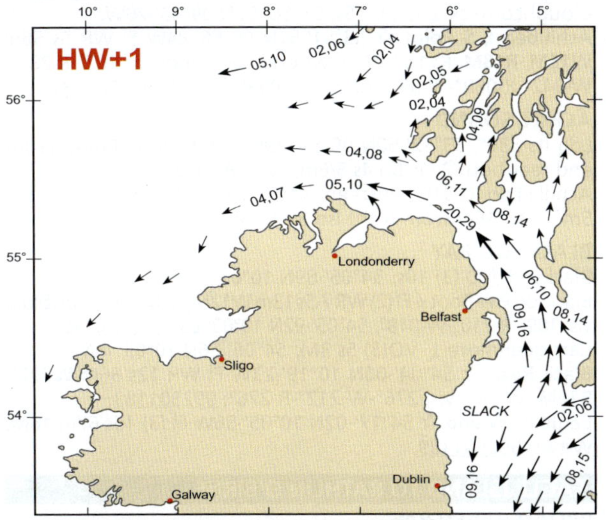

1 Hour after HW Dover (0110 after HW Belfast)

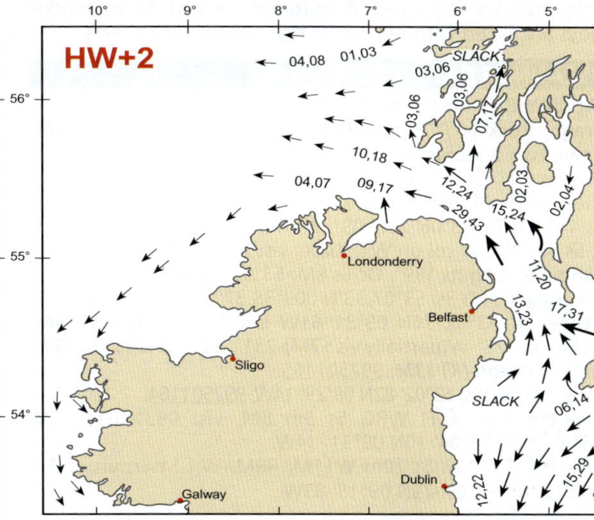

2 Hours after HW Dover (0210 after HW Belfast)

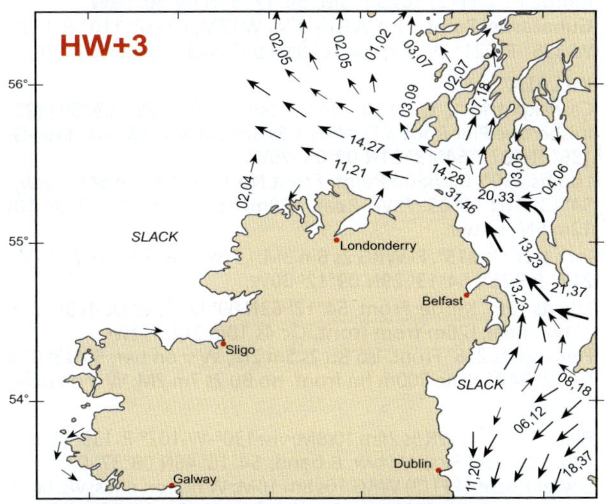

3 Hours after HW Dover (0310 after HW Belfast)

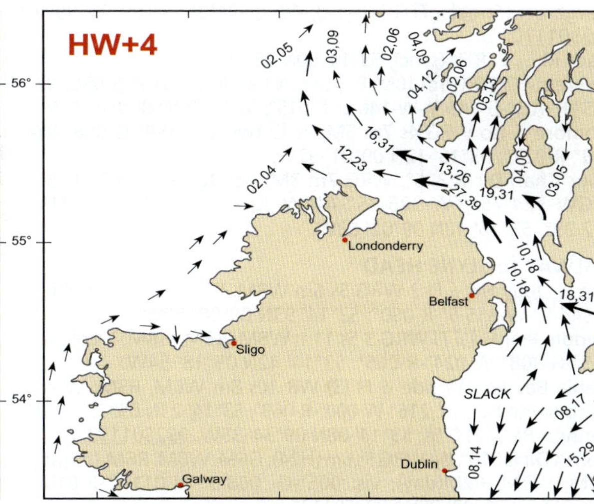

4 Hours after HW Dover (0410 after HW Belfast)

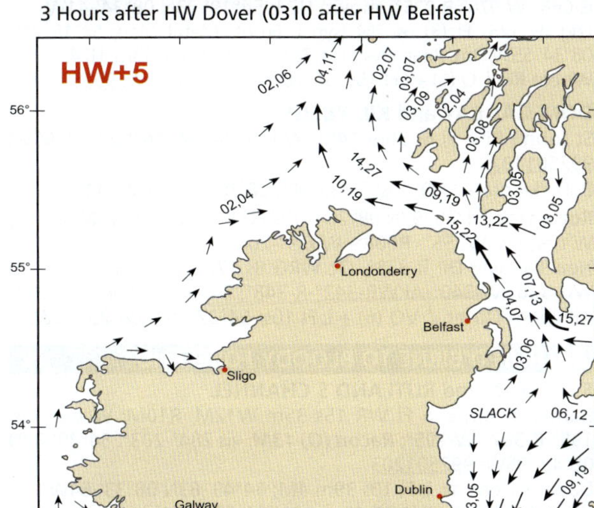

5 Hours after HW Dover (0510 after HW Belfast)

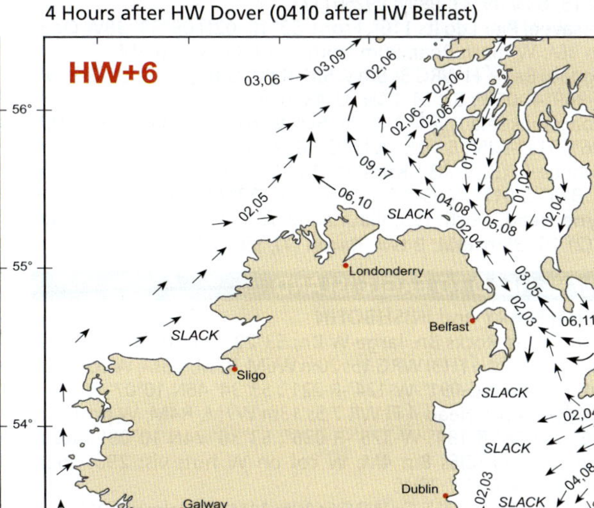

6 Hours after HW Dover (0610 after HW Belfast)

6.3 LIGHTS, BUOYS AND WAYPOINTS

Bold print = light with a nominal range of 15M or more. CAPITALS = place or feature. *CAPITAL ITALICS* = light-vessel, light float or Lanby. *Italics* = Fog signal. ***Bold italics*** = Racon. Many marks/buoys are fitted with AIS, MMSI No; see relevant charts.

LISCANNOR BAY TO SLYNE HEAD

GALWAY BAY and INISHMORE

Eeragh, Rock Is ☆ 53°08′·91N 09°51′·39W Fl 15s 35m **18M**; W twr, two B bands; vis: 297°-262°; 992501172.
Straw Is ☆ Fl (2) 5s 11m 12M; W twr; 53°07′·08N 09°37′·82W.
Killeany Ldg lts 192°. Front, Oc 5s 6m 3M; W col on W □ base; vis: 142°-197°, 53°06′·25N 09°39′·74W. Rear, 43m from front, Oc 5s 8m 2M; W col on W □ base; vis: 142°-197°.
Inishmaan, Ldg lts 199°, Oc 6s 8M; 53°06′·08N 09°34′·77W.
Killeaney Fl G 3s; 53°07.33′N 009°38.37′W; 992501166.
Inisheer ☆ 53°02′·76N 09°31′·61W Iso WR 12s 34m **W16M**, R11M; vis: 225°-W(partially vis >7M)-231°, 231°-W-245°-R-269°-W-115°; ***Racon (K) 13M***; 992501165.
Finnis Q (3) 10s; 53°02′·82N 09°29′·14W, 992501164.
Ballyhees Pier ☆ Fl WRG 5s 3m 8M, vis: 093°-G-150°-W-226°-R-290°; 53°04′·10N 09°31′·34W.
Black Hd ☆ Fl WR 5s 20m W11M, R8M, W □ twr; vis: 045°-R268°-276°; 53°09′·25N 09°15′·83W.

GALWAY

Margaretta Shoal Fl G 3s (sync); *Whis;* 53°13′·68N 09°05′·99W, 992501170.
Black Rk Fl R 3s (sync); 53°14′·00N 09°06′·55W.
Leverets ☆ Q WRG 9m 10M; B □ twr, W bands; vis: 015°-G-058°-W-065°-R-103°-G-143·5°-W-146·5°-R-015°; 53°15′·33N 09°01′·90W.
Rinmore ☆ Iso WRG 4s 7m 5M; W □ twr; vis: 359°-G-008°-W-018°-R-027°; 53°16′·12N 09°01′·97W.
Appr Chan Dir lt 325°, WRG 7m 3M; vis: 322·25°-FG-323·75°-AlGW-324·75°-FW-325·25°-AlRW-326·25°-FR-331·25°-FlR-332·25°; 53°16′·12N 09°02′·83W.

GALWAY to SLYNE HEAD

Barna Quay Hd ☆ Fl 2 WRG 5s 6m W8M, R5M, G5M; vis:250°-G-344·5°-W-355·5°-R-090°; 53°14′·93N 09°08′·90W.
Spiddle Pier Hd ☆ Fl WRG 3·5s 11m W8M, R8M, G8M; Y col; vis: 265°-G-308°-W-024°-R-066°; 53°14′·42N 09°18′·54W.
Cashla Bay Ent, W side ☆ Fl (3) WR 10s 8m W6M, R3M; W col on concrete twr; vis: 216°-W-000°-R-069°; 53°14′·23N 09°35′·20W.
Cannon Rk Fl G 5s; 53°14′·08N 09°34′·35W, 992501173.
Lion Pt Dir lt 010°, Iso WRG 5s 6m (H24), G6M, W8M, R6M,(night), G2M, W3M, R2M(day); vis: 005°-G- 008·5°-W-011·5°-R-015°; 53°15′·83N 09°33′·98W; 992501171.
Rossaveel Pier Ldg lts 116°. Front, 53°16′·02N 09°33′·38W Oc 3s 7m 3M; W mast. Rear, 90m from front, Oc 3s 8m 3M.
Kiggaul Bay ☆ Fl WRG 3s 5m W5M, R3M, G3M; vis: 310°-G-329°-W-349°-R-059°; 53°14′·03N 09°43′·02W.
Croaghnakeela Is ☆ Fl 3·7s 7m 5M; W col; vis: 034°-045°, 218°-286°, 311°-325°; 53°19′·40N 09°58′·21W.
Inishnee ☆ Fl (2) WRG 10s 9m W5M, R3M, G3M; W col on W □ base; vis: 314°-G-017°-W-030°-R-080°-W-194°; 53°22′·75N 09°54′·53W.
Slyne Head, North twr, Illaunamid ☆ 53°23′·99N 10°14′·05W Fl (2) 15s 35m **19M**; B twr; ***Racon (T)***; 992501175.

SLYNE HEAD TO EAGLE ISLAND

CLIFDEN BAY and INISHBOFIN

Carrickrana Rocks Bn, large W Bn; 53°29′·24N 10°09′·48W.
Cleggan Point ☆ Fl (3) WRG 15s 20m W6M, R3M, G3M; W col on W hut; vis: shore-G-091°-W-124°-R-221°; 53°34′·48N 10°07′·69W.
Inishlyon Lyon Head ☆ Fl WR 7·5s 13m W7M, R4M; W post; vis: 036°-W-058°-R-184°-W-325°-R-036°; 53°36′·74N 10°09′·56W.
Gun Rk ☆ Fl (2)6s 8m 4M; W col on W hut; vis: 296°-253°; 53°36′·59N 10°13′·22W.
Inishbofin Dir lt 021°, Oc WRG 6s 10m 11M; W pole; vis: 015·75°-G-020·75°-W-021·25°-R-026·25°; 53°36′·78N 10°13′·16W.

CLEW BAY and WESTPORT

Roonagh Quay Ldg lts 144°. Front 53°45′·75N 09°54′·23W. Rear, 54m from front, both Iso Bu 10s 9/15m.
Inishgort ☆ L Fl 10s 10M; 53°49.59′N 009°40.25′W; 992501179.
Cloughcormick Q (9) 15s; 53°50′·56N 09°43′·20W.
Achillbeg I, S Point ☆ 53°51′·51N 09°56′·84W Fl WR 5s 56m **W16M**, **R18M**, R11M; W ○ twr on □ building; vis: 262°-R-281°-W-342°-R-060°-W-092°-R(intens)-099°-W-118°; 992501181.

ACHILL SOUND

Ldg lts 330°, 53°52′·50N 09°56′·89W Whitestone Point. Front and rear both 2 Oc Bu 4s 5/6m; W ◊, B stripe.
Achill I Ldg lts 310°, Purteen, 53°57′·81N 10°05′·96W, Iso Bu 6s 5m. Rear, 46m from front Iso Bu 6s 6m.

BLACKSOD BAY

Blacksod Q (3) 10s; 54°05′·89N 10°03′·01W.
Blacksod Pier Root ☆ Fl (2) WR 7·5s 13m W12M, R9M; W twr on bldg; vis: 189°-R-210°-W-018°; 54°05′·92N 10°03′·63W; 992501186.
Carrigeenmore VQ(3) 5s 3M; 54°06′·56N 10°03′·4W.
Black Rock ☆ 54°04′·06N 10°19′·23W Fl WR 12s 86m **W20M, R16M**; W twr; vis: 276°-W-212°-R-276°; 992501183.
Eagle Is, W end ☆ 54°17′·02N 10°05′·56W Fl (3) 15s 67m **18M**; W twr; 992501189.

EAGLE ISLAND TO RATHLIN O'BIRNE

BROAD HAVEN BAY

Rinroe Pt ☆ Fl (2) 10s 5m 3M; 54°17′·83N 09°50′·59W.
Gubacashel Point ☆ Iso WR 4s 27m **W17M**, R12M; 110°-R-133°-W-355°-R-021° W twr; 54°16′·06N 09°53′·32W; 992501190.

KILLALA

Carrickpatrick Q (3) 10s; 54°15′·56N 09°09′·17W; 992501192.
Inishcrone Pier Root ☆ Fl WRG 1·5s 8m 2M; vis: 098°-W-116°-G-136°-R-187°; 54°13′·21N 09°05′·79W.
Ldg lts 230°. Rinnaun Point. Front No 1, Oc 10s 7m 5M; □ twr; 54°13′·21N 09°05′·79W. Rear, 150m from front, No 2 Oc 10s 12m 5M; □ twr.
Inch Is Dir lt 215°, Fl WRG 2s 6m 3M; □ twr; vis: 205°-G-213°-W-217°-R-225°; 54°13′·29N 09°12′·30W.
Ldg lts 196°. Kilroe. Front, 54°12′·63N 09°12′·33W Oc 4s 5m 2M; □ twr. Rear,120m from front, Oc 4s 10m 2M; □ twr.
Pier Ldg lts 236° Front, Iso Bu 2s 5m 2M; W ◊ on twr; 54°13′·02N 09°12′·84W. Rear, 200m fm front, Iso Bu 2s 7m 2M; W ◊ on pole.

SLIGO

Black Rock ☆ Fl WR 5s 24m 10/8M; vis: 130°-W-107°-R-130° (R over Wheat + Seal Rks); W twr, B band; 54°18′·46N 08°37′·06W.
Lower Rosses ☆ Fl (2) WRG 10s 8m 10M; W hut on piles; vis: 061°-G-066°-W-070°-R-075°; shown H24; 54°19′·73N 08°34′·41W.
Ldg lts 125° Fl (3) 6s 7M (sync). Front, Metal Man; 54°18′·24N 08°34′·55W, 3m. Rear, Oyster Is, 365m from front, 13m; H24.
Wheat Rk Q (6) + LFl 15s; 54°18′·84N 08°39′·10W; 992501196.

DONEGAL BAY and KILLYBEGS

St John's Pt ☆ Fl 6s 30m 14M; W twr; 54°34′·16N 08°27′·66W; 992501197.
Bullockmore Q (9) 15s; 54°33′·98N 08°30′·14W; 992501198.
Rotten I ☆ 54°36′·97N 08°26′·41W Fl WR 4s 20m **W15M**, R11M; W twr; vis: W255°- R008°- W039°-208°.
New Landing Dir lt 338°, Oc WRG 8s 17m; vis: 328°-G-334°-Al WG-336°-W-340°-Al WR-342°-R-348°; 54°38′·14N 08°26′·38W.
Killybegs Outer VQ (6) + L Fl 10s; 54°37′·92N 08°29′·15W.

RATHLIN O'BIRNE TO BLOODY FORELAND

S of ARAN and RUTLAND S CHANNEL

Rathlin O'Birne ☆ Fl WR 15s 35m W12M, R10M**;** W twr; vis: 195°-R-307°-W-195°; ***Racon (O) 13M***, vis 284°-203°. 54°39′·82N 08°49′·95W; 992501203.
Dawros Head ☆ L Fl 10s 39m 4M; 54°49′·63N 08°33′·64W.
Wyon Point ☆ Fl (2) WRG 10s 8m W6M, R3M; W □ twr; vis: shore-G-021°-W-042°-R-121°-W-150°-R-shore; 54°56′·51N 08°27′·54W.

BURTONPORT
Ldg lts 068·1°. Front , FG 17m 1M; Gy Bn, W band; 54°58′·95N 08°26′·40W. Rear, 355m from front, FG 23m 1M; Gy Bn, Y band.

N SOUND OF ARAN and RUTLAND N CHANNEL
Rutland I Ldg lts 137·6°. Front, 54°58′·97N 08°27′·68W Oc 6s 8m 1M; W Bn, B band. Rear, 330m from front, Oc 6s 14m 1M.
Inishcoo Ldg lts 119·3°. Front, Iso 6s 6m 1M; W Bn, B band; 54°59′·43N 08°29′·63W. Rear, 248m from front, Iso 6s 11m 1M.
Ldg lts 186°. Front, Oc 8s 8m 3M; B Bn, W band; 54°58′·94N 08°29′·27W. Rear, 395m from front, Oc 8s 17m 3M; B Bn.
Aranmore, Rinrawros Pt ☆ 55°00′·90N 08°33′·69W Fl (2) 20s 71m **18M**; W twr; obsc by land about 234°-007° and about 013°. Aux lt Fl R 3s 61m 13M, same twr; vis: 203°-234°; 992501205.

OWEY SOUND to INISHSIRRER
Cruit Is. Owey Sound Ldg lts 068·3°. Oc 10s. Front, 55°03′·06N 08°25′·85W. Rear, 107m from front.
Rinnalea Point 55°02′·59N 08°23′·72W Fl 7·5s 19m 9M; □ twr; vis: 132°-167°.
Gola Is Ldg lts 171·2°. Oc 3s 2M (sync). Front, 9m; W Bn, B band; 55°05′·11N 08°21′·07W. Rear, 86m fm front, 13m; B Bn, W band.
Glassagh. Ldg lts 137·4°. Front, Oc 8s 12m 3M; 55°06′·83N 08°18′·97W. Rear, 46m from front, Oc 8s 17m 3M; synch.
Inishsirrer, NW end Fl 3·7s 20m 4M; W □ twr vis: 083°-263°; 55°07′·40N 08°20′·93W.

BLOODY FORELAND TO INISHTRAHULL

BLOODY FORELAND to SHEEPHAVEN
Bloody Foreland Fl WG 7·5s 14m W6M, G4M; vis: 062°-W-232°-G-062°; 55°09′·51N 08°17′·03W.
Tory Island ☆ 55°16′·36N 08°14′·96W Fl (4) 30s 40m **18M**; B twr, W band; vis: 302°-277°; ***Racon (M) 12-23M***; 992501211.
West Town Ldg lts 001° Iso 2s 9m 7M △ on Y structure R stripe; 55°15′·79N 08°13′·50W. Rear Iso 2s 11m 7M ▽ ditto (sync).
Inishbofin Pier Fl 8s 3m 3M; 55°10′·14N 08°10′·01W.
Ballyness Hbr. Ldg lts 119·5°. Front, Iso 4s 25m 1M; 55°09′·06N 08°06′·98W. Rear, 61m from front, Iso 4s 26m 1M.
Portnablahy Ldg lts 125·3°. Front Oc 6s 7m 2M; B col, W bands; 55°10′·79N 07°55′·65W. Rear, 81m from front, Oc 6s 12m 2M; B col, W bands.

MULROY BAY
Limeburner Q Fl; 55°18′·54N 07°48′·40W; 992501214.
Ravedy Is Fl 3s 9m 3M; vis 177°-357°; 55°15′·14N 07°46′·90W.

LOUGH SWILLY, BUNCRANA and RATHMULLAN
Fanad Head ☆ 55°16′·57N 07°37′·92W Fl (5) WR 20s 39m **W18M**, R14M; W twr; vis 100°-R-110°-W-313°-R-345°-W-100°; 992501215.
Swillymore Fl G 3s; 55°15′·12N 07°35′·79W; 992501216.
Dunree Fl (2) WR 5s 49m W12M, R9M; vis: 320°-R-328°-W-183°-R-196°; 55°11′·89N 07°33′·24W; 992501217.
Buncrana Pier near Hd Iso WR 4s 11m W13M, R10M; R twr, W band; vis: R shore- over Inch spit, 052°-W-139°-R-shore over White Strand Rock; 55°07′·60N 07°27′·88W.
Rathmullan Pier Fl G 3s 5M; vis: 206°-345°; 55°05′·70N 07°31′·66W.
Inishtrahull ☆ 55°25′·89N 07°14′·63W Fl (3) 15s 59m **19M**; W twr; obscd 256°-261° within 3M; ***Racon (T) 24M 060°-310°***. Fog Det Lt VQ; 992501229.

INISHTRAHULL TO RATHLIN ISLAND

LOUGH FOYLE
Foyle L Fl 10s; 55°15′·32N 06°52′·62W; ***Racon (M)***; 992501230.
Tuns Fl R 3s; 55°14′·00N 06°53′·46W; 992501232.
Inishowen Dunagree ☆ 55°13′·60N 06°55′·70W Fl (2) WRG 10s 28m **W18M**, R14M, G14M; W twr, 2 B bands; vis: 197°-G-211°-W-249°-R-000°. Fog Det lt VQ 16m vis: 270°.
Greencastle S Bkwtr Dir lt 042·5° Fl (2) WRG 3s 4m W11M, R9M, G9M; vis 307°-G- 040°-W-045°-R-055°; 55°12′·17N 06°59′·13W.
McKinney's Fl R 5s; 55°10′·9N 07°00′·5W.
Moville Fl WR 2·5s 11m 4M; W house on G piles vis: 240°-W-064°-R-240°; 55°10′·99N 07°02′·12W.

RIVER BANN, COLERAINE and PORTRUSH
River Bann Ldg lts 165°. Front, Oc 5s 6m 2M; W twr; 55°09′·96N 06°46′·23W. Rear, 245m from front, Oc 5s 14m 2M; W □ twr.
W Mole Fl G 5s 4m 2M; vis: 170°-000°; 55°10′·25N 06°46′·45W.
Portstewart Point Oc R 10s 21m 5M; R □ hut; vis: 040°-220°; 55°11′·33N 06°43′·26W.
N Pier Hd Fl R 3s 6m 3M; vis: 220°-160°; 55°12′·34N 06°39′·58W.
Skerries Fl R 5s; 53°13′·90N 06°36′·90W; 992351096.

RATHLIN ISLAND
Rathlin W ☆ (½M NE of Bull Pt) 55°18′·05N 06°16′·82W; Fl R 5s 62m **18M**; W twr, lantern at base; vis: 015°-225°; H24. Fog Det Lt VQ; 992351000.
Drake Wreck 55°17′·00N 06°12′·48W Q (6) + L Fl 15s.
Manor House Oc WRG 4s 5M; vis: 020°-G-023°-W-026°-R-029°; 55°17′·52N 06°11′·73W.
Rue Pt Fl(2) 5s 16m 14M; W twr B bands; 55°15′·52N 06°11′·46W; 992351131.
Altacarry Head ☆ 55°18′·11N 06°10′·31W Fl (4) 20s 74m **18M**; W twr, B band; vis: 110°-006° and 036°-058°; ***Racon (G) 15-27M***; 992320707.

FAIR HEAD TO LAMBAY ISLAND

RED BAY, CARNLOUGH and LARNE
Red Bay Pier Fl 3s 10m 5M; 55°03′·93N 06°03′·19W.
Carnlough Hbr N Pier Fl G 3s 4m 5M; 54°59′·59N 05°59′·29W.
East Maiden ☆ Fl (3) 15s 32m **18M**; ***Racon (M) 11-21M;*** W twr, B band; 54°55′·74N 05°43′·65W. Aux lt Fl R 5s 15m 8M; same twr vis:142°-182° over Russel and Highland Rks, H24; 992351110.
N Hunter Rock Q; 54°53′·04N 05°45′·13W.
S Hunter Rock VQ(6) + LFl 10s; 54°52′·69N 05°45′·22W; 992351007.
Larne No 1 QG; 54°51′·68N 05°47′·67W; *AIS*.
Chaine Twr ☆ Iso WR 5s 23m **W16M,** R12M; Gy twr; vis: 232°-W-240°-R-000° (shore); 54°51′·27N 05°47′·90W.
Larne Ldg lts 184°, No 11 Front, 54°49′·60N 05°47′·81W Oc 4s 6m 12M; W 2 with R stripe on R pile structure; vis: 179°-189°. No 12 Rear, 610m from front, Oc 4s 14m 12M; W 2 with R stripe on R □ twr; synch with front, vis: 5° either side of Ldg line.

CARRICKFERGUS
Black Hd ☆ 54°46′·02N 05°41′·34W Fl 3s 45m **27M**; W 8-sided twr; 992351002.
Marina Ent Appr Dir Oc WRG 3s 5m 3M; vis: G308°- W317·5°-R322·5°-332°; 54°42′·58N 05°48′·78W.

BELFAST LOUGH and BANGOR
Mew Is ☆ NE end 54°41′·92N 05°30′·82W F Fl (4) 30s 35m **18M**; B twr, W band; ***Racon (O) 14M***; 992351109.
Belfast Fairway Iso 4s; 54°42′·32N 05°42′·30W; ***Racon (G)***; *AIS*.
Kilroot Fl QG (sync); 54°42′·85N 05°42′·85W.
Helen's Bay QR (sync); 54°41′·86N 05°42′·85W.
No 1 Fl G 2s (sync); 54°41′·67N 05°46′·51W.
No 2 Fl R 2s (sync); 54°41′·55N 05°46′·43W.
Briggs Q; 54°41′·18N 05°53′·73W; 992351133.

DONAGHADEE
Merandoragh Fl (2) G 6s (sync); 54°39′·84N 05°32′·24W.
Foreland Spit Fl (2) R 6s (sync); 54°39′·64N 05°32′·31W.
Governor's Fl G 3s (sync); 54°39′·36N 05°31′·99W; 992351134.
Riggs Bank ⊙ V–AIS PHM; 54°38′·63N 05°27′·10W; 992356011.
Donaghadee ☆, S Pier Hd 54°38′·70N 05°31′·86W Iso WR 4s 17m **W16M**, R10M; twr; vis: shore-W-326°-R-shore; 002320792.

BALLYWATER and PORTAVOGIE

Ballywater, Bkwtr Hd Fl WRG 3s 4m 9M; vis: 240°-G-267°-W-277°-R-314°; 54°32'·68N 05°28'·83W.

Skulmartin Fl (2) R 6s 10s; 54°32'·39N 05°24'·91W; 992351022.
Portavogie Bkwtr Hd Iso WRG 5s 6m WRG 5M; □ twr; vis: shore-G-262°-W-272°-R-350°; 54°27'·44N 05°26'·14W.
Plough Rock 54°27'·40N 05°25'·12W Fl R 3s.
South Rock Fl (3) R 30s 9M 54°24'·48N 05°21'·99W; ***Racon (T)***; 992351004.

STRANGFORD LOUGH

Strangford L Fl 10s; 54°18'·63N 05°28'·69W; 992351028.
Butter Pladdy Q (3) 10s; 54°22'·45N 05°25'·74W.

Bar Q (6) + L Fl 15s; 54°19'·34N 05°30'·51W; 992351135.
Dogtail Pt Ldg lts 341°. Front, Iso 4s 2m 5M; G Bn; 54°20'·79N 05°31'·84W. Rear, Gowlands Rk, 0·8M fm front, Iso 4s 6m 5M; W twr, G top, B base.

Swan Is Q (3) 5m; BYB brick twr; 54°22'·38N 05°33'·16W.
Strangford East Ldg lts 256°. Front, Oc WRG 5s 6m W9M, R6M, G6M: vis: 190°-R-244°-G-252°-W- 260°-R-294°; 54°22'·29N 05°33'·27W. Rear, 46m from front, Oc R 5s 10m 6M; vis: 250°-264°.
Portaferry Pier Hd Oc WR 10s 9m W9M, R6M; Or mast; vis: W335°-R005°-W017°-128°; 54°22'·82N 05°33'·03W.

ARDGLASS

Inner Pier Hd Iso WRG 4s 10m W8M, R7M, G5M; twr; vis: shore-G-308°-W-314°-R-shore; 54°15'·79N 05°36'·33W.

DUNDRUM BAY

St John's Point ☆ 54°13'·61N 05°39'·61W Q (2) 7·5s 37m **25M**; B twr, Y bands. **Auxiliary Light** ☆ Fl WR 3s 14m **W15M**, R11M; same twr, vis: 064°-W-078°-R-shore; Fog Det lt VQ 14m vis: 270°; 992351005.

DZ East Fl (2) Y 10s; 54°12'·05N 05°45'·30W.
DZ West Fl Y 5s; 54°11'·84N 05°50'·82W.

ANNALONG

E Bkwtr Hd Oc WRG 5s 8m 9M; twr; vis: 204°-G-249°-W-309°-R-024°; 54°06'·51N 05°53'·73W.

KILKEEL

Pier Hd Fl WR 2s 8m 8M; vis: R296°-W313°-017°; 54°03'·46N 05°59'·30W; 992356010 (emergency AIS 992356008).

CARLINGFORD LOUGH and NEWRY RIVER

Hellyhunter Q(6) + LFl 15s; 54°00'·35N 06°02'·10W; 992351009.
Haulbowline 54°01'·19N 06°04'·74W Fl (3) 10s 32m 10M; Grey twr; 992501235.

Ldg lts 310·4° Front, Oc 3s 7m 11M; R △ on twr; vis: 295°-325°; 54°01'·80N 06°05'·43W; 992501237. Rear, 457m from front, Oc 3s 12m 11M; R ▽ on twr; vis: 295°-325°; both H24.
Newry River Ldg lts 310·4°. Front, 54°06'·37N 06°16'·51W. Rear, 274m from front. Both Iso 4s 5/15m 2M; stone cols.

DUNDALK

Imogene Fl (2) R 10s; 53°57'·41N 06°07'·02W; 992501238.
Pile Light 53°58'·56N 06°17'·71W Fl WR 15s 10m 10M; W Ho.
Dunany Fl R 3s; 53°53'·56N 06°09'·47W; 992501243.

SKERRIES BAY

Cardy Rks Q(3) 10s; 53°37'·91N 06°10'·86W.
Skerries Pier Hd Oc R 6s 7m 7M; W col; vis: 103°-R-154°; 53°35'·09N 06°06'·49W.

DROGHEDA to LAMBAY ISLAND

Drogheda Dir lt WRG 10m **W19M, R15M, G15M**; vis: 268°-FG-269°-Al WG-269·5°-FW-270·5°-Al WR-271°-FR-272°; 53°43'·30N 06°14'·73W.
Balbriggan Fl (3) WRG 10s 12m W13M, R10M, G10M; W twr; vis: 159°-G-193°-W-288°-R-305°; 53°36'·76N 06°10'·80W.

Rockabill ☆ 53°35'·81N 06°00'·30W Fl WR 12s 45m **W17M, R13M;** W twr, B band; vis: 178°-W-329°-R-178°; 992501246.
Skerries Bay Pier Hd Oc R 6s 7m 7M; W col; vis: 103°-154°; 53°35'·09N 06°06'·49W.

6.4 PASSAGE INFORMATION

Admiralty Leisure Folio 5612 covers Carlingford to L Foyle. The latest Irish Cruising Club Sailing Directions are recommended for all Irish waters (www.irishcruisingclub.com), particularly on the N and W coasts where other information is scarce. They are published in two volumes, *E and N coasts of Ireland* and *S and W coasts of Ireland*. (Available from Imray or Todd Chart Services, Bangor, Co Down, ☎028 9146 6640 (www.toddchart.com).)

CROSSING THE IRISH SEA

(AC 1123, 1121, 1411) Passages across the Irish Sea range from the fairly long haul from Land's End to Cork (140M), to the relatively short hop from Mull of Kintyre to Torr Pt (11M). Such distances are deceptive, because the average cruising yacht needs to depart from and arrive at a reasonably secure hbr. See 0.32 for distances across the Irish Sea. Submarine exercise areas are at 2.15.

► *Tidal flow in North Channel may cause heavy overfalls.* ◄

Many yachts use the Land's End/Cork route on their way to and from the delightful cruising ground along the S coast of Ireland. Penzance Bay or one of the Scilly Islands' ⚓s are convenient departure points, with good lights. Although the Celtic Sea is exposed to the Atlantic, there are no dangers on passage and the tidal streams are weak.

Landfall between Ballycotton and Old Hd of Kinsale (both have good lights) presents no offlying dangers, and in poor vis decreasing soundings indicate approach to land. Outward bound under sail, it is likely that the boat will be on the wind – a possible benefit on the return passage. If the wind serves, and if it is intended to cruise along the southern coast, a landfall at the Fastnet with arrival at (say) Baltimore will place the yacht more to windward, for a little extra distance (170M). From Land's End another likely destination is Dun Laoghaire. A stop at Milford Haven enables the skipper to select the best time for passing the Smalls or Bishops (see 4.4) and roughly divides the total passage into two equal parts of about 100M. From S Bishop onwards there are the options of making the short crossing to Tuskar Rk and going N inside the banks (theoretically a good idea in strong W winds) or of keeping to seaward.

► *In bad weather the area off Tuskar is best avoided; the tide is strong at Sp and the sea can be very rough.* ◄

Holyhead/Dun Laoghaire is another typical crossing (56M) and with relatively straightforward landfalls either end. Beware the TSS off The Skerries and Kish Bank wind farm.

►*The tide runs hard round Anglesey at Sp, so departure just before slack water minimises the set N or S.*◄

Harbours on the Isle of Man provide convenient staging points for cruising in the Irish Sea, wherever bound.

CROSSING TO/FROM SCOTLAND

(AC 2198, 2199, 2724) Between Scotland and Ireland there are several routes, but much depends on weather and tide. Time of departure must take full advantage of the stream, and avoid tide races and overfalls (see 2.4). Conditions can change quickly, so a flexible plan is needed. The distance to Mull of Kintyre from Belfast Lough entrance is about 35M.

▶ *Departure at local HW (also HW Dover) provides at least 6hrs of N-going tidal stream, and fair winds allow passage past the Mull or Sanda Is on one tide. To be sure of reaching Gigha or Port Ellen, a departure from Glenarm Marina or Red Bay at HW makes a shorter passage with better stream. The inshore side of the TSS bounds the race SSW of the Mull of Kintyre; this runs from HW Dover +0430 until +0610 when a local S-going stream opposes the main N-going stream.* ◀

LISCANNOR BAY TO SLYNE HEAD

(AC 2173) The coast NE of Liscannor Bay is devoid of shelter. O'Brien's Tower conspic is just N of the Cliffs of Moher (199m). Eastward from Black Hd there are many bays and inlets, often poorly marked, but providing shelter and exploration.

Galway is a commercial port, with a small marina. 3M SE, New Harbour (AC 1984) is a pleasant ⚓ with ▲ off Galway Bay SC. Usual approach to Galway Bay is through South or North Snd. South Snd is 3M wide, with no dangers except Finnis Rk (0·4m). North Snd is 4M from Eagle Rk / dangers offlying Lettermullan, to banks on S side where seas break in strong winds. Other channels are Gregory Sound (1M wide) between Inishmore and Inishmaan, and Foul Sound between Inishmaan and Inisheer. The latter has Pipe Rock and the reef inshore of it, extending 3ca NW of Inisheer. Inishmore, disused Lt ho (conspic) has the only feasible harbour in the Aran Islands, at Kilronan (Killeany Bay) but this is exposed to E winds. The N side of Galway Bay is exposed, as far W as Rossaveel.

In good visibility the Connemara coast (AC 2709, 2096) and Aran Islands (AC 3339) give excellent cruising. There are few navigational marks, many rks and offlying dangers. A tower (24m, conspic) on Golam Hd is prominent. Going W better harbours are Cashla, Greatman, Killeany, Cashel and Roundstone Bays. Keep well seaward of Skerd Rks.

SLYNE HEAD TO EAGLE ISLAND

(AC 2420) This coast has many inlets, some sheltered, but few lights and marks. Refuelling opportunities are few. Slyne Hd Lt ho marks rocks and islets extending 2M WSW from coast.

▶ *Here the stream turns N at HW Galway –0320, and S at HW Galway +0300. It runs 3kn at Sp and in bad weather causes a dangerous race; keep 2M offshore.* ◀

Seas break on Barret Shoals, 3M NW of Slyne Hd. Cleggan B is a passage ⚓ open to NW. High Is Sound is usual route, not Friar Is Sound or Aughrus Passage. Clifden Bay (AC 2708) has offlying dangers with breakers; enter 3ca S of Carrickrana Bn and ⚓ off Drinagh Pt, in Clifden Hbr or Ardbear Bay.

Ballynakill Hbr (AC 2706), entered either side of Freaghillaun South, has excellent shelter; Tully mountain is conspic to N. Beware Mullaghadrina and Ship Rk in N chan. ⚓ in Fahy, Derryinver or Barnaderg Bays. There is ⚓ on S side of Inishbofin (lit), but difficult access in strong SW wind or swell. Rocks and breakers lie E of Inishbofin and S of Inishshark; see AC 2707 for clearing lines. Lecky Rks lie 1M SSE of Davillaun.

Carrickmahoy is a very dangerous rock (1·9m) between Inishbofin and Cleggan Pt. Killary (AC 2706) and Little Killary Bays both have good ⚓s in magnificent scenery. Consult ICC SDs, and only enter in fine weather and good visibility.

Caher, Ballybeg, Inishturk (⚓ on E side) and Inishdalla islands have few hidden dangers. Keep 1·5M off mailand coast in calm weather; in strong winds seas break much further off. Beware Meemore Shoal 1·5M W of Roonagh Hd. 2M further W is the isolated rock Mweelaun. Two Fathom Rk (3·4m) lies 5ca NW of Clare Is, and Calliaghcrom Rk 5ca to the N; a passage ⚓ is to the NE side of the island.

Clew Bay Newport and Westport (AC 2667, 2057) need detailed pilotage directions. Achill Sound (ACs 2667/2704) is entered close N of Achillbeg Is and extends N for about 8M to Bull's Mouth. Passage is possible at HW for shallow draught craft (<2m) via a swing bridge, which is rarely opened. ⚓ at either end of Sound, but the stream runs strongly. Rough water is likely off Achill Hd (highest cliffs in the British Isles).

Blacksod B (AC 2704) is accessible H24 and good shelter. In the appr Black Rk (lit) has rocks up to 1·25M SW. From N, in good weather, a chan runs between Duvillaun Beg and Gaghta Is, but in W gales beware breakers 1M SE of Duvillaun More.

Keep 5ca off Erris Hd; further in bad weather. Unless calm, keep seaward of Eagle Is (lit) where there is a race to the N. Frenchport (AC 2703) is good temp ⚓ except in strong W'lies. Inishkea Is (AC 2704) can be visited in good weather; ⚓ N or S of Rusheen Is, otherwise keep clear 5ca W to avoid overfalls if wind against tide. Avoid Pluddany Rk (6ca E of Inishkea N) when transitting Snd off Mullett Peninsula.

EAGLE ISLAND TO BLOODY FORELAND

Broad Haven (AC 2703) is good ⚓ and refuge, but in N/NW gales sea can break in ent. In approach beware Slugga Rk with offlier on E side, and Monastery Rk (0·3m) on S side.

The coast E of Broad Haven is inhospitable. Only Portacloy and Belderg give some shelter. The Stags, 1M N of Buddagh, are steep-to and high. Killala B has temp'y ⚓ 1M S of Kilcummin Hd, to the W side. Beware St Patrick's Rks off Killala. The ent is well marked, but the bar is dangerous in strong NE'lies. Keep well clear of coast N from Sligo in onshore winds, and beware of lobster pots. Inishmurray is worth a visit in good weather, ⚓ off S side. There are shoals close E and NE of the Is, and Bomore Rks 1·5M to N.

In Donegal Bay (AC 2702) ⚓ off Mullaghmore or pick up YC ● in fair weather with winds from SE through S to NW. Donegal Hbr is an estuary with (AC 2715) with fair access, but Killybegs has better shelter and is always accessible. Beware uncharted rocks W of Teelin, a natural hbr exposed to S/SW.

Rathlin O'Birne Is has steps E side; ⚓ SE of them 100m offshore. Sound is 5ca wide; hold Is side to clear rks off Malin Beg Hd. On S side of Glen Bay ⚓ (but not in W or NW winds) just E of Rinmeasa Pt. Boylagh B has shoals and rocks N of Roaninish Is. Connell Rk (0·3m) is 1M N of Church Pool, a good ⚓, best approached from Dawros Hd 4·5M to the West. Behind Aran Is are several good ⚓s. Use N entrance, since S one is shallow (AC 2792). Rutland N Chan is main appr to Burtonport.

NE of Aran Is (AC 1883) an inshore passage avoids offlying dangers on which seas can break: Stag Rks 2M NNW of Owey Is and Bullogconnell 1M NW of Gola Is. ⚓s include Bunbeg, Gweedore Hbr, and Cruit Bay which has easier access. Bunaninver and Brinlack shoals, lie NE of Inishsirrer. Off low-lying Bloody Foreland there is often heavy swell.

BLOODY FORELAND TO FAIR HEAD

(AC 2723, 5612) This is a good cruising area, under the lee of land in SW'lies, but very exposed to NW or N. Beware fishing boats and nets in many places and the North Channel TSS.

(AC 2752) Between Bloody Foreland and Horn Hd are three low-lying islands: Inishbofin, Inishdooey and Inishbeg. The first is joined to the shore by a sand strand with a temp'y ⚓ on S side. A more sheltered ⚓ on NE side is in Toberglassan Bay. 6M offshore is Tory Is (Fl 4 30s) with rocks 5ca off SW side. Hbr in Camusmore Bay provides the best shelter on this coast.

▶ *In Tory Sound the stream runs W from HW Galway +0230, and E from HW Galway –0530, Sp rates 2kn.* ◀

Enter Sheep Haven between Horn Hd and Rinnafaghla Pt; good ⚓ except in strong NW or N winds; there is a ● in Downies Bay. Beware Wherryman Rks, dry 1·5m, 1ca off E shore. An inshore passage between Guill Rks and Carnabollion S of Frenchman's Rk leads from Sheep Haven to Mulroy Bay in good weather, otherwise keep 1M offshore. Mulroy Bay has good ⚓ but needs accurate pilotage (see ICC SDs). E to Lough Swilly the coast is very foul. Beware Limeburner Rk (2m), 6·8M WNW of Fanad Hd.

Entrance to L Swilly is clear except for Swilly Rks off the West shore, SSE of Fanad Hd. From Dunaff Hd keep 5ca offshore to Malin Hd (**buoyage changes**). Trawbreaga Lough (AC 2697) gives shelter, but is shallow, and seas break on bar; only appr when there is no swell, at half flood.

Garvan Is, Tor Rks and Inishtrahull lie E/NE of Malin Hd. Garvan Sound can be used safely in daylight avoiding two sunken rks, one 1½ca NE of Rossnabarton, the other 5ca NW. Inishtrahull is lit, about 1M long; Blind Rks extend 3ca N into Tor Sound. In bad weather pass at least 3M N of Tor Rks.

▶ *W of Malin Hd W-going eddy starts at HW Galway +0400, and E-going one at HW Galway –0300. Inishtrahull Snd, between Inishtrahull and Garvan Is, is exposed; tidal streams up to 4kn Sp can raise a dangerous sea with no warning. Stream also sets hard through Garvan Isles. The main stream runs W for only 3hrs, from HW Galway –0500 to –0200.*◀

Enter Lough Foyle by either the North Chan W of The Tuns, or S chan passing 2ca N of Magilligan Pt allowing for set towards The Tuns on the ebb (up to 3·5kn). Proceeding to Portrush, use Skerries Sound in good weather. Beware the Storks to the E, which dry, marked by a NCM. Pass outside Carrickmannanon Rk (0·3m) and Sheep Is. Small hbrs lie at Church Bay (Rathlin Is) and Ballycastle.

▶ *A fair tide is essential through Rathlin Sound, as Sp rates reach 6kn, with dangerous overfalls. The main stream sets W from HW Dover +0030 for 5hrs, and E from HW Dover –0530 for 5hrs. The worst overfalls are S of Rue Pt (Slough-na-more) from HW Dover +0130 to +0230, and it is best to enter W-bound at the end of this period, on the last of fair tide. E-bound enter the Sound at HW Dover –0500. Close inshore between Fair Hd and Carrick-mannanon Rk a counter eddy runs W from HW Dover –0030, and an E-going eddy runs from HW Dover +0200 to +0300.* ◀

FAIR HEAD TO LAMBAY ISLAND

(AC 2199/8, 2093, 44) Fair Hd is a bold 190m headland, steep-to all round, but with extensive overfalls in Rathlin Sound. The coast is steep-to except in larger bays, particularly Dundalk.

▶*Streams in North Channel reach more than 4½kn. S of Belfast L they are weaker, running up to 2·5kn S of Rockabill.*◀

⚓ in offshore winds in Cushendun Bay, 5M NNW of Garron Pt, and in Red Bay 4M further S. They provide respite on passage to/from the Clyde or Western Is. Glenarm Marina provides good shelter for small craft and is useful for on passage to the W coasts of Scotland or Ireland.

(AC 2198) 4M N of Larne are the Maidens, two dangerous groups of rks extending 2·5M N/S; E Maiden is lit. Hunter Rk (0·8m), S of the Maidens, is marked by N/S cardinals. North of Belfast, Muck Island is steep-to on its E side, as is Black Hd.

Three routes lead into Belfast Lough from the south:

a. E of Mew Is.

▶*Beware Ram Race (N'thly on ebb and S'thly on flood).*◀

b. Copeland Sound, between Mew Is and Copeland Is, is passable but not recommended.

▶*Here the stream runs SSE from HW Belfast +0420 and NW from HW Belfast –0115.*◀

c. Donaghadee Sound is buoyed and a good short cut for small craft (see AC 3709).

▶*Here the stream runs SSE from HW Belfast +0530 and NW from HW Belfast –0030, 4·5kn max. An eddy extends S to Ballyferris Pt, and about 1M offshore.*◀

Numerous rocky dangers lie close inshore between Belfast Lough and Strangford Lough, but is reasonably clear keeping 2M offshore. In fair weather and good vis, there is a passage between North Rocks and South Rock, otherwise pass to the E using South Rock superbuoy as a guide. Pass E of Butter Pladdy and 5ca off Ballyquintin Point.

▶*The tidal cycle is approx 3hrs later than in the N Channel. Flood runs for 6hrs from HW Belfast –0330 (HW Dover –0345), with a maximum rate of 7.5kn at Rue Point. The strong flow flattens the sea in onshore winds and entrance can be made in strong winds. The ebb runs for 6hrs from HW Belfast +0230 (HW Dover +0215), max rate 7.5kn, E of Angus Rk. If entering against ebb use West Channel with care. Smoothest water near Bar Pladdy Buoy when leaving.*◀

Ardglass marina is 5M SSW of the ent to Strangford Lough.

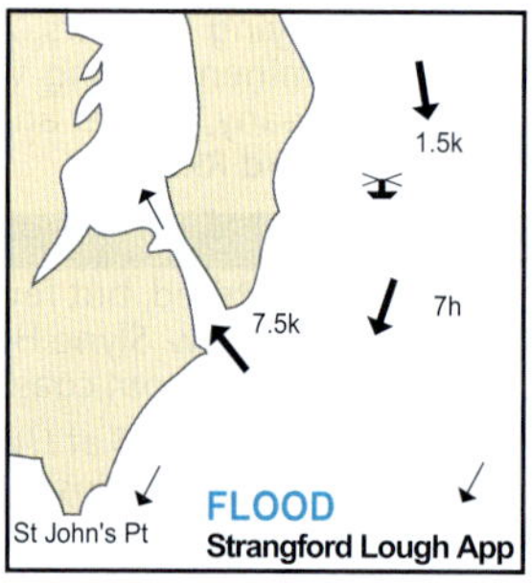

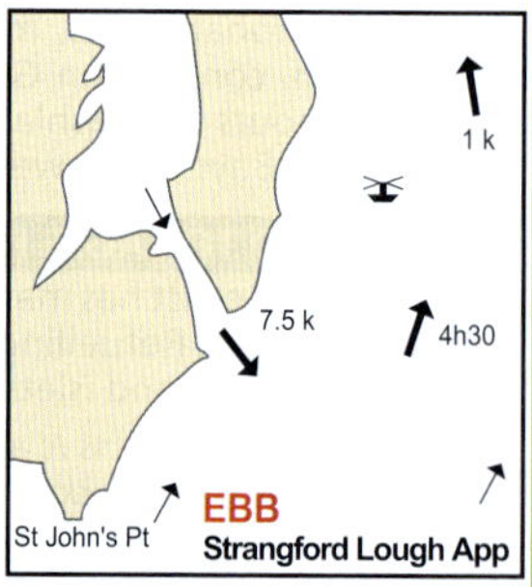

There are no offshore dangers SW to Carlingford Lough. Skerries Islands (Colt, Shenick's and St Patrick's) are 1M E and SE of Red Island, to E of Skerries hbr. Shenick's Island is connected to shore at LW. Pass between Colt and St Patrick's Islands, but the latter has offliers 3ca to S. Rockabill, two steep-to rks with Lt ho, is 2·5M E of St Patrick's Island. Lambay Is (private) is steep-to except to the W, where there can be overfalls.

6.5 SPECIAL NOTES FOR IRELAND: See 5.5

ANCHORAGES ADJACENT TO GALWAY BAY

ARAN ISLANDS Inishmore: Killeany Bay with harbour at Kilronan. 8 Y ⛵s available, ⚓ S of Kilronan pier or ⚓ E of Killeany Pt, but exposed to E/NE wind. Killeany hbr ldg lts 192° Oc 5s. Facilities: HM ☎099 20946 ⛽ ⚓ ✉ 🛒; Ferry to Rossaveel.

Inishmore: Eeragh Island (Rk Is) Fl 15s 35m 23M, W tr, B bands. Straw Is, Fl (2) 5s 11m 17M. In good weather ⚓ at Portmurvy.

Inishmaan: Ldg lts 199°, Oc 6s 8M, lead into small harbour with 3·5m and good shelter. Ferries have priority for ⏜, but do not stay overnight.

Inisheer: Iso WR 12s 34m 20/16M, Racon, vis 225°-W-245° (partially obscd 225°-231° beyond 7M), R sector covers Finnis Rk. Ballyhees Pier, Fl WRG 5s 8M 3m, vis: 093°-G-150°-W-226°-R-290°.

The better ⚓s in outer Galway Bay northward to Slyne Head are:

Greatman Bay: English Rk dries 1·2m, Keeraun Shoal –1·6m breakers. Avoid Arkeena Rk, Trabaan Rk, Rin and Chapel Rks. ⚓ off Natawny Quay (E side), or 4 Y⛵s off Maumeen Quay (dries), ⏜ possible.

Kiggaul Bay: Easy ent, H24; ⚓ close W /NW of lt Fl WRG 3s 5/3M , 329°-W-359°-R-059°; depth 3–4m; exposed to S/SE winds.

Kilkieran Bay: Easy entry abeam Golam Tr (conspic). 12 Y ⛵s off Kilkieran. Many ⚓s in 14M long, sheltered bay.

Roundstone Bay: AC2709 (Off chartlet at 53°23'N 09°54'·5W). Safe shelter/access, except in SE'ly. 4 Y ⛵s are 5ca SSE of Roundstone, or ⚓ in 2m off N quay. Other ⚓s E in Bertraghboy and Cashel Bays. Croaghnakeela Is Fl 3·7s 7m 5M. Inishnee lt Fl (2) WRG 10s 9m 5/3M, W sector 017°-030°.

Bunowen Bay: (53°24'·6N 10°06'·9W). Sheltered in W–NE winds; unsafe in S'ly. Easy appr with Bunowen House brg 000°, leaving Mullauncarrickscoltia Rk (1·1m) to port. ⚓ in 3-4m below Doon Hill.

6.6 GALWAY BAY

Galway **53°12′N 09°08′W**

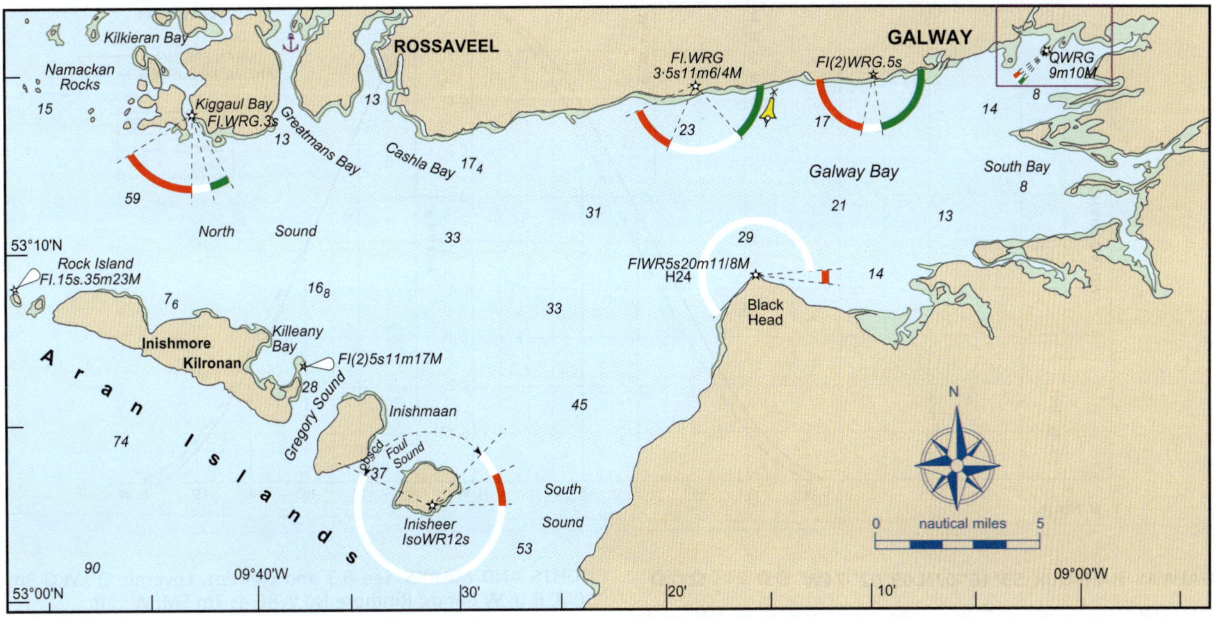

CHARTS AC 2173, 3339, 1984,1904; Imray C55, C54

TIDES –0555 Dover; ML 2·9; Duration 0620

Standard Port GALWAY (⟶)

Times				Height (metres)			
High Water		Low Water		MHWS	MHWN	MLWN	MLWS
0600	1100	0000	0700	5·1	3·9	2·0	0·8
1800	2300	1200	1900				
Differences KILKIERAN COVE							
+0005	+0005	+0016	+0016	–0·3	–0·2	–0·1	–0·2
ROUNDSTONE BAY							
+0003	+0003	+0008	+0008	–0·7	–0·5	–0·3	–0·3
KILLEANY BAY (Aran Islands)							
0000	0000	+0001	–0001	–0·1	+0·1	+0·1	+0·2
LISCANNOR							
–0003	–0007	+0006	+0002	–0·4	–0·3	ND	ND

SHELTER Galway Bay is sheltered from large swells by Aran Is, but seas get up in the 20M between the Aran Is and Galway. Beware salmon drift nets in the apps to many bays. On the S Shore:

Kinvarra, Aughinish, South and Ballyvaghan Bays between Black Hd and Galway have rocks and shoals, but give excellent shelter. Enter Kinvarra B with caution on the flood avoiding rks. Berth in small drying hbr. Beware fish farm in South Bay. Ballvaghan Bay, entered either side of Illaunloo Rk, leads to two piers (both of which dry) or ⚓ close NE in pool (3m). Best access HW±2.

On the N coast there is no safe hbr from Galway to Cashla (20M).

Cashla Bay: Easiest all-weather entry on this coast. To the East **Rossaveel** RosaveelFHC@agriculture.gov.ie is a sheltered but busy fishing hbr, with 2 marinas, To the West 8 Y 🅐s lie off Struthan Quay.

NAVIGATION Enter the Bay by one of four Sounds:

- North Sound between Inishmore and Golam Tr (conspic), 4½M wide, is easiest but beware Brocklinmore Bank in heavy weather.
- Gregory Sound between Inishmore and Inishmaan, is free of dangers, but give Straw Island a berth of 2-3ca.
- Foul Sound between Inishmaan and Inisheer; only danger is Pipe Rock (dries) at end of reef extending 3ca NW of Inisheer.
- South Sound between Inisheer and mainland. Finnis Rock (dries 0·4m) 4½ca SE of E point of Inisheer (marked by ECM buoy Q (3) 10s). From S, beware Kilstiffin Rocks off Liscanor Bay.

LIGHTS AND MARKS Black Head lt Fl WR 5s 20m 11/8M H24, vis 045°-W-268°-R (covers Illanloo Rk)-276°. Killeen Pt Fl (3) WR 10s 6/3M; Lion Pt Dir lt 010°, Iso WRG 4s 8/6M, 008·5°-W-011·5°.

FACILITIES

Cashla Bay: **Carraroe** (1M SW) Hotel. **Costelloe** (1½M E) ✉.

Rossaveel Marina ☎091 560506,

N Marina 2.6m below CD; 116

S Marina 2.0m below CD, 44

Town ✉ Ⓑ ✕ (1M). Ferry to Aran Is.

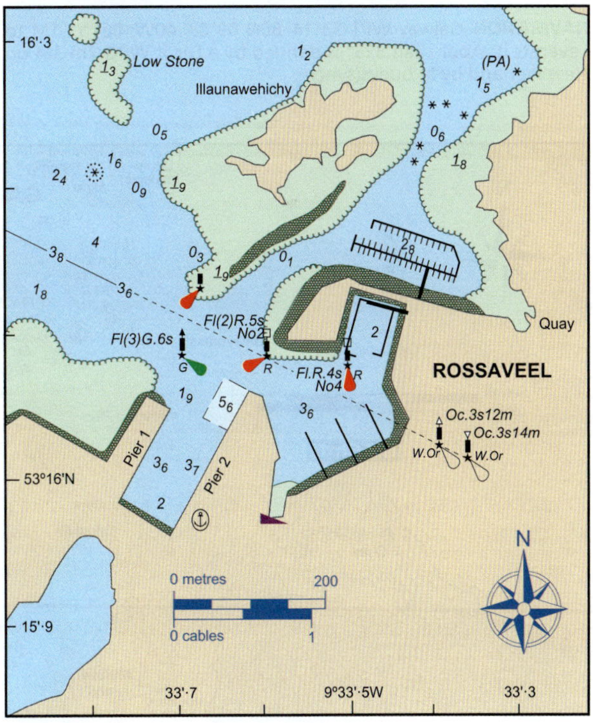

FACILITIES Nearby

Greatman Bay: Maumeen (1M).

Kiggaul Bay: (no ☎), shop at Lettermullen (1M).

Kilkieran Bay: Bus to Galway.

Roundstone Bay: ✉ Bus to Galway.

Bunowen Bay: No facilities.

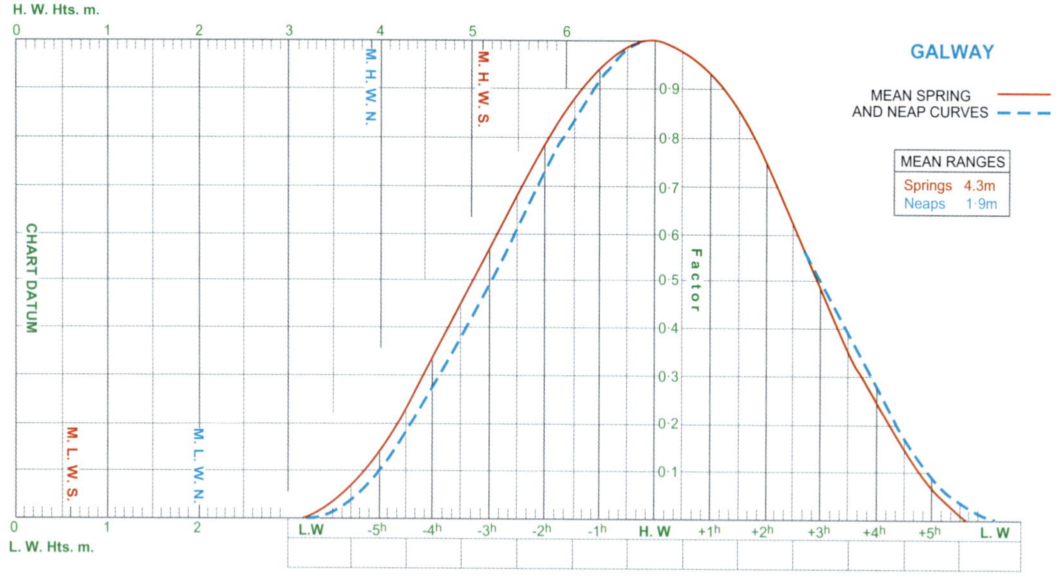

GALWAY HARBOUR **53°16'·07N 09°02'·74W**

SHELTER Very good in Galway hbr, protected from SW'lies by Mutton Island. Dock gates open HW–2 to HW. The approach channel is dredged to 3.4m. Enter Galway Dock and secure in SW corner of basin where there is a 31-berth marina, or ask HM for waiting berth on lead-in pier. In the 'Layby' (a dredged cut NE of New pier) an additional 8 berths are available on a 60m pontoon. New Harbour (2·5M ESE and home of Galway Bay SC) is nearest safe ⚓ to Galway.

NAVIGATION Galway WPT 53°14'·80N 09°03'·40W, 061°/1·1M to Leverets lt. Appr chan 325° is defined by a Dir lt WRG 7m 3M on New Pier and by lit buoys(sync).

LIGHTS AND MARKS See 6.3 and chartlet. Leverets Q WRG 9m 10M; B tr, W bands; Rinmore Iso WRG 4s 7m 5M; W □ tr.

COMMUNICATIONS (Code 091) Coast Rescue Service (099) 61107; Police 538000; Dr 530054. HM 561874.

Galway Harbour Radio VHF Ch **12** 16 (HW–2½ to HW+1). Call Galway Pilots on VHF Ch **12** in case ship movements are imminent or under way and follow their instructions on berthing.

FACILITIES **City Marina**: www.galwayharbour.com ☎091 561874, 31 €2/m if space available, (by r/tanker). **Galway YC** ; **Galway Bay SC** ☎794527, . **Galway Boatbuilding** ☎086 3379304, (18t). **Town** ACA Kos Ⓑ .

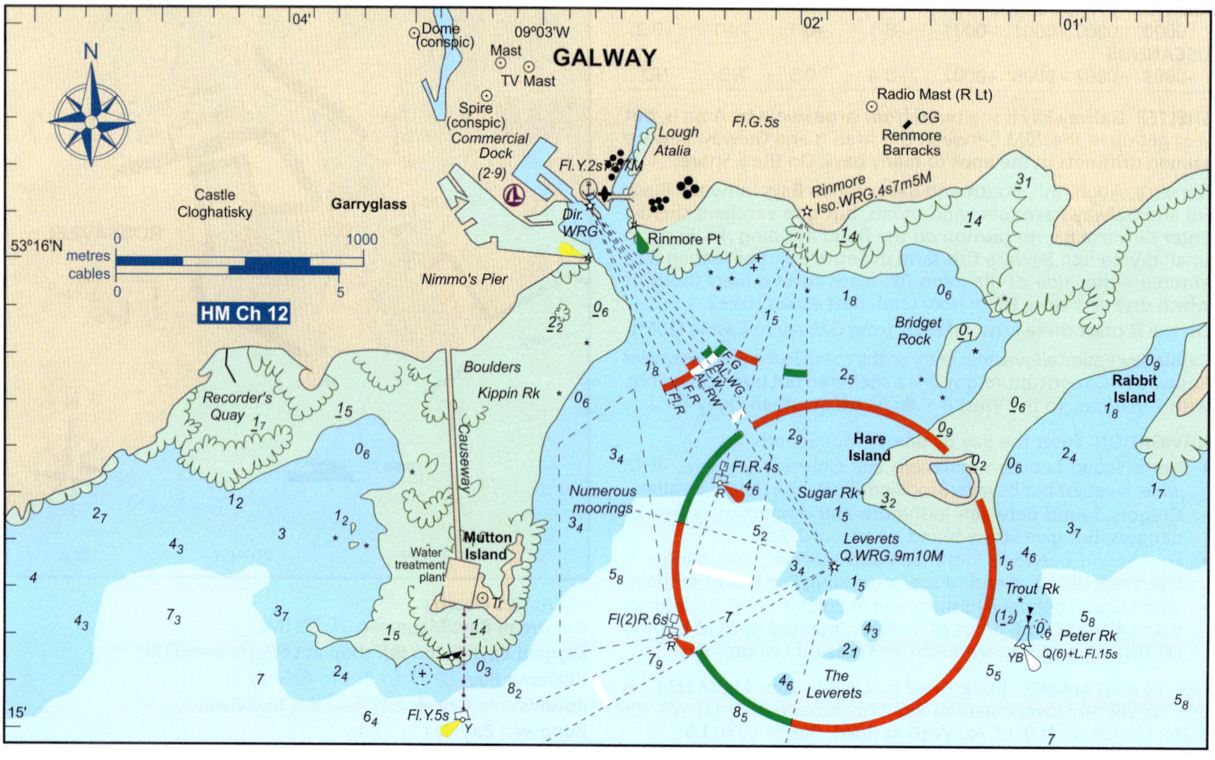

STANDARD TIME (UT)
For Summer Time add ONE hour in **non-shaded areas**

GALWAY LAT 53°16'N LONG 9°03'W

TIMES AND HEIGHTS OF HIGH AND LOW WATERS

Dates in red are SPRINGS
Dates in blue are NEAPS

YEAR **2024**

JANUARY

Date	Time	m	Date	Time	m
1 M	0146	1.7	16 TU	0203	1.1
	0819	4.6		0834	5.2
	1415	1.5		1432	0.9
	2052	4.4		2108	4.8
2 TU	0225	1.9	17 W	0254	1.3
	0901	4.4		0926	4.9
	1457	1.7		1523	1.2
	2135	4.2		2201	4.5
3 W	0308	2.1	18 TH	0351	1.6
	0946	4.2		1022	4.6
	1542	1.9		1621	1.5
	2223	4.1		◐ 2300	4.3
4 TH	0359	2.2	19 F	0457	1.8
	1036	4.1		1128	4.3
	1637	2.0		1728	1.8
	◑ 2315	4.0			
5 F	0508	2.3	20 SA	0011	4.2
	1131	4.0		0616	1.9
	1753	2.1		1248	4.1
				1850	1.9
6 SA	0012	4.0	21 SU	0129	4.2
	0639	2.3		0741	1.9
	1233	4.0		1404	4.2
	1910	2.0		2008	2.0
7 SU	0113	4.1	22 M	0234	4.3
	0742	2.1		0851	1.7
	1341	4.1		1505	4.3
	2007	1.9		2107	1.8
8 M	0213	4.3	23 TU	0328	4.5
	0834	1.9		0945	1.5
	1442	4.3		1557	4.5
	2055	1.7		2154	1.7
9 TU	0304	4.6	24 W	0414	4.7
	0921	1.6		1027	1.3
	1534	4.6		1641	4.7
	2139	1.5		2231	1.5
10 W	0352	4.9	25 TH	0455	4.9
	1005	1.3		1101	1.2
	1622	4.8		1722	4.8
	2222	1.3		○ 2304	1.4
11 TH	0439	5.1	26 F	0533	5.0
	1048	1.0		1131	1.1
	1710	5.0		1800	4.9
	● 2304	1.1		2337	1.3
12 F	0525	5.3	27 SA	0610	5.1
	1131	0.8		1201	1.0
	1757	5.1		1835	4.9
	2347	1.0			
13 SA	0611	5.4	28 SU	0010	1.2
	1215	0.6		0645	5.0
	1843	5.2		1233	1.0
				1911	4.8
14 SU	0031	0.9	29 M	0043	1.3
	0659	5.5		0719	4.9
	1258	0.6		1306	1.1
	1931	5.1		1944	4.7
15 M	0116	1.0	30 TU	0116	1.4
	0746	5.4		0753	4.8
	1344	0.7		1339	1.2
	2018	5.0		2018	4.6
			31 W	0149	1.5
				0826	4.6
				1413	1.4
				2054	4.4

FEBRUARY

Date	Time	m	Date	Time	m
1 TH	0226	1.7	16 F	0316	1.4
	0903	4.4		0949	4.6
	1450	1.6		1542	1.6
	2135	4.2		◐ 2216	4.3
2 F	0307	1.9	17 SA	0421	1.8
	0947	4.2		1050	4.1
	1533	1.8		1651	2.0
	◑ 2223	4.1		2322	4.0
3 SA	0355	2.1	18 SU	0546	2.0
	1042	4.0		1224	3.9
	1624	2.1		1820	2.2
	2319	4.0			
4 SU	0453	2.3	19 M	0110	3.9
	1145	3.9		0720	2.1
	1727	2.2		1357	3.9
				1949	2.2
5 M	0022	4.0	20 TU	0227	4.1
	0637	2.3		0851	1.8
	1256	3.9		1501	4.1
	1940	2.2		2100	2.0
6 TU	0132	4.1	21 W	0321	4.3
	0817	2.0		0942	1.6
	1412	4.1		1549	4.3
	2043	1.9		2145	1.8
7 W	0239	4.4	22 TH	0405	4.6
	0911	1.6		1018	1.3
	1517	4.4		1630	4.6
	2132	1.6		2218	1.5
8 TH	0335	4.8	23 F	0443	4.8
	0958	1.2		1045	1.1
	1610	4.8		1706	4.8
	2216	1.2		2247	1.3
9 F	0425	5.2	24 SA	0518	5.0
	1041	0.8		1109	0.9
	1657	5.1		1740	4.9
	● 2257	0.9		○ 2316	1.1
10 SA	0511	5.5	25 SU	0552	5.0
	1121	0.5		1136	0.8
	1741	5.3		1813	4.9
	2337	0.7		2346	1.0
11 SU	0556	5.7	26 M	0624	5.0
	1201	0.3		1205	0.8
	1825	5.4		1844	4.9
12 M	0016	0.5	27 TU	0016	1.0
	0641	5.7		0656	5.0
	1240	0.3		1235	0.8
	1909	5.4		1915	4.8
13 TU	0057	0.6	28 W	0047	1.0
	0725	5.6		0724	4.8
	1321	0.4		1306	1.0
	1953	5.2		1944	4.7
14 W	0139	0.7	29 TH	0119	1.2
	0810	5.4		0752	4.7
	1403	0.7		1339	1.1
	2037	5.0		2014	4.5
15 TH	0225	1.0			
	0858	5.0			
	1449	1.1			
	2124	4.6			

MARCH

Date	Time	m	Date	Time	m
1 F	0154	1.3	16 SA	0246	1.3
	0823	4.5		0921	4.4
	1415	1.4		1509	1.7
	2050	4.3		2140	4.3
2 SA	0234	1.6	17 SU	0354	1.8
	0905	4.2		1020	4.0
	1456	1.7		1624	2.1
	2136	4.1		◐ 2239	3.9
3 SU	0318	1.9	18 M	0525	2.0
	1001	4.0		1209	3.7
	1543	2.0		1758	2.3
	◑ 2235	3.9			
4 M	0413	2.1	19 TU	0056	3.7
	1110	3.8		0654	2.0
	1643	2.3		1347	3.8
	2344	3.8		1921	2.3
5 TU	0527	2.2	20 W	0212	3.9
	1226	3.7		0841	1.8
	1927	2.3		1445	4.0
				2037	2.0
6 W	0101	3.9	21 TH	0303	4.2
	0805	1.9		0922	1.5
	1355	4.0		1530	4.3
	2032	1.9		2119	1.7
7 TH	0221	4.3	22 F	0345	4.5
	0859	1.4		0950	1.3
	1507	4.4		1608	4.5
	2120	1.5		2151	1.4
8 F	0321	4.8	23 SA	0421	4.7
	0944	0.9		1014	1.0
	1556	4.8		1642	4.7
	2201	1.0		2220	1.2
9 SA	0409	5.2	24 SU	0455	4.8
	1024	0.5		1039	0.9
	1639	5.2		1713	4.8
	2240	0.6		2249	1.0
10 SU	0453	5.6	25 M	0527	4.9
	1102	0.2		1106	0.7
	1721	5.5		1744	4.9
	● 2317	0.3		○ 2318	0.8
11 M	0536	5.8	26 TU	0558	4.9
	1139	0.0		1135	0.7
	1802	5.6		1814	4.9
	2355	0.2		2348	0.8
12 TU	0618	5.8	27 W	0628	4.9
	1216	0.1		1204	0.8
	1843	5.5		1843	4.9
13 W	0033	0.3	28 TH	0019	0.9
	0702	5.6		0656	4.8
	1253	0.3		1235	0.9
	1924	5.3		1910	4.8
14 TH	0113	0.5	29 F	0052	1.0
	0746	5.3		0723	4.6
	1333	0.7		1309	1.1
	2007	5.0		1939	4.6
15 F	0156	0.9	30 SA	0128	1.1
	0831	4.9		0754	4.5
	1417	1.2		1346	1.3
	2051	4.6		2014	4.4
			31 SU	0208	1.4
				0837	4.2
				1427	1.6
				2100	4.2

APRIL

Date	Time	m	Date	Time	m
1 M	0253	1.7	16 TU	0502	1.9
	0935	3.9		1140	3.6
	1515	2.0		1732	2.3
	2203	3.9			
2 TU	0350	1.9	17 W	0018	3.7
	1047	3.7		0617	1.9
	1619	2.2		1319	3.7
	◑ 2316	3.8		1844	2.3
3 W	0509	2.1	18 TH	0141	3.8
	1206	3.7		0728	1.8
	1907	2.2		1415	3.9
				1947	2.0
4 TH	0035	3.9	19 F	0233	4.0
	0745	1.7		0826	1.6
	1340	4.0		1500	4.2
	2012	1.8		2037	1.7
5 F	0200	4.3	20 SA	0315	4.3
	0838	1.2		0903	1.3
	1448	4.4		1537	4.4
	2058	1.3		2115	1.4
6 SA	0300	4.7	21 SU	0351	4.5
	0921	0.8		0935	1.1
	1534	4.9		1610	4.6
	2138	0.8		2148	1.2
7 SU	0347	5.2	22 M	0424	4.6
	1000	0.4		1005	1.0
	1615	5.2		1640	4.7
	2216	0.5		2219	1.0
8 M	0430	5.5	23 TU	0456	4.7
	1036	0.1		1035	0.9
	1655	5.5		1711	4.8
	● 2253	0.2		○ 2250	0.9
9 TU	0513	5.6	24 W	0528	4.8
	1112	0.1		1104	0.8
	1735	5.5		1741	4.9
	2330	0.2		2320	0.8
10 W	0556	5.6	25 TH	0559	4.8
	1148	0.2		1134	0.9
	1816	5.5		1811	4.8
				2353	0.9
11 TH	0009	0.3	26 F	0630	4.7
	0639	5.4		1208	1.0
	1226	0.5		1841	4.8
	1858	5.3			
12 F	0050	0.6	27 SA	0029	0.9
	0724	5.1		0702	4.6
	1306	0.9		1244	1.1
	1940	5.0		1914	4.7
13 SA	0134	0.9	28 SU	0108	1.1
	0810	4.7		0740	4.4
	1351	1.4		1324	1.4
	2025	4.6		1954	4.5
14 SU	0226	1.4	29 M	0151	1.3
	0900	4.3		0826	4.2
	1445	1.8		1408	1.6
	2114	4.2		2043	4.3
15 M	0337	1.7	30 TU	0240	1.5
	0958	3.9		0925	4.0
	1607	2.2		1502	1.9
	◐ 2210	3.9		2145	4.1

N Ireland

Chart Datum: 0·20 metres below Ordnance Datum (Dublin). HAT is 5·9 metres above Chart Datum.

STANDARD TIME (UT)
For Summer Time add ONE hour in **non-shaded areas**

GALWAY LAT 53°16'N LONG 9°03'W

TIMES AND HEIGHTS OF HIGH AND LOW WATERS

Dates in red are SPRINGS
Dates in blue are NEAPS

YEAR **2024**

MAY

Date	Day	Time	m
1		0341	1.7
		1033	3.8
	W	1613	2.1
		◑ 2255	4.0
2		0501	1.8
		1148	3.8
	TH	1803	2.1
3		0011	4.1
		0706	1.5
	F	1312	4.1
		1939	1.7
4		0131	4.3
		0806	1.2
	SA	1417	4.5
		2028	1.3
5		0232	4.7
		0851	0.8
	SU	1506	4.8
		2110	0.9
6		0322	5.0
		0931	0.5
	M	1549	5.1
		2150	0.6
7		0407	5.3
		1009	0.4
	TU	1630	5.3
		2229	0.4
8		0452	5.3
		1046	0.4
	W	1711	5.4
		● 2309	0.4
9		0536	5.3
		1124	0.6
	TH	1753	5.3
		2350	0.5
10		0621	5.1
		1205	0.9
	F	1835	5.1
11		0033	0.8
		0707	4.9
	SA	1247	1.2
		1919	4.9
12		0120	1.1
		0754	4.6
	SU	1334	1.5
		2005	4.6
13		0213	1.4
		0843	4.3
	M	1429	1.9
		2053	4.3
14		0317	1.6
		0937	4.0
	TU	1541	2.1
		2146	4.1
15		0428	1.8
		1042	3.8
	W	1656	2.2
		◐ 2248	3.8
16		0534	1.9
		1222	3.7
	TH	1801	2.2
17		0040	3.8
		0635	1.8
	F	1328	3.9
		1900	2.1
18		0146	3.9
		0729	1.7
	SA	1416	4.0
		1952	1.8
19		0232	4.0
		0816	1.5
	SU	1455	4.2
		2036	1.6
20		0311	4.2
		0856	1.4
	M	1529	4.4
		2114	1.4
21		0347	4.4
		0931	1.2
	TU	1602	4.6
		2149	1.2
22		0421	4.5
		1004	1.1
	W	1635	4.7
		2222	1.1
23		0456	4.6
		1036	1.1
	TH	1708	4.8
		○ 2256	1.0
24		0532	4.7
		1109	1.1
	F	1743	4.9
		2333	0.9
25		0609	4.7
		1147	1.1
	SA	1820	4.8
26		0012	1.0
		0649	4.6
	SU	1227	1.2
		1900	4.8
27		0056	1.0
		0733	4.5
	M	1312	1.4
		1945	4.7
28		0143	1.1
		0822	4.3
	TU	1401	1.5
		2036	4.5
29		0235	1.3
		0917	4.2
	W	1458	1.7
		2133	4.4
30		0334	1.4
		1018	4.1
	TH	1605	1.8
		◑ 2236	4.3
31		0442	1.4
		1126	4.1
	F	1721	1.8
		2345	4.3

JUNE

Date	Day	Time	m
1		0559	1.4
		1238	4.2
	SA	1843	1.6
2		0058	4.4
		0717	1.3
	SU	1343	4.4
		1950	1.4
3		0203	4.6
		0816	1.1
	M	1437	4.7
		2042	1.1
4		0258	4.8
		0903	1.0
	TU	1524	4.9
		2128	0.9
5		0348	4.9
		0946	0.9
	W	1609	5.1
		2212	0.8
6		0436	5.0
		1028	0.9
	TH	1653	5.1
		● 2255	0.8
7		0523	5.0
		1109	1.0
	F	1737	5.1
		2339	0.8
8		0609	4.9
		1151	1.2
	SA	1820	5.0
9		0022	0.9
		0654	4.8
	SU	1234	1.4
		1904	4.9
10		0107	1.1
		0739	4.6
	M	1318	1.6
		1947	4.7
11		0153	1.3
		0824	4.4
	TU	1405	1.8
		2032	4.5
12		0243	1.5
		0911	4.2
	W	1459	2.0
		2120	4.3
13		0337	1.7
		1000	4.0
	TH	1601	2.1
		2210	4.1
14		0437	1.8
		1054	3.9
	F	1708	2.2
		◐ 2305	3.9
15		0538	1.9
		1154	3.9
	SA	1810	2.1
16		0007	3.8
		0637	1.9
	SU	1300	3.9
		1906	2.0
17		0120	3.9
		0730	1.8
	M	1355	4.1
		1956	1.9
18		0217	4.0
		0818	1.7
	TU	1440	4.3
		2041	1.7
19		0303	4.2
		0900	1.6
	W	1521	4.5
		2123	1.5
20		0346	4.4
		0939	1.4
	TH	1600	4.7
		2202	1.3
21		0427	4.5
		1016	1.3
	F	1640	4.8
		2241	1.1
22		0510	4.7
		1055	1.2
	SA	1722	4.9
		○ 2322	1.0
23		0553	4.7
		1136	1.2
	SU	1805	5.0
24		0004	0.9
		0637	4.8
	M	1219	1.2
		1849	5.0
25		0048	0.8
		0723	4.7
	TU	1305	1.2
		1935	5.0
26		0135	0.8
		0811	4.6
	W	1353	1.3
		2024	4.9
27		0224	0.9
		0901	4.5
	TH	1446	1.4
		2117	4.7
28		0317	1.1
		0956	4.4
	F	1544	1.5
		◑ 2214	4.5
29		0415	1.2
		1056	4.3
	SA	1648	1.6
		2317	4.4
30		0518	1.4
		1202	4.3
	SU	1758	1.6

JULY

Date	Day	Time	m
1		0027	4.3
		0628	1.5
	M	1311	4.3
		1914	1.6
2		0140	4.3
		0743	1.5
	TU	1414	4.5
		2023	1.4
3		0242	4.4
		0845	1.5
	W	1509	4.6
		2119	1.3
4		0338	4.6
		0936	1.4
	TH	1558	4.8
		2208	1.1
5		0428	4.7
		1021	1.3
	F	1644	4.9
		● 2251	1.0
6		0515	4.8
		1102	1.3
	SA	1728	5.0
		2332	1.0
7		0559	4.8
		1140	1.3
	SU	1809	5.0
8		0009	1.0
		0641	4.8
	M	1217	1.3
		1850	5.0
9		0046	1.0
		0721	4.7
	TU	1255	1.4
		1929	4.8
10		0123	1.1
		0800	4.6
	W	1333	1.5
		2008	4.7
11		0202	1.3
		0839	4.4
	TH	1412	1.7
		2048	4.5
12		0242	1.5
		0920	4.2
	F	1453	1.9
		2131	4.3
13		0323	1.7
		1004	4.1
	SA	1539	2.0
		◐ 2217	4.1
14		0410	1.9
		1052	4.0
	SU	1637	2.2
		2308	3.9
15		0509	2.0
		1145	3.9
	M	1804	2.2
16		0005	3.8
		0635	2.1
	TU	1244	4.0
		1918	2.1
17		0111	3.9
		0744	2.0
	W	1347	4.1
		2015	1.9
18		0219	4.0
		0838	1.8
	TH	1444	4.3
		2105	1.7
19		0316	4.2
		0925	1.6
	F	1533	4.6
		2150	1.4
20		0406	4.5
		1007	1.4
	SA	1620	4.9
		2233	1.1
21		0452	4.7
		1048	1.2
	SU	1705	5.1
		○ 2314	0.8
22		0537	4.9
		1128	1.0
	M	1749	5.3
		2355	0.6
23		0621	5.0
		1210	0.9
	TU	1834	5.3
24		0036	0.5
		0706	5.0
	W	1252	0.8
		1920	5.3
25		0119	0.5
		0751	5.0
	TH	1336	0.9
		2006	5.2
26		0204	0.6
		0837	4.8
	F	1424	1.1
		2054	5.0
27		0251	0.9
		0927	4.6
	SA	1516	1.3
		2147	4.7
28		0344	1.2
		1021	4.4
	SU	1616	1.6
		◑ 2247	4.4
29		0444	1.6
		1125	4.2
	M	1727	1.8
30		0001	4.1
		0557	1.8
	TU	1246	4.1
		1854	1.8
31		0126	4.0
		0725	1.9
	W	1402	4.2
		2020	1.7

AUGUST

Date	Day	Time	m
1		0238	4.1
		0842	1.8
	TH	1503	4.4
		2123	1.5
2		0334	4.3
		0936	1.7
	F	1553	4.6
		2210	1.2
3		0422	4.5
		1017	1.5
	SA	1637	4.8
		2248	1.1
4		0505	4.7
		1052	1.3
	SU	1718	5.0
		● 2319	0.9
5		0544	4.8
		1123	1.2
	M	1755	5.0
		2347	0.9
6		0621	4.8
		1155	1.1
	TU	1831	5.0
7		0017	0.9
		0656	4.8
	W	1227	1.1
		1905	4.9
8		0050	0.9
		0730	4.7
	TH	1300	1.2
		1939	4.8
9		0123	1.1
		0803	4.6
	F	1333	1.4
		2013	4.6
10		0156	1.3
		0839	4.4
	SA	1408	1.6
		2050	4.4
11		0232	1.5
		0918	4.2
	SU	1447	1.8
		2133	4.1
12		0312	1.7
		1004	4.1
	M	1532	2.0
		◐ 2223	3.9
13		0359	2.0
		1057	3.9
	TU	1627	2.2
		2322	3.8
14		0456	2.2
		1157	3.9
	W	1841	2.3
15		0028	3.7
		0720	2.2
	TH	1304	4.0
		1958	2.0
16		0145	3.9
		0824	2.0
	F	1415	4.2
		2052	1.7
17		0258	4.2
		0913	1.7
	SA	1514	4.6
		2138	1.2
18		0350	4.5
		0956	1.3
	SU	1602	5.0
		2220	0.8
19		0435	4.9
		1036	0.9
	M	1647	5.3
		○ 2300	0.5
20		0518	5.1
		1114	0.7
	TU	1730	5.5
		2338	0.2
21		0600	5.3
		1152	0.5
	W	1814	5.6
22		0016	0.2
		0642	5.3
	TH	1231	0.5
		1858	5.6
23		0055	0.2
		0725	5.2
	F	1312	0.6
		1942	5.4
24		0137	0.5
		0808	5.0
	SA	1357	0.8
		2029	5.0
25		0221	0.9
		0855	4.7
	SU	1446	1.2
		2120	4.6
26		0312	1.3
		0946	4.4
	M	1547	1.6
		◑ 2220	4.2
27		0415	1.8
		1049	4.1
	TU	1708	1.9
		2344	3.9
28		0540	2.1
		1232	3.9
	W	1847	2.0
29		0126	3.8
		0718	2.2
	TH	1359	4.0
		2029	1.8
30		0237	4.0
		0841	2.0
	F	1458	4.3
		2124	1.5
31		0328	4.3
		0929	1.7
	SA	1544	4.6
		2202	1.2

Chart Datum: 0·20 metres below Ordnance Datum (Dublin). HAT is 5·9 metres above Chart Datum.

STANDARD TIME (UT)
For Summer Time add ONE hour in **non-shaded areas**

GALWAY LAT 53°16′N LONG 9°03′W

TIMES AND HEIGHTS OF HIGH AND LOW WATERS

Dates in red are SPRINGS
Dates in blue are NEAPS

YEAR **2024**

SEPTEMBER

Date	Day	Time	m	Time	m	Time	m	Time	m
1	SU	0410	4.5	1004	1.4	1624	4.8	2232	1.0
2	M	0448	4.7	1032	1.2	1700	5.0	2254	0.8
3	TU	0522	4.8	1059	1.1	1734	5.0	● 2318	0.8
4	W	0555	4.9	1127	1.0	1806	5.0	2346	0.7
5	TH	0626	4.9	1157	0.9	1838	4.9		
6	F	0016	0.8	0657	4.8	1228	1.0	1909	4.8
7	SA	0047	0.9	0728	4.7	1300	1.1	1939	4.6
8	SU	0120	1.1	0759	4.5	1335	1.4	2011	4.4
9	M	0155	1.4	0835	4.3	1413	1.6	2051	4.1
10	TU	0234	1.7	0919	4.1	1456	1.9	2143	3.9
11	W	0319	2.0	1015	3.9	1549	2.1	◐ 2248	3.7
12	TH	0416	2.3	1120	3.8	1701	2.3	2359	3.6
13	F	0705	2.4	1232	3.9	1942	2.0		
14	SA	0123	3.8	0809	2.0	1352	4.2	2035	1.5
15	SU	0247	4.2	0857	1.6	1456	4.6	2120	1.0
16	M	0334	4.6	0938	1.1	1543	5.1	2200	0.6
17	TU	0415	5.0	1015	0.7	1626	5.4	2237	0.2
18	W	0454	5.3	1051	0.4	1708	5.7	○ 2313	0.0
19	TH	0534	5.5	1128	0.2	1750	5.7	2350	0.0
20	F	0615	5.5	1207	0.3	1833	5.6		
21	SA	0027	0.2	0657	5.4	1247	0.5	1919	5.4
22	SU	0108	0.6	0740	5.1	1331	0.8	2006	4.9
23	M	0152	1.1	0825	4.7	1421	1.2	2057	4.5
24	TU	0244	1.6	0916	4.3	1526	1.7	◑ 2158	4.0
25	W	0355	2.0	1018	4.0	1658	2.0	2338	3.7
26	TH	0529	2.3	1225	3.8	1832	2.0		
27	F	0121	3.8	0658	2.3	1346	4.0	2021	1.7
28	SA	0223	4.0	0821	2.0	1440	4.3	2104	1.5
29	SU	0309	4.3	0905	1.7	1523	4.5	2135	1.2
30	M	0348	4.5	0937	1.4	1601	4.7	2159	1.0

OCTOBER

Date	Day	Time	m	Time	m	Time	m	Time	m
1	TU	0423	4.7	1004	1.2	1635	4.8	2222	0.9
2	W	0454	4.8	1031	1.0	1707	4.9	● 2247	0.8
3	TH	0525	4.9	1059	0.9	1738	4.9	2315	0.8
4	F	0555	4.9	1129	0.9	1809	4.9	2345	0.8
5	SA	0624	4.9	1200	0.9	1840	4.8		
6	SU	0015	0.9	0654	4.8	1232	1.1	1909	4.6
7	M	0049	1.1	0724	4.6	1307	1.3	1941	4.4
8	TU	0125	1.4	0758	4.4	1346	1.5	2021	4.1
9	W	0204	1.7	0842	4.2	1430	1.8	2116	3.9
10	TH	0251	2.0	0941	4.0	1525	2.0	◐ 2223	3.7
11	F	0351	2.3	1050	3.8	1641	2.1	2336	3.6
12	SA	0640	2.4	1203	3.9	1918	1.9		
13	SU	0102	3.8	0745	2.0	1324	4.2	2011	1.4
14	M	0222	4.3	0832	1.5	1430	4.7	2055	0.9
15	TU	0308	4.7	0912	1.0	1518	5.1	2133	0.5
16	W	0348	5.1	0949	0.6	1601	5.4	2209	0.2
17	TH	0427	5.4	1026	0.4	1644	5.6	○ 2245	0.2
18	F	0508	5.5	1104	0.3	1727	5.7	2322	0.2
19	SA	0549	5.5	1144	0.3	1812	5.5		
20	SU	0001	0.5	0632	5.4	1225	0.6	1859	5.2
21	M	0043	0.9	0716	5.1	1311	0.9	1947	4.8
22	TU	0130	1.3	0802	4.8	1404	1.3	2040	4.4
23	W	0224	1.8	0853	4.4	1514	1.7	2141	4.0
24	TH	0341	2.2	0953	4.1	1639	1.9	◑ 2318	3.8
25	F	0507	2.3	1148	3.9	1757	1.9		
26	SA	0053	3.8	0622	2.3	1315	4.0	1914	1.8
27	SU	0152	4.0	0729	2.1	1410	4.2	2012	1.6
28	M	0238	4.2	0820	1.8	1454	4.3	2049	1.4
29	TU	0317	4.4	0859	1.6	1531	4.5	2119	1.2
30	W	0351	4.6	0931	1.3	1605	4.7	2147	1.1
31	TH	0422	4.7	1002	1.2	1637	4.8	2216	1.0

NOVEMBER

Date	Day	Time	m	Time	m	Time	m	Time	m
1	F	0452	4.9	1032	1.1	1709	4.8	● 2246	1.0
2	SA	0523	4.9	1103	1.0	1742	4.8	2317	1.0
3	SU	0555	4.9	1136	1.0	1815	4.7	2349	1.1
4	M	0626	4.8	1210	1.1	1848	4.6		
5	TU	0024	1.3	0658	4.7	1248	1.3	1924	4.4
6	W	0103	1.5	0735	4.5	1329	1.4	2007	4.2
7	TH	0145	1.7	0821	4.3	1416	1.6	2100	4.0
8	F	0236	2.0	0918	4.2	1513	1.8	2204	3.9
9	SA	0340	2.2	1024	4.1	1628	1.9	◐ 2313	3.8
10	SU	0511	2.2	1134	4.1	1825	1.7		
11	M	0030	4.0	0703	1.9	1249	4.3	1934	1.4
12	TU	0143	4.3	0757	1.5	1357	4.7	2021	1.0
13	W	0235	4.7	0842	1.1	1451	5.0	2102	0.8
14	TH	0320	5.1	0923	0.8	1538	5.3	2142	0.6
15	F	0402	5.3	1003	0.6	1624	5.4	○ 2221	0.5
16	SA	0445	5.4	1044	0.5	1710	5.4	2301	0.7
17	SU	0528	5.4	1127	0.6	1757	5.3	2343	0.9
18	M	0613	5.3	1212	0.8	1844	5.1		
19	TU	0027	1.2	0658	5.1	1300	1.0	1934	4.8
20	W	0115	1.5	0745	4.8	1353	1.3	2025	4.5
21	TH	0210	1.8	0835	4.5	1454	1.6	2121	4.2
22	F	0316	2.1	0929	4.3	1604	1.8	2227	4.0
23	SA	0429	2.2	1032	4.0	1712	1.9	◑ 2352	3.9
24	SU	0537	2.3	1209	3.9	1813	1.9		
25	M	0101	3.9	0638	2.2	1321	4.0	1910	1.8
26	TU	0154	4.1	0732	2.0	1412	4.1	1958	1.7
27	W	0237	4.3	0818	1.8	1454	4.3	2039	1.5
28	TH	0313	4.4	0859	1.6	1530	4.4	2116	1.4
29	F	0346	4.6	0935	1.4	1606	4.6	2150	1.3
30	SA	0420	4.8	1010	1.3	1642	4.7	2223	1.3

DECEMBER

Date	Day	Time	m	Time	m	Time	m	Time	m
1	SU	0455	4.9	1044	1.2	1718	4.7	● 2256	1.3
2	M	0530	4.9	1119	1.2	1756	4.7	2332	1.3
3	TU	0605	4.9	1157	1.2	1833	4.7		
4	W	0010	1.4	0643	4.9	1237	1.2	1914	4.6
5	TH	0052	1.5	0723	4.8	1321	1.3	1958	4.4
6	F	0137	1.6	0809	4.6	1408	1.4	2047	4.3
7	SA	0228	1.8	0901	4.5	1502	1.5	2143	4.2
8	SU	0328	1.9	1000	4.4	1604	1.6	◐ 2245	4.1
9	M	0436	1.9	1104	4.4	1713	1.6	2352	4.2
10	TU	0552	1.9	1213	4.4	1829	1.5		
11	W	0102	4.4	0709	1.7	1324	4.5	1939	1.4
12	TH	0204	4.6	0810	1.4	1427	4.8	2034	1.2
13	F	0256	4.9	0902	1.2	1521	5.0	2121	1.1
14	SA	0345	5.1	0949	1.0	1611	5.1	2207	1.1
15	SU	0431	5.2	1035	0.9	1700	5.1	○ 2251	1.1
16	M	0517	5.3	1121	0.9	1748	5.1	2335	1.2
17	TU	0602	5.3	1205	0.9	1834	5.0		
18	W	0018	1.3	0647	5.2	1249	1.0	1921	4.9
19	TH	0102	1.5	0730	5.0	1334	1.2	2006	4.7
20	F	0147	1.7	0815	4.8	1421	1.4	2053	4.4
21	SA	0236	1.9	0900	4.5	1512	1.6	2140	4.2
22	SU	0331	2.1	0949	4.3	1609	1.8	◑ 2231	4.1
23	M	0436	2.2	1042	4.1	1711	2.0	2327	4.0
24	TU	0542	2.3	1142	4.0	1813	2.0		
25	W	0032	4.0	0644	2.2	1255	3.9	1911	2.0
26	TH	0136	4.1	0740	2.1	1402	4.0	2003	1.9
27	F	0227	4.2	0829	1.9	1453	4.2	2049	1.8
28	SA	0311	4.4	0914	1.7	1537	4.4	2132	1.7
29	SU	0351	4.6	0955	1.5	1618	4.5	2211	1.5
30	M	0431	4.8	1034	1.3	1659	4.7	● 2248	1.4
31	TU	0510	5.0	1112	1.2	1740	4.8	2325	1.3

Chart Datum: 0·20 metres below Ordnance Datum (Dublin). HAT is 5·9 metres above Chart Datum.

6.7 WESTPORT (CLEW BAY)

Mayo **53°47'·85N 09°35'·40W** ✿✿✿✿✿✿✿

CHARTS AC 2667, 2057; Imray C54

TIDES –0545 Dover; ML 2·5; Duration 0610

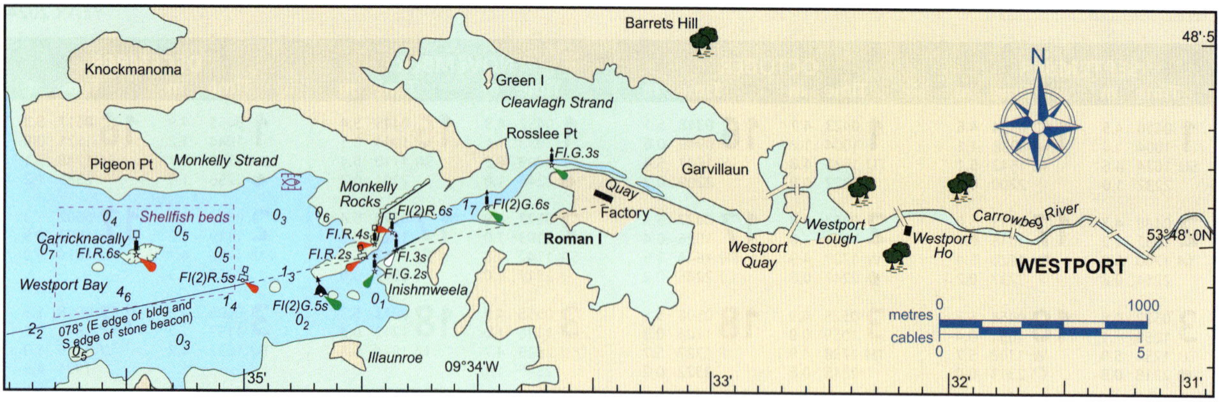

Standard Port GALWAY (⟵)

Times				Height (metres)			
High Water		Low Water		MHWS	MHWN	MLWN	MLWS
0600	1100	0000	0700	5·1	3·9	2·0	0·8
1800	2300	1200	1900				
Differences BROAD HAVEN							
+0035	+0035	+0040	+0040	–1·4	–1·0	–0·6	–0·2
BLACKSOD QUAY							
+0025	+0035	+0040	+0040	–1·2	–1·0	–0·6	–0·4
CLARE ISLAND							
+0015	+0021	+0039	+0027	–0·6	–0·4	–0·1	0·0
INISHGORT/CLEW BAY							
+0035	+0045	+0115	+0100	–0·7	–0·5	–0·2	0·0
KILLARY HARBOUR							
+0021	+0015	+0035	+0029	–1·0	–0·8	–0·4	–0·3
INISHBOFIN HARBOUR							
+0013	+0009	+0021	+0017	–1·0	–0·8	–0·4	–0·3
CLIFDEN BAY							
+0005	+0005	+0016	+0016	–0·7	–0·5	ND	ND

SHELTER Secure ⚓s amongst the islands at all times, as follows: E of Inishlyre in 2m; 2ca NE of Dorinish More, good holding in lee of Dorinish Bar (dries); 6 Ⓐs in Rosmoney Hbr 53°49'·75N 09°37'·34W; Westport Quay HW±1½, to dry out on S side; Newport Hbr (dries) can be reached above mid-flood with careful pilotage (AC 2667); dry out against N quay or ⚓ at E end of Rabbit Is.

NAVIGATION WPT 53°49'·20N 09°42'·10W, 071°/1·2M to Inishgort lt ho. Approaches to Westport Channel between Monkellys Rks and Inishmweela are well marked by lit PHMs and SHMs. Beware fish farms E of Clare I and in Newport Bay. Do not ⚓ or ground in the Carricknacally Shellfish Bed Area.

LIGHTS AND MARKS Westport Bay ent via Inishgort lt, L Fl 10s 11m 10M (H24), and a series of ldg lines, but not advised at night. Final appr line 080° towards lt bn, Fl 3s. but beware of drying patches on this lead inwards from Pigeon PHM. Chan from Westport Bay to Westport Quay, 1½M approx, is marked by bns.

COMMUNICATIONS (Code 098) ⊜ (094) 9021131; Police 9025555; Ⓗ (094) 9021733. No VHF.

FACILITIES **Westport Quays** Kos Ⓔ; **Town** Ⓑ (Galway/Knock). **Mayo SC Rosmoney** ☎9026160; **Glénans Irish SC** ☎9026046 (Collanmore Is).

OTHER ANCHORAGES FROM SLYNE HEAD TO EAGLE ISLAND

CLIFDEN BAY, Galway, **53°29'·40N 10°05'·90W**. AC 1820, 2708. HW –0600 on Dover; duration 0610. Tides at 6.7.

Identify conspic W bn on Carrickrana Rks prior to entry; ldg marks: W bn at Fishing Pt on 080° with Clifden Castle (ruin). Avoid Coghan's and Doolick Rks to the E and beware bar 2·4m off Fishing Pt.

8 Y Ⓐs are 3ca S of Castle ruins, or ⚓ NE of Drinagh Pt. Beware ruined training wall In the drying creek to Clifden; dry out against the quay or enter Ardbear Bay to ⚓ SE of Yellow Slate Rks in 3·4m. Keep clear of fish farms. Facilities: **Town** Kos Ⓑ Dr Ⓗ bus to Galway.

BALLYNAKILL, Galway, **53°34'·95N 10°03'·00W**. AC 2706. Tides as Inishbofin/Killary. Easy appr between Cleggan Pt, Fl (3) WRG 15s and Rinvyle Pt. Then pass N of Freaghillaun South Is, E of which is good passage ⚓ in 7m. Further E, Carrigeen and Ardagh Rks lie in mid-chan. Keep N for ⚓ in Derryinver B. S chan leads to ⚓s: off Ross Pt; S of Roeillaun; in Fahy Bay with 8 Y Ⓐs sheltered by bar dries 0·2m. No facilities.

INISHBOFIN, Galway, **53°36'·60N 10°13'·20W**. AC 1820, 2707. HW –0555 on Dover; ML 1·9m. Very safe inside narrow ent. Daymarks 2 conspic W trs lead 032° and Dir RWG lt leads 021° at night to increase separation from Gun Rock, Fl (2) 6s 8m 4M, vis 296°-253°. ⚓ between new pier and Port Is. Old pier to the E now refurbished and dredged may provide. (on both piers) / B&B: ☎(095) 45829.

KILLARY HARBOUR, Mayo/Galway, **53°37'·83N 09°54'·00W**, 4ca W of Doonee Is. AC 2706. Tides 6.7. A 7M long inlet, narrow and deep. Caution fish farms, some with Fl Y lts. Appr in good vis to identify Doonee Is and Inishbarna bns, both LFl G, ldg 099° to ent. ⚓s off Dernasliggaun, Bundorragha and, at head of inlet, Leenaun with 8 Y Ⓐs. (**Village** hotel.) Enter **Little Killary Bay** 4ca S of Doonee Is; drying rks at ent. Good ⚓ in 3m at head of bay.

INISHTURK, Mayo, **53°42'·3N 10°05'·2W**. 8 Y Ⓐs Garranty Hbr sheltered SW to NNW winds. quay 6Ⓐs on E side.

CLARE ISLAND, Mayo, **53°48'·1N 09°56'·7W**. 6Ⓐs on SE side untenable in E winds. Hotel some shops.

BLACKSOD BAY, Mayo, **54°05'·00N 10°02'·00W**. AC 2704. HW –0525 on Dover; ML 2·2m; Duration 0610. See 6.7. Easy appr, accessible by night. Safe ⚓s depending on wind: NW of Blacksod Pt 6 Y Ⓐs in 3m; at Elly B in 1·8m; Elly Hbr 6 Y Ⓐs; Saleen Bay (ldg lts 319°, both Oc 4s, lead to pier); N of Claggan Pt. Beware drying rk 3·5ca SSE of Ardmore Pt. Lts: Blacksod Pt, Fl (2) WR 7·5s 13m 9M, see 6.3. ECM buoy Q (3) 10s. Ldg lts 181°, Oc W 5s, lead to Blacksod pier hd. Few facilities; nearest town is Belmullet.

ACHILL SOUND ⚓s at each end sheltered by Achill Is. Mayo Co Council (+353 (0)97 81004) requires 2 days' notice to open bridge.

PORTNAFRANKAGH Mayo, **54°14'·95N 10°06'·00W**. AC 2703. Tides approx as Broadhaven. A safe passage ⚓, close to the coastal route, but swell enters in all winds. Appr towards Port Pt, thence keep to the N side for better water; middle and S side break in onshore winds. ⚓ in 4–5m on S side, close inshore. at new pier. Unlit, but Eagle Is lt, Fl (3) 15s 67m 26M H24, W tr, is 2M N. No facilities; Belmullet 4M.

BROAD HAVEN, Mayo, **54°16'·00N 09°53'·20W**. AC 2703. A safe refuge except in N'lies. Easy appr across Broadhaven Bay to the ent between Brandy Pt and Gubacashel Pt, Iso WR 4s27m 12/9M, W tr. 7ca S of this lt is Ballyglas Fl G 3s on W side. ⚓ close N or S of Ballyglas which has pier (2m) and 8 Y Ⓐs. In E'lies ⚓ 3ca S of Inver Pt out of the tide. Further S off Barrett Pt, the inlet narrows and turns W to Belmullet. Facilities: .

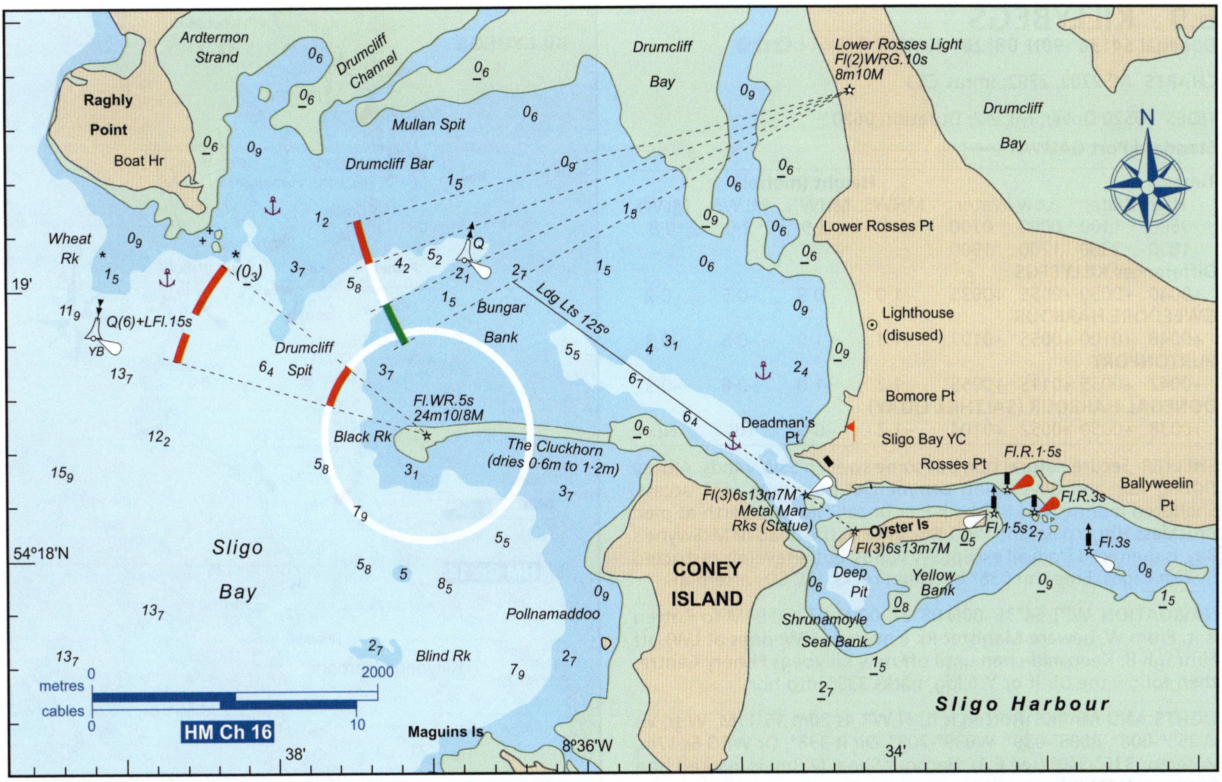

6.8 SLIGO

Sligo **54°18'·30N 08°34'·70W** ❀❀◊◊✿✿

CHARTS AC 2767, 2852; Imray C54

TIDES –0511 Dover; ML 2·3; Duration 0620

Standard Port GALWAY (⟵)

Times				Height (metres)			
High Water		Low Water		MHWS	MHWN	MLWN	MLWS
0600	1100	0000	0700	5·1	3·9	2·0	0·8
1800	2300	1200	1900				
Differences SLIGO HARBOUR (Oyster Is)							
+0043	+0055	+0042	+0054	–1·0	–0·9	–0·5	–0·3
MULLAGHMORE							
+0036	+0048	+0047	+0059	–1·4	–1·0	–0·4	–0·4
BALLYSADARE BAY (Culleenamore)							
+0059	+0111	+0111	+0123	–1·2	–0·9	ND	ND
KILLALA BAY (Inishcrone)							
+0035	+0055	+0030	+0050	–1·3	–1·2	–0·7	–0·4

SHELTER The lower harbour is fairly exposed; ⚓ along N side of Oyster Island, or proceed 4M (not at night) up to the shelter of Sligo town; 2nd berth below bridge for yachts.

NAVIGATION WPT 54°19'·15N 08°36'·77W, 125°/1·6M to front ldg lt.

- The passage between Oyster Island and Coney Island is marked 'Dangerous'.
- Pass N of Oyster Is leaving Blennick Rks to port. Passage to Sligo runs between training walls. Appr quays at HW–3 or higher.
- Some perches are in bad repair. Pilots at Raghly Pt and Rosses Pt. *Tide Tables* (based on Inishraher/Inishgort, published by Westport Hbr Comm.) available locally.

LIGHTS AND MARKS See 6.3 and chartlet. Bungar Bank NCM marks turn on approach; channel to Sligo Quay is well marked.

COMMUNICATIONS (Code 071) ⊜9161064; Police 9157000; Dr 9142886; ⊞9171111. Hbr Office 9111236.
Pilots VHF Ch 12 16. HM Ch 16.

FACILITIES 60m visitors pontoon, 20-30ft €19.00; ⛽ (15t) ; **Sligo YC** ☎9177168, ⚓s ⛽ . **Services** . **Town** ✉ Ⓑ ✕ ⇌ Irish Rail ☎9169888, Bus ☎9160066, ✈ Londonderry/Derry or Knock, Co Mayo (60-70M).

MINOR HARBOUR/ANCHORAGE TO THE WEST

KILLALA BAY, Sligo/Mayo, **54°13'·02N 09°12'·80W**. AC 2715. Tides, see 6.18. The bay, open to the N-NE, is entered between Lenadoon Pt and Kilcummin Hd, 6M to the W. 1·1M W of Kilcummin Hd are 8 Y ⚓s off Kilcummin pier, well sheltered from W'lies. Carrickpatrick ECM lt buoy, in mid-bay marks St Patrick's Rks to the W. Thence, if bound for Killala hbr, make good Killala SHM lt buoy, 7½ca to the SSW. The Round Tr and cathedral spire at Killala are conspic. Four sets of ldg bns/lts lead via a narrow chan between sand dunes and over the bar (0·3m) as follows:

- 230°, Rinnaun Pt lts Oc 10s 7/12m 5M, □ concrete trs.
- 215°, Inch Is, □ concrete trs; the rear has Dir lt Fl WRG 2s.
- 196°, Kilroe lts Oc 4s 5/10m 2M, W □ trs, which lead to ⚓ in Bartragh Pool, 6ca NE of Killala hbr; thence
- 236°, Pier lts Iso 2s 5/7m 2M, W ◊ daymarks, lead via narrow, dredged chan to pier where is possible in about 1·5m.

Facilities: ⛽ in town ½M.

Other hbrs in the bay: R Moy leading to Ballina should not be attempted without pilot/local knowledge. Inishcrone in the SE has a pier and lt; see 6.3.

MINOR HARBOUR ON S SIDE OF DONEGAL BAY

MULLAGHMORE 54°27'·90N 08°26'·80W. AC 2702. Tides see 6.8. Pierhead lit Fl G 3s 5m 3M. Fair weather ⚓ in 2-3m off hbr ent, sheltered by Mullaghmore Head, except from N–NE winds. For ⚓s near hbr ent, call Rodney Lomax, ☎071 9166124, mobile 0872 727538. Keep close to N pier to avoid shingle bank drying 1m, ⅔ of the way across the ent towards the S pier. Take the ground or dry out against the piers inside hbr berth on pontoon on bkwtr (min 1m at MLWS). Access approx HW±2 when least depth is 2m.

Communications: VHF Ch 16, 8, 6.

Facilities: ⛽ at S Pier and on bkwtr, ✕ .

6.9 KILLYBEGS

Donegal **54°36′·90N 08°26′·80W**

CHARTS AC 2702, 2792; Imray C53

TIDES –0520 Dover; ML 2·2; Duration 0620

Standard Port GALWAY (⟵)

Times				Height (metres)			
High Water		Low Water		MHWS	MHWN	MLWN	MLWS
0600	1100	0000	0700	5·1	3·9	2·0	0·8
1800	2300	1200	1900				
Differences KILLYBEGS							
+0040	+0050	+0055	+0035	–1·0	–0·9	–0·5	–0·2
GWEEDORE HARBOUR							
+0048	+0100	+0055	+0107	–1·3	–1·0	–0·5	–0·3
BURTONPORT							
+0042	+0055	+0115	+0055	–1·2	–1·0	–0·6	–0·3
DONEGAL HARBOUR (SALTHILL QUAY)							
+0038	+0050	+0052	+0104	–1·2	–0·9	ND	ND

SHELTER Secure natural hbr, but some swell in SSW winds. A busy fishing hbr and developing commercial port with H24 access. Sheltered marina N of Black Rk Pier or call HM and berth at pier. **Bruckless Hbr**, a pleasant ⚓ in 1·8m, 2M E at the head of McSwyne's Bay, is sheltered from all except SW winds, but is severely restricted by fish cages. Enter on 038° between rocks; ICC SDs essential.

NAVIGATION WPT 54°36′·00N 08°27′·00W, 022°/0·94M to Rotten Is lt. From W, beware Manister Rk (covers at HW; dries at LW) off Fintragh B. Keep mid-chan until off new Killybegs Fishery Centre, then follow the Dir lt or Y ◊ ldg marks 338° into hbr.

LIGHTS AND MARKS Rotten Is lt, Fl WR 4s 20m 15/11M, W tr, vis W255°-008°, R008°-039°, W039°-208°. Dir lt 338°, Oc WRG 6s 17m; W sector 336°-340° (see 6.3). Harbour Shoal (2·3m) is marked by a SCM and NCM lt buoy.

COMMUNICATIONS (Code 07497) MRCC (01) 6620922/3; Bundoran Inshore Rescue ☎(071) 9841713; 31070; Police 31002; Dr 31148 (Surgery). HM 31032.

HM Ch **14**; essential to request a berth.

FACILITIES **Marina** 65 inc 4 €2/m (6-H24 min charge €15); short stay (<6hr) €10 (berth to be vacated by 1700), (card system) available from marina office (development ongoing).

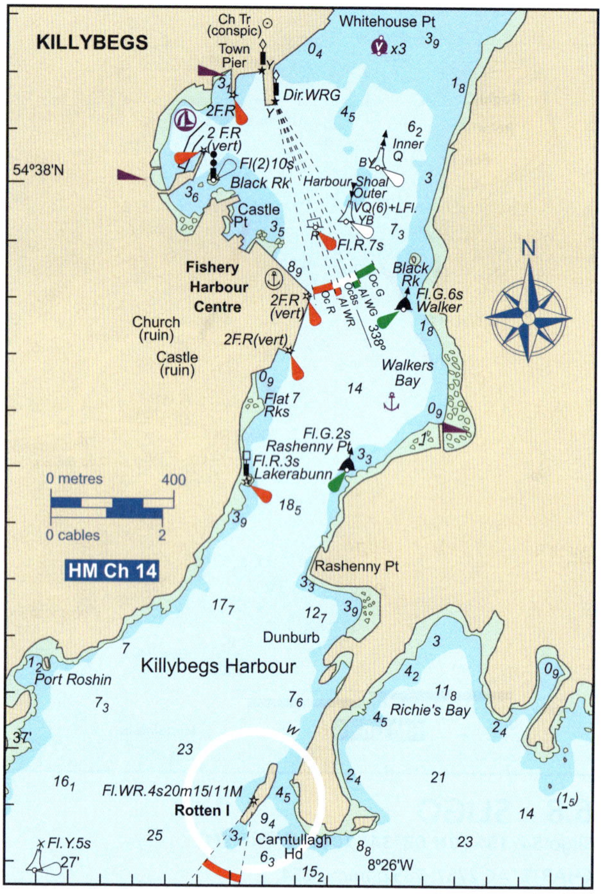

Town Pier ☎31032 (free) Kos (12t).

Black Rock Pier

Town Ⓔ Ⓑ (bus to Sligo).

OTHER HARBOURS AND ANCHORAGES IN DONEGAL

TEELIN HARBOUR, Donegal, **54°37′·50N 08°37′·87W**. AC 2792. Tides as 6.9. A possible passage ⚓, mid-way between Rathlin O'Birne and Killybegs. But Hbr is open to S'ly swell and prone to squalls in NW winds. Ent, 1ca wide, is close E of Teelin Pt lt, Fl R 10s, which is hard to see by day. 4 Y s and ⚓ on E side in 3m to N of pier, or ⚓ on E side near pier. Many moorings and, in the NE, mussel rafts. Facilities: , at Carrick, 3M inland.

INISHKEEL, Donegal, **54°50′·82N 08°26′·50W**. AC 2792. 6 Y s in Church Pool, 3ca E of Inishkeel. Open to N/NE'lies.

BURTONPORT, Donegal, **54°58′·93N 08°26′·60W**. AC 1879, 2792. HW –0525 on Dover; ML 2·0m; Duration 0605. See 6.9. Only appr via N Chan marked by lit bns. Entry safe in all weathers except NW gales. Habour busy, no space to ⚓; berth on local boat at pier or go to Rutland Hbr or Aran Roads: 6 Y s 250m NE of Black Rks, Fl R 3s. Ldg marks/lts: N Chan ldg lts on Inishcoo 119·3°, both Iso 6s 6/11m 1M; front W bn, B band; rear B bn, Y band. Rutland Is ldg lts 138°, both Oc 6s 8/14m 1M; front W bn, B band; rear B bn, Y band. Burtonport ldg lts 068°, both FG 17/23m 1M; front Gy bn, W band; rear Gy bn, Y band. HM ☎(075) 42155 (43170 home); VHF Ch 06, 12, **14**, 16. Facilities: (root of pier), (½M inland). **Village** Kos .

GWEEDORE HARBOUR/BUNBEG, Donegal, **55°03′·75N 08°18′·87W**. AC 1883. Tides see 6.9. Gweedore hbr, the estuary of the R Gweedore, has sheltered ⚓s or temp at Bunbeg Quay, usually full of FVs. Apprs via Gola N or S Sounds are not simple especially in poor visibility. N Sound is easier with ldg lts 171°, both Oc 3s 9/13m 2M, B/W bns, on the SE tip of Gola Is. (There are ⚓s on S and E sides of Gola Is.) E of Bo Is the bar 0·4m has a Fl G 3s and the chan, lying E of Inishinny Is and W of Inishcoole, is marked by a QG and 3 QR. SHM QG marks ent to Bunbeg. Night ent not advised. Facilities: at quay; Ⓑ at village ½M.

SHEEP HAVEN, Donegal, **55°11′·00N 07°51′·00W**. AC 2699. HW –0515 on Dover. See 6.10. Bay is 2M wide with many ⚓s, easily accessible in daylight, but exposed to N winds. Beware rks off Rinnafaghla Pt, and further S: Black Rk (6m) and Wherryman Rks, which dry, 1ca off E shore. ⚓ or 8 Y s in Downies Bay to SE of pier; in Pollcormick inlet close W in 3m; in Ards Bay for excellent shelter, but beware the bar in strong winds. Lts: Breaghy Hd LFl 10s 3m 6M, Portnablahy ldg lts 125°, both Oc 6s 7/12m 2M, B col, W bands; Downies pier hd, Fl R 3s 5m 2M, R post.

Facilities: **Downies** EC Wed; .

MULROY BAY, Donegal, **55°15′·30N 07°46′·30W**. AC 2699; HW (bar) –0455 on Dover. See 6.10. Beware Limeburner Rk, (NCM buoy, Q) 3M N of ent and the bar which is dangerous in swell or onshore winds. Obtain local advice as the depths on the bar change considerably. Ent at half flood (not HW); chan lies between Bar Rks (Low Bar Rk Fl G 2s) and Sessiagh Rks, it is rep'd to run along the alignment of the charted drying spit thence through First, Second (under bridge 19m) and Third Narrows to Broad Water. HW at the head of the lough is 2¼hrs later than at the bar. ⚓ Close SW of Ravedy Is (Fl 3s 9m 3M); Fanny's Bay (2m), excellent; Rosnakill Bay (3·5m) in SE side; Cranford Bay; Milford Port (3-4m). Beware cable 6m, over Moross chan, barring North Water to masted boats. Facilities: **Milford Port**, pier derelict, ⚓; **Fanny's Bay** Mevagh Boatyard, 074 9154470 / 087 8355373, mevaghboatyard@gmail.com wooden, GRP and steel repairs, ; hotel at Rosepenna (¾M).

6.10 LOUGH SWILLY

Donegal **55°17'N 07°34'W**

CHARTS AC 2697; Imray C53

TIDES –0500 Dover; ML 2·3; Duration 0605

Standard Port GALWAY (⟵)

Times				Height (metres)			
High Water		Low Water		MHWS	MHWN	MLWN	MLWS
0200	0900	0200	0800	5·1	3·9	2·0	0·8
1400	2100	1400	2000				
Differences INISHTRAHULL							
+0100	+0100	+0115	+0200	–1·8	–1·4	–0·4	–0·4
TRAWBREAGA BAY							
+0115	+0059	+0109	+0125	–1·1	–0·8	ND	ND
FANAD HEAD							
+0115	+0040	+0125	+0120	–1·1	–0·9	–0·5	–0·3
RATHMULLAN							
+0125	+0050	+0126	+0118	–0·8	–0·7	–0·1	–0·3
MULROY BAY (BAR)							
+0108	+0052	+0102	+0118	–1·2	–1·0	ND	ND
SHEEP HAVEN (DOWNIES BAY)							
+0057	+0043	+0053	+0107	–1·1	–0·9	ND	ND

SHELTER Good, but beware downdrafts on E side. ⚓s N of 55°05'N may suffer from swell. ⚓s from seaward: Ballymastocker Bay, also 8 Ⓥs, but exposed to E'lies; inside Macamish Pt, sheltered from SE to N; Rathmullan Roads N of pier, where yacht pontoon lies N/S in 3·6m MLWS; Fahan Creek is buoyed by local YC and marina ent at HW–1, but dredging is irregular and depths variable.

NAVIGATION WPT 55°17'·00N 07°34'·20W, 180°/5M to 5ca W of Dunree Hd lt. Entrance is easy and dangers are well marked. Off W shore: Swilly More Rocks, Kinnegar Spit and Strand; off E shore: Colpagh Rocks, White Strand Rocks and Inch Spit/Flats. Fahan Creek is buoyed; there is a shallow bar S of Inch Spit PHM and Inch Flats dry. Entry should not be attempted before LW+2. Numerous marine farms / shellfish beds run S from Scraggy Bay.

LIGHTS AND MARKS Fanad Hd lt, Fl (5) WR 20s 38m 18/14M, touching Dunree Hd lt, Fl (2) WR 5s 46m 12/9M, leads 151° into the Lough. Thence Ballygreen Point and Hawk's Nest in line 202°.

COMMUNICATIONS (Codes: both sides of lough 074); Police 9153060 (Milford) and 074 9320540 (Buncrana); Dr 9153500 (Rathmullan), 1850 400911 (out of hours), and 9363611 (Buncrana); Rathmullan Pontoon 9158131, 9158315 (eves). No VHF.

FACILITIES Portsalon Tamney Health Centre (4M), ☎0749159060

Rathmullan Pontoon (Easter–October) ☎087 2480132, €20/craft, season ticket €150 at pierhead, Kos ✉ Hotel ✕.

Ramelton (drying) Kos ✉ Ⓒ ✕.

Lough Swilly Marina www.loughswillymarina.com ☎9360008 mob 0861082111, 200 some Ⓥ; €3/m.

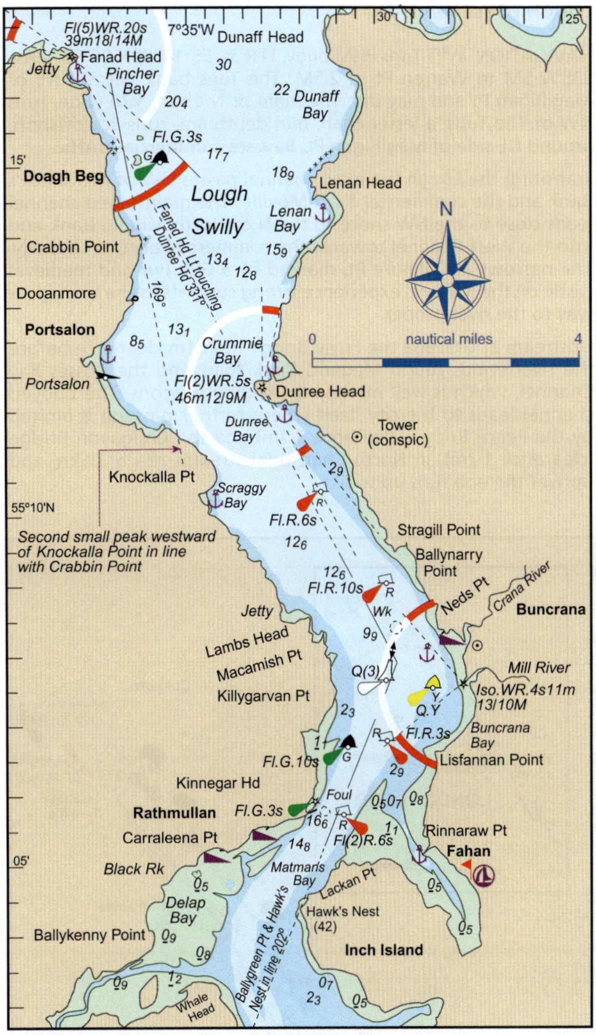

Fahan ✕ **Lough Swilly YC** www.loughswillyyc.com (1M SE): ⇄ ✈ (Londonderry 10M bus/taxi).

Buncrana (busy) Kos ✉ Ⓑ Hotel ✕ @ (library).

Dunree, Small concrete pier S of Dunree Head gives access to Fort Dunree Military Museum (✕) in settled weather in winds N through E to SE. Beware Dunree Skellig on approach. Tide gauge.

6.11 LOUGH FOYLE

Londonderry/Donegal **55°14'N 06°54'W**

CHARTS AC 2723, 2798, 2511, 2510, 5612; Imray C53, C64

TIDES

Standard Port RIVER FOYLE (LISAHALLY) (⟶)

Times				Height (metres)			
High Water		Low Water		MHWS	MHWN	MLWN	MLWS
0100	0800	0200	0700	2·6	1·9	0·9	0·4
1300	2000	1400	1900				
Differences WARREN LIGHTHOUSE							
–0055	–0115	–0155	–0117	–0·3	0·0	ND	ND
MOVILLE							
–0042	–0057	–0127	–0058	–0·3	0·0	+0·1	0·0
QUIGLEY'S POINT							
–0020	–0027	–0040	–0027	–0·3	–0·1	0·0	–0·1
LONDONDERRY							
+0033	+0035	+0032	+0032	+0·1	+0·2	+0·3	+0·2

Warren Point: –0430 Dover
Londonderry: –0255 Dover;
Moville: –0350 Dover
ML 1·6; Duration 0615

SHELTER The SE side of the Lough is low lying and shallow. The NW rises steeply and has several village hbrs between the ent and Londonderry (often referred to as Derry).

White Bay: close N of Dunagree Point is a good ⚓ in settled weather on passage.

Greencastle: Seasonal Ⓥ pontoon May-Sep 200m S of hbr, open to NE–SE and subject to swell, not advised in strong E'lies. Busy fishing hbr, open to swell in winds SW–E.

Moville: a quaint resort on the western shore. A concrete pier, with 1·5m at the end, is near the village (shops closed all day Wed), but is much used by FVs. ⚓ outside hbr is exposed; inside hbr for shoal draught only. 8 Y Ⓥs are about 600m upstream.

Carrickarory: pier/quay is used entirely by FVs. ⚓ in bay is sheltered in winds from SW to NNW. Plans for possible new marina.

Culmore Bay: good shelter. ⚓ 1½ca W of Culmore Pt in pleasant cove, 4M from Londonderry. *Continued overleaf*

LOUGH FOYLE *continued*

NAVIGATION WPT Tuns PHM buoy, Fl R 3s, 55°14′·00N 06°53′·49W, 235°/2·5M to Warren Pt lt, 2·5M. The Tuns bank lies 3M NE of Magilligan Pt and may dry. The main or N Chan, ¾M wide, runs NW of The Tuns; a lesser chan, min depth 4m, runs 3ca offshore around NE side of Magilligan Pt. **Beware commercial traffic**.

Transiting the Lough the main channel passes NW of McKinney's Bank and the commercial ⚓ off Moville. The maintained channel leads close to the NW shore to the N of North Middle Bank and into the West Channel towards the commercial port of Lisahally. The narrows at Culmore Pt, marked by a GW Twr and medieval castle on the N shore, experience strong currents as the Loch gives way to the river proper.

Upstream at Gransha the Foyle Bridge has 31m clearance before the river winds round Madams Bank following the Rosses Bay Channel, which is well marked by leading beacons. The buoyed channel leads to the city itself where further passage is limited by the Peace Bridge (clearance 3·7m) and the Craigavon Bridge (clearance 1·2m). In North Chan tidal streams reach 3½kn, and upriver the ebb runs up to 6kn.

LIGHTS AND MARKS Inishowen Fl (2) WRG 10s 28m 18/14M; W tr, 2 B bands; vis 197°-G-211°-W-249°-R-000°. Warren Pt Fl 1·5s 9m 10M; W tr, G abutment; vis 232°–061°. Magilligan Pt QR 7m 4M; ✕ structure. The main chan up to Londonderry is very well lit. Foyle Bridge centre FW each side; VQ G on W pier; VQ R on E.

COMMUNICATIONS (Code 028) ⊖ 7126 1937/Eire (353) 749 326324; Police 101; Dr 7126 4868; Ⓗ 7034 5171. HM (at Lisahally) 7186 0555. *Harbour Radio* VHF Ch **14** 12 16 (H24). Traffic and nav info Ch 14.

FACILITIES **Culdaff Bay** (10M W of Foyle SWM buoy) 6 Y ⚓s at 55°18′N 07°09′·1W, off Bunnagee Port. HM ☎7601 1281

Greencastle Ⓥ Pontoon 10€ Eu <12m; HM Kevin McNellis Ch 16 ☎ (0)877174724. McDonald Boats, ☎074 9381420/087 0640526.

Lisahally is the commercial port (55°02′·6N 07°15′·6W).

Londonderry Foyle Marina (pontoon) www.londonderryport.com billmccann@londonderryport.com, ☎71860555, mob 078 41580590 ⛵ in 5-7m, £15-£21/night, ♿ 🚿 ⛽£3, adjacent to city centre. Yachts are to call *Harbour Radio* on Ch 14 for berthing directions at Foyle Marina; payments can be made online through PayPal.

Prehen Boat Club (above Craigavon Bridge) ☎7034 3405.

City Ⓟ Ⓓ 🔧 ⚙ ✉ Ⓑ 🛒 ✕ 🍷 ≷ ✈.

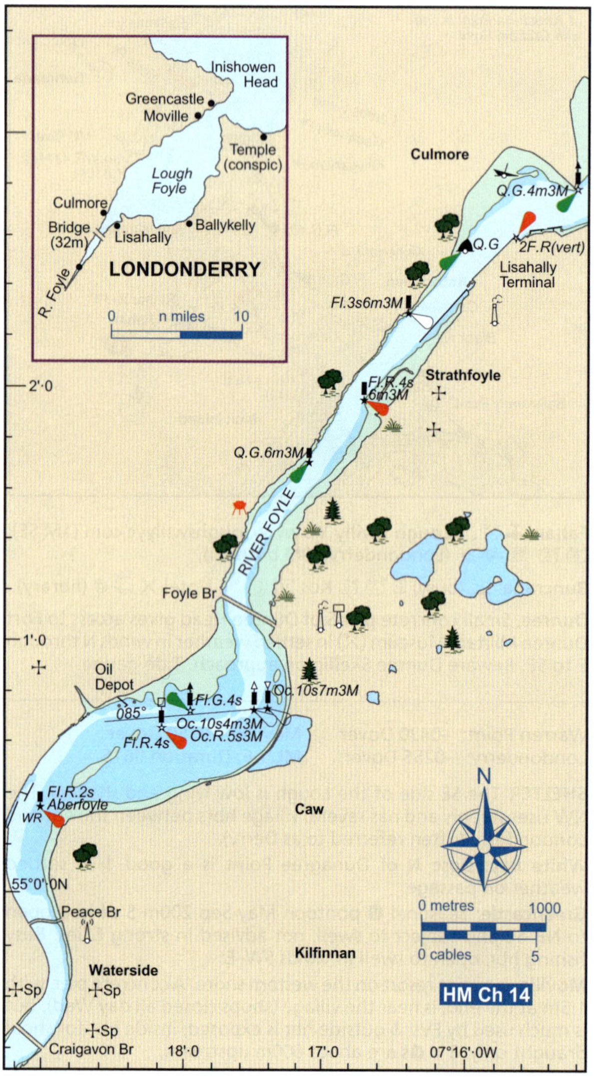

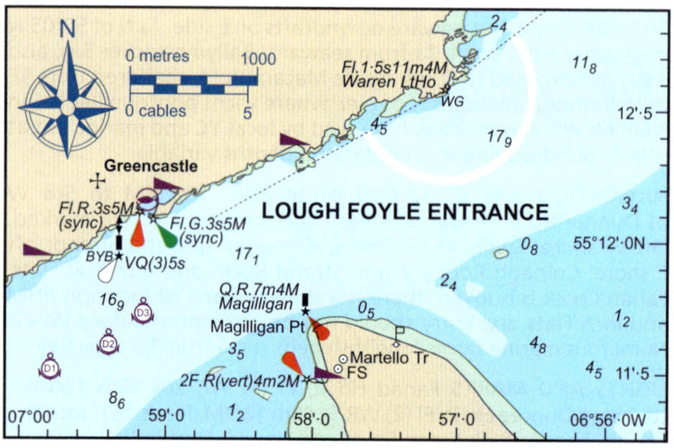

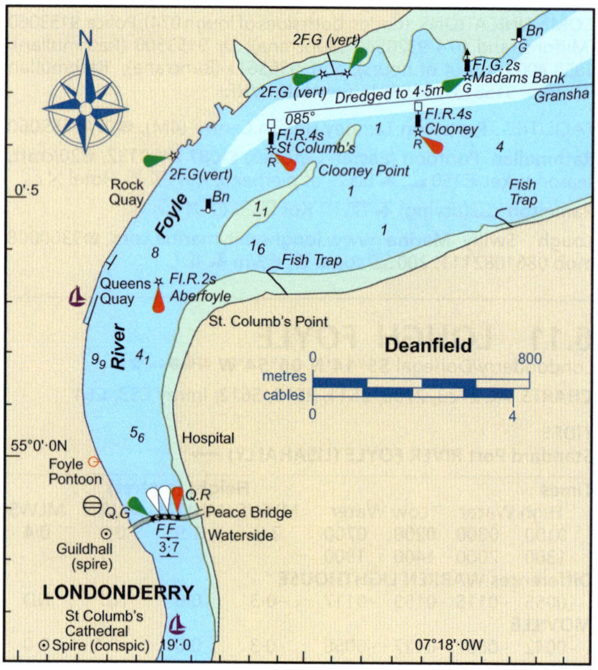

STANDARD TIME (UT)
For Summer Time add ONE hour in **non-shaded areas**

RIVER FOYLE LAT 55°03′N LONG 7°16′W

TIMES AND HEIGHTS OF HIGH AND LOW WATERS

Dates in red are SPRINGS
Dates in blue are NEAPS

YEAR **2024**

JANUARY

Day	Time	m	Day	Time	m
1 M	0421 1040 1734 2312	0.7 2.3 1.0 2.0	16 TU	0500 1110 1747 2331	0.5 2.8 0.6 2.2
2 TU	0500 1122 1822 2359	0.7 2.2 1.0 1.9	17 W	0545 1205 1837	0.6 2.6 0.8
3 W	0545 1214 1917	0.8 2.1 1.0	18 TH ◐	0023 0639 1312 1934	2.0 0.7 2.4 0.9
4 TH ◑	0100 0641 1326 2017	1.8 0.9 2.0 1.0	19 F	0135 0749 1430 2040	1.9 0.9 2.3 1.0
5 F	0212 0746 1440 2118	1.8 1.0 2.0 0.9	20 SA	0306 0920 1546 2154	1.9 1.0 2.2 1.0
6 SA	0321 0853 1541 2218	1.9 1.0 2.1 0.9	21 SU	0437 1046 1658 2302	2.0 0.9 2.2 1.0
7 SU	0422 0959 1635 2313	2.0 1.0 2.2 0.8	22 M	0540 1149 1755 2355	2.1 0.8 2.3 0.9
8 M	0513 1102 1725	2.2 0.9 2.3	23 TU	0625 1240 1841	2.3 0.7 2.3
9 TU	0000 0559 1159 1813	0.7 2.4 0.8 2.4	24 W	0039 0702 1325 1921	0.8 2.5 0.7 2.3
10 W	0045 0642 1253 1900	0.6 2.6 0.7 2.4	25 TH ○	0118 0736 1407 1956	0.7 2.5 0.7 2.3
11 TH ●	0129 0724 1345 1947	0.6 2.8 0.6 2.5	26 F	0155 0808 1446 2028	0.6 2.6 0.7 2.3
12 F	0212 0807 1437 2033	0.5 2.9 0.5 2.5	27 SA	0228 0839 1522 2058	0.5 2.6 0.7 2.3
13 SA	0255 0851 1527 2119	0.4 3.0 0.5 2.5	28 SU	0300 0908 1553 2128	0.5 2.5 0.7 2.3
14 SU	0337 0936 1614 2203	0.4 3.0 0.5 2.4	29 M	0330 0938 1623 2200	0.5 2.5 0.7 2.3
15 M	0418 1022 1700 2246	0.4 2.9 0.5 2.3	30 TU	0402 1009 1653 2234	0.5 2.4 0.7 2.2
			31 W	0436 1043 1729 2313	0.6 2.2 0.8 2.1

FEBRUARY

Day	Time	m	Day	Time	m
1 TH	0516 1121 1813 2359	0.7 2.1 0.9 1.9	16 F ◐	0609 1231 1842	0.7 2.2 0.9
2 F ◑	0603 1210 1909	0.8 2.0 0.9	17 SA	0029 0718 1401 1946	1.9 0.9 2.0 1.1
3 SA	0103 0705 1323 2013	1.8 0.9 1.9 1.0	18 SU	0238 0915 1540 2115	1.8 1.0 1.9 1.1
4 SU	0227 0814 1454 2124	1.8 1.0 1.9 1.0	19 M	0437 1051 1700 2243	1.9 0.9 2.0 1.0
5 M	0346 0926 1616 2242	1.9 1.0 1.9 0.9	20 TU	0538 1151 1755 2340	2.1 0.8 2.1 0.9
6 TU	0452 1044 1723 2345	2.1 0.9 2.0 0.8	21 W	0619 1237 1837	2.3 0.7 2.1
7 W	0545 1158 1817	2.3 0.8 2.2	22 TH	0024 0654 1316 1912	0.7 2.4 0.6 2.2
8 TH	0035 0631 1255 1903	0.6 2.5 0.6 2.3	23 F	0104 0725 1354 1943	0.6 2.5 0.5 2.3
9 F ●	0121 0714 1347 1945	0.5 2.7 0.4 2.4	24 SA ○	0140 0753 1429 2009	0.5 2.5 0.5 2.3
10 SA	0204 0755 1434 2025	0.4 2.9 0.3 2.5	25 SU	0214 0818 1500 2033	0.4 2.5 0.5 2.3
11 SU	0245 0836 1517 2103	0.2 3.0 0.3 2.5	26 M	0243 0843 1527 2100	0.4 2.5 0.5 2.4
12 M	0324 0917 1557 2140	0.2 3.1 0.3 2.5	27 TU	0311 0910 1551 2129	0.4 2.4 0.5 2.4
13 TU	0402 0959 1635 2216	0.2 3.0 0.4 2.4	28 W	0340 0939 1616 2200	0.4 2.4 0.5 2.3
14 W	0441 1042 1713 2253	0.3 2.8 0.5 2.2	29 TH	0413 1010 1645 2234	0.5 2.2 0.6 2.2
15 TH	0521 1130 1753 2334	0.5 2.5 0.7 2.0			

MARCH

Day	Time	m	Day	Time	m
1 F	0449 1044 1721 2312	0.6 2.1 0.7 2.0	16 SA	0548 1159 1756 2350	0.7 2.0 0.9 1.9
2 SA	0533 1124 1808	0.7 1.9 0.9	17 SU ◐	0704 1341 1858	0.9 1.8 1.0
3 SU ◑	0003 0631 1224 1916	1.9 0.9 1.8 1.0	18 M	0232 0919 1523 2034	1.8 0.9 1.7 1.1
4 M	0132 0745 1420 2038	1.8 1.0 1.7 1.0	19 TU	0414 1040 1641 2212	1.9 0.8 1.8 1.0
5 TU	0318 0906 1618 2221	1.8 0.9 1.7 0.9	20 W	0513 1135 1734 2312	2.1 0.7 1.9 0.8
6 W	0432 1048 1727 2331	2.0 0.8 1.9 0.8	21 TH	0555 1216 1814 2358	2.2 0.6 2.0 0.6
7 TH	0528 1200 1814	2.3 0.6 2.1	22 F	0630 1253 1848	2.3 0.5 2.1
8 F	0020 0614 1251 1854	0.6 2.5 0.4 2.2	23 SA	0038 0700 1328 1917	0.5 2.3 0.4 2.2
9 SA	0104 0655 1336 1930	0.4 2.7 0.2 2.4	24 SU	0115 0726 1401 1941	0.4 2.4 0.4 2.3
10 SU ●	0145 0734 1417 2004	0.2 2.9 0.1 2.5	25 M ○	0148 0749 1431 2004	0.3 2.4 0.3 2.4
11 M	0224 0814 1455 2037	0.1 3.0 0.1 2.5	26 TU	0218 0812 1456 2029	0.3 2.4 0.3 2.4
12 TU	0302 0853 1530 2111	0.0 3.0 0.1 2.5	27 W	0246 0840 1519 2058	0.3 2.4 0.4 2.4
13 W	0340 0933 1603 2145	0.1 2.9 0.3 2.4	28 TH	0315 0910 1541 2129	0.4 2.3 0.4 2.4
14 TH	0418 1015 1636 2220	0.2 2.7 0.4 2.3	29 F	0348 0943 1608 2202	0.4 2.2 0.5 2.3
15 F	0459 1101 1712 2259	0.4 2.4 0.7 2.1	30 SA	0426 1018 1640 2240	0.5 2.1 0.6 2.1
			31 SU	0510 1059 1721 2329	0.7 1.9 0.8 1.9

APRIL

Day	Time	m	Day	Time	m
1 M	0608 1158 1820	0.8 1.7 0.9	16 TU	0209 0853 1442 1948	1.8 0.9 1.6 1.0
2 TU ◑	0052 0726 1402 1955	1.8 0.9 1.6 1.0	17 W	0329 1001 1555 2126	1.9 0.8 1.7 0.9
3 W	0251 0857 1559 2148	1.9 0.8 1.6 0.9	18 TH	0428 1054 1654 2231	2.0 0.6 1.7 0.8
4 TH	0403 1036 1705 2301	2.1 0.7 1.8 0.7	19 F	0515 1138 1738 2321	2.1 0.5 1.9 0.6
5 F	0459 1140 1751 2351	2.3 0.5 2.0 0.5	20 SA	0553 1217 1813	2.2 0.4 2.0
6 SA	0546 1229 1829	2.5 0.3 2.2	21 SU	0003 0625 1252 1843	0.5 2.2 0.4 2.1
7 SU	0035 0628 1310 1904	0.3 2.7 0.1 2.3	22 M	0041 0651 1326 1908	0.4 2.2 0.3 2.2
8 M ●	0116 0709 1349 1936	0.1 2.9 0.1 2.5	23 TU ○	0114 0714 1356 1933	0.4 2.3 0.3 2.4
9 TU	0157 0748 1425 2009	0.0 3.0 0.1 2.5	24 W	0145 0741 1422 2001	0.4 2.3 0.3 2.4
10 W	0236 0829 1459 2043	0.0 2.9 0.1 2.5	25 TH	0216 0812 1447 2031	0.4 2.3 0.3 2.5
11 TH	0316 0910 1531 2119	0.1 2.8 0.3 2.5	26 F	0249 0846 1513 2105	0.4 2.3 0.4 2.4
12 F	0357 0953 1604 2156	0.3 2.5 0.4 2.3	27 SA	0326 0924 1543 2141	0.4 2.2 0.5 2.3
13 SA	0442 1041 1640 2238	0.5 2.2 0.6 2.1	28 SU	0409 1006 1618 2223	0.5 2.1 0.6 2.2
14 SU	0538 1140 1723 2339	0.7 1.9 0.8 1.9	29 M	0458 1055 1659 2318	0.6 1.9 0.7 2.1
15 M ◐	0706 1314 1820	0.9 1.7 0.9	30 TU	0600 1159 1756	0.7 1.7 0.8

Chart Datum: 1·37 metres below Ordnance Datum (Belfast). HAT is 3·1 metres above Chart Datum.

STANDARD TIME (UT)
For Summer Time add ONE hour in **non-shaded areas**

RIVER FOYLE LAT 55°03′N LONG 7°16′W

TIMES AND HEIGHTS OF HIGH AND LOW WATERS

Dates in red are SPRINGS
Dates in blue are NEAPS

YEAR **2024**

MAY

Date	Day	Time	m	Time	m	Time	m	Time	m
1	W	0041	2.0	0718	0.7	1341	1.6	◑ 1923	0.9
2	TH	0220	2.0	0841	0.7	1514	1.6	2104	0.8
3	F	0327	2.2	0958	0.5	1623	1.8	2218	0.6
4	SA	0424	2.3	1102	0.4	1716	2.0	2315	0.4
5	SU	0514	2.5	1154	0.3	1758	2.1		
6	M	0003	0.3	0601	2.7	1238	0.2	1836	2.3
7	TU	0047	0.2	0644	2.8	1318	0.2	1911	2.4
8	W	0130	0.1	0726	2.8	1355	0.2	● 1946	2.5
9	TH	0213	0.1	0809	2.7	1430	0.2	2022	2.5
10	F	0257	0.3	0852	2.6	1505	0.3	2101	2.4
11	SA	0342	0.4	0938	2.3	1540	0.4	2142	2.3
12	SU	0433	0.6	1028	2.1	1617	0.5	2229	2.2
13	M	0534	0.7	1125	1.9	1658	0.7	2339	2.0
14	TU	0652	0.8	1234	1.7	1748	0.8		
15	W	0126	1.9	0809	0.8	1346	1.6	◐ 1855	0.8
16	TH	0238	1.9	0909	0.7	1453	1.6	2021	0.8
17	F	0336	2.0	1001	0.7	1555	1.6	2136	0.8
18	SA	0426	2.0	1049	0.6	1649	1.7	2234	0.7
19	SU	0508	2.0	1132	0.5	1731	1.9	2321	0.6
20	M	0541	2.1	1212	0.4	1804	2.0		
21	TU	0000	0.5	0610	2.1	1248	0.4	1835	2.2
22	W	0036	0.5	0640	2.2	1321	0.4	1905	2.3
23	TH	0112	0.4	0713	2.2	1352	0.4	○ 1938	2.4
24	F	0149	0.4	0750	2.3	1423	0.4	2012	2.5
25	SA	0230	0.4	0831	2.3	1455	0.4	2050	2.5
26	SU	0314	0.5	0916	2.2	1531	0.4	2132	2.4
27	M	0403	0.5	1004	2.1	1610	0.5	2220	2.3
28	TU	0458	0.6	1057	1.9	1654	0.6	2318	2.2
29	W	0600	0.6	1158	1.8	1748	0.7		
30	TH	0029	2.2	0707	0.6	1309	1.7	◑ 1900	0.7
31	F	0146	2.2	0813	0.5	1425	1.7	2023	0.7

JUNE

Date	Day	Time	m	Time	m	Time	m	Time	m
1	SA	0251	2.3	0917	0.5	1535	1.8	2137	0.6
2	SU	0350	2.3	1019	0.5	1638	1.9	2241	0.5
3	M	0445	2.4	1117	0.4	1730	2.0	2336	0.4
4	TU	0537	2.5	1207	0.4	1813	2.2		
5	W	0026	0.3	0625	2.5	1251	0.3	1854	2.3
6	TH	0113	0.3	0712	2.5	1332	0.3	● 1932	2.4
7	F	0200	0.3	0757	2.4	1410	0.3	2011	2.5
8	SA	0248	0.4	0843	2.3	1447	0.4	2052	2.4
9	SU	0338	0.5	0929	2.2	1523	0.4	2135	2.4
10	M	0429	0.6	1015	2.1	1559	0.5	2222	2.2
11	TU	0522	0.7	1101	1.9	1637	0.5	2316	2.1
12	W	0617	0.7	1149	1.8	1718	0.6		
13	TH	0022	2.0	0715	0.7	1242	1.7	1808	0.7
14	F	0134	1.9	0809	0.7	1342	1.6	◐ 1911	0.8
15	SA	0235	1.9	0901	0.7	1445	1.6	2021	0.8
16	SU	0327	1.9	0953	0.6	1548	1.7	2129	0.8
17	M	0413	1.9	1043	0.6	1643	1.8	2228	0.7
18	TU	0454	2.0	1130	0.5	1729	2.0	2319	0.7
19	W	0533	2.0	1213	0.5	1808	2.2		
20	TH	0004	0.6	0613	2.1	1252	0.4	1845	2.3
21	F	0048	0.6	0655	2.2	1330	0.4	1923	2.4
22	SA	0134	0.5	0739	2.2	1409	0.4	○ 2002	2.5
23	SU	0223	0.5	0826	2.2	1448	0.4	2044	2.6
24	M	0315	0.5	0914	2.2	1528	0.4	2129	2.6
25	TU	0407	0.4	1002	2.1	1609	0.4	2217	2.5
26	W	0458	0.4	1050	2.1	1652	0.4	2308	2.5
27	TH	0550	0.4	1140	2.0	1739	0.5		
28	F	0006	2.4	0644	0.5	1233	1.9	◑ 1836	0.6
29	SA	0111	2.3	0740	0.5	1337	1.8	1945	0.6
30	SU	0218	2.3	0839	0.6	1450	1.7	2102	0.7

JULY

Date	Day	Time	m	Time	m	Time	m	Time	m
1	M	0323	2.3	0942	0.6	1607	1.8	2218	0.6
2	TU	0425	2.2	1047	0.6	1715	2.0	2323	0.6
3	W	0525	2.3	1145	0.6	1807	2.1		
4	TH	0018	0.5	0620	2.3	1234	0.5	1850	2.3
5	F	0110	0.5	0709	2.3	1318	0.5	● 1930	2.4
6	SA	0200	0.5	0755	2.3	1358	0.4	2009	2.5
7	SU	0248	0.5	0837	2.2	1436	0.4	2047	2.5
8	M	0334	0.5	0917	2.2	1511	0.4	2125	2.4
9	TU	0417	0.6	0954	2.1	1544	0.4	2203	2.3
10	W	0457	0.6	1030	2.0	1616	0.4	2241	2.2
11	TH	0536	0.6	1107	1.9	1651	0.5	2322	2.1
12	F	0618	0.7	1148	1.8	1732	0.6		
13	SA	0010	1.9	0704	0.7	1238	1.7	◐ 1823	0.7
14	SU	0112	1.8	0756	0.7	1341	1.7	1926	0.8
15	M	0220	1.8	0851	0.7	1453	1.7	2034	0.9
16	TU	0320	1.8	0951	0.7	1602	1.8	2141	0.9
17	W	0416	1.9	1052	0.7	1702	1.9	2246	0.8
18	TH	0511	1.9	1146	0.6	1750	2.1	2346	0.7
19	F	0602	2.0	1235	0.5	1833	2.3		
20	SA	0040	0.6	0651	2.1	1319	0.4	1914	2.5
21	SU	0133	0.5	0738	2.2	1401	0.4	○ 1954	2.6
22	M	0225	0.4	0823	2.2	1442	0.3	2036	2.7
23	TU	0314	0.4	0906	2.3	1522	0.2	2118	2.8
24	W	0400	0.3	0948	2.3	1601	0.2	2201	2.8
25	TH	0444	0.3	1028	2.2	1640	0.2	2247	2.7
26	F	0527	0.4	1109	2.1	1721	0.3	2336	2.5
27	SA	0612	0.5	1154	2.0	1808	0.5		
28	SU	0035	2.3	0703	0.6	1249	1.8	◑ 1911	0.7
29	M	0148	2.2	0801	0.7	1411	1.7	2037	0.8
30	TU	0306	2.1	0909	0.8	1555	1.8	2214	0.8
31	W	0422	2.1	1027	0.8	1722	2.0	2327	0.7

AUGUST

Date	Day	Time	m	Time	m	Time	m	Time	m
1	TH	0531	2.1	1133	0.7	1813	2.2		
2	F	0022	0.6	0625	2.1	1224	0.6	1853	2.3
3	SA	0111	0.5	0710	2.2	1308	0.5	1929	2.4
4	SU	0157	0.5	0749	2.2	1348	0.4	● 2002	2.5
5	M	0239	0.5	0823	2.2	1423	0.3	2034	2.5
6	TU	0318	0.5	0854	2.2	1456	0.3	2104	2.5
7	W	0353	0.5	0924	2.2	1525	0.3	2134	2.4
8	TH	0424	0.5	0955	2.2	1554	0.3	2204	2.3
9	F	0454	0.6	1027	2.1	1625	0.4	2236	2.2
10	SA	0526	0.6	1104	2.0	1701	0.6	2313	2.0
11	SU	0606	0.7	1147	1.9	1745	0.7		
12	M	0000	1.8	0656	0.8	1245	1.7	◐ 1844	0.9
13	TU	0113	1.7	0756	0.8	1409	1.7	1955	1.0
14	W	0244	1.7	0905	0.8	1534	1.8	2110	1.0
15	TH	0402	1.8	1024	0.8	1644	1.9	2231	0.9
16	F	0510	1.9	1131	0.7	1737	2.1	2345	0.7
17	SA	0604	2.0	1222	0.6	1820	2.3		
18	SU	0041	0.6	0649	2.1	1306	0.4	1900	2.6
19	M	0131	0.4	0730	2.2	1348	0.3	○ 1938	2.8
20	TU	0217	0.3	0808	2.3	1427	0.2	2017	2.9
21	W	0300	0.2	0844	2.4	1505	0.1	2056	3.0
22	TH	0340	0.2	0921	2.4	1542	0.1	2136	3.0
23	F	0417	0.2	0957	2.4	1619	0.1	2219	2.8
24	SA	0455	0.4	1034	2.3	1657	0.3	2305	2.6
25	SU	0534	0.5	1114	2.1	1742	0.5		
26	M	0001	2.3	0620	0.7	1204	1.9	◑ 1846	0.8
27	TU	0126	2.0	0720	0.9	1350	1.8	2038	0.9
28	W	0303	1.9	0842	1.0	1607	1.9	2224	0.9
29	TH	0426	2.0	1014	0.9	1720	2.1	2328	0.7
30	F	0528	2.0	1119	0.8	1804	2.3		
31	SA	0017	0.6	0616	2.1	1208	0.6	1841	2.4

Chart Datum: 1·37 metres below Ordnance Datum (Belfast). HAT is 3·1 metres above Chart Datum.

STANDARD TIME (UT)
For Summer Time add ONE hour in **non-shaded areas**

RIVER FOYLE LAT 55°03′N LONG 7°16′W

TIMES AND HEIGHTS OF HIGH AND LOW WATERS

Dates in red are SPRINGS
Dates in blue are NEAPS

YEAR **2024**

SEPTEMBER

Date	Day	Time	m	Time	m	Time	m	Time	m
1	SU	0100	0.5	0655	2.2	1250	0.5	1913	2.5
2	M	0139	0.5	0729	2.2	1328	0.4	1942	2.5
3	TU	0216	0.4	0758	2.3	1403	0.3	● 2009	2.5
4	W	0250	0.4	0824	2.3	1433	0.3	2034	2.5
5	TH	0320	0.5	0850	2.4	1501	0.3	2059	2.4
6	F	0346	0.5	0918	2.3	1528	0.4	2126	2.4
7	SA	0410	0.6	0948	2.3	1557	0.5	2156	2.2
8	SU	0437	0.6	1021	2.2	1632	0.6	2228	2.1
9	M	0511	0.7	1058	2.0	1713	0.8	2306	1.9
10	TU	0556	0.9	1146	1.9	1808	0.9		
11	W	0005	1.7	0658	1.0	1318	1.7	◐ 1923	1.0
12	TH	0221	1.6	0817	1.0	1510	1.8	2049	1.0
13	F	0358	1.7	1000	0.9	1620	2.0	2234	0.9
14	SA	0503	1.9	1111	0.8	1713	2.2	2340	0.7
15	SU	0551	2.0	1200	0.6	1756	2.5		
16	M	0029	0.5	0631	2.2	1242	0.4	1835	2.7
17	TU	0113	0.3	0707	2.3	1322	0.2	1912	2.9
18	W	0153	0.2	0741	2.5	1401	0.1	○ 1950	3.1
19	TH	0232	0.1	0815	2.6	1439	0.0	2029	3.1
20	F	0308	0.2	0849	2.6	1516	0.1	2109	3.0
21	SA	0343	0.3	0924	2.6	1554	0.2	2151	2.8
22	SU	0418	0.4	1001	2.4	1635	0.4	2237	2.5
23	M	0455	0.6	1042	2.2	1723	0.7	2335	2.2
24	TU	0538	0.8	1134	2.0	1835	0.9	◑	
25	W	0113	1.9	0638	1.0	1357	1.9	2050	1.0
26	TH	0253	1.9	0810	1.1	1546	2.0	2214	0.9
27	F	0408	1.9	0947	1.0	1651	2.2	2311	0.7
28	SA	0505	2.0	1050	0.8	1736	2.4	2355	0.6
29	SU	0550	2.1	1139	0.7	1813	2.5		
30	M	0033	0.5	0627	2.2	1221	0.5	1845	2.5

OCTOBER

Date	Day	Time	m	Time	m	Time	m	Time	m
1	TU	0109	0.5	0659	2.3	1300	0.4	1913	2.5
2	W	0143	0.4	0725	2.4	1334	0.4	● 1936	2.5
3	TH	0214	0.4	0750	2.5	1403	0.4	1959	2.5
4	F	0242	0.5	0815	2.5	1430	0.4	2024	2.5
5	SA	0305	0.5	0843	2.5	1458	0.5	2052	2.4
6	SU	0328	0.6	0914	2.5	1529	0.6	2122	2.3
7	M	0354	0.6	0946	2.4	1605	0.7	2155	2.2
8	TU	0426	0.8	1022	2.2	1647	0.8	2234	2.0
9	W	0506	0.9	1106	2.1	1742	1.0	2329	1.8
10	TH	0600	1.0	1220	1.9	1857	1.1	◐	
11	F	0146	1.7	0721	1.1	1433	2.0	2032	1.0
12	SA	0330	1.7	0907	1.0	1542	2.1	2208	0.8
13	SU	0432	1.9	1030	0.9	1636	2.4	2311	0.6
14	M	0520	2.1	1124	0.6	1722	2.6		
15	TU	0000	0.4	0600	2.3	1209	0.4	1803	2.8
16	W	0042	0.3	0637	2.5	1250	0.3	1844	3.0
17	TH	0121	0.2	0711	2.6	1331	0.2	○ 1923	3.1
18	F	0159	0.2	0746	2.7	1411	0.1	2003	3.1
19	SA	0235	0.3	0822	2.8	1451	0.2	2045	3.0
20	SU	0310	0.4	0859	2.7	1533	0.4	2129	2.8
21	M	0345	0.5	0938	2.6	1619	0.6	2217	2.5
22	TU	0423	0.7	1022	2.4	1713	0.8	2317	2.1
23	W	0506	0.9	1122	2.2	1837	1.0		
24	TH	0049	1.9	0601	1.0	1336	2.1	◑ 2029	1.0
25	F	0218	1.8	0722	1.1	1502	2.2	2141	0.9
26	SA	0327	1.9	0900	1.0	1606	2.3	2234	0.8
27	SU	0426	2.0	1008	0.9	1656	2.4	2318	0.7
28	M	0513	2.1	1101	0.8	1736	2.4	2357	0.6
29	TU	0552	2.2	1146	0.7	1810	2.4		
30	W	0032	0.6	0624	2.3	1225	0.6	1838	2.5
31	TH	0106	0.5	0651	2.4	1259	0.6	1901	2.5

NOVEMBER

Date	Day	Time	m	Time	m	Time	m	Time	m
1	F	0137	0.5	0717	2.6	1329	0.6	● 1925	2.5
2	SA	0204	0.5	0745	2.6	1358	0.6	1952	2.5
3	SU	0229	0.6	0815	2.7	1430	0.6	2024	2.5
4	M	0254	0.6	0848	2.7	1505	0.7	2059	2.4
5	TU	0324	0.7	0923	2.6	1545	0.8	2138	2.2
6	W	0358	0.8	1002	2.4	1632	0.9	2223	2.1
7	TH	0439	0.9	1051	2.3	1729	1.0	2323	1.9
8	F	0530	1.0	1200	2.2	1841	1.0		
9	SA	0100	1.8	0639	1.0	1343	2.2	◐ 2004	0.9
10	SU	0238	1.8	0810	1.0	1457	2.3	2122	0.8
11	M	0347	1.9	0934	0.9	1555	2.5	2227	0.7
12	TU	0442	2.1	1040	0.7	1647	2.7	2321	0.5
13	W	0527	2.3	1133	0.5	1733	2.9		
14	TH	0007	0.4	0608	2.5	1220	0.4	1818	3.0
15	F	0049	0.4	0646	2.7	1305	0.3	○ 1901	3.0
16	SA	0129	0.4	0724	2.8	1349	0.3	1944	3.0
17	SU	0207	0.4	0802	2.8	1434	0.4	2028	2.8
18	M	0244	0.5	0842	2.8	1520	0.6	2114	2.6
19	TU	0322	0.6	0925	2.7	1610	0.7	2203	2.4
20	W	0400	0.7	1013	2.5	1708	0.9	2300	2.1
21	TH	0442	0.8	1115	2.3	1821	1.0		
22	F	0008	1.9	0529	0.9	1248	2.2	1944	1.0
23	SA	0122	1.8	0627	1.0	1410	2.2	◑ 2051	1.0
24	SU	0230	1.8	0743	1.1	1514	2.2	2145	0.9
25	M	0331	1.9	0904	1.0	1609	2.2	2232	0.8
26	TU	0426	2.0	1011	1.0	1655	2.3	2315	0.8
27	W	0511	2.1	1103	0.9	1731	2.3	2354	0.7
28	TH	0548	2.3	1145	0.8	1801	2.3		
29	F	0029	0.6	0620	2.4	1222	0.8	1827	2.4
30	SA	0102	0.6	0651	2.6	1256	0.7	1856	2.4

DECEMBER

Date	Day	Time	m	Time	m	Time	m	Time	m
1	SU	0133	0.6	0722	2.7	1332	0.7	● 1929	2.5
2	M	0203	0.6	0756	2.7	1409	0.7	2006	2.5
3	TU	0235	0.6	0833	2.7	1451	0.7	2048	2.4
4	W	0309	0.7	0912	2.7	1537	0.8	2133	2.3
5	TH	0347	0.7	0956	2.6	1627	0.8	2222	2.2
6	F	0429	0.8	1046	2.5	1722	0.8	2317	2.1
7	SA	0517	0.8	1145	2.4	1824	0.9		
8	SU	0022	1.9	0616	0.9	1259	2.4	◐ 1930	0.8
9	M	0141	1.9	0728	0.9	1413	2.4	2037	0.8
10	TU	0255	1.9	0846	0.9	1518	2.5	2142	0.7
11	W	0401	2.1	1000	0.8	1616	2.6	2244	0.7
12	TH	0458	2.2	1105	0.7	1711	2.7	2338	0.6
13	F	0547	2.4	1201	0.6	1801	2.8		
14	SA	0025	0.6	0630	2.6	1251	0.6	1848	2.8
15	SU	0108	0.5	0712	2.7	1340	0.6	○ 1934	2.7
16	M	0149	0.5	0753	2.8	1428	0.6	2020	2.6
17	TU	0229	0.5	0835	2.8	1517	0.7	2105	2.5
18	W	0307	0.6	0918	2.7	1606	0.8	2150	2.4
19	TH	0344	0.6	1003	2.6	1655	0.9	2235	2.2
20	F	0421	0.7	1050	2.5	1745	0.9	2320	2.0
21	SA	0500	0.8	1144	2.3	1839	1.0		
22	SU	0009	1.9	0544	0.9	1253	2.2	◑ 1939	1.0
23	M	0110	1.8	0637	1.0	1409	2.1	2038	1.0
24	TU	0219	1.8	0742	1.0	1513	2.1	2134	1.0
25	W	0325	1.9	0854	1.1	1608	2.1	2227	0.9
26	TH	0425	2.0	1003	1.0	1653	2.1	2314	0.8
27	F	0513	2.2	1102	1.0	1730	2.2	2357	0.8
28	SA	0554	2.3	1150	0.9	1804	2.2		
29	SU	0035	0.7	0631	2.5	1234	0.8	1841	2.3
30	M	0113	0.7	0708	2.6	1318	0.8	● 1920	2.4
31	TU	0150	0.6	0745	2.7	1403	0.7	2001	2.4

Chart Datum: 1·37 metres below Ordnance Datum (Belfast). HAT is 3·1 metres above Chart Datum.

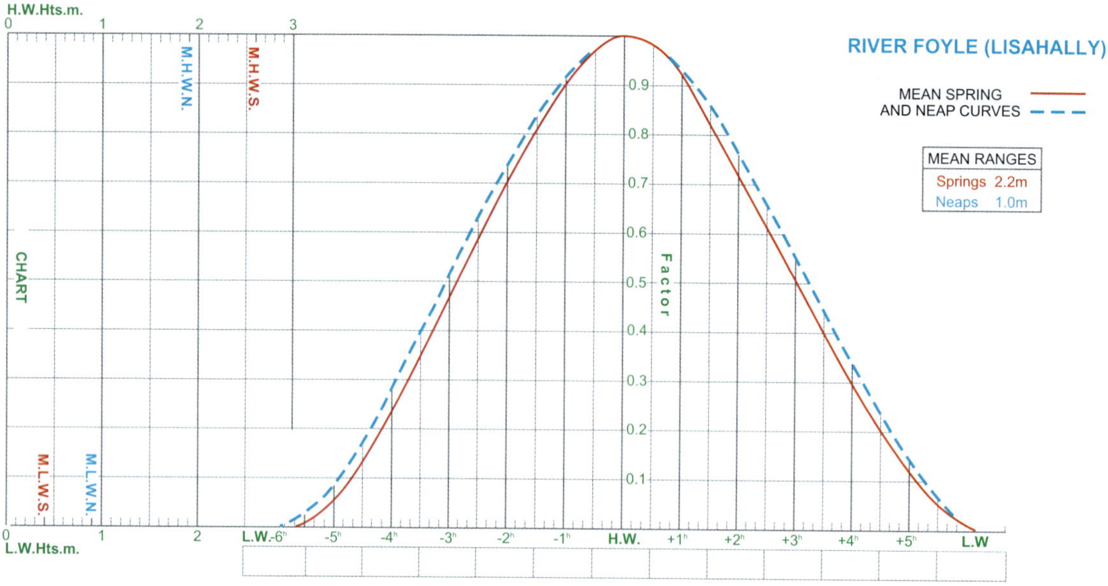

6.12 RIVER BANN AND COLERAINE

Londonderry/Antrim **55°10'·32N 06°46'·35W**

CHARTS AC 2723, 2798, 2494, 5612; Imray C53, C64

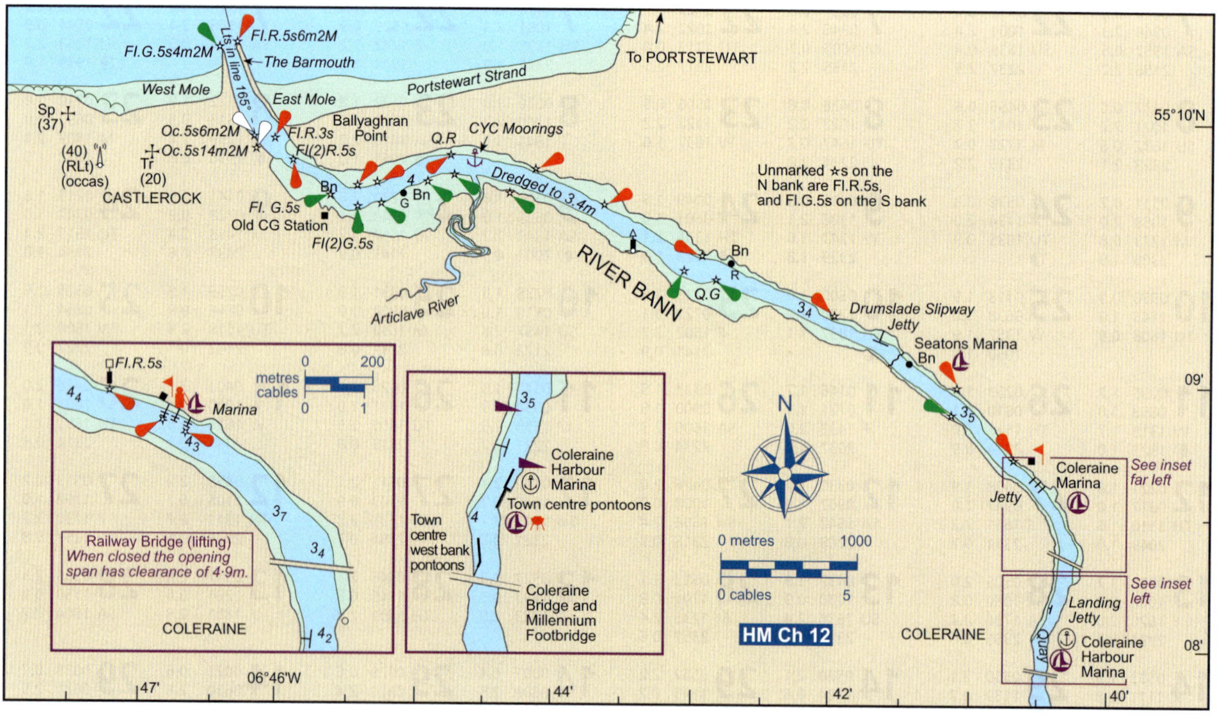

TIDES −0345 Dover (Coleraine); ML 1·1; Duration 0540

Standard Port RIVER FOYLE (⟵)

Times				Height (metres)			
High Water		Low Water		MHWS	MHWN	MLWN	MLWS
0100	0800	0200	0700	2·6	1·9	0·9	0·4
1300	2000	1400	1900				
Differences COLERAINE							
−0004	−0106	−0109	−0005	−0·4	−0·1	0·0	0·0

SHELTER Good, once inside the river ent (The Barmouth) between 2 training walls, extending 2ca N from the beaches. Do not try to enter in strong onshore winds or when swell breaks on the pierheads. If in doubt call Coleraine Hbr Radio or ring HM at Harbour Marina in town centre. ⚓ upstream of old CG stn, or berth at Seaton's, Coleraine or Town Centre marinas, 3½M, 4½M and 5M from ent, on NE bank. The last has berths on both banks between the railway and Millennium bridges.

NAVIGATION WPT 55°11´·00N, 06°46´·65W, 165°/0·72M to ent. Appr from E of N to bring ldg lts into line at bkwtr ends. The sand bar is constantly moving but ent is dredged to approx 3·5m. Beware commercial traffic, which runs up to Coleraine Harbour (town centre). This facility is accessed via the lifting railway bridge. Contact HM to arrange opening prior to arrival.

LIGHTS AND MARKS Ldg lts 165°, both Oc 5s 6/14m 2M, front on W pyramidal metal tr; rear W □ tr. Portstewart Pt, Oc R 10s, is 2M ENE.

COMMUNICATIONS (Code 028) CGOC 91463933; Police 101; Ⓗ 70344177; Dr 70344831; HM ☎ 70342012, mob 07742242788; Railway Bridge 70325400.

Coleraine Hbr Radio and Town Centre Marina Ch 12 (Mon-Fri: HO and when vessel due); Coleraine Marina Ch M.

FACILITIES **Coleraine Hbr (town centre)** ☎70342012, slip, E Bank 10 ⓥ, W Bank 7 ⓥ, £10; (40t) WC.

Coleraine Marina ☎70344768, slip 90+5ⓥ £21, (H24) (12½t).

Seatons Marina ☎70832086 mob 07718 883099, slip (£3) (12t).

Coleraine YC ☎70344503.

Town Ⓔ Ⓑ ✕ ⇌ ✈ (Belfast).

MINOR HARBOUR TO THE EAST

Portstewart, Antrim, **55°11'·21N 06°43'·21W**. AC 2494, 5612. Tides as for Portrush. A tiny hbr 1·1ca S of Portstewart Pt lt, Oc R 10s 21m 5M, vis 040°–220°, obscd in final appr. A temp, fair weather berth (£10) at S end of inner basin in 0·8–1·7m; the very narrow ent is open to SW wind and swell. Visitors should obtain fuel at Portrush before proceeding to Portstewart. Beware rocks close to S bkwtr. Facilities: ✕ @ at library.

6.13 PORTRUSH

Antrim **55°12'·34N 06°39'·49W**

CHARTS AC 2798, 2494, 5612; Imray C53, C64

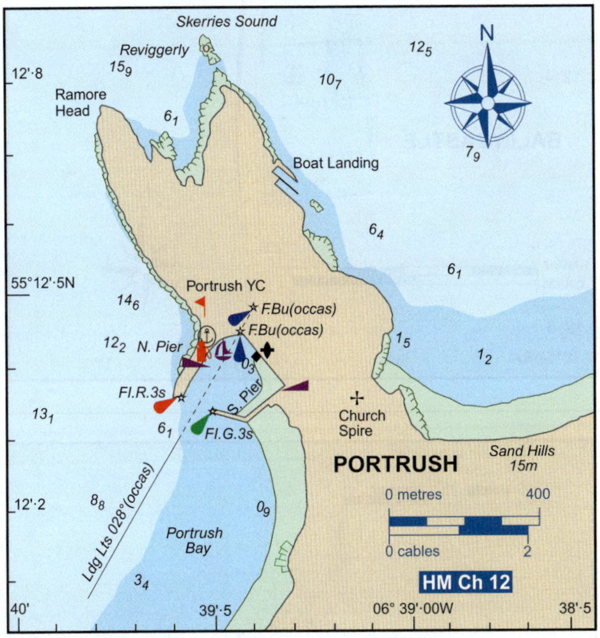

TIDES –0400 Dover; ML 1·1; Duration 0610

Standard Port RIVER FOYLE (←)

Times				Height (metres)			
High Water		Low Water		MHWS	MHWN	MLWN	MLWS
0100	0800	0200	0700	2·6	1·9	0·9	0·4
1300	2000	1400	1900				
Differences PORTRUSH							
–0046	–0052	–0117	–0057	–0·5	–0·3	+0·1	+0·1

SHELTER Good in hbr, except in strong NW/N winds. Berth on N pier or on pontoon at NE end of it and see HM. A mooring may be available, but very congested in season. ⚓ on E side of Ramore Hd in Skerries Roads 1ca S of Large Skerrie gives good shelter in most conditions, but open to NW sea/swell.

NAVIGATION WPT 55°13´·00N 06°41´·00W, 128° to N pier lt, 1·1M.

Ent with onshore winds >F 4 is difficult. Beware submerged bkwtr projecting 20m SW from N pier. Depth is 2·8m in hbr entrance.

LIGHTS AND MARKS Ldg lts 028° (occas, for LB use) both FR 6/8m 1M; R △ on metal bn and metal mast. N pier Fl R 3s 6m 3M; vis 220°-160°. S pier Fl G 3s 6m 3M; vis 220°-100°.

COMMUNICATIONS (Code 028) Dr 7082 3767; Ⓗ 7034 4177. HM 7082 2307.

VHF Ch 12 16 (0900-1700LT, Mon-Fri; extended evening hrs June-Sept; Sat-Sun: 0900–1700, June-Sept only).

FACILITIES Hbr slip (£3) £14, (0900-1800) Ⓔ; Portrush YC ☎7082 3932; **Town** Ⓑ ✕ @ Library ⇌ ✈ (Belfast). Giant's Causeway is 10M ENE.

HARBOURS & ANCHORAGES BETWEEN PORTRUSH & LARNE

RATHLIN ISLAND, Antrim, **55°17′·47N 06°11′·78W**. AC 2798, 2494, 5612. HW sp –0445, nps –0200 on Dover. Small harbour in NE corner of Church Bay, sheltered from winds NW through E to SSE. Ferries run from the the Inner Harbour to Ballycastle. Beware sp streams up to 6kn in Rathlin Sound (6.14) and the North Channel TSS, just 2M NE of the island. Pass N or E of a wreck 6ca SW of hbr, marked on its SE side by a SCM lt buoy. When clear, appr on NNE to the W and S piers which form an outer hbr. The white sector of Manor House lt, Oc WRG 4s, leads 024·5° to Inner Harbour (2m) ent via channel dredged to 3·5m (2013). on yacht pontoons just S of Inner Harbour. Outside hbr, close to W pier ⚓ possible in about 5m, but holding poor in rock/weed. Facilities: Church Bay ⊠ ✕ ferry to Ballycastle.

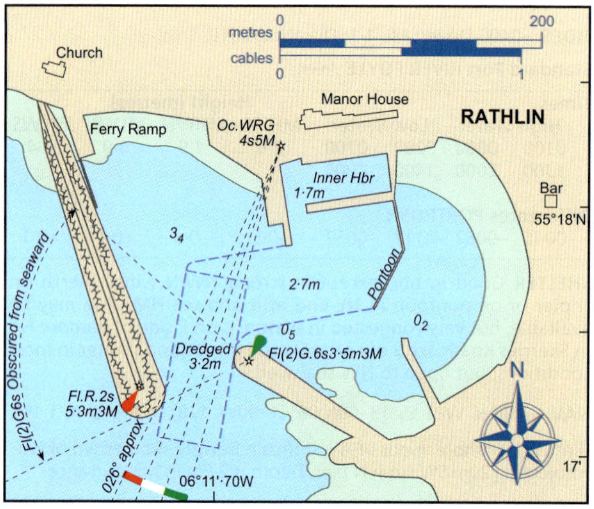

BALLYCASTLE, Antrim, **55°12′·47N 06°14′·27W**. AC 2798, 2494, 5612. Tides as for Rathlin Is; ML 0·8m; –0320 on Dover. Ferries to Rathlin Island berth inside the N breakwater; RoRo disused. The marina is in the S part of the harbour with 2·3m. Outside the harbour is a fair weather ⚓ clear of strong tidal streams, but liable to sudden swell and exposed to onshore winds. Lights: see chartlet and 6.3. CG ☎20762226; Ⓗ 20762666. **Marina** ☎(028) 20768525, mob 07803 505084 74 £2·10, short stay £4/hr. **Town** ⊠ Ⓑ ✕.

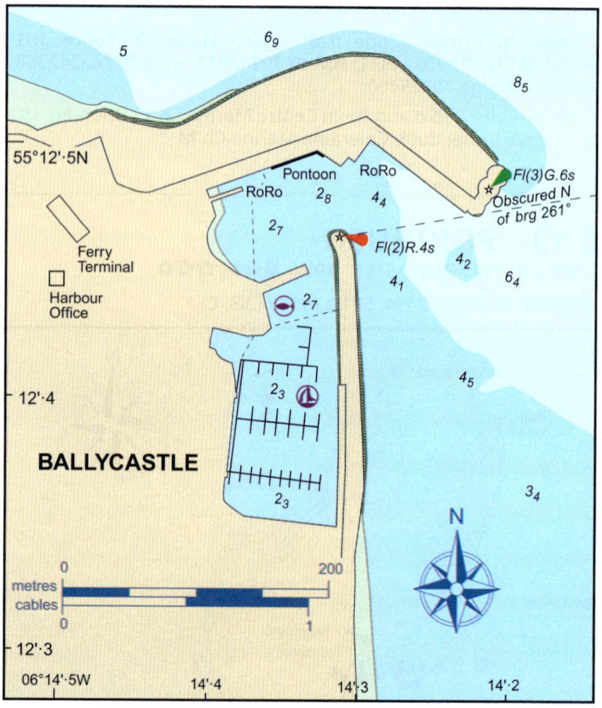

RED BAY, Antrim, **55°03′·91N 06°03′·13W**. AC 2199, 5612. HW +0010 on Dover; ML 1·1m; Duration 0625. See 6.15. Good holding, but open to E winds. Beware rocks, 2 ruined piers W of Garron Pt and on S side of bay, approx ½M from shore, fish farms, marked by lit buoys. Glenariff pier is lit Fl 3s 10m 5M. In S and E winds ⚓ 2ca off W stone arch near head of bay in approx 3·5m; in N or W winds ⚓ S of small pier in 2–5m, ½M NE of Glenariff (Waterfoot) village. **Waterfoot** ✕ ⊠.
Cushendall (1M N of pier) ⊠ ✕.

CARNLOUGH HARBOUR, Antrim, **54°59′·87N 05°59′·20W**. AC 2198, 5612. HW +0006 on Dover, +0005 on Belfast; HW –1·6m on Belfast; ML no data; Duration 0625. Good shelter, except in SE gales; do not enter in fresh/strong onshore winds. Entrance shoaling due to build up of kelp, minimum depth 1m (2004). Ldg marks 310°, Y ▽s on B/W posts. N pier lt, Fl G 3s 4m 5M; S pier Fl R 3s 6m 5M, both lts on B/W columns. Beware fish farms in the bay marked by lt buoys (unreliable); and rocks which cover at HW on either side of ent. Small harbour used by yachts and small FVs; visitors welcome. HM mob 07703 606763.
Quay £1, (see HM) (by arrangement).
Town ⊠ ✕.

GLENARM, Antrim, **54°58′N 05°57′W**. AC 2198, 2199, 5612. HW +0006 on Dover, +0005 on Belfast; HW –1·6m on Belfast; ML no data; Duration 0625. Good shelter in marina, which reports 3m at LW. Hbr ent lts G.3s 3M and R.3s 3M. Beware fish farm about 0·5M NE of entrance. HM / Marina ☎028 2884 1285, Mob 07703 606763.
Marina 40 inc 10 Ⓥ in 4-6m, £2.20.
Village.

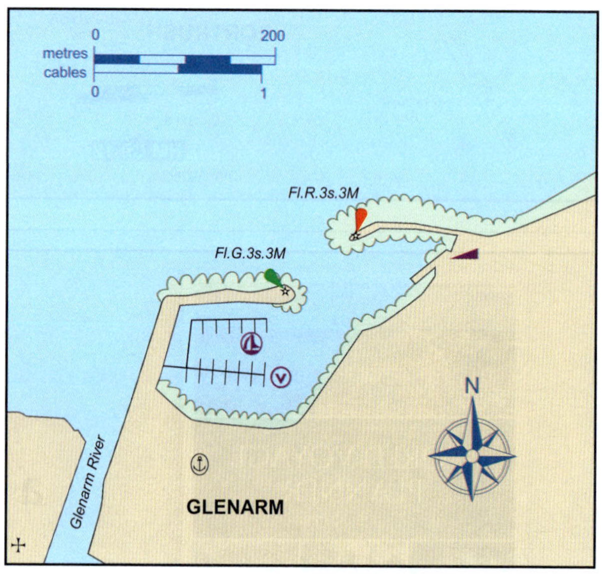

6.14 TIDAL STREAMS AROUND RATHLIN ISLAND

North Ireland 6.2
North Irish Sea 3.2
Off Mull of Kintyre 2.10
SW Scotland 2.2
South Ireland 5.2

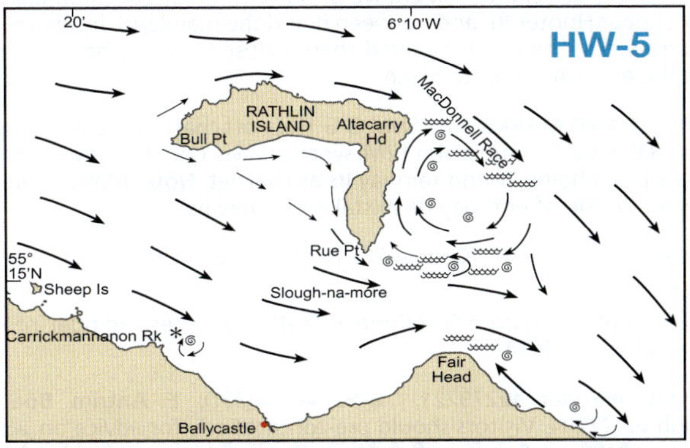

5 Hours before HW Dover (0605 after HW Greenock)

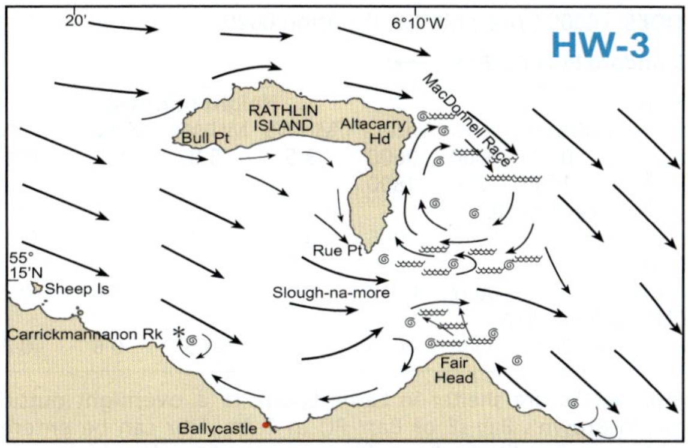

3 Hours before HW Dover (0420 before HW Greenock)

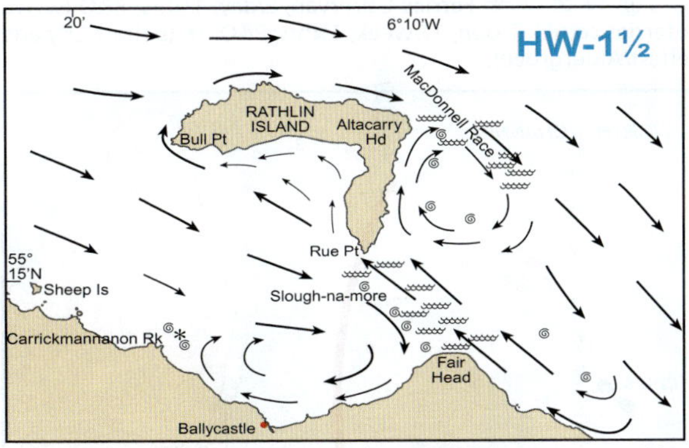

1½ Hours before HW Dover (0250 before HW Greenock)

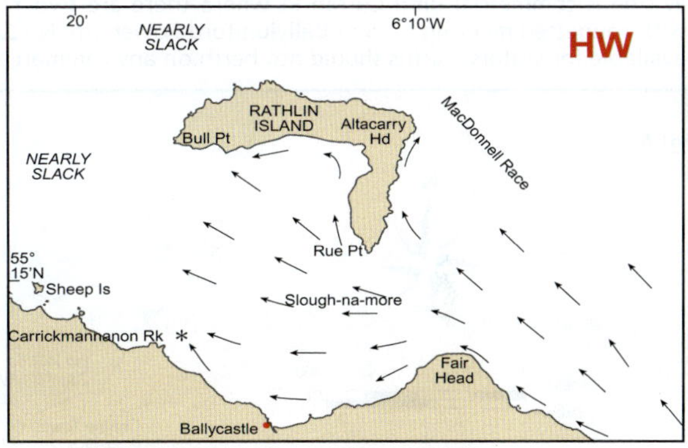

HW Dover (0120 before HW Greenock)

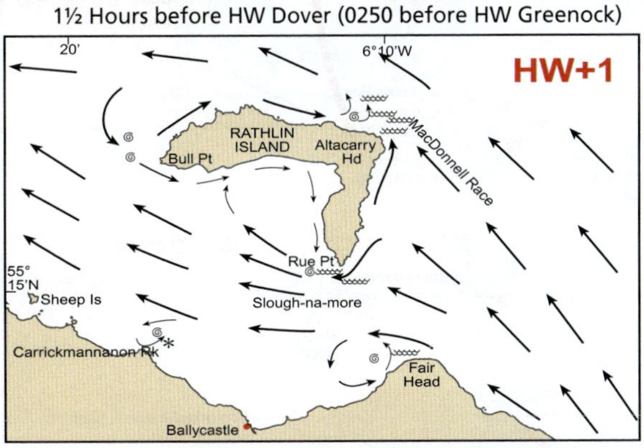

1 Hour after HW Dover (0020 before HW Greenock)

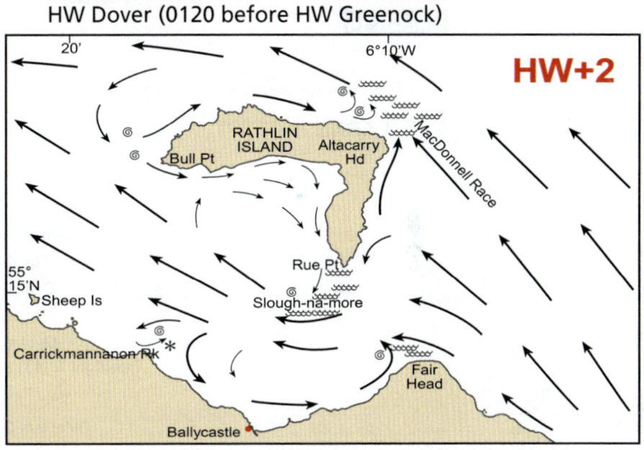

2 Hours after HW Dover (0040 after HW Greenock)

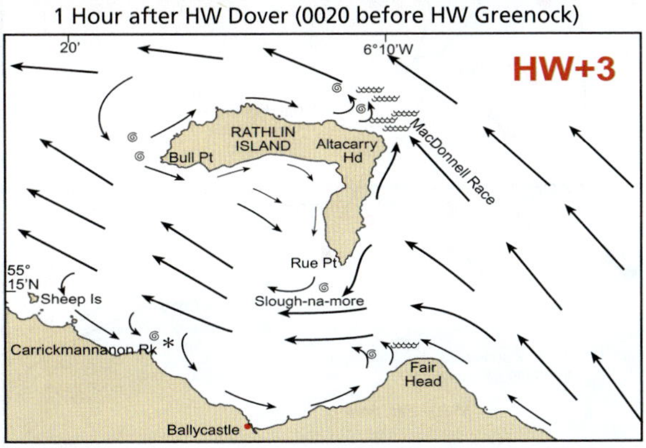

3 Hours after HW Dover (0140 after HW Greenock)

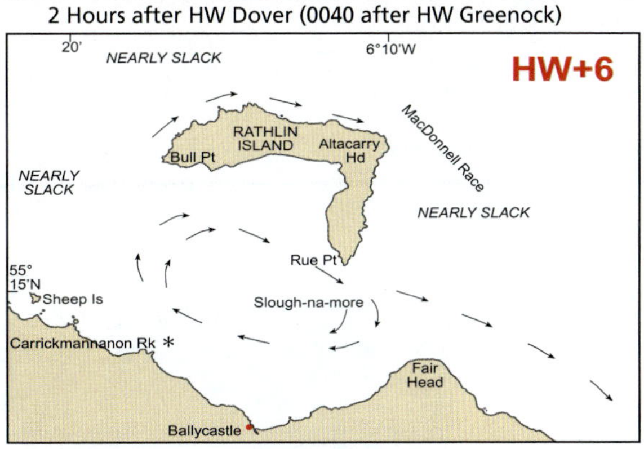

6 Hours after HW Dover (0440 after HW Greenock)

6.15 LARNE

Antrim **54°51'·20N 05°47'·50W** ❀❀❀◊◊✿✿

CHARTS AC 2198, 1237, 5612; Imray C62, C64, C69

TIDES +0005 Dover; ML 1·6; Duration 0620

Standard Port BELFAST (⟶)

Times				Height (metres)			
High Water		Low Water		MHWS	MHWN	MLWN	MLWS
0100	0700	0000	0600	3·5	3·0	1·1	0·4
1300	1900	1200	1800				
Differences LARNE							
+0005	0000	+0010	−0005	−0·7	−0·5	−0·3	0·0
RED BAY							
+0022	−0010	+0007	−0017	−1·9	−1·5	−0·8	−0·2
CUSHENDUN BAY							
+0010	−0030	0000	−0025	−1·7	−1·5	−0·6	−0·2

SHELTER Secure shelter in Larne Lough or ⚓ overnight outside hbr in Brown's Bay (E of Barr Pt) in 2-4m. Hbr can be entered H24 in any conditions. Larne is a busy commercial and ferry port; W side is commercial until Curran Pt where there are two YCs with congested moorings. ⚓ S of Ballylumford Power Stn. No ⚓ available for visitors. Yachts should not berth on any commercial quays, inc Castle Quay, without HM's permission. Boat Hbr (0·6m) 2ca S of Ferris Pt only for shoal draft craft.

NAVIGATION WPT 54°51'·70N 05°47'·47W, 184°/2·1M to front ldg lt. Beware Hunter Rk 2M NE of hbr ent. Magnetic anomalies exist near Hunter Rk and between it and the mainland. Inside the narrow ent, the recommended chan is close to the E shore. Tide in the ent runs at up to 3½kn.

LIGHTS AND MARKS No1 SHM Q G 1½ca off chartlet N edge; Ldg lts 184°, Oc 2.5s 6m / 5s14m 12M, synch and vis 179°-189°; W ◊ with R stripes. Chaine Tr and fairway lts as chartlet. Note: Many shore lts on W side of ent may be mistaken for nav lts.

COMMUNICATIONS (Code 028) Pilot 273785; Dr 275331; HM 872100.

VHF Ch **14** 11 16 *Larne Port Control*. Traffic, weather and tidal info available on Ch 14.

FACILITIES **Pier** ☎279221, (33t); **E Antrim Boat Club** ☎277204, Visitors should pre-contact Sec'y for advice on ; **Services** . **Town** (delivered, tidal) ✉ Ⓑ ✕ **⇄ Ferries** Cairnryan; 8/day; 1¾hrs; P&O (www.poferries.co.uk). Troon; 17/week; 1¾hrs; P&O. ✈ (Belfast City and Belfast/Aldergrove).

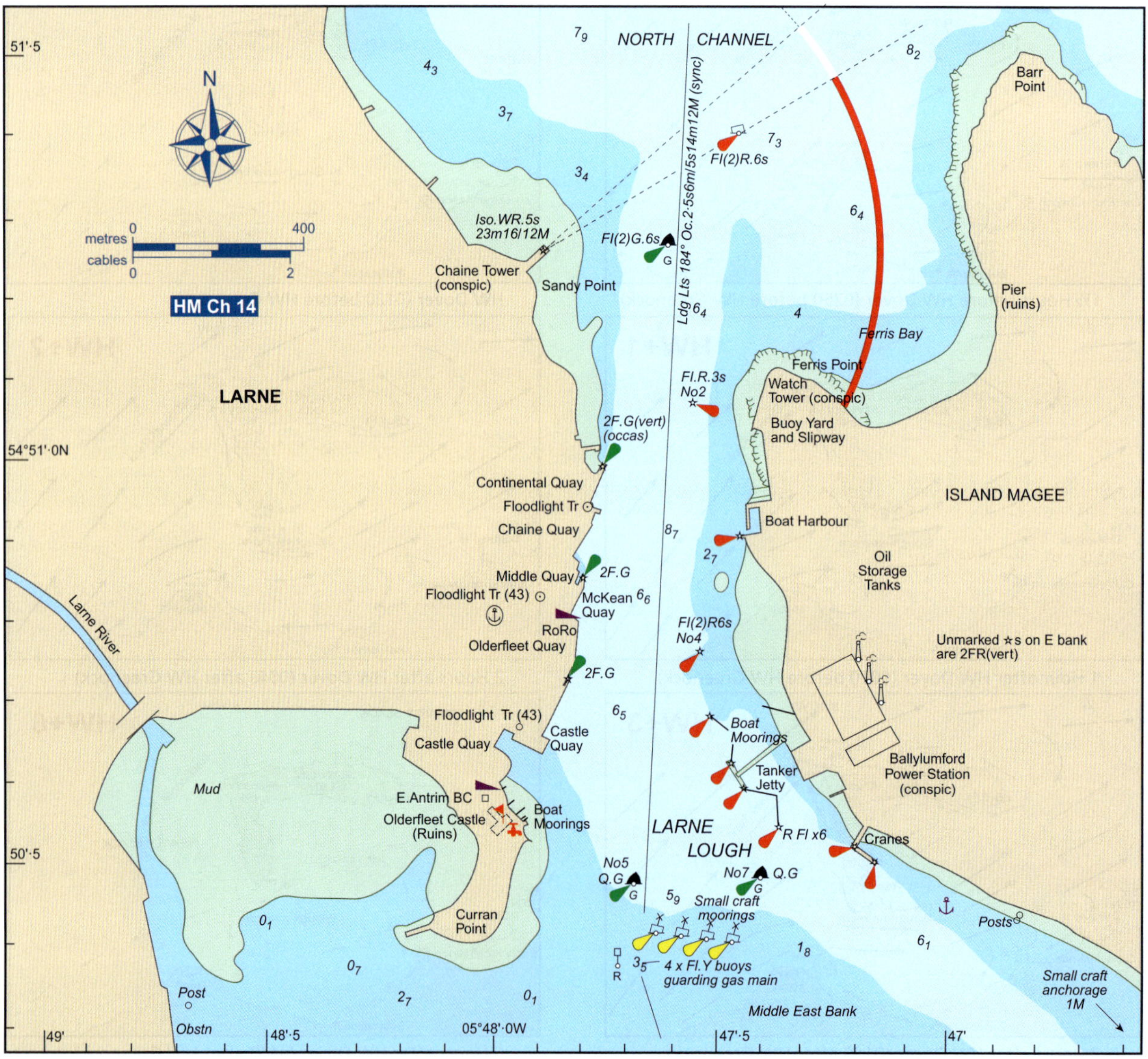

6.16 BELFAST LOUGH

County Down and County Antrim **54°42'N 05°45'W**

Bangor ❀❀❀◊◊◊✿✿; Carrickfergus ❀❀❀◊◊◊✿✿

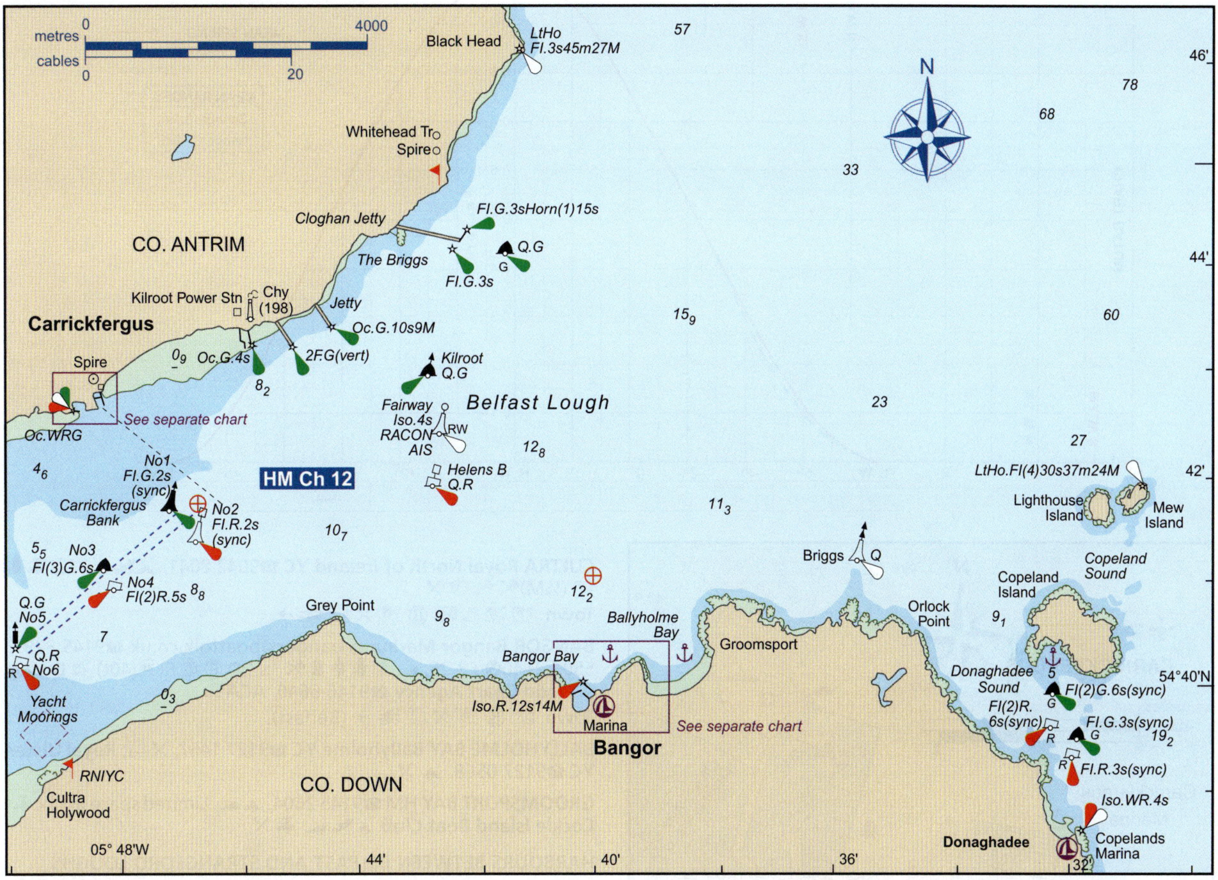

CHARTS AC 2198, 1753, 1752, 5612; Imray C62, C64, C69

TIDES +0007 Dover; ML Belfast 2·0, Carrickfergus 1·8; Duration 0620

Standard Port BELFAST (⟶)

Times				Height (metres)			
High Water		Low Water		MHWS	MHWN	MLWN	MLWS
0100	0700	0000	0600	3·5	3·0	1·1	0·4
1300	1900	1200	1800				
Differences CARRICKFERGUS							
+0005	+0005	+0005	+0005	–0·3	–0·3	–0·2	–0·1
DONAGHADEE							
+0020	+0020	+0023	+0023	+0·5	+0·4	0·0	+0·1

SHELTER Main sailing centres, clockwise around Belfast Lough, are at Bangor, Cultra and Carrickfergus.

Groomsport: small hbr sheltered by Cockle Is at SE ent to the Lough.

Ballyholme Bay: good ⚓ in offshore winds.

Bangor: exposed to N winds, but well sheltered in marina (depths 2·9m to 2·2m). Speed limits: 4kn in marina, 8kn between Luke's Pt and Wilson's Pt.

Cultra: in offshore winds good ⚓ and moorings off RNoIYC.

Belfast Harbour is a major commercial port, but there are 40 berths in Abercorn Basin, just NE of Lagan Bridge, in the River Lagan.

Carrickfergus: very good in marina, depths 1·8–2·3m (2015). The former commercial hbr has 10 yacht berths on the W quay. A stub bkwtr, marked by 2 PHM bns, extends NNE into the hbr from the W pier. The ent and SW part of the hbr are dredged 2·9m (2015); the NE part of the hbr dries 0·7m. Good ⚓ SSE of Carrickfergus Pier, except in E winds.

NAVIGATION Belfast Fairway SWM buoy, 54°42'·32N 05°42'·30W, Traffic passes inbound to N between SWM and Kilroot SHM, outbound between SWM and Helens Bay PHM. The Lough is well marked. WPT Carrickfergus 54°41'·71N 05°46'·16W, marks start of the buoyed chan to Belfast Hbr. It bears 121°/301° from/to Carrickfergus Marina, 1.7M. Carrickfergus Bk liable to shift. Deep draught yachts should not enter/leave before LW±2. Beware HSS ferry operation. WPT Bangor 54°41'·00N 05°40'·00W, 190°/1M to bkwtr lt. Rounding Orlock Pt beware Briggs Rks extending ¾M offshore.

LIGHTS AND MARKS Chan to Belfast Hbr is well marked/lit by buoys and bns. Beyond No 12 PHM bn it is dangerous to leave the chan. Carrickfergus is easily recognised by conspic castle to E of Marina. On Marina Bkwtr, 30m W of the ☆ QR 7m 3M, is a Dir lt 320°, Oc WRG 3s 5m 3M, (H24).

COMMUNICATIONS (Codes: Belfast 028) (08494) 22339; Dr 91468521. HM Bangor 91453297; HM Belfast 90553012; Belfast VTS 9055 3504. 0845 600 8000.

Bangor Marina Ch **80** M (H24); Bangor HM Ch 11 (H24). Royal N of Ireland YC (at Cultra) Ch **16**; 11 (H24) 80. *Belfast Port Control* (at Milewater Basin) Ch **12** 16 (H24); VTS provides info on request to vessels in port area. The greater part of Belfast Lough is under radar surveillance. Carrickfergus Marina Ch M, 80, M2.

FACILITIES Anti-clockwise around the Lough:

CARRICKFERGUS Marina www.carrickfergus.org/site/marina ☎93366666; entry H24; 300 inc ♥ £3·00, short stay (max 6hrs) £9·00 Ⓔ. **Carrick SC** ☎351402.

Hbr: 10 (45t).

Town Ⓑ (Belfast).

BELFAST Abercorn Basin www.belfast-harbour.co.uk 40 £16.80 inc; short stay (5hrs) £8.

City all facilities.

Ferries Stranraer; 6/week; 2½hrs; Stena (www.stenaline.co.uk). Liverpool; 2/day; 8hrs.

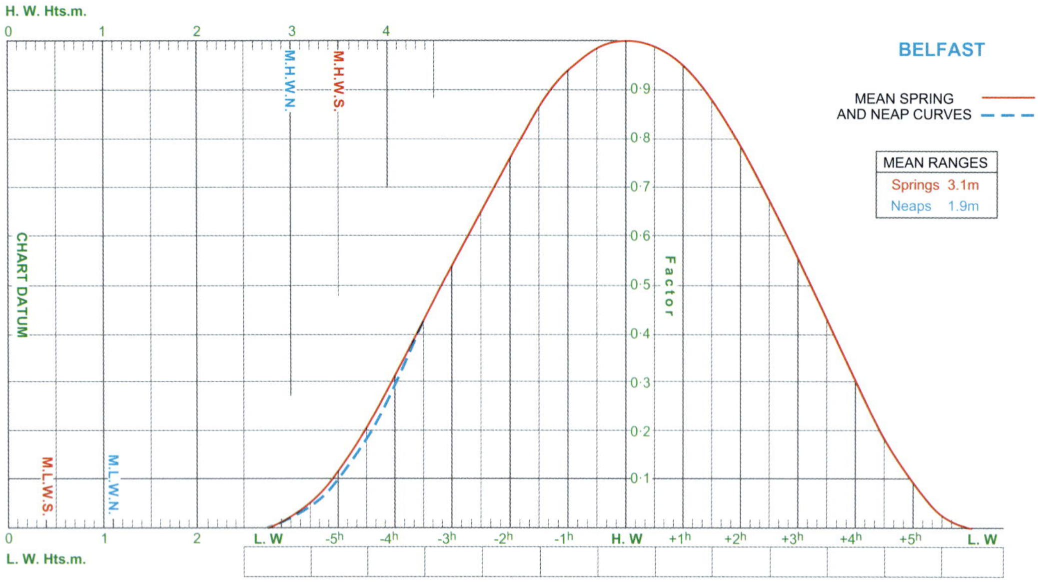

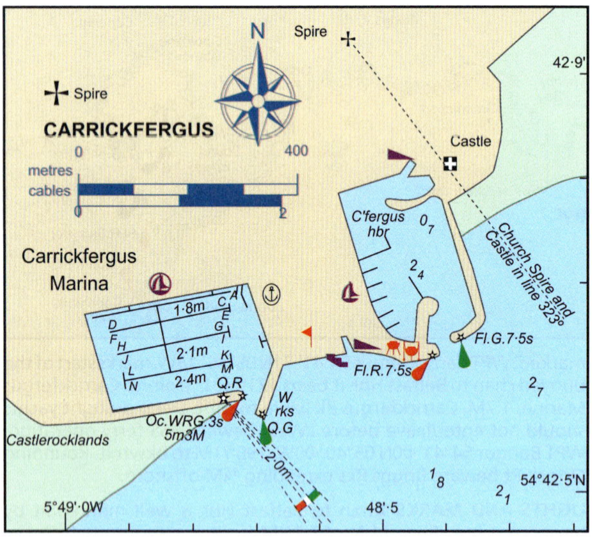

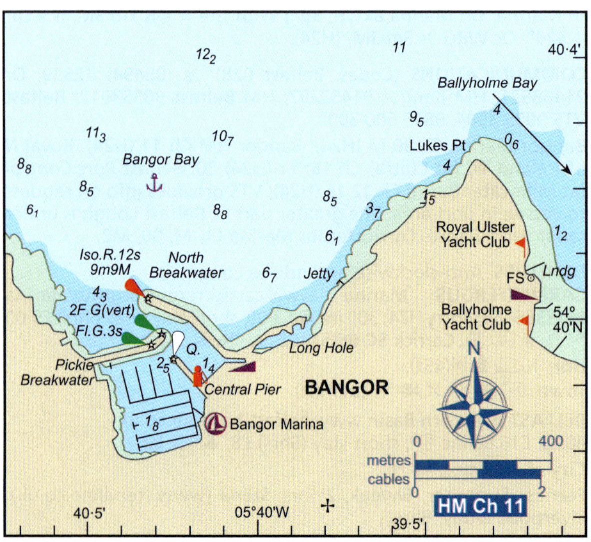

CULTRA Royal North of Ireland YC ☎9042 8041, (½M).

Town ✉ Ⓑ ✈.

BANGOR Bangor Marina bangor@boatfolk.co.uk ☎9145 3297, 550+40 £3·25, Ⓔ (40t) Diving. **Todd Chart Agency** ☎9146 6640, ACA.

Town ✉ Ⓑ ✈ (Belfast).

BALLYHOLME BAY Ballyholme YC ☎9127 1467, ; **Royal Ulster YC** ☎9127 0568, .

GROOMSPORT BAY HM ☎9145 2604, Limited space in hbr. **Cockle Island Boat Club** .

HARBOURS BETWEEN BELFAST AND STRANGFORD LOUGHS

DONAGHADEE, Down, **54°38´·71N 05°31´·85W**. AC 1753, 5612. HW +0025 on Dover; see 6.16; ML no data; Duration 0615. Excellent shelter and basic facilities in tiny marina, access HW±1 over sill; covers approx 1m at half tide. Appr on about 275° on ldg marks, orange △s to tricky ent with sharp 90° port turn into marina (pilots available). Appr in strong winds or at night not advised. 3ca to the N, the Old Hbr is small and very full; scend often sets in. Beware rocky reef with less than 2m extends 1·5ca ENE from S pier hd. Max depth in hbr is approx 2·5m, dries at SW end; best berth alongside SE quay. S pier lt, Iso WR 4s 17m 18/14M, W shore–326°, R326°–shore. HM ☎9188 2377. Police 101. Facilities: **Copelands Marina** ☎9188 2184, mob 07802 363382; VHF Ch **16** 11 80; for 6 (20t). **Old Hbr** £4. **Town** ✉ Ⓑ (Bangor), ✈ (Belfast).

BALLYWALTER HARBOUR, Down, **54°32´·68N 05°28´·84W**.
BALLYHALBERT HARBOUR, Down, **54°29´·46N 05°26´·45W**.
AC 2156. Both drying harbours set amongst rocky outcrops. These are run by Ards and North Down Borough Council, together with **DONAGHADEE, GROOMSPORT** and Cook St Quay, **PORTAFERRY**. HM William Angus at Donaghadee; mob 07718579105; facilities are limited but they provide a welcome stopover if tide allows.

PORTAVOGIE, Down, **54°27´·45N 05°26´·08W**. AC 2156, 5612. HW +0016 on Dover; ML 2·6m; Duration 0620. See 6.17. Good shelter, but hbr so full of FVs as to risk damage; best only for overnight or emergency. Entrance dangerous in strong onshore winds. Beware Plough Rks to SE marked by PHM buoy, Fl (2) R 10s, and McCammon Rks to NE of ent. Keep in W sector of outer bkwtr lt, Iso WRG 5s 6m 5M, shore-G-262°-W-272°-R-350°. Inner bkwtr 2 FG (vert) 6m 4M. Monitor VHF Ch **14** on entry/exit. (Mon-Fri: 0900-1700LT). HM ☎(028) 4277 1470. Facilities: (on central quay). **Town** ✉.

STANDARD TIME (UT)
For Summer Time add ONE hour in **non-shaded areas**

BELFAST LAT 54°36′N LONG 5°55′W

TIMES AND HEIGHTS OF HIGH AND LOW WATERS

Dates in red are SPRINGS
Dates in blue are NEAPS

YEAR **2024**

JANUARY

Day	Time	m	Time	m	Time	m	Time	m
1 M	0217	3.0	0806	1.0	1431	3.5	2030	0.8
2 TU	0301	3.0	0848	1.1	1512	3.4	2112	0.8
3 W	0348	2.9	0933	1.1	1557	3.3	2159	0.9
4 TH	0439	2.9	1023	1.2	1647	3.2	◑ 2252	1.0
5 F	0534	2.8	1122	1.3	1745	3.1	2354	1.0
6 SA	0632	2.9	1233	1.3	1847	3.1		
7 SU	0103	1.0	0731	2.9	1344	1.2	1949	3.1
8 M	0203	1.0	0826	3.1	1441	1.1	2046	3.2
9 TU	0255	0.9	0917	3.2	1531	0.9	2137	3.3
10 W	0341	0.8	1002	3.3	1617	0.7	2225	3.4
11 TH	0426	0.7	1045	3.5	1702	0.6	● 2312	3.4
12 F	0510	0.7	1128	3.6	1746	0.4	2359	3.4
13 SA	0555	0.7	1213	3.7	1832	0.4		
14 SU	0047	3.4	0642	0.7	1259	3.7	1920	0.3
15 M	0138	3.3	0730	0.7	1348	3.7	2009	0.3
16 TU	0230	3.3	0820	0.7	1439	3.7	2100	0.4
17 W	0324	3.2	0911	0.8	1532	3.6	2155	0.5
18 TH	0419	3.1	1006	0.8	1628	3.5	◐ 2257	0.6
19 F	0518	3.1	1109	1.0	1734	3.3		
20 SA	0005	0.8	0623	3.0	1222	1.0	1851	3.2
21 SU	0113	0.9	0731	3.0	1335	1.0	2006	3.1
22 M	0215	0.9	0835	3.1	1442	1.0	2110	3.1
23 TU	0311	0.9	0931	3.3	1541	0.8	2204	3.2
24 W	0359	0.9	1020	3.4	1629	0.7	2251	3.2
25 TH	0441	0.9	1104	3.5	1709	0.7	○ 2333	3.1
26 F	0519	0.8	1143	3.6	1744	0.6		
27 SA	0009	3.1	0554	0.8	1218	3.6	1817	0.6
28 SU	0042	3.0	0628	0.8	1252	3.6	1849	0.6
29 M	0114	3.0	0701	0.8	1326	3.5	1921	0.6
30 TU	0147	3.0	0735	0.8	1359	3.5	1955	0.6
31 W	0221	3.0	0812	0.8	1433	3.4	2032	0.6

FEBRUARY

Day	Time	m	Time	m	Time	m	Time	m
1 TH	0257	3.0	0852	0.9	1509	3.3	2113	0.7
2 F	0336	2.9	0935	1.0	1552	3.2	◑ 2158	0.9
3 SA	0425	2.9	1026	1.1	1647	3.0	2253	1.0
4 SU	0528	2.8	1131	1.3	1756	2.9		
5 M	0004	1.1	0637	2.8	1308	1.3	1909	2.9
6 TU	0134	1.1	0745	2.9	1421	1.1	2018	3.0
7 W	0238	1.0	0849	3.0	1517	0.8	2120	3.1
8 TH	0329	0.8	0943	3.2	1606	0.6	2212	3.2
9 F	0415	0.7	1029	3.4	1650	0.3	● 2259	3.3
10 SA	0458	0.6	1113	3.6	1733	0.2	2344	3.4
11 SU	0541	0.5	1158	3.7	1816	0.1		
12 M	0030	3.4	0624	0.4	1243	3.8	1900	0.1
13 TU	0117	3.3	0708	0.4	1331	3.8	1944	0.1
14 W	0205	3.3	0754	0.4	1419	3.7	2031	0.3
15 TH	0254	3.2	0841	0.5	1509	3.6	2121	0.5
16 F	0344	3.2	0933	0.7	1602	3.4	◐ 2220	0.7
17 SA	0437	3.0	1035	0.9	1703	3.1	2335	0.9
18 SU	0540	2.9	1158	1.0	1823	2.9		
19 M	0049	1.1	0700	2.9	1318	1.0	1955	2.8
20 TU	0158	1.1	0817	3.0	1432	0.9	2102	2.9
21 W	0300	1.0	0916	3.2	1536	0.8	2155	3.0
22 TH	0350	0.9	1005	3.3	1622	0.6	2238	3.0
23 F	0429	0.8	1047	3.4	1655	0.6	2316	3.0
24 SA	0501	0.7	1124	3.5	1723	0.5	○ 2350	3.0
25 SU	0531	0.7	1158	3.5	1750	0.5		
26 M	0019	3.0	0602	0.7	1228	3.4	1820	0.5
27 TU	0045	3.0	0633	0.6	1255	3.4	1850	0.5
28 W	0109	3.0	0705	0.6	1323	3.4	1921	0.5
29 TH	0135	3.1	0738	0.6	1354	3.4	1955	0.5

MARCH

Day	Time	m	Time	m	Time	m	Time	m
1 F	0207	3.1	0815	0.7	1430	3.3	2033	0.6
2 SA	0245	3.0	0855	0.8	1514	3.2	2116	0.8
3 SU	0329	2.9	0942	1.0	1608	3.0	◑ 2208	1.0
4 M	0427	2.8	1045	1.1	1720	2.8	2317	1.2
5 TU	0548	2.7	1242	1.2	1839	2.8		
6 W	0111	1.2	0708	2.7	1403	0.9	1956	2.8
7 TH	0222	1.0	0822	2.9	1500	0.6	2104	3.0
8 F	0315	0.8	0922	3.2	1549	0.3	2156	3.2
9 SA	0400	0.6	1010	3.4	1632	0.1	2240	3.3
10 SU	0441	0.4	1054	3.6	1713	0.0	● 2323	3.4
11 M	0521	0.3	1138	3.7	1753	0.0		
12 TU	0007	3.4	0602	0.3	1223	3.8	1834	0.0
13 W	0052	3.4	0643	0.3	1310	3.7	1916	0.1
14 TH	0138	3.4	0727	0.3	1358	3.6	2001	0.3
15 F	0225	3.3	0813	0.4	1448	3.5	2049	0.6
16 SA	0312	3.2	0905	0.6	1540	3.2	2146	0.9
17 SU	0403	3.1	1008	0.8	1638	3.0	◐ 2303	1.1
18 M	0502	3.0	1135	1.0	1800	2.7		
19 TU	0022	1.2	0622	2.9	1257	1.0	1942	2.7
20 W	0134	1.2	0752	2.9	1414	0.9	2047	2.8
21 TH	0240	1.1	0853	3.1	1517	0.7	2136	2.9
22 F	0331	0.9	0941	3.2	1558	0.6	2216	3.0
23 SA	0408	0.8	1021	3.3	1627	0.5	2250	3.0
24 SU	0437	0.7	1057	3.4	1652	0.5	2321	3.0
25 M	0505	0.6	1129	3.3	1719	0.5	○ 2349	3.0
26 TU	0534	0.6	1156	3.3	1748	0.5		
27 W	0010	3.1	0605	0.6	1219	3.3	1818	0.5
28 TH	0030	3.1	0636	0.6	1247	3.3	1849	0.5
29 F	0058	3.2	0709	0.6	1322	3.3	1923	0.6
30 SA	0133	3.2	0744	0.6	1402	3.2	2002	0.7
31 SU	0213	3.1	0825	0.7	1449	3.1	2046	0.8

APRIL

Day	Time	m	Time	m	Time	m	Time	m
1 M	0258	3.0	0914	0.9	1548	2.9	2140	1.0
2 TU	0356	2.9	1020	1.0	1701	2.8	◑ 2251	1.2
3 W	0515	2.8	1222	1.0	1819	2.7		
4 TH	0043	1.2	0639	2.8	1341	0.8	1938	2.8
5 F	0158	1.0	0757	3.0	1437	0.5	2044	3.0
6 SA	0252	0.8	0858	3.2	1525	0.2	2133	3.2
7 SU	0338	0.6	0947	3.5	1608	0.0	2217	3.4
8 M	0419	0.4	1031	3.6	1648	0.0	● 2259	3.4
9 TU	0458	0.3	1116	3.7	1727	0.0	2343	3.5
10 W	0538	0.3	1202	3.7	1807	0.1		
11 TH	0027	3.5	0620	0.3	1249	3.6	1850	0.3
12 F	0113	3.4	0705	0.3	1338	3.5	1935	0.5
13 SA	0159	3.4	0752	0.4	1428	3.3	2024	0.8
14 SU	0246	3.3	0845	0.6	1520	3.1	2121	1.0
15 M	0335	3.2	0949	0.8	1617	2.8	◐ 2232	1.2
16 TU	0430	3.1	1109	0.9	1732	2.6	2347	1.3
17 W	0537	2.9	1225	0.9	1914	2.6		
18 TH	0056	1.3	0710	2.9	1335	0.8	2018	2.7
19 F	0201	1.2	0817	3.0	1434	0.7	2105	2.8
20 SA	0254	1.0	0907	3.1	1516	0.6	2143	2.9
21 SU	0334	0.9	0947	3.2	1548	0.6	2216	3.0
22 M	0406	0.8	1022	3.3	1617	0.5	2246	3.1
23 TU	0436	0.7	1053	3.3	1646	0.5	○ 2313	3.1
24 W	0507	0.6	1121	3.3	1717	0.6	2336	3.2
25 TH	0538	0.6	1147	3.3	1748	0.6		
26 F	0000	3.2	0612	0.6	1219	3.3	1822	0.6
27 SA	0032	3.3	0646	0.6	1259	3.3	1858	0.7
28 SU	0111	3.3	0724	0.6	1344	3.2	1940	0.8
29 M	0155	3.2	0809	0.7	1437	3.1	2029	0.9
30 TU	0245	3.1	0904	0.8	1539	2.9	2127	1.1

Chart Datum: 2·01 metres below Ordnance Datum (Belfast). HAT is 3·9 metres above Chart Datum.

STANDARD TIME (UT)
For Summer Time add ONE hour in **non-shaded areas**

BELFAST

LAT 54°36′N LONG 5°55′W

TIMES AND HEIGHTS OF HIGH AND LOW WATERS

Dates in red are SPRINGS
Dates in blue are NEAPS

YEAR **2024**

MAY

Day	Time	m	Day	Time	m
1 W	0344 1016 1648 ◑ 2239	3.0 0.9 2.8 1.2	16 TH	0457 1143 1810	3.1 0.9 2.6
2 TH	0454 1153 1802	3.0 0.8 2.8	17 F	0008 0603 1246 1926	1.3 3.0 0.9 2.7
3 F	0005 0613 1309 1916	1.2 3.0 0.6 2.9	18 SA	0109 0717 1341 2016	1.2 3.0 0.8 2.8
4 SA	0121 0730 1406 2017	1.0 3.1 0.4 3.1	19 SU	0205 0816 1428 2057	1.1 3.0 0.7 2.9
5 SU	0219 0832 1455 2107	0.8 3.3 0.2 3.3	20 M	0251 0902 1506 2132	1.0 3.1 0.7 3.0
6 M	0309 0923 1540 2152	0.6 3.5 0.2 3.4	21 TU	0331 0941 1541 2206	0.9 3.2 0.6 3.1
7 TU	0354 1010 1621 2236	0.5 3.6 0.2 3.5	22 W	0406 1017 1614 2238	0.8 3.3 0.6 3.2
8 W	0437 1056 1703 ● 2321	0.4 3.6 0.3 3.5	23 TH	0441 1050 1648 ○ 2308	0.7 3.3 0.6 3.3
9 TH	0520 1143 1745	0.4 3.6 0.4	24 F	0517 1123 1724 2338	0.7 3.3 0.7 3.3
10 F	0005 0604 1230 1830	3.5 0.4 3.5 0.6	25 SA	0554 1201 1802	0.6 3.3 0.7
11 SA	0051 0650 1319 1917	3.5 0.4 3.3 0.7	26 SU	0015 0634 1244 1844	3.4 0.6 3.2 0.8
12 SU	0136 0738 1408 2006	3.5 0.5 3.2 0.9	27 M	0058 0717 1334 1931	3.4 0.6 3.2 0.8
13 M	0222 0830 1459 2100	3.4 0.6 3.0 1.0	28 TU	0145 0806 1429 2024	3.4 0.6 3.1 0.9
14 TU	0309 0929 1552 2200	3.3 0.7 2.8 1.2	29 W	0236 0904 1529 2122	3.3 0.6 3.0 1.0
15 W	0400 1035 1653 ◐ 2305	3.2 0.8 2.7 1.3	30 TH	0332 1009 1633 ◑ 2225	3.3 0.6 2.9 1.0
			31 F	0434 1121 1741 2332	3.2 0.6 2.9 1.0

JUNE

Day	Time	m	Day	Time	m
1 SA	0544 1230 1847	3.2 0.5 3.0	16 SU	0008 0613 1245 1902	1.2 3.0 0.9 2.8
2 SU	0039 0700 1331 1947	0.9 3.2 0.5 3.1	17 M	0111 0714 1338 1956	1.2 3.0 0.9 2.9
3 M	0143 0806 1424 2040	0.8 3.3 0.4 3.2	18 TU	0207 0811 1424 2044	1.1 3.0 0.8 3.0
4 TU	0241 0902 1513 2129	0.7 3.4 0.4 3.3	19 W	0255 0901 1506 2128	1.0 3.1 0.8 3.1
5 W	0333 0953 1600 2216	0.6 3.5 0.4 3.4	20 TH	0339 0946 1546 2208	0.9 3.2 0.7 3.2
6 TH	0422 1042 1645 ● 2303	0.6 3.5 0.5 3.5	21 F	0420 1027 1626 2245	0.8 3.3 0.7 3.3
7 F	0509 1130 1730 2349	0.5 3.4 0.6 3.5	22 SA	0501 1107 1707 ○ 2322	0.7 3.3 0.7 3.4
8 SA	0555 1217 1815	0.5 3.3 0.8	23 SU	0543 1148 1749	0.6 3.3 0.7
9 SU	0033 0641 1303 1901	3.6 0.5 3.2 0.9	24 M	0001 0626 1233 1835	3.4 0.5 3.2 0.8
10 M	0117 0726 1349 1947	3.6 0.6 3.1 0.9	25 TU	0046 0711 1323 1923	3.5 0.5 3.2 0.8
11 TU	0200 0811 1435 2033	3.5 0.6 3.0 1.0	26 W	0133 0800 1416 2014	3.5 0.4 3.1 0.8
12 W	0244 0858 1523 2120	3.4 0.7 2.9 1.1	27 TH	0223 0852 1512 2107	3.5 0.4 3.1 0.8
13 TH	0330 0948 1613 2210	3.3 0.8 2.8 1.1	28 F	0315 0947 1611 ◑ 2202	3.5 0.4 3.1 0.8
14 F	0420 1043 1707 ◐ 2306	3.2 0.9 2.7 1.2	29 SA	0411 1048 1711 2301	3.4 0.5 3.0 0.9
15 SA	0514 1145 1804	3.1 0.9 2.7	30 SU	0515 1154 1813	3.3 0.6 3.0

JULY

Day	Time	m	Day	Time	m
1 M	0006 0628 1259 1916	0.9 3.2 0.6 3.1	16 TU	0003 0621 1238 1903	1.2 2.9 1.0 2.9
2 TU	0115 0742 1400 2016	0.9 3.2 0.6 3.2	17 W	0122 0724 1345 2000	1.2 2.9 1.0 3.0
3 W	0221 0847 1455 2111	0.8 3.2 0.7 3.3	18 TH	0225 0826 1439 2054	1.1 3.0 0.9 3.1
4 TH	0321 0944 1546 2203	0.8 3.3 0.7 3.4	19 F	0317 0921 1526 2141	0.9 3.1 0.8 3.2
5 F	0414 1035 1633 ● 2251	0.7 3.3 0.7 3.5	20 SA	0404 1009 1610 2224	0.7 3.2 0.8 3.3
6 SA	0503 1123 1718 2336	0.6 3.2 0.8 3.5	21 SU	0447 1052 1653 ○ 2304	0.6 3.3 0.7 3.4
7 SU	0547 1207 1801	0.6 3.1 0.8	22 M	0530 1135 1735 2346	0.4 3.3 0.7 3.5
8 M	0017 0628 1247 1842	3.6 0.5 3.1 0.9	23 TU	0612 1219 1820	0.3 3.3 0.6
9 TU	0057 0706 1326 1920	3.6 0.6 3.0 0.9	24 W	0030 0656 1306 1905	3.6 0.2 3.3 0.6
10 W	0137 0742 1406 1958	3.5 0.6 2.9 0.9	25 TH	0116 0740 1356 1952	3.6 0.2 3.2 0.6
11 TH	0216 0818 1448 2036	3.5 0.6 2.9 0.9	26 F	0205 0827 1447 2041	3.6 0.3 3.2 0.6
12 F	0257 0856 1533 2117	3.4 0.7 2.9 1.0	27 SA	0255 0918 1541 2132	3.6 0.4 3.2 0.7
13 SA	0340 0939 1621 ◐ 2203	3.3 0.8 2.9 1.1	28 SU	0348 1014 1637 ◑ 2229	3.5 0.5 3.1 0.8
14 SU	0427 1027 1711 2256	3.1 0.9 2.8 1.2	29 M	0447 1122 1738 2339	3.3 0.7 3.1 0.9
15 M	0520 1125 1806	3.0 1.0 2.8	30 TU	0559 1235 1846	3.1 0.9 3.0
			31 W	0057 0726 1343 1957	1.0 3.0 0.9 3.1

AUGUST

Day	Time	m	Day	Time	m
1 TH	0211 0841 1444 2100	0.9 3.0 0.9 3.2	16 F	0202 0754 1418 2021	1.1 2.9 1.1 3.0
2 F	0317 0940 1537 2154	0.8 3.1 0.9 3.4	17 SA	0259 0900 1509 2116	0.9 3.0 0.9 3.2
3 SA	0412 1030 1624 2240	0.7 3.1 0.9 3.5	18 SU	0347 0952 1554 2202	0.6 3.2 0.8 3.4
4 SU	0457 1114 1705 ● 2322	0.6 3.1 0.8 3.5	19 M	0430 1035 1635 ○ 2244	0.4 3.3 0.6 3.5
5 M	0534 1153 1741	0.6 3.1 0.8	20 TU	0511 1116 1716 2326	0.2 3.4 0.6 3.7
6 TU	0000 0607 1227 1815	3.5 0.6 3.0 0.8	21 W	0551 1159 1756	0.1 3.4 0.5
7 W	0035 0637 1300 1847	3.5 0.6 3.0 0.8	22 TH	0010 0631 1243 1839	3.7 0.1 3.4 0.5
8 TH	0109 0706 1333 1920	3.5 0.6 3.0 0.8	23 F	0056 0713 1330 1924	3.8 0.1 3.4 0.5
9 F	0144 0738 1408 1955	3.4 0.6 3.0 0.8	24 SA	0144 0757 1419 2011	3.7 0.3 3.3 0.6
10 SA	0219 0812 1446 2034	3.4 0.6 3.0 0.9	25 SU	0234 0845 1511 2101	3.6 0.5 3.3 0.7
11 SU	0255 0850 1527 2116	3.3 0.7 3.0 1.0	26 M	0327 0939 1605 ◑ 2200	3.4 0.7 3.2 0.8
12 M	0335 0933 1614 ◐ 2204	3.2 0.9 2.9 1.1	27 TU	0426 1050 1706 2319	3.2 1.0 3.1 1.0
13 TU	0426 1024 1710 2304	3.0 1.0 2.9 1.3	28 W	0539 1216 1819	3.0 1.1 3.0
14 W	0531 1131 1813	2.9 1.2 2.8	29 TH	0047 0720 1330 1942	1.1 2.8 1.2 3.1
15 TH	0042 0643 1311 1918	1.3 2.8 1.2 2.9	30 F	0207 0837 1436 2047	1.0 2.9 1.1 3.2
			31 SA	0317 0933 1531 2139	0.8 3.0 1.0 3.4

Chart Datum: 2·01 metres below Ordnance Datum (Belfast). HAT is 3·9 metres above Chart Datum.

STANDARD TIME (UT)
For Summer Time add ONE hour in **non-shaded areas**

BELFAST LAT 54°36′N LONG 5°55′W

TIMES AND HEIGHTS OF HIGH AND LOW WATERS

Dates in red are SPRINGS
Dates in blue are NEAPS

YEAR **2024**

SEPTEMBER

Date	Day	Time	m	Time	m	Time	m	Time	m
1	SU	0408	0.6	1018	3.1	1614	0.9	2223	3.5
2	M	0445	0.6	1057	3.1	1647	0.9	2302	3.5
3	TU	0512	0.6	1131	3.1	1716	0.8	● 2337	3.5
4	W	0536	0.6	1202	3.1	1744	0.8		
5	TH	0007	3.5	0603	0.6	1228	3.1	1814	0.8
6	F	0036	3.4	0630	0.6	1254	3.1	1845	0.8
7	SA	0105	3.4	0700	0.6	1322	3.1	1919	0.8
8	SU	0137	3.4	0733	0.7	1354	3.2	1955	0.8
9	M	0212	3.3	0810	0.7	1430	3.1	2035	0.9
10	TU	0252	3.2	0851	0.9	1514	3.1	2122	1.1
11	W	0344	3.0	0940	1.1	1611	2.9	◐ 2221	1.3
12	TH	0454	2.9	1045	1.3	1726	2.8		
13	F	0007	1.3	0612	2.8	1236	1.4	1841	2.9
14	SA	0140	1.1	0729	2.8	1357	1.2	1951	3.0
15	SU	0237	0.8	0839	3.0	1450	1.0	2051	3.3
16	M	0325	0.5	0931	3.2	1534	0.8	2138	3.5
17	TU	0407	0.3	1013	3.4	1613	0.6	2221	3.7
18	W	0446	0.1	1053	3.5	1651	0.5	○ 2304	3.8
19	TH	0524	0.1	1135	3.5	1730	0.4	2349	3.8
20	F	0602	0.1	1219	3.5	1812	0.4		
21	SA	0035	3.8	0644	0.2	1305	3.5	1857	0.5
22	SU	0124	3.7	0728	0.4	1353	3.5	1944	0.6
23	M	0215	3.6	0816	0.7	1444	3.4	2036	0.7
24	TU	0310	3.4	0910	1.0	1538	3.3	◑ 2138	0.9
25	W	0410	3.1	1024	1.2	1638	3.2	2304	1.1
26	TH	0527	2.8	1154	1.4	1752	3.1		
27	F	0032	1.1	0712	2.8	1310	1.4	1920	3.1
28	SA	0154	1.0	0823	2.9	1419	1.2	2025	3.2
29	SU	0300	0.8	0915	3.0	1513	1.1	2115	3.4
30	M	0346	0.7	0956	3.1	1553	1.0	2158	3.5

OCTOBER

Date	Day	Time	m	Time	m	Time	m	Time	m
1	TU	0418	0.6	1031	3.1	1622	0.9	2235	3.5
2	W	0439	0.6	1103	3.2	1648	0.9	● 2308	3.5
3	TH	0502	0.7	1130	3.2	1715	0.8	2337	3.5
4	F	0529	0.7	1154	3.2	1744	0.8		
5	SA	0002	3.4	0557	0.7	1216	3.3	1815	0.8
6	SU	0029	3.4	0627	0.7	1243	3.3	1848	0.8
7	M	0102	3.4	0700	0.8	1316	3.3	1924	0.9
8	TU	0141	3.3	0737	0.8	1355	3.3	2005	0.9
9	W	0226	3.2	0820	1.0	1439	3.2	2053	1.1
10	TH	0321	3.0	0911	1.2	1535	3.1	◐ 2155	1.2
11	F	0431	2.9	1018	1.4	1649	3.0	2334	1.2
12	SA	0548	2.8	1153	1.4	1807	3.0		
13	SU	0110	1.0	0705	2.9	1325	1.3	1922	3.1
14	M	0208	0.7	0813	3.1	1421	1.0	2024	3.4
15	TU	0256	0.5	0904	3.3	1506	0.8	2114	3.6
16	W	0338	0.3	0948	3.5	1546	0.6	2159	3.8
17	TH	0417	0.2	1029	3.6	1625	0.5	○ 2244	3.9
18	F	0455	0.2	1112	3.7	1706	0.5	2330	3.9
19	SA	0536	0.3	1156	3.7	1749	0.5		
20	SU	0017	3.8	0619	0.5	1242	3.7	1836	0.5
21	M	0108	3.7	0705	0.7	1331	3.6	1925	0.6
22	TU	0201	3.5	0754	0.9	1422	3.5	2019	0.8
23	W	0256	3.3	0851	1.2	1514	3.4	2123	0.9
24	TH	0356	3.0	1002	1.4	1611	3.3	◑ 2243	1.0
25	F	0510	2.8	1122	1.5	1718	3.2		
26	SA	0001	1.1	0645	2.8	1234	1.5	1841	3.1
27	SU	0115	1.0	0754	2.8	1341	1.4	1950	3.2
28	M	0218	0.9	0844	3.0	1436	1.2	2043	3.3
29	TU	0303	0.8	0924	3.1	1518	1.1	2126	3.4
30	W	0335	0.8	0958	3.2	1550	1.0	2203	3.4
31	TH	0401	0.8	1029	3.3	1619	0.9	2236	3.5

NOVEMBER

Date	Day	Time	m	Time	m	Time	m	Time	m
1	F	0429	0.8	1058	3.3	1649	0.9	● 2306	3.4
2	SA	0458	0.8	1124	3.4	1720	0.9	2334	3.4
3	SU	0529	0.8	1149	3.4	1753	0.9		
4	M	0003	3.4	0601	0.8	1218	3.5	1828	0.9
5	TU	0040	3.4	0636	0.9	1254	3.5	1905	0.9
6	W	0123	3.3	0716	1.0	1336	3.4	1948	0.9
7	TH	0212	3.2	0802	1.1	1423	3.3	2039	1.0
8	F	0308	3.1	0857	1.2	1518	3.2	2144	1.1
9	SA	0414	3.0	1003	1.3	1622	3.2	◐ 2305	1.0
10	SU	0525	2.9	1120	1.4	1735	3.1		
11	M	0027	0.9	0638	3.0	1237	1.2	1850	3.3
12	TU	0129	0.7	0743	3.2	1340	1.1	1955	3.4
13	W	0221	0.5	0835	3.4	1433	0.9	2050	3.6
14	TH	0307	0.4	0922	3.5	1520	0.7	2139	3.7
15	F	0350	0.4	1007	3.6	1604	0.6	○ 2227	3.8
16	SA	0432	0.4	1052	3.7	1649	0.6	2315	3.7
17	SU	0516	0.6	1138	3.7	1735	0.5		
18	M	0004	3.7	0602	0.7	1225	3.7	1823	0.6
19	TU	0055	3.5	0649	0.9	1314	3.7	1914	0.6
20	W	0147	3.4	0740	1.0	1402	3.7	2007	0.7
21	TH	0240	3.2	0834	1.2	1452	3.6	2106	0.9
22	F	0335	3.0	0934	1.3	1543	3.4	2211	1.0
23	SA	0435	2.9	1039	1.4	1640	3.3	◑ 2317	1.0
24	SU	0547	2.8	1145	1.4	1743	3.2		
25	M	0021	1.0	0701	2.8	1247	1.4	1854	3.2
26	TU	0119	1.0	0756	2.9	1345	1.3	1955	3.2
27	W	0209	1.0	0841	3.0	1434	1.2	2044	3.3
28	TH	0250	0.9	0919	3.2	1516	1.1	2127	3.3
29	F	0325	0.9	0954	3.3	1552	1.0	2205	3.4
30	SA	0359	0.9	1028	3.4	1627	0.9	2241	3.4

DECEMBER

Date	Day	Time	m	Time	m	Time	m	Time	m
1	SU	0433	0.9	1101	3.5	1702	0.9	● 2315	3.4
2	M	0508	0.9	1131	3.5	1739	0.8	2348	3.4
3	TU	0545	0.9	1203	3.5	1817	0.8		
4	W	0026	3.3	0624	0.9	1240	3.5	1859	0.8
5	TH	0110	3.3	0707	1.0	1323	3.5	1944	0.8
6	F	0200	3.2	0755	1.0	1410	3.5	2035	0.8
7	SA	0254	3.1	0848	1.1	1501	3.4	2132	0.8
8	SU	0352	3.1	0946	1.1	1558	3.4	◐ 2235	0.8
9	M	0456	3.0	1048	1.2	1701	3.3	2342	0.8
10	TU	0603	3.1	1155	1.1	1813	3.3		
11	W	0048	0.7	0708	3.2	1301	1.1	1925	3.4
12	TH	0147	0.7	0807	3.3	1404	1.0	2028	3.5
13	F	0241	0.6	0900	3.4	1501	0.8	2124	3.5
14	SA	0331	0.6	0950	3.5	1553	0.7	2216	3.6
15	SU	0418	0.7	1039	3.6	1642	0.6	○ 2307	3.5
16	M	0505	0.7	1127	3.7	1730	0.6	2357	3.5
17	TU	0552	0.8	1214	3.7	1818	0.6		
18	W	0045	3.3	0639	0.9	1259	3.7	1905	0.6
19	TH	0133	3.2	0725	1.0	1344	3.7	1952	0.7
20	F	0220	3.1	0811	1.1	1428	3.6	2038	0.7
21	SA	0306	3.0	0857	1.1	1514	3.5	2126	0.8
22	SU	0353	2.9	0945	1.2	1602	3.4	◑ 2218	0.9
23	M	0444	2.9	1039	1.3	1654	3.2	2316	1.0
24	TU	0539	2.8	1143	1.3	1751	3.1		
25	W	0019	1.1	0638	2.9	1250	1.3	1852	3.1
26	TH	0117	1.1	0738	2.9	1350	1.3	1954	3.1
27	F	0209	1.1	0833	3.1	1442	1.2	2049	3.2
28	SA	0254	1.0	0921	3.2	1528	1.0	2138	3.2
29	SU	0335	0.9	1005	3.3	1609	0.9	2221	3.3
30	M	0415	0.9	1043	3.4	1649	0.8	● 2301	3.3
31	TU	0454	0.9	1118	3.5	1728	0.7	2338	3.3

Chart Datum: 2·01 metres below Ordnance Datum (Belfast). HAT is 3·9 metres above Chart Datum.

STRANGFORD LOUGH

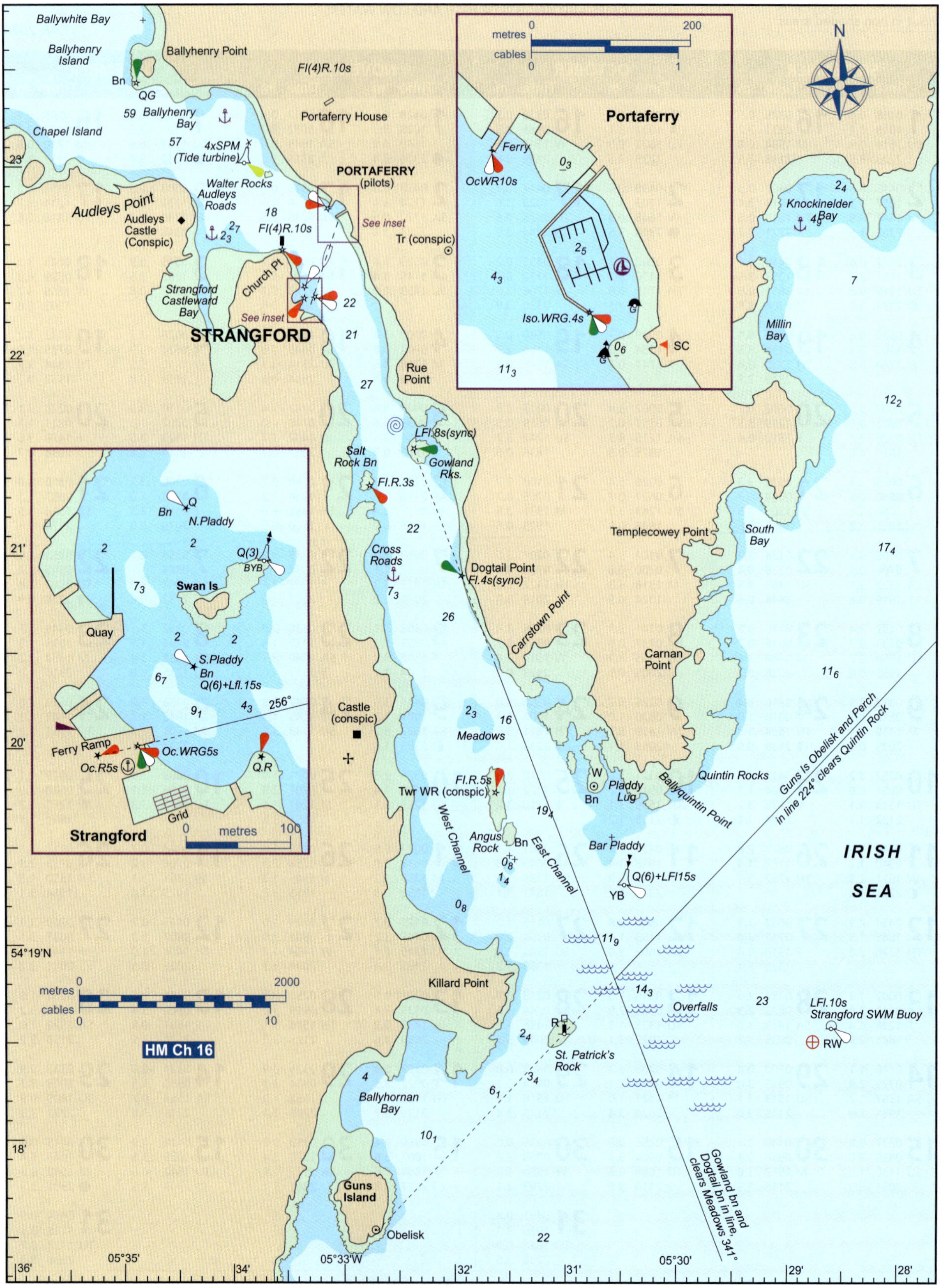

6.17 STRANGFORD LOUGH

Down **54°19'·33N 05°30'·85W** (Narrows)

CHARTS AC 2156, 2159, 5612; Imray C62, C69

TIDES Killard Pt 0000, Strangford Quay +0200 Dover; ML 2·0; Duration 0610

Standard Port BELFAST (⟵)

Times				Height (metres)			
High Water		Low Water		MHWS	MHWN	MLWN	MLWS
0100	0700	0000	0600	3·5	3·0	1·1	0·4
1300	1900	1200	1800				
Differences STRANGFORD (The Narrows)							
+0147	+0157	+0148	+0208	+0·1	+0·1	–0·2	0·0
KILLARD POINT (Entr)							
+0011	+0021	+0005	+0025	+1·0	+0·8	+0·1	+0·1
QUOILE BARRIER							
+0150	+0200	+0150	+0300	+0·2	+0·2	–0·3	–0·1
KILLYLEAGH							
+0157	+0207	+0211	+0231	+0·3	+0·3	ND	ND
SOUTH ROCK							
+0023	+0023	+0025	+0025	+1·0	+0·8	+0·1	+0·1
PORTAVOGIE							
+0010	+0020	+0010	+0020	+1·2	+0·9	+0·3	+0·2

SHELTER Excellent; largest inlet on E coast. ⚓ in the Narrows at Cross Roads, off Strangford clear of moorings, in Audley Roads (in about 5m) and in Ballyhenry Bay. Limited moorings at Strangford; moorings may be available in Audley Roads (check with Sailing Club). Small marina at Portaferry, where stream runs fast; best to enter near slack water. Many good ⚓ (NB Marine Nature Reserve) and some 🅥s up the lough, by villages and YCs.

NAVIGATION WPT: SWM buoy, L Fl 10s, 54°18'·63N 05°28'·69W, 306°/2·04M to Angus Rk lt twr Fl R 5s 5M. Visitors should use E Chan. Disregard W Chan ≠ 320·5° shown on old editions of AC 2159. Beware St Patricks Rk, Bar Pladdy and Pladdy Lug; overfalls occur in the SE apprs and at the bar, which can be dangerous when ebb meets the NW set outside. Strong tidal streams (7kn at sp) in the Narrows. The bar is passable during the flood; best to enter on young flood or at slack water. The flood starts in the Narrows at HW Belfast –3½ and runs for about 6hrs; the ebb starts at HW Belfast +2½. Beware car ferry between Strangford, S and E of Swan Is, and Portaferry. Swan Island, seen as a grassy mound at HW, is edged with rks and a reef extends 32m E ending at W bn, Q (3). Further up the lough, despite improved marks and lights, unmarked drying shoals (pladdies) abound; AC 2156 or equivalent is essential.

LIGHTS AND MARKS Turbine 1¾ca WNW of Walter Rks marked by 2 pair Y SPM; outer pr Fl Y 10s, inner pr Fl Y 5s.

COMMUNICATIONS (Code 028) Medical Clinic 4488 1209. HM at Strangford Ferry Terminal 4488 1637.

HM Ch 16 (Mon-Fri 0900-1700). Some YCs Ch **80** M.

FACILITIES Strangford, Portaferry and Killyleagh are easy to access and offer good shops, pubs and restaurants.

STRANGFORD 25m 🅥 pontoon, 3🅥; Cuan Inn.

PORTAFERRY Marina portaferrymarina.co.uk, mob 7703 209780, (limited) £1·50. **Village** Ⓑ.

Cook St Pier (2ca S), see **DONAGHADEE** ☎9188 2377, HM mob 07718579105; limited.

QUOILE RIVER: Quoile YC ☎4461 2266.

KILLYLEAGH Kos (Irish Spars & Rigging ☎9751 2830, Ⓑ.

Killyleagh YC ☎07801 291410, N of village.

East Down YC ☎4482 8375, (about 1M NE of town).

RINGHADDY QUAY CC, drying.

SKETRICK ISLAND In White Rk Bay.

Strangford Lough YC ☎9754 1883.

Down CC (Old Lightship to NW in Dorn).

KIRCUBBIN (tidal) Ⓑ.

6.18 ARDGLASS

Down 54°15'·63N 05°35'·96W

CHARTS AC 2093, 633, 5612; Imray C62

TIDES HW +0025 Dover; ML 3·0; Duration 0620

Standard Port BELFAST (⟵)

Times				Height (metres)			
High Water		Low Water		MHWS	MHWN	MLWN	MLWS
0100	0700	0000	0600	3·5	3·0	1·1	0·4
1300	1900	1200	1800				
Differences KILKEEL							
+0040	+0030	+0010	+0010	+1·2	+1·1	+0·4	+0·4
NEWCASTLE							
+0025	+0035	+0020	+0040	+1·6	+1·1	+0·4	+0·1
KILLOUGH HARBOUR							
0000	+0020	ND	ND	+1·8	+1·6	ND	ND
ARDGLASS							
+0010	+0015	+0005	+0010	+1·7	+1·2	+0·6	+0·3

SHELTER Good, except in strong winds from E to S. It is the only all-weather, all-tide shelter between Howth and Bangor. Phennick Cove/Ardglass marina is on W side of hbr, with depths 1·0m to 2·8m. Visitors should check depth of berth offered by marina against depth drawn. The busy fishing port is in South Hbr, with quays (2·1m) on inside of extended S pier. At NW end of hbr, old drying N Dock is also used by FVs.

NAVIGATION WPT 54°15'·30N 05°35'·32W, 131°/5ca to hbr ent. Appr 311° in W sector of WRG Dir lt. Depth in chan 2·4m. Off the tip of the inner breakwater the buoyed marina channel commences in a depth of 1.3m. It is marked by lit PHM and SHM (not shown on chartlet) and turns sharply to port to approach the marina on a heading of 230°. Do not cross the drying SW portion of inner bkwtr, marked by two unlit SCM perches.

LIGHTS AND MARKS Dir lt, 311°, conspic W tr at inner hbr, Iso WRG 4s 10m 8/7/5M, 308°-W-314°; reported hard to see against shore lts. S bkwtr Fl R 3s 10m 5M. W roof of shed on S bkwtr is conspic. If entering S Hbr, avoid Churn Rk, unlit SCM bn. Entrance to marina is buoyed. Castle, spire and water tr (off plan) are conspic to W.

COMMUNICATIONS (Code 028) Dr 9084 1242. HM 4484 1291, mob 07790 648274.

Monitor VHF Ch **12** on entry/exit. Marina Ch 80.

FACILITIES

Ardglass Marina www.ardglassmarina.co.uk ☎44 842332, (£8·00) 55 inc 22🅥 £3·00 inc.

Town

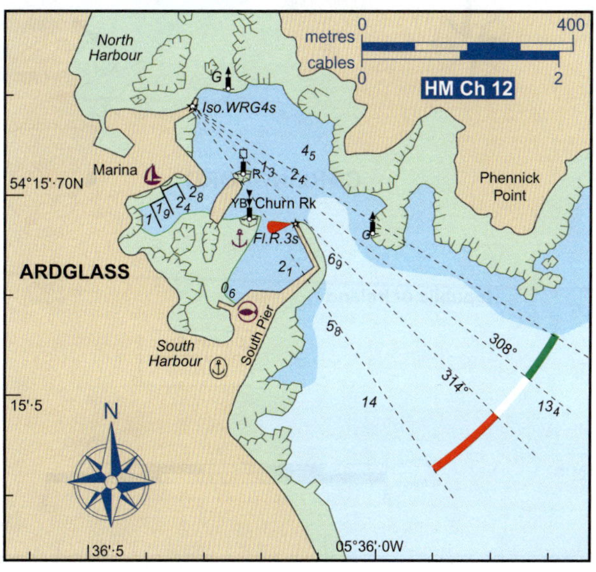

MINOR HARBOURS SOUTH OF ARDGLASS

DUNDRUM BAY, Down. AC 44, 5612. Tides see 6.18. This 8M wide bay to the W of St John's Pt is shoal to 5ca offshore and unsafe in onshore winds. The small drying hbr at **Newcastle** (54°11'·8N 05°53'·0W) is for occas use in fair weather. HM ☎(02843) 722804, mob 07803 832515. **Dundrum Hbr (54°14'·2N 05°49'·4W)** No longer used by commercial tfc and only to be used with caution, provides ⚓ in 2m for shoal draught; the bar carries about 0·3m. A steep sea can run at the bar in onshore winds. HW Dundrum is approx that of HW Liverpool; see also 6.18 Newcastle. *The Irish Cruising Club's Sailing Directions* are essential for the 1M long, buoyed approach channel. 2 lit DZ buoys offshore are part of the Ballykinler firing range, 2M E of hbr; R flag/lts indicate range active.

ANNALONG HBR, Down, **54°06'·50N 05°53'·65W**. AC 44, 5621, 5612. Tides as Kilkeel, see 6.7. Hbr closed 2018, North Wall Pier rebuilt in 2021, but pontoon and gates yet to be renewed. Appr in W sector of S breakwater light, Oc WRG 5s 8m 9M, vis 204°-G-249°-W-309°-R-024°. Hug N side of the breakwater to avoid rocky shore to starboard. IPTS shown at entrance. HM mob 07739 527036. Facilities: 🛒 📖 ✉.

KILKEEL, Down, **54°03'·47N 05°59'·26W**. AC 44, 2800, 5612. HW +0015 on Dover; ML 2·9m; Duration 0620. See 6.18. Do not appr in E–SW winds >F4. Inner basin is sheltered, but crowded by FVs; depth off quays approx 1m. Secure in inner basin and see HM. There are drying banks both sides of ent chan and SW gales form a sandbank across ent. This is dredged or slowly eroded in E winds. S bkwtr lt Fl WR 2s 8m 8M, 296°-R-313°-W-017°, storm sigs. Meeney's pier (N bkwtr) Fl G 3s 6m 2M. Monitor VHF Ch **12** on entry/exit. HM ☎(028 417) 62287. Facilities: on quay, (between fish market and dock). **Town** (¾M) ✉ 🛒 ✕ 📖.

6.19 CARLINGFORD LOUGH

Louth/Down **54°01'·25N 06°04'·30W** ✿✿✿

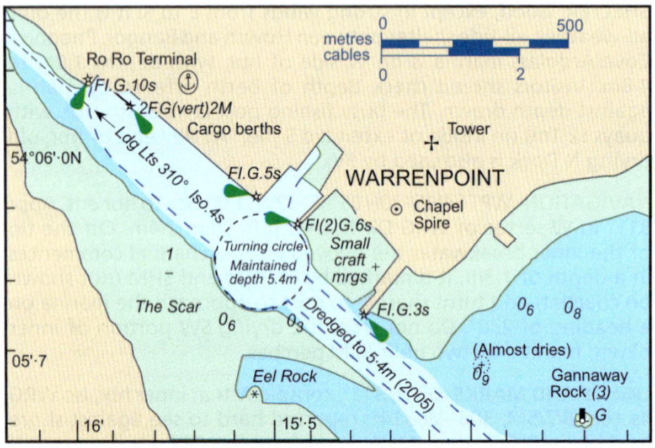

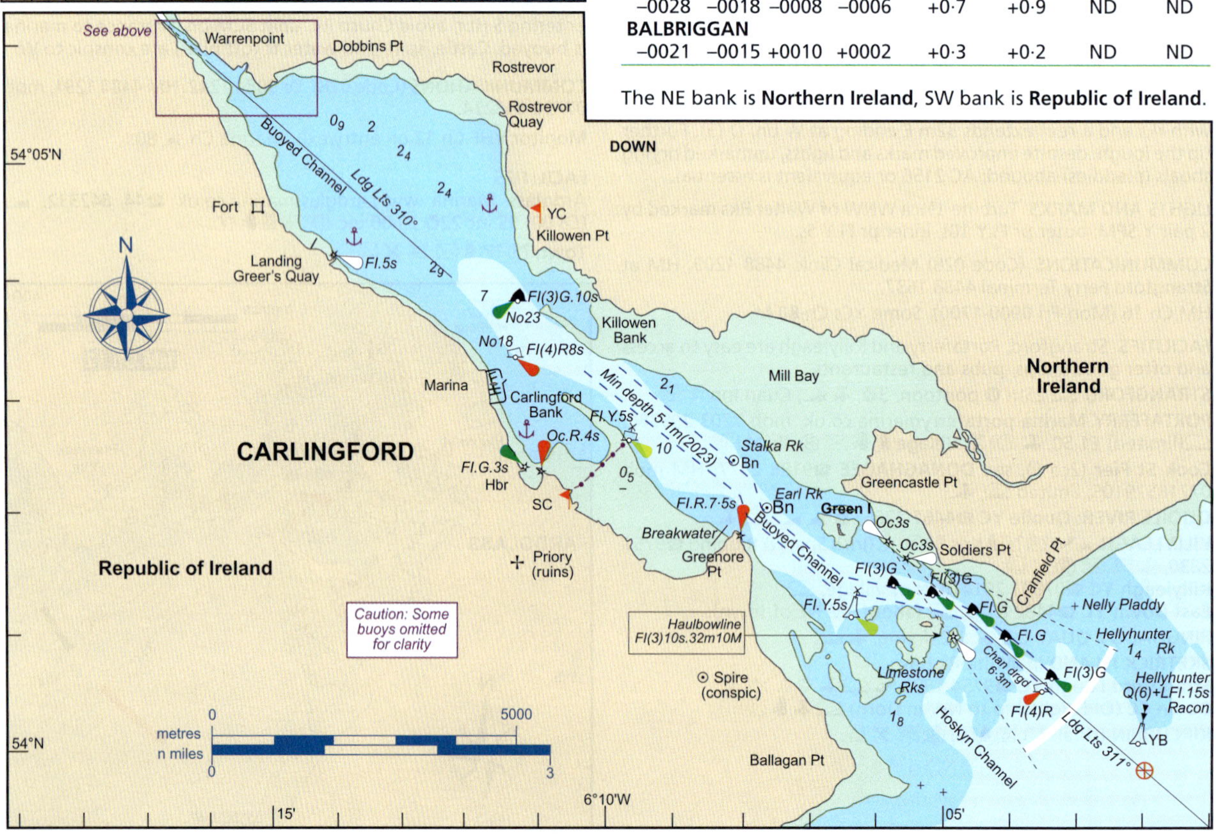

CHARTS AC 44, 2800, 5621, 5612; Imray C62

TIDES Cranfield Pt +0025 and Warrenpoint +0035 Dover; ML 2·9; Duration Cranfield Pt 0615, Warrenpoint 0540

Standard Port DUBLIN (NORTH WALL – AREA 5) (⟵)

Times				Height (metres)			
High Water		Low Water		MHWS	MHWN	MLWN	MLWS
0000	0700	0000	0500	4·1	3·4	1·5	0·7
1200	1900	1200	1700				
Differences CRANFIELD POINT							
–0027	–0011	+0005	–0010	+0·7	+0·9	+0·3	+0·2
WARRENPOINT							
–0020	–0010	+0025	+0035	+1·0	+0·7	+0·2	0·0
NEWRY (VICTORIA LOCK)							
+0005	+0015	+0045	Dries	+1·2	+0·9	+0·1	DR
DUNDALK (SOLDIERS POINT)							
–0010	–0010	0000	+0045	+1·0	+0·8	+0·1	–0·1
DUNANY POINT							
–0028	–0018	–0008	–0006	+0·7	+0·9	ND	ND
BALBRIGGAN							
–0021	–0015	+0010	+0002	+0·3	+0·2	ND	ND

The NE bank is **Northern Ireland**, SW bank is **Republic of Ireland**.

SHELTER

Carlingford Marina is protected on S side by sunken barge; depths 1·5m at LW (check with Marina). Appr from N with Nos 18 and 23 buoys in transit astern 012°, to clear the tail of Carlingford Bank (dries) and beware of marine farms in vicinity. Ⓥ on C pontoon.

Carlingford Hbr (dries 2·2m), at piers.

Warrenpoint has small pontoon NW of breakwater (Fl G 3s); access dredged 1·1m. Ⓥ pontoon at Town Dock Marina run by port authority www.warrenpointport.com WC. ⚓s clockwise from ent include: off Greenore Pt, between SW end of quay and bkwtr, in 3m clear of commercial traffic; off Greer's Quay in 2m; off Rostrevor Quay, Killowen Pt (YC) and off derelict pier at Greencastle Pt (beware rks). Limited space may be available for short-stay visits in the mussel fishing complex (approx £15/night). Call at least 24hrs before arrival.

NAVIGATION WPT 54°00´·09N 06°02´·00W, (2½ ca S of Hellyhunter SCM lt buoy) 311°/1M to first chan buoys. The main chan is Carlingford Cut (6·3m), about 3ca SW of Cranfield Pt, and passing 2ca NE of Haulbowline lt ho. Drying rocks and shoals obstruct most of the entrance. Small craft should at all times keep clear of commercial shipping in the narrow dredged channel.

The entrance is impassable in strong onshore winds. The lough becomes choppy in S'ly winds and, due to the funnelling effect of the mountains, NW winds can cause a higher sea state within the lough than outside it.

Tides run up to 5kn off Greenore Pt through a channel with a minimum depth of 5.6m. Entry is impracticable against the ebb. Beware sudden squalls and waterspouts.

Extensive shellfish beds exist along the NE side of the lough; give fishing vessels on both sides of the channel a wide berth.

LIGHTS AND MARKS Haulbowline Fl (3) 10s 32m 10M; granite tower. Ldg lts 310°26′: both Oc 3s 7/12m 11M, vis 295°-325°; R △ front, ▽ rear, on framework trs. Greenore Pier Fl R 7·5s 10m 5M. Newry R: Ldg lts 310°, both Iso 4s 5/15m 2M, stone columns. Channel from Green Is to Warren Pt marked by lit lateral buoys. Ferry route fm Greenore to Greencastle slip follows marked channel E of Green Is past Small Flat and Half Tide Rock.

COMMUNICATIONS (Code Greenore/Carlingford 042; Warrenpoint 028). Irish ⊜: Dundalk (042) 34114; Dr (042) 73110; Ⓗ Newry (028) 3026 5511, Dundalk (042) 34701; Police Newry 101, Dundalk (042) 9373102.

Greenore (*Ferry Greenore*) Ch 12 16 (HJ). Carlingford Marina Ch **M (37)** 16. Warrenpoint Ch 12 16 (H24); call Ch 12 at By No 23 to enter dredged chan. Dundalk Ch 14 16 (HW±3).

FACILITIES **Carlingford Marina** www.carlingfordmarina.com ☎0429373072, mob 087 652 4820, 290 inc Ⓥ €25·00/boat, short stay <5hrs €10, HO 0900-1800LT (Summer 2100 Thu-Sat) (50t) (Indian) @.

Services ☎0872 301319, ☎(048)44 828882, Divers.

Carlingford YC ☎(041) 685 1951.

Carlingford Hbr Kos.

Village Ⓑ.

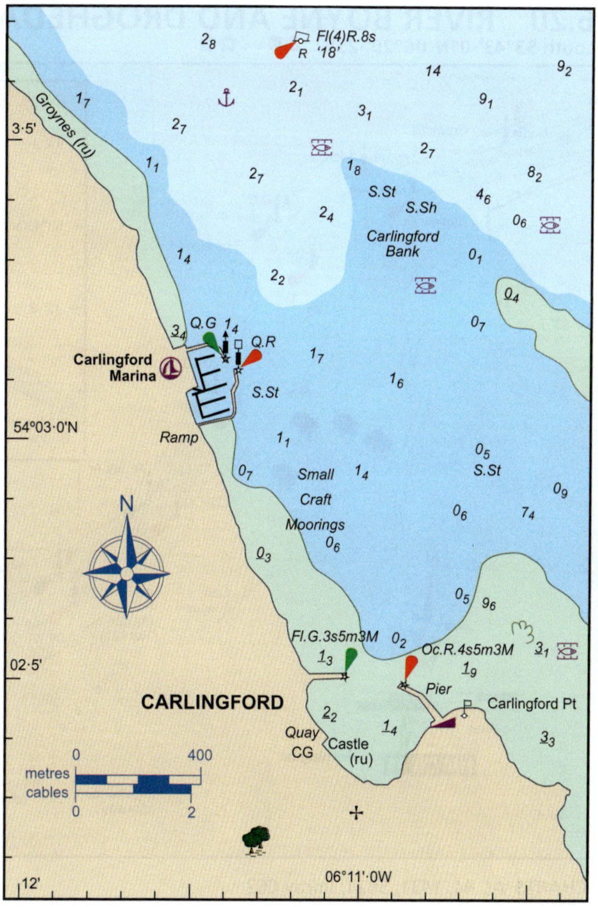

Warrenpoint HM ☎(02841) 752878; (but no access at LW) also at Rostrevor, Ⓑ also Dundalk, (Dundalk, Newry), (Dublin).

MINOR HARBOURS AND ANCHORAGES BETWEEN CARLINGFORD LOUGH AND RIVER BOYNE

PORT ORIEL, Louth, **53°47'·94N 06°13'·37W.** AC 44. Tides see 6.19 (Dunany Pt). Good shelter in small new harbour except in strong ENE winds when a dangerous scend can enter the harbour. Entry reported to be difficult in strong NE winds. Approach from NE on leading marks 174·9°, front and rear Fl 3s (sync) avoiding Wk 1·6m 2.7ca from entrance; Pier Head Light Mo(A) R 9s. on pier in 4m, €25.00/craft, or dry out in inner harbour. HM ☎087 2628777. No facilities; by tanker, in Clogher Head village (1·2M).

6.20 RIVER BOYNE AND DROGHEDA

Louth **53°43'·01N 06°20'·25W**

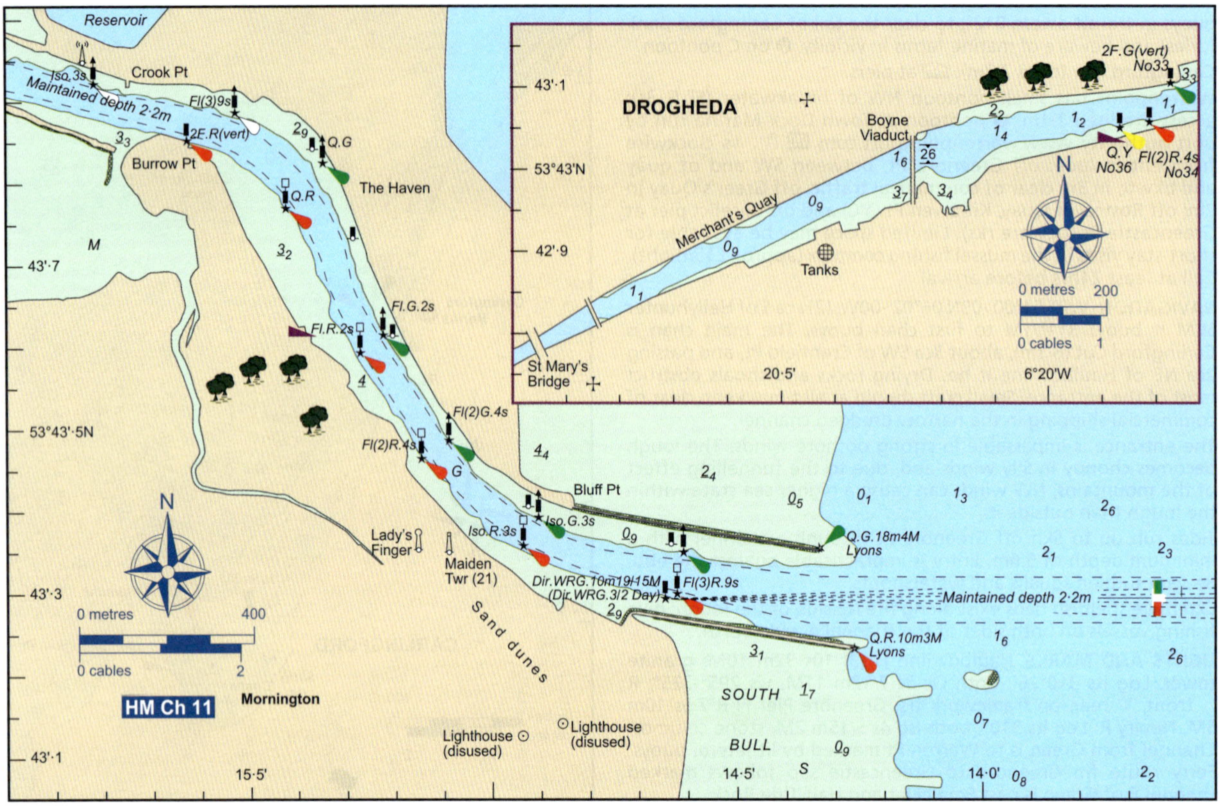

CHARTS AC 44, 1431, 5621; Imray C62

TIDES +0030 Dover (Ent); ML 2·8; Duration 0620

Standard Port DUBLIN (NORTH WALL – AREA 5) (←)

Times				Height (metres)			
High Water		Low Water		MHWS	MHWN	MLWN	MLWS
0000	0700	0000	0500	4·1	3·4	1·5	0·7
1200	1900	1200	1700				
Differences BOYNE BAR							
–0015	–0009	–0001	+0005	+0·9	+0·6	+0·2	+0·1

SHELTER Good, once inside the river ent between 2 training walls, extending 3ca E from the beaches. Drogheda lies 7km upstream from the bar. There are no suitable ⚓ in the river below the viaduct, 400m above which is Fiddle Case Pier, a dedicated 40m open pile pier for yachts and leisure craft.

NAVIGATION WPT 53°43´·31N, 06°10´·00W, 270°/2·5M to ent. Appr from E on Dir lt between sandbanks North and South Bull in chan which extends 700m seaward. B'waters either side of river ent marked by lit bns. Lateral bns mark channel upstream to Drogheda. Best entered on latter part of inbound stream (HW Dublin –0300, HW Dover +0220). Maintained depth 2.2m to Tom Roes Pt terminal, thereafter 1.6m below CD to town centre quay. Air draft beneath viaduct 26m, Hugh de Lacy Br upstream limit.

LIGHTS AND MARKS Dir lt 270°, between b'water lts, N Aleria Bn QG (N), Lyons QR (S). Two disused Lt ho lie S of ent on golf course. Inside ent at Mornington Maiden Twr conspic 21m and Lady's Finger.

COMMUNICATIONS (Code 00353 41) Ⓗ 9837601; Drogheda Port Co 9838378; HM 838385 mob 086 2547827.

Drogheda Radio Ch 11 (HW-3 to HW+1 or when vessel due).

FACILITIES Fiddle Case Pier N Bank 10-12 ⓥ; WC.

Town Ⓔ ✉ Ⓑ ✕ ⇌.

ADJACENT ANCHORAGE

SKERRIES, Dublin, **53°35'·09N 06°06'·49W**. AC 633. Tides as Balbriggan, 6.19. E and SE of Red Island (a peninsula) lie Colt, Shenick's and St Patrick's Islands, the latter foul to S and SW. Inshore passage between Colt and St Patrick's Is uses transit/brg as on chart to clear dangers. Good shelter and holding in 3m at Skerries Bay, W of Red Is. Approach from E or NE outside PHM buoy, Fl R 10s, off Red Is. ⚓ WNW of pier, Oc R 6s 7m 7M, vis 103°-154°; clear of moorings. Most facilities; Skerries SC ☎1 849 1233, (HW±3). Rockabill Lt, Fl WR 12s 45m 17/13M, is conspic 2·4M ENE of St Patrick's Is.

Index

Index

PANTAENIU
SAIL & MOTOR YACHT INSURAN
INSURANCE
YOU CAN
RELY ON
Talk to the boat insurance experts.
Get your quote today!
01752 223656
quotes@pantaenius.co.uk
PANTAENIUS.CO.UK
Motor Boat
Sailing Yacht
RIB
Motor Cruiser
Sailing Boa
Pantaenius UK Ltd is authorised and regulated by the Financial Conduct Authority (Authorised No. 308688)